Beethoven

Also by Jan Swafford

The Vintage Guide to Classical Music
Charles Ives: A Life with Music
Johannes Brahms: A Biography

Beethoven

Anguish and Triumph

A BIOGRAPHY

Jan Swafford

Houghton Mifflin Harcourt
BOSTON · NEW YORK

For information about permission to reproduce selections from this book,
write to Permissions, Houghton Mifflin Harcourt Publishing Company,
215 Park Avenue South, New York, New York 10003.

www.hmhco.com

Library of Congress Cataloging-in-Publication Data
Swafford, Jan.
Beethoven : anguish and triumph : a biography / Jan Swafford.
pages cm
Includes bibliographical references and index.
ISBN 978-0-618-05474-9
1. Beethoven, Ludwig van, 1770–1827.
2. Composers — Germany — Biography. I. Title.
ML410.B4S94 2014
780.92—dc23
[B]
2014011681

Printed in the United States of America
DOC 10 9 8 7 6 5 4 3 2

Could a historiographer drive on his history, as a muleteer drives on his mule, — straight forward; — for instance, from Rome all the way to Loretto, without ever once turning his head aside either to the right hand or to the left, — he might venture to foretell you an hour when he should get to his journey's end; — but the thing is, morally speaking, impossible: For, if he is a man of the least spirit, he will have fifty deviations from a straight line to make with this or that party as he goes along, which he can no ways avoid. He will have views and prospects to himself perpetually soliciting his eye, which he can no more help standing still to look at than he can fly.

— LAURENCE STERNE, *Tristram Shandy*

Fame is a form of incomprehension, perhaps the worst.

— JORGE LUIS BORGES

My custom even when I am composing instrumental music is always to keep the whole in view.

— BEETHOVEN

Contents

Introduction *xi*

1 BONN, ELECTORATE OF COLOGNE 1

2 FATHER, MOTHER, SON 21

3 REASON AND REVOLUTION 40

4 LOVED IN TURN 56

5 GOLDEN AGE 69

6 A JOURNEY AND A DEATH 84

7 *BILDUNG* 95

8 STEM AND BOOK 112

9 UNREAL CITY 132

10 CHAINS OF CRAFTSMANSHIP 145

11 GENERALISSIMO 166

12 VIRTUOSO 186

13 FATE'S HAMMER 207

14 THE GOOD, THE BEAUTIFUL, AND THE
   MELANCHOLY 242

15 THE NEW PATH 269

16 OH, FELLOW MEN 301

17 HEAVEN AND EARTH WILL TREMBLE 331

18 *GESCHRIEBEN AUF BONAPARTE* 370

19 OUR HEARTS WERE STIRRED 402

20 THAT HAUGHTY BEAUTY 436

21 SCHEMES 462

22 DARKNESS TO LIGHT 484

23 THUS BE ENABLED TO CREATE 516

24 MYTHS AND MEN 544

25 MY ANGEL, MY SELF 580

26 WE FINITE BEINGS 613

27 THE QUEEN OF THE NIGHT 657

28 WHAT IS DIFFICULT 697

29 THE SKY ABOVE, THE LAW WITHIN 738

30 *QUI VENIT IN NOMINE DOMINI* 789

31 YOU MILLIONS 826

32 *ARS LONGA, VITA BREVIS* 857

33 *PLAUDITE, AMICI* 898

Appendix 937

Works Cited 946

Notes 956

Index 1055

Introduction

❧

There has always been a steady trickle of Beethoven biographies and always will be, as long as the fascination of the music and the man endures. That bids to be a long time. Like Shakespeare, Rembrandt, and a few other figures in our creative history, Beethoven has long since been a cultural artifact, woven into our worldview and into our mythologies from popular to esoteric.

A few miles from where I write, his is the only name inscribed on a plaque over the proscenium of Boston Symphony Hall, built at the end of the nineteenth century. In our time, a performance of the Ninth Symphony celebrated the fall of the Berlin Wall. In Japan, important occasions such as the opening of a sumo arena are marked by a performance of *Daiku, the Big Nine*. Around the world, the Fifth is seen as the definition of a Classical symphony. When I taught in a conservatory, there were few days when we didn't hear Beethoven drifting down the hall. My Beethoven seminars were full of young musicians whose professional lives were going to be steadily involved with the composer.

There is, of course, great danger in that kind of ubiquity. To become more of an icon than a man and artist is to be heard less intimately. Unlike others of his status, Beethoven has been relatively immune to the usual historical ebbs and flows of artistic reputations. That has happened partly because in the decades after his death the concert hall evolved into more of a museum of the past than an explorer of the present. That situation too has its dangers. Instrumental music is in many ways a mysterious and abstract art. With Shakespeare and Rembrandt, we can be anchored in the manifest passions in their works, their racy jokes, their immediacy. It is that immediacy that is all too easy to lose when confronting iconic musicians like Beethoven, Bach, and Brahms.

In the two-century course of Beethoven's fame, he has inevitably been batted about by biographers and other writers. He was born during the Aufklärung, the German embodiment of the Enlightenment, and came of age during the revolutionary 1780s. Many in his time saw him as a musical revolutionary and connected him to the spirit of the French Revolution. By the time he died in 1827, he was already a Romantic myth, and that is what he stayed through the nineteenth century: Beethoven the demigod, a combination of suffering Christ figure and demonic icon. In his person rough, crude, and fractious, in his music everything from crude to transcendent, he became the quintessential Romantic genius in an age that established a cult of genius that lingers on, for well and ill.

Critical reframings and reinterpretings are inevitable, and like everything in the arts they reflect the temper of their times. After the lingering decay of Romantic myths in the twentieth century, writing on Beethoven during the past decades has largely risen from the academy, so it reflects the parade of fashions and shibboleths of that industry. Many present-day books concern ideas about Beethoven rather than Beethoven himself. The assorted theoretical postures of late twentieth-century academe took some heavy shots at him, but do not seem to have dislodged him from his unfortunate pedestal, which I believe lodges him too far from us.

I suspect many people still feel that in some ways the most effective Beethoven biography remains the massive late nineteenth-century one by Alexander Wheelock Thayer. That American writer set out with the goal of assembling every available fact about Beethoven and putting it down as clearly as possible. "I fight for no theories and cherish no prejudices," Thayer wrote. "[M]y sole point of view is the truth." In the 1960s, the book was corrected and updated, with a similarly direct agenda, by Elliot Forbes. For me it is within Thayer's Victorian language that Beethoven casts the strongest shadow as a person, where I catch glimpses of him walking down the street, joking with friends, thumping the table as he composes, tearing into his fish dinner.

Without aspiring to the voluminousness of Thayer, the book you are reading was written in his spirit. Now and then in the course of an artist's biographical history, it comes time to strip away the decades of accumulated theories and postures and look at the subject as clearly and plainly as possible, without prejudices and preconceptions. That as biographers we all have agendas, both known and unknown to us, does not change the value and necessity of getting back to the human reality of a towering figure. This book is a biography of Beethoven the man and musician, not the myth. To that end I have relegated all later commentary to the endnotes. I want the book to stay on the ground, in his time, looking at him as directly as possible as he walks, talks, writes, rages, composes.

We will see that Beethoven was in some ways a hard man. The troubling parts of his personality, the squalor he lived in, his growing paranoia and delusions of persecution, his misanthropy, and later his double-dealings in business will be on display here roughly in the proportion that they were on display in his life. Likewise the plaintive history of his deafness and illness and his failed love affairs. Still, I believe that in the end there was no real meanness in Beethoven. He aspired to be a good, noble, honorable person who served humanity. At times he could be entirely lovable and delightful in his quirks and puns and metaphors and notions, even in his lusty sociopolitical rants. There was something exalted about him that was noted first in his teens and often thereafter. He was utterly sure of himself and his gift, but no less self-critical and without sentimentality concerning his work.

To the degree that I have a conscious agenda, it is this: I am myself a composer, both before and after being a biographer, so this is a composer's-eye view of a composer, written for the general public. When I look at Beethoven I see a man sitting at a table, playing the piano, walking in fields and woods doing what I and a great many others have done: crafting music one note, one phrase, one section at a time. I hear the scratch of a quill pen on lined music paper. I see a work coming into focus in page after tumultuous page of sketches. I see a man in the creative trance all of us work in — but Beethoven's trance deeper than most, and the results incomparably fine and far-ranging.

In Beethoven I see, in other words, a person leading what is to me the familiar life of musician and composer, and so he will be viewed here. Like many composers of his time and later, he cobbled together a living from this and that, and he was deeply involved in the skills and traditions of his trade. The main difference is how thoroughly he mastered those skills, on the foundation of a gigantic inborn talent. In the course of my work I came to realize that Beethoven was in every respect a consummate musician, whether he was writing notes, playing them, or selling them. The often shocking incompetence of the rest of his life was familiar to history, to his friends, and to himself. That too was the incompetence of a man, not a myth.

I had drafted a good part of this book before I realized that in the text proper I was shying away from two words that are all too familiar in biographies of artists: *genius* and *masterpiece*. The first word I use only in quotations from Beethoven's time. The latter word I don't use at all. In regard to *genius,* this was not because I don't believe in its existence, but rather that I simply didn't need the word. This book is a portrait of a consummate musician creating his work, playing the piano, finding his voice, finding his niche, selling his wares, courting patrons and champions and publishers, falling in love, pleasing his audience here and provoking them there; and in his art pushing every envelope with incomparable courage and integrity.

My problem with the word *genius* is not with the concept but with the way it has been slung around over the last two centuries. It is one of those words like *spiritual, profound, incredible, amazing, masterpiece,* and so on that tend to be wielded vaguely and carelessly. I use some of those words now and then, I hope not carelessly. Even though I never use the word *genius,* however, the book assumes Beethoven's genius and constitutes an ongoing examination of what that might mean.

To begin, I'll attempt a nutshell definition. For me genius is some-

TALENT

thing that lies on the other side of talent. In my life I've encountered a good deal of talent but no genius, because it is a rare quality. Talent is largely inborn, and in a given field some people have it to a far higher degree than others. Still, in the end talent is not enough to push you to the highest achievements. Genius has to be founded on major talent, but it adds a freshness and wildness of imagination, a raging ambition, an unusual gift for learning and growing, a depth and breadth of thought and spirit, an ability to make use of not only your strengths but also your weaknesses, an ability to astonish not only your audience but yourself. Those kinds of traits that lie on the other side of talent. The sense of the word *genius* underwent a change between the Classical eighteenth century and the Romantic nineteenth. The age of Haydn and Mozart defined genius as something one *possessed.* The Romantics defined genius as something you innately *were,* which possessed you and made you something on the order of a demigod. My sense of the idea is closer to that of the eighteenth century: I believe in genius, but not in demigods.

By the postmodern end of the twentieth century, the word *genius* had evolved again, the concept becoming a sociopolitical outrage to be pulled from its pedestal and smashed. I am not a postmodernist any more than a modernist or a neoromantic; I am neither conservative nor liberal. I try to look at things with as few preconceptions as possible and see what is actually there (without holding any illusion that this is ultimately achievable). That truth and fact and objectivity are all unreachable is no reason not to struggle toward them — to the death, if necessary.

So when it comes to history and biography, I believe, submission to objective fact is, for all its limitations, what the discipline is about. "Interpretation" comes in second to that, and for me a distant second. A biography is mainly a narrative of a life, not an interpretation of it. Nor do I pick and choose from my subject's life to make a tidy literary form. Our lives are not like a book; real lives drift, and my books drift along with them. Anyway, I usually find facts more interesting than interpretations, also more dramatic and unexpected and funny. I believe that most of the time, interpretation in a biography is best left up to you, dear reader. I supply the material for you to work with.

All my biographies have been written on the basis of that philosophy. I look for fact, however impossible the quest. For me, the idea of spending one's life chasing something impossible is simply normal, necessary, even a touch heroic. It is what artists do all the time. In one of his rare poetic moments in words, Beethoven put it in a nutshell: "The true artist has no pride. He . . . has a vague awareness of how far he is from reaching his goal; and while others may perhaps admire him, he laments the fact that he has not yet reached the point whither his better genius only lights the way for him like a distant sun." To me, art is when you make things up, so I call biography a craft rather than an art. But in both endeavors the impossibilities are alike.

The preceding thoughts are said in relation to my subject's life, not his music. I don't believe any person's life is lived to be "interpreted," by strangers, for money. Every person's life is ultimately a mystery, even to him- or herself. That is the moral source of the humility with which I write biography. But art is created to be enjoyed, to move, to excite, to soothe and provoke, to teach, to be discussed, indeed to be interpreted. While I will submit judgments and interpretations of Beethoven's life only when they seem to me obvious, in the book there will be a good deal of interpretation of the music. Composers hear music one way, performers another way, listeners another, scholars another. I hear mainly as a composer. In the conservatory where I taught, the focus was not on our art as an abstract theoretical study but on *making* music. I have taught musical composition and theory and history in hopes of helping my students become better performers and composers. That is the angle of view in this book: Beethoven as a maker of music.

As a composer, I like to see how a thing was made, and I hope to convey that fascination to my readers. I ask for a bit of patience from nonmusicians for technical moments here and there. I have tried to keep these to a minimum, placing a lot of the technical matters in the endnotes (which are designed to be browsed and are largely directed to musicians and scholars). Beethoven's pieces will be treated as they come up in the course of his story. This is not so much a "life and works" as a "works as part of a life." Still, I will by no means try to cover every piece he wrote but rather the important ones and minor ones of particular interest.

I will be steadily interested in what my subject seems to have intended in his music; at the same time, my analyses are ultimately my own. I know that most of the labor in creating a work of art is unconscious and instinctive. Art is too complex to be done any other way. All the same, though Beethoven's creative trances were deep, I have found him to be an unusually conscious craftsman. By the time sketches for a work were well under way, what we see in the sketchbooks is not as much the *creation* of a work as the *realization* of a fundamental conception that was already in place, with a firm sense of the leading ideas and of what the whole was "about." Beethoven kept at a piece as long as it took, but until the late music he usually composed quite fast. Still, the details were mutable, and he considered everything provisional to the end. A fine conception for a work is not enough; one has to make it happen, note by note. That is an exacting and sometimes excruciating process, and it cannot be done without a steady supply of inspiration.

In Beethoven's day, most music was put together with reference to existing models. The period he grew up in, what we call the Classical era in music, established formal outlines for composition that he largely adhered to — freely and creatively. The book will therefore be much involved with traditional forms such as sonata and sonata-rondo and variations and how he interacted with them. Because this issue is important, the appendix explains those musical models. I suggest reading the appendix before the book proper. Those not interested are welcome to skip it — but the book will make more sense if you read it.

It is clear that Beethoven considered music a language conveying emotion and character, and he expected sensitive listeners to understand it in those terms. His favorite critics of his work were notably flowery and imaginative to our ears. In fact, I find the feelings and "narratives" in his instrumental music more transparent than in, say, Mozart or Brahms.

After the emotional part of music comes the formal, the abstract, the structural scaffolding. In my discussions of Beethoven's music I don't play the influences game as much as many writers do. Saying that this tune echoes Mozart, that keyboard figure Clementi, and so on, may often be true, but that does not tell us much about the work at hand. Each work is conceived as an individual by a composer who was, in his more serious efforts, trying to do something new. For me every one of Beethoven's major works is a boldly painted individual with an unforgettable profile. I'll note influences here and there, but on the whole with each piece I'll mainly be interested in what is special, not what is typical.

Likewise, in much commentary there is a tendency to look at every work in a given form, such as sonata form, as just one more example of that form, perhaps with a few quirks. From a composer's perspective, that is a backward view of the matter. For a composer of Beethoven's era, the *idea* of a work comes first, and then it is mapped into a familiar form that has to be cut and measured to fit the idea. The "quirks" in a given piece are clues to the distinctive nature of that piece. Sometimes for the composer the fundamental idea is such that a new, ad hoc form has to be invented.

Like many musicians I consider our art ultimately an emotional language beyond words — which is to say, a mystery. I hope I have conveyed that too. The success of a given work is ultimately unanalyzable. A clever scaffolding can hold up a dull building just as well as a beautiful one. I'll also admit that the kind of analysis I indulge in, Beethoven himself didn't care for. He considered his workshop a private matter, and I have some appropriate regret at having snooped into it. But I've spent the writing part of my career trying to explain music and musicians to nonmusicians, and that effort continues in this book, whose research and writing consumed some dozen years of my life.

I add that I don't expect anyone to take my interpretations and analyses of the music as any sort of final word. No reader will have precisely the same responses I do. Music is not mathematics. The individuality of responses to music is one of its greatest virtues. While I talk sometimes about Beethoven's creative process — indeed, a central chapter is devoted to the *Eroica* — when I envision him creating, I am not saying *it happened like this* but rather *it happens like this* and *something in this direction seems to have given rise to this idea, this piece.*

I offer my interpretations and analyses of the music as a point of view, and as a gesture in the direction of what I believe Beethoven expected his listeners to do: be sensitive and knowledgeable enough to sense the spirit in which his music was offered, then respond to it creatively, as an individual. I consider it my job here to get as far as I can in understanding what Beethoven had in mind before his work reached the public, to report the response of his audience mainly via contemporary critics, then to add my own responses. What an artist thinks he or she is doing, what the general public thinks they are doing, and what I surmise they are doing are three different things. Biography, I believe, is properly concerned with all three.

My own encounters with Beethoven were early and deep, as with most musicians. He is so ingrained that most of us don't entirely remember how his work and his story reached us. In classical music I was first involved with Brahms and Copland and Handel and Bach, because they are what I first happened to encounter. But I knew Beethoven was supposed to be great, so when one day in my teens I ran across a record of the *Eroica* sitting inexplicably in a rack at Pruitt's Supermarket in Chattanooga, Tennessee, I bought it, took it home, and eagerly listened. It went in one ear and out the other. I kept listening, a couple of dozen times as I remember, until it started to make sense.

Around that time I read Romain Rolland's legendary study, *Beethoven the Creator*. In it, every sketch of the *Eroica* becomes a heroic act. Undoubtedly, that book and its high-Romantic image of Beethoven helped nurture in me a desire to compose. Otherwise it was, in fact, not a useful model. It inflicted on me ambitions beyond my age and skill, a conviction that every idea must be born in suffering and voluminous sketches, and so on. When later I read Stravinsky saying something to the effect that "Every great genius does great harm," I knew what he was talking about. Schubert had been one of the first composers to groan, "Who can do anything after Beethoven?" Thousands have echoed him since. In order to write my own music less encumbered, I had to divest myself of the Romantic myth of Beethoven. Only later did I come to a more thoughtful critique of that myth.

I'll add one more personal detail. The mother of my grandfather Lawrence Swafford came from a western Tennessee family of dirt farmers named Edgemon. Their ancestry is Dutch, and their name is a southernized version of "Egmont." From that, I've long noted with due irony, I possess a family relationship to a play by Goethe and an overture by Beethoven. Given that I set out to be a composer and teacher and nothing else, who knew that someday I would write about both of them in a book.

For my thanks, I'll begin with writers who have inspired me, above all Thayer as amended and expanded by Elliot Forbes (under whose baton I sometimes played trombone at Harvard). I have made ample use of classic studies including the irreplaceable but long out of print *Der Junge Beethoven* by Ludwig Schiedermair, and H. C. Robbins Landon's collection of original sources in *Beethoven*. Recent biographies and studies by William Kinderman, Lewis Lockwood, Barry Cooper, Leon Plantinga, and Maynard Solomon have been valuable as sources of information, correction, and thought. Thanks to Beata Kraus of the Beethovenhaus in Bonn, who directed me to the sixty-volume collection of regional historical studies never mined in English biographies, the *Bonner Geschichtsblätter*. In those studies I found answers to a good many questions about Beethoven's youth and *Bildung*. Belated thanks to the late Dorothy DeLay, celebrated Juilliard violin teacher, who in a long interview gave me her thoughts about and experiences with musical prodigies. That interview has informed all my biographies. The operative line of hers: "They know how to play the piano or the fiddle, but they never learn how to live."

    Thanks to my musicologist readers Teresa Neff and Elizabeth Seitz, who vetted the book and saved me from any number of blunders. The remaining ones are entirely my responsibility. Thanks to Ben Hyman for consistently astute editing. Writer friend Zane Kotker contributed many suggestions, Boston Conservatory colleague Jim Dalton gave me advice on matters of tuning, and my German Ivesian friend Dorothea Gail found me items from the Bonn newspaper of the day. My brother Charles Johnson contributed his verbal expertise. Conductor and Ives editor James Sinclair looked over chapters and cheered me on. Marc Mandel, my editor for Boston Symphony program notes, was encouraging and understanding when he knew that my Beethoven notes were really aimed at this book. Thanks to the people at *Slate* for permission to use bits and pieces of articles I wrote for them. Michael and Patricia Frederick of the Frederick Historic Piano Collection provided invaluable information on and recordings of Michael's exquisitely restored period instruments. My pianist friend Andrew Rangell is an endless source of fascinating and provoking late-night conversations about Beethoven and music in general. My students in Beethoven classes over the years have provided a steady flow of ideas in every direction. I have fine memories of an afternoon with Beethoven editor Jonathan Del Mar, talking shop and looking over his materials.

Finally, I thank and apologize to the authors and friends whose ideas I have made use of without realizing it. What I know about Beethoven goes back some fifty years, research for the book goes back a dozen years, and in some cases I no longer know where an idea came from, whether it is my own or something I encountered a long time ago.

This book is dedicated to the late painter Frances Cohen Gillespie, who inspired me, as she did all her friends, with the passion, commitment, and beauty of her work. Of all the artists I've known personally, Fran most reminds me of Beethoven. During the long labor of this book, I lost more friends and inspirations whom I'd like to remember here: writer Norman Kotker; composer and hiking partner Dana Brayton; teaching colleague and hiking partner Ginny Brereton; physicist and oldest friend Mike Dzvonik; singer, violist, and cousin Cathy Bowers. They are all remembered and mourned by their family and friends, and all of them have echoes in this book.

I'll finish with one more personal detail. Some years ago I ordered a used copy of the rare Schiedermair *Junge Beethoven* and received a nearly century-old book. Only months later did I open to the first page and discover it was once owned by Elliot Forbes. I like to call that a good omen.

Beethoven

1

Bonn, Electorate of Cologne

As he lay dying, he remembered Bonn.

I N THE FREEZING entrance of St. Remigius, the family watches the priest make the sign of the cross on the baby's head and on his breast as he mewls in his grandfather's arms. It is the newborn's name day, when his name is registered in the book of the church and eternally in the book of heaven.

The priest breathes three times on the face of the infant to exorcize the Demon, acknowledging the presence of original sin. After the first exorcism, the blessed salt is placed in the mouth of the child, so he may relish good works and enjoy the food of divine wisdom. Prayers, the second exorcism. "Credo in Deum," the priest chants, "Patrem omnipotentem, Creatorem caeli et terrae." I believe in God, the Father almighty, Creator of heaven and earth.

The family shuffles into the chapel behind the priest. To complete the third exorcism he moistens his right thumb with spittle and, in the form of the cross, touches the right and left ear of the child, proclaiming, "Adaperire." Be opened.

The group arrives at the massive marble christening font. This is not the first Ludwig van Beethoven to be baptized in this family; it is the third. The elder Ludwig van Beethoven stands as godfather to his newborn grandson and namesake. Both grandfather and godfather, the older man is the distinguished figure among them. As godmother stands not old Ludwig's sad wife, the baby's grandmother, but a neighbor's wife. The mother Maria, the father Johann shift on their feet in the cold as the priest drones on, his hands moving over the child, weaving ancient spells.

Inescapably the family feels hope and also fear for this baby. Half or more of one's children will die in infancy. The year before, there had been another baptism, of Ludwig Maria van Beethoven, named both for the patriarch of the family and for the baby's mother and grandmother. That second Ludwig lived six days. When Maria was seventeen, her first child had died before his first birthday, followed a year later by her first husband. Three deaths. Now with hope and fear Maria watches the christening of her third child, the second Ludwig, with her second husband. In two days, Maria van Beethoven will be twenty-four years old.

The first anointing, the profession of faith, the holy water poured three times: "Ludovicus, ego te baptizo in nomine Patris, et Filii, et Spritus Sancti." I baptize thee in the name of the Father, and of the Son, and of the Holy Spirit. The second anointing, the lacy baptismal cap placed on the infant's head. "Go in peace," the priest concludes, "and the Lord be with thee."

The name day of the composer Ludwig van Beethoven is December 17, 1770. The mother is Maria Magdalene van Beethoven, born Keverich, formerly Leym. The father is Johann van Beethoven, thirty, tenor in the court chapel choir under his father, *Kapellmeister* Ludwig van Beethoven. The date of the composer's birth, a day or two before his name day, is lost to a history that will be interested in everything to do with this child. He will grow up nominally Catholic and, in his fashion, close to God, but he will be no lover of priests, ritual, or magic. Near the end, through the words of the liturgy, Beethoven will proclaim his credo in the maker of heaven and earth that, like everything else in his life, is an image of his own imagining.

• • •

The first Ludwig (or Louis, or Lodewyck, or Ludovicus) van Beethoven that history documents, grandfather of the composer, was Flemish, born in the town of Malines, or Mechelen, in the duchy of Brabant. His father Michael van Beethoven began his career as a baker but then developed a prosperous business in luxury goods. Michael and his wife had four sons, of whom Ludwig and brother Cornelius survived. Backward from that point the family history is uncertain.

In Brabant the name Beethoven was common in assorted spellings: Betho, Bethove, Bethof, Bethenhove, Bethoven.[1] Most of those bearing the name were tradesmen, tavern keepers, and the like. The origin of the name is obscure. An area near the town of Tongeren was called Betho, which might account for it. In Flemish, *beet* means "beetroot" and *hof,* "garden," so the name could mean "beet garden," a farmer's name. It could be derived from Flemish words meaning "improved land."[2] The Flemish *van* means "from," implying a place one hails from. So the Flemish *van* nominally means the same as the German *von.* But the German word implies "from the house of" and therefore indicates nobility, which *van* does not. One day that difference in one letter would cause the composer Ludwig van Beethoven a great deal of trouble.

The youth of the elder Ludwig van Beethoven is traced in church records starting in many-steepled Malines, a town celebrated in his time for the blaze of its carillons and the glory of its church music.[3] This Ludwig was baptized at St. Katherine's Church on January 5, 1712. At age five he became a choirboy in the cathedral of St. Rombaut. When Ludwig was thirteen, his father hired the town's leading organist to give the boy keyboard lessons.[4] Ludwig must have demonstrated impressive ability in both music and leadership; at nineteen he became a singer and substitute *Kapellmeister* — music director — at St. Peter's in Louvain. A year later he was listed as a singer at St. Lambert's in Liège, where his admirers may have included Clemens August, Archbishop Elector of Cologne, Lord of the Electoral Residence in Bonn.[5]

In 1733, Elector Clemens August summoned Ludwig van Beethoven to become a singer with his court chapel in Bonn. In September of that year, settling into his new home, the first Ludwig married a young woman from an old Bonn family, Maria Josepha Poll. Then twenty-one, Ludwig would serve the Bonn court under two Electors for the next forty years.

A fine bass singer, able keyboard player, formidable presence in the chapel or on an opera stage, Bonn's first Ludwig van Beethoven became a fixture at the palace, where music had a long history as part of the splendor of the Electoral Court. When Ludwig arrived in Bonn, the town was undergoing a glorious makeover under the reign of his employer, the gracious and sublime Prince-Archbishop Elector of Cologne, Clemens August.

The title Elector meant that the Archbishop of Cologne, residing in Bonn, belonged to the group of traditionally seven princes granted the privilege of voting for the emperor of the Holy Roman Empire, whose throne lay in Vienna. Though the Holy Roman emperor was therefore elected and not hereditary, the throne had been held by Habsburgs in all but a few years since 1438. The polyglot Habsburg Empire included Hungary, lands in Italy, and in the future Belgium and Yugoslavia.

In the eighteenth century there had never been a country of Germany or Austria. Rather there was a mélange of three hundred mostly small German-speaking states ruled by 250 sovereigns. These states contained around twenty million German speakers, some Catholic and some Protestant. The Holy Roman Empire, which geographically had nothing to do with its name, was a regime based in Vienna that mediated among and protected the German states but exercised little control over them. Most of the states ruled themselves and took pride in their own history and heritage, their food and wine and traditional dress. Most minted their own currencies, maintained their own police and armies. Most considered themselves specially smiled upon by God.

For centuries the sovereigns of each German state had possessed the privilege to spend and enjoy, to erect and tear down, to exalt and execute, tax and torture their subjects, as they pleased. The Holy Roman Empire traced its lineage back to Charlemagne in the ninth century; the Electorate of Cologne dated from the thirteenth century. As the prince-bishop of little Speyer instructed his people, "The commanding will of his majesty is none other than the commanding will of God himself." Outside their territories, few of these proud princes ever had any power at all.[6] A progressive spirit emanating from Vienna challenged traditional staples of the social order like torture and feudalism; but no more than anyone challenged the church did anyone question the existence of the thrones or the expenditures of the ruling princes.

All the same, the patchwork of states that constituted Germany under the banner of the Holy Roman Empire never constituted any kind of rational order. The welter of small German states were like bubbles on the surface of history. They existed because they apparently had always existed, so surely they were there by the will of God. Of the German states, sixty-three were ecclesiastical, ruled by an abbot, bishop, or archbishop. These prince-bishops had the same sorts of privileges and powers as secular rulers of the Holy Roman Empire.

The most prominent ecclesiastical states lay on the Rhine, the main trade artery of German lands: the electorates of Mainz, Trier, and Cologne. The latter city had thrown out its archbishop in 1257, to preserve its status as a "free city." The archbishop's successors had since ruled their lands and cities from nearby Bonn, upriver to the south. For centuries the people of sunny and progressive Bonn and those of conservative and priest-ridden Cologne (which gave its name to the Electorate) had despised each other. The atmosphere of old Cologne was captured in a bit of doggerel by an English visitor, Samuel Taylor Coleridge:

> *In Köhln, a town of monks and bones,*
> *And pavements fang'd with murderous stones,*
> *And rags, and hags, and hideous wenches;*
> *I counted two and seventy stenches.*

Because there could be no legitimate heirs to thrones held in the ecclesiastical states by Catholic clerics, the Archbishop Electors, all of noble birth, were placed in power not by vote or by rising through the ranks but through the machinations of powerful families and ministers. Elector Clemens August, the first Ludwig van Beethoven's employer, had from childhood been groomed for power by his family, the Wittelsbachs of Bavaria, who had supplied the previous four Electors of Cologne.

Clemens's forebears were distinguished, and his immediate family remarkable: his mother was the daughter of King Jan Sobieski of Poland, who defeated the Turks at the gates of Vienna in 1683, whom the pope then hailed as "the savior of Western European civilization." Clemens's father was Elector of Bavaria, his uncle Elector of Cologne. He was educated in Rome by Jesuits, learned something of music and astronomy and architecture in addition to his numbers and letters.[7] At age sixteen, he was invested as Bishop of Regensburg, at nineteen Bishop of Münster and Paderborn, at twenty-three Archbishop Elector of Cologne, and so on.[8]

None of this had anything to do with the man's talent, intelligence, or reason. In each of his exalted posts, Clemens August was splendidly brainless and incompetent, not the least interested in governing anything. As Elector in Bonn, his attention would be given largely to pleasure in the forms of ladies, music, dancing, and erecting monuments to his glory and munificence. A 1754 report to the papal nuncio noted that if you wanted to get anywhere with the Bonn court, you had to deal with the ministers. As for the Elector: "In short, prattle and yet more prattle."[9] Clemens did enjoy or at least tolerate the endless round of court and church ceremonies; he played viola da gamba, presided over Mass in his chapel every morning.[10]

History remembers the reign of Clemens August as the most glittering of its time in western Germany, and ranks his orchestra among the finest German princely ensembles. In his court theater Clemens watched Italian operas, French plays, concerts and ballets; he threw epic masked balls during Karneval.[11] If he was not gifted in policy, statesmanship, or brains, Clemens was not idle. He had traveled Europe and had seen Versailles; he imported French art and architects and demanded the same style at home. Most of the buildings worthy of being seen in Bonn for the next two centuries would be his doing. On foundations laid by his predecessor, he finished and grandly decorated the Electoral Residence facing the Rhine; built the multicolored

Rathaus (Town Hall) presiding over the market square; built Michael's (later Koblenz) Gate; enlarged the Poppelsdorf Palace (aka Clemensruhe, "Clemens's Rest") for his summer residence; and built the high-rococo Holy Steps on the Kreuzberg Church, where the pious would *Rococo* ascend on their knees to the top of the stairs, which led nowhere but back down.

The creation closest to Clemens August's heart was his country palace, the Augustusburg, in nearby Brühl, like a miniature Versailles flanked by French gardens, the palace classical and stately outside but writhing with rococo ornament inside. In Brühl an alley of trees led out to Falkenlust, one of Clemens's several grand hunting lodges.

Clemens August was determined to make Bonn glorious. It had long been called beautiful, part of a storied landscape spreading from the banks of the storied Rhine. Travelers arriving on the tree-lined river saw the grand Electoral Residence presiding over spreading French gardens, behind the palace the spires of churches, in the distance a windmill looming over the town. Poppelsdorf Allée, the tree-lined walk from the residence to the summer palace of Poppelsdorf, was declared by a visitor "the most pleasant [walk] in lower Germany. Quiet joy seems to permeate the whole landscape and a sweet pleasure fills the soul."[12]

Bonn's cathedral, the Romanesque five-towered minster, was started in the eleventh century. Within the remains of the old city walls, the lanes where much of the populace lived were close and dirty and unpaved, the paved streets black-surfaced with lava stone. As everywhere in Europe, the streets stank mightily from garbage and sewage tossed from windows. But most of the houses were of brick, roughly plastered and brightly painted, and all were close to attractive squares and gardens and parks.

On the Rhine, the city's lifeblood, flowed a steady traffic of commercial and pleasure boats, under sail or oar or towed from the banks. The banks were covered with vineyards, the high roads in the countryside planted with fruit trees for the refreshment of travelers. Much of the quality of life in Bonn came from its location and its status as an ecclesiastical state. Taxes were moderate, there was little military presence or impressment, the land was fertile, prosperity flowed in from the river.[13] It was a landscape to kindle the imagination, full of beauties a later age would call Romantic. Lying picturesquely across the Rhine was a series of rolling hills, the Siebengebirge.[14] An English visitor described the Siebengebirge as "awful," meaning inspiring awe. Three of the hills were topped by the stark towers of ruined castles, including Drachenfels, where legend said the hero Siegfried slew a dragon and bathed in its blood to become invincible.

The Rhine landscape, full of legends, enchanted a Romantic visitor of the nineteenth century, Victor Hugo:

> An entire population of imaginary creatures in direct communication with beautiful ladies and handsome knights was scattered throughout the Rhine Valley: the oreads, who seized the mountains and forests; the undines, who took possession of the waters; the gnomes, who captured the inside of the earth; the spirit of the rocks; the spirit-rapper; the Black Hunter, who roamed the thickets mounted on a huge stag with sixteen antlers . . . there is nothing in the woods, crags, and vales but apparitions, visions, stupendous combats, diabolical pursuits, infernal castles, sounds of harps in the thickets, melodious songs chanted by invisible singers, hideous laughter emitted by mysterious wayfarers.[15]

In its dream of the triumph of reason and science, the Enlightenment of the eighteenth century failed in its hope of sweeping away old legends and superstitions like these — partly because the next generation, the Romantics, would condemn the reign of reason and embrace the ancient, the wild and mysterious, the mingling of fear and awe they called the sublime.

In 1790, Bonn contained some twelve thousand souls, nine hundred of them registered as master craftsmen.[16] The people had the usual character of Rhinelanders: lighthearted, not overly hardworking, not too impressed by rank, with an appreciation of a good joke and a good comeback. The roads in German lands were terrible and travel on land or water expensive, so most Bonners stayed home in their pleasant backwater, their town largely out of history and out of mind of the rest of the world. With nowhere else to go for amusement, Bonners loved dancing and music; their religious holidays were more worldly than pious. They loved beef and beer and Rhine wine, and their cooking was liberal with vinegar, too sour for the palates of some visitors.[17] On feast days, the gentry and nobility blossomed in multicolored finery, the men in wide-flapped waistcoats enlivened by satins and silks and silver belt buckles and ruffled sleeves, topped by great powdered wigs and cocked hats, with a sword to the side, perhaps a scarlet cloak over the ensemble. The ladies sported long narrow bodices and sweeping robes and long silk gloves, tottered on huge high heels under a cloud of artfully enhanced hair.[18]

Music was everywhere. The French traveler and memoirist Madame de Staël wrote of the Rhineland: "Townspeople and country folk, soldiers and laborers *nearly all know music* . . . I have entered wretched cottages blackened with smoke, and suddenly heard the mistress, and the master of the house too, improvising on the harpsichord . . . On market days players of wind instruments perform on the town hall balcony over the public square."[19] Presiding over the airy market in the middle of town, the Rathaus made a splendid polychrome town hall, topped by the arms of Bonn, below them two lusty fauns flanking the town clock.

In Clemens August's reign as Elector, Bonn was thriving and peaceful. Its only significant business was the court. "All Bonn," the proverb ran, "is fed from the Elector's kitchen." The irrationality of the system was not an issue when you could find work at court in one of the myriad titled positions: a Lackey, a Page, a Window Cleaner, a Fowl Plucker, a Master of the Cellar, an Equerry in the Stables, one of the army of Bakers and Cooks, a Minister, a Musician.[20] Clemens August's theater and opera productions alone cost upwards of 75,000 florins a year. (The average yearly salary of a court musician: less than 250 florins.) Expenditures for theatrical productions were nothing compared to those for furniture, paintings, objets d'art, and above all buildings. All this splendor was financed by insatiable borrowing from France and elsewhere.[21]

While the reign of Clemens August slipped toward catastrophic debt, he maintained a facade of grandeur and prosperity, and for it he was loved by his subjects. That would be in contrast to his successor, whose regime had to clean up the financial mess Clemens left behind.

In 1761, after nearly four decades as Elector, Clemens August died in royal fashion. During a trip to visit relatives in Munich he was stricken with illness on the road, barely making it to his fellow Elector's palace at Ehrenbreitstein. Too sick to eat, Clemens still could not resist attending the evening's ball. Once there, he had to dance eight or nine turns with a charming baroness, and naturally could not deny that pleasure to other ladies. At some point he sank to the floor in a faint, and the next day he gently expired. It would be said of Clemens, he danced out of this world into some other.[22] After sumptuous funeral ceremonies, his estate from jewels to paintings to porcelain to fiddles was auctioned off, the proceeds applied to his debts.[23] Clemens's corporeal remains were graciously divided among his subjects: his body went to the Cologne Cathedral, heart to a church in Altötting, entrails to St. Remigius in Bonn.[24]

Clemens's successor Maximilian Friedrich was not a Bavarian Wittelsbach like the last five Electors but rather came from the old Swabian house of Königsegg-Rothenfels. The man whose gift for backstage machinations put Max Friedrich on the electoral throne became his chief minister and de facto ruler of the Electorate: the wily, brilliant, hated, and feared count Caspar Anton von Belderbusch. Among his accomplishments, Belderbusch was to be the hero and protector of the Beethoven family.

When the new Elector took over in 1761, Belderbusch was quick to impose austerities, because it fell to him to get the state out of debt. In that he succeeded, meanwhile lavishly feathering his own nest. Belderbusch laid the foundation of Bonn's golden age at the end of the century, but he was never able to make the genial and retiring Max

Friedrich as popular as his predecessor. A series of natural disasters did not improve the temper of the town. As the ditty ran:

> *With Clemens August one wore blue and white,*
> *Then one lived as in paradise.*
> *With Max Friedrich one wore black and red,*
> *And suffered hunger and may as well be dead.*

When the new regime trimmed the ranks of court musicians and cut the salaries of the ones remaining, *Kapellmeister* Touchemoulin departed. Court bassist Ludwig van Beethoven saw his opportunity and petitioned the Elector in terms duly outraged yet properly groveling:

> May it please Your Electoral Grace to permit a representation of my faithfully and dutifully performed services for a considerable space as vocalist as well as, since the death of the Kapellmeister, for more than a year his duties in Dupplo, that is to say by singing and wielding the baton . . . Inasmuch as because of particular recommendation Dousmoulin [*sic*] was preferred over me, and indeed unjustly, I have been forced hitherto to submit to fate . . .
>
> There reaches Your Electoral Grace my humble petition that you may graciously be pleased . . . to grant me the justice of which I was deprived on the death of Your Highness's antecessori of blessed memory, and appoint me Kapellmeister . . . For which highest grace I shall pour out my prayers to God for the long continuing health and government of your Electoral Grace, while in deepest submission I throw myself at your feet.[25]

The Elector smiled on the petition. Ludwig served as court *Kapellmeister* for the next dozen years. The music-loving chief minister Belderbusch was a reliable patron of the Beethoven family, who repaid him with loyalty and, it appears, a little spying on their neighbors.

If Ludwig's salary became more pleasant with his new position, his life was not the least pleasant. By the time of his ascension to the post of *Kapellmeister,* Ludwig had a son singing in the chapel choir, but in his house he no longer had a wife. She had been shut away as an alcoholic, out of sight and past hope, and their only child possessed a relentless wanderlust.

From his first years in the Bonn court *Kapelle,* the elder Ludwig van Beethoven was greatly valued and paid accordingly. He entered service at 400 florins a year, a generous salary for a musician.[26] Like other local musicians in a town full of musical amateurs and aspiring professionals, he would have added to his income by giving private lessons. His elevation to *Kapellmeister* in 1761 made him the preeminent musician in Bonn and overseer of the *Kapelle,* the court musical establishment, with a salary of nearly 800 florins.

The duties of a *Kapellmeister* joined leadership to artistry. Ludwig directed the chapel choir, and the chorus and orchestra when they performed together (otherwise the orchestra was directed by the concertmaster, who ranked below the *Kapellmeister*). He did the hiring and firing, oversaw the careers of his musicians, arbitrated disputes. Ordinarily *Kapellmeisters* were also expected to supply new music to the court, in the same way that its bakers supplied bread and its hunters meat. Ludwig was not a composer, but he remained the leading bass soloist in the *Kapelle,* performing in everything from cantatas and oratorios to leading roles in operas.[27]

From his parents, who had traded in fine goods, the elder Ludwig seems to have inherited an interest in business as well. He leased two apartments and rented out one of them. More profitably, he started a trade buying local Rhine wine and shipping it in bulk back to his native Brabant; in town, he rented two cellars from which he sold wine by the barrel. In a census of the 1760s, Ludwig is listed not as a musician but as a wine dealer.[28] Later he added a sideline lending money to local citizens.[29]

For many years off and on, two generations of Beethovens lived in rented rooms on the second floor of a Rheingasse house called Zum Walfisch (the Whale), owned by baker Johann Fischer and then by his son Theodor, who marked the fourth generation to sell baked goods from the ground floor of the house.[30] (Theodor's son Gottfried, who wrote memoirs of the Beethoven family, marked the fifth generation of bakers.) The Beethoven flat in the Fischer house was a spacious suite of six rooms.[31] The Fischer children remembered it as a vision of prosperity, filled with Flemish luxuries inherited from Ludwig's family: elegant furniture, paintings on the walls, a cupboard sparkling with silver and porcelain and glass, on the table fine linen drawn through polished silver rings.[32]

Ludwig and his wife, Maria Josepha, had three children, of whom only the last survived: Johann, born around 1740. Like most Bonn children, he was taken out of school early and reared for the family trade, his father teaching him keyboard and singing. To be the child of a craftsman, cook, musician, or the like could virtually guarantee a position at court; the same family names turned up through generations in the same jobs.

Court records from 1752 show Johann van Beethoven entering the choir as a boy soprano; as his voice changed, he dropped to alto and finally to tenor. At first he was unpaid, which was usual with children and teenagers in the *Kapelle;* if a child proved capable and dutiful, he or she would eventually claim a salary. At the beginning of 1764, when Johann was about twenty-four and had sung in the choir some dozen years, he petitioned for a salary and his father followed with a request that he get 200 florins. Johann was granted 150.[33] In those days children of the working classes were reared to contribute to the family labors and income, so Johann would also have worked in his father's wine business. And if music was the Beethoven family's route to respect and prosperity, wine was their undoing.

All the Beethovens had a thirst. While old Ludwig was a connoisseur of wine, his wife and son took more interest as consumers. Memoirist Gottfried Fischer recalled that Johann "early got expert in wine-tasting, and became a good wine drinker."[34] Bonn would know Johann as a tippler the whole of his life, though alcohol fully claimed him only in his last years. His mother, Maria Josepha, was not so lucky.

Particular stories of the disintegration of the Beethoven family have not come down, but they would have been much the same as in any family. Old Ludwig was not the sort to keep his feelings quiet. In childhood Johann had to watch his parents play out scenes violent and pathetic, had to hear screams and accusations, watch repentances and relapses, his mother sodden with drink. That part of their life ended when Maria Josepha was taken to Cologne and shut away in a cloister. What kind of life she led in that limbo can hardly be imagined. It lasted until she died, still sequestered, some twenty years later.[35]

Theodor Fischer's daughter Cäcilie remembered *Kapellmeister* Ludwig van Beethoven as "a very respectable man in his dealings, a good-hearted man."[36] Another family friend recalled him as a "bull of vitality, a picture of strength."[37] Others see an echt-Flemish personality: independent, concrete and forceful, hardheaded and sometimes uncouth, aggressive and violent in temper. That description would also apply to his son Johann and to his grandson Ludwig.[38]

It is said that often in a family, talent skips a generation. Old Ludwig trained Johann to be a competent musician within the range of his limited gift and mediocre voice. Otherwise, he appeared to have viewed his only surviving child with something near contempt. When his father was away it was Johann's habit to bolt the house and roam around nearby towns, carousing with friends. Once, the Fischers heard Ludwig declaiming a nasty little set piece to his son: "There are altogether three Johnnys in one, like a cloverleaf. The apprentice is Johnny the glutton [*Johannes der Fräßer*], that you see eating all the time. And the journeyman in the house is Johnny the loudmouth [*Johannes der Schwätzer*]." Here, he pointed to his son: "And then there's Johnny the runner [*Johannes der Läufer*]. You keep running, keep running; someday you'll run to your grave."[39] *Johannes der Läufer* is a bitter pun on *Johannes der Täufer*, John the Baptist.

If there was never a complete break between father and son, there seems to have been little peace either. The closest to a break came when Johnny the runner's rebelliousness and wanderlust climaxed with marriage.

During one of his jaunts in neighboring towns, Johann met Maria Magdalena Leym, born Keverich, in Ehrenbreitstein. She was from a prominent family; her father had been overseer of the kitchen for the Elector of Trier, an important position among court servants. Her ancestors included councillors and senators. At sixteen, Maria made a fortunate marriage to Johann Georg Leym, a valet of the Elector. By eighteen she was widowed, their only child dead. When Johann van Beethoven began courting her, some two years later, Maria was living in an inn with her mother.[40]

Johann was in his mid-twenties then and had been prospecting for a wife. He and baker Theodor Fischer, friendly competitors in all things, had vowed to "set sail on the sea of love" and see who reached port first.[41] Johann was a passably handsome man, with strong features and broad shoulders, sociable and full of *Lebenslust* in the way of Rhinelanders, and he sported a repertoire of songs he sang and played on keyboard and fiddle and zither. Maria was slender, blond, and pretty, though her face was serious and over the years only became more so. However and whyever, Maria accepted Johann's hand. Then he informed his father.

Somehow Ludwig had the impression that the woman his son wanted to marry was a chambermaid, though she was not. Ludwig was outraged, not interested in explanations. He was heard shouting at Johann, "I would never have thought that of you, never expected you would stoop so low!"[42] He did not forbid the marriage but refused to attend the wedding unless it was kept short and held in Bonn. Maria would not forget that she was cheated of the fine wedding in Ehrenbreitstein that her mother would have given her.[43] Eventually it became Maria's stated opinion that from the wedding day forward, married life was a downhill course.

After a honeymoon in Ehrenbreitstein, Johann and Maria moved to a garden house behind 515 Bonngasse, a street full of court musicians. Neither humble nor elegant, spacious nor cramped, the house was a squat three floors, the windows flanked by shutters, the stucco probably painted yellow.

The first two of their children were born in the Bonngasse house: the Ludwig who died and the Ludwig who lived, the latter born December 16 or 17, 1770, in a top-floor garret barely high enough to stand up in. In England that year, steam power began to create an industrial revolution; across the ocean, the Boston Massacre helped trigger a political revolution; in France, the dauphin married Marie Antoinette, daughter of the Holy Roman emperor; in Königsberg, Immanuel Kant became a professor. Though the Beethoven family did not yet figure in history and lived in the garden house on Bonngasse only a few years, that ordinary dwelling would in due course become a shrine, the composer born there the main reason most of the world would ever think of Bonn at all.

While Maria was pregnant with her second Ludwig, Johann suddenly declared to his employers that he had received an offer to work in the cathedral of Liège, where his father had once sung. Johann produced a letter from the cathedral making the offer; the salary offered was considerably better than Johann was making in Bonn.[44] In light of his later history, the letter and the offer were probably bogus. It was a characteristic ruse of Johann to extract a raise from the court, and it didn't work—also characteristic. If Johann did forge the document, it would not be his last time.

The period after Ludwig the younger was born was a time of relative peace and prosperity in the family. There is little doubt that old Ludwig doted on his grandson and namesake: his wife was a phantom, his son a disappointment. The Fischers remembered the grandfather, for all his strength and willfulness, as jolly with children, bouncing their daughter Cäcilie on his knee and pulling faces to scare her.[45] The toddler Ludwig lost his grandfather early but never forgot him as a wellspring of love and kindness, his features a model for his own face, his career and character likewise a model for his own. But the later Ludwig van Beethoven's tangible connection to his grandfather would be in the form of a singular painting.

In 1773, worn down and no longer able to sing, old Ludwig commissioned a portrait of himself. The artist was Amelius Radoux, a fellow Fleming employed by the court as a sculptor and wood-carver.[46] Though this was to be his only known painting, Radoux did a handsome job. The finished piece was a collaboration between artist and subject.

In his portrait as he was in life, *Kapellmeister* Ludwig van Beethoven is a commanding figure. The canvas depicts him as strong-featured, high-browed, fleshy, and ruddy. He wears a fur cap and an elegant tasseled jacket. His piercing eyes fix the viewer. It is the picture of an imperious and prosperous professional, a leader.

It is also a portrait of anguish and endurance. This was the statement *Kapellmeister* van Beethoven, feeling himself near the end, wanted to leave posterity about his life. Every element of the picture forms a symbolic narrative. On the table to the viewer's left lies a decorated strip of fabric; it is the traditional "husband's band" that a bride-to-be made for her fiancé. Looking up from the embroidered band, the viewer finds a dark cape falling from Ludwig's shoulders, the clothing of a man in mourning. Its fall evokes his escape from the darkness that had enveloped him.

With a decisive gesture Ludwig's arm emerges from the cape; the forefinger of his right hand points to the left hand, which is turning the pages of a musical score. Here is the heart of the painting's message. It says, This engagement with my art is what brought me out of darkness; this is what saved me from the tragedy of my marriage. The notes on the pages of music amplify the message. The score is part of an aria from Giovanni Pergolesi's famous opera *La serva padrona,* which had been performed at the court theater, likely with Ludwig singing the principal role of Umberto. The snippet of text from the aria is "If love . . . If love . . ." In the story at that moment, the singer is trying to decide what to do about a woman who is driving him to distraction.[47]

Ludwig van Beethoven's grandson kept that painting near him to the end of his life, telling friends stories about his grandfather, proudly pointing out their resemblance in the shape of their faces, their animated eyes. The painted image of his grandfather was a talisman of his heritage as a musician. There is no indication that Ludwig the younger understood the story secreted in the painting, so much like the covert and sometimes tragic stories adumbrated in his own music. In telling friends stories about his grandfather, Beethoven perhaps did not point out that his hero and model, the man he honored in place of his father, died when his grandson was barely three years old. The painting was their main connection.

It was less the memory of his actual grandfather that Beethoven treasured, more the idea and ideal of his grandfather represented by

art. As man and artist, the younger Ludwig van Beethoven was someone for whom ideas, ideals, and art outshone people in the flesh. And,
like his grandfather, the composer Ludwig van Beethoven saw music
as his salvation.

The day before Christmas 1773, after suffering a stroke, *Kapellmeister*
Ludwig van Beethoven died. Despite his objections to Johann's marriage, he had been generous to the couple; he left them a substantial
inheritance in money and finery, much of the latter brought years before from his Flemish homeland. Meanwhile, when Ludwig died, a
number of people owed him money. He had been making unsecured
loans and selling wine on credit.[48] With the family patriarch and benefactor gone, Johann bestirred himself to improve his situation. He petitioned the court for a raise, "since the death of my father has left me
in needy circumstances my salary not sufficing."[49] Perhaps he was not
as needy as all that. He went after his father's debtors and collected
from them. One debt amounted to some 1,000 florins, a sum a frugal
family could live on for three years.[50] The Beethovens, however, did
not prove frugal.

If Johann van Beethoven did not inherit a full measure of his father's musicality or intelligence, he still had some of Ludwig's energy
and ambition. In practice, that meant Johann was a perennial schemer
and opportunist, if usually an unsuccessful one. (The court again
turned down his petition for a raise.) There were successes sometimes,
in a manner of speaking. When he married Maria, Johann acquired
from her mother 450 florins. This money was sometimes described
as a dowry, but more likely it constituted his mother-in-law's savings,
and Johann pinched it.[51] (A petition to the Court of Trier declared that
the mother was impoverished because of her daughter's "ill-advised
marriage.")[52] After her daughter left home, the mother's mind seems
to have faltered; she was reported standing in front of a church in Ehrenbreitstein through wind and rain and winter nights.[53] She died in
miserable circumstances in 1768.

When old Ludwig died prosperously, besides chasing down his father's debtors, Johann looked out for himself in other ways. Ludwig

had been close to the power behind the throne at the Bonn court, music-loving chief minister Caspar Anton von Belderbusch, and Johann cultivated that important connection.

After his father died, Johann aspired to succeed him as *Kapellmeister*. His salary at that point was hardly enough to sustain his family, and Maria was pregnant again. As importantly, Johann imagined himself becoming the leading musician at court, which would make him the most prominent musician in Bonn. To that end, he primed Belderbusch with valuables from old Ludwig's estate, mostly Flemish antiques: a standing clock; fine glassware and porcelain; an illuminated Bible; and paintings, including a descent from the cross — all valued at some 650 florins, two years' living for a musician.[54]

For weeks officials of the court put off Johann's petition to replace his father as *Kapellmeister*. He took the delay as promise of a favorable outcome, but that was a forlorn fantasy. By then, Johann was a familiar part of the musical life of the town, a tenor competent to handle minor roles in opera, a respected teacher, a convivial fellow who had befriended important people both musical and otherwise. But in temperament, talent, and intelligence Johann van Beethoven was not the least prepared to run a musical establishment, a fact probably obvious to everyone but him.

In May 1774, it was announced that the new *Kapellmeister* would be Andrea Luchesi, a conductor and well-known opera composer, who brought some luster of fame and a welcome Italian influence to the court. The *Kapelle* then was a choir of nine and an orchestra of fourteen, plus an organist and the trumpeters and drummers required for festive occasions. Court musical forces grew steadily from that point. They were kept busy providing music in church, concert room, and theater for daily masses, balls, theatrical productions, concerts, and the yearly calendar of twenty high holidays.[55]

Possibly Johann van Beethoven understood that when his father died and he was brushed aside as *Kapellmeister*, he lost his best chance to become an important man in town, with a comfortable income. He was destined for the life of an ordinary music teacher and member of the choir. But Johann did not give up. He remained a loyal protégé of Belderbusch (who did not deign to return the articles constituting the attempted bribe). Johann did not treat new *Kapellmeister* Luchesi as a rival but instead befriended him. As for his further ambitions in court and in the world, Johann turned, with a vengeance, to his little son Ludwig.

2

Father, Mother, Son

OST OF THE time the extraordinary begins in the ordinary. The son reared in the family business. The father who has extravagant dreams for his child. The father who is mediocre in his trade and discovers his son is talented, so drives him all the harder. The father who expects his son to realize his own frustrated dreams. The father who drinks and lashes out. The son who is helpless to resist. The father who does not know how to express love. The mother who watches and tries to soften the blows. The wife who makes her accommodations with the wrong husband and preserves herself and her children as best she can. The wife and mother who wishes none of it had happened. All these are old, ordinary stories.

When a child is reared in a supremely difficult discipline such as music, the great plan, the impetus, usually comes from a parent.[1] The child will do this and that, will do it when he is told, and will excel — or else. There is only the question of method. Johann van Beethoven knew one way to keep his son in line, and that was with shouts, threats, beatings, locking the little scamp in the basement. Perhaps his own father had trained the young Johann in music with the same hardness. In any case, Johann had the impatience and the explosive temper of his father, as would his son. The Fischer children remembered a small boy standing on a low bench to reach the keyboard, crying as he played while his father loomed over him.[2]

Johann began teaching his son, beating music into him, when Ludwig was four or five. First, history says, the boy was taught "clavier." Given that this word encompasses any kind of keyboard instrument, which one is meant is not certain. The pianoforte was still expensive and relatively undeveloped when Ludwig was a child, though soon it would push the old harpsichord into obsolescence. But Bonn was still a backwater, not a center of piano development like Vienna, so Ludwig learned his notes on harpsichord or clavichord.

In those days children often started on the smaller and quieter clavichord, which had a particular advantage: whereas the mechanism of the harpsichord plucked the strings always at the same volume, each key of the clavichord was joined to a small metal hammer that struck the string, so subtleties of touch and volume were available on the clavichord that were not possible on the larger instrument. If Ludwig started on clavichord, he was already learning nuances of touch that would translate to the pianofortes of that time, which were no larger than a harpsichord and had a far more delicate touch than the instruments of a century later.

Clearly Johann's idea was to rear Ludwig as a court musician so he would be employable as soon as possible and earn his keep. Johann had been reared to that same end by his father. As it had been with Johann, musical teenagers from the families of court musicians might have to work for years before being paid—but if Ludwig could become a clavier soloist by his teens, he might command a salary right away.[3] When the boy had learned his notes at the clavier, Johann began to teach him violin and viola so he could play in the court orchestra. Eventually, most likely, the goal was that Ludwig would become *Kapellmeister*, like his grandfather—the post his father had failed to achieve.

Early on, the boy wanted to make up his own music. Once when his father caught Ludwig improvising on violin, he was heard to shout, "What stupid stuff are you scratching at now? You know I can't stand that. Scratch on the notes or you'll never get anywhere!" But the boy kept at it; again Johann caught him playing his own tunes. "Haven't you heard what I said?" he demanded.

On his fiddle the boy played a phrase he had invented and asked, "But isn't this beautiful?"

"That's another matter entirely," Johann said. "This is just something you made up yourself. You're not to do that. Keep at your clavier and violin and play the notes correctly, that's what will get you somewhere. When you've learned enough then you can and you will play from your head. But don't try it now. You're not ready for it."[4] Inevitably the boy continued making up music, but now in secret, as something private and forbidden.[5]

As a musician, at least, Johann was no fool. Before long he would have realized that this son was remarkably gifted. At that point it appears his plans broadened toward a splendid new horizon. He began to imagine that Ludwig might be in the same category as the most famous musical phenomenon of the age, a child of freakish talent named Mozart.

More benignly, there were memories of Ludwig sitting on his father's lap at parties, and accompanying while Johann sang. A lot of people liked Johann van Beethoven, or at least enjoyed his and the family's hospitality. Musicians and court figures were in the house constantly. From the cradle, Ludwig heard music all the time, from the songs and keyboard and chamber works of famous masters to folk music and dances and hunting songs and wedding songs.[6] Holidays were celebrated with food, drink, and lots of music.

Every year saw a family festival on Maria van Beethoven's name day. On that day, at least, she was coddled and adored. Court musicians showed up with music stands from the *Kapelle,* and chairs were lined up along the walls in one of the large street rooms of the Beethoven flat. The men set up a canopy decked with laurel branches and flowers and foliage; inside the canopy they hung the portrait of the patriarch, old Ludwig. Maria was ushered in, and the celebration began with a burst of music. Then came more than enough food and wine, and dancing late into the night in stocking feet so as not to wake the neighbors.[7]

At Christmas, Johann ordered a pig slaughtered and had a court butcher make holiday wurst. The court musicians served at midnight Mass in the chapel, the Archbishop Elector presiding, the bodyguards and the regiment appearing in full dress, the choir hoping to shine on the most joyous of holidays. After the services ended with volleys of muskets and cannons, Johann and his friends tramped home in the cold and sat down to wine, punch, coffee, a table heaped with food, and singing and playing.[8] One thing seems to have been appreciated about Johann and Maria van Beethoven: they knew how to throw a party.

Johann's schemes and machinations, of course, had to do with money. To support a family, his pay as a minor member of the court *Kapelle* was modest (by then about 315 florins),[9] and while he busied himself teaching private students, there was not much profit in it. Meanwhile, by the time Ludwig was six there were five mouths in the family to feed.

Ludwig's brother Caspar Anton Carl had been christened on April 8, 1774, Nikolaus Johann on October 2, 1776. Caspar was named for Chief Minister Caspar Anton von Belderbusch, who agreed to serve as godfather for his namesake. As godmother stood the chief minister's mistress, Caroline von Satzenhoven, abbess of a home for elderly gentlewomen in Vilich. (The abbess also generously served as mistress of Maximilian Friedrich, the current Elector). To the actual christening of Caspar Anton Carl van Beethoven the distinguished godparents naturally sent deputies of lower rank.[10]

As Ludwig van Beethoven of five and six years old occupied his time with clavier and violin and viola practice and started school, outside there were signs of change everywhere. The indolent and pleasure-loving new Elector, Max Friedrich, nevertheless abstained from the kind of extravagance for which his predecessor Clemens August was famous. There were no more grand new building projects in Bonn; the books were heading toward balance.

The governing style of Max Friedrich and Belderbusch was at least partly philosophical. For centuries, the lives of all people under feudalism had existed to serve the prosperity and pleasure of their superiors, that obligation starting from the serf's toward the lord of the manor, the lord's toward his count or duke, and so on in a ladder of fealty rising through the ranks to the divinely ordained throne, which answered to no one but God. In the middle of the eighteenth century, the first of the German "enlightened despots," Frederick the Great of Prussia, began to mediate those centuries of privilege, changing the ancient paradigm of the state as essentially the vassal of the sovereign. Frederick denied that he ruled by divine right and called himself "the first servant of the state." A rationalistic and humanistic spirit was gathering across Europe and across the Atlantic. Enlightenment — in German, Aufklärung — was the name for the spirit of the times.

In the Electorate of Cologne, the reign of Max Friedrich by way of Belderbusch amounted to a transition from the old model of absolute power to the progressive model of an enlightened ruler, a process the next Elector would complete.[11] An English traveler of 1780 described the government of Bonn as "the most active and most enlightened of all the ecclesiastical governments of Germany. The ministry of the court in Bonn is excellently composed . . . The cabinet . . . is singularly happy in the establishment of seminaries of education, the improvement of agriculture and industry, and the extirpation of every species of monkery."[12]

In 1773, the pope dissolved the Jesuits, ending their traditional monopoly on education, after several countries had already banned them. The dissolution of the order was seen as a triumph of the Enlightenment. (Like many other triumphs of Enlightenment, it was short-lived, and the Jesuits eventually revived.)[13] Chief Minister Belderbusch oversaw turning the Jesuit school in Bonn into a new state school, the Academy, and the regime began to enact reforms — part of the movement around Germany to restrain the power of the clergy and to put education in secular hands.

Outside backwater Bonn, after centuries of slumber in literature and thought, by the 1770s Germany was awakening in a precipitous flowering of drama, fiction, and philosophy. Francophile Frederick the Great wrote in 1780, "The Germans up to now know nothing except to eat, drink, make love, and fight . . . We have no good writers whatever: perhaps they will arise when I am walking in the Elysian Fields."[14]

1770

But Frederick did not have to die for German literature to flourish. In the 1770s, the language's first important playwright, Gottfried Ephraim Lessing, was in his prime, his plays including *Nathan der Weise,* which preached tolerance toward Jews. The fame of young poet, novelist, and playwright Johann Wolfgang von Goethe was rising toward the point that an entire period in Germany would be remembered as the Goethezeit, the age of Goethe. In spring 1775, Bonn's newspaper, the *Intelligenzblatt,* published a review of "Herr Goethe's newest tragedy *Clavigo* . . . One will know from the earlier plays of this author that . . . his pieces will transgress against once-accepted rules in almost every respect, but the reader will be compensated by many inimitable beauties." The paper tracked the course of the American Revolution, the first political fruit of the Enlightenment.

At the same time, every age contains the seeds of its own destruction. If the Enlightenment and its cult of science and reason was the triumphant ideology of the eighteenth century, in Germany of the 1770s a literary countercurrent flowered that exalted the violent, excessive, and subjective. In 1774, Goethe published his epochal novel *The Sorrows of Young Werther,* whose hero kills himself over a frustrated love. The work that gave the anti-Enlightenment movement its name came from a Friedrich Maximilian Klinger play about the American Revolution: *Sturm und Drang* (Storm and Stress).

It was a movement of angry young men, determined to follow not chilly reason but their inner convictions, their personal storms and stresses. They idealized lonely and even violent outsiders.[15] Perhaps the climax of Sturm und Drang came with the 1782 premiere of Friedrich Schiller's play *Die Räuber* (The Robbers). Its hero is a son who is cheated of his inheritance and, in a transport of fury both moral and nihilistic, determines to become a king of robbers. In the premiere, after the horrifying denouement, an eyewitness recalled, "The theater was like a madhouse — rolling eyes, clenched fists, hoarse cries in the auditorium. Strangers fell sobbing into each other's arms, women on the point of fainting staggered towards the exit."[16]

The spirit of Sturm und Drang was too frenzied and irrational to last long. It flared and dimmed in little more than a decade. Its traces turned up for a few years in Haydn's music, among that of other com-

*Romantic
? ? ?*

posers. Goethe and Schiller both washed their hands of Sturm und Drang, and it never really challenged the Aufklärung. But its echoes helped create the period that came to be called Romantic, which loved the demonic and excessive, and which would endure. That was the atmosphere in which the grown Ludwig van Beethoven created, following his own singular star.

One episode of storm and stress the six-year-old Beethoven witnessed was not a literary but a literal firestorm. During the night of January 15, 1777, the Electoral Residence, the Elector's palace, lit up in flames. Fueled by heavy winds, the conflagration raced to the powder magazine, which exploded thunderously.[17] The town fire drum began to beat. It beat continuously for two days as fire consumed most of the palace, whose massive, stately front commanded the southern border of the city.[18]

In their flat next to the palace, the Beethovens heard the cries, the drums, the explosion. Like most of the town, they came out to watch the spectacle: amid roaring flames, frantic figures ran with water while others dashed in and out of the building attempting to save papers and valuables. The injured and dead were laid out in the courtyard. Dozens of court servants and officials risked their lives to pull art, furniture, clocks, and vases from the building.[19] Among the spectators, court musician Candidus Passavanti was heard to cry, "Oh, my poor contrabass, that I brought with me from Venice!"[20]

Hofrat Emanuel Joseph von Breuning collected eleven men and with *Breunings* them was hauling state documents out of the burning palace when a wall collapsed on them. All but Breuning died on the spot. Terribly injured, Breuning was brought to his house, where the next day, at age thirty-seven, he slipped away in the circle of his family, leaving his wife, Helene, twenty-seven, and four small children. The Breunings had been one of the most literary and cultured families in Bonn. Under the widow they continued to be so, and a number of townspeople, including Beethoven, were the better for it.

The ruins of the Electoral Residence were still smoldering five days later. By then, the town rumor mill had flared up, its theme apparently that the fire was welcomed by, perhaps even started by, the all-powerful Belderbusch to obliterate the evidence of his embezzlements and intrigues, and that the valuables salvaged from the residence ended up gracing the palace of Belderbusch in town. Elector Max Friedrich decreed the rebuilding of the residence, but on a more modest scale, with less lavish gardens.

In the three years since old Ludwig van Beethoven died, the family had changed its lodgings three times. With inheritance in hand, Johann had moved the family out of the modest house on Bonngasse, where young Ludwig was born, to a spacious flat on Dreieckplatz. From there, they had returned to baker Theodor Fischer's house on Rheingasse, where Johann had lived with his father. Then, shortly before the fire, Maria had insisted that they move to a smaller flat on Neugasse, because it was close to the market and church and Electoral Residence.

When the residence caught fire, Johann appeared at the door of the Fischer house in tears, begging to come back because the Beethovens' flat was threatened by the conflagration. On Fischer's agreement, Johann rounded up men to spirit the family belongings out of Neugasse and back to Rheingasse while the flames raged behind them. For the Beethoven children, the spectacle of those days must have been thrilling. Gottfried Fischer recalled the boys declaring it was good to come back to Rheingasse, because there was plenty of water in the river to put out a fire.[21]

Ludwig van Beethoven spent most of his childhood in the tall, narrow Fischer house, Zum Walfisch. There his father supervised his lessons, his mother did her sewing and her other daily chores, the maids cooked and washed and watched the children. In the small area of the inner city, Johann van Beethoven's face was familiar, seen on the go every day: his broad forehead, scarred but not unpleasant face, round nose, hair gathered into a thin pigtail, serious eyes, and air of being perennially late for something.[22] Although the family was not prosperous, they generally got by in the flat at the Fischers', their flat spacious with two rooms on the street, four in the back, plus a kitchen and servant's room. It seems that Johann kept up with his bills. Old Ludwig's inheritance may have leaked away, but there is no record that in those years the family fell into serious debt.[23]

The bustling street that the Fischer house fronted on, Rheingasse, was the town's main commercial avenue from the river. Goods came in at the Rhine Gate and were hauled to the market in the middle of town, where at the Rathaus they were weighed, taxed, and offered for sale in the square. The inside of the Beethoven house bustled with music and family, the outside bustled with wagons and horses and men. Maria van Beethoven and Frau Fischer, Theodor's wife, consulted on matters of child rearing. Frau Fischer provided a remedy for Ludwig's bed-wetting and advised about treating an abscess on Nikolaus's head (he grew up crooked in face and frame). The Beethoven and Fischer children played piggyback in the courtyard, alternated on the swing. (Theodor Fischer and his wife had nine children, of whom five died early — a normal percentage.)

With Johann usually out of the house and Maria busy, their three boys were often left to the care of servants. It was Frau Fischer who alerted Maria that the maids carelessly let the boys play in the street, where the commercial traffic from the Rhine flowed past. Maria, like the rest of the family, had a temper, and sometimes she flared at suggestions about, for example, how she should rear her children. Usually, soon after a ruckus Johann and Maria would turn up together to apologize to the Fischers.[24]

Most days, Johann ran from appointment to appointment, sang tenor in the court choir, taught voice and clavier to Bonn children and the children of English and French and German envoys.[25] On days when he had to sing at court, he sucked a raw egg or ate prunes for his throat.[26] As a musician and teacher, despite his well-known propensity for carousing, Johann in those years was, on the whole, hardworking and respected. Still, his modest talent and the mediocrity of his voice meant that his career would go only so far.

Johann did a great deal more for his son than drumming keyboard and violin into him. He became a canny promoter of Ludwig's embryonic career as a soloist. From early on, Johann had the boy playing at court, and he made it his business to see that everyone musical in Bonn knew about his child. In 1778, Johann made a bid to establish Ludwig as a marketable prodigy.

His inspiration was Wolfgang Amadeus Mozart, the prodigy of prodigies. Wolfgang and his sister had been trained from early childhood by their violinist father, Leopold. The boy composed his first pieces at five, and by age six, with his father and nearly equally talented sister, he toured Europe giving performances that quickly slipped into legend: improvising on given themes, playing blindfolded and with a cloth over the keys. The Mozart family had appeared in Bonn in 1763, and it is unlikely that Johann and his father missed the show.[27] In 1770, the year Ludwig was born, Mozart, at age fourteen, was in the middle of another tour of the musical capitals of Europe.

If Johann had a conception of what he was doing with his son, it was surely that he imagined himself to be another Leopold Mozart, who reared a phenomenon and made sure the world heard about it. Johann was determined to do whatever was necessary to foster the gift he saw in his son and cash in on it. With visions of glory dancing in his mind, Johann rented a hall in Cologne to present one of his pupils, the teenage contralto Helene Averdonk, and Ludwig. The newspaper notice ran thus:

> Today, March 26, 1778, in the musical concert-room in the Sternengass the Electoral Court Tenorist, BEETHOVEN, will have the honor to produce two of his scholars; namely, Mdlle. Averdonc, Court Contraltist, and his little son of six years. The former will have the honor to contribute various beautiful arias, the latter various clavier concertos and trios, in which he flatters himself that he will give complete enjoyment to all ladies and gentlemen, the more so since both have had the honor of playing to the greatest delight of the entire Court.[28]

At that point, Ludwig was seven. Johann advertised him as a year younger to enhance the aura of prodigy — and maybe to remind readers of Mozart, who was six when he came to fame.[29] Ludwig, a little figure sitting confidently at the keyboard, likely looked the age he was advertised to be. No report survives of whether Ludwig played harp-

sichord or pianoforte at the concert, or how the performance was received. The overall results can be seen in the absence of any report.
The boy was wonderfully talented, a budding prodigy of Mozartian
dimensions, but his father was no Leopold Mozart.

Johann's premature bid for fame and money for his son having come
to nothing, he turned to less dramatic endeavors to promote Ludwig's
career. He had him perform in the house, in court, and in the great
houses of the town, and showed him off on jaunts around the region.

Johann knew that eventually his son needed more sophisticated
keyboard and violin teachers than his father. In the next years under
those teachers, Ludwig would ascend extraordinarily in skill and in
reputation, and in the process he would make his escape from his father's ambitions into his own. Then, unlike Mozart, who remained
loyal and more or less compliant to his father, Ludwig would feel scant
loyalty or love toward his first mentor and teacher. From others, the
grown-up Beethoven did not countenance criticism of his father or
any of his family; others had no right to that. He did his duty as oldest son, whatever it cost him; to Beethoven, family was family. But he
had been reared harshly by a father whose own father had more or
less done the same, and his resentments were inevitable. Beethoven's
relation to his brothers conformed to the pattern he had learned: fierce
loyalty, blind rage, and the occasional motivation of a fist.

Around 1778, Johann van Beethoven began to mine his musical acquaintances as teachers for his son. The first appears to have been ancient Gilles van den Eeden, a Fleming born in Liège. At that point, van
den Eeden had been a court organist for some fifty-five years and had
been acquainted with the Beethoven family at least since he witnessed
old Ludwig's wedding, in 1733. For a short while, van den Eeden gave
young Ludwig keyboard lessons.[30]

From early on, Ludwig was a pianist rather than a harpsichordist,
becoming one of the first generation to grow up as pure pianists from
close to the beginning of their studies. Van den Eeden may also have
taught the boy his first lessons in thoroughbass, giving him a foundation in harmonic practice by way of learning to read the numerical figures that indicate the chords to be played above a bass line.[31] Most solo

BASSO CONTINUO

works of that time consisted simply of a melody and figured bass, the keyboardist improvising an accompaniment from the given harmonies. Learning the art of harmony via thoroughbass was a foundation of both composition and improvisation.

Among Johann's circle of friends was actor and theater manager Gustav F. W. Grossmann, who came to Bonn in 1778 to run the court's new National Theater. Grossmann was a sophisticated artist and man, and he was fond of or at least amused by Johann van Beethoven. The two became friends. As a teacher for Ludwig to replace the aged and ailing van den Eeden, Grossmann recommended a broadly talented, also splendidly eccentric young newcomer named Tobias Friedrich Pfeifer. He was something of an unclassifiable man. As part of Grossmann's theatrical company, Pfeifer served in the capacities of actor, pianist, oboist, and flutist (appropriately, his name means "piper"). He took up residence in the Beethovens' flat at the Fischer house and started teaching Ludwig clavier, meanwhile carousing with Johann. The two endeavors mingled in ways that created new miseries for the boy, but Ludwig seems to have made considerable progress under Pfeifer.

The Fischer family was tormented by Pfeifer pacing around his room through the night in heavy boots. When Theodor Fischer complained, Pfeifer responded by removing one boot at night but not the other. One day, the house was startled by the sound of a barber hurtling down the stairs, whence Pfeifer had thrown him. Pfeifer and Johann were both given to flirting with teenage Cäcilie, the fetching Fischer daughter. Pfeifer would cry, "Here comes my darling girl! I love you, you'll be my wife, I'll take you with me to Saxony!" Cäcilie replied that her father had told her musicians were people who blew with the wind.

In the end, everyone in the house seems to have been fond of Tobias Pfeifer except the Beethovens' maid, who complained that at all hours he ordered coffee, wine, beer, and brandy, which she was convinced he mixed and drank together. Ludwig's lessons were as irregular as his teacher, taking place whenever Pfeifer was in the mood. Sometimes he felt in the mood after midnight, when he and Johann arrived home from the tavern. They would shake the boy awake and drag him to the keyboard, where he was forced to play into the early hours. Ludwig also began to play chamber music with Pfeifer on flute and court violinist Franz Georg Rovantini, a man shy and religious, the opposite of the flighty insomniac Pfeifer. Rovantini, who was distantly related to Maria van Beethoven, gave Ludwig violin and viola lessons. (He was another of Cäcilie Fischer's admirers.) As the three played trios in a front room of the Beethoven flat, passersby would stop in the street, exclaiming that they could listen for hours.[32]

The widespread musicality of Bonners that struck visitors like writer Madame de Staël had its roots in a lower Rhine musical culture that went back centuries.[33] The court added more impetus and professionalism to the picture. At the Electoral Residence, music was required in the chapel, theater, concert room, and ballroom; the town calendar included some twenty high holidays with special services and music. Max Friedrich allowed the court orchestra to give two public concerts a week in the Rathaus, where they also played for the all-night Shrovetide balls.[34] If in the larger world Bonn was too much a backwater for a musician to find wide fame, it was still a town as good as any in which to learn the art. Beethoven was not the only virtuoso to emerge from Bonn as if out of nowhere to dazzle the capitals of music.

In those days, the pursuit of music was perceived in a pair of dichotomies. Listeners were divided into amateurs and connoisseurs, performers into *dilettanti* and *virtuosi*. As in C. P. E. Bach's keyboard sonatas for *Kenner und Liebhaber,* composers generally wrote with those divisions in mind. In 1782, Mozart wrote his father about his new concertos, "[H]ere and there connoisseurs alone can derive satisfaction; the non-connoisseurs cannot fail to be pleased, though without knowing why."[35] That defined the essentially populist attitude of what came to be called the Classical style: composers should provide something for everybody, at the same time gearing each work for its setting, whether it was the more intimate and complex chamber music played by enthusiasts in private homes, or public pieces for theater and larger concerts, which were written in a more straightforward style.

In Bonn, music was heard in houses from low to high, and often the skills of dilettantes rivaled those of professionals. Chief Minister Belderbusch employed a wind quintet of his own; his nephew's wife was an able keyboard player.[36] A daughter of the Viennese ambassador

Count Metternich was called the best clavier player in town.[37] (This was the Metternich family whose son later rose to power in Vienna and gave his name to a political era.)

Finance Minister J. G. von Mastiaux was among the most perfervid of the aristocratic music fanciers at court. He maintained a Haydn cult, corresponding with the master, acquiring all the Haydn scores he could get his hands on including eighty symphonies and thirty quartets, and he had a huge library of music by a range of contemporary composers.[38] Mastiaux and his five children all played; his instrument collection included a pyramid-shaped piano that people came from miles around to admire.[39] There were regular concerts in his music room, which had space for a small orchestra and dozens of listeners.

In those days, private houses were the primary venue where secular music was heard. Public concerts in large halls were less common, largely reserved for orchestral and large choral works.[40] From childhood on, Beethoven made his reputation as a performer mainly in the setting of house music, and that situation hardly changed through his career. Solo pieces and chamber music, in other words, were played in chambers, much of the time by amateur musicians for audiences of family and friends. Programs were a mélange of genres and media; a concerto might be followed by a solo piece, followed by an aria, the musicians alternately playing and listening. The audience typically wandered in and out of the room, sometimes chatted and played cards. This pattern for concerts both private and public also lasted through Beethoven's lifetime — though he demanded to be listened to attentively. Only once in his life was one of his piano sonatas played in a public concert.[41]

Elector Max Friedrich was well on in his seventies when Belderbusch turned his thoughts and intrigues toward a successor. Bonn had traditionally been oriented toward France, but Belderbusch hated the French and they hated him in return.[42] To secure the next Elector, he decided on a bold move toward Vienna. Maximilian Franz von Habsburg-Lothringen, the youngest sibling of Holy Roman Emperor Joseph II, had as yet no throne to his name. Securing Max Franz for Elector would make a profitable connection between Bonn and Vienna and would also bring the influence of Joseph himself, one of the most progressive "benevolent despots" of the age.

Belderbusch began to lobby in Vienna and succeeded on his usual scale. Max Franz would become "coadjutor" of the Electorate of Bonn, the appointed heir to the throne. Besides agreeing to the electoral scheme, Vienna promised the Bonn court a yearly subsidy of 50,000 florins and a one-time "present" of 100,000 florins. Meanwhile, another 100,000 florins was allocated to Belderbusch himself, plus the title Graf (Count) for him and his three nephews.[43] (Again, a basic year's salary for a court musician was 250 florins.)

News of the (pro forma) election of the coadjutor was celebrated in Bonn with cannons and bells, a solemn *Te Deum* in the minster, an illumination of the whole city that His Electoral Grace "condescended to view," a great banquet at the Electoral Residence, and a masked ball open "to all respectably dressed citizens" that went on until 7 o'clock in the morning.[44] All that would be as nothing compared to the celebration when Max Franz made his first appearance.

So it came to pass that in October 1780, Bonn witnessed the triumphal entry of the coadjutor. The arrival of Max Franz was chronicled in a series of pictures by the court painter: the coadjutor's fleet of boats is greeted with gunfire and trumpets and drums on the river; his carriage and train progress through the market before the eyes of the town, whose citizens are dressed in multicolored finery, many waving handkerchiefs and weeping for joy; Max Franz greets Elector Max Friedrich and his retinue outside the Electoral Residence. There followed a two-week whirl of masked balls, banquets, hunting, operettas, comedies, galas, grand promenades, dinners "with ladies," and church ceremonies.[45] Despite his impressively portly frame, future Elector Max Franz held up manfully under it all.

For the Beethovens, the beginning of 1779 climaxed with the birth of the family's first daughter, Anna Maria Franziska, in February. Violinist and family friend Franz Rovantini served as her godfather. The baby died in four days, the first death in the family that the boys had to witness.

Johann kept at his daily round of singing and lessons. If he was no longer Ludwig's main teacher, he was still the enforcer. Now it was younger brother Caspar Carl undergoing their father's regime. Carl grew up playing and eventually taught a little piano, but he never amounted to much as a musician. There is no indication that youngest brother Nikolaus Johann was taught music. He was remembered as mild and good-natured — unique in that family — and a bit dim. In the end, however, Nikolaus Johann made more money than the rest of his family put together.

Johann van Beethoven was recalled as much for his merrymaking as for his professionalism. The Fischers remembered him and his prime drinking companion, fishmonger Klein, across the way, toot-tooting through their fists at each other from the windows. With a few glasses in him, Johann could be jolly or mean, and the children knew he was always ready with the back of his hand. Theodor Fischer recalled that on hot days Johann went to a tavern next door and ordered a flask each of wine and water, then returned and strolled about swigging from them, singing away, to a mixture of amusement and scorn from his wife.[46]

Maria van Beethoven was remembered as a good and kindly woman, though like the rest of the Beethovens she had a formidable temper. When she died, her son Ludwig called her his best friend. She knew how to handle a troublesome husband, how to talk to those both high and low, how to give a clever comeback. She managed the household, the endless bills, and the knitting and sewing, though cleanliness was not her strong suit with either the house or the children. The boys were often grubby.

Maria was her children's mentor in morals. "From childhood on," Beethoven later wrote, "I learned to love virtue."[47] One of Maria's sayings comes close to a prophecy of the life of her composer son and his ethos: "Without suffering there is no struggle, without struggle no victory, without victory no crown."

Family friends remembered Maria's thin face full of care, her serious eyes. She endured. Above all, she felt a rankling sense of regret. Working with Cäcilie Fischer one day, Maria told the teenager that their violinist friend Franz Rovantini was enamored of her and would like to marry her. And he was a fine man. But, Maria continued, "[i]f you want my good advice, stay single. Then you'll have the best, most peaceful, most beautiful, most enjoyable life you can have. Because what is marriage but a little joy, then afterward a chain of sorrows. And you're still so young . . . So many sorrows come that unmarried people have no idea of . . . One should weep when a girl is born into the world."[48]

Having buried a well-to-do husband and a child before she was twenty, now Maria had to live with a husband who drank too much and was never going to prosper. Her mother had died impoverished and mad. Maria knew she would most likely bury half or more of her children before they came of age. Maria van Beethoven had a ready wit and enjoyed a party, but Cäcilie Fischer could not remember ever seeing Maria laugh.

Maria seemed more amused than outraged at her husband's flirting with Cäcilie Fischer. As she fended Johann off, Cäcilie would protest, "I'm not a girl for kissing! You have your wife to kiss!" Once, there was enough of a tussle in the kitchen that they fell onto the stove and knocked the pipe out of the wall. It clattered to the floor, at which everyone broke up laughing. Johann declared he'd learned his lesson; Maria told Cäcilie she'd handled it well.[49]

None of it seemed to interfere with the easy relations of the Beethovens and the Fischers. Cäcilie was so named because she had been born on the festival day of the patroness of music, St. Cecilia. On Cäcilie's name day, the Beethovens would come to offer their congratulations, and in honor of the saint all would retire to a tavern with Johann's musical friends and get merry enough that the children would have to help their father home.[50]

So a marriage endured with its ordinary sorrows and tragedies and passing amusements and guilty pleasures. The stories of Ludwig and his brothers in childhood are no less ordinary. The maids take them to play in the garden of the Electoral Residence. From there they can run over to the rampart of the Old Toll and look out over the Rhine to the Siebengebirge. When guests are in the house, Johann dispatches the boys to the ground-floor bakery, where the young ones crawl around the stone floor unsupervised and Nikolaus cracks his head, developing the aforementioned abscess, which leaves him scarred. Ludwig steals eggs from Frau Fischer's chickens and gets caught. The boys steal a neighbor's chicken and have the maid cook it; they don't get caught but beg a Fischer son who'd figured it out, "Don't tell Papa and Mama or we'll have to run away from home."

When Gottfried Fischer was little, the Beethoven boys naturally tormented him. "Listen, Gottfried, your father is a fisher."

"My father is not a fisher, he's a baker! He bakes bread!"

"Listen, Gottfried, your father catches fish at night and bakes fish."

"No, my father is a baker, not a fisher! My mother bakes fish in the kitchen, not my father."

"Listen, Gottfried, you and your father, both of you fishers, when you're big you'll have to catch fish at night and bake them."

"No, when I'm big I'm going to be a baker, not a fisher!" This kept up until Gottfried was furious and hitting at them; then they'd relent and reassure him that his papa was a baker after all.[51]

From the big attic of the Fischer house, you could see down the Rhine in one direction and the Siebengebirge in the other. In the attic stood two telescopes owned by the landlords. In youth, Ludwig spent much time there alone, peering at the landscape up and down the river and over to the hills. "The Beethovens," Gottfried recalled, "loved the Rhine."[52]

At Easter 1780, the family said goodbye to Tobias Pfeifer, who was leaving town after less than a year. The grand eccentric had proved an able teacher for Ludwig and a reliable drinking companion for Johann. Now, at age nine (and still advertised as a year younger), Ludwig was starting to attract attention from connoisseurs, had become the star of house concerts, and in that capacity was ready to make money.[53]

Having suggested Pfeifer as teacher for the boy, Johann's actor friend Grossmann provided another one, a man who had recently arrived in Bonn to become music director of the court theater. This teacher turned out to be an irreplaceable figure in Ludwig's life: Christian Gottlob Neefe, a composer, organist, writer, poet, biographer, and enthusiast for Aufklärung. No one person shaped the child who grew up into Ludwig van Beethoven, but Neefe would be his most important mentor.

• • •

Much of what this teacher would have to work with was already settled. A pattern had formed in Ludwig's childhood. From his fourth or fifth year, music was beaten into him. It was misery, but whether he chose it or not, music had been from early on what his life was about. Childhood brought good times as well as bad, times when his father was laughing and proud of him, and when he received the steady wisdom and solace of his mother. He enjoyed tramps in the lovely landscape and pranks and games with his brothers and the Fischer children. It was at least a measure of an ordinary childhood. His early years also laid the foundation of a phenomenal resilience and courage.

On the other side of the misery of his training, there was the ecstasy of music itself. When he escaped from his father's regime and found better teachers and discovered his own ambitions, the teenage Beethoven still sought solitude, hours when he could be alone with music and pore over his own creations. Even though he was performing constantly in public, the rest of the world and everybody in it could not reach him in that solitude.

Music was the one extraordinary thing in a sea of the disappointing and ordinary. Reared as he was in a relentless discipline, instinctively responsive to music as he was, the boy never truly learned to understand the world outside music. Nobody ever really demanded that of him until, disastrously, near the end of his life. Nor did he ever really understand love. He could perceive the world and other people only through the prism of his own consciousness, judging them in the unforgiving terms he judged himself.

Otherwise Beethoven had little grasp of the world at all. In childhood he did not truly comprehend the independent existence of other people. He never really did. He reached maturity knowing all about music, from writing notes to selling them, but otherwise he did not know how to live in the world. In the ideals he lived by in his solitude, instead of human beings there would be an exalted abstraction: Humanity.

3

Reason and Revolution

WHEN AT ABOUT ten years old he began studying with Christian Neefe, Ludwig van Beethoven was already a musician people noticed. They paid to hear him play in the house concerts his father produced in the front rooms of the Fischer house. Johann had dropped his objections to the boy's making up his own notes; Ludwig was teaching himself to compose, following where his ears and his inner singing took him. He understood harmony instinctively. "I never had to learn how to avoid mistakes," he later wrote. "From my childhood I had so keen a sensibility that I wrote correctly without knowing it had to be that way, or could be otherwise." None of his earliest creative attempts would survive, but at ten he was not far from his first publication, and it was not the work of a beginner. Still, Beethoven's reputation then and for a long time after was founded on his playing.

After his lessons with van den Eeden and Pfeifer on keyboard and Rovantini on strings, Ludwig began to study organ with Franciscan Friar Willibald Koch. Soon he was playing organ for the 6 a.m. mass at the Minorite Church. One of the Minorite order, an organist named Father Hansmann, was taken by the boy's playing and followed him home, haunting the Beethoven house concerts. Unaccustomed to devotees and their usefulness, Ludwig was only annoyed. He told Fischer daughter Cäcilie, "That monk who's always coming around, he'd be better to stay in his cloister and pray over his breviary."[1]

Ludwig was attending a Latin school called the Tirocinium, reaping the benefit of the progressive educational initiatives of the Max Friedrich regime. After the reign of the Jesuits in education ended, the teaching of children became more secular and enlightened, less dogmatic and brutal. In school, Beethoven absorbed a little French and Latin and learned to write in an elegant hand that he retained into his twenties, only then lapsing into a skittering scrawl. In school he learned to add but never to divide or multiply. To the end of his life, if he needed to multiply 62 by 50, he did it by writing 62 in a column 50 times and adding it up.

To schoolmates, Beethoven at age ten appeared a cipher: grubby, taciturn, and withdrawn, always walking angled forward as if impatient to get away from wherever he was. He had no friends at school. Because of his dark complexion, his family and neighbors took to calling him *der Spagnol,* "the Spaniard," painting him with a touch of the exotic. When the boy was not quite eleven, Johann decreed he was learning nothing useful and took him out of school — as most Bonn parents did at about that age, as Johann had been himself.[2] At eleven, it was time for a boy to concentrate on a trade. From here on, Ludwig was expected to think and do little but music. That suited him fine.

At home he played with his brothers and the Fischer children and sat for hours with his mother. He could talk more easily and happily to her than to anyone else. Father Johann was his manager and promoter, but otherwise Ludwig was slipping away from him. In his art he gained applause and praise, a chorus of admiration that would continue to the end of his life. He seems to have taken it for granted as his due. Eventually his admirers in Bonn drew him out to a degree; at last he learned to make friends. Even then, on his own path with its own horizon, praise hardly reached him.

Early on, he took for granted that he was destined to be somebody. Once when Cäcilie Fischer lectured him, "How dirty you're looking again! You ought to keep yourself properly clean," he told her, "What's the difference? When I become a gentleman nobody will care."[3]

Once, Johann van Beethoven had been derided by his father as "Johnny the runner" for his restless wandering. In adulthood he did not lose his wanderlust. Every summer, when the Elector went on his annual visit to Westfalen in his capacity as prince-archbishop of Münster, the Bonn court *Kapelle* had its vacation. During the break of 1781, Johann made another of his escapes from home, taking with him Ludwig and the boy's string teacher, violinist Franz Rovantini.

If Ludwig had not inherited Johann's mediocrity, neither did he inherit his father's sociability. A lot of people liked Johann van Beethoven, and most of his friends appear to have been musicians and music lovers. In the fair weather of 1781, father and son and violinist wandered from town to town and house to house in the Rhineland, on the lookout for music fanciers with influence, money, and a clavier in the house. Back home, Maria van Beethoven told Cäcilie Fischer that with the men and their commotion out of the way, she was a happy straw widow and could do what she liked.[4]

These summer jaunts of father and son were working vacations. Ludwig's instinctive love of nature burgeoned as they traveled in slow rattling wagons from one sleepy town to another: Flamersheim, Ahrweiler, Bad Neuenahr, Ersdorf, Odendorf, Röttgen.[5] Ludwig and Rovantini played in hoary, creaking half-timbered houses and in country palaces. Among those visited on this and later trips was the wealthy and aristocratic banking family Meinertzhagen of Oberkassel, whose patriarch frequented the boy's performances in Bonn. In Bensberg, Ludwig played for C. J. M. Burggraf, who owned the second-largest Baroque palace north of the Alps. The boy became accustomed to being welcomed in great houses. As the weather turned toward autumn, it became the season for Johann's most beloved dish (later one of his son's as well): *Krammetsvögel,* made from a thrush whose flesh was infused by the juniper berries it had fattened on.[6]

In autumn 1781, they returned home to a city in the grip of a dysentery epidemic. Soon the illness claimed their traveling companion and the boy's teacher, the much-admired Franz Rovantini. Johann and Maria did what they could for him, but the day came when Rovantini told Maria he'd dreamed of his grave and was resigned. "Dreams are foolishness!" Maria exclaimed. Back at the house her report was grim.

In the hour Rovantini died, Cäcilie Fischer, whom he had loved, heard a familiar step behind her in the kitchen and turned to find no one. In affectionate fun, Rovantini had often sneaked up behind Cäcilie and hoisted her into the air. The *Kapelle* gave him a musical send-off. Maria wrote the news to Rovantini's sister, a cousin of Maria's, in Rotterdam.[7] Eventually, that connection was to produce another adventure for Ludwig.

The 1780s witnessed the height of Enlightenment and Aufklärung optimism and activism. Above all, at the end of the decade the widespread revolutionary fervor climaxed with revolution in France. The year 1781 alone was extraordinary. It saw the premiere of Schiller's cathartic drama *Die Räuber*, which embodied the turbulent spirit of Sturm und Drang. In Vienna, Holy Roman Emperor Joseph II issued decrees that abolished serfdom in Austria and proclaimed religious tolerance. Immanuel Kant published *Critique of Pure Reason*, which turned a page in the history of philosophy. Haydn published his *Russian* String Quartets; Mozart premiered his finest tragic opera, *Idomeneo*. And that year a new esoteric society calling itself the Order of Illuminati issued its general statutes. As a significant footnote in history, around 1781 Beethoven began his studies with Christian Gottlob Neefe.

A native of Chemnitz in Saxony, Neefe (pronounced *Nay*-feh) had come to Bonn in 1779, at age thirty-one, to serve as music director of his friend G. F. W. Grossmann's theater troupe, which was installed at the theater of the Electoral Residence. The cosmopolitan, enlightened, highly musical atmosphere of Leipzig had shaped Neefe. The son of a poor and devout tailor, he spent seven years getting a law degree at the University of Leipzig to satisfy his parents. But music was Neefe's passion; he had composed since age twelve, teaching himself from books. After finishing his law examinations, Neefe turned entirely to music. His particular interest lay in the theatrical side of the art, which brought together a mixture of his musical and literary passions.[8] His first works, from the early 1770s, were comic operas and operettas.

Neefe's mentor in Leipzig was composer and writer on music J. A. Hiller, a successor of J. S. Bach as cantor of St. Thomas Church and founder of the historic Gewandhaus concerts. The city was a breeding ground of progressive social and artistic ideas. Mentor and student shared a vision of creating a German national opera and reforming musical pedagogy, bringing to their agenda an exalted idealism about music, theater, literature, Aufklärung, and personal growth. Duty was a relentless imperative that Neefe preached, the point being to serve God by serving humanity.

Neefe's enthusiasms were equally literary, and his taste began with the pious lyrics and ingenuous moral fables of Christian Fürchetegott Gellert, whose homely inspirational works were at the time second in popularity only to the Bible in Germany. A leading voice of the Aufklärung, Gellert was both symptom of and contributor to the burgeoning German obsession with the Good, the True, and the Beautiful, which aspired to be a kind of science of morality and ethics. As Gellert also demonstrates, music and the other arts of the Aufklärung were marked by a populist sensibility and a deliberate artlessness: even the highest art should aim for the direct, the natural, the broadly communicative. In keeping, Neefe was an enthusiast for German folk poetry and song, composing his own faux-naïf imitations of both: "The Saxon maids are sweet and smart; / But I'll take no Saxon Maiden to wife" begins his lyric *To the Bonn Girls*. After a tour of Bavarian, Swabian ("A Swabian maid, a delightful thing! / She'll trip in a dance *hop sie sa sa!*"), and other flavors of the fair sex, he concludes, "So only a Bonn girl will I marry / A Bonn maid alone will make me tarry."[9] (Neefe's actual wife was a singer from Leipzig.)

Central to Neefe's influence on Beethoven was Leipzig's living memory of two towering composers who had lived and worked in the city: J. S. Bach, some of whose students were still active when Neefe studied in the city, and his son C. P. E. Bach. During his later years in Berlin and Hamburg, C. P. E. became the prime musical representative of the aesthetic called *Empfindsamkeit,* a cult of intimate feeling and sensitivity. Along with his brother J. C. Bach, C. P. E. helped create the early Classical style in music, but his introverted sensibility and capricious imagination made him also a prophet of Romanticism. In his treatise *Toward the True Art of Clavier Playing,* C. P. E. declared that moving the heart was the chief aim of music, and to do that one had to play from the heart and soul. Haydn called that book "the school of schools." While outside Leipzig J. S. Bach's reputation languished in the shadow of his famous sons, Neefe understood the elder Bach's stature and the importance and the synoptic quality of his *Well-Tempered Clavier*, a work in those years known only to a cultish few.

The voices and ideals of Hiller and C. P. E. Bach, more than any others, echo in Neefe's music and aesthetic writings. Through him, those passions touched his student Beethoven. At the same time, Neefe promoted new literature; he read Goethe and Schiller and the poets and dramatists of the Sturm und Drang.[10]

An echt Aufklärer, Neefe declared himself "no friend of ceremony and etiquette . . . detestable flatterers and informers . . . The great men of earth I love when they are good men; I honor their laws when they work best in civil society." In his youth he scorned religion, but finally he became Calvinist and declared he hoped "to die a proper Christian."[11] (Not lacking in practicality, he had his children who were born in Bonn baptized as Catholic, to pacify local sensibilities.) Neefe's writings range from idealistic to pedantic. Believing poetry should be a kind of national institution to promote virtue, he wrote music and lyrics for a *Song in Praise of Potatoes*. His *Song for Those Looking for a Job* warned against "the dire consequences of idleness."[12]

Which is all to say that Neefe's enthusiasms were diffuse, likewise his creativity: he was a composer of sonatas, concertos, singspiels, and operas; writer of inspirational homilies, biographies, and autobiographies; critic and aesthetician of music; journalist; translator of librettos; and poet. Everything Neefe did was worthy and engaging, if a bit fearfully earnest. If nothing close to an original genius, he was one of the more interesting German creators of his time. By the end of his career he had a considerable reputation in Germany, both musically (his "Turkish" opera, *Adelheit von Veltheim*, was performed widely) and literarily (Goethe's mother was one of his admirers). Carl Friedrich Cramer's *Magazin der Musik*, to which Neefe contributed, listed him along with C. P. E. Bach, Hiller, and a few others as one of "our Matadors in tonal art."[13]

A portrait of Neefe captured him as well as, years before, a painter had captured Ludwig van Beethoven the elder. The painter of old Ludwig pictured an imposing figure looking the viewer in the eye. The painter of Neefe pictured a dreamer. The face is mild and pleasant, the feelings shrouded, the eyes intelligent, the gaze searching somewhere beyond the viewer. In life, Neefe was depressive and hypochondriacal; he leaned and limped from a deformity. His description of himself: "a small, dry, gaunt little man."[14] Yet he was insatiably involved with life, an intellectual and spiritual man of action, curious about everything.

In a word, Neefe was the definition of what Germans call a *Schwärmer*, one swarming with rapturous enthusiasms. The breadth of his outlook on life, art, and ideas was unique in Bonn and rare among musicians anywhere. Like many in his time, he was intoxicated with hope for a humanity living in the new age of science and freedom, and he dedicated his life to the service of enlightened ideals. As for himself, he wrote in a poem:

> *I wish only*
> *To be a man among men, and to be clear in head and heart,*
> *And to find my happiness in good deeds.*[15]

His pupil Beethoven was to echo those thoughts and many others of Neefe's — always in his own fashion. Like Neefe too, Beethoven grew up a man of the Enlightenment. At the same time he became a creator unlike his teacher, broad and rich enough to galvanize the musical re-action against the Enlightenment.

What is Enlightenment? Near the end of his life as the most visible representative and court jester of the Enlightenment, after his famous cry of "Crush infamy!" after his declaration "If God did not exist, it would be necessary to invent Him," Voltaire felt hopeful. In the article on God for his *Philosophic Dictionary*, he wrote, "Year by year the fanaticism that overspread the earth is receding in its detestable usurpations . . . If religion no longer gives birth to civil wars, it is to philosophy alone that we are indebted; theological disputes begin to be regarded in much the same manner as the quarrels of Punch and Judy at the fair. A usurpation odious and injurious, founded upon fraud on one side and stupidity on the other, is being at every instant undermined by reason, which is establishing its reign." Shortly before he died, Denis Diderot, editor of the revolutionary *Encyclopedia,* prophesied that everywhere, the eons of submission to religion and princes were about to end once and for all.[16]

Of course, these French philosophes could not have been more wrong. Reason would not reign, princes did not depart, the Punch-and-Judy quarrels of theology endured. But for a few decades in the eighteenth century, an overwhelming sense of hope gave the Enlightenment a singular radiance. The age envisioned the end of fanaticism and tyranny, when not only would the understanding of nature be completed by science and reason, but government, society, humankind itself would be perfected. Philosophers spoke of the "science of government," the "science of man." When humanity illuminated by reason was free of the chains of superstition and submission to tyranny both secular and sacred, when every individual was free to find his or her way to happiness, then, as Schiller and Beethoven sang, earth would become an Elysium.

In the 1780s, that spirit reached a climax. There was a fever of revolution in the air, an intoxication of hope, a conviction that humanity was about to turn a corner into an exalted age, the birth of true civilization and a final understanding of the universe.[17] Hope and excitement vibrated everywhere, in philosophy and literature and poetry and in the pages of the *Intelligenzblatt,* the town paper in Bonn.

Just after Immanuel Kant published *Critique of Pure Reason,* in 1781, which set philosophy on a new course of asking what is possible to truly know on earth, the philosopher wrote a popular article on the topic, "What Is Enlightenment?" He answered:

> *Enlightenment is mankind's exit from its self-incurred immaturity. Immaturity* is the inability to make use of one's own understanding without the guidance of another. *Self-incurred* is this inability if its cause lies not in the lack of understanding but rather in the lack of the resolution and courage to use it without the guidance of another. *Saper aude!* Have the courage to use your *own* understanding! is thus the motto of Enlightenment.

Kant continued: "Rules and formulas, these mechanical instruments of a rational use (or rather misuse) of [humankind's] natural gifts, are the fetters of an everlasting immaturity."[18] Could "a society of clergy-men," he asked, demand an unquestioning obedience to dogma?

> I say that this is completely impossible. Such a contract, concluded for the purpose of closing off forever all further Enlightenment of the human race, is utterly null and void even if it should be confirmed by the highest power . . . It is absolutely forbidden to unite . . . in a permanent religious constitution that no one may publicly doubt, and thereby to negate a period of progress of mankind toward improvement.

Beyond this resounding credo that freedom of thought and rejection of religious dogma are the essence of Enlightenment, Kant in his work put an end to the traditional muddling of philosophy and natural science. He made the declaration, at once radical and commonsensical, that while the objective world certainly exists, we can never truly comprehend it, because as human beings, we are limited in the means we possess to grasp reality. We can think only in *appearances* that make sense to us. We can make representations of the world only in terms of time, space, causality, and our other human categories, which may or may not apply to any *Ding an sich,* thing-in-itself.[19]

The implications of these ideas were epochal not only in philosophy but also in the realm of ethics, aesthetics, and morals. The essence of the things outside ourselves that humanity cannot understand is God. "The desire to talk to God is absurd," Kant wrote. "We cannot talk to one we cannot comprehend — and we cannot comprehend God; we can only believe in Him." For that reason, we also cannot accept the unquestionable authority of scripture or any other dictates divine or earthly. We must live by our own free and individual understanding, discover our own rules for ourselves. As Beethoven later put it, "Man, help yourself!" If we are believers, then, how do we serve God? When men "fulfill their duties to men, they fulfill thereby God's commandments; that they are consequently always in the service of God, as long as their actions are moral, and . . . it is absolutely impossible to serve God otherwise."

So as individuals on our own, Kant asked, what can we truly know, and how can we know it? By what ethics and morals can we find our way for ourselves? What are the Good, the True, the Beautiful? For Kant, the moral part came down to what he called the "categorical imperative": every person must "act only in accordance with that maxim through which you can at the same time will that it become a universal law." Every act should be done with the conviction that if everyone did likewise, life would be good. Each person's actions become a mirror of all moral law, and thereby each finds freedom and happiness apart from the dictates of gods or princes. And to serve humanity is to serve God.

Kant touched off a revolution in humanity's sense of itself and its imperatives. In Bonn, as in other German intellectual centers, Kant was in the air thinkers and artists breathed. The people around Beethoven were aflame with these ideas. In the end, Kant the man of the eighteenth century became the bridge between the Enlightenment and the Romantic era — which is to say, in the early nineteenth century, Kant occupied the position in philosophy that Goethe did in literature and Beethoven in music.

The first practical political fruit of the Enlightenment was the American Revolution, its eternal expressions of enlightened ideals laid out in Thomas Jefferson's Declaration of Independence: "We hold these truths to be self-evident, that all men are created equal, that they are endowed by their Creator with certain inalienable Rights, that among these are life, liberty, and the pursuit of happiness." That sentence distilled the secular and humanistic ethos of the age. Jefferson's words echoed philosopher David Hume: "Every man . . . proceeds in the pursuit of happiness, with as unerring a motion, as that which the celestial bodies observe." "The entire pursuit of reason," wrote Kant, "is to bring about . . . one ultimate end — that of happiness." This made human well-being a joining of head and heart, a spiritual quest for joy not in heaven but on earth.[20]

Jefferson's declaration also shows that the Enlightenment did not do away with God but rather placed Him at a remove from His creation: the Creator as cosmic watchmaker who crafted the perfect machinery of the universe and sat back to let His cosmic experiment run, like a wise parent leaving humanity free to find its own path. The goal of life is the pursuit of *happiness,* here and now. Religion and state are different realms.

The Enlightenment's determination to separate church and state was a radical departure in any society, Western or otherwise, but, as the founding fathers of the United States recognized, it was a fundamental principle of an enlightened state. An established church and enforced dogma were a guarantee of tyranny, and tyranny of any stripe was anathema to Aufklärers. "To do good wherever we can," Beethoven would say, "to love liberty above all things, and never to deny truth though it be at the throne itself."

To the philosophes, God was a figure beyond the stars, watching all and knowing all, a transcendent moral influence, but one who did not deign to meddle with the perfection of His physics to make miracles. Science had opened the path to that conviction. Isaac Newton made the epochal discovery that the physical laws that rule the whole universe are the same that rule our lives on earth. For the first time in history, the heavens and the earth became part of the same immutable mechanism.[21]

If the Enlightenment was Christian in its foundation and in much of its tone, no longer was any religion presumed to have a monopoly on the divine. Religions were unique to the cultures that shaped and sustained them; in their myriad voices, all religions worshiped the same transcendent and unknowable reality. For the mainstream of the Enlightenment, the most immediate revelation of divinity was in nature, and the truest scripture was found not in a book but in science.[22] Let God rest out beyond the stars in His sublime perfection; it is up to us to understand ourselves and rule ourselves. "Know then thyself, presume not God to scan," wrote Alexander Pope. "The proper study of Mankind is Man."

This rationalistic, antidogmatic, searching, secular humanist sense of the divine came to be called "deism." The term helps describe the convictions of Voltaire and Rousseau, Jefferson and Franklin — and, to a degree, Beethoven. He was no churchgoer; in his maturity, he studied Eastern religion and scripture. "Only art and science," he wrote, "can raise men to the level of gods."[23] He never claimed that God imbued him with his gifts. He believed his talent came from nature — God's nature, to be sure. At the same time, Beethoven would be no more a conventional deist than he was a conventional anything else, and his ideas of God evolved along with his life and art. The older he got, the more he turned toward faith in a God who was present and all-seeing, who listened to prayers (though none of this was anathema to deists).

All eras pass, and in the end, the Enlightenment's dream of an earthly Elysium did not endure. It was overturned in Europe by forces including the limitations of science, the limitations of reason, the fear of social chaos, the resistance of religions to giving up their monopoly on truth. The Enlightenment's shibboleth of reason toppled at last. The founding Romantic poet and philosopher Novalis condemned the "harsh, chilly light of the Enlightenment" and exalted the mythical and mystical.[24] Beethoven, for his part, did not share that spirit; he never really absorbed the Romantic age. At the same time the Enlightenment birthed ideas whose reverberations would not disappear in the world, or in Beethoven's mind and music.

So many excesses of the Enlightenment, in all its forms great and terrible, rose from excesses of hope.

If the methods of reason and science that were applied (and often misapplied) to all things united the whole of the Enlightenment — and among progressives everywhere there was a sense of boundless human potential about to be unleashed — there were still essential differences between the way the Enlightenment was translated and transposed in France, England, and America, and how it took form in German lands: Aufklärung.

In most regions, philosophical and ethical ideals quickly became political. In an age that prided itself on rationality, it was natural to conclude that the institutions and extravagances of the ancient courts had little reason behind them. Enlightenment criticism of church and aristocracy, the unchallenged privilege once granted to Electors and petty princes, and the power wielded and abused by the clergy would, in France, lead to revolution, then to an avalanche of murder and an attempt to wipe away the aristocracy and the church. But, like most of Germany, Bonn never challenged the system of princes and courts. In stark contrast to the French, German Aufklärers wanted strong governments, efficient bureaucracies, strong armies, powerful and enlightened princes. The German ideal of enlightened reform was top-down, achieved by edict.

Thus the celebration of what came to be called "benevolent despots," most famous among them Frederick the Great in Berlin (for whom Voltaire was house philosopher) and Joseph II in Vienna. In a letter, Frederick wrote a virtual definition of enlightened despotism: "Philosophers should be the teachers of the world and the teachers of princes. They must think logically and we must act logically. They must teach the world by their powers of judgment; we must teach the world by our example."[25]

While Aufklärers often tended to the anticlerical, they were not against religion. By the time Beethoven left Bonn, he had experienced little but cultured and enlightened aristocrats and clerics, many of them his admirers and patrons. Partly for that reason, he never despised the church and nobility in their existence — or at least he held them in no special contempt compared to the rest of the world. His disgust with the Viennese aristocracy would be based on its behavior. In any case, nobles paid much of his rent.

In a later century, the trust in bureaucracy and armies and despots benevolent or otherwise would lead Germany to catastrophe, but still a monumental achievement of the Aufklärung was the science of government. Progressive ideas created state bureaucracies in Vienna and Berlin and elsewhere that supported, at first, the liberal goals of the Aufklärung — and only later the goals of police states. It was the time of the rise of the *Hofrat,* the court privy councillor, and a welter of other titles. The courts' demand for skilled administrators in turn created a new educated and ambitious middle class, hungry for power and also hungry for literature and ideas and music. This bureaucratic middle class was a primary engine of the Aufklärung in German lands.[26]

In the age of reason, German literature bloomed, some of it in the spirit of Aufklärung and some opposing it — one example of the opposition being the Sturm und Drang decade of the 1770s. The next generation in Germany turned against it all. If the resonating ideas of the Enlightenment were reason, truth, nature, order, and objectivity, those of the coming Romantics would be the subjective, the instinctive, the uncanny, the sublime, and nature in its great and terrible face. As one essential Romantic writer, E. T. A. Hoffmann, put it, "Beethoven's music sets in motion the mechanism of fear, of awe, of horror, of suffering, and wakens just that infinite longing which is the essence of Romanticism." The Aufklärung looked to a radiant future of social and scientific perfection; the Romantics looked to the fabled, mysterious, unreachable past. The eighteenth century longed for freedom and happiness. The nineteenth century was caught up not in longing toward an end but in longing for the delirium and pain of longing itself.

In 1785, in the middle of a decade with a fever of revolution in the air, Friedrich Schiller caught the spirit of the age in ecstatic verses called "An die Freude" (Ode to Joy). The poem's essence was the Enlightenment cult of happiness as the goal of life, the conviction that the triumph of freedom and joy would bring humanity to an epoch of peace and universal brotherhood, the utopia he called Elysium:

Joy, thou lovely god-engendered
Daughter of Elysium.
Drunk with fire we enter,
Heavenly one, thy holy shrine!
Thy magic reunites
What fashion has broken apart.
Beggars will be princes' brothers
Where thy gentle wing abides . . .

Be embraced, you millions!
This kiss for the whole world!
Brothers! over the starry canopy
A loving Father must dwell!
Whoever has had the great success
To be a friend of a friend,
He who has won a sweet wife,
Join our jubilation! . . .

Brothers, drink and join the song,
All sinners shall be forgiven,
And Hell shall be no more.

Schiller's poem is in the tradition of a German *geselliges Lied*, social song, intended literally or figuratively to be sung among comrades with glasses raised.[27] The verses themselves are drunken and reeling with hope. In dozens of musical settings, *An die Freude* was sung in Freemason lodges all over Germany and by young revolutionaries in the streets.[28] For Beethoven and for many of his era, these verses were the distillation of the revolutionary 1780s. By the end of his teens, Beethoven was determined to do his own setting of the poem. Perhaps he did, but if so, the attempt did not survive. When he took up *An die Freude* again, decades later, those verses still rang for him with what they meant to his youth, and to the Aufklärung.

At the center of the Rhenish Aufklärung lay Bonn, already in the 1770s, under Elector Maximilian Friedrich, called "the most Enlightened ecclesiastical city in Germany."[29] A decade later, under new Elector Maximilian Franz, it would be still more so. Even the Rhenish clergy were devotees of Aufklärung. A liberal Catholic journal in Bonn railed at the "crude, uncouth manners and great stupidity" of the monks in conservative Cologne.[30]

In the Aufklärung, encompassing what came to be called the Classical period in music, the art was called a wonderful, even exalted entertainment. It would be the Romantics, in search of the transcendent, who placed instrumental music at the summit of the arts, and Beethoven at the summit of instrumental music. If he had grown up in Cologne (or perhaps anywhere but in Bonn in the late eighteenth century), he might have been great in his art but he would have been a different and likely a lesser artist — not the demigod to bestride the nineteenth century that demanded bestriding demigods.

In the revolutionary 1780s, these tides, personified in Beethoven's teacher Neefe and later in his Bonn circle, whirled around the teenager, part of his daily experience and conversation. Even as he stubbornly resisted any shaping but his own, the age still molded him, leaving him with ideals and ambitions about being a composer that no one had ever had before. He never quite spelled out those ideals in words. They would be found in his music, and in the lyrics he chose to embody in music — above all, *An die Freude*.

As for Bonn and places like Bonn, these little ecclesiastical states and principalities had existed for centuries with their customs and costumes and dialects, their courts sometimes progressive and cultured and sometimes moldering and repressive, their princes sometimes benign and sometimes tyrannical. It was all a world that was passing, to be swept away by revolution and change, dying piece by piece sometimes over decades, sometimes in days. In the course of the next century, Bonn and the absurd patchwork of other ancient little German principalities that Beethoven knew would drift and vanish like summer clouds.

4

Loved in Turn

ROUND THE BEGINNING of 1783, the firm of Goetz in
Mannheim published a work whose elegantly engraved title
page declares, "Variations pour le *clavecin* Sur une Marche
de Mr. Dresler, Composeés et dediées à Son Excellence Madame la
Comtesse de Wolfmetternich nèe Baronne d'Asseourg, par un jeune
Amateur Louis van Betthoven, agè de dix ans."[1] The publication had
been the doing of Beethoven's teacher Christian Neefe. He advertised
it himself, in third person, in a report on Bonn music and musicians in
Cramer's *Magazin der Musik:*

> Louis van Betthoven, son of the tenor singer mentioned, a boy of
> eleven years and of most promising talent. He plays the clavier very
> skillfully and with power, reads at sight very well, and . . . plays chiefly
> *The Well-Tempered Clavier* of Sebastian Bach, which Herr Neefe put
> into his hands. Whoever knows this collection of preludes and fugues
> in all the keys — which might almost be called the *non plus ultra* of
> our art — will know what this means. So far as his duties permitted,
> Herr Neefe has also given him instruction in through-bass. He is now
> training him in composition and for his encouragement has had nine
> variations for the pianoforte . . . engraved in Mannheim. This youth-

ful genius . . . would surely become a second Wolfgang Amadeus Mozart were he to continue as he has begun.[2]

These were not idle opinions and prophecies. Neefe had come from Leipzig, where Bach's music was still alive decades after his death, and his student's keyboard studies were centered on *The Well-Tempered Clavier*, in those days more a work known to the occasional connoisseur than something active in the repertoire. Neefe understood its synoptic quality, its incomparable survey of the depth and breadth of what music can do both technically and expressively. Beethoven was perhaps the first musician outside the Bach family to grow up playing the *WTC*, imprinting that music in his fingers and his heart and his very sense of music. Perhaps here he began to learn what Bach called "invention," in which the whole of a piece elaborates a single idea. Here, for the first time, this giant of the past nourished a budding giant. Teaching the boy the *WTC* from the age of ten or eleven may have been the single most important thing Neefe did for him.

Now Beethoven had been called in print a genius for the first but hardly last time, and the magical connection to Mozart was invoked for the first but hardly last time. The title page of the variations declares that the composer is age ten; he was, in fact, twelve when they were published. Abetted by his father, his confusion about his age had settled in.

The *Dressler* Variations are in C minor, on a funeral march by the eponymous composer. The piece is slight and conventional, reasonably impressive in imagination, harmony, and keyboard technique for a boy of Beethoven's years. At the same time, this earliest-known Beethoven work is rich in prophecy not only in its musical substance but also in its existence in print: already Neefe and others were inspired to feats of generosity for this brilliant but oblivious student.

Beethoven pursued the variation genre from now to the end of his life. The idea of theme and variations is to start with a short piece of music by oneself or someone else (often a well-known melody) and to transform and reimagine it in a series of vignettes. These may be based on the theme's melody, harmony, bass line, or some combination of them. The variation form is an ideal learning exercise for a student, because it amounts to studying a fundamental element of what *composition* is about: taking a piece of material, an idea, and transforming it into new passages that share an underlying essence but sound different. So a student learns that an essential part of composing is a matter of contrast and diversity founded on unity and invention: fashioning many things from one thing. If Bach was a model of invention, writing variations put the idea into practice. From here on, the concept and technique of variation lay at the core of Beethoven's art in whatever genre he took up.

Already in the *Dressler* Variations, he understood that a sequence of variations should not be random or static; there needs to be a sense of growth from first variation to last. Beethoven already knew, in other words, that there needs to be an overarching plan. On this first attempt, the variations do not entirely add up and some are oversimilar, but still a pattern is evident: starting from the stolid pace of the march, he animates the music by degrees — using the old technique of *division,* decorating the theme with faster notes — until the concluding allegro variation, the first in C major, erupts in ebullient virtuosity.

In that may lie a story. These variations on a funeral march in C minor (foreshadowing Beethoven's future funeral marches and other darkly expressive works in that key) might form a memorial for the boy's recently passed, still-lamented teacher and friend Franz Georg Rovantini. If so, the final variation conveys a triumph over sorrow and fate — another narrative to which Beethoven returned throughout his life.[3]

The young composer, of course, knew none of these prophecies. He knew he had made a start in the larger world of music. In the next two years, two rondos for piano saw print, along with two songs, *Description of a Girl* and *To an Infant*. From this starting point in his creative life, not yet in his teens, Beethoven was already fashioning pieces that would be played in places he would never see, by people he would never know.

These were the years when Beethoven's life came intensely into focus around music at a professional level, from soloing to playing in the orchestra pit. This student that Christian Neefe inherited was unpromising in every way but musically: morose, intractable, deficient in hygiene. But it was after the advent of Neefe as his teacher that the pace of Beethoven's life, musical and otherwise, gained momentum, if not yet in any definable direction.

As Neefe said in his published note, he was teaching the boy composition as much as keyboard. The technical part of Beethoven's keyboard studies appears to have been concentrated on organ. Neefe was an able keyboard player, but no notable virtuoso. What he did more importantly was to introduce the boy to a wealth of musical literature, centered on German composers, that had been neglected in a court that preferred Italian music.[4] (There were a number of Italians in the *Kapelle,* starting with *Kapellmeister* Andrea Luchesi.) Besides *The Well-Tempered Clavier,* Neefe introduced the boy to the intimately expressive keyboard works of C. P. E. Bach, to Haydn and Mozart, and to a new generation of piano-oriented composers including Sterkel and Clementi.

The 1780s marked the decade when the pianoforte — still in the middle of its evolution, still marked by significant differences among regional schools and individual makers — finally triumphed over the harpsichord. With its hammers striking strings rather than the strings being plucked, as with the harpsichord, the piano could create a far wider range of volume and touch than older keyboard instruments. In turn, this changed the kind of keyboard music being written. New kinds of figuration, written articulations, pedal effects, and dramatic contrasts of volume began to appear in keyboard music, which in turn urged composers toward more intense kinds of expression.

By his mid-teens, Beethoven was thoroughly a piano player and composer. Neefe held out, preferring the more intimate clavichord, though eventually he embraced the newer instrument. So at the piano Beethoven may have been mainly his own teacher; or perhaps he and his teacher together worked out how to play this instrument, as distinct from the harpsichord and clavichord. Beethoven developed his playing in the same way he developed his composing: by experimenting and by studying other accomplished musicians. Throughout his life, in all things musical he modeled what he did on what he perceived to be the best of its kind, then took the models in his own direction.

When Ludwig's first teacher, Giles van den Eeden, finally died in June 1782, after fifty-nine years as court organist, Neefe took over the position. He found his ascension surprising, because he was Protestant and the court Catholic. The day after he assumed the job, Neefe followed Elector Max Friedrich to Münster and left Beethoven as his substitute.[5] At age eleven, the boy was capable of filling in at the most important organ position in town. Soon he was regularly substituting for Neefe at the organ in the chapel, at the clavier in the court orchestra, and in rehearsals at the theater, where Neefe remained music director.

Earlier, Chief Minister Belderbusch had decreed that the small theater of the Electoral Residence was to be a national theater, like the one Joseph II established in Vienna. The larger agenda of the theater was didactic, high-minded, high-Aufklärung: it would endeavor "to raise German theatrical art to an ethical school for the German people."[6] To head it, Belderbusch brought in the Grossmann-Hellmuth Company, its leading member the actor, director, playwright, and friend of the Beethoven family G. F. W. Grossmann. The idea was not only to present a wide variety of theatrical art but also to emphasize German playwrights and composers.

The theater's ambitions expanded. Grossmann's production of Schiller's *Fiesko* in 1783 may have been its premiere; he mounted Schiller's *Räuber* and *Kabale und Liebe*; Shakespeare's *Macbeth*, *King Lear*, and *Hamlet*; works by Molière, Voltaire, Beaumarchais, the Italians Goldoni and Gozzi; and his own plays. He produced *The Abduction from the Seraglio*, the greatest success of Mozart's life, soon after its premiere in Vienna, and that season mounted nineteen other operas and operettas and melodramas. Beethoven would have seen most or all of these productions. Soon he was a rehearsal pianist at the theater and, after that, a member of the orchestra.

As Beethoven entered his early teens, there were other influences as important to him as his teacher Neefe and the town's newly rich offerings of opera and theater. Other people began to reach him. For all his roughness, the fractiousness he inherited from his family, his tendency to drift off in his own thoughts, he was attracting the ears and the admiration of the town's most sophisticated connoisseurs. These were aristocrats, civil servants, clerics, and educators who could discern talent when they saw it and who had the vision to see uncommon qualities of spirit beneath a raw exterior. Now Beethoven found friends and champions. From his teens on, these champions tended to be exceptional people — though none more exceptional than himself, as Beethoven knew, perhaps, too well.

The first of his lifelong friends was medical student Franz Wegeler. They met when Ludwig was twelve (as Wegeler remembered it) or thirteen. Wegeler was five years older. One of the first things the older boy noticed about Beethoven was that he talked enthusiastically about his grandfather and his mother, hardly at all about his father. He was always after his mother to tell him stories of his grandfather, old Ludwig. His teacher Neefe, the boy told Wegeler with some bitterness, had been harsh in criticizing his first compositions.[7] Here also appears a lasting pattern: Beethoven was generally to be fondest of friends, family, and benefactors who were distant or, like his grandfather, dead. With those he saw intimately and regularly, sooner or later there would usually be trouble.

But Beethoven and Wegeler got along from the start and never ceased to. It was Wegeler who recommended his younger friend to a wealthy local family named Breuning as a piano teacher. Daughter of the Elector's personal physician, Helene von Breuning was the widow of *Hofrat* Emanuel Joseph von Breuning, who had died from trying to save court records in the conflagration at the Electoral Residence. From that point, Helene reared their four children with the help of her brother-in-law Canon Lorenz, one of the liberal, enlightened clergy of Bonn.[8] Beethoven was engaged to teach piano to daughter Eleonore, called Lorchen, a year younger than him, and to Lorenz, called Lenz, youngest of three brothers.

The Breuning house was a stately three-story mansion on Münsterplatz, facing the cathedral. Helene was admired for her fine aristocratic features, her wisdom and patience with children, her intellectual curiosity and broad culture. When Beethoven came into the Breuning family circle, he joined a stream of court officials, artists, and intellectuals who frequented the house. Its tone of Rhenish joie de vivre was enlivened by the racket of four boisterous children playing games and music upstairs. Second son Stephan von Breuning was to be one of Beethoven's lifelong friends, despite quarrels and long estrangements. Stephan studied with *Kapelle* violinist Franz Anton Ries and sat in occasionally with the court orchestra. Oldest son Christoph, like the rest of the family, was a passionate reader and wrote poetry.

What probably began as a simple matter, the hiring of a talented local boy to teach keyboard to children under the eyes of their benevolent and formidable mother, developed over the next years into an irreplaceable part of Beethoven's *Bildung,* that German word meaning not only schooling but also growth in experience, maturity, understanding. Beethoven came into the orbit of a family that gave him something like the nurturing home he never really had and provided him with books and ideas that stayed with him.

In 1783, once again with Neefe pulling strings, Beethoven, at twelve, published three clavier sonatas dedicated to Elector Max Friedrich. Remembered as the *Electoral* Sonatas, they are a leap beyond the slight *Dressler* Variations of a year before. Under Neefe's tutelage, the boy was learning composition at a tremendous pace. He was also going furiously at the technical aspects of writing not for clavier in general, like most keyboard publications of the time, but specifically for the pianoforte. The *Dresslers* have no volume markings and few articulation marks; they are harpsichord pieces. The *Electoral* Sonatas bristle with pianistic effects.

Each sonata has its own personality. The opening movement of no. 1, in E-flat major, has an atmosphere stately, aristocratic, fashionably *galant,* and a little pompous; its tone may have been a tribute to the Elector. No. 2, in F minor, starts with a slow and fraught introduction, then launches into an intense (or would-be) Allegro assai. It is followed by an Andante strikingly poignant for a boy of twelve, and a perfunctory Presto finale. No. 3, in D major, the strongest of the set, suggests Haydn at his most vivacious. Its jolly outer movements frame the most striking formal idea of the sonatas, a minuet followed by six variations. Most prophetic is the unfolding of the F Minor Sonata:

it begins with a somber introduction that leads to a driving Allegro theme, and features an unusual repeat of the slow introduction and another return of that introduction before the recapitulation. All this is to say that Beethoven's first minor-key sonata is the embryo of his future op. 13, the *Pathétique* Sonata, which treats its introduction the same way.

The *Electoral* Sonatas reveal that, by age twelve, Beethoven knew correct harmonic practice, modulation, and the traditional formal models of sonata movements — a more sophisticated matter than the genre of theme and variations. He could write sparkling and idiomatic virtuoso passages. He knew about the emotions and characters one weaves into music and wielded these expressive and traditional topics effectively: the gestures and mood of the *galant*, the tone of the elevated and aristocratic, the gay, the poignant, the comic, and so on through the emotions as represented in music. He had the beginnings of his sense of the character of particular keys: E-flat major, aristocratic and expansive and noble; F minor, dark and *furioso*; D major, bright and ebullient. Maybe most surprising of all, in these early sonatas Beethoven is already in the habit of connecting his themes by means of small motives, such as the rising and falling thirds heard throughout the E-flat Sonata and the rising tonic triad outline that begins each movement. Consciously or instinctively, Beethoven already grasped not only that a multimovement work needs a unity of mood but also that it can be based on a unified collection of ideas, just as a set of variations are all based on one theme.

At the same time, the *Electoral* Sonatas reveal the elements of his craft that Beethoven had not mastered as he entered his teens. If his themes are attractive, they are also conventional, some of them shapeless and static. It is hard to tell whether his departures from standard forms are imaginative or naive; he has not learned the inner logic of form, how to make the material inflect a shape and sit convincingly within it.

Most strikingly, in his determination to write pure piano music using the full range of the instrument's volume and touch, the twelve-year-old goes over the top with fussy, awkward, sometimes impossible dynamics and articulations. Some markings have to be ignored: say, the intricate articulations on fast sixteenth notes, the wild up-and-down dynamics.[9] Especially in the first two sonatas, ideas tend to be presented and then dropped. Only in the D Major does he begin to grapple with the sophisticated discipline of sustaining an idea: if the *furioso* first theme of the F Minor Sonata did not soon collapse into bland octave passages, it might have approached the intensity of its descendent the *Pathétique*.

The dedication to Elector Max Friedrich that prefaces the printed score of the sonatas is significant in itself:

> Gracious One!
>
>   Since my fourth year, music has been the first of my youthful pursuits. Having become acquainted early on with this dear muse that called forth pure harmonies in my soul, I grew to love it, and, as it often appeared to me, it grew to love me in turn. Now I have reached my eleventh year; and ever since, in hours of blissful solitude, my muse has often whispered to me: "Try to write down the harmonies of your soul!" Eleven years — I thought — and how would the author's role suit me? And what would men of our art say to it? I was almost shy. Yet, it was the will of my muse — I obeyed and wrote.
>
>   And may I now, Gracious One! dare to put my first youthful works at the foot of Your throne? And may I hope that You will grant them the encouraging approval of Your gentle fatherly eye?[10]

These words may have been written by Beethoven, but the style and the moony idealism are Christian Neefe's. Beethoven would never write words quite like these again. By adulthood, the fastidious schoolboy lettering disappeared from his handwriting, and his language became concrete and to the point. The harmonies of his soul would speak in his art, rarely in his words.

In 1783 there was a small fourth brother in the Beethoven household: Franz Georg van Beethoven, named in honor of the late violinist Franz Georg Rovantini. In March the toddler died at age two. There was a consequence of the earlier death. Rovantini's sister Maria Magdalena, a cousin of Maria van Beethoven, came from Rotterdam to visit her brother's grave. While she was at it, she wanted to take in the sights around Bonn and the Rhineland. She was accompanied by a wealthy widow and her daughter, for whom Maria Magdalena worked as governess. The well-to-do trio from Rotterdam stayed with the Beethovens for a month, and made later visits.[11]

To Rotterdam

In turn, Maria's cousin and her employer invited the Beethovens to Rotterdam and arranged for aristocratic performance venues for Ludwig, including the royal court at the Hague. Johann was not able to get released from his court duties in Bonn, so, toward the end of 1783, Maria van Beethoven and Ludwig set off north down the Rhine to Holland. The weather was so cold that on the boat, Maria held Ludwig's feet in her lap to keep them from freezing. It turned out to be one of the longest journeys of his life. At the concert, before an audience of nobles in the Hague, he found great success playing a concerto in E-flat of his own.[12] Beginning with a flavor of hunting call–cum–march (the march an abiding topic in his future concerto first movements), it is a lively and eclectic piece that showed off his virtuosity.

Playing a solo work on the same program was the Mannheim-born composer, violinist, and violist Carl Stamitz, then living in the Hague. Known for his *symphonies concertantes* and concertos, he likely became the first internationally famous composer the young Beethoven met. For his concerto performance, Ludwig was paid the unusually high fee of 63 florins, nearly 50 florins more than the distinguished Stamitz. (Perhaps because his mother was there, on the court's payment record Beethoven was listed at his correct age of twelve.)[13]

Apparently Ludwig and his mother stayed with Maria's cousin for a while, the boy concertizing in grand houses, before returning to Bonn.[14] In Holland, he had found favor with both his composing and his playing, met a celebrated composer, and saw a great European city for the first time. There is no indication what he thought of any of it, but probably he was not impressed. If he had ever felt daunted to be performing before, say, a roomful of aristocrats and a famous composer in the splendid music room of a palace, he appeared no longer daunted and never would be. He simply saw it as his job and his due. All Beethoven is recorded to have said about his Rotterdam journey is this: "The Dutch are skinflints, they love money too much, I'll never visit Holland again." His fee for playing his concerto, 63 florins, would have meant several months' living to a member of the Bonn *Kapelle*. He never did visit Holland again.

January 1784 brought the first herald of a new era in Bonn. For twenty years chief minister and power-behind-the-throne Count Caspar Anton von Belderbusch, moving force behind the founding of the National Theater and of the Academy, which he was preparing to turn into a university, and music-loving patron of the Beethoven family, died from an overdose of emetic. Bonners had seen him as a corrupt minister mainly concerned with feathering his nest. Hearing the news of his death, the city danced in the streets.[15]

Around that time, Beethoven received a review of his first published compositions. This first notice of his career was a bad one: the *Musikalischer Almanach* dismissed the *Dressler* Variations and *Electoral* Sonatas, saying they "perhaps could be respected as the first attempts of a beginner in music, like an exercise by a third- or fourth-form student in our schools." Beethoven may have hoped to get the E-flat Major Piano Concerto published; if so, he dropped the idea.[16]

Besides being Neefe's assistant organist, the boy had taken over for his teacher as rehearsal pianist in the theater. In February, Neefe petitioned Elector Max Friedrich to make the boy's organ position official and salaried. Relaying Neefe's petition, lord high steward and *Musikintendant* Sigismond gave the Elector a summary of where Beethoven and his family stood at that point:

> The supplicant's father served Your Electoral Grace and Your Grace's predecessors for 29 years, and his grandfather for 46 years [*sic* — it was 40 years] . . . the supplicant has been sufficiently tested in the past and has been found capable of playing the court organ, which he has often done in the absence of the organist Neefe, as well as at rehearsals of plays and at various other functions, and will do so in such cases in the future; . . . Your electoral Grace has most graciously provided for his care and contingent subsistence (which his father is absolutely no longer able to do) . . . the supplicant well deserves to have graciously

bestowed upon him the position of assistant at the court organ, in addition to a small increase of remuneration.[17]

The petition got nowhere for the moment, swallowed by events at court. Meanwhile, it reveals that <u>Johann van Beethoven was becoming useless as a provider, on the way to being a charity case.</u> Belderbusch, the family's champion at court, was dead. If anyone was going to support the Beethovens now, it had to be oldest son Ludwig. His father had been making 450 florins a year, to which he added with private lessons, to which Ludwig added with proceeds from his performances, gifts for dedications, and the like — a trickle that helped keep the family going but was at the same time unpredictable. By then Maria van Beethoven was weary and perhaps ill, Johann sinking deeper into the bottle. The Electoral Court, for its part, had lost its leader Belderbusch and had further troubles of its own.

For Elector Max Friedrich, 1784 was another unfortunate year, though it would be his last bad one. His regime had already seen a grueling famine and a fire that all but destroyed the Electoral Residence, and he and Belderbusch were, in some degree, blamed for both. Now, after the death of Belderbusch, who had run the government, the court being rudderless under an Elector unused to governing, nature with a certain touch of biblical poetry followed fire and famine with flood.

On February 27, a thaw and heavy rain broke up the ice covering the Rhine, which that winter had been thick enough to support the market and its trade. When the river ice broke, a wave of ice and water engulfed the town. At the Fischer house, the baker's family hauled their valuables and furniture from the ground-floor bakery to the attic. As the water climbed to four feet on the next floor, Maria van Beethoven was heard to say, "What flood? . . . In Ehrenbreitstein we had lots of floods, so this one doesn't impress me." When the water reached the bottom of their third-floor stairs, Maria was impressed. The Beethovens also dragged their belongings to the attic, where they and the Fischers conferred and decided to get out. They exited the house on a ladder, parents carrying children; ran along boards placed in the courtyard; and ended up in a house on higher ground in Stockenstrasse to wait out the disaster. It was the worst flood Bonn had seen since 1374. City walls on the river were damaged and more than a hundred houses destroyed, but the Fischer's Zum Walfisch survived.[18]

On March 3, while ice and water still stood in the streets, Elector Maximilian Friedrich died. As usual on the death of an Elector, the theater company and musicians and other artists were dismissed with a month's pay. National Theater director Grossmann left Bonn never to return, and most of his actors were dispersed. Christian Neefe lost his position as theater music director and had nothing to do but play organ in the chapel.[19]

Once coadjutor, now Elector, Maximilian Franz arrived in Bonn late at night on April 27, 1784, without fanfare but, he declared, "with the most lively feelings of joy." He was like an ambitious young scientist taking over a splendid laboratory. His assumption of the throne marked the full flowering of Bonn's golden age. That apotheosis would not be found in the palaces and monuments of electoral glory but in art, poetry, philosophy, music, and the ideals behind them: in Aufklärung.

5

Golden Age

FOR COURT ACTORS and musicians, the death of an Elector was a time of sorrow, however they felt about the glorious deceased. They were all dismissed, to be rehired or not at the pleasure of the next regime. In June 1784, a court official wrote for new Elector Maximilian Franz a "Respectful Pro-memoria Regarding the Electoral Court Musique." Its summary of the members of the *Kapelle* included these items:

8. Johann Beethoven has a definitely decaying voice; he has been long in service, is very poor, of respectable conduct and married.

13. Christian Neefe, the organist, according to my unprejudiced judgment, could be relieved of this post since he is not particularly accomplished on the organ, is moreover, a foreigner of no particular *merriten* and of the Calvinist religion.

14. Ludwig van Beethoven, a son of Beethoven sub no. 8, receives no stipend but, in the absence of Kapellmeister Luchesy [*sic*], has taken over the organ. He has good ability, is still young and his conduct is quiet and upright.[1]

The next month, a depressed Christian Neefe wrote a letter to his old friend and employer Grossmann, who had left town with the regime change and closing of the National Theater. Knowing cabals in the court were against him, Neefe was desperate to find a job away from Bonn: "Your letter, my dearest Grossmann, has contributed much, much to reassure me . . . Take the warmest thanks of this friend trusting you for work. I will never forget this noble prompting of your heart." Neefe tells Grossmann that his friends have advised him to be patient and hopeful, and have found him piano students. To Neefe, at age thirty-six, that feels like he is going back to the drudgery of age sixteen, teaching keyboard to children. He adds about his situation: "Betthoven [sic] will be the happiest, but I doubt very much that he'll draw much actual benefit from it."[2] Beethoven, at age thirteen, had just been officially appointed Neefe's second at the court organ, his new salary of 150 florins taken out of his teacher's stipend. Between that reduction and the ending of his theater position, Neefe had lost most of his income and was close to losing it all.[3]

Does Neefe's curt observation that Beethoven will be pleased at his demotion show a break between them? Not necessarily; only that Neefe knew that the officials were trying to replace him as organist with his more tractable and less expensive student. Beethoven had no hand in that, nor did his father — Neefe was a friend of the Beethoven family and a frequent visitor in the house. But surely Beethoven had some idea of what was going on, that he was caught unpleasantly between his teacher's future and his own need to earn a salary. He was in the process of becoming the main support of his family. There the situation sat for months, uncomfortable for everyone concerned.

Beethoven had better reasons to be happy. With no duties in the theater and court music at low ebb for the moment, he had lots of time to practice piano, and for the first time in his life he was earning a regular paycheck. Meanwhile, through Neefe's interests outside music, Beethoven was going to acquire more ideas and ideals that would endure in his life.

· · ·

For Neefe, there would be no theatrical work forthcoming from Gross- [Freemasons]
mann. He had to struggle on in Bonn. In the meantime, he worked on
a collection of ethical and aesthetic writings. Neefe had long been an
enthusiast, a *Schwärmer,* for Aufklärung. That had led him to the Freemasons, the international secret society founded early in the century.
Besides numbers of the aristocracy, civil service, and clergy, its membership included progressive leaders and thinkers around the West:
George Washington, Benjamin Franklin, and thirteen of the signers
of the U.S. Constitution were Freemasons; likewise Goethe, Lessing,
Gluck, and Frederick the Great of Prussia. Friedrich Schiller was not a
member but was close to Masonic circles. Haydn and Mozart became
lodge members in Vienna.

One of the outcomes of Mozart's membership was his Masonic op- [Magic Flute]
era *Die Zauberflöte* (The Magic Flute), whose final chorus proclaims,
"Strength, Beauty, and Wisdom have attained the crown of victory!"
Strength, Beauty, and Wisdom were the symbolic pillars upholding
Masonic lodges.[4] The trials of Mozart's lovers Pamina and Tamino
echo Masonic initiation rituals. One day, *Die Zauberflöte* would be
Beethoven's favorite opera, because of its humanistic ideals as much as
its music.

Dramatist G. E. Lessing summarized the Masonic agenda: "By the [Masonic agenda]
exercise of Brotherly Love we are taught to regard the whole human
species as one family, the high and the low, the rich and the poor, created by one Almighty Being and sent into the world for the aid, support and protection of each other. On these principles Masonry unites
men of every country, sect and opinion, and by its dictates conciliates
true friendship among those who might otherwise have remained at
a distance."[5] When Haydn was initiated, in 1785, a lodge brother congratulated him for his Masonic conception of instrumental music: "If
each instrument does not consider the rights and properties of other
instruments in relation to its own rights, if it does not diminish its own
importance considerably, so as not to detract from the expression of its
companions, the aim, which is beauty, will not be achieved."[6]

Freemasonry was the first international organization whose agenda
was not economic, governmental, or religious. Its social network-

ing and its association with Enlightenment ideals — equality, morality, tolerance, the brotherhood of humanity — brought in thousands
of members. By the end of the eighteenth century, in Germany alone
there were upwards of three hundred lodges peopled by more than
fifteen thousand brothers, including most of the progressive leaders
and thinkers of the time.[7] The incessantly proclaimed essence was the
conception of brotherhood. The very word *brother* took on an enlightened, Masonic overtone (as someday the word *citizen* would take on a
revolutionary overtone). But, if lodges were democratic in spirit, they
were elite in practice: the membership was middle and upper class,
with few tradesmen and fewer women.

"Mankind in East and West" ran a line in a popular lodge song.[8] That
the lodges were an international humanistic institution independent
of church and state was a prime reason churches and states loathed
them. Catholics, especially Jesuits, declared the Masons antireligious
and atheistic. Yet plenty of religious men, including practicing Jews
and Catholics (Mozart and Haydn among the latter), were Freemasons
in good standing. "We regard all men as our brothers," said a speaker
in 1742. "The doctrines of the law of nature, the prime uniter of human
society, do not permit us to enquire as to the religious beliefs of those
we choose to be our brothers."

Masonic rites and activities had a peculiar dichotomy: on one side,
a murky mysticism, with esoteric rituals and talk of Solomon's Temple and the Knights Templar, of Isis and Osiris and Brahma; on the
other side, practical and educational endeavors. Lodge brothers were
steeped in Enlightenment convictions flowing from the scientific revolution: the Science of Man and the Science of Morality, but also practical science and common sense. In more worldly respects, Masonic
lodges amounted to a circle of people who socialized and helped one
another, in career terms no less than high-minded ones. And in the
end, despite propaganda to the contrary, no unified Masonic program
of action aspired to bring about an enlightened world by revolution.
The transformation the Masons preached was personal and social.[9]

Christian Neefe joined a lodge and wrote Masonic songs, but he
wanted to go further toward reform and revolution not only within
himself but in the whole of society. That brought him to one of the

near-mythical sideshows of the Aufklärung: the Bavarian Order of *ILLUMINATI*
Illuminati. The order was a secret society like the Freemasons and
shared many of their ideals, but the younger organization aimed for
something bigger and more radical. Its members intended to save
the world and had a plan to do it. The order was proclaimed in 1776
by Adam Weishaupt, a professor at the University of Ingolstadt. As
Weishaupt laid it out, the order was a mélange of ancient mystery cults,
Jesuit-style organization, and quasi-Masonic ritual.[10] As of 1783, the
height of its strength and influence, there were perhaps twenty-five
hundred members, most of them from the same elite classes and professions that filled the much larger membership of the Freemasons.[11]

The secrecy of the Illuminati was deeper than that of the Masons,
their grades more rigorous, their mysteries more arcane, their agenda
more radical. Their style is shown in a model for questions and answers for those aspiring to the grade of Illuminatus Major:

> *Where have you come from? / From the world of the first chosen.*
> *Whither do you want to go? / To the innermost sanctum.*
> *What do you seek there? / He who is, who was, and who shall*
> *always be.*
> *What inspires you? / The light, which lives in me and is now*
> *ablaze in me.*[12]

As a result of their arcana and their secrecy, the Illuminati acquired
an aura of the uncanny or the insidious, or both. Secrecy at all levels was obsessive, starting with code names for everybody and everything: Weishaupt was "Spartacus," the secret group of directors the
"Areopagus." For a few years, the order spread modestly but steadily.
Like the Freemasons, the Illuminati did not preach violent revolution.
They were concerned, first, with the development and enlightenment
of individual members: moral reform one person at a time. That, however, was only the first step. Eventually the order intended to form an
elite cadre that would infiltrate bureaucracies everywhere, becoming
a covert but pervasive influence on governments, leading ultimately
to the unification and perfection of all human societies. Wrote Adam
Weishaupt, "Princes and nations shall disappear from the face of the

earth peacefully, mankind shall become one family, and the world shall become a haven of reasonable people. Morality shall achieve this transformation, alone and imperceptibly."[13] While its agenda was progressive and humanistic, the order was elitist by definition: the transformation of society was to be carried out by the secret male group of the illuminated.[14]

In practice, the Illuminati amounted to a sort of activist left wing of the Freemasons. A certain number of Freemasons were drawn to the order; illustrious Illuminati included possibly Goethe and, by some reports, Mozart.[15] Friedrich Schiller was suspicious of the secrecy and moralistic flummery of the Illuminati. All the same, in Dresden Schiller was close to the Illuminatus Christian Gottfried Körner, and the order's intoxicating dream of the brotherhood of humanity creating an Elysium on earth appears to have inflected "An die Freude."[16]

Education was a prime concern of the order. Every member was expected to recruit promising youths between fifteen and twenty years of age and inculcate them in Illuminist ideals.[17] Neefe was relentlessly devoted to duty, so for a while he would have groomed Beethoven for the order, though the boy was too young to join a lodge. The goals of the Aufklärung and Illuminati were imparted with homilies and maxims, like Neefe's own published homilies. Some of the maxims advised a youth to keep his distance from women romantically, to view them with the purest ideals but not expect them to be intellectual equals. Neefe wrote in an article, "They don't think much, the female souls . . . To think is virile."[18] These attitudes pointed Beethoven toward the prudish and idealistic, as opposed to realistic, attitude toward women that he showed throughout his life.

In 1781, an Illuminati lodge formed in Bonn, called the Minervalkirche Stagira, the Minerval Church of Stagira (named for the birthplace of Sophocles). Neefe was a founding member, along with his actor friend Grossmann.[19] Members from the court *Kapelle* were horn player Nikolaus Simrock and Beethoven's violin teacher and court concertmaster, Franz Anton Ries, along with a collection of progressive civil servants and artists including J. F. Abshoven, publisher of the town *Intelligenzblatt,* and Bonifaz Oberthür, later the first rector of the University of Bonn. So the lodge was woven into the artistic and intellectual leadership of the town. The Minerval Church met at the house of widow Anna Maria Koch in the market square, where she kept a wine bar and rented rooms.[20] Widow Koch eventually added a bookstore; under the name of Zehrgarten, her establishment became the nexus of Aufklärers in Bonn. All these currents swirled around the young Beethoven as they swirled around the whole town.

Neefe received his order name, "Glaucus," from the Greek word for "brightly shining." At meetings, members heard lectures on books, philosophy, science.[21] Neefe had to write an autobiographical piece subjecting his own character and ideals to a rigorous examination. There was a list of one hundred questions he must answer. They began, "What do you wish to be the purpose of the Order?" Neefe replied: "Thorough and particular connection of men with God, Nature, and themselves. Especially: The implementation of the Rights of Man."

The hyperbolic style of the Illuminati and the order's ultra-Aufklärung agenda seemed a perfect fit for Neefe the *Schwärmer*, who believed that true artists were likewise a cadre of the elect. Brother Glaucus had a precipitous rise in the order. In only four weeks, he attained an advanced grade. Two years later, in 1783, he became prefect of the Stagira lodge.[22] He was involved in creating and writing for the lodge's weekly journal, *Contributions to the Spread of Useful Knowledge,* which carried articles on everything from Eastern religions to husbandry. "Morality," declared the journal, "is the science of the happiness of every single individual . . . Politics, however, has the happiness of a whole nation, even . . . of all nations as its object; it is accordingly the science of citizenship."[23] For Illuminati, as for all Aufklärers, *science* was the great shibboleth.

The year 1785 turned out to be critical for Neefe in a number of directions. In February, after a trial of his playing before new Elector Max Franz, he was restored to his full salary as court organist, Beethoven remaining his assistant.[24] Max Franz was agreeable to Neefe's idea that religious services at court should be based more on German choral music, accompanied by smaller instrumental forces, a change from the former Italian orientation of court music.[25]

That year Neefe also published his collection of prose sketches, modestly called *Dilettanterien,* which open a window into his personality, his ideals, his teaching. Widely read around Germany, the book was made up mostly of homely reflections with Masonic and Illuminist overtones, such as his response to seeing a broken bottle on the street: "Think of so many other frustrated designs and collapsed hopes of men, of friendships ruined, riches lost, courtiers fallen, empires vanished, or on the becoming and passing of nature, or on the vanity of all things . . . And then turn your gaze upwards!"

In the *Dilettanterien,* Neefe also addresses matters technical and aesthetic relating to his profession, including his article "Characteristics of Instrumental Music":

> Sulzer, one of our greatest philosophers, and probably the greatest aesthetic thinker of our time, complains about the carelessness of the endeavor to make instrumental music more important . . . There is more to [composing] than the art of putting one note after another according to the rules of thorough bass and singing . . . which any village schoolmaster can easily learn. A fiery imagination, a deep penetration into the sanctuary of harmony that is only granted to a few initiates, fervent inner feeling, insight into the nature and capacities of the various instruments, an understanding of the whole substance of music, an ability to develop that substance according to forms and models, a meticulous acquaintance with the various characters [of men], with the physical and moral aspects of mankind, with the passions . . . [are required] if music is to be no empty cling-clang, no sounding brass or tinkling cymbal . . . One observes the nuances of feelings, or the point where one passion changes into another . . . The mob of listeners the composer doesn't need to worry about; they never know what they want, and never truly understand anything . . . Woe to the composer who heeds such men! He will deny his talent . . . and must compose minuets, polonaises, and Turkish marches. And then — good night Talent, Genius, and Art! The great composer doesn't get drawn into the mob. He goes calmly and unimpeded on his way to musical eloquence. It is enough for him that here and there unnoticed in some corner a better educated listener can be found who understands his language.[26]

Neefe preached this idealistic *Schwärmerei* about art and the initiated few to his pupil Beethoven, along with the broader Aufklärung ideals of reason, freedom, duty to humankind, the pursuit of happiness. Neefe also preached a relentless sense of duty to one's talent: _what gifts you possess are owed to humanity._ And, as an Illuminatus, he proclaimed the imperative of morality and how it must shape one's life and work: _to be a good artist, you must first be a good man._

In his essay on instrumental music, the man Neefe calls one of the greatest philosophers was Johann Georg Sulzer, whose *Allgemeine Theorie der schönen Künste* (General Theory of the Fine Arts) was one of the celebrated treatises concerning aesthetics in the German Aufklärung. Sulzer's ideas are as idealistic as Neefe's but more concrete, less rhapsodic. Whether or not Neefe gave Beethoven his book, he taught from it in important ways. Many of Sulzer's ideas read like a prophecy of Beethoven's mature music in its conceptions, its technique, its methods. In adulthood, he owned a copy of Sulzer and consulted it. Sulzer wrote,

> The most important service the fine arts can offer to man consists without doubt in the well-ordered dominating desires that it can implant, by which the ethical character of man and his moral work is determined. [To the end, Beethoven called himself a servant of humanity.]
>
> Every individual part of a work that is conceptually ill-suited to the whole, that possesses no relation with the other parts and thus stands in opposition to the unity, is an imperfection and blemish . . . There has to be a thread drawing together the many different things so that they are not arbitrarily joined, but rather have a natural connection to one another. Variety must appear as the constantly varied effects of a single cause. [Beethoven's sketchbooks are an illustration of this search for unity within variety.]
>
> In any sketch . . . one's complete attention must always be focused upon the whole so that one can see how every section fits in. [Later Beethoven said, "It is my habit . . . always to keep the whole in view."]
>
> The most important forms in which beauty ascends to the sublime, are those in which beauty is united with both functionality and

a moral essence, where the matter conveys an impression of spiritual power, where the soul becomes visible, so to speak. [Later Beethoven said, "Only art and science can raise man to the level of the divine."]

A musical composition written for many instruments, or one to be performed outside or in a large hall should not be so elaborated as a trio. [Beethoven had a strong sense of the differing styles of orchestral and chamber music.]

The composer would do well to imagine some person, or a situation or passion, and exert his fantasy to the point where he can believe that this person is ready to speak . . . He must never forget that music that expresses no kind of passion or sentiment in a comprehensible language is nothing but sheer noise. [Later Beethoven said that all his music was written with some idea, story, or image in mind.]

The main theme is commonly termed the *thema*. Mattheson justly compared it to the Biblical verses upon which a sermon is based, and which must contain in a few words all that will be developed more fully in the course of the sermon . . . The main theme is always the most important element. [This is a definition of Beethoven's procedure in his mature music: Everything flows from *das Thema*.][27]

Through Neefe, the ideals of both Freemasons and Illuminati reached his pupil, and to some degree these ideals stayed with Beethoven to his last symphony and his last days. But these influences did not play out in predictable ways. Contra Neefe, he composed, for example, plenty of minuets, polonaises, Turkish marches, and the like, the sort of commercial items his teacher deplored. Anyway, neither as a teenager nor later did Beethoven uncritically accept anyone else's ideas about his art. Everything had to be transformed into his own terms. Though he sympathized with Freemasons and benefited from their network, there is no record he ever belonged to a lodge. Joining groups of any kind was not his style. Yet even as he resisted authority, he also had a German respect for authority, for precedent, for the scholarly and theoretical.

In other words, when all was said and done, Beethoven was not only incapable of taking any path but his own, he was incapable of *understanding* any path but his own. If this is true of most teenagers, he never moved beyond that stage. At the same time, there was a fruitful paradox in Beethoven's relations to the world. For all his fierce independence and his obliviousness unto scorn regarding much of the life around him, from his youth on, musically and otherwise, he still took in everything significant he encountered and made use of it. Most of what he did as an artist was based on models in the past; but he had to make those models his own.[28]

Beethoven learned and grew extraordinarily through the course of his life and music, but his bedrock remained the intellectual and spiritual atmosphere of Aufklärung Bonn, and part of that comprised the teachings musical and otherwise of Christian Neefe. Among the elements that inflected Beethoven's sense of his mission was the Illuminist (and *Zauberflötean*) sense of a cadre of the enlightened, initiates into the Mysteries and covert leaders of humanity in the direction of Elysium. The boundless optimism of the Aufklärung applied to music as well: the arts were to have a higher development, both in their creation and in the perception of them, and so would be part of the progress of humanity toward the light. Musically and otherwise, Neefe was a patient teacher. In contrast to Beethoven's first teacher, his father, Neefe was encouraging rather than bullying, firm and frank, but he allowed his pupil to find his own ways and means. Neefe preached his social and spiritual ideals gently, likewise his teaching of composition.

As Neefe had written, he knew he had on his hands a student of Mozartian dimensions. Even if Neefe possessed a higher opinion of his own talents than history would, he had to have understood how far this boy's gifts stretched beyond his own. At the same time, Neefe had enough experience to understand that talent is not enough, that in the end few prodigies amount to much. There must also be an unusual adaptability, a drive to learn, toughness, courage, tenacity, ambition, fire in the belly, none of which can be taught, all of which Beethoven possessed boundlessly. Neefe suggested, guided, critiqued, shaped, but he also gave the boy rein to follow where his gifts led him. By 1785, they led Beethoven to three works of remarkable maturity and skill.

The idea for the three Piano Quartets WoO (works without opus) 36 — in E-flat major and minor, D major, and C major — smacks of an assignment a teacher gives a student: use particular works of a master as models for pieces of your own; follow the models as you like, but keep close to them as a formal, expressive, tonal, and gestural scaffolding. Whether the idea was assigned by Neefe or by himself, and without having much practice in composition since writing the *Electoral* Sonatas, in these quartets Beethoven made another exponential leap in his apprenticeship.

In the massive Adagio assai that begins the Piano Quartet in E-flat Major, listeners then and later could only be stunned at the subtlety and depth of feeling, call it a certain wistful pathos, coming from a composer of age fourteen. This does not sound like learned rhetoric, like everything he had written before; it sounds like music from the heart. What had he experienced to arrive at such an outpouring? All that can be certain is that he had experienced his model, Mozart's Violin Sonata in G, K. 379. In his opening, Beethoven follows Mozart's introduction closely. The gestures and the low, close harmonies are Mozart's, and so is the Mozartian tone: languid, seemingly suspended between conflicting emotions, peculiarly shadowed for the major mode.

For all their modeling, these works are closer than Beethoven had ever been to the composer the world would know. While he based each of them on a particular Mozart violin sonata, his imitation became freer, more his own, as he went. He began making the models his own with his choice of medium: the virtually unknown piano quartet instead of solo sonata.[29] If in all the quartets he generally follows Mozart's forms, meters, and key relations, he extends everything; his quartets are longer and more substantial than the Mozart solo sonatas. The C Major Quartet has the dancing gaiety of its model in Mozart's C Major Sonata, K. 296, though Beethoven's is more madcap.[30] Like Mozart, Beethoven concludes the piece grandly, with double-stops on the strings — but Beethoven's finish is longer and louder than Mozart's.

After his introduction to the E-flat Quartet, Beethoven, like Mozart, launches into minor mode, but more so: a fiercely driving Allegro con spirito. The most striking thing is the key. After Mozart's G-major beginning, the Allegro is in an unexpected G minor, but that key itself is common, and a resonant one for the violin because it involves the open strings. In his quartet, Beethoven makes the same turn to the parallel minor, but that puts him in the outlandish key, at the time almost unknown, of E-flat minor — unresonant and ungratifying for the strings, but giving them and the untempered keyboard a singular shadowed coloration. (E-flat minor was familiar, though, to someone who knew *The Well-Tempered Clavier*.)[31] Here begins Beethoven's life-long attraction to unusual keys, often ones in the deep-flat direction, like the six flats of E-flat minor.

In the fourth bar of his Allegro, Mozart introduces a dissonance, a diminished-seventh chord. Beethoven makes the same harmonic move in the same place, but his dissonance is more stark, a D diminished seventh clashing with a tonic pedal, and he prolongs the tension for four bars to Mozart's one. In volume, Mozart never goes beyond *forte* and *piano;* right away, Beethoven crescendos from *forte* to *fortissimo* on the dissonant chord. Beethoven's piano part is harder to play than Mozart's, challenging the fingers of amateur musicians.

Foreshadowed here is another of Beethoven's lifelong patterns. He pushes every envelope, makes his models his own partly by doing everything *more:* volume levels both louder and softer than his models, everything more intense, more poignant, more driven and dramatic, more individual, longer and weightier, with heightened contrasts and greater virtuosity. There is an attempt to give each piece a higher profile, a more individual personality than in the past. Mozart and Haydn shared motives among their movements; Beethoven took that unifying device further, creating intricate interconnections of melody, harmony, key, and gesture throughout a work.

The other two piano quartets are based less directly on Mozart's notes, more on the violin sonatas' tone and especially their forms. Maybe here was the essential point of this assignment: not just to study in Mozart the common layout of Classical forms — sonata form, theme and variations, rondo — but also to understand how malleable these formal models not only can be but must be, for a composer who wants to say something fresh, to make forms motivated from within rather than by rote.

The signs of immaturity in the Piano Quartets are less glaring and pervasive than in Beethoven's earlier pieces. Here, his age is shown in the restricted string writing, the cello usually stuck fast to the bass line.

A testament to how close to his later voice these quartets are is that he used ideas from them in three works graced with opus numbers: the C Minor Piano Trio, op. 1, no. 3, and two of the Piano Sonatas op. 2.[32]

There would be another legacy of these Piano Quartets. They were breakthroughs for him, and the spark of that breakthrough was Mozart. Through Mozart, Beethoven began to discover himself. Mozart was to remain his prime talisman, the model to whom he would return year after year for ideas and inspiration. On a 1790 sketch in C minor, Beethoven broke off and wrote, "This entire passage has been [inadvertently] stolen from the Mozart Symphony in C [the 'Linz']." He then reworked the passage slightly and signed it "Beethoven himself."[33] At the same time that Mozart became a talisman, he became a challenge, another father from whom Beethoven needed to escape.

For Christian Neefe, 1785, the year of his student's Piano Quartets, his reinstatement as full court organist, and the publication of his *Dilettanterien* was also the year when it became clear that whatever his strengths were, whatever his devotion to the goals of the Aufklärung and Illuminati, his talents did not include leadership. As prefect of the Minerval Church, Neefe had earned enemies.

In a written denunciation, some lodge members, among them court official Clemens August von Schall and *Kapelle* hornist Nikolaus Simrock, declared brother Glaucus to be a failure as prefect. Joseph Eichoff, eventually one of Beethoven's closet friends in Bonn, penned a devastating appraisal. Neefe is a good musician, Eichoff wrote, but he is proud and opportunistic, and he insults people we don't need as enemies. Specifically, Eichoff cited a row of moral faults: *Self-regard.* Neefe believes all his works are masterpieces, and when people are looking at his things, he watches them intently, waiting for praise. He cavalierly wrote a satire of Count Belderbusch and read it out in a beer hall. *Pride.* He is a name-dropper and presumes inappropriate intimacy with people. *Thirst for power.* He is argumentative, can't stand being contradicted, believes as leader he can do no wrong. *Talkativeness.* He likes to gossip over a glass of wine at Widow Koch's wine house.[34]

Whether or not the accusations against Neefe were fair, they were believed. By 1786, Bonn's Minerval Church of Stagira had collapsed. By that point, in any case, the Order of Illuminati had been outlawed in Bavaria, and its eight-year career was essentially over. But the passion for Aufklärung had not dampened among progressives in Bonn. Many Illuminati members, including Neefe, soon joined a new, less radical, but in the end more broadly influential organization, the Lesegesellschaft, or Reading Society.

Later Neefe wrote of this period in his life with regret but remarkably little bitterness: the ideas of the order were splendid, he said, "but in the results I discovered many gaps, many personal weaknesses, and still worse things that convinced me to remove myself."[35] The "science" of moral self-improvement had turned out more elusive than expected.

If with the collapse of the Illuminati lodge Neefe failed in his most ambitious endeavor to promote Aufklärung, Beethoven's Piano Quartets represent what may have been the last major creative collaboration between Neefe and his pupil. Though in his mid-teens, Beethoven was now a rival to Neefe on the organ bench at court and some of his friends were sworn enemies of his teacher, the two remained colleagues, and the older man continued his paternal interest in the younger. At court, they worked peaceably side by side.

In any case, after the Piano Quartets, Beethoven seems to have largely put composition aside for several years, giving his energy to keyboard practice.[36] By the time he left Bonn, he would be one of the finest piano players alive. And in his last years in Bonn, new mentors and champions shaped him.

6

A Journey and a Death

CONCEIVED AND DECREED under the reign of Elector Maximilian Friedrich, the University of Bonn was inaugurated in November 1786, under new Elector Maximilian Franz. He decreed a grand Rhenish celebration. The town was decked with flags, and bells rang the hours through three days of ceremonies. There were processions, church services, and speeches; public debates were held around a triumphal arch erected for the occasion.[1] In his inaugural proclamation to the faculty, Max Franz laid out an agenda for the school by way of citing his brother the emperor in Vienna: "Joseph, who knew how to value men and the benefits of the Aufklärung, gave them to you in the confidence that you will live up to his high intentions."[2]

A certain symbolism figured in the first location of the university. It took over the Bonn Academy, the former gymnasium of the Jesuits, who for years had imposed a conservative Catholic education across Bonn, as across most of Germany. The first rector of the university was liberal theologian Bonifaz Oberthür, once a brother in the Illuminati lodge.[3] The reactionary clerics and professors of Cologne, nominally subjects of Max Franz, understood that this new university was a progressive rival to the University of Cologne, so they made themselves the first line of resistance against the liberal and anticlerical spirit flowing from Bonn. If the intellectual vanguard of the University of Bonn did not comprise the godless revolutionaries they were painted as, they constituted a true hotbed of Aufklärers, committed to all things rational and practical, their religion tending to Protestant and deist.

The founding of the university epitomized the golden age of old Bonn's intellectual and artistic life. It was as a representative figure of that high-Aufklärung era and a contributor to it that Beethoven came of age. The early faculty included physician and Beethoven's friend Franz Gerhard Wegeler. Teaching classics was Eulogius Schneider, a former monk who was heading away from the church and toward revolution. The philosophy of Immanuel Kant became a staple of the university. Among the early students was Bartholomäus Fischenich, later professor of natural law and human rights, who became friends with Friedrich Schiller over their mutual fervor for Kant.[4] The galvanizing force of the Aufklärung ferment in Bonn flowed not just from the university, however, but also from the new Elector and his court.

Maximilian Franz hardly looked the part of a thinker or a dynamic leader. He adored music and dancing, but his principal enthusiasm was the table: one of the heroic trenchermen of his time, Max Franz is said eventually to have weighed upwards of 480 pounds. The sight of the Elector heaving his prodigious avoirdupois into motion on the dance floor earned him the nickname *L'abbé sacrebleu,* "Father Omygod."[5] In manner usually jovial and easygoing if oddly affected, Max Franz gave audiences in a worn black uniform and wandered the streets of his capital in the early morning wrapped in a dirty topcoat.[6] In those and other aspects of style and substance he echoed his brother Emperor Joseph II in Vienna. Growing up in Vienna under the rule of his formidable mother, Empress Maria Theresa, Franz took up Joseph's high-Aufklärung ideals. In 1770, the year Beethoven was born, Franz's mother sent his sister Marie Antoinette off to France to become queen beside Louis XVI. On Max Franz's one visit to his sister in France, his lack of polish — perhaps also his girth — embarrassed Marie Antoinette and created a rift between them. In Vienna, he had befriended Mozart, and for a while Mozart envisioned himself the future court *Kapellmeister* in Bonn. But by 1781, Mozart was fed up, writing his father, "Stupidity stares out of his eyes. He talks and pontificates incessantly, always in falsetto."[7]

Still, behind this Elector's outlandish facade lay convictions that bore vitally on Bonn and its life practical, philosophical, and artistic. He wrote, "To rule a land and people is a duty, a service to the state. I must make everything depend on making my people happy." If his table was excessive, he was generally frugal in matters of spending and ceremony. The extravagant building projects with which Elector Clemens August had once nearly bankrupted the state were anathema to Max Franz. If he made a show of anything, it was austerity.

Generous, open-minded, sometimes absurd, the Elector was still firm and tart in his opinions. In 1786, he wrote in a letter, "I was never and never will be a Freemason, because I've always considered Freemasonry a useless game of tricks and ceremonies to pass the time for bored minds."[8] When the local painter brothers Kügelgen exhibited their work in the Rathaus, he observed, "I understand absolutely nothing about art, but I can see that they are splendid fellows," and he gave them a stipend to go study in Rome, expecting them to come back to Bonn and adorn the court and town with their art (which they did). Max Franz proved similarly generous with Beethoven, with the same sort of hopes.

Music was the Elector's favored art. In Vienna, he had studied voice and viola and followed Italian opera, Gluck's reform opera, German singspiels, church music old and new, and the chamber and orchestral music of Viennese salons and public concerts.[9] As Elector, he built up the forces of the Bonn court *Kapelle;* the orchestra became one of the finest in German lands. He liked to read through opera scores at the piano; in 1788, he reopened the National Theater, with an emphasis on opera productions. Under his influence, private music making flourished even more than before in the houses of the nobility and the middle classes. Though he kept on the Italian Andrea Luchesi as his *Kapellmeister,* he and Christian Neefe turned the traditional Italian orientation of court music toward Germany and Vienna. That change influenced the musical taste of the whole town — and likewise the taste of teenage Beethoven.

At the end of 1787, Max Franz also lent his imprimatur to the founding of Bonn's Lesegesellschaft (Reading Society). Given the collapse of the Illuminati and the official suspicion lingering over the Freemasons, the accumulating Aufklärung fervor of the thinkers and clergy of Bonn needed new outlets. In an era when books were too expensive for many, the Lesegesellschaft proposed to be a repository of liberal and practical literature, newspapers, and journals concerning not only news and politics but also geography, history, agriculture, everything practical and progressive. With the Elector's blessing, the Lesegesellschaft established its meeting rooms at the center of Bonn in the Rathaus, the Town Hall that presided over the market. In the inaugural ceremonies, Max Franz's portrait was ceremoniously installed in the society's main reading room, accompanied by verses from Eulogius Schneider, the university professor and one of Bonn's *Schwärmers* for all things progressive. Schneider hailed the Elector as "protector of the Lesegesellschaft" and the town's symbol of Aufklärung.

In the end, the golden age of Bonn that Max Franz galvanized in scholarship, ideals, and the arts turned out to be a short interlude in the life of a rather small town. While the university ascended to an important position among German institutions, it never rivaled the ideas coming out of Leipzig University, where the high-Aufklärung figure Christian Fürchtegott Gellert lectured on philosophy; of Königsberg, where Kant presided; of Weimar, where Goethe and Schiller lived; or of the enlightened courts of Joseph II in Vienna and Frederick the Great in Berlin. Bonn remained a backwater where the progressive spirit was reflected, not formulated. The effects of its golden age fell mainly on the lives of strong but ultimately obscure individuals. The only figure from the heady period of Max Franz's Bonn to live prominently in history would be Beethoven.

During the festivities that inaugurated the university, a procession ended at a ceremony with a uniformed Beethoven, age fifteen, at the organ.[10] By then, his family had moved out of the Fischer house to a spacious flat on Wenzelgasse. Baker Theodor Fischer had finally gotten tired of all the music upstairs while he was trying to sleep, and politely gave them notice. The Beethovens' new flat did not entirely reflect the family's fortunes or happiness. Maria van Beethoven had given birth to Maria Margaretha Josepha, her seventh child, but the mother had also contracted tuberculosis, in those days generally a death sentence.

Johann, about to be forcibly retired and hapless in dealing with an ailing wife, her medical bills, a new baby, and two vigorous younger sons, was sinking into the bottle. He began to sell off family effects and pawn others; in a petition of July 1787, with Maria in desperate condition, he begged the court for an advance on his salary. Apparently, it was not granted.[11]

Desperate to turn his fortunes around and regain some control in the slide of events, Johann cooked up another of his schemes. He sued the estate of the late Count Belderbusch for the return of valuables he had given the minister after old Ludwig died in hopes of securing the position of *Kapellmeister*. In other words, Johann wanted back his unsuccessful bribe, which mostly consisted of antiques and heirlooms his father had brought from Flanders: paintings, a clock, porcelain, laces, a fine Flemish Bible, and so on, the collection valued at hundreds of florins.

If there was some justice in Johann's demand, there was no intelligence in the way he went about it. He forged the signature of a local lawyer on a legal document and got caught. Shown the document, the lawyer wrote on it, "The above signature is not in my hand and I have not the slightest knowledge of this document, with all its vilenesses."[12] Thereby Johann van Beethoven ended his last economic initiative in a muddle of delusion, dishonesty, and ineptitude.

Ludwig at fifteen and sixteen was steadily busier at court, bustling between theater and chapel, giving keyboard lessons to children of the nobility and officialdom, playing in chamber groups and as soloist with the orchestra. The pace of his days was much as his father's had been, both of them overworked employees of the *Kapelle*. At that time, Beethoven was small and thin but solidly built, maybe less unkempt than before because he had to keep up his court musician's uniform: sea-green frock coat with matching breeches, white or black silk stockings, shoes tied with black bows, embroidered vest with gold cord, crush hat carried under the arm, wig curled with a braid in back, a little sword hanging on a silver belt.[13] He had become more at ease with people, acquiring a circle of friends. But still he craved solitude, to be at home alone with music, to roam the woods and hills on the banks of the Rhine.

In his composing he did not follow up the stunning advance of the Piano Quartets with more ambitious works, but rather fell into occasional pieces, songs, experiments, sketches. The dozens of pages of surviving Bonn sketches include experiments in piano figuration and texture, probably jotted down as he improvised. He made a start at a C-minor symphony that went nowhere.[14] He taught piano to Maria Anna von Westerholt, daughter of an official of the electoral stables. In 1785 or the next year, perhaps for her and her family, he wrote a slight, Mozartian trio for piano, flute, and bassoon. For the same instruments and orchestra, he produced a triple concerto he called *Romance cantabile,* his largest orchestral effort to date; it appears to have been played at court.[15]

By then, Beethoven was making sketches on loose sheets that he carried with him for the rest of his life. He worked out his completed pieces in these pages, preserving unused sketches as an accumulating mine of ideas. For several years beginning in 1785, though, piano would be his main focus. He planned a career as a composer and pianist, his performing as important to him as his writing. Later, he said that in those days he practiced "prodigiously," often well into the night, and he speculated that it damaged his health. In any event, if excessive practicing did not affect his health, something did.[16]

In the later 1780s, Max Franz gave Beethoven more time to practice by frequently going out of town; during his absences, court music making slowed.[17] The Elector was musical enough to understand what kind of talent was blooming in his young assistant organist. So, with the Elector's financing, Beethoven was dispatched, aged sixteen and alone, on the most ambitious journey of his life to that point: to Vienna, the capital of German lands and Europe's capital of music.

The purpose of his journey to Vienna is not altogether clear — whether to study or to play concerts or simply to absorb the atmosphere in the city. The leading musician in town then was Mozart, and certainly Beethoven hoped to meet him, play for him, perhaps have some lessons. Mozart had been a mentor at a distance; Beethoven wanted him in person.

In spring 1787, Ludwig said farewell to his suffering mother, to his brothers, to bleary father Johann. He left Bonn around March 20, setting out on rough and muddy roads in a jolting coach. En route, he seems to have stayed in Augsburg, where he met Johann Andreas Stein, maker of his favored pianos, and daughter Maria Anna, called Nannette, who was to follow her father's trade in Vienna.[18] Eventually both of them were numbered among the finest instrument makers of their time, and among Beethoven's friends. In Augsburg, he stayed with *Hofrat* Joseph von Schaden and his wife, another Nannette. She was a well-known pianist and singer, her husband a Freemason and one-time Illuminatus. Impressed with this teenager, the couple accompanied Beethoven as far as Munich and gave him names of Freemasons to look up in Vienna.[19] The boy was learning the value of Masonic connections. On April 1, he appeared in a Munich newspaper's list of arrivals as "Herr Peethofen, musician of Bonn via Cologne."[20] The spelling shows one of the many pronunciations of his name.

After some eighteen days on the road, Beethoven reached Vienna around April 7. Shortly after, someone brought him to Mozart. The go-between may have been another Masonic connection, because Mozart was a fervent lodge brother.

The one-time prodigy of prodigies was now one of many musicians in Vienna with a wife and children, trying to keep his head above water. At that point Mozart was as admired as any composer alive, but his wife was constantly and expensively ill, and he was unwell himself. Meanwhile, he had been receiving distressing reports about his father back home in Salzburg. (Leopold Mozart had only weeks to live.) Around the time Beethoven arrived, Mozart had just returned from Prague, where the public adored him more unequivocally than the Viennese did, and he was in the middle of composing *Don Giovanni*. It could hardly have been a worse time for a musician of sixteen to introduce himself to a famous, busy, and worried man. But Mozart received the teenager from Bonn and agreed to hear him play. Or so the story goes.

Who knows what Beethoven thought of his first sight of this living legend. In those days Mozart looked like a fat little bird, with bug eyes and aquiline nose and a formidable head of hair that he had dressed daily. He was always on the move, fidgeting or tapping his feet. When it came to musicians, Mozart was exceedingly hard to impress. The endeavors of others generally only reminded him of his own superiority. As he wrote his father about the acclaimed Muzio Clementi, one of Beethoven's models for piano composition, "About the Clementi Sonatas. They are valueless as compositions as everyone who plays or hears them will recognize. Clementi is a charlatan like all Italians."[21]

Beethoven was fortunate that he did not know how brutal Mozart could be in his judgments. The whole story of their meeting is a matter of myth, which accumulated roughly like so: The teenager played some of his showpieces and Mozart was, as usual, unimpressed: at sixteen, he had been miles ahead of this youth from the provinces. Maybe Beethoven showed him the Piano Quartets, which had been based on Mozart's violin sonatas. Maybe the older man took that as a compliment and noticed how precocious they were. At last Beethoven asked the master to give him a theme he could improvise on. Mozart obliged. Listening to the results, he was finally impressed. He strolled out of the music room and observed to some other guests, "Keep your eyes on him — someday he'll give the world something to talk about."

Thus rose a foundation myth, a passing of the torch, the sort of thing the coming generations of Romantics elevated to scripture. Possibly it happened that way, equally possibly it did not, because Beethoven was not yet the improviser he later became.[22] But his talent could not have been lost on Mozart. Afterward there may have been something on the order of lessons, or not. In later years, at one time and another Beethoven said he never heard Mozart play, also that he heard him several times. If the latter, Beethoven had only one comment on the great man's piano performance: "He had a fine but choppy way of playing — no legato." Which is to say, he found Mozart outdated, a harpsichord player rather than a true pianist who could produce a singing legato.

Beethoven's dismissive comment on Mozart's playing is virtually the only thing he is recorded to have said about his first sight of Vienna and his encounter with his chief artistic model. At that time, the walled

city with its twisted streets had around two hundred thousand inhab-
itants, a larger percentage of them musicians than in most places of
the world. It was a bustling, cosmopolitan, polyglot center on a far
grander scale than Bonn. The court of Holy Roman Emperor Joseph II
sponsored much of the important music, opera, and theater in town.
Beethoven presumably took in some of the splendors of churches and
palaces, heard as much music as he could, maybe played in some gilded
salons, but there is no record of what he did or what he thought about
it. There is also no record of whether he encountered the fury of the
Viennese, both highborn and low-, against Joseph's high-Aufklärung
social and political agenda, promoted by dictate, which had struck at
the ancient powers of the aristocracy and the church and imposed rational austerities that the Viennese hated.

The idea was probably for Beethoven to stay in Vienna for a while, take
in the scene, have some lessons with Mozart if possible, make some
connections, all this at the Elector's expense, and pay his way with the
proceeds of his performances. As it turned out, he stayed in Vienna
less than two weeks. A letter came from his father saying that Maria
van Beethoven was failing and he must come home at once.

He hastened back to Bonn, hastening in those days meaning more
than a week of travel on wretched roads. On the way back he again
stayed over in Augsburg with lawyer von Schaden and his wife, borrowing money from them to get home. He discovered the truth when
he arrived: Maria von Beethoven coughing blood, suffering the tuberculosis victim's final torment of slow suffocation. The physicians of
that time had no concept of the causes of tuberculosis and no treatment for it. He saw his younger brothers traumatized, his father drunk
and helpless, useless doctors filing in and out, friends gathering to help
as best they could, a baby in the house who still needed the breast: all
ordinary horrors of the age, no less terrible for that.

Ludwig watched his beloved mother suffer for more than two weeks
before she was released, on July 17, 1787, from a life of many cares and
few satisfactions. Having buried her first husband and four children,
Maria van Beethoven died at forty years old. Feeling lost and devastated, sixteen-year-old Ludwig was now the only capable person in the

family. Father Johann, for his part, did the only thing he knew how to do: he gathered up his wife's good clothes and went out to sell them. Cäcilie Fischer was shocked to see those familiar fineries, with their memories of holidays and happy times, for sale on the street. She ran home in tears to tell her parents.[23] *Kapelle* concertmaster Franz Ries, who had taught Ludwig, stepped in with help and money. Beethoven remembered Ries's kindness warmly and long.

Two months later, after the first shocks had receded, Beethoven wrote to his new friend Joseph von Schaden in Augsburg. Written in a neat schoolboy hand, this letter is the first personal correspondence of his that survives. He begins politely and properly, and then sorrow takes over:

Most nobly born and especially beloved Friend!

I can easily imagine what you must think of me. That you have well founded reasons not to think favorably of me I cannot deny. However, before apologizing I will first mention the reasons . . . I must confess that as soon as I left Augsburg my good spirits and my health too began to decline. For the nearer I came to my native town, the more frequently did I receive from my father letters urging me to travel more quickly than usual, because my mother was not in very good health. So I made as much haste as I could, the more so as I myself began to feel ill . . . I found my mother still alive, but in the most wretched condition. She was suffering from consumption and in the end she died about seven weeks ago after enduring great pain and agony. She was such a good, kind mother to me and indeed my best friend. Oh! who was happier than I, when I could still utter the sweet name of mother and it was heard and answered; and to whom can I say it now? To the dumb likenesses of her which my imagination fashions for me? Since my return to Bonn I have as yet enjoyed very few happy hours. For the whole time I have been plagued with asthma; and I am inclined to fear that this malady may even turn to consumption. Furthermore, I have been suffering from melancholia, which in my case is almost as great a torture as my illness . . . I shall hope for your forgiveness for my long silence. It was extraordinarily kind and friendly of you to lend me three carolins when I was at Augsburg. But I must beg you to bear with me a little longer, for my journey has cost me a good deal and I cannot hope for any compensation here . . . Fortune does not favor me here at Bonn.[24]

That does not sound like a letter of a boy of sixteen, even a grieving one, but like that of an older man with a devastating burden on his shoulders. And the letter sounds themes that will be reprised, with variations, for the rest of Beethoven's life. He mentions no one but himself and his mother, depicting her suffering largely in terms of its effect on him. He responds to her decline and death with illness and depression of his own. He calls his town indifferent and useless to him. He is alone with his suffering, overwhelmed by melancholy. (Before long, melancholy, "La Malinconia," would become a powerful theme in his work. Christian Neefe had taught him to observe human feelings as subjects for his work — starting with his own feelings.) At least in the long chronicle of Beethoven's illness and anguish that begins with this letter, there would be no further mention of asthma. It was as if his mother's choking had, for the moment, stolen his own breath.

Elector Max Franz remembered Beethoven's excursion to Vienna very well. He remembered that it produced more debts than results. If that abortive journey did not represent the hoped-for turn in the young musician's fortunes, however, they were about to turn anyway, decisively and at home.

7

Bildung

IN EARLY 1788, a new figure arrived at the Bonn court: a young nobleman, handsome and charming, very greatly promising. Count Ferdinand Ernst Joseph Gabriel Waldstein was of an old and influential Bohemian lineage. The year before, he had joined the Order of Teutonic Knights, and he came to Bonn at the summons of Max Franz, who, like his predecessors, was Grand Master of the order. By his first summer in Bonn, at age twenty-six, Waldstein had been knighted and was serving as a trusted envoy and companion of the Elector.[1]

A connoisseur, a capable amateur pianist, and an occasional composer, Waldstein joined the ranks of aristocratic musical *Schwärmers* in Bonn. He would have come to town relishing how liberal politically and also how musical was his new post. He looked over the local talent, perhaps hoping to discover a protégé in whom to invest attention and money. In any case, he was quick to find Bonn's leading prodigy and to take him up.

Beethoven's childhood friend Franz Wegeler would call Waldstein the teenager's "first, and in every respect most important, Maecenas."[2] Probably he was not the first: when, at around age seventeen, Beethoven first met Waldstein, he already had admirers among the nobility and the bureaucratic middle class. But in Bonn he never had a socially more exalted, musically more sophisticated, more generous and influential champion and mentor than Waldstein.

It was the beginning of Beethoven's lifetime of association not only with well-placed music lovers but also with the higher nobility, of the kind who could open golden doors to him. His ascent would be charted by the status of the people who lionized him. For years he accomplished that rise without kowtowing unduly to the nobility or even acknowledging their admiration, and often despite their annoyance at his lack of deference and his manners of an unlicked bear — the legacy of an early childhood where he was taught music, not grooming and graces. In his childhood nearly everything but music and the love of his mother had been shabby, grueling, and ordinary.

On the whole, Beethoven ascended in the world not because he courted the great but because of his gifts, combined with an indefinable aura of inner grace and a relentless ambition to learn and to rise in every sense of the term. Waldstein understood this protégé and helped the boy become what nature had fitted him to be. The brilliant and sociable Waldstein rose as well, for a while, serving for ten years in the British army, then becoming Commander of the Teutonic Order at Virnsberg. Later, in Vienna, he served as exchequer to the emperor.[3] He began his career young, at the top of his form. Then, after a couple of decades of glory in high posts, his recklessness and his passion for gold speculation mastered him. In the end Waldstein lost everything he had: the affection of the Elector to a political quarrel, his wife to death, his fortune, his houses, the respect of his peers. The destiny of Waldstein was to die wretchedly in Vienna a few years before Beethoven, long out of touch with the man who he had once prophesied was to inherit the genius of Mozart.[4]

When he took up the teenage Beethoven, Waldstein was in his prime, generous with funds and influence, a Freemason with close ties to liberal aristocratic and Masonic circles in Vienna. With gentle irony, Waldstein called the happiness of humankind "my favorite chimera."[5] He began to slip Beethoven small sums, letting the proud teenager believe they were gratuities from the Elector. He encouraged the youth not only in his performing and composing but also in his improvising.[6]

There was nothing unusual in a performer taking up improvisation. For centuries, many composers had been instrumental virtuosos as well, and in both capacities they were expected to extemporize. A visitor to Venice in the early eighteenth century recalled with awe the violin improvisations of Antonio Vivaldi; J. S. Bach's improvisations were celebrated in his time, his admirers including Frederick the Great. In his Vienna years, Beethoven's extempore playing would be compared to memories of Mozart's. Here as otherwise, his conception of his apprenticeship in music had to do with first mastering, then personalizing the traditional skills and techniques of being a composer: figured bass, instrumentation, vocal setting, counterpoint. But the leading edge in establishing his reputation would be improvisation.

As he settled into Bonn, Count Waldstein naturally gravitated to the circle of Helene von Breuning, who had been serving not only as a patron of Beethoven but also as a substitute mother. At Helene's big house on the Münsterplatz, Beethoven was still teaching piano to her daughter Lorchen and youngest son Lenz. Meanwhile, he served as Helene's showpiece among the cultured circle who gravitated to her. A silhouette of the Breuning family made by a local artist has Lorchen pouring tea for her mother as the latter reads a book; her son Christoph also reads, while Lenz plays violin and Stephan toys with a bird in a cage; also in the picture stands Helene's brother-in-law, Canon Lorenz von Breuning, a prominent name among progressive clergymen in Bonn.[7] All the children would be close to Beethoven in his teens, and Stephan survived just long enough to tend to his friend on his deathbed. The silhouettist of the Breunings also did a likeness of their protégé Beethoven at about sixteen, his first portrait.[8] It shows a fleshy profile, his father's blunt nose, a thin wig with a ribbon-tied pigtail.

Later Beethoven called the Breunings "the guardian angels of my youth." Even before Maria van Beethoven died, Ludwig spent many nights in the house on Münsterplatz. He submitted to Helene's efforts to mitigate his stubbornness and his hot temper, to civilize and socialize him.[9] Franz Wegeler, who brought him into the Breuning circle, wrote that Beethoven's youthful exuberance first bloomed in that lively and sophisticated atmosphere.[10] Beethoven was not a gracious companion and never would be, but he was no longer the sullen and taci-turn child he had been. He could be funny and sociable, and he turned his relentless will to learn and to raise himself in every dimension.

Performing regularly at the Breunings for a salon of knowledge-able and admiring listeners, Beethoven played Haydn and Mozart and Bach, his own pieces, improvisations. Often he was asked to im-provise a character portrait of one of the Breuning circle.[11] That came naturally to him; Christian Neefe had taught him that music was mod-eled not only on forms but also on passions and characters. Young Beethoven joined in the ongoing dialogue over the Good, the True, and the Beautiful. He read books he heard spoken of in the house: Homer and Plutarch and Shakespeare, the current German poems of Klopstock, and works of the young Goethe and Schiller. He soaked up the Aufklärung ferment that was a constant presence.[12]

In childhood, Ludwig's father had loomed over him; in his early teens, Christian Neefe was his mentor and champion. Beethoven and Neefe still worked together daily at court, but his mentors and cham-pions now were Waldstein and the Breunings and the cultured young intellectuals his age and older who befriended him when he emerged from his childhood shell.

Now Beethoven was old enough to fall in love, too, though he would be constrained in his romantic affairs by a puritan idealistic streak about women, maybe absorbed in part from the antifeminist doctrines of the Freemasons and Illuminati around him.[13] He and Stephan von Breuning shared their first love, for a music-loving, delicately blond girl from Cologne named Jeanette d'Honrath, who frequented the Breunings. This presumably decorous passion ran its course with no visible scars.[14] Sooner or later, Beethoven likely fell in love with his student Lorchen von Breuning; that ended with a quarrel before he left Bonn. (Lorchen finally married his friend Franz Wegeler.)

It was Helene von Breuning who gave a name to Ludwig's tendency to drift off into his thoughts and become oblivious to everything and everybody. His landlord's daughter Cäcilie Fischer recalled that once she spoke to Ludwig and, staring into space, he did not seem to hear her. When Cäcilie demanded a reply, he came to and explained, "I was just occupied with such a lovely, deep thought, I couldn't bear to be disturbed."[15] When the like happened around Helene, she would say, "He has his *raptus* again today."[16]

The *raptus* became a little legend in his circle. It was not different in kind from that of other artists, most of whom create in something on the order of a trance. But Beethoven's trance was profound, a withdrawal into his mind that echoed his steady physical isolation from the world. Alone in rooms, alone in nature, alone in his *raptus*, Beethoven was happiest and always would be. For his friends, the *raptus* was most familiar when he improvised, falling into the music that flowed from his fingers as if he were falling into a dream.

In June 1788, Count Waldstein petitioned the court to increase Ludwig's salary. The family was still living on Wenzelgasse, where Maria van Beethoven had died, followed four months later by her last child, Maria Anna. Ludwig was receiving 150 florins as assistant organist, father Johann 300 florins plus three measures of grain. Without the rudder and goad of his wife, Johann was drinking heavily, losing much of the vivacity and joie de vivre that had once made him so many friends. He was rearing Ludwig's brother Carl as a musician, though this son had no notable talent. Probably Ludwig gave him lessons, though that may have been a fraught situation: Carl was even more hotheaded than Ludwig. Mild-tempered brother Nikolaus Johann was apprenticed to an apothecary.

The more Johann van Beethoven's fortunes and spirits fell, the more Ludwig at seventeen and eighteen had to take over as head of the family, overseer of his younger brothers and finally of his father. Ludwig got in the habit of managing his brothers' lives. From that point he essentially never lost the conviction that it was his duty to shepherd them. Count Waldstein's petition to the court for a raise in pay for Ludwig, despite the latter's mounting burdens and responsibilities, was turned down.

With the university under way, the Elector turned his attention to reviving the court theater and to expanding and deepening his *Kapelle*. The National Theater was reopened, with a stronger focus on musical productions; that made Bonn an important center for opera in German lands. Christian Neefe served as theater pianist and stage manager of the reconstituted theater. Directing the orchestra, and soon the opera and concert and chapel ensembles as well, was Bohemian-born cellist Joseph Reicha, who had arrived in Bonn in 1785 to work in the *Kapelle*. He oversaw a record expansion of the orchestra.[17] With him he brought his young nephew flutist and violinist Anton Reicha, who wanted to be a composer. Anton studied with his uncle and then with Neefe.

Beethoven and Anton Reicha became close. Reicha recalled, "Like Orestes and Pylades, we were constant companions during fourteen years of our youth."[18] If Reicha was not as gifted as Beethoven and was destined to be frustrated in his dreams of fame as a composer, he was still a talented and ambitious musician. The two became young artists together, talking music and politics and aesthetics, sharing adventures in and out of the *Kapelle*.

Making use of his early training in strings, as his father had intended, Beethoven joined the viola section of the court orchestra.[19] From his position in the center of the string section, he absorbed the orchestral and operatic repertoire from the inside and learned the art of scoring for orchestra in the most practical way. In the course of performances in theater and concert and dance rooms and in the chapel, he also developed a feeling for musical genres: the functional and stylistic differences between a symphony and an overture, between incidental music for plays and scores for singspiels and operas and ballets, between sacred and secular music, between the traditions of opera seria and opera buffa. During 1789 and 1790, the court opera mounted productions of Mozart's *The Abduction from the Seraglio*, *The Marriage of Figaro*, and *Don Giovanni*.[20]

Of the musicians in the orchestra, then numbering thirty-one and rising, many, including Anton Reicha and Beethoven, went on to fame of one kind and another, Reicha more as a musical theorist. The cousins Andreas (violin) and Bernhard (cello) Romberg found solid success as soloists and composers, Bernhard also as a cello pedagogue.[21] Old Beethoven family friend and *Kapelle* concertmaster Franz Ries was a widely respected violinist and might have had a solo career if he had not preferred to stay in his hometown. Horn player Nikolaus Simrock founded a historic music publishing house. In his teens, Beethoven gained a great depth of experience among first-rate musicians and a first-rate orchestra, comparable to what had been available to Haydn and Mozart in their formative years.[22]

Now there was a good deal besides music in his life. Along with most of the creative and cultured people of Bonn, Beethoven frequented the wine house, bookshop, and rooming house Zum Zehrgarten, run by widow Anna Maria Koch in her house on the market square. By the late 1880s her place had become the epicenter of the town's endless talk of philosophy, science, music, politics, literature, and drama, plus a generous helping of local gossip. The popularity of the Zehrgarten owed much to the daughter of the house, Barbara Koch, called Babette, the belle of Bonn, who made the Aufklärung atmosphere still more attractive. University professor and philosopher Bartholomäus Fischenich, one of many of Babette's admirers, boarded in the Zehrgarten: "In that house I spent a lovely part of my life and many happy hours. It was once the center of all intellectual and social pleasures in Bonn."[23]

Beethoven numbered among Babette's admirers, who for that matter included many of the professors, officials, musicians, and students in town. Though Babette was musical, she appears to have been too busy with business and beaux to reciprocate Beethoven's interest; he was a face in a crowd. The conviviality of the Zehrgarten regulars is seen in a day in summer 1789 when "the whole table from Koch's house" went on an excursion to the Elector's palace, the Augustusburg, and its French gardens at Brühl.

In May of that year, Anton Reicha, Beethoven, and Karl Kügelgen, one of the painter twins whom the Elector supported but admitted he did not understand, enrolled in the university. There is no record what if any classes or other school activities Beethoven attended. He resisted Franz Wegeler's attempts to sign him up for lectures on Immanuel Kant, the philosopher of the day.[24] For Beethoven, enrolling in the university was probably a gesture in the direction of broader education rather than a commitment to it. In his new responsibilities at court and in his private attention to his art as well as his social life, he was an extraordinarily busy eighteen-year-old. Beethoven was entering the heart of his *Bildung*.[25] By his teens, he was impressing the adults around him by the force of his spirit as well as by his music.

Europe itself entered a creative and catastrophic era of *Bildung* in 1789. After a decade of revolutionary fever, the long-anticipated day of wrath against the old order arrived on the fourteenth of July, when an armed mob of Parisians stormed the dungeon fortress of the Bastille, which had become a symbol of the tyranny of the ancien régime. In August the new National Assembly published the Declaration of the Rights of Man, proclaiming that not just French men but people everywhere had a natural right to liberty, property, security, happiness, equality, opportunity, and freedom from oppression.[26]

The shock wave flew around Europe, and the reverberations amplified as the French Revolution took shape. For devotees of Enlightenment, there was a dazzling sense of *It has happened!*, the tide of humanity turning once and for all in the direction of reason and freedom, of *liberté, egalité, fraternité*. Edmund Burke wrote in England in 1790 that the Revolution "is the first example of a government based on principles and a coherent and consistent system."[27] America had mounted the first Enlightenment revolution and fashioned the first rational and representative government. But America was far away. This was here and now. For the first time in Europe, a government was going to be created on practical and egalitarian principles, an answer to the thrones that had ruled because they had always ruled, and for no better reason.

The French Revolution aspired to wipe away the past and replace it with a future fashioned by and for the people. Wrote one contemporary in 1798, "If suddenly . . . the Alps would collapse from the Montblanc to Istria, if all of England would be swallowed by oceans . . . such a revolution in the physical world could not be greater, nor would the familiar shape of Europe suffer more from change, than the Revolution . . . brought to the political world."

There was joy unto ecstasy in Freemason lodges and Lesegesellschafts all over Germany. Philosophers Kant and Herder, writers Schiller and Klopstock, and a chorus of other German artists and thinkers were quick to hail the Revolution. Klopstock cried to Germans, "France free — and you hesitate? Are silent?" To many in that intoxicating early period, it seemed that the Elysium of brotherhood and happiness that Schiller had prophesied in his "An die Freude" was taking shape. The French National Assembly declared Schiller and Klopstock, along with Americans George Washington and Thomas Paine, honorary French citizens. Goethe, skeptical of chaos, held back his approval: "Sudden action is for the masses, thus they command respect. In judgment they are pitiful."[28]

Inevitably the response of the Austro-German ruling class was muted. Even so, many progressive nobles and clergy and bureaucrats applauded the unfolding events in France. In Germany and Austria there had already been a movement to curtail the unbounded powers of the nobility and end feudalism. Besides, German princes might conclude that a blow against the proud and powerful French throne was to Germany's advantage. Or so it appeared at the time.

In Vienna, a reaction to reform and revolution was gaining strength. Yet the reality was that if most progressive Germans approved the Revolution at first, they were still largely not radicals, not Jacobins, not haters of princes and nobles. In German lands, there would be no active revolt against their own ancient regimes and marginal agitation in that direction, though some of that agitation would be heard, ringingly, in Bonn. Most German Aufklärers still wanted not an end to princes but better ones: benevolent despots, like Joseph II in Vienna.

The revolutionary enthusiasm of many German artists and thinkers ended with the fall of the guillotine on Louis XVI and his Austrian queen, Marie Antoinette. The Jacobin-inspired Terror that ensued galvanized reactionaries. From that point in the courts of Vienna and elsewhere commenced a relentless campaign to crush anything smacking not only of Jacobinism but also of Josephinism or republicanism.

Beethoven's circle was among those electrified by the advent of the French Revolution, but between his duties in the viola section of the court orchestra, his piano performing and practice, the increasing helplessness of his father, and the overseeing of his brothers, he had little leisure to ponder France and the future of Europe.

It was past time for Johann van Beethoven to retire. His voice had been shot for years, and he had fallen into a sad and public soddenness. When Johann was a child he had watched the bottle master his mother. Now his sons watched him lose the same battle, if indeed Johann put up a fight at all. There were the usual scenes, the ordinary tears. The children appeared at the tavern at night to pull at his coattails: "Papächen, Papächen, come home." There were nights when Johann collapsed on the street and Ludwig wept and pleaded with the police not to arrest him, then had to drag his reeking and ranting father back to the house.

Around November 1789, Ludwig petitioned the Elector to retire his father and pay him Johann's salary so he as oldest son could feed and clothe his family and pay off his father's debts.[29] When the decree came back it had a provision to send Johann away, as once his mother had been sent away to oblivion:

Johann Retires

> Because His Serene Electoral Highness has graciously granted the request submitted by the supplicant and has henceforth entirely dispensed with the further services of his father, who is to withdraw to a country village in the electorate of Cologne, it is most indulgently commanded that in the future he be paid, in accordance with his wish, only 100 Reichsthalers of the annual salary that he has received until now . . . that the other 100 Thalers be paid to his supplicating son in addition to the salary that he already enjoys, as well as three measures of grain annually, for the upbringing of his brothers.[30]

With this decree, the humiliation of Johann van Beethoven was nearly complete. His son of eighteen was now the recognized breadwinner and head of the family; by the decree, it would be Ludwig handing Johann half of his pension. They both knew what most of that would be spent on. It seems to have been understood, though, that the order to exile Johann from Bonn was for the moment a threat, something to hold over him if he were not cooperative with the court and his son.

Before Ludwig could present the decree to the court official and receive his pay, Johann pleaded to let him collect the salary so he would not have to endure the shame. Johann pledged to hand over to his son the ordained half of every salary payment. Ludwig agreed and, perhaps to the surprise of both, Johann lived up to that promise. Now, with half his father's pay added to his salary as organist, Ludwig was making the equivalent of 300 florins a year, a living slim but workable for the upkeep of himself and his brothers. He added to it with earnings from lessons and performances. And his father did not have to beg him for wine money.

If Beethoven did not issue many ambitious pieces in the several years before 1790, he still sketched ideas on paper and improvised constantly. Then as later, improvisation was not only his main road to fame but his prime creative engine. He was building a fund of ideas and techniques on which a career would be founded. Since his occasional Trio for Piano and Winds of 1786, he had apparently finished little: perhaps two preludes (later op. 39) and a piano concerto in B-flat major eventually, much worked over, to become Concerto No. 2. He was still Neefe's assistant as court organist and one of the four violists in the orchestra, performing a steady diet of orchestral works and operas. By that year the number of vocal and instrumental musicians employed by the court *Kapelle* had expanded to forty-nine.[31]

What revived the teenage Beethoven as a composer was urgent news that arrived in Bonn on February 24, 1790: four days earlier, Holy Roman Emperor Joseph II, older brother and inspiration of Elector Maximilian Franz, had died in Vienna. One of the most progressive leaders of the age, the model of an enlightened despot, Joseph died exhausted and embittered, despairing of the reforms that had become a movement bearing his name: Josephinism.

His mother, Empress Maria Theresa, had undertaken modest reforms and among her sixteen children gave birth to a quartet of future crowned heads: Joseph, Marie Antoinette, Maximilian Franz, and Joseph's successor, Leopold. When Joseph came into sole possession

Josephism

of the throne after his mother's death in 1780, he issued a blizzard of decrees, finally totaling six thousand in his ten-year reign. Most were issued in the name of reason and progress; many earned him more enemies than admirers. He expanded the University of Vienna and established the German National Theater in the palace's Burgtheater (both endeavors were echoed in Bonn). He issued the Code of Civil Law. He liberated the serfs, decreed Jewish emancipation, and, with the Edict of Toleration, allowed free practice of religion. He mounted initiatives to improve public health, abolished the death penalty and torture (the regime of his mother, Maria Theresa, had published an illustrated manual of torture techniques for officials).[32] Whereas his mother had tried to stamp out Masonry, Joseph had Freemasons as advisers. He was vitally interested in the arts, including music, and if he had not appreciated and championed Mozart as much as he might have, he had still allowed and perhaps even encouraged the court production of Mozart's *The Marriage of Figaro,* based on a notorious Beaumarchais play that, under the cloak of a sex comedy, amounts to an indictment of aristocratic tyranny.

Joseph's campaign to bridle the church was more draconian. A Catholic like all Holy Roman emperors before him, he was still virtually anticlerical and antipapist. A personal visit and plea from Pope Pius VI did not prevent Joseph from dissolving more than seven hundred contemplative monasteries that he deemed were not doing useful work for society. The immense fortune generated by the sale of monastery lands was largely devoted to education. What priests remained were placed under the tight control of the government, creating something close to a state church.[33]

On the other side of the equation, Joseph's foreign policy ended disastrously when he joined an ill-fated alliance with Russia in a war against Turkey. His meddling with the church turned many citizens against him, including former serfs he had liberated. As Joseph returned from the battlefield to die in Vienna, deserted by friends and family, there were uprisings of nobles and peasants around his lands.

By the time of his death, more of his subjects hated Joseph than loved him, and the reaction against Josephinism was in full fury in Austria. Besides his habit of stepping on toes in every direction, both high and low, it had been noted that most of his endeavors in one way or another enhanced the power of the throne. He had abolished many religious holidays, which had the effect of reducing everyone's leisure. His expansion and refinement of the Austrian bureaucracy turned out to serve the interests of repression better than it served progress. Even his personal austerities — his order that no one should bow to him on his walks, his old coat with patches on the elbows — only annoyed the Viennese, who loved imperial ceremony and finery, and called him stingy.[34] In the misery of his last months, Joseph declared as his epitaph, "Here lies a prince who had the best of intentions and whose plans were all doomed to failure."

But in Bonn, Josephinism had taken root because Joseph's brother Max Franz was Elector and because there was little resistance to progressive initiatives: few people outside Bonn cared much what happened in that city, though the relations between liberal Bonn and conservative Cologne remained poisonous. In Bonn, at least, Joseph was mourned as a hero, the incomparable champion of Aufklärung in his time.

When Joseph died the Lesegesellschaft planned an elaborate memorial program. The spearhead of the memorial was Eulogius Schneider, one-time Franciscan monk at odds with his church, lecturer on Greek literature at the university, and one of its fire-breathing radicals. Among the minority of Germans who were true Jacobins, Schneider was the first to translate *La Marseillaise* into German. He not only endorsed but served the French Revolution through its self-devouring course, until it devoured him.[35]

As Schneider began working on his ode to Joseph II, to be declaimed at the memorial, he proposed that the ceremony should include a funeral cantata written by one of the leading musicians in Bonn. Schneider put forward a cantata text by a protégé of his, Severin Anton Averdonk. This young theology student was younger brother of the late contralto Johanna Helene Averdonk, the student of Johann van Beethoven who had made her debut alongside seven-year-old Ludwig in their Cologne recital of 1778.[36] To compose the cantata Schneider probably had in mind Christian Neefe or Joseph Reicha, leader of the court orchestra. Besides the usual musical challenges, there was hardly

more than two weeks to write the piece so it could be copied and rehearsed for the March 19 festivities. In the event, perhaps because of
the urging of Neefe or Count Waldstein or both, Beethoven was assigned the task. He went to work furiously, setting Averdonk's impassioned verses.

Then two days before the ceremony, the Lesegesellschaft drily announced, "The recommended cantata cannot be performed for various reasons." The reasons seem to have been mainly twofold: the piece
was not finished, and in any case the music the teenager was writing
was too hard to pull together in the available time. Beethoven probably
finished it that summer.[37]

There is no record that Beethoven was upset that his *Cantata on the
Death of Emperor Joseph II* was not performed. He may have hoped it
would have a chance later. And he may have sensed its immaturity;
he never published or performed the cantata himself, and it was lost
for many years. All the same, in terms of his career, he would scarcely
write anything more important.

The text of the cantata is overwrought as can be, and a high-
Aufklärung manifestation: a funeral cantata written by a theology student that does not mention God until the third number, and then only
in passing; only toward the end does it give lip service to paradise and
immortality. In this cantata death is nothing but tragic, and Joseph's
main immortality is his legacy on earth, not his bliss in heaven. It begins portentously, with all nature theatrically in mourning:

> *Dead! Dead! Dead!*
> *Dead, it is groaned through the desolate night,*
> *and the echoing rocks cry it back!*
> *And you waves of the sea howl it in your deeps:*
> *Joseph the Great is dead!*[38]

And so on. Beethoven's setting also pulls out all the stops, revealing
that at age nineteen he had a number of stops to pull. If he pulled too
many, that is a sign of his youth, but already the expression is powerful,
the handling of the orchestra effective and expressive, the voice unmis-

takably his own. As a sign of that dynamism, he mined ideas from this cantata again and again in later years.[39]

The opening pages, scored for an orchestra of strings and doubled winds, are momentous in sound and import: an ominous low C answered by whispered high chords, a halting and sobbing flute solo, an atmosphere new to music in its very sound and texture.[40] The high wind chords become the chorus's cry of "Dead! Dead!" This opening movement has a tragic depth hardly heard since the high Baroque. That tone would be heard again in Mozart's *Requiem* the next year, and after that not again perhaps until the Largo e mesto movement of Beethoven's Piano Sonata op. 10, no. 3.[41] One of Beethoven's most significant contributions to the music of his time was to rediscover a true tragic style that had bordered on foreign to the elegant, ironic, restrained temper of Haydn and Mozart and their time. That tragic style reawakened with the opening of the *Joseph* Cantata.

The overall approach in the choruses and the arias is operatic, from a youth who had heard a good deal of Mozart and Gluck from the orchestra pit. In the opening chorus we find another prophecy of future dark-toned Beethoven works in C minor. At the same time, in the course of incessant chromatic restlessness and piercing suspensions, he lands on the uncommon deep-flat keys he favored: B-flat minor, and the E-flat minor he had used in the first Piano Quartet. In other words, prophesied in the opening of the *Joseph* Cantata are both a Beethoven C-minor mood and a more shadowed E-flat-minor mood, slower in tempo, whose pathos recalls Bach's E-flat Minor Prelude in *The Well-Tempered Clavier*.[42]

The first movement reaches a depth of sorrow stunning for a teenager, if beyond what its maudlin text deserves. The same applies to the following recitative, "Die Ungeheur" (The Monster), its *furioso* accompaniment outracing the fingers of many string players of the time. The monster in question is a familiar Aufklärung bête noire:

A monster, its name Fanaticism,
Rose from the depths of hell,
Stretched itself between earth and sun
And it became night!

Joseph's assault on the power, privileges, and, by implication, dogmas of the church — the monster of fanaticism — is the single specific
thing he is hailed for in the cantata text. In the next aria with chorus,
Joseph brings sunlight to humanity via D major, though the music
maintains its restless and rambling chromaticism. (This seems to be
the main device the teenage Beethoven knew to express sorrow.)

The cantata's steady diet of modulations is over the top, some of
the word setting awkward, all of it overscored. If the opening chorus
is equal to the occasion, it overmatches the text; the rest of the cantata
shows a manifest straining and stretching for effect, with little sense of
the appropriate length to fit the material, the text, the sentiment. Still,
there is a mature sense of rhythm; the teenage Beethoven knew how
to keep a long movement in motion with expressively apt accompaniments. The soaring lyric melody of the soprano aria, "Then men rose
to the light," he would remember in *Fidelio,* in which men again rise to
the light.

With the crowning of Joseph's brother Leopold II as Holy Roman emperor, in October 1790, Beethoven was supplied with another cantata
text for the occasion. The second imperial cantata shared the same fate
as the first; it was too hard for the court orchestra to play. In the *Cantata on the Accession of Emperor Leopold II,* Beethoven reveals even
more clearly that he is a youth of remarkable technique but with a
shaky sense of form and proportion. He sets to music what he wants
the text to be rather than what it is, with its flights of angels and "smile
of humanity floating" on Leopold's lips. In the soprano aria "Flow,
tears of Joy!" he prolongs the first syllable of *Segen,* "blessings," for a
page and a half of virtuosic melisma, to unintentionally comic effect.
Before that the soprano has to hold her joyful tears through nearly five
pages of introduction to her aria. Beethoven has not yet grasped the
importance of proportion.

In their texts both cantatas were forlorn gestures to a dying age. The
time of benevolent despots in German lands died with Joseph. Leopold II, his brother and heir to the throne, recoiled at the bloody revenge the French Revolution was taking on the aristocracy. He started
the process of dismantling Josephinism once and for all.

The *Imperial* Cantatas of 1790 reveal Beethoven as a splendid young talent flexing his creative muscles, showing off a precocious knowledge of harmony, the orchestra, and operatic-style expressiveness. They also show the nearest approach yet to his mature voice. At the same time, they show that he had a good deal to learn about doing more with less —one of the main lessons he was to learn in the next decade. Besides the *Joseph* Cantata's prophecies of his later music, there is at least one in the *Leopold.* At the beginning of the finale the chorus proclaims, "Stürzet nieder, Millionen," "fall to your knees, you millions." That line echoes, surely deliberately, a familiar line from Schiller's "An die Freude," a leading motif not just of Beethoven's youth but of his entire life.

8

Stem and Book

A S OF DECEMBER 16, 1790, Beethoven was twenty years old, a young talent much remarked on, and naturally there were young women in the picture. His piano student Lorchen von Breuning sent him a birthday card containing a little poem wishing him long life and "forbearance and patience," the latter applying for some reason to her. The printed poem uses the familiar *du* form of address, her signature the formal *Sie*. Beethoven may have been in love with Lorchen at this or some point, but probably not helplessly so.

There was another girl who had moved him, Madame Baroness de Westerholt, his piano student and daughter of an official of the electoral stables with a musical family. A few years before, Beethoven had written for the family the Trio for Piano, Flute, and Bassoon. This year he sent the baroness a card with a printed French verse ending, "For you, my very dear friend! / My heart will never change, / And will cherish you forever."[1] Years later Bernhard Romberg remembered this infatuation as a "Werther love," which is to say desperate and frustrated, like that of Goethe's doomed hero.[2] If so, Beethoven did not seem to suffer for long, and in any case, like most of his loves to come, the baroness was above his station. While his collection of friends and objects of affection was growing, he still loved solitude as much as he did a woman, still fell into his *raptus* when he became oblivious to everything except what was singing in his head.

As he left his teens Beethoven was small, swarthy, and slim, with a large head and a short neck and the piercing and expressive dark eyes he would possess until illness dimmed them in his last years. Perhaps he did not yet strike women as ugly, as later he generally did. Beethoven's adult face bore what appeared to be smallpox scars, but there is no record of when or whether he had that often-fatal disease in youth.[3] Some of the social rough edges had been knocked off him by Helene von Breuning. Now he could conviviate in company, laugh with the rest of them. With those of more or less his own age and station he freely used the *du* form of address indicating sworn friendship. Still, Count Waldstein, the Breunings, and his other mentors and friends in Bonn valued him despite his personality more than because of it. Yet even as a teenager Beethoven somehow radiated an aura of a great and noble nature that marked not only his music but him personally.

This year, along with many of his friends, he subscribed to a collection of poems political, erotic, and antipapist by the town's resident radical professor, Eulogius Schneider, who had conceived the plan for the *Imperial* Cantatas.[4] In Schneider's book, Beethoven read the poet's paean to the French Revolution:

> *Fallen now are the despot's chains,*
> *Happy people! by your hand;*
> *The prince's throne is your free abode,*
> *The kingdom become the fatherland.*
>
> *No stroke of the pen, no: This is our Will,*
> *Decrees again the citizen's fate.*
> *Lo, in ruins the Bastille lies,*
> *Freedom today is the Frenchman's state!*[5]

For all the liberalism of Bonn, Schneider's poems caused rumbles in high places. Max Franz kept out of it but let his censor suppress the book in the electorate. In June 1791, the university had had enough and

fired the irrepressible Schneider. He went to Strasbourg, where he became public prosecutor, equipped himself with a portable guillotine,
and began serving the Revolution by chopping off heads.[6] The Terror
was adding its bloody caveat to Enlightenment dreams of reason and
freedom. But powers that reigned now in Paris were displeased, and
these men were not the sort benignly to let Schneider flee out the back
door again. Louis Saint-Just and Philippe Lebas wrote Robespierre,
"We are delivering the public prosecutor of the Strasbourg Revolutionary Tribunal to the Committee of Public Safety . . . We do not believe
in this cosmopolitan charlatan and we trust only ourselves."[7] Schneider went to the guillotine in Paris in 1794.

Schneider had been one of the most radical voices in Bonn, and
an electrifying speaker. The town had never gone Jacobin, which is to
say radical and in sympathy with the Terror, but Schneider had still
found more listeners in Bonn than he would have in most of Germany.
Beethoven was among those listeners; maybe Schneider contributed to
the perennial resonance in his mind and in his music of the word *freedom*. One instance is Beethoven's 1792 song *Wer ist ein freier Mann?*
(Who Is a Free Man?), the text set in a melodically and harmonically
straightforward, declamatory style to which he later returned for similar texts:

> *Who is a free man?*
> *The man to whom his own will alone,*
> *And not any overlord's whim,*
> *Can give him the law.*
> *That is a free man! . . .*
>
> *Who is a free man?*
> *The man for whom neither birth nor title,*
> *Nor velvet coat nor workman's smock,*
> *Can conceal the presence of a brother.*
> *That is a free man! . . .*

For musical citizens in town, the great event at the end of 1790 was the
appearance in December of the Bonn-born, London-based violinist

and musical impresario Johann Peter Salomon, accompanied by someone as close to a living legend as a musician could get in those days: Joseph Haydn. As composer, conductor, *Kapellmeister,* opera producer, and conductor, Haydn had labored in the palaces of the Hungarian princes of Esterházy for nearly thirty years as a valued household servant, but a servant all the same. Before he gained his freedom, he wrote a female admirer, after he returned from a journey, "I did not know for three days whether I was Kapellmeister or Kapellservant . . . It is indeed sad to be a slave."[8] Now pensioned off and prospering from commissions and publications, Haydn had moved to Vienna, happy to be, at age fifty-eight, his own man for the first time in decades and creatively at the top of his form.

Soon Haydn was surprised to find Salomon knocking at his door in Vienna, presenting him with a virtual demand: Haydn was to come with him to London to compose, perform, and be celebrated. Extravagant sums of money were specified for various services while in England, including a commission for six symphonies. Haydn was agreeable to the scheme. Before leaving for London he said farewell to his admired younger colleague and fellow Freemason Mozart. The legend ran that when Mozart cautioned, "You don't know the language," Haydn replied, "My language is understood all over the world." The legend continues that both men wept and Mozart said, "We shall not see each other ever again."[9] In the event, they did not.

En route to London, Salomon and Haydn made a stop in Bonn on Christmas Day 1790. The impresario still had family and friends in the town where he was born and learned his trade. Before becoming a promoter in England, he had established himself as one of the leading violin virtuosos in Europe.

On Sunday, Salomon brought his prize catch to High Mass at the Bonn court chapel, where Haydn was surprised and pleased to hear the choir singing one of his masses. At the end of the service he was led to the oratory, where, to his further surprise, the gigantically portly Max Franz was waiting for him, beaming. Taking Haydn's hand, the Elector declared to the assembled musicians of the court, "Here I make you acquainted with the Haydn whom you revere so highly." During Haydn's first sojourn in Bonn, Beethoven surely got a chance to shake the great man's hand and get his first look at him, wearing an old-fashioned wig and clothes, long of torso and short of leg, his face large-nosed and homely but kind. Haydn's musicians at the palace had affectionately called him "Papa." A later age would call him "father of the string quartet" and "father of the symphony."

After a short stay in Bonn, the travelers set off for London, where Haydn was to discover that he was more famous than he could have imagined. There his fortune and his glory reached their zenith, where they resided for the rest of his life.

Beethoven's two *Imperial* Cantatas of 1790 opened a new vein of creativity. Having concentrated on piano for several years, now he returned to composing steadily. The pieces of 1790–92 included the first movement of a violin concerto in C (it apparently did not get past the draft of a first movement, scored for orchestra), songs and sets of variations, dances commissioned by Count Waldstein, and some piano variations on an Italian opera tune that stand as the most sophisticated work he completed in Bonn. Elsewhere 1791 saw momentous events: in Paris, the massacre of the Champ de Mars; Thomas Paine's *The Rights of Man,* defending the French Revolution; Goethe's becoming director of the court theater in Weimar; and the appearance of two operas that would be galvanizing to Beethoven — Cherubini's *Lodoïska* and Mozart's *Die Zauberflöte* (The Magic Flute).

The commission from Beethoven's chief patron Waldstein was a peculiar one. Beethoven was to write some little orchestral dances for a Waldstein-created event in the court theater to mark the end of Karneval. The nobility would attend in medieval German dress and watch a ballet featuring old-fashioned tunes — a march, drinking song, hunting and war songs, and so on.[10] Since the count dabbled at composing, the music was to be billed as his work.

The resulting *Ritterballet,* or *Knight's Ballet,* premiered on March 6, 1791. The miniatures that make it up, the longest about a minute and a half, reveal that Beethoven knew how to write lilting and attractive dances in traditional style. The score implies he had most of the court orchestra at his disposal. He used it artfully, his scoring full and colorful: string writing in rich octaves, martial effects of winds and brass and timpani, hunting horns in the "Hunting Song," a droll piccolo solo in the "Drinking Song" (the last two pieces in particular echo Mozart's *Abduction from the Seraglio*). The town *Theaterkalendar* gave a gushy review of the evening, saying that "Waldstein's" piece reflected "the chief proclivities of our ancestors for war, the chase, love, and drinking . . . It was also noticeable that the ladies would lose none of their charms were they to return to the costumes of antiquity."[11]

That same year, Beethoven wrote and published a D-major set of piano variations of immense confidence and maturity, rich with prophecies for his future. For a theme he chose a popular operatic aria, the "Venni amore" of Vincenzo Righini. The Italian's theme, two eight-bar periods, each repeated, is jaunty and slight. Beethoven transforms it into a virtuosic exploration of pianistic colors and effects on a more imaginative scale than anything in his piano writing so far.

The echoes of the *Righini* Variations stretch to the end of Beethoven's life, to his late piano music and last set of variations: the comic tone with moments of pathos and lyricism, the sudden changes of direction, the wide spaces between the hands, a variation glittering with trills that are not surface decorations but part of the music's substance. Also present are his offbeat accents and his trademark device of a crescendo to a *subito piano*.[12] In sound, the variations are singular individuals set off from their fellows by contrasts of all sorts: volume, rhythm, texture, register, and varieties of touch ranging from gently flowing to marchlike to staccato octaves dashing up and down the keyboard.

Beethoven again shows off his formidable talent and technique along with his inexperience. The proportions seem too short and too predictable, most of the variations sticking to the theme's two brisk periods, each relentlessly repeated. A variation has too little time to make its point before it is gone. Only the extended fantasias of the last two variations escape that problem. The first is a poignant and richly decorated Adagio sostenuto that recalls C. P. E. Bach's soulful and inward *empfindsamer* style. The last variation is a return to the theme's jaunty Allegro that amounts to a recall of earlier variations (the true Beethoven formal touch). He thought enough of the *Righinis* to use them during the next years as a showpiece, and was not embarrassed to republish them a decade later.[13]

The vision of the greater musical world that Haydn brought to Bonn and to Beethoven continued in an extended excursion of autumn 1791, when Max Franz sailed up the Rhine to the ancient town of Mergentheim for a meeting of the Teutonic Knights. The recent Electors of Cologne had served as Grand Masters. Like his predecessors, Max Franz basked in the pomp and ceremony of the militant religious order whose symbol was the sharp-pointed Teutonic cross. Formed in the twelfth century and having been a leading force in the Crusades, the order acquired vast wealth and power. In the sixteenth century, the Grand Magistry of the now-secularized order was established in a medieval castle in Mergentheim, near Württemberg on the Rhine. As late as the eighteenth century, knights still appeared now and then on the battlefield, but by that point the Teutonic Order amounted to a legendary anachronism. As with the courts of Europe, the order endured because it had seemingly always been there, its power gone but its self-importance undimmed.[14]

In their capacity as Grand Masters, the Electors of Cologne periodically journeyed to their official residence at Mergentheim for convocations. Max Franz arrived in the middle of September 1791, the knights of his retinue including Count Waldstein. He brought most of the *Kapelle* to help pass the time and to show off his musical establishment. His court actors and musicians — among them twenty-five men of the orchestra — traveled up the Rhine and Main Rivers in two large boats with mast and sail, installed in comfortable cabins. As a joke, the singer and comic actor Joseph Lux had been declared monarch of the journey for the artists; he appointed Beethoven and Bernhard Romberg his kitchen boys.

In childhood Beethoven had made a freezing winter journey down the river to Rotterdam, and his father had taken him on summer tours around the countryside. Now in the best of spirits and in jolly company, he was sailing up the Rhine in lovely weather, watching the slow slipping past of vineyards and medieval towns, stone towers and ancient walls and hoary half-timbered houses presided over by castles

on hilltops. Beethoven recalled the trip as "a fruitful source of loveli-
est visions." Where the river narrowed dangerously at the Bingerloch,
the Bonn artists disembarked and climbed to the Niederwald, where,
on the heights above Rüdesheim, "King" Lux presented Ludwig with
an ornate faux diploma officially promoting him in the kitchen ranks.
Years later his friend Wegeler found that Beethoven had preserved the
diploma as a memory of splendid days.

There was a stop in Aschaffenburg-am-Main, at the summer palace
of the Electors of Mainz. Working there was a then-celebrated pianist
and composer whose keyboard music Beethoven had played and profited from, Abbé Sterkel. Like Muzio Clementi and a few others, Sterkel
had made important contributions to the new repertoire specifically
created for the pianoforte.

Concertmaster Franz Ries and horn player Nikolaus Simrock took
Beethoven to meet Sterkel. The famous man played for his guests in
his famous manner. Beethoven found the playing refined but precious—"ladylike" was the term Wegeler recalled. In turn, Sterkel
wanted to hear the young composer of the newly published *Righini*
Variations. Beethoven resisted playing until Sterkel provoked him by
expressing doubt that he could manage the most difficult of his own
variations. Beethoven replied by sitting down and playing most of the
piece from memory, continuing on with equally virtuosic improvised
variations. This was impressive enough, but there was more: as Simrock recalled, rather than in his usual style, Beethoven "played them
completely in the manner of the Herr Kapellmeister with the utmost
daintiness and brilliant lightness . . . The Herr Kapellmeister was unbounded in his praises."[15]

When they reached Mergentheim, the musicians and actors of the
Bonn court were featured in a round of evening entertainments whose
pleasures must have been exhausting. One week's listing shows the kind
of marathon entertainment schedule courts were given to on holiday:
a ball on Monday night, singspiel Tuesday, big concert Wednesday,
comedy Thursday, operetta Saturday.[16] In Mergentheim, the orchestra made an attempt to perform one of Beethoven's *Imperial* Cantatas,
probably the *Joseph,* but it was no-go. "We had all manner of protests
over the difficult places," recalled Nikolaus Simrock, "and [Beethoven]

asserted that each player must be able to perform his part correctly; we proved we couldn't, simply because all the figures were completely unusual."[17] For another joke during the trip, some musicians arranged for a waitress in a pub to flirt with Beethoven. Outraged, he boxed her ears.

Among those admiring the Bonn *Kapelle* was amateur musician and writer Karl Ludwig Junker, chaplain at nearby Kirchberg. He traveled to Mergentheim to hear the Bonn musicians and wrote an account for a musical journal. "Here I was also an eyewitness to the esteem and respect in which this Kapelle stands with the Elector," Junker wrote. He described an after-dinner orchestral concert, one of the time's marathon evenings of music. The seven major works started with a Mozart symphony, included a single and a double cello concerto from the Rombergs, and ended with a symphony by the *Kapellmeister* of Wallenstein.

Junker rhapsodized over the orchestra's playing: "It was not possible to attain a higher degree of exactness . . . the members of the Kapelle, almost without exception, are in their best years, glowing with health, men of culture and fine personal appearance. They form truly a fine sight, when one adds the splendid uniform in which the elector has clothed them — red, and richly trimmed with gold." Junker noted that the orchestra members were jammed together in the small room and sweated mightily as they played, but "one saw no unhappy faces among them." He was surprised by the liberal temper of the court of the Elector of Cologne: "Before this one was apt to think of Cologne as a land of darkness, in which the Aufklärung had not found a foothold. One gets a quite different sense when one enters the Court of the Elector. Especially among the orchestra players I found quite enlightened, sound-thinking men."[18]

The one Bonn musician Junker singled out with particular warmth and admiration was Beethoven. This sophisticated dilettante would tell history a good deal about Beethoven as a virtuoso of age twenty. That the young man's pride and his rough edges were scarcely showing to this new acquaintance indicates what a fine mood Beethoven was enjoying on that visit, how pleased at what people were making of him. Junker understood the singular quality of Beethoven's playing, the result of years of not only practicing the pianoforte but also thinking about how it should be played, as distinct from a harpsichord or a clavichord:

> I heard also one of the greatest of pianists — the dear, good Bethofen ... true, he did not perform in public, probably the instrument here was not to his mind. It is one of Spath's make, and at Bonn he plays upon one by Steiner. But ... I heard him extemporize in private; yes, I was even invited to propose a theme for him to vary. The greatness of this amiable, light-hearted man, as a virtuoso, may in my opinion be safely estimated from his almost inexhaustible wealth of ideas, the altogether characteristic style of expression in his playing, and the great execution which he displays ... Even the members of this remarkable orchestra are, without exception, his admirers, and all ears when he plays. Yet he is exceedingly modest and free from all pretension. He, however, acknowledged to me, that, upon the journeys which the Elector had enabled him to make, he had seldom found in the playing of the most distinguished virtuosi that excellence which he supposed he had a right to expect. His style of treating his instrument is so different from that usually adopted, that it impresses one with the idea, that by a path of his own discovery he has attained that height of excellence whereon he now stands.[19]

In December 1791, just after his twenty-first birthday, Beethoven was back playing his viola in the orchestra pit of the court theater, at the beginning of the fourth season since Max Franz had revived the opera. As history transpired, it turned out to be the last opera season in Bonn. Again, part of the repertoire was the biggest success of Mozart's life, the exotic singspiel *The Abduction from the Seraglio.*[20] Surely musicians mounted a memorial for Mozart, who had died in Vienna at age thirty-five on December 5. Hearing the news in London, Haydn was inconsolable.

The hit of the opera season was Dittersdorf's mellifluous *Das rote Käppchen,* or *Little Red Riding Hood.* Beethoven wrote two jovial sets of variations on tunes from the opera, one for keyboard and the other for piano trio. Around the same time came a piano trio in E-flat, with *Scherzo* his first known movement called "scherzo."[21]

In Vienna Leopold II died after a short reign and was succeeded by his son Franz II, twenty-four, who appointed conservative to reactionary advisers and a cabinet that began to dismantle Joseph's reforms in earnest and to turn Austria into a police state. On April 20, France declared war on Austria, Prussia, and Sardinia. For the next twenty-three years, Austria and its allies would alternate between fighting the French and licking their wounds while preparing for the next war.

With armies on the march and travel uncertain, in July 1792, Joseph Haydn stopped in Bonn on the way back from his eighteen-month sojourn in England. His success had been monumental; he returned home a far wealthier man than he had left. His music, including the six new symphonies Salomon commissioned, had been featured in some two-dozen grand concerts and any number of smaller performances, and he had been awarded an honorary doctorate by Oxford University. He had gained a collection of new friends and thousands of admirers, and the particular admiration of a handsome widow. He luxuriated in his new life: "Oh, my dear gracious lady!" he wrote a friend from London. "The realization that I am no longer a bond-servant makes ample amend for all my toils."

During the visit Haydn had worked himself nearly to exhaustion, but in the end the only thing that truly sullied his triumph and his pleasure in it was the blow of Mozart's passing. Haydn wrote to their mutual friend and fellow Freemason Johann Michael Puchberg, "For some time I was beside myself about his death and could not believe that Providence would so soon claim the life of such an indispensable man."[22] What Haydn would not have calculated but was nonetheless true was that in Vienna, Europe's capital of music, after Mozart's death there was no longer an apparent heir to his legacy. As Haydn approached his sixtieth birthday, the position of Mozart's musical heir, the new indispensable man, lay open.

During Haydn's brief second sojourn in Bonn, the *Kapelle* orchestra members invited him to breakfast in nearby Godesberg. For some time the village had been known for its mineral waters, and the Elector was busy turning it into a spa. Among the first efforts in that direction was to build a theater and beside it a middle-sized but elegant building in subdued classical style called La Redoute, the Ballroom. Already in the theater and the still-unfinished Redoute there were plays, performances by the *Kapelle* orchestra and theater troupe, and balls twice a week featuring ladies boated in on the Rhine. The Redoute was where the orchestra's gala breakfast for Haydn was held. There came the definitive meeting between Haydn and Beethoven.[23]

Beethoven played and did what an aspiring young composer does: put some scores before the master. Mainly it seems to have been the *Joseph* Cantata. It is unlikely that Beethoven yet knew the story of Haydn's triumph in England, but the young man knew quite well that he was in the presence of the reigning composer in the world, in person old and old-fashioned but vigorous, kindly, and without pretension. Haydn had been no child prodigy and was never a virtuoso performer, but he knew a prodigy when he saw one. He was powerfully impressed with what he heard from the young man. Perhaps, among other things, in the opening of the *Joseph* Cantata he saw a tragic voice in music beyond anything conceived in a long time, and an imagination capable of conjuring powerful expression out of sheer instrumental color, from a leap from low to high, from silence.

Noting the dramatic style of the cantata, Haydn seems to have concluded that this young man should be writing operas — more or less the king of genres at that time.[24] For much of his career, Haydn had considered opera his main métier, until the advent of Mozart revealed to Haydn his limitations as a composer for the stage. Nor was vocal music in general going to be Beethoven's true forte.

All that understanding lay in the future. The immediate matter of the meeting was for Beethoven to ask for lessons. The old man agreed. Beethoven was ready to finish his apprenticeship, and the Elector encouraged artistic youths to complete their studies out of town, to get a more cosmopolitan perspective. There were consultations, an appeal to the Elector for permission, and soon Beethoven had been granted leave to go to Vienna to study with Haydn. After acquiring his final polish there as an employee of the Elector, he was expected to return to Bonn, perhaps eventually to become court *Kapellmeister* like the first

Ludwig van Beethoven. What would intervene in that plan was, for once, not the younger Beethoven's recalcitrance but history: history in the streets, history at your door.

What happened among Beethoven, his family and friends in the next weeks transpired virtually under the gun. In April 1792, France declared war on the Habsburg Empire; the Legislative Assembly vowed "aid and fraternity to all peoples wishing to recover their liberty." Meanwhile a Prussian invasion of France, with the intention of restoring Louis XVI to the throne and thereby striking a blow at the Revolution, was stopped by the French in September at the Battle of Valmy. Everyone understood what that meant: the Revolution would go forward, and the king of France and his family might be doomed. Goethe was present at Valmy. Riding onto the front with French shells howling around him, for a moment he believed he saw the earth turn red. At the end of the day Goethe declared to a group of officers, "From this place, and from this day forth begins a new era in the history of the world, and you can all say you were present at its birth."[25]

In late October, Max Franz and his retinue, fearful of the French approach in the Rhineland, vacated Bonn for several weeks. With hostile armies close and anxiety in the air, Beethoven prepared to leave for Vienna. His circle at the Zehrgarten wrote their farewells to Ludwig in a *Stammbuch*, an album assembled by his friends Matthias Koch and Johann Martin Degenhart. One of them likely drew the portentous picture on the first page, a moldering gravestone topped by an urn in a wild and tumbled forest. The inscription on the stone reads, "My friends," and at the bottom is written "Ludwig Beethoven": no *van* among friends.

Stammbuch means "stem-book," not only a record of friendship but also a testament to a person's roots. The farewells in the *Stammbuch* are earnest and serious, most of the men using the familiar form of address *du,* the women the more proper *Sie.* Most of the handwriting is in the exquisitely neat form taught to boys and girls in school, which Beethoven also possessed in those days. The entries are largely in verse, some original and so more personal, some quoted from poets including Klopstock and Schiller (there are three quotations from *Don*

Carlos). There are no passionate declarations of eternal friendship and nothing approaching levity. A few amount to curt aphorisms: "Investigate and choose."

Lorchen von Breuning had sent Beethoven warm birthday cards in the last years, which he would preserve. But now Lorchen penned only a few distant and ambiguous lines from Herder: "Friendship with one who is good / Grows like the evening shadows / Until the sun of life sets." He and Lorchen had quarreled. She and Christoph von Breuning signed the book, but, surprisingly, their mother, Helene, and brother Stephan did not, though they were the two people in the family closest to Beethoven. Widow Koch contributed, along with two of her children, but not the adored Babette. There is nothing from Christian Neefe and nothing from the *Kapelle* members, which is all not as surprising as the missing name of Franz Wegeler, his oldest friend.[26]

The verse farewell of Johann Martin Degenhart provides a sense of how the circle looked at the improvisations of their most musical member — with understanding, awe, and a touch of fear:

> *Sometimes, as you coax love, anger, and subtle jokes,*
> *Mighty Master of Music!*
> *You coax passions and caprice from the string,*
> *With truth and accuracy,*
> *Such as the devil himself would treasure.*

The inscription that history would most remember is from Count Waldstein, written in a bold hand on a page facing his silhouette perched on a pedestal. Like the others more about music than friendship, it is not a poem but a prose prophecy by a man who knew music, knew about Beethoven's abortive encounter with Mozart in Vienna, and knew what kind of potential this protégé had in him:

Dear Beethoven!

You are now going to Vienna in fulfillment of your long-frustrated wishes. Mozart's genius still mourns and is weeping over the death of its pupil. In the inexhaustible Haydn, it had found refuge but no occupation; through him it wishes to form a union with another. Through uninterrupted diligence you shall receive *Mozart's spirit from Haydn's hands.*

> Your true friend,
> Waldstein[27]

These few words say a great deal. Unlike most of his friends in the *Stammbuch,* Waldstein uses the formal *Sie* address, appropriate for an aristocrat addressing a commoner however well regarded. His conception of genius is that of the eighteenth century: a metaphor for a transcendent spirit that moves among and inhabits great creators, genius as a spirit one *possesses,* rather than the coming Romantic cult of genius as something one *is* in one's very being, which elevates a person to the state of a demigod.[28] Waldstein depicts the genius of Mozart as in mourning, surviving in the old Haydn but waiting to be handed off to a new young avatar.

History would remember Waldstein's prophecy because, on the whole, it came to pass. Except Beethoven would not claim Mozart's genius quite as anybody expected him to. His genius would turn out to be to take the lessons of the past and make them into something boldly and singularly new: it could be called a revolution, but it was better an *evolution* from within tradition rather than against it. Now Mozart was dead. In part, Beethoven's coming career as a composer would be predicated on having no real rival in his own generation.

His youth was over now, everything focused on the future. Beethoven never found another circle of friends and mentors and admirers like the ones he had in Bonn — cultured, serious but lively, liberal unto radical, given to high-flown discourse — who understood and admired him but also saw him in terms of equality as well as fraternity. The effect of that loss on his creative life can be summarized briefly: little to none. Beethoven craved companionship, love, stimulation intellectual and spiritual, but other than people to play and publish and listen to his music, for most of his life he would never truly *need* anybody. He was to spend the rest of his years in Vienna, in a city and among a people he despised as fickle and frivolous. That also would have little or no discernible effect on his music.

On the evening of November 1, 1792, as Widow Koch noted in

the *Stammbuch*, the Zehrgarten saw Beethoven's farewell party. At 6 o'clock the next morning he loaded his effects into the coach and the driver cracked his whip. Ahead of him was the prospect of more than a week of wretched roads, some of them filled with marching armies.

He said goodbye to his brothers and to his father, who wrote no poems of farewell and who had been living for years in the shadow of his son. He had given the boy his first training, had spent years patiently showing him off to patrons at court and among the gentry. If Johann's efforts had not made Ludwig the phenomenon Mozart had been, still they had effectively launched him.

Beethoven was already far beyond his father's reach, Johann too weary and bleary to reach for much beyond what was at hand. His son did not love him, wanted only to get away from him, now that his brothers could more or less fend for themselves. But it was well. As Johann watched his son disappear in the coach to Vienna, he knew he had accomplished one great thing in his life that could never be lost to him. That and the bottle were his solace. "My Ludwig!" Johann van Beethoven would crow to whoever was listening. "He is my only joy now, he has become so accomplished in music and composition that everyone looks on him with wonder. My Ludwig! My Ludwig! Someday he will become a great man in the world. You who are here today, remember what I have said!"[29]

Other than a few possessions and a pile of manuscripts and sketches, what did Beethoven carry with him from Bonn to Vienna? He carried the musical talent he had inherited from his family and also the family temper, explosive and aggressive. For well and for ill, he would meet all challenges and challengers with attack — sometimes followed, as was his mother's style, by heartfelt apology. He had the family love of wine but the force of will to keep it at bay. His phenomenal discipline was his own. Then and later, he considered himself responsible for his younger brothers.

When he left Bonn, Beethoven was nearly twenty-two and as much pianist as composer. It was evident to him and to many others that he was one of the finest virtuosos alive, and he was an improviser of tremendous power. He had not written a great deal of music compared to what Mozart had done by that age, and his output in the next few years would be spotty. Still, he had taken tremendous strides as a composer, nearly every major effort leaping beyond the last. He knew that as well as anyone. Since his childhood, people had told him he was extraordinary, and he never had reason to doubt it.

So he carried to Vienna an ineradicable sense of his gift, the conviction that someday he would have momentous things to say in music and that people would listen to him. They always had. Yet he seemed in no hurry to find what he had to say, feeling that eventually it would be there. Likewise there is no sign that he ever worried about his performances, ever had to contend with nerves. He appeared to be devoid of doubts about himself. He was capable of self-criticism, in fact ruthlessly self-critical, but his terms were his own.

Part of his gift was the *raptus,* that ability to withdraw into an inner world that took him beyond everything and everybody around him, and also took him beyond the legion of afflictions that assailed him. Improvising at the keyboard and otherwise, he found solitude even in company. Solitude his steadiest and most welcome companion.

Beethoven's worldly ambitions matched his gift. But if he was determined to rise in the world, he also believed, as Christian Neefe and his other mentors had taught him, that it was his sacred duty, not only to God but to the world, to place his gift at the service of humanity. His duty was to take in the whole of life and embody it in music, then to give that music back to its source so humanity might better know who and what it is. In his last, wretched decade, he would write this consolation: "God, who knows and understands my deepest self, you know how I fulfill my sacred duties presented by mankind, God, and nature." There was his personal trinity. In return for performing his duty to humanity, he expected applause, fame, a good living, and that relatively new ambition for a mere musician, immortality for his work and his name. It was a legitimate bargain and he largely achieved it. But the applause and fame and the livelihood were not enough, never enough.

He left Bonn believing that his capacities made him the equal of anyone, one of the world's elite. He looked at the aristocracy not just as his equals but also as his patrons and his natural milieu. The aristocracy he had known had largely been musical, liberal, approving, and generous. When it came to religion, his attitudes were open, evolving, emotional rather than rational. If not a conventional Enlightenment deist, he was still no churchgoer or conventional Catholic. Already in youth he had come to feel closer to the divine in nature than in church or scripture. For the rest of his life he would have little to do with churches and priests. He preferred to deal with God directly, man to man. If he believed in eternal life, he did not unequivocally speak of it. Like most progressives of his time, he had no use for dogma concerning religion, art, or anything else. Dogma was a variety of tyranny, and as an Aufklärer he despised tyranny.

Humanity, as the philosophers of the day taught him, had to find its own way upward, as individuals and as a species. *Freedom* was the vehicle. As someday he would put it, "Man, help yourself!" and, "Only art and science can raise man to the level of gods." As far as the record shows, the day of his baptism may have been the last time before his deathbed that he was subjected to the ancient shibboleths, submitted to the old spells. In the end he would return on his own terms to the Latin rite by way of a titanic musical mass, his own credo, and turn to God as consolation and companion.

He had been taught that the path to greatness starts inside, with the cultivation of morality, duty, discipline, and courage. The Masons and the Illuminati said that the rise of humankind to Elysium begins by remaking oneself and then goes out into the world. So personal virtue, rather than skill and technique, was the true foundation of any worthy endeavor. In practice, however, he was obsessed with his craft and always would be, although the effort to sustain his moral convictions would require him constantly to believe that he was more virtuous than he actually was. When he arrived in Vienna he was not a complete man or musician, and he knew that perfectly well.

Beethoven left Bonn with a sense that revolution was under way in the world — in motion both figuratively, within the human spirit, and literally, in new societies and marching armies. His art would be called revolutionary, but for himself he never expressed any such intention. He wanted to make art better, thereby humanity better. While absorbing ideas and influences from around Europe and beyond, he would remain true to his heritage in the forms and genres of the Viennese masters: Mozart his prime model, Haydn his mentor and rival.

These were his foundations. Though in the course of his life Beethoven grew and changed as much as any creator ever has, he never slipped off those foundations in the Bonn Aufklärung. What they added up to was this: when young Beethoven left Bonn, he already had ideals and ambitions about being a composer that no one had ever had before, and he knew beyond doubt that he had the gifts to realize those ideals and ambitions.

There was one more thing Beethoven carried inside that would never leave him: the source of a lifetime of illness and physical misery, and the ruin of his most precious faculty, his hearing. This physical and mental suffering would mount a sustained assault on his sense of discipline and duty, his gigantic ambition.

There was little medical science worthy of the name in those days, so the reasons for Beethoven's physical trials may never be known for certain. One possibility is that from cooking utensils, or from adulterated wine, or from spa waters or some other source he may have ingested a great deal of lead. If so, it came to rest in his bones and slowly leaked out, ravaging his digestive tract. In his teens he was already familiar with the lacerating seizures of stomach pain and diarrhea that would never leave him, exacerbating his incipient tendencies to paranoia and misanthropy. He served humankind but never understood people, and though he yearned with all his heart for love and companionship, year after year he could bear humanity less and less in the flesh.

His own flesh became a fearful and relentless enemy. "Already," he wrote at age thirty, "I have cursed my Creator and my existence." If the main source of his misery was not lead poisoning, it was something else, or a combination of assaults with similar effects of chronic and painful illness, on top of which would be laid a progression of passing illnesses. So as Beethoven left Bonn with confident and entirely justified hopes for glory, he was destined both for triumph and for anguish.

• • •

After he left in December 1792, University of Bonn professor and Kant scholar Bartholomäus Ludwig Fischenich wrote Charlotte, wife of his friend Friedrich Schiller:

> I am enclosing with this a setting of the "Feuerfarbe" on which I would like to have your opinion. It is by a young man of this place whose musical talents are universally praised and whom the Elector has sent to Haydn in Vienna. He proposes also to compose Schiller's "Freude" . . . I expect something perfect, for as far as I know him he is wholly devoted to the great and sublime. Haydn has written here that he would put him at grand operas and soon be obliged to quit composing. Ordinarily he does not trouble himself with such trifles as the enclosed, which he wrote at the request of a lady.[30]

In October of the next year a notice appeared in the *Berliner Musik-Zeitung*: "Ludwig van Beethoven, assistant court organist and now unquestionably one of the foremost pianoforte players, went to Vienna at the expense of our Elector to Haydn in order to perfect himself under his direction more fully in the art of composition." It cites a letter from Beethoven to his teacher saying, "I thank you for your counsel very often given me in the course of my progress in my divine art. If I ever become a great man, yours will be some of the credit." The notice was placed by Christian Neefe.[31]

Some two weeks after Beethoven arrived in Vienna, Elector Maximilian Franz and his court fled Bonn for the second time as the French overran the Rhine and occupied Mainz. Following a French retreat, Max Franz would return again in the spring, but the Electorate of Cologne, more than five hundred years old, and the Bonn Beethoven knew were nearing their last days. The Aufklärung ideals that had brought Bonn to its splendid brief flowering led to little in the world except in the individual lives they had shaped. In history the most significant of those individuals would be Beethoven.

9

Unreal City

"G ERMANY," WROTE A British visitor in the eighteenth century, "claims the pre-eminence for badness of roads & the most tormenting construction of vehicles."[1] Heading southeast toward Vienna with oboist Georg Liebisch from the Bonn *Kapelle*, Beethoven tracked his journey of December 1792 in a notebook where he kept minute accounts of their expenditures. When they parted, their joint expenses had been a frugal 35 florins.

Jolting over rutted roads in freezing weather, the coach hauled the travelers through storied and picturesque towns. At Koblenz, Beethoven crossed to the east side of the Rhine for good; at Maria van Beethoven's hometown of Ehrenbreitstein, her son saw his beloved river for the last time. Soon the coach was picking its way around a French army. On the road to Montabaur their driver was fearless when he found German troops filling the road. Beethoven wrote in his notebook, "Tip because the fellow drove us at the risk of a beating through the Hessian army going like the devil — one small thaler." Now Beethoven had seen armies bustling and rattling on the march. He would not forget the sight and sound. As the coach rolled on, more old towns passed before his weary eyes: Limburg, with its half-timbered houses; Würges, where his companion went his way; Regensburg, where he again saw the Danube; Linz, just over the Austrian border. From there it was some 130 long miles to Vienna.[2]

After Linz, the roads ran along the meandering Danube. For a traveler from the west the great sight on the way to Vienna was the Wachau Valley, starting below the looming cloister at Melk. Along the road lay medieval towns and villages and the fortress of Dürnstein, where once Richard the Lion-Hearted was imprisoned. In summer, in that landscape where someday Beethoven would spend the last summer of his life, the Wachau would be covered with flowers and grapevines and apricots. Now as the coach started the long downhill to Vienna, the valley was locked in winter and a cold wind stirred the sluggish Danube.

Around December 10, he was watching the suburbs of Vienna flow past. From Bonn, he had traveled more than 550 miles, his journey with overnight stops at inns averaging about three miles an hour. He would never travel that far again. As he crossed the southern arm of the Danube and approached Vienna, the bastions of the fortress city loomed in the winter gray. The coach bounced across the open meadow of the encircling Glacis, passed through a gate, and stopped at the customs office. Police examined this foreigner's papers and belongings and scrutinized him to see if he looked like a Jacobin. Then he could find someplace to lie down.

That place turned out to be what Beethoven would recall as a miserable garret, owned by a bookbinder on the Alservorstadt.[3] Immediately he got down to business equipping himself, made an appointment for a lesson with Joseph Haydn, looked over his list of contacts gleaned from Count Waldstein and other patrons. He knew most of the people he needed to meet in Vienna would be Freemasons, like his Bonn patrons; several were friends and relatives of Count Waldstein. He also knew that if these people were truly musical, all he needed to do was sit down at the piano and play, and they would know what he was worth.

When it came to musical matters he seemed to take no time to think or to plan. He already knew what he was going to do. In a new city one is usually a stranger feeling one's way, but Beethoven seems to have felt no uncertainty. He was used to quick conquests. As it turned out, his teenage successes in the provinces along the Rhine would be duplicated in the most musically sophisticated city in the Western world.

Meanwhile he discovered that, having spent his life in the Rhineland hearing his name pronounced *Biet*-hoffen, in Viennese dialect he was going to be Herr Be-*toof*-fen.[4] He would not have liked the sound.

In Beethoven's notebook the expenditures of the journey were followed by a shopping list: "wig-maker, coffee, overcoat, boots, shoes, pianoforte-desk, seal, writing-desk, pianoforte-money." Then a note: "Andreas Lindner, dancing-master, lives in the Stoss am Himmel, No. 415." He had been advised that if you wanted to get ahead in Vienna, you had to know how to dance. (There would be no record of whether he actually took lessons. Later Carl Czerny reported that Beethoven could not for the life of him keep time while dancing, any more than he could sing or play the violin in tune.) In his notebook follows another list of expenses: "Black silk stockings, 1 ducat [ca. 4½ florins], 1 pair of winter silk stockings, 1 florin, 40 kreuzers [60 kreuzers to a florin]; boots, 6 florins," and so on. He bought a piano for a modest 6 florins, 40 kreuzers.[5] On December 12, he noted the price of his first lesson: "Haidn 8 groschen." As he tended to do with nonaristocratic students, the old master was teaching this youth for a token sum.

Beethoven's obsession about money down to the last groschen came from the uncertainty of living in a foreign city on a tight budget. Vienna was far more expensive than Bonn. The only saving grace for an austere income was that food in the city was blessedly cheap. In a restaurant one could have a meal of two meat dishes, soup, vegetables, unlimited bread, and a quarter liter of wine for 31 kreuzers, about half a florin.[6] But for a lower-middle-class man to get by for a year without frills, in Bonn a matter of some 300 florins, Vienna required at least 1,000.[7] And Beethoven was still responsible for his brothers back home. He got a shock when the first stipend he received from Bonn was his quarterly salary rather than what he had expected, his full yearly 400 florins, to get him settled in Vienna. At least he had brought from home some money saved from lessons, gifts, and the like.[8] While he was trying to cope with finances that December of 1792, he received

LEARN TO DANCE

more bad news: his father had died on the eighteenth. The cause was given as "dropsy of the chest," probably indicating heart failure, surely rising in some degree from a lifetime of indulgence.[9]

Johann van Beethoven was around fifty-three when he died. He had lived his last years on his slim pension, his wife dead, his famous son supporting the family, his life a shambles. Memoirist Gottfried Fischer remembered sad encounters with the specter of the once vigorous and vivacious Johann weaving down the street, always in the same shabby brown topcoat.

"Where've you been?" the old man would ask.

"I'm coming from school," Gottfried would answer.

"Well, you learn, then you can do something. Give my greetings to your father Theodor Fischer and your mother."[10] And that would be that.

Johann's death was commemorated by Elector Max Franz in a sardonic note to Court Marshal von Schall: "The revenues from the liquor excise have suffered a loss in the deaths of Beethoven and Eichhoff." Ludwig did not return home for the funeral. After his mother died, Beethoven had written an anguished letter to an acquaintance. After his father died, there were probably no tears and a quite different sort of letter. He wrote the Elector, hoping to seize this opportunity to improve his finances. The letter reviews how a few years before, he and his father had split Johann's original court income. Now he petitioned to have his father's share paid to him, for the support of himself and his brothers.[11]

There followed months of uncertainty and extensive borrowing from Haydn. The Elector's reply to Beethoven's petition did not arrive until the following May, because of the second significant piece of news Beethoven received that December. When the French overran the Rhine and took Mainz that month, Max Franz and much of the Bonn court fled for the second time. Since his electorate was not far from the French border, Max Franz was desperately trying to keep Bonn neutral. Given that he ruled a strategically significant German territory on the crucial artery of the Rhine, that option was a forlorn hope.

By May 1793, the Elector was back in Bonn and on the job, be-

stowing his grace on his future *Kapellmeister* in Vienna. He granted
Beethoven the requested additional 300 florins in quarterly payments,
and "he will further receive the three measures of grain most kindly
bestowed upon him for the education of his brothers."[12]

As regards money, Beethoven may have felt on the verge of desperation as he turned twenty-two in December 1792. But it would take
him less than a year to establish a reputation in Vienna comparable
to what he had enjoyed in the Rhineland. And a reputation in Vienna
was worth far more in the city Mozart once described to his father as
"Clavierland."

Beethoven's new home was a legendary capital city of stone palaces,
of parks and churches, all still enclosed in the old walls built to keep
out the Turks. (The question of the hour was whether they would keep
out the French.) Said a British visitor, "I never saw a place so perfectly
delightful as the faubourg of Vienna. It is very large and almost wholly
composed of delicious palaces."[13] The aristocracy spent their winters
in the city, then departed for summer palaces in the country. In fact,
anyone who could afford it left the city in the summer, when the traffic and the heat became nearly unbearable. Horse-drawn fiacres were
taking over from the old sedan chairs, and in the summer their traffic
and the horses' leavings covered the city with choking brown dust.[14]

The Hofburg, the emperor's residence in the city, was not an integral
design like the Electoral Residence in Bonn but a sprawling complex of
buildings from different eras — a hodgepodge, like the polyglot empire
itself. Most Viennese lived along dark, cramped, muddy streets, where
there was a chronic shortage of living space. But the parks were open
to all, including the wooded Prater between the Danube arms, once
the emperor's hunting preserve but given to his people by Joseph II, for
which his people were briefly grateful at best.

Vienna was the most musical city in Europe, perhaps in the world.
For musicians themselves, it was the best and the worst of places.
While the Viennese loved music extravagantly, most of them didn't
care what kind of music it was: an opera, a song in the street, an organ
grinder, a concerto in the park — it was all the same. For all the music demanded by the Viennese, there were still too many musicians

in residence, among them too many virtuosos. As had once afflicted Mozart, competition was merciless, complete with rivalries and feuds and cabals. *SECRET POLITICAL CLIQUE OR FACTION*

When Beethoven arrived, Vienna had some two hundred thousand people, twenty times more than Bonn. The capital of the Holy Roman Empire had Poles and Bosnians and Turks parading the streets in native garb, gypsies playing soulful music in the parks and cafés, diplomats and nobles in residence with names like Lichnowsky, Razumovsky, Zmeskall, Esterházy, Guicciardi, Swieten. The absurd title "Holy Roman" reflected the sprawling pointlessness of the empire and Habsburg holdings accumulated haphazardly over the centuries. Emperor Franz II, who had ascended when his father, Leopold II, died after two years on the throne, ruled over twenty-seven million people in Bohemia, Moravia, Hungary, Croatia, Slavonia, part of Poland, the future Belgium and Luxembourg, and parts of Italy. He was meanwhile the nominal head of the myriad small German states.

Franz II had been tutored by his uncle Joseph II in the enlightened ideals that came to be called Josephinism. Not notably intelligent or curious, by nature conservative and fearful of change, the boy absorbed some of that spirit, but not the more progressive parts. Franz took the throne in 1792 opposed to democracy and fascinated by the potential of secret police and censorship to keep his subjects in line. When King Louis XVI was beheaded in Paris in January 1793 and the Terror rolled into motion, Franz responded by declaring any hint of freedom of speech or popular rule a spark to be stamped out. Vienna became the first modern police state, less murderous than later ones but just as relentless, and more efficient than most.

Viennese officialdom lived in fear of "Jacobins," the term coming to designate anyone who believed in popular constitutional rule or who leaned left in any fashion. In fact, there was a cadre of French sympathizers in Austria, but they were not murderously inclined toward the aristocracy like the French. Some of them were highborn themselves. In any case, authentic German Jacobins were few and powerless. Still, the very existence of French sympathies was perceived as a mortal threat to the throne and to the privileges of the aristocracy.

Soon anyone wearing side-whiskers was viewed as a potential revolutionary. The emperor complained that too many people were reading newspapers.[15] The police would establish relentless control over the newspapers, too.

Eventually Austria became a place where intellect, creativity, any kind of independent thought was officially held to be somewhere between suspect and criminal. One day the emperor declared, concerning Beethoven, "There is something revolutionary in that music!"[16] In practice, though, Viennese composers would be among the few beneficiaries of the all-encompassing repression. Try as they might, the police could find no grounds to censor instrumental music, which had always been the city's chief glory. In the end, symphonies, string quartets, piano concertos, and the like became virtually the only kind of free speech left in Austria.

For the middle class and up, Vienna remained on the surface prosperous and merry. Emperor Franz appreciated that a fun-loving people devoted to appearances is easier to keep in line. He made a point of mastering Wienerisch, the town dialect made up of bits and pieces of languages from around the empire; he rode his carriage modestly in the Prater alongside the grandees of the town. The city called him "Franz the Good." While once Emperor Joseph's benevolence had left his people unsatisfied, Franz's show of modesty and generosity screened a true despotism fixed on suppressing all opposition and preserving the powers and privileges of the throne.

Beethoven grasped the city's style soon enough. In a time of mounting repression, censorship, and arrests in 1794, he wrote Nikolaus Simrock in Bonn, "We are having very hot weather here; and the Viennese are afraid that soon they will not be able to get any more ice cream. For, as the winter was so mild, ice is scarce. Here various important people have been locked up; it is said that a revolution was about to break out — But I believe that so long as an Austrian can get his brown ale and his little sausages, he is not likely to revolt."[17]

He had grasped the Viennese devotion to pleasure. It included a love of shows of every kind: music and theater; jugglers, acrobats, clowns, and puppet shows in the streets; and a compulsion for showing off. Aristocrats and the prosperous middle class promenaded along the six miles of ramparts, the men in tight blue riding coats and white trousers and stovepipe hats, the women with corkscrew curls and flowery dresses with wide hoops and deep-cut bodices. On summer nights, throngs streamed out of the city gates onto the Glacis, once a moat encircling the walls but now a broad meadow where soldiers paraded, where there were circuses, vendors of ice cream and sausages and wine from endless sources.[18] Surrounding the Glacis began the suburbs and the vineyards that flowed up into the hills of the Vienna woods.

Dancing was everywhere. Every year, Karneval and the days between Epiphany and Ash Wednesday in January saw an orgy of dancing. Dance fashions evolved continuously, though the courtly minuet featuring solo couples lingered well into the nineteenth century. But more vigorous and populist styles had arrived, including the contra dance called *anglaise* or *englische.* In this line dance everyone regularly changed partners, so the *englische* had a democratic frisson: the changing couples created a literal mingling of classes. On the rise by 1800 was the swirling and scandalous three-beat waltz, the first dance in which couples actually embraced. Vienna and the waltz were made for each other. The waltz craze in the city would be addressed by prodigious new dance halls; one, the Apollo, could accommodate six thousand people in motion.[19]

Some dance halls offered more intimate services. In a society where men tended to rise slowly in professions and marry late, prostitution flourished. When it was suggested to Joseph II that brothels be licensed, he replied with sour irony, "The expense of roofing would be ruinous, for it would be necessary to put a roof over the whole city."[20] With most of the populace forced to live in cramped and stuffy housing, everyone spent leisure hours in cafés, sipping coffee — which the Viennese had been the first Westerners to discover, in the tents of the conquered Turkish army — and indulging in the confections for which the city was famous. Each level of society had its own cafés and its own brothels, from the dives of workingmen and the haunts of soldiers to elegant establishments for the nobility.[21] Besides coffee, the Viennese were drinkers of wine more than beer; the Vienna woods were full of little inns serving new wine and simple food.

None of this was quite what it appeared. If gaiety and a fickle search for pleasure marked the Viennese, it was a heavy kind of high spirits rising from an undercurrent of frustration and anxiety. The city's pursuit of mirth stood in for the pursuit of happiness. "The situation is desperate," runs an old Viennese saying, "but not serious."

Viennese commoners had plenty of diversions but no voice. It was not so different at the top of the social scale. Emperor Joseph II had hamstrung the aristocracy and concentrated power in the throne, with the censors, bureaucracy, and police as enforcers. Though Franz II restored some aristocratic privileges, all but returning farmers to serfdom, the nobility still had little real power. The result was that there was little to keep them occupied other than private amusements. Wrote Madame de Staël,

> All the best people go en masse from one salon to another, three or four times a week. Time is wasted on getting dressed for these parties, it's wasted on travelling to them, on the staircases waiting for one's carriage, on spending three hours at table; and in these innumerable gatherings one hears nothing but conventional phrases . . . The great lords parade with magnificent horses and carriages in the Prater, for the sole pleasure of recognizing there the friends they have just parted from in a drawing-room. These seigneurs, the richest and most illustrious in Europe . . . even allow miserable fiacres to hold up their splendid conveyances. The Emperor and his brothers take their place in the queue and like to be considered as simple individuals.[22]

The priesthood, their liturgy and influence tightly controlled by the state, lived similarly to the nobility. An Italian visitor wrote, "A host of priests say Mass daily and receive a florin for it. The rest of the time they seek distractions, particularly with the fair sex . . . Libertinage is enormous in Vienna and the women are very coquettish."[23] And a British visitor: "No city perhaps can present such scenes of affected sanctity and real licentiousness."[24]

Many of the nobles' amusements naturally ran to display and dissipation, but they also ran to music. "Music," wrote a visitor of the 1780s, "is the only thing in which the nobility shows good taste."[25] In Vienna as in Bonn, but on a far grander canvas, the Viennese musical aristocracy was passionate unto obsessive. A number of Beethoven's admirers and patrons were capable amateur performers who could manage a Mozart sonata or a Haydn quartet. A few aristocratic amateurs were true virtuosos, and their ranks included many women. Later Beethoven's favorite performer of his sonatas would be a baroness. There were some three hundred professional pianists in town, many capable amateurs, and upwards of six thousand piano students.[26]

Around Germany and Austria in the eighteenth century, the main impetus of music making and music supporting had shifted from the church to the courts, of which the *Kapelle* of Bonn and Haydn's employers, the Esterházy princes, were examples. In Haydn's day as *Kapellmeister,* the Esterházy Palace musical establishment had included a resident orchestra and opera troupe, visiting theater and dance companies, an opera house seating five hundred, and a splendid puppet theater.[27] The arts were a means for princes to show off their wealth and taste and to one-up their rivals. The Vienna *Hofkapelle,* the court orchestra, had a nearly three-hundred-year tradition. In Vienna by the 1890s, most of the palace orchestras outside the Hofburg had been disbanded as too expensive and no longer fashionable, but the yen for music still ran strong.

So then and for decades after, the main venues for music making in Vienna were private, in parlors of the middle class and the ornate music rooms of palaces. For all its musicality, however, Vienna was rich in dance halls but poor in music halls. In the eighteenth century, public performances and dedicated halls had sprung up in London, in Paris, in Leipzig, and elsewhere around Europe, but in Vienna the nobility liked to keep music for themselves. Wrote a correspondent from Leipzig, where public concerts in the Gewandhaus were an institution, "It is astonishing that in this munificent city of Emperors, where the passion for music is cultivated to the highest degree, there is no suitable concert hall at all, neither one which is acoustically favorable nor one which can accommodate a sizeable number of listeners."[28]

So while music was heard all the time everywhere, public concerts had to rely on any space where there was enough room for the requisite seats. Likewise opera, which along with theater was a citywide obsession. In just over a year before December 1792, 180 Italian operas were mounted in Vienna, plus 163 ballets. Most were produced in two venues. The Burgtheater, a legendary old hall attached to the Hofburg, had seen the premieres of three Mozart operas. It was small and stuffy, but the acoustics were good. The Kärntnertortheater, next to the Kärntner Gate, was roomier but barnlike in its acoustics. Both halls were administered by the court and used for plays and concerts as well as opera.

Across town, the huge ramshackle residence called the Freihaus included a theater run by impresario and actor Emanuel Schikaneder, famous as the cocreator of, and first Papageno in, Mozart's *Die Zauberflöte*. He presented a variety of entertainments, including opera. Just after Beethoven arrived in Vienna, Schikaneder announced his hundredth performance of that singspiel (this was, however, a public-relations fib — it was more like the sixtieth). At the turn of the century, Schikaneder moved his troupe to the new Theater an der Wien, the largest hall in the city, and above the entrance he placed a statue of himself as Papageno. He understood that was his immortality.[29]

Otherwise, orchestral music was heard in restaurants, University of Vienna halls, the large and small ballrooms of the Hofburg. Public concerts were at least on the rise in the 1790s.[30] In summer they were given inside or outside a pavilion, or else a restaurant, in the Augarten, a park north of the city. Though the Burgtheater had a good orchestra in residence, it was used mainly for plays and operas. Besides the private orchestras lingering in a few palaces, there were no standing ensembles in town and no subscription series. Orchestras were assembled ad hoc, mostly staffed by amateurs. Yet Vienna was overflowing with able musicians, enough to fill several orchestras.[31] The amateurs were often able players and intrepid sight-readers, necessary in a milieu where most concerts were put together in one rehearsal.

One reason the majority of performers were part-timers was that pay for professional musicians was miserable. At the summer palace of the Esterházy princes, for whom Haydn worked, 6,000 florins were once spent on a single puppet play, while the *Kapelle* members, who all together made not much more than 600 florins in half a year, were housed in plain quarters two to a room, forbidden to have their families in residence. Haydn, as *Kapellmeister,* was granted three modest rooms.[32] Yet the Esterházy orchestral and opera establishment was one of the finest in Europe before it was dissolved by a new prince who was indifferent to music.

If you were a composer or performer wanting to show your wares in Vienna, you rented the hall yourself, put together the chamber ensemble or orchestra and paid them, and often sold advance tickets out of your own apartment. Mozart prospered in Vienna for a while, mounting one-shot subscription concerts, the subscribers being mostly from the nobility. That system was moribund by the time Beethoven arrived. For his whole career in Vienna, he produced his own concerts and pocketed the occasionally handsome proceeds. But most of the time he lost money, and sometimes lost disastrously.

The exception to that pattern was charity concerts of various kinds, which paid nothing but were a good showcase for a musician. The one organization putting on regular public concerts was the Tonkünstler Society, an organization benefiting the widows and orphans of musicians. The group mounted two pairs of charity concerts a year, during Lent and Christmas, when theater productions were forbidden. The programs leaned to symphonies and concertos, later to oratorios.

In Vienna, Beethoven would cobble together a living the same way that most of his contemporaries did, from a combination of composing, teaching, and performing. In that respect, there was nothing exceptional about his career in his years as a keyboard virtuoso — performing was the best way to earn quick money. Beethoven never pursued the traditional avenues of writing sacred music and/or working as a *Kapellmeister* for church or court, though he thought he wanted to. Mozart had been part of a growing trend of composers as freelancers. That had not been the plan in his youth. Leopold Mozart wrote his young son that the goal of an ambitious composer was to become "a famous Kapellmeister about whom posterity will read in books."[33] By the time Beethoven arrived in Vienna, the glory days of court and chapel *Kapellmeisters* like his grandfather were waning.

At the turn of the nineteenth century, the center of European musical development was concentrated in German-speaking lands, and the epicenter of German music was Vienna. The city's singular joining of fantastic wealth, the general powerlessness of the aristocracy and middle class, the passion for music, the constant demand for glitter and show to cover lacerating realities created a cloud of unreality that marked Vienna for the better part of two centuries. Viennese folk and popular music had a singular quality of world-weary, desperate gaiety, a mood that sometimes carried over into the more serious music.

For Beethoven, high-talking Bonn had spoiled him intellectually. To most of these aspects of Viennese life — the endless frivolity, the bittersweet music, the dance-till-you-drop holidays, the open sexuality — he would never be anything but indifferent unto hostile. He frequented cafés and restaurants, drank the beer and wine, enjoyed the music and theater, was lionized in palaces, but essentially he had no sympathy for the city and the people among whom he lived for more than half his life. "From the Emperor to the bootblack," he declared in old age, "all the Viennese are worthless." He never again found the kind of idealism and high talk he was reared on in Bonn.

At the same time, living for decades in a place he held largely in contempt, where there was no standing orchestra or subscription concerts or real concert hall, had no great impact on him. Not many artists could flourish in a situation like that, but Beethoven did. Ultimately, he needed no one but himself, and in some degree, sooner or later, he would have despised anyplace he came to rest.

When he had established himself, he would not kowtow to the Viennese but demanded they kowtow to him. To a surprising degree, they did. Nor would the Viennese hold his contempt for them against him particularly. The best explanation for that might be a simple one: when all was said and done, a good many Viennese appreciated great talent when they found it and extraordinary music when they heard it.

10

Chains of Craftsmanship

DURING HIS FIRST months in Vienna, starting in late 1792, Beethoven kept up his notebook of expenses, not omitting after-lesson treats at the café: "22x, chocolate for Haidn and me . . . Coffee, 6x for Haidn and me."[1] The meetings with Haydn, scheduled and unscheduled, had two aspects. One was informal advice on pieces Beethoven was working on, at that point minor efforts drafted or sketched in Bonn including an oboe concerto (later disappeared), a highly Mozartian octet, and a big piano concerto in B-flat, written and perhaps performed in Bonn, with which he would tinker for years.

Haydn was now at the height of his fame and essentially a free man, somewhere between on call and pensioned off by his employer of twenty-eight years, the house of Esterházy. He retained his salary and his title of *Kapellmeister*. Industrious as always, in the fertile decade of the 1790s Haydn produced some of his finest work, including symphonies and string quartets that would be models for every composer in those genres to come. When Beethoven began working with him, Haydn was working on commissions that would be due when he returned to England for his second visit.

As a teacher, Haydn was patient and kindly, as he was in most things except when he felt his honor or his status in music questioned, or his pocketbook threatened. Someone left an account of him teaching composition (not to Beethoven) in the later 1790s. Looking over a symphony by the student, Haydn saw a line of rests for the winds and quipped, "Rests are the hardest things of all to write." Looking further, he frowned. "I don't find anything wrong in the part writing. It's correct. But the proportions are not as I would like them to be: look, here's an idea that is only half developed; it shouldn't be dropped so quickly; and this phrase connects badly with the others. Try to give the whole a proper balance; that can't be so hard because the main subject is good." However, added the observer, "This was all spoken with charm."[2]

These are perennial issues between teachers and students of composition: don't overscore, learn to sustain, don't drop ideas before they've made their point, pay attention to proportion and continuity. Studying Beethoven's pieces, Haydn would have said the same kinds of things. In the Bonn scores, Haydn noted that Beethoven already had the habit of generating new themes in a work from earlier ones. For some time, Haydn had been composing with tiny melodic and rhythmic motifs, matters of two or three or four notes presented at the beginning, then wielded with endless subtlety and imagination to build themes through the course of a piece. Beethoven picked up Haydn's motivic technique, though it may have been more a matter of refining and extending what he was already doing.

In their discussions, Haydn surely deepened Beethoven's conceptions of form. The model that a later time named "sonata form," for nearly a century used in most first movements and often elsewhere, had been brought to maturity more by Haydn than by anyone else, and had been certified by Mozart. Looking over his student's pieces, Haydn would have noted a precocious understanding of form. But he would also have found certain problems, including overwrought harmonies, miscalculations of emphasis and scale. The *Imperial* Cantatas often meander. Like most imaginative young composers, this one needed to learn how long to run with an idea and when to stop. He needed to learn the power of simplicity.

There is no record of what transpired in their lessons. But it can be said that at least by his op. 2 Sonatas, composed in 1794–95, Beethoven was showing the fruits of his studies in a startlingly mature way. After his months with Haydn, Beethoven emerged a far more sophisticated composer. To mention only one issue: Before Haydn, Beethoven had a shaky idea of proportion, might write an introduction to an aria that was a quarter its length. After he finished the lessons with Haydn, he had one of the most refined senses of proportion of any composer — a sense of it, in other words, at the level of Haydn.

Still, the extent of the debt Beethoven owed his teacher he never understood, or anyway never acknowledged. To all and sundry for the rest of his life, he would declare he had learned nothing from Haydn, nothing from anybody but himself, and from studying the music of the masters.[3]

For Beethoven, whom someday everyone would declare a revolutionary, the process of becoming a proper composer was not to come up with revolutionary conceptions but something like the opposite: to base the future on the past, to master the traditional crafts of the art and then to embody that knowledge in his own way. From beginning to end, but especially in the early Vienna years, Beethoven was obsessed with technique. He also sensed that his creative road had to lead through Vienna, above all studying what Mozart and Haydn had done. Which is to say: the Classical high-Viennese style was Beethoven's route to understanding himself as a composer.

In Bonn he had learned harmonic practice, how to build chords and chord changes and changes of key over a bass line by way of studying "thoroughbass." This was a practical matter for an organist and pianist, because sometimes one was required to extemporize an accompaniment from a bass line, but it also imparted a good sense of managing harmony. He had learned to make new material out of a given idea by writing variations on a theme. He had absorbed conventional formal models and instrumentation.

When he arrived in Vienna, the aspect of craft Beethoven knew to be his weakest suit was counterpoint, the art of weaving melodies together. Neefe had never really taught him counterpoint, which was regarded as an abstruse but nonetheless valuable study for a composer. Thus the period's term for contrapuntal music: the "learned style," with its overtone of pedantry. During his first year in Vienna, largely putting away ambitious creative work, Beethoven turned his full attention to counterpoint, turning out dozens of exercises.

What that study amounted to, for any composer of that time and long after, was something on the face of it absurd: a systematic, minutely rule-bound course of study in the style of Renaissance choral music in general, Palestrina in particular. In other words, one of the essential paths to becoming a serious composer in the eighteenth century was to master the skills of the fifteenth and sixteenth centuries. The particular hurdle Haydn, Mozart, and Beethoven had to clear was a 1725 treatise by Viennese court *Kapellmeister* Johann Joseph Fux (pronounced *fooks*) called *Gradus ad Parnassum,* or *Steps to Parnassus.* The original had been an imaginary quasi-Socratic dialogue, in Latin, between a teacher and his student. Haydn, like Mozart with his pupils, used his own adaptation of the treatise.

Fux laid out the path to mastery of counterpoint in a series of "species," each exercise starting with a given melody in long notes called a *cantus firmus,* "fixed song." Writing counterpoint — one or more new melodies — around a preexisting cantus was a technique going back to the Middle Ages, but Fux put the practice into a rationalized and systematic method. In first species the student composes a new melody under or on top of a cantus, one note for each note of the cantus. In second species there are two notes per note of the cantus, in third species four notes, and so on. The species proceed in increasingly elaborate stages until one is writing four-part counterpoint in a kind of abstraction of Renaissance–Palestrina style, using the old church modes as well as modern major and minor scales. Each stage of the process accumulates rules governing the relation of every note to every other note. By the point of writing in four parts, the maze of notes and rules has become head-splitting. In the original Fux, the teacher reassures the suffering student that if he can do this, everything else in music will seem easy.[4]

Why did generations of students submit to this torturous study in an archaic style? For several reasons. It teaches a young composer to make notes do what the composer wants rather than follow where they lead. Fux lectures his imaginary student that to make it work, you have to think ahead, not jump on a solution before you know where you are going. Every note matters, and every note has to be seen in the context of the whole. For a composer like Beethoven, who learned harmony by means of thoroughbass — thinking from chord to chord — species counterpoint led him to understand the long-range movement of melodic lines. Which is to say that he learned a central principle: the lines create the harmony rather than submit to the harmony. (Even when composers of that era seemed to be writing simple melody and accompaniment, they were thinking contrapuntally.)

There is another insight to be gained in doing species exercises. As you learn one rule after another, you also learn that the rules are not immutable but form a hierarchy. You give up one rule for the sake of a higher rule, and ultimately what determines that choice is your taste, ear, and sensitivity. So the later stages of species counterpoint approach the subtle relativity of decisions that is free composition. Submitting to Fux's rules carries over into finding and following your own rules, and also into knowing when to break them.

These are the conceptions and skills Beethoven willed himself to master — these, and the more practical matter of being fluent at the learned style when he needed it. The early Classical *galant* style had viewed counterpoint as old-fashioned, inexpressive, charmless, as symbolized by C. P. E. Bach's nickname for his father: "the Old Wig." The mature Viennese Classical style shaped by Haydn and later Mozart put counterpoint back into the picture, especially with fugal passages and movements integrated into the new formal models. Mozart's discovery of J. S. Bach was also a discovery of the power of counterpoint; it helped lead him to his greatest music. So the richness of the Viennese Classical style had much to do with both overtly contrapuntal episodes and steady contrapuntal undercurrents.

Steeped in Haydn and Mozart, Beethoven took as self-evident that he needed the learned style to be a true craftsman. Yet in the end his mighty efforts to master counterpoint never entirely took. It was not his kind of discipline. On the page as at the keyboard, his forte was improvisation, the lightning flash of inspiration. He would never be a natural contrapuntist, never completely fluent though he wrote a great deal of counterpoint, some of it splendid. Yet exactly because counterpoint remained a struggle, it was also an endless challenge and fascination. "Whatever is difficult," Beethoven would write, "is good." He never forgot Fux, never forgot Palestrina, never forgot the old church modes. Eventually all these elements, and Bach, found their places in his art.

As for the great Haydn as a teacher, Beethoven was soon disgusted. Correcting counterpoint exercises is a tedious business; the best counterpoint tutors tend to be pedants, and Haydn was anything but. "Art is free," he said, "and is not to be diminished by any chains of craftsmanship."[5] In Beethoven's exercises, Haydn missed more mistakes than he caught, and Beethoven knew it. That his teacher had his own urgent projects would not have mattered to this pupil. Haydn seems to have remained patient, or maybe the word is *dogged*. But it is not entertaining to work with a student, however talented, who clearly considers you a sloppy teacher at the same time that he hates being told what to do.

There was another issue Beethoven would probably not have cared about, if he knew of it. At the end of January 1793, a month after the lessons began, Haydn lost one of his most treasured friends when Marianne von Genzinger died at age forty-three. She was a married woman with whom he had carried on a platonic relationship, much of it through letters in which he poured out his feelings. Haydn had a spouse, but she was impossible and they had separated long before. (Haydn referred to her in a letter as "my wife, that infernal beast.")[6] For that matter, Haydn was juggling a long-time mistress from his Esterházy Palace days, plus a new mistress in London. But nobody could replace Mme Genzinger in his life. After she died, friends noted that Haydn became less warm, more sarcastic.[7] For a number of reasons, then, Haydn would be no lasting mentor for Beethoven. Like most younger people, Beethoven called the old man "Papa," but he had little affection to spare for father figures.

Beethoven's formal lessons with Haydn probably lasted only through spring 1793, but there would be contacts and consulting between them in the coming years, and now and then they appeared in concerts together. There was a curious postscript to his counterpoint studies. Some years after Beethoven died, a venerable Viennese composer and teacher named Johann Baptist Schenk stepped forward with a startling account of that period. Frustrated with Haydn's carelessness, Schenk recalled, Beethoven had come to Schenk behind Haydn's back to cor- rect his counterpoint exercises first, which Schenk was happy to do. Wrote Schenk, "I pointed out to him, however, that our work together must forever remain a secret." But a year later, Schenk continued, Haydn found out about the deception and was furious, which put a permanent crimp in relations between teacher and student.

?TRUE?

The trouble is, Schenk's yarn does not add up. For one thing, Beethoven seems to have saved all his exercises, as he apparently tried to save every page he put pen to. The 245 pages that survived show a steady trickle of mistakes that had not been corrected by anybody. Only 42 pages show any corrections at all.[8] Is it conceivable that in his old age Schenk, a distinguished composer and teacher, would cook up the story? It is more than conceivable; it was standard practice. The science of history was still taking shape in the early nineteenth century, and there was little sense of the primacy of fact. To make up things about one's relationship with a historic figure like Beethoven was a convenient way to engrave one's name in history. It was also a good way to settle scores. Schenk hated Haydn, declaring to a friend, "Mozart was a good soul, but Haydn was false through and through."[9]

In any case, there never was a complete break between Haydn and Beethoven. The old master was patient and generous, the young man not so stupid as to openly insult the leading composer in the world. In May 1793, Haydn took Beethoven with him to the Esterházy Pal- ace in Eisenstadt, to acquaint his employer Prince Nikolaus with this new talent. Beethoven returned to Vienna, while Haydn stayed on in Eisenstadt, working intensively on the pieces for England.[10] Haydn was frantically busy when he returned in the fall, so it is likely the regular lessons never resumed.

Beneath the cordiality, a degree of tension simmered between the two, most of it on Beethoven's side. They were separated by two generations. Beethoven had found a quick success in Vienna, where Haydn had for decades been brushed aside (Joseph II had declared his music "tricks and nonsense").[11] Haydn could accept the younger man's boldness only so far, and that would rankle Beethoven. Meanwhile the

older man understood perfectly well the nature of the ego he was dealing with. To a degree, it amused him. Behind Beethoven's back, Haydn
took to calling him *die große Mogul,* "the Great Mogul" — in the phrase
of a later time, "the Big Shot." When Beethoven largely stopped coming to call in later years, Haydn would ask visitors, "How's it going
with our Big Shot?" More seriously to a devout man, Haydn reportedly
declared Beethoven an atheist.[12]

If it took some years for the Viennese to realize that the heir of Haydn
and Mozart had arrived as a composer, it took little time for Beethoven
to establish his primacy among pianists. For the better part of his first
decade in Vienna he remained, in the eyes of the public and himself,
a composer-pianist as Mozart had been, as many composers were.
Beethoven had given more of his teens to the keyboard than to composing. (Haydn was a competent pianist and played violin, but he was
unusual among composers of the time in being, as he put it, "no magi-
cian" on any instrument.) Besides the brilliance of Beethoven's playing
in general and the unprecedented fire of his improvising, there were
really no serious piano rivals in sight when he arrived in town.

There were, of course, those who imagined themselves to be rivals.
One established entertainment in the salons of music fanciers was the
piano duel, in which virtuosos would present their repertoire and be
handed challenges of sight-reading and improvisation. In 1782, Mozart reported to his father a duel before Joseph II with his rival Muzio
Clementi: "After we had stood on ceremony long enough, the Emperor
declared that Clementi ought to begin ... He improvised and then
played a sonata. The Emperor then turned to me: '*Allons,* fire away.' I
improvised and played variations. The Grand Duchess produced some
sonatas by Paisiello ... , of which I had to play the Allegros and Clementi the Andantes and Rondos. We then selected a theme from them
and developed it on two pianofortes."[13]

On the street sometime around 1793, the father of pianist Carl
Czerny ran into Abbé Joseph Gelinek, a leading virtuoso of the city,
dressed up and headed for a piano duel at a reception. His opponent
was a young foreigner. "I'll fix him," Gelinek assured the elder Czerny.

The next day Czerny ran into the abbé again and asked how the duel went. Gelinek's response was awestruck. "Yesterday was a day I'll remember! That young fellow must be in league with the devil. I've never heard anybody play like that! I gave him a theme to improvise on, and I assure you I've never heard even Mozart improvise so admirably. Then he played some of his own compositions which are marvelous — really wonderful — and he manages difficulties and effects at the keyboard that we never even dreamed of."

"I say," said Czerny the elder, "what's his name?"

"He's a small, ugly, swarthy young fellow, and seems to have a willful disposition . . . His name is Beethoven."[14]

Besides improvising, Beethoven had probably played his *Righini* Variations, brilliant and virtuosic in the extreme, his showpiece during his first months in Vienna. It would take little time for the wealthy music fanciers of the town to try to capture him for their music rooms, and little time for Beethoven to capture the most storied and generous of Viennese connoisseurs.

Soon after arriving in Vienna, Beethoven had found better lodging than the garret he started in, moving to a less miserable garret at 45 Alstergasse. Before long he was given a comfortable room on the first floor of the house. The owner of the building was Prince Karl Alois Johann Nepomuk Vinzenz Leonhard Lichnowsky, who kept an apartment in the building for his own use. As it happened, if there was any music-fancying prince in Vienna whom Beethoven most needed to know, it was Lichnowsky.

From a recently ennobled Prussian family of music patrons going back generations, Karl Lichnowsky was one of the most important connoisseurs and patrons in the city, spending great swaths of his considerable fortune on his passion. His circle had long amounted to a nexus of Viennese musical life. Liberal-minded, a lover of Voltaire, a competent pianist, Lichnowsky had been a patron, student, and Masonic lodge brother of Mozart — and, like Mozart, possibly an Illuminatus.[15]

Lichnowsky's wife, Princess Maria Christiane, had once been among the "Three Graces," sisters called the most beautiful women in Vienna.[16] She had also studied with Mozart and was one of the better amateur pianists in the city. Prince Karl's brother Moritz was another Mozart pupil and a fine pianist. Karl was an old friend of Count Waldstein, Beethoven's patron in Bonn, and Christiane was a cousin of Waldstein. Her sister was married to Count Razumovsky, the Russian ambassador to Vienna, another patron who was to play a historic role in Beethoven's life. Christiane's mother, Countess Thun, had been a friend of Mozart; he wrote his father that the countess was "the most charming and most lovable lady I've ever met."[17]

For Beethoven, who needed to establish himself in Vienna, the interconnections of people and interests emanating from the Lichnowskys did not end there. Lichnowsky had studied in J. S. Bach's home of Leipzig and developed a taste for the work of the elder Bach; he had a long correspondence with son C. P. E., from whom Lichnowsky obtained the elder Bach's manuscripts in a time when little of the music was in print.[18] Every Friday, Karl and Christiane gave a musicale at their palace for friends and cognoscenti, who included Haydn. Beethoven's playing of Bach's *Well-Tempered Clavier* was one of the things that endeared him to the Lichnowsky circle. One day an elderly guest declared that he had once heard J. S. Bach himself play, and Beethoven sounded, the visitor said, just like Bach.[19]

In short, the first patrons Beethoven acquired in Vienna could hardly have been more cultured, connected, rich, and generous. His quick triumph sprouted mainly from Haydn and the Lichnowskys and their influence. Karl Lichnowsky, rather than Haydn, would be the dedicatee of opus 1. For years Beethoven kept a bust of the prince in his rooms; the princess gave him an elegant desk clock that he kept by him the rest of his life. From that point on, Beethoven moved in aristocratic circles as an admired artist and more or less an equal. There was an abiding irony in that situation. Part of his success came from three letters: the *van* in his name that many of the aristocracy assumed indicated that he came from a noble background.

The Lichnowskys' shared passion for music did not translate into a happy married life. An acquaintance noted that Christiane always looked sad.[20] She had a sickly constitution; in a time without anesthetics, both her breasts had been removed in fear of cancer. The main source of her unhappiness was not her health, however, but her husband. In every respect, Karl Lichnowsky was a piece of work. Swaggering and domineering, with a brassy voice, Lichnowsky womanized constantly, which endlessly tormented his wife (even though infidelity was common practice in the Viennese nobility). In her diary, the ever-catty Countess Lulu von Thürheim pitied Christiane and loathed Karl, calling him a "a cynical rake and shameless coward."[21] All the same, Christiane Lichnowsky was a formidable figure in her own right. Thürheim wrote that the countess combined "a good heart and Christian forbearance with violent prejudices." People whom Christiane didn't like she went out of her way to damage in the elegantly vicious world of Viennese high society.[22]

In a miserable marriage, music was Christiane's solace. Her admiration for Beethoven was boundless and forgiving. Though only five years older than her protégé, she began, to his annoyance, to mother him. Karl behaved likewise. Beethoven had a standing invitation for lunch at 4 p.m. "I would have to be home by half past three every day," he complained to his visiting Bonn friend Wegeler, "change into something better, see that I was properly shaved, etc. — I can't stand all that!" So he usually ate at a tavern, whether or not he could afford it. At some point the prince notified his servants that if he and Beethoven rang for them at the same time, they were to answer Beethoven first. Hearing about it, Beethoven went out that day and hired himself a servant.[23]

Karl's brother Moritz and Christiane Lichnowsky were both more able pianists than Karl; they could actually play Beethoven's keyboard works rather than play at them. Yet Karl steadily reassured Beethoven that he did not have to write down to amateurs.[24] It was up to the players to cope with what he gave them. Before long, many did, in a time when some of the best pianists were amateurs, and piano sonatas were played not in public concerts but in private gatherings or alone for the pianist's private pleasure.

The connection of Beethoven to the brothers and Princess Lichnowsky was a virtually ideal patron-and-protégé relationship, but it could endure only up to a point. The abiding threat to their relations was that Beethoven and Prince Karl were both imperious and proud men and not in the habit of keeping their feelings to themselves. Inevitably, there were clashes, and sooner or later one of their shouting matches was likely to lead to a break. Eventually one did, but not before years of fruitful partnership. Karl's brother, the more talented and more amiable Moritz Lichnowsky, remained close to Beethoven to the end.

The Lichnowskys' Friday musicales were frequented by leading musicians and connoisseurs, and the level of performing was about as good as could be found anywhere. There Beethoven encountered a broad repertoire of chamber music and connected with more musicians and patrons. One was a brilliant violinist and conductor named Ignaz Schuppanzigh. As a teenager he was already first violin in a string quartet that played at the Lichnowsky musicales. Schuppanzigh's place in history would be secure twice over. He became a lifelong champion of Beethoven, playing the string quartets, conducting the orchestral music, serving as concertmaster in the premiere of every Beethoven symphony. Meanwhile, with an evolving collection of players, Schuppanzigh established and led the first standing professional string quartet in Europe, which mounted the first public performances.

Before Beethoven and Schuppanzigh, quartets were designed, like all chamber music, to be played privately, mainly by amateurs. By the time Beethoven and Schuppanzigh were done, they left the medium of string quartet in a quite different place, carried on by specialists. Yet their long collaboration never became a real friendship. Through the years they addressed each other as *Er*, in third person, a patronizing form used with children and servants. Beethoven relentlessly teased the portly Schuppanzigh about his girth, gave him the nickname "Falstaff," after Shakespeare's fat, hard-drinking buffoon. Schuppanzigh was no intellectual companion, and Beethoven was more interested in politics, literature, and ideas than in talking shop. In other words, Beethoven vitally needed Schuppanzigh and at the same time never seemed to regard him as anything but a servant of his will. An equally enduring and relatively warmer connection that Beethoven made at the Lichnowskys' was Baron Nikolaus Zmeskall von Domanovecz. A lifelong bachelor, described by an acquaintance as "a very precise gentleman with abundant white hair," Zmeskall served as an official of the Hungarian chancellery. Otherwise he was an amateur cellist good enough to sit in with the Schuppanzigh quartet, said to be a capable composer of quartets himself but shy about publishing them.[25] In summer 1793, Zmeskall received the first of Beethoven's wry and affectionate notes summoning him for one task or another. Over the next decades the baron carefully preserved those dozens of notes. With his connections, his cello, his own chamber music soirees, and especially with his deft hand at cutting quill pens, for year after year bustling and efficient Zmeskall felt happy to be at Beethoven's beck and call.

A third patron Beethoven gained through Lichnowsky and/or Haydn was the legendary and formidable Gottfried Freiherr van Swieten. His father had been a physician brought from Holland by Empress Maria Theresa to be her personal doctor and to reform the Viennese medical establishment. For his success the family was ennobled by the empress. Son Gottfried became a diplomat and finally librarian for the Viennese court. Swieten lived and held forth in his lavish rooms, one a music room, on the third floor of the court library.[26]

Another of the crowd of obsessives in the musical landscape of Vienna, another Aufklärer and Freemason, Swieten had a particular obsession with resurrecting old music, forming an aristocratic Society of Associated Cavaliers to produce performances.[27] But during that era when most music heard and published was by living composers, "old" music usually meant less than a hundred years old. It had been Swieten who drilled into Mozart, with historic results, the significance of Handel and J. S. Bach. Later he became a friend and patron of Haydn and, with mixed results, Haydn's librettist.

In those days, J. S. Bach's music had something of a cult status among connoisseurs, while Handel's work had never faded in popularity. He was the first composer in Western history who never had to be "rediscovered." In other words, Handel, who died in 1759, when Haydn was in his twenties and Mozart a toddler, gave the first inkling that there could be such a thing as a permanent repertoire. One of the things that made Beethoven what he became was the understanding, still relatively novel at the time, that one's music could not only bring fame in life but also write one's name on the wall of history.

That does not happen on its own. Every artist needs champions, needs them when alive and even more when dead. Gottfried van Swieten spent his life championing the past. "My consolation," he declared, "above all is Handel and the Bachs, and with them a few masters of our day, who walk the path of these masters of truth and beauty."[28] Swieten also owned a collection of old-master paintings, one of them *An Artist in His Studio,* by the then-obscure Vermeer.[29] It may well have been that Mozart and Beethoven performed in Swieten's music room beneath that sublime picture of an artist in the first moment of creation, painting a Muse.

By the time Beethoven met him, Swieten was an aging, lugubrious, autocratic patriarch of music in Vienna. If he heard someone talking at a concert, he would rise grandly to his feet and stare the person down.[30] As he said, though, his devotion to "ancient" music did not keep him from championing living and breathing composers he approved of. In December 1794, Swieten sent a note to Beethoven to come Wednesday evening "with your nightcap in your bag."[31] The occasion may have been to celebrate Beethoven's name day. He played a great deal in Swieten's music room — Swieten especially appreciated Beethoven's Bach playing — and there heard Handel oratorios that helped move him toward his eventual conviction that Handel was the greatest of all, his only superior.

Haydn, the three Lichnowskys, Zmeskall, Swieten, Schuppanzigh — these musicians and cognoscenti were the leading edge of Beethoven's triumph in Vienna. Some of them commissioned works, and he dedicated pieces to all of them except Schuppanzigh. Beyond that touch of immortality, the main thing Beethoven bequeathed to these champions in return for their generosity was to be who he was, and do what he did.

As his reputation ascended in Vienna, Beethoven did not forget friends in Bonn. He appeared to regard those back in the Rhineland — Wegeler and the Breunings, though not Christian Neefe — as his real friends. To him Bonn and the Rhine were still home. They always would be.

In November 1793, he wrote a long letter to Eleonore von Breuning, daughter of the family that had practically adopted him, once his piano student, whom he had probably loved, from whom he had parted on a sour note — there had been a fight. It is a prime example of the abjectly apologetic letters in which Beethoven specialized in those years.

He addresses her, "Most estimable Leonore! My most precious friend!" . . . "You have been constantly and most vividly in my thoughts," he reassures her,

> but — whenever I did so I was always reminded of that unfortunate quarrel; and my conduct at that time seemed to me really detestable. But what was done could not be undone. Oh, I would give a great deal to be able to blot out of my life my behavior at that time, a behavior which did me so little honor and which was so inconsistent with my usual character . . . I am inclined to think that the chief obstacle to a harmonious friendship between us was the fact that third parties were whispering to us the remarks which each of us was making about the other. Each of us thought at the time that he or she was speaking with true conviction. Yet it was only fomented anger; and we were both deceived.

He tells her she is about to receive a dedication from him. It was some light variations for piano and violin on Mozart's "Se vuol ballare" from *The Marriage of Figaro*, which he had begun in Bonn. Now it was being published by Artaria in Vienna — one of Haydn's publishers, the connection perhaps Haydn's doing. In the letter Beethoven begs Leonore to "please accept this trifle and bear in mind that it comes from a friend who admires you." The variations are "a small token to recall the time when I spent so many and such blissful hours in your home. Perhaps it will continue to remind you of me until I return to Bonn, though indeed that will not be for some time. But oh! my beloved friend, how happy our meeting will be! For you will then find me a much more cheerful person; and you will see that time and more favorable circumstances have smoothed out the wrinkles produced by my earlier unpleasant experiences." He asks Leonore to knit him a new angora waistcoat. A coat she had made him earlier "is so out of fashion that I can only keep it in my wardrobe as a very precious token from you, my beloved friend." Then a coy confession: "There is a touch of vanity fundamentally connected with my request. For I want to be able to say that I've received a present from one of the best and most adorable girls in Bonn."[32]

His campaign to get back in Leonore's good graces did not succeed. The next spring she sent him a handsome knitted cravat, but evidently (the letter did not survive) she was having none of his apologies. "Oh, if you could have witnessed what I felt yesterday on the arrival of your gift," he wrote her in return,

> you would certainly not think that I exaggerate when I tell you that your remembrance made me tearful and very sorrowful. — However little, in your opinion, I may deserve to be believed, yet I beg you to believe, <u>my friend</u> (please let me continue to call you friend), that I have suffered greatly . . . from the loss of your friendship. I shall never forget you and your dear mother . . . I know what I have lost and what you have meant to me . . . However little I may mean to you, please believe that I entertain just as great a regard for you and your mother as I have always done.

<u>As always, he dwells on the effect on him, not on her and her family, of their late friendship.</u> All the same, with the letter he enclosed the printed "Se vuol ballare" Variations dedicated to Leonore, and in a PS reverted to his role as teacher, giving her advice, then going on to his trademark paranoia:

> The v[ariations] will be rather difficult to play, and particularly the trills in the coda . . . you need only play the trill and can leave out the other notes, since these appear in the violin part as well. I should never have written down this kind of piece, had I not already noticed fairly often how some people in Vienna after hearing me extemporize of an evening would note down on the following day several peculiarities of my style and palm them off with pride as their own . . . I resolved to forestall those people. But there was yet another reason, namely, my desire to embarrass those Viennese pianists, some of whom are my sworn enemies. I wanted to revenge myself on them in

this way, because I knew beforehand that my variations would . . . be put before the said gentlemen and that they would cut a sorry figure with them.[33]

Still, as a later wise man would note, even paranoids have enemies. In the roiling competitive arena of Viennese pianists, Beethoven was the new threat, and they would not watch his rise without trying to steal what they could while doing their best to shoot him down.

In November 1793, Haydn and Beethoven wrote coordinated letters to Elector Max Franz in Bonn, by way of a progress report and entreaty. Beethoven's letter is gracious and flattering. Haydn's long, fulsome letter arrived with "several musical pieces, namely a Quintet, an eight-voiced Parthie, an Oboe Concerto, Variations for the Piano, and a Fugue, composed by my dear student." Haydn adds, "Connoisseurs and nonconnoisseurs must impartially admit, from the present pieces, that in time Beethoven will fill the position of one of the greatest musicians in Europe, and I shall be proud to be able to call myself his teacher; I only wish that he might remain with me a considerable time longer."

Then Haydn goes into financial matters. He notes that Beethoven was getting only 500 florins from the Elector and needed 1,000 to get through the year. The young man had been forced to borrow 500 florins from Haydn, which was accumulating interest. Haydn signed the letter with his official title: *Kapellmeister* of Prince Nikolaus Ester-házy.[34]

In regard to the "considerable time longer" Beethoven would need for study, Haydn did not mention that in a couple of months he was leaving for a long stay in England. In fact, the situation outlined in both these letters to the Elector was more than a little dodgy. Beethoven sent the Elector what was supposedly the product of his year's work in composition. All the pieces were minor, hardly anything to promise the glorious future Haydn prophesied. And though Beethoven may have finished or revised the pieces under Haydn's tutelage, they were mostly things written or begun earlier. Beethoven had spent the year mainly playing piano, going to musicales, and turning out counterpoint exercises.

Elector Max Franz was not fooled and not happy. His chilly reply to Haydn arrived in December: "I received the music of the young Beethoven that you sent me, along with your letter. Since, however, this music, except for the Fugue, was composed by him here in Bonn, and was performed before he undertook this, his second journey to Vienna, it can be no proof for me of the progress that he has made in Vienna."

In response to Haydn's concern over Beethoven's inadequate stipend from the court, Max Franz points out that while this student was indeed getting only 500 florins specifically for his Vienna studies, that was in addition to his ongoing court salary of 400 florins. That made a total of 900 a year, which couldn't be so bad — and which Beethoven apparently had not mentioned to Haydn. The Elector curtly concluded, "I wonder, therefore, whether he should not begin his return journey here ... for I very much doubt that he will have made any important progress in composition and taste during his present stay, and I fear that he will bring back only debts from his journey, just as he did from his first trip to Vienna."[35]

The Elector had a long memory, though he did not take note of the reason Beethoven had aborted his Vienna visit five years before: his mother had been dying. In any case, it appears that Haydn had been taken for something of a ride by his student, and made to look duped or dishonest before His Serene Electoral Highness.

Haydn cannot have been pleased about all this. What transpired between him and Beethoven as a result was not recorded. Beethoven may actually have been finished taking lessons by this time anyway, and Haydn was scrambling to finish three symphonies in the weeks before he left for England. Given their more or less placid future relations, Haydn's departure may have helped calm the situation. In any case, there was no action on the Elector's threat to bring Beethoven back to Bonn. Max Franz had his own problems. He was desperately campaigning to keep his electorate out of the burgeoning conflict with France, and he went to Vienna to plead his case with the emperor.

On January 19, 1794, Haydn departed for his second visit to England. He would be gone the better part of two years. Even before Beethoven left Bonn, there had been a suggestion that he might accompany

Haydn on this second English trip. In the farewell *Stammbuch,* Christoph von Breuning had declared in a poem, "Albion [England] long beckons to you, O friend." It may have been that Haydn decided not to take Beethoven with him because of friction between them.[36] In any event, the old man set out accompanied only by his copyist. *ALBRECHTSBERGER*

Haydn arranged for Beethoven to begin counterpoint lessons with the *Kapellmeister* of St. Stephen's Cathedral, Johann Georg Albrechtsberger. Beethoven understood that Albrechtsberger was a hoary pedant who would never understand somebody like him, but he wanted the old man to hold his feet to the fire more than Haydn had. Albrechtsberger would attempt to do so. From his own adaptation and extension of Fux's *Gradus,* Albrechtsberger drilled this student in more species counterpoint, in fugue, in invertible counterpoint at the octave, tenth, and twelfth.

In a surviving note, it appears that in handing over his pupil Haydn sent some practical advice to Albrechtsberger: "Another six months in c[ounterpoint] and he can work on whatever he wants."[37] Music in those days remained in many ways a trade like others, in which one did one's apprentice work, learned the requisite skills and disciplines to attain mastery, and then in the fullness of time produced a "masterpiece" to demonstrate one's competence. Beethoven took it for granted that he must go through that process.

The lessons with Albrechtsberger went on for more than a year, three lessons a week; 160 exercises would survive.[38] Through it all, Beethoven proved just as imperious and recalcitrant with this teacher as he had been with Haydn. Later Albrechtsberger recalled this student as "always so stubborn and so bent on having his own way that he had to learn many things through hard experience."[39] Beethoven, of course, knew no way to learn anything other than his way — the hard way.

As he seemed to resist everything and forget nothing, Beethoven remembered parts of Albrechtsberger's counterpoint text, particularly a passage where the teacher lists a series of devices to vary a fugue subject: augmentation (lengthening the theme rhythmically), diminution (shortening the theme), abbreviation, syncopation, and stretto (the overlapping of entries of the fugue subject). Albrechtsberger ends by noting that it is quite rare for all these devices to be combined in a single fugue. Many years later, in Beethoven's most ambitious fugue, he more or less did so.[40] Meanwhile from here on, the old devices of rhythmic augmentation and diminution became a constant feature of Beethoven's rhythmic style, as they had been with Haydn and Mozart, whether or not the music was overtly contrapuntal.

Albrechtsberger and Beethoven struggled on doggedly together. Later there were reports of mutual behind-the-back sniping. Albrechtsberger dismissed one of Beethoven's op. 18 Quartets as "trash"; Beethoven declared his teacher's compositions "musical skeletons."[41] Yet as with Haydn, on the surface he and Albrechtsberger stayed friendly. For years Beethoven visited the old pedant and sent him students to be subjected to the tortures of counterpoint.

For all he learned in Vienna, Beethoven never forgot the people he had known and the ideals he had absorbed in Bonn, or the high-Aufklärung talk he loved there. He had not dropped his determination to set Schiller's "An die Freude," and was possibly working on a setting. In May 1793, in the album of a merchant named Volcke, he wrote an entry with a quote from Schiller's *Don Carlos*: "I am not wicked — Hot blood is my fault — my crime is that I am young. I am not wicked, truly not wicked. Even though wildly surging emotions may betray my heart, yet my heart is good — / Precepts. To do good whenever one can, to love liberty above all else, never to deny the truth, even though it be before the throne."[42] He signed it "Ludwig Beethoven from Bonn near Cologne." (His Bonn friends had often skipped the *van*.) His inscription is echt Aufklärung, echt Bonn.

Count Waldstein showed up in Vienna in early 1794, and presumably they had a reunion.[43] But their relations did not revive. For Beethoven by that time, Waldstein appears to have been a figure of his past, not his future.

As 1794 appeared, Beethoven was working on some piano trios intended to be his most ambitious works yet. Around the beginning of that year, perhaps on New Year's Day, he wrote down a memo for himself: "Courage. In spite of all weaknesses of the body, my spirit shall rule. You are 25 years old [in fact, he was 23]; this year must determine the complete man — nothing must remain undone."[44]

He had been taught that to be a complete artist he must be a complete man. Now he willed himself to become that man. This is the first recorded sweeping resolution of his life. There would be more. Unlike most such resolutions by most people, Beethoven's would mark turning points in his life and his work. All of them are a summoning of discipline and determination, despite all obstacles to remake himself and to do something new in music, new in the world.

11

Generalissimo

A T THE BEGINNING of 1793, Beethoven had been one more new virtuoso in a town teeming with the species. By the beginning of 1794, he was the hottest pianist in Vienna and protégé of the powerful Lichnowskys — the definition of a lionized and cocky young artist. Now with something like a generalissimo's strategy, he turned the full fury of his attention to showing the public what he was made of as a composer.

Artaria published the "Se vuol ballare" Variations as op. 1 against his wishes. This coup, a piece placed with the leading house in Vienna, the main publisher of Haydn and Mozart, only annoyed him. Beethoven would never have a problem putting minor rent-paying items in print, but more than any composer before him he crafted the progress of his first opus numbers. (He would also be the first composer to be published constantly from the beginning to the end of his mature work.) The pieces with opus numbers were to be only serious ones, the choice of medium and genre and the order and variety of pieces within each opus carefully calculated. In 1794, the main project was to finish the three piano trios slated to be the real op. 1.

As he moved forward in the early Vienna years, Beethoven composed with reference to the past, and not only in terms of studying traditional form and craft. He was intensely aware of where the past left him more room and where less. The most pressing parts of the past were the immediate ones: the superb Mozart, always looming over him as a model and challenge but safely dead; Haydn, still alive and evolving in unpredictable and potentially threatening directions.

Beethoven understood which media and genres Haydn and Mozart were supreme in, and which ones had been less important for them. He charted his path with that in mind, genre by genre. Both his predecessors had spent much of their careers composing for harpsichord, while Beethoven was a pure pianist and piano composer. There he could be bold. When it came to idiomatic piano writing — exploiting the full range of touch, articulation, volume, texture, and color available to the piano as opposed to the harpsichord — one of his prime models was *CLEMENTI* Muzio Clementi, who wrote one of the first substantial bodies of work for piano. At the same time, as a composer in general Clementi posed no threat to Beethoven. Clementi wrote attractively and idiomatically for the piano, Mozart and Haydn beautifully in general, but as far as Beethoven would have been concerned, the first truly significant repertoire for the piano as such was waiting to be written. He intended to write that repertoire.[1]

At the same time, as a young composer finding his way in the 1790s, *STRING QUARTET* Beethoven knew excruciatingly well that when it came to the string quartet, Haydn owned that territory, had all but singlehandedly created the genre in its modern form. Mozart's mature quartets and string quintets followed in Haydn's footsteps and were likewise virtually unchallengeable. With quartets, Beethoven had to step carefully. If he could not outdo Haydn and Mozart here, he had to wait until he could find a path of his own. Sometime in 1793–94, he copied out the whole of Haydn's String Quartet op. 20, no. 1, to see what he could learn. But finding a territory of his own in quartets would not happen soon.[2] As for symphonies — well, he would have to wait and see what Haydn came up with. Haydn had fathered the modern symphony as well.

When it came to the medium of piano trios, Beethoven felt himself *PIANO TRIOS* on relatively firm ground. Haydn and Mozart had written delightful ones, but for those men the trio was not a particularly ambitious effort. Here also, he had room. It helped that the trio was founded on the piano, his own instrument. He would make his piano trios expansive and ambitious. All the same, Beethoven did not barge in but stayed on a line. First in op. 1 would be two cautious and accessible trios, in E-flat and G major; then he would finish the opus with a bold work in C minor. That one, as it turned out, left him and Haydn at a greater distance.

In January 1794, Beethoven said farewell to Haydn, who set off on his second visit to England. Probably at some point during the first months of the year, Beethoven paid his respects to Elector Max Franz, who was in Vienna to plead for his regime's neutrality, trying to act as a mediator between Austria and France.[3] That initiative would get nowhere. Holy Roman Emperor Franz II was part of an international coalition against France and spoiling for a fight. Soon the Electorate of Cologne would be forced to contribute troops to the coalition.[4] That marked the end of Bonn's neutrality, and soon the end of the electorate. In March Beethoven's support from Bonn stopped, though not his nominal connection to the court: an autumn 1794 memo from the exiled Elector described Beethoven as "without salary in Vienna, until recalled."[5] Beethoven showed no anguish at losing his Bonn stipend of 900 florins a year. He had his own resources now, including the generous Prince Lichnowsky.

That spring Carl van Beethoven, Ludwig's red-haired and choleric middle brother, moved to Vienna. Likely with Ludwig's help, he first set up as a piano teacher, trying a little composing himself, though he was not cut out to be a professional musician. Before long Carl became Ludwig's agent and go-between with publishers, to unfortunate effect. When he arrived, Carl told Ludwig that back home, Nikolaus Simrock, once a horn player in the Bonn *Kapelle* and now proprietor of a music-publishing house, was putting into print some four-hand piano variations that Ludwig had written on a theme of Count Waldstein. For the second time, this time without his knowledge or approval, a set of variations Beethoven considered a trifle was going to come out before he had put anything ambitious into print.

Simrock was an old family friend, so in a letter Beethoven settled for a gentle chiding: "I am inclined to think that you should have taken the trouble to consult me about this. What would you think of me if I were to act in the same way and sell these v[ariations] to Artaria, although you are now engraving them? However, do not let this cause you any anxiety." He said he would send Simrock a manuscript with some improvements. "The fact is," he added, "I had no desire to publish any variations at the present moment, because I wanted to wait until some more important works of mine, which are due to appear very soon, had first been given to the world."[6] He meant the piano trios. Nothing this composer of age twenty-three said shows more succinctly the boundlessness of his confidence.

Beethoven had settled in as one of the stars of the Friday-morning musicales at the Lichnowskys. In that sociable and informal atmosphere, with food and wine and conversation accompanying the music, he played his pieces, improvised, tried out works in progress for an audience of leading dilettantes and professionals, probably read through other composers' works. Among the pieces played were his new trios, with Beethoven on piano and probably Ignaz Schuppanzigh on violin and one of the father-and-son Krafts on cello. After one reading, the elder Kraft said that the finale of the G Major would be more lively and effective if written in 2/4 rather than 4/4, and a couple of passages in the finale of the C Minor should indicate *sul C* for the cello, because the passages would sound best on the C string.[7] Beethoven took both pieces of advice.

One of the visitors in the Lichnowsky soirees of those years was a Frau von Bernhard, who left a description of the scene and of Beethoven's style in it. She describes a man "small and plain-looking with an ugly red, pock-marked face, dark shaggy hair and commonplace clothes," with a provincial dialect spoken in "a rather common manner." By that point, Beethoven had shed the old courtly wig and was wearing his hair in the fashionable French neoclassic style.[8] On arrival, he would stick his head in the door of the music room to see if anyone he hated was present. If someone was, he vanished. This new virtuoso was "unmannerly in both gesture and demeanor." On one occasion, the mother of the hostess, Countess Thun, once admired by Mozart, got down on her knees begging him to play, and Beethoven haughtily refused.

Frau Bernhard remembers legendary visitors to the salon, Haydn and court *Kapellmeister* Antonio Salieri, who had once been a rival of Mozart (and was rumored to have poisoned him): "I still remember clearly both Haydn and Salieri sitting on a sofa on one side of the small music-room, both carefully dressed in the old-fashioned way with peruque, shoes and silk hose, whereas even here Beethoven would come dressed in the informal fashion of the other side of the Rhine, almost ill-dressed."[9]

In Viennese salons of those years, war competed with art in conversations. The French were a threat not only in their armies but also in the march of the democratic and republican ideals they represented. After the Terror broke out and the French turned to conquest, Holy Roman Emperor Franz II's hatred of democracy or of any change in the status quo, and his fear of secret societies, became an obsession. The Freemasons and all other secret societies had already been effectively banned in 1793.[10] Now writings on politics were seized, some private social and intellectual salons shut down. The discovery of a conspiracy was announced, Jacobins were arrested, some of them publicly pilloried for three days and some hanged, others given life terms in prison. The emperor ordered the police to set up a system "to secure the most absolute stability which ingenuity could devise."[11]

During this time Beethoven wrote Nikolaus Simrock in Bonn, with political matters passing through his letter as lightly as the practical and romantic: "I promised to send you some of my compositions, and you treated my statement as if it were merely the fine phrase of a courtier . . . Fie, who in these democratic times of ours would indulge in that kind of talk . . . Well, in order to clear myself of the epithet . . . you are to receive . . . something which you will certainly engrave." He goes on to another pressing subject: "If your daughters are now grown up, do fashion one to be my bride. For if I have to live at Bonn as a bachelor, I will certainly not stay there for long."[12] If he was not entirely serious about Simrock's daughters, now that he had found some success he was thinking about marriage.

His expectation of returning to Bonn was in the process of becoming moot. With the French advancing in the Rhineland again that autumn, Max Franz readied his third departure. This time it was clearly a more serious matter. He called up seven ships on the Rhine, onto which palace servants loaded records and treasures of the Electoral Court: furniture, silver, the library, the cream of the wine cellars. At the beginning of October 1794, from the steps of the Rathaus in the market, the last Elector of Cologne said farewell to his people and vowed to return. Most of the nobility and well-to-do commoners who could afford to escape fled to various havens on the east bank of the Rhine.[13] On October 8, the French marched unopposed into the town. Two weeks after the Elector fled, his sister Marie Antoinette went to the guillotine in Paris. Killing first a king and now a queen, the Revolution was burning its bridges.

Now every person in Bonn was of the same rank: citizen. The French authorities decreed the assignat as currency, and with military pomp erected a Freedom Tree in the market. Few townsfolk attended the ceremony, though in fact there was a good deal of sympathy for the Revolution. Religion was roughly handled; the French turned the Jesuit church into a horse stall. The inevitable requisitions began. Before long, it sank in that Max Franz was never going to return and the town's only real industry, the court, was finished. The Electorate of Cologne, more than five hundred years old, had evaporated like a summer cloud.

The French made a mess of the occupation.[14] Between their harsh and incompetent rule and the collapse of the economy with the fall of the court, within a year Bonn was in shambles. So was the career of Christian Neefe, whom the French drafted to be a municipal official and paid starvation wages. Neefe was seriously ill. He and his wife began selling their possessions to stay alive. In 1795, Neefe wrote a friend that he was "weak in my limbs, apprehensive in my breast, alarmed at every sound, my arm and leg trembling — I'm almost useless for anything." Finally allowed to leave Bonn in 1796, he went to work for the court theater in Dessau. But Neefe the well-regarded composer and writer, the *Schwärmer* and leader of the Illuminati, the teacher of Beethoven the phenomenon of his generation, was a broken and nearly forgotten man. He died in Dessau in January 1798.[15] There would be no record of Beethoven's response to the news.

FRANZ
WEGELER   Among other refugees from the French was Beethoven's oldest
           friend, physician Franz Wegeler. He had experienced a remarkable rise
    ↓   and a disastrous fall. In 1793, at age twenty-seven, Wegeler had been
VIENNA   elected rector of the University of Bonn. At the approach of the French
army, he signed a resolution forbidding students to have any contact
with French prisoners being marched through town. The order was
issued for health reasons, in fear of students catching typhus. But the
resolution was interpreted as antirevolutionary, and as the French approached, Wegeler had to flee to keep his head.[16] In Vienna, he and
Beethoven had a warm reunion. Among other things, Wegeler served
as somebody Beethoven could vent his complaints to: "He developed
. . . an aversion to being asked to play at social occasions. Many times
he came to me, gloomy and upset, complaining that he was forced to
play even if the blood burned under his nails."[17]

Soon enough there was a blowup between them, followed by one of
Beethoven's hyperbolic apologies:

> What a horrible picture you have shown me of myself! Oh, I admit
> that I do not deserve your friendship. You are so noble and well-
> meaning; and this is the first time that I dare not face you, for I have
> fallen far beneath you. Alas! For eight weeks now I have been a source
> of distress to my best and noblest friend. You believe that my good-
> ness of heart had diminished. No, thank Heaven, for what made me
> behave to you like that was no deliberate, premeditated wickedness
> on my part, but my unpardonable thoughtlessness . . . Yet, oh do let
> me say this in my defense, I really was always good and ever tried to
> be upright and honorable in my actions. Otherwise how could you
> have loved me?[18]

It should not be doubted that this letter, and all the letters like it that
Beethoven wrote over the years, was sincere. It was characteristic of
him that when the fury passed he was, sometimes, ready to listen to
the remonstrations of a friend. Whether or not his goodness of heart
was exactly as he painted it in the letter, Beethoven was nonetheless
correct that there was nothing premeditated in his rage and vitupera-
tion. There is no record that he ever deliberately set out to hurt or

betray a friend, though he fought with most of the friends he ever had. In Wegeler's case the prodigal was forgiven, the friendship restored. Nothing shook it again before Wegeler left Vienna, in 1796; after that he never saw Beethoven in the flesh again. At that point of complete separation their friendship became, for Beethoven, perfect and unassailable.

All of Beethoven's testimonials to his goodness had to do less with what he truly was than with what he believed he had to be. If he was not mean, he was still proud, suspicious, paranoid, contemptuous of much of humanity. In youth he had been taught by the ancients and by the Freemasons and Illuminati around him that the foundation of wisdom is "know thyself." As his letters show over and over, his self-knowledge ranged from insightful to delusional. Even less did he understand anybody else. What he did understand, as fully as anyone ever had, was music and its connection to the heart and soul.

In his diary, Beethoven had decreed 1794 as the year when he must become a whole man, which also meant getting his career properly under way not only as a virtuoso but also as a composer. The collapse of the Bonn court lost him a good deal of income but was otherwise a gift, freeing him from having to account to anybody for anything he was doing. He would never have to report upward again. For better and for worse, he was his own man, with patrons and income from publishers and performers. Though he disliked teaching, he took on piano students, especially aristocratic ones who could pay well, also particularly talented ones whom he would teach for little or nothing. Young female students, talented or not, he taught with special attention.

What mainly made up 1794 for Beethoven was continuing contrapuntal studies with Albrechtsberger, practicing piano intensively, and working on the new piano trios and piano sonatas. He continued to revise the B-flat Piano Concerto, probably adding a new slow movement. Soon he would write a concerto in C major, more mature than the earlier one but still more conventional than otherwise. Beethoven was cagey in these years, more himself in smaller works than in larger.

In 1795 he was ready to place the previous year's projects before the public. At the beginning of March, for a gathering at the palatial home

of Prince Franz Joseph Maximilian von Lobkowitz, Beethoven played
a program including perhaps one of the concertos, perhaps an improvisation. "One named Beethoven touched everybody," wrote a member of the audience.[19]

This new patron, Prince Lobkowitz, was two years younger than
Beethoven, another indefatigable aristocratic music fancier, from one
of the most prominent and influential families in Austria.[20] Suffering
from a deformity that required him to use a crutch, he was not able
to take on the usual military or diplomatic careers of men of his class,
so he turned to the arts. An able bass singer and violinist, Lobkowitz
in 1796 founded a private orchestra that traveled with him among his
palaces and country houses; he was one of the last of the Viennese nobility to follow that outdated fashion.[21] He made his musicians and his
home available to composers for programs and tryouts of new pieces.
Sometimes there would be multiple rehearsals going on in different
rooms of his palace.[22] In her memoir, Countess Lulu von Thürheim
had a touch of sympathy for this prince: "In his castle at Eisenberg the
door was open to artists and the dinner table was laid uninterruptedly
. . . He himself composed several operas and, although he walked with
a crutch, he took an active part in the performances. Even though he
was himself a spendthrift, his purse was open to all and sundry who
called on him for help."[23]

As he did with Prince Lichnowsky, Beethoven would quarrel periodically with Lobkowitz, and like Lichnowsky, this prince had his
eccentricities: he would let mail go years unopened, spent weeks in
total seclusion, obsessively watched people on the street by way of a
mirror.[24] But in contrast to the imperious and demanding Lichnowsky,
Lobkowitz was a mild and forgiving sort, especially when it came to
first-rate musicians. When he and Beethoven fought, they fought as
equals.[25]

Beethoven's private concert for Lobkowitz at the beginning of March
1795 may have been a warm-up for a major part of his campaign that
came at the end of the month: his public debut in Vienna. He took part
in three benefit concerts in three days, the first two for the Tonkünstler
Society at the venerable Burgtheater. Two days before the first concert,
Franz Wegeler visited his old friend and witnessed a sight he never for-

got. Beethoven was composing the finale for the C Major Piano Concerto, handing each page of score with the ink still wet to four copyists sitting in the hall, who were writing out the instrumental parts for a rehearsal the next day. At the same time Beethoven was wretchedly sick to his stomach, a familiar condition for him. So Wegeler watched his friend finish a rondo finale for piano and orchestra virtually in one sitting, his work interspersed with violent fits of vomiting. The next day Wegeler heard the concerto rehearsed with the whole, presumably small, orchestra crammed into Beethoven's flat. Here Beethoven produced another feat. Finding that his piano was a half-step flatter than the winds, he played his solo part in C-sharp major.[26]

On March 29, 1795, the Viennese musical public heard Beethoven premiere the concerto in a program including an oratorio by Herr *Kapellmeister* Kartellieri called *Joas, King of Judah.* The next day he did an improvisation at the second Tonkünstler benefit. On the thirty-first, he played a Mozart concerto during a performance of Mozart's opera *La Clemenza del Tito,* in a program for the benefit of the composer's widow Constanze.[27] Which Mozart he played was not noted, but it was likely the D Minor, Beethoven's favorite, the most dramatic, demonic, call it *Beethovenian* of Mozart concertos.[28] In the *Wiener Zeitung* of April 1, there was a notice of the first Burgtheater concert: "As an intermezzo . . . the celebrated Herr Ludwig van Beethoven reaped the unanimous applause of the audience for his performance on the pianoforte of a completely new concerto composed by him."[29]

The first two piano concertos are exercises in the style of the day, no less telling for that. Beethoven took up each musical genre individually, distinctly, with reference to its literature and traditions. In comparison to the bold personalities of some works, such as the sonatas and trios from op. 1 on, the relatively well-behaved first two concertos suggest that, so far, he was inclined to view the genre in terms more practical than ambitious. As with Mozart's concertos, these were vehicles for his career as a virtuoso. In any case, he was not yet ready to challenge Mozart's supremacy.

Because they were vehicles for himself, Beethoven did not regard his earlier piano concertos in the same terms as a sonata or symphony or string quartet. The latter were genres to be composed, premiered, perhaps touched up, then published as soon and as profitably as possible. His piano concertos were items to play around with for a while, revising as he went, the solo part evolving, the cadenzas left for improvisation.[30] None of this is to say that he considered his first concertos potboilers, or that he did not take pains with them. As he performed them over the months before publication he polished them, in the process learning a good deal about the colors and balances of the orchestra. And as with other of his less overtly brash works in these years, the concertos have beautiful slow movements that are more original than their surroundings.

The Piano Concerto No. 2 in B-flat, written first but published second, as op. 19, started life in Bonn around 1790. The first movement, much revised, was likely the only surviving element of the original version. A new rondo finale finished its evolution around 1798.[31] Its opening movement has a military air, like G. B. Viotti's and many concertos in that era, eventually including all Beethoven's solo concertos. (If a convention suited his purpose, he used it.) For a main theme he juxtaposed brisk fanfares with lyrical phrases, both rather on the conventional side. As occurs often in Mozart, after an extended orchestral tutti the soloist first enters with a quasi-new idea derived from earlier material. The soloist emphasizes the lyrical aspect of the material, providing some quite lovely stretches.

In the end, the opening movement of the B-flat is grand and effective, but it still adds up to one of the most routine orchestral movements Beethoven ever published. It features rough transitions, stolid block scoring in the winds, and a drifting quality recalling a young small-town composer following his nose — and a mature composer who didn't have the time or patience to fix everything. Beethoven surely understood that. It didn't bother him excessively. When he first presented the B-flat to a publisher, he introduced it as a work "which I do not claim to be one of my best." Yet as in the early violin sonatas and string quartets, beneath a not particularly bold surface, his searching nature can't help showing itself. The first movement of the B-flat Concerto has startling tonal excursions: after some nervous modulations, the second theme arrives with a leap into D-flat major. In the recap, that theme returns in an even more peculiar G-flat major, another distinctively spiced key when pianos were not tuned in equal temperament.

The next two movements sound more mature, more Viennese. The Adagio in E-flat major is Mozartian in conception — it echoes the preciousness of the eighteenth-century *galant* mood and the lofty choruses of Mozart's *Magic Flute* — but more nearly Beethovenian in tone, with an elegantly nocturnal atmosphere. The keys include a strikingly dark B-flat minor, and the handling of the piano is fresh and brilliant. Traditionally, concerto finales were lively and witty sonata-rondos — another convention, and Beethoven invariably conformed to it. The soloist ends the piece with a blaze of double trills in the right hand, a specialty of his at the keyboard.

While the B-flat Concerto developed over the better part of a decade before he was ready to put it in print, the later C Major, published as Piano Concerto No. 1, op. 15, was a quicker and more confident affair. Beethoven had noted down a few ideas for it in 1793, including the rondo theme, then perhaps drafted the three movements sometime around the end of 1795. It was the completion of the finale, under trying circumstances, that Franz Wegeler witnessed.

Op. 15 turned out to be another well-behaved item, predictable in much of its material, including its foursquare military first movement, its droll rondo finale, its slow movement ornamenting an elegantly *galant* theme. If in his person Beethoven had left behind the courtly wig for a fashionable French-style hairdo, in his concertos he had not yet taken the wig off.

Again, but no more so than in the B-flat, this concerto works in some tonal experiments — in a C-major first movement, the second theme lands on E-flat.[32] The more subtle experiment in the first movement is that its main theme is more a rhythm than a tune. Its marching tread, especially its opening long–short–short–long tattoo, Beethoven used as a scaffolding for themes throughout the concerto, starting with the first movement's second theme and including the main theme of the next movement.

In the C Major, the character of the soloist is more distinctive than in the B-flat. Bringing the piano out of the militant opening tutti with a sweeping lyrical turn, Beethoven gave the soloist the character of, say, a jolly lieutenant in the regiment, sentimental but well muscled and his own man. For all his flamboyant passagework, he never plays the martial opening theme. The Largo second movement, in A-flat major — unusual for a work in C major — is atmospheric and introspective, gradually passionate. In the rondo finale the soloist is a rambunctious lad, with his floor-shaking dance that defies us to find the beat. On its last appearance he brings in the rondo theme in the wrongest of wrong keys, B major, before getting chased back to a proper C major. The style of this finale amounts to a playful version of the usually more placid dance called the *englische*, a genre that in a few years would come to preoccupy Beethoven.

In August Haydn arrived back in town from his second visit to England, which had been a still-greater triumph than his first. He had premiered six new symphonies of the total of eleven he wrote for his two visits. British music lovers had found their greatest hero since Handel. Once there had been a mutual influence between Haydn and the younger Mozart. Now maybe the old master was looking to keep up with the new man on the scene, to show that he could still learn and change and show the Great Mogul a thing or two.

Beethoven would have been quick to study Haydn's new symphonies. With these and Mozart's later ones, the symphony had effectively become the king of musical genres. It needed only a few more fresh and ambitious examples to secure it on the throne. As of 1795, it seemed likely that Haydn was about to make that happen. But he never wrote another symphony. Instead, he turned to genres traditionally considered more important: mass and oratorio. The reasons for that turn were simple: Haydn wrote only on commission, and from the later 1790s on, his commissions were for choral music. He looked at those masses and oratorios as the crown of his work. In the domain of the symphony, now the road was open for Beethoven to pick up where Haydn left off.

The month after Beethoven's concerto performance, another notice appeared in the paper: local publisher Artaria invited the public to buy advance subscriptions to Herr van Beethoven's new piano trios.

Beethoven made sure that in the future, the published "Se vuol ballare" Variations were demoted to "No. 1" on the title page, so the Artaria edition of the trios would have the honor of being op. 1.

After airings of the piano trios at the Lichnowsky musicales, in musical Vienna there was a buzz of excitement over the publication. The price for a subscription to the trios was steep, yet when they came out in July there were 123 subscribers, including much of the cream of Viennese nobility. Karl Lichnowsky claimed twenty copies for himself and his wife. In fact, without telling his proud protégé (who would have been furious), Lichnowsky quietly slipped publisher Artaria 212 florins to cover the cost of engraving the plates. Other aristocratic subscribers made their debuts as important Beethoven patrons: Count and Countess Browne, Haydn's employer Prince Nikolaus Esterházy, Prince Lobkowitz, Count and Countess Razumovsky, Countess Thun.[33]

Beethoven had made an unprecedented deal with Artaria, saying that he could keep most of the profits of the first four hundred copies of the trios sold. From the subscriptions and sales, he pocketed some 800 florins, the better part of a year's living. That coup, however, gave him an unrealistic impression of his prospects: he would not make that much on a publication again for thirty years.[34] As Mozart had discovered, when you were no longer the hot new virtuoso in Vienna, you found your affairs becoming more difficult.

Soon after Haydn got back to Vienna, he came to one of the Friday-morning musicales at the Lichnowskys', to be hailed as conquering hero by the cream of Viennese cognoscenti. There the just-published Beethoven trios were played for him. Later Beethoven told his student Ferdinand Ries that Haydn "said many fine things about the trios, but also cautioned that he would not have advised his pupil to publish No. 3, the C minor." The public, Haydn declared with the weight of his experience and fame, would not understand or accept that work.[35]

Beethoven was stunned and outraged. He knew the C Minor was the best of the three, the boldest and most personal. Given the way Beethoven thought, Haydn's response could mean only one thing: his teacher was another rival, jealous and conniving, who wished him ill, who wanted to suppress the very work that could put Beethoven on the map.

The public response proved Beethoven right and Haydn wrong, but that the C Minor was the sensation of the trios did not calm Beethoven's resentment. Soon appeared another matter equally galling. Having written the most ambitious of his symphonies for England, Haydn in the next years produced an oratorio of Handelian dimensions on a suitably epic subject: the Creation. His magnum opus, *The Creation,* would be received rapturously by the musical world.

When it came to his few keyboard rivals, Beethoven could be generous and friendly. But having an unassailable old-master composer as a rival ate at him. The struggle between the artistic debt and the veneration he owed Haydn and his uncontrollable jealousy would never be resolved. Until this rival was in his grave, after the affair of the C Minor Trio Beethoven had very little good to say about Haydn or his music. One element inspiring his works to the end of his life (among many other elements) would be the rankling drive to challenge and outdo Haydn.

In the event, Beethoven for once bit his tongue. There was no blowup over the C Minor Trio; relations between the two men remained polite, if strained. Soon they were collaborating in concerts — only there was more distance than before. Haydn had expected Beethoven to put "pupil of Haydn" on the cover of his first published opus. Most of his students, after all, were proud to name their teacher publicly. Beethoven refused. As far as he was concerned, he told people, he had learned nothing from Haydn.[36] Op. 1 was dedicated to Prince Lichnowsky, Beethoven's most generous patron. Op. 2 would have a dedication to Haydn, but there would be nothing about his "pupil."

If in those years Beethoven plotted his career like a generalissimo, if he composed with reference to the past, present, and future, he still composed with fierce attention to the shaping of the work at hand. So it was with the op. 1 Trios. Two are ingratiating, one aggressive, though to the ears of the time the first two sounded up-to-date enough. From a broader perspective, the word for op. 1 is *uneven.* There is a precocious sophistication of structure and tonal organization, and Beethoven had learned much about proportion, but all is inconsistent.[37]

In these trios Beethoven wanted to be expansive, both within the movements and in the pieces as a whole, and he made them rich and brilliant in sound. He wanted, in other words, to write the most ambitious piano trios to that time. They are the first to have four movements. Two have a scherzo, meaning "joke," a genre Haydn invented, a three-beat form modeled on the stately minuet but sped up into a dashing and often witty movement (though like a minuet, a scherzo can have many moods). Trio No. 3 has a minuet, but it is closer to a scherzo in tempo.

Beethoven composed the trios in order, learning and growing as he went. Sketches for no. 1 may have gone back to Bonn.[38] Call its tone stately and high-Classical, Haydnesque in its nimble dancing rhythms, its coy flourishes recalling Mozart. It is the kind of piece listeners and critics of the eighteenth century called "pleasing." For many in those days, pleasing was the main thing music was supposed to be. Changing that aesthetic would be one of Beethoven's essential tasks, but that came later.

In op. 1, Beethoven already shows tremendous thematic discipline. There would be no apprentice works in any of the opus numbers. In the E-flat Trio, the first theme of the first movement, which Beethoven and his time called *das Thema, the* theme, lays out the leading ideas of the piece melodically, rhythmically, harmonically, gesturally, and expressively. The first idea in a work is *das Thema* of the whole in the same way that the first passage of an essay expresses the theme of the essay, though in music the theme is worked out in ways that are not expected to be perceived so much as sensed by listeners, conveying a sense of rightness and wholeness.[39] Whether or not a work possessed "unity" was a leading motif of the time among connoisseurs, critics, and aestheticians. Much of the critical debate over Beethoven's music would turn on judgments relating to questions of organic unity versus caprice, whether he was provoking for the sake of provocation.

In the E-flat Trio the opening upward-dancing arpeggio returns in varied forms in every movement. (The gesture would have been familiar to Beethoven as the traditional "Mannheim rocket" theme also used by Mozart.)[40] At the same time, showing a pattern Beethoven would follow for the rest of his life, an equally significant motif is rhythmic: the Haydnesque *rum-tum-TUM* of bars 2 and 3 is as important to the music as any melodic motif. Augmented (slowed), it is the rhythm of the second theme; the first bar of movement 2 varies it; it is echoed in the repeated chords of the scherzo; it turns up in the second theme of the finale.[41] Beethoven improvised on the page as he improvised in performance, but in all cases he improvised on specific ideas. In the first movement, one echt-Beethoven touch is the expansive coda, lingering far longer than most codas in Haydn and Mozart. Beethoven would write the longest codas of any music to his time (he would prove equally given to the abrupt, before-you-know-it ending). Already he was beginning to reconfigure the weights and balances of the formal models he inherited from Haydn and Mozart.

His youth and inexperience show in material that is lively and ingratiating while at the same time amorphous and generically eighteenth century. Beethoven had already found elements of his mature voice, but he was not yet settled into that voice — which is to say, he had not yet picked out his essential voice from the competing ones in his music. To Beethoven at twenty-three and twenty-four, what the future would recognize as "Beethovenian" was simply one direction of his work, the part that escaped the safe and conventional, the part that more and more he would be drawn to.

There are other signs of immaturity and caution in the trios. Like piano trios of the past, the first two are heavily weighted to the piano, the cello much of the time anchored to the bass line and only occasionally soaring on its own. The violin is mostly written down in the staff, as if Beethoven were uncertain about taking it high on the E string.

In the E-flat, after a pleasing if passionless first movement comes a slow movement of stunning depth, the music singing and inward, strangely shadowed for a major-key movement. From a poignant but simple beginning, with a touch of the *galant* style, the movement finds its way to a place haunting and fresh.[42] The middle lands on the deep-flat minor keys that, for Beethoven, were touched with brooding and sorrow — A-flat and E-flat minor — with a surging, yearning expression that a later time would call Romantic. That freshness carries into the scherzo, with its blend of dancing merriment and quietly pensive long notes. The sonata-form last movement is mainly devoted to Haydnesque whimsy, and also recalls Haydn's freedom in treating form: the recapitulation is much recomposed, more than Beethoven would tend to do in the future.

Trio No. 2 in G Major begins with an extended Adagio introduction that prefigures two things: the violin presents a slow version of the coming Allegro theme, and the introduction as a whole foreshadows the poignant atmosphere of the second movement. Otherwise, the outer movements of the G Major are nimble and witty and large scale; but, in his drive to expand the material, Beethoven did not notice that he expanded it further than it deserved. He would rarely commit the sin of padding, but in these two fast movements he padded lavishly. The slow movement is as fresh and inwardly expressive as the previous trio's, once again strangely affecting for a piece in a major key.

No. 3 in C Minor is the first work to demonstrate how that key galvanized him: a repertoire of effects in the direction of fierce and implacable, what would come to be called his "C-minor mood." It begins tentatively, with quiet sighs recalling some of Mozart's soft beginnings of intense pieces — say, the C Minor Concerto, K. 491. Then a searing theme in a relentlessly repeating rhythm breaks out to define the dynamic, driven, and obsessive core of the work. In every way, this last of the op. 1 trios outdoes the others: in focus, in intensity, in the growing liberation of the cello from the bass line and the violin from the staff line.

But the main effect of the C Minor Trio is visceral. Having rambled and padded and pleased to various degrees in the first two trios, here Beethoven reached out and seized his listeners by the throat. He shows a mature skill in the difficult art of sustaining high intensity from the beginning to end of a movement, providing a few calm passages for the listener to catch a breath.[43] His dark key of E-flat minor makes an appearance on the second page. As a sign of its demonic provenance, the first movement and the whole trio return again and again to the tritone, an interval so ambiguous and fraught that its traditional name was *diabolus in musica,* "the devil in music."[44]

With the slow movement's variations on an Andante cantabile theme, Beethoven took up the genre with which at that point he had more experience than with any other, his row of keyboard variations going back to his first published work. Like the slow movements of the previous trios, this one is in a shadowed major key. The shadow lingers through the variety of texture and mood of the first three variations and deepens in the E-flat-minor fourth variation. The main theme of the third-movement minuet is in a driving C minor, its quiet intensity broken by *fortissimo* chords and offbeat accents.

The finale does not so much begin as pounce on the listener. We are off in another fierce and obsessive C-minor movement that stops only for charged silences that are shattered by new explosions of energy. The feeling of the finale is like an echo of the first movement, with a similarly gentle E-flat-major second theme that briefly quiets the whirlwind. The coda seems almost to unravel, ending on vacantly repeated notes *pp* in the strings, the piano slithering upward in C-major scales that sound not hopeful and resolving but exhausted and defeated.

The publication of op. 1 did for Beethoven what he intended it to do. The opus represented his first large-scale essay in what amounted to a high-Viennese style and genre, and it caused a stir in Vienna that spread from there. As he also hoped and expected, it was the C Minor Trio that most seized players and listeners, except the backward-looking ones like Haydn. In the next years Beethoven would sometimes please the old master with a piece, but with the C Minor Trio he had staked his own territory. And that was the work which, as far as Beethoven was concerned, Haydn wanted to suppress.

At the same time, a mutual acquaintance of Haydn's and Beethoven's recalled that in the next years Beethoven felt "a sort of apprehension, because he was aware that he had struck out a path for himself which Haydn did not approve of."[45] Beethoven did not like having apprehensions like that. In his long and unforgiving memory, the image of Haydn gained a permanent niche near the center of his creative consciousness. Even beyond the grave, Haydn would remain a goad, a judge, and a rival.

Listening to the fiery C Minor Trio, sitting in Lichnowsky's music room wearing his old-fashioned knee breeches and wig, Haydn had plenty of reason for concern. This youth with no charm and no deference to his betters or his teacher, with no wig and wild hair: who knew what he might perpetrate? In his long experience of art and of the world, Haydn perhaps understood what was happening. It is what happens to most great artists who live into their own legend among creative progeny who are struggling to get out from under them. Even though he was at the summit of his fame and with splendid works still ahead of him, Haydn had to sense that now he was the past and this youth was the future. That future was audible, enough to trouble the old man, in the C Minor Piano Trio.

When he published the op. 1 Trios, the Great Mogul was twenty-four years old.

12

Virtuoso

TOWARD THE END of 1795, Beethoven fell into a flurry of activity. In November came the annual ball for the pension fund of the Society of Plastic Artists, held in the large and small *Redoutensaals* (ballrooms) of the Hofburg, the imperial palace. For the occasion, he composed twelve minuets and German dances. Haydn and Mozart had supplied music for earlier balls. The announcement for this year's read, "The music for the Minuets and German Dances for this ball is an entirely new arrangement. For the larger room they were written by Royal Imperial Kapellmeister Süssmayr; for the smaller room by the master hand of Hr. Ludwig van Beethoven out of love for the artistic fraternity." These little occasional pieces marked Beethoven's Vienna debut as an orchestral composer and as a conductor.[1] Three weeks later, on December 16 (probably his twenty-fifth birthday), Beethoven performed in a Haydn concert in the small *Redoutensaal.* Haydn conducted three of his *London* Symphonies, Beethoven contributed the Piano Concerto in C Major and perhaps an improvisation on a Haydn theme. In January the two collaborated in another concert.[2]

On the day after Christmas, youngest brother Johann Nikolaus van Beethoven arrived in Vienna. In contrast to brother Carl Caspar, who was small, volatile, and unhandsome, and at that point attempting a musical career, Johann was tall, dandyish, not bad-looking despite uneven features, even-tempered if not notably bright, and he had no particular interest in music. In Vienna, Johann continued his chosen profession, going to work at an apothecary shop.[3] He arrived in town with two more Bonners, Stephan von Breuning and his younger brother Christoph. Matthias Koch, brother of Babette of the Zehrgarten, was already in town visiting Franz Wegeler. It was a cheery time for Beethoven, his career humming and hometown friends around him.[4] Of the Bonn friends, only Stephan von Breuning remained in Vienna for long. Relations between him and Beethoven also cycled up and down, as they did among the Beethoven brothers.

After the second concert with Haydn, Beethoven and his patron Prince Karl Lichnowsky set out on a pleasure trip and concert tour initiated and arranged by Lichnowsky. The prince was recapitulating a trip he had taken with Mozart seven years before. He and his new protégé were hoping for a similar success. Though Beethoven was not given to magical thinking of any sort, perhaps it seemed to both of them that there was a power in following Mozart's footsteps.

By the middle of February 1796, the two were in Prague, where once *Prague* *Don Giovanni* had found a sensational premiere. They got a room in the inn Zum Goldenen Einhorn, the Golden Unicorn, where Lichnowsky and Mozart had also stayed. It would have been like the prince to see to it that Beethoven got the same bed Mozart had slept in. When Lichnowsky departed, this protégé stayed on in Prague, secured a piano, and got to work. In a fine frame of mind, Beethoven wrote brother Johann: "First of all, I am well, very well. My art is winning me friends and renown, and what more do I want? And this time I'll make a lot of money. I'll stay here for a few weeks longer and then travel to Dresden, Leipzig, and Berlin . . . I hope you will enjoy living in Vienna more and more. But do be on your guard against the whole tribe of bad women . . . And now I hope that your life will become more and more pleasant and I trust that I shall be able to contribute to your happiness."

Along with the boasting, there is a bit of affection in the letter, as well as the big-brother admonitions that Beethoven was given to, especially when it came to women. As a teenager he had been his

brothers' keeper, and he had not given up the role. At the end of
the letter he adds, "My greetings to our brother Caspar." (In Bonn,
Beethoven's younger brothers had gone by their first names, Caspar
and Nikolaus. In Vienna, for some reason, both began to use their
second names. Beethoven had not made the switch.) Then Ludwig
violently crossed out his middle brother's name.[5] In letters it was as
if he could not bear to write the name of a person he was angry at.
More than once, he left an empty space to represent the name. Sometimes Nikolaus would be the void, sometimes Caspar. This time he
relented: after crossing out Caspar's name, he underscored it with a
wavy line, indicating it was to be put back in, Caspar for the moment
forgiven.

In Prague Beethoven worked on some Goethe settings, tinkered
with the Symphony in C, composed six German dances, an easy piano
sonata that would eventually become op. 49, no. 2, and a wind sextet
eventually op. 71 (he claimed to have written the latter in one night).
He also dashed off some weightless and charming mandolin pieces for
Countess Josephine de Clary, who played the instrument. On February 11, he gave a concert to benefit the Poor Institute, and gave another
concert in March.[6]

The most ambitious and entertaining product of the Prague sojourn
was a large concert scena for soprano on an Italian text: *Ah! perfido*.
The text is deliciously melodramatic, demanding quick shifts of direction and mood. Addressing the lover who threw her over, the singer
begins *furioso*: "Ah, faithless liar, vile deceiver, thou leavest me?," and
so on. Suddenly her rage melts into despair: "I am unchanged; I have
lived for him — let me die for him!" At the end, with a certain air of
voilà, she calls on her very suffering to move him: "Am I not worthy of
compassion?"[7]

There is a feeling that Beethoven had great fun with this piece and
did not feel compelled to be original. In it he largely submitted to Mozartian and Italianate operatic conventions, underlining emotions in a
barrage of vocal pyrotechnics and colorful instrumentation. There are
a few peculiar touches, including wild octave-and-a-third virtual glis-
sandos on the word *affando*, "affliction," and a few bars in the bizarre
key C-flat major. The scena is modeled on the "Bella mia fiamma" Mo-

zart had composed for his friend Josefa Duschek. Beethoven, in other words, was continuing in Mozart's footsteps, and not only in the music. Mme Duschek was still active, and though the piece is dedicated to Countess Clary (who also sang), Beethoven wrote it with Duschek and her celebrated dramatic skills in mind. She premiered it in Leipzig that November.[8]

While Beethoven was happily occupied playing and composing on the road that spring, his future and the future of Europe were taking shape far to the south. A new commander arrived to take over the French army in Italy. He was Napoleon Bonaparte, then twenty-six, who had recently earned the gratitude of the ruling Directory by using cannons to cut down a royalist revolt in the streets of Paris. In Italy on March 28, 1796, in his first address to an army under his command, Napoleon cried, "Soldiers, you are naked, badly fed . . . Rich provinces and great towns will be in your power, and in them you will find honor, glory, wealth. Soldiers of Italy, will you be wanting in courage and steadfastness?" His soldiers would not be found wanting in thumping the Austrians. When regions of Italy were free of Austria and under French rule, Napoleon would turn his implacable ambition toward Vienna.

That March, the three piano sonatas of op. 2 were published. Now in contrast to the piano trios Beethoven was writing for his own instrument, solo. As he worked on the music at the keyboard, the products of improvisation, his main idea engine, could go onto the page without having to be translated into catgut and horsehair.

As a whole, op. 2 plays out in a direction similar to, and as calculated as, op. 1. If none of the sonatas has the visceral impact of the C Minor Trio, they are altogether more focused and more consistently original. As with op. 1, Beethoven presented two pieces in major keys, one in minor; all have four movements; all tend toward a big, quasi-orchestral sound. By op. 2, no. 2, Beethoven had mostly escaped conventional eighteenth-century gestures and style. He made each sonata a distinct individual with its own sonority, which is to say, each has its own kind of pianism, its particular handling of the instrument.

· · ·

The taut and sinewy first movement of no. 1, the Sonata in F Minor, sounds Mozartian, not only because the darting upward arpeggio of its beginning recalls the "Mannheim rocket" figure Mozart used in the G Minor Symphony but also because it sounds like harpsichord music, with spare textures, forthright rhythm, and variety of articulation. In contrast to all the other pieces in the first two opuses, this sonata is relatively compact, with regular recaps and no codas at all. The tonal personality of the first movement comes mainly from a tendency to flavor major-key passages with a tincture of minor, what the Germans call *moll-Dur,* "minor-major." Only at the last cadence of the first movement does Beethoven bring in full, two-fisted, entirely pianistic sonorities.[9] The second movement is another of his poignant and soulful slow movements in a major key, its opening another of his looks back to the eighteenth-century *galant* atmosphere. In fact, for its theme he dipped into his mine of ideas from Bonn, here reworking an idea from the slow movement of his old C Major Piano Quartet.

As a theme for the finale of the F Minor, Beethoven did something singular: he took the crashing chords from the end of the first movement and made them into the leading theme of the finale. It is as if the finale picks up where the first movement left off, raising the intensity. In contrast to the bony, constrained, backward-looking sound of the opening, the driving and implacable finale is rich in sound, full of extreme volume jumps, unmistakably pianistic. The A-flat-major central section recalls the first movement in a different way, with the same rising arpeggio and left-hand rhythm as at the beginning, now smoothed and gentled. At the end, instead of the expected turn to a resolving and hopeful F major, there is a headlong F-minor plunge from the top to nearly the bottom of the keyboard.

Did Beethoven intend some sort of symbol with the F Minor Sonata? In this first published solo sonata of his adulthood, it is as if in the opening movement he says farewell to the harpsichord and to the past, and in the finale brings us once and for all into the world of the piano, which for Beethoven was not Haydn's or Mozart's world but the future: *his* world.

He shaped the Sonata in A Major, op. 2, no. 2, to be as mercurial and expansive as no. 1 was lithe and taut. By the second line of the

A Major, he has presented four ideas: a downward hop, a downward swoop, a downward stride (each of these a development of the hop), and an answer in the form of flowing contrapuntal lines rising upward. These gestures, and their tendency to playful, ebullient juxtaposition, will be prime ingredients of the sonata to come. But then Beethoven plays a wild card: the E-minor second theme breaks into high spirits as something suddenly troubled, surgingly (and pianistically) passionate: Romantic.[10] So the narrative he fashioned for the A Major Sonata is marked by gaiety periodically interrupted by incipient anxiety or melancholy. Contradiction will abide in the sonata. This quality explains the way the ending of the first movement, on the way to being loud and assertive, suddenly falls into a soft and ambiguous halt.

Here already, we find a distinctive Beethoven pattern: the expressive effect, the dramatic narrative, is embodied in a sonority particular to this piece. From this beginning onward, each Beethoven piano sonata would be a singular emotional world expressed by a singular approach to the instrument. In the sonatas of his full maturity, that quality would only be intensified.

In the A Major, Beethoven virtually embodied his generating idea of contradiction in the sound of the second movement, which combines what seems like a sustained string chorale in the upper voices with a pizzicato bass accompaniment. The flighty A-major main theme of the scherzo is answered by a dark and intense A-minor trio. In format, the finale is a traditional sonata-rondo, but rather than the usual high-spirited rondo, he marked this *grazioso,* "gracefully," the main theme warmly singing. The contradiction, the incipient darkness that has dogged this piece, returns and boils over into fury in the driving, pounding A-minor middle of the finale. The last pages seem to attempt a resolution of the stark dichotomies in the piece, but the attempt fails: the sonata ends as if with a rising cry sinking to a sigh. Already in op. 2, Beethoven is capable of great psychological subtlety in painting his tonal pictures, what Christian Neefe had taught him was the task of the composer: to study human characters and passions and embody them in tones.

•   •   •

If his first two piano concertos had on the whole turned out well behaved and comfortably late eighteenth-century, what Beethoven really had in him for concertos is first suggested in the Sonata in C Major, op. 2, no. 3. In this brilliant and thematically tight-knit piece, he alternates quiet, inward music with explosions of virtuosity, the whole seeming to be a two-handed version of a piano concerto, complete with cadenzas at the end of the first and last movements. His soft beginning sounds rather like a string introduction, into which a virtual soloist bursts with a bravura *fortissimo* passage. With these sorts of shifts of texture and color, he gives the C Major a kaleidoscopic quality.

Beethoven was thinking intensively about what kinds of ideas hold a work together. He was already adept in wielding small, two-to-four-note motifs like Haydn, to build themes through a piece. As early as the old Piano Quartets and more so now, he showed his characteristic (if likely unconscious) propensity: take what Haydn and Mozart did and do it *more*. As with Haydn, Beethoven's motifs are the simplest and most common things in music: an interval between two notes, a scrap of scale, an arpeggio, a note out of key, a turn figure, a rhythmic figure. Because his building blocks are so simple, so innate to music itself, they can be woven constantly into a musical fabric that seems free unto capricious. As Haydn demonstrated over and over, *the ability to be surprising yet logical was a prime Classical quality:* the surprise in Haydn's *Surprise* Symphony is carefully prepared but still makes listeners jump out of their seats. That kind of surprise is something else Beethoven learned from Haydn. And from opp. 1 and 2 on, there is an overriding principle: *Beethoven never sacrificed the technical for the expressive, or the expressive for the technical* (at least, hardly ever). Both sides worked together, to the same ends.

How he would choose and develop his material would change and deepen over time. In any case, behind all his piano works lay thousands of hours of improvising at the keyboard, engendering an enormous fund of ideas and textures and colors that lay at hand for him. Eventually, he would thematize nearly every element of music, including single chords, single notes, and silence. One of the leading motifs in the Sonata in C Major, for example, is the opening gesture, which amounts to a slow trill. The trill becomes a theme that stretches all the way to the electrifying triple trills of the end.[11] That highly difficult combination of trills, two of them in the right hand, was part of Beethoven's bag of tricks as a virtuoso.[12]

With the three piano sonatas of op. 2, Beethoven began a long journey no one could have foreseen at that point, he no more than anyone else. In the history of keyboard music there had been only one truly synoptic body of keyboard works, a collection that showed not just the full range of what an instrument can do but the full depth and breadth of what music itself can do and can be. That collection was J. S. Bach's *Well-Tempered Clavier,* which as has been noted, Beethoven grew up playing. By the time his journey was done, the second great synoptic body of keyboard music would be his piano sonatas, a journey through the possibilities of music and emotion, finishing in territories of feeling and spirit and sonority unknown and unimagined until Beethoven found them.

His eternal obstacles in that journey would be, first, the limitations of the human body and mind and creative potential against which he struggled relentlessly, and second, the limitations of the instrument he was writing for. He would never be satisfied with his pianos or with the piano itself, though it would evolve considerably during his lifetime — that evolution partly flowing from him.

In 1796, the year of his tour, Beethoven wrote two letters to Johann Andreas Streicher, a well-known piano maker who had recently set up shop in Vienna. Streicher had married a woman equally distinguished in the trade: Nannette Stein, daughter of piano maker Johann Andreas Stein of Augsburg. Beethoven had gotten to know father and daughter Stein en route to Vienna on his first visit. In one letter to Streicher, from Pressburg during the tour, Beethoven pays a backhanded compliment to a piano Streicher had sent him: "I received the day before yesterday your fortepiano, which is really an excellent instrument. Anyone else would try to keep it for himself; but I — now you must have a good laugh — should be deceiving you if I didn't tell you that in my opinion it is far too good for me, and why? — Well, because it robs me of the freedom to produce my own tone. But, of course, this must not deter you from making all your fortepianos in the same way. For no doubt there are few people who cherish such whims as mine."[13]

In fact, Beethoven was beginning a campaign to do exactly what he

improve Pianos disclaims doing. He wants to press Streicher to move his instruments toward a more robust weight and sound. His next letter to Streicher shows his agenda. He softens the blow by starting with a personal matter:

> Your little pupil, dear St, apart from the fact that when playing my Adagio she drew a few tears from my eyes, has really astonished me . . . I am delighted that this dear little girl, who is so talented, has you for her teacher . . . There is no doubt that so far as the manner of playing it is concerned, the fortepiano is still the least studied and developed of all instruments; often one thinks that one is merely listening to a harp. And I am delighted, my dear fellow, that you are one of the few who realize and perceive that . . . one can also make the pianoforte sing. I hope that the time will come when the harp and the pianoforte will be treated as two entirely different instruments.[14]

Though he writes in terms of the "manner of playing" that makes the piano sound like a harp, he implies that the real problem is the instrument itself. It is especially hard to make a singing adagio if the sustain of each note is hardly longer than the plink of a harp. And the all-wooden instruments were still delicately built, like a harpsichord. Once, back in Bonn, Beethoven had furiously plowed through a Mozart concerto, breaking strings as he went, while Anton Reicha frantically pulled the broken strings out and disentangled the hammers. What Beethoven wanted from pianos, as he wanted from everything, was *more:* more robust build, more fullness of sound, a bigger range of volume, a wider range of notes. As soon as new notes were added to either end of the keyboard, he used them, making them necessary to anyone wanting to play his work. There would be moments in his piano music when a pattern would surge up to the top note on the keyboard and then, almost with an audible curse, fall back.[15] From early on, piano makers asked for Beethoven's opinion, and they listened to what he said.

Dresden The next stop on what was becoming an improvised extended tour was Dresden. In that beautiful, ornately Baroque city, Beethoven spent a profitable week. He was used to arriving at a town a stranger and soon having listeners at his feet. He had been doing that since he was a boy. Bonn official August von Schall was in Dresden and sent two reports to exiled Elector Max Franz on this musician still considered to be an employee, pending the return of the court to Bonn. "Young Beethoven arrived here yesterday," Schall wrote. "He's said to have gotten enormously better and to compose well." Later he reported, "Beethoven was here for about eight days. Everyone who heard him play on the clavier was delighted. With the Elector of Saxony, who is a connoisseur of music, Beethoven had the privilege of playing quite alone and without accompaniment for some one and a half hours. His Grace was exceptionally satisfied and gave him the present of a gold snuffbox."

From there, Beethoven went on to Berlin via Leipzig, where C. P. E. Bach had worked for the court of Frederick the Great. The current Prussian king, Frederick William II, was the nephew and successor of Frederick and equally enthusiastic about music, with more progressive tastes than his uncle had. During Mozart's tour of 1789, Frederick William had given him a commission totaling nearly 4,000 florins.[16] Beethoven knew about this king's interest in music, and about his generosity. He would linger in the Prussian capital for a highly profitable two months, June and July of 1796.

The best-known musicians associated with the Prussian court were pianist Friedrich Heinrich Himmel and the Duport brothers, Jean-Louis and Jean Pierre, both of them cello virtuosos. The king himself was a cello player and commissioned works from Luigi Boccherini, who was living in Spain on a pension from the Spanish court. Soon, apparently, Beethoven had a commission from the king to write two pieces for one or both of his house cellists. The results, two sonatas, would be the main finished products from the tour, for that matter the most ambitious pieces Beethoven finished that year. In Berlin he also wrote part of the eventual op. 16 Quintet for Piano and Winds, started sketching a third piano concerto, worked more on the Symphony in C Major, and finished a small set of variations for cello and piano on a theme from Handel's *Judas Maccabaeus;* soon they would be joined by variations for cello and piano on Papageno's song from *Die Zauberflöte,* "Ein Mädchen oder Weibchen."

Otherwise Beethoven played at court and in noble houses, showed off his improvisation, and performed his new cello sonatas, all of which would have caused a sensation. He played before the venerable Singakademie, then some ninety voices strong, and made the acquaintance of composers Carl Friedrich Christian Fasch and Goethe's future friend and musical adviser Carl Friedrich Zelter (he would long resist Beethoven's music but end up an admirer). Later, to Goethe, Beethoven recalled his annoyance when, at the end of one of his Berlin performances, people crowded around him in tears. "That's not what we artists wish," he complained. "We want applause!"[17] Nor Tears

Mightily impressed with this latest genius, King Frederick William appears to have asked Beethoven to stay on at the Prussian court, but Beethoven declined what could have been quite a plush job. The explanation is contained in a description of his improvisation written years later by Carl Czerny:

> His improvisation was most brilliant and striking. In whatever company he might chance to be, he knew how to produce such an effect upon every hearer that frequently not an eye remained dry, while many would break out into loud sobs; for there was something wonderful in his expression in addition to the beauty and originality of his ideas and his spirited style of rendering them. After ending an improvisation of this kind he would burst into loud laughter and banter his hearers on the emotion he had caused in them. "You are fools!" he would say. Sometimes he would feel himself insulted by these indications of sympathy. "Who can live among such spoiled children?" he would cry, and only on that account (as he told me) he declined to accept an invitation which the King of Prussia gave him after one of the extemporary performances above described.[18]

If Beethoven's episodes of rudeness, petulance, and scorn ever seriously alienated his audiences, there is no record of it. From early on, his temperament was part of his reputation.

Beethoven got on well with the Duport brothers, absorbed the personality and playing style of Jean-Louis, and wrote him into the new cello sonatas.[19] Things went less well with Friedrich Himmel, royal pianist and composer. Himmel was described by one acquaintance as "that dissolute eccentric who now lives almost perpetually in a state somewhat between being drunk on champagne and cheerless sobriety."[20] Beethoven and Himmel decided to improvise for each other. Beethoven played, then it was Himmel's turn. As he had exerted himself to his utmost, he heard Beethoven snap, "Well, when are you going to start?" There was some unpleasantness over that, finally smoothed over. ("I thought Himmel had just been preluding a bit," Beethoven explained.)

When a musician performed for royalty, it was customary to maintain a facade that one was playing out of deference and gratitude, with nothing so vulgar as payment involved, but it was expected that gifts would be forthcoming. The king presented Beethoven with a golden casket filled with Louis d'or. In later years Beethoven declared with pride that the casket was "no ordinary box but one suitable for presentation to ambassadors."[21]

The cello sonatas in F major and G major that Beethoven wrote in Berlin and premiered with Jean-Louis Duport were published the next year as op. 5, dedicated to King Frederick William II of Prussia. It would be no surprise that these sonatas turned out confident, ebullient, fresh, and youthful. At this point in his life, Beethoven had every reason himself to feel the same. He was lionized and well paid everywhere he went. He felt completely healthy, which was not common with him. He was writing pieces inspired by two of the finest cellists in the world, for a cello-playing king who admired his music and wanted to sponsor new cello literature.

Best of all, in writing sonatas for cello and piano Beethoven had a genre virtually to himself. He did not have to look over his shoulder, because Mozart and Haydn had never written for this combination, nor had anyone else written serious works for cello and piano as more or less equals. Beethoven knew that if he wrote ambitious and successful cello sonatas, they would be embraced by every cellist who cared about the status and the future of the instrument. The cello was coming into its own, detaching from its traditional role of reinforcing the bass in orchestral music, becoming a solo instrument and equal partner in chamber music. Coming into his own himself, Beethoven leaped at the chance to help emancipate an instrument.

Op. 5 seems to ride on its own joy of discovery. The form Beethoven devised for these sonatas is particular to the genre he was creating. Both are in two large movements, the first movements beginning with long introductory fantasias that are essentially slow movements. Then in each come an Allegro and a dancing rondo finale. The Allegro of No. 1 in F Major has a foursquare theme, but neither here nor anywhere else in these pieces is eighteenth-century style much present. Rather, he found a voice neither backward-looking nor proto-Romantic.

As much as anything, the sonatas are about the instrument, the cello's colors, moods, big range, singing voice, and robust staccato. Though there is no sense of tragedy troubling the sonatas, the introduction of No. 2 in G Major is dark and brooding, leading to an Allegro molto of churning intensity that ends nonetheless with a big joyous coda, followed by a genial and puckish rondo finale.[22] Inevitably, there are prophecies of later works, but on the whole, Beethoven wrote no other pieces quite like them, perhaps because never again would he find himself happy and hearty and fathering a medium he knew he would, in a way, own forever.

By late November 1796, Beethoven was back in Vienna, taking up a busy schedule of piano students and new projects, rejoining old friends. The teasing and affectionate relationship he had fallen into with Zmeskall is shown in a note of this year to the baron, who had perhaps gotten tiresome, but Beethoven was in a jovial and forgiving mood: "From today the Count of Music has been dismissed with ignominy. — The first violin is being transported into the wilds of Siberia. For a whole month the Baron has been forbidden to put any more questions or to commit any more precipitate actions or to interest himself in anything but his ipse miserum" — his "miserable self," in bad Latin.[23]

When Beethoven's twenty-sixth birthday arrived, in December, he received an invitation from his counterpoint tutor Albrechtsberger: "My very best wishes for your name-day tomorrow. May God give you health and satisfaction and grant you much good fortune. My dear

Beethoven, if you should happen to have an hour at your disposal, your old teacher invites you to spend it with him."

Stephan von Breuning wrote of Beethoven to Bonn family and friends, "In my opinion . . . the journey (or perhaps the outpouring of friendship upon his return!) has made him more stable, or actually a better judge of men, and has convinced him of the rarity and value of good friends. A hundred times, dear Wegeler, he has wished you were back with us, and he regrets nothing more than that he did not follow many of your suggestions."[24]

But Stephan von Breuning was premature in judging Beethoven changed. He was not a better judge of men or a better friend; he was simply in the best of health and the best of moods. None of that would last in the coming year, least of all the good health.

Still, luck and talent had given Beethoven a splendid year. Music in Vienna in 1796 was summed up for the public by publisher Johann Ferdinand Ritter von Schönfeld in *A Yearbook of the Music of Vienna and Prague*. After listing some of the "Special Friends, Protectors, and Connoisseurs in Vienna," including Princess Lichnowsky and Baron van Swieten, Schönfeld profiles leading composers and performers, noting their styles and quirks and making some critical points. In regard to St. Stephen's *Kapellmeister* Albrechtsberger, "His main subject is church music, and his fugues are exceptional. He is no friend of modish music in the *galant* style." The article on Haydn is extensive and mixed: "His symphonies are unequaled and, as many imitators have found, inimitable, it is equally true that they are his greatest works . . . But there is many a man of taste who will listen to his older products of this kind with greater pleasure than to his younger ones. Perhaps he has been wanting to show that he too can wear the garments of the latest musical fashion."

As for "Bethofen," "a musical genius who has chosen to live in Vienna for the last two [*sic*] years,"

He is generally admired for his extraordinary speed and the ease with which he plays extremely difficult [music]. He seems recently to have entered deeper into the inner sanctum of music, and one notices this particularly in the precision, feeling, and taste of his work. It has heightened his fame considerably. His true love of art is revealed by the fact that he has become a student of our immortal Haydn, to be initiated into the sacred mysteries of composition . . . We already have several beautiful sonatas from him; the most recent are particularly outstanding.[25]

It is hard to imagine Beethoven could have been anything but pleased about this sort of attention, but given his nature, that is no guarantee that he actually was.

The year 1797 started with another concert. It was a benefit for the string-playing and composing cousins Andreas and Bernhard Romberg, more refugees from Bonn, the French occupation, and the breakup of the court *Kapelle*. There had been friction over planning the program, as there tended to be when Beethoven was involved. Apparently Haydn had promised to supply a symphony and then reneged. Beethoven wrote Lorenz von Breuning, "We spoke yesterday, although I almost find it shameful that he might give a symphony of his or not."[26] After the concert, Lorenz von Breuning reported to Franz Wegeler, who had returned to Bonn, "Beethoven is . . . the same as of old and I am glad that he and the Rombergs still get along . . . Once he was near a break."[27]

In February 1797, the cello sonatas were published, and soon other products of the previous year: a four-hand piano sonata, op. 6; and *Twelve Variations on a Danse Russe,* dedicated to Countess von Browne, who as a token of thanks gave Beethoven a horse. Beethoven found a stable for the horse, rode it a few times, then forgot about it. In the absence of the owner, a stable hand began renting out the horse and pocketing the profits. Some time later, Beethoven received a huge feed bill, at which he was astonished and infuriated.[28]

Another publication that winter would turn into one of the abiding successes of his life, the song *Adelaide*. Beethoven obviously loved the sentimental verses of poet Friedrich von Matthisson. He labored on the setting of the poem "Adelaide" for more than two years. The

poem's four stanzas conjure up images of the beloved inspired by nature, each verse ending with a rapturous refrain of her name: "Adelaide!" In the last verse, the poet imagines his tomb and a purple flower
growing out of the ashes of his heart, each petal inscribed "Adelaide."
Beethoven laid out the song through-composed in three sections, like
a small solo cantata. For it, he created a singular style, limpid and direct, though with far-roaming modulations.[29] Like the cello sonatas
and other works of his early maturity, it is a style if not quite "Beethovenian," not derivative either. Matthisson received the dedication and,
in 1800, a copy of the song with an admiring and pleading letter from
Beethoven: "My most ardent wish will be fulfilled if my musical setting
of your heavenly 'Adelaide' does not altogether displease you and if, as
a result, you should be prompted to write another similar poem . . . I
will then strive to compose a setting of your beautiful poetry."[30]

Beethoven's romantically themed songs would sometimes be addressed to women in his life. Was he singing to a woman with the perfervid *Adelaide*? Possibly, in his fashion. As is perennial with bards and
musicians, Beethoven had begun to attract female attention. When
Franz Wegeler was in Vienna, he was amazed at his old friend's romantic life. In his teens Beethoven had been quick to fall in love, though
also prudish, and in any case unsuccessful in his attempts. Wegeler had
found, as he would recall, "Beethoven was never not in love and was
usually involved to a high degree." In Vienna he "was always involved
in a love affair, at least as long as I lived there, and sometimes made
conquests which could have been very difficult indeed, if not impossible, for many an Adonis."[31] How platonic or otherwise Beethoven's
"affairs" and "conquests" were, Wegeler does not note. At least among
Bonners, it was a discreet age.

Adelaide might, in fact, have been written as part of Beethoven's
courting of Magdalena Willmann, a beautiful and talented contralto
whom he had known in the Bonn *Kapelle* and who had come to Vienna
to sing at Schikaneder's theater. Beethoven began the song around the
time Willmann arrived in Vienna, and she sang a song of his, likely
the recently published *Adelaide,* at a concert of April 1797. Around the
same time, he wrote a combined setting of two poems, "Sighs of an

Unloved One" and "Reciprocated Love." (He would recycle the tune of the latter years later, in the *Choral Fantasy*.) But the adorable Willmann would not be one of his conquests. He proposed to her that year and she turned him down, one would hope with more gentle reasons than the ones she gave her daughter years later: when he courted her at age twenty-six, she said, Beethoven had been "ugly and half crazy."[32] These would be recurring themes among women he was in love with.

In later 1796 and into the next year, the French were devouring Austrian territory in Italy. Kaiser Franz II sent a giant army south, but Napoleon outgeneraled the Austrians in a series of battles. At Arcole in November, he raced alone ahead of his army to plant the flag on a bridge, then, surrounded by the enemy, was rescued by his troops (or so the myth ran). The climactic disaster was the Battle of Rivoli, in January 1797, when the Austrians lost fourteen thousand men to France's five thousand. When afterward Franz II rejected the terms of surrender, Napoleon declared to his troops, "Soldiers! You have been victorious in 14 pitched battles, 70 actions; you have taken 100,000 prisoners . . . Of all the foes who conspired to stifle the Republic in its birth, the [Holy Roman] Emperor alone remains before you."[33] With the hated Austrian yoke off their backs, many Italians cheered the French army as liberators. Of that moment Stendhal wrote in *The Charterhouse of Parma*: "The departure of the last Austrian regiment marked the collapse of the old ideas . . . It was necessary to love one's country with real love and to seek heroic actions. They had been plunged in the darkest night by the despotism of the Habsburgs; they overturned it and found themselves flooded with daylight."[34]

For those who had hailed the French Revolution, Napoleon was becoming its embodiment and fulfillment, the man who would liberate nations and spread republicanism across Europe. Taking shape at the same time were the fever and mythology called nationalism that would inflame the next two centuries. While Italians erupted in nationalist and Jacobin sentiments, planning revolutions, harassing priests, threatening to disenthrone the pope, Napoleon set his army marching for the Austrian border.

In Vienna there was a convulsion of Austrian patriotism, to which Beethoven contributed with a pair of war songs. In the autumn of 1796, he wrote *Farewell of Vienna's Citizens* to the troops. In the spring came the *Kriegeslied der Oesterreicher:* "We are a great German people; / we are powerful and just. / You French, do you doubt it? / You French, you understand us badly! / For our prince is good, our courage sublime." That spring, the not-so-sublime Austrians and the French struck a deal that, for the moment, staved off an invasion. (Lacking enough reinforcements made Napoleon conciliatory.) In October, the Peace of Campo Formio declared, among other provisions, that the east bank of the Rhine, including Bonn and most of the former Electorate of Cologne, now belonged to France.[35] A Bonner wrote sadly, "With the Court, both luster and employment have gone."[36] What no one could have imagined is that the Treaty of Campo Formio also served as overture to the finish of the thousand-year history of the Holy Roman Empire.[37]

Beethoven's war songs were unapologetic exercises in popular patriotism. The more enduring musical responses to the time were Haydn's. He had been commissioned to write masses for the name day of Prince Nikolaus Esterházy; two of them would be the *Mass in Time of War* (also known as the *Paukenmesse* [Mass with the Kettledrum], for the drums of its beginning) and the *Missa in Angustiis* (Mass for Times of Distress). The latter became known as the *Nelson* Mass, in honor of British admiral Horatio Nelson, who shortly before the piece premiered destroyed the French fleet in the Battle of the Nile. Nelson heard the premiere of the mass while visiting the Esterházy Palace, and he and Haydn struck up a friendship. In a larger sense, what Haydn had done was to join his music to a historical moment. Beethoven would not miss the implications of that.

Previously, at the Burgtheater on February 12, 1797, Franz II had been greeted on his birthday by an anthem newly composed by Haydn: *God Protect Franz the Kaiser*. It was inspired by the British national anthem, *God Save the King*, which Haydn had admired during his time in England. His song would become the unofficial Austrian national anthem. Its melody is one of Haydn's finest, with a quality of timelessness, naturalness, and a touching and noble simplicity, like so much of his work. France had *La Marseillaise,* and now Austria had its anthem. Haydn's pride in having written it would be a solace for him in his sad last years. For Beethoven, the fact that Haydn and not Beethoven had written such an anthem would burn in him until his own last years.

In February 1798, General Jean Baptiste Jules Bernadotte arrived in Vienna as the new French minister. He had been Napoleon's aide-de-camp in the Italian campaign.[38] Young, handsome, and fiery, a zealot with a revolutionary tricolor plume on his hat and pistol-shaped sideburns, Bernadotte was well received by everyone at court, including the kaiser, and he raised a sensation among the ladies. Bernadotte had been ordered that he was not to recognize "any other official rank than that of citizen." In theater performances he ordered his staff to hiss at every cry of "Long live the emperor!"

Bernadotte's service in Vienna would last only a couple of months, up to the point when he ordered the tricolor to be flown over his hotel. It was a deliberate provocation, and the results followed suit. A stone-throwing mob of Viennese gathered while Bernadotte grasped his sword and cried, "What's this rabble up to? I'll kill at least six of you!" He was saved by Viennese cavalry, while the crowd burned the French flag in the Schottenplatz. Napoleon wrote one of his generals, declaring that if the Viennese government was involved, such behavior might leave him "only one course of action, and that would be to blot out a number of Europe powers, or to blot out the house of Austria itself."[39] But Napoleon had already declared Bernadotte to be somewhere between hotheaded and crazy, and ordered him back to Paris.[40]

Bernadotte was a connoisseur of music and had in his entourage the famous French violinist and composer Rodolphe Kreutzer. Prince Moritz Lichnowsky introduced the general and the violinist to Beethoven.[41] The three struck up a friendship, Beethoven soaking up Bernadotte's stories of Napoleon and armies and battles. Naturally they talked music too, and Kreutzer had something interesting to show Beethoven: a published collection of works written for revolutionary *fêtes* by composers including F. J. Gossec, E. N. Méhul, and Kreutzer himself.

This music was aimed for broad appeal, some of it part of outdoor celebrations that might include thousands of performers and tens of thousands of listeners. Given that this was music of revolution and struggle, funeral marches were a favored genre. The style was straight-forward and powerful, with clear lines and no counterpoint, often martial in tone, with much use of wind instruments. It enfolded ele-ments of folk and military music, the straightforward operatic music of Gluck, and the sober, simple, nobly humanistic music Mozart wrote for Masonic ceremonies and for the enlightened brotherhood in *Die Zauberflöte*.[42] The central element was strong, memorable melody de-signed to be grasped and sung by the people. It was massive music to elicit mass emotions, art as communal ritual.

For the Festival of the Supreme Being, part of the Revolution's campaign to replace the church with a state religion, Robespierre had wanted not only the chorus of twenty-four hundred but every citizen present to join in singing Gossec's *Hymn to the Supreme Being*. He sent music teachers all over France to impart the words and melody to as many people as possible: "Father of the Universe," went the deistic text of Marie-Joseph Chénier, "Your temple is on the mountain, in the heavens, on the waves. / You have no past, you have no future; / And living not in time, you fill the entire universe, / which cannot contain you."[43]

In a way no government had done before, the French Revolution placed music near the center of public life as an essential element of education, morality, enlightenment, and propaganda. During the Rev-olution, the spine-chilling melody and words of *La Marseillaise* ("Let impure blood water our furrows," and so on) had been a galvanizing force, a virtual weapon. Poring over the music for *fêtes* with Rodolphe Kreutzer and General Bernadotte, Beethoven found not only a monu-mental humanistic style but something like an ethos of music — an ethos exalted but secular, epic in its ambitions: music as revolutionary ritual, part of the remaking of humanity. Here joined together were art, life, progress, history. "The basis of all human institutions is mo-rality," wrote Chénier, "and the fine arts are essentially moral because they make the individual devoted to them better and happier. If this is true for all the arts, how much more evident is it in the case of music."

A train of thought began to take shape in Beethoven's mind and eventually in his work. By 1798, the first parts of a great puzzle were falling into place for him. The parts included the enlightened and revolutionary ideals of his childhood in Bonn, the French Revolution, the rise of Napoleon, the new idea of revolutionary and national anthems, Haydn's masses reflecting the historical moment, and the collection of revolutionary music shown to him in Vienna by Kreutzer and Bernadotte. These things would contribute to solving a looming crisis in Beethoven's work: How and in what terms could he get past the plateau where he was languishing? How could he lift his art to a new level, to the territory of scope and ambition where he had always expected it to live? How could he step out of the role of entertainer and into the stream of history?

13

Fate's Hammer

B Y THE END of 1797, Beethoven had gone through a serious illness, what may have been typhus. That would have meant weeks of pain, fever, coughing, stupor, even delirium. The disease is a terrific shock to the body and nervous system, in those days often a killer. And it can affect the hearing.

But he remained basically robust and, when he was not prostrate, apparently indefatigable. Once back on his feet, he leaped back into composing and performing. He finished some smaller pieces — light variations on Mozart's "La ci darem la mano" from *Don Giovanni,* and an easy piano sonata, later op. 49. A symphony in C major and a long-planned piano concerto in C minor were simmering. In a rush, he completed what became four opus numbers: three string trios; three piano sonatas op. 10; a clarinet trio; and violin sonatas op. 12. The patterns of relative boldness and cautiousness in these pieces are complex. Collectively, they may have cleared the decks for a bombshell of a piano sonata that he called *Pathétique.*

Earlier in 1797, he had finished the *Grande Sonate,* op. 7, in E-flat major, dedicated to a piano student, the teenage countess Babette Keglevics. She lived across the street from Beethoven and recalled that he would show up for her morning lessons in a peaked sleeping cap,

dressing gown, and slippers. Later she got the dedication of his variations on a Salieri theme; the First Piano Concerto; and, after she had
married the musical prince Innocenz d'Erba-Odescalchi, the important op. 34 Variations. If that were not enough to indicate Beethoven's
feelings toward her, there was the character of op. 7. The longest piano
sonata he would write until his later years, it is rich in texture and innovative in its pianism. Its turbulent emotions earned it the nickname
Die Verliebte, "The Beloved." The soulful dissonances and eloquent silences of its second movement foreshadow his slow movements long
into the future. In these years, Beethoven remained more often prophetic in slow music than in fast.

Before undertaking the perilous journey of writing string quartets
that were going to be competing with those of Haydn and Mozart,
Beethoven studied writing for strings by way of the less fraught ensemble of string trio. As op. 3, he had published a light and lively six-
movement Trio in E-flat, in the spirit of eighteenth-century diverti-
mentos in general and Mozart's great E-flat Divertimento in particular.
Beethoven's op. 8 Serenade for String Trio in D major, finished early in
1797, was another multimovement divertimento. The glory of op. 8 is a
movement in which a quasi-aria of tragic cast alternates with a scherzo.
This juxtaposition of comic and tragic was much on Beethoven's mind
in those days.

In duration, the three string trios of op. 9 are all shorter than op. 8
but manifestly more serious. All are four-movement pieces whose ambition is on the order of the op. 1 Piano Trios. Though Mozart had
written splendid string trios, there was no extensive and intimidating
repertoire Beethoven had to bow to. So as in the cello sonatas, his op. 9
Trios are all fresh, looking toward his mature voice. He wrote them fast
and fearlessly.

Trio No. 1 in G major is lively and ingratiating, a touch bold if not
yet "Beethovenian," at times gently poignant; No. 2 in D major is more
sober, stylistically more current than forward-looking; No. 3 is an intense piece in C minor, a key Beethoven was defining in a way unique
to himself.[1] This C-minor outing echoes the raging C-minor piano trio
of op. 1 — less demonic but still driven and dynamic, though its finale
turns up in a good-humored, entirely undemonic C minor.

When he sent the op. 9 Trios to their dedicatee, Count Johann Georg von Browne-Camus, he called them "la meilleure de [mes] oeuvres" and declared the count, for the moment, "the foremost Maecenas of my muse." Browne came from an old Irish family. An acquaintance described him as "one of the strangest of men, on the one hand full of excellent talents and splendid qualities of heart and mind, and on the other full of weaknesses and depravity." He was headed eventually for a mental breakdown and a sojourn in an institution, but he and his wife would be steady supporters of Beethoven and repeated dedicatees.[2] The countess received the dedication of the op. 10 Piano Sonatas.

Publication of op. 9 was announced in June 1798. By that point, with five string trios under his belt, Beethoven had taken a metaphorical deep breath and was well into sketches of a string quartet in D major. Prince Lobkowitz had commissioned a set of six quartets each from Beethoven and Haydn. As Beethoven started to work on the second quartet, he sketched on a random collection of loose sheets. Such sheets formed an unwieldy pile of material dating back some dozen years, which he ferried around with him from flat to flat. Now he bought himself a sketchbook made of stitched-together sheets of printed music paper, and began working in it.

From then on, these books, sometimes purchased and sometimes sewn together from loose sheets by himself, contained most of his jottings and drafts. At first they were large, for working at home. Later he also made smaller books that could fit in his coat pocket, for sketching during his daily walks and rambles. The sketchbooks may have helped to give him more focus. Now a work in progress was something he could hold in his hand, leaf through.[3] They became indispensable companions through the day. In that first one, he worked on a broad spectrum of pieces: a piano sonata in E major, eventually op. 14, no. 1; the string quartet in D major, eventually the third of the Lobkowitz set; revisions of the B-flat piano concerto. He also did the first work on the Septet op. 20 and the eventual first of the Lobkowitz quartets, in F major.

In the middle of these multilayered projects, in 1798, Beethoven acquired a friend closer than any he had found since Bonn. Karl Friedrich

rich Amenda came from Courland, then part of western Russia. Born a year after Beethoven, he had been something of a violin prodigy, but felt a call to the ministry and got his degree in theology. Amenda arrived in Vienna in the spring of 1798, worked a while for Prince Lobkowitz, and eventually found a job teaching music to the children, with her second husband, of Mozart's widow Constanze. Amenda's time in Vienna was a testament to his amiable and earnest character; despite his severely pockmarked face, people were drawn to him.

Amenda was one of the people who in those years were already seized by Beethoven's music. Several times when he spotted his hero in a restaurant, Amenda tried to make conversation, but he could not break through Beethoven's reserve. One day he was playing first violin in a quartet at Constanze Mozart's house, and a hand kept appearing to turn his pages. At the end of the piece he looked up from the music to discover that his page-turner was Beethoven. The next day, at a dinner party, the host declared, "What have you done? You've captured Beethoven's heart! Beethoven requests that you rejoice him with your company." The next morning, Amenda hurried to his hero's flat; after a warm greeting, Beethoven suggested they play through some violin and piano music. They went on for hours, probably reading through new Beethoven and old Mozart pieces. (Beethoven was working on op. 12, his first set of violin sonatas.) Finally Amenda left, but Beethoven followed him home; there were more hours of music making, then back to Beethoven's flat for the same, well into the night.

The two men became inseparable, seen around town together so much that when one appeared alone on the street, passersby would shout, "Where's the other one?" In Amenda, Beethoven found an idealist of his own stripe, an able violinist, a *Schwärmer* for music and literature and philosophy and aesthetics, voluble in the high-Enlightenment talk Beethoven had missed since his Bonn days. Here was somebody he could embrace and admire, who admired him in return and understood him as a man and an artist.

They made music and had fun. Once, Amenda declined to believe Beethoven's modest description of his own violin playing and demanded to hear him play the solo part in one of his sonatas. After a few bars of intolerable sawing, Amenda cried, "Have mercy—stop!" and they both broke up laughing. Another time, after Beethoven had improvised at the piano for Amenda alone, his friend said it was sad that such glorious music should be lost to the world. "There you're mistaken," Beethoven said, and played the whole thing again, note for note.[4]

The quality of their relationship, and of Amenda's insight, is found in a fervent letter he wrote Beethoven the next year, after the death of his brother called him back to Courland. For address, Amenda uses the intimate *du*, "thou," reserved for close friends, an intimacy always mutually and ceremonially agreed to.

> My Beethoven,
>
> I still approach you with the same heartfelt love and esteem that the value of your heart and of your talent irresistibly and eternally demand of me . . . Friend! grant to very many other friends of music the good fortune of becoming acquainted with you better. You are responsible not only to yourself and to them, but indeed to the general progress of your art . . . Outside of Vienna, believe me, the musical public is still too backward . . . to be able to evaluate your beautiful compositions according to their worth. You yourself must play for them, and compose for them pieces of all sorts according to their prevailing comprehension; [you] must educate them to your level, as you have done with me and others in Vienna.[5]

He goes on to promise that he will acquaint "rustic Courland" with Beethoven's music, and rhapsodizes about a girl who "has captured your Amenda." In the letter, Amenda essentially charts a course for Beethoven, or confirms a course Beethoven was already on. Don't neglect sometimes to write broadly, Amenda said, not just for connoisseurs. After his serious first two opus numbers, Beethoven would issue a steady stream of lighter pieces in a range of media, some earning opus numbers and some not. At the same time, Amenda goes on, for your most important works, "you must educate them to your level." In other words, Beethoven needed to teach people how to listen to his music. Haydn and Mozart had done the same in their day, but Beethoven's challenge to eighteenth-century taste was more aggressive than theirs.

The fervor of Beethoven's friendship with Amenda can be contrasted with the social divides and the tensions of his relations with aristocratic patrons like Lichnowsky and Lobkowitz, with his tendency to view performers like Ignaz Schuppanzigh as hardly more than servants, and with his bantering relationship with faithful minion Baron Zmeskall von Domanovecz: "Will the very high born personage, the Zmeskality of H[err] von Zmeskall, graciously condescend to decide where he can be spoken to tomorrow — We are quite damnably devoted to you." In another note of 1798: "My cheapest Baron! See to it that the guitarist [a friend of Amenda's] shall come to me today for certain. Amenda instead of paying amends ... for his failure to observe rests, must let me have this [admirable] guitarist." For whatever reasons, surely fondness among them, Beethoven was patient with the baron. They would never have a real fight, but now and then Zmeskall had to be taken down a notch:

> My very Dear Baron Muckcart-driver,
>   Je vous suis bien oblige pour votre faiblesse de vos yeux. — By the way, I refuse in future to allow the good humor, in which I sometimes find myself, to be destroyed. For yesterday thanks to your Zmeskall-Domanoveczian babble I became quite melancholy. The devil take you, I refuse to hear anything about your whole moral outlook. *Power* is the moral principle of those who excel others, and it is also mine; and if you start off again today on the same line, I will thoroughly pester you until you consider everything I do to be good and praiseworthy ... Adieu Baron Ba ... ron ron/nor/orn/rno/onr/ (Voilà quelque chose out of the old pawnshop).[6]

That mock-offended but mostly jovial note is striking in several dimensions. The reference in bad French to the baron's eyes has to do with a viola-and-cello piece Beethoven had written for the two of them, *Duet with Two Obbligato Eyeglasses,* since both of them required spectacles to play it. The last line in parentheses indicates that the duet is enclosed by means of an arcane pun on *versetzen,* which can mean "to transpose" (as with music) or "to pawn." The line about power as the moral principle of the superior man may reflect a philosophy or a momentary mood — Beethoven seems never to have written a sentiment quite like it again. Near the end of the note, he composes an alphabetical theme and variations on Zmeskall's noble title. These notes to Zmeskall are among many that suggest Beethoven tended to write letters later in the day, after composing, in high spirits from a glass or several glasses of good cheer. Wine had made his father merry sometimes, volatile at other times. His son followed suit. Quite unlike his father, however, nobody ever reported Beethoven as a sloppy or abusive drinker or found him passed out in the street.

In August 1798, Napoleon Bonaparte's inexorable rise was halted for the moment when British admiral Horatio Nelson destroyed a French fleet in the Battle of the Nile. That galvanized a new coalition of Britain, Austria, Russia, and Turkey, which for a while promised to end the French rampage. There is no record of how Beethoven viewed all this trouble, though he could hardly have been unaware of it. He remained happily and profitably at work that year.

There was a flurry of piano sonatas, natural enough given that it was his instrument, that piano sonatas were among his most salable items, and that he did not feel intimidated by precedents in Haydn, Mozart, Clementi, or anybody else. Piano sonatas were also laboratories where he could experimnt with new ways of putting pieces together, with new sonorities and new voices. So it was with the three modestly scaled but significant sonatas of op. 10. All of them have a singular expressive pattern: sprightly-unto-joking outer movements set off by second movements of a poignancy and depth that intensify throughout the opus.

Op. 10, no. 1, in C minor, amounts to another stage in Beethoven's ongoing process of finding his sense of this key. To a degree, he would discover who he was as an artist by way of C minor. Still, the Beethoven voice the world would come to know is not quite that of this sonata — the fiercer moments of the op. 1 Trio in C Minor are closer. The C Minor Sonata has an opening theme darting upward in dotted rhythms answered by a quiet, poignant gesture, introducing a movement largely impulsive and headlong, spaced by flowing lyrical interludes, while the gentle slow movement in A-flat major is a touch backward-looking, *galant*, its themes sprouting ornaments in Mozartian fashion. A short finale turns the driving force of the first movement into fun and games, the themes scampering along. At the coda, there is a quiet and thoughtful moment recalling the second movement.

No. 2, in F major, begins with a little hop and proceeds in a series of fits and starts, characterizing a movement wry and lively, with moments ironically grand and *furioso*. Rather than a slow movement, what follows is an oddly pensive and flowing, at times haunted, un-scherzo punctuated with offbeat accents. Whatever griefs shadow those pages are eased by a good-humored finale, the main theme folk-like and stamping.

Then comes the stunning D-major, no. 3 in the set, the finest sonata and one of the most individual works he had produced yet. The progress of its four movements echoes the expressive shape of the previous two, but the comedy in the first and last movements is ratcheted higher, framing an unforgettable song of sorrow in the slow movement. Part of the humor in the outer movements is the stinginess of material: the first four notes of the dashing opening theme (a bit of descending scale) will dominate the first movement to a point of absurdity; the next three notes (a rising half step, then jump of a third) will dominate the finale.

The twitchy and obsessive opening movement is rarely able to escape its scrap of scale, whether it is running up or running down. The last rush to the cadence is laugh-out-loud funny. (Whether intentional or not, that ending is also a near-quote of the opening of Mozart's light-hearted Piano Concerto in B-flat, K. 450.)

The D-minor slow movement is marked Largo e mesto, slow and mournful. That describes one of the most mournful works of music written to its time. It seems locked in a trance of sorrow, at once individual and world-encompassing. Moments of hope soon sink; the main relief is in bleak, trembling silences. What follows, a delicate *minuetto*, feels like a pulling together after the suffering of the slow movement.

Then the droll finale, an Allegro rondo, begins with a couple of can't-get-started stutters followed by sort of a sneeze. The stuttering figure is relentless and steadily funnier; earlier movements are recalled in more sober moments that don't impede the high spirits.

What did Beethoven mean by these experiments in antithetical emotions? A number of things beyond a simple desire to intensify contrasts. In the world at large, this kind of juxtaposition was a leading topic of debate among German thinkers. It was an aspect of Shakespeare's tragedies that, with the advent of new German translations, had troubled German eighteenth-century aesthetics: how can a mingling of tragedy and comedy be said to have unity when they are in the same work? For his part, Beethoven did not make contrasts for the sake of momentary effects, without reference to the whole. Already in op. 1, he was shaping his works as a single narrative, a coherent journey through a series of characters and emotional states. In the D Major Sonata, that paradoxical journey has particularly significant implications.

Again, the very beginning of the D Major's comic first movement sets up two motives that will dominate the piece. The theme of the tragic slow movement is made from those two motives:

Largo e mesto

Finale motif — First-movement motif

Who knows what Beethoven thought of the motivic connections among these contradictory worlds of first and second movements. But what the D Major Sonata suggests, in terms philosophical and psychological, is that the material of comedy and tragedy is the same, that joy and suffering are made of the same things. Here is something articulated in tones that reaches a far-sighted human wisdom.

In the elegant and ingratiating (à la Mozart, in his light vein) op. 11 Trio for Piano, Clarinet, and Cello, there is no attempt at wisdom or innovation. The clarinet serves in the usual position of the violin in a piano trio. (In hopes of better sales, Beethoven supplied an optional violin version of the clarinet part.) For a finale, he wrote variations on a well-known perky tune from an opera by Joseph Weigl, earning the piece the nickname *Gassenhauertrio,* or "Popular Melody Trio."

The presence of Mozart also hovers over the more substantial, yet nonetheless still cautious, three violin sonatas of op. 12. Here, as usual, Beethoven used what he considered the best models for a given medium and genre, and, as usual, they left traces in the music. Mozart was the main model, because his violin sonatas were supreme in the repertoire.[7] There would be no record of a commission for these pieces. It appears Beethoven wrote them because he wanted to try his hand at the medium. They may also have been helped along by his acquaintance with the French virtuoso Kreutzer in Vienna in early 1798. Kreutzer and Beethoven gave a private concert at Prince Lobkowitz's in April, and Beethoven was duly impressed with this celebrated exemplar of the French violin school.[8] That violin tradition would remain another model for him. Around the time of the Kreutzer concert, he finished the second and third sonatas.

To ears schooled in later Beethoven, op. 12 would sound like relatively light excursions in a current style. Beethoven was, in other words, still not ready to mount a challenge in a medium that Mozart dominated. All three violin sonatas are in major keys and in three movements, in tone ranging from lighthearted to playful, though no. 2 has a beautiful, melancholy slow movement and no. 3 is a degree more serious. As he had done in earlier, more backward-looking works like the first two piano concertos, Beethoven slipped into these pieces some startling harmonic excursions. In the first movement of Sonata No. 1 in D Major, he surrounds the main key with mediants, keys a third away in each direction: B-flat and F. In the fairly short course of the first-movement development section of No. 3 in E-flat, he ranges into the wilds of flat keys: C minor, G minor, B-flat minor, E-flat minor (his old favorite), even C-flat major.[9] That was pushing things in those days, and he would get slapped for it in one of his first important reviews. The premiere of one or more of the sonatas probably came in a Vienna concert of March 1798, Beethoven and Ignaz Schuppanzigh presiding.[10]

In one way and another, creatively and professionally, the ground was prepared for another piano sonata finished in 1798, the first work of Beethoven's to bid for the term *epochal.* It was published the next year as op. 13, *Grande Sonate Pathétique.*

From its glowering opening chords, the *Pathétique* paints pathos like no work before: naked and personal. Here Beethoven found a kind of music that seems not like a depiction of sorrow but sorrow itself:

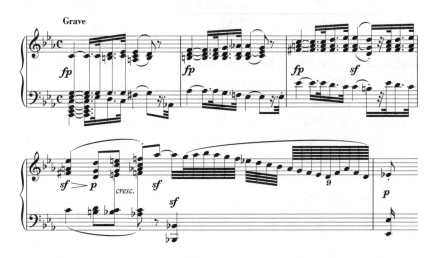

Still, this music of great originality does not discard traditional form or even familiar modes of representing sadness. There are half steps everywhere in music, but the particular descending half step on the third beat of the *Pathétique* is unmistakably pathetic. The gesture has a tradition going back to Bach and beyond.[11] It is the *voice* that is new in this sonata, the emotional immediacy. The *Pathétique* did not initiate so much as confirm that Beethoven was bringing to music a new immediacy and subjectivity. As a revelation of individual character and emotion (what a later age would call "expressing oneself"), it was a kind of democratic revolution in music. And as such, the kind of expression exemplified in the *Pathétique* became a founding element of the Romantic voice in music.[12]

There had never been a more grave Grave in music than the one that opens this work about melancholy, resignation, and defiance. In an essay called "On the Pathetic," Schiller wrote that when suffering is depicted in art, it must be resisted, transcended. As a matter of ethical necessity, pain and despair cannot win.[13] Whether or not Beethoven knew that decree of Schiller's, he conformed to it here — in his own way.

In the *Pathétique* the full force of Beethoven's C-minor mood is unleashed. Here is a shining prophecy of what he was to call a New Path, the direction that would bring him to his full maturity.[14] While his earlier sonatas had been in some degree singular, the *Pathétique* is among the first of his works in any medium to stand from beginning to end as an unforgettable individual. Like the earlier sonatas, it has a singular sonority, an approach to the instrument special to the work and its emotional world, but now the sonority has a sharper and more distinctive profile than in the earlier ones.

What seized the imagination of his contemporaries in the mournful harmonies of the Grave introduction is that sense of intimate pain. The opening passage flows into a rising, hopeful song, outlining the essential dramatic narrative of the *Pathétique*: varying responses to melancholy. Then erupts the furious, relentless Allegro di molto e con brio. From that point there is no break in the surging energy, except that twice, in the middle and near the end, the music of the Grave interrupts. Which is to say: for all the sound and fury of the Allegro, the inner melancholy remains.[15]

Bringing back the slow introduction in the course of a fast movement was a striking formal innovation. Yet Beethoven had already done that, innocently, at age eleven in the F Minor *Electoral* Sonata that was the predecessor of the *Pathétique*. Now he bent a formal tradition knowingly. Meanwhile the second theme of the first movement is the seed of the finale's main theme. Beethoven would be increasingly concerned with tightening connections among movements.

The A-flat-major slow movement of the *Pathétique* is one of Beethoven's uncannily beautiful stretches, noble and resigned in tone, its material simple and songful. (As such, it is foreshadowed from the beginning, in the hopeful, rising E-flat-major passage of the opening Grave.) That movement defines what would become his familiar A-flat-major mood. Its form is a slow rondo: ABACA Coda. Triplets enliven the return of the A theme: for the moment, melancholy is defeated. The rondo finale, however, turns out neither triumphant nor lighthearted. Returning to C minor and to the driving intensity of the first movement, the tone now is of defiance, a shouting refusal to give in. There are moments of peace, notably in the coda, with its gentle recollection of the middle movement. The very end, though, takes no hopeful turn but races to a pealing, angry C-minor cry.

The *Pathétique* made an immediate and enduring sensation. Played in parlors and private halls, it helped carry its composer's name around Europe. It would endure as the first fully formed avatar of the tension and dynamism Beethoven found in C minor. Still, for him there was no epiphany, no sense that at the time he said, *Eureka! This is who I am.* For the time being, this voice would be one of several Beethoven wielded — some current, some prophetic, some backward-looking. And he never entirely stopped looking backward for inspiration and instruction.

The idea that a given key had a particular emotional resonance was hardly unique to Beethoven. Just as there were long-standing associations of musical gestures with particular emotions, like the mournful descending half steps in the *Pathétique,* there were also associations with keys. This was not entirely an arbitrary matter, because it had partly to do with the tuning of keyboard instruments. Nature perversely makes it impossible to get more than one key at a time even near in tune on a keyboard. For abstruse physical reasons, when it comes to tuning, nature's math does not add up: stacking a series of mathematically perfect intervals does not produce a perfect interval. If you tune a piano with perfect intervals of a fifth up the keyboard, the fifths get sharper and sharper until they are impossibly out of tune.

The only way around this situation is to cheat somehow. Systematic adjustments are required to temper the tuning of intervals. The musical term for this is *temperament.*[6] In the most common tuning systems from the eighteenth into the nineteenth centuries, a given interval, say, a whole step, ended up being slightly different sizes in different parts of the keyboard. Thus "unequal temperament." The result of all the older tuning systems was to give each key a subtle coloration, a personality of its own.

For centuries, the dominant philosophy of keyboard tuning had been to get a certain range of keys passably well in tune and simply not use any other keys, because they were unbearably out of tune. So for centuries, most keyboard music was written in keys between three sharps and three flats. But the unavailable keys were a standing frustration for composers. The long-known tuning called "equal temperament," in which the intervals between notes are mathematically the same, makes every scale equally in, and slightly out of, tune. J. S. Bach may have had equal temperament in mind when he wrote in all possible major and minor keys in *The Well-Tempered Clavier*—but probably not. It is more likely that Bach intended a tuning system that was serviceable but not equal, preserving some of the old individual personalities of keys but still making all of them usable. The name for Bach's kind of unequal tuning is "well-tempered."[17] Well-tempered tunings would have been familiar to Beethoven since childhood, when he was playing *The Well-Tempered Clavier*.[18]

There were many unequal tuning systems around in the eighteenth and nineteenth centuries, each with fierce partisans and enemies (tuning has always been a spur for fanaticism). Beyond loose traditions of emotional associations, a good deal of the contemporary theorizing about the characters, call them the "colors," of the various keys came from the nature of unequal temperament. An eighteenth-century theorist said of his preferred tuning, "If an organ or clavier is tuned according to this temperament . . . each key receives its own special character, on account of its individual chords."[19]

Traditional expressive associations had collected around the keys, though in practice commentators interpreted them differently. Most tended to see D major, for example, as a bright, pure key for bright feelings. It was, wrote one theorist, "the perfect key for funny pieces and joyful dances . . . The key of triumph, of Hallelujahs, of war-cries, of victory-rejoicing."[20] Theorists' responses to G minor are more varied and flowery: "It is suited to frenzy, despair, agitation, etc."; "the lament of a noble matron, who no longer has her youthful beauty."[21]

Italian violinist and pedagogue Francesco Galeazzi published an interpretation of keys in 1796. C major, said Galeazzi, was "a grandiose, military key, fit to display grand events, serious, majestic." As for C minor, it was "a tragic key . . . fit to express grand misadventures, deaths of heroes, and grand but mournful, ominous, and lugubrious actions." D minor was "extremely melancholy and gloomy"; B-flat major, "tender, soft, sweet, effeminate, fit to express transports of love, charm, and grace"; E major, "very piercing, shrill, youthful, narrow and, somewhat harsh";[22] E-flat major, "a heroic key, extremely majestic, grave, and serious: in all these features it is superior to that of C"; A major, "totally harmonious, expressive, affectionate, playful, laughing, and cheerful." Whether or not Beethoven studied Galeazzi's characterizations, they are close to the way he tended to interpret those keys.[23]

So partly because in unequal keyboard temperaments C major is usually the key most nearly in tune, it was widely seen as a key of equanimity, of the grand but also the placid. (This surely also has to do with how it looks on the page, innocent of sharps or flats.) C, D, and G majors, all close to ideally in tune, were called "pure" keys. These, wrote one theorist, "are little suited to pathetic expressions; on the contrary, they are best used for amusing, noisy and martial expressions, for pleasing, tender and playful expressions, or often for merely serious expressions. The less pure keys are, [they are] always more effective for mixed feelings."[24] Beethoven's First Symphony in C Major is often noisy and martial. His tragic and passionate pieces are typically in more flavorful keys, usually ones in the flat direction, with an unusual preference for deep-flat keys like A-flat minor and E-flat minor. Here and there a phrase ends up in the outlandish key of C-flat major (which no theorist mentioned at all).

When it came to A-flat major, theorists tended to throw up their hands in dismay. That was the key usually least in tune on a well-tempered keyboard. Galeazzi called it "a gloomy key, low, deep, fit to express horror, the silence of night, stillness, fear, terror."[25] Another theorist is even more aghast: "Death, grave, putrefaction, judgment, eternity lie in its radius."[26] Yet A-flat major was a favorite key of Beethoven's, his interpretation of it his own. He saw it as a tonality of noble and resigned emotions, as in the slow movement of the *Pathétique* and the solemnly beautiful opening of the op. 26 Piano Sonata. As for Beethoven's much-loved E-flat minor, Galeazzi echoes those few who deal with it at all: "little practiced on account of its great difficulty in performance, it is extremely melancholy and induces sleep."[27] Keys with a number of sharps and flats tend to get the fingers snarled in the black keys of the piano, but that impracticality never seemed to concern Beethoven.

In other words, like most things in his art, Beethoven's sense of keys was partly traditional and partly personal. In his mind and ear C minor, the key of the *Pathétique,* was the most charged and dynamic. That sonata also shows his sense of C minor in fast tempo as driving, relentless, implacable, like some great mechanism of will, fate, or rage. In slow tempos, his C minor is tragic: the funeral march of the *Eroica* is an example. His E-flat-minor mood seems close to Galeazzi's description, which in turn is close to the mood of the E-flat Minor Prelude in *The Well-Tempered Clavier:* melancholy, inward, peculiarly shadowed not only in keyboard tunings but also on string instruments, where the E-flat-minor scale involves only one open string (D, the leading tone). E-flat major, meanwhile, was rich in associations: a heroic mode, as Galeazzi says, the key of one of the greatest of Mozart's late symphonies, No. 39, the preferred key in his music for Masonic services, the home key of *Die Zauberflöte.* Many issues, in other words, affected a composer's sense of the characters of keys. It was not a question of objective reason but a mingling of individual responses to tunings and a matter of tradition, habit, presence in the repertoire, and instinct.

So 1798 was a busy and prolific year, Beethoven's confidence and reputation ascending together. He appeared chipper and optimistic; socially he was very much part of the Viennese musical fraternity and a favorite of the music-loving aristocracy. He kept in touch with Haydn, visiting the master and showing him new work. Probably in this year, he began to study vocal composition in Italian with court *Kapellmeister* Antonio Salieri, then forty-seven, once called "the musical pope of Vienna" and famously a rival of Mozart. Salieri was still turning out old-school operas and was active as a conductor and teacher.

The reason for this surprising study was pragmatic: Beethoven was looking toward opera, planning someday to take on the medium Vienna loved beyond all others. Opera was considered essentially an Italian art, so he went to an Italian-born master to study it. As thanks to

Salieri, Beethoven dedicated the op. 12 Violin Sonatas to this, his last teacher. As with his counterpoint masters, in his dealings with Salieri Beethoven was a willful student even as he dutifully set his assigned old-fashioned Italian texts in a suitable style. One day Beethoven ran into Salieri in the street after the teacher had thrashed one of those efforts. Salieri complained that he hadn't been able to get the tune out of his head. "Then, Herr von Salieri," Beethoven grinned, "it can't have been so utterly bad."[28]

He enjoyed being generous. One of his nonmusical friends was the celebrated actor J. H. F. Müller, at whose house Beethoven met a young aristocratic amateur pianist named Carl Friedrich, Baron Kübeck von Kübau. Beethoven agreed to hear the youth play, to which he responded as kindly as possible, "My dear fellow, you have no particular talent for music. Don't waste too much time on it. You do not lack, however, a certain facility." He hired the baron to coach one of his students, a thirteen-year-old girl who was a few years too young to arouse Beethoven's special interest.

Kübau retained vivid and unsentimental memories of Beethoven: "He was a small man with unkempt, bristling hair with no powder, which was unusual. He had a face deformed by pock-marks, small shining eyes, and a continuous movement of every limb in his body . . . Whoever sees Beethoven for the first time and knows nothing about him would surely take him for a malicious, ill-natured and quarrelsome drunk who has no feeling for music . . . On the other hand, he who sees him for the first time surrounded by his fame and his glory, will surely see musical talent in every feature of an ugly face." Years after their association, the baron was surprised to see Beethoven hustling toward him "in his loping genius-gait, and [he] expressed his pleasure at seeing me again. We talked about all sorts of things . . . he embarked on his favorite subject, politics, which bores me very much."[29] All this he recalled with a certain affection.

It appears to have been in the midst of this sociable and productive bustle that fate's hammer fell.

It began, he would recall, with a transport of rage. In his flat he had been arguing over some music with a tenor, who left and then returned to pound on the door as Beethoven was busy composing. He jumped up from his desk, so furious that he was struck with a fit and fell face-down to the floor, landing on his hands. When he got up, he said, "I found myself deaf, and have been so ever since."[30]

That fit of rage would have been the trigger, not the cause, of his deafness. By that point he may have had lead poisoning, maybe gotten from the lead salts commonly added as a sweetener to cheap wine, or from lead wine containers, or from the waters of spas. Lead or something equally insidious was ravaging his gut. But lead does not usually attack the ears. That had another cause. Beethoven was doomed to go deaf by something that occurred before, maybe typhus or one of the other illnesses of his past years, or childhood smallpox — in any case, something that had passed but left behind a terrible legacy.

If that moment of fury was when deafness first manifested itself, he was not entirely deaf, or only briefly. His hearing returned, but not all of it. Now what he heard was accompanied by a maddening chorus of squealing, buzzing, and humming that raged in his ears day and night. Frantic, he fled to doctors. They reassured him, gave him medicine. One doctor after another, one remedy after another. None of it accomplished anything.

Medicine was half a century or more away from being able to treat or understand a disability like his. Doctors in those days knew virtually nothing about the true sources of disease. Despite the advent of the scientific method, medicine had made little progress since the Middle Ages. Viruses and the effects of bacteria were unknown, antiseptics unknown, the structure of the nervous system and function of the digestive system unknown. The stethoscope was not invented until 1816. There was no anesthetic for operations; surgeons cut open their patients with furious speed, trying to finish before the screaming victims died of shock. Most medicines did no good at all, and some did great harm.

For Beethoven, the horror in his ears came on top of old, chronic miseries, the periods of vomiting and diarrhea that had assaulted him since his teens. In his profession he saw enemies all around him. Now his body became his most virulent, most inescapable enemy. His livelihood, his creativity, his spirit were under siege by a force that did not care about his music, his talent, his wisdom: the force of fate that had claimed his infant brothers and sisters in childhood, his teacher Franz Rovantini, his mother.

He was twenty-seven years old. At first there had to have been disbelief, a young man's refusal to countenance what was happening to him. It was imperative to hide the decline of his hearing, to hide his panic and depression. He feared it would ruin his career if it came out, and that fear was entirely reasonable. He had to hide everything, turn the old confident and robust face to the world. For the moment he told no one — not Amenda, not Franz Wegeler or Stephan von Breuning. When he did not respond or hear properly, people would think he was absentminded, lost in thought. Let them think that. Meanwhile he would find a cure. He *must* find a cure.

So he went to doctors, one after another. Beethoven was the worst imaginable patient, unable to maintain any regime of medicine or diet for long, furious if results were not immediate. Doctors resorted to leeching, bleeding, lukewarm baths and cold baths, painful and dangerous applications of tree bark tied to his arms, little of it with any solid scientific basis.[31] Medicine had learned, at least, that cheap wine with lead salts could have terrible effects on the digestive system and on the personality: it could make a victim irritable and paranoid (and Beethoven was irritable and paranoid enough already). Leaded wine was illegal but still common. Maybe Beethoven knew about these dangers, maybe not. If he did know, it was too late.

Inevitably, the burden of his health entered his music. Perhaps the slow movement of the op. 10 D Major Sonata was a first intimation, or the *Pathétique*. He had composed tragic pages before, but not as intense as those. As a teenager, in the *Joseph* Cantata he wrote powerfully about death because he had seen it. His teacher and a row of siblings had died; he watched his mother succumb by inches. For everyone in that era, death was all around, everyone's life like a battlefield. But for Beethoven this new threat was different, a decay from within: a slow death, the mind watching it, helpless before the grinding of fate. Fate would become an abiding theme for him, its import always hostile.

There must have been days, his ears howling and his body racked by vomiting or diarrhea or both, when he lay in a blinding transport of misery and despair. Beyond the specter of deafness, the kind of incessant and maddening tinnitus Beethoven suffered can by itself drive victims to suicide. Yet when he could work at all he worked with his old energy, with undimmed brilliance and confidence. He met extraordinary suffering with extraordinary endurance and courage. He needed that strength. Other than death itself, going deaf is the worst thing that can happen to a musician. That is easy to understand, terrible to bear.

After the first onslaught, it was some time before he arrived at the realization that there could be no cure, only a steady slide into silence. His days as a virtuoso were numbered. It was well that he did not understand that right away. It is well that a sick man cannot see the future.

Beethoven did not pull back from society, not yet, or from performing. In October 1798, he made another tour, to Prague, where he gave two public concerts featuring the first two piano concertos and improvisations, and some private performances. One of those who came to hear was the Czech virtuoso and composer Wenzel Johann Tomaschek. After the first experience of this newcomer, Tomaschek was not just impressed, he was devastated: "Beethoven's magnificent playing and particularly the daring flights in his improvisation stirred me strangely to the depths of my soul; indeed I found myself so profoundly bowed down that I did not touch my pianoforte for several days."

Tomaschek dragged himself to a second concert that afflicted him equally. Then after a concert at the home of a "Count C.," he drew some consolation after hearing Beethoven improvise and play pieces including the "graceful Rondo from the A major sonata," op. 2, no. 2. In his response, Tomaschek, younger than Beethoven but with an older sensibility, showed the distinction between an eighteenth-century musical consciousness and a progressive one: "This time I listened to Beethoven's artistic work with more composure. I admired his powerful and brilliant playing, but his frequent daring deviations from one motive to another, whereby the organic connection, the gradual development of ideas was broken up, did not escape me. Evils of this nature frequently weaken his greatest compositions ... The singular and original seemed to be his chief aim."[32] Here were charges that would turn up in criticism regularly in the coming years: Beethoven was capricious, he provoked for the sake of provocation, in his work he leaped from idea to idea with no sense of unity or organic unfolding.

By the end of October 1798, he was back in Vienna, playing one of his concertos in a program. Despite the threat to his hearing, he was still an active virtuoso, still practicing intensely, still growing as a performer. But he had taken his next-to-last concert tour.

Later he said that his hearing bothered him most in company, least when he composed. Sunk in his *raptus,* he could shut off the chaos in his ears and hear only what he was improvising on the piano or in his head, sketching on the page. The year 1799 turned out unhappy but richly productive. In the early months he filled his second sketchbook with ideas and drafts toward a string quartet in F major, eventually no. 1 of the set commissioned by Prince Lobkowitz. Through page after page, he drafted variations on an obsessive figure, laying out a nearly monorhythmic kind of first movement that he would often return to in the future. His composing process alternated stretches of improvising at the keyboard with the scratch of a quill pen racing across the page at the table he kept beside the piano. Once or twice a day, in all weathers, he set off on a brisk walk around the city walls, his head ringing with music as he hustled unseeing past palaces and bastions and strolling Viennese. So his creative rhythm was set. Day after day, year after year: improvise, sketch at the table, go out and walk. Walking was as much a part of the process as the rest of it.

Haydn was once asked whether he ever composed with a story in mind. He said he thought he had once, something about a man's confrontation with God, but he couldn't remember which piece. Beethoven told an admirer that there were always stories or images behind his music. Unusually in one case, he admitted the inspiration when somebody guessed it. He played over the slow movement of the F Major String Quartet for Amenda. His friend said it sounded like the parting of two lovers. It's based on the ending of *Romeo and Juliet,* Beethoven said. Sketches for the last part of the movement show a close attention to the story: with a dramatic *fortissimo* "he enters the tomb"; a sweeping figure is noted as "despair"; at "he kills himself," the music sinks to empty single notes; descending figures represent "the last sighs."[33] But in the final version of the movement, Beethoven took out all those pictorial gestures in the sketches. What remains is a mood, a sense of encroaching threat: the rushing figure he called "despair" became a whirlwind that appears in the middle of the movement and rises to the end like doom.

Except for a few pieces whose character or scene he would label — *Pathétique, Pastoral, Das Lebewohl* — he rarely again spoke to anyone about his images and stories, and few hints show up in his sketches. Even on the page he kept his cards close. Sometimes the stories were a starting point, something to get the notes flowing, like the old days in Bonn when he improvised musical portraits of his friends. Stories, characters, images helped him shape a piece and find evocative ideas, helped keep the narrative and feeling focused. But that was a matter of the workshop, and Beethoven rarely talked about his workshop. And while he was obsessed with technique, he did not appreciate anybody else talking about it: technical analysis was mere "counting syllables," he would say, as if describing the meter of a poem could explain what the poem is about.

His craftsmanship was nobody's business but his own. He wanted his listeners to create their own stories, their own poetry, their own fantasias from his poems in tone. Eventually he came to call himself not a *Komponist* but a *Tondichter,* a tone poet. In his scale of values, poets were more important than musicians, superior beings all around. In later years, if there was any man alive whom Beethoven placed on a higher plane than himself, it was the poet and writer Goethe.

Beethoven spent most of thirty pages of the new sketchbook on the F Major Quartet, as usual largely working through one movement before going to the next. At the end of the main work on the F Major, he continued on to quartets in G and A major, a septet that was eventually op. 20, and some piano variations, among a miscellany of pieces large and small, finished and unfinished.[34] His anxiety about his hearing apparently did not slow him so much as a step.

CRIMES
IN PRINT

From now on, the stages in Beethoven's career would be tracked by critics in print. There had long been music critics and critical journals; an ambitious new one appeared at the end of 1798: the *Allgemeine Musikalische Zeitung* (*General Musical Magazine*), produced by the Leipzig music-publishing firm Breitkopf & Härtel. Though it was in effect a house journal, Breitkopf gave it considerable editorial latitude and named an able first editor, Johann Friedrich Rochlitz. He had studied music in Leipzig, then turned to theology and Kantian aesthetics.[35] Rochlitz would make the *AMZ* into the most important musical journal of its time, its format large and double-columned like a newspaper, its stable of writers keeping music lovers apprised of the publications and the doings of famous musicians.

Naturally the journal kept readers apprised of the most dynamic of the younger pianist-composers, Beethoven. By this point he had a serious keyboard rival in Vienna. One of the first extended *AMZ* pieces involving Beethoven, in May 1799, describes a duel with Joseph Wölffl. Originally from Salzburg, Wölffl had studied violin in childhood with Leopold Mozart; later he was a friend and perhaps piano and composition student of Wolfgang. Wölffl was yet another eccentric virtuoso and looked the part: gaunt and tall, his clothes flapping around him. Wenzel Tomaschek described Wölffl's fingers as "monstrously long," giving him a huge reach on the keyboard. He had the peculiar habit of sometimes playing melodies, even quite fast ones, with one finger.[36]

It was an age when for many listeners the polish and virtuosity of pianists were at least as important as the music they played. Competing virtuosos were treated like rival athletes. The piano enthusiasts of Vienna split into Beethoven and Wölffl camps. Between the two men, however, the rivalry stayed friendly. Beethoven tended to be more generous to competitors (except overrated ones) than Mozart had been. After all, in his generation he knew he still had no real peer as a composer. Wölffl for his part dedicated his op. 6 Piano Sonatas to Beethoven.

Inevitably when they were in Vienna together, there would be a duel. It took place before a packed audience at the home of wealthy businessman and one-time Mozart patron Baron Raimund Wetzlar. Beethoven's patron Prince Lichnowsky sat in the front row; host Baron Wetzlar was a devotee of Wölffl. The two contenders played their own music, improvised alone, and, seated at two pianos, tossed ideas for improvisation back and forth in mounting waves of virtuosity.[37] The favored, Mozartian style of playing in those days was Wölffl's: lucid, concise, subtle. A favored term of approval was a "pearly" sound, each note delicate and distinct. Beethoven, in comparison, was less precious, more fiery, technically dazzling with his blinding scales and double and triple trills. In his youth he had spent a great deal of time teaching himself to play the piano as distinct from the harpsichord and clavichord. He had a rare gift for a singing legato at the piano, achieved partly by his prophetic technique: he held his fingers bent and close to the keys, his body still, his fingers sometimes hardly seeming to move. During loud passages, though, he might break hammers and strings on the delicate, harpsichord-like pianos of the time.

Most reviews of his playing pointed out these things in one way or another. After the duel, a summary of the opinions of local cognoscenti was included in an *Allgemeine Musikalische Zeitung* article of May 1799 called "The Most Famous Female and Male Keyboard Players in Vienna." After commending a couple of women virtuosos, the anonymous writer compares the styles of the two leading "gentlemen":

> Beethoven and Wölffl cause the most sensation. Opinions about preferences for one over the other are divided. Nevertheless, it seems as if the majority is inclined toward [Wölffl] . . . Beethoven's playing is extremely brilliant but less delicate, and it occasionally crosses over into the obscure. He demonstrates his greatest advantage in improvisation. And here it is really extraordinary with what ease and yet steadiness in the succession of ideas B. does not just vary the figurations of any given theme on the spot . . . but really performs it. Since the death of Mozart . . . I have never found this kind of pleasure anywhere to the degree provided by Beethoven. Here, Wölffl is inferior to him. However, Wölffl has . . . fundamental musical learning and true dignity in composition, plays passages that seem impossible to execute with astonishing ease, precision, and clarity . . . Wölffl gains a special advantage because of his unassuming, pleasant bearing over Beethoven's somewhat haughty manners.[38]

Another and more Romantic account came, years later, from conductor and composer Ignaz von Seyfried. He witnessed this duel or another one like it between Beethoven and Wölffl and recalled his impressions of these "athletes" and "gladiators." He declared it was "difficult, perhaps impossible, to award the palm of victory to either one." In his lavishly metaphorical description, there is, as in the *AMZ* account, an implication that Beethoven was a composer and player for the few rather than the many:

> In his improvisations even then Beethoven did not deny his tendency toward the mysterious and gloomy. When once he began to revel in the infinite world of tones, he was transported above all earthly things;—his spirit had burst all restricting bonds, shaken off the yokes of servitude, and soared triumphantly into the luminous spaces of the higher aether. Now his playing tore along like a wildly foaming cataract, and the conjurer constrained his instrument to an utterance so forceful that the stoutest structure was scarcely able to withstand it; and anon he sank down, exhausted, exhaling gentle plaints, dissolving in melancholy. Again the spirit would soar aloft, triumphing over transitory terrestrial sufferings, turn its glance upwards in reverent sounds and find rest and comfort on the innocent bosom of holy nature. But who shall sound the depths of the sea? It was the mystical Sanskrit language whose hieroglyphs can be read only by the initiated. Wölffl, on the contrary, trained in the school of Mozart, was always equable; never superficial but always clear and thus more accessible to the multitude.[39]

In these responses, one finds an important element of the critical debate that marked Beethoven's public career. The ideal of the later eighteenth century, the age of reason, placed a supreme value on transparency, coherence, and restraint: the art that hides art, the "organic," the elegance and irony that mask emotion while subtly revealing it. It was a time when the tragic voice in music (heard mainly in opera and religious works) felt detectably forced and stylized. Mozart's greatest operas were comedies, which suited the temper of the time and the temper of its music.[40] Originality was valued, but only in good measure. In search of the "natural," "pleasing," and "accessible," the later eighteenth century dismissed the creations of the previous era as "baroque," a word actually meaning a misshapen pearl, made into a term for art overdecorated and overcomplex (in musical terms, too densely contrapuntal). As a pejorative, the term *baroque* was allied to "bizarre," meaning deliberately provocative, irrational, *unnatural*. (The modern, nonpejorative use of the word *Baroque* as the name of a period in the arts came much later.)

Another characteristic complaint visited on Beethoven was that his sonatas were "fantastic." *Fantasia* was the time's term for a genre in a quasi-improvisatory style outside the usual formal models, free in meter, tempo, form, and character, "in which," wrote a theorist of the time, "the composer arranges the images of his imagination without an evident plan, or with a certain level of freedom, and thus sometimes in connected, at other times in quite loosely ordered phrases."[41] Mozart had written famous fantasias.

To compose fantasias was acceptable to the aesthetic sensibility of the time; to call them sonatas was not. Beethoven founded everything he did on models from the past, but many musicians and critics did not understand or approve of the ways he pushed tradition. In fact, he was pushing his models in directions innate to them: he used contrast, but sharper contrasts; a variety of keys, but a broader variety; developments and codas, but longer and more varied ones; transitions, but sometimes longer transitions than usual and sometimes none; and so on through every dimension of music. Those who could not hear the connections to the past accused Beethoven of making his sonatas too much like fantasias: loose, incoherent, beyond all decorum.

Charles Burney, in *General History of Music* of 1776 had defined the attitude of the high Enlightenment: music was "an innocent luxury, unnecessary, indeed, to our existence, but a great improvement and gratification to the sense of hearing." A few years later Mozart wrote to his father, "Passions, violent or not, must never be expressed to the point of disgust, and music must never offend the ear . . . but must always be pleasing." Mozart epitomized the Enlightenment's musical aesthetic in the letter describing some of his new works: "These concertos are a happy medium between what is too easy and too difficult; they are very brilliant, pleasing to the ear, and natural, without being vapid. There are passages here and there from which connoisseurs alone can derive satisfaction; but these passages are written in such a way that the less learned cannot fail to be pleased, without knowing why."[42]

When Ignaz von Seyfried wrote about Beethoven's music using terms such as "mysterious," "gloomy," "Sanskrit," "hieroglyphs," "the initiated," he drew a line between Beethoven and the eighteenth-century taste for subtlety, restraint, irony, broad appeal, the happy medium. In order to make his way, Beethoven had to change that aesthetic. That task would not be entirely his job, however. As of 1798, there was a new spirit in the air that was to foster an audience for whom words like "mysterious," "hieroglyphs," "fantastic," even "bizarre" would be terms of praise. This was the movement that named itself Romantic, which came to embrace Beethoven as its essential musical voice. Even though the Romantic sensibility was abroad in the land by the end of the eighteenth century, it had not yet made its way to music. When Beethoven's music and that sensibility connected, his ascent toward the status of demigod began. The contest between Beethoven and Wölffl in a crowded eighteenth-century Viennese music room was, in a real sense, a duel between the past and the future of music.

In June 1799, a hapless critic of the *Allgemeine Musikalische Zeitung* with little to no experience of Beethoven was assigned to review the op. 12 Violin Sonatas. Contemplating these pieces so mild, so beholden to Mozart (and to a later age so barely Beethovenian), this befuddled listener could only splutter:

> After having arduously worked his way through these quite peculiar sonatas, overladen with strange difficulties, he must admit that . . . he felt like a man who had thought he was going to promenade with an ingenious friend through an inviting forest, was detained every moment by hostile entanglements, and finally emerged, weary, exhausted, and without enjoyment. It is undeniable that Herr van *Beethoven* goes his own way. But what a bizarre, laborious way! Studied, studied, and perpetually studied, and no nature, no song. Indeed . . . there is only

a mass of learning here, without good method. There is obstinacy for which we feel little interest, a striving for rare modulations . . . a piling on of difficulty upon difficulty, so that one loses all patience and enjoyment.[43]

He relents enough to suggest that "this work shouldn't be thrown away because of these complaints. It has its value . . . particularly as a study for experienced keyboard players. There are always many who love excessive difficulties in invention and composition, that which one could call perverse." He ends these backhanded compliments by hoping the composer will "follow the path of nature," when he will "certainly provide us with quite a few good things for an instrument over which he seems to have extraordinary control."

Beethoven generally read everything he could find written about himself. He would have read that review with blood boiling. Soon he would find a way to twist Breitkopf & Härtel's arm to assign him more sympathetic reviewers. Within a few years, he had the satisfaction of seeing op. 12 go through several reprintings by Artaria in Vienna, and further editions in Paris and London.[44] Meanwhile he issued works designed to show critics and the public that, when he wanted, he could write as pleasingly as you like.

On March 19, 1799, Joseph Haydn publicly unveiled the work he considered his magnum opus, the oratorio *The Creation,* on a libretto by Baron van Swieten. Haydn considered oratorios and masses the most important musical genres and the crowns of his work, and he wanted to leave behind something to place beside the Handel oratorios, above all *Messiah,* which he had come to admire in London. The old master worked slowly and carefully on the piece, praying to God for inspiration as always, but now sketching more elaborately than he had done in his decades as a palace servant, when he had to turn out a constant stream of works to order.[45]

Presumably Beethoven attended the premiere of *The Creation* at the Burgtheater. He subdued his jealousy as best he could, admired the scope and splendor of the music as best he could. His agitated state of mind around the premiere is perhaps indicated by a rare wrangle he had with Zmeskall over tickets, the only time on record when there were strong words between them. "You seemed to be offended with me yesterday," Beethoven wrote, "perhaps because I declared rather heatedly that you had acted wrongly in giving away the tickets . . . etc., etc." *The Creation* drew the largest crowd ever seen in the court theater. Its legendary opening masterstroke is the hair-raising proclamation of "Let there be light!" in a great C-major effulgence bursting from the depiction of Chaos. It was an effect not only in music but in his audience that Haydn had calculated as precisely as the eponymous *fortissimo* explosion in the *Surprise* Symphony. Knowing that moment would begin the piece with a coup de théâtre, Haydn swore the musicians and choir to secrecy. At the premiere it caused the sensation he knew it would. The oratorio went on to be, for many years, one of the most popular large choral works in the repertoire.

Jammed in amid the throng of adoring listeners in the Burgtheater, Beethoven might have sensed with a touch of relief that the wild acclaim was not quite earned. The music had manifold splendors, but when all was sung and done, vocal works of Handelian scope were not really Haydn's forte any more than opera had been, and the style of *The Creation* was generally operatic. The aria depicting the creation of the earth, for one example, starts in a *furioso* mode suitable for a revenge aria on the stage. In the end, Haydn was at his best on a more immediate and intimate scale: a string quartet, a piano sonata, a symphony whether witty or elegant or judiciously Sturm und Drang.

It would not have required an inordinate gift of prophecy for Beethoven to foresee that this kind of scope and ambition was actually his own forte, even if he did not yet know when and how he could manage it. For him, when great works were in question, Handel would become the prime model and challenge, not Haydn (given that Beethoven and his time hardly knew the large works of J. S. Bach). Nor would it have been especially humbling for Beethoven to realize that he might never write a better string quartet than Haydn's greatest ones, and several of those greatest ones were brand-new.

The Creation would remain with Beethoven as a challenge and a goad. For the rest of his life, the oratorio weighed on his mind, along with Haydn's Austrian national anthem, until at last he found his own ways — not in oratorio but in more congenial genres — to respond to them.

The main threat to Beethoven's productivity was hardly the challenge of Haydn but rather the financial necessity of teaching piano. It was a job he hated except when it involved exceptionally talented students or attractive young females of whatever talent. Exemplars of the latter appeared in spring 1799. They were Therese and Josephine, two of three teenage daughters — Charlotte was the third — of Countess Anna von Brunsvik. At that point, the family was visiting Vienna for only some eighteen days.

Therese von Brunsvik showed up at Beethoven's flat in St. Peter's Square with his op. 1 Trios under her arm, sat down, and played away at his out-of-tune piano, singing the string parts as she went. Beethoven was hopelessly charmed by this teenager. For the moment, he largely gave up work on the string quartets to go to the family's hotel and give lessons to Therese and her sister Josephine, turning up faithfully sixteen days in a row. "He did not tire," Therese perhaps innocently recalled in her memoirs, "of holding down and bending my fingers, which I had been taught to raise and hold flat." The lessons were nominally an hour long, but he often stayed three or four hours. Therese was delicate and had a deformed spine.[46] His main attention fell on the more attractive Josephine. That interest would keep simmering while Josephine, under fierce pressure from her mother, made a forced and loveless marriage with Count Joseph Deym.

When Therese and her family left town, Beethoven got back to the string quartets and other pieces, putting aside anxieties about his hearing. He endured an emotional loss in June when his beloved friend Karl Amenda left Vienna for good, to take care of family matters back home in Courland. As a testament to their friendship, Beethoven gave Amenda the manuscript of the F Major Quartet, eventually no. 1 of the set. For the moment he considered the piece finished, but he changed his mind about that.

In October he delivered to Prince Lobkowitz the first three of the commissioned six quartets and received a fee of 200 florins.[47] Work on the next three was sporadic for a while as he turned to other projects needing attention, including sketches for a C-major symphony that for years had refused to take wing.

 Another keyboard rival, nearly the same age as Beethoven, arrived in Vienna for an extended stay in autumn 1799. This was Johann *Cramer* Baptist Cramer, German born and reared in England, where he had studied with Clementi. Cramer was a prolific if unoriginal composer, then in the process of becoming the supreme piano virtuoso of his generation in Europe. Cramer's admirers soon included Beethoven, who coveted the fineness and control of his touch. Having just lost the friend he felt closest to, Beethoven embraced this new acquaintance, who was one of the few musicians he felt he could learn from, and a man to whom he could expose his (never very profound) insecurities. An old story has them walking together in the Prater park and in the distance hearing the haunting Mozart C Minor Piano Concerto, K. 491. Beethoven stopped, swaying to the music (his failing ears still permitted him to hear it), and groaned, "Cramer, Cramer! We'll never be able to do anything like that!"

Apparently Beethoven was generous toward Cramer's music too, but that part of the relationship was not reciprocated. Later Cramer would give his famous friend mixed reviews. As a player, he said, Beethoven could be brilliant and focused one day, eccentric and confused the next. (Confused with the aid of wine, perhaps. It hardly seems likely that Beethoven composed with a glass at hand, but he may have played after a few glasses sometimes.) Cramer later told his students, If you haven't heard Beethoven improvise, you have never heard improvisation at all. One day he had turned up to visit Beethoven and stopped in the anteroom when he heard him improvising alone in the next room. Cramer stood listening for a half hour, enthralled. Finally, knowing Beethoven did not like to be overheard, he left without a greeting.[48] But Cramer's admiration was limited. He was among the musicians who were not prepared to follow Beethoven into new territories of sound and feeling. Though he did play some of the Beethoven sonatas, Cramer's idols were Handel and Mozart. To a student enthusiastic about Beethoven's works, he scoffed, "If he emptied his inkstand on a piece of music paper, you'd admire it!"[49]

Which is all to say that as the new sensation, the new controversy, the new rebel, Beethoven and his music and motives were always questioned. There would always be the unconvinced, the bad reviews, the outright enemies. But as a new century approached he found more admirers, more enthusiasm. Looking over the op. 10 Piano Sonatas in autumn 1799, the *Allgemeine Musikalische Zeitung* reviewer confessed,

> It is not to be denied that Hr. v B. is a man of genius, has originality and goes his own way. In addition, his unusual thoroughness in the higher manner of writing and his own extraordinary command of the instrument he writes for unquestionably assure him of his rank among the best keyboard composers and performers of our time. His abundance of ideas . . . still too often causes him to pile up ideas without restraint and to arrange them in a bizarre manner so as to bring about an obscure artificiality or an artificial obscurity . . . [Yet] this critic . . . has learned to admire him more than he did at first.[50]

Early next year the *AMZ* response to the *Pathétique* was still warmer and more insightful: "This well-written sonata is not unjustly called pathetic, for it really does have a definitely passionate character. Noble melancholy is announced in the effective . . . and flowingly modulated *Grave* in C minor, which occasionally interrupts the fiery Allegro theme that gives much expression to the very vigorous agitation of an earnest soul."[51] The tastes of reviewers were broadening, though it would be a while before the *AMZ* found critics whose prose could evoke this new music.

The two piano sonatas that followed the *Pathétique* as op. 14 were another pulling back to warmer and lighter music: each comprises three concise movements with no foreboding, no slow movements, no virtuosity, and overall a delicious playfulness and joie de vivre — yet they are no less fresh in their pianism than the sonatas that precede and follow them. A feature of no. 1, in E major, is a new, urgent theme in the first-movement development. That had been part of the conception from the beginning: Beethoven wrote on an early sketch, "zweiter Theil, ohne das Thema durchzuführen" (second part [i.e., the development], without working out the theme). He was aiming for a more through-composed effect. The opening motif of op. 14, no. 2, in G major, is a wry little fillip containing an octave leap and a three-note hook figure that will mark themes throughout the sonata, down to a droll final gurgle in the bass.

One chilly winter day around 1800, a father brought his ten-year-old son to play for Beethoven. The boy was Carl Czerny, and he carried with him the music for *Adelaide* and the newly published *Pathétique*, which he had already learned. Father and son were shepherded by an early Beethoven devotee, violinist Wenzel Krumpholz. He had at some point given fiddle lessons to Beethoven (to apparently little effect: in adulthood, Beethoven was a laughable violinist). They spent much time together, Beethoven playing new pieces and improvising, poking fun at Krumpholz's ecstatic responses. In the habit of giving nicknames to his friends, Beethoven dubbed this disciple his "court jester"; the two stayed close for many years. Besides his fondness for the man, Beethoven appreciated the value of having a champion like Krumpholz in the ranks of leading Viennese performers.

When Czerny father and son turned up, Beethoven was living in a fifth- or sixth-floor flat on Tiefer Graben, near the Hofburg — the imperial palace — in the center of town. After Krumpholz had the Czernys climb what seemed like endless creaking flights of stairs, a shabby-looking servant showed them in. There they found their genius inhabiting a bare room with bare walls, the floor littered with boxes, clothes, and papers, with few places to sit other than a rickety chair parked before a Walter piano (the leading Viennese make of the day, once Mozart's favorite). Several people were present, including the celebrated Mozart pupil Franz Süssmeyer, violinist Ignaz Schuppanzigh, and one of Beethoven's brothers (probably Carl, who was not at this point on Beethoven's enemies list).

Young Czerny knew about Beethoven's dangerous reputation. His works, Czerny later recalled, "were totally misunderstood by the general public, and all the followers of the Mozart-Haydn school opposed them with the most intense animosity." That may have been an exaggeration, but not by much. Czerny wrote that his first sight of Beethoven reminded him of Robinson Crusoe: brown in complexion, his stubble of whiskers reaching nearly to his eyes, his thick hair coal-black and bristling. That day he wore a dark gray morning coat and matching trousers. Young Czerny noticed a strange detail: Beethoven had his ears stuffed with cotton stained by some yellowish medicine.

Beethoven agreed to hear the boy play. Shoving down his anxiety, Czerny started with the solo part of the Mozart C Major Concerto, K. 503. Soon Beethoven stepped to the piano and began playing bits of the orchestral part around the boy's hands. Reassured, Czerny went on to play the *Pathétique* and to accompany his father in *Adelaide*.

Once, Beethoven had himself been a ten-year-old prodigy, so he was not inordinately impressed. His response was matter-of-fact: "The boy has talent. I will teach him myself and accept him as my pupil. Send him to me several times a week. First of all, however, get him a copy of Emanuel Bach's book on the true art of piano playing, for he must bring it with him the next time he comes." Here began a historic career. As Czerny's teacher, Beethoven shaped not only a musician and a disciple, but what became a lasting school of piano pedagogy.[52]

Some other new acquaintances from this period also bore fruit in one degree or another. Beethoven got to know pianist and composer Johann Nepomuk Hummel, once Mozart's favorite pupil. There are two notes Beethoven wrote around 1799 whose addressee tradition would assign to Hummel. The first dismisses him in contemptuous third person: "Don't come to me anymore. He is a false dog, and may the hangman do away with all false dogs." Then on the next day: "Dear Little 'Nazy of my Heart! You are an honest fellow and I now realize that you were right. So come to me this afternoon. You will find Schuppanzigh here too and we shall both blow you up, batter and shake so that you will have a thoroughly good time. Kisses from your Beethoven, also called Dumpling."[53]

Beethoven was still outgoing and sociable in this period, interested in any new musical phenomenon that turned up. Another traveling virtuoso visiting Vienna in 1799 was double bass soloist Domenico Dragonetti, acclaimed for transforming a workaday instrument into a thing of beauty. As one critic said, Dragonetti "by powers almost magical, invests an instrument, which seems to wage eternal war with melody . . . with all the charms of soft harmonious sounds."

When Dragonetti arrived in Vienna, his fame preceding him, he and Beethoven naturally wanted to get acquainted. The defining moment in their acquaintance came when the two read through the Cello Sonata op. 5, no. 2, Dragonetti playing the cello part on his bass. At the end a delighted Beethoven jumped up from the piano and embraced player and instrument together.[54] From that point on, Beethoven had a new appreciation of the orchestra's basement. That inspiration, put into the pages of his symphonies, would oppress generations of orchestral bass players who had enjoyed their anonymity on the generally easy bass line. In his visits to Vienna, Dragonetti proved an amiable companion as well, going on about his collections of instruments, his paintings and musical manuscripts, snuff boxes and dolls.[55] Dragonetti had more money than Beethoven ever did, and unlike Beethoven he knew how to have fun with it.

Dec 1799

In December 1799, the French Constitution of revolutionary year VIII declared Napoleon Bonaparte First Consul. He was now de facto dictator of the country. He soon returned to the battlefield, leading his armies in Italy against the Second Coalition, in which Austria was again the major player.

As the new century began, Beethoven had a thick portfolio of works newly or nearly done. It was time to make his bid to become First Consul of music in Vienna.

14

The Good, the Beautiful, and
the Melancholy

18 00

THE PROGRAM READ, "Today, Wednesday, April 2nd, 1800, Herr *Ludwig van Beethoven* will have the honor to give a grand concert for his benefit in the Royal Imperial Court Theater beside the Burg." At age twenty-nine, after more than seven years of living in Vienna, Beethoven was mounting his first concert in the city for his own benefit. For it he had secured the theater of the Hofburg, the imperial palace, which numbered among its legendary premieres Mozart's *Figaro* and the recent one of Haydn's *Creation*. His conquest of Vienna as a virtuoso had been quick and relatively easy. Now he needed to establish his name as a composer.

The evening was one of the long patchwork programs of the time, seven numbers beginning with "a grand symphony by the late Kapell-meister Mozart." Second and fifth were arias from *The Creation* by "the Princely Kapellmeister Herr Haydn." With the orchestra, Beethoven played one of his first two piano concertos, probably the C Major. In central place was the public premiere of the new Septet for three winds and four strings, "most humbly and obediently dedicated to Her Majesty the Empress." Ignaz Schuppanzigh handled the nimble first-violin part. Before the final work, Beethoven improvised at the piano. For a finish, he premiered "a new grand symphony" in C major, his first.[1]

Haydn was probably present. It was a program he would approve of, one that acknowledged Beethoven's roots.

The size and enthusiasm of the audience was not reported in the *Allgemeine Musikalische Zeitung* notice. The reviewer concentrates on the strong and weak suits of the program. Declaring it "probably the most interesting public concert for a long time," he never quite gets around to explaining why. He gives passing praise to the concerto, the Septet, and Beethoven's "masterly" improvisation. In the symphony he finds "very much art, novelty, and a wealth of ideas. However, the wind instruments were used far too much." That means he found the symphony overscored — which, on the whole, it is.

The main trouble, the reviewer continues at greater length and greater heat, was not the music but the musicians. He cites wrangles over who was to conduct; the players came close to rebelling at Beethoven's choice. In the concerto the performers "did not make any effort to pay attention to the soloist. As a result there was no trace of delicacy in the accompaniment." In the new symphony, "they became so lax that in spite of all efforts, no fire could any longer be brought forth in their playing ... With such behavior, what use is any amount of skill ... ?"[2] It was a lukewarm review of a less-than-splendid evening, but still the concert did Beethoven more good than harm. In the next years, the C Major Symphony proved a popular addition to the orchestral repertoire, alongside those of Haydn and Mozart and a row of lesser lights.

Beethoven's gambit on this first outing was to be strong but not provocative. One item was manifestly designed to be a hit: the Septet, a divertimento in six movements, moderate and mellifluous, not too hard for amateurs to play or to hear. In short, meant to "please." It begins with a stately introduction on a tone of high-Mozartian elegance, a mood from which it never strays. No formal experiments, no renegade keys, little break in the silken surface. It is glowingly scored, with a lively and memorable clarinet part as foil to the first violin.

Later, prodding a publisher to rush it out, Beethoven complained, "Do send my septet into the world a little more quickly — because the rabble is waiting for it."[3] Asked for a piece by impresario Johann Salomon in London, he sent off the Septet as his British debut.[4] In his effort to please and to make a few florins, though, Beethoven succeeded too well. Published as op. 20, the Septet became, to his eternal annoyance, the biggest success of his life. From then on, conservative critics would use it as a cudgel with which to belabor his more adventurous pieces. The C Major Symphony would serve a similar function. Which is to say that Beethoven was subject to a classic dilemma of the artist with early success: as a young composer, he had to put up with being compared unfavorably to Haydn and Mozart; as a mature composer, he would have to endure unfavorable comparisons to his younger self.

Symphony No. 1 in C Major, op. 21, is larger and in theory more ambitious than his chamber works, at the same time geared to appeal to an audience reared on Haydn and Mozart. For years Beethoven had been sketching at a symphony in that key. Now, wanting a big finish for his concert, he brushed aside his uncertainty and pulled the piece together quickly. He took what had been some ideas for a first movement and gave them to the finale, then composed three new movements. Because of the weight of those transferred ideas, this symphony points in the direction Beethoven was to pursue: the finale became the heaviest and most serious, rather than the first movement carrying the main weight as in symphonies of the past.[5]

In tone, the First Symphony recalls Haydn more than Mozart. The beginning of the Adagio molto introduction is a series of wind chords that bend a couple of rules, if gently: it commences on a dissonance and in the wrong key. Only in the fourth measure does the music arrive at a chord that reveals the piece is in C major. As the *AMZ* critic noted, it is overrich in tuttis from beginning to end, which makes for an orchestral sound tending to monochromatic — a mistake Haydn and Mozart did not make, and Beethoven never made again.

The main motif of the symphony is the ascending half step heard over and over in the beginning of the introduction. After that Beethoven runs up and down a scale, foreshadowing the introductory scale figure in the last movement (for which he already had the leading ideas). Then follows a vigorous, military-toned Allegro con brio, its phrasing foursquare, its modulations modest, its development and coda not excessively long. Much of the movement is *forte* or *fortissimo*, most of it scored for the whole band. Whether or not the material itself has great impact, he wanted to make some noise with it. C major had a reputation as a key for sentiments from the moderate to the elevated and grand, not bold or passionate, and so it is here. As for the second movement (in a slightly unusual sonata form), Beethoven would never get closer to the elegantly precious mood of the eighteenth-century *galant*, still current in those years. However far from his own temperament, the *galant* was a tone he could wield when he wanted to.

The third movement he called "Minuetto," but its tempo of Allegro molto e vivace reveals it as a scherzo. This one is dashing, as scherzos are supposed to be; in practice, it's one of the least distinctive he ever wrote. The tone of gaiety-in-moderation is maintained in the finale, which begins like the first movement, with an Adagio introduction. There is a clear family resemblance in the opening themes of all the movements; by now those kinds of intermovement relations were old habit to Beethoven.

The C Major Symphony was fresh enough for the first reviewer to call it "novel," without putting too fine a point on it. How novel could it be if the critic found nothing but its scoring to complain about? It was one of the most overtly crowd pleasing, most resolutely eighteenth-century of Beethoven's works in this period, crafted with his usual skill but less personal in material than some of the early piano sonatas, piano trios, and string trios. When he wrote it he was not far from having composed the *Pathétique,* a harbinger of his mature voice. But with this symphony, the Septet, and the other works on the program, he stepped gently before the Viennese public. For the moment, as a composer of symphonies and concertos he would rest patiently in the shadow of Haydn and Mozart and experiment with voices while he waited for his muse to show him a more adventurous path.

Beyond that cautiousness, by this point a pattern had emerged: Beethoven tended to follow more aggressive and challenging works with milder, more attractive, more "pleasing" ones. As with the Septet, there would also be a steady sprinkling of manifestly commercial items. When it came to the symphony, he made his debut with a work of modest scale and ambition. Having entered the fray, his ambitions for the genre would mount precipitously.

• • •

At the turn of the new century, piano performing held its place in Beethoven's income and identity. He had worked hard and long to become the virtuoso he was, spending much of his teens practicing deep into the night. He liked the immediacy of performance and of applause, so different from the lonely business of scribbling notes on paper in hopes, someday, of gaining something from it. But the racket in his ears, his declining ability to hear soft passages and nuances of color, could only erode his playing.

His performing was receding now, though there was still the occasional public appearance. In April 1800, he gave a program at the Burgtheater with visiting Bohemian horn virtuoso Wenzel Stich, who called himself Giovanni Punto (both last names mean "engraving," respectively, in German and Italian). Call Punto the Dragonetti of the horn: he had reached a new level of virtuosity on what by the later eighteenth century had become a workaday instrument. Among his admirers had been Mozart, who raved in a letter, "Punto blows magnifique."[6] His instrument was still essentially the old *Waldhorn,* or hunting horn, which had no valves and so ordinarily could play only a restricted range of notes, like a bugle. Besides mastering the usual elements of virtuoso horn playing — accuracy of pitch, rapid tonguing, a beautiful singing tone — Punto had developed unprecedented skill in hand stopping, a technique of shoving the hand in the bell to change the pitch, thereby producing a greater range of notes.

Delighted to meet another virtuoso who was expanding the possibilities of an instrument, Beethoven dashed off a horn and piano sonata in F major, published the next year as op. 17, for their concert. Later he claimed to have written the whole piece the day before the performance (possible, but only just). The sonata is largely devoted to enjoying Punto's playing in styles from singing to bravura. The second movement is in F minor, requiring steady hand stopping. Besides changing the pitch, stopped notes have muted sound, veiled when soft, metallic and piercing when loud. These are qualities to be exploited by a composer who knows the instrument. At the premiere, the audience response to the sonata was so enthusiastic that they played the whole thing again (movements or even entire pieces were often encored in those days).

The next month Beethoven and Punto performed in Budapest and planned to continue traveling and concertizing together. But there was a squabble, as often happened when dealing with Beethoven. Punto went on alone while Beethoven stayed in Budapest for a while.[7] The next year they reunited to put on a charity concert in Vienna.[8] What Beethoven retained from this encounter, as with Dragonetti and the bass, was a sense of how the capabilities of an instrument could be extended beyond the norm. As with his new respect for the bass, that experience led him to strain the capacities and the patience of his orchestral horn players.

Around this period, the visit of another virtuoso became the occasion for an unplanned piano duel. This was not, like the Wölffl evening, a duel of respectful rivals but a thoroughly unpleasant business. Pianist and composer Daniel Steibelt, a handsome and canny showman, had developed a fervent following. He concertized with his wife, a virtuosa of the tambourine, for whom he wrote showpieces that were wildly applauded. (After a performance, he would auction off the tambourine.)[9] Beethoven's admirers worried that this glamorous soloist might eclipse their hero.

When he arrived in Vienna, Steibelt did not deign to pay his respects to Beethoven. That was his first mistake. At an evening concert in the music room of a Count Fries, with Steibelt in the audience, Beethoven presented his op. 11 Trio for Piano, Clarinet, and Cello.[10] Steibelt listened distractedly and made a few airy compliments. Another mistake. Then the visitor presented a quintet of his own, followed by an improvisation featuring his trademark *tremolando,* a fluttering effect new to most listeners of that time.[11] Listening to this new idol, Beethoven concluded that the man was a charlatan.

A week later, at another Count Fries evening with Beethoven attending, a Steibelt piece garnered much applause. He went on to play a showy "improvisation," clearly prepared ahead, on a theme Beethoven had used for variations in the Trio. That was a calculated challenge, and his last mistake with Beethoven. Naturally when Steibelt was done the crowd demanded a response. Beethoven resisted as usual but finally rose, provoked in the extreme. On the way to the piano he picked up the cello part of Steibelt's piece. Slumping down at the keyboard, he made a show of turning the part upside down on the music stand.

With one finger, he plunked out a few upside-down notes at random. With those notes as a theme, he began to improvise.

It may well have been a phenomenal performance. His later student Ferdinand Ries noted that Beethoven played best when he was either in an especially good mood or when he was angry.[12] This was the latter sort of occasion. Czerny said Beethoven used to emphasize the leading motifs when he played; in this case the motif was a pure insult.[13] And as usual with both composing and improvising, Beethoven would have stuck closely to his random *Thema.* Thereby he indicated to this would-be rival, *At any moment I can take any idea, any damned thing at all, and make more out of it than anything you've ever done.*

Steibelt got the point. When Beethoven was finished, his rival had vanished from the hall. In the future Steibelt would demand that anyone who desired his presence would not invite Beethoven. Shortly before, in Prague, Steibelt had made the dazzling sum of 1,800 florins for a single concert. Then, reported pianist Wenzel Tomaschek with relish, "[h]e went to Vienna, his purse filled with ducats, where he was knocked in the head by the pianist Beethoven."[14]

At the beginning of August 1800, Beethoven wrote his letter to Friedrich von Matthisson, enclosing his setting of "Adelaide" dedicated to the poet, with thanks for the inspiration. The song had become one of his best-selling items. Beethoven had an abiding respect for poets, their words, and their wisdom. To this fellow artist he unburdened himself a little, by way of almost apologizing for the song: "You yourself are aware what changes a few years may produce in an artist who is constantly progressing. The greater the strides he makes in his art, the less he is satisfied with his earlier works."[15]

He felt more and more restless, searching for a way forward. Beyond that, his hearing and health kept him on edge, anxious for the future. So far he had found extraordinary success in everything he had done. Inevitably there were plenty of people who did not like his work, but plenty of others were buying his music, and that was not lost on publishers. Another pleasant sign of success turned up this year when his most powerful patron, Prince Lichnowsky, granted him an annuity of 600 florins, to be renewed until he had found a permanent position (most likely as a *Kapellmeister*, most likely in Vienna).[16] That was more or less half a year's workable income. Lichnowsky gave Beethoven another gift that in terms of a later time would be incredible: a quartet of string instruments, including a violin and a cello made by the legendary Guarneri, another violin by the legendary Amati.[17] Since this gift was not made to a true string player, it amounted to a token of respect in anticipation of string quartets to come.

Still, Beethoven had not yet settled on the kind of music he imagined writing, that reached beyond the confines of patrons' music rooms, that mattered the way Handel and J. S. Bach and Haydn and Mozart mattered. The dissatisfaction he expressed in the letter to Matthisson followed directly on the completion of the most sustained and ambitious project of his life, the six string quartets commissioned by Prince Lobkowitz. They had been Beethoven's major project for some two years; there is nothing comparable to their scope in the sketches of middle 1798 to late 1799.[18] Aware of the looming presence of the Haydn and Mozart quartets, painfully aware that Haydn had recently written some of his greatest ones, Beethoven composed the set with the most meticulous care. Having drafted them to the end, he returned to the F Major and G Major and possibly D Major and revised them with the advice of Viennese composer Emanuel Aloys Förster, a respected old hand with quartets.[19] (In the 1790s, Beethoven was a regular at Förster's twice-weekly quartet parties.)[20] Having given the manuscript of the first version of the F Major to Karl Amenda, Beethoven dispatched a letter to his distant friend, saying, "Be sure not to hand on to anybody your quartet, in which I have made some drastic alterations. For only now have I learned how to write quartets."[21]

All the op. 18 quartets turned out strong and listenable. As was second nature to him, each is knit together by patterns of keys, melodic and rhythmic motifs, gestural shapes. If they tend to be reminiscent of Haydn and Mozart, and well within the tradition of quartets written for amateurs, none of them are blandly conventional and all of them have probing ideas, even if sometimes the impact of the ideas does not rise to the level of the craftsmanship.

In other words, he composed the set cautiously, with Haydn and Mozart figuratively looking over his shoulder, knowing he was going to be submitting these pieces to Haydn's judgment in person. Haydn was, of course, no ordinary judge of string quartets. He had virtually invented the modern idea of the genre: a four-movement piece for instruments treated more or less equally (superseding the older, first-violin-dominated pieces). Under Haydn's nurturing, the string quartet had become the king of chamber-music genres, though still aimed toward skilled amateurs playing at home. As of 1800, there was no such thing as an established professional string quartet playing regular public concerts.

Haydn described his six quartets of op. 33, published in 1782, as written "in a new and special manner." Besides a more near equality of the instruments, central to that new manner was systematic thematic work — using a few small, recurring motifs to build themes — and a new wealth of expressive variety, integrating music in high style with folksy and comic material. Inspired mainly by op. 33, in the next years Mozart issued his splendid set of six quartets dedicated to Haydn. By then quartets were one of the most salable of genres, with enthusiasts everywhere and composers supplying those enthusiasts with hundreds of works. The quartet had become the chamber medium par excellence for connoisseurs and for fanatics, in a period when the favored amateur instruments were strings, not yet the piano. All over Europe, families and groups of friends played quartets together to entertain themselves and their circle. So quartets, like the other chamber genres, were private and social, in contrast to the more public and popularistic genres of symphony and opera.

Again mainly because of Haydn, there was a sense that quartets were the ultimate test not only of a composer's craft but of his heart and soul, his most refined and intimate voice. It was understood that in composing a quartet it was appropriate to be more subtle, idiosyncratic, and complex than in big public pieces. The strange, chromatic beginning of Mozart's C Major Quartet, the last of the Haydn-dedicated set, earned it the nickname "Dissonant." A beginning that, harmonically gnarly, would have been out of place in a symphony, even for Beethoven.

As he began work, Beethoven knew that Haydn was working on his own set of six quartets also commissioned by Prince Lobkowitz.[22] As it turned out, Haydn was able to finish only two of the quartets and part of a third (the latter op. 103).[23] Age was unkind to Haydn. But as far as

Beethoven knew, with his first quartets he would be competing with new Haydns written at the top of the old master's form. For the moment, then, Beethoven conceded the field. At the same time, he did his preparatory work, studying Haydn quartets and copying out the whole E-flat Quartet from op. 20.[24]

Thus the contemporary rather than prophetic tone of the op. 18 Quartets. In later years, it would be written of them that Beethoven was "learning his craft," "mastering form," "finding his voice," "looking backward." None of that applies. The quartets show him as already a master craftsman, already with a mature understanding of form and proportion (though that understanding would greatly deepen and broaden), a composer who had already found much of his voice (though he had not fully settled into it).[25] Still, for all their relative modesty and eighteenth-century tone, the op. 18 quartets are ambitious in their way: well written for the instruments, widely contrasting in mood and color, at least as varied as any set by Haydn or Mozart, and full of ideas particular to Beethoven.

After reading through the quartets with his group, violinist Ignaz Schuppanzigh advised placing the F Major, the second composed, as no. 1 in the published set.[26] Beethoven agreed. The F Major has the most arresting opening, perhaps is the most consistent throughout the set. It starts with a sober movement driven by an obsessive repetition of a single figure whose significance is rhythmic as much as melodic.

In coming years Beethoven would return to similar monorhythmic movements, but later he tended to use repeated figures to sustain a sense of relentlessness, whether a mood of irresistible fate, or the spell of dance, or the blissful trance of a summer day. In the first measures of the F Major, the figure is presented blankly in quiet unison, then in a yearning phrase, then in a more aggressive *forte*. The obsessive theme is a blank slate on which changing feelings are projected. This being Beethoven, the opening idea also unveils the leading motif of the whole quartet, a turn figure. Between the published version of the F Major and the original version in Amenda's copy, with advice from old hand Emanuel Förster, Beethoven went back and made dozens of large and small changes in details compositional, textural, thematic:

extending thematic connections, tightening proportions and tonal relations (he transposed long stretches of the development).[27] In the process he trimmed the appearances of the turn figure from 130 repetitions to 104.[28]

The second movement of the F Major is one of the most compelling movements in op. 18. This is the music that Beethoven told Amenda was based on *Romeo and Juliet*. It is in D minor, the same as the Largo e mesto movement of op. 10, no. 3, so in a key in which Beethoven found a kind of singing, tragic quality. Here it is marked Adagio affettuoso ed appassionato: slow and warmly impassioned, the main theme a long-breathed, sorrowful song. In the middle of the movement a new figure intrudes, like the whirling of fate that swells relentlessly to a deathly end. There follow a brilliant and delightful scherzo and a briskly racing, perhaps a bit wispy finale that leaves listeners pleased, if perhaps puzzled as to how all this adds up.

The next quartet in the set, no. 2 in G Major, is jaunty and ironic from beginning to end, starting with the three distinct gestures of its opening, each like a smiling tip of the hat to the eighteenth century. Its slow movement starts elegantly *galant*, in 3/4, but that tone is punctured by an eruption of mocking 2/4 serving as trio. No. 3 in D Major was the first to be written — in other words, the first full string quartet of Beethoven's life. If the opening movement seems featureless to a degree, the finale manages to be an effervescent romp full of Haydnesque rhythmic quirks.[29] Its slow movement, in a dark-toned B-flat major, branches into deep-flat keys including E-flat minor. That movement shows off Beethoven's sensitivity to the contrast between keys involving open strings and keys that avoid open strings; to great effect, he juxtaposes dark and bright string keys throughout. No. 4 in C Minor is the only minor-key work in the opus, this one more aspiring to than attaining the dynamism of his C-minor mood.[30] The first movement has some apprentice echoes, awkward harmonic and phrasing jumps rare in his music.[31] Its gypsy rondo of a finale is the (relative) glory of this number. No. 5 in A Major has its quirky pleasures, including a dashing, as if opera buffa, finale.

No. 6 in B-flat Major was written last. Here more overtly and eloquently than in any of its neighbors in op. 18, Beethoven showed his hand in wanting to say something beyond music. To that end, he shaped a narrative both personal and universal. Its subject is the encroachment of depression.

When Beethoven was his student in Bonn, Christian Neefe had written that a composer must be a student not just of notes but of humanity. You need "a meticulous acquaintance with the various characters [of men] … with the passions … One observes the nuances of feelings, or the point where one passion changes into another."[32] So Beethoven had been taught. In himself he had watched the nuances of feeling. Now he began putting that knowledge to use in ways that took him, in a work on the surface not notably "Beethovenian," closer to his full maturity.

The quartet begins on a striding, muscular theme, buffa in tone, even a touch generic and foursquare. It is a Haydnesque theme, and Beethoven is going to play a Haydnesque game with it: set up the listener's expectations, then subvert them.

Whereas Haydn usually pursued that game with a wink for the connoisseurs who would get it, Beethoven plays it in fierce earnest. What the listener expects after the beginning of the B-flat Quartet is for the music to remain in uncomplicated, eighteenth-century high spirits. The second theme starts off in the expected second-theme key of F major, the tone elegant and refined, the rhythm with a touch of marching tread.

Then something intrudes, a shadow. The elegant march strays into unexpected keys, arriving with a bump on the chromatic chord called the Neapolitan, a harmonic effect that often has something unsettling about it.

After a few seconds, the shadow seems to pass, the music shakes itself back into F major, all is well again. Nothing really troubles the movement further until the recap, except that in the development the jolly tone gets sometimes a touch harsh, and in a couple of places the music trails off strangely into silence, like it has lost its train of thought. In the recap of the second theme, the harmony veers into B-flat minor and E-flat minor, then shakes off the shadow again.

The second movement begins in a blithe and galant mode, but that is a mood made to be spoiled. In the middle part, the music slips again into E-flat minor, one of Beethoven's most fraught keys, usually implying inward sorrow. Here it is, an eerie, spidery, keening whisper, all of it based on a twisting motif:

Then, as in the first movement, there is a sudden clearing back to the elegant mood of the opening. Near the end, preceded by explosive chords, the eerie whispering returns. The *galant* theme rises again, tentatively, and the music collapses into silence.

With its intricate cross-accents that defy the listener to find the meter or even the beat, the scherzo plays another Haydn game, his fool-the-ear rhythms. Yet as the music goes on, the tone begins to feel excessive unto obsessive: not innocent gaiety but manic gaiety. So it is not entirely an intrusion when, at the end of the trio, the music suddenly falls for a moment into a strange, shouting B-flat minor before the repeat back into the scherzo and its madcap (too madcap) fun.

Then comes the most arresting and significant page in op. 18, a slow passage serving as extended introduction to the last movement. Over it Beethoven placed an Italian title: *La Malinconia,* or "Melancholy." More than a small movement, striking in itself, this is the heart of a story that began with a few passing shadows in movement 1, expanded to a mysterious, spidery whispering in movement 2, and sent the scherzo reeling nearly out of control.

His portrait of melancholy's devious onset begins mildly, in B-flat major:

It is an echo of the second theme in movement 1, with a smoothing out of the same marching figure, the mood again elegant, like a gesture with a lace handkerchief at an aristocratic ball. The phrase ends with a little *galant* turn. It is repeated. As it repeats, the cello begins to sink chromatically; as in the second theme of movement 1, there is a sudden darkening. This time the darkness lingers. The music falls into a slow, steady tread. The little turn comes back, repeating. The key drifts aimlessly. A new section begins, its theme a slow, lugubrious version of the twisting motif in the middle of movement 2.

The once-elegant little turn comes back, whispering and crying over and over like some inescapable bête noire, the harmony oozing around it (touching on E-flat minor and B-flat minor).[33]

In rhythm, harmony, and melody, *La Malinconia* had been foreshadowed from the beginning, starting with a darkness that shadows the second theme of the first movement. After the scherzo, when we are expecting an allegro finale, melancholy seems to arise suddenly. But it had been lurking even in the blithe moments, as melancholy does in life. In the music it is present in strange diversions in harmony, in thoughts trailing off, things manically exaggerated. Again and again in the piece, an elegant and conventional surface slips to reveal a darkness beneath, until the melancholy reveals itself in its full malevolence. The *Malinconia* movement ends with a high cry and a dying sigh.

The finale breaks out *attacca subito,* with a driving, dancing gaiety that we take for an escape from melancholy. The music is in the mode of a spirited German dance called the *alla Tedesca* or *Deutsche.* Yet something is subtly off. The color and the rhythm are wrong. The main theme is carried in the first violin mostly on the darker and milder middle strings rather than on the bright and brilliant E string. The rhythm is at odds: the violin starts off dividing the measure equally in two, while the accompaniment, rather than flowing with the meter, has lurching accents on the offbeats. Eventually, the music does dash up into high, bright regions, but only briefly before falling back into the low register.

Suddenly, a crashing halt. *La Malinconia* returns with its deathly tread, its nasty little turn figure, its convulsive cries. It sinks, the dance tries to start up again, fails. Melancholy takes another step, pauses, waits. Tentatively, searching for the right key, the dance tries again until it finds its proper key. It will not be stopped this time, or not quite: before the end there is a slowing, a few turns quiet and hesitant, inward. Then a fierce rush to the cadence, *fortissimo.* Melancholy is banished for the moment, but only for the moment.

Melancholy was an old, familiar companion to Beethoven. After his mother died when he was sixteen, he wrote in a letter that he had asthma, but also that "I have been suffering from melancholia, which in my case is almost as great a torture as my illness." He knew the demon of melancholy like he knew the arcana of harmony and counterpoint. He knew that in the midst of dancing and gaiety, the demon can always come back.

For Beethoven, the Quartet in B-flat, op. 18, no. 6, is in both technical and psychological dimensions a manifestly mature work and a gathering of prophecies musical, dramatic, and expressive. Its prophecies will play out in the way a middle movement returns to trouble the triumphant finale of the Fifth Symphony, in more explorations of despair and tragedy unprecedented in style, including the slow movement of the Seventh Symphony. The long-range psychological unfolding in the B-flat Quartet will be repeated in works to the end of his life, in steadily more profound and subtle ways. The prophecy will play out in his life too: a slowly insinuating shadow that suddenly descends overwhelmingly, all at once, and the world goes dark.

All the same, on the whole, op. 18 was not intended to challenge anything or anybody. If as of 1800 Beethoven had known where he wanted to take the genres of symphony and string quartet, he would have taken them there. But he did not know yet where he wanted to go with the two genres he took most seriously — and took seriously because Haydn and Mozart had made them serious. So he proceeded warily.

As he finished the quartets and turned thirty in December 1800, Beethoven had to wonder when he would come into his own, find out who he was. In retrospect the clues were there, especially in the *Pathétique* and some slow movements in the first dozen opuses. But that is retrospective. His perspective on the ground was far less broad, far less certain. He was trying one thing and another, one voice and another, and biding his time.

If Beethoven was not yet exactly a darling of publishers (he was a difficult darling in any situation), he was still in demand. In 1800, publisher and composer Franz Anton Hoffmeister moved from Vienna to Leipzig as a base for his operations. This entrepreneur knew Beethoven personally; Hoffmeister & Kühnel had put out the first edition of the *Pathétique*.[34] Beethoven was fond of Hoffmeister, and they had friendly business relations for a while before the inevitable break. When he was settled in Leipzig, Hoffmeister wrote Beethoven asking for pieces. Beethoven replied in December, apologizing for a delay: "I am dreadfully lazy about writing letters." There follows a gentle rebuke:

> I am very sorry that you, my beloved and worthy brother in the art of music, did not let me know something about this sooner, for I could have brought to your market my quartets [op. 18] and also many other works which I have already disposed of. But if our worthy brother is as conscientious as many other honorable engravers who hound us poor composers into our graves, no doubt you too will know what advantage to draw from these works when they appear. — Hence I will jot down briefly what works my worthy b[rother] can have from me.

The letter is written in what was becoming a characteristic tone of Beethoven's with publishers, at once imperious and friendly (his address to Hoffmeister as "brother in the art" is both a compliment and a take on the way a Freemason would address a brother). He proffers the Septet, "which has been very popular"; the First Symphony; "a grand solo sonata" for piano, in B-flat; and a piano concerto, "which, it is true, I do not make out to be one of my best [the B-flat]; and also another [the C Major Concerto]." As a sign of favor to Hoffmeister, he finishes, "You yourself when replying may fix the prices as well; and as you are neither a Jew nor an Italian and since I too am neither, no doubt we shall come to some agreement."[35] (The anti-Semitic and anti-Italian touches at the end of the letter are rare for Beethoven, but this is not his last ethnic snipe.) Hoffmeister took all the pieces. The Piano Sonata in B-flat, published as op. 22, is a big, four-movement work of which Beethoven was fond, even though its style is more contemporary than forward-looking — his last one of which that could be said.[36]

Beethoven's procedure toward publishing his works amounted to this: he gave everything he had, heart mind and soul, to the creation of anything he considered serious. Once done, it became stock-in-trade, for which he wanted the best price and the most favorable terms he could find. Of the hundreds of letters of his that survive, the majority would be to publishers: stroking, pitching, complaining, correcting proofs. No composer before Beethoven published as continuously from the beginning as he did, and few if any before depended so much on income from publishing.[37] As soon as he was through with a piece and contractually able to, he would offer it to one or more publishers. Before that point there had to be an intermediary, a copyist. For some twenty years his favored copyist was one Wenzel Schlemmer, who was adept at tracking Beethoven's notes through the sometimes battlefield conditions of the manuscripts.[38] When the piece was accepted by a publisher, the real misery began. Proofreading the invariably faulty engravings and dealing with corrections would consume a crushing amount of Beethoven's time, an endless necessity and an endless frustration.

For better and for worse, a freelance composer of that era was subject to the market. Unless he had one of the increasingly hard-to-find positions as *Kapellmeister* in court or church, he had to cobble together a living from a grab bag of sources: commissions, publishing, part-time jobs in church or court, teaching, performing, patronage from the nobility.[39] Like most of his brothers in art, Beethoven pursued all those avenues. (In his mix of incomes, only the guaranteed 600-florin stipend from Prince Lichnowsky was unusual — a stipend with no stated duties.)

If one had talent in music and resourcefulness in business, this was a workable way to live. If one built a reputation and a demand, publishing could be a steady source of income and also a spur to creativity. Beethoven would prove a generally sharp and competent businessman, the sales dimension being, for him, another part of the job that he was determined to master. This was in contrast to his general incapacity with everything else having to do with money, including his inability to divide or multiply sums.

Music publishing gathered momentum in the later eighteenth century. As the middle class expanded, the market for music grew along with the market for every other leisure endeavor. The growth continued through the next century, tracking the burgeoning number of amateurs and professionals demanding new pieces to play. Another reason was the development of engraving on pewter and copper plates, which made publishing faster and cheaper. Music was incised on the plates backward by skilled (and wretchedly paid) craftsmen, and run off on a handpress.[40]

There were no royalties for composers; you sold your work to a publisher for a flat fee. For his part, the publisher put out a pile of copies of a new piece, hoping to sell as many as possible as soon as possible because, since there was also no copyright, any successful composer's work would immediately be pirated. The first pirates of your work might be your own copyists, who would secretly make a second copy and run to a publisher with it. If you were not careful, the pirated edition might come out before the legitimate one. Mozart dealt with that problem by making his copyists work in his apartment, so he could keep an eye on them.[41] Once Haydn had begun publishing, a thriving trade in fake Haydn sprang up. That at least was considered reprehensible, likewise plagiarism. But musical forgery, plagiarism, and piracy were none of them against the law. Beethoven was aggressive in fight-

Publishing cont'

ing back against his pirates, but lacking legal means, he had to use threats to publishers and notices in the papers.

Payments were small, so one had to turn out a good deal of music to get by. Haydn discovered a clever and profitable way to market his work: he would contract a piece or an opus simultaneously to two or more publishers in different countries, giving each limited but exclusive territory. That meant he could be paid for a given piece more than once (all this was done openly). Beethoven eventually took up that procedure and found himself bedeviled with its innate problem: to keep pirates at bay as long as possible, a given piece had to come out in every country at the same time. But in an era of slow mail and slower travel, coordinating publishing dates across Europe and England was a dicey affair. Beethoven made use of another kind of contractual arrangement with patrons who commissioned from him: on delivering the piece to the person who commissioned it and collecting his fee, Beethoven would put off publication and give the person exclusive rights to the work in manuscript for a stated time (usually six months to a year); then he would be free to sell it at will.

Years before, Beethoven had written his brother that for anything he wrote he had his pick of publishers, who paid whatever he asked (though he did not usually demand extravagant prices). Even though he changed publishers often, he would rarely have much trouble getting things in print, if not always with the houses he wanted. Which is to say that as of the new century he remained in pleasant professional circumstances; he would remain so for the next decade. The counters to the rosy prospects were his declining hearing and his health. He was miserably ill through much of the winter of 1800–1801 with what he described as "frightful attacks" of vomiting on top of his old chronic diarrhea; and at the same time, he wrote, "my ears hum and buzz day and night."[42]

The Holy Roman Empire was having a hard winter of its own. In the ongoing War of the Second Coalition, Austria suffered another mauling from the French at the Bavarian village of Hohenlinden. The hospitals of Vienna filled up with wounded soldiers — gratifying to musicians at least, because benefit concerts would be needed.[43] The Battle of Hohenlinden forced the Habsburgs to make peace, which meant the end of the latest coalition against France. In the Treaty of Lunéville, signed in February 1801, Austria conceded all its territories in Italy except for Venice. The thousand-year-old Holy Roman Empire was not just shrinking; it was dying.

In the middle of January 1801, Haydn conducted his *Creation* at a benefit for wounded soldiers in the *Grosser Redoutensaal* of the Hofburg. In another benefit at the end of the month, Beethoven felt well enough to play his Horn Sonata, now in print as op. 17, with Giovanni Punto. Haydn conducted two of his symphonies on that program.

Beethoven had other matters on his mind. In January he wrote another long letter to publisher Franz Anton Hoffmeister in Leipzig, laying on his respect, pleasure, gratitude, humility, etc. If he was in demand, he still felt the need to court publishers vigorously. As a practical item, he offers to make a piano arrangement of the Septet. He names his prices for the pieces accepted: 20 ducats (around 100 florins) for the Septet arrangement; the same for the C Major Symphony (a shockingly low price); the B-flat Piano Concerto for a bargain 50 florins. He also asks 100 florins for the big B-flat Piano Sonata, reassuring Hoffmeister, "This sonata is a terrific piece, most beloved and worthy brother." He goes on to give quite lucid reasons for the prices, in effect telling the publisher his business: "I find that a septet or a symphony does not sell as well as a sonata. That is the reason why I do this, although a symphony should undoubtedly be worth more ... I am valuing the concerto at only [45 florins] because, as I have already told you, I do not consider it to be one of my best concertos ... I have tried to make the prices as moderate for you as possible."

At the end he emits an inked sigh for having to make these mundane arrangements: "Well, that tiresome business has now been settled. I call it tiresome because I should like such matters to be differently ordered in this world. There ought to be in the world a market for art, where the artist would only have to bring his works and take as much money as he needed. But, as it is, an artist has to be to a certain extent a business man as well." The market idea is neither irrational nor insincere. Beethoven was thinking of similar organizations proposed during the French Revolution.[44] It was not, however, an idea a publisher would conceivably be receptive to.

Beethoven includes an aside showing that the recent middling-to-bad reviews in the *Allgemeine Musikalische Zeitung* were still eating at his mind: "As for the Leipzig r[eviewers], just let them talk; by means of their chatter they will certainly never make anyone immortal, nor will they ever take immortality from anyone upon whom Apollo has bestowed it."[45] As the bestower of immortality he cites not the Christian God but Apollo. Since he does not believe God makes miracles or meddles in one's born gifts, he resorts to a metaphor.

At the end of his letter to Hoffmeister, Beethoven adds, "For some time I have not been well; and so it is a little difficult for me even to write down notes and, still less, letters of the alphabet." Perhaps, but he had taken on a commission to write the music for a ballet called *Die Geschöpfe des Prometheus* (The Creatures of Prometheus). For this apparently merely commercial job, he dropped every other project and jumped in.

The *Prometheus* ballet and its story were the creation of dancer, choreographer, composer, and impresario Salvatore Viganò, the recently appointed ballet master of the Vienna court. Viganò was one of the premiere dancers and choreographers in Europe, in those days at least as famous as Beethoven.[46] Viganò's approach to ballet was reformist and controversial. He was given to storytelling with pantomime and tableaux, as it would be with *Die Geschöpfe des Prometheus*. He had the usual problems of reformers. As one of his admirers described it, "There was something disconcerting in suddenly seeing dramatic action, depth of feeling, and pure plastic beauty of movement in a particular form of spectacle in which one was hitherto accustomed to seeing nothing but leaps and contortions, constrained positions, and contrived and complicated dances."[47]

On the face of it, Viganò's plot for this new ballet was chimerical. The figure of Prometheus, in Greek myth the demigod punished by Zeus for bringing fire to humanity, was not exactly the same character as the hero of the ballet. Viganò took a newly invented Prometheus myth from an eighteenth-century French novel and adapted it to his Enlightenment taste. As the playbill explained, Viganò's new Prometheus was "a sublime spirit, who came upon the men of his time in a state of ignorance, who refined them through science and art, and imparted to them morals."

Prometheus carves stone statues of a man and a woman and magically brings them to life, only to discover that his creatures are alive but not yet human. They have no spirit, no soul. In order to teach them feelings, wisdom, and moral awareness, Prometheus takes them to Apollo on Parnassus. The god commands his subjects to humanize the creatures by bringing them to understand music, drama, and dance, each represented by its respective deity. At the end, Apollo commands "that Bacchus [performed by Viganò himself] make known the heroic dance that he invented."[48]

The idea of humanity being illuminated by art and science is a high-Aufklärung theme that struck deep resonances in Beethoven. He would later write, from the same kind of conviction, "Only art and science can raise men to the Godhead." That the arts were necessary to become fully human was an idea that reached back to the core of his *Bildung* in Bonn, where, for one example, the goal in founding the National Theater had been to create "an ethical school for the German people." But there was a more specific body of thought relating to ethics, morality, and art that Viganò may have drawn from: the recent philosophical writings of Friedrich Schiller.

Schiller had been one of the artists and thinkers who hailed the French Revolution. He had virtually prophesied it in his most famous poem, "An die Freude." He had been declared an honorary citizen of France. But the coming of the Reign of Terror horrified Schiller. After the execution of Louis XVI he wrote, "I haven't been able to look at the papers for the last fortnight, I feel so sickened by these abominable butchers . . . The [revolutionary] attempt of the French people . . . has plunged not only that unhappy people itself, but a considerable part of Europe and a whole century, back into barbarism and slavery."[49] Schiller remained true to the Enlightenment principles of the Revolution, but he recoiled from endorsing, as some did, what became of the Revolution in France. And despite all the rage against tyranny in his early plays — *The Robbers, Fiesco, Don Carlos* — Schiller retained a characteristically German-Aufklärung faith in enlightened princes who had the power to impose reform from above.[50]

Schiller   In the 1790s, after devoting years to studying Kant's philosophy,
Schiller issued what amounted to his answer to the Terror and the fail-
On the   ure of the Revolution to establish a rational society: *On the Aesthetic*
Aesthetic
Ed. of Man *Education of Man.* The essence of that book, which had a wide and lasting influence, is that the ideal society cannot rise from revolution but
only from education in aesthetics — in other words, from an appreciation of the Good, the True, and the Beautiful, and their embodiment
in Art. "Art is a daughter of freedom," Schiller wrote; and, "It is only
through Beauty that man makes his way to Freedom"; and, "The way
to the head must be opened through the heart."[51] Earlier he had been
fervent about the Aufklärung *Glückseligkeitphilosophie,* the philosophy of happiness as the goal of life. The ideal society, in which brotherhood and freedom make happiness possible, Schiller called Elysium.
This was the essence of "An die Freude": "Joy, thou god-engendered
daughter of Elysium." That poem, rising from the revolutionary (and
Masonic and Illuminist) spirit of the 1780s, was part of his path to the
Aesthetic Education.

Whether Viganò read this work of Schiller's or whether he and
Beethoven absorbed their ideas from the zeitgeist, these kinds of ideals were the foundation of *Die Geschöpfe des Prometheus:* learning of
beauty and art makes a human being free, moral, and ethical, thereby
able to mold lives and societies that are harmonious and happy. The
story of the *Prometheus* ballet would be a representation of that ideal
in sound and movement.

The depth and breadth of these ideas, however, are not particularly audible in the tone of Beethoven's music, which on the whole is
in conventional ballet style. Like most composers of his time, he was
schooled in the traditions of genres: how a symphony is distinct from
a quartet, how the tone of an overture to an opera is distinct from the
first movement of a symphony. To study composers as models for his
works was also to study how they handled genres. He had spent the
last decade exploring and mastering one medium and genre after another. Now he tried his hand at ballet music, which required a certain
elegance and lightness of touch, and he conformed to that expectation
as best he could.

After his latest siege of illness, complaining of exhaustion, Beethoven got to work. In the first two months of 1801, he wrote an hour's worth of orchestral music — overture, introduction, and sixteen numbers. The job appealed to him beyond the commission fee and his attraction to the story and ideas. It was a way of making himself better known to the Viennese court and getting practice in theatrical music. He was not a beginner in writing for dance; there had been the *Ritterballet* in Bonn and ballroom dances for Vienna. In style, this music for the theater would be entirely distinct from his work for the concert hall and his other theatrical music. The *Prometheus* Overture, elevated and Mozartian in tone, begins dramatically, with dissonant chords punctuating silence. From there, he kept the ballet music graceful, tuneful, light and pleasing even in its sterner moments (though as it turned out, not light enough for reviewers). Given the speed at which he had to produce the score, there was little time for rumination in any case.

Still, what mainly galvanized Beethoven were the humanistic implications of the ballet, in particular its finale. After much dancing by the gods of the various arts, in which the new creatures join in, to the horror of his children Prometheus is killed by a wrathful Melpomene, Muse of tragedy. But luckily Thalia, Muse of comedy, is on hand to cheer everybody up and bring the demigod back to life.[52] And so, "amid festive dances the story ends." The particular festive dance that Beethoven and Viganò chose for a finale was one of the most popular dances of the time: the *anglaise* or *englische.*

Beginning as an English country dance, the *englische* had spread across Europe. There were regional variations, but it was always done as a contra dance: a line of women and a line of men changing partners during its course. By 1800, the Viennese form of the dance was accompanied by a suite of short tunes in changing meters: say, a touch of minuet in three-beat, a two-beat segment, and so on. It ended with a waltzlike segment.[53]

Dances usually have symbolic dimensions that are part of their image and popularity. The *englische* contra dance had uniquely progressive implications. The constant change of partners as one danced down the line produced a literal mingling of classes; a nobleman might end up hand in hand with a merchant's daughter. This was not a small thing. It was something new in public social life, even radically new.

In the *englische* each participant was, for the duration of the music at least, an equal *citoyen* of the dance, and for that reason the *englische* acquired a frisson of democracy. In turn, for some thinkers that situation made the *englische* into a symbol of an ideal society. One of those caught up by that symbol was Schiller, who wrote in a letter,

> I can think of no more fitting image for the ideal of social conduct than an English dance, composed of many complicated figures and perfectly executed. A spectator ... sees innumerable movements intersecting in the most chaotic fashion ... yet *never colliding* ... it is all so skillfully, and yet so artlessly integrated into a form, that each seems only to be following his own inclination, yet without ever getting in the way of anybody else. It is the most perfectly appropriate symbol of the assertion of one's own freedom and regard for the freedom of others.[54]

So, the "festive dances" that end the *Prometheus* ballet are more than a formal conclusion. Choosing an *englische* for the finale made the end and goal of the story a symbol something like Schiller's image of "one's own freedom and regard for the freedom of others." The music for this finale begins innocuously enough, with a lilting two-beat tune, distinctively an *englische*. A simple bass line anchors the simplest possible harmonies. Yet over the next two years that little tune and its bass line would come to obsess Beethoven, for their simplicity that held enormous musical potential and for the harmonious society this dance represented to him, to Schiller, and to many others.

Here burgeoned a train of thought that took Beethoven and music itself to a new place. By means of this ballet, he began to understand how he could join his art to the social, ethical, moral, and spiritual ideals of the age. That train of thought took him beyond youthful brilliance and craftsmanship to his full maturity.

In this period, Beethoven revised his 1794 setting of Matthisson's "Opferlied" (Song of Sacrifice). Its Schilleresque last lines became a touchstone with him: "Give me, as a young man and as an old man ... O Zeus, the Beautiful together with the Good." In autograph albums, he would quote that indispensable joining of the sensuous and ethical: *the Beautiful together with the Good.*[55]

15

The New Path

A T ITS PREMIERE, *Die Geschöpfe des Prometheus* had a middling reception, the reaction to the dance more middling than to the music. One J. C. Rosenbaum reported to his diary, "The ballet did not please at all, the music a little . . . At the end the ballet was more hissed than applauded."[1] Most ballet aficionados wanted their leaps and positions rather than Salvatore Viganò's high-minded pantomime. The *Allgemeine Musikalische Zeitung* reviewer summarized: "As much dignity and artistic design as it had . . . it nevertheless was not liked in general . . . The music also did not entirely live up to expectations, even though it possesses more than *ordinary* merit . . . However, that he wrote *too learnedly* for a ballet, and with too little regard for the dance, is certainly not subject to doubt."[2] All the same, there would be a respectable fourteen performances of *Prometheus* in 1801, more the next year.

After the premiere Beethoven ran into Joseph Haydn on the street. The old man greeted him with, "Now, yesterday I heard your ballet and it pleased me very much."

Beethoven attempted to be gracious: "Oh, my dear Papa, you're very kind, but it's a long way from being a *Creation*!"

Confused about what that meant, Haydn replied, "That is true, it is not yet a *Creation,* and I very much doubt whether it will ever succeed in being." And they took their leave, both of them baffled and annoyed.[3]

If Haydn's reply to Beethoven's attempted compliment meant anything, it was not the absurd statement that *Prometheus* could never turn into a *Creation* but that its composer would never rise to a *Creation.* Haydn kept up with what Beethoven was putting out, and he could not have liked much of what he heard.

Haydn had his own frustrations as of 1801. He had been seriously ill in the winter of 1800–1801 and was worn down by his labors on another giant oratorio from a text by Baron von Swieten, *The Seasons.* He was disgusted with himself for taking on the project and for giving in to Swieten's pressure to put into the piece literalistic depictions of flora and fauna, not omitting croaking frogs. The public would eat up the representations of nature in the oratorio, but Haydn dismissed some of those passages as "Frenchified trash." Though after its premiere, in May 1801, *The Seasons* would find nearly as much popularity as *The Creation,* Haydn was nearly exhausted as a composer. "*The Seasons,*" he said, "has finished me off."[4] He would not complete the set of string quartets commissioned like Beethoven's op. 18 by Prince Lobkowitz, with which he surely had intended to show his one-time pupil a thing or two. He had a visiting card made that said, quoting one of his song texts, "Gone forever is my strength, old and weak am I."[5] Senility was overtaking one of history's supreme musical minds.

As Haydn sank, Beethoven rose. After the short but intense labor on the ballet, he got back to practical business. Time he had once spent practicing piano was now going into the unending nuisance of publishers and publications. In a letter to Hoffmeister in Leipzig regarding ongoing projects, he apologized for not writing sooner to "my dear brother": "I was ill, and in addition, I had a great deal to do . . . Perhaps the only touch of genius which I possess is that my things are not always in very good order . . . I have composed a ballet; but the ballet-master has not done his part very successfully."

Another element holding up his dealings with Hoffmeister was that he had begun what became an extended courtship of Breitkopf & Härtel. The firm, founded in 1719, was the leading music-publishing house in Europe. Beethoven wanted its celebrated imprint on his works. If he thought the firm paid better than lesser publishers, however, he was to learn otherwise.

There was another matter between him and Breitkopf & Härtel. He wanted to strike back at the humiliating reviews of his music in its journal, the *Allgemeine Musikalische Zeitung*. Beethoven was becoming a hot name in print, and he knew it. So he was ready to issue a little warning to a house that wanted his music. With great precision of purpose, he wrote to Gottfried Christophe Härtel, head of the company. The pans of his op. 12 Violin Sonatas and other pieces had galled him, and he was already anticipating future nasty notices:

> Please be so kind just to inform me what types of composition you would like to have from me, namely, symphonies, quartets, sonatas and so forth, so that I may be guided by your wishes . . . I merely point out that <u>Hoffmeister</u> is publishing <u>one of my first concertos,</u> which, of course, is not <u>one of my best compositions.</u> Mollo is also publishing a <u>concerto which was written later</u> . . . Let this serve merely as a hint to your Musikalische Zeitung about reviewing these works . . . Advise your reviewers to be more circumspect and intelligent, particularly in regard to the productions of younger composers. For many a one, who perhaps might go far, may take fright. As for myself, far be it from me to think that I have achieved a perfection which suffers no adverse criticism. But your reviewer's outcry against me was at first very mortifying. Yet when I began to compare myself with other composers, I could hardly bring myself to pay any attention to it but remained quite calm and said to myself: "They don't know anything about music." And indeed what made it easier for me to keep calm was that I noticed how certain people were being praised to the skies who in Vienna had very little standing among the best local composers . . . However, pax vobiscum — Peace between you and me.[6]

Settling down, Beethoven then offers to donate something for the benefit of the indigent last daughter of J. S. Bach, whom he calls, with his underline accent, "<u>the immortal god of harmony.</u>" The gist of his message to Härtel concerning reviewers was this: if you want my things, call off your dogs. And Gottfried Härtel, who did want Beethoven in his catalog and had sent him a query about it, did call them off. Though the *AMZ* would have plenty more criticism for Beethoven over the years, there would be no more snarling reviews like the one that greeted op. 12. Härtel did not necessarily direct the critics to go easy; rather he found more progressive and sympathetic reviewers to assign to the Great Mogul. The tone of the *AMZ* reviews shifted decisively toward a tempered respect. And so it came to pass that a historic turnaround of opinion concerning Beethoven in Germany's leading musical journal was stage-managed behind the scenes by Beethoven himself.

One of the first visible results of his maneuver was the *AMZ* review of the opp. 23 and 24 Violin Sonatas. The judgment of the last set had been on the order of "strange sonatas, overladen with difficulties." This time, it was a mixed notice, including even a swipe at the last reviewer: "The original, fiery, and bold spirit of this composer, which . . . [earlier] did not find the friendliest reception everywhere because it occasionally stormed about in an unfriendly, wild, gloomy, and dreary manner, is now becoming more and more clear, begins more and more to disdain all excess, and emerges more and more pleasant without losing anything of his character . . . The less he strives to impress and glorify himself . . . the more he will work for the satisfaction of the better people and at the same time for his own permanent fame."[7] Call this review transitional. When the value of "pleasing" declined and the values of "original, fiery, and bold" ascended, Beethoven criticism came of age. The sonatas themselves are transitional, perhaps the last time Beethoven was detectably cautious, with Mozart's violin sonatas hanging over him. These are patently ingratiating pieces. Beethoven had settled into his pattern of periodically courting listeners and critics with more agreeable items. If the intent was in some degree practical, even commercial, the motivation was not purely venal. He was, after all, a servant not only of the Good and the True but also of the Beautiful.[8]

There are bold touches as well, say, the consistently contrapuntal quality of the op. 23 in A Minor and its experiments with form (the recapitulation in the first movement arrives on the "wrong" theme, a rarity with Beethoven).[9] Op. 24, his first violin sonata in four movements, is sunny and lyrical enough eventually to earn the title *Spring* Sonata. The dewy loveliness of its opening is carried on in a second movement that seems almost like a parody of an eighteenth-century *galant* aria, until some late modulations take it in a memorably poignant direction. In keeping, the finale starts like an echo of Mozart and then ventures into territory not at all Mozartian (this following a wry scherzo whose tininess — just over a minute — is part of the joke).

If opp. 23 and 24 are the freshest of Beethoven's violin sonatas so far, they hardly hint at the creative tide that was rising in him. Still less do they reveal his gathering despair.

By this time, Beethoven had said any number of literal and symbolic farewells to his youth in Bonn. Another milestone came when in July 1801 Bonn's exiled Elector Maximilian Franz died at age forty-five near Vienna in Hetzendorf, where he had lived out his last decade dreaming of reclaiming his throne. Beethoven had planned to dedicate his First Symphony to his old sovereign and employer, but now there was nothing to be gained from it. On the title page he scribbled out the dedication to Max Franz and wrote in the name of a living and still useful patron, Gottfried van Swieten. For the summer he retired, as it happened, to Hetzendorf. He had acquired the Viennese habit (for those who could afford it) of leaving the reeking, dusty, sweltering city for a summer in the country.

Meanwhile friends from Bonn were arriving in Vienna. Stephan von Breuning, son of his one-time champion and mentor Helene, came to town in the summer of 1801 and settled permanently. "We meet almost every day," Beethoven reported to Franz Wegeler. "It does me good to revive the old feelings of friendship. He has really become an excellent, splendid fellow, who is well-informed and who, like all of us [Bonners] more or less, has his heart in the right place."[10] Beethoven would soon change his tune about Stephan's temperament. Composer Anton Reicha, Beethoven's closest friend in his later teens, came to Vienna for a while in 1802. These companions had to compete for Beethoven's time with his more celebrated Viennese friends and patrons, but he had a special fondness for friends of his youth — though that did not forestall the usual frictions.

1802

Another refugee from Bonn around the beginning of 1802 was pianist, violinist, and composer Ferdinand Ries. His father Franz had been concertmaster of the Bonn orchestra. Ferdinand was a child when Beethoven left Bonn. Now eighteen, he arrived at Beethoven's door destitute, with a letter of introduction from his father, having spent the last year in Munich copying music for pennies and nearly starving.[11] He hoped to study piano and composition, and to find a savior. Beethoven brushed aside the letter with, "I can't answer your father now, but write to him that I could not forget how my mother died." He had not forgotten, that is to say, how Franz Ries helped the family in the aftermath of losing Maria. Beethoven would become a generous mentor and keyboard teacher to Ries, but he refused to teach him theory or composition. For theory studies, he sent the youth to his old counterpoint master Albrechtsberger. As for composition, Ries would have to teach himself, with informal coaching from Beethoven.

Ries would become, like Carl Czerny, a long-term disciple; like Czerny, he had been something of a prodigy as a pianist and composer. In 1803, Ries wrote publisher Nikolaus Simrock in Bonn, "Beethoven takes more pains with me than I would ever have believed possible. I have three lessons a week usually from one o'clock till half past two. I shall soon be able to play his *Sonate pathétique* in a manner that will please you, for the accuracy on which he insists is beyond belief."[12] Czerny was dubious about this would-be rival: "Ries played very fluently, clear but cold." Czerny also recalled Beethoven saying of Ries's music, "He imitates me too much."[13] No one in Beethoven's life in that period spent as much time with him as Ries, who outside his studies became a reliable helper, amanuensis, and sounding board.

Through this period, Beethoven's spirits seem to have been divided between exhilaration and suppressed depression over his hearing and health. The exhilaration of the 1790s had come from his quick success, the enthusiasm of audiences and patrons, the attention from publishers. The exhilaration of 1801 into 1802 seems to have been more an excitement of discovery, a sense that his ideas were moving toward something new as his attention to performing receded. This mingling of antithetical feelings can be seen in a long reply of July 1801 to Franz Wegeler. Here Beethoven returns not only to the intimacy of childhood friends but to the high idealism of the Bonn years. The Rhineland remained, as far as he was concerned, at the core of his identity. He begins, as often with people he respects, with an abject apology.

MY DEAR KIND WEGELER,

I do thank you most warmly for your remembrance of me which I have so little deserved or even endeavored to deserve where you are concerned. Yet you are so very good; you allow nothing, not even my unpardonable carelessness to put you off; and you are still the same faithful, kind and loyal friend — But you must never think that I could ever forget yourself and all of you who were once so dear and precious to me . . . For my fatherland, the beautiful country where I first opened my eyes to the light, still seems to me as lovely and as clearly before my eyes as it was when I left you. In short, the day on which I can meet you again and greet our Father Rhine I shall regard as one of the happiest of my life — When that will be I cannot yet tell you. But indeed I can assure you that when we meet you will certainly see that I have become a first-rate fellow; not only as an artist but also as a man you will find me better and more fully developed. And if our Fatherland is then in a more prosperous condition, my art will be exercised only for the benefit of the poor.

This is as Bonn taught him: to be a first-rate artist, you must be a first-rate fellow. The essence of both is duty to humankind. Now and always, Bonn would represent to him peace and escape — an escape he never took. Next he allows himself to crow a little, before confessing for the first time his greatest anxiety:

You want to know something about my present situation. Well, on the whole it is not at all bad. For since last year Lichnowsky who . . . was always, and still is, my warmest friend (of course we have had some slight misunderstandings, but these have only strengthened our friendship), has disbursed for my benefit a fixed sum of 600 [florins]

... My compositions bring me in a good deal; and I may say that I am offered more commissions than it is possible for me to carry out. Moreover for every composition I can count on six or seven publishers ... People no longer come to an arrangement with me, I state my price and they pay. So you see how pleasantly situated I am ... I have given a few concerts.

But that jealous demon, my wretched health, has put a nasty spoke in my wheel; and it amounts to this, that for the last three years my hearing has become weaker and weaker. The trouble is supposed to have been caused by the condition of my abdomen which, as you know, was wretched even before I left Bonn, but has become worse in Vienna where I have been constantly afflicted with diarrhea and have been suffering in consequence from an extraordinary debility. Frank [a Viennese doctor] has tried to tone up my constitution with strengthening medicines and my hearing with almond oil, but much good did it do me! His treatment had no effect, my deafness became even worse and my abdomen continued to be in the same state as before ... A more sensible doctor, however, prescribed the usual tepid baths in the Danube. The result was miraculous; and my insides improved. But my deafness persisted, or, I should say, became even worse. During this last winter I was truly wretched, for I had really dreadful attacks of colic and again relapsed completely into my former condition ... [Dr. Vering] succeeded in checking almost completely this violent diarrhea.

This was the bursting of the dam. He had to talk to someone, and Wegeler, as both childhood friend and physician, was the logical choice. Wegeler would have read these words with a chill in his heart. A deaf composer. It was unthinkable. The glorious hopes for his old friend's career appeared to be collapsing.

Beethoven praises his new doctor, Vering, who prescribed the Danube baths, gave him pills and "strengthening ingredients" and an infusion for his ears. And he says he had been feeling better, though "my ears continue to hum and buzz day and night." Since Wegeler might have something to offer him medically, he goes into the symptoms:

Nor Deaf But Hearing Impaired

I must confess that I lead a miserable life. For almost two years I have ceased to attend any social functions, just because I find it impossible to say to people: I am deaf . . . And if my enemies, of whom I have a fair number, were to hear about it, what would they say? — In order to give you some idea of this strange deafness, let me tell you that in the theater I have to place myself quite close to the orchestra in order to understand what the actor is saying, and that at a distance I cannot hear the high notes of instruments or voices. As for the spoken voice it is surprising that some people have never noticed my deafness; but since I have always been liable to fits of absent-mindedness, they attribute my hardness of hearing to that. Sometimes too I can scarcely hear a person who speaks softly . . . but if anyone shouts, I can't bear it. Heaven alone knows what is to become of me. <u>Vering tells me that</u> <u>my hearing will certainly improve, although my deafness may not be</u> <u>completely cured.</u>

Makes sense.

He liked the new doctor because this one gave him hope. Already, though, there is the encroaching fear that there was no hope, that fate had ordained this cross. He puts down some bitterly prophetic words, based on his childhood reading of the ancients: "Already I have often cursed my Creator and my existence. <u>Plutarch</u> has shown me <u>the path of resignation.</u> If it is at all possible, I will bid defiance to my fate, though I feel that as long as I live there will be moments when I shall be God's most unhappy creature."

This is no self-dramatizing rhetoric. Beethoven was beginning to understand what he faced, one element of which could be the end of his performing career. He asks Wegeler to consult with Dr. Vering. He talks about coming to the Rhineland and "in some beautiful part of the country and then for six months I will lead the life of a peasant." Maybe the country life would cure him. But he knew how bleak a consolation Plutarch's message was: "Resignation, what a wretched resource! Yet it is all that is left to me." Resignation had its own heroism, but that was no philosophy for a young man, and in any case too passive for Beethoven. His mode of response to any challenge was defiance and aggression.

Dropping the train of sorrows, he tells Wegeler about Stephan van Breuning's arrival, about his nice rooms overlooking the battlements. He offers a gift for a service: "If you let me know how to set about it, I will send you all my works, which, I must admit, now amount to quite a fair number . . . in return for my grandfather's portrait, which I beg you to send me by the mail coach as soon as possible. I am sending you the portrait <u>of his grandson,</u> of our ever loyal and warm-hearted Beethoven." The memory of old Ludwig van Beethoven remained for him a fundamental connection to his homeland and his artistic heritage. He wanted Grandfather Ludwig's imperious gaze watching over him as he worked. Finally in the letter to Wegeler he sends a greeting to Helene von Breuning, one of the irreplaceable figures of his youth. "Tell her," Beethoven writes, "that I still now and then have a raptus."[14] (Wegeler was now married to Lorchen von Breuning, one of Beethoven's first loves.)

The curtain he had drawn over his affliction was parted. Two days after writing Wegeler, he sent another long confessional letter, this one to Karl Amenda in distant Courland. Amenda was a minister, and to him Beethoven recounted not his medical but his spiritual malaise:

MY DEAR AMENDA, MY KIND AMENDA, MY
WARM-HEARTED FRIEND!

I received and read your last letter with intense emotion and with mixed feelings of pain and pleasure — To what shall I compare your loyalty to me, your affection for me? . . . You are no <u>Viennese friend,</u> no, you are one of those such as my native soil is wont to produce. How often would I like to have you here with me, for yo<u>ur B is lead-</u> <u>ing a very unhappy life and is at variance with Nature and his Creator.</u> Many times already I have cursed Him for exposing His creatures to the slightest hazard, so that the most beautiful blossom is thereby often crushed and destroyed. Let me tell you that <u>my most prized pos-</u> <u>session, my hearing,</u> has greatly deteriorated . . . You will realize what a sad life I must now lead, seeing that I am cut off from everything that is dear and precious to me and, what is more, have to associate with such miserable egoists as Zmeskall, Schuppanzigh, and the like. I may say that of all of them Lichnowsky has best stood the test. During the last year he has disbursed for my benefit 600 [florins]. This sum and the steady sale of my works enable me to live without financial anxiety . . . Well, to comfort me somebody has returned to Vienna . . . one of the friends of my youth, and several times I have told him about you . . . He too does not care for Z[meskall], who is and always will be too weak for friendship. I regard him and S[chuppanzigh] as merely instruments on which to play when I feel inclined. But they can never be noble witness to the fullest extent of my inward and outward activities, nor can they ever truly share my life. I value them merely for what they do for me.

Having dismissed as hardly more than self-important servants his most devoted Viennese friend and his most skillful interpreter, Beethoven adds a forlorn hope that he and Amenda can rejoin soon. He intends to make more concert tours: "I shall then travel (when I am playing and composing, my affliction still hampers me least; it affects me most when I am in company) and you must be my companion. I am convinced that my luck will not forsake me. Why, at the moment I feel equal to anything."[15] That boast was not idle.

November 1801 saw another long letter to Wegeler, partly to report on his medical treatments. Dr. Vering had subjected him to the misery of tying the bark of the daphne plant to his arms. The bark blistered his skin and kept him from playing: "The humming and buzzing is slightly less than it used to be, particularly in my left ear, where my deafness really began. But so far my hearing is certainly not a bit better." His stomach continued to improve after tepid baths. He would try Wegeler's suggestion of applying herbs to his belly, but he had turned against the latest doctor: "Vering won't hear of my taking shower baths. On the whole I am not at all satisfied with him. He takes far too little interest in and trouble with a complaint of this kind." He asks Wegeler's opinion of galvanism, treatment with electricity: "A medical man told me that in Berlin he saw a deaf and dumb child recover its hearing and a man who had also been deaf for seven years recover his." (These treatments were all useless, and every part of a daphne plant is poisonous.)

A rising peroration that would live in legend shows Beethoven had not lost hope or courage, at least not on the day of this letter: "If only I can be partially liberated from my affliction, then — I will come to you as a complete and mature man ... You will find me as happy as I am fated to be on this earth, not unhappy — no, that I could not bear — I will seize Fate by the throat; it shall certainly not bend and crush me completely — Oh, it would be so lovely to live a thousand lives."

The letter goes on to a different kind of confession. In this period he still taught students, and to a degree he had returned to socializing:

> You would find it hard to believe what an empty, sad life I have had for the last two years. My poor hearing haunted me everywhere like a ghost; and I avoided — all human society. I seemed to be a misan-thrope and yet I am far from being one. This change has been brought about by a dear charming girl who loves me and whom I love. After two years I am again enjoying a few blissful moments; and for the first time I feel that — marriage might bring me happiness. Unfortunately she is not of my class — and at the moment — I certainly could not marry — I must still bustle about a good deal.[16]

The dear charming girl was most likely his new piano student, the seventeen-year-old countess Giulietta Guicciardi, called Julie. Staying in Vienna in the 1790s, Wegeler had found his old friend, then the new keyboard lion in town, getting a lot of attention from women. No details of those encounters would survive, in itself a sign that Beethoven did not take these flirtations or affairs seriously. He could fall in love as precipitously as tripping over a cobblestone, but this is the first time his letters show any evidence of it. Julie was the daughter of Countess Susanna Guicciardi, sister-in-law to Countess Anna Brunsvik, who was mother of Josephine and Therese. Beethoven fell for at least two of those musical young cousins, Julie and Josephine, and possibly with all three of them.

Julie Guicciardi was remembered as delightful to look at, modestly bright and talented, well aware of her charms. Early in 1801, there was a catty letter from Josephine Brunsvik to her sister: "Julie Guicciardi is creating a furore here. They refer to her only as the beautiful Guicciardi, and you know that she understands how to capitalize on it."[17]

Julie was surely flattered to have the attention of Beethoven, among others, and he would not have been subtle about it. But whatever his fantasies might have been, there was no realistic chance of marriage. A woman of the nobility who married a commoner lost the privileges of her class; her children could not inherit her title. Few noblewomen were prepared to give up so much, least of all to marry a freelance composer of uncertain income, however celebrated, who was meanwhile homely, hot-tempered, utterly self-involved, and afflicted with chronic diarrhea. The other matter, his growing deafness, he would have kept hidden from Julie.

If Beethoven was strict with his women students, he was surely milder than with the young males. One of those boys ran home crying from a lesson after Beethoven whipped his fingers with a steel knitting needle.[18] (That was Johann van Beethoven's teaching style.) In later years Julie Guicciardi remembered that he insisted on a light touch and drilled her on interpretation to the last detail: "He himself was often violent, throwing the music around and tearing it up." He would not take any payment except linen, if she promised she had sewn it herself. She found he did not particularly like to play his published pieces and preferred to improvise. (For him improvising was the creative future, old pieces were the past; they were merchandise.) He was, she recalled, "very ugly, but noble, sensitive, and cultured. Most of the time he was shabbily dressed."[19] They had proper lessons, perhaps flirted, she gave him an ivory medallion with her picture, he fell into transports. An old tradition says that eventually he proposed, and not Julie but one of her parents squelched it.[20] In any case, her parents married her off to Count Wenzel Robert Gallenberg, a minor composer, in what turned out to be another loveless aristocratic union. Beethoven kept the medallion of Julie Guicciardi in his collection of talismans for the rest of his life.

Standing between Beethoven and the women he yearned for were his health, his high-mindedness, their social position, his eccentricity. Just how outlandish he could be sometimes is seen in a letter he wrote to Julie's mother, Countess Susanna, who had sent him a present as thanks for the free lessons to her daughter. Perhaps in his cups, he dashed off a long, semicoherent, partly ironic complaint. The gist of it seems to be that to pay him for what he considered a gift was to treat him as a common music teacher in it for the money:

> It seemed to me that you wanted to humble my pride by wanting to show me that you wished . . . to put me in your debt than to have the appearance of being in mine. What, after all, did I do to deserve anything like this? None of the time I ever spent at your house was for gain . . . The talent of your daughter and your social ease make me glad to be in your house; why drag in any other whys? No . . . I can't ever completely forgive you for now robbing me entirely of the pleasure of ever giving at least the appearance of seeming an unselfish person. But I shall plan my revenge; this shall consist of my thinking of nothing else than of how to put you so much in my debt . . . that it won't even occur to you to reflect how it would even be possible to dispose of me again in this way.[21]

Here on display is one of the essential factors of Beethoven's life: for well and ill, his response to every challenge was outsized. The greater the challenge, the more aggressive his response. He fought with most of his friends. He often improvised best when he was angry at the audience. He fell in love with unavailable women. His outsized reactions made him a chronically difficult man to get on with. That same drive to overreaction also, more than once, saved his art and saved his life.

His fancied courtship with Julie Guicciardi lingered on into 1802, perhaps until the announcement of her engagement the next year. Whatever feelings of passion and loss he experienced did not slow the tide of ideas washing over him. A nagging dissatisfaction had been growing in his mind for some time, the realization that he had not entirely freed his work of the eighteenth century, had not put any lasting stamp on the music of his time. For whatever reasons, he looked over what he had done and saw it was not good enough. He was still young. He did not realize yet that it would never be good enough.

Sometime in 1801 or 1802, he arrived at another of those reckonings when he willed a change in his life and his art. In his usual laconic fashion he announced to his violinist disciple Wenzel Krumpholz, "I'm not satisfied with what I've composed up to now. From now on I intend to embark on a new path."22

This declaration came not just from dissatisfaction, and it was not that Beethoven had forsworn one path for another. The reality was that, to that point, there had been no path. He had been trying one thing and another, one voice and another. Now he intended to put that wandering behind him, because he had begun to understand who he was as man and artist, which is to say, now he *saw* a path lying before him. It would be in the direction of the voice he wielded in the C Minor Piano Trio of op. 1, in the D Major Piano Sonata of op. 10, and in the *Pathétique*. (Always, though, he would wield more than one voice.) Before long, the New Path would lead him to an overarching and defining metaphor, the figure of the hero.

In other words, Beethoven was ready to become what he had imagined becoming, a figure in the world and in history, and he had begun to see how that could be done on the page. He told Amenda that despite illness and deafness he felt equal to anything. The sureness of purpose he had always possessed amid the contrapuntal uncertainties of life and art was still with him, only now the direction was visible. The works of 1801–2 stand as the first avatars of the New Path.

Those pieces came in the most natural medium for him, in the piano sonatas of opp. 26–28, all from 1801. In that year when he wrote his anguished and defiant letters to Wegeler and Amenda, he was extraordinarily full of creative juice. These first hints of a maturity that would be named for a heroic voice, however, were characterized less by aggressiveness than by a beauty sometimes verging on the uncanny. At the same time, in the piano sonatas of 1801, he mounted singular experiments with the genre and its forms.

In the Grand Sonata in A-flat Major, op. 26, Beethoven fully possessed the voice history would know him by, and at age thirty he was writing music that would place him once and for all in the history of his art. Everything about this sonata seems to be more than anything in the works before: more personal; more innovative in the approach to form (there are no movements in sonata form); more varied in the expressive scope, with fresh kinds of unity. Not least, starting from the gentle beginning, the A-flat Major finds heights of individuality and sheer beauty of expression beyond anything he had reached before. That key at the farthest usable limits of the unequal keyboard tunings of the time, dismissed by theorists as expressing mainly horror, inspired Beethoven to feelings of tenderness, nobility, resignation.

As here, he scaled those heights often with simple means employed with incomparable subtlety. The opening Andante con variazioni of op. 26 is unforgettable in its serene songfulness. (He would have recalled another piano sonata with a beautiful first-movement set of variations: Mozart's A Major, K. 331. But his main model for variations was always Haydn.) The ensuing variations are mostly subdued and inward but with a gathering momentum and great variety of color and texture. The first movement also sets up one of the generating conceptions of op. 26: no overt motivic connections, no steady dramatic unfolding, but rather *the idea of variation itself* as a unifying element. The opening theme sets the pattern by itself infolding a variation:

He placed the scherzo second — a genial and flowing one, its main theme involving continuous variation of its opening measures.

Alongside the sketch for the first-movement theme, Beethoven had written, "[V]aried at once — then Minuetto or some other character piece like for example a March in A♭ minor and then this," followed by a sketch, soon rejected, for the last movement. (He returned to an earlier idea for the finale, which had been the first notation for the sonata in that sketchbook.)[23] Typically, before he got to work on the music for a movement, he could not work properly until he knew its key. To decide on the tonality for a piece was, for him, to decide on its expressive quality. That "character piece" in A-flat minor turned out to be the *Marcia funèbre sulla morte d'un eroe*.

By a character piece he meant something that had an overt topic (military, funereal, pastoral, or the like) from which it did not depart. To write a funeral march was nothing surprising in wartime, with Vienna full of wounded and dying soldiers. At the beginning of 1801, Beethoven had played in a charity concert for the wounded. Specifying "on the death of a hero" was another matter: in the era of the Napoleonic Wars, when funerals were everywhere, Beethoven was beginning to think about heroes and heroism. And funeral marches were a familiar and popular genre in the French revolutionary style.

The main theme of the op. 26 *Funeral March* is not a melody so much as a variation on its dotted rhythm, in dark A-flat minor, its middle section a stretch of musical pictorialism evoking drumrolls and, perhaps, musket shots.[24] Beethoven was to write two more funeral marches in his life, each of them also for soldiers: heroes. The purposeful miscellany of movements in op. 26 comes to rest on a lithe and brilliant rondo made largely from continual variations of its opening figure. The effect is of pulling back from the somber funeral march into something animated but impersonal, like a cleansing rain.

Beethoven hardly took a breath between the remarkable sonatas of that year. Published next would be the two of op. 27, both of them titled *Sonata quasi una fantasia*. By that he implied that they were in the style of a relatively free-form improvisation.[25] Variation and improvisation remained at the core of his creativity, now highlighted in pieces that helped give birth to the New Path. Instead of the usual Allegro, both sonatas open with slow movements, each enigmatic in its way; there are no sonata-form movements in either; in both sonatas the movements run together and the finale is the most intense (the first of his works decisively to take that end-directed shape). Beethoven may have been thinking of the critics who wrote that all his sonatas were wild and formless, like fantasias. Now he intended to demonstrate how a fantasia was done.

Op. 27, no. 1, in E-flat major, ended up the lesser-known of the two, but like all his sonatas it has a singular personality, from stately to haunted to ebullient. Its opening Andante is something of a blank sheet, offering little in the way of melody or passion but a great deal of pregnant material: an opening short–short–long rhythm that will resonate throughout, a falling third and rising fourth that will do likewise. In the middle of this ABA movement, a dashing figure runs amok in glittering roulades. Again a scherzo is placed second, this one in C minor, strange unto ghostly with its falling chromatic whispers punctuated by pouncing *fortes*. An Adagio con espressione lies somewhere between a solemn and aria-like slow movement — with the first sustained melodies in the piece — and a long introduction to the finale. He finishes with a buoyant Allegro vivace rondo with fugal tendencies. Startlingly, the slow movement intrudes again near the end, before a laughing Presto coda that recalls both the rondo theme and the start of the first movement. Thus he ties the knot in drawing the whole together. The point was that, for Beethoven, if a fantasia on paper was not a standard form but a style, an atmosphere, a quasi-improvisation, it still had to be unified.

On publication, the first movement of the *Sonata quasi una fantasia* of op. 27, no. 2, eventually misnamed the *Moonlight*, ascended quickly to feverish popularity, on its way to becoming one of the most famous pieces ever written. Its mythical status was well established in Beethoven's lifetime. The reason is the rapt and dolorous atmosphere unlike anything heard before — and no less the ease with which the opening movement lies under the fingers and within the affections of amateur pianists.

The key is C-sharp minor. C. F. D. Schubart, a poet and aesthetician whose work Beethoven consulted (though hardly followed slavishly), called this rare and solemn tonality suitable for "[p]enitential lamentation, intimate conversation with God . . . signs of disappointed friendship and love."[26] Any or all of these descriptions are appropriate to the uncanny poetry of this work. Nearly everyone who knows music would come to know that first movement, impossible to forget from the first hearing, its endlessly murmuring triplets and hazy colors tinged with mysterious yearning and sorrow. The sonata is dedicated to Julie Guicciardi, and if it is Beethoven's farewell to her, it is a heart-breaking one — but it ends in fury and defiance. Beethoven here gave to music a piercing emotional rhetoric never imagined before.[27] He directs the whole first movement to be played with the sustain pedal down, so the harmonies overlap, one fading into the next, the resonances in the instrument building up as each chord is dwelled on.[28]

By way of relief comes a relaxed scherzo with elegant and winsome themes. Then the most shocking movement of that year's pieces: the finale is marked Presto agitato, which conveys its implacable ferocity. The whispering arpeggios of the first movement have become a torrent of arpeggios that rise to whiplash offbeat chords. As in the previous sonata, the finale is the focus and payoff of the whole. The mystery and incipient tragedy of the first movement have boiled into fury, expressed in a virtuosity that is the antithesis of the first movement's simplicity.

Now, having that year written three sonatas each of which takes a radically distinct direction and embodies a formal experiment, with op. 28, in D major, Beethoven added another whose regular form belied another complete departure. There would be no better demonstration of his unremitting search for variety and contrast than the comparison of this halcyon work to the tumults and innovations of the previous sonatas. The title *Pastoral* was a later publisher's invention, *Pastoral* but at least this time it fits the music, which largely unfolds in sunny serenity. At the beginning, over a long tonic drone a falling melody spins out lazily, repeats, is answered by a companion melody that rises and also repeats, giving notice that this sonata will take its time about things and not depart too far from its basis on the simple tonic triad. After a misty and babbling second theme (actually starting in C-sharp major), the *Durchführung,* the "working out" of themes, falls into a mounting agitation that seems to be suddenly soothed when the da capo, the recapitulation, arrives like a rediscovery of bliss.

There is no real slow movement in the *Pastoral* Sonata but rather a bustling one that combines textures: legato and singing in the right hand, staccato and bouncing in the left. Maybe because of that tricky mingling of touches, Beethoven especially liked to play this second movement.[29] The middle is cheery, but toward the end clouds seem to gather into troubled and ambiguous last measures. A drily witty scherzo shoos the clouds away. The rondo finale's theme recalls the first movement's start, its drones now loping along in a droll, donkey-cart gait, with flowing and yodeling lines above. The intervening sections seem to be trying to get excited about something, but they are tamed by the calming return of the A theme and its donkey cart. Finally the suppressed excitement bursts out in a ebullient, virtuosic coda.

Beethoven's concern with unifying the whole of his pieces does not always show clearly in his sketches. Often what is most fundamental in a piece is what a composer does not need to write down, because it is innate in the conception. But in this case, after jotting an idea for the second movement, Beethoven immediately added a few bars of sketch for a finale, both sketches turning around a galvanizing idea, the fifth D to A in melody and accompaniment.[30] The theme in both sketches begins with a descent from A to D.

The three sonatas of opp. 26–27 were the most stunning items of 1801, but there was more. Among other works of that year came the only string quintet Beethoven completed as such, published as op. 29 in C Major. From his years of listening to chamber music in aristocratic parlors and the readings he mounted in his own rooms, Beethoven knew intimately the Mozart string quintets, the greatest ones in that sonorous medium, some of the few quintets ever to challenge the string-quartet repertoire. It is indicative of Beethoven's burgeoning confidence that his Quintet is not particularly beholden to Mozart. It is a warmly songful work that for all its lightness of spirit has a singular voice and some startling experiments — it amounts to a covertly radical outing. Its broadly flowing opening theme modulates three times in the first eight measures, beginning a piece marked by restless modulations and prophetic tonal patterns — a second theme in A major, a moment in the recapitulation in which the music modulates stepwise, C major–D minor–E minor–F major–G major–A minor: six keys in eight bars.

After a rather *galant* nocturnal slow movement in F major and a frantic C-major scherzo, the Quintet's finale begins on a main theme that amounts to a tremolo shiver plus falling swoops in the violins.

Twice in the course of the finale a new piece of music turns up like an unknown guest at a wedding: a jaunty minuettish tune in 3/4 marked *andante con moto e scherzoso,* the last word indicating "jokingly."[31] A striking work that attracted comparatively little attention in its time or later, the Quintet in the next year was to bring Beethoven a monumental amount of annoyance.

If the Quintet is marked by playfulness of material, key, and form, another work of 1801 is a world away: the cycle of six Gellert lieder, on poems of the pious Leipzig pastor and professor who was one of the *[802* beloved voices of the German Aufklärung. The score is dated March 8, 1802, but ideas for the songs went back several years.[32] Beethoven's settings match the earnest simplicity of the lyrics: mostly simple, short, syllabic, the accompaniments restrained until the climactic last song. That Beethoven turned to the artless North German piety of these poems, and set them in a style more interested in declaiming the words than in waxing lyrical, is another indication of his state of mind. If doctors could not help him, maybe God could, at least in giving him consolation. These songs come from the heart of his anguish and incipient depression:

> *O God, look also upon my lamentation.*
> *My supplication, my sighing are not concealed from You,*
> *and my tears are laid before You.*
> *Oh, God, my God, how long must I be careworn?*
> *How long will You withdraw Yourself from me?*

At the end of 1802, a journal called the *Historic Pocketbook* looked back at the year in music, revealing where Beethoven's First Symphony had ended up in the repertoire. It was "a masterpiece that does equal honor to his inventiveness and his musical knowledge . . . there prevails in it such a clear and lucid order, such a flow of the most pleasant melodies, and such a rich . . . instrumentation that this symphony can justly be placed next to Mozart's and Haydn's." As usual, the newer pieces would have to make their way against a resisting tide: "Impartial connoisseurs were not as pleased with Beethoven's most recent fortepiano works that . . . conspicuously strove to be unusual and original, only too often at the cost of beauty." "Pleasing," for this reviewer, was still the highest praise. Excessive originality earned the terms "peculiarity, which verges on the fantastic."

The *Allgemeine Musikalische Zeitung*, however, had now put more progressive critics on Beethoven's case. The review of the three sonatas of opp. 26 and 27 in June says,

> They are a true enrichment and belong among the few products of the present year that will hardly ever become obsolete; certainly [the *Moonlight*] can never become obsolete . . . This fantasia is one solid whole from beginning to end; it arises all at once from an undivided, profound, and intimately excited heart and is cut, as it were, from one block of marble. It is probably not possible that any human being to whom nature has not denied inner music should not be stirred by the first *Adagio* . . . and be guided higher and higher, and then as intimately moved and as highly elevated by the *Presto agitato* as free-composed keyboard music can elevate him. These two principal movements are written in the terrifying key of C♯ minor with consummate reason.

Less than a year old, the *Moonlight* Sonata was ascending toward ubiquity and legend. And now "terrifying" could be a term of approval. Necessary to Beethoven's triumph was a new generation that expected more from music than the "innocent luxury" Charles Burney had called it a quarter century before. One voice of the new generation, Wilhelm Wackenroder, wrote in a novel about his hero's feeling for music: "Many passages were so vivid and engaging that the notes seemed to speak to him. At other times the notes would evoke a mysterious blend of joy and sorrow in his heart, so that he could have either laughed or cried. This is a feeling that we experience so often on our path through life and that no art can express more skillfully than music . . . That is the marvelous gift of music, which affects us the more powerfully and stirs all our vital forces the more deeply, the vaguer and more mysterious its language is."[33] There is no record of whether Beethoven read these words or what he knew at this point about the Romantic sensibility. If he did read them, they must have reassured him that there were people out there ready to understand him.

Around April 1802, on the advice of his new favored doctor, Johann Adam Schmidt, Beethoven retired for a planned stay of six months to quiet and beautiful Heiligenstadt, one of the villages amid the trees and vineyards of the Vienna woods, a few miles from the city. He took rooms upstairs off the courtyard of a peasant-style house at 13 Herrengasse (later Probusgasse), his outside windows looking to hills and fields and the Danube, in the distance the Carpathian Mountains. The mineral baths of the spa were a few minutes' walk away.[34] His doctor wanted him to rest his ears and regain some health and strength, but he was planning no vacation. Heiligenstadt was close enough for friends and family to visit; among those who came were Ferdinand Ries and brother Carl. Beethoven arrived eager and full of hope that this cure amid the beauty of nature would restore his health and his spirit, maybe even arrest the decline of his hearing.

His ongoing creative fury burned even brighter during this nominal vacation that climaxed in one of the devastating moments of his life. The Heiligenstadt summer of 1802 was blisteringly productive. With him he had brought sketchbooks filling up with ideas and drafts and the nearly finished Second Symphony, a work that, for all its laughter, is far weightier, bolder, and more mature than the First. As he got down to work, his daily walks were not around the battlements of Vienna but through woods and vineyards and alongside brooks.

Trying to gain more time to write and to free himself from selling his notes, he handed off some of his dealings to an agent, writing Breitkopf & Härtel in March 1802, "I propose, sir, to write to you myself very soon — a good deal of business — and also a great many worries — have rendered me for a time quite useless for some things — Meanwhile you can rely entirely on my brother — who, in general, attends to all my affairs."[35] As an agent, Caspar Carl van Beethoven, now working as a minor tax official in Vienna, proved a slowly unfolding disaster. Carl had the family impatience and quick temper with little of Ludwig's intelligence and still less of his talent. Chipping in, Carl wrote Härtel, "At present we have three sonatas for the piano and violin, and if they please you, then we shall send them. My brother would have written to you himself, but he is not inclined to do anything just now, because the Theater Director Baron von Braun, who is known to be a stupid and crude fellow, has refused him the Theater for his concert and has rented it to the most mediocre artists."[36]

One of Carl's initiatives was nearly to double the asking prices for Ludwig's pieces, and he had success in some quarters — though at the same time Carl's initiatives largely quashed the interest of Breitkopf & Härtel, who wanted things as cheap as possible. Ludwig had sold the First Symphony and the Septet for 90 florins each; Carl demanded and got some 170 florins for the String Quintet. On his own initiative, he tried to persuade Härtel to pay for a series of arrangements of pieces certified by Ludwig but not written by him. Härtel rejected the idea, and Ludwig actually wrote Härtel commending his judgment: "Concerning the arrangements of the pieces, I am heartily glad that you rejected them. The unnatural rage now prevalent to transplant even pianoforte pieces to stringed instruments, instruments so utterly opposite to each other in all respects, ought to come to an end. I insist stoutly that only Mozart could arrange his pianoforte pieces for other instruments, and also Haydn."[37] All the same, in coming years Beethoven would follow the fashion of the time in issuing multiple versions of many of his works, often advertised as *arrangé par l'auteur même,* when in fact that was true of only a few. Earlier ones included an arrangement of the Septet for piano trio and the Piano Quintet with winds turned into a piano quartet with strings. His student Ferdinand Ries recalled that many pieces "were arranged by me, revised by Beethoven, and then sold as Beethoven's by his brother."[38]

Carl apparently got into the habit of rummaging in Ludwig's manuscripts and sending stray items to publishers on his own; some of those pieces Ludwig had no desire to let see the light of day. There were other wrangles over practical matters. When Ludwig finished the piano sonatas of eventually op. 31 that summer of 1802, the brothers had an ongoing argument about which publisher to give them to. Beethoven had promised them to Nägeli in Zürich, and was outraged when he found Carl had offered them to Breitkopf & Härtel in hopes of more money.

It was over the op. 31 Sonatas that Heiligenstadt was entertained one day by the sight of the Beethoven brothers slugging it out on the street. The next day Ludwig, nursing his bruises, ordered Ferdinand Ries to send the sonatas to Nägeli. He also gave Ries a letter for Carl with a "beautiful sermon" about Carl's behavior: "First he showed him the true, despicable character of his conduct, then forgave him completely, but also predicted a miserable future for him if he did not radically change his life and behavior."[39] At least so recalled Ries, who despised both Beethoven's brothers. The following year Ries wrote to Simrock back in Bonn, "Charl [*sic*] Beethoven is the biggest skinflint in the world — for a single ducat he would take back 50 words of promise, and his good brother makes the greatest enemies because of him." In any case, Carl continued his efforts as before. When questioned or criticized about it, Beethoven was quick to defend him, explaining, "After all, he is my brother."[40]

In the first weeks the sun and serenity of Heiligenstadt seemed to have a vitalizing effect on Beethoven. Between March and May he drafted the three violin sonatas of op. 30. All are relatively good-natured pieces, even no. 2, in C minor, only modestly fiery compared to the storms that that key usually roused in him. All in all, these are the freshest of his violin sonatas so far. Here he stands at the point of making his escape from Mozart in a medium in which he had always kept his audacity under wraps.

Nonetheless, once again, violin sonatas provoked him to wide-ranging tonal excursions. The development of the C Minor, no. 2, first movement touches on nine keys before making its way back to the tonic. Perhaps the glory of the set is the slow movement of no. 2, a touching Adagio cantabile with no lingering hints of the eighteenth-century *galant* but rather an inward and spiritual atmosphere of wonderful beauty. This movement owes little to the expressive rhetoric of the past; there is a sense of a powerful, fresh, and authentic music emerging that Beethoven was still learning to manage. If not that movement, the crown of the set might be the opening of no. 3, in G major, which begins with a swirling unison followed by a lilting (and a touch tipsy) theme, complete with hiccup in the violin.[41] The rondo of the G Major is one of the most deliciously whimsical finales he ever wrote, its theme a spinning folk tune over a bagpipe drone, starting a brilliant and smile-inducing movement unlike anything else in his work. Call it Haydnesque wit and folksiness gone deliriously over the top.

For the first sonata, in A Major, Beethoven drafted a finale he concluded was too long and obstreperous for the piece. He replaced it with a theme and variations, and put the rejected finale on the shelf in hopes it might serve something sometime. It certainly did. He dedicated op. 30 to the newly crowned tsar Alexander I. Reared by his grandmother Catherine the Great, Russia's own benevolent despot, Alexander was a sovereign of liberalizing ambitions and at that point a professed admirer of Napoleon. Beethoven's dedication, then, was deliberately to a figure famously allied to enlightened ideals — who might also be moved to do something for a composer now and then.

Then Beethoven returned to keyboard works. The three piano sonatas of op. 31 that he wrote that summer would all be historic, each innovative in a distinctive way, the outer ones vivacious and the middle one tragic.

Each begins with a gesture unprecedented in the literature. No. 1 in G Major starts with a ripping downward scale followed by two-fisted chords that seem to be a joke about pianists who can't get their hands together. Myriad variants of ripping scales and arpeggios and out-of-sync chords constitute much of the material of a jovial first movement. The following Adagio grazioso seems retrospective, gracefully spinning out into a long, mellifluous nocturne whose main theme recalls Mozart at his more decorative, but the rest is Beethovenian in its far-ranging moods, rich harmonies, and dazzling pianistic colors. The warmth of the slow movement seems to merge into a gracious finale, alternately flowing lazily and dashing spiritedly, sometimes uniting those qualities. A few pensive moments drift by, but it ends with gleeful shouts and whispers.

In forging op. 31, no. 2 in D Minor, Beethoven had to have known he was playing with fire. For all its fury and fatefulness, he made sure it was nonetheless taut. This was to be one of the works that cemented his reputation for the dark, the unique in voice, the incomparably dramatic. It provided for listeners, critics, perhaps for Beethoven himself an unmistakable signpost toward the New Path he was setting out on. Later dubbed *The Tempest,* more for its stormy atmosphere than for a connection to Shakespeare's romantic drama (though a story lingered that he related it to the play), the sonata is an unforgettable human document.[42]

With a disquieting quietness, *The Tempest* begins on a whispering arpeggio of uncertain tonality that erupts into a driving Allegro. Quiet descends abruptly again, then the pattern repeats with insistent but still more ambiguous harmonies. From the beginning Beethoven does violence to the formal traditions of an eighteenth-century first movement, with its expected clear first and second themes and unequivocal tonal outline. Instead, here the form asks questions: Is the first harmony here the tonic chord? (No, it is a V6.) Are the opening arpeggio and first Allegro a theme or an introduction? (They are either or both.) What is the first theme proper? (It is probably the whirling, driving theme of measure 21, which starts with the first clear D-minor cadence in the piece.)[43] The indistinct form amplifies the uncertainties of the nervous rhythms and themes. This is *expressive form.* The movement takes an enigmatic course that includes a constant background of driving, demonic energy, with the development section a period of comparative calm. The recapitulation falls into moments of mournful quasi-recitative, as if the music were struggling for words that cannot be spoken.

Another quiet arpeggio opens a time-stopping slow movement, dark and fateful despite its major key, troubled by distant drums, its moments of hope fraught and inconclusive. The end of the movement is a chilling evocation of emptiness. Later Carl Czerny said the finale was inspired by a horse galloping past Beethoven's window. If so, in this music horse and rider are spreading alarm. The finale is relentless, obsessive, virtually monothematic, with a churning intensity like some unstoppable machinery of fate. There ends a sonata as intense as any ever written to that time, as bold and innovative as any, yet executed with the most luminous clarity of means and purpose. From this point forward, that joining of passion and lucidity would mark most of Beethoven's highest achievements.

Then, the opposite. Beethoven begins op. 31, no. 3 in E-flat, with a harmony so strange that it would have earned him more cries of *bi-zarre* from critics if it did not commence a work of surpassing warmth, wit, and winsomeness.[44] The beginning is an invitation, like a hand extended in friendship or love. That drifts into a blithe and whimsical first theme, a recall of the invitation, and a flowing and almost child-like second theme whose rippling delight simply wants to keep going. The coda seems to reflect contentedly on the invitation figure and the cheery second theme.

What amounts to a scherzo for the second movement is in a bouncy two-beat instead of the usual quick three-beat, its main theme a lurch-ing and comical tune with Beethoven's trademark offbeat accents. Fol-lowing the scherzo, most unexpectedly, comes a graceful and lyrical minuet — he wanted no slow movement to trouble the warm weather of this sonata. For conclusion, a tarantella marked Presto con fuoco, with the fire appropriate to that old whirling dance in which, once upon a time, you hoped to survive the bite of the tarantula by dancing to exhaustion.[45] Its tireless churning is the equivalent of the same in the D Minor Sonata, but here to ebullient ends.

At the same time that Beethoven worked on the opp. 30 and 31 sona-tas, he wrote two deliberately groundbreaking sets of piano variations, opp. 34 and 35. The first, in F major, is a smaller work on a delicately wistful theme of his own. The tone of the whole is lighthearted, but in its way it fractures the decorum of its formal model as decisively as did *The Tempest*. Traditionally a set of variations sticks to the key of the theme, with perhaps an excursion to the parallel minor. Here Beethoven presents each variation in its own key, and those keys form a descending chain of thirds: F–D–B-flat–G–E-flat–C minor, then back to F for a joyous and nostalgic close.[46] Changing keys in a set of variations was, for Beethoven, necessarily a matter of changing char-acters as well, or rather reinforcing the traditional changes of charac-ter in variations. Each key had its distinctive tuning on the keyboard and an allied expressive feel, for example, the G-major variation racing and gay, the E-flat stately, the C-minor fateful (though here detectably ironic, faux fateful).

In the op. 35 Variations, Beethoven took up the bass line and *eng-*

lische melody from the end of the *Prometheus* ballet (by then also used as a theme in a set of contredanses). The unique idea here, as he labeled the first sections in the score, is to start the piece with only the naked bass line of the theme: *Introduzione col Basso del Tema.* Then follow a series of variations adding a voice at a time, labeled *a due, a tre, a quattro,* until we arrive in variation 4 at music under the heading *Thema (aus dem Ballet "Die Geschöpfe des Prometheus").*

Here again in pieces of summer 1802, the nature of the form poses a fundamental question: what actually *is* the theme — the bass line, or the treble *englische* melody that does not turn up until the fourth variation? Or to put it another way, this is a singular set of variations that amounts, in the beginning, to a bass line searching for its melody as a kind of fulfillment. The rest of the piece proceeds with a sense that the abiding, generating presence is the *basso* that flaunts its elemental simplicity. For Beethoven, that blunt and ingenuous little bass theme already seemed to possess an iconic significance, not just in its structure but in its character — not just a dance but some kind of ethos.

The next variations spin Bachian counterpoint around the bass theme, which rises an octave on each iteration. A neo-Bachian flavor turns up again in the canonic variation 7.[47] When the *englische* melody turns up it is presented straightforwardly, as a lilting dance with oompah accompaniment. As with op. 34, the tone of the set is generally cheerful; Beethoven gets some high comedy out of the thumping B-flats in the theme's refrain. The pianism is as brilliant and imaginative as anything he had done. It ends with a grand Bachian fugue on the *Prometheus* theme. In the middle of the last section, the unadorned *englische* theme puts in a final, nostalgic appearance before the bravura finish.

When he first sent the new variations to Breitkopf & Härtel, Beethoven included some uncharacteristic but not exaggerated boasting about their innovations:

> As my brother is writing to you, I am just adding the following information — I have composed two sets of variations . . . Both sets are worked out in quite a <u>new manner,</u> and each in a <u>separate and different way.</u> I would infinitely prefer to have them engraved by you, <u>but</u>

on no other condition than for a fee of 50 ducats [ca. 250 florins] for both sets — . . . Usually I have to wait for other people to tell me when I have new ideas, because I never know this myself. But this time — I myself can assure you that in both these works the method is quite new so far as I am concerned —

This was perhaps the worst way to pitch the piece to this publisher. Härtel had already revealed himself as uninterested in taking risks, and his offers had been low. Much as Beethoven wanted the Breitkopf & Härtel logo on his music, however, he was having none of that: "What you wrote to me once about the endeavor to sell my works I cannot endorse. Surely it is an outstanding proof of the excellent sale of my works that nearly all foreign publishers are continually writing to me for compositions, and that even those who pirate engraved works, about whom you rightly complain, are to be found among this number."[48]

In the midst of all this work, a letter arrived from publisher Hoffmeister in Leipzig. An aristocratic lady had offered to commission the famous composer to write a "revolutionary sonata." Clearly the musical world had come to associate Beethoven with that spirit. In his high-ironic, figuratively or literally intoxicated reply to Hoffmeister, full of dashes like hiccups, Beethoven first scoffs at the lady's offer, then accepts it:

Has the devil got hold of you all, gentlemen? — that you suggest that I should compose such a sonata — Well, perhaps at the time of the revolutionary fever — such a thing might have been possible, but now, when everything is trying to slip back into the old rut, now that Bonaparte has concluded his Concordat with the Pope — to write a sonata of that kind? — If it were even a Missa pro Sancta Maria a tre voci, or a Vesper or something of that kind — In that case I would instantly take up my paintbrush — and with fat pound notes dash off a Credo in unum. But, good heavens, such a sonata — in these newly developing Christian times — Ho ho — there you must leave me out — you won't get anything from me — Well, here is my reply in the fastest tempo — The lady can have a sonata from me, and, moreover, from an aesthetic point of view I will in general adopt her plan —

but without adopting — her keys — The price would be about [250 florins].[49]

When his reply including the asking price was relayed to the lady, a Countess von Kielmansegge, she took back the offer indignantly, writing to Hoffmeister's partner, "You yourself will see, dear Herr Kühnel, how much Herr Beethoven has demanded and how unreasonable this is."[50]

Beethoven's puckish letter about the proposed sonata is remarkable on the face of it and, in some immeasurable degree, historic in its aftermath. As far as he was concerned, the revolutionary period was dead; that was the 1780s, his youth, climaxed by the French Revolution. Now it seemed to him pointless to write a piece of music on a social or political theme that was old news — and that also might draw the attention of the police in Vienna. If he was going to write a politically inspired piece, he wanted the political import to be current.

It seems also that for the moment he was not buying the idea of Napoleon as the fulfillment of the Revolution. Things were going back to "the old rut." With his anticlerical instincts, Beethoven scorned the Concordat signed by Pius VII in July 1801, in which Napoleon declared that the French government would end the official separation of church and state that the Revolution had imposed. While not agreeing to a state religion as such, and reserving the right of the government to appoint bishops, Napoleon conceded Catholicism to be "the religion of the majority of the French people." With the Concordat, Napoleon adroitly took from French conservatives and counterrevolutionaries their main issue, the suppression of the church.[51] Privately, Napoleon said, "They will say I am a papist, but I am nothing at all. In Egypt I was a Muhammedan; here I will be a Catholic, for the good of the people."[52]

Beethoven hints that he'd be ready to write a sacred work if commissioned, even though he also has minimal personal interest in that idea "in these newly developing Christian times" — developing, he appears to mean, in the direction of cynical expediency. In this analysis of the current state of politics — what an acquaintance called his "favorite subject" — he was, as usual, informed and astute.

Yet the lady's offer had money attached; he was not ready to reject it out of hand. She could have her sonata not about revolution specifically but along those lines, "aesthetically," in the tone of the music. So the historic part of the lady's offer and Beethoven's reply is that they may have brought him another step toward a characteristic piece with a revolutionary flavor but a more contemporary subject. In those days he was finishing his Second Symphony, perhaps working on a piano concerto in C minor, taking up the *Prometheus* material again for some piano variations, and writing piano works that showed the world what his New Path amounted to. Likely by the time he finished the *Prometheus* Variations he had decided to use the theme of *Prometheus* as the finale of another work, not a sonata but a symphony, with which he intended to show the world what a revolutionary symphony was.

Beethoven had come to Heiligenstadt full of hope, and there in the summer of 1802 he was breathtakingly productive. His letters in those months reflect his usual tone, being businesslike, chipper, wry, and full of beans. He was jousting with publishers more than ever, trying to parlay the boiling fever of his inspiration into fortune and fame. He was creating some of the most extraordinary music of his life, or anyone's life. But all that together could not save him from the crash that was waiting for him. The medical advice to rest in the country came to nothing. His hearing got worse. After years of denial and defiance and desperate appeals to doctors, his curtain of defenses slipped, fate turned its full malevolent gaze on him, and his spirit filled with despair unto death.

16

Oh, Fellow Men

THE LETTER BEETHOVEN wrote in Heiligenstadt to his brothers Johann and Caspar is dated October 6, 1802. The three pages and later addendum, written in his upstairs room looking out to autumnal fields and hills, were apparently never mailed. Though the letter was torn from his heart, it was not scribbled down like most of his correspondence, but considered, sketched, then written out in fair copy. It may have been intended to be found after his death from age or illness or accident, or sooner by his own hand. After it was read by his brothers he hoped it would be published, to enlighten people about how they had scorned and misunderstood him. So it was a letter to the world too. Three times he left a blank space representing the name Johann. Always Ludwig detested writing a name or even a word that pained him, so it seems that at the time brother Johann pained him.

The letter became one of the talismans he kept always with him, perhaps the most important of those talismans. The others were keepsakes from lost loves. This was a keepsake from lost joy in life. Likely over the years he took the letter out of its hiding place in his desk, unfolded it, and read it over to remind himself what he had resolved his life was to be and why, and how close he had come to death before he created his true work.

He begins the letter with a review of his goodness, his bitterness, his ambition, his loneliness. His state of mind at that moment is that of the human soul he had painted earlier that summer, in the D Minor Piano Sonata: a moment of intense despair in contemplating the mechanism of fate, and also a moment of intense clarity:

For my brothers Karl and   Beethoven.

Oh you men who think or say that I am malevolent, stubborn or misanthropic, how greatly do you wrong me. You do not know the secret cause which makes me seem that way to you. From childhood on my heart and soul have been full of the tender feeling of goodwill, and I was ever inclined to accomplish great things. But, think that for 6 years now I have been hopelessly afflicted, made worse by senseless doctors, from year to year deceived with hopes of improvement, finally compelled to face the prospect of a lasting malady (whose cure will take years, or perhaps be impossible). Though born with a fiery, active temperament, even susceptible to the diversions of society, I was soon compelled to withdraw myself, to live life alone. If at times I tried to forget all this, oh how harshly was I flung back by the doubly sad experience of my bad hearing. Yet it was impossible for me to say to people, "Speak louder, shout, for I am deaf."

Ah, how could I possibly admit an infirmity in the one sense which ought to be more perfect in me than in others, a sense which I once possessed in the highest perfection, a perfection such as few in my profession enjoy or ever have enjoyed. — Oh I cannot do it, therefore forgive me when you see me draw back when I would have gladly mingled with you. My misfortune is doubly painful to me because I am bound to be misunderstood; for me there can be no relaxation with my fellow-men, no refined conversations, no mutual exchange of ideas . . . I must live almost alone like an exile.

. . . Thus it has been during the last six months which I have spent in the country. By ordering me to spare my hearing as much as possible, my intelligent doctor almost fell in with my own present frame of mind, though sometimes I ran counter to it by yielding to my desire for companionship. But what a humiliation for me when someone standing next to me heard a flute in the distance and I heard nothing, or someone heard a shepherd singing and again I heard nothing. Such incidents drove me almost to despair, a little more of that and I would have ended my life.

It is no surprise that his affliction brought him to the brink of suicide. It would be surprising if it did not. If he was to live, he must understand that he would live in misery, and there must be a reason to endure that misery:

φ suicide

It was only my art that held me back. Oh, it seemed impossible to me to leave this world before I had produced all that I felt capable of producing, and so I prolonged this wretched existence — truly wretched for so susceptible a body that a sudden change can plunge me from the best into the worst of states.

He recapitulates what he had written to Wegeler and Amenda about his illness: the pathetic consolation of patience is his only choice. He drifts back to the feeling that he is wronged and misunderstood. He invokes God, turns the letter into a will, becomes the wise and magnanimous big brother, recalls other friends and his most valued worldly possessions, the quartet of string instruments Prince Lichnowsky had given him. At the moment, he believes he is three years younger than he actually is.

Patience, they say, is what I must now choose for my guide, and I have patience done so — I hope my determination will remain firm to endure until it pleases the inexorable Parcae to break the thread. Perhaps I shall get better, perhaps not, I am ready. — Forced to become a philosopher already in my 28th year, oh it is not easy, and for the artist much more difficult than for anyone else. — Divine One, thou seest my inmost soul, thou knowest that therein dwells the love of humanity and the desire to do good — Oh fellow men, when at some point you read this, consider then that you have done me an injustice . . .

You my brothers Carl and　　　as soon as I am dead if Dr.

Schmidt is still alive ask him in my name to describe my malady, and attach this written document to his account of my illness so that so far as it is possible at least the world may become reconciled to me after my death. — At the same time I declare you two to be the heirs to my small fortune (if it can be called that); divide it fairly: bear with and help each other. What injury you have done to me you know was long ago forgiven.

To you, brother Carl I give special thanks for the attachment you have shown me of late. It is my wish that you may have a better and freer life than I have had. Recommend <u>virtue</u> to your children; it alone, not money, can make them happy. I speak from experience; this was what upheld me in time of misery. Thanks to it and to my art I did not end my life by suicide — Farewell and love each other.

I thank all my friends, particularly <u>Prince Lichnowsky</u> and <u>Professor Schmidt</u> — I would like the instruments from Prince L to be preserved by one of you, but not to be the cause of strife between you, and as soon as they can serve you a better purpose, then sell them. How happy I shall be if I can still be helpful to you in my grave — so be it —

He would not kill himself — not yet — but still, with great clarity, he understood how much death could relieve him of, even at the moment when he knew he was rising toward his best work:

<u>With joy I hasten to meet death — If it comes before I have had the chance to develop all my artistic capacities</u>, it will still come too soon despite my harsh fate and I should probably wish it later — yet even so I should be happy, for would it not free me from a state of endless suffering? — Come <u>when</u> thou wilt, I shall meet thee bravely — Farewell and do not wholly forget me when I am dead, I deserve this from you, for during my lifetime I was thinking of you often and of ways to make you happy — please be so —
Ludwig van Beethoven

Beethoven folds the letter the world will someday name the Heiligenstadt Testament and presses his seal to the wax. He notes the place and time. He addresses it "For my brothers Carl and   to be read and executed after my death." Three days later, he adds a frenzied addition on the outside of the letter. He falls into his dashes, his breathless mode, as if gasping — or drunk. This has not been part of the draft, part of the plan. This is the true cry from the cross:

∅ Cure

> Heiglnstadt [*sic*], October 10th, 1802, thus I bid you farewell — and indeed sadly — yes, that fond hope — which I brought here with me, to be cured to a degree at least — this I must now wholly abandon. As the leaves of autumn fall and are withered — so likewise my hope has been blighted — I leave here — almost as I came — even the high courage — which often inspired me in the beautiful days of summer — has disappeared — Oh Providence — grant me at last but one day of <u>pure joy</u> — it is so long since real joy echoed in my heart — Oh when — Oh when, Oh divine One — shall I feel it again in the temple of nature and of mankind — Never? — No — Oh that would be too hard.[1]

He means the joy that was more than the pleasures of a good life. For an Aufklärer, joy was at the center of everything: life, liberty, and the pursuit of happiness; Schiller's god-engendered daughter of Elysium. Or call it peace, hope, joie de vivre, joy in work and in love. The things chronic pain and disease rob you of. That is the subject of his frantic last words, because that is what he feared most.

This was his last word, after he had written into the letter proper the idea that would sustain him: *It was only my art that held me back. Oh, it seemed impossible to me to leave this world before I had produced all that I felt capable of producing, and so I prolonged this wretched existence.* There was no posturing in those words. It was the truth. At some point he would no longer be able to function properly at the keyboard. He could have little hope for an end to deafness and painful illness. He had no children or anyone who truly needed him. Art was all he had left.

Here with passion, anguish, clarity, and insight, Beethoven wrote of what lay on his heart. There is one thing he did *not* say that tells a great deal about him. Twice he calls on God, who sees and understands what he suffers. He believes in God, he believes God sees his heart and understands. But he does not say, "I must do what God put me here to do." His gifts come from nature; the will to accomplish great things is his own. He does not believe God is chastising him. As authors of his fate he names the mythical Parcae. He does not pray for miracles because he does not believe in them — even if only a miracle could restore his health. His relationship to God would change and deepen over the years, he would draw closer, he would pray. But years later when a protégé wrote on a score, "Finished with the help of God," Beethoven wrote under it, "O Man, help yourself!"

It is easy enough to declare, *Help yourself*. But to suffer without hope, without believing that the suffering has some larger meaning and purpose, requires great courage. For an artist to continue growing and working at the highest level without hope takes still greater courage. Beethoven had something near as much courage as a human being can have. From this moment on, without hope and, he feared, without joy, he needed to be heroic just to live and to work. The Heiligenstadt Testament shows that he understood this with excruciating clarity. True heroism is usually called for in the face of suffering and death. It is rarely joyful. But in the letter Beethoven vowed to live with suffering and for his art, and he kept vows like that. His crisis had little observable effect on his output. In his work he had been soaring, and he was about to soar higher.[2]

After the Heiligenstadt Testament, that moment of clarity, what happened in Beethoven's life and work? The pattern of his life changed once and for all. His posture in the world had been as a budding master of his art, a virtuoso, a generalissimo, a conqueror laughing at the admiration he aroused. Now he was at the mercy of something he had never encountered before, a malevolent fate beyond the force of his will. It would not be long before the hopeless path of resignation turned to a path of fist-shaking defiance, and that was the right path for him as a still-young man.

On the most elemental level, the decline of his hearing meant that he had to let go of a long-cherished view of himself as pianist-composer. Since childhood he had devoted much of his time and energy to making himself the virtuoso he was. Much of his reputation in Vienna and elsewhere had come from his playing. In losing his hearing, not only was he losing his most prized sense but with the end of his performing career he also was going to lose part of his identity and half or more of his income.

In the next years, while his hearing was in some degree still functional, he would perform on occasion, if rarely publicly. But in 1802, the prospect of having someday to let go of the piano was part of his anguish. At around this point, it appears, he stopped practicing. He had written twenty piano sonatas, most of them in some eight years. He would write only a dozen more, and only two more violin sonatas. The prospect of having to earn a living as purely a freelance composer may have frightened him, as it should have. Bach, Mozart, Haydn — none of them had lived mainly on their earnings as a composer. He could sell anything he wrote, but the fees were small. His most ambitious pieces, concertos and symphonies and choral works, paid proportionately worst of all because they were the least salable.

In all this may lie one fundamental aspect of the stupendous level of creativity he was about to launch into. The crisis of October 1802 confirmed that now Beethoven's life was composing and nothing else. Another element had to do with despair. The reality of being an artist, for most artists, is that it must be on the order of a life-and-death matter or it will not succeed at the highest level a given creator can achieve, whatever that may be. An artist needs to cling to art like a survivor clings to a spar in the middle of the ocean. That was the position Beethoven now found himself in.

The crisis did not forge the New Path but rather made it mandatory. There would be no more of trying this and that. It was do or die, and for Beethoven now that was no metaphor, it was the simple truth. He was not above writing commercial pieces, but to devote most of his time to them was not an option for him. In his serious work, for the first time he had in his grasp *how* to do what he needed to do. By the time he wrote the unmailed letter to his brothers and to the world, he was planning a concert in Vienna that in effect drew a line between the past and the future. He already saw the next step after that: the Third Symphony.

In all things with Beethoven the stronger the challenge, the more

aggressive and outsized his response. The depth of his despair was answered by the opposite forces of his will, his courage, his defiance of
fate.

Soon after writing the Heiligenstadt Testament, Beethoven returned
to Vienna and got back to work — on the surface, at least, as if nothing
had happened. For the moment, for some incomprehensible reason,
given the state of his hearing, he had taken a corner house on the Pe-
tersplatz, where his ears would be assaulted by the bells of St. Stephen's
on one side and St. Peter's on the other.³ Friends including Carl Czerny
and Anton Reicha visited him. He heard about *Lodoïska,* the new opera from France by Luigi Cherubini that had made a sensation in Vienna. He got busy looking for a libretto for himself.

For his upcoming benefit concert, Beethoven decided to write an
oratorio on the passion of Christ. He pitched the new piano variations
to Breitkopf & Härtel. He placed in the town paper, the *Wiener Zeitung,* a scathing notice that a string-quartet arrangement of his op. 20
Septet, by then a big success, was pirated.⁴ At that point he was not the
most popular and performed composer in Vienna, but he was becoming the most circulated of his generation in print.⁵

Then arrived a proper public row to rouse his fighting instincts. At
the beginning of November 1802, he got a letter from Breitkopf & Härtel giving him hope that his months-long campaign to get them committed to his work was paying off. Having already taken on the new
String Quintet, they agreed to publish the piano variations, opp. 34 and
35, and to pay for them a decent if not generous 225 florins (some three
months' food and shelter). In the letter, Gottfried Härtel notes that
they would like to publish more of his music. "Unfortunately, however,
it has come to pass in Germany, with [the appearance of] every interesting new work, the pirate reprinters now often follow suit, so that the
legitimate printers ... often cannot sell a tenth as many copies as the
pirate can." (This was hardly news to Beethoven.) Härtel went on to
say the String Quintet op. 29 was engraved and the proofs forthcoming, and he enclosed an opera libretto for Beethoven to consider (he
sent it back). For good measure, Härtel turned down the two violin
Romances Beethoven had offered; they eventually became opp. 40 and

50.[6] The Romances are lyrical and manifestly beautiful, but Härtel did not want to pay for engraving an orchestral work of unusual genre, with many times the notes of a piano piece.

Then to his astonishment and outrage, Beethoven learned that Artaria, his first publisher in Vienna, was about to put out the String Quintet without his knowledge. Its dedicatee and probably commissioner, Count Fries, had given his copy of the piece to Artaria, and the company essentially stole it. This put Beethoven in a nasty bind with Breitkopf & Härtel, threatening to destroy his carefully cultivated relationship with them. He informed Gottfried Härtel of the atrocity by "the archvillains Artaria . . . the whole affair is the greatest swindle in the world."[7] Härtel was duly appalled: "That Artaria came by the manuscript of your Quintet is certainly only your own fault; since you assured us in writing that this work should be our exclusive property . . . you alone are responsible if serious consequences arise from it."[8] Now, Beethoven was facing a costly debacle because of his own popularity. Carl hardly calmed the waters with a complaint to Härtel about the tone of the letter to his brother:

> You have written my brother a letter that, if necessary at all, is more appropriate to a schoolboy but not an artist like Beethoven. You would not dare write such a letter to Herr Haydn . . . I have already endured two violent storms on your account, because I explained to him that [the letter] which you wrote was done only in the first heat and was not very prudent . . . Also I am sending you the enclosed *Revers* [retraction] signed by Artaria for your inspection. This *Revers* cost my brother seven days, during which he could do nothing [else], and [it cost] me innumerable trips and unpleasantnesses, and the loss of my dog.[9]

With no legal recourse for Artaria's piracy, Beethoven blasted the company with everything he could think of. He demanded and got the *Revers,* the signed statement Carl mentioned, admitting that its printing was unauthorized, and an assurance that its edition would not come out until two weeks after Breitkopf & Härtel's edition reached the shelves in Vienna. Receiving fifty copies from Artaria for proofing, which in fact were wretchedly engraved, Beethoven instructed his pupil Ferdinand Ries to make so many and elaborate corrections that the copies would be unusable.[10] Having made sure Artaria's printed copies were ruined, he put a notice in the paper saying its edition was "extremely faulty, inaccurate, and quite useless for the performer, whereas Herren Breitkopf & Härtel, the lawful owners of this quintet, have done their utmost to produce the work as handsomely as possible." This in turn outraged Artaria, which instituted and won a suit that required Beethoven to publish a retraction. He never got around to it. The affair trickled out in 1803.[11]

Despite everything, Härtel asked to see more music. In November, Carl offered two large works that had yet to be premiered: "At present . . . we have nothing but a Symphony and a grand Concerto for Piano; the former is 300 florins, the latter is the same price." He mentions three piano sonatas, perhaps not yet composed; or, astoundingly, he may be inviting Härtel to print the op. 31 Sonatas that Ludwig, after their fistfight in the street, had sent to Nägeli in Zürich. And that's it for sonatas, Carl adds, "because my brother no longer troubles himself very much with such trifles, and writes only oratorios, operas, etc."[12]

At the same time, Beethoven had reason to regret giving op. 31 to Nägeli. When the proofs of nos. 1 and 2 arrived from the publisher, he asked Ries to sit at the piano and play over the proofs for him while he worked at his desk. Ries's reading uncovered a pile of engraving mistakes in no. 1. The climax came when Ries played a bland little phrase and found Beethoven rocketing out of his chair crying, "*Where the hell does it say that?*" Beethoven all but shoved Ries away from the piano to have a look at the page.[13] To the disbelief of both men, Nägeli had added four bars to the music, to even out a phrase or to make a correct cadence. In a fury, Beethoven first tried to get the *Allgemeine Musikalische Zeitung* to publish a notice with corrections. When that failed, he had Ries send the proofs with a list of eighty mistakes to Simrock in Bonn, who published an at least marginally improved printing of the sonatas with, as Beethoven demanded, *Edition très correcte* on the title page — except as coda to this comedy of errors, that very phrase came out with a typo: *Editiou très correcte.*[14]

• • •

Around the middle of February 1803, Carl van Beethoven came down with rheumatic fever. Since they were at that point living together, this inevitably claimed some of Ludwig's time and energy. Dealing with the contrapuntal distractions of business, his brother's illness, and his own health had to have been grueling. Beethoven was as busy as a musician and impresario could be. He had just gotten an appointment as composer in residence of the new Theater an der Wien; he and Carl had moved into a cramped apartment there in January. The position came through its artistic director, Emanuel Schikaneder. Though he was not the owner as such, Schikaneder had essentially built the Theater an der Wien; over the entrance he placed a statue of himself as Papageno. He knew Beethoven from concerts in his old Theater an der Weiden and from the *Prometheus* ballet, and he knew a hot property when he saw one.

The arrangement between them was that Beethoven would compose an opera on a Schikaneder libretto and could use the theater for his own benefit concert in April.[15] (He had failed in an attempt to secure a theater for the end of 1802.) It appeared that the new position with Schikaneder happily addressed several issues: Beethoven's yen to write opera, his need for a venue to present his new works, and his anxiety over money given that his hearing threatened his performing and Austria was in the throes of inflation.[16]

For his benefit concert he planned three major premieres. The last was to be a new oratorio written for the occasion: *Christus am Ölberge* (Christ on the Mount of Olives). It could serve the dual purposes of providing a grand finish for his concert and give him some practice in the direction of opera. To that end he had concluded his years-long desultory studies in Italian vocal composition with Antonio Salieri with a sort of graduation piece, the duet *Nei giorni tuoi felici*.[17] A good deal of what he had absorbed in those studies with Salieri would go, for better and for worse, into *Christus*.

In terms of his reputation and prosperity at that point, Beethoven had little to complain about (though he would always find something to complain about). In his thirty-second year he was well established, [Age 32] his music moved off the shelves, and he was generally understood to be the inheritor of the mantle of Mozart and Haydn as an instrumental

1803

composer. The attention paid to his work was rising in quantity and quality. An overview of the Viennese musical scene and Beethoven's reputation in 1803 came from a new polemical journal of the arts called the *Freymüthige*. It was founded by the politically reactionary playwright August von Kotzebue, who had been carrying on a public feud with Goethe. Kotzebue was director of the Burg Theater, the rival house to Schikaneder's. An article probably written by Kotzebue, "Amusements of the Viennese after Carnival," surveyed many of the amusements involving music in the salons:

> Amateur concerts at which unconstrained pleasure prevails are frequent. The beginning is usually made with a quartet by Haydn or Mozart, then follows, let us say, an air by Salieri or Paër, then a pianoforte piece with or without another instrument *obbligato,* and the concert closes as a rule with a chorus or something of the kind from a favorite opera. The most excellent pianoforte pieces that won admiration during the last carnival were a new quintet by Beethoven [probably the light op. 16 for piano and winds], clever, serious, full of deep significance and character, but occasionally a little too glaring. . . Beethoven has for a short time past been engaged, at a considerable salary, by the Theater an der Wien, and will soon produce at that playhouse an oratorio of his composition . . . Schuppanzigh performs quartets very agreeably . . . Great artists on the pianoforte are Beethofen [*sic*], Hummel, Madame Auernhammer and others.[18]

An *Allgemeine Musikalische Zeitung* note on Beethoven at the end of 1802 shows how much the critics there had moved to accommodate him. It is also a meditation insightful enough in regard to musical form in general and to Beethoven's sense of it to suggest that it came from editor Friedrich Rochlitz, who had studied Kantian philosophy and would have kept up with Schiller's recent contributions to aesthetics:

> An artist like [Beethoven] can really do nothing better than remain faithful to himself. This character and manner have been stated in these pages so precisely, and the composer already has such a respect-

able public throughout the entire musical world, that little remains for the advertiser of new works to say than, they are there . . . For, in the end, what is the result if one praises or censures individual things in works of art? . . . In art, as it should be, details do not remotely make up the total work. They can constitute an interesting product, but they never constitute a complete work, which must exist in the meaning of the total work.[19]

This echoes Schiller's treatise *On the Aesthetic Education of Man:* "In a truly successful work of art the contents should affect nothing, the form everything; for only through the form is the whole man affected . . . Herein, then, resides the real secret of the master in any art: *that he can make his form consume his material.*"[20] Schiller did not apply this conception to music particularly, but it defines the effect of much music by Beethoven, Haydn, and Mozart, particularly their works in what the future would name *sonata form.* Haydn often presented material that appeared plain and unpromising; it was the totality of the work, the whole of the form, that gave the material vitality and meaning. This was perhaps one of the deepest lessons Beethoven learned from Haydn, whether it had come directly from his teacher or from studying his music. Now, in the leading musical journal of the time, Beethoven read that he embodied this sense of form.

In another journal, the *Musikalisches Taschenbuch* of 1803, Beethoven likely read another article that surveyed the current state of the symphony as a genre. The symphonies universally called the greatest up to that time were first Haydn's, then Mozart's — even though neither of those men saw symphonies as his most significant work. For Mozart his main focus had been operas; for Haydn the late oratorios and masses. After his symphonies conquered London, Haydn never wrote another one, even as he was called the father of the genre. Yet the critic of the *Taschenbuch* wrote,

Symphonies are the triumph of this art. Unlimited and free, the artist can conjure up an entire world of feelings in them. Dancing merriment, exultant joy, the sweet yearning of love and profound pain, gentle peace and mischievous caprice, playful jest and frightful gravity pour forth and touch the sympathetic strings of the heart, feeling, and fantasy . . . Also, these gigantic works of art are subject to the necessary conditions of the mutual determination of content and form and of unity in diversity . . . *Mozart* and *Haydn* have produced works of art in this genre of instrumental music that deserve great admiration. Their great, inexhaustible genius, their profundity and universality, their free, bold, vigorous spirits are expressed more purely therein. Mozart's symphonies are colossal masses of rock, wild and abundant, surrounding a gentle, laughing valley; Haydn's are Chinese gardens, created by cheerful humor and mischievous caprice . . . *Beethoven,* a novice in art who is, however, already approaching the great masters, has in particular made the great field of instrumental music his own. He unites Mozart's universality and wild, abundant boldness and Haydn's humoristic caprice; all his compositions have abundance and unity.[21]

There was more inspiration. Back in Bonn, Christian Neefe had given his student J. G. Sulzer's *Allgemeine Theorie der schönen Künste*. Now Beethoven returned to it. He read again these meditations on the symphony:

The allegros of all the best . . . symphonies contain profound and clever ideas, a somewhat free treatment of the parts, an apparent disorder in the melody and harmony, strongly marked themes of different types, robust melodies and unison passages . . . free imitations of a theme (often in fugal style), sudden modulations and digressions from one key to another that are all the more striking the more distant their relation, distinct gradations of loud and soft, and especially the crescendo . . . Such an allegro is to the symphony what a Pindaric ode is to poetry; it elevates the soul of the listener.[22]

Reading these words as a teenager, Beethoven could hardly have imagined where these ideas could take him, how music could become like elevated poetry. Now he could imagine. Planning a third symphony but diverted in early 1803 by his impending concert and opera project, these perorations could have seemed like a call to produce the symphony he had already conceived and to make it as bold, as free, as mischievous and frightful and elevated as he wanted. As for unity within diversity, which is the primacy of form over content, he struggled for greater unity and at the same time for greater diversity than any composer had aspired to before. He could only have felt the time was right. After the darkest night of the soul he had experienced in Heiligenstadt, the world of music seemed to be holding out its arms and beckoning him to the future.

5 April Benefit Concert

As of early 1803, lying between Beethoven and his New Path was the April 5 benefit concert, the program constituting premieres of the Second Symphony and the Third Piano Concerto, another airing of the First Symphony, and the oratorio *Christus am Ölberge* that he had somehow to finish in February and March.

Inevitably, by the time April arrived things were frantic. In Vienna in those days, assembling orchestras and choruses and rehearsing them was a catch-as-catch-can affair, the available forces a mélange of professionals and amateurs. In this case, as often, the single rehearsal for Beethoven's concert started the morning of the performance day. They began at 8 a.m. The vocal soloists would have studied their parts and the chorus probably rehearsed ahead, but there was a long struggle to get the pieces ready. After hours of coping with the *Christus* oratorio, the First and Second Symphonies, and the Third Concerto, most of the music new to the players, the troops were exhausted by what Ries recalled as a "dreadful" ordeal. Prince Karl Lichnowsky hovered over the rehearsal, in midafternoon producing great baskets of bread and butter, cold meat, and wine for everybody. This restored spirits and the rehearsal went forward, even including the prince's request for another run-through of the oratorio. When rehearsal ended shortly before the doors opened for the 6 p.m. concert, the singers and players had been rehearsing for nearly ten hours.

A day or so before the concert Ries had arrived at Beethoven's flat at dawn to assist him and found him in bed scribbling on sheets of paper. "What is it?" Ries asked. "Trombones," Beethoven said. The trombones played from those parts in the premiere of *Christus*.[23] Beethoven had doubled and tripled the usual ticket prices but still got a full house for a long and variegated program. The performers trudged through the two symphonies and the concerto, Beethoven soloing, and only after some hour and a half started the eventful *Christus,* itself more than an hour long.

Based on later response, the music was decently represented and no audience or later critical outrage reported. There was, in fact, as in Beethoven's previous concert in Vienna, nothing terribly provocative on this program, though the big new symphony in D major had to have been a challenge on first hearing. The First Symphony had by then become an audience favorite. The Third Piano Concerto is audibly in Mozart's orbit and safely in his shadow (but with prophecies of concertos to come).

The Second Symphony is an extravagantly comic piece, but there had been one private joke in the course of the program. Beethoven had not had time to write down the piano part of the Third Concerto before the concert — only the orchestral parts. So the solo music existed only in his head, to be fleshed out with improvisation en route. No one in those days publicly played from memory. Beethoven arrived onstage, took his bow, sat down at the piano, and placed a sheaf of music on the stand. Young conductor Ignaz von Seyfried, who had helped out through the marathon rehearsal, was the designated page-turner. When Beethoven opened the solo part, Seyfried discovered that the pages were largely full of empty measures, with only a few "Egyptian hieroglyphs" to remind the composer of passages. Seyfried spent the concerto riveted in fear, watching Beethoven for his nodded cues to turn the pages of invisible music. At dinner afterward Beethoven had a large helping of laughter over Seyfried's anxiety.[24]

Reports of the audience response varied, likewise the review in the local *Zeitung für die Elegante Welt:* "The pieces performed consisted of two symphonies of which the first [the by-then-popular C Major] had more worth than the second [the new D Major] because . . . in the second [there was] a striving for novel and striking effects . . . It goes without saying that neither was lacking striking and brilliant qualities of beauty. Less successful was the next concerto, in C minor, which Mr. v B., who otherwise is known as a first-rate fortepianist, also performed not to the complete satisfaction of the public." Besides the unenthusiastic welcome for the Third Concerto, this was one of the most critical reviews a Beethoven keyboard performance had ever received. Whether his skills were on the wane at that point can't be said. What can be said is that thereafter he never again played the C Minor Concerto in public, or any other concerto except the premiere of his G Major, No. 4.

The reviewer of the concert went on to declare that *Christus am Ölberge* "was good and contains a few first-rate passages . . . A number of ideas from Haydn's *Creation* seem to have found their way into the final chorus." Beethoven would not have been pleased about that comparison, though it was manifestly true. The last chorus was not the only bit of Haydn lifted for the oratorio, and Mozart had been plundered as well. The reviewer sardonically quoted some lines from the weakest among the oratorio's weak suits, its libretto: "'We have seen him. / Go toward that mountain, / Just take a left, / He must be quite near!' And the rest is also written in this poetic spirit."[25]

Beethoven later claimed that *Christus* was thrown together in some two weeks, on a text hurried out by a local opera librettist, Franz Huber. (Earlier, Huber's anticlericalism and enthusiasm for the French Revolution got him in trouble with the police — and probably earned him Beethoven's approval.)[26] Huber seems to have written the libretto on Beethoven's scenario and with the composer at his elbow. The story is centered unusually not on the crucifixion but on Christ's anguish in the Garden of Gethsemane. It is likely that after his Heiligenstadt crisis of the previous autumn, Beethoven felt a personal relationship to the suffering he was depicting, starting with Christ's first words: "Jehovah! Thou my father! O send me consolation and strength and steadfastness." His first aria ends, "Take this cup of sorrow from me."[27]

Regardless of how much of his own cup of sorrows Beethoven poured into the libretto of *Christus,* the result showed more professionalism than inspiration. To compose an hour-long work for major forces at headlong speed generally involves compromises, shortcuts, having to make do with the first ideas that come to mind. (Handel, Haydn, Mozart, and Beethoven succeeded splendidly at that sometimes, but not always.) Though *Christus* has its striking moments and is nothing but skillful, it was then and would remain one of the most misconceived, inauthentic, undigested large works Beethoven ever wrote.

The conventionality of most of the music is matched by the boilerplate pieties of the text: "Woe to those who dishonor the blood that flowed for them. The curse of the Judge will strike them; damnation is their lot." Beethoven was not conventionally religious, not a churchgoer, not interested in judgment and damnation. As to the music, in his haste he made a fundamental decision that put the work on the wrong foot, where it remained: he cast much of it in the kind of eighteenth-century operatic style he had studied with Salieri, with ample and not always apt contributions from Haydn and Mozart.

It begins well enough. The long introduction in his high-tragic key of E-flat minor is an effective stretch of scene setting that calls to mind the opening of another of the oratorio's predecessors — the *Joseph* Cantata from Bonn. Then Jesus Christ, a bravura tenor, takes the stage. His first recitative and C-minor aria depicting his anguish at imminent crucifixion are the sort of thing one would expect from an operatic hero lamenting frustrated love or lost honor, complete with high-range pyrotechnics. At a reference to "the world that burst forth from chaos" at God's command, there is a C-major blaze of light straight from Chaos in Haydn's *Creation*. A seraph (coloratura soprano) appears to succor Christ in his sorrow. She and the Son of God have a duet that resembles all too much a pair of lovers commiserating — say, cousins of Pamina and Tamino in the fraught stretches of *Die Zauberflöte*. There are fugues. There are fervent *Heils*. In the choruses of soldiers coming to arrest Christ, there are unfortunate echoes of the "Turkish" choruses in Mozart's *Abduction from the Seraglio*. At the conclusion there is a solemn hallelujah chorus owing more to Haydn than Handel.

None of this is to say that *Christus am Ölberge* was a failure with the public. Mounted in Vienna in 1803 and again in 1804 with some revisions (not the last ones), it found considerable popularity in the next decades. For Beethoven's audiences, its operatic style was simply normal. It was the usual mode for second-rate religious works, for that matter not so far from the sacred style of Haydn and Mozart. A critic of the *AMZ* wrote, "[I]t confirms my long-held opinion that Beethoven in time can effect a revolution in music like Mozart's. He is hastening toward this goal with great strides."[28]

Beethoven himself never had any illusions about *Christus*. His admissions and excuses were issued piecemeal over the next decade before it was published: I was rushed, my brother was sick, the libretto is bad. All true. But he was quite prepared to make money from the piece, if a publisher would take it on. In any case, *Christus* did him a great service in at least two directions. For one thing it was a step, however faltering, in the direction of opera. At the same time, if he did not yet know what he wanted for a sacred style, now he knew what he did *not* want. Once and for all, he swore off writing a religious work in conventional operatic mode: "What is certain," he wrote later, "is that now I should compose an absolutely different oratorio from what I composed then."[29] Which left the question: if not operatic, what? That question would occupy him for much of the next two decades.

The Second Symphony in D Major, op. 36, was a different matter: ambitious, carefully crafted, well digested. If when he began it in 1800 Beethoven did not quite know what he wanted a symphony to be, he leaped into this one with both feet. The First Symphony had been something of a rush job like *Christus,* to provide a big finish to a concert, but in that case he had been tinkering for years with ideas for a C-major symphony — in other words, grappling with the genre. The First Symphony amounted to a clearing of the throat, if still more satisfying than *Christus.* The Second has a much richer and fresher treatment of the orchestra, adding up to high comedy on a grand canvas. The D Major may be, in fact, the longest symphony written to that date.

More specifically, as the expansive and kaleidoscopic introduction lays out, the tone of the work is of an operatic comedy. *Christus* was a kind of trial run at opera seria, the Second Symphony perhaps a warm-up for buffa. Call it Mozart intensified: more brash, rollicking, and youthfully raw than Mozart's time would have found decorous. The introduction lays out a series of contrasting ideas like a collection of characters: a pouncing *fortissimo* unison, a tender moment, a

comic tripping figure, and so on. There is a sense of breadth in the
ideas and in the orchestral sound quite different from the rather generically eighteenth-century character and orchestra of the First Symphony. In the introduction we seem to hear a story being laid out, the
essential character jovial but with hints of intrigue and romance, in a
palette of offbeat accents and *subito* eruptions that will mark the whole
symphony. An Allegro con brio breaks out with a dashing theme that
gathers energy toward a racing climax. The second theme strikes an
ironic military note, say, Beethoven's version of Mozart's Cherubino,
off to war. The whole of the movement is muscular, leaping, explosive,
brillante, its engine less melodic than rhythmic.

Grace and charm were not constant qualities with Beethoven as
they had been with Mozart. In his earlier opuses, when he was aiming
for charm he often resorted, as in the First Symphony, to the *galant*
mode of the previous century. But in this second movement he was
beginning to discover his own kind of charm. It is a long movement
in full-scale sonata form, wistful and nostalgic, lyrically lovely despite
a moment of operatic *tristesse* and hand-wringing in the development
— when, say, our heroine does not find her lover at the masked ball.
All ends well, if with a final sigh.

Once again, for the third movement Beethoven takes up the scherzo
form. This time he labeled it as such and made it driving and pouncing,
with nimble banter between the orchestral choirs. Its trio alternates a
phrase of warmly eighteenth-century elegance with faux-*furioso* interruptions.

The finale begins with an absurd giant hiccup that dissolves into
skittering comedy. Before long, astute listeners would have realized
that, believe it or not, this is actually the rondo theme; the hiccup is developed diligently. The second part of the opening section is flowing,
more of an A theme proper, but the hiccup cannot be forsworn. The
qualms and shadows that have turned up periodically in this summery
romp make a final appearance in the coda, which begins with a tone of
whispering intrigue. Here as in Mozart and Shakespeare, comedy and
sorrow are close companions. But the spirit of fun wins the day, and
the curtain comes down on a scene of laughter with troubles resolved
and glasses raised.[30]

And that was the end of that train of thought. Beethoven never wrote another piece that much resembles the Second Symphony, not even in his theater music, where he had to find a way to escape from Mozart. For him the D Major was a way station en route to somewhere he did not know when he began it, but perhaps had begun to understand by the time he finished it.

Ferdinand Ries, watching Beethoven at work, was always astonished at how his mentor's compositions reached the heights they did, given what he knew of their inception. "This *Larghetto*," Ries recalled of the second movement, "is so beautifully, so purely and happily conceived and the melodic line so natural that one can hardly imagine anything in it was ever changed." But Ries had seen the manuscript with the accompaniment revised so heavily that the final version could hardly be made out in the splotch of notes. Hoping for a lesson in craft, Ries asked about the changes. "It's better this way," was all Beethoven had to say about it.[31] "Better" was all he or anyone needed to know.

If the premiere of the Concerto No. 3 in C Minor got mixed reviews, that was in part because, in contrast to the relatively conventional first two concertos, this one summarized the past in the stream of Beethoven's music while no less pointing to the future. If he began extricating himself from the looming shadow of Mozart in the violin sonatas of op. 30, here is where he made a broad step toward the same with concertos.

He had been thinking about the piece since at least 1796, when during his Berlin stay he jotted on a sketch, "For the Concerto in C minor kettledrum at the cadenza." At that point he had been near the height of his piano career, and for him concertos were as much a matter of practicality as of aesthetics: a repertoire of concertos by oneself and by others was required to establish a reputation as a virtuoso. Now his virtuoso career was winding down. He began working on the C Minor intensively perhaps in 1800, perhaps sometime in the next two years.[32] It was still in flux at its premiere, as one observes from the absence of a written solo part.

Beethoven's only minor-key concerto does not exactly have the driving and demonic tone of the *Pathétique* and other examples of his

C-minor mood; neither is it the full-blown "heroic" style of the coming New Path. The quiet stride of the beginning sets a tone stern and dramatic. Its military-march aspect was familiar in concertos by Mozart and many others, including Beethoven. The atmosphere, scoring, and opening emphasis on a rising figure involving C, E-flat, and A-flat all suggest Mozart's C Minor Concerto hovering in the background. At the same time, the concerto is full of fresh ideas.[33]

He made the music taut and the material tight, beginning with a rising figure in the first measure, a down-striding scale in the second. The third measure introduces a dotted drumbeat figure; the concerto will turn steadily around that essential rhythmic idea, as well as the melodic and harmonic ones from the previous two measures.[34] The most important motif, as it turns out, is the drumbeat. The opening string phrase is echoed a step higher by the winds, which add another fundamental idea with their line rising up to a piercing dissonance on A-flat. In various guises, that A-flat (and its equivalent G-sharp) will resonate throughout the concerto.

The second theme of the orchestral exposition is the expected lyrical contrast to the sternly militant opening. After a couple of subthemes, we arrive at the end of the first exposition and the piano's first entrance on an explosive, uprushing scale (an idea that marks the solo voice throughout). Rather than entering with a new and distinctive theme as Mozart tended to, the soloist takes up the main theme, establishing a commanding personality in the dialogue with the orchestra. It is as if the music has found its leader. With piano and orchestra in close dialogue, the effect is as much symphonic as concerto-like.

Much of the music from the solo entrance on, especially the development section, is dominated by the drumbeat figure in constantly new forms. After the piano's concluding cadenza, the rhythmic motif turns up in the timpani, as if emerging in its true guise as a drumbeat, in a duet with the piano. As Beethoven jotted down in 1796, "For the Concerto in C minor kettledrum at the cadenza." That striking moment involving timpani was one of the germs from which the concerto grew.

The second-movement Largo arrives with a sense of something otherworldly, both because of its exquisite theme and because it is in E major, about as distant from C minor as a key can be. The unforgettable first E-major chord in the rich lower register of the piano arrives magically out of nowhere and lingers for two slow beats. The main connection between C minor and E major is A-flat/G-sharp, the note singled out by the winds at the beginning of the concerto. Beethoven had been experimenting with extended key relations for years, but rarely so strikingly as here. These sorts of forays into wide-ranging key relations were to be a thumbprint of much of his music to come.[35]

The form of the middle movement is a simple ABA, the piano still the commanding presence, now with an air of rapturous improvisation. Carl Czerny recalled that Beethoven played the entire opening with the sustain pedal down, giving it a kind of acoustic halo. The piano figures are like breezes, garlands, butterfly wings. From his memory of Beethoven's playing, Czerny said the slow movement should evoke "a holy, distant, and celestial harmony." Here was a moment when in a stretch of sublime beauty Beethoven floated free of the past in one more genre. His trajectory as a composer coming fully into his own was still sharply rising in those months of early 1803. And with his most innovative music, he was beginning to earn extraordinary critical superlatives. Already in 1805, a critic of the *Allgemeine Musikalische Zeitung* called the concerto's second movement "one of the most expressive and richly sensitive instrumental pieces ever written."[36]

The final chord of the second movement places G-sharp on the top in strings. The piano picks up that note and turns it back into A-flat to begin what will be a lilting and playful rondo, despite the C minor. Again the piano leads the symphonic dialogue; we hear echoes of the first movement in dotted rhythms, down-striding figures, uprushing scales from the soloist. A couple of times, the piano interrupts with mini-cadenzas before the middle section in A-flat major — the starring note now with its own key. As a kind of musical pun, Beethoven turns the A-flat back into G-sharp and on that pivot thrusts us for a moment into E major, the key of the slow movement, and for that moment the music recalls that movement. In the expansive coda, the 2/4 main theme is transformed into a *presto* 6/8, driving to the end in C-major high spirits. The main feature of this new incarnation of the rondo theme is a wry flip on G-sharp–A, the last disguise of the leading pitch, finally resolving into C major.

In the aftermath of his benefit concert, Beethoven had much to be pleased about. The music had gone well enough, and after expenses were settled he pocketed the inspiring sum of 1,800 florins. Publications were steady, and Prince Lichnowsky added his annual stipend of 600 florins. In the year after the worst crisis of his life, this was a most gratifying kind of success. Beethoven probably understood what his audience of April 1803 could not know, that with this slate of pieces he had cleared the decks, drawn a line in his life and art between the old, wandering paths and the New Path.

After those exhausting months of production around the beginning of 1803, Beethoven's energy did not flag. A couple of weeks after the concert, Prague physician Johann Held met him on the street and was invited to a soiree at the flat of violinist Ignaz Schuppanzigh. They were rehearsing string-quartet arrangements of Beethoven's piano music. "His piquant conceits," the doctor recalled of Beethoven, "modified the gloominess, I might say, the lugubriousness, of his countenance. His criticisms were very keen."[37] There Dr. Held met Beethoven's violinist disciple Wenzel Krumpholz and a visiting violinist and composer named George Polgreen Bridgetower.

This twenty-four-year-old former prodigy had made a sensation in Vienna. Prince Lichnowsky introduced him to Beethoven, who was suitably impressed. In childhood, Bridgetower may have lived in the Esterházy Palace, and he claimed to have studied there with Haydn. Years later, as a rising young virtuoso living in England, he appeared in Haydn's London concerts. Among his mentors and admirers was Giovanni Battista Viotti, which connects Bridgetower with the heart of the French violin school and its kaleidoscopic effects based on the new "Viotti" bow.[38] Besides the brilliance of his playing, Bridgetower came with a multicultural and mixed-race background that gave him an exotic cachet. His father was West Indian, his mother European. Happy to exploit his background for publicity, he billed himself as "son of the African Prince" (probably not strictly true). A triumph in Dresden, where he was visiting his mother, gained Bridgetower connections to the musical aristocracy in Vienna, thus to Lichnowsky, thereby to Beethoven.

The two struck up a friendship. On one of their first evenings Beethoven brought the violinist along for a dinner at Countess Guicciardi's, and he helped introduce the younger man to useful patrons.[39] In their time away from the piano the two men seem to have caroused vigorously. At some point the violinist asked his new friend if they could mount a joint concert, perhaps premiere a piece. Though there was little time, Beethoven did not need persuading. Apparently he had been sketching some ideas for a violin sonata, with the notion that its finale would be the one discarded from the A Major Violin Sonata, op. 30. Since Beethoven was not given to throwing movements together casually, that meant that he based the new movements on material from the existing finale — so, in a way, composed the piece back to front.

The concert date in Vienna was set for May 22, 1803, but it was postponed to the twenty-fourth, likely because the new movements of the sonata, which Beethoven had been writing at top speed with Bridgetower prodding him, were not finished. By the hour of the concert, the first movement had only a sketchy piano part on the page, and the slow movement had to be read from the manuscript with the ink barely dry.[40]

No matter. The recital, in the big pavilion of the Augarten, seems to have been a grand occasion for both men. Their easy camaraderie was demonstrated when, on a soaring C-major arpeggio in the first-movement Presto, Bridgetower answered the piano's figure with an improvised arpeggio of his own. Ordinarily that sort of thing would have brought an explosion of wrath from Beethoven. This time he jumped up from the piano in delight, embraced Bridgetower, and cried, "Once again, my dear boy!" Bridgetower recalled Beethoven's playing of the slow movement as "so chaste, which always characterized the performance of all his *slow movements,* that it was unanimously hailed to be repeated twice."[41]

Despite the haste of its creation, what came to be called the *Kreutzer* Sonata amounted to a defining, even galvanizing work of the New Path: another leap in maturity and confidence, a moment where in one more genre he escaped his model Mozart. Beethoven was in a remarkable creative ferment that year, but part of the sonata's hot-blooded nature surely had to do with the circumstances of its creation: his encounter with this professedly "exotic" virtuoso of impulsive personality in his playing and in his person.

This sonata was to become an obsession of the new Romantic generation. The whole is splendid, but its legend rests on the breathtaking first movement. There is a kind of improvisatory excitement and immediacy about it, a breadth and variety of ideas that surprise and dazzle at every turn. At the same time, it is an exercise in sustained intensity of which few composers other than Beethoven were capable. Which is to say, it is in the category of works to come like the *Waldstein* and *Appassionata* Sonatas.

In a subtitle Beethoven notes that the A Major Sonata was written in a style "like that of a concerto." It begins Adagio sostenuto with an impassioned and virile violin solo in A major, slashing across the strings. The piano answers the violin with a pensively ambiguous and minorish phrase, setting up an essential counterforce. The Presto breaks out in A minor with a seething dynamism that never flags, though for contrast there is a meltingly lovely second theme. The opening gesture of the Presto in the violin is a surge from E to F; that stroke from consonant to dissonant touches off the high tension of the music to come — and also foreshadows the significance of the key of F (and that "sore" pitch) in the course of the first movement, in the entire second movement, and in the middle of the finale. The development manages to ratchet the excitement still higher as it rages through keys and brilliant figures. Near the end, there is a quiet *adagio* moment that will be echoed in the following movements.[42]

Next, a set of decorative F-major variations on a gently pulsing theme. Trills near the end of the theme are one of the main ideas to be developed, subsumed into florid figuration. The tone of the variations shifts slowly from playful to more serious, the last one quietly reflective. The finale erupts as a 6/8 tarantella in A major, in which the driving intensity of the first movement is transformed into an exhilarating frolic. As in the first movement there is a suddenly slow and lyrical second theme and a retrospective moment near the end (in practice, these being ideas on which the preceding movements were built).

Beethoven's affection for George Bridgetower is reflected in a joking inscription in improvised Italian that he scrawled on the sonata's manuscript, maybe during an evening of carousing. Roughly translated, it reads, "Mulattic sonata written for the mulatto Brischdauer, a complete lunatic and mulattic composer." Bridgetower seems to have been an exciting violinist and a brash and lusty personality, and so was his sonata. Who knows to what degree Beethoven was galvanized by some fanciful association of the violinist's African heritage and carnality. If Beethoven's music encompasses the range of human characters and feelings, one category of feeling he usually left out was the sexual. He was powerfully drawn to women but at the same time prudish. He did not consider the erotic a proper subject for art and criticized Mozart for the racy plots of his comic operas. Perhaps the surging passions of the *Kreutzer* constitute the exception to the rule.[43]

In the end Beethoven and Bridgetower broke up for a time as friends and colleagues over what the violinist recalled as "some silly quarrel about a girl."[44] So the dedication of the A Major Sonata went to another violinist, Rodolphe Kreutzer, whom Beethoven had met and come to admire in 1798, when Kreutzer was in the entourage of the French minister, General Bernadotte. In regard to the publication and dedication, Beethoven wrote Nikolaus Simrock in 1804, "This Kreutzer is a dear kind fellow who during his stay in Vienna gave me a great deal of pleasure. I prefer his modesty and natural behavior to *all the* exterior without *any* interior, which is characteristic of most virtuosi — As the sonata was written for a competent violinist, the dedication to Kreutzer is all the more appropriate."[45] What Beethoven did not know was that Rodolphe Kreutzer had no use for Beethoven's music and apparently never performed the work that made his name immortal. Kreutzer told Hector Berlioz that he found the sonata "outrageously unintelligible."[46]

For Beethoven the following summer continued at an exuberant, breakneck creative pace hard to conceive for a man who a year before had been ready to kill himself. If his public performances on piano had begun to recede, as a composer he was juggling more schemes and projects than ever. He still had a flat in Schikaneder's Theater an der Wien as nominal house composer (he spent the summer in Baden and Oberdöbling). Supposed to be supplying operas, he took up the impresario's libretto of ancient Rome, *Vestas Feuer*, and began sketching at it, with little enthusiasm. His seven Bagatelles for piano, a mellifluous and delightful grab bag of miniatures, were published as op. 33. He received a letter from the Scottish publisher George Thomson wanting to commission six sonatas. Beethoven asked for more than 1,300 florins, Thomson offered half that, and there the matter rested.[47]

A story Ferdinand Ries recalled from 1803 shows the easy relations Beethoven enjoyed with the nobility. He and Ries were the evening's entertainment at the home of his patron Count Browne. Ries missed a note playing the op. 23 Sonata and Beethoven tapped him on the head, only to show his pupil that he had noticed. At that, Princess Browne, leaning on the piano, smiled mischievously. Later when Beethoven was playing *The Tempest* he made a slip of the fingers that sounded, Ries remembered, "like a piano being cleaned." The princess rapped him several times on the head, saying, "If the pupil received one tap of the finger for one missed note, then the Master must be punished with a full hand for worse mistakes." On that occasion, Beethoven chose to laugh, started the sonata again, and "performed marvelously. The Adagio in particular was incomparably played."[48]

In August the piano maker Érard of Paris sent Beethoven a gift of a piano, state of the art, part of that being more notes at the top — its range was five and a half octaves, stretching beyond the usual top F above the staff up to C — and with a heavier action and more robust British-style sound in comparison to the delicate Viennese pianos. Beethoven was reported to be "enchanted" with the Érard. Soon with its help he produced epochal works. Later, perhaps inevitably, he became disgruntled with the heavy action and tried to have it lightened. Still, the Érard would be his main instrument for years.[49]

Carl van Beethoven was nearing the end of his usefulness as an agent and go-between. Ries wrote publisher Simrock a sarcastic warning: "The second Beethoven will soon do you the honor of visiting you. You can very much look forward to this, for all the publishers in

Vienna fear him worse than fire, because he is so terribly rude." Relations with Breitkopf & Härtel had cooled because of Carl's style.[50]

The difference between Ludwig's dealings with publishers, with which he was perennially annoyed but patient, and Carl's style is seen in the difference between letters each wrote to Breitkopf & Härtel in the autumn of 1803. Beethoven was seething at the firm's house journal for its lukewarm review of his concert. In ironic mode, he wrote Gottfried Härtel, "Please convey my most respectful thanks to the editor of the [*Allgemeine Musikalische Zeitung*] for his kindness in allowing such a <u>flattering report</u> on my oratorio to be inserted, which contains such <u>blatant lies about the prices I fixed</u> and treats me in such a degrading manner . . . What nobility of character is expected of a true artist, and certainly not entirely without good reason! On the other hand, how detestably, how meanly people proceed to attack us without the slightest hesitation."

Härtel already knew that Beethoven was going to return fire when he got bad reviews in the *AMZ*. Nonetheless, Beethoven was offering the house his new piano variations on *God Save the King* and *Rule Britannia* and some smaller works — which Härtel turned down.[51] In October 1803, Carl, while offering Härtel major works including a triple concerto (probably not even begun at that point), demanded ominously to know the name of the *AMZ* reviewer: "The reason for this has nothing to do with whether my brother is disgraced in your <u>Zeitung</u> or not, because the greatest proof that the opposite is the case comes from the quantity of orders that we receive from everywhere. But I find it very remarkable that you accept such crap in your <u>Zeitung.</u> My brother does not know that I want to learn the identity of the reviewer; therefore be so kind as to enclose a little note to me in your reply."[52] It is unlikely Härtel was so kind.

In late summer of 1803, Ries wrote Simrock the surprising news that Beethoven was settled on moving to Paris within a year and a half, "which I am extraordinarily sorry about."[53] It was a strange determination, and it is hard to conceive what might have come of it, but it was strong. Did Beethoven hope to meet Napoleon, did he imagine himself as one in the French conqueror's stable of artists like composer Étienne-Nicolas Méhul and painter Jacques-Louis David?

In any case, a good deal of Beethoven's effort was now devoted to a multifront campaign to prepare this relocation. One item was the dedication of the new violin sonata to a leading French virtuoso, Kreutzer. Another, perhaps, was the plan to compose a French-style triple concerto. Another was that he was about to put aside Schikaneder's opera libretto in favor of a French one; he knew that writing opera was the best route to fame in Paris.[54] Still another, his main project of that summer and fall, was a work he had started sketching in summer 1802, before his Heiligenstadt crisis, directly after the pages devoted to the *Prometheus Variations.*[55] It was a symphony dedicated to the most famous of Frenchmen.

17

Heaven and Earth Will Tremble

HOW DOES A composer forge a great symphony, with its span of nearly an hour and its myriad notes? Among human endeavors, shaping a long work of music is one of the hardest things to do well. Very few people have ever been consistently good at it. No matter how long the piece takes to write, every note has to be marshaled to the same purpose, and in performance it should unfold as effortlessly as an improvisation. From the outside, the job seems superhuman. As Beethoven saw it from the inside, it was done one quilled note, one theme, one phrase, one transition, one section, one movement at a time.

Often the creation of great things begins with small things: an itch in the mind, a scrap of material, a train of thought that seems on its own to leap into motion. This time, an epic work began with a bit of dance tune.

The *englische* bass and theme from *Prometheus* obsessed him:

There was the protean quality of the *Basso del Tema,* anchoring the simplest harmonies but with a hint of something beyond — a little chromatic slide of three notes, the smallest touch of seasoning. The bass line was something next to nothing that could be the foundation of anything. Yet its implications reached far. Bass and tune formed the image of a dance that for Beethoven had come to represent something in the direction of Schiller's "most perfectly appropriate symbol of the assertion of one's own freedom and regard for the freedom of others." An image, in other words, of an ideal society.

It was in summer of 1802, in Heiligenstadt before his crisis, around the same time as he worked on the *Prometheus* Variations, that on a couple of pages Beethoven made exploratory sketches for the first three movements of a new symphony, probing for a sense of its character and leading ideas. Most of the sketches are toward the exposition section of a first movement. None of them ended up in the finished piece.

Though it does not appear in those first sketches, the implicit galvanizing element was the *Prometheus* theme. He kept its E-flat major as the key of the symphony. In his time this was called a noble, heroic, humanistic, echt-Aufklärung tonality: as said before, the main key of Mozart's Masonic pieces and of *Die Zauberflöte.* For the beginning of the piece, at this point Beethoven imagined a solemn, slow introduction based on another simple idea, an ascent on a triad. A few bars labeled *seconda* were a try at a slow movement in C major and 6/8 meter. Toward a third movement were a couple of lines he labeled *Minuetto serioso.* He wrote down nothing specific for the finale; he already knew it would be based on the *Prometheus* material, in a similar direction as the piano variations.[1]

Around June of 1803, he rented three rooms in what had been a winegrower's house in Oberdöbling, a village up the hill from Heiligenstadt. It was the kind of simple place he liked, in the countryside. The house was surrounded by gardens and vineyards and sat beside the solitary Krottenbach gorge that separates Döbling from Heiligenstadt.[2] It was a countryside to beckon the wanderer. In that setting he returned to the symphony in a new sketchbook.

For Beethoven a big work was a dramatic and emotional narrative, also a moral and ethical one. At the same time, for him and his age music was called a kind of rational discourse on stated themes, a wordless rhetoric like an oration, or like a sermon founded on its verse of scripture.[3] At some point since the previous year's sketches, he had done significant work on the new symphony. Among other things, he had found *das Thema*, the all-important leading theme.

He had also settled on the symphony's subject. It was to be what he and his time called a "characteristic" piece and what the future would call a "program" piece, based on some sort of story or image usually conveyed by a title. The subject of this symphony inspired by the *Prometheus* music was to be another Promethean figure, the only man in Europe who appeared to deserve that description as a benefactor of humanity: Napoleon Bonaparte, who had begun his self-willed ascent as "the little corporal" and now was the conqueror and benevolent despot who proposed to bring Europe peace, republican governments, the rule of law, and an end to ancient tyrannies. Hegel declared him a "world spirit on horseback."[4] One Prometheus suggested another. The Third Symphony was to be called *Bonaparte*.

A composer asks of a conception, *What can I do with this? What sort of ideas express it? Where do these ideas want to go?* The answers to these questions are sequences of sounds. Chains of ideas and associations gathered in his mind, rising from the intersection of the *Prometheus* dance and the French conqueror. The symphony would be not only dedicated to Napoleon but also in some way modeled on his character and career and on the larger image of a hero who has the vision and capacity to create a new order, a just and harmonious society: as Schiller said, free and respecting freedom.

As usual, the project was not all abstractions and ideals. Self-promotion was woven into all of it. If Beethoven was going to make his long-planned move to Paris, a *Bonaparte* symphony could be a calling card to the French government, even to Napoleon himself. The political atmosphere made that scheme workable. The 1802 Treaty of Lunéville ended the War of the Second Coalition and inaugurated a hiatus in hostilities between France and its prime antagonist, Austria. For the moment, Holy Roman Emperor Franz II was staying neutral, resisting Russian and English pressure for a new alliance. There was actually talk of a pact between Austria and the French republic. After all, the effects of the Lunéville treaty had been bearable, losing Austria only distant territories and the left bank of the Rhine. To the delight of liberal and anticlerical circles, the treaty also abolished the ecclesiastical states, including Bonn.[5] Now in Austria Napoleon was called a peacemaker, even a bastion against radical Jacobinism.

In August 1802, the French Senate proclaimed Napoleon First Consul for life. At this point he was in all but title an absolute monarch, a dictator — just like Holy Roman Emperor Franz II. A German journal of the time declared that Napoleon "had subdued the warring peoples of Europe and Asia, and by his laws made himself loved by those he had conquered."[6] Napoleon declared that he intended to deliver Europe from "the terrible pictures of chaos, devastation and carnage" that war — lately his wars — had brought.[7] Millions in the occupied territories were jubilant over their liberation from Austrian rule. In practice, Napoleon was managing another of his balancing acts: keeping progressives around Europe convinced that he was a liberator and the fulfillment of the Revolution while convincing the reactionary rulers in Vienna that he had put revolution to rest.

In the *Bonaparte* Symphony Beethoven wanted to evoke the character and story of a conqueror and the moral dimension of what the French were creating across Europe. Napoleon appeared to have achieved in war and diplomacy the kind of transformations that had escaped Joseph II in Vienna and Maximilian Franz in Bonn.[8] At this critical moment in Beethoven's career, to go to France, perhaps to charm the First Consul in person, was to attach himself to the most powerful and dynamic figure alive, the incarnate spirit of the age. In the process he placed himself alongside Napoleon as an embodiment of the age. This would be his means of stepping out of the role of servant in court and parlor and attaching himself to history as an actor rather than an entertainer. In an ideal sense, Beethoven might imagine becoming the kind of ethical and spiritual leader he recognized in poets and philosophers like Goethe and Schiller. *Bonaparte* was aimed toward lifting him to such heights. In the process, it would show the world what a *sinfonia grande* could truly be and do. Here was a conception worthy of the Aufklärung and of his gifts and ambitions.

In these months he had to have felt himself imbued with a sense of possibility, discovery, inevitability. Perhaps he felt (he had reason to feel) that this was meant to be, that a new humanistic spirit had given birth to this music. Napoleon revitalized the Aufklärung ideals Beethoven had grown up with. Now he understood how to attach those ideals to his music. His teacher Christian Neefe wrote, "A meticulous acquaintance with the various characters [of men], with the physical and moral aspects of mankind, with the passions . . . [is required] if music is to be no empty cling-clang." Beethoven remembered the Aufklärung dream of happiness and brotherhood that the Freemasons and Illuminati proclaimed, that Schiller called Elysium. (It appears that in this period he returned to an old ambition and made a setting of "An die Freude" — or a second setting — but he held it back.)[9] These and more threads reaching from the present back to his childhood gathered to make the fabric of *Bonaparte*.

In a winegrower's cottage in Oberdöbling in summer of 1803, he settles down to work. As epic dreams unroll before his imagination, he rushes to realize them on the keyboard, in his head, in notes scratched onto the page. He spends hours lost in his *raptus,* improvising at the keyboard, ideas flowing from his fingers into sound, sketchbook on a table beside him to fix the sounds before they are gone. As he writes out the sketches he drums the beat with his hands and feet, cursing the notes for their recalcitrance. For Beethoven composing is a process physical as well as mental; his whole body is involved in it. Every day in all weathers he walks in hills and woods and country lanes, growling and howling and waving his arms conducting the music in his head, stopping to pencil ideas in the pocket sketchbooks he carries with him.

The dots quilled and penciled on the page define an accumulating and clarifying vision of the work. Beethoven has never seen a battle, but years before, on the road from Bonn to Vienna, he encountered armies, heard the bustle and rattle of troops on the march, the bugle calls and martial music. Since then Vienna has been full of armies in parades and exercises, preparing to fight the French. After the battles the city streets filled with soldiers wounded and dying, with funerals and mournful music. These scenes will find a place in the symphony. At the same time his sense of heroes and battles is founded on the ancients, on Plutarch and his exemplary men, Homer and the battle for Troy. So his larger subject will be heroes contemporary and ancient: Napoleon and his fellow benevolent despots Joseph II and Frederick the Great, Hector and Achilles and Odysseus — not only *a* hero but *the Hero* as archetype: Napoleon as man and myth.

The overarching conception and the minutiae of melody and rhythm and harmony feed on one another. As usual, he conceives his ideas in terms of familiar formal outlines. For the first movement he needs a *Thema* for the opening, then what he calls the *mitte Gedanke,* subsidiary ideas. Then he needs ideas for the *Durchführung,* his term for the development section, then a transition to the da capo, the recapitulation.[10] His forms are not molds to be filled with notes but general guidelines to help organize a conception. This time the conception has a name: *Bonaparte.* Whatever the form becomes, it has to be measured and cut to that subject.[11]

He wears out one quill pen after another, notes spreading over empty staves, pages accumulating in the sketchbook. The conception will not be complete in his mind, not completely grasped, until the end is in place or at least in sight. But as usual, by the time sketches are seriously under way, he already has a sense of what the thing is about, what the leading ideas are, a plan for where *das Thema* is headed and why.

But finding material is not a mechanical or mathematical process. Musical ideas, when they come, are like characters in a novel; each appears to the writer with a face and a personality and begins to speak.

Beethoven keeps the reins tighter on his ideas than most artists, but he still has to wait for what the Muse, the unconscious, the angels, God — whatever it is — bestows on him.[12] Sometimes the ideas come fast, sometimes they have to be courted at length. For Beethoven the process is harder than for most creators, because he demands that every idea has to submit to the plan, to leading motives of pitch and rhythm, the character, flow, key scheme, harmony. It is no easy job to make the wild horses of imagination run on a narrow track. Nonetheless, work on the *Bonaparte* proceeds fast.

What does Beethoven know about *Bonaparte* in these early stages? Mainly he knows that it will be in E-flat major and it will end with a variation movement, based on the dance from the *Prometheus* ballet — like the *Prometheus* piano variations but recomposed for orchestra. Though using a naked bass line as a theme for variations is unheard of, a variation movement in a large work is nothing new.[13] Haydn and Mozart did it — but as a middle movement in a quartet or sonata or symphony, or more rarely as a first movement. In the *Bonaparte* Symphony the variations on the *englische* are to be the finale, and a symphonic finale has to be pointed and climactic in a way that variations ordinarily are not. For the finale, then, he will have to fashion a new kind of form, a hybrid variation movement.

The finale and its heroic key are the first elements he sees more or less clearly. So in a way he composes the symphony back to front, as he did with the *Kreutzer* Sonata. But finalizing the last movement has to wait. He needs to write the beginning before he writes the ending. For the listener, the finale can't be a beginning, can't be *das Thema*. That has to be the leading theme of the first movement, which sets up the primal sense of the work, its affect, tone, motifs, harmonies. The opening *Thema* begins the story. It needs to be compelling in itself, rich in potential for development and for growing subsidiary themes. At the same time this particular beginning has to contain the germ of the ending already settled on: variations on the *basso* and the *englische* tune.

The way he does that is to base the beginning on the ending. A work feeds on itself. To get to the next step, you stand on what you have. So he derives his first-movement *Thema* from the last-movement *Pro-*

metheus ideas. This is no great trick, a familiar process for him: taking a piece of material and making something new out of it. Once he has his opening *Thema* he can compose forward, working out the finale in detail at the end of the process.

To do that, he has to consider, *What sort of* Thema *for the beginning?* In the sketch with ideas for the first three movements that he jotted down in summer 1802, he makes what appear to be two attempts to fashion a new theme out of the bass:[14]

From Lockwood, *Beethoven: Studies in the Creative Process*

With these perhaps first attempts to turn the end into a beginning, he has already come to a surprising decision about the first movement. This evocation of a military hero, of campaigns and battles, will be in 3/4 time rather than in the 2/4 or 4/4 march time of military music. The music of the opening movement will have no literal evocation of marches or pageantry at all. It will be in a meter and in a lilting triple rhythm suggesting a dance — say, a waltz — rather than the military tread that marks the openings of his concertos. The symphony's first movement is to be a kind of abstraction of heroism in the meter and rhythm of dance: a dance of destruction and creation in 3/4 time.

To make his *Thema* he squeezes the *Prometheus* scraps for everything they hold. Since for Beethoven what comes first is usually most important, the first four notes of the *basso* are the prime issue: the move from tonic to dominant and back, the octave outline of the two B-flats. The rising chromatic slide in the middle of the *basso* will also serve.

Finally, to make the opening theme he adds the note G to the scaffolding of the *basso* and inverts the direction of the two B-flats. To that he appends the three-note chromatic slide, this time going not up but down: E-flat–D–C-sharp. The first three notes of the resulting *Thema*, a major third up and back down, E-flat–G–E-flat, are the same as the first three notes of the *englische* tune. The new theme and the *englische* share a trochaic rhythm, long–short, long–short, and a wavelike shape:

In other words, the new opening starts by outlining an E-flat-major chord, a triad, filling in the outline of the bass theme and forming the familiar figure of a horn call. A triadic horn call, then, is the essence of *das Thema*. Taking the most common chord in music as the leading motif is an utterly Beethovenian way to proceed. Surely from Haydn he had learned that he could start with something nearly meaningless and fill it with meaning through the course of a work.

At some point before summer 1803, he has fashioned that triadic opening *Thema*. When he has settled on his theme, in a new sketchbook he begins to shape all the themes of the movement on or around a triad. As it turns out, his leading idea is not really a theme in the usual sense but simply a triad followed by a chromatic figure. Those motifs will turn up separately and together in evolving forms and permutations.

While Beethoven improvises at the keyboard — and scribbles and walks, howls, conducts, stamps his feet and pounds the table — technique, story, symbol, and expression take shape together. Call the symphony's opening theme "the Hero." It is hardly a melody, less a theme in the usual sense than (like the *basso*) a kind of primal gesture. And this protean scrap of material has not just an abstract but a symbolic dimension: in the same way that the Hero theme generates the subsidiary themes of the first movement, the spirit of the Hero imbues his soldiers and his campaigns.[15]

• • •

With his *Thema* in hand, Beethoven can go forward from the opening movement's first part to *Durchführung* to da capo and coda—in the terms of a later time, exposition, development, recapitulation, coda. Amid the ragged tumult of ideas spilling into the sketchbook, he begins to make longer continuity drafts of the exposition. As in all his sketches, a single line of melody or figuration stands in for the full ensemble he hears in his mind.

Feeling his way into the exposition section, he is already working with quite particular concepts. The first continuity sketch looks like this:

Much of that sketch will fall by the wayside, but already it has elements that will endure: (1) an opening on two monumental chords slashed onto silence, similar to the beginning of the *Prometheus* Overture (but not the same chords or the two downbeats he finally settles on); (2) the Hero theme fully formed in its dancelike 3/4, with a chromatic slide down to an out-of-key C-sharp that throws the harmony into uncertainty;[16] (3) several variants of that chromatic slide; (4) a flowing second theme in B-flat built on the triadic motif of the Hero theme; (5) a skittering theme built on a descending triad (the theme will remain, but the harmony will change); and (6) a modulation to the distant key of D-flat, an enharmonic echo of the C-sharp in measure 7 (but the key of D-flat not in its final position in the movement). This continuity sketch spawns variants of some of its segments, some of those side sketches representing discoveries, some of them dead ends.

In this first attempt at the exposition, he is already creating a sense of restless flux: in the middle of the first continuity sketch (marked X), the Hero theme climbs stepwise through a row of keys, B-flat to C to D-flat to E-flat. He will end up placing that idea later, in the development. Already, subsidiary themes are proliferating beyond the conventional one or two or three.

In an addendum to the first continuity sketch, he arrives at another significant idea, another resonance that will start on the first pages: the idea of drifting. The quiet first statement of the Hero theme drifts off into uncertainty (the C-sharp) before righting itself back in E-flat. The second statement of the theme starting in the solo horn drifts, with an upward chromatic slide, into F minor in the violins. Eventually the third statement of the theme will be a *fortissimo* eruption in E-flat for full orchestra — which quickly drifts into *piano*. No point of arrival holds steady. Already, this drifting conjures the image of a protagonist in motion, advancing but not yet arriving.

In another sketch he finds the hemiola figure that will be a steady feature of the movement: superimposing two-beat patterns over the three-beat meter, generating energy by striding across the bar line.[17] In a further sketch, Beethoven discovers another idea for the first page that will have great import: the unsettling syncopations of the violins moving from G to A-flat and back. That pair of notes will have a long career in the symphony.

Already, then, he has one of the central conceptions: he wants his exposition restless and searching, so its themes need to be fragmentary, incomplete, constantly in flux. From the first airing of the Hero theme forward, each idea will start decisively and then drift, avoiding a sense of closure or clear formal articulation. Everything points forward rather than feeling like an arrival. He wants that incessant nervous energy as an evocation of a military campaign or a battle: great forces on the move not only across a landscape but across the mind and across history. At the head of those forces, their driving energy: the Hero.

Which is all to say that *he fashions the exposition as if it were a development.*[18] This will be music about a process of *becoming*. Here is another element both abstract and symbolic: the Hero striving *toward* something. Call it *victory;* call it *coming into his own.*[19]

In the sketchbook, the second extended concept sketch is longer, a try at the whole exposition. Now he is up to five themes and has realized that if he wants that many ideas in an exposition, he needs to give each of them a distinctive character, rhythmic profile, and orchestral color. Eventually, there will be effectively six themes in the exposition, all of them less themes in the usual sense than protean gestures. The second concept sketch:

From Nottebohm, *Two Beethoven Sketchbooks*

He will throw out the last of those themes as irrelevant. In this continuity sketch also appears a hint of the loping scale figures he will use to link sections. And generally, from here on, each theme will be characterized not only by a distinctive rhythm but also by the way it interacts with or against the meter. Most of the themes (except, significantly, the Hero theme) break free of the bar line in one way and another.

He is well into the opening movement now, forging symbol and narrative into notes and form.[20] In his primal-triad theme and its avatars in all the other themes, the Hero is a galvanizing presence, able to bring freedom because he has freed himself. As a self-created man, the Hero transcends convention, shatters barriers, electrifies every soldier and *citoyen* with the force of his will. This is the image of an enlightened leader Beethoven learned in Bonn: to remake the world, you must remake yourself first. It is the figure he celebrated in the *Joseph* Cantata and in his song from that period *Who Is a Free Man?*: "The man to whom only his own will, and not any whim of an overlord, can give laws."[21]

In sketching the exposition, he has kept his proliferating themes fluid, like the arrival of the second theme proper (measure 57). It feels tender and breathless after the perorations of the Hero theme. But the arrival of that leading secondary idea is veiled; he is more interested in flow than in eighteenth-century formal clarity. So rather than the usual clear contrast of a first and second theme, there is a welter of contrasts, flowing, pulsing, and declaiming, moving restlessly around in the meter, every moment swallowed by the relentless onwardness, the constant sense of becoming.

By the time he writes down a fourth continuity sketch of the exposition, he is close to what he is looking for.[22] As transitions the loping scales are in place. Another transition in the middle features wide leaps, which will flower later in the movement. The Hero theme is always present, either overtly in its opening triadic horn call or in the triadic scaffolding of themes that seem independent but are avatars of the Hero theme. Sections of the long drafts that are not working he takes up and revises through page after page. The end of the exposition gives him trouble. A series of sketches probes how to end the first part and usher in the *Durchführung,* the development section's quasi-improvisation on themes from the exposition.[23]

●　　●　　●

Like any mature artist, Beethoven understands that a splendid conception and an effective realization are different things. The struggle to realize a conception on the page is an attempt to turn productive ideas into compelling material and self-generating form: the organic, coherent, gripping play of parts and whole. In the sketchbook, he began with a narrative conception on the order of *the nature and character of the hero Napoleon, and his journey*. He has turned that idea into themes, rhythms, phrasing, orchestral colors, a singular extension of the usual sonata-form model of a first movement. In this symphony, the guidelines and signposts of that model are expanded, blurred, subverted by the working out of the conception at hand. *Bonaparte* is to be new from top to bottom, in its material and in its form, the sounding image of the free man.

As was said earlier, for a craftsman of Beethoven's level, not only melodies and harmonies are expressive and meaningful; the whole of the form is expressive and meaningful. Here ideas form and dissolve, searching for stability and completion, everything *becoming*. A characteristic gesture in the first movement is its heavy-striding hemiola passages, their two-beats contradicting the three-beat meter, breaking the bar line. The strings respond to the disorienting C-sharp on the first page with a flurry of syncopations, unsettling the rhythm; harmony and rhythm regain their footing only to drift again. All the subsidiary themes, which are variegated avatars of the Hero, break out of the boundary of the meter in one way and another, most of them by way of displaced downbeats.

Hemiola

Displaced downbeats

Music and symbol feed on one another. In the struggle to come into his own, *the Hero shatters boundaries and conventions and makes things anew.* The exposition is as unpredictable, searching, dynamic, unstable as a development, as dynamic as a hero. In the exposition *the Hero is still uncertain, not fully formed.*[24] The task of the development proper will be to portray his struggle for completion, his triumph, his coming into his own.

With the exposition largely settled, Beethoven begins to hammer out his development. One of the first ideas he writes down for it is not the beginning but the aftermath of its climax: a flowing line in the distant key of E minor, a new theme that will stand as the most sustained melody, the most themelike passage in the movement. Before he begins detailed work on the development, then, he already has in hand its goal, what will become one of the most startling and striking episodes in the movement.[25]

Another early idea for the development will become the most notorious moment of all, what for more than a century will often be called an oversight, a mistake, even evidence of incipient madness. But Beethoven works out this idea through a dozen sketches, all on the same conception: while a string harmony in whispering tremolos prepares the recapitulation on a dissonance, a solo horn enters early on the Hero theme in E-flat, making an outlandish clash of harmonies:

From Nottebohm, *Two Beethoven Sketchbooks*

So before he starts working out the development in detail, he knows that its climax is going to be followed by a new theme in E minor. He also knows that the Hero theme will burst into the recapitulation prematurely, in the home key of E-flat, in its essential voice in the horn, over the wrong chord.[26] The premature *Thema* shatters the arrival of the recapitulation, as if the Hero has escaped the shackles of form and forces the music to sanction his transgression. *The Hero is a free man; it is his nature to break out of boundaries.*

As Beethoven gropes his way forward he faces a quandary: he has developed his themes from the beginning, made his exposition like a development. What, then, should he do in the development section itself? By the time he begins grappling with that problem, he has in hand the new E-minor theme and the recapitulation as targets to aim for. He settles on the idea of shaping the development as a series of waves surging toward the new theme, like armies surging toward the crux of a battle. The main element is the triadic head motif of the Hero theme rising implacably step by step in the bass, dragging the harmony upward from C minor to C-sharp, D, E, then G and A minor, and finally back to C minor. This generates a relentless, call it *fateful*, momentum different from the kaleidoscopic exposition.

For the second part of the development he feints at a fugue on a wide-striding subject that batters against the meter. But the fugue breaks down under hammer-blow hemiola chords. Those chords rise to a shattering harmony, horrifying to the ears of the time — an evil chord, not just a climax but a catastrophe:[27]

Following a crunching stride of dissonance in low strings, the crisis gives birth to the new theme in E minor, at the furthest remove from the home key of E-flat. This theme amounts to a new avatar of the Hero, built on his primal triad and the chromatic slide — the latter on the same pitches but in a new context. It is the moment of triumph, when *the Hero comes into his own.*

In using the Hero theme as scaffolding for this new development theme, the most sustained melodic passage in the movement, Beethoven makes the theme integrative. It represents coming into one's own not as a cry of victory but as a matter of grace under pressure; the new theme is inward in tone, and it flows with the meter as smoothly as a waltz. It seems almost to dance away from the crisis. All the same, this theme, like all the others, is not complete. Like everything in the movement, it also drifts off, swept up in the flux.

Beethoven's sketches for the new development theme all concern what ends up as its lower voice, derived from the Hero theme. In the final version he adds a counterpoint above it. In the end the new idea becomes *a double theme.* If its lower voice is built on the scaffolding of the Hero theme, the upper voice is integrative in a different way, looking forward more than backward. In the first pages of sketching the opening movement, he has already made a first attempt at a leading idea for the *second* movement, which is to be a funeral dirge.[28] The opening phrase of the *Funeral March* theme is settled from the first sketch, because he bases it on bars 5–7 of the *Prometheus* bass. The upper voice of the new development theme in the first movement is also based on that figure. So besides being integrative in relation to the first movement, *the upper line of the new development theme foreshadows the* Thema *of the* Funeral March. And it is played by the oboe, which will be its main avatar in the *Funeral March.*[29]

The new, integrative double theme soars away from the development's climax, its quiet song of triumph somehow encompassing the crisis that engendered it. The next phrases develop the new theme, emphasizing its upper and lower voices in alternation (the upper voice foreshadowing the theme of the second movement). Finally he arrives at the next attack on his listeners' ears with the horn, the sounding image of the Hero, jumping in early over the wrong chord and forcing the recapitulation.

The recapitulation Beethoven keeps fairly regular but still unresolved. The coda is fashioned as an enormous, slowly gathering, five-part conclusion nearly as long as the exposition. In the coda he knows the cognoscenti among his listeners will expect a resolution of the movement's conflicts and uncertainties. But that is not his intention. Already in the decade before, Beethoven had begun to rearrange the proportions of the first-movement form he inherited from Haydn and Mozart, mainly by extending the length and intensity of the development section and of the coda. Long or short, a coda can do several things. First and most traditionally, it is there to make a decisive final assertion of the home key, especially if there is thematic material that was never resolved to the tonic key. In that regard it can have a sense of thematic fulfillment or completion, as when he proclaims *das Thema* in glory. Second, a coda can pick up ideas and issues from the development and carry them further, functioning like a second development. Third, a coda can in one way and another prepare the next movement.[30] The coda of *Bonaparte's* first movement does all three, yet it still eludes a sense of completion.

He makes several small sketches and three extended drafts for the coda, none of them entirely like the final version.[31] There after a grandly sonorous D-flat chord, the music falls into a lilting new themelet placed over the first bars of the Hero theme, which rises step by step as it did in the development. A central point is that he wants the coda to return to the flowing new development theme and weave it fully into the fabric of the movement, resolving it into the home key of E-flat (though E-flat minor, not major). Again, that theme foreshadows the theme of the *Funeral March*.

Then he shapes a long windup to a final peroration of the Hero theme, beginning not with a triumphant blaze but rather quietly. It arrives in E-flat major, the home key, for the first time extended into something like a real theme in two regular four-bar phrases, played by its destined avatar the horn. What comes then is his most graphic representation of the Hero as leader. The music swells in a rising wave, at first around a trio of horns on the Hero theme, instruments joining in until all is *tutti fortissimo.* The effect is like a throng of people gathering behind the leader and moving toward some great act, some final victory. But the climactic *fortissimo* collapses after only two bars.[32] For the last time the music drifts off, going suddenly quiet with a return of the second theme. Once again, he pulls back from finality. The end of the first movement leaves a sense of final victory incomplete, unfulfilled. A giant-striding hemiola challenges the bar line to the last, until with two *fortissimo* yet oddly inconclusive chords the movement ends with an echo of its beginning. The rest of *Bonaparte* will constitute a search for the E-flat-major certainty of its opening chords.

In terms of the symphony's narrative, *the hero has come into his own, but his task is unfinished.*[33] At some point Beethoven decides that the paying off of the ideas and energies of the first movement, the completion of the Hero's task, will not happen until the finale. In fact, the final triumph and true conclusion will not take place until the last pages of the *Bonaparte* Symphony.

When it is time to realize the sketches in score, Beethoven finds a new richness in his handling of the orchestra. The scoring of the symphony needs to be as kaleidoscopic as the notes, from tender passages to brassy perorations. He begins work on this, like other pieces, by doing some groundwork. He studies an *Allgemeine Musikalische Zeitung* article about the natural horn, taking pages of notes.[34] His encounter with the horn virtuoso Giovanni Punto plays its part. The scale and sophistication of the symphony's horn writing are beyond anything he has done, and he adds a third horn to the usual two of the eighteenth-century orchestra. He conceives more elaborate clarinet parts than before. He gives the cellos an unprecedented independence, starting on the first page, where perhaps for the first time in a symphony they alone present the *Thema.* Again and again the cellos rise from their traditional place on the bass line to become a leading voice.

Besides giving a distinctive orchestral color to every theme and section in the first movement, he makes each succeeding movement distinctive in sound: the often-monolithic effect of the first movement spaced with lyrical moments, ideas restlessly passing from voice to voice in the orchestra; the shadow and light of the second movement, with imitations of drums and cannons; the darting, quicksilver sound of the scherzo and its hunting-horn trio; the sometimes chamberlike scoring of the finale, but including massive, brilliant tuttis. Meanwhile, if the horn is the protagonist of the first movement, of the trio of the scherzo, and of much of the finale, the voice of the oboe, from plaintive to incisive, is the first of the woodwinds, a second orchestral protagonist.

He finishes the first movement knowing it is the longest, most ambitious, most complex first movement of any symphony: a movement in the image of a great and unbridled hero.[35] The second movement will be no less remarkable.

The dramatic point of a second movement titled *Marcia funèbre* in a symphony called *Bonaparte* is plain enough: after the battle, in victory or defeat, the first task is the burial of the dead, with the requisite mourning and commemoration. Beethoven may have considered this a funeral for the masses of dead, or one for the martyred hero himself.

In the background of this solemn and elegiac C-minor second movement is the one Beethoven wrote for the op. 26 Piano Sonata titled "Funeral March for the Death of a Hero." Further in the background are funeral marches written in France in the wake of the Revolution, some of them well known in Vienna. For revolutionary festivals, French composers developed a grand popular style, simple and songful, often using massive sonorities featuring the military instruments of brass and drums.[36] For listeners of the day, this was the sounding image of revolution. Rodolphe Kreutzer had shown Beethoven collections of this music in 1798, at the residence of the French minister;

Beethoven registered it with his steel-trap mind for what might suit his purposes. Now in composing the whole of *Bonaparte* but most overtly in the second movement, he takes the revolutionary style and carries it far beyond his models.

He has kept the thematic ideas of the first movement fragmentary, protean, like voices rising and disappearing in the flux. Now as he sketches toward the main theme of the *Marcia funèbre,* he is looking for a piercing tragic lament, a dirge that will be the touchstone of the movement, never far away. With that kind of ambition weighing on it, the melody does not come easily. He decides to start without introduction. The dotted pickup and first two bars, the melodic shape extracted from the *Prometheus* bass and foreshadowed in the first movement's E-minor development theme, are settled right away. After that he wrestles with the dirge bar by bar, sketch after sketch, until it has found the depth and tragic scope he requires for *das Thema* of a movement about burial, sorrow, mourning, and apotheosis:[37]

The beginning of the movement he shapes as an archetypal funeral march from the Revolution, from all wars: a mournful dirge in the darkest register of the violins, the basses evoking muffled drums. In the mind's eye, troops slowly march behind the catafalque, the masses gathered to watch the procession and to grieve. The dirge rises to a piercing dissonance on A-flat, falling to G, which captures the pathos of the scene (as falling half steps did in the *Pathétique*). Those two pitches, singled out on the first page of the symphony, will play a steady role in the movement. The opening dead march is answered by a consoling E-flat-major theme in richly scored strings, echoing (whether or not he realized it) the well-known *Marche lugubre* of François-Joseph Gossec, who had been in the vanguard of French revolutionary composers.[38]

Once again Beethoven has to be a psychologist in tones. He wants this music to enfold the whole process of mourning, which is not one event and one emotion but a mingling of events and emotions: formal public mourning and inchoate private sorrow, and the exaltation of the dead as martyrs patriotic and transcendent. Meanwhile the end of burial and elegy is to honor the dead and also to give completion. In those terms humanity endures tragedy and lays it to rest. The hope of mourning is to reclaim joy. All those things he enfolds in this music that is based on French models but still sounds sui generis. → OF IT'S OWN KIND

Ø Hymn
To God   From beginning to end there is a missing element in this funeral service: there is no hymn to God. It is a secular humanist ceremony, as it would have been in revolutionary France.[39]

To encompass the stages of burial and mourning, Beethoven again has to bend formal traditions, this time nearly beyond recognition. The basic form is on the order of a march with trio, ABA. But he needs more perspectives than ABA can give him. To that pattern he adds interludes, constant variations of the material, internal repeats that evolve into a complex and unprecedented form dominated by the rondo-like return of the dirge — six returns, four of them varied, moving between C minor and F minor.

After the flowing beginning of the middle section in C major (with perhaps representations of cannon shots) and the return of the dirge in C minor, he takes up a solemn and majestic double fugue. It rises to a transcendent climax in the high-humanistic key of E-flat: horns soar upward accompanied by strings striding up and down. It is a moment of heart-filling grandeur that Beethoven will never surpass and hardly equal. It is not a paean to God but a hymn to humanity.[40] Then the music falls back to earth, to the burial of the dead: a crashing low A-flat chord, drums and cannons, lacerating bugle calls. It dies away to a return of the dirge over an ominously surging bass; that resolves to the consolation of the B theme, but the bass and dirge return, and the drums and bugles.[41]

He begins the coda in D-flat, as he did the coda of the first movement, here with a fragile but hopeful new theme like the sun breaking out over a scene of mourning. It does not last. The anguish returns, cadencing back to C minor with the snarl of a low stopped horn and wind figures like distant wails. Composing the end takes him hours, perhaps days of improvising at the keyboard and singing and walking, some eight drafts on the page to discover what he wants.[42] The result is extraordinary, unprecedented. The music is no longer the picture of a march or a funeral cortege. It is inside now, in the heart, and there the dirge falls into sighs and fragments. The movement ends with a distant cry, sinks again to deathly silence.

In summer 1803, Beethoven begins work on the third movement with an idea for its ending. At the head of the sketch is "M.," meaning "minuetto." The summer before, he had made an initial sketch for the movement labeled Minuetto serioso. But in these years he is apt to be vague in what he calls a "minuet" and a "scherzo." It is not clear when he begins seeing these ideas in fast scherzo tempo rather than slower minuet. He continues with a peculiar note: "M[inuetto] at the end of the Coda a strange vo[ice]" — *eine fremde St[imme].*[43] The "strange" (meaning foreign-to-the-movement) voice in question involves a rising three-note chromatic line, the chromatic slide that he established in the first movement as a central motif. That *fremde Stimme* will indeed end up in the coda of the movement.

Soon, he finds the dashing, folklike melody of the scherzo, whether he sees it yet as scherzo or minuet. A long continuity sketch adds an introduction to the E-flat theme and makes some stabs at the trio. Then something takes hold. He sketches a rushing figure leading up to the folk theme and notes the tempo as *presto.* Whether or not he had been before, now he is composing not a minuet but a scherzo. Now he has the ideas that will dominate the movement: a rushing figure of indecipherable meter sounding like a teeming host (the hemiolas of the first movement becoming manic) and his bit of piping folk tune:

From there the scherzo takes shape quickly.[44] The two basic ideas of rushing figure and folk tune (most essentially in the oboe), steadily varied, modulating, sometimes taking the form of intricate chromatic windings, will be material for the movement proper. The movement is dashing, impetuous, quicksilver, the form taking shape with reference to traditional minuet-scherzo form, adapted and expanded. One singular feature is that after an opening indistinct murmur in E-flat, the music moves to B-flat and first presents its little oboe tune in that key,

(*continued from previous page*)

then in F, then in B-flat again. Only then, *tutti fortissimo,* horns leaping upward, basses following the theme in canon, does the tune arrive
in the home key of E-flat with a joyous sense of *Aha!* The model for
this procedure is the first movement, where the Hero theme is heard
quietly twice before its *tutti fortissimo* eruption.[45] In some ways, the
3/4 scherzo is an echo of the 3/4 first movement lightened, accelerated,
electrified.

In the trio section of the scherzo, he revels in his trio of horns in
their primeval role as hunting horns. The classically virile, crowing
theme is based on a triad, making it another avatar of the first movement's Hero theme:

The coda begins with a *pianissimo* whisper, and there he places (from measure 425) the "strange voice" he had noted in the first sketch:

The keening chromatic slide D-flat–D–E-flat does sound like a voice from somewhere outside the scherzo (though its notes are already there in the violins a few measures earlier). And indeed, the figure is from outside: the "strange voice" answers the downward chromatic slide E-flat–D–C-sharp on the first page of the symphony that created a harmonic kink, the C-sharp a sore note that has resonated ever since. Here, at the end of the scherzo, after its adventures as both C-sharp and D-flat, the sore note resolves up to the tonic note. From there, the music gathers strength and intensity, just as did the coda of the first movement, up to a *tutti fortissimo* finish in three curt staccato chords. (All the movements end with staccato chords.)

From the sketches, then, it appears that he started the third movement at first with little clear sense of it, either its material or perhaps even its genre — not sure whether it was minuet or scherzo.

But when the ideas appear and become *presto,* the movement takes shape as a stretch of effervescent exhilaration. As the *Marcia funèbre* followed the battle, the scherzo follows as the end of burial and mourning: the return to life and to joy. That journey, from suffering to joy, is a story Beethoven enacted over and over in his music, and in the whole of his life.

For Beethoven to begin work on the finale is to arrive in familiar territory: the *basso* and *englische* themes he has handled three times before and decreed from the beginning will be the goal of *Bonaparte.* He knew from the beginning that his approach here would echo the treatment in the *Prometheus* Variations for piano: after a new introduction in the context of the symphony, he will start with the *Basso del Tema* and add voices until the *englische* tune arrives. He will quote none of the variations from the piano version, only the *basso* and tune. The variations have to be redone for orchestra and for a new purpose — at once an arrival, a fulfillment, and an apotheosis.[46]

The qualities musical and humanistic that Beethoven found in the *englische* are manifest in its being the foundation of two major sets of variations, one for piano and now this one for orchestra. After the rise and victory of the Hero, the burial of the dead, and the scherzo's return to life and joy, the music arrives at the gift the Hero has given to the world. Recall Schiller's words on the *englische*:

> I can think of no more fitting image for the ideal of social conduct than an English dance, composed of many complicated figures and perfectly executed. A spectator . . . sees innumerable movements intersecting in the most chaotic fashion . . . yet *never colliding* . . . It is all so skillfully, and yet so artlessly, integrated into a form, that each seems only to be following his own inclination, yet without ever getting in the way of anybody else. It is the most perfectly appropriate symbol of the assertion of one's own freedom and regard for the freedom of others.[47]

Here is the meaning of the simple contredanse that underlies a heroic symphony: the *englische* as image of the ideal society, the conquering

Hero's gift to humanity. As in the other movements, it is a dramatic and symbolic image adumbrated in musical form.[48]

Like the scherzo, the finale falls quickly into place for him. The first sketch is the first four notes of the *basso*, the head motif that in much of the movement will stand for the whole of the theme, as the first four notes of the Hero theme often served in the first movement. Next he writes down a rushing passage in sixteenths, in G minor. It evolves into the G-minor eruption that will begin the finale.[49]

In the end that manifestly militant introduction storms only briefly. By the end of the first phrase, the music has turned into the familiar mode of an introduction to a dance, and the variation-finale proper is under way. The music conjures the atmosphere of the *Prometheus* ballet, the *Basso del Tema* run through alone and echoed jauntily in the winds. As in the ballet version, a suddenly loud three-eighth tattoo serves as a kind of refrain to the *basso*.[50] Its ending starts with the A-flat–G figure and brings the music back to the tonic, the home key. Like most sets of variations, and also like the music for an *englische* at a dance, the finale will have a series of contrasting sections with changes of mood and tempo.

He gathers the variations over the *basso* as he did in the piano version: the music first in two parts, then three, then four. In the third variation he arrives at what the music was searching for, the sprightly little *englische* tune, first in the light mode of a dance, then suddenly loud, assertive, undergirded with rocketing bass lines. From its beginning, *the goal of the symphony is the* englische. Which is to say, this dance and the ideal society for which it is a symbol are going to be exalted. The idea of an apotheosis in dance was implicit from the beginning. The Hero theme of the first movement was not a martial figure but a dance on the order of a waltz, and its half-and-quarter trochaic rhythm foreshadowed the dotted-quarter-and-eighth trochees of the *englische*. At the same time, the first three notes of the Hero theme are the same as the beginning of the *englische*: E-flat–G–E-flat.

Once more Beethoven fashions a singular, ad hoc form for the finale, less a series of variations in discrete blocks than a movement that will gather, swell, intensify toward the end. In his sets of variations

Kapellmeister Ludwig van Beethoven the elder, as he wished to be remembered.
© *Alfredo Dagli Orti / The Art Archive / Corbis*

View of Bonn from the Rhine, with the Electoral Residence in the left middle.
Stadtarchiv und Stadthistorische Bibliothek Bonn, Grafiksammlung

Beethoven's birthplace in Bonn.
Beethoven-Haus Bonn

Silhouette of Beethoven at around sixteen, probably made at Frau von Breuning's house.
Beethoven-Haus Bonn

Beethoven's teacher Christian Neefe, the dreamer and *Schwärmer*.
Beethoven-Haus Bonn

Bonn's Elector Maximilian Franz, brother of Emperor Joseph in Vienna.
Beethoven-Haus Bonn

The marketplace in Bonn, with Elector Maximilian Friedrich's monument to himself in the middle, the Rathaus in the rear, and Frau Koch's Zehrgarten wine bar on the right.
Stadtarchiv und Stadthistorische Bibliothek Bonn, Grafiksammlung

Count Waldstein, Beethoven's most important patron in Bonn.
Österreichische Nationalbibliothek

View of Vienna, showing the grassy Glacis, the old walls, and St. Stephen's Cathedral in the middle.

Fine Art Images / Superstock

The imperious Prince Karl Lichnowsky, Beethoven's first powerful patron in Vienna.

Getty Images

Prince Joseph Lobkowitz, another important patron, who bankrupted himself with his passion for music.

Österreichische Nationalbibliothek

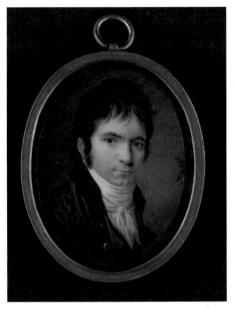

Ivory miniature of Beethoven in 1802.
Beethoven-Haus Bonn, Collection H. C. Bodmer

Ivory miniature of Julie Guicciardi, Beethoven's first serious love in Vienna.
Beethoven-Haus Bonn, Collection H. C. Bodmer

View of rural Heiligenstadt, with the village in the distance.
The Art Archive / Superstock

Violinist Ignaz Schuppanzigh, Beethoven's "Mylord Falstaff" and his irreplaceable partner in remaking the string quartet.

Beethoven-Haus Bonn

Violin virtuoso George Polgreen Bridgetower, for whom Beethoven wrote the *Kreutzer* Sonata. Bridgetower billed himself as the "son of the African Prince."

© The British Library Board, P.P. 1931 pcx, vol. 182, p. 296

since childhood, he has imposed overarching plans, and so it is here. It is the particularities of the plan, the interweaving of material, the gathering of threads from earlier movements, the multidimensional form, that make this movement unprecedented, more pointed and forceful than variations tend to be. The finale will be kaleidoscopic, like the first and second movements. Like the first movement it will be a kind of ongoing process, but with more sustained themes and a sense of stylistic evolution and transformation.

Within the overall process of intensification, he lays out the finale in four large sections, though the effect is more continuous than strongly marked. The first section reaches the *englische* and develops it at length. The second section (from measure 117) leaves E-flat for C minor, starting as a double fugue (constituting variation 4) on a motif from the first variation combined with the *basso* (this recalls fugues in the *Marcia funèbre* and in the first movement). The fugue dissolves into variation 5, a quiet recall of the *englische* in distant B minor / D major. That reversion to a dance style leads to a climactic *fortissimo* in triplets, reminiscent of the scherzo. Variation 6 is a real march at last, the first one in this work whose subject is a military hero: a "Turkish"-tinged march in G minor, the style familiar from the military music of the day, the effect like a passing parade of soldiers in a peaceful time.

The third section of the finale builds to an apotheosis of the *Basso del Tema*. It starts with variation 7, another quiet recall of the *englische* in C major. Variation 8 is another *fugato* over the *basso*, in E-flat major. With that Beethoven makes a peculiar decision, to return to the home key in the middle of a section, *pianissimo*.[51] But this is a return of many things, another gathering of threads. Figures in the *fugato* recall the C-sharp/D-flat sore note and G–A-flat motif going back to the first page of the symphony.

During the *fugato* the *basso* theme is inverted — turned upside down. Inversion is an old contrapuntal device, but Beethoven does not make this inversion casually: the scaffolding of the Hero theme was an inversion of the *basso*. In the middle of the *fugato,* the flutes dart in with the beginning of the *englische* theme, E-flat–G–E-flat–D. Then the horns enter on the same, but with a new last note suiting their nature as horns: E-flat–G–E-flat–B-flat. Those four notes are, of course, the head motif of the first movement's Hero theme. Here Beethoven "explains" where that motif came from.[52] With his theme, the Hero is present, in person or in recollection. The section ascends to a climax, the *basso* in glory pealing out in the horns.[53]

He has shaped the finale as a steady intensification from the light style of a dance to a heroic voice, and has placed the exaltation of the *Basso del Tema* at the end of the third section. The fourth and last section of the finale is the apotheosis of the *englische* melody. Rather than carrying its accustomed lilt, it appears solemnly, *poco andante*. Here he transforms the *englische* into a hymn, its poignant leading voice the oboe that has been the main wind protagonist all along. At this moment near the end of the symphony, he makes his little dance tune into a song of great tenderness and compassion. As in the *Funeral March,* this is a hymn not to God but to Humanity. At the same time he gathers up more threads. In a web of subtle allusions in the third section, he recalls themes, colors, textures, feelings from the *Marcia funèbre:* the martyrs to freedom are recalled, woven into the pattern of life.[54] Now the music has moved from a heroic voice to one inward, contemplative, commemorative. In that way the finale retraces the journey from first to second movement, from victory to mourning, outward to inward. Once again he builds to a *fortissimo* climax, the horns pealing out the *englische* theme.[55] Slowly the music sinks from that peak to stasis and anticipation.

So ends the finale proper. Throughout the symphony, Beethoven has suppressed a sense of completion and closure. For that he has reserved the very end, an explosion of jubilation that is the climax not only of the finale but of the whole of *Bonaparte.* Mozart wrote that when he reached the end of a work he felt the whole of it resounding in the last chord. So it is here. The final pages are what the unfulfilled end of the first movement was waiting for, the true victory, the completion of the Hero's task. The coda is presented like the denouement of a great ceremony vibrant with horns and trumpets — like throngs, like all humanity exulting in a revolution triumphant, with a joy that obliterates everything else. The theme the horns proclaim is Hero and *englische,* leader and people united; the harmony is nothing but the tonic and dominant of the *basso.* The end celebrates humanity's imagined triumph, and no less Beethoven's real one.

[handwritten: 3rd Symphony EROICA]

There are many resonances social and musical in the densely woven fabric of movements Beethoven fashioned in 1803, which was finally published in 1806 as a symphony now called *Eroica*. With it he reached his full maturity by joining his Aufklärung ethos with his music. In the framework of metaphors and symbols conveyed by means of a few words — *Bonaparte, Marcia funèbre, Eroica* — and otherwise in notes, shapes, forms, analogies, there is a final crucial point. *Das Thema* of the first movement was made from the finale's *Prometheus* bass and the *englische* melody. If the theme of the first movement is the Hero, call its source in the finale's *englische* dance tune the People, who are humanity.

Whether or not Beethoven saw it consciously as such, here is an overarching metaphor. Like Napoleon, this enlightened Hero does not rise from aristocracy or from accident of birth but is self-created from his origin in the People, just as his theme is created from its origin in the *englische*. Thereby the self-created hero becomes a paradigm of all human potential. To exalt this kind of Hero is to exalt the People, the common clay. The Hero theme turns that idea into sound: it is based on a triad, one of the simplest and most common things in music. From that common clay, the theme is exalted. *[handwritten: A CHORD OF 3 NOTES - A GIVEN NOTE TO A 3RD + 5TH ABOVE IT]*

In autumn of 1803, back in his flat in the Theater an der Wien, Beethoven wrote out the orchestral score of the Third Symphony. Its *[handwritten: fall 1803]* flowery title page proclaimed, *Sinfonia grande / intitulata Bonaparte / del Sigr. / Louis van Beethoven*. Then he turned his pen to other projects nearly as extraordinary. He knew beyond doubt that this was the best thing he had done. He hoped it would have a brilliant future. But he could hardly have imagined the implications of that future. The *Eroica* reframed what a symphony, and to a degree what music itself, could be and achieve. It would stand as one of the defining statements of the German Aufklärung and of the power of the heroic leader, the benevolent despot, to change himself and the world. No less is its exalting of such an individual a prophecy of the Romantic century, whose cult of genius would declare Beethoven the true hero of the *Eroica*.[56]

Before long this symphony took its place as one of the monumental humanistic documents of its time, and of all time. Its purpose is not to praise God but to exalt humanity. It is a vision of what an enlightened leader can do in the world. But Beethoven had not forgotten God. Some two decades later, in his last symphony, he would return to the question of the ideal society, the search for Elysium under the starry heavens. And again and again in his music he returned to an ending in joy.

At age thirty-two, Beethoven had once again mobilized a gift he had possessed since childhood, of making prodigious advances in a short period. In the genre of symphony he had made three leaps in less than four years whose scope is larger than most artists travel in a lifetime. Starting with, in his terms, the cautious and conservative First Symphony, by the Third he had created a work that, when its import and impact played out in the next years, remade the genre of symphony once and for all. In some quarters, at least, the symphony had already been declared the first of genres, based on what Haydn and Mozart had made of it. Beethoven had taken the development of the Classical symphony where Haydn and Mozart pointed it but in directions neither of them could have imagined. A new scope and ambition had entered the symphonic genre, and it would stay there.[57]

For Beethoven himself, the *Bonaparte* (eventually *Eroica*) Symphony did not so much begin the New Path as confirm and epitomize it. What did the New Path, his full maturity, amount to? In the long view, it was no complete departure. Rather, he took up his boldest and most personal mode, heard in the *Pathétique* and the op. 31 Sonatas, among other works, as his essential voice. By the force of his personality he went on to move the mainstream of music toward that voice.

But what one conceives oneself to be doing and what one is perceived by one's public to be doing are two different things. For Beethoven the New Path (what later history would name the Second, or "Heroic," Period) was mainly a private matter between himself and his Muse. For the public it was a different and grander issue. After the inevitable inertia of opinion, a growing chorus of musicians, listeners, and critics called the *Eroica* unprecedented, magnificent, terrifying, exalted: *revo-*

New Path = Second or Heroic Period

lutionary and before long *Romantic.* Yet while many of his audience joined Beethoven to the spirit of the French Revolution, he never said anything to that effect (though never denied it, either).

In his *Bildung* and in his temperament, Beethoven was not a Romantic, and he never called himself a revolutionary. He based much of what he did on tradition, models, and authorities, and he never intended to overthrow the past. He was an evolutionist more than a revolutionist. Call him a *radical evolutionary,* one with a unique voice.

In practice, then, the New Path was not entirely new but more of a stylistic and technical consolidation. In terms of technique, he intensified the drive to integration, making more elements thematic throughout a work. His major works had always seemed distinctive, individual. Now they became intensely more so, each work a strong-featured and unforgettable personality not only in its material but in its very sound and fundamental conception.[58]

In *The Tempest* and the *Eroica* and the coming works of the New Path, Beethoven intensified and consolidated a particular conception of theme and form. Rather than following his usual procedure — learned mainly from Haydn and Mozart — of starting with extended themes from which he extracted motifs as building blocks, now sometimes he treated motifs as protean elements in the foreground. So he might conceive movements without themes in the usual sense, which is to say, he used motifs *as* themes, like the mysterious arpeggio that begins *The Tempest,* which seems like an introduction but turns out to be a generating idea, or the triad and chromatic slide that constitute the Hero theme of the *Eroica.*[59] (The distillation of this motif-as-theme trend would be the Fifth Symphony.) Beethoven had begun to think of any element of music as potentially thematic; not only traditional melodic and rhythmic figures but even a single chord like a Neapolitan or a diminished seventh could be a unifying motif. Likewise a texture, a trill, a single pitch, silence — the simplest and most common elements of music. For him this desire to treat anything as a potential leading motif was not new on the New Path, but the tendency intensified categorically.

Now his handling of form became not so much more varied or experimental as more expressive, more flexible and responsive to the conception at hand. In practice, though, after the *Eroica* his forms largely became more regular than before. Which is to say that as the ideas themselves became bolder and more pointed (other times more lyrical and pointed) and his rhythm more dynamic, the formal outline became more individual and expressive, though not usually more complex or experimental — until the late music.

When he finished the *Eroica,* Beethoven was no longer looking cautiously over his shoulder at the past. Now he saw himself as the peer of Haydn and Mozart. At the same time, his relation to the public had changed. He would never stop producing items designed for popular appeal, but in his major works he no longer worried about challenging his audience (though he still loathed bad reviews). Now he was prepared to make demands. If the *Bonaparte* Symphony was beyond his audience on first hearing, he expected them to listen again, and again and again. Here was a sea change from the attitude of Haydn and Mozart, who by and large wrote for the immediate pleasure of audiences and performers while incorporating subtleties for the delectation of connoisseurs.

Part of what was truly new in the New Path was a joining of Beethoven's art and his Aufklärung consciousness. His music became more personal and intense partly because he found ways to connect his work to intensely held ideals, at the top of them freedom and joy. His politics were not revolutionary, not Jacobin, not even democratic, but very much republican: he believed in the sovereignty of constitutions and laws, like the British parliamentary system (with its king and its Houses of Lords and Commons). At the same time, like many liberal Germans he still had the echt-Aufklärung belief in the strong man, the benevolent despot, which is to say, the Hero. Even if some of his personal heroes, like Elector Max Franz and Holy Roman Emperor Joseph II, were born to their thrones and he had no dispute with aristocracy in theory, his image of the hero was not in itself aristocratic in the hereditary sense. He believed in an aristocracy of mind and talent and spirit.

It was central to Beethoven that Napoleon was not highborn but self-made — the first such man in European history to wield such power. For all his eventual disgust at the dictator, that admiration endured. A French visitor of 1809 reported, "He was uncommonly preoccupied with Napoleon's greatness and often spoke to me about it. Although he was not well-disposed towards him, I noticed that he admired his rise from such a lowly position."[60] (Actually Napoleon's "lowly" origin was partly a myth. His family came from minor rural nobility; his father was a lawyer.) Now at the end of 1803, still determined "irrevocably" to go to Paris, Beethoven had a symphony worthy and appropriate to lay at Napoleon's feet, whether figuratively or literally.

But for him the heroic image did not apply only to political and military leaders; it applied to anyone self-made, self-generated, capable and courageous, rising above the crowd and therefore a natural leader: a "free man." Napoleon was that kind of free man and, inescapably, Beethoven perceived himself to be the same. He would model some — by no means all — of the works of the coming decade on the image of the hero, in many guises: the great leader, the strong man, hope of the people, or, as in the Fourth Piano Concerto, the brooding loner. So inevitably Beethoven, leading music on the New Path that he saw opening before him, became one of the heroes in his own stories.[61] And part of his heroic voice was built on the French revolutionary style.[62] For him a free society was one that allows a Napoleon and a Beethoven to rise as far as their natural gifts can take them. In France it had taken a revolution to make that possible. In German lands, however, by the time the *Eroica* appeared that dream of freedom had come to seem a dead relic of the past. In Austria particularly, society and social mobility were frozen in place, freedom of thought under relentless assault.

The later Romantic generations of the nineteenth century saw his intensely personal music, and saw it rightly, as a revelation of the individual consciousness and personality: the individual as hero, fundamental to the Romantic vision of the world. To the degree that in his youth Beethoven absorbed the Kantian ideas that were in the air, he learned that freedom is required to become a complete human being and that every free person must think and judge for himself as an individual. That, Kant said, is the essence of Enlightenment. He also said that the world as it is perceived and interpreted by each person is all that is possible for human beings to know. The self is essentially the world. And like the Hero's journey in the *Eroica*, that self is continually in flux, continually becoming.

Christian Neefe and the other Freemasons and Illuminati around Beethoven taught that the foundation of changing the world is first to remake yourself. While the Romantics mythologized the supreme Self, they rejected the Aufklärung delusion that individuals and societies can be perfected. Aufklärers proclaimed the triumphs they believed to be imminent under the rule of a free, rational, enlightened humanity grounded in the rule of enlightened leaders. The Romantics turned away from what Novalis called "the cold voice of Reason" and exalted the passionate, the unattainable, the unimaginable, the sublime, the great and terrible. (Given the reaction and repression that happened after the fall of Napoleon, there was little to exalt anyway but the unattainable.)

Beethoven would be *the* composer for the coming Romantic generation, who resonated with his proclamation of the individual as if it were a democratic revolution in tones. But Beethoven was not a Romantic, not a revolutionist, not a democrat. He was a republican who came of age in the revolutionary 1780s, all for *fraternité* and *liberté*, not remotely for *egalité*.[63] The people as a whole were rabble to him. "Vox populi, vox dei," he said late in life, "I never believed it." In practice, the models of *egalité* he grew up with were those of the Freemasons and Illuminati, an equality of middle-class artists and bureaucrats and midlevel aristocracy — the society he lived in most of his life.

It is unanswerable to what degree the sense of humanistic individualism in his mature music, in the heroic style and otherwise, was a conscious matter or simply Beethoven being Beethoven, an individual to the point of solipsism. That was who he was, and his music came out of who he was. But as with any artist of any value, his art was a great deal bigger than he was. No better example of that than the *Eroica*. His individualism, his engagement with the zeitgeist, and his determination to serve humanity (despite his disdain for most of humanity in the flesh) made his music imperative for the Romantic generations — even the egalitarian Romantics. For his time and later, his music breathed a new sense of the individual engaged with the world, like a dancer caught up in the whirling patterns of the *englische*. With the New Path and the *Eroica* he unleashed emotional forces that had been unknown to music, of a raw power and individuality the eighteenth century had never imagined. He became a new kind of composer writing a new kind of music, yet he did it without pulling up his roots in the eighteenth century.

To discover new means of expression is to discover new territories of the human. It seems that such an ideal, not revolution, was what Beethoven considered to be his task, his duty. He had always believed he had it in him to do something like that. The difference now was that he knew how to do it.

In October 1803, Ferdinand Ries wrote to publisher Simrock in Bonn, "He wants to sell you the Symphony for 100 gulden. In his own opinion it is the greatest work that he has yet written. Beethoven played it for me recently, and I believe that heaven and earth will tremble when it is performed. He is very much inclined to dedicate it to Bonaparte, but because Lobkowitz wants to have it for half a year and will give 400 gulden, then he will entitle it 'Bonaparte.'"[64]

In Beethoven's sketchbook, after the last of the *Bonaparte* pages the creative juices were still running high. In the middle of the symphony sketches he noted down a folk-dance tune that would serve in the scherzo of the Sixth Symphony, along with two sketches trying to capture the sound of a murmuring brook, with a note: "the bigger the brook the deeper the tone." There was a sketch for the Schikaneder opera *Vestas Feuer;* its melody would end up in *Fidelio.* Bonn had been on his mind through these months. Directly after the *Bonaparte* pages, with no pause for breath, he jotted down ideas for an epochal piano sonata that came to be named for its dedicatee from the Bonn days: *Waldstein.*

18

Geschrieben auf Bonaparte

IN LATE 1803, Beethoven returned to his cramped quarters as house composer in the Theater an der Wien. There Stephan von Breuning brought to see him a young Rhinelander named Willibrord Joseph Mähler. He was a civil servant of various artistic leanings: amateur singer, poet, songwriter, and portrait painter. Beethoven was generally pleased to make the acquaintance of anyone from his homeland. Even more to his credit, Mähler had been born in Ehrenbreitstein, hometown of Beethoven's mother. When Mähler asked to hear something, Beethoven obliged, playing the variation-finale of the *Bonaparte* Symphony. When he got toward the end of the movement he kept playing, improvising new variations for two hours.

"There was not a measure which was faulty," Mähler recalled, "or which did not sound original." As much as the music, he remembered Beethoven at the keyboard, "with his hands so very still; wonderful as his execution was there was no tossing of them to and fro, up and down; they seemed to glide right and left over the keys, the fingers alone doing the work."[1] That day Mähler did not see the performer who broke hammers and strings with a power beyond the capacities of his instruments. Beethoven also had a most delicate legato. Carl

Czerny noted that he often played his best in slow, soulful music; his "playing of adagio and legato . . . has yet to be excelled."[2]

Given that Mähler was an amiable young man and a native of, as far as Beethoven was concerned, the best place on earth, in the next year he was able to persuade the impatient and fidgety composer to sit still for a portrait. The painting turned out odd and memorable, a companion to the Bonn portrait of old Ludwig, the composer's grandfather. Both paintings are interpretations of the life of a musician. Grandfather Ludwig had himself rendered as an imperious man of importance, turning the pages of a score. Mähler painted Ludwig van Beethoven the younger as an icon of Genius.

In his left hand this icon holds a lyre, symbol of a musician in general and of Apollo the singer in particular. The right hand is extended and splayed in a peculiar way, which the painter described "as if, in a moment of musical enthusiasm, he was beating time." He had learned that Beethoven was given to startling musical enthusiasms, vocally and physically. He also noted Beethoven's blunt, square hand. For his portrait Beethoven is neatly and fashionably dressed, his hair cut in the French neo-Roman style. The face is impassive, the eyes piercing. This too is well observed: others noted that in public Beethoven's face was often reserved and blank, his feelings visible mainly in the flash of his small brown eyes. In private, over a glass of wine, he might become jolly and teasing. In both public and private he rose easily to fury.

The background of the painting is as telling as the figure. To the left of the picture, Mähler explained, is a temple of Apollo.[3] On the other side, behind Beethoven, looms a dark forest with a dead tree at the top. For the sunlit temple, read the Classical past, both of antiquity and of the eighteenth century that exalted reason and restraint: the rational. For the dark forest, read the wild, the mysterious, the emotional, the Romantic: the irrational. Which is to say that in the first years of the nineteenth century, at the moment Beethoven had embarked on the New Path, this artist already portrayed him as a bridge between Classical and Romantic. If Mähler was not a great painter, he was a keen observer of his subject as a man and as an incipient icon and myth. This would be Beethoven's favorite portrait of himself, the one he kept with him alongside the portrait of his grandfather: two musicians in ideal and in action.

As winter came on in 1803, Beethoven involved himself with finalizing the *Bonaparte* Symphony and exploring what it had unleashed, where it pointed on his New Path. The implications unfolded in a scarcely believable rush over the next few years, producing some works in the heroic vein, some not, but all of a phenomenal strength and freshness. The main project of that year's end was a *Grande Sonate* for piano in C major. It would be dedicated to his Bonn patron and mentor Count Ferdinand Waldstein, at that point away from the Continent serving in the British army. This sonata was the repayment of an old debt for the man who as much as any had helped launch Beethoven, a mentor and patron for the teenager and then a connection to important Viennese patrons. The two must have met after Bonn, but no record remained of it.

So op. 53 came to be called the *Waldstein*. Beethoven wrote it with the inspiration of his new French Érard piano and its four pedals and extended range, its action heavier and its sound bigger than the Viennese pianos he was used to. It had a foot pedal to raise the dampers, rather than the traditional knee lever, making pedal effects more inviting.[4] With his usual forcefulness he told an acquaintance that he was "so enchanted with it that he regards all the pianos made here [in Vienna] as rubbish."[5] Perhaps for that reason, this twenty-first of his published piano sonatas would be the one most thoroughly involved to that point with exploring and expanding the instrument, in music of vibrant coloration. The very nature of the piano became the vehicle of a heroic journey that ends in overflowing exaltation.

The *Waldstein* Sonata leaps into life in medias res, with a sense of restless energy that will hardly flag throughout. Above the pounding rhythms are only scraps of motifs; at first the music is like an accompaniment in search of a theme.[6] Mainly the effect is of a surging and singularly pianistic dynamism. The C-major opening immediately strays to G major, then drops to B-flat major straying to F, searching for resolution. The main relief from the irresistible drive is the sudden peace of the chorale-like second theme in a radiant E major, which sprouts a babbling variation in triplets. Perhaps the most remarkable thing about the movement is that, for all its energy, most of it is soft: crescendos often lead to a *subito piano* marking; the few loud moments are placed in transitional sections or quickly choked off. The movement surges and drives, but most of it is actually *piano* to *pianissimo*. The governing idea is power under restraint, generating a fund of energy that never dissipates and never climaxes. As in the Third Symphony first movement, everything points forward.[7]

In the *Waldstein* Beethoven invented fresh colors and textures for the piano and at the same time took a fresh look at C major. As the key most in tune on the keyboards of the time, it usually represented the mean, the restrained, a tonality suitable for equanimity or for grandeur, even military pomp, but not for passion or excitement. Now Beethoven made it sonorous and intense, partly by surrounding it with surprising tonalities. The drop to B-flat in the beginning foreshadows a sonata written largely in flat keys. Into that mix of darker flat keys he drops two brilliant sharp ones: the E major of the second theme, which comes around in the recapitulation in an equally breathtaking A major. (Only in a reminiscence in the coda does the second theme find its resolution into C major.)

As a second movement he drafted a long, tranquil, quite beautiful Andante grazioso con moto that he was especially fond of. But when he played the completed sonata for one of his friends (it is not recorded which one), the friend declared the middle movement too long. Beethoven responded angrily. Soon after, he decided the friend was right. He took the long movement out of the *Waldstein* and published it as *Andante favori* ("favorite andante"), because it was a piece he liked to play at soirees.[8] With its warmly proto-Romantic tone, it became a favorite of many besides the composer.

With that friend's help, he had realized that the long Andante would have been a critical miscalculation. In the first movement he had deposited a great deal of energy in a kind of savings account, waiting to pay off. A long middle movement would have dissipated that energy. So to replace the Andante he wrote a short, transitional slow movement in F major—a shadowed, minorish major. As counterpoise to the driving and extroverted outer movements, this middle passage is

inward, chromatic, searching, full of silences, unfolding like an improvisation. Midway it finds an exquisitely poignant melody, only to see it
evaporate. It is a short stretch of reverie and anticipation.

That short slow movement or long introduction segues into the
rondo finale, the long-delayed climax that unfolds as one of the most
ecstatic of all movements for piano. It begins, again, quietly, in a surging whisper that slowly rises to a series of climaxes that mount higher
and higher until it seems they can go no further — then they go further. The climaxes of this movement are physical, like a gust of wind
that shocks the listener into a sense of the joyous effervescence of life.
With its simple, folklike main theme surrounded by sparkling figuration, Beethoven completes the sonata's process of pushing the expressive and sonorous possibilities of the piano further than they had ever
gone, the searching energy of the beginning paying off in the finale
with pealing rapture, a resplendent and unprecedented texture of trills
and whirling scales.[9]

The *Waldstein* took its place as one of the defining works of the
Second Period in its heroic mode, but it is much more than that. For
Beethoven in the white-hot years of his full maturity, this sonata was
a feat of disciplined craftsmanship that would have been practically
unimaginable if he had not done it. Enforcing a relentless economy of
material, he marshaled every element of music — melody, harmony,
rhythm, volume, register, timbre, form, proportion, key — to create the
effect of a twenty-minute crescendo of intensity and excitement on an
instrument of limited pitch, color, and volume. In every dimension
— expressive, technical, pianistic — here is a defining demonstration
of what musical *composition* is about. Only Beethoven was capable of
doing it, and only he was capable of surpassing it. A year later, with a
work called *Appassionata*, he did just that.

By December 1803, Beethoven was busy sketching the opera he owed
Schikaneder by contract, on the impresario's ancient-Rome libretto *Vestas Feuer*. At the same time, he told friend George August Griesinger, a
diplomat, agent for publisher Breitkopf & Härtel, and longtime Haydn
devotee, that he was keeping an eye out for "reasonable texts."[10] It could
not escape his attention that *Vestas Feuer* lacked anything close to aes-

thetic or ethical depth. Perhaps as he contemplated setting the text to music, he rationalized that not so long ago Mozart had taken on an outlandish Schikaneder idea called *Die Zauberflöte* and made something out of it. Still, he pushed Schikaneder to find a better writer to tone up the text.

Meanwhile the more tangible business of the profession went on. Toward the end of November, Carl van Beethoven wrote Breitkopf & Härtel, having offered the firm the Second and Third Symphonies, "At this time I cannot accept your recent offer of 500 florins. I am sorry about this, but you may regret it in the future, because these symphonies are either the worst that my brother has written or the best."[11] This was another bit of evidence that Ludwig, himself so careful and patient in cultivating publishers, exercised no oversight in how Carl pitched the music. A few weeks later, pupil Ferdinand Ries was writing Simrock in Bonn, "Beethoven will absolutely not sell his new symphony, and will reserve it for his tour, for which he is also composing another one now."[12] The tour in question seems to have tapped Beethoven's ongoing determination to go to Paris, which as late as the next spring he declared "irrevocable." Those sorts of declarations, so dependent on financial and political matters, rarely work out, and that one did not.[13] But as a further element of his French campaign, at the end of the 1803 sketchbook where he had laid out most of the Third Symphony, he began sketching a triple concerto in French style.

It was in this period that a practical joke went awry, with unpleasant results. Beethoven had played over the *Andante favori* for Ries and Wenzel Krumpholz, who liked it so much they pressed him to play it again. On the way home, Ries stopped by Prince Lichnowsky's to tell him about this new piece, and played as much of it as he could remember for the prince, who picked up some of it. Next day Lichnowsky visited Beethoven and in the course of their conversation said he'd composed a little number of his own. Over Beethoven's groans, he insisted on playing it.

When Beethoven heard Lichnowsky start the *Andante favori* he was not in the least amused. Innocently, Ries and Lichnowsky had inflamed his deep-lying paranoia about his ideas being stolen — a not entirely irrational fear in Vienna. Beethoven took his rage out on Ries, refusing ever again to play when his student was present. If Beethoven was asked to perform in company, Ries had to leave the room. Beethoven held to that policy from then on.[14] For well and for ill, when he got something into his head, there was no budging it unless somebody could convince him he was in the wrong.

Still, for all the friction, there was no break between composer, student, and patron. The latter two understood that with Beethoven, friction was going to be part of the picture. Ries was functioning as an assistant now, probably in exchange for lessons (they remained purely piano, not composition). The following year, the student took a calculated risk in their relationship when he soloed in the Third Piano Concerto. To that point the solo part of the Third Concerto had never been written down. Beethoven wrote it out especially for Ries's performance.

For Ries this was a defining moment: his first public appearance as Beethoven's pupil, with Beethoven conducting. The occasion was one of the public concerts produced by Ignaz Schuppanzigh in the Augarten pavilion. Ries asked his teacher to write a cadenza for him. Beethoven declined, saying Ries was a composer and ought to write his own, but that he would vet it. When Ries showed his cadenza to Beethoven, he was told to rework a particularly hard passage. Ries didn't; then in a play-over he bungled the passage and again was ordered to change it. He duly wrote an easier version but did not feel happy with it. At the concert, as Beethoven settled into a chair to listen to the first-movement cadenza, Ries decided on the spot to play the harder version. When he launched into it he saw Beethoven nearly jump out of his chair. Ries managed to bring it off well enough. Beethoven joined the bravos at the end, then afterward said, "But you're stubborn all the same! If you'd missed that passage I would never have given you another lesson."[15] Ries knew he meant it, that their relationship turned on that cadenza.

Ries in those days was spending perhaps more time with Beethoven than anyone else. He recorded a number of such moments. At one point Beethoven got his student a job for Count Johann Georg Browne and his wife, for years some of his most generous patrons. Ries's duties consisted largely of playing Beethoven's music hour after hour for the couple and their guests. One night in Baden, tired of it all, he improvised a little march of his own. A visiting "old countess" fell into raptures, thinking it was a new work of Beethoven's. Ries went along with it as a joke on her. Then to Ries's horror Beethoven arrived in Baden the next day, appeared at the Brownes', and found the countess raving about his wonderful new march.

With no other choice, Ries pulled his master aside and told him he had intended to "make fun of her foolishness." Since Beethoven couldn't stand this particular lady, who was always after him about something, he didn't mind at first. Ries was forced to repeat the march and fumbled through it, Beethoven standing beside him. When a new chorus of praises broke out at the end, Ries saw Beethoven's fury rising — then he suddenly dissolved in laughter. "There you see, my dear Ries!" he said later. "Those are the great connoisseurs who aspire to judge all music so correctly and astutely. Just give them the name of their darling; more than that they do not need." In a more productive response to that bit of comedy, Count Browne commissioned Beethoven to write four marches for four-hand piano that became op. 45.[16]

These episodes were all symptomatic. Beethoven could ride roughshod over people, he could be thoughtless, he could be distracted and forgetful, his responses were always unpredictable, but he was not intentionally mean and he liked to be generous. Yet as his old teacher Haydn fell into a sad decline, Beethoven was not notably thoughtful, visiting the ailing and depressed master less and less. Already in 1799, Haydn had written publisher Gottfried Härtel, "Every day the world compliments me on the fire of my recent works, but no one will believe the strain and effort it costs me to produce them. Some days my enfeebled memory and the unstrung state of my nerves crush me to the earth to such an extent that I fall prey to the worst sort of depression, and am quite incapable of finding even a single idea for many days thereafter; until at last Providence revives me, and I can again sit down at the pianoforte and begin to scratch away."[17]

The failing and forgetful old man was disappointed that Beethoven made himself increasingly absent. Haydn opined to their mutual friend Griesinger that it was "on account of his great pride." Even so, Haydn still asked his musical visitors what the Great Mogul was up to. In 1803, Haydn sent Beethoven a libretto for a proposed oratorio, asking what he thought of it. Beethoven looked it over and advised against taking it on. He may have understood that the old master did not have another oratorio in him. In fact, Haydn's work had drifted to a halt except for some folk-song arrangements for Scottish publisher George Thomson, who also aspired to have Beethoven working for him.[18]

By the latter part of December 1803, Beethoven, after drafting eighty-one pages of the first scene, had given up Schikaneder's *Vestas Feuer* in favor of a new story that had seized him.[19] He wrote Friedrich Rochlitz, editor of the *Allgemeine Musikalische Zeitung*, who had just plied him with a libretto of his own,

> If the subject had not been connected with magic, your libretto might have extricated me this very moment from a most embarrassing situation. For I have finally broken with Schikaneder, whose empire has really been entirely eclipsed by the light of the brilliant and attractive French operas . . . I hoped at least that he would have the verses and the contents of the [*Vestas Feuer*] libretto corrected and considerably improved by someone else, but in vain . . . Just picture to yourself a Roman subject . . . and language and verses such as could proceed only out of the mouths of our Viennese apple-women — Well, I have quickly had an old French libretto adapted and am now beginning to work on it.

This "old French libretto" had been floating around since the mid-1790s and had already been set by three composers.[20] It was *Leonore, ou l'amour conjugal*, by J.-N. Bouilly, librettist of Luigi Cherubini's *Les deux journées*, which had made a sensation in Vienna a couple of years before. The same composer's *Lodoïska* and *Faniska* had fared the same. These works initiated a craze for French opera in Vienna. Bouilly claimed that both his librettos were based on actual incidents during the Reign of Terror. They were part of a genre that came to be called "rescue opera," which with its themes of heroism and liberation had a connection in the public mind with the French Revolution. This story concerned a woman named Leonore whose husband Florestan is a political prisoner. In the dungeon he is being starved to death on the orders of the prison's governor, Pizarro, whose crimes Florestan has denounced. Leonore dresses up as a young man named Fidelio, gets a job at the prison, and finally manages to expose Pizarro to the minister Don Fernando and liberate her husband. Librettist Bouilly claimed that the story was based on a real incident, and he himself had played the part of Don Fernando in the event.[21]

For Beethoven, taking up this fashionable libretto accomplished several things at once. The Bouilly gave him an alternative to *Vestas Feuer* that he could actually embrace with pleasure—a story of triumph over tyranny. (He said later that he considered Bouilly's *Les deux journées* to be one of the best librettos ever written.)[22] Schikaneder's annoyance he would deal with in due course, but *Leonore* would also fulfill his contract. Rescue operas were now the rage in Vienna; he counted on that to help launch the piece. At the same time, this French story and the influence of Cherubini gave him another route of escape from, on the one hand, the conventions of Italian opera he had studied with Salieri, and on the other, the influence of Mozart that he had been trying to hold at bay for years. Neither of those influences had done much good for *Christus am Ölberge*. Now for opera and theater music Beethoven could embrace a current, fresh, popular model: Cherubini, Italian born but long in Paris, whom Beethoven admired more than any other living composer, whose brilliant orchestral style he appropriated as part of his own theatrical voice.[23] In one more medium, he had found his way around the looming presence of Mozart: instead of Mozartian domestic comedy or fantastical singspiel, he would compose revolutionary French opera.

Finally, in its story *Leonore* galvanized Beethoven. Here was a woman whose devotion to her husband leads to an extraordinary act of heroism, who stands up to tyranny as an individual and triumphs. It was a contemporary, realistic tale; he could use spoken dialogue—like a singspiel—rather than the traditional operatic recitative that he found artificial. Around the time he took up the *Leonore* libretto, two other composers produced versions of it in Italian. As part of his general preparation he got himself a copy of one of those, the *Leonore* of

Ferdinando Paer, though what his study of it contributed to his own version would be harder to detect than the pervasive influence of Cherubini — with, inevitably, contributions from Mozart as well.[24]

As for the whole idea of taking on an opera, Beethoven seems to have pursued it the way he pursued every other genre, as a problem to attack and solve with the help of models in other composers. But opera was going to make demands on him that he never had to cope with before. He knew a great many operas, his experience starting with his years in the orchestra pit and rehearsal stage of the opera in Bonn. In Vienna he constantly attended the theater in search of entertainment and ideas. Still, for all that experience Beethoven was not a man of the theater in the way Mozart had been. Where Mozart had started writing opera at age eleven and worked up step by step to the climactic productions of his last years, *Leonore* was Beethoven's first attempt. The oratorio *Christus* had been his closest approach to opera, and from it he had mainly learned what not to do.

Beyond all that, Mozart's letters document a man fascinated with people and their doings, full of arch, catty, earthy observations of parties and musicales and their denizens. That sensitivity to character and behavior flowed into Mozart's operas, along with his innate comic and theatrical instincts that Beethoven did not possess. Beethoven mastered instrumental music quickly because that was where his gifts and his instincts lay. He could shape a gripping dramatic line in a string quartet or a piano sonata, but the pacing and the arc of a story in words and actions onstage were nearly a closed book to him. Likewise, other people, their passions, their lives, their ideals and quirks — also virtually closed to him.

What is emotionally profound and universal in Beethoven's music is what he observed in himself. He approached opera the same way. In the story of *Leonore* he was interested in ideas, ideals, feelings, not so much in behavior or in characters, though he knew he had to portray those elements and he did, with spotty results. In the first act he resorted to Mozartian conventions of comic opera that hardly suited the story. Still, from the beginning he kept his eye on where the opera's dramatic climax lay and knew what would express it. The whole story would turn on a single transformative moment: a bugle call.

Meanwhile he always had more trouble writing vocal music than instrumental. In a sketchbook for *Leonore* there are eighteen differ- ent beginnings to Florestan's aria "In des Lebens Frülingstagen" and ten for the chorus "Wer ein holdes Weib."[25] From choosing a key to shaping a melody, he struggled with setting words. Partly for just that reason, as with counterpoint, he attacked the problem with implacable determination. When all was done, his commitment to write opera, for reasons both careerist and personal, was one more decision he made and stuck to wherever it took him and whatever it cost him. Like other such decisions in his life, it cost him a great deal.

To translate and adapt the French libretto of *Leonore,* Beethoven recruited a friend he judged to be a reliable collaborator. Joseph von Sonnleithner was a lawyer and son of a lawyer who had also been a composer; this son was a diplomat and music lover interested in composers of the past. He had made a nearly three-year tour of Europe gathering rare old scores for study and publication. Besides his profession as a bureaucrat, Sonnleithner was a founding partner in a music-publishing firm with the anomalous name of Bureau des arts et d'industrie, which published a good deal of older music by J. S. Bach and others, and by 1814, forty-four works by Beethoven.[26] Just as usefully, as he worked with Beethoven customizing the libretto of *Leonore,* Sonnleithner served for several months as artistic director of the Theater an der Wien, after that for ten years as secretary of the court theaters.[27] In a country where everything in life and art was of concern to the censors, and arts involving words, with their infinite capacity for subversion, were of most special concern to the censors, a high-level bureaucrat like Sonnleithner was a good man to have on one's side. That weighed as heavily as his skills as a librettist, which at that point were largely untested anyway.

Sonnleithner's short tenure as director of the Theater an der Wien resulted from a shake-up that resolved Beethoven's sticky contract situation with his nominal employer and ex-librettist Schikaneder. In the beginning of 1804, Baron Peter Anton Braun, who managed both court theaters, bought the Theater an der Wien. Shortly after, Braun fired Schikaneder as director of the theater, whose statue as Papageno presided over the entrance. At that point Beethoven's contract with

Schikaneder for an opera was terminated, and he had to move out of the theater. That solved the friction over *Vestas Feuer,* but it was a setback for *Leonore.* Beethoven had been going at the opera full tilt, composing scenes as fast as he could get words from Sonnleithner.

Beethoven had already had run-ins with Baron Braun over performance venues and considered him an enemy. He wrote Sonnleithner, "I know in advance that if everything depends again on the worthy Baron's decision, the answer will be no . . . his treatment of me has been persistently unfriendly — Well, so be it — I shall never grovel — my world is the universe . . . I do not want to spend another hour in this wretched hole."[28] Soon after, he moved out of the theater and into a flat in the building where his childhood friend Stephan von Breuning lived, known as *das rothe Haus* (the Red House) and belonging to the Esterházy estates. Before long he moved in with Stephan. At that point the two hotheaded Rhinelanders began to work out whether they could get along as roommates.[29]

By around April 1804, the score of *Bonaparte* was copied and ready. Prince Lobkowitz had given Beethoven a splendid 1,800 florins for exclusive access to the symphony for six months and made his house orchestra available for trial run-throughs to be heard by invited guests. Beethoven had to have been concerned about the fate of a symphony he knew tested so many boundaries. He was becoming resigned to the deterioration of his hearing and the steady drain of illness. As for *Leonore,* he was uncertain about its performance possibilities as he continued desultorily to work on it.

At the same time, publishing was going well and likewise his reviews, so he had reason to be hopeful about the reception of the symphony. In nearly the whole of an issue with Beethoven's picture on the cover, the *Allgemeine Musikalische Zeitung* hailed the publication of the *Prometheus* Variations in these kinds of terms: "inexhaustible imagination, original humor, and deep, intimate, even passionate feeling are the particular features . . . from which arises the ingenious physiognomy that distinguishes nearly all of Herr v. B's works. This earns him one of the highest places among instrumental composers of the first rank."[30] When the Second Symphony appeared the journal called it "a noteworthy, colossal work, of a depth, power, and artistic knowledge like *very* few . . . it demands to be played again and yet again by even the most accomplished orchestra, until the astonishing number of original and sometimes very strangely arranged ideas become closely enough connected, rounded out, and emerge like a great unity." More and more the elements that were special, unusual, even bizarre about his music were becoming the things most admired about it, at least in progressive circles. In other words, critics were beginning to let Beethoven be Beethoven, to sense the unity that lay under the bewildering diversity of his surfaces.

If his musical enemies were fading in strength, his body remained his greatest enemy. Around the time Beethoven moved in with Breuning, he became frighteningly ill. When he recovered from the worst of it, he was left with a fever that lingered for months. He began to be attacked by abscesses in his jaw and finger, and a septic foot; eventually the finger problem nearly led to an amputation.[31] To be so physically beset in the middle of preparing for the symphony readings and trying to keep *Leonore* afloat made him more brittle than usual. And there were other projects demanding attention. In the middle of sketches for the opera he jotted down two ideas, one the beginning of a piano concerto and the other the beginning of a symphony, one idea gentle and the other dynamic but sharing a common rhythmic motif. Here he found the leading ideas for his greatest concerto and eventually his most famous symphony.

The first four bars of the G Major Piano Concerto:

Sketches for the first movement of the Fifth Symphony:

From Nottebohm, *Two Beethoven Sketchbooks*

As plans heated up for readings of the new symphony and other new pieces with Lobkowitz's orchestra, in late May of 1804, Ferdinand Ries turned up at Beethoven's flat with stunning news: the puppet French Senate had just declared Napoleon Bonaparte to be emperor of France. For Beethoven this was not just an interesting or shocking piece of information; it concerned him intimately. Ries had seen the copyist's score of the new symphony lying on a table in his room, with its title page: at the top, *Bonaparte;* at the bottom, *Luigi van Beethoven.*

Now Beethoven heard that the hero he had admired as a liberator, so much that he shaped his most ambitious work around him, had made himself an emperor. Beethoven did not stop to think about the practical questions, did not try to gloss over the import of this news. He grasped quite clearly what it meant. Napoleon was no liberator but was in it for his own power and glory. In a transport of rage, Beethoven cried to Ries, "So he too is nothing more than an ordinary man! Now he also will trample all human rights underfoot, and only pander to his own ambition. He will place himself above everyone else and become a tyrant!" He snatched up the title page of the symphony, ripped it in two, and threw it to the floor.[32]

If that was said and done as Ries remembered it years later, Beethoven was correct in every respect. In his response, the news hit him in terms of ideals and history. He understood that now the revolutionary dreams of the 1780s were finished, because Napoleon had been the only man able to realize them. The Revolution is dead; long live the Revolution.

But of course, Beethoven did not throw out the Third Symphony. When the parts were published in 1806, the title would read *Sinfonia eroica, composta per festeggiare il sovvenire d'un grand'uomo:* "Heroic symphony, composed to celebrate the memory of a great man." It was a finely considered title. The great man in memory was the beau ideal Beethoven and so many others had taken Napoleon to be. That imaginary hero was dead and buried, while Napoleon himself continued to triumph on the battlefield. More than the death of a hero, now the symphony marked the death of a dream.

But the vanished title did not erase the connection of the symphony to Napoleon in its foundation and in Beethoven's mind. It did not even fully erase his name from the manuscript. In August 1804, offering the symphony and a pile of other new works to Breitkopf & Härtel, Beethoven noted, "[T]he title of the symphony is really <u>Bonaparte</u> . . . I think that it will interest the musical public." A title page of the symphony survived, with a date of that same month in another hand. On the top of the page, the words *Intitulate Bonaparte* have been erased so violently that some of it has chewed right through the paper. <u>When</u> <u>Beethoven was enraged at a thing or a person, he hated to see the very</u> <u>name or word.</u> Yet at the bottom of the page, in pencil in Beethoven's own hand, are the words *Geschrieben auf Bonaparte*, "written on Bonaparte," and that has not been erased. Here is a graphic representation of the ambivalence that was seen all over Europe. Napoleon himself defined it: "Everybody has loved me and hated me," he said. "Everybody has taken me up, dropped me, and taken me up again."[33]

His enthronement, the central symbolic event of Napoleon's career, elevated to myth the day it happened, came on December 2, 1804. Amid stupendous pomp and ceremony in the Cathedral of Notre Dame in Paris, in the presence and with the blessing of Pope Pius VII, Napoleon placed the Charlemagne Crown on his head as emperor of France.[34] That he crowned himself was the ultimate symbol of this self-made conqueror, now a self-made emperor. With that he declared himself Charlemagne's successor, and thereby symbolically erased the thousand-year succession of emperors of the Holy Roman Empire down to the present Emperor Franz II. Napoleon was no longer the dictator of a nominal republic; he was the founder of a new hereditary line of sovereigns, on the model of the ancien régime that the Revolution believed it had annihilated once and for all.

Among the French government's decrees of the next months was <u>an Imperial Catechism,</u> which the church was directed to teach to all children of the soi-disant republic that was in fact a dictatorship. This new catechism included these responses:

> Q. Why are we obliged to all of these duties to our Emperor?
> A. First, because God, who created empires and distributes them according to His will, in heaping on our Emperor gifts, both in peace and war, has established him as our sovereign and rendered him the minister of his power and image on earth. To honor and serve

our Emperor is thus to honor and serve God himself.

Q. What should one think of those who fail in their duty to the Emperor?

A. According to the Apostle Saint Paul, they would be resisting the order established By God Himself, and would render themselves worthy of eternal damnation.

Q. What is forbidden to us by the Fourth Commandment?

A. We are forbidden to be disobedient to our superiors, to injure them, or to speak ill of them.[35]

This is, of course, the definition of tyranny worldly and spiritual. Yet while Napoleon had only briefly been a Jacobin, was a dictator in every sense, and had essentially put aside the French republic, there were still progressive elements in his agenda. In spring of 1804, his regime issued the Code Napoleon, a set of civil laws that enshrined some foundations of the Revolution: personal liberty, freedom of conscience, and property rights. The ancient nobility and class privileges were abolished and the government declared to be entirely secular. The influence of the code would be immense and lasting.[36] Yet beside its progressive clauses were ones reflecting Napoleon's hatred of democracy. The code suppressed the rights of women and gave precedence to landowners and to employers at the expense of employees. Napoleon held to Enlightenment beliefs in science and reason, but he had nothing but contempt for popular will or parliamentary debate. In those respects he stood not so far from German Aufklärers, including Beethoven (also no believer in democracy, even if he admired parliaments).

So with Beethoven and many others over the next decades, the habit of dropping and taking up Napoleon continued. In more practical terms, after a couple of years of the French fighting only the British, the rapprochement with Austria was crumbling and a new coalition against France on the horizon, so in any case it was no longer safe to premiere a symphony called *Bonaparte*. The renewal of war, meanwhile, scuttled Beethoven's "irrevocable" plans for a French tour or relocation. For such reasons, the world would know the Third Symphony as *Eroica*. But as Beethoven wrote his publisher, it is really *Bonaparte*.

•   •   •

Around the middle of 1804, Beethoven worked on two new piano sonatas and an orchestral work. The first sonata is on the order of what
gardeners call a "sport": a surprising deviation of type in a species. He
laid out the Piano Sonata in F Major, op. 54, in two droll and inexplicable movements. The first begins with a lazily lilting tune that repeats
a couple of times before pounding triplets erupt and clatter along *forte*
for two pages, after which the lazy friend returns. Their connection is
sealed in a coda that marries the two contradictory ideas. The finale
takes shape as a mostly monothematic *moto perpetuo* that threads a
virtuosic course through dazzling changes of texture and key. To later
times, op. 54 would be remembered as the valley between the summits
of *Waldstein* and op. 57, the *Appassionata.* Beethoven began the latter
in 1804 as well, interrupting work on *Leonore,* which for the moment
had no performance possibilities.[37]

A second curious manifestation of that period was the Triple Concerto op. 56 for orchestra and a trio of violin, cello, and piano, dedicated to Prince Lobkowitz. Beethoven called it a *Konzertant,* relating it
to the genre of *symphonie concertante* fashionable in France. So for him
it likely amounted to another salute and calling card to the French, to
prepare his journey. That in turn might explain, if anything does, the
singular and sometimes backward-looking style of the music. Some of
it looks back as far as the Baroque concerto grosso for multiple soloists
—though a piano trio was an unusual, perhaps unprecedented, solo
group.[38] In effect, Beethoven here returned to a pattern of the years before the New Path, producing a stylistic experiment that had no progeny in his work. Gorgeous but peculiar, expensive and impractical to
perform, the Triple Concerto would never really catch on. Beethoven
himself scarcely promoted it, though he was quick to sell it—the 1807
publication came out, as far as history knows, before the piece was
premiered.

Despite distractions including lingering illness in the middle of
1804, Beethoven's ideas still ran strong. But life was ganging up on
him. He had to have been on edge, and that goes partway to explaining a nasty row between him and Stephan von Breuning in early July.
Tensions had been brewing between the roommates for a while; what
touched it off was practically nothing. Beethoven learned that the care-

taker of the building had not gotten proper notice that he had vacated the other flat to move in with Stephan, so Beethoven was still liable for the rent. Over dinner the visiting Carl van Beethoven, provoking as usual, blamed the oversight on Breuning. Ludwig tried to defuse the situation by jokingly blaming it on Ries, but Breuning boiled over, jumped up, and shouted that he would send for the caretaker on the spot. Beethoven was having none of that. He also shot up, sending his chair flying, and bolted the house. Soon he bolted all the way to Baden.[39]

A hail of recriminations followed. Breuning wrote a conciliatory note, but Beethoven was having none of that either. He wrote Ries, "As Breuning by his behavior has not scrupled to present to you and the caretaker my character from an aspect in which I appear to be a wretched, pitiable, and petty-minded fellow, I am asking you ... to give my answer verbally to B ... I have nothing more to say to Breuning — His thoughts and actions — prove that there should never have been a friendly relationship between us and will certainly never be again." A few days later he wrote to Ries again:

> My sudden rage was merely an explosion resulting from several previous unpleasant incidents with him. I have the gift of being able to conceal and control my sensitivity about very many things. But if I happen to be irritated at a time when I am more liable to fly into a temper than usual, then I erupt more violently than anyone else. Breuning certainly has excellent qualities . . . yet his greatest and most serious faults are those which he fancies he detects in other people. He is inclined to be petty, a trait which since my childhood I have despised . . . And now our friendship is at an end! I have found only two friends in the world with whom, I may say I have never had a misunderstanding. But what fine men! One is dead, the other is still alive.[40]

The two friends he meant were the long-departed Amenda and the late Lorenz von Breuning, Stephan's brother. (He forgot to number Stephan's brother-in-law Franz Wegeler among the friends he had never seriously fought with.) In any case, a couple of months later Beethoven and Stephan met by chance on the street and fell into each other's arms. Beethoven sent him an ivory miniature of himself and a rhapsodic letter of reconciliation:

> Behind this painting my dear good St, let us <u>conceal</u> forever what <u>passed between us</u> for a time — I know that I have wounded <u>your heart;</u> but the emotion within me, which you must certainly have detected, has punished me sufficiently for doing so. It was not <u>malice</u> which was surging in me against you, no, because in that case I would no longer have been worthy of your friendship. It was passion, both <u>in your heart</u> and <u>in mine.</u> — But distrust of you began to stir in me — People interfered between us — people who are far from being worthy of <u>you</u> or of <u>me</u> [probably Carl van Beethoven was the "people"] ... You know, of course, that I always meant to give [the enclosed portrait] to someone. To whom could I give it indeed with a warmer heart than to you, faithful, good and noble Steffen — Forgive me if I hurt you. I myself suffered just as much. When I no longer saw you beside me, for such a long time, only then did I realize fully how dear you were to <u>my</u> heart, how dear you always will be.[41]

The old friendship returned to its course, for a time. Stephan remained a close and critical student of his friend. In November, Stephan wrote Wegeler,

> He who has been my friend from youth is often largely to blame that I am compelled to neglect the absent ones. You cannot conceive, my dear Wegeler, what an indescribable, I might say fearful effect the loss of hearing has had upon him. Think of the feeling of being unhappy in one of such violent temperament; in addition, reservedness, mistrust (often toward his best friends), and in many things indecision! For the greater part ... intercourse with him is a real exertion, at which one can hardly trust oneself ... I took him into my rooms. He had hardly come before he became severely, almost dangerously ill, and this was followed by a prolonged intermittent fever. Worry and the care of him took quite a lot out of me. Now he is completely well again. He lives on the ramparts ... and since I am running my own household, he eats with me every day.[42]

Beethoven was not as well as Stephan thought. By that point, still beset by fevers, he had spent most of the summer in Oberdöbling. In the fall he moved into a large, grand apartment building called the Pasqualati House, on the Mölkerbastei. From the fourth floor he had a view over the eponymous Mölker bastion, across the broad green Glacis to the Vienna suburbs and the mountains beyond. Ries had found the place for him.[43] Lichnowsky lived a few houses away. Beethoven would keep that apartment for years as he continued his restless roaming.

Apparently that summer saw the first private *Eroica* readings at Prince Lobkowitz's palace.[44] The orchestra of twenty-five to thirty and the listeners were crowded into the narrow music room with gray marble walls and golden-painted ceiling, twenty-four by fifty-four feet, intended mainly for chamber music.[45] The orchestra sat on a low podium behind a balustrade. The invited guests lounged on red-upholstered benches, sat in adjoining rooms, strolled around as they listened to the players stumble through the strangest music any of them had ever heard. At the rehearsals it was noticed that Beethoven sometimes had trouble hearing the wind parts.[46]

Ries was present and recalled that the first reading of the symphony went "appallingly." It may have been this occasion when Beethoven began conducting one of the hemiola passages, superimposed on the three-beat meter in a two-beat pattern that confused the orchestra so much that they had to start the movement over again. It did not help when the orchestra came to the first movement's peculiar retransition, when a solo horn seems to come in with the theme early, over the wrong chord, and Ries exclaimed to Beethoven, "That damned horn player! Can't he count! — It sounds terrible!" Ries said Beethoven looked close to hitting him, and "he was a long time in forgiving me."[47]

Before the Third Symphony, symphonies and concertos had largely been considered public and in some degree popularistic pieces written to be put together in a hurry, sometimes more or less sight-read in performance. Haydn and Mozart had written tremendous works under those constraints. Beethoven was in the process of changing that pattern. Gradually, through reading after reading, this unprecedented music sank into the players' minds and fingers. Other works were read over — the Triple Concerto, a piece by Salieri — while the listening connoisseurs murmured and stroked their chins. In the Third Symphony, so much was being put before them for the first time: difficulties of playing, difficulties of understanding for the audience. It seemed as if this piece demanded new kinds of musicians and listeners, new kinds of criticism and poetry and philosophy. And this symphony seemed in some way the embodiment of the revolutionary spirit, coded in instrumental music and so lying beyond the clutches of the ubiquitous Viennese censors. The private readings went on in various Lobkowitz palaces, Beethoven in no hurry to put the symphony before the public until the players knew it thoroughly. In any case, the prince owned the piece exclusively for six months.

Meanwhile, that August there was another turnover of regime at the Theater an der Wien, Schikaneder being reinstated and Beethoven's contract with him likewise. Beethoven moved back into the theater, still paying rent for his new flat at the Pasqualati House, and went at *Leonore* with renewed vigor aided by his recovery — not a lasting one — from months of debilitating illness. As if he did not already have enough trouble that year, he had also fallen in love.

As a virtuoso of passionate cast, Beethoven naturally attracted female attention. Wegeler and Breuning both left testimony to his "success" with women, his "conquests." What they meant by success and conquest was left unsaid. Bachelors in those days tended to visit brothels and Beethoven likely did, but there is no record of that in these years, or of who his conquests were, or what they amounted to. As has been noted before, it was a discreet age on matters sexual and romantic.

One speculation is that when women were drawn to Beethoven because they were aroused by his music, he responded but did not take them seriously. His ideas about women were puritanical, but his instincts robust. Ries remembered that "Beethoven very much enjoyed looking at women; lovely, youthful faces particularly pleased him. If we passed a girl who could boast her share of charms, he would turn around, look at her sharply through his glass, then laugh or grin when he realized I was watching him. He was very frequently in love, but usually only for a short time."

Ries's definition of "love" is more flexible than Beethoven's. His real loves were few; the rest were passing. One day in Baden, Ries stumbled into a situation that gives a portrait of Beethoven's style with amours of the moment. Ries appeared for a lesson and found his master sitting on the sofa with an attractive young woman. Embarrassed, he turned to leave, but Beethoven cried, "Sit down and play for a while!" Ries did as ordered, facing away from the pair and playing bits of Beethoven pieced together with his own transitions. Suddenly Beethoven called out, "Ries, play something romantic!" Then, "Something melancholy!" Then, "Something passionate!" Finally Beethoven jumped up and theatrically exclaimed, "Why, those are all things I've written!" This, hoping the young lady would be impressed. Instead, she seemed offended by something and left abruptly.

Amused, nonplussed, whatever he felt, Ries asked the lady's name. Beethoven had no idea. She had knocked on his door wanting to meet him, and in the heat of the moment he never got around to asking. The two set out to follow her, but she was lost in the darkness. They continued their walk into a moonlit valley, talking of all sorts of things, but Beethoven's last word was, "I must find out who she is, and you must help me!" Ries proved not much help. Afterward he learned she had been the mistress of a foreign prince in Vienna. To this recollection Ries added that he never had so many visits from Beethoven as during a period when he lived in a house owned by a tailor with three daughters, all beautiful but unfortunately "irreproachable." Beethoven wrote Ries in a teasing letter, "Do not do too much tailoring, remember me to the fairest of the fair, send me half a dozen sewing needles!"[48] There were presumably other female enthusiasts who turned up at Beethoven's door, and presumably not all of them fled.

The women Beethoven fell for seriously were a different matter. The pattern was clear: most of them were quite young, all of them musical in some degree, most of them celebrated beauties, all of them highborn. The one who obsessed him in the middle years of the decade was Josephine Deym, née Brunsvik. He had met the three musical Brunsvik sisters in 1799, when Therese showed up at his door, and he was soon giving long lessons to the sisters during their family's short visit to Vienna. Their cousin was Julie Guicciardi, Beethoven's love of 1801. Besides his varying attractions to Therese and Josephine Brunsvik, Beethoven also became a friend and mentor of their brother Franz, who was an expert amateur cellist.

The Brunsvik children had been shaped by an idealistic, music-loving, Americanophile father; they were brought up, Therese wrote, "with the names of Washington and Benjamin Franklin."[49] Hampered by a deformed spine, Therese became fiercely religious, never married, vowed to make herself a "Priestess of Truth."

From the beginning, sister Josephine, an excellent pianist, was ecstatic about the Beethoven works that she heard at family musicales. She declared the op. 18 String Quartets "the *non plus ultra* of musical compositions"; later she said the op. 31 Piano Sonatas "annul everything he has written until now" (overstated, but astute). With her marriage in 1799, at age twenty, Josephine's life took a downward slant from which it never recovered. Her mother had pressured her to marry the supposedly rich Count Joseph Deym, who was nearly thirty years older. A forced marriage based on money and position was an old, ordinary story among the aristocracy. When it was too late, they discovered Deym was heavily in debt and anxious to claim her dowry —which her mother refused to give him.

Count Deym opened a wax museum next to St. Stephen's in the middle of town, modeled on Madame Tussaud's in London. His exhibits included an effigy of Emperor Joseph II in his tomb and a mechanical organ for which Mozart had composed pieces (Beethoven also wrote for it, in 1799). More morbidly, Deym exhibited a wax impression of the dead Mozart.[50] His waxworks became celebrated and popular but never made enough money to support the family. Josephine did find a place in her heart for Deym, and for a while, in defiance of his situation, they lived the elegant aristocratic life, full of balls and fine clothes and musicales, in some of which Beethoven performed. Therese's diary reports that on their promenades, onlookers would call out to Josephine, "Beautiful as an angel and ready to paint!"[51]

After more than four years of an anxious and financially disastrous marriage, Josephine's husband died of pneumonia in January 1804, before the birth of their fourth child.[52] She fled to stay with sister Charlotte in Hietzing. Beethoven was summering nearby and visited, solicitous for Josephine. He wrote her in autumn, sending a copy of the op. 31, no. 3 Sonata that she requested, asking, "I must earnestly beg you not to give it to anyone. For, if so, it might fall into the hand of a Viennese publisher ... All my best greetings to Count Franz."[53] Beethoven and Josephine's musical brother Franz had a *du* ("thou") relationship, showing a closeness not common among Beethoven's aristocratic friends. Then and later, though, in letters he and Josephine used the formal *Sie*. For a male commoner to use the intimate form with an aristocratic woman was beyond the pale, except in the unlikely event they were actually engaged.

The widowed Josephine returned to Vienna and took up the exhausting task of running her late husband's business; at the same time, she rented out some eighty rooms in the building, all as she reared four young children. Surely she had no idea what she was in for when she welcomed Beethoven's attentions. In September 1804, she wrote him, "Dear kind Beethoven! According to my promise, you are receiving a report from me on the first post day after my arrival. How are you? What are you doing? These questions occupy me rather often, very often." The letter is cheery and affectionate, but that month Josephine fell into what Charlotte reported to Therese as a "dreadful nervous breakdown; sometimes she laughed, sometimes wept, after which came utter fatigue and exhaustion."[54] Later in a memoir in her old-maid years, Therese ruefully recalled her and her sisters' earlier life, in the time when they first met Beethoven, before everything came down on them: "We were young, cheery, beautiful, childish, naïve. Whoever saw us, loved us."[55]

In November some musical evenings with Beethoven in attendance helped lift Josephine's spirits. Now he was giving her lots of lessons. This was not the first time that teaching led to his falling for a student. The situation began to alarm Charlotte. "Beethoven comes quite frequently," she wrote Therese. "[H]e is giving Pepi lessons, it is a bit dangerous, I must confess." Soon after: "Beethoven is with us almost daily, gives lessons to Pipschen — *vous m'entendez, mon coeur!*"[56]

As winter came on, Josephine still seemed to be encouraging, or Beethoven convinced himself she was. Nonetheless, he did not neglect passing fancies. Around that time he wrote to Willibrord Joseph Mähler, who had finished his painting of Beethoven: "I most urgently request you to return my portrait to me . . . I have promised it to a stranger, a lady who saw the portrait at my place, so that she may have it in her room during her stay of a few weeks in Vienna — and who can resist such <u>charming</u> advances?" The charming lady was apparently not Josephine, who nonetheless had begun to obsess him. In the same period he wrote her, "Yesterday I did not pay proper attention to what you were saying. <u>Did you not say</u> that I was to dine with you? — If you <u>really said it,</u> then I will come." The note is friendly and only that, but he impulsively signed it, "Your BEETHOVEN who worships you."[57]

In January 1805, he wrote asking if Josephine would give a recommendation of his brother Carl for a job "in some quarter . . . Although <u>wicked people</u> have spread a rumor that he does not treat me honorably, yet I can assure you that all that is not true, but that he has always looked after my interests with sincere integrity. He used to have <u>something uncouth</u> in his behavior and that is what put <u>people</u> against him. But he had completely lost <u>all that</u> as the result of some <u>journeys</u> he has undertaken on behalf of his office." (Since 1800, Carl had been working in a government tax bureau.)[58]

By then Beethoven was courting Josephine in earnest. Courting as a composer, he presented her with a song: *An die Hoffnung* (To Hope). Now the family was truly alarmed, Josephine feeling herself under siege. She admired Beethoven as much as any man alive, maybe more than any, but she was in delicate shape, desperately trying to hold the museum and boardinghouse and family together. Her feelings for Beethoven seem to have been spiritual and admiring, not romantic, still less sexual. Moreover, Josephine was of the nobility. If she were to marry a commoner like Beethoven, she would lose her title and privileges. Legally he could not even serve as guardian to her children.[59] This was the way of the world. In great anxiety Therese again wrote Charlotte: "But tell me, Pepi and Beethoven, what shall become of it? She should be on her guard! . . . <u>Her heart must have the strength to say No,</u> a sad duty, if not the saddest of all!!!"[60]

An die Hoffnung, his song for Josephine, is simple, polite unto decorous, strophic (three verses to the same music), setting stanzas by
Christophe August Tiedge. It is a song for a young woman to play and
sing, designed not to frighten her away in the sense that the setting is
not as fervent as the text, which addresses a personification of hope
in the same way that *An die Freude* addresses a personification of joy:
"O Hope, let the patient sufferer, uplifted by You, understand that up
above an angel counts his tears!" This follows an introduction that
babbles up heavenward. The relation of poem and setting is not unlike his polite and practical letter to Josephine signed "BEETHOVEN
who worships you." Because of the dedication, the pretty little song
would become another element raising consternation in the ranks of
his patrons and friends, not to mention his beloved. But even as he lost
himself in love, there was still the matter of the public premiere of the
Third Symphony.

The premiere was set for April 7, 1805, at the Theater an der Wien. It
was part of a benefit for violinist Franz Clement, a friend of Beethoven's
and director of the house orchestra. By the premiere there had been
four or more readings of the piece in Lobkowitz palaces and at least
one in another music lover's house, all before invited guests.[61] During
the rehearsals, Beethoven had made a number of experiments and revisions. A letter of Carl van Beethoven to Breitkopf & Härtel, trying once
again to sell the score, says, "Before he had yet heard the Symphony,
my brother believed it would be too long if the [exposition] of the first
movement were repeated, but after several performances he found it
disadvantageous if the first part were not repeated."[62] Beethoven had
worried that the length of the movement would weary listeners, but in
the end he went with what he decided the music needed.

Word went around that something unusual was coming. Old Haydn
friend and new Beethoven acquaintance Georg August von Griesinger
wrote a report to publisher Gottfried Härtel: "The Symphony has been
heard at Academies at Prince Lobkowitz's and at an active music-lov-
er's named Wirth, with unusual applause. That it is a work of genius,
I hear from both admirers and detractors of Beethoven. Some people
say that there is more in it than in Haydn and Mozart, that the Sym-

phony-Poem has been brought to new heights! Those who are against it find that the whole lacks rounding out; they disapprove of the piling up of colossal ideas."[63] The first critic of the *Allgemeine Musikalische Zeitung* to comment on it, still before the official premiere, was less generous:

But

> This long composition, exceedingly difficult to perform, is actually a very broadly expanded, bold, and wild fantasia. It is not at all lacking in startling and beautiful passages in which the energetic and talented spirit of its creator must be recognized; however, very often it seems to lose itself in irregularity . . . The reviewer certainly belongs to Mr. v. Beethoven's most sincere admirers. However, in this work he must confess to finding much that is strident and bizarre, so that an overview of the whole is obscured and the unity is almost completely lost.[64]

Once again Beethoven was accused of writing a fantasia, a formless and rambling piece full of bizarre ideas in a genre where such freedom was not appropriate. Most of the early reviews would follow suit.

At the public premiere in the Theater an der Wien on April 7, 1805, the audience had to have been befuddled. One could not have imagined how much of the future of music lay in this puzzling and profligate work. There were no program notes to give them a handle on it, and at this point it had neither the name *Bonaparte* or *Eroica*. As always, Beethoven's conducting was outlandish: during loud passages, he rose up on his toes, windmilling his arms as if he were trying to take wing; in soft passages he all but crept under the music stand. The playing, by the house orchestra laced by Lobkowitz's musicians, who knew the piece well by then, would have been better handled than at most of his premieres. The audience sat through the strange, epic first movement that then and later was nearly impossible to digest at first hearing. Connoisseurs lost track of the seemingly half-formed themes bustling past, waited for familiar formal landmarks that never clearly appeared, for resolutions and climaxes that never quite happened. They heard the horn entrance over the wrong chord before the recapitulation and assumed it was an embarrassing mistake. Carl Czerny was present and reported that somewhere in the middle somebody yelled, "I'll give another kreuzer if the thing will only stop!"[65] Since a kreuzer was worth hardly more than a penny, however, it was not a serious offer.

Listeners found the *Marcia funèbre* easier to grasp. If the form is unusual, it is not as complex as the first movement, and anyway they would recognize it as a French-style funeral march. Those who knew the op. 26 Piano Sonata might recall the funeral march in that piece and surmise that this symphony was a similar sort of thing, a set of character pieces. The manifestly delightful scherzo might have garnered some applause. For those ears, though, the finale variations with their tone of mingled ballet music and heroic perorations would have been the strangest of all. At the end, Beethoven was visibly piqued by the scanty applause and refused to acknowledge it.

Then he waited to see what the world would make of it. The initial reviews were surprising only in their attempts at balance and generosity. First came an extensive, skeptical, but respectful notice in *Der Freymüthige*:

> A new symphony in E♭ by Beethoven was performed here, over which the musical connoisseurs and amateurs were divided into several parties. One group, Beethoven's very special friends, maintains that precisely this symphony is a masterpiece, that it is in exactly the true style for more elevated music, and that if it does not please at present, it is because the public is not sufficiently educated in art to be able to grasp all of these elevated beauties. After a few thousand years, however, they will not fail to have their effect. The other group utterly denies this work any artistic value and feels that it manifests a completely unbounded striving for distinction and oddity, which, however, has produced neither beauty nor true sublimity and power. Through strange modulations and violent transitions, by placing together the most heterogeneous things, as when for example a pastorale is played through in the grandest style, with abundant scratchings in the bass, with three horns and so forth, a true if not desirable originality can indeed be gained without much effort. However, genius does not pro-

claim itself by simply bringing forth the unusual and the fantastic, but rather by creating the beautiful and sublime. Beethoven himself has demonstrated the truth of this statement in his earlier works. The third, very small group stands in the middle; they admit that the symphony contains many beautiful qualities, but admit that the context often seems completely disjointed, and that the endless duration of this longest and perhaps also most difficult of all symphonies exhausts even connoisseurs, becoming unbearable to the mere amateur. They wish that Mr. v. B. would use his well-known great talent to give us works that resemble his first two Symphonies in C and D, his graceful Septet in E♭, the spirited Quintet in D Major, and others of his earlier compositions, which will place B. forever in the ranks of the foremost instrumental composers. They fear, however, that if Beethoven continues on this path, both he and music will come off badly . . . The public and Herr v. Beethoven, who conducted the work himself, were not satisfied with each other this evening. To the public the symphony was too difficult, too long, and B. himself was too impolite, since he did not nod in acknowledgement of those who did applaud.[66]

Really, for a review of the premiere, Beethoven could hardly have hoped for anything better. But he would not have seen the review that way, and neither would the next generations who read it. In later times critics like this one would stoke the Romantic myth that genius and revolution are never understood in their own time. But the evolution of the symphony's reviews over the next few years shows the opposite. (After 1806, critics could study the printed parts, which were now titled *Eroica*.) The second *Allgemeine Musikalische Zeitung* notice was by the same critic:

At this concert I heard the new Beethoven symphony in E♭ . . . conducted by the composer himself, and performed by a very well-comprised orchestra. But this time as well I found no reason at all to change the judgment that I had already formed about it. To be sure, this new work of B. has great and daring ideas, and, as one can expect from the genius of this composer, great power in the way it is worked out; but the symphony would improve immeasurably (it lasts an entire hour) if B. could bring himself to shorten it, and to bring more light, clarity, and unity into the whole.[67]

It is actually 40–45 minutes. Beethoven was said to observe, "If *I* wrote a symphony an hour long it will be found short enough."[68] He means he will write pieces as long as he likes, and the public will accept it — as, on the whole, it did.

The incomprehension was repeated in other cities. The *Berlinische Musikalische Zeitung* wrote in May 1805, "A new Beethoven Symphony in E♭ is so shrill and complicated that only those who worship the failings and merits of this composer with equal fire, which at times borders on the ridiculous, could find pleasure in it."[69] But critical perceptions began to evolve quickly. A January 1807 *AMZ* review after a Mannheim performance and publication of the parts: "The first movement is impressive and full of power and sublimity . . . The funeral march is new and bears the character of noble melancholy. As long as it is, even in relation to the other movements, we are still glad to linger in the emotion it arouses . . . The scherzo menuetto is a piece full of lively, restless motion, against which the sustained tones of the three horns in the trio contrast exceptionally well . . . The finale has much value . . . however, it cannot very well escape from the charge of great bizarrerie."[70] Only a month later, the *AMZ* was calling the second movement a "triumph" that could not "be conceived, born, and raised with such perfection by any person without true genius."[71] In the *AMZ*, April 1807, after a Leipzig performance:

> The most educated friends of art in the city were assembled in great numbers, a truly solemn attentiveness and deathlike silence reigned . . . Each movement unmistakably had the effect that it should have, and each time at the end of the entire piece loud demonstrations of applause gave vent to well-founded enthusiasm. The orchestra had voluntarily gathered for extra rehearsals without recompense, except for the honor and special enjoyment of the work itself . . . And so this most difficult of all symphonies . . . was performed not only with the greatest accuracy and precision . . . After this study, and after hear-

ing the work repeatedly at rehearsals and public performances, we would simply like to add to this that the first, fiery, magnificent allegro, in its astounding many-sidedness within the greatest unity, in its clarity and purity within the most extensive complications, and its irresistible enchantment throughout its great length, has become and remained our favorite of all the movements.[72]

That complete reversal of opinion evolved in two years. Critics and often audiences responded with mounting enthusiasm for this most difficult of symphonies, one that for the first time in history demanded to be heard in multiple performances and perhaps even to be studied on the page to be properly understood. But in its style and scope and unprecedented ambition, the *Eroica* resonated with the Napoleonic era, and the era was quick to understand that and to embrace it. In 1807, the magazine of trend and fashion *Journal des Luxus und der Moden* (Journal of the Luxurious and the Fashionable) echoed fashionable opinion in calling it "the greatest, most original, most artistic and, at the same time, most interesting of all symphonies."[73] A few years later, the Third Symphony had become a byword. The *AMZ*, February 1810: "It would be superfluous here to say anything about the value of this artistically rich and colossal work."[74] The repercussions of the *Eroica* would roll through the rest of the century and into the next. Ferdinand Ries had said he thought heaven and earth would tremble when the symphony was played. Metaphorically speaking, his prophecy was correct.

For Beethoven, the repercussions were more immediate and personal. He would always have enemies, and bitter ones — though he always believed them to be more numerous and bitter than they actually were. But if triumphs are never complete, this could still only be called a triumph of the highest order, exactly as he had hoped, exactly as he deserved. At least until the Ninth, he would name the *Eroica* his favorite of his symphonies. But it was still not good enough, never good enough. He did not know whether he could surpass the *Eroica*, but he intended to try, and in quite different directions.

19

Our Hearts Were Stirred

BY THE TIME the Third Symphony had its public premiere in April 1805, Beethoven's art and life had heated up to what would seem an unbearable degree. But he was capable of bearing extraordinary burdens, including the ones he heaped on himself. One of them was the height of the bar the new symphony set in his work. Another was the maddening and often debilitating state of his health: recurring fevers, painful and frightening abscesses, headaches that assaulted him for months, on top of his long-standing episodes of vomiting and diarrhea and the ongoing deterioration of his hearing. In spring 1805, the opera *Leonore* and other projects demanded attention. Amid it all, he was boiling with passion for Countess Josephine Deym.

This newly widowed woman with four children had welcomed the kindness and attention of a person she profoundly admired. Josephine soon learned what kind of whirlwind she had opened her door to. Beethoven went at love the way he went at music, with implacable determination. Beyond the question of what Josephine and her children would lose if she married a commoner, beyond his temperament, his utter self-absorption, his ugliness of face and unpleasant chronic ailments, his passion itself became frightening to her.

After writing a paean to love in *Leonore,* he yearned with all his heart for his own devoted wife, his own *Retterin:* his savior. He had written Josephine the song *An die Hoffnung* (To Hope) and dedicated it to her. The song became one more misery for both of them. She learned that Prince Lichnowsky had seen it and its dedication, and that alarmed her. If word got out about it, she could be compromised. She refused to accept the dedication and likewise the proffered *Andante favori.*[1] In spring 1805, Beethoven wrote her a rambling attempt at reassurance, his letter full of echoes of the Heiligenstadt Testament. It begins rationally and ends in ecstasy:

> As I said, the affair with L, my beloved J, is not as bad as was made out to you — Quite by chance L had seen the song <u>"An die Hoffnung"</u> <u>lying about at my place</u> . . . <u>And he said nothing about it.</u> But he gathered from this that I must surely have some affection for you. And then when <u>Zmeskall went to him</u> . . . he asked him if he knew whether I went to see you <u>fairly often.</u> Zmeskall said neither yes nor no. After all, there was nothing he could say, for I had dodged his vigilance as much as possible . . .
>
> L himself said that so far as he was concerned he had far too great a feeling of delicacy to <u>mention</u> a single word, <u>even if he had assumed</u> <u>with certainty the existence of a more intimate association between</u> <u>us</u> — On the contrary, there was nothing which he desired more than the formation of such an association between you and me, if it were possible. For [given] what had been reported to him <u>about your char-</u> <u>acter,</u> such a friendship could not but be advantageous to me . . .
>
> Well, it is true that I have not been as diligent as I ought to have been — but a <u>private grief</u> — robbed me for a long time — of my usual intense energy. And for some time after the feeling of love for you, my adored J, began to stir within me, this grief increased even more — As soon as we are together again . . . you shall hear all about my real sorrows and the struggle with myself between death and life . . . for a long period a certain event made me despair of ever achieving any happiness <u>during my life on this earth</u> — but now things are no longer so bad. I have won <u>your heart.</u> O, I certainly know <u>what value</u> I ought to attach to this. My activity will again increase and — here I give you

a solemn promise that in a short time I shall stand <u>before you</u> more worthy <u>of myself and of you</u> . . .

O, beloved J. It is no desire for the other sex that draws me to you, no, <u>it is just you, your whole self</u> with all your individual qualities — that has compelled my regard . . .

Long — long — of long duration — may our love become — For it is so noble — so firmly founded upon mutual regard and friendship . . . Oh, you, you make me hope that <u>your heart</u> will long — beat for me — <u>Mine</u> can only — cease — to beat for you — when — <u>it no longer beats.</u>[2]

His letter crescendos to a breathless climax, words and phrases blurted between dashes like gasps. The line about standing "<u>before you</u> more worthy <u>of myself and of you</u>" carries the old Bonn tone: the duty of self-improvement to make himself worthy. His *raptus* on the page reached its climax in another letter, which survives in a fragment copied by Josephine. Here his passion makes him virtually incoherent, his words gushing into rhythm and sound, into music:

Why is there no language which can express what is far above all mere regard — far above everything — that we can ever describe — Oh, who can name <u>you</u> — and not feel that however much he could speak about <u>you</u> — that would never attain — to <u>you</u> — only in music — Alas, am I not too proud when I believe that music is more at my command than words — <u>You, you,</u> my all, my happiness — alas, no — even in <u>my music</u> I cannot do so, although in this respect thou, Nature, hast not stinted me with thy gifts. Yet there is too little for <u>you.</u> Beat, though in silence, poor heart — that is all you can do, nothing more — for <u>you</u> — always for <u>you</u> — only <u>you</u> — eternally <u>you</u> until I sink into the grave — My refreshment — my all. Oh, Creator, watch over her — bless her days — rather let all calamities fall upon me —

Even if you had not fettered me again to life, yet you would have meant everything to me —[3]

How could Josephine answer this delirium? How reply when a man like Beethoven says she is saving his life? (In the Heiligenstadt Testament it had been his art. Now it is Josephine.) His art and his well-being meant a great deal to her. At the same time, her morals, her position in the aristocracy, her children, her lack of attraction to him all made an affair unthinkable. Marrying him could be disastrous, not only personally but legally. She had to keep him at bay. At first she tried an affectionate but firm tack:

> You have long had my heart, dear Beethoven; if this assurance can give you joy, then receive it — from the purest heart. Take care that it is also entrusted into the purest bosom. You receive the greatest proof of my love [and] of my esteem through this confession, through this confidence! . . . I herewith [give] you — of the . . . possession of the noblest of my Self . . . will you indicate to me if you are satisfied with it[?] Do not tear my heart apart — do not try to persuade me further. I love you inexpressibly, as one gentle soul does another. Are you not capable of this covenant? I am not receptive to other [forms of] love for the present.[4]

This got her nowhere. His passion was more than words on paper. There were anger, accusations, probably wretched fumbling moments with her having to push him away. His accusations had to do with a shadowy count who had been courting her — egregiously enough to prompt sister Therese to warn her about "keeping two cavaliers on a string."[5] Later, Therese would write that the relationship deteriorated because Beethoven "did not know how to act" with women. She may not have understood that he never really knew how to act with anyone.

When notes resisted him or life resisted him, Beethoven's response was anger and attack — and when it came to people, suspicion and accusation. All this trouble broke over Josephine in a time when she was trying to recover from a nervous breakdown in the wake of losing her husband, having to assume his debts and run his business and rear their children. She became desperate herself: "Even before I knew you, your music made me enthusiastic for you — the goodness of your character, your affection increased it. This preference that you granted me, the pleasure of your acquaintance, would have been the finest jewel of my life if you could have loved me less sensually. That I cannot satisfy this sensual love makes you angry with me, [but] I would have had to violate solemn obligations if I gave heed to your longings."[6]

His longings did not ebb. Finally Josephine was also at her wit's end:

> You do not know how you wound my heart — you treat me entirely wrong —
>
> You do not know <u>what</u> you often do! — How deeply I feel — If my life is dear to you, then treat me with more consideration, and above all, <u>do not doubt me.</u> I cannot express how deeply hurtful it is, with my inner consciousness, with so much sacrifice for virtue and duty, to be compared to lowly creatures, if only in [your] thoughts and quiet suspicion.
>
> <u>Believe me, d[ear] k[ind] B, that I</u> suffer <u>much more, much more</u> than you do — <u>much more!</u>
>
> It is this suspicion that you so often, so hurtfully intimate to me, that pains me beyond all expression. Let this be far from me — I abhor these low, extremely low devices of our species. They are far below me . . .[7]

> I love you and value your moral character. You have shown much love and kindness to me and my children; I shall never forget that, and as long as I live, I shall constantly take interest in your destiny, and contribute what I can to your success.[8]

Beethoven may not have understood the last letter for what it was, a respectful fare-thee-well. There, apparently, for the moment, it rested. In the fall Josephine left Vienna at the approach of the French and spent the winter in Budapest, out of reach.[9] None of this appears to have interrupted his work on *Leonore*, his concern with publication, his other initiatives. Nothing in love or war or illness, nothing short of death could slow the tide of his art in those years.

Still, he wrote another song that appears to relate to Josephine: *Als die Geliebte sich trennen wollte* (When the Beloved Wished to Part), with its lines "The last ray of hope is sinking" and "Ah, lovely hope, return to me."[10]

· · ·

A quietly historical moment was caught in an *Allgemeine Musikalische Zeitung* of March 1805: "Last winter a musical institute was formed . . . which in its way is truly perfect. These are quartets, which are played in a private house in such a way that the listener always pays five gulden in advance for four productions. Schuppanzigh, the entrepreneur, knows how to enter precisely into the spirit of the composer with his superb quartet performance and how to bring that which is fiery, powerful, or finer, tender, humorous, lovely or playful so significantly to the fore that the first violin [part] could hardly be better occupied."[11] Here was the formation of the first professional string quartet presenting a more or less public subscription series. The rest of the group were musicians who had been performing with Schuppanzigh for years. The series later moved out of the private house to a restaurant, a common venue of the time. Given the size of the spaces, audiences numbered less than a hundred.[12] The subscription series did not last long, but change was coming to the way chamber music was presented. Haydn's string quartets had been directed to players as much as to audiences.[13] Schuppanzigh was intruding on the long-standing tradition of private amateur quartet playing; Beethoven's contribution to that evolution would be his first quartets in years.

Publication remained an ongoing necessity and misery for him. For months he had been pushing Breitkopf & Härtel to publish his backlog of large works; he sent them three sonatas, the Third Symphony, the perhaps-still-unperformed Triple Concerto, and *Christus am Ölberge*. They balked at the oratorio and were not offering what he wanted for the rest. Moreover, Gottfried Härtel was fed up with brother Carl's machinations and rudeness. In June, Härtel washed his hands of the current business: "Approximately nine months have passed since your first negotiation with us concerning the five new works that you offered us, without reaching our goal . . . Although our esteem for your art remains great, this dubious situation has become very unpleasant for us . . . Hence we prefer to relinquish these works . . . We repeatedly assure you that it will give us honor and pleasure to publish your works, only we must request . . . that it be done without the intercession of a third party."[14] In other words, no Carl. Beethoven replied with due heat but still, for him, great restraint:

Though I can fully understand the connection between your Paris letter and the long delay in your latest reply — Yet the whole procedure is
altogether far too humiliating for me to waste even one word on it . . .
If any mistake was made, then it was due to the fact that my brother
was wrong <u>about the time</u> which the copying took — The <u>fee</u> is much
lower than what I usually accept — Beethoven is no braggart and he
despises whatever he <u>cannot obtain solely</u> by his art and his own merits — Send me back, therefore, all the manuscripts you have had from
me . . . I cannot and will not accept a lower fee.[15]

All the pieces but *Christus* went to the Bureau des arts et d'industrie,
owned partly by Beethoven's friend and operatic collaborator Joseph
Sonnleithner. This earned the short-lived publishing company its
place in history. Breitkopf & Härtel dropped out of contention for the
moment but still hoped to secure something. Critics of its journal, the
Allgemeine Musikalische Zeitung, were still boggling at Beethoven's
bolder productions, as seen in a virtually schizophrenic August 1805
review of the newly published *Kreutzer* Sonata:

This strange work . . . has extended the boundaries of the type . . .
The reviewer believes, after becoming carefully acquainted with this
composition, that one has to have limited one's love of art to just a
certain realm of the more ordinary, or be strongly prejudiced against
Beethoven if one does not recognize this piece of music . . . as a new
demonstration of the artist's great genius, his vivid, often glowing fantasy, and his broad knowledge of deeper harmonic art. Also, however,
one must be possessed by a type of aesthetic or artistic terrorism or be
won over to Beethoven to the point of blindness, if one does not find
in the work a new, blatant proof . . . that for some time now this artist
had indeed been dead-set on using the most exquisite gifts of nature
and his diligence to simply shift toward the greatest arbitrariness, but
above all else to be entirely different from other people.[16]

This review could not have improved Beethoven's mood, given that he
was <u>temperamentally incapable of enjoying critical incomprehension.</u>
After a period of avoiding people because of his deafness, he was

getting sociable again. He wrote on a manuscript this year, "Just as you are now plunging into the whirlpool of society — just so is it possible to compose works in spite of social obstacles. Let your deafness no longer be a secret — even in art."[17] At a Sonnleithner soiree in July, he met his current operatic hero, Luigi Cherubini. One report of the meeting said he doted on the French master, but Cherubini told Czerny that he had not gotten a friendly reception.[18]

Just before Beethoven left Vienna for the summer, he met another celebrated figure in old Ignaz Pleyel, a publisher and piano maker in addition to a composer, considered by some a rival of his teacher Haydn. At a Lobkowitz soiree, Beethoven listened to new Pleyel string quartets, after which some ladies dragged him to the piano. Annoyed as usual in those situations, he did the same thing he had once done to his would-be rival Daniel Steibelt: on the way to the piano, he picked up a Pleyel second-violin part and based his improvisation on a few notes chosen at random. Czerny was present and reported it as one of his more remarkable efforts. Meanwhile, Czerny said, "Throughout the whole improvisation the quite insignificant notes . . . were present in the middle parts, like a connecting thread or a cantus firmus, while he built upon them the boldest melodies and harmonies in the most brilliant [concerto] style."

It was another demonstration of how Beethoven composed on the page as well as how he improvised: never lose sight of *das Thema*, and emphasize its elements in the playing; but what it gives birth to, the whole of the piece, is more important than the *Thema* itself. The last time he pulled that trick before a composer at a party, his rival Daniel Steibelt had left in outrage. This victim responded quite otherwise. Czerny recalled that Pleyel "was so amazed that he kissed Beethoven's hands. After such improvisations, Beethoven used to break out laughing in a loud and satisfied fashion."[19] Beethoven wrote Zmeskall of the occasion, "I wanted to entertain Pleyel in a musical way — But for the last week I have again been ailing . . . and in some ways I am becoming more and more peevish every day in Vienna."[20]

He was generally less peevish in the country, and friends liked to visit him there. For his summer sojourn in 1805, he headed to Hetzendorf, another suburb of Vienna, where his main project was to finish *Leonore.* One frequent visitor was Ferdinand Ries, who came for lessons and for company. In early 1805, Beethoven may have finished work on the op. 57 Piano Sonata that would be named (by a later publisher) *Appassionata.*

The previous summer in Baden, Ries had watched him at work on it. He arrived at his teacher's door for a lesson and heard Beethoven inside playing short passages at the piano over and over with improvised adjustments. When he got up from the keyboard to open a window, Ries knocked and entered, finding his master in a fine mood. "We won't have a lesson today," Beethoven said. "Instead let's take a walk together, the morning is so beautiful." They were soon strolling in the hills around Baden, enjoying the day and letting the words and the paths find themselves. Then Beethoven stopped talking, began humming tunelessly to himself, the swirling contours reminding Ries of what he had heard earlier from the piano.

They sat down in a meadow, Beethoven sunk in thought. Suddenly from the opposite hillside rose the keening of a shawm, an oboe-like folk instrument. A herder or a shepherd was playing it. Moved by this unexpected rough music, Ries called Beethoven's attention to it. He watched as Beethoven listened intently, clearly not able to hear a thing. It was the first time Ries witnessed his teacher's deafness, though he had suspected it. To try to protect Beethoven's feelings, Ries declared the playing had stopped, though in fact he still heard it clearly. They returned home, Beethoven once again humming and singing to himself, Ries feeling oppressively sad. When they reached the house, Beethoven sat down at the keyboard and said, "Now I'll play something for you." With what Ries remembered as "irresistible fire and mighty force," he tore through the vertiginous last movement of the *Appassionata,* which he had just pulled together in his head. It was a moment Ries never forgot.[24]

As revolutionary as the *Waldstein* in its expression, its pianism, its relentless power, its dramatic unity from tragic beginning to malevolent end, the *Appassionata,* op. 57, is the shadowed counterpart to the earlier sonata. The *Waldstein* ended at the height of joy music can contain; here it comes to the deepest anguish. The *Appassionata* is a story of voids, abysses, dashed hopes. In those years, in the middle of his all-but-superhuman productivity, holding at bay the gnawing miseries of his health and deafness and his frustrated love for Josephine Deym, incipient despair was Beethoven's most intimate companion. But he had vowed to live for his art, and as long as his art ran strong he never contemplated breaking that vow. Now as with all artists, his own suffering became grist for the mill.

A *pianissimo* F-minor arpeggio plunges down to the bottom note of his keyboard and rises back up, answered by a little ambiguous turn figure. Together these constitute the essential *Thema;* the whole *Appassionata* flows from them, along with a fateful four-note tattoo on D-flat–C in the bass.[22] From the beginning this piece neither sounds nor looks on the page like any other work for piano. While the *Waldstein* filled up the texture with brilliant figuration, much of the *Appassionata* first movement is involved in emptying out the texture with ominous silences, murmurs, pulsations with enigmatic wisps of gestures above and below. There are three themes in the exposition: call them fateful in F minor, briefly hopeful in A-flat major, driving and demonic in A-flat minor. For the first time in a Beethoven sonata, there is no repeat of the exposition, as if such sorrows would be unbearable to revisit. The end is a stride up to the top of the keyboard, then back down to the abyss, and a whispering exhaustion. (One sketch had been for a *fortissimo* conclusion, but likely that seemed too defiant, too hopeful for this piece.)

As happens other times in Beethoven (the *Pathètique* an example), the response to suffering is a noble, hymnlike middle movement, this one Andante con moto variations on a somber and almost immobile D-flat-major theme. The four variations describe an upward rise to the brilliant top of the keyboard, but after a coda returning to the opening theme there is no harmonic resolution. Instead the slow movement flows into the finale, which begins with an angry, dissonant pounding on a diminished-seventh chord. Then a consuming whirlwind rises and seems to steadily gather momentum in its rush deathward.[23]

Beethoven had an incomparable skill for raising a movement to what seems an unsurpassable peak of excitement or tension, then to surpass it. He did that at the end of the *Waldstein* finale; he will do it in the coda of the Fifth Symphony's first movement. So it is at the end of the *Appassionata* as well. In the coda a weird, stamping dance breaks out, like a maddened attempt at defiance, but the whirlwind rises again, more furious than ever, as if it were beating the piano to pieces. With that, the last hope is snuffed out.[24] There ends one of the supreme tragic works in the piano literature: the dark side of the heroic. Beethoven would have read a relevant sentiment in his Shakespeare, from *King Lear:* "As flies to wanton boys are we to the gods; / they kill us for their sport." The critic of the *Allgemeine Musikalische Zeitung* seemed divided between shock and awe regarding this piece:

> In the first movement of this sonata [Beethoven] has once again let loose many evil spirits, such as are already familiar from other grand sonatas of his. In truth, however, it is here worth the effort to struggle not only with the wicked difficulties, but also with many a sudden impulse of indignation over learned peculiarities and bizarreries! These oddities of the master's fancy have been discussed so often, however, that the reviewer does not wish to say another word more about them. He will only remark that precisely for that reason he also can say nothing about the details of this entire long movement, because almost everything is saturated by these oddities.[25]

In relation to the new piano music and in all else, Beethoven's own self-criticism was as relentless as his creativity. On a *Leonore* sketch of this period he wrote, "Finale always simpler. All pianoforte music also. God knows why my pianoforte music always makes the worst impression [on me], especially when it is badly played."[26]

On August 9, 1805, England, Russia, and Austria formed a Third Coalition and declared war. It was destined to be the shortest and, for the allies, the most humiliating of eight coalitions against the French. Quickly the fighting bore down on the Viennese, the price of food going up and availability going down. In Vienna a mob stormed a bakery, breaking down the fence and door and cleaning out the shop. On August 25, Napoleon's army left Boulogne for Germany. Poet Heinrich Heine remembered the spectacle of troops marching through Düsseldorf that he saw at age five: "The drumming in the streets continued, and I stood before the house door and looked at the French troops marching, those joyous and famous people who swept over the world singing and playing, the merry serious faces of the grenadiers, the bearskin shakoes, the tricolor cockades, the glittering bayonets."[27]

To his horror Ferdinand Ries, as a citizen of Bonn now under French rule, found himself conscripted into the French army. Beethoven wrote a letter to Princess Josephine, wife of Field Marshal von Leichtenstein, asking her to help: "Poor Ries, who is a pupil of mine, must shoulder his musket in this unfortunate war and — as he is a foreigner, must also leave Vienna in a few days . . . He is compelled to appeal for help to all who know him."[28] He asks her to give the young man some money. Ries reported for duty as ordered but, to his immense relief, was turned down because childhood smallpox had claimed the sight in one eye. Soon he fled to Paris, where he subsisted for nearly three years in poverty and depression.[29]

Out in rural Hetzendorf, Beethoven kept his attention on *Leonore*. In late summer of 1805, he prodded librettist Sonnleithner: "I'm quite ready now — and am waiting for the last four verses — for which I have already thought out the theme provisionally — It is my definite purpose to write the overture during the rehearsals and not until then." (This in fact was the usual procedure for opera composers.) He returned to Vienna in September, the opera nominally ready for rehearsal. He arrived in no better mood than he had left in, and he had not forgotten his anger at Ries over the *Andante favori* joke. One day after a breakfast including Lichnowsky, Ries, and Beethoven, the company retired to Beethoven's flat to hear him play through the opera. Once there, he refused to play until Ries left the room. Ries, about to leave for Bonn and an uncertain fate, exited in tears. Lichnowsky followed Ries and told him to wait, he'd settle the matter, but his angry remonstrations with Beethoven had no effect.[30]

All the same, next month Beethoven wrote Josephine, "My dear L[ichnowsky] is leaving tomorrow — In spite of many rough passages which we are encountering on the path of this friendship, yet now that he is leaving Vienna I feel how dear he is to me — and how much I owe him." He ends on a note of affection and hope: "Tomorrow evening I shall see my dear, my beloved J[osephine] — Tell her that to me she is far more dear and far more precious than anything else —."[31]

Uncertain fate was the motif of these weeks. Before the court opera production of *Leonore* could go forward, as with every opera in Austria, every play, novel, poem, painting, any artistic production involving words or stories or images, the libretto had to be approved by the censors. Their rules were many and intricate. There were to be no religious or current political themes. The military must be treated in a positive manner; the very mention of cowards and deserters was forbidden. A couple could not leave the stage together without a chaperone. Certain words, such as *freedom, equality,* and *enlightenment,* could be permitted only in particular and rare circumstances.[32] Everyone involved knew that *Leonore* was going to be a hard sell, given that it had to do with prisoners, tyranny, liberation, climaxes on the word *Freiheit* ("freedom"), and other subversive elements. Inevitably, the setting of Bouilly's original story was changed from France to Spain.

Sure enough, the change didn't help. The censors banned the production. At that point librettist Sonnleithner, who was Imperial Royal Court Theater secretary at the time, pulled strings as Beethoven surely counted on him to do. Sonnleithner submitted a petition to the censors with a series of points, starting with his best: the empress herself knew the libretto and "had found the original very beautiful and assured me that no opera subject had ever given her so much pleasure." Second, the Paer version of the story had already been given in Prague and Dresden. Third, "Herr Beethoven has spent over a year and a half with the composition of my libretto and . . . has already held rehearsals, and all other preparations have been made, since this opera is supposed to be given on the Name Day of Her majesty the Empress." Fourth, the story after all took place in Spain in the sixteenth century. Fifth, it presented "the most touching description of wifely virtue, and the malicious governor exercises only a private revenge."[33]

At the same time, Sonnleithner went over the censors' heads with an urgent plea to a well-placed friend, State Councillor von Stahl, concluding, "This piece, which is moral in the highest degree, will make a good impression, and recommend it to your love of justice."[34] On

October 5, the censors approved the production. They decreed minor changes in "the most offensive scenes," which Beethoven and Sonnleithner duly made. They had no choice. A police official would be present at all performances, libretto in hand, to make sure the text was performed to the word as the censors approved it (no alteration of any text was allowed on a public stage). The holdup had set back the copying, rehearsals, and other preparations, so it forced a delay of five weeks for the production. Beethoven kept working on the music. In November, he wrote stage manager (and first Pizarro) Friedrich Meyer: "The quartet in the third act is quite correct now . . . I'll send again for Acts I and II because I also want to go through these myself—I can't come, because since yesterday I have been suffering from colic pains—my usual complaint."[35]

Eight days after the ban on *Leonore* was lifted, the French army reached Vienna. It had taken Ulm and Salzburg at the end of October, and the city was left essentially undefended. At the approach of the French, the court and the aristocracy packed up and left, "sending everything away," wrote a diarist, "even bedwarmers and shoe-trees. It looks as if they have no intention of ever coming back." The emperor provided a hundred horses in the Josephsplatz to pull carriages loaded with the possessions of the wealthy; eventually he added a fleet on the Danube for the same purpose, and guaranteed they would be protected.

On November 13, fifteen thousand French troops marched into the city in ranks with banners flying and bands playing. The Viennese turned out to watch as if it were a holiday parade. They found the grenadiers grand with their high caps and breastplates, but it was noticed that the common soldiers were shabby, and many of them marched with strips of confiscated lard, hams, and chunks of meat dangling from their belts.[36] On the fifteenth, Napoleon issued the usual proclamation from the emperor's palace at Schönbrunn, where he had taken up residence. His troops generally behaved well, but they were allowed to appropriate every bit of food they could find and every horse in town.

Hundreds of officers were billeted inside the city walls and thousands of ordinary soldiers in the suburbs, all in commandeered private homes. The markets emptied and the banks closed. Most of the population stayed home. The rattle of coaches and throngs of pedestrians disappeared and a strange calm reigned, the streets populated mostly by French soldiers.[37] Baron Braun announced to the performers and employees of the court theaters that, by imperial order, the theaters were to remain open unless there was a bombardment, in which case everyone was permitted to run for their lives.[38]

Under those conditions, rehearsals for *Leonore* resumed in an atmosphere far worse than the usual pre-premiere anxiety. At one point Beethoven was fuming about a missing third bassoon and Prince Lobkowitz made a joke about it. Passing the prince's palace on his way home, Beethoven was heard to shout, "Lobkowitzian ass!"[39] A week after the occupation began, the opera premiered at the Theater an der Wien. The title role was handled by twenty-year-old Anna Milder, for whom Beethoven had written the part. She was talented, also young and inexperienced.[40] Over Beethoven's protest the title was given as *Fidelio,* to avoid confusion with the Paer version.

The circumstances of launching a serious and ambitious opera low in action and high in ideals could hardly have been worse. For three nights, it played to almost empty houses made up mainly of French officers, a few Beethoven friends including Lichnowsky, and a smattering of tourists and brave souls willing to leave their homes. "Except for whores," wrote one theatergoer, "one sees very few women at the theaters."[41]

The audience watched the story advance on its slow course with its spotty cast: an overture that begins gloomily, evoking Florestan singing in his chains; the opening scene with Leonore disguised as a young man named Fidelio, working in the prison where her husband is starving in the dungeon. There are the awkward touches of comedy as she fends off the attentions of the jailer's daughter Marzelline, who is in love with this youth; the prisoners' moment in the sun, singing of sunlight and freedom; Pizarro's vow that this will be his prisoner's last day. Fading in his chains, Florestan remembers his love and the springtime of his life. Leonore finds her way to the dungeon, helping the jailer dig her husband's grave. Gun in hand, she cries to an incredulous Pizarro, "First kill his wife!" The minister's trumpet calls, the villain is exposed, the lovers freed, and Leonore hailed in music of resplendent celebration: *Retterin!* Savior![42] At the second performance Stephan von Breuning distributed to the minuscule audience a poem he had written hailing the work, overoptimistically: "Our hearts were stirred, elated, pierced in turn / By Leonore's courage, love, and tears; / Now jubilant echoes vie to praise her faith / And dread anxiety gives way to bliss."[43]

There was the potential for a great and moving opera in this story, and Beethoven's music was equal to it. But this was his first attempt at the stage, and even if it had been an ideal performance, the opera was not ready to sail. A Viennese reported to his diary, "In the evening I went to W. Th. to hear Louis Beth.'s opera . . . The Opera has pretty, ingenious, difficult music and a tedious libretto of little interest. It had no success and the theater was empty." Reported a visiting British doctor, "The story and plan of the piece are a miserable mixture of low manners and romantic situations; the airs, duets and choruses equal to any praise . . . Beethoven presided at the pianoforte and directed the performance himself. He is a small dark young-looking man, wears spectacles . . . Few people present, though the house would have been crowded in every part but for the present state of public affairs."[44]

The reviews followed suit, everybody noting that the music was in some degree splendid, the story slow and clichéd. "Both melody and characterization," said the *Freymüthige*, "failed to achieve that happy, striking, irresistible expression of passion that grips us so irresistibly in Mozart's and Cherubini's works. The music has several pretty spots, but it is still far from being a perfect work or even a successful one."[45] The *Allgemeine Musikalische Zeitung* was more blunt: "Until now, Beethoven had so often paid homage to the new and strange at the expense of the beautiful; one would thus expect above all to find distinctiveness, newness, and genuine, original creative flair . . . and it is precisely these qualities that one encounters in it least."[46] The visiting Cherubini took in the opera and declared the overture so chromatic that he had no idea what key it was in, and that Beethoven had little conception of writing for the voice.[47]

Immediately Beethoven's friends began a campaign to persuade him to rework it. Singer and stage manager Friedrich Meyer invited the new house tenor, Joseph August Röckel, to a meeting in the music room of Lichnowsky's palace, where a circle of friends and admirers were assembling to demand revisions. Everybody but Beethoven agreed that the slow and ponderous first act had to be shortened, mainly by cutting three numbers. Meyer advised Röckel that there was going to be a storm. He was right. The occasion, in December 1805, went on from seven in the evening until two in the morning in an atmosphere of rage, hysteria, and implacable determination from Beethoven's friends.

Röckel recalled that those present, mostly of Beethoven's inner circle, included Prince and Princess Lichnowsky, brother Caspar van Beethoven, Stephan von Breuning, poet and playwright Heinrich von Collin (whose play *Coriolan* had stirred Beethoven), actor Joseph Lange (Mozart's brother-in-law), Friedrich Meyer (another Mozart brother-in-law), playwright G. F. Treitschke (who later worked on the final version of the opera), and theater concertmaster Franz Clement. Under the many-candled chandeliers of the Lichnowsky music room, surrounded by silken draperies and old-master paintings in golden frames, they began going through the opera number by number. Princess Lichnowsky played piano from Beethoven's enormous manuscript score while violinist Clement, famous for his recall, provided a distillation of the string parts from memory. Meyer and Röckel covered the singing parts, male and female. They played and sang through the first two of the three acts, making suggestions as they went, all of which Beethoven rejected. Before long the company discovered that while most of them had experienced his fury, they had never seen anything like the apoplectic heights he attained when they brought up the issue of cutting three numbers. He attempted to seize the score and run off with it but was prevented by the princess, who placed her hands over the music and refused to give it up. They continued on to the third act, Röckel sight-reading the part of Florestan (his effort earned him the part in the next production).

It was well past midnight when they finished the reading. "And the revisions, the cuts?" Princess Lichnowsky asked Beethoven. "Do not insist on them!" he declared. "Not a single note must be missing!" This called for desperate measures. The frail princess hurled herself at his feet, crying, "Beethoven! No — your greatest work, you yourself shall not cease to exist in this way! God who has implanted those tones of purest beauty in your soul forbids it, your mother's spirit, which at this moment pleads and warns you with my voice, forbids it! Beethoven, it must be! Give in! Do it in memory of your mother! Do it for me, who am only your best friend!"

Stunned, Beethoven stood still for a moment, turned his eyes upward, and burst into sobs. "I will — yes, all!" he gasped. "I will do all, for you — for your — for my mother's sake!" Gently he pulled the princess to her feet.

By then it was nearly two in the morning, everyone completely exhausted. Not another word was spoken about the opera. Doors were flung open, revealing the dining room spread with a sumptuous dinner. As they sat down Beethoven was suddenly in the best of moods. Gaily he asked Röckel what the tenor had just devoured from his plate. Röckel said he had no idea, he had been so ravenous. "He eats like a wolf," Beethoven roared, "without knowing what! *Ha!*"[48]

From that point Beethoven took the revisions in his own hands. Behind librettist Sonnleithner's back, he had Stephan von Breuning work over the libretto. He wrote disingenuously to Sonnleithner, "I particularly request you to give me a short written statement permitting me to have the libretto with its present alterations printed again under your name ... Three acts have been reduced to only two. In order to achieve this and to make the opera move more swiftly I have shortened everything as much as possible." In regard to the libretto changes, he wrote, "I have made them myself."[49] That was essentially a lie, perhaps to protect Sonnleithner's feelings. The matter of adjusting the timing and the dramatic arc of a play or opera is a craft that has to be learned by a combination of experience and trial and error. By the end Beethoven had surgically excised more than five hundred bars, reduced the first two acts to one, and cut jailer Rocco's comic (and not very amusing) aria "Hat man nicht auch Gold."[50]

All this was carried on in the middle of the continuing French occupation. During it Beethoven entertained some visiting French officers by playing through the entire Gluck opera *Iphigénie en Tauride* from the orchestral score while the Frenchmen provided the arias and choruses. Czerny, who was present, recalled that the soldiers sang "not at all badly."[51]

The occupation was relatively peaceful, with the occasional pleasant moments like that one, but outside the gates of the city there was nothing but disaster for Austria. On December 2, 1805, in the greatest victory of his career, Napoleon's 68,000 troops crushed the Austro-Russian army of 90,000 at Austerlitz, near Brno in Moravia. He lured Russian tsar Alexander I into a trap, cut the allied army in two, and by midday the French, with minimal losses, had killed or wounded 15,000 enemy and captured 11,000, totaling nearly a third of the allied forces. In spite of the October Battle of Trafalgar, in which Admiral Nelson wiped out most of a Franco-Spanish fleet and ensured Britain's command of the sea, the Third Coalition could not survive Austerlitz. The tsar took his army back to Russia. "We are babies," he said, "in the hands of a giant." Austria was forced to sign the humiliating Treaty of Pressburg, ceding cities and vast territories to France and Bavaria and recognizing Napoleon as king of Italy. Napoleon also required Austria to pay 40,000 gold francs in indemnity. That contributed to a rising financial crisis in Austria that came to a head years later.

The next July, in 1806, Napoleon joined sixteen German states into the Confederation of the Rhine, with himself as "protector," for the first time reducing the number of small principalities. Nearly two dozen states eventually joined. The new entities soaked up smaller states around them. All members of the confederation were obliged to supply Napoleon with troops, as was Austria. These developments inflamed Prussia, which joined Britain and Russia in a new coalition. That ended quickly with French victories in the battles of Jena and Friedland in October 1806. (On hearing about Jena from friend Wenzel Krumpholz, Beethoven quipped, "It's a pity I don't understand the art of war as well as I do the art of music. I would conquer him!") At the end of the year, Napoleon imposed on his subject territories the Continental System, which amounted to a gigantic embargo on trade with Britain. It was ineffective and did harm to everyone involved, including France, but it lasted until 1814.

Acting on the inevitable, in August 1806, Franz II declared the dissolution of the Holy Roman Empire. He retitled himself Franz I, first emperor of Austria. So came the final collapse of the union that traced its ancestry back a thousand years to Charlemagne. This was the summit of Napoleon's career, when a born nobody, a "little corporal" of genius, unbounded ambition, and remarkable luck, wiped away a millennium of history. He was a tyrant with the blood of millions on his account by the time he was done, but there had never been anyone like him. For all the disgust and betrayal felt by Beethoven and myriad others, they knew the simple fact that Napoleon existed made him an irrevocable part of history.

With the premiere of the reworked version of the opera set for March 1806, new Florestan Joseph Röckel was summoned to Beethoven's flat to pick up some revisions. He was confronted by an elderly servant. In the next room he heard splashing as the great man washed himself to the accompaniment of mighty groans. Finally persuading the servant he was supposed to be there, Röckel entered and beheld the fabled Beethoven household chaos: a chair held some pages of the *Eroica,* pages of the opera were scattered like leaves over furniture and floor for the ink to dry, and in the middle of assorted piles of music, Beethoven stood before his washstand naked or nearly so, groaning as he poured cascades over himself, the water running through the floorboards to the apartments below. Röckel was struck by Beethoven's powerful build; he looked indestructible. That day he was in a kindly mood. As he dressed, he went on about how he had copied out the new version of Röckel's part himself from the illegible draft.[52] He gave Röckel the music and sent him on his way.

Just before the premiere of the revival, Prince Lobkowitz sponsored a performance of the Paer version of *Leonore* in his palace.[53] It is not recorded why he did that; maybe it was to show connoisseurs how much better Beethoven's setting was. The three airings of the revised *Leonore* at the end of March and into April were a quite different matter from the original production. The French were gone, the nobility returned from their hiding places. The streets filled up again with Viennese desperate for entertainment and distraction. "The people are indifferent upon every topic but mere idle objects of amusement," wrote an English visitor, "and the new ballet or play, the dress of the bourgeois, the parade of their emperor's return, etc., is more eagerly talked about than the miserable treaty of peace, the loss of an army, or the overthrow of an empire. The subject is '*traurig*' [sad], they say, and in this world we ought to amuse ourselves."[54]

The first performance was fairly well attended. Stephan von Breuning distributed a new poem of praise. The orchestra, however, had gotten their parts at the last minute and stumbled through the music. Not the least sympathetic, Beethoven wrote stage manager Meyer to have house conductor Ignaz von Seyfried handle the next performance, because "I want to see and hear it myself today at a distance. At all events my patience will not then be so severely tried as it would be if I were near the orchestra and had to listen to the murder of my music! . . . All desire to compose anything more ceases completely if I have to hear my work performed like that!"[55] He was equally furious that his preferred title of *Leonore* — a title focused on the real heroine rather than the disguised one — had once more been rejected, and the production was again billed as *Fidelio*.[56]

He had written a new overture for this production, roughly the same length as the first, and likewise in C major, but more focused and forceful. (Later, in a confused chronology, the original came to be called *Leonore* No. 2, the second No. 3, and one for an abortive 1808 Prague performance No. 1.) The first two overtures give a kind of self-contained musical summary less of the action of the opera than of its emotional unfolding, from suffering to salvation to celebration. In other words, rather than the expected operatic curtain raiser, the *Leonore* overtures amount to what a later time would call a "program piece" or a "symphonic poem," a work painting pictures and tracing a narrative.

In these first of his mature overtures, Beethoven indulged his love of musical storytelling. Connoisseurs of the time, himself included, deplored descriptive instrumental music as in bad taste. Yet Beethoven wrote many such pieces anyway — for example, most of his overtures. Like the earlier overture, No. 3 begins memorably, with a descent into the darkness and despair of the dungeon, wandering through inchoate harmonies until suddenly we are in A-flat major, Florestan's key, and we hear a moment of his aria "In des Lebens Frühlingstagen" (In the Springtime of Life). Here is the essence of the opera, its ethos, its utterly Beethovenian idea: a hero dying in a tyrant's dungeon, singing in his chains of a better life. After the extended Adagio of the introduction, a surging and hopeful Allegro begins. In contrast to *Leonore* No. 2, No. 3, like his later overtures, is laid out in a clear and direct sonata outline. The orchestral sound is brilliant and muscular, Cherubini-esque, in contrast to Mozart's darting, quicksilver textures. Here is the theatrical version of Beethoven's heroic style, which is the French revolutionary style: grand, spacious, forceful, direct, popularistic. The minister's trumpet is the turning point of the overture, as of the opera; then there is a coda of overflowing jubilation.

In the theater, neither of the first written overtures worked. They overwhelmed the light, almost buffa tone of the opera's opening, and by anticipating the climax and its trumpet call, they weakened that climax. A new approach Beethoven drafted for the abortive performance in Prague in 1808 he shelved unheard.

After the premiere of the revised opera, more people showed up for the next two performances. The applause burgeoned, the press reviews turned warmer. After so much labor and frustration, a success appeared to be brewing. Then everything went up in smoke. Waiting outside the office of court theater manager Baron von Braun, tenor Röckel heard shouting break out behind the door. Beethoven had gotten an unprecedented deal giving him a direct percentage of the gate, and he refused to believe the figures he was getting for his share of the receipts. Braun had aroused Beethoven's perennial conviction that everybody was swindling him.

Patiently Braun explained that while the expensive seats had been full, the galleries were not. Stalking up and down the room, Beethoven cried, "I don't write for the multitude—I write for the connoisseurs!" The baron replied with something he should have known better than to say to Beethoven: "But the connoisseurs alone do not fill our theater. We need the multitude to bring in money, and since in your music you have refused to make any concession to it, you yourself are to blame . . . If we had given Mozart the same percentage of the receipts of his operas [that we gave you], he would have been rich."

That was the last straw. "I want my score!" Beethoven bellowed, his face crimson. "My score at once!" The baron rang for a servant and had him fetch the music. When he returned, the baron tried to calm the raging composer: "I'm sorry, but I believe on calmer reflection —." Beethoven snatched the score from the servant's hand and fled, running past Röckel outside without seeing him. Röckel went in to find Braun distraught. "Beethoven was excited and overhasty," Braun said. "You have some influence with him. Try everything — promise him anything in my name, so that we can save his work for our stage!" Röckel hurried out to try to persuade Beethoven, but he would not discuss the matter. The score went into the drawer and stayed there.[57]

Thus out of pride and paranoia, Beethoven himself sank his opera for what turned out to be the better part of a decade. There was talk of a performance at Prince Lobkowitz's palace, but apparently nothing came of it; likewise the 1808 Prague performance.

If the collapse of *Leonore* was his own doing, he was still terribly depressed about it. "Probably nothing," Stephan von Breuning wrote Wegeler in Bonn, "has caused Beethoven so much grief as this work, whose value will be fully appreciated only in the future."[58] During this period Beethoven copied out some lines from a book that gave him inspiration for years, Rev. Christian Sturm's reflections on the tangible presence of God in nature: "Thou has tried all means to draw me to Thee. Now it hath pleased Thee to let me feel the heavy hand of Thy wrath, and to humiliate my proud heart by manifold chastisements. Sickness and misfortune has Thou sent to bring me to a contemplation of my digressions. But one thing only do I ask, O God, cease not to labor for my improvement. Only let me, in whatsoever manner pleases Thee, turn to Thee and be fruitful of good works."[59] By whatever agency, that prayer was answered in 1806, a year when Beethoven was chronically ill, crushed over the collapse of his opera, disappointed in love, and fruitful beyond belief in good works.

That spring, brother Carl van Beethoven married Johanna Reis, daughter of a prosperous upholsterer. Ludwig considered her a contemptible tramp. Carl's position with the Office of Revenue kept him busy, and he was near the end of his service as his brother's agent. Their son Karl was born just over three months after the ceremony.[60]

The day after Carl's ill-omened marriage, Beethoven started the first of three string quartets that had been commissioned by Count Andreas Kyrillovich Razumovsky, the Russian ambassador to Vienna. Apparently Beethoven had been planning new quartets for some time.[61] Part of the commission agreement seems to have been that each quartet would include a Russian folk tune. He secured a collection of national songs and combed it for material. When in the previous decade he had accepted the commission from Prince Lobkowitz for the six quartets that became op. 18, he had been a young composer feeling his way into territory owned mainly by Haydn, then still in his prime as a composer. Now Beethoven had come fully into his own and Haydn's creative career was closed. He began these quartets feeling free and fearless.

This patron, Count Razumovsky, was known to Vienna as one of the most extravagant princes in a city full of the breed. He came from a musical family. His father and his father's brother had started as singers in the Russian court and were ennobled in fond gratitude for their services, mainly of an intimate nature, to the future empresses Elizabeth Petrovna and Catherine the Great.[62] Like Lichnowsky and Lobkowitz, Razumovsky was another aristocrat mad for music who played an instrument well. As a violinist he had been tutored in Haydn's quartets by Haydn himself, and he often sat in at second violin in house performances. In 1800, he asked Beethoven for lessons in quartet writing and was sent to Aloys Förster, Beethoven's mentor in the medium.[63]

Like Lichnowsky, Razumovsky was a prince of the decadent variety in his private life. An acquaintance described him as "enemy of the revolution, but good friend of the fair sex." He pursued women as avidly as music, among his conquests in the high nobility being the queen of Naples. Meanwhile he married into the highest Viennese nobility: Elizabeth, Countess Thun, sister of Prince Karl Lichnowsky. As an ambassador, it appears that he paid more attention to his own affairs, in every sense, than to affairs of state, but his position was secure under his patron, Tsar Alexander.[64]

Whatever Razumovsky's appeal to women, it did not seem to lie on his surface. While his manners were impeccable, he was said to have the pinched and malevolent face of a Russian police interrogator.[65]

Wrote one acquaintance, Baroness du Montet, "He radiates pride in all things; pride in his birth, his rank, and his honor, . . . in his bearing, in his speech."[66] The Razumovsky Palace, finished in 1808, sat imperiously on a hill in the suburb of Landstrasse, built in a mixture of Empire and Renaissance styles, flaunting its roof garden, library, art gallery, and hall of sculptures by Canova. Given his interest in music and his connection to the Lichnowskys, Razumovsky naturally had made Beethoven's acquaintance early on. They seemed to have gotten along with less friction than Beethoven did with Lichnowsky and other patrons.[67]

The quartets for Razumovsky went quickly. In August 1806, Beethoven notified publisher Gottfried Härtel that brother Carl was coming to visit (at which Härtel would have groaned) and wrote, "You may discuss with him the question of new violin quartets, one of which I have already finished; and indeed I am thinking of devoting myself almost entirely to this type of composition."[68] Neither of those statements was necessarily true. Beethoven was given to telling publishers he had works in hand that were not finished, sometimes not even begun. That he was thinking of devoting himself to string quartets may have been equally exaggerated, or may have been a symptom of the joy and sense of discovery he was finding in working on Razumovsky's commission. The Muse kept passionately by his side in those days.

At the end of his letter to Härtel, he unleashed another of his broadsides about bad reviews in the Breitkopf & Härtel house journal: "I hear that in the musikalische Zeitung someone has railed violently against the [Third] symphony, which I sent you last year and which you returned to me. I have not read the article. If you fancy that you can injure me by publishing articles of that kind, you are very much mistaken. On the contrary, by so doing you merely bring your journal into disrepute." The Third was published that year under the title Eroica. In fact the AMZ reviewers had been inevitably baffled but scrupulously fair. Beethoven's return fire concerning reviews was generally excessive. And he probably had read the reviews.

Around the end of August he and Prince Lichnowsky, still his most powerful patron, still supplying him with a stipend of 600 florins a year, went together for a stay at the Lichnowsky castle in Grätz, Silesia (later part of the Czech Republic). This working vacation proved fateful in several directions. Beethoven brought with him ideas in various states of completion for a symphony (eventually the Fifth) and a fourth piano concerto; in Grätz, he wrote most of a violin concerto, in addition to working on the quartets for Razumovsky. At the castle he could spend his time as he wished. A servant, asked later about his impressions of the famous visitor, said Herr Beethoven struck him as not in his right mind. He would dash around the castle and grounds for hours on end, bareheaded in the cold and rain; other times, he would shut himself up in his room for whole days, not seeing anyone.[69] What the servant was seeing amounted to an extended creative *raptus*. Beethoven was writing work after work, most of them remarkable, at a clip that would strain anyone's sanity.

Not long after Beethoven arrived, Lichnowsky took him out to meet his friend Count Franz Joachim Wenzel Oppersdorff, who had a castle near Ober-Glogow stocked with one of the last private orchestras maintained by the aristocracy of those days. His musicians doubled as household officials. Oppersdorff and Beethoven hit it off from the beginning, especially after the house orchestra played the Second Symphony.[70] It seems likely that Beethoven headed back to Grätz with a commission for two symphonies. Putting the other projects aside, he scraped together some ideas and plunged into a symphony in B-flat.

In a letter of September 3, he offered the new symphony, three Razumovsky quartets, *Leonore*, and *Christus am Ölberge* to Breitkopf & Härtel "immediately." Despite all the frustrations, he was still doggedly courting the most prestigious publishing house in Europe. Probably only the last two pieces were finished by then, but he apparently did write the symphony in a matter of weeks. By the end of the year the Fourth Symphony, Fourth Piano Concerto, *Razumovsky* Quartets, and Violin Concerto would all be more or less finished, all of them largely completed in the preceding six months. There were also minor works from 1806, including the Thirty-Two Variations for Piano, WoO 80, which he dashed off and forgot about. Later he happened to overhear the daughter of the piano maker Streicher playing the variations and asked her who wrote them. Told he was the culprit, he exclaimed, "Such nonsense by me? Oh, Beethoven, what an ass you were!"

Then in late October, in the middle of this rush of work, once again he managed one of his self-inflicted disasters. Beethoven and Lichnowsky, both of them egotists of a major order, had a fractious history. The year before, Beethoven had written Josephine Deym, "In spite of many rough passages which we are encountering on the path of this friendship . . . I feel how dear he is to me."[71] What touched off this scuffle was the visit of some French officers, who were at their leisure after their army's thrashing of the Austrians and Russians at Austerlitz. Lichnowsky arranged a musicale for the visitors, to show off his prize protégé. He may have known Beethoven had recently hobnobbed with French officers, playing through a Gluck opera, so there was no reason to expect a storm.

What happened survived only in rumors and echoes. Beethoven refused to play, declaring that he was no servant and would not be ordered to perform for enemies of his country. Lichnowsky admired and understood Beethoven perhaps as well as anyone, but he was also a prince, imperious in nature, used to being obeyed. He did not enjoy being humiliated in front of foreign dignitaries, least of all by a commoner who had enjoyed his generosity for years. He demanded that Beethoven play, was refused, demanded again. In one story Beethoven locked himself in his room and Lichnowsky kicked the door in. In another version Beethoven was swinging a chair over his head and had to be restrained from braining the prince by Count Oppersdorff. There may have been a threat of jail, by way of a joke Beethoven did not appreciate. There may have been worse threats from Lichnowsky. Later in a letter, Beethoven referred to "people who like to belabor their friends with flails."[72]

It appears that, in the wake of the ruckus, Beethoven gathered up his manuscripts, bolted the Lichnowsky castle, and walked some five miles to a nearby village. From there he found a cart and made the 140-mile, three-day journey back to Vienna. During a rainstorm on the trip, some of his music, including the manuscript of the *Appassionata*, got wet in his trunk, damaged but not destroyed. Two legends of the aftermath may or may not be true: one, that when Beethoven got home he smashed on the floor a plaster bust of Lichnowsky he had been given; two, that he wrote a note to Lichnowsky saying, "Prince! What you are, you are by circumstance and by birth. What I am, I am through myself. Of princes there have been and will be thousands. Of Beethovens there is only one." Whether or not he actually wrote those words, it was surely what he believed, and he had every reason to.

But moral and financial issues are two quite different things. Whatever satisfaction Beethoven found in his rages and revenges, he soon realized that this paroxysm had cost him Lichnowsky's stipend of 600 florins a year. Having sunk his opera in a fit of paranoid rage, now Beethoven had tossed out a quarter or more of his income. (For a landed aristocrat like Lichnowsky, the stipend was pocket change.) He and the prince eventually reconciled to some degree, but they were never really close again, and the stipend was gone for good.[73] Beethoven, for his part, learned the relevant lesson. He never made that kind of mistake again with a patron. This was his last major indulgence in self-damaging fury.

Yet after the fight he arrived back in Vienna in high spirits. Sometimes fits of wrath seemed to leave him refreshed. He was laughing when he showed the still-wet *Appassionata* manuscript to Paul Bigot, Count Razumovsky's librarian. Bigot's wife Marie, a fine pianist, insisted on playing over the sonata on the spot. Beethoven was delighted with her sight-reading of the water-stained manuscript in his scratchy hand (though his fair copies could be legible enough). After the sonata reached print, he submitted to Marie's plea and made her a gift of the manuscript. The Bigots, especially Marie, were becoming highly appreciated friends.

At the beginning of November, a new offer arrived from Scottish publisher George Thomson. In 1803, he had asked Beethoven for six sonatas based on Scottish themes, but Beethoven's price had been too steep. A later request for chamber pieces had also gone nowhere. Thomson was a promoter and publisher of Scottish and other regional folk music. Now he offered Beethoven some piecework: arranging folk songs for a modest fee each, but with the promise of a steady supply of material. Earlier Thomson had commissioned Lord Byron, Sir Walter Scott, and Robert Burns to supply words for existing melodies. Some of the results were historic, the Burns lyrics including those to *Auld lang syne*. For arrangements, Thomson had hired German composers including Pleyel and Haydn.

Now that Haydn was no longer able to manage even piecework, Thomson turned to the newest famous German composer. The arrangements he wanted from Beethoven varied between ones for solo voice and piano to more elaborate ones for multiple voices, sometimes including obbligato parts for other instruments. Thomson insisted the arrangements had to be playable by amateurs.[74] It was never entirely clear why Beethoven agreed to take on commercial items like this that took up time and paid skimpily. The loss of Lichnowsky's stipend may have had something to do with it. In any case, whatever the constraints, Beethoven agreed, writing Thomson, in French, "I will take care to make the compositions easy and pleasing as far as I can and as far as is consistent with that elevation and originality of style, which, as you yourself say, favorably characterize my works and from which I shall never stoop. I cannot bring myself to write for the flute, as this instrument is too limited and imperfect." It would be another four years before he sent Thomson the first consignment, of fifty-three melodies. They constitute the beginning of one of the most extensive, also nearly negligible, bodies of work in his career.

The first public manifestation of what Beethoven had accomplished in this almost-inconceivable year came when the Violin Concerto was premiered by Franz Clement in a benefit concert for himself on December 23, 1806. Along with the Fourth Symphony, most of the concerto had been written at a gallop in the autumn, the finale finished, it was said, two days before the premiere. Clement may have sight-read the finale in the concert. The former child prodigy was at the peak of his fame, not a traveling virtuoso but a much-admired concertmaster and soloist in Vienna. When Clement was a prodigy of fourteen, in 1794, Beethoven had written in an album, "Go forth on the way in which you hitherto have travelled so beautifully, so magnificently. Nature and art vie with each other in making you a great artist."[75] In the next decade he and Beethoven had come to an easy and mutually admiring professional relationship, and the concerto was written for him. Beethoven's affection for Clement was shown in one of his wry annotations on the manuscript, with a trademark pun: *Concerto par Clemenza pour Clement,* "Concerto for Clemency from Clement."

In his most recent violin sonatas, Beethoven had been inspired by the modern French school, which had created a revolution in playing based in part on the relatively new Tourte, or "Viotti," bow. Its inward arc, rather than the Baroque outward-arced bow, made possible a stronger tone and a wider range of effects. The French style was familiar to Beethoven through the playing of Rodolphe Kreutzer and George Bridgetower, and through the well-known concertos of Giovanni Battista Viotti, like Cherubini an Italian-born composer who found his fame in Paris. Viotti's concerto style, which came to be known as simply "the French violin concerto," involved bravura effects, forceful attacks, and a greater repertoire of slurs, all enabled by the new bow. These concertos also expected a more robust tone from the soloist. All this in turn helped associate French concertos in the audience's mind with the atmosphere of the Revolution. Along with the development of the modern bow, pre-1800 violins, even the most precious Stradivaris and Guarneris, were being taken apart and fitted with longer fingerboards, a higher bridge, and a thicker sound post inside. In addition to the new bow, these adaptations gave the violin more power and brilliance, even though the strings remained the traditional gut.

Still, as with Viennese piano makers, violinists in Vienna were slow to adopt new trends. Beethoven's string players in those days probably used a mixture of old- and new-style instruments and bows. Clement himself was an old-fashioned player who played on a traditional fingerboard with a traditional bow. He was noted more for his elegance and delicacy, and his sureness in the difficult high register, than for flash and power.[76] So the concerto Beethoven wrote for him had little of the dramatic cross-string chords and virtuosic bow work of the more French-style *Kreutzer* Sonata. Inspired by Clement, the concerto did involve a great many passages in the high reaches of the E string (which Beethoven had avoided in the early violin sonatas). The stratospheric violin writing was perhaps a progressive element in the Violin Concerto, but otherwise the piece was largely devoted to a lyrical style, which Beethoven, writing as fast as he could get the notes down, pushed into a new dimension in concertos.

The Violin Concerto is unique from the first sound: it begins unprecedentedly with a timpani solo marking the four beats of the first measure and the downbeat of the second, where the winds enter on a quietly soaring theme marked *dolce*, "sweet."[77] The opening gesture says two important things about the music to come: first, that timpani rhythm is going to be a leading motif of the first movement; second, its simplicity heralds a piece that is going to be made of radically simple elements: rhythms largely in quarters and eighths, most of the phrasing in four bars, flowing melodies made largely out of scales. Many of Beethoven's themes had always been fashioned from bits of scales; here that is carried to a transcendent extreme. In keeping, the harmony is simple but with touches of striking color, unexpected shifts of key, excursions into minor keys that arrive not like dark clouds but as colorations and intensifications. The lucidity and simplicity of the material contribute to the singular tone, serene and sublime, marked by the soloist singing on top of the orchestra in the highest range of the instrument.

All that is to say, this is not a heroic or a particularly virtuosic or dramatic concerto. The opening timpani stride might imply a military atmosphere like the openings of his piano concertos, but the music does not go in that direction. And there is no readily discernible dramatic narrative of the kind in which the contemporary Fourth Piano Concerto is so rich. Call the main topic of the Violin Concerto *beauty* in the visceral and spiritual sense that the time understood it.

When things are stripped down to the simple and direct, every detail takes on great significance. So it is in the enormous first movement, with its sure-handed proportions, its subtle touches of color and contrast that keep the music riveting and moving. The orchestral exposition unveils three rather similar themes, all of them flowing up and down a D-major scale. The quarter-note tattoo introduced by the timpani underlies everything, including patterns that speed it up to eighths and sixteenths.

An out-of-nowhere D-sharp intruding on the placid D major creates more color than drama. That pitch will summon later harmonies and keys (mainly B-flat) in the movement. In the orchestral exposition, the main contrasting keys are B-flat and F, surrounding the home key not with the expected dominant but rather with thirds above and below

—an increasingly common Beethoven pattern. Here they are placid mediants in the flat direction, generating warmth rather than tension. The unusual element is the lack of tonal movement, each theme first heard in D major, the second one feeling more like the *Thema* proper of the movement.

The violin enters on bravura octaves that soar from the bottom of the instrument up into the high range, where the soloist will live much of the time, devoted more to spinning out lace than thematic work. This is a symphonic concerto in which the soloist is not a heroic or even distinctive personality so much as a kind of ethereal presence floating through and above the orchestra. After an improvisatory quasi-cadenza, the violin seems to improvise on the first theme high in the clouds while the winds play it straight. The development section is striking mainly in its placidity and its melodiousness, in contrast to the usual fragmentation and drama of developments. The first movement, like the others, requires a cadenza; Beethoven supplied none of them.

If it is possible, the gentle second movement is even more exquisitely lyrical than the first. Its form takes shape both simply and unusually as a serene theme over a repeating bass pattern, variations that are largely rescorings of the theme to which the soloist adds quasi-improvisatory filigree. After three variations, two new themelets, call them B and C, stand in for a couple of variations, and an extension of C serves as coda.[78]

An old Viennese legend says that the leaping 6/8 "hunting" theme of the rondo finale was written by violinist Clement. That makes sense for two reasons: Beethoven had to write the finale in a tremendous hurry and may have seized the nearest thing to work with; and in style, the tune seems a throwback to the gay and slight rondo finales of his youth. Still, his treatment of the theme is fresh despite its conventions (including a hunting episode for horns). The total length is only about a third that of the first movement.[79] Its vigorous joyousness is the pay-off of a work of serene beauties.

The enormous program in Vienna, where the concerto premiered, had the time's usual mixture of genres and media. It included overtures by Méhul and Cherubini, a Mozart aria, a Cherubini vocal quartet, and vocal pieces by Handel. In the middle of the Beethoven concerto Clement performed one of his trademark tricks, playing a piece on a violin with one string, upside down. A review in the *Wiener Zeitung* said, "The superb violin player Klement [*sic*] also played, among other exquisite pieces, a violin concerto by Beethhofen [*sic*], which was received with exceptional applause due to its originality and abundance of beautiful passages. In particular, Klement's proven artistry and grace . . . were received with loud bravos." That said, the reviewer turned the back of his hand:

> The educated world was struck by the way that Klement could debase himself with so much nonsense and so many tricks . . . Regarding Beethhofen's concerto, the judgment of connoisseurs is undivided; they concede that it contains many beautiful qualities, but admit that the context often seems completely disjointed and that the endless repetition of several commonplace passages can easily become tiring. They maintain that Beethhofen should use his avowedly great talent more appropriately and give us works that resemble his first two Symphonies in C and D, his graceful Septet in E♭, the spirited Quintet in D major, and various others of his earlier compositions, which will place him forever in the ranks of the foremost composers.[80]

Beethoven was very tired of the Septet, the Quintet, and the first two symphonies being held over him as the unsurpassable master-pieces of his life. After all, he had once said to a publisher in regard to the Septet, "The rabble are waiting for it." The "commonplaces" cited in the review of the concerto probably referred mostly to the finale, also to the violin figuration and other ideas borrowed from the concertos of Viotti, Kreutzer, and Clement himself.[81] The reviews did not mention how awkward and unviolinistic was much of the solo writing. Beethoven had once played violin and viola, but hardly at a soloist's level. The speed of the concerto's composition carried over into a muddle in the publication, when advice from Clement about the violin writing, which may have been included in the performance, did not get into the published score. In general, the score as the world would know it remained riddled with mistakes and ambiguities.[82] Poorly received in its time, the concerto did not become part of the repertoire until decades later.

Over the years Beethoven produced a number of works that amounted to last-minute, back-to-the-wall professionalism, and in one way and another all those pieces left traces of their haste. When composing at top speed you have to follow your instincts fearlessly on the fly. Beethoven had incomparable instincts and no fear. The miracle is that a few of those pieces, among them the *Kreutzer* Sonata and the Violin Concerto, turned out to be among his most inspired works. On the face of it the Violin Concerto had no reason to be what it was to become well after Beethoven was gone: one of the most beautiful and beloved of all concertos. Its greatness, said a later champion, lay not in its technique but in its cantabile, its singing.[83]

For Beethoven, 1806 had been a marvel of a year. In a rush of inspiration scarcely equaled in the history of human creativity, while struggling with crushing physical and emotional pain, he wrote or completed the epochal three *Razumovsky* Quartets, the Fourth Symphony and much of the Fourth Piano Concerto, the second and third *Leonore* overtures and the revised *Fidelio,* and the Violin Concerto. History would confirm each of those works as standing among the supreme examples of their genres in the entire chronicle of music.

20

That Haughty Beauty

1807

By THE BEGINNING of 1807, Beethoven had a backlog of works he was desperate to put before the public. That remained no simple matter in Vienna, where the limited space for concerts was controlled by an obdurate and omnipresent bureaucracy. His published chamber and orchestral music turned up in concerts regularly in Vienna and elsewhere, but there were no royalties for those performances. Public programs were not only his preferred medium for premieres, they were also his most direct way to raise cash.

He could have made a good income touring as a soloist, but his hearing hobbled his playing now, and his health made tours risky. Besides, public performance hardly interested him anymore. He preferred to improvise in private for himself and a few listeners. He still had piano students, still participated in charity benefits, still could rely on his patrons' private soirees to air new chamber pieces. But when it came to ready money, he needed concerts for his own benefit. Securing the best halls, especially the Theater an der Wien, required months if not years of scheming and wheedling the bureaucracy. It was as if he were carrying his works on his back, begging in the street.

Baron Braun had recently resigned from a long tenure as head of the two court theaters. That could only have been gratifying for

Beethoven, who considered the baron a nemesis. Braun was replaced by a consortium of nine aristocrats who included Beethoven's old patron Prince Lobkowitz. This group leased the two court theaters and the Theater an der Wien and rented them out for concerts and operas.[1] Beethoven surely expected that the new regime would open its arms to him, but in the spring, yet another initiative for a benefit fell through.[2] He snarled about the "princely rabble" he had to deal with. Early in 1807, he added to his orchestral backlog a new overture called *Coriolan,* used for the revival of the play of that name by his friend Heinrich von Collin. After a single performance in April, Collin's once-popular play sank out of sight, but the overture took off on its own.

In March a brief review appeared in the *Allgemeine Musikalische Zeitung:* "Three new, very long and difficult violin quartets by Beethoven, dedicated to the Russian ambassador Count Razumovsky, also attract the attention of all connoisseurs. They are deep in conception and marvelously worked out, but not universally comprehensible, with the possible exception of the third one, in C major, which by virtue of its individuality, melody, and harmonic power must win over every educated friend of music."[3] At some point the new quartets had premiered in Vienna, likely in Ignaz Schuppanzigh's short-lived public quartet series. The pieces were shaped not just with history in mind but with that virtuoso ensemble in particular. With these quartets, a historic turn in chamber music had begun, away from private amateur performance and toward programs played by professionals for the broad public.

In some six years, between the completion of the op. 18 and the op. 59 *Razumovsky* Quartets, Beethoven had gone from a young composer trying on voices and attempting to escape from the shadow of Haydn and Mozart, to an artist in his prime widely called their peer. With those two men as models, in op. 59 he made another medium his own.

Throughout his journey with quartets, Beethoven's partner, champion, and inspiration remained violinist, conductor, and entrepreneur Schuppanzigh, the first musician in history to make his main reputation as a chamber-music specialist.[4] One of the notable things about Schuppanzigh was how little he looked like an artist. Czerny described him as "a short, fat, pleasure-loving young man . . . one of the best violin-players of that time . . . unrivaled in quartet playing, a very good concert artist and the best orchestra conductor of his day . . . No one knew how to enter into the spirit of this music better than he." The visiting composer Johann Friedrich Reichardt praised Schuppanzigh's clarity and his "truly singing and moving" cantabile playing, at the same time groaning over his "damnable habit . . . of beating time with his foot."[5] Beethoven teased Schuppanzigh endlessly about his weight and his love of a good time. In 1801, Beethoven presented Schuppanzigh with a piece entitled *Lob auf den Dicken* (Praise to the Fat Man), and he wrote equally tongue in cheek to Ries that "Mylord Falstaff" "ought to be grateful if all my insults have caused him to lose a little weight."[6] It is recorded that once, Schuppanzigh coaxed his composer to try some Falstaffian entertainment and accompany him to a whorehouse. It did not go well. Schuppanzigh had to avoid the wrathful Beethoven for months afterward.[7]

If there had been no leader like Schuppanzigh and no professional quartet at the level of his group, the *Razumovsky* Quartets would have been different pieces — which is to say that Beethoven's evolution and the later history of the string quartet would have been different. This portly, silly-looking violinist was the indispensable partner in Beethoven's remaking of the medium.

Another way to put it is that the presence of Schuppanzigh and his men allowed Beethoven to take quartets wherever he wanted to go with them. He wrote the op. 59 *Razumovskys* in a rush of inspiration and enthusiasm, probably between April and November of 1806, interrupted by the Fourth Symphony and maybe the Violin Concerto. With the quartets he intended to repeat what he had done with the symphony in the *Eroica*: to make a familiar medium bigger, more ambitious, more varied, more individual, more personal.[8] Once, at Czerny's flat he had picked up the Mozart A Major Quartet, K. 464, and exclaimed, "That's what I call a work! In it, Mozart was telling the world: 'Look what I could do, if you were ready for it!'"[9] Now, Beethoven was going to show the world what he could do with the quartet, and he did not particularly care whether the world was ready for it.

The most immediate revolution in op. 59 had to do with the scope of the difficulties. In scale and ambition they are the most symphonic quartets to that time, harder on both players and listeners than any quartet before, even in a medium traditionally meant for connoisseurs. Their progress in the world would be tenuous for years, more so than many of Beethoven's major works of that period. In comparison, it took the *Eroica* only a couple of years to make its point. But there is no mystery in the slow reception of these quartets. The electricity, aggressiveness, and in some ways sheer strangeness of the *Razumovskys* are collectively breathtaking. Even some of their beauties are strange. If in his heart Beethoven remained not a revolutionary but a radical evolutionary, these pieces were still an unprecedented challenge to the public.

But revolutionary does not always equal loud. The beginning of no. 1 in F major is a quiet pulsation in the upper strings while the cello sings a spacious, flowing, gently beautiful tune rather like a folk song. There is a breezy, outdoorsy quality that will be amplified in the "horn fifths" idea that follows, and later in bass drones in open fifths.[10] At the time, an extended lyric line for the cello under barely moving harmony was simply outlandish. As he had already been doing in his piano sonatas, from here on Beethoven began each string quartet with a distinctive color and texture. Theme and harmony and rhythm are no longer the exclusive subjects of a work; now its very sound is distinctive, as if with each quartet he set out to reinvent the medium from the ground up.[11] The three numbers of op. 59 are a collection of unforgettable characters: one singing, one mysterious, one ebullient.

As he had done in the *Eroica,* then, in the F Major he takes an unprecedented step in giving the opening *Thema* to the cello. He continues his campaign to free the instrument from a life mainly toiling on the bass line. Meanwhile, placing the leading theme in the lowest instrument of the quartet pulls the rug from under the harmony, creating a shifting foundation that destabilizes everything. A melodic cello will be a steady feature of this quartet.[12]

As Beethoven began work on the F Major, he pored over his collection of Russian folk songs in order to comply with Razumovsky's commission requirement, picking a tuneful one to use as the theme for the finale. So as in the *Eroica,* he wrote this piece in some degree back to front, basing the opening *Thema,* with its vaguely folk-song quality, on the Russian tune of the finale. That tune is a touch modal, suggesting natural minor on D. What Beethoven picked up to use in the *Thème russe* was mainly its beginning: the first four notes of the Russian tune, C–D–E–F, became the opening notes of his first-movement theme. The first two notes of the *Thème russe,* the falling step D–C, linger throughout as a primal motif.[13] The note D plays a pivotal role throughout the quartet.

The opening presents three distinct, contrasting ideas. But in practice most of the first movement, like the finale, will be involved with the flowing *Thema,* mainly its rising-fourth figure and its 1234 1 rhythmic motif.[14] The second theme, by now rather unusually for Beethoven, is in the conventional dominant key, C major. It extends the rising-fourth scale line to an octave in another flowing theme, the cello again waxing melodic rather than anchoring the bass. Here might be a fundamental conception of this quartet, and not a new one for Beethoven: the idea of *redefinition,* placing the opening idea in a variety of tonal and emotional contexts.[15] (He had played that game with the obsessive little theme in the first movement of the String Quartet op. 18, no. 1, also in F major.)

After a gentle closing theme starting over a rustic drone, connoisseurs would hear the expected repeat of the exposition, returning to the cello theme. But it's a feint, a false return; there will be no conventional repeat.[16] From that point the development spins through a winding course involving some dozen keys, coming to rest for a moment on a section of double fugue in his old admired key of E-flat minor — here not in its usual poignant-unto-tragic vein but rather driving and intense.[17]

The recapitulation is as singular as the false repeat of the exposition. It arrives back in F major not with the expansive cello theme but with the first subtheme, then wanders off harmonically. At length, a grand C-major scale brings in the recapitulation proper but overlaps the return of the cello theme. All this is done to blur the moment of recapitulation. Beethoven wanted the form of the movement fluid, suppressing the formal landmarks to make a more continuous, fantasia-like effect. Finally in the coda of (for Beethoven) modest length, the main theme returns in glory, pealed out in the high violin over droning fifths in the bass, and so finds a stable harmonic foundation at last. At the end there is a quiet touch of modal cadence on the primal D–C before the official *fortissimo* cadence to F major.

All the movements are in sonata form. The following Allegretto vivace e sempre scherzando ("vivacious and always playful") was for its time the most scandalous movement of all, its personality and leading idea so eccentric that many never grasped how playful it is. (He never wrote another movement like it.)[18] It occupies the place of a scherzo but has little to do with conventional scherzo style or form. It starts, like the first movement, with the cello, this time alone with a bouncing rhythm on the note B-flat, followed by a little dancing figure in the violin; call them the drumbeat and the pirouette.[19] They will be nearly the entire melodic subjects of the movement, taken through a variegated course of keys and moods echoing the development of the first movement. (There are a couple of flowing ideas for contrast.)

To use a one-note rhythmic figure as a theme defines what critics of the time decried as "bizarre." On first playing over the movement in Moscow, cellist Bernhard Romberg, Beethoven's old Bonn friend, was so outraged by it that he threw the music to the floor and stamped on it, calling it an undignified joke.[20] In fact the idea is simple in conception, if singular in effect: a naked rhythm treated as a theme, first presented as if it were drummed out, then redefined during a long, romping, kaleidoscopic journey. Already by this point in op. 59, Beethoven seems to be reveling in his emancipation from Haydn, his freedom to bend melody and harmony and form any way he wants, his confidence that Schuppanzigh and his men could handle anything he asked of them.

Nothing quite prepares listeners for the F-minor Adagio molto e mesto third movement, *mesto* meaning "mournful." It begins in medias res, with its twisting, anguished *mesto* aria. On a sketch, Beethoven wrote, "A Weeping Willow or Acacia Tree over my Brother's Grave."[21] That is a poetically apt evocation of the mood, if a mystery in terms of his life: both his brothers were still alive.[22] The second theme is a sorrowfully arching melody that begins in a spidery texture of violin and cello. Unlike his earlier *mesto* in op. 10, hopefulness lingers amid the sadness, the cello turning its theme to A-flat major. In the development comes a poignant, whispering D-flat arioso, like a tentative answer to pathos, a wounded consolation.[23]

The last movement's Russian folk tune is dutifully titled *Thème russe* on the page, in case we might miss it. The music is jaunty and ironic, verging on monothematic, like the first movement, beginning with its vaguely modal tune on the cello — also like the first movement. If there is no overt lingering of the sorrows of the *mesto*, repeated notes in a segment near the end of the exposition recall the second movement. The main concern of the short development is a sustained march toward an expansive D-minor treatment of the chattering second theme; there, the starring pitch, D, having hung around in the background, finds its moment of glory. As another example of redefinition, the recapitulation begins in the wrong key, B-flat major (with a flat sixth). The *Thème russe* has to start with its first notes harmonized in B-flat until the music rights itself into F major.[24] As in all the movements,

the form is fluid. A racing and raucous *fortissimo* final page is interrupted by a gently chromatic *adagio* that recalls the atmosphere of the
slow movement; then high spirits bubble up. So ends a quartet fresh,
fascinating, galvanizing to the future of the medium, at the same time
emotionally elusive, with little of the transparent beginning-to-end
narrative arc that Beethoven was usually given to.[25]

Again, as it had been with Haydn and Mozart and his own earlier procedure, in issuing sets of pieces Beethoven provided a variety of keys
and moods. No. 2 of the *Razumovsky* set is normal in being a contrasting piece in E minor. What surprises in this generally surprising opus
is the intensity of the contrast. There are also some tonal connections
that suggest these three quartets may have been intended as a complete
concert program.

   Where no. 1 was expansive and extroverted, the beginning of no. 2
in E minor paints a character inward and unpredictable: two slashing chords by way of introduction, then keening wisps of melody
and silences to start a compact exposition. The beginning is as curiously fragmentary as the previous quartet's was curiously sustained.
The opening E–B fifth in the violin is one primal motif, the cello's
E–D-sharp another. On the second line a passionate theme breaks out
only to go up in smoke, starts again only to be erased by a *fortissimo*
outburst. The feeling of the minor mode here is not tragic but mysterious, with startling harmonic jumps. The opening whispered E-minor
figure moves, after a rest, to the same figure a half step higher, on F major, the Neapolitan — the key of the previous quartet. So we start with
a jump from E minor to F with only silence as transition. That half-
step harmonic motion will mark the whole piece. So will silences.[26]
Beethoven remains as completely a master of the expressive pause as
of expressive notes.[27] The rests here are fraught and questioning. And
the overall progress of the quartet, as in no. 1, is not a clear dramatic
narrative but something more intangible, abstract, even esoteric.

   The G-major second theme is contrasting, gracious, sustained, the
exposition's closing theme a burst of ebullience. Here as he did in the
F Major Quartet's first movement, he introduces the second theme in
the conventional key, as if to provide a lifeline in the larger tonal tur-

bulence. After a brief development, the music reaches the home key of E minor several bars before the recapitulation proper, so the development flows unbroken into the recapitulation (he blurred the formal lines similarly in the F Major). The compact development is answered by a highly uncommon repeat back to its beginning, making the movement expansive after all. In the coda, the attempts at a sustained theme heard on the first page flower into a passionate stretch of melody that rises to a *fortissimo* peak and sinks back to quietness.

Carl Czerny recalled Beethoven saying that the E-major second movement fell into his mind "when contemplating the starry sky and thinking about the music of the spheres" — for Beethoven the Aufklärer, an evocation of the divine. It is a sonata-form movement of tender, long-breathed melodies in a poignant E major.[28] Inevitably the future would see this stretching for the ethereal and sublime as a prophecy of his late music.[29] The droll and quirky scherzo is again in E minor. Its theme smacks the second beat, giving the music a gimpy tread, and it plays with ideas from the quartet's opening including the E–B fifth, the B–C, and E–D-sharp figures. The second period makes the quartet's trademark jump from E minor to F major. A jovial and fugal E-major trio gives this quartet's Russian tune a whirl. There have been various foreshadowings of this tune from the beginning (its first two notes, for example, are E–B), but on the whole this Russian theme sounds as if it were in ironic quotation marks. Beethoven offers it without all that much attempt to integrate it.[30]

In tonal terms, call the sonata-rondo finale ironically perverse: the rondo theme is in the wrong key, C major (so a prophecy of the key of the next quartet in the set). It is a romping and raucous march with some sort of exotic overtone — Turkish, or Gypsyish. Against that C major the proper key, E minor, struggles to assert itself. In the developmental middle section a fugue pops up, its quick entries and mock-scholarly inversions of the theme reinforcing the comic mood. The overall tonal point is going to be, in the coda, a grand resolution of C down to B and D up to D-sharp and so finally, belatedly, to E minor. Yet at the beginning of the coda, the rondo theme turns up yet again in its C-major effrontery until, with a *più presto,* the theme settles on the right key in a frenetic E-minor peroration — with a last whiff of F major. In a way, the games with keys in the E Minor Quartet amount to comedy for connoisseurs, who know a peculiar tonal leap when they hear one, and who know that a rondo theme is supposed to be in the home key.

The introduction of the last of the op. 59 quartets, no. 3 in C major, seems to announce the strangest, most chromatic piece of the set: wandering harmonies starting with a diminished-seventh chord and suggesting no key at all — a little harmonic labyrinth.[31] Yet that introduces an Allegro vivace that could serve as a definition of *vivace*, lively, and of C major in its most ebullient mood. Connoisseurs would immediately identify where this paradoxical juxtaposition came from: Mozart's famous quartet nicknamed the "Dissonant" because it has the same effect of a chromatic and gnarly introduction to a largely carefree C-major movement. In the context of the *Razumovsky* set, it is as if with this high-spirited and ingratiating personage Beethoven offered a panacea for players and listeners boggled by the first two quartets. Sure enough, no. 3 was the first to catch on, as its first reviewer implied: "[B]y virtue of its individuality, melody, and harmonic power [it] must win over every educated friend of music."[32]

This was another of the 1806 works written at a gallop. Like the Violin Concerto and Fourth Symphony, it is absolutely of a piece and a splendid piece, but more compact in material than its colleagues in the set, with less complex interrelations than the others. Its conservative elements, however, do not imply a retreat to the eighteenth century. All the *Razumovskys* are distinctive pilgrims on Beethoven's New Path.

After the introduction, the Allegro vivace starts with a sharp little pickup away from the tonic to a downbeat dominant-seventh chord, creating much energy with a flick of the pen. Upbeat figures mark most of the themes in this quartet — with steady variations on the idea. Another abiding motif from the first-violin solo is a zigzag shape, figures that tend to go up, down, up, down, in chains. The long solo for the first violin presages a piece with concerto-like overtones, bravura solos handed around generously. The first theme proper has the same key as the rondo theme in the finale of no. 2 and starts with the same notes in the same register. It's as rambunctious as its predecessor, in a more loping rhythm. The rippling second theme presents its own version of the upbeat and the zigzag. As in all the *Razumovsky* first movements, the second theme debuts in the conventional key, here G major:

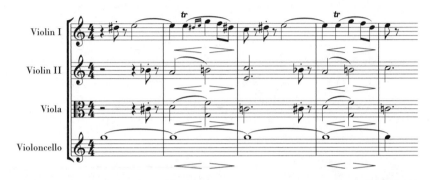

All this is to say that this is the least searching, least eccentric member of op. 59. The development mainly concerns itself with the Allegro's opening violin solo, its pickup figure and dotted rhythms. The recapitulation plunges into the dancing first theme proper, refurbished with scintillating rhythms in gorgeous sonorities. The coda starts with a section of nothing but pickup figures in one form and another.

There appears to be no quote of a Russian tune in no. 3. For the second movement, there is what Beethoven may have conceived as an evocation of a slow Russian song or dance. Marked Andante con moto quasi allegretto and in sonata form, it is one of those sui generis pieces he pulled out of the air now and then, haunting and beautiful in its quiet obsessiveness, its rocking barcarole rhythm, its key of A minor rare and special for Beethoven.[33] The flavor is hard to trace because it sounds not all that Russian. If there is a nameable overtone, call it Jewish soulfulness, or a lament of some imaginary tribe. The tone is muted and brooding rather than tragic, with a suddenly gay C-major second theme.

In the third movement Beethoven looks back to the past in terms of his own present with a Minuetto grazioso that once again defines its heading. It is a minuet without lace, with only a distant echo of the *galant* tone, its mellow and unassuming gracefulness nearly as singular as in the previous movement. Then, having started with an Allegro much like the previous quartet's finale, for the Allegro molto finale in C major, he leaps into a madcap quasi-fugue, continual variations of its quirky and comical opening theme dashing through keys in company with a series of countersubjects. It is one of his less substantial but most effervescent finales, the kind of thing he could write in a burst of compositional virtuosity, a movement skating headlong on its own constantly renewing energy:

With his commission, Count Razumovsky surely got more than he expected, certainly far more than he paid for. He got in many ways the three most original, most idiosyncratic, most expansive and ambitious string quartets ever written to that time — in their brilliance and in their eccentricities the only ones among the hundreds of that era that stand up to Haydn and Mozart. After they settled in, they would prove to be inescapable influences on virtually every future string quartet by every future composer. For Beethoven's part, having cleared his throat with op. 18, with op. 59 he was ready to stand up to his predecessors and models, ready to prove he was their equal on their home ground. In his bargain, Count Razumovsky also commissioned immortality for himself. He became one more of those great and glorious noblemen whom history remembers only for their connection to the commoner Ludwig van (not von) Beethoven.

In quality and in quantity, the standard of work Beethoven established in 1806 could hardly be matched by any mortal, including himself. By that standard, 1807 was a calmer year in creative terms, at the same time richer in incident on both sides of the ledger. He and Lichnowsky had more or less made up after their battle royal of the previous year, though they were never as intimate again. In April, Beethoven came near to losing another important friend, this time because of carelessness more than pride.

He had become close to pianist Marie Bigot and her husband Paul Bigot de Morogues, Count Razumovsky's librarian.[34] This couple was not rich and powerful, like his aristocratic patrons, but simply people he liked and appreciated. Marie he admired for her playing, which she had showed off in reading through the water-stained *Appassionata* manuscript at sight. As a performer Marie is recorded as being not only technically brilliant but also imaginative and individual. In 1805, when she first played for Haydn, the old man threw his arms around her and exclaimed, "Oh, my dear child, I did not write this music — it is you who have composed it!" In the same spirit, Beethoven said after listening to her render a sonata of his, "That's not exactly the character I wanted to give this piece, but go right ahead. If it isn't entirely mine, it's something better."[35] As musicians sometimes say of a conductor or a coach, Beethoven let his performers *play,* gave them the reins if they were artists he respected. When he said to Marie Bigot, "[I]t's something better," he meant *better for you, because it's yours.*

He much admired Marie's person, beyond her talent. Soon, maybe too soon, Beethoven fell into an affectionate relationship with the Bigots, and with Marie a flirtatious one. "Kiss your wife very often," he wrote Paul. "I could not blame you for it." Probably Paul got less and less amused by this sort of thing. That he was more than twenty years older than Marie would not have increased his patience with younger men's attentions to her.[36]

Maybe a blowup was inevitable. It was sparked by an invitation. "My dear and much admired Marie!" Beethoven wrote her at the beginning of April. "The weather is so divinely beautiful . . . So I propose to fetch you about noon today and take you for a drive — As Bigot has presumably gone out already, we cannot take him with us, of course . . . Why not seize the moment, seeing that it flies so quickly?"[37] And so on. An anxious Marie declined the invitation and showed the letter to her husband, who was duly outraged.

There was a face-to-face confrontation that Beethoven did not handle well — it seems in fact that he was speechless. What Paul Bigot said is not recorded, but Beethoven's chagrin when he got home produced two of his longest and most convoluted letters of apology. Even if he had no improper designs on Marie, he realized he had stepped over the line. Still, he felt the need to explain himself:

> I can well believe that my strange behavior has startled you . . . At the same time you would be wrong to think that my behavior was prompted to any extent by my displeasure <u>at the refusal of my request to Marie</u> — True enough, I cannot deny it, I felt very much hurt; and the reason why I did not speak to you was in order not <u>to display my feelings</u> . . . I am so very fond of you all, and why should I not confess it; indeed you are the <u>dearest</u> people I have met since I left my native town . . . I still cannot understand why it would have been improper if Marie and Caroline [her sister] had come out driving with me — But we shall talk about this . . . You cannot conceive the pain it causes me merely to think that I have given you an unpleasant moment.

Directly after, in a letter addressed to both Marie and Paul, he has become more embarrassed, but still not abject:

> Not without experiencing the deepest regret have I been made to re-alize that the purest and most innocent feelings can often be misun-derstood . . . dear M, I never dreamed of reading anything more into your behavior than the gift of your friendship . . . Besides, it is one of my chief principles <u>never to be in any other relationship than that of friendship with the wife of another man</u> . . . Possibly once or twice I did indulge with Bigot in some jokes which were not quite refined. But I myself told you that sometimes I am very naughty — I am ex-tremely natural with all my friends and I hate any kind of constraint.

He explains at length that there was nothing in the invitation for a ride other than friendship and the beautiful day — probably true enough. And after all, he had included her sister in the invitation. There is the inevitable turning back to how the situation has affected him, to ill-ness, to protests of his goodness:

> <u>Never, never</u> will you find me dishonorable. Since my childhood I have learned to love virtue — and everything beautiful and good — Indeed you have hurt me very deeply — but your action will only serve to strengthen our friendship more and more — I am really not very well today and it is difficult for me to see you. Since the performance of the [*Razumovsky*] quartets yesterday my sensitiveness and my imagina-tion have been constantly reminding me that I have made you suffer. I went last night to the ballroom in order to amuse myself . . . and the whole time I was reminded that "the Bigots are so good and are suffer-ing perhaps through your fault" . . . Write me a few lines.[38]

Beethoven and the Bigots smoothed it over. He would be careful about displays of affection to Marie. But he had coached her in his music, she had become one of his chosen interpreters, and for him that was a matter equally important as a rich patron and far more im-portant than flirting. The previous year's near break with Lichnowsky soon after his own explosion of rage sank *Fidelio* may have, in fact, scared him. He did not want to lose the Bigots as friends, or Marie as an ally. In 1809, the Bigots moved to Paris, where Marie became an important champion. One of her later students was Felix Mendelssohn, and she inculcated that budding talent in the doctrine of Beethoven.

As antidotes to the passing storm with the Bigots, to a mysterious string of headaches that went on for months, to the collapse of hopes for yet another concert, all on top of his declining hearing and chronic digestive afflictions, other developments that spring were more to the good. Nikolaus, the fourth Esterházy prince to employ Joseph Haydn (now incapacitated but still nominally court *Kapellmeister*), commissioned a mass from Beethoven to honor the name day of the princess. Haydn had already provided six celebrated masses for that occasion. Beethoven remained vitally interested in sacred music, a field he had yet to conquer, partly because he had yet to find his own path into it. At the same time, he wanted to find an alternative to Haydn's approach and to the generally operatic Viennese mass — which is to say, something other than the style of his own *Christus am Ölberge*. What came of this commission would be one of the real experiments of his life.

In performances of his music in Vienna, Beethoven often presided on the podium and at the keyboard. March 1807 saw two all-Beethoven concerts for an invited audience in Prince Lobkowitz's music room. The programs included the first four symphonies, the Fourth Piano Concerto (which had to wait another year for its public premiere), arias from *Leonore,* and the overture *Coriolan.* By then the first two symphonies were well established and popular, the *Eroica* riding a wave of acclaim. The Fourth Symphony, overture, and concerto were new to Vienna. In its review of the concerts, the *Journal des Luxus und der Moden* declared, "Richness of idea, bold originality and fullness of power, which are the particular merits of Beethoven's music, were very much in evidence to everyone at these concerts; yet many found fault with lack of a noble simplicity and the all too fruitful accumulation of ideas which . . . were not always adequately worked out and blended, thereby creating the effect more often of rough diamonds."[39]

The inexorable necessity and misery of publication at least tended to be more profitable in these years. For Beethoven the central busi-

PUBLISHER in ENGLAND
MUZIO
CLEMENTI

‑ness development of 1807 was centered in the appearance of Muzio Clementi, celebrated piano virtuoso, also piano maker, pedagogue, and publisher. As a pioneering composer for the piano, he had been a formative influence on the young Beethoven, because Clementi was among the best available models for how to write idiomatically for the instrument. Now retired from performing, Clementi lived in England and prowled the Continent looking for music to publish and customers for his pianos. He made several visits to Vienna.

Naturally he was eager to court Beethoven, and Beethoven eager to find a British publisher. Yet an absurd contretemps had developed when Clementi came to town in 1804. Beethoven told brother Carl that he wanted to call on Clementi. Carl insisted that that was beneath his dignity; it must be the publisher who called first. Beethoven agreed. Then gossip started going around that he was snubbing the older man, and Clementi got wind of it, which offended his own sense of pride and propriety. The result was that, despite their pressing mutual interests, the two men never spoke, even on occasions when they were eating at the same long table in the Swan restaurant.⁴⁰

When Clementi returned to Vienna in 1807, all that was forgotten, as he reported to his partner in London. The letter, written in English, shows Clementi's puckish spirit:

I have at last made a complete conquest of that haughty beauty Beethoven, who first began at public places to grin and coquet with me, which of course I took care not to discourage; then slid into familiar chat, until meeting him by chance one day in the street.

"Where do you lodge?" says he, "I have not seen you this long while!" — upon which I gave him my address.

Two days after, I find on my table his card, brought by himself, from the maid's description of his lovely form. This will do, thought I.

Three days after that, he calls again and finds me at home. Conceive, then the mutual ecstasy of such a meeting! I took pretty good care to improve it to our house's advantage . . . In short, I agreed with him to take in manuscript three quartets [the *Razumovskys*], a symphony [the Fourth], an overture [*Coriolan*], a concerto for the violin which is beautiful and which, at my request, he will adapt for the pianoforte . . . , and a <u>concerto for the pianoforte</u> [the Fourth], for <u>all</u> of which we are to pa<u>y him one hundred pounds sterling.</u> The property, however, is only for the British Dominions . . . The Symphony and the overture are wonderfully fine, so that I think I have made a very good bargain. What do you think? I have likewise engaged him to compose two sonatas and a Fantasia for the pianoforte.[41]

Beethoven cobbled together the promised piano arrangement of the Violin Concerto, at the same time revising the hastily written solo-violin part. Despite an elaborate new first-movement cadenza, the solo part of the piano version is remarkably sketchy. Beethoven packed off the Fourth Piano Concerto, the Fourth Symphony, and *Coriolan* to Clementi as a first installment, but the package got waylaid by the on-going war and never arrived.[42] Eventually Clementi put out the first British editions of the *Razumovsky* Quartets and the Violin and Fourth Piano Concertos; during 1810–11, he issued ten Beethoven works. Clementi's commission for piano sonatas became opp. 78–79.[43] His conquest of the haughty beauty had been gratifying on both sides.

At the same time, <u>Clementi's understanding that his edition was going to be only for Britain reflects Beethoven's pursuit of the kind of multiterritory publishing deals Haydn had arranged (and for which Beethoven had once criticized Haydn).</u> In April Beethoven wrote his publisher friend Simrock in Bonn, "I intend to sell the following six new works to a firm of publishers in France, to one in England, and to one in Vienna simultaneously." He offered the French rights for all the pieces to Simrock (who finally published only the quartets) — Bonn now being, thanks to Napoleon, part of France. With this method one could be paid for the same piece two or more times. It was all above-board but tricky to manage. To forestall piracy, all the editions needed to come out virtually on the same day, but in practice they rarely did. In any case, Beethoven was exhilarated by the prospects when he wrote Count Franz Brunsvik, Josephine's brother, in Buda. He seems to have picked up some of Clementi's hilarity:

I am to get 200 pounds sterling — and, what is more, I shall be able to sell the same works in Germany and France . . . so that by this means

I may hope even in my early years to achieve the dignity of a true artist — So, <u>dear B,</u> I need the <u>quartets.</u> I have already asked your sister
[Josephine] about this . . . If you can arrange for the Hungarians to
invite me to give a few concerts, please do so — you can have me for
200 gold ducats . . .

Whenever <u>we</u> . . . drink your wine, we souse you, i.e. we drink
your health — All good wishes. Hurry — hurry — hurry and send
me the quartets . . . Schuppanzigh has got married — <u>to somebody</u>
<u>very like him</u> [in girth], I am told — what will their family be like????
Kiss your sister Therese and tell her that I fear that I shall have to
become a great man without a monument of hers contributing to my
greatness — send me tomorrow, send me immediately the quartets
— quar-tets-t-e-t-s.[44]

The quartets were the *Razumovskys;* he had lent the manuscripts to
Franz. His reference to Therese von Brunsvik probably refers to her
hobby of painting portraits. She never did his.

The current object of his attentions in Vienna was *Fidelio* librettist
Joseph Sonnleithner's publishing house, Bureau des arts et d'industrie.
By this point his volunteer agent was no longer brother Carl, and
brother Johann made some attempts in that direction that only provoked hostility between them. Now his go-between was Ignaz von
Gleichenstein, to whom Beethoven wrote that summer, "You may tell
my brother [Johann] that I shall certainly never write to him again
— Of course I knew the reason for his behavior. It is this: because he
has lent me money and has formerly spent a little for me he is (<u>I know</u>
<u>my brothers</u>) probably worried because I cannot yet repay the sum;
and the other one [Carl], moved by a spirit of revenge against me, is
probably egging him on too."[45]

Gleichenstein, soon to be made a baron, was another music-loving
amateur, a friend of Haydn's, a cellist, and a colleague of Stephan von
Breuning at the War Ministry. He and Beethoven had known each
other for some time; by this summer they used the intimate *du* address. Gleichenstein had been witness for the signing of the contract
between Beethoven and Clementi. As an agent he proved a great deal
more expedient than Beethoven's brothers.

GLEICHENSTEIN = AGENT

As for Johann van Beethoven, he badly needed the money he had lent Ludwig and was cannily making his demand for payment when he knew his brother was doing well. Johann was about to buy an apothecary shop in Linz, at a bargain but still beyond his means. Gleichenstein secured the payment from the Bureau des arts et d'industrie, for the same six pieces sold to Clementi, and used the money to pay off the debt to Johann — who the following year took possession of the apothecary shop so desperate for cash that he sold the iron gratings off the windows.[46] Johann's business, however, thanks to the French army, was about to bring him a comfortable fortune.

Beethoven spent the first part of summer 1807 in Baden, working and taking the waters for the headaches that had bedeviled him for months, then went to Heiligenstadt.[47] When he informed Prince Nikolaus Esterházy that the commissioned mass was nearly done, he explained that the headaches "prevented me at first from working at all and even now [have] allowed me to do very little work." As evidence he enclosed a letter from Dr. Schmidt. His physician had given up treatment with leeches and prescribed spurge-laurel bark to be applied to his arms. One remedy was as useless as the other.[48]

1807

It was actually a productive if physically miserable summer, with at least one comic interlude. Beethoven got into the habit of stopping during his walks to admire a comely young farmer's daughter as she worked in the fields. They never spoke, and Fräulein Liese was not pleased to be ogled by this unhandsome stranger. When her father was arrested for a drunken brawl, Beethoven showed up to remonstrate with the village council and for his vociferousness nearly got himself thrown in jail.[49]

Despite the ongoing headaches, he worked with something like his usual discipline, indoors and out, on long walks in the hills and fields. He heard from Count Oppersdorff, who declared himself pleased with the Fourth Symphony he had commissioned and was ready to pay 500 florins for a fifth. Beethoven finished the Esterházy mass, picked up some symphonic sketches from several years back, and plunged in.

As autumn arrived, he had to break off composing and travel to the Esterházy Palace at Eisenstadt for the premiere of the Mass in C on

September 13, celebrating the name day of the princess. He found the attitude of the singers and musicians presaging a fiasco; at the dress rehearsal four of the five altos in the choir did not show up.[50] Meanwhile Beethoven discovered that he was not, as he was accustomed to, getting a room to himself in the palace but was relegated to sharing a dank apartment in town with the court secretary of music.

Who knows what sort of mass Prince Nikolaus and his court expected from Beethoven. Based on precedent, they might have anticipated one of three things: the full operatic, bravura treatment, as in *Christus am Ölberge*, by then a fairly popular piece; an operatic/symphonic mass on the Haydn model; or perhaps something excitingly bold, Beethovenian. That summer he had humbly written Nikolaus, "I shall hand you the Mass with considerable apprehension, since you, most excellent prince, are accustomed to have the inimitable masterpieces of the great Haydn performed for you—."[51] In terms of formal outline, there were no rules or standards in mass settings, only precedents, and on the whole Beethoven followed Haydn's models in layout.[52] In the end, though, he was looking for something quite new, but this time new in the direction of subtlety and simplicity.

With due anticipation, the audience for the premiere assembled in the glittering music room of the Esterházy Palace, scene of any number of Haydn triumphs. Beethoven gave the downbeat for the mass, bringing in the basses on their unaccompanied and almost inaudible Kyrie. As the underrehearsed, apathetic performance unfolded, the prince and princess, the court, and the cognoscenti alike would have been befuddled. What they heard was a mass compact, chaste, sometimes ingenuous unto childlike, with echoes of the past from Haydn back to the Renaissance yet largely unlike any other sacred music they had ever heard.

Beethoven was still searching for a fresh and direct sacred style, far from *Christus*. On a sketch of the Agnus Dei he wrote, "Utmost simplicity, please, please, please."[53] As he worked he copied out for study passages from Haydn's *Creation* Mass. If in some respects he followed his old master's model, the music hardly sounded like it.[54] The court expected brilliant perorations, high drama, suffering, exaltation, all the moods of the text in high-Beethovenian style. What it got was a work gentle, devotional, ceremonial. Often the choir sings in block harmonies, the orchestra is subdued, the music full of exquisite small moments and subtleties that require a loving and nuanced performance — exactly what the premiere was not.

For a composer, a fiasco is a uniquely traumatic experience, emotionally and physically, even worse when one is on the podium. It plays out excruciatingly slowly as the piece goes on and on and the fidgets and whispers grow in the audience. A bad performance amplifies the misery. Beethoven would have finished the performance in high dudgeon. Nikolaus, meanwhile, was not the liberal and tolerant sort of nobleman Beethoven was used to but an old-fashioned prince who considered composers to be servants. To be served badly by a mere musician sullied his court and his princely dignity.

After the performance, the cognoscenti and musicians gathered to talk over the music and to give the usual ceremonial congratulations to the composer. When Beethoven appeared, Nikolaus turned to him and barked, "But, my dear Beethoven, what is this you have done?" Presumably he went on to more pointed complaints. Nearby stood court *Kapellmeister* Johann Nepomuk Hummel, Mozart's most famous pupil and a more or less friendly rival of Beethoven. Beethoven saw Hummel chuckle at the prince's response — for all Beethoven knew, chuckled with schadenfreude.[55] Based on precedent, what ensued would have been an unpleasant scene and a precipitous flight on Beethoven's part, as had taken place the year before at the Lichnowsky Palace and at the Theater an der Wien. Legend would have it that he left the palace immediately in a huff. In fact, there was no unpleasant scene. He lingered at the palace for several days, hoping for a performance of a concerto, parts for which had been specially copied for the occasion.

Nothing came of the concerto and little from the mass, and there would be no more commissions from the house of Esterházy. Another attempt to find his voice as a sacred vocal composer had come to little. Beethoven spent years trying to sell the mass to one publisher after another, finally giving it to Breitkopf & Härtel for free. Prince Nikolaus wrote a friend, "Beethoven's mass is unbearably ridiculous and detestable, and I am not convinced that it can ever be performed properly. I am angry and mortified." But this time Beethoven had held his tongue

PLEASURE DERIVED BY SOMEONE
FROM ANOTHER PERSON'S MISFORTUNE

and burned no bridges. In 1808, Nikolaus sent him 100 florins to help out with a performance of parts of the mass in Vienna.[56]

Beethoven added to the pile one more unhappy experiment with sacred music and bided his time. The Mass in C stood, in the end, as something of a disengaged work, like *Christus,* however contrary in style. Both came from a man who since childhood had rarely been found inside a church. For Beethoven, God was a constant presence, but religious dogma, the liturgy, the kind of incantations chanted over him at his baptism had long since lost their magic. He was, all the same, fond of the piece. "I do not like to say anything about my Mass or myself," he wrote Breitkopf & Härtel, "but I believe I have treated the text as it has seldom been treated."[57] Certainly he had. It is a unique and beautiful work — only not a particularly exciting one.

In the midst of this creative frustration, Beethoven returned to a still-simmering romantic frustration, in the form of Countess Josephine Deym. Around the time of the mass performance she wrote him a friendly if guarded note apologizing for some unintended slight and adding, "For a long time I had indeed wished to have news of your health, and I would have inquired about it long ago if modesty had not held me back. Now tell me how you are, what you are doing . . . The deep interest that I take in all that concerns you, and shall take as long as I live, makes me desire to have news about these things. Or does my friend Beethoven, surely I may call you thus, believe that I have changed?"[58] They had been in Baden at the same time in July but apparently did not meet. She surely hoped that he had calmed down, was ready to be friend rather than suitor. His response of September 20, from Heiligenstadt, showed otherwise. His passion flared up, along with his breathless dashes on the page:

> Dear, beloved and only J! Again even a few lines, only a few lines from you — have given me great pleasure — How often have I wrestled with myself, beloved J, in order not to commit a breach of the prohibition which I have imposed upon myself [not to see her] — But it is all in vain. A thousand voices are constantly whispering to me that you are

my only friend, my only beloved — I am no longer able to obey the rule which I imposed upon myself. Oh, dear J, let us wander unconstrainedly along that path where we have often been so happy — Tomorrow or the day after I shall see you ... Until now my health has continued to be very poor, but it is slowly improving ... I returned from Eisenstadt a few days ago. I had hardly been back in Vienna for a day when I called on you <u>twice</u> — but I was not so fortunate — as to see you — That hurt me deeply — and I assumed that your <u>feelings</u> had <u>perhaps</u> undergone some change — But I still hope ... Do not forget — do not condemn / your ever faithfully devoted / Bthvn / I am just coming into town today — and I could almost deliver this letter myself — if I did not suspect that I might for the third time fail to see you.[59]

His letter of the next month reveals that Josephine had ordered her servants not to let him in the house. Whatever it took, however she admired him as an artist, she was not going to be tormented by the fury of his love anymore. He learned, if he had not before, that the intimate feelings of women were a quite different matter from the enthusiasm of admirers. It is notable that he never questioned Josephine's right to make her own decisions and run her own life, even if one of those decisions was to turn him away. There is a wan resignation in his last two surviving letters to her:

Since I must almost fear that you no longer <u>allow yourself to be found</u> by me — and since I do not care to put up with the refusals of your servant any longer — well then, I cannot come to you any more — unless you let me know what you think about this — Is it really <u>a fact</u> — that you do not want to see me any more — if so — do be <u>frank</u> — I certainly deserve that ... When I kept away from you, I thought I must do so, because I had an idea that you desired it — although when doing so I suffered a good deal — yet I controlled my feelings — but it occurred to me again later on that — I was mistaken in you ... Do let me know, dear J — what you think. Nothing shall bind you — In the circumstances I can and certainly dare not say anything more to you.

And shortly after, still more sadly:

> Please deliver this sonata to your brother, my dear Josephine [the *Ap-passionata*, dedicated to Franz Brunsvik] — I thank you for wishing still to appear as if I were not altogether banished from your memory . . . You want me to tell you how I am. A more difficult question could not be put to me — and I prefer to leave it unanswered, rather than — to answer it too truthfully.[60]

With that, at least for the foreseeable future, he put Josephine aside, his hopeless dream of marriage one more thing to endure with everything else he had to endure. It was not just that he had fallen helplessly in love with a woman; it was that, perhaps for the first time, he *needed* a woman, not just a nice wife at his side and some nice children. He felt desperately that he needed love to save him, because he was not so sure he could save himself. But the love he needed did not transpire, and he was left with only himself. Despite all he had been through, he was just beginning to discover how much courage and resilience he was going to require.

How did he endure the end of this dream? From around this time there would be rumors of a suicide attempt. One story had it that Beethoven went to Countess Erdödy's estate in Jedlersee and suddenly disappeared. It was assumed he had gone back to Vienna, but after three days a servant found him huddling in the distant parts of the palace garden, apparently trying to starve himself to death.[61]

Josephine for her part went on to a second and unmitigatedly disastrous marriage with Baron Christoph von Stackelberg — the marriage having been precipitated by her pregnancy.[62] The handsome baron combined qualities of the domineering, the incompetent, and the sinister, with a gift for sowing misery and disaster around him. It was one more aristocratic marriage of the worst kind, with money at the center of it — he had none, and he wanted hers. They became estranged; he appropriated Josephine's inheritance, having gone through his own; he virtually kidnapped their children and left her to die alone. "What Josephine suffered and endured after her marriage to Stackelberg," Therese wrote, " — entire books could be written about it."[63] Beethoven remained in touch with Therese and through her received occasional, never good, reports about Josephine. There is no record of whether he and Josephine ever met or corresponded again — though that does not mean it could not have happened.

His physical headaches, at least, were receding. He was working on Count Oppersdorff's commission for a fifth symphony, a work he would not give a name but which concerned something in the direction of fate and triumph. When that symphony was done, without stopping for breath he would take up some ideas from the sketchbooks and finish a sixth symphony, that work concerned with peace, contentment, and God.

21

Schemes

AROUND THE END of 1807, Beethoven wrote an elaborate petition to the directors of the Theater an der Wien. His old patron Prince Lobkowitz, now one of the directors of the theater, had encouraged him to try it. His letter to "The Worshipful R. I. Theater Direction" begins,

> The undersigned flatters himself that during his sojourn in Vienna he has won some favor and approval not only from the high nobility but from the general public as well, and that he has secured an honorable acceptance of his works at home and abroad. Nevertheless, he has been obliged to struggle with difficulties of all kinds and has not yet been able to establish himself here in a position which would enable him to fulfill his desire to live wholly for art, to develop his talent to a still higher degree of perfection, which must be the goal of every true artist . . .
>
> Inasmuch as the undersigned has always striven less for a livelihood than for the interests of art, the ennoblement of taste and the uplifting of his genius towards higher ideals and perfection, it necessarily happened that he often was compelled to sacrifice profit and advantage to the Muse.[1]

Here is a sign of a new vision: to live wholly for his art, to secure a steady position and income and to be relieved of the wretched uncertainties of freelancing. In the petition he lays out his proposals and blows his own horn with proper restraint. He applies to himself the word *genius,* not in the Romantic sense but in the Classical, eighteenth-century sense: a spirit that animates a person's character, gifts, capacities; not so much what one *is* but a quality one *possesses* to a greater or lesser degree.[2] So Beethoven uses the term in the sense he grew up with, in the sense Haydn and Mozart used it.

Further in the letter, Beethoven notes — or rather threatens — that he is on the verge of being driven from Vienna, a city "more estimable and desirable to him than any other." If other declarations in the petition are earnest enough, that one is balderdash. He still had no love for Vienna and the Viennese and never would. He was entirely open to offers from elsewhere.

He proceeds to make two concrete and yet, given the direction of his career and the nature of his genius, unlikely suggestions. If the Worshipful Direction will grant him "the means of a comfortable livelihood favorable to the exercise of his talents"... He promises and contracts to compose every year at least one grand opera ... [for] a fixed remuneration of 2400 florins per annum and the gross receipts of the third performance of each such opera." Second, he proposes to supply, gratis, any small operettas, divertissements, choruses, or other occasional pieces desired by the Direction. The idea of his producing "at least" an opera a year plus potboilers to order was one of his regular overestimations of what he could produce — well beyond the stupendous quantity and quality of what he actually was producing in those years. He was slow to pull an opera together and highly choosy about librettos. But his proposal to the theater shows that he believed it was worth devoting most of his time to. In Vienna as in much of Europe, composing opera remained the most direct route to fortune for a composer.

At the end he adds, with a nod to the likely outcome, "Whether or not the Worshipful Direction confirms and accepts this offer, the undersigned adds the request that he be granted a day for a concert in one of the theater buildings." In the end, even though the directors included his old patron Prince Lobkowitz, they approved neither the residency nor the concert. They knew Beethoven's history with opera; it had not been pleasant or profitable. Three of the directors were Esterházys, one of them Prince Nikolaus, who had been "angry and mortified" over the mass he commissioned from Beethoven.[3] Of course, if Beethoven was the loser in this situation, music may have been the winner. His principal gift was for instrumental music; writing for voices was a perennial struggle for him. If the management of the Theater an der Wien had accepted his proposal and he had actually devoted himself to opera more or less full-time, the future history of opera might have been less enriched than the future history of instrumental music would have been impoverished.

In any case, Beethoven's hopes for a benefit had fallen through again. Each failure outraged him more. "I have already become accustomed to the basest and vilest treatment in Vienna," he wrote playwright friend Heinrich Collin. "I have altogether five written statements about a [concert] day which has never been allotted to me . . . and indeed I have discussed this point with a lawyer — And why should I not do so? . . . Away with all consideration or respect for those vandals of art —."[4]

Beethoven had every reason to be furious over his treatment by the theater management and the rest of the bureaucracy. All the same, those vandals were doing their best for art in other respects. Toward the end of 1807, a group of aristocrats including Lobkowitz founded a subscription series that came to be called the Liebhaber Concerte, Concerts for Enthusiasts. They mounted twenty programs between November 1807 and the next March, giving each one a generous allotment (for those days) of two rehearsals. There was an orchestra of around fifty-five, largely made up of experienced amateurs; the audience was mostly of the nobility. For the final evening of the series they planned a gala performance of Haydn's *Creation.* "Every concert," the directors declared, "must be distinguished by the performance of significant and decidedly splendid music, because the institute has the intention to uphold the dignity of such art and to attain an ever higher perfection."[5]

Half the twenty concerts had Beethoven works, and some of them, including the *Eroica,* were performed twice.[6] For a moment it appeared that Vienna was finally catching up to London and Paris, where public concerts were a normal part of musical life. But like Schuppanzigh's public quartet series, this one soon collapsed. Vienna remained Europe's capital of music and also remained conservative, hidebound, existing under the burden of an omnipresent bureaucracy at the service of a reactionary court. A rich and sophisticated private musical life continued to outstrip public life, and Beethoven's symphonies, ascending in performances and popularity elsewhere, were only occasionally put before the public.[7] In fact, during this period symphonies were generally out of fashion in Vienna. Only a few by all composers together were heard in the city. Between 1808 and 1811, not a single Mozart symphony was performed. At the same time, Haydn's massive oratorio *The Creation* had thirty-one performances in Vienna during the decade after its 1798 premiere.[8]

Despite all Beethoven's complaining, his patrons continued to favor him above any other composer. In 1808, Prince Razumovsky established a standing string quartet in his palace. At the head, naturally, was Ignaz Schuppanzigh. Often as not the prince sat at second violin. Conductor Ignaz Seyfried wrote of that period, "Beethoven was, as it were, cock of the walk in the princely establishment; everything that he composed was rehearsed hot from the griddle and performed to the nicety of a hair . . . just as he wanted it and not otherwise, with affectionate interest, obedience and devotion such as could spring only from such ardent admirers of his lofty genius, and with a penetration into the most secret intentions of the composer."[9] In that same period, Beethoven was more fed up with the city than ever and scheming to get out of it — or to stay and secure a steady income.

His health treated him even less kindly than the Viennese. After the slim year of 1807, his production shot up again despite continuing illness and the climax of a series of infections; he came close to having a finger amputated. "My colic is better," he wrote Collin. "But my poor finger had to undergo a drastic nail operation. When I wrote to you yesterday it looked very angry. Today it is quite limp with pain."[10]

1808

In March 1808 came the gala Liebhaber performance of Haydn's *Creation,* celebrating the composer's seventy-sixth birthday. The concert was an extraordinary honor for an artist who had spent much of his active career neglected by the Viennese while his music spread around the world. Everyone who knew the master understood that any performance could be his last. Three years before, a visitor reported in a letter, "We found him very weak . . . He told us that he was only 74 years old [in fact he was 73] and looks as if he were eighty . . . We found him holding a rosary in his hands, and I believe he passes almost the whole day in prayer."[11] Every day the nearly toothless invalid sat down at the keyboard and devoutly played over his Austrian anthem. It was the only thing musical he could still manage.

Haydn had to get permission from his doctor to attend the concert, and the doctor accompanied him. His nominal employer Prince Nikolaus Esterházy sent his personal carriage to bring his *Kapellmeister* to the door of the packed university hall. Four men carried him in lifted high on an armchair. To a flourish of trumpets and drums and cries of "Long live Haydn!," he was set down next to Princess Esterházy. Noticing he was shivering, the princess wrapped her shawl around him. Other aristocratic ladies followed suit, until Haydn was swathed in elegant robes. As he waited for the oratorio to begin he was handed poems in his honor.

Antonio Salieri conducted. The orchestra whispered its evocation of Chaos. Finally came the moment everybody waited for: Haydn's great coup, the explosion of C major on the words "And there was *light*." Here was a central metaphor of the age, a joining of freedom, Aufklärung, and the divine. (In *Fidelio*, Beethoven had composed that same image with his chorus of prisoners emerging into the sun.) Ecstatic applause broke out in the hall. Unbearably moved, Haydn raised trembling hands heavenward toward the source of all creation.[12] At intermission his doctor declared the old man could take no more excitement. As the bearers prepared to lift him, Beethoven pushed through the crowd, kissed his teacher's forehead and hands, knelt at his feet. It was a time to put aside the resentments, the disappointments, the gnawing rivalry Beethoven felt for his teacher. If there were ever a moment the torch was passed from the old master to the Great Mogul, here it was.

* * *

Despite the ongoing deterioration of his hearing, Beethoven still stood before the public. In a charity concert of April 1808, he conducted — rather than soloed in — the Third Piano Concerto, the *Coriolan* Overture, and the Fourth Symphony. The next month saw what appears to have been the public premiere of the four-year-old Triple Concerto, which had already been published (in parts, not score) the previous year.[13] The Fourth Symphony and *Coriolan* had been privately premiered in March 1807, at the Lobkowitz Palace.[14]

The three works in this charity concert form a rich pattern of relationships to the future and the past in Beethoven's music. The Third Concerto sits on the divide between the old way and the New Path. The others lay out his future.

In the summer and fall of 1806, he had written the Fourth Symphony in B-flat Major, op. 60, virtually in one breath, hard on the heels of finishing the revised version of *Leonore*. For the Fourth Symphony he put aside work on the Fifth. As with the Second, an operatic quality hovers over the Fourth. (The first sketches appear in the middle of ones for *Leonore*.)[15] If it is less mercurial and buffa than the Second, it is no less vivacious. Meanwhile its opening melodic gambit traces the same motif as the opening of the Fifth Symphony, in a dramatically different atmosphere. Both symphonies begin with two falling thirds joined by a rising step, but where the Fifth is driving and dynamic out of the gate, in the Fourth that motif begins a darkly *misterioso* introduction.[16] Call it a nocturnal scene as prelude to a romantic-comic opera.

The Fourth conjures a series of atmospheres, from nocturnal to romantic to rambunctious. Two elements of its opening will abide: one is the falling third from B-flat to an out-of-key G-flat. Both notes turn up in various situations and guises, memorably as F-sharp and A-sharp toward the end of the development, bringing the music to distant B major. The other element is falling thirds joined by a step, the motif of the first bars. That motif is going to be sped up and otherwise played with rhythmically, used as a seed to grow new themes.

The darkness of the introduction sinks into silence. Then in a flash the music takes a turn to gaiety with a series of driving up-rips, as if a door were thrown open to a brightly lit ballroom. And from the opening up-rips, echoing ones Mozart used in the *Jupiter* Symphony and elsewhere, to the bouncing comic gait of the first allegro, the rhythmic quality is Mozartian — operatically Mozartian.[17] Like the Violin Concerto, written equally fast just after this symphony, the thematic material is generally simple and without contrapuntal elaboration. There was not much time for complexities. Like the Violin Concerto's opening on a timpani pulse, as in the Third Piano Concerto's thematic timpani figure, in the Fourth the timpani sometimes steps into the foreground as a kind of protagonist, transcending its old association with military and festive music. At the end of the development, as a joke for connoisseurs, the music ends up in B major, but the fixed-tuning timpani insists that the A-sharp is really B-flat and so prepares the recapitulation.

A long, drifting melody of ineffable tenderness begins the second movement. For its accompaniment Beethoven mobilizes one of his first symphonic monorhythmic stretches: a lilting dotted figure that a future time would call a tango rhythm. The figure goes on and on, gentle and then insistent, an accompaniment developed like a theme. At the end of the movement the tango motif comes to rest in the timpani, playing quietly unaccompanied, like a dancer taking a few wistful turns alone at the end of the evening. At the close of the first movement of the *Eroica*, the Hero theme finds its rightful place in the home key, in its proper instrument, the horn. In the Fourth Symphony, the second movement's rhythm finally arrives in the timpani alone. In both cases it is as if an idea were searching through the course of a movement not only for its home key but also for its true instrumental avatar, and finds it at the end as another kind of homecoming. This is a kind of musical and psychological logic that Beethoven surely invented. The Fourth's third movement is a romping scherzo, its two-beat theme kicking against the three-beat meter. The finale is a breathless, madcap *moto perpetuo,* like the gayest of final tableaux in a comic opera.

With the Fourth Symphony Beethoven confirmed his pattern of maximal contrast in pairs of symphonies: dramatic unto tragic in the odd-numbered, joyful unto comic in the even-numbered; muscular and bold scoring in the odd-numbered, warm and rich scoring in the even (though each of the symphonies has its distinctive orchestral sound). In other words, the Fourth Symphony is virtually the anti-Third. It would be the same with the Fifth and Sixth.

As stunning as any of the dichotomies of the Third and Fourth is the simplification of form, texture, and material represented by the new symphony. One might think that the Fourth is more transparent in form and material than the Third mainly because it was written fast. But the Fifth and Sixth have the same quality. Starting with the *Eroica*'s enormous, multithemed opening, all the movements of that symphony are complex and unusual in form. Now Beethoven turned from a radical complexity to a radical simplicity, but with a defining new element: simplicity plus a new driving energy. This will be one of the thumbprints of the heroic style. Once he had written on a sketch, "simple and always more simple." He aspired to the directness of voice he admired in Handel, which Haydn also possessed: the ability to get big effects with the most direct means. Not until his last symphony would he return to movements as complex in form as the *Eroica*'s.

Beethoven inherited a tradition that said a symphony ought to be a more public, more populist, less complex genre than chamber music, which is more for connoisseurs. After the *Eroica*, Beethoven submitted to that tradition but reimagined it from within, as he had done before in genre after genre. After the Fourth, the next four symphonies would be, each in its own way, largely lucid and transparent in form, the material emotionally direct, the whole broadly communicative whether bringing a sob or standing the hair on end, whether conveying a dig in the ribs or a strike at the jugular.

When Beethoven took up his friend Heinrich von Collin's play *Co-riolan* in 1807 and agreed to write an overture for its revival, he was working with a story he already knew from two sources: Shakespeare's *Coriolanus,* and Shakespeare's source in Plutarch's *Parallel Lives,* where the Greek historian examines celebrated or notorious Roman and Greek figures and draws conclusions about character and morality. Collin used the same plot outline as Shakespeare. After experiencing insults to his pride in Rome, the leading general Coriolan goes over to the enemy Volscians. Then, on the eve of battle, in a confrontation with his mother, Volumnia, and his wife, he is dissuaded from leading an attack on Rome. He pays for that second change of heart with his life. Beethoven, feeling daily insults from the Viennese and yearning to be somewhere else, had to have resonated with this story.

Collin's play is more introspective than Shakespeare's version, concerned with the interior struggle of Coriolan, who finally falls on his sword in despair. That intimate moral and ethical debate also appealed to Beethoven, perennially concerned with those matters. At the same time, his overture suggests he was also thinking of Shakespeare's more dynamic, more theatrical version of the story.

Collin's play vanished from the boards after the revival, but the *Coriolan* Overture soon became a favorite on orchestral programs. With this piece Beethoven more or less invented what came to be called the "concert overture," and no less what was to be called the "symphonic poem." Since the overture needed to evoke the story somehow, and since it was intended to have its own life outside the play, Beethoven could indulge in program music with less risk of being condemned for it. As in the *Leonore* overtures, he does not so much preface the story as embody it in the music.

Coriolan was in his current theatrical style, modeled on Cherubini rather than Mozart, lucid and colorful in orchestration, simple in material and structure but starkly powerful in effect. It begins with low-C unisons answered by crashing high chords, each followed by a violent silence. Charged silence is one of the leading motifs of the piece. The music's cries and silences echo two other evocations of death in his music: the dungeon scene in *Leonore* and before that the beginning of the *Joseph* Cantata. Meanwhile we are in Beethoven's heroic and darkly dynamic C-minor mood, defined earlier in the *Pathétique* Sonata and other works.

The introduction gives way to a restless figure that surges on for pages, at once portraying the implacable spirit of Coriolan and foreshadowing his doom. Like the other Beethoven overtures, this one is laid out in sonata form. The lyrical second theme in E-flat major stands for the pleading Volumnia. Their debate grows progressively more heated and never resolves. After a short but tumultuous development section suggesting Coriolan's inner battle, Beethoven manages a dramatic and psychological masterstroke with the recapitulation. Coriolan's theme is truncated, harmonically unstable, out of balance: he has lost himself. Volumnia's theme is extended, more and more urgent as it drives into a coda reprising the fateful introduction, with its glowering low Cs and crashing chords and electric silences. His mother's anguish is now inside Coriolan, creating a fatal inner conflict.

At the end we hear the spiritual and physical death of the hero in the dissolution, the bleeding away of his theme, until it sinks to emptiness. The essence of the drama is captured in the journey from the violent silences of the beginning to the deathly silences of the end.[18] With *Coriolan* under his belt, one of the most searingly intense things he had written yet, in his next symphony Beethoven would return to C minor on a larger canvas.

An *Allgemeine Musikalische Zeitung* review of a Leipzig performance is warmer and more astute than many early reviews of his pieces: "Beethoven's overture to Collin's *Coriolan* ... is once again a very significant work, written more in the manner of Cherubini than that of B's previous orchestral works. The character of this overture is grand and serious, to the point of gloominess. It is strictly and learnedly written ... and is calculated besides to produce much more of a profound than a radiant effect."[19]

The belated premiere of the Triple Concerto in 1808 might imply several things about it, including ambivalence on the part of the composer. Beethoven was an unsentimental and unforgiving judge of his own work, though always ready to make some florins on nearly anything he had in stock. He sold the concerto sometime before getting it played in public (there had been private readings). He had to have known, though, that besides its surprising style, the Triple Concerto was an expensive and impractical number to put on, given that it required three times the usual soloists.

The first movement, marked Allegro, deals out an intriguing hand in the expression: the opening theme is declaimed quietly in unaccompanied basses, giving it a fateful cast despite the C major. The music brightens and gathers momentum to the first solo entrance, on cello alone. The cello is the main protagonist of the solo trio; its gift for poignant lyricism will be central to the piece. Each soloist enters dutifully on the main theme, and so begins a movement long, rambling, and elegantly beautiful. Beethoven explores solos, duets, and trios with the group, avoiding cadenzas and other soloistic heroics. There is an operatic quality that perhaps spilled over from *Leonore*.

Where the first movement's touches of expressive ambiguity were headed becomes manifest in the second movement, in A-flat major, surely one of the saddest major-key movements ever written. The solo cello sings eloquently throughout. The movement is almost choked off by a quick transition to a finale headed Rondo alla Polacca. The title implies an energetic outing recalling the Polish polonaise. It arrives at the kind of games audiences expected from a rondo finale, including a loping middle section like a parody of a polonaise.

The *Allgemeine Musikalische Zeitung* reviewer knew something was puzzling about this piece, and he didn't much care for it: "In our judgment . . . this concerto is the least of those by Beethoven in print. In it the composer has loosed the reins of his rich imagination, all too ready to luxuriate exuberantly in its richness."[20] Listeners were used to mainstream Beethoven now, and resistant to anything else. The Triple Concerto never caught on in his lifetime, and scarcely later.

Of the four large orchestral pieces written between 1804 and 1807, in the wake of the *Eroica* — Fourth Symphony, Violin Concerto, Triple Concerto, *Coriolan* — only the last is in the heroic style, with that effect of dynamism and struggle on an epic canvas. Of the three equally significant chamber works Beethoven finished in 1807, none is heroic, but all are close to the level of the *Razumovskys* in boldness, freshness, and scope. All of them trace more complex emotional arcs than much of his earlier work. In contrast to the symphonies, it becomes harder in the chamber pieces of these years to find a clear expressive line from beginning to end. The narrative becomes more mysterious, more like poetry than storytelling.

With the Sonata for Cello and Piano in A Major, op. 69, Beethoven returned for the first time since op. 5 to a genre he more or less invented and still more or less owned. The A Major has an air of something settled and incontrovertible. With a quiet, epigrammatic opening theme starting with cello alone, he establishes the central elements. The opening cello line contains in embryo all the themes of the so-

‿nata‿ The piano supplies the second phrase of the theme, setting up a partnership of equals who complete one another's thoughts. For all its impact, much of the work will be subdued and introspective in tone. Cello and piano inject small cadenzas into the music, as if reflecting on its course. The straightforward A major of the first page is compromised by a turn to a passionate A minor, and that change echoes through the first movement: the expected E major of the second theme is prepared by E minor, and the E major is oddly unsunny. So the essential dynamic of the sonata unfolds as a dialogue of bright and dark, inward and outward.

By the end of the exposition the music has turned pealingly triumphant. That triumph, however, is the last for a while. The development section is largely quiet, minor key, undramatic except for a *furioso* E-minor outburst in the middle. (The autograph of the development is a maze of scribbling out. Beethoven essentially wrote a revised version of the development on top of the first one, improvising on the page.)[21] The recap is expanded and recomposed, developmental, yet for much of it the tone is still quiet and introspective. By the end the music has taken on a quality of reflection and retreat.

The scherzo in A minor is rhythmically quirky, ironically demonic, irresistible. In the main theme the piano and cello seem unable to agree on the downbeat. It ends nearly inaudibly in sighs and fragments. An aria-like slow movement suddenly breaks off, and we find it was an introduction to the Allegro vivace last movement, which begins with a broad, serene A-major theme that echoes the opening of the first movement. Once again, much of the music is quiet where we expect otherwise. Has the moment of triumph from the first movement vanished for good? No: after a muted and expectant opening of the development, the music finds that tone again. In the coda racing joy is unleashed and prevails to the end, with an introspective *pianissimo* before the crashing last chords.

Around this time Beethoven tested the possibilities of a genre he had not touched on since op. 1. His first piano trio in a decade, op. 70, no. 1 in D Major begins precipitously with an energetic unison stride downward on a four-note motif, slams to a halt on an out-of-key

F-natural, then picks up into a quiet, coiled-spring whirlwind notably vehement even for a major-key movement. Beethoven's response to D major, from the model in his op. 10, no. 3, piano sonata, had been a mixture of traditional and personal. That key, wrote a theorist of the time, "is suited to noisy, joyful, warlike, and rousing things." So it would be in opp. 10 and 70, but the later work is richer in its emotional and thematic profile. In both pieces Beethoven contrasts the comic ebullience of the outer movements with a radical shift in the middle: the op. 10 slow movement keeningly tragic, the ghostly op. 70 slow movement in D minor another of his sui generis essays. His D-minor mood tended toward deep darkness.

He had lived and learned a great deal since the op. 10 D Major, one of the finest of his early piano sonatas. In the op. 70 Trio, the tight motivic relations of the early work have been expanded into underlying patterns of rhythm, melodic shape, gesture, psychological consistency. With the F-natural on the first line of the trio he foreshadows tonal excursions throughout the piece to F major, B-flat major, and D minor (so the ebullient first line of the piece is already haunted by a touch of D minor).[22] The first movement's exposition is compact, but it ends up expansive because at the end of the recap it repeats back to the spiky and relentless development. That expansiveness prepares the immense slow movement that occupies the middle of the trio. Early on, that movement gave the work its subtitle of *Ghost,*

To say it again, in background and temperament Beethoven was no Romantic, even if in practice he was by 1808 the essential composer for Romantics. If the tone of the weird and the uncanny was central to Romanticism, it was not central to Beethoven. But in the Largo of the *Ghost* Trio, he set the mark for the weird and uncanny. Much as in the op. 10 Sonata, a downward-fourth motif from the first movement is taken up and made into something a world away. This movement, with its obsessive concentration on one motif, its strange whisperings and flutterings, its spare and bizarre textures, its utterly eerie ending, may have originated as an idea for Collin's libretto of the Shakespeare *Macbeth.* If so, this music would have been for the witch's-cauldron scene that begins the play. It would have made that scene as darkly unforgettable as Florestan's dungeon in *Fidelio.*

In the sketches he took much trouble to make an ending for the ghostly movement that would not resolve the tension but carry it into the finale that follows — no scherzo would fit this piece.[23] With a flowing and lighthearted finale the music appears to escape the shades, but in a uniquely organic way: the genial main motif echoes the slow movement's theme. Dark obsession turned into sunny escape might be an example of Beethovenian dramatic shape, but the reality is not so simple. In the finale something lingers from the shivery second movement, a tone gay on the surface but unsettled beneath. It ends with a triplet fillip echoing the obsessive theme of the "ghost" movement. Ghosts haunt the gaiety. Here Beethoven returns to the psychological subtlety of the op. 18 Quartet in B-flat, where a dancing finale cannot entirely banish *La Malinconia*.

If op. 70, no. 1 became famous for its weird middle movement, the whole of no. 2, in E-flat, is quietly, subtly enigmatic. Its color and character are unique in Beethoven, and it lies at a far remove from a heroic E-flat major. The introduction begins with a spare four-part canon, setting up a work with much imitative material and a sometimes archaic tone. An emotional ambiguity hovers, moving unpredictably between tension and warmth. The tone has partly to do with a peculiarity of the violin part: hardly at all in the first movement and only occasionally later does the violin make it up to the bright E string. Beethoven keeps the cello mostly in its low to medium register as well. (Both trios confirm the emancipation of the cello from the bass line that he began in op. 1.) The register of the strings gives the whole piece an oddly subdued effect. At the same time the piano has a good deal of high passagework, making for striking textures of low strings and high, brilliant piano. The first movement turns to deep-flat keys, including E-flat and A-flat minor and C-flat major, all unbrilliant in the strings. So even what would seem to be the bouncy and happy 6/8 of the first movement's main theme is strangely inflected by the instrumental coloration.

The two middle movements are both marked Allegretto, in C major and A-flat major. The second movement is double variations on contrasting themes that still share material, including a "Scotch snap" figure. The first theme flows, the second has a bit of driving "Turkish" tone. Structured like a scherzo but muted and introspective, the third movement is in a flowing three-beat, with two appearances of a trio. The dashing finale returns to brilliant piano figures but remains mostly low and subdued in the strings. A dashing, full-throated coda ends what is, in its subtle way, one of the more unusual pieces of Beethoven's life.

A cello sonata and two piano trios, each a distinct personality. All these chamber pieces form an illustration of something Beethoven said more than once: he based all his pieces on a story or an image and wrote the music to fit it. Recall the *Romeo and Juliet* backstory in his first string quartet. But in all but a few cases, Beethoven as a matter of policy did not tell the world what his model stories were. They were his own business, another part of his workshop that he did not want the world snooping in. He wanted his listeners to write their own stories, their own poems, to his work. Which is to say that he was too wise in his art to compromise one of the important things about music, perhaps the most important of all: its mystery.

Summer 1808 found Beethoven on Kirchengasse in Heiligenstadt, his main project to finish the Sixth Symphony. (He did not hold his crisis of 1802 against the rural spa town.) He seems to have finished the Fifth Symphony early that year, after nearly four years of off-and-on work on it. His room looked out to the street. The inner rooms, around a garden, were rented to the Grillparzer family, whose son Franz was a budding poet. He had encountered Beethoven before, at the home of his uncle, Beethoven's librettist Joseph Sonnleithner. Grillparzer recalled that in this summer his mother took to standing in the courtyard listening to Beethoven play as he composed. When he caught her at it, he did not play another note aloud all summer.[24] This female enthusiast became another victim of Beethoven's iron unforgivingness.

Just as he always had pieces in progress, he also generally had schemes going. He returned to his dogged campaign to sell pieces to Breitkopf & Härtel. "The tutor of the young Count Schönfeld," he wrote Gottfried Härtel in June, ". . . assures me that you would again like to have some of my works—Although, since our relations have been broken off so frequently, I am almost convinced this resumption . . . will again lead to nothing." He offers them the two new symphonies, the cello sonata, the Mass in C. Other publishers would be happy to take them, he says, but "I would prefer your firm to all others." On one point he is particularly insistent: "You must take the Mass or else I can't give you the other works — for I pay attention not only to what is profitable but also to what brings honor and glory."[25] The particular honor and glory he may have had in mind was putting his mass up against Haydn's — a delusional idea, if he hoped to challenge their popularity.

At that point Härtel was not remotely interested in the mass. He would take a great deal of convincing. In another letter Beethoven offered it to him for nothing and said he would pay to have it copied. Härtel did not budge. (He finally published it, grudgingly, in 1812.) Soon Beethoven gave up on the mass. Breitkopf & Härtel received the Fifth and Sixth Symphonies, the op. 69 Cello Sonata, and the two Piano Trios op. 70 — every one of them among the greatest examples of their genre. The price Beethoven asked was 600 florins; he got a little over 400, three months' living at best.[26] Later when he received the proofs of the Cello Sonata from Härtel, he discovered they were unbelievably infested with mistakes. In a letter he meticulously corrected them. The corrections were ignored.

That summer he wrote Collin hoping for another opera libretto, only "I should like this time a libretto without dancing and recitatives." He may have been sketching on Collin's *Macbeth*, but that never got far, though the ideas perhaps served for the *Ghost* Trio. He had gently put off the playwright's *Bradamante* because it had magical elements, which appealed to him even less than dancing and recitatives. "I cannot deny that on the whole I am prejudiced against this sort of thing," he wrote, "because it has a soporific effect on feeling and reason." (True, Mozart's *Zauberflöte*, the definition of a magical opera, was his favorite. But he had no intention of competing with Mozart in that kind of story, still less in his trademark sex comedies.) "In any case," he sighed, "I think that we shall probably have to wait a bit; for that is what those worshipful and high and mighty theatrical directors have decreed — I have so little reason to expect anything favorable from them that the thought that I shall certainly have to leave Vienna and become a wanderer haunts me persistently."[27]

Back in Vienna he moved into the Krügerstrasse apartment of another patron, the Hungarian countess Anna Marie Erdödy. Lichnowsky had an apartment in the same building, but the resentments of their 1806 quarrel lingered and they saw little of each other. There seems to have been nothing romantic between Beethoven and the countess — they would have been more circumspect if there had been. But they were on easy terms and stayed that way, except for the usual quarrel that arose sooner or later with anyone in Beethoven's proximity. Erdödy gave him a patient and sympathetic ear; he called her his *Beichtvater,* his father confessor. He gave her the dedication of the op. 70 Trios, finished at her house. In many ways, the countess's story was similar to Beethoven's other aristocratic patrons, only more so: she was a fine amateur pianist and a grand eccentric, having been relieved by separation of an unhappy marriage to a Hungarian count, and with three children to rear.

Like Josephine Deym, this countess was a celebrated beauty. Unlike Josephine, she was comfortably rich, and more or less an invalid. A chronic condition swelled her feet and kept her often in bed. Much of her activity involved limping painfully from one piano to another, often to play Beethoven in musical soirees at her house. She was reported to be, in spite of everything, cheerful and high-spirited. Police reports of the time, however, describe her as "depraved." That may have meant something as simple as her being denounced by a spy for criticizing the government. Or Erdödy may have taken opium, a common painkiller in those days.[28]

Around October Beethoven suddenly received an offer to become *Kapellmeister* for the soi-disant king of Westphalia in Cassel, which lay in northwestern Germany. This king was none other than Jérôme Bonaparte, youngest brother of the French conqueror, who had established his family in similar positions all over the map. Jérôme had led a rambling youth. Sent off to sea by Napoleon in 1800, he stopped for two years in the United States and, to the consternation of his family, married the daughter of a Baltimore millionaire. (He was expected to marry into the European nobility.) Napoleon had the marriage annulled and banned the woman from any of his territories. Jérôme protested, to no avail; his American wife bore his son in London and never saw him again.

Effective service in the Prussian campaign of 1806 got Jérôme back in Napoleon's good graces. He was installed in Westphalia and supplied by his brother with a more appropriate mate, Princess Catherine of Württemberg, a cousin of Tsar Alexander I. "The wellbeing of your people is important to me," Napoleon wrote him in a cautionary letter, "not only for the influence that it will have on your glory and mine, but also for the prospect of Europe as a whole." (Note the order of values.) "It is essential that your people enjoy a liberty, an equality, a wellbeing unknown to the people of Germany." Jérôme remained something of a loose cannon. Even for a ruler of the time, he was excessively fond of military pomp and finery, of parties and mistresses. His subjects dubbed him *König Lustig,* "King Merry." But his imposition of Napoleonic reforms, including the Civil Code and a parliament, made him popular, for a time, with his people.

Jérôme's offer to Beethoven was not a sign of his musical sophistication. It was designed to bring luster to a puppet court. He already had the services of the finest painters in Napoleonic France to glorify himself and his queen, and he had extravagant architectural plans for his capital. As the offer to Beethoven stated, the only duties of the court *Kapellmeister* were to conduct a few concerts and play occasionally for the king. Beethoven would have unlimited access to the court orchestra and freedom to travel and pursue his own projects. The proffered salary was a handsome 600 gold ducats, around 2,700 florins, plus 1,000 more for travel expenses.[29] Perhaps Beethoven knew and approved that the court's religious commissar, one Wuerschmidt, was a proud Freemason and former Illuminatus.[30] Such things on an official's resume were unthinkable in Vienna.

Now Beethoven had an escape route from Vienna, if he chose to take it. At the beginning of November he wrote Count Oppersdorff, commissioner of the Fourth and Fifth Symphonies, "I have been offered an appointment as Kapellmeister to the King of Westphalia and it may well be that I shall accept this offer." With that he left the door open to a better offer. It is entirely possible that he kept Jérôme Bonaparte on the line as a bargaining chip. Did he really believe he could be happy as a servant in a gaudy French puppet court? Did he consider the job a way of reaching Napoleon himself?

In March he had written Oppersdorff a jovial letter about "your symphony": "The last movement of the symphony has three trombones and a piccolo — and, although, it is true, there are not three kettledrums, yet this combination of instruments will make a more pleasing noise than six kettledrums."[31] Then he began putting off Oppersdorff concerning the disposal and dedication of the symphonies the count had commissioned. He wrote in the November letter, "You will probably have formed an unfavorable impression of me. But necessity drove me to hand over to someone else the symphony which I composed for you [the Fifth], and another one as well [the Sixth] — Rest assured, however, that you will soon receive the symphony which is specially intended for you [the Fourth]."[32] Oppersdorff naturally expected dedications for the Fourth and Fifth in return for commissioning them. In the end both Fifth and Sixth ended up dedicated to older and more generous patrons, Princes Lobkowitz and Razumovsky, and the Fourth to Oppersdorff. He may have formed the unfavorable impression Beethoven was concerned about, because there is no indication of further business or communication between them.[33]

By early November Beethoven had agreed to conduct an orchestral concert of his works — including the popular *Coriolan* but none of the new pieces — for a benefit at the Theater an der Wien. There commenced the hectic slate of arrangements and complaints and threats that accompanied all his public endeavors. During the month he wrote promoter and friend Count Moritz Dietrichstein:

> I could not get the concerto. And even if I had got it, it would have been no good. For at the Theater . . . I have had the experience of hearing performers play from rough copies. You cannot ask me to expose my compositions to the uncertainty of a performance which is likely to fail. I will come to the meeting on Monday, although indeed I know that my presence is quite unnecessary, because people never pay any attention to what I say . . .

[A few days later:] If I have to experience a repetition of what happened at the rehearsal on Saturday, nobody will ever persuade me to have anything more to do in the slightest way with this unfortunate concert.[34]

But he did conduct at the unfortunate charity concert, and the upshot of it was that the "Worshipful Direction" of the Theater an der Wien finally, after he had spent two years begging them, allowed him a concert on December 22 — just over a month from the charity concert. Both programs were a testament to the speed at which orchestral programs could be pulled together in those days.

To add to the frenzy, as he had done in his earlier Vienna benefits Beethoven decided to compose a new work to make a grand finale for the concert. The previous hasty productions had been the First Symphony and *Christus am Ölberge*. Why he needed a splashy finish for a program that already was to include the premieres of the Fifth and Sixth Symphonies and Fourth Piano Concerto is hard to conceive. But as always, his resolve once made was implacable. He began to cobble together a fantasia for solo piano, orchestra, and chorus using an old tune from the sketchbooks, and found a poet to whip up a text about the splendors of music. The opening of the piece would be a piano solo he would improvise on the spot.

His letters in this month of frantic labors are some of the cheeriest he had written in years. As part of his attempt to secure soprano Anna Milder, his first Leonore, he wrote his old Florestan, Joseph August Röckel, "Be sure to make a very good arrangement with Milder . . . tomorrow I will come myself to kiss the hem of her garment." He was still promising Collin to compose the playwright's libretto *Bradamante*: "Great and Enraged Poet!!!!! Give up Reichardt — and use my notes for your poetry. I promise that . . . immediately after my concert which, to counterbalance its purpose of putting some money into my pocket, is robbing me of a good deal of my time, I will go to you, and then we will start work on the opera at once." He deplored the magical elements in *Bradamante* and had no real intention of setting it. But he liked Collin and probably considered him the best available prospect to produce a workable libretto.

Beethoven knew that Collin, frustrated with being put off, had
shown the libretto to visiting composer Johann Friedrich Reichardt,
who was anxious to set it (and eventually did, with no success). Reichardt, then fifty-six and well known, had just arrived in Vienna eager
to take in its musical atmosphere and perhaps to make himself part
of it. One of his first endeavors was to seek out Beethoven at Countess Erdödy's. (As his letter shows, they had met before at some point.)
Reichardt was a sharp observer of people and events, and his letters,
which he soon got in print, paint a vivid portrait of Beethoven and
Vienna in the months Reichardt visited there:

> I have also sought out and visited the good Beethoven. People pay so
> little attention to him here that no one could tell me where he lives,
> and it entailed quite a lot of trouble on my part to locate him. [The
> difficulty was more likely due to Beethoven's constant relocations.] Fi-
> nally I found him in a large, desolate and lonely apartment. At first he
> looked as dark as his own lodgings, but soon became more cheerful
> and even seemed as pleased to see me again as I was heartily glad to
> see him. He also told me a lot of things which were important for me
> to know, all in a very frank and agreeable manner. His is a powerful
> nature, like a Cyclops in appearance but at the same time very inti-
> mate, hearty, and good. He lives and spends a good deal of time with
> a Hungarian Countess Erdödy who lives in the front part of the large
> house. But he has become quite estranged from Prince Lichnowsky
> who lives in the upper part of the same house.[35]

Among the things Beethoven told Reichardt about was the offer
from Cassel. This was a considerable shock to the visitor, because as
far as Reichardt knew he currently occupied that position himself.[36]
Though he had not been happy in Cassel and may have had no intention of going back, he did not appreciate being replaced without
notice. Reichardt advised Beethoven in the strongest terms not to take
the job.

In early December Reichardt attended a house concert:

> The whole pleasant impression was once more destroyed by Bee-
> thoven's overwhelming, gigantic overture to Collin's *Coriolan*. My

brain and my heart almost burst from the hammer blows and shrill-
ness within the narrow rooms, especially as everyone tried . . . to increase the noise in view of the fact that the composer was present.
It gave me great pleasure to see dear Beethoven being much fêted,
particularly because he has the unfortunate, hypochondriac whim
that everyone here persecutes and despises him. His highly obstinate
character may well scare off many of the kind-hearted and gay Viennese . . . It really upsets me very deeply when I see this basically good
and remarkable man looking gloomy and suffering. Although I am
convinced, on the other hand, that his best and most original works
can only be produced when he is in a stubborn and deeply morose
state of mind.[37]

A couple of weeks later, on December 22, 1808, Reichardt was sitting in Prince Lobkowitz's box when, at 6:30 p.m., in the unheated
Theater an der Wien, Beethoven gave the downbeat for the premiere
of the Sixth Symphony, commencing one of the most remarkable and
outlandish concerts in the history of music. Reichardt and Lobkowitz
were among the shivering survivors still in their seats when the concert ended at 10:30.

22

Darkness to Light

NEAR THE END of 1808, the *Weiner Zeitung* ran an advertisement for a "musical *Akademie*" whose scope and ambition were extraordinary to the point of absurd:

> On Thursday, December 22, Ludwig van Beethoven will have the honor to give a musical *Akademie* in the R. I. Priv. Theater-an-der-Wien. All the pieces are of his composition, entirely new, and not yet heard in public . . . First Part: 1, A Symphony, entitled: "A Recollection of Country Life," in F major (No. 5). 2, Aria. 3, Hymn with Latin text, composed in the church style with chorus and solos. 4, Pianoforte Concerto, played by himself.
>
> Second part. Grand Symphony in C minor (no. 6). 2, Hymn, with Latin text composed in the church style with chorus and solos. 3, Fantasia for Pianoforte alone. 4, Fantasia for the Pianoforte which ends with the gradual entrance of the entire orchestra and the introduction of choruses as a finale.[1]

Beethoven placed the notice himself. The program was only the third he had mounted for his benefit since he arrived in Vienna, and it had been five years since the most recent concert. For the last two of those years, his creativity had burned at white heat while the Viennese bureaucracy kept him waiting for a venue. The result was an overstuffed program, compounded by his decision to present solo and choral pieces to contrast the orchestral ones, and his determination to whip up the stem-winding *Choral Fantasy* to end the evening.

His claim that all the pieces were "entirely new" is, of course, not entirely true. Four were premieres and three not. The numbering of the symphonies is the reverse of the order in which he finally published them. The two movements of the Mass in C are called "hymns," because music from the Latin liturgy was not allowed in secular concerts; the texts had to be translated into German. In all that planning Beethoven paid no attention to the time and the season. The concert amounted to some four hours of what was doomed to be underrehearsed music in an unheated hall in the dark of winter.

The run-up to the program had witnessed more Beethovenian sound and fury. In the charity program of the previous month at the Theater an der Wien he managed to offend the house orchestra. Concertmaster Franz Clement and conductor Ignaz Seyfried took his side, but in December the rank and file at first refused to play under his baton. Striding up and down in rage and anxiety, Beethoven "listened" to the rehearsals from an anteroom (given his hearing, he heard very little). He had also somehow alienated the brilliant young soprano Anna Milder, his first Leonore, who declined to sing the aria. Her replacement in *Ah! perfido* was the inexperienced Josephine Killitschgy, sister-in-law of concertmaster Ignaz Schuppanzigh.

At the last minute the orchestra relented and allowed Beethoven onstage for the concert. It was a stressful evening for all. Unnerved by the difficult and unvocal solo part, Killitschgy succumbed to stage fright and muffed the performance. During the *Choral Fantasy* Beethoven realized some players had miscounted rests and a crash was imminent. He stopped the music, shouting angrily, "Quiet, quiet, this isn't working! Once again!"[2] He probably had no choice, but the orchestra was once again furious. (This time he took the political route and apologized to the players.)

Those not used to Beethoven's singular conducting style had much to enjoy outside the music, what with his leaping and crouching and wild gesticulations on the podium. The month before, conducting one of his concertos from the keyboard, to mark a *sforzando* in the orchestra he swept his arms wide and knocked off the candles that were lighting his music stand. The audience was much amused. To forestall that sort of thing two choirboys were sent to stand at the sides of the piano and hold the candles. The orchestra started again. In the same spot Beethoven made the same gesture and smacked one of the boys in the face while the other one ducked. This inspired general hilarity. Beethoven was so furious that when he tried to start again at the piano, he broke several strings on the first chord.[3]

At the December concert visiting composer Johann Reichardt was marooned in Prince Lobkowitz's box. While many of the audience trickled away, neither of them could decently leave even if they wanted to, because the box was in front of the hall, in view of the audience. The performing forces were heterogeneous, he noted, all the pieces difficult and unusual, and there had never been a complete rehearsal. Reichardt experienced, he wrote, "that one can easily have too much of a good thing—and still more of a loud."[4]

On December 22 the program began with the *Pastoral* Symphony and finished with the *Choral Fantasy,* the latter cobbled together in one of Beethoven's last-minute marathons. At the first rehearsal the ink was barely dry on the vocal parts. The fantasy has a kind of ingenuous charm. The text, by a local poet, was written to fit the tune of an old unpublished song of Beethoven's called *Gegenliebe.* The lyrics, an ode to music, set forth a train of unions that bestow gifts on humanity. It begins—

> *Flatteringly lovely and fair are the sounds*
> *of our life's harmonies,*
> *and from our sense of beauty there arise*
> *flowers that blossom eternally.*

In the next stanzas, "peace" and "joy" are wedded to bring exaltation, "music" and "words" wedded to turn the storms of life into light (once more that echt-Aufklärung image). "Outward repose" and "in-

ward rapture" engender yet more light. The last stanza calls on enlightened humanity to embrace the final union:

> *And so, noble souls, accept*
> *gladly the gifts of beautiful art.*
> *When love and strength are wedded,*
> *the favor of the gods rewards mankind.*

The *Choral Fantasy* takes shape as an ad hoc form, an accumulation: long piano solo, orchestra brought in bit by bit, soloists brought
in bit by bit, then a rapturous coda with full choir. The opening solo
is a solemn C-minor fantasia — not at all a tragic C minor. Beethoven
improvised it at the 1808 performance and in the published version
likely recreated and touched up what he remembered of it. In the piece
the piano soloist perhaps represents the spirit of music itself. It begins
with massive handfuls of chords striding up and down the keyboard:
"lovely and fair are the sounds / of our life's harmonies." Finally after
a stretch of quasi-improvisation, the piano issues a glittering deluge
of notes rising from bottom to top, the strings commence a dialogue,
and that coaxes the leading theme from the piano. It is a forthright,
declamatory kind of tune that since his teens (as in the song *Who Is a
Free Man?*) Beethoven had associated with high-Aufklärung humanism. For him that humanistic style had been broadened and intensified
by the example of the populistic music of the French Revolution. No
less, the theme's folklike style and stein-thumping rhythm evoke a *geselliges Lied,* the kind of exalted drinking song exemplified by Schiller's
poem "An die Freude."

In several ways, Beethoven later remembered this grandiose if mid-
dleweight excursion when he came to compose his last symphony and
returned to *An die Freude.* For one example, from the beginning of
the *Choral Fantasy* there is a sense of searching for something. That
destination turns out to be the main theme, its contours suggested in
veiled form in the prefatory music. In his last symphony as here, the
instruments would find the staunch main theme before the voices enter, and extend it into a series of variations. In the *Choral Fantasy* there
is a "Turkish"-style variation; in his last symphony Beethoven remem-

bered that idea too. Meanwhile the second variation is fronted by a dancing flute solo that operagoers at the time would have recognized as an echo of Mozart's eponymous magic flute. In Mozart's *Zauberflöte* and its echo here in Beethoven, the flute represents the magical power of music.

The voices enter piecemeal: a trio of women then a trio of men race through five stanzas until the chorus arrives to drive home the final verse, the one Beethoven most cared about. He extends that text for page after page, homing in on key words and the key idea: the marriage of "love" and "strength," through whose union in art "the favor of the gods rewards mankind." There is a hair-raising moment when the choir falls from G major to a brilliant E-flat chord on the word *strength.* Beethoven most especially would remember that chord change in his second mass and in his last symphony, where it proclaims the love and strength of God. That magical chord change echoes Haydn's "Let there be light!" in *The Creation.*

The end of the *Choral Fantasy,* like the endings of *Leonore* and the *Eroica,* rises to unbounded joy: "Götter-Gunst!" ("the favor of the gods!"). Clearly, the text had been put together with the composer whispering in the ear of the poet, because the final stanza amounts to a description of Beethoven's art. In the *Choral Fantasy* that ideal was set forth in a thin vessel turned out in a hurry. It would prove a model for the greater but fundamentally similar work to come. The Ninth Symphony also involves unions and marriages, but on a universal scale: music about things far beyond music.

The Third Piano Concerto had not entirely freed itself of Mozart and the eighteenth century, and it was still the vehicle of a virtuoso. The Fourth Piano Concerto in G Major, op. 58, was entirely Beethoven's concerto, in the sense that the *Razumovskys* had declared his mature voice with quartets. The premiere of the Fourth in the concert of December 1808 marked the last time Beethoven played a concerto in public. Maybe in part for that reason, since concertos were no longer a practical part of his portfolio, in this piece he felt unconstrained in remaking the genre, as he had done with other genres, by intensifying its singularity, sharpening its profile as an individual.

The Fourth Concerto begins with the piano unaccompanied. The soloist is discovered brooding and soliloquizing alone, like a Romantic hero, in a phrase of inward and reverberant simplicity:[5]

Its thunder stolen, the orchestra enters quietly but in a very wrong key, distant B major, and not even with the soloist's theme but with a variation of it. Soon the orchestra finds its way back to G major and something closer to the soloist's theme, but from those opening gestures a divide is established that will mark the whole of the Fourth Concerto: soloist and orchestra are on different planes, sometimes complementary, sometimes opposing, sometimes mutually oblivious. Here is the essential gambit of the Fourth Concerto.[6] The solo has its version of *das Thema,* the orchestra has its version, and the two never quite agree on it. In fact, the soloist's version will be heard only once more. So which version of the theme is the "real" one? There is no answer to that question.

Meanwhile the air of brooding nobility that the soloist establishes in the beginning is not otherwise his mood in the first movement, where he is playful, flighty, even mocking. The beginning foreshadows his inner voice, his mood in the second movement, where he and the orchestra will be at odds to a degree that threatens to shatter the integrity of the music.

At the same time the soloist's opening soliloquy establishes a melodic and also a rhythmic motif that will rarely be absent from the first movement. That conception was there from what may have been the first idea for the concerto, in the 1803 sketchbook largely devoted to the *Eroica.* In the wake of his breakthrough symphony, Beethoven's imagination had been racing toward the future. As of 1803 he had found the leading idea for what became the Fifth Symphony, not only its leading motif but the central conception that it would rage on relentlessly. In a sketch he takes the motif down a chain of descending thirds:

From Nottebohm, *Two Beethoven Sketchbooks*

Then something struck him. On the opposite page from that sketch he jotted down an idea in G major:

From Nottebohm, *Two Beethoven Sketchbooks*

There is the melodic line, virtually intact, of the opening piano soliloquy of the Fourth Piano Concerto. The sketch continues with a passage for orchestra, not immediately in B major, like the final score, but including a jump to B major. Already he had conceived the harmonic dissonance between solo and orchestra.

What unites these sketches for a symphony and a concerto is a contrasting interpretation of the same rhythmic motif. The three-note upbeat to a longer note had been a favorite of Beethoven's for a long time, a motif that served him well. There is something innately propulsive about it, the strength of the propulsion depending on how it is presented. In the Fifth Symphony that motif, sped up, is driving and ferocious. Slowed in the first movement of the Fourth Concerto, it creates a gentle lilt, strung along and ending with a sigh:

The commission for the Fourth Symphony and the other rush of works of 1806 broke off work on both the C Minor Symphony and the Fourth Concerto. He picked up the concerto again and had it finished by spring 1807, then returned to the Fifth Symphony. Before the premiere of December 1808, the concerto likely had a private reading or two, hosted by Prince Lobkowitz.[7]

Czerny recalled that in the premiere of the concerto Beethoven handled the solo part freely, with a good deal more embellishment than ended up in the published score. That was fitting to the personality of the concerto soloist: when he is expected to echo or to lead the orchestra, he is apt instead to break into glittering roulades. Most especially, this notably flighty soloist is not interested in the military direction the orchestra takes in the A-minor second theme and its lead-in. All this foreshadows the calls and nonresponses that will mark the second movement. Solo and orchestra are on two different tacks, if in the first movement in the same general direction.

The second entrance of the soloist, in the normal concerto position beginning the second exposition, hints at his attitude in a series of tritones, C–F-sharp, the old *diabolus in musica* Beethoven had singled out as early as the op. 1 Trio in C Minor. The implication here is not tragic or demonic but contrarian: at his second entrance in the piece the piano declares neither his own version of *das Thema* nor the orchestra's but rather offers up a bouquet of flowers. From that point on, their interaction is a series of frustrated expectations, the soloist remaining neither a follower nor a leader — though he does manage a more embroidered version of the orchestral *Thema:*

Soon after, while the bassoon plays a lyrical line, the piano surrounds him in mocking dissonances:

Throughout this game the overall tone is stately, lyrical, only occasionally military. The orchestra's exposition does fall into a tranquil and lovely interlude in B-flat that the piano succumbs to later. During the development there is no particular hostility between the forces, but suddenly at the recapitulation the soloist bursts out *fortissimo* with his original version of *das Thema*, which has not been heard since the opening soliloquy. It is as if he were shouting, *No! This is the way it goes! This is my idea that you stole and never got right!*[8] Then the piano retreats to *pianissimo,* the tension ebbs, the combatants return to their places, and the exact solo version of the *Thema* disappears again. In the cadenza the soloist must work hard to outdo all the virtuosity that has preceded it.[9] The coda builds to a grand *fortissimo* finish, the soloist joining the massive chords of the close.

The rift between solo and orchestra comes to a head in the E-minor second movement: alternating phrases, never together, the orchestra insistent, the soloist oblivious, inward, lost in some kind of *raptus* — but also calming and cajoling. While the basis of this dramatic tableau is simple enough, there had never been anything like it, because its fundamental conception negates the very idea of unity of affect and material. At the beginning the strings play a quiet, dotted military figure, ending on a harmonically open note: an invitation. Then, silence. The soloist responds quietly, *molto cantabile,* as if singing to himself. He has returned to the chordal texture and the brooding tone of his soliloquy that opened the piece. As in the first movement, he is not interested in the military tread that the strings try to force on him in phrases of mounting belligerence. The soloist sighs, retreats, breaks out in roulades, screams tritones (A–D-sharp) in a small cadenza. The strings retreat with a last marching tread, *pianissimo,* then slide into a sigh much like the soloist's. He echoes it. With that the movement ends, if not in resolution, then in some kind of truce.[10]

In the beginning of the concerto, the strings first entered on the not-quite-right piano theme, in the wrong key. The strings kick off the Vivace finale with a dashing rondo theme again in the wrong key, C major. It also happens to be a tune that the soloist cannot play: a piano is not capable of comfortably executing those fast repeating notes that are natural for a bowed instrument. Echoing the theme, all he can do is turn it into a piano version:

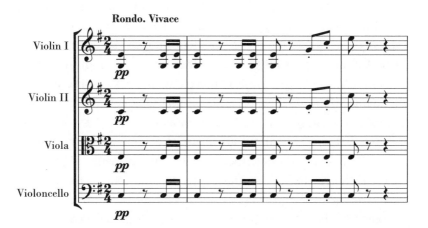

In other words, topsy-turvy. In the first movement the strings can't get the piano theme right; in the finale the piano can't precisely play the string's rondo theme at all. In the slow movement the two forces reach a tentative rapprochement only in the last bars. In the finale the original rivalry endures, the sense of call-and-unreliable-response, but now the game is played as comedy. By the third line the strings even present a coy little bit that the piano *can* play exactly. The piano is back to its glitter-and-be-gay mood, but now there is a sense that the two forces are completing one another's thoughts rather than contradicting them. The piano presents a beautifully lyrical B theme that the strings gently second. Still, the music has a lot of trouble settling on the actual key, G major, until the final appearance of the flowing B theme, and that long-delayed resolution gives the moment a throat-grabbing poignancy. In the coda the A theme insists on coming back in C major but finally agrees to end in the proper key, G.

One of the striking qualities of the Fourth, eventually to be numbered among the finest of all concertos, is that its disputes, its debates, its mutual lacks of understanding, whatever one wants to call them, are carried on in the outer movements largely in a tone of play, most playfully in the finale. And the finale's denouement comes well before the coda, in a sudden and sublime stretch of singing E-flat major, *pianissimo,* in divided violas, with gentle piano garlands above. It is as if piano and orchestra have decided together that wrong keys are a fine thing.[11]

It is hard to conceive what that first audience in 1808 made of the Fifth Symphony in C Minor, op. 67, as they sat shivering in the cold theater having already heard nearly two hours of scrambling performances of new and strenuous music. How many listeners heard an epoch beginning at the first performance of the *Eroica*? Something of nearly that order was happening again. By comparison to the Fifth Symphony, the Third is almost esoteric. The Fifth reaches out and shakes you, then for solace presents you with the most exquisite beauties.

The Third Symphony is in E-flat major, to Beethoven most often meaning an echt-Aufklärung, humanistic, heroic piece (though he explored other moods of that key).[12] The Fifth is in C minor, therefore driving, portentous, fateful. First conceived and sketched in the same burst of creative fire as the *Eroica*, the Fifth unfolds in a different world from that of the Third, but it has the same kind of dramatic narrative.

Only this time Beethoven did not give a name to the story. At some early point in the sketching, he decided on or sensed something like this: *The C Minor Symphony will be more unified in its narrative and in its material than any symphony before, beyond anything I or anybody else has done. The essence of that unity will be conveyed by the simplest thing possible: a four-note tattoo, a primal rhythm. That rhythm will saturate the first movement and return in new guises to the end. How the motif is transformed will be the essence of the narrative. So the leading idea will be not a "theme" but a motif. And I will treat that tiny motif in the same way I treat any opening theme: everything will flow from it.*

Later Beethoven's amanuensis Anton Schindler told the world that

Beethoven said of the symphony's opening thunderclap, *Thus fate knocks at the door.* Beethoven was excruciatingly familiar with that knock. But Schindler was a chronic liar, and there is no way to know whether Beethoven truly said that (assuming that, now and then, Schindler uttered something true). At the same time, Schindler was an accomplished musician and what he said about Beethoven's music was often astute, whether factual or not. Which is to say that here Schindler was right: the first movement implies a story about something on the order of the action of fate on the life of an individual, an assault that cannot be turned back but can only be borne, resisted, transcended from within.[13]

So in Beethoven's mind there was presumably some dramatic scenario behind the Fifth Symphony, but he decided that, like most of his works, this one did not need to be nailed to a stated narrative. For those equipped to understand it, the gist would be clear enough in the notes. That story would be as direct as the rest of the symphony: a movement from darkness to light, from C minor to C major, from the battering of fate to joyous triumph.

The compaction of material flows from the first gesture, that unforgettable explosion of three Gs and an E-flat. Once again, for Beethoven the opening idea, *das Thema,* is the embryo of a work. Here he boils down *das Thema* to just four notes that still function like a *Thema:* they are the symphony in essence.

In the symphony's first moment, in that percussive *da-da-da-dum*, we hear the primal rhythmic figure that will dominate the first movement and persist as motif and rhythmic scaffolding to the end. We sense the force-of-nature energy of the movement. We hear the bluntness of effect, the simplest harmonies proclaimed as if discovered for the first time. We hear the muscular quality that will mark the orchestral sound. We are misled by the key; it seems to be E-flat major but is actually C minor; that ambiguity creates tension.[14] The propulsive effect of the primal "&-2-& 1" rhythmic tattoo comes from its beginning on a void, a charged rest on the beginning of the 2/4 measure, then three eighth notes driving into the next measure, in which a new start of the figure is usually overlapped to drive forward again. Call the effect of this tattoo dominating the movement a *monorhythm*.

At the same time, besides that dominating rhythmic motif, we are presented with a more subtle undercurrent: the opening pitches G–E-flat–F–D form an S shape, down-up-down, that will serve as scaffolding for all the themes in the symphony.[15]

A rhythm, a shape, a dynamism moving from darkness to light, from C minor to C major, a determination to knit the piece tightly from beginning to end — these are essential conceptions of the Fifth Symphony. They are not different in kind from what Beethoven had done before. For that matter, they are not different in kind from Haydn and Mozart. They are different in intensity and concentration, in force and fury, in how thoroughly they permeate the music. Now instead of using a rhythmic motif as a background device for moving the music forward, Beethoven places the motif in the foreground as the substance of the music. To the ears of the time the result was strange and breathtaking in a way that later listeners, for whom the Fifth became ubiquitous in the repertoire, a kind of sacred monster, would hardly be able to reclaim.

The blunt simplification of gesture and sound, the monorhythm, and the simple, stripped-down sonata form of the first movement are shaped to convey something ferocious, inescapable: a force of nature, a relentless drumming of fate. Once again Beethoven shows off his incomparable skill at creating and sustaining tension, one of the hardest things to do in music that has to be worked out over months and sometimes years, penned one note at a time.

The singing second theme is bound to the basic ideas. It is introduced by a pealing horn call on B-flat–E-flat–F–B-flat — the S shape, the intervals expanded from the beginning. Those notes in turn are used as scaffolding for the second theme:

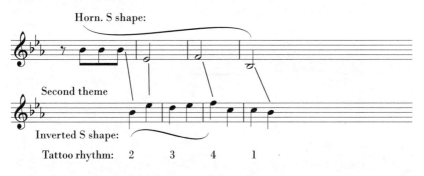

As has been noted, the *phrasing* of that theme is 2-3-4 1, augmenting the primal rhythmic tattoo. The basses under the second theme inject the original tattoo. The primal figure gets into everything: the rhythms on the surface and the phrasings under the surface.

To say it again: For Beethoven the elements of a piece are not just abstractly logical, they are also expressive, full of feeling and meaning from the level of the individual gesture to the whole of the form.[16] In the first movement he intensifies the effect of something inescapable by a simplification of form: only the primal motif for first theme; the short, contrasting second theme in the usual key, the relative major; in the development not a wide range of keys (mostly G minor). No subthemes, no formal ambiguities, a regular recapitulation. (The whole of the symphony is one of his shortest, some thirty-four minutes, but its impact makes it feel much longer.) The simplification of outline is part of its fatalism. It is as if there were *no way out* of the dictates of the form.

So the form is simple and regular — except for one giant peculiarity: the retransition to the recapitulation. Ordinarily for Beethoven that is a point of high anticipation. Instead, here at that point the music drifts into a fog, vague pulsations of strings and winds calling to one another. The shouting horns that herald the recapitulation burst out of that fog. The haze will return in the movements to come. Another unusual element in an otherwise straightforward recapitulation is a brief, poignant oboe soliloquy that interrupts the flow. The oboe appears like an individual standing frail and alone, singing in the midst of a storm. Here again logic and emotion work together: the oboe retraces the descent from G to D in the first four bars of the movement; at the same time, in its flowing descents the soliloquy foreshadows the themes of the second movement.

The final novelty is an immense coda, equal in length to the exposition and to the development. As he had done in the *Waldstein* and the *Appassionata,* here again Beethoven manages the feat of ratcheting enormous tension still higher; the music becomes an all-consuming rampage. The climax, strings and winds again calling to one another, is a sweeping downward scale tracing a sixth. That downward sixth, from E-flat to G, will become a refrain in the second movement. So the coda is at once an intensification of the drama, a thematic completion, a continuation of the development, and a foreshadowing of the slow movement.[17] Yet the coda generates so much energy that the curt final chords cannot resolve the tension. As in the *Eroica* and the *Waldstein,* resolution and completion will have to wait until the finale.

After the tempest of the first movement and its climax in the coda, the second movement arrives suddenly, in medias res, its lilting theme in the cellos like an oasis and a solace. (Its key of A-flat major served the same function of release from C-minor tension in the *Pathètique.*) Beethoven labeled the first sketch of the main theme Andante quasi minuetto. For all its gentle charm, the cello line has a strangely angular configuration, partly because it is built in several ways on the scaffolding of the S shape, the intervals expanded (see earlier example). In the second movement the driving tattoo from the opening bars is tamed. On the first page of the symphony it is a driving upbeat figure: &-2-& 1. In the second movement it often forms a more flowing figure starting on a downbeat: 1-2-3 1. In bars 14–16 of the second movement we hear the figure in both forms at four speeds, underlying a phrase of ineffable tenderness that echoes the descent from E-flat to G in the coda of the first movement:

In its form the Andante con moto is lucid but singular: alternating double variations, first on the cello theme with its tender refrain, then a B theme that begins quietly in A-flat and then flares into a pealing, brassy C major. Eventually that C-major fanfare will be transformed into the first blaze of the finale. (In sketches Beethoven first made it quite close to the opening of the last movement, then tempered the resemblance to a premonition.)[18] The fog of the first-movement retransition turns up again; at the end of each pair of variations, the music retreats into a mist, as if it has lost its thought. The first variation on theme A is drifting and beautiful, like a fair-weather cloud in summer. But near the end, after more exchanges of the two themes, the final variation of theme A is a strange staccato march of woodwinds, in affect somewhere between parodistic and ominous. Both those qualities foreshadow the next movement.

That movement, in C minor, is a scherzo in meter and tempo and form (scherzo-and-trio), but in tone hardly the usual playful outing; it is tinged with Beethoven's C-minor mood. There is a whispering bass oration, then a peal of horns and answering winds on a sternly aggressive theme:

That theme is another expression of the 1-2-3 1 version of the primal rhythmic motif, and its C minor returns the music to something like the fateful tone of the first movement. But now the moods drift, there is no monorhythm, no sense of something inescapable. So the first part is capable of giving way to a jovial C-major trio whose main theme strides continually down in thirds:

There is a farcical moment when the basses set out on a racing line and stumble, stop, try it again, stumble again, and finally get it right. Besides providing a comic interlude in the expressive narrative, there may be a private joke here: Beethoven retaliating against perennial grumbles over the difficulties of his bass parts. The trio also previews leading melodic ideas of the finale, so it amounts to a prophecy of the triumph of C major.

Here ambiguity creeps in. The C-minor nonscherzo comes back altered, the bass theme turned into a staccato parody — the same thing that happened to the main theme in the previous movement. Then, as in both earlier movements, fog rolls in, truncating the varied repeat.[19] The music falls into a mysterious texture of strings and thrumming timpani.[20] Its ancestor is Haydn's "Chaos," which prepares the emergence of light.[21]

From that quiet chaos bursts the C-major blaze of the finale, whose essence lies in the brass. Its style recalls the simple and straightforward manner of French revolutionary music, the feeling like a cry of freedom and release. Enhancing the weight and flexibility of the brass, to the horns and trumpets Beethoven adds trombones for one of the first times in a symphony.[22] Their throaty blare gives the finale not only weight but a distinctive coloration. To extend the orchestra's compass upward, he adds a piccolo.

Call the finale a triumphant recomposition of the first movement, without the fateful monorhythm but with the same kind of relentless intensity — now a joyful intensity. The materials of first and last movements are the same. The primal rhythmic tattoo is first enfolded in scales dashing upward. The main motif of the movement itself is a three-note up-striding figure, prophesied in the brass theme of the second movement:

The &-2-& 1 and 1-2-3 1 motifs turn up in various avatars, likewise the S shape (see earlier example).[23]

Like the first movement the layout is straightforward sonata form, but with more variety of themes and keys. The development starts loud, calms down, builds with mounting excitement toward the recapitulation. But at the moment of return, when we expect the brass to break into their heroic shout, abruptly the music pulls back into a shrouded place, as it did several times in the earlier movements. What happens then is beyond anticipation: the comic/ominous theme of the third movement returns in a staccato tread. The effect is much like something Beethoven had done years before: the racing finale of the op. 18 B-flat Major Quartet invaded by *La Malinconia*. This time there is no label on the page, and the effect of the nonscherzo invading the finale is ambiguous. But in both pieces the gist is the same: *The joy and the triumph will not be unsullied, not be complete.* Beethoven knew that triumph is never final. The demon can always come back.[24]

After a truncated recall of the foggy transition to the finale the recapitulation erupts in full force, as if the interruption had never happened. In the coda, Beethoven wanted, as he had done in the first movement, to raise the intensity even higher. There the intensity of fate, here the intensity of joy. He returns to the monorhythm of the first movement, in a steadily ascending figure. Here is the final transformation of the primal rhythm: in the beginning of the symphony it was a fatefully falling figure, here a triumphantly rising one:

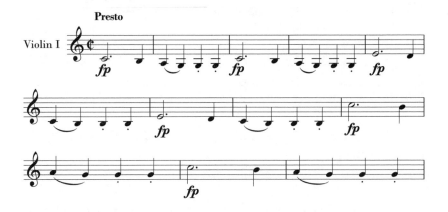

The effect is similar to the end of the *Eroica*, but the implications are quite otherwise. The *Eroica* adumbrated a story of a hero's victory and the blessings he brings the world; it conveyed that narrative in complex forms and a welter of ideas. The *Fifth* tells a story of personal victory and inner heroism, painted in broad strokes on an epic canvas. The ecstasy at the *Eroica*'s end is humanity rejoicing. The ecstasy at the end of the Fifth Symphony is a personal cry of victory.

That journey from despair to victory was Beethoven's own. As his mother taught him: without suffering there is no struggle, without struggle no victory, without victory no crown. But Beethoven was not a Romantic, and he was not mainly concerned with "expressing himself." As in all his music, even if there were echoes of his own life the goal was not autobiography but a larger human statement. The *Eroica* exalts a benevolent despot as a human ideal. The Fifth Symphony makes that heroic ideal individual, inward, but no less universal. The *Eroica* exalts the conquering hero as bringer of a just and peaceful society. The Fifth proclaims every person's capacity for heroism under the buffeting of life, a victory open to all humanity as individuals. The later course of Beethoven's music amplified that journey inward. As he would put it one day: through suffering to joy.[25]

The Fifth would stand as a thunderclap in musical history. With the Sixth Symphony in F Major, op. 68, Beethoven took a turn equally drastic, as drastic as any in his career. On the face of it, the Sixth echoed something he had done before: follow an aggressively challenging work with a gentler and more popularistic one. The Fifth is ferocious and has no stated program. The Sixth is a sunny walk in the fields, equipped with a title: *Pastoral*, each movement with a subtitle relating to a day in the country. But again it is a matter of degree, of the intensity of the contrast: the Sixth Symphony is the anti-Fifth.

From older sketchbooks Beethoven picked up some sketches toward the *Pastoral* and finished it in spring 1808, directly after the Fifth, in the middle of trying to extract another benefit concert from the court bureaucracy. In the *Pastoral* we see one of the more transparent demonstrations of how he turned an idea into sound: the idea inflecting melody, harmony, rhythm, and color. His inherited formal outlines he cut and shaped and sometimes broke to fit the idea.

The Sixth's first germ was perhaps a sketch conjuring the sound of a brook. His thought process evolved toward the idea of an orchestral work about a visit to the country. It was not to be an overture or a single movement or some kind of free-form orchestral fantasia. It was to be a real symphony: a "pastoral" symphony. The pastoral mode had been done many, many times before. Like the popular pieces picturing battles, pastorals were largely a trivial genre. Handel, however, had placed a lovely interlude called "Pastoral Symphony" in his *Messiah*. More to the point, Haydn had woven natural scenes and sounds into his *Creation* and *Seasons*. History had accumulated a repertoire of conventional pastoral gestures, such as bagpipe drones, folk tunes, simple harmonies, lilting music in 6/8 or 12/8, country dances, bird-songs, placid keys like B-flat major and F major, an air of gentleness and artless simplicity.[26] How, Beethoven reflected, can you map these kinds of effects and moods into the forms and the movements of a symphony? How can you set down the necessary clichés and not have them add up to a cliché?

The idea he settled on was this: *Each movement will be a vignette from a day in the country.* The symphony would depict one mid-summer day, morning to sunset. No conventional "four seasons," no clever incidents, no pictures. Only vignettes and feelings. He jotted on a sketch, "effect on the soul." He searched for corollary ideas to fill out the overriding idea. He called the first movement "Awakening of cheerful feelings on arriving in the country."[27] The city gives way to fields and woods; the feelings are rapturous. The listener is, say, riding in a cart, flowing into the beauty and the warmth, the timelessness, the holiness. The key would be F major, the same that Haydn used for pastoral movements in his oratorios. But the 2/4 tempo would not race — not like the Fifth. Everything the Fifth was, this would be the opposite.

The first movement will follow the usual outline with its themes, *Durchführung*, and so on. But no drama, no feverish excitement this time. No *fate*. Glorious sunshine, not even a passing cloud. No suffer-ing, no triumph, but fulfillment. Themes like folk tunes, a shepherd's pipe, flowing rhythms. Minor keys all but banished (only three bars in minor), scarcely even a minor chord. Most of it soft. A peaceful de-velopment.[28] Waves of exaltation passing over the soul. As Beethoven said: every tree and hill shouting, *Holy! Holy!* Ultimately it is to be about stepping into holiness, about beholding God.

For the slow movement he returns to the sketch from years before, trying to capture the sound of a brook in notes. He calls it "Scene by the brook." Flowing, babbling. A sense of endlessness: the first move-ment the arrival; the second movement the being there, the trance, the drifting ecstasy. Not a contrast to the first movement but a fulfillment of it. The warmth of low strings with divided cellos.

A symphony needs a scherzo or a minuet. Call this one a country dance in the outdoors, "Merry gathering of the countryfolk." A dance in the late afternoon, after work in the fields. He remembered an idea in 2/4, a quote or imitation of a country dance jotted in the sketchbook of the *Eroica*. That serves as a trio. He remembered a country band he saw at a dance, the oboist who couldn't find the downbeat, the sozzled bassoonist who kept dozing off and awoke now and then to blat out a few notes. They go into the scherzo.[29]

He had vowed to avoid pictures and events, but all the same there had to be a storm, a staple of the pastoral genres. This would be a good one for a change. He'd show them how violence was done, not like the polite primal "Chaos" in Haydn's *Creation* but rain and lightning and thunder. (Still, the storm in the "Summer" of Haydn's *Seasons* would be a model.)[30] Kant said that the works of God in the world are the visible sublime, but that we can conceive them only inside ourselves, as feeling. *Effect on the soul.* A *real* storm. All the harmonies unsettled. Bring in trombones!

But how would all this thunder and lightning fit into a symphony? A separate movement? That had been done a thousand times. What about this: *The storm interrupts the repeat of the scherzo,* as if it has broken up the dance and sent the peasants running for shelter. But how to make that work? What could make a transition from a jolly dance to raging chaos? Well, after all . . . a storm *happens.* There is no logical transition in God's nature, so why should Beethoven have to make a transition? The storm interrupts the form just as it interrupts the dance. The storm *breaks* the form.

For the last movement, the storm is over, the sun comes out, God smiles. Beethoven jotted on a sketch, "O Lord we thank thee," but the published version leaves that implicit.[31] "Shepherd's song. Happy and grateful feelings after the storm." The idyll returns. The folk emerge into the sunset with relief and thanks. He wouldn't make it the usual fast finale, and certainly not a heroic one. This called for thankfulness, not dancing. A prayer of thanks in the glow of the sunset after the storm. Start with an alpenhorn sounding in the distance, calling in the herds.[32] Not so slow as an *adagio,* but flowing and peaceful and beautiful, in 6/8, the old pastoral meter, almost all the movement in F major.

Now find the notes. Throughout the symphony he wanted listeners to sense the consuming beauty, peace, and holiness of the country, feel it not just in the senses but in the soul. The rhythms needed to be gently loping like a horse cart, or babbling like a brook. Long repetitions of figures as in the Fifth, but to the opposite end: there fierce and fateful, here a trance of beauty. Themes like folk songs and country dances. In the harmony use more peaceful subdominants than dynamic dominants. Let them feel the timelessness, hear the shepherd's pipe in the oboe. The sound of the orchestra spacious and warm, not hard and muscular like the Fifth or monumental like the *Eroica*. The feeling simple, flowing and piping and singing. Lots of woodwinds, not much trumpet. Save the trombones for the storm. The warmth of violas and divided cellos. Alpenhorn calls in the winds and horns. A portrayal of sensation and emotion without, however, the sensation of boredom. How to make the notes do these things, be that simple without boredom, was very, very difficult. Beethoven had always known this: the simpler, the harder. But difficult was good. Make it unmistakably pastoral but *new*.[33]

In terms something like these the *Pastoral* Symphony took shape, flowing from its fundamental idea: what Beethoven's time called a "character piece" and a later time called a "program piece." For him that meant not a detailed portrayal of episodes but broader scenes and feelings, as in his funeral marches, which were not marches in detail but moods (still, with trumpets and drums and cannons). Here the point was not to paint pictures (though in fact he painted them) but to bring the listener to a particular kind of reverie, an exaltation that he knew intimately. Years later he wrote in a diary, "My decree is to remain in the country . . . My unfortunate hearing does not plague me there. It is as if every tree spoke to me in the country, holy! holy! / Ecstasy in the woods! Who can describe it? If all comes to naught the country itself remains . . . Sweet stillness of the woods!"[34] And in a letter: "Surely woods, trees, and rocks produce the echo which man desires to hear." He meant an echo of all creation, a yearning for the divine.

These yearnings and intuitions rose from the Aufklärung, which saw nature as the revelation of the divine and science as the truest scripture. In that respect Beethoven had a more immediate inspiration for his ecstasies and his symphony in what may been his favorite and most-read book: *Reflections on the Works of God and His Providence Throughout All Nature.* Its author was Rev. Christoph Christian Sturm, a Lutheran theologian and preacher. Published first in 1785, Sturm's book was widely read, reprinted, and translated. In a series of 365 meditations, one for each day of the year, keyed to the seasons, Sturm tours much of the day's scientific knowledge while turning each entry into a little homily on the grace and goodness of God. For an example, here is Sturm's paean to the seasons:

> If we examine the works of God with attention, we shall find . . . many subjects which may lead us to rejoice in the goodness of the Lord, and to exalt the miracles of his wisdom. During the budding spring, the bountiful summer, and the luxuriant autumn, when Nature . . . assumes her gayest and most splendid robes, hardened and callous, indeed must be that heart which does not throb with pleasure, and pulsate with gratitude, for such choice gifts. But when the north wind blows, when a biting frost stiffens the face of the earth, when the fields . . . present one wild and desolating view, then it is that men . . . will sometimes forget to be grateful. But is it true that the earth at this season is so utterly destitute of the blessing of Heaven . . . ? Certainly not.

Sturm's inspirational perorations are boilerplate and his attitude relentlessly Panglossian: everything God has created is perfect and good, and only our blindness and ingratitude can picture it otherwise: "All the arrangements of thy Providence, however extraordinary they may appear to my feeble intellects, are full of wisdom and goodness." Still, Sturm's torrents of facts from science and natural history are thorough and up to date for his time:

> In the center of the planetary system, the Sun, more than a million times larger than our earth, and at the distance of 82 millions of miles, rolls his majestic orb, round which revolve seven planets with their attendant satellites, all deriving their luster from the central luminary . . . Of these, the nearest to the sun is Mercury; it is much smaller than

the earth, its diameter being only 2600 miles, and from its proximity
to the sun, round which it performs its course in eighty-eight days,
rolling at the rate of 95,000 miles an hour, is seldom visible to our eye.

In Sturm Beethoven read similar accounts of the planets and the universe, the discoveries of the microscope, the formation of minerals
and strata and fossils in the earth, the construction of the human eye
and ear and heart, how tides and earthquakes happen, how fog forms
and sap circulates, magnets, the structure and elements of blood, navi-
gation and sunspots and hair, the population of the earth, husbandry,
the lives of the bees, the forms of plants, the nature and properties of
sound and how it is transmitted by air, the statistics of infant mortal-
ity, the structure of comets, the span of the Milky Way, the harsh but
admirable lives of the Laplanders, the life of the herring, the marvels
of the lobster. In the book Beethoven read of resurrection but not of
damnation, nothing of miracle beyond the entire miracle of the universe. He read a survey of human anatomy that omits the generative
organs, as if they did not exist. He found a condemnation of astrology
not because it was heretical but because it was unscientific. He did not
find much moralizing as such.

Sturm's book amounts to a general education in the sciences in 365
lessons, a high-Aufklärung endeavor in practical knowledge. His essential message is the perfection of nature, every part and particle of
which is a revelation of God and a reason for rejoicing: "Wherever
we direct our attention, whether to examine the beautiful and grand
objects diffused over the face of nature, or whether to penetrate within
the interior of the earth, we perceive that every thing is arranged with
wisdom, and we everywhere discover the legible character and broad
stamp of an Infinite, Almighty, and Supreme Being." Sorrow and tumult are passing disturbances, themselves part of the divine order:
"When the storm and the tempest have threatened, how soon has light
been restored to the heavens, and joy and gladness again smiled on the
earth!" In those terms Beethoven's peasants rejoice in the finale of the
Pastoral Symphony. Ultimately, Sturm preaches, the whole of creation
is a sublime unity: "Every thing in the universe is connected together,
and concurs to the preservation and perfection of the whole." The mi-

crocosm of a musical form, Beethoven would surely have agreed, aspires to the divine unity of the macrocosm.[35]

Whether or not Sturm's treacly spirituality appealed to Beethoven, in its survey of science he gained a broad general education and an attitude toward the world, a vision of nature as divine revelation, as visible scripture and an endless hymn of praise: a holiness he found outside of scripture and churches. All this, fashioned in his own way as always, helped form the foundation of the *Pastoral* Symphony and a great deal of his music to follow.

But it was not all spiritual. It rarely is with an artist, least of all with Beethoven. The motivations galvanizing a work of art are a mingling of ideal and practical, spiritual and worldly, generous and competitive, high and low. With the Sixth Symphony Beethoven intended to show the world that Haydn, in *The Creation* and *The Seasons,* was not the only master of painting nature. Haydn was part of the inspiration for the *Pastoral,* in the sense that here, as in other works to the end of his life, Beethoven's rivalry with his teacher was part of his creative ferment. (Mozart haunted him. Haydn dogged him.) *Beethoven generally wrote in reaction to something.* Sometimes it was in reaction to the past in various ways; here it is in reaction to Haydn and the pastoral genre going back at least to Handel's "Pastoral Symphony" in *Messiah.* Sometimes Beethoven wrote in reaction to himself, as the Sixth is the anti-Fifth.

But he did not intend to show himself to the world as a tasteless hack. In those days cognoscenti deplored pictorial music, those stacks of battle pieces, nature pieces, and their dismal kin — all drivel as far as Beethoven was concerned, likewise Haydn's croaking frogs and crowing cocks in *The Seasons.* In the end Haydn himself had declared those pages of his oratorio "Frenchified trash." Beethoven's pupil Ries recalled, "He [Beethoven] frequently laughed at musical paintings and scolded trivialities of this sort. Haydn's *Creation* and *The Seasons* were frequently ridiculed."

He laid out the *Pastoral* Symphony in clear traditional forms — except where he needed to break those forms.[36] No pictures! Except for some pictures. As noted before, Beethoven was afflicted here with a certain aesthetic divide. He loved painting musical pictures, loved telling stories in music. Most of his overtures, including the ones to his own opera, outline the drama from beginning to end. His vocal music depicts nearly every illustratable image in his text. In other words, Beethoven loved doing things he considered to be tasteless, the kind of thing he laughed at in Haydn.

So he created the *Pastoral* trying to convince himself and the world that he was not doing what he was doing. His ambivalence is captured in prose jottings on the sketches: "One leaves it to the listener to discover the situation . . . Also without descriptions the whole will be perceived more as feeling than tone painting . . . Who treasures any idea of country life can discover for himself what the author intends . . . All tone painting in instrumental music loses its quality if it's pushed too far."[37] To underline his point he titled the Breitkopf & Härtel first edition "Pastoral Symphony or Recollection of Country Life, an expression of feeling rather than a description." Certainly in the end, though, he made his intended point, in part: feelings trump pictures.

The challenge of the *Pastoral* was to evoke timelessness and pastoral scenes without resorting to cliché more than necessary to establish the mood and the genre, and without eliciting boredom. Into that sense of timeless peace he intended to drop, virtually without preparation, the most violent and form-destroying music he knew how to write. So the voluminous sketches for the symphony, some of the most extensive for any of his works *(simple is hard)*, are in part a record of battle with himself. It was as if his sensibility refused to recognize what his hand was writing as it put down ideas and identified them: "thunder," "lightning," and eventually (a later idea) the carefully labeled birdcalls that end "Scene by the brook."[38] (The literalistic birdcalls interrupt the coda of the second movement just as the literalistic storm interrupts the scherzo.) The many sketches — probably done fast — also reflect the fact that much of the *Pastoral* depends on timing, on the most minute details. There would be many repetitions of figures, he decreed, but how many? (His teacher Christian Neefe had written an article on the uses and abuses of repetition in music.) How should the birdcalls be done, in what succession and juxtaposition? Pages of sketches are devoted to that issue. The birds he chose all have traditional symbolism:

the nightingale represents love, the cuckoo is the harbinger of summer, the quail associated with divine providence in the Bible.

In part he intended the *Pastoral* to challenge the nature scenes in
Haydn's oratorios, its storm to outdo Haydn's "Chaos." But his was a
covert battle waged not in the form of an oratorio but on Beethoven's
home ground, the symphony, and in the traditional formal outlines of
a symphony — including the storm, his own version of chaos to echo
and, he hoped, outdo Haydn's. And there was a larger, more spiritual
purpose. He had tried oratorio with *Christus am Ölberge,* and it had
not worked so well. He had written a quite-fresh Mass in C that he
loved, but of all his large works, it had been the hardest to sell and the
least liked. With the *Pastoral* he approached God from a new direction. Call the Sixth Symphony another experiment, not his last but his
most successful yet, toward a new kind of sacred music.

The Fifth and Sixth Symphonies are more direct in their personalities than the *Eroica* and in that respect closer to the public, popularistic tradition of the symphony. The Sixth was made to be embraced
and loved. Responses to the Fifth were less a matter of confusion than,
for those immune to it, of fear and outrage. Basing a movement on
a little motif was so outlandish that for years some took it as a joke
unbearably prolonged. Some found the emotional world of the Fifth
provocative and dangerous. For the many who thrilled to it, the Fifth
was the essence of revolutionary and Romantic élan. Yet nothing in
the Fifth Symphony contradicts Haydn and Mozart. Beethoven took
the essential nature and formal outlines of the symphony he inherited
and dramatized and intensified them, to a degree that might as well
be called revolutionary. But he continued his radical evolution from
within tradition.

The first *Allgemeine Musikalische Zeitung* review of the concert was
commonsensical, the critic realizing that he had heard only a vague
approximation of far too much music: "It is all but impossible to pro-
nounce judgment upon all of these works after a single first hearing,
particularly since we are dealing with works of Beethoven, so many
of which were performed one after another, and which were mostly
so grand and long ... In regard to the performances at this concert,

however, the concert must be called unsatisfactory in every respect."[39]
He goes on to describe the breakdown of the *Choral Fantasy*.

Soon enough, both symphonies triumphed, each in its own way.
The incomparable Fourth Concerto had another fate. It received in the
Allgemeine Musikalische Zeitung one of the most rapturous reviews of
Beethoven's life: "the most wonderful, unusual, artistic, and difficult
[concertos] of all those that B. has written . . . [the second movement
is] uncommonly expressive in its beautiful simplicity, and . . . the third
. . . rises up exuberantly with powerful joy."[40] Yet the concerto lay in
obscurity for a long time, mainly because Beethoven no longer played
his concertos, and virtuosos usually played their own. The performance of the Fourth and the improvisation of December 1808 mark
the close of Beethoven's two-decade career as a virtuoso.

In the case of the Fifth Symphony, so much involved with echoes
of French revolutionary style, history records two representative responses. In the midst of an early French performance, a soldier of
the Napoleonic Guard jumped up in the audience and cried, "C'est
l'empereur! Vive l'empereur!"[41] And the composer Jean-François
Lesueur, teacher of Berlioz, after the final chords emerged from the
hall so excited and upset that when he tried to put on his hat, he could
not locate his head.[42]

The concert of December 1808 marked the end of some eight years
of fertility hardly equaled in the history of human creative imagination. As of 1799, Beethoven had been a lionized young keyboard virtuoso whose boldest and best-known works were for solo piano and
chamber groups with piano — and his most celebrated performances
improvisations at the keyboard. In the eight years since then he had
finished six symphonies and the *Choral Fantasy,* four concertos,
eleven piano sonatas, nine string quartets, an opera, a mass, a collection of overtures, a variety of chamber music destined to live among
the most powerful and innovative works of their genres, and a stream
of other works from important to potboiling. In the process he had
transformed most of those genres: symphony, string quartet, concerto,
piano sonata, cello sonata, violin sonata, piano trio, and theme and
variations would all bear his thumbprints from then on. In achieving

that Beethoven had to overcome devastating disappointments in love, the assaults of painful and debilitating illness, and the steady decline of his hearing.

For centuries to come, careers, triumphs, failures, and myths would be founded on the man and musician Beethoven became between 1800 and 1808. The concert of 1808 drew another line in his life and work, and stands as a defining reason why the young Franz Schubert, one of the most profound born talents in the history of the art, groaned, "Who can do anything after Beethoven?" For Beethoven himself, a similar question loomed in 1808: *What now?*

23

Thus Be Enabled to Create

IN EARLY JANUARY 1809, Beethoven accepted the offer to become *Kapellmeister* of the court of Jérôme Bonaparte in Cassel.[1] He had always wanted to be a *Kapellmeister* like his grandfather and namesake, one of the few steady jobs available for a composer. But by now he knew he would probably not go to Cassel, if he ever actually wanted to in the first place. Instead, he was busily involved in plans to secure a permanent annuity from a collection of Viennese patrons. The idea, and the outline of the agreement, had originated with Beethoven himself and had been promoted by Baron Gleichenstein and Countess Erdödy. Its gist was that in return for staying in Vienna, Beethoven asked to receive a yearly sum simply for plying his trade as he saw fit. The amount he hoped to receive was roughly the same as he had been offered in Cassel.

Archduke Rudolph, the leading force in the agreement, was then twenty-one and about to become the most loyal, important, and demanding patron Beethoven ever had. As half brother of the reigning emperor Franz I, Rudolph was a prime catch. He had been reared with the usual princely curriculum of languages, court protocol, fencing, and dancing, but his passion was for music. Not satisfied with the palace music teacher, Rudolph began studying piano with Beethoven as early as 1804 (the exact date fell by the wayside), and he wanted to compose. By 1808, he had earned enough of Beethoven's gratitude to get the dedication of the Fourth Piano Concerto, the first of many dedications to him.

The archduke's health had always been delicate, and he suffered from the old Habsburg affliction of epilepsy. As a result, the chubby and good-natured youth had been directed away from the usual military career of men in the royal family. (His brother Archduke Karl was commander in chief of the Austrian army.) Rudolph chose the only other real option he had, the church. He took minor orders in 1805, at age seventeen, and gained the right of succession as archbishop of Olmütz. Rudolph's interest in music was another royal tradition, but he pursued it with unusual dedication. He could have succeeded to the archbishopric in 1811, but passed it up likely because he wanted to concentrate on his studies.[2] If it was considered proper for an archduke to amuse himself playing the piano and composing, however, there was no question of his becoming a professional musician. Rudolph was born into a family of emperors; that was his profession.

Rudolph assembled a music library that by 1814 had some 5,700 pieces by 825 composers, and it grew from there.[3] Early on he opened his library to Beethoven. Most likely Rudolph had met Beethoven at musicales in which he performed at Prince Lobkowitz's palace.[4] Visiting composer J. F. Reichardt heard Rudolph and was impressed both by his handling of Mozart and by his personality: "The Archduke is so modest and unassuming in his whole demeanor, and so informal, that it is easy to be near him."[5]

So this gentle brother of an emperor was the galvanizing figure, both with money and influence, in the initiative to keep Beethoven in Vienna. By early February 1809, the annuity agreement was in the polishing stage. Beethoven wrote his friend Baron Gleichenstein, "His Lordship Archduke Rudolph again wanted to insert a few more items such as and, but, and whereas — Please make the whole statement refer exclusively to the true practice of my art in a way that will suit me."

[margin note: 1 March 1809]

When Rudolph's *and*s and *but*s were in place, the formal contract was dated March 1. It begins,

> The daily demonstrations which Herr Ludwig van Beethoven gives of his extraordinary talent and genius as a musical artist and composer have aroused the desire that he may surpass the great expectations warranted by the experiences heretofore achieved.
>
> Since, however, it has been demonstrated that only a man as free from cares as possible can devote himself to one profession excluding all other occupations, and thus be enabled to create great and sublime works ennobling the arts, therefore the undersigned have come to a decision to place Herr Ludwig van Beethoven in the position wherein his most pressing requirements will not be of embarrassment to him, nor in any way inhibit his powerful genius.

[margin note: 4000 florins yr]

The undersigned were three: His Imperial Highness Archduke Rudolph, who guaranteed 1,500 florins per annum; the noble Prince Lobkowitz, who added 700; and the noble Prince Ferdinand Kinsky, who took the leading part at 1,800, all totaling 4,000 florins a year. This was not the kind of money one built palaces with, but it was some four times the salary of a middle-class civil servant. To it Beethoven could add fees from commissions, publications, and students. The stipend more or less made up, then, what he had lost in earnings for keyboard performances because of his encroaching deafness. Besides, in theory, the annuity was a reliable sinecure, while income from performing had always been dicey.

At the same time, for some unknown reason Beethoven expected soon to be named imperial *Kapellmeister*. He agreed that if he were so appointed, his salary at court would be deducted from the annuity. Probably understanding that this was not likely to happen, that Beethoven could never be a courtier and a composer on call, the sponsors agreed that "should such an appointment not come about" or if he were incapacitated, the stipend would continue for life. In return, Beethoven promised nothing except that he would not move out of Austria or travel out of the country without permission from the contracting parties.[6]

That Rudolph and Lobkowitz signed the contract is as expected. That the names of Razumovsky and several other important patrons are missing is surprising. Prince Lichnowsky contributed nothing, perhaps a sign of lingering tension over the fracas of 1806 that ended Lichnowsky's own annuity to Beethoven. Curiously, the largest share in the new annuity came from Prince Ferdinand Johann Nepomuk Kinsky. The contract of 1809 is the first surviving evidence of any connection between Beethoven and that prince. Nor is the then-twenty-seven-year-old Kinsky on record as being an active patron of musicians. He was an officer in the Austrian army. Soon after signing the contract he left town to fight the French and apparently forgot all about the annuity.[7]

At age thirty-eight, Beethoven had secured something few artists ever enjoy: a guarantee of a prosperous and independent life devoted to his work. It seemed almost too good to be true — and as it turned out, it was too good, too easy. After a brief period of elation, Beethoven sank into depression. His work began a long decline — less in quality than in quantity. He would never again approach the nearly superhuman level of production he had sustained since the Heiligenstadt crisis of 1802. And watching his annuity being eroded from a combination of happenstance, economics, and death, Beethoven would come to see the contract as a millstone around his neck.

Around this time Beethoven fell into in a wrangle with Countess Erdödy, one of the contract's first promoters. It was a fine mess of misunderstanding seasoned by Beethoven's paranoia. Since fall 1808, he had been living in rooms in her apartment. The cause of the fight is obscure, but it had to do with a male servant on the countess's staff who was working for Beethoven and whose income, it appears, she covertly supplemented. It may have been a matter as simple as Beethoven's offended pride that a patron would keep a servant on the job by adding to the salary he was paying. Given the mysteries of the countess, however, he may have suspected something more sinister. On a sketch of his current project, the Fifth Piano Concerto, he wrote in fury, "Beethoven is no servant. You wanted a servant, now you have one . . . Indeed you have gotten a servant in place of the master. What a replacement!! What a magnificent exchange!!!!" From that it seems he had concluded that the countess was paying the man for more intimate services than housework.[8]

Beethoven usually fled after these blowups, and so he did again. He took the first flat in Vienna he could find, which happened to be a residence on Walfischgasse that also sported a brothel. He began a torturous campaign to find a better apartment, Baron Zmeskall scouting places and getting himself tied up in Beethovenian knots.

Before long Beethoven was persuaded that Countess Erdödy had actually been bribing the servant so the man would put up with his troublesome employer. Beethoven felt, he wrote to Zmeskall, "compelled to believe in this generosity, but I refuse to allow it to be practiced any longer."[9] Erdödy duly received one of his apologies: "I have acted wrongly, it is true — forgive me. If I offended you, it was certainly not due to deliberate wickedness on my part — Only since yesterday evening have I really understood how things are; and I am very sorry that I behaved as I did — Read your note calmly, and then judge for yourself whether I have deserved it and whether you have not paid me back sixfold for all I have done . . . Do write just one word to say that you are fond of me again. If you don't do this I shall suffer infinite pain."[10] This had become his formula for telling people they were important to him, and for manipulating them: *Do what I ask or you will cause me pain.* Even though he and Erdödy were soon back on friendly footing, he did not move back into her comfortable flat, but in April he escaped the rooms over the brothel for a nicer place. Even when he took comfortable and elegant lodgings, however, he had a gift for turning them into depressing hovels.

He had hardly run out of bile. This winter he was also feuding with Carl, who remained, in practice, the most fractious of the Beethoven brothers. Ludwig wrote Johann, "If only God would give to our other worthy brother instead of his heartlessness — some feeling — he causes me an infinite amount of suffering. Indeed with my poor hearing I surely need to have someone always at hand." Married, working as a clerk in the Department of Finance, and with a young son, Carl had largely bailed out of serving as Beethoven's agent and lackey. The details of this friction are also obscure, but it may have stemmed from a set-to involving Stephan von Breuning, who had heard doubts about Carl's integrity from a colleague at the Ministry of War. Stephan told Ludwig, who told Carl, who pitched a fit with the originator of the story. Among the three of them, old wounds reopened.[11]

The blows kept coming. In this period Breuning, one of Beethoven's oldest friends, lost his young and talented wife of less than a year, Julie von Vering. Beethoven had been fond of Julie, often played piano duets with her, and dedicated to her the piano version of the Violin Concerto (the violin version is dedicated to Stephan). After Julie died, Beethoven wrote his friend Baron Gleichenstein, "I find it impossible to resist my impulse to tell you of my fears about Breuning's hysterical and feverish condition and at the same time to beg you so far as possible to attach yourself to him more closely . . . My circumstances allow me far too little time to discharge the supreme duties of friendship. So I beg you . . . to shoulder the burden of this anxiety which is really torturing me."[12] In other words, Beethoven was asking a proxy to do his consoling for him. Again, his main plea was based on the pain it caused him. Still, this amounted, in his fashion, to an act of kindness to Stephan.

Despite all this trouble, work on the Fifth Piano Concerto went well, perhaps marking a burst of creative energy after signing the annuity contract. Even with signs of war on the horizon, music in Vienna was bustling as usual. In early March, Beethoven's op. 69 Cello Sonata had its premiere, the cello played by Schuppanzigh's quartet-playing colleague Nikolaus Kraft, the piano by Baroness Dorothea von Ertmann. The baroness, probably once a pupil of Beethoven's, had become one of his favored keyboard interpreters.[13] His pet name for her was "Dorothea-Cäcilia," after the patron saint of musicians.[14] In one of his reports on the Viennese musical scene, J. F. Reichardt raved about Ertmann, "A lofty noble manner and a beautiful face full of deep feeling increase my expectation still further at the first sight of the noble lady; and then as she performed a great Beethoven sonata I was surprised as almost never before. I have never seen such power and innermost tenderness combined even in the greatest virtuosi; from the tip of each finger her soul poured forth . . . Everything that is great and beautiful in art was turned into song."[15] In those days women instrumentalists were still effectively banned from the public stage, but they were central to private musical life, which remained the most important avenue for chamber and solo music. As has been noted before, only once in Beethoven's lifetime was a sonata of his performed in public. And he valued a powerful champion when he heard one.

Ertmann was not in Beethoven's intimate circle, but there was an enormous respect and sympathy between them. At one point when she had lost a child, Beethoven invited her over, sat down at the piano, and said, "Now we will converse in music." For more than an hour he improvised for her. "He said everything to me," Ertmann later told Felix Mendelssohn, "and finally gave me consolation."[16] It must have been a heartrending scene, Beethoven making music for a bereaved woman who played and understood his work as well as anybody alive. He gave voice to her grief and offered her hope. Here was a microcosm of what all his music does: it captures life in its breadth of sorrow and joy, spoken to and for the whole of humanity. Beneath the paranoid, misanthropic, often unbearable surface, Beethoven was among the most generous of men.

Shortly after he signed the annuity contract in March 1809, Beethoven sent a copy to Gleichenstein and observed gaily,

> You will see from the enclosed document, my dear, kind Gleichenstein how honorable my remaining here has now become for me — Moreover the title of Imperial Kapellmeister is to follow . . . now you can help me look for a wife. Indeed you might find some beautiful girl at F[reiburg] where you are at present, and one who would perhaps now and then grant a sigh to my harmonies . . . If you do find one, however, please form the connection in advance — But she must be beautiful, for it is impossible for me to love anything that is not beautiful — or else I should have to love myself.[17]

In those days a man usually married only after settling into a profession. Beethoven was feeling relatively healthy and after the annuity relatively prosperous, so it was a natural time to think again of marriage. His flippancy quickly receded when he was faced with the reality of courtship and the discouraging prospect of what he really had to offer.

In Vienna the more pressing concern of March 1809 was Austria's latest declaration of war on France. Napoleon was at the zenith of his career, absolute dictator of his country and unrivaled on the battlefield. In 1806, he imposed the Continental System on his territories, the massive — and generally ineffective — blockade of Britain. He had neutralized the Russians by an arrangement with Tsar Alexander, and controlled most of the German states under the Confederation of the Rhine. His brother Louis ruled Holland; brother Jérôme, Westphalia; brother Joseph, Spain; and a stepson, most of Italy. Pope Pius VII had excommunicated Napoleon and stood as a powerful voice of resistance in Italy. To address that problem, in July 1809, French troops broke into the Vatican and kidnapped the pope. He was held in luxurious exile for five years.

The new coalition against the French joined Austria and Great Britain, with the support of occupied but rebellious Spain. A familiar story commenced. Once again the French army marched toward Vienna, once again the imperial family and much of the aristocracy packed up and fled. Among them was Archduke Rudolph. Beethoven drafted a sonata movement as an affectionate farewell, calling it *Das Lebewohl,* "The Farewell." He waited until after Rudolph returned to finish more movements.

As the French neared Vienna, Rudolph's brother Archduke Maximilian proposed to defend the city with sixteen thousand troops, one thousand conscripted students and artists, some militia, and other rags and tatters of forces. Reaching the walls of the city, the French demanded surrender. Maximilian declined. The French parked twenty howitzers on the heights of the Spittelberg and began shelling. Once again the Viennese sprinted for cover in vaults and cellars. Vienna had cannons on the bastions of the town, but apparently they never fired a shot. During the barrage, Beethoven retired to brother Carl's basement, where he huddled miserably with pillows over his ears as explosions lit up the city.

Meanwhile Napoleon ordered a bridge of boats over the Danube, and his troops entered town by way of the Prater park, outside the walls.[18] After a day's charade of resistance the white flag went up on the walls of Vienna. By May 13, Napoleon was back in his old headquarters in the emperor's summer palace at Schönbrunn. A Count Andréossy issued a proclamation to the Viennese: "An aggression as unjust as unforeseen, and the chances of war have brought before your eyes for the third time, the Emperor NAPOLEON, King of Italy, Protector of the Confederation of the Rhine . . . I shall prove myself to be faithful to his plans . . . striving incessantly for the maintenance of order, for the repression of all unjust acts, and in a word, for all that will assure your tranquility."[19] This second French occupation was again relatively gentle, unlike in Spain where the French met fierce resistance and atrocities were ongoing on both sides. In Vienna the French were quick to impose not only restrictions but pointed new freedoms. A newspaper notice said, "All persons who have forbidden books on deposit at the former Censorship Bureau may now claim them." Banned plays, including Schiller's *Don Carlos* and *Wilhelm Tell* and Goethe's *Egmont*, returned to the Viennese stage.[20]

There were relatively few casualties in the bombardment of Vienna. They included a perhaps delayed one. On May 12 a shell exploded outside Haydn's house with a concussion that shook the place and scared the wits out of his servants. The old man heaved himself up and cried defiantly, "Children, don't be frightened. Where Haydn is, nothing can happen to you!" But the shock left him prostrate. On May 26, in the new occupation, a French officer called and in a strong voice sang him an aria from *The Creation*. In tears, Haydn declared that he had never heard it sung so beautifully. Later that day he assembled the household and, at the piano, played for them, three times over, with all the passion he had left in him, his simple and eloquent Austrian anthem. The next day he took to bed, whispering, "Children, be comforted, I am well," and began to drift in and out of consciousness. Haydn died peacefully on May 31, at seventy-seven.[21] He had been an honorary member of the French Institute of Arts and Sciences, and many French soldiers and officers were in the funeral train. In the ceremonies at the Schottenkirche the music was the Requiem of his beloved friend Mozart.[22] Now, Beethoven was the only peer of Haydn alive. And only now did he begin to speak with admiration of his teacher.

. . .

During the occupation Beethoven was visited by a music-loving French diplomat, Baron de Trémont, who found the composer in a good mood. He reported the visit in a memoir. Before going to Vienna, he had asked Luigi Cherubini in Paris for a letter of introduction. "I will give you one to Haydn," Cherubini said, "and that excellent man will make you welcome, but I will not write to Beethoven. I should have to reproach myself that he refused to receive someone recommended by me. He is an unlicked bear!" Beethoven's once-inseparable Bonn friend Anton Reicha, now also in Paris, wrote a letter for Trémont but warned that Beethoven hated the French and was, moreover, "morose, ironical, misanthropic."

Once in Vienna, Trémont set out for the visit with little hope of success. To make things worse, when he reached Beethoven's street he found French troops trying to blow up stretches of the city walls under Beethoven's windows.[23] Neighbors gave the French officer directions but warned, "He is at home . . . but he has no servant at present, for he is always getting a new one, and it is doubtful whether he will open." After Trémont had rung Beethoven's bell three times and was about to give up, the door opened and "a very ugly man of ill-humored mien" asked what he wanted.

"Have I the honor of addressing M de Beethoven?" Trémont asked.

"Yes, Sir!" Beethoven answered in German. "But I must tell you that I am on very bad terms with French!" Hoping Beethoven meant the language, not the people, Trémont assured him that his German was equally bad. For some reason, Beethoven let him in. They spent the next hours talking pidgin German and French, the Frenchman shouting because of Beethoven's bad hearing. Trémont observed a good deal and wrote one of the most vivid firsthand descriptions of the Beethoven household style (worse than usual at that point because he had no servant):

Picture to yourself the dirtiest, most disorderly place imaginable — blotches of moisture covered the ceiling; an oldish grand piano, on which the dust disputed the place with various pieces of engraved and manuscript music; under the piano (I do not exaggerate) an unemptied chamber pot; beside it, a small walnut table accustomed to the frequent overturning of the secretary placed upon it; a quantity of pens encrusted with ink . . . then more music. The chairs, mostly cane-seated, were covered with plates bearing the remains of last night's supper, and with wearing apparel, etc.

Taken with this enemy diplomat or anyway intrigued by him, Beethoven invited Trémont back several times and spent hours improvising for him at the piano. "I maintain," Trémont recalled, "that unless one has heard him improvise well and quite at ease, one can but imperfectly appreciate the vast scope of his genius." They talked philosophy, Greek and Latin authors, and Shakespeare, "his idol." Trémont noted Beethoven's style of conversation, animated and full of singular conceits — always on, always thinking and shaping to his own designs: "Beethoven was not a man of *esprit,* if we mean by that term one who makes keen and witty remarks . . . His thoughts were thrown out by fits and starts, but they were lofty and generous, though often rather illogical."

Their conversations showed that Beethoven had never stopped thinking about the man whose name he removed from the Third Symphony: "His mind was much occupied with the greatness of Napoleon, and he often spoke to me about it. Through all his resentment I could see that he admired his rise from such obscure beginnings." The baron tried to get Beethoven to agree to a French visit, which he had the power to facilitate. Beethoven said he was tempted, but produced a row of objections that Trémont tried to answer. Finally, they shook hands on the promise of a visit. Then the baron's work took him away from Vienna for good, war continued, and Beethoven never got to France.[24]

In July 1808, Napoleon inflicted a devastating defeat on the Austrians at Wagram, smashing the fifth coalition against him. In an all-out battle between the two largest armies in European history, the Austrians lost fifty thousand killed or wounded. Having been lenient in his previous victories, with the ensuing Treaty of Schönbrunn Napoleon intended to cripple and humiliate this enemy that would not stay prostrate. He demanded a massive indemnity that would necessitate imposing new taxes on an Austrian population already reeling from inflation. Bits of Austria including Salzburg and the southern Tyrol were hacked off and taken over by France and its subject states. Austria was required to join the Continental System.

All this impacted everyone in the country, including artists. But inevitably some profited from the war, and that included Ludwig's brother Johann, who had spent his last florins to buy a pharmacy in Linz. He secured some contracts to furnish the French army with medical supplies and from them made a small fortune.

Still, in victory Napoleon did not unseat the Habsburgs. After all, now he was at the peak of his power and confidence, made emperor by his own hand, and really lacked only two things: a truly unshakable grip on the Continent, and an heir to take the throne of France. Napoleon's wife, Josephine, had been unable to conceive. He attacked both problems in a startling but characteristic way: he made himself part of the Habsburg family.

In 1810, having brought Austria to heel, Napoleon put Josephine aside and married Marie Louise, the eighteen-year-old daughter of Emperor Franz I. "I am marrying a belly," he observed with incomparable cynicism.[25] Already wed by proxy, Marie Louise arrived in Paris with three hundred attendants in eighty-three equipages. Napoleon all but raped her on the stairs leading up to the nuptial chamber. (He claimed that her response to this greeting was, "Do it again.") Yet somehow their union turned out affectionate. Marie Louise gave him the son he demanded, François Joseph Charles Bonaparte.

If Beethoven's response to the shelling, occupation, and military defeat of Austria was mostly related to himself, he was not entirely oblivious to the general suffering. Having finally succeeded in placing major works with Breitkopf & Härtel, he began writing Gottfried Härtel as if the publisher were a friend and confessor. After finishing the Fifth Piano Concerto in April, Beethoven found himself at loose ends. He wrote Härtel a long, rambling letter:

> You are indeed mistaken in supposing that I have been very well. For in the meantime we have been suffering misery in a most concentrated form. Let me tell you that since May 4th I have produced very

little coherent work, at most a fragment here and there . . . The existence I had built up only a short time ago rests on a shaky foundation — and even during this last short period I have not yet seen the
promises made to me completely fulfilled — So far I have not received
a farthing from Prince Kinsky, who is one of my patrons . . . What
a destructive, disorderly life I see and hear around me, nothing but
drums, cannons, and human misery in every form . . . I had begun to
have a little singing party at my rooms every week — but that accursed
war put a stop to everything.[26]

At the singing parties he and his friends had been going through
repertoire, Beethoven looking not only for pleasure but for ideas. In
the letter he asks Härtel for scores from the publisher's catalog and offers to pay for them — whatever Härtel has of Haydn's masses. He asks
Härtel to send greetings to a writer he admires, adding, "One thing
more: there is hardly a treatise which could be too learned for me. I
have not the slightest pretension to what is properly called erudition.
Yet from my childhood I have striven to understand what the better
and wiser people of every age were driving at in their works. Shame
on an artist who does not consider it his duty to achieve at least as
much —" There is no exaggeration in that. He had always sought out
the best of its kind, in every medium.

Instead of the regular and comfortable income Beethoven had
hoped for from the annuity, his patchwork career continued. He sent
the finished score of the Fifth Piano Concerto to Breitkopf & Härtel
in April 1809, and in November received new editions from the same
publisher of the Fifth and Sixth Symphonies and the op. 70 Trios. (He
found everything distressingly error-ridden.) Meanwhile, another
publisher stepped up with an offer of piecework not extravagantly paid
but at least steady. Scottish publisher George Thomson, having stalked
Beethoven for years, sent him forty-three mostly Welsh and Irish folk
songs that Beethoven had agreed to arrange, including preludes and
postludes and parts for optional violin and cello. Thomson noted in
his letter that he had sent twenty-one melodies to Beethoven nearly
three years before but had no idea whether they were received.

Likely what most appealed to Beethoven about the folk-song settings was the idea of something regular in the midst of his freelance uncertainties, which were particularly unpleasant at this point. Prince Kinsky had not paid his part of the annuity (his being the largest contribution), and Beethoven still had not been paid for the six pieces Clementi published three years before. Clementi was outraged about the delay, writing his business partner, "A most shabby figure you have made me cut in this affair! — and with one of the foremost composers of this day!"[27] Beethoven finally received his money from Clementi in 1810.[28]

Besides the attractiveness of steady work for Thomson, Beethoven clearly enjoyed these Welsh, Scottish, and Irish tunes, all of which he generally referred to as "Scottish." They gave him a supply of classic melodies to work with, and like anything else musical, they might serve as grist for the mill. When it came to sheer beauty and facility, his melodic gift was not the equal of Mozart's and Handel's, at least, and with his fine judgment he may have understood that. But eventually melody was going to have to carry more weight in his work than it had before. The folk-song arrangements helped him along in that direction.

In his letter Thomson offered 100 ducats (over 500 florins) for the forty-three airs, plus 120 ducats more for three quintets for varied instruments and three violin sonatas. Nothing came of the latter commission. Thomson added a caution that was to become an invariable refrain: "I permit myself the liberty to request that the composition of the accompaniment for the piano to be the most simple and easy to play, because our young ladies, when singing our national airs, do not like and hardly know how to play a difficult accompaniment."[29] Beethoven had written plenty of music playable by young ladies of modest skill, including the first movement of the *Moonlight* Sonata, but he had never done it to order. He replied patiently but firmly to Thomson: "You are dealing with a true artist who likes to be paid honorably, but who likes glory and also the glory of art even more — and who is never content with himself and tries always to go further and make yet greater progress in his art." He got to work on the songs right away but did not finish them until the next year. He finally sent the lot in July 1810, noting in his cover letter that he had done them "con amore."[30] Perhaps. In any case, many of his accompaniments did prove too hard for the young ladies who were Thomson's main concern.

Beethoven had every reason to worry about money. In Vienna prices had inflated some 300 percent in the last years. War taxes and requisitions affected everybody, and there was little hope of relief.[31] In addition to taking on this piecework in a time of mounting financial catastrophe in Austria, Beethoven decided to reduce his expenses by eating at home rather than in restaurants. This would entail hiring an extra servant as cook. Restaurant food was relatively cheap, but servants were cheaper. Beethoven wrote Zmeskall, "Cursed tipsy Domanovetz — not count of music, but Count of gluttony — Count of dinner, Count of supper and the like . . . I must have someone to cook for me, for as long as our food continues to be so bad, I shall always be ill." (He was suffering from abdominal miseries that went on for weeks.)[32] A couple briefly and unhappily worked for him, the husband doing the chores and the wife the cooking. Before long he was writing Zmeskall, who had handled their pay, "I simply cannot see that woman at my rooms again; and although she is perhaps a little better than he is, I don't want to hear anything more about either of them . . . Both of them are wicked people."[33] This period marks the beginning of an endlessly frustrating search, which lasted to the end of his life, for servants whom he found to be other than contemptible.

Creatively speaking, war-troubled 1809 was not the nearly wasted year Beethoven declared it, even if his output was modest by his standards of the last eight years. Quick on the heels of completing the *Emperor* Concerto, at Baden in the fall, he finished the gentle and agreeable String Quartet in E-flat Major and six songs, op. 75, that he dedicated to Princess Caroline Kinsky, wife of the benefactor who was too busy at war to see to his part of the annuity. Also in this year Beethoven finished four piano works including his first sonatas since the epic *Appassionata* of 1805.

Around the end of 1809, Beethoven spent a good deal of time collecting instructional material to use for Archduke Rudolph's lessons in piano, theory, and composition. Beethoven had a broad knowledge of the musical theoretical literature. Now he put together a thick pile of material including works of his old teacher Albrechtsberger; of Fux, who devised the study of counterpoint in species; of the theorist and

J. S. Bach disciple Kirnberger; and from the classic *True Art of Clavier Playing,* by C. P. E. Bach.[34] For the archduke, the only student he had left, he intended to be as good a pedant as Albrechtsberger.

Rudolph was not only the most generous and loyal patron of Beethoven's life but also the most powerful. Beethoven was determined not to estrange an important patron again. If he was resentful of the demands on his time, if he was careless about proper etiquette in visiting the residence of the archduke (who told his servants to ignore it), Beethoven would, as best he could, humble himself when appropriate. There would be no blowups between them, something that could be said of few people in Beethoven's life. In that regard it helped that Rudolph was one of the less imperious examples of his class. It also helped that he had some talent, more than most students. With Beethoven's coaching and meticulous editing, he eventually produced a trickle of respectable work.

How much of Beethoven's relations with Rudolph rose from fondness and how much from calculation is impossible to untangle. After Rudolph returned to town with the royal family, at the end of January 1810, Beethoven finished the three-movement sonata he called *Das Lebewohl,* "The Farewell," and presented the archduke with the manuscript inscribed to him: "The Farewell, Vienna, May 4, 1809, on the departure of his Imperial Highness the revered Archduke Rudolph," and at the finale, "The Arrival of His Imperial Highness the revered Archduke Rudolph, January 30, 1810."[35]

The *Lebewohl* had been preceded by two relatively low-key but not inconsiderable piano sonatas. Surrounded by war and occupation and bedeviled by digestive miseries toward the end of 1809, Beethoven did not try to outdo the *Appassionata,* which he called his best sonata, but produced some works of youthful, almost dewy freshness. Creatively, he had begun a period of marking time, but marking time at the height of his powers.

In this period he also fulfilled Muzio Clementi's commission for a piano fantasia. The one-movement Fantasia, op. 77, begins with two startling swoops down the keyboard, like the clusters of notes Beethoven sometimes smashed out before beginning an improvisation. The swoops return as a kind of curtain device in a work of playful and enigmatic charm. The key is given as G minor, that being more or less where it starts, but the Fantasia goes through a patchwork of keys and ideas and ends up with a long stretch of quasi-variations in B major. The capricious spirit of C. P. E. Bach hovers in the background. For Beethoven this potpourri also might have represented a portrait of his scattered life at the time. In any case, it does what a fantasia is supposed to do, which is to be exploratory and quasi-improvisational.

Beethoven still had his French Érard. Though he had paid twice, without success, to have its touch lightened to the style of Viennese pianos, he still appreciated the more robust sound of the Érard, which was close to the sound of British pianos. He had been leaning on local piano maker Streicher to depart from the more delicate Viennese build and sound. Wrote J. F. Reichardt, "Streicher has abandoned the soft, overly responsive, bouncing, and rolling [character] of the other Viennese instruments and — upon Beethoven's advice and request — has given his instruments more resistance and elasticity in order to enable the virtuoso . . . to have more control over the instrument's sustaining and carrying [power], and for the subtle emphases and diminuendos."[36] Behind England and France as usual, and with Beethoven's prodding, Vienna took another belated step toward the future, in this case the future of an instrument.

At some opposite extreme from the Fantasia is the tightly woven op. 78 Sonata, in two movements and in the eccentric and finger-tangling key of F-sharp major. With the music as evidence, for Beethoven this key possessed great charm and melting tenderness. The dedication to Therese Brunsvik, the more ascetic sister of Beethoven's hopeless love Josephine, might explain some of its singular spirit. It begins with four *adagio cantabile* measures that are part introduction, part a source of motivic material, part an almost prayerful meditation that inflects everything that follows, starting with the wistful and flowing theme of the Allegro non troppo. The second theme is largely butterfly flutters. Both movements make their points succinctly and exquisitely and move on. In the second movement, alternately dashing and absurdly chirping, Czerny saw wit and childlike mischief.[37] Beethoven was fond of this sonata, not because it was heroic or ambitious but because it was unique — "really something different," he said.

He preferred it to the *Moonlight,* which lies in the equally eccentric key of C-sharp minor.

Like the two sonatas of op. 49 from ten years before, the three-movement Sonatine in G Major, op. 79, is nominally a short, attractive, reasonably easy outing for amateurs. But for Beethoven, simple in 1809 is not the same thing as it was ten years before: there is more depth, more personality, more quirkiness, and it's not all that easy to play. A folksy mood predominates. The first movement is a vivacious and headlong Presto alla tedesca, a *tedesca* being a fast German dance in triple time. The second movement, in G minor, is a sort of song without words, like an aria in a "Turkish" opera, the melodies exotic and infectious. The last movement is a breezy, charming, finally laugh-out-loud rondo Vivace.

His piece for Archduke Rudolph, *Das Lebewohl,* op. 81a in E-flat Major, is one of the few overtly autobiographical works of Beethoven's life. It can be added to the list of his "characteristic" pieces and to his responses to E-flat major that depart from a heroic tone. The sonata forms a simple story of departure, absence, and return, each movement so labeled in the manner of the *Pastoral* Symphony, but the music is not as ingenuous as the *Pastoral.* In any case, what on the surface appears to be an occasional work for a patron becomes a distinctive form, a narrative that as always with Beethoven is addressed not just to a particular occasion but to the ages. The music is inspired by the story, but the story does not entirely generate the music.[38]

The atmosphere and the pianism of op. 81 are as individual as in any of his sonatas. It begins with a solemn three-note horn call. So we can't miss the point, Beethoven writes over these notes *Le-be-wohl.* After a poignant and searching *adagio* introduction a pealing Allegro breaks out, everything pervaded with the *Lebewohl* motif.[39] We can interpret the movement, if we like, as the bustling preparations for a journey. The sadness of departure arrives with the coda, which ends with fading farewells echoing into the distance, the harmonies overlapping in a singular way, like horn calls echoing across a valley.

Next comes "Absence," with its trancelike atmosphere, sorrow and hope locked in an unresolved cycle that can be broken only by "The Return," which serves as finale. It starts with a jubilant shout of greeting that takes up and embroiders the *Lebewohl* motif, then sinks to a calm joy expressed in brilliant and inventive piano sonorities. Echoing the end of the first movement, the coda has a wonderful warmth, with echoes of the farewell motif resolved into the settled happiness of reunion.

History would mostly remember op. 81a with a French title, *Les adieux,* because Breitkopf & Härtel first published it that way. Beethoven was put out about the change. To Härtel he made an insightful linguistic point, noting that the German farewell is more intimate and significant than the French: "I have just received the 'Lebewohl' and so forth. I see that after all you have published other c[opies] with a French title. Why, pray? For 'Lebewohl' means something quite different from 'Les Adieux.' The first is said in a warm-hearted manner to one person, the other to a whole assembly, to entire towns."[40] Here was another small battle with a publisher in which Beethoven was entirely in the right, and which he lost.

After this effusion of solo piano music in 1809–10, he put away sonatas for another five years.

Another product of 1809, a year Beethoven said in June was producing only "a fragment here and there," was the warm and ingratiating String Quartet in E-flat Major, op. 74, eventually dubbed the *Harp* for its striking pizzicatos. For some reason Beethoven had gotten stuck on E-flat major. Between 1809 and early 1811, he wrote four major works in that key: the *Emperor* Concerto, *Harp* Quartet, *Lebewohl* Sonata, and *Archduke Trio.* Only the *Lebewohl* carried Beethoven's own title, and none of the pieces are in a "heroic" E-flat major.

The *Harp* begins with a gentle, flowing introduction, harmonically and metrically wandering but untroubled, that keeps turning up a foreign D-flat in the middle of what purports to be E-flat major. Here is a "sore" note, the same pitch as in the *Eroica* Symphony, also important to the *Serioso* Quartet, that will again have its resonances. But in keeping with the untroubled mood of this quartet, it is not a *particularly* sore note. A forthright Allegro breaks out with an eighteenth-century atmosphere, until the transition to the second theme injects some pizzicatos rare for the time in being in the foreground of the music rather than an accompaniment.[41] As with the first two piano sonatas of the year, the exposition and whole first movement are compact and without formal or, for that matter, emotional ambiguities.

Beethoven made the opening movement gracious, elegant, beautiful, but not in the vein of the Beautiful as an aesthetic study. Here beauty is as unassuming as everything else in the music. It is that quality which makes the *Harp* fresh in Beethoven's work in general and his quartets in particular, especially compared to the aggressively radical *Razumovskys*. All the same, he remains determined to give every piece not only distinctive material but also a distinctive sonority. The pizzicatos are a way to do that simply and directly, and they were unusual enough to give a name to the quartet. After a cheery and only modestly eventful development and fairly literal recapitulation (though the pizzicatos are extended), there comes a surprise in the form of an enormous coda that starts with frenetic and exciting cross-string fiddling from the first violin while the main theme surges beneath; then comes a section of accelerating pizzicatos. In other words, as usual with Beethoven, the pizzicatos are not just a color or a passing fancy but a motif to be developed and paid off.

In his music he was searching, so he would not have known yet that one of the places he was headed toward was a poignant and broad songfulness like the Adagio ma non troppo second movement. Its key is A-flat and the key of its second section D-flat, both echoes of the D-flat in the introduction to the first movement. The main point of the second movement is to present its long, lovely melody and two ornamented versions of it, spaced by two equally lyrical and barely contrasting sections. The contrast comes with the scherzo, marked Presto, one of his most boisterous C-minor excursions, more delicious than demonic. Its exhilarating rhythmic thrust comes from a nimble alternation of three-beat (2+2+2) and two-beat (3+3) within the bar. The scherzo section alternates with a manically contrapuntal C-major trio, marked *più presto quasi prestissimo*, that comes back twice.[42]

The movement finishes with a preparatory chord that instead of ending the scherzo ushers in the finale. The fact that this is a work more conciliatory than provocative finds its denouement in Beethoven's only variation finale in a quartet. Its theme is a bouncy little Allegretto of unpretentious charm. His variations do not play Haydn's game of inflating a modest tune into something grand but rather ornament the theme in six simple and graceful variations. The end becomes suddenly playful, then ebullient, and finally *fortissimo*, only to pull back to a quiet and once again modest departure.

All this is to say that the *Harp* Quartet is another work, like the piano sonatas that preceded it, that is no lapel grabber, that for all its freshness smacks of nothing "revolutionary." This and the other pieces of 1809–10 were intended not to make strides but to bide time. Moreover, in the procession of his quartets, Beethoven may have wanted to give the public and musicians a rest after the strenuous workout of the *Razumovskys*.

The absence of great strides, meanwhile, is a symptom of what may have been coming over him in this period, when he had a nominally guaranteed income and was expected to repay it by surpassing himself. For the first time in some nine years, after a series of extraordinary effusions, Beethoven no longer knew as clearly as he once had what direction he was headed in. His situation may have been worse than that. He may have begun to wonder not only where he was headed but why he was headed anywhere at all. Still, the subtle and unassuming *Harp* would not be his only musical response to his situation. His next quartet boils with fury.

In letters of April 1810, Beethoven made three, for him startling, requests. He asked Zmeskall for the loan of a looking glass, because his was broken. He sent Baron Gleichenstein 300 florins for shirts and neckcloths, to be picked out by the baron. "Not only do I understand nothing whatever about such matters" of fashion, he wrote, "but also such matters are very distasteful to me."[43] Around the same time, he wrote Wegeler in Bonn asking for a copy of his baptismal certificate. Here were signs and portents that, once again, Beethoven was courting.

And once again, the object of his affections was young, attractive, musical, and above his station. She was Therese Malfatti, seventeen, one of two strikingly beautiful daughters of a wealthy and cultured family. Gleichenstein had introduced Beethoven to Jakob Friedrich Malfatti von Rohrenbach zu Dezza and his family in February. Jakob was cousin to Beethoven's new physician, Johann Malfatti, who had taken over this difficult patient after the death of Beethoven's long-time doctor Johann Schmidt. Even though Beethoven was more than twenty years older than Therese and chronically ill, in visits to the family he was quick to fall for this lively and talented girl. He hoped his art and fame, in lieu of looks and charm, might bring her to him.

This time, however, his courtship would not be the near-crazed whirlwind of passion he inflicted on Josephine Deym. He used Gleichenstein as a go-between and proceeded cautiously. He sent Therese music, writing to the baron, "Here is the s[onata] which I promised Therese. — As I cannot see her today, do give it to her — My best regards to them all. I am so happy when I am with them. I feel somewhat that the wounds which wicked people have inflicted on my soul could be cured by the Malfattis. Thank you, kind G, for introducing me to that house — Here are another 50 gulden for the neckcloths. Let me know if you need more."[44]

He became a regular visitor to the Malfatti house, sporting his new neckcloths and shirts, his hair combed carefully in his new mirror. They could not have been long in realizing what was going on. In May he wrote to Therese, who was in Mödling on her family's estate. He enclosed a piece he wrote especially for her. His tone is tender and avuncular:

In this letter, beloved Therese, you are receiving what I promised you. And indeed, if the most powerful obstacles had not prevented me, you would be receiving still more, if only to show you that I always <u>do more for my friends than I promise</u> . . . No doubt I should be counting too much on you or valuing my worth too highly if I were to apply to you the saying [from Goethe's *Egmont*], "People are united not only when they are together; even the distant one, the absent one too is present with us." Who would apply such a saying to our volatile T who treats so lightheartedly all the affairs of life? — In connection with your pursuits be sure not to forget the pianoforte or, in general, music as a whole. You have such a splendid gift for music, why don't you cultivate it seriously? You who have so much feeling for all that is beautiful and good, why will you not direct it to discerning in such a glorious art what is fine and perfect, a quality which in its turn ever radiates beauty upon us? — I am leading a very lonely and quiet life. Although here and there certain lights would like to awaken me, yet since you all left Vienna, I feel within me a void which cannot be filled and which even my art, which is usually so faithful to me, has not yet been able to make me forget.[45]

He had picked out a piano for her. He recommends to her Goethe's *Wilhelm Meister* and Schlegel's translations of Shakespeare. He asks her to "forget my mad behavior." He asks whether he might visit her, if only for a half hour: "You see that I want to bore you for as short a time as possible." The piece he had written for her is a wistful and yearning A-minor tune he called simply *Für Elise,* that presumably being her pet name.[46] Beethoven would have been astounded and probably outraged to know that eventually this little courtship item became one of the most famous things he ever wrote.

Maybe Therese did, as he had put it, grant a sigh to his harmonies. But the courtship was soon suppressed. The Malfattis were not high nobility, but they were too high for Beethoven to marry into without consequences, and exquisite young Therese was hardly likely to feel an attraction for this middle-aged, unhandsome, deaf, ill, and eccentric suitor, no matter how famous. In any case her parents would never give consent. Beethoven had planned to go to the Malfattis and propose to Therese, but he didn't have the courage to face her eyes looking at him.[47] Instead he asked Baron Gleichenstein to sound out the family (actually, the baron was courting Therese's younger sister Anna, whom he eventually married). Gleichenstein's report does not survive, but Beethoven's anguished reply to him does:

Your news has again plunged me from the heights of the most sublime ecstasy down into the depths — And why did you add the remark that you would let me know when there would be music again? Am I then nothing more than a music-maker for yourself or the others? . . . Well, so be it. For you, poor B[eethoven], no happiness can come from outside, you must create everything for yourself in your own heart; and only in the world of ideals can you find friends — I beseech you to set my mind at rest by letting me know whether I was to blame yesterday. Or if you cannot do that, tell me the truth. I am as glad to hear it as I am to speak it.[48]

He had been somehow egregious around the Malfattis, or perhaps all he had done was to declare himself to Therese or her parents. Their response was apparently to forbid him from visiting the house except as a performer.[49] He was plunged to the depths, lovesick, also physically sick with violent attacks of vomiting. As always, he stumbled on. He finished a commissioned overture and vocal solos for Goethe's *Egmont*, whose Vienna production was recently unbanned thanks to the French occupation, but his music came too late for the opening. He went on to a trilogy of songs on Goethe lyrics: *Wonne der Wehmut, Sehnsucht*, and *Mit einem gemalten Band*.

In the fall Stephan von Breuning wrote Wegeler in Bonn not to worry that Beethoven didn't thank him for finding the birth certificate: "I believe his marriage project has fallen through."[50] Beethoven wrote Gleichenstein ruefully, "You are either sailing on a calm and peaceful sea or are already in a safe haven [the engagement to Anna Malfatti], — You do not feel the anguish of a friend who is struggling against a tempest . . . My pride is humbled."[51] In the letter asking for his birth certificate he had written Wegeler, "Who can escape the onslaughts of tempest raging around him? Yet I should be happy, perhaps one of the happiest of mortals, if that fiend had not settled in my ears — If I had not read somewhat that a man should not voluntarily quit this life so long as he can still perform a good deed, I would have left this earth long ago — and what is more, by my own hand — Oh, this life is indeed beautiful, but for me it is poisoned forever." In the letter to Wegeler he notes that "I lived for a while without knowing how old I was." But in fact he was still wrong about his age.[52]

Ultimately Beethoven could live with bad health and without love, but all the new tempests were heaped on top of the humiliating fiend in his ears. Thoughts of suicide were again eating at his mind. It was inevitable that he would be depressed about this new collapse of his romantic dreams. There is no record of friends helping him through this convulsion of despair. "Only in the world of ideals," he wrote Gleichenstein wretchedly, "can you find friends." The next years show that in music he was searching for some new path and not finding it, though his production ran strong for a while, if not nearly as voluminous as it had been. In the wake of one more romantic failure he desperately needed new reasons to live — which is to say, new reasons to make music.

The sketchbooks of the years after 1808 suggest that now Beethoven was having more and more trouble getting pieces off the ground.[53] Yet as of 1810, his star was high and rising. "Every day," he wrote Zmeskall with a mingling of pride and bitterness and a strange humility, "there are fresh inquiries from foreigners, new acquaintances, new circumstances connected with my art . . . Sometimes I feel that I shall soon go mad in consequence of my unmerited fame, fortune is seeking me out and for that very reason I almost dread some fresh calamity."[54] The last calamity, presumably, was Therese, though his health was also bedeviling him: fevers, headaches, a crippling foot problem, on top of his chronic vomiting and diarrhea and the demon in his ears.

It was that year when his music finally found a reviewer equal to it. Ernst Theodor Amadeus Hoffmann was a critic, composer, painter, and in his later years creator of fantastical tales that made him one of the most celebrated German authors. Hoffmann wrote operas and after he died had an opera written about him, *Tales of Hoffmann*. He had changed his name to include Mozart's middle one. In all capacities he was a defining voice of the Romantic spirit. His two *Allgemeine Musikalische Zeitung* articles of July 1810 on Beethoven's Fifth Symphony live in history as the first important exposition of the Romantic sense of music. Which is to say that they were the first major steps in turning Beethoven the man and musician into Beethoven the demigod and myth. Here the Fifth Symphony itself ascended to the realm of archetype. Here appears the Romantic conception of instrumental music in particular as the supreme art, not in spite of its indefinable nature but because of it.

Part of the myth-making drive of the Romantics was to make myths of themselves. The Romantic era was the first cultural-aesthetic period in history to name itself. Many of Hoffmann's critical writings are concerned with the question of what is, and who is, Romantic. In his review of the Fifth all these elements of Hoffmann's personality and ideas, including his distinctive jumble of the factual and the fabulous, are extravagantly on display. He was yet to write the literary fantasies that established his fame, but these articles were among the most influential writings of his life.

He begins with a couple of pages about music in general that laid the foundation for the century's dominating myth of Beethoven as the archetypal genius:

> The reviewer has before him one of the most important works of that master whom no one will now deny belongs among the first rank of instrumental composers. He is permeated by the topic that he is to discuss, and no one may take it amiss if, stepping beyond the boundaries of the customary critique, he strives to put into words what this composition made him feel deep within his soul.
>
> When music is being discussed as a self-sufficient art, this should always be understood to refer only to instrumental music, which, disdaining all help, all admixture of any other art, purely expresses the peculiar essence of this art . . . [Instrumental music] is the most Romantic of all the arts — one almost wishes to say the only one that is *purely* Romantic. Orpheus's lyre opened the gates of the underworld. Music reveals an unknown kingdom to mankind: a world that has nothing in common with the outward, material world that surrounds it, and in which we leave behind all predetermined, conceptual feelings in order to give ourselves up to the inexpressible . . .
>
> The magical power of [instrumental] music works like the wondrous elixir of the wise, by means of which various mysterious ingredients make every drink delicious and magnificent. Every passion — love — hate — anger — despair etc., . . . is clothed by music in the purple shimmer of Romanticism, and even that which we experience in life leads us out beyond life into the kingdom of the infinite . . .
>
> The expression of a childlike, happy soul dominates in Haydn's compositions. His symphonies lead us into a vast, green meadow, into a joyous, colorful crowd of fortunate people. Youths and maidens glide by in round dances; laughing children, listening beneath trees,

beneath rose bushes, teasingly throw flowers at each other. A life full of love, full of blessedness, as though before sin, in eternal youth ... Into the depths of the spirit kingdom we are led by Mozart. Fear surrounds us: but, in the absence of torment, it is more a foreboding of the infinite. Love and melancholy sound forth in charming voices, the power of the spirit world ascends in the bright purple shimmer, and we follow along in inexpressible longing behind the beloved forms ... flying through the clouds in the eternal dance of the spheres ...

In this way, Beethoven's instrumental music also opens up to us the kingdom of the gigantic and the immeasurable. Glowing beams shoot through this kingdom's deep night, and we become aware of gigantic shadows that surge up and down, enclosing us more and more narrowly and annihilating everything within us, leaving only the pain of that infinite longing ... Beethoven's music moves the lever controlling horror, fear, dread, pain, and awakens that infinite longing that is the essence of Romanticism.[55]

Hoffmann goes on to print snippets of the Fifth Symphony with commentary in the manner of the time, citing the ideas with little attempt at analysis. Analysis and niceties of craftsmanship were not high-Romantic concerns. But Hoffmann does note, citing the first bars, "The beginning of the Allegro [the first 21 bars] determines the character of the entire piece," and he observes without giving examples that "it is primarily the intimate relationship that the individual themes have to one another that produces that unity that holds the listener's soul firmly in a *single* mood." He cites the "terrifying effect" of the mysterious whispers in the retransition to the recapitulation. Terror, longing, spirits, and the infinite make regular appearances. By the end, he promises, the listener "will not be able to depart from the wonderful spirit kingdom, where pain and joy surrounded him in musical form."

Beethoven surely read those words, as he appears to have read everything he could find about himself, especially in the *Allgemeine Musikalische Zeitung*. Hoffmann's prose fantasia was unlike anything Beethoven had seen written about his music, hardly like anything he could have read about any music. Beethoven was a man of the Aufklärung, the age of reason, used to thinking in concrete terms. Now he was confronted with what amounted to a manifesto of a new age that rejected reason, a manifesto that happened to be inspired by his art. He read about the inexpressible, about unknown kingdoms, the bright purple shimmer of Romanticism, the dance of the spheres, infinite longing, the lever of horror and fear. All of them were called part of his music. What was he to think?

In the Romantic century instrumental music was going to take center stage as the supreme art, and Beethoven's music was going to be central to that process. When he read Hoffmann's words Beethoven could not have understood much of this, at least not yet. But he had to be interested in Hoffmann's reviews, because they were the most admiring and by far the most imaginative ones he had ever received, and in the most important musical journal in Europe. It set forth a brave new world of some kind that he had helped create. And he tended to appreciate it when his poetry in tones inspired poetic responses, especially when they outstripped his own few and fumbling words about music.

For Beethoven Hoffmann's fantasies may have been the first clues pointing toward a second New Path, for which he did not yet know he was searching. At the height of the Aufklärung, Christian Neefe and others had taught him that instrumental music should paint characters, emotions, scenes, implicit but coherent dramas. Beethoven had always written his works at the service of images and stories, though he usually kept those models to himself. Hoffmann provided him a clue that instrumental music did not have to be so specific, so definable. Maybe "the inexpressible" and "infinite longing" were qualities worth capturing, just as worthy as the Aufklärung's Good, True, and Beautiful. That, in any event, was the direction Beethoven was headed. It lay years ahead, on the other side of great acclaim and great suffering.

It was in the middle of his courtship of Therese Malfatti and just before Hoffmann's articles appeared that Beethoven met another avatar of the zeitgeist who was destined for fame. Even better, Bettina Brentano was a dazzling young woman, and she worshiped Genius.

24

Myths and Men

1810

I N MAY 1810, as Beethoven sat working at the piano, he felt a
touch at his shoulder. A voice shouted in his ear, "My name is
Brentano!" He turned to find a young woman with fathomless
brown eyes looking at him. A smile lit up his bulldog face. Gallantly he
offered his hand and said, "I've just written a fine song for you." With
that he took, so to speak, the bait.

Bettina
Brentano
Age 25

In his harsh voice he began to sing and play his setting of "Kennst
du das Land," a lyric sung by the little Italian dancer Mignon in
Goethe's *Wilhelm Meister.* Beethoven did not know that Goethe, that
book, that character, that lyric lay at the center of Bettina Brentano's
existence.

Goethe

> *Do you know the land where the lemon trees bloom*
> *And oranges glow from the leaves' dark gloom*
> *and a soft wind wafts from a cloudless sky . . .*
> *You must know that land?*
> *It is there, there, I long to go with you, my beloved.*

He sang, she remembered, "not meltingly, not softly . . . far beyond
cultivation and the desire to please." At the end he asked her if she

liked it. She nodded. He offered another Goethe lyric, "Do not dry the tears of eternal love."

By then Bettina's cheeks were glowing. Neglecting her for a moment, he leaned over a sketchbook and jotted down ideas for the song. As he wrote, she stroked his hair, arranging the disorderly locks. In his *raptus*, did he notice? When he was done he rose and kissed her hand, and when she turned to leave he came along. "Music is the climate of my soul," he told her as they walked. "Few realize what a throne of passion each single musical movement is — and few know that passion itself is music's throne." He sensed she already knew all this. He spoke, she wrote, "as though I had been his intimate friend for years."[1]

At least, that is how Bettina Brentano recalled their meeting, years later, before her connections and correspondence with celebrated men made her famous, and also infamous.

Bettina was about to turn twenty-five when she met Beethoven. She would not have been the first young female enthusiast to appear in his rooms. It happened now and then, maybe more than now and then. His friend Wegeler mentioned his "conquests," without giving details. There was the time some years before when his student Ferdinand Ries intruded on a scene of Beethoven romancing a young woman on the couch, whose name he hadn't thought to ask. On that occasion, Beethoven seemed to know what he was doing, at least up to the point that she jumped up and fled. Of the women who appeared at his door, only Bettina would be remembered to history by name.

When Beethoven read E. T. A. Hoffmann's articles on his music, he encountered a defining Romantic figure in print. In his connection with Bettina Brentano, he was stirred by an embodiment of the Romantic spirit in the form of a bewitching young woman. Bettina made it her business to bewitch, and she brought a kind of genius to the endeavor. In her singular and diffuse way, Bettina was talented. She drew beautifully, studied music, sang her own songs in a rich contralto, accompanying herself on guitar. People described her singing as unforgettable. Often she improvised her performances. Eventually she published a collection of songs that show manifest technical deficiencies but a distinctive voice. In later years she became notorious for her liberal politics in a reactionary age. She campaigned against anti-

Semitism; she befriended Franz Liszt, the brothers Grimm, Karl Marx, Robert and Clara Schumann, Ralph Waldo Emerson. In her youth Bettina set out to be a muse to great men, to recast them and their lives as myths in her personal pantheon.

Artists and muses of the Brentano family were celebrated before Bettina. Her maternal grandmother, Sophie de la Roche, wrote popular novels and kept a salon. Before he became the titan of German letters, the young Johann Wolfgang von Goethe frequented those salons. In turn, Sophie's daughter Maximiliane became one of the first of Goethe's long string of sweethearts. He gave her black eyes to Lotte in his epochal novel *The Sorrows of Young Werther*.[2] After bearing eight children in an unhappy union in Frankfurt, Maximiliane Brentano died in 1793. Her seventh child, Elisabeth Catharina Ludovica Magdalena, called Bettina, was five when her mother died. Bettina and her sisters were packed off to a convent, her older brother Clemens sent to live with an aunt.[3]

Bettina remembered the main privation in the convent to be the lack of mirrors. In her teens, now living with her grandmother, she returned with gusto to life outside.[4] Her real first love was for an older girl, the poet Karoline von Günderrode. They exchanged extravagant letters that Bettina published decades later. "I can't write poetry like you, Günderrode," Bettina wrote, "but I can talk with nature when I am alone with her . . . And when I come back . . . we put our beds side by side and chat away together all night long . . . great profound speculations that make the old world creak on its rusty hinges."[5] Günderrode took up with a married man, who promised her everything and then went back to his wife. One day as they sat on the bank of the Rhine Günderrode opened her dress and showed Bettina the place on her breast where a surgeon had told her a knife would find her heart.

After her lover left her Günderrode went to the Rhine and plunged a knife into that place on her breast. (Goethe visited the scene and made literary use of the story.) Bettina's friend had fallen to the dark, suicidal side of Romanticism. Soldiering through the next decades with reaction and repression surrounding her, Bettina would continue to embody the sunny, idealistic side of the age, which never gave up

on the dreams of spiritual and political freedom that had created the
Enlightenment and the French Revolution.[6]

When Bettina was around twelve, her brother Clemens suddenly
turned up. She had not laid eyes on him for seven years. He was then
twenty, growing toward the important Romantic artist he was to become — as lyric poet, a rival of Goethe. Clemens encouraged Bettina
to read Goethe. She promptly went mad for the dancer Mignon in *Wilhelm Meister*. In dress and manner she became the elfin, inexplicable
Mignon. She began to conceive a passion for Goethe himself, seeing
him as a kind of family property and part of her destiny.

Bettina eventually published the letters between her and Clemens.
They reveal an ongoing spiritual battle. Clemens was at once fascinated
and repelled by his sister's independence. He wanted her to give up her
chimeras and become a proper hausfrau. "In heaven's name," he wrote
Bettina, "don't become a . . . seeress . . . If you knew that . . . witches of
former centuries were none other than the victims of constipation, you
would take more care to avoid falling into over-sensibility." And worse:
"If you cannot avoid being singular then you had better avoid society
altogether . . . Best of all you should be taken for a good quiet girl."[7]

Then and later, Bettina's conception of male and female was fluid
and unique to herself, and she had a horror of domesticity. For all her
love of Clemens, her defiance was intractable: "My soul is a passionate
dancer; she dances to hidden music which only I can hear . . . Whatever police the world may prescribe to rule the soul, I refuse to obey
them."[8]

By Bettina's teens, Goethe was settled into his fame as something on
the order of the Shakespeare of German letters. He lived in Weimar,
where he was a court minister, friend of the king, and resident genius. Bettina finally ran him to ground when she was twenty-one and
he fifty-eight. When his long-ago love's daughter stood before him,
Goethe asked what interested her. "Nothing interests me but you," Bettina said. Goethe invited her onto his knee and put his arms around
her. She went to sleep, then awoke, she recalled, "to a new life." For
hours Bettina extolled and chastised Goethe. Then in a fallow creative
period, always susceptible to young beauty, he was thunderstruck. He

told her he would like to have her always around so he would never get old.[9] Their exchange of letters began soon after. Published after he died as *Goethe's Correspondence with a Child*, the book made Bettina famous. That she was hardly a child when they met indicates the kind of adjustments to reality she made in her books of correspondence. But in the end Goethe had not been just an aging bard dazzled by youth. There was more to Bettina than her sparkle. She wrote to him early on (unless she actually wrote these words in middle age) this remarkable piece of poetic world-weariness: "I cannot deny the presentiment that ... this world, in which my senses are alive, is going to perish; that what I ought to shield and protect, I will betray; that where I ought to patiently submit I will take revenge; and when childlike wisdom artlessly beckons, I will act defiant and claim I know it all. But the saddest thing is that I will label with the curse of sin what is not sin, just as they all do. And I will be justly punished for it."[10]

But Bettina was not all high ideals. In January 1810, some two years after their meeting, she wrote her idol an only lightly veiled proposition: "The time will come when I will repay you, beloved Goethe; by repayment, I mean that I will embrace you with my warm loving arms."[11] To a poet friend, on the way to their first meeting, she had declared: "You know, Tieck, I have got to have a child by Goethe at all costs — why, it will be a demigod!"[12]

In August of that year there was finally a heated encounter between them. As Bettina described it, they were standing at dusk before an open window. Her arms lay around his neck, she was looking deep into his eyes. Goethe said, "Why not open your breast to the evening breeze?" She did not resist as he undid her bodice and kissed her breast and laid his head on it. "He showered kisses on me, many, many violent kisses ... I was frightened," she recalled. Finally he said to her, "And will you remember that I should like to cover your bosom with as many kisses as there are stars in heaven?" And there it ended — or so Bettina told it.[13]

Experienced in these matters, Goethe realized soon enough that for the sake of his marriage and his peace of mind he had better keep Bettina at a distance. Another writer who was not Bettina's friend wrote, "If I didn't resist, Bettina would turn me entirely into her slave ... She always wants something from the man who is with her, she wants to admire him and use him and tease him, or be admired, used, teased by him . . . The charming, sensitive and brilliant Bettina is brazen and shameless in lying."[14]

Brother Clemens, perhaps more fascinated and alarmed by Bettina than anyone else, called her "[h]alf witch, half angel . . . half seeress, half liar; half cat, half dove; half lizard, half butterfly; half morning dew, half fishblood; half chaste moonlight, half wanton flesh," and so on for a dozen more lines.[15] In Bettina's maturity, in a dark time, an observer of her own sex wondered, "What's the use of an elf in a commercial age? Who wants her trick dances, her treetop games and flowery palaces?"[16]

This was the young woman who shouted in Beethoven's ear in May 1810. It was a meeting of two transcendently self-centered people, two forces of nature, from two eras. Beethoven had grown up in the Aufklärung and came of age in the revolutionary 1780s. He built on that foundation while the artistic world around him was engulfed in the Romantic tide that he observed from a distance. But Beethoven resonated with the zeitgeist all the same, and so he resonated with Bettina Brentano, who was the zeitgeist embodied. Like many liberals of his time, after Napoleon's betrayal, he had buried revolutionary dreams for the foreseeable future. Just out of her teens, Bettina mounted her own revolution and never gave up her dreams. Like Beethoven's old teacher Christian Neefe but more vibrant, she was a person of swarming enthusiasms, a *Schwärmer* of *Schwärmers*. Unlike Neefe, she set out to mold the world to her imagination.

If eventually Bettina alarmed Goethe, she never seems to have alarmed Beethoven. If he had some practice in the art of seduction, he did not have Goethe's practiced wariness. It never occurred to him to be frightened of anyone, least of all a small, shapely young woman with deep brown eyes, not so much beautiful in the usual way as riveting in her whole being.

Whatever her later adjustments to her encounters with Beethoven and others, Bettina had an acute eye and understanding of the people she dealt with. Beethoven talked to her about his music and his ideas and showed her his work. Soon after their meeting, she wrote a straightforward account to a friend:

> I did not make Beethoven's acquaintance until the last days of my stay [in Vienna]. I very nearly did not see him at all, for no one wished to take me to meet him, not even those who called themselves his best friends, for fear of his melancholia, which so completely obsesses him that he takes no interest in anything and treats his friends with rudeness rather than civility . . .
>
> His dwelling-place is quite remarkable: in the front room there are from two to three pianos, all legless, lying on the floor; trunks containing his belongings, a three-legged chair; in the second room is his bed which . . . consists of a straw mattress and a thin cover, a wash basin on a pinewood table, his night-clothes lying on the floor . . .
>
> In person he was small (for all his soul and heart were so big), brown, and full of pockmarks. He is what one terms repulsive, yet has a divine brow, rounded with such noble harmony that one is tempted to look on it as a magnificent work of art. He had black hair, very long, which he tosses back, and does not know his own age, but thinks he is fifty-three.

This largely rings true except for the last detail, which Bettina misheard or misremembered. Beethoven might have guessed forty-three for his age; in fact, he was thirty-nine. In her later account of their meeting not all the pianos are legless, because he was playing one of them. She says that he accompanied her back to where she was staying with her half brother Franz Brentano and sister-in-law Antonie. They managed to induce him to play for them. Bettina hardly comments on the music. She goes on to report that for the rest of her stay in Vienna Beethoven came to see her every night.

In the letter she contrasts Beethoven's way of working with another composer she has been studying with: "He does not follow Winter's method, who sets down what first occurs to him; but [Beethoven] first makes a great plan and arranges his music in a certain form in accordance with which he works."[17] Whether Beethoven had told her how he proceeded or she observed it herself, Bettina had grasped one of the central elements of his method: the plan for a piece was made early in the process, and the material he invented had to submit to it.

Before that matter-of-fact letter, though, Bettina had written Goethe in the rhapsodic mode she reserved for him:

> When I saw him of whom I shall now speak to you, I forgot the whole world . . . It is Beethoven of whom I now wish to tell you, and how he made me forget the world and you . . . I am not mistaken when I say — what no one, perhaps, now understands and believes — he stalks far ahead of the culture of mankind. Shall we ever overtake him? . . .
>
> Everything that he can tell you about is pure magic, every posture is the organization of a higher existence, and therefore Beethoven feels himself to be the founder of a new sensuous basis in the intellectual life . . .
>
> He himself said: "When I open my eyes I must sigh, for what I see is contrary to my religion, and I must despise the world which does not know that music is a higher revelation than all wisdom and philosophy, the wine which inspires one to new generative processes, and I am the Bacchus who presses out this glorious wine for mankind . . . I know that God is nearer to me than to other artists; I associate with him without fear; I have always recognized and understood him and have no fear for my music . . . Those who understand it must be freed by it from all the other miseries which the others drag about with themselves . . .
>
> "Speak to Goethe about me . . . tell him to hear my symphonies and he will say that I am right in saying that music is the one incorporeal entrance into the higher world of knowledge which comprehends mankind but which mankind cannot comprehend . . . The encased seed needs the moist, electrically warm soil to sprout, to think, to express itself. Music is the electrical soil in which the mind thinks, lives, feels. Philosophy is a precipitate of the mind's electrical essence; its needs which seek a basis in primeval principle are elevated by it . . . Thus every real creation of art is independent, more powerful than the artist himself and returns to the divine through its manifestation. It is one with man only in this, that it bears testimony of the mediation of the divine in him . . . Everything electrical stimulates the mind

to musical, fluent, out-streaming generation. I am electrical in my nature."

Bettina ends, "Last night I wrote down all that he had said; this morning I read it over to him. He remarked: 'Did I say that? Well, then I had a *raptus!*'"

In time those lines written to Goethe became the most celebrated words Beethoven ever spoke about music, a cornerstone of the myth for which Bettina Brentano, E. T. A. Hoffmann, and other high Romantics were laying the foundation. But whose words were they? If they were Beethoven's, they have a tone of visionary *Schwärmerei* that he never, as far as history would know, quite wrote or spoke with anyone else: "I am the Bacchus who presses out this glorious wine for mankind." As a matter of principle, he rarely spoke or wrote about his music at all. In some degree, then, all this has to be the Romantic spirit speaking through Bettina: music is a higher revelation than all wisdom and philosophy; it unifies the sensuous and the intellectual; it electrifies and liberates the spirit and the soul.

And yet, and yet: Bettina adjusted, she embroidered, but not as much as history accused her of. In his heart Beethoven was as extravagantly idealistic as the man she painted, but ordinarily he articulated it only in music. To Goethe she cites his *raptus,* a word Beethoven and his friends used for his creative seizures. Bettina could have learned about his *raptus* only from Beethoven, just as he told her about his compositional process. That raises still another provoking, unanswerable question: as Bettina claims, did he actually read over those words of his that she reported to Goethe? If he did not actually speak those high-flown phrases but signed off on them, was he letting her speak for him?[18]

There is no way finally to know. When Bettina entered Beethoven's life, she brought an element of mystery that would endure. But again, while she had a creative sense of reality she did not tend to make up things out of whole cloth. A number of the letters she later published between her and Goethe, and two she said were written to her from Beethoven, did not survive; all of hers to Beethoven were lost. But the Goethe letters she published that did survive reveal that her adjustments were partly to make a better and more coherent story, partly to attribute to him some of her own politics, partly to weave in a fascination with herself more outspoken than Goethe actually expressed.[19] The one letter to her from Beethoven that survived is exactly as she published it. In other words, the essence of what she published, invented or not, was not so far from the truth.

All this is to say that Bettina's embroideries were founded on an uncommon understanding of the lives and minds of her subjects, interwoven with her conviction that she was born to be adored by great men. Did Beethoven imagine a new integration of the sensuous and the intellectual, or was that Bettina speaking? If those were her words and he read and consented to them, did they strike a chord in him?

Beethoven had made the acquaintance of an endlessly fascinating and ambitious young woman, a virtuoso muse. How did she feel at this point about him? Was he a friend, a lover, a prospective mate? What can be said for certain is that Bettina made it her project to bring together the two demigods of her acquaintance, Goethe and Beethoven. Beethoven was excited to meet the man he felt to be the greatest of Germans, because he believed poetry to be a higher calling than music. And he had more than one offering to Goethe, not only three lieder on Goethe lyrics but also a new overture and incidental music for the play *Egmont*. That summer Goethe wrote Bettina saying he and Beethoven might get together at the Karlsbad spa.[20] "It would give me great joy," he concluded, "if Beethoven were to make me a present of the two [*sic*] songs of mine which he has composed." (They would be played for him by his friend and musical adviser, composer Carl Friedrich Zelter — in those days not the Beethoven admirer he later became.) Plans for a meeting of the titans went forward sporadically for the next two years.

Beyond achieving the opening to Goethe, had Beethoven fallen for Bettina? Ordinarily, men who were not frightened by her might well fall for her, and at the time she met Beethoven she was available. But when he met Bettina, in May 1810, Beethoven was not exactly available. He was still in the middle of courting Therese Malfatti, had just written *Für Elise* for her, was sending her warm letters, had asked Wegeler in Bonn to find his birth certificate in preparation for an offer of marriage. Not until July did he write Gleichenstein, who had been deputized to convey the marriage offer, "My pride is humbled . . . if you would only be more candid." Around the end of that summer Stephan von Breuning wrote Wegeler, "I believe his marriage project has fallen through."[21]

All these frustrations and uncertainties contribute to an accumulating mystery. Even for Beethoven, whose emotions were as fickle as the breeze, it was not like him to fall in love with one woman while he was seriously courting another. At the same time, it is hard to imagine he was not fascinated by Bettina. However these questions took shape in his mind, however much Bettina had to do with it, that spring and summer he began an emotional odyssey that came to its bitter climax in the spa of Teplitz in the summer of 1812.

Another part of the emotional turmoil of those months was that through Bettina, Beethoven met another woman who would become important to him. He may already have known Antonie Brentano, Bettina's sister-in-law, through her family in Vienna.[22] Antonie, called Toni, had been born Antonie Birkenstock, daughter of a distinguished Austrian statesman and art collector. As so often happened in those days, her father married her off to a prosperous man fifteen years older, Frankfurt merchant Franz Brentano. He was half brother of Bettina and Clemens, to both of whom Antonie became close. As corollary of the familiar, sad story, Antonie's was a largely loveless marriage, though it amounted to less of a disaster than Beethoven's old love Josephine Deym's two marriages, or the misery of the womanizing Prince Lichnowsky's home life.

Antonie Brentano at least appreciated her husband, called him "the best of all men," but she felt no passion for him.[23] Franz was absorbed in his business and often went back to the office after dinner. She hated living in drab Frankfurt and longed for her hometown of Vienna. As the years went by she slipped into a trance of frustration and sorrow. Clemens Brentano wrote in 1802, "Toni is like a glass of water that has been left standing for a long while." From 1806 on, her health declined; she was tormented by headaches and a nervous condition. She wrote to Bettina's sister, "A deathly silence reigns within my soul."[24] In only one of her several portraits is there a hint of a smile trying to break through. The earliest portrait, painted when she was twenty-eight, just after her marriage, shows a melancholy beauty with a long, pale neck.[25] Not so charitably, Bettina wrote in 1807, "Toni . . . has rouged and painted herself like a stage set, as though impersonating a haughty ruin overlooking the Rhine toward which a variety of romantic scenes advance while she remains wholly sunk in loneliness and abstraction."[26]

In 1809, Antonie's father lay dying. She moved to Vienna with her four children, back into the grand house of her childhood that was crammed with art and memorabilia. Franz followed and set up a branch of his business in town. There were concerts and parties. After connecting with the couple through Bettina, Beethoven became a regular visitor and played piano regularly, something people found increasingly harder to coax him into.

It was Antonie's task, after her father died, to organize his collection, get myriad items appraised, and auction them off. The process took more than three years. The whole time she dreaded the return to Frankfurt that would come when the house was empty. In that period, she recalled late in life, her main consolation was Beethoven. She had touched his abiding vein of empathy—at least that, if not something deeper in him. They found a "tender friendship," she recalled. He would "come regularly, seat himself at a pianoforte in her anteroom without a word, and improvise. After he had finished 'telling her everything and bringing comfort' in his language, he would go as he had come." He presented her with manuscripts including the song *An die Geliebte* (To the Beloved). The manuscript bears a note in her hand: "Requested by me from the author on March 2, 1812."[27]

Antonie was not the only admired woman friend Beethoven comforted with music in a time of sorrow whether or not he felt a romantic interest in them. He did the same with Baroness Dorothea Ertmann, who was not an intimate but a pianist he admired. What sort of intimacy did Antonie and Beethoven form in this hectic period when on top of his work he hopelessly courted Therese Malfatti and met Bettina Brentano, all while coping with overlapping illnesses? What place in his heart was open to ailing, melancholy Toni? Was it love and hope for reciprocation? He knew and liked her businessman husband Franz. Was he capable of making a play for the wife of a friend, even if the marriage was unhappy? The unanswerable questions of his relations with Antonie Brentano only intensify the mystery of those years that for him were brimming with pain and disappointment, perhaps also touched by hope.

If Beethoven was not a Romantic artist setting out mainly to express himself, it is still hard not to connect his emotional storms of 1810 with the String Quartet in F Minor, completed that summer and eventually published as op. 95. It is one of the singular works of his life. After the warm and engaging *Harp* Quartet of the previous year, now he produced a challenge and an enigma. There was no commission; op. 95 is dedicated not to an exalted patron but to his old Viennese helper Baron Zmeskall. It is one of the handful of works to which he gave titles: *Quartetto serioso.*

The *Serioso* is beyond "bold," deeper than "experimental." For Beethoven F minor seems to have been a darkly expressive key, more raw, more nakedly tragic than tumultuous C minor. It is the key of the *Appassionata,* of the dungeon scene in *Fidelio,* of the overture to Goethe's *Egmont* written that year. The distilled essence of his sense of F minor is the first movement of the *Serioso,* which seems to involve something on the order of a confrontation between love and rage.

A simple description may be the best representation in words. A grinding *furioso* phrase answered by a violent silence. An eruption of stark octaves in jolting dotted rhythms. Another glowering silence. A wrenching harmonic jump from F minor to G-flat major, the key of the Neapolitan chord but in a tender phrase, quickly shattered by the return of the *furioso* figure.[28] After a first theme of twenty bars, which contain those three distinct, starkly contrasting ideas with only silence as transition, there is a short bridge to a second theme in D-flat major that sounds evanescent, breathless, unreal.[29]

That moment of melting beauty is again invaded by the grinding figure and by the intrusion of uprushing *fortissimo* scales in inexplicable keys.[30] In this movement there is more confrontation than transition, no normal key relations, wrenching jumps from key to key, the sonata form so condensed as to be desiccated. There is no repeat of the exposition before the development, because in this movement the material is always volatile, all development. At the same time the music cannot escape from the opening *furioso* figure, which grinds through most of the twenty-two bars of a truncated development. The coda jumps from F minor to D-flat major, rising to a scream and a fall to exhaustion.

A startling jump from F minor to D major, beginning with an enigmatic lone cello stride, begins the Allegretto ma non troppo second movement. Its main theme is of a profound but fragile beauty.[31] In its middle comes a strange fugue whose falling chromatic subject feels like an endless descent into melancholy. Among fugues it is one of the most poignant, a quality rarely heard in that disciplined contrapuntal form.

There is no slow movement, nor a scherzo or minuet. In meter and tempo the third movement stands in place of a scherzo. So that there can be no mistake about its import, it is marked Allegro assai vivace ma serioso, very lively but seriously. The movement has an aggressive drive, with its relentless dotted rhythms and blunt silences. In contrast, the two trios are lyrical and soaring, recalling in their tone and keys (G-flat and D-flat) the tender moments of the first movement.

A softly poignant phrase introduces an Allegro agitato finale that is nearly as tight and taut as the first movement. Its main theme begins curt, desiccated, half made of rests, until it reaches a surging, quietly agitated song. The penultimate page dies into silence, stasis, whispers. Then as perhaps the strangest stroke of all comes a coda that seems intended to wipe away all sadness. It is a burst of F-major ebullience like the end of a comic opera, yet still short and curt, ending with an uprushing scale that recalls the peculiar ones in the first movement. If the coda is a resolution to hope, it is an oddly choked-off one — but hope all the same.

Whether the fury and the tenuous moments of hope in the *Serioso* represent Beethoven's state of mind that year is another of that year's elusive questions. But there is no question that the *Serioso* sounds like a cry from the soul. In 1810, he had experienced his second devastating marriage rejection. At the same time, in two new women acquaintances, both of them named Brentano, he perhaps found some possibility of the emotional and family life he yearned for. He knew this quartet was going to be a puzzle for listeners, perhaps enough to do him harm. He did not publish it for six years and in an 1816 letter made an extraordinary declaration: "The Quartet is written for a small circle of connoisseurs and is never to be performed in public."[32]

In any case, if the *Serioso* is a cry from the soul that seemed to him too intimate to be made public, it is a tightly disciplined cry, a systematic experiment with the musical norms and forms Beethoven inherited. In that respect it amounts to something he could not have understood yet: a prophecy of music he was going to be writing a decade later. Surely the music of that coming decade rose in part from the issues and feelings of the *Serioso* brewing in his mind.

In his work Beethoven was entering a protracted search for a second New Path, a new vision of the nature and purpose of music — which is to say, a new vision of the human. Whether or not he ever realized it, the *Serioso* was a clue, a step toward that path. But more than ever before, his struggle toward a new vision would have to be carried on alongside a still more grueling struggle with his health, his hearing, his state of mind.

If 1810 was fertile for Beethoven, his productivity still did not approach the all-but-superhuman years before 1808 and never did again. Except for the *Serioso,* which had no immediate ramifications, there were no great bold strides but rather works exercising the imagination and mastery he could always rely on.

The less music he wrote, meanwhile, the more letters. As always most of them were practical, like the prodding one of this year to Viennese piano maker Johann Andreas Streicher, who apparently had asked for endorsements:

> Here, dear Streicher, are the letters . . . But I do ask you to ensure that the instruments do not wear out so quickly — You have seen your instrument which I have here and you must admit that it is very worn out . . . You know that my sole object is to promote the production of good instruments. That is all. Otherwise I am absolutely impartial.

Here you must not be annoyed at hearing the truth from your most
devoted servant and friend
   Beethoven

He was trying to get from Streicher a piano that pleased him, but
the reality was that no instrument pleased him for long. The Érard
from Paris, sent him as a gift, which had helped inspire the *Waldstein*
and *Appassionata,* was now finished for him: "My motto," he wrote
Streicher, "is either to play on a good instrument or not at all — As for
my French piano, which is certainly quite useless now, I still have mis-
givings about selling it, for it is really a souvenir such as no one here
has so far honored me with." He adds that he was suffering from a new
complaint, an infection or abscess: "On account of my foot I cannot yet
walk so far."[33]

   Still more letters were directed to publisher Gottfried Härtel, who
had finally agreed to take the Mass in C, though not to pay for it. (In-
credibly, in October Beethoven jotted down, "The mass could perhaps
be dedicated to Napoleon.")[34] There were steady misunderstandings
and wrangles over the mass. "For God's sake publish the mass just as
you have it," he wrote Härtel, "without waiting for the organ part . . .
The general character of the Kyrie . . . is heartfelt resignation, deep sin-
cerity of religious feeling . . . Gentleness is the fundamental characteristic . . . cheerfulness pervades this mass. The Catholic goes to church
on Sunday in his best clothes and in a joyful and festive mood."[35] (Here
is another of the few times he revealed an underlying conception of a
piece.) After one particularly egregious train of engraving errors that
he had meticulously corrected, he wrote Härtel with exasperation and
remarkable restraint:

   Mistakes — mistakes — you yourself are a unique mistake — Well I
   shall have to send my copyist to Leipzig or go there myself, unless I
   am prepared to let my work — appear as nothing but a mass of mistakes — Apparently the tribunal of music at Leipzig can't produce one
   single efficient proofreader; and to make matters worse, you send out
   the works before you receive the corrected proofs . . . Please note that
   a whole bar is missing from the pianoforte arrangement of the over-

ture to Egmont . . . All the same I do esteem you very highly. As you
know, it is the custom with human beings to esteem one another for
not having made even greater mistakes — [36]

All his courting of Härtel over the years, all his patience and determination were finally negated by an overcautious publisher afraid
that Beethoven would lose him money. After taking on a few works,
including the *Harp* Quartet and the *Emperor* Concerto, the *Egmont*
music, op. 84, was the last new Beethoven work Breitkopf & Härtel
published.[37] In 1815, Beethoven finally settled a row of pieces on the
Viennese publisher Sigmund Anton Steiner, whose house became
his principal outlet for years.[38] But he doggedly kept pitching ideas to
Härtel.

The endless drain of proofreading and contending with publishers was hardly Beethoven's only distraction. When Archduke Rudolph
was in town he expected several lessons a week in piano and composition, and they dragged on for hours. In this period began a major
motif of Beethoven's letter writing for years to come: notes begging
off a lesson with Rudolph because of ill health. In early 1811, he wrote,
"For over a fortnight now I have again been afflicted with a headache."
A few days later: "I am better and in a few days I shall again have
the honor of waiting on you and of making up for lost time — I am
always desperately worried if I cannot be zealous in your service and
if I cannot be with Your Imperial Highness as often as I should like.
It is most certainly true to say that this privation causes me very great
suffering."[39] The latter sentiment is most certainly not true; clearly, to
Rudolph he exaggerated his physical travails to escape lessons. But
in his notes he took pains not to cause offense. He was no longer the
brash young lion treating his aristocratic admirers imperiously. He
had come to understand the importance of hanging on to this loyal
and royal friend. With Rudolph there would be no break like the violent argument that ended the earlier stipend from his once-leading
patron, Prince Lichnowsky.

But why did Rudolph, an accomplished musician and one of the
most admiring, talented, and generous noblemen Beethoven ever

knew, make such demands? As a composer himself, he understood that Beethoven needed all the time he could get for his work. Furthermore, though Rudolph was a fine pianist and worked hard at his music, to have professional ambitions in the field would have been unthinkably beneath his station.

There is no evident reason for Rudolph's demands other than that he was high aristocracy and when all was said and done, Beethoven for him was still a kind of servant — a well-paid one at that. (Beyond his contribution to Beethoven's yearly stipend, Rudolph likely paid separately for the lessons.) Commoners enjoying one's patronage were expected to be at one's beck and call. As mild, good-natured, unpretentious, and relatively enlightened as Rudolph was, his demands had the authority of centuries, of eons. Beethoven served, groveled, made excuses, kept his feelings to himself. Much of the year, at least, Rudolph was out of town.

Beethoven's private feelings, however, were hardly groveling. At the end of 1811, a visitor reported him declaring, "From the Emperor to the shoeshine boy, all the Viennese are worthless." His contempt for the Viennese was undimmed after nearly twenty years in the city. The visitor went on to say that Beethoven "has only one [student], who gives him very much trouble and whom he would gladly be rid of, if he could." Asked by the visitor who that might be, Beethoven was not shy in saying: "The Archduke Rudolph."[40] But for the rest of his life, he and Rudolph stayed true to each other, in their fashions.

Keeping the pot boiling on another front, in summer 1810 Beethoven sent off fifty-three British Isles folk-song arrangements to publisher George Thomson in Edinburgh. So among publishers, patrons, hackwork, illness, and romantic tumult, his days were consumed.

The lasting testaments to Rudolph's favor were the string of major works dedicated to him. Beethoven announced a new one in a letter of March 1811. After noting the headache that had afflicted him for weeks, he wrote Rudolph, "I began to work rather hard; and one of the fruits of this diligence is a new pianoforte trio." In light of its stately opening theme and its dedication to Rudolph, the Piano Trio in E-flat Major,

op. 97, came to be known as the *Archduke*. It is an indicative product of these years: brilliant, attractive, and safe (except for the *Serioso*
Quartet).

Still, the *Archduke* is hardly a simple bow to a patron; it is a huge
— some forty-five minutes — four-movement work of surprising contrasts. The mellifluous and expansive opening evaporates momentarily
when the strings enter on a poignant note. That habit of withdrawing
inward is central to the overall tone of the trio. It is seen throughout
the gentle development section of the first movement, the opposite
of the familiar dramatic Beethovenian development. It flows without
fanfare into a varied recapitulation of the main theme. The scherzo is
placed second in line, rather than the usual third, and involves one of
Beethoven's jokes for connoisseurs: the theme starts with a bald B-flat-
major scale, rhythmized. The mood is one of delight, and that persists through the middle trio section, which expands the joke: after
the scherzo theme made from a major scale, the trio theme outlines a
slithering chromatic scale. That idea alternates with buoyant bursts of
waltz.[41]

For the slow movement he made a warm and gorgeous set of variations, its theme one of the long-lined, singing chorale melodies that
were to become a signature of his late style. Here the inward moments
of the earlier movements flower. If this is not quite so ethereal as his
later *andantes*, it still has some of his future style's expansiveness and
also the experiments in texture, where the appearance of the pages
starts to become complex unto spiky — but no less singing in sound.
The movement ends with a varied and affecting return of its opening,
as if recalled in memory.

By now it had become normal for Beethoven not only to interweave
the keys and thematic material of a work throughout its course but
also to join movements, especially the last two. So the Andante flows
into a sparkling, dancing finale with dynamic dotted figures, the rondo
theme uniting the scale motifs of earlier movements with the melodic
shape of the work's opening measures. The mood is cinched at the
end, when the 2/4 theme is remade into a dashing, scherzolike 6/8,
and the movement races to a scintillating conclusion. It would not be
a stretch to imagine the *Archduke* as taking shape in Beethoven's mind

as an idealized portrait of the archduke himself, or a portrait of their relationship — from the sunny side of the picture.

With his two major instrumental pieces of 1810–11, the *Serioso* Quartet and the *Archduke* Trio, a desert and an oasis as starkly contrasting as any adjacent works of his life, Beethoven returned again to an old pattern of his: an aggressive and challenging piece followed by a more approachable one. Always he had an acute sense of the effect of his music on his listeners. In the brusque, enigmatic, prophetic *Serioso*, he pushed technical and expressive norms, and the sympathy of his listeners, close to their breaking points. In the *Archduke* he returned to the relatively normative and genial with all the mastery at his command.

Josephine Deym remained on his mind into 1811. In January, he wrote to Therese Brunsvik, Josephine's sister: "I do request you . . . to send me again that little sketch which I have been unfortunate enough to lose. An eagle was gazing at the sun, that was the subject. I can never forget it. But you must not assume that in this connection I am thinking of myself, although such a thought has already been imputed to me. Why, many people surely like to witness an act of heroism without being in the very least like heroes."[42] Beethoven liked to keep inspirational items on his desk and piano, that image of aspiration being one of them. Therese copied Beethoven's letter and sent it to Josephine, who was living in Vienna, newly and disastrously married to Baron Christophe von Stackelberg. But though Beethoven might still have been carrying a torch for Josephine, there is no record or much likelihood of contact between her and Beethoven at this point — she was not yet separated from Stackelberg. Eventually, the baron absconded with her children and left her alone and desperate.[43]

A month after writing to Therese, Beethoven sent Bettina Brentano a rambling and affectionate letter:

Dear, Dear Bettine!

I have already received two letters from you, and see from your letter to "die Tonie" [Antonie Brentano] that you still think of me, and far too favorably at that. I carried with me your first letter all summer long, and it has often made me very happy . . . although if I haven't written you often, and although you don't see anything of me at all, in thought I write to you a thousand times. Even though you haven't written to me about it, I can imagine how you have to put up in Berlin with those "worldly" good-for-nothings — much chatter about art but no action!!!! . . .

You are getting married, dear Bettine, or maybe it has already happened, yet I haven't even been able to see you beforehand; nevertheless may all blessings that marriage offers stream down upon you and your husband . . .

What can I say about myself? "Pity my fate!" I exclaim with poor Johanna [referring to a character in a Goethe poem]. If I am granted a few more years of life, I shall thank the all-embracing almighty for it, whether those years be ones of contentment or pain.

If you write to Goethe about me, try to use words that will convey to him my most profound respect and admiration for him. I am just about to write to him myself about Egmont which I have set to music, quite literally out of love for his poetry, which makes me very happy; but who can thank enough a great poet, the most precious jewel that a nation can possess?

And now I must close, dear good B. I did not get back home until 4 this morning from a drunken party that made me laugh heartily, and for which I am now tempted to cry nearly as much. Uproarious jollity often drives me back into myself. Many thanks to Clemens for his kind interest; as for the Cantata [Clemens had sent him a libretto] the topic is not important enough for us here; it's otherwise in Berlin — as for affection, the sister has such a large part of it that not much is left over for the brother . . .

And now goodbye, dear, dear B., I kiss you on the forehead, and thus press on it as with my seal all my thoughts for you. Write soon, soon and often to your friend

Beethoven[44]

In the letter his feelings for Bettina are obvious, but there is none of the breathless rapture that used to mark his letters to Josephine Deym. He seems not particularly anguished at the news that she is marrying

Achim von Arnim. (Arnim was a prominent poet and a friend of her brother Clemens. She had worked with them on their later legendary collection of German folk poetry, *Des Knaben Wunderhorn.*) He wants Bettina to recommend him again to Goethe, and he invites her to make up words for him that will please the poet. So he knows Bettina's propensity for invention but trusts her to invent for him, because his own words will not do. There is love in his letter, but it is not disappointed love, not the anguish of love lost. It concludes with a rueful story about a hangover and a polite rejection to relay to her brother. The most essential point of the letter, in fact, may be to prod Bettina to continue her campaign to bring him and Goethe together.

Yet his tone of warm but restrained affection is inflected by two striking details. Near the end, after the words "I kiss you," Beethoven has stricken out "with pain." Then in the last sentence, he uses the intimate *du* for "you." Earlier, through all the raptures of the letters to Josephine Deym, Beethoven had always used *Sie,* the formal "you." These details may be clues to his feelings for Bettina — or not. He may have stricken out "with pain" because it seemed to him improper for a now-married woman. In any case, the phrase is hardly a cry from the soul, and it could be ironic: one may write such words gallantly to tell a woman she is desirable without putting too fine a point on it. As for the *du* to Bettina and the *Sie* to Josephine, that may be a sign of overflowing affection to Bettina.[45] Or it could be only a reflection of the reality that Bettina was a commoner and Josephine an aristocrat, for whom a commoner could never properly use the intimate pronoun unless the two were virtually betrothed.

Finally, after months of the two men turning their thoughts warily toward one another from a distance, Beethoven wrote a gushing letter to Goethe in April. He used the proper form of address for Goethe's position as an official of the Weimar Court.

To Goethe

Your Excellency! The pressing opportunity afforded me by a friend of mine and a great admirer of yours (as I am also), who is leaving Vienna very soon, allows me only a moment in which to thank you for the long time I have known you (for that I have done since my childhood) — That is so little for so much — Bettina Brentano has assured me that you would receive me kindly, or, I should say, as a friend. But how could I think of such a welcome, seeing that I can approach you only with the greatest reverence and with an inexpressibly profound feeling of admiration for your glorious creations! — You will shortly receive from Leipzig through Breitkopf and Härtel my music for Egmont, that glorious Egmont on which I have again reflected through you, and which I have felt and reproduced in music as intensely as I felt when I read it — I should very much like to have your opinion on my music for Egmont. Even your censure will be useful to me and my art and will be welcomed as gladly as the greatest praise. —

Your Excellency's profound admirer
Ludwig van Beethoven[46]

The letter was hand-delivered to Goethe in Weimar by Franz Oliva, a bank clerk and amateur pianist who was becoming Beethoven's new unpaid secretary and go-between — now that brother Caspar was married, working in the Austrian bureaucracy, and rearing a child.[47] Goethe's encouraging reply to Beethoven came in June:

With great pleasure, my most highly esteemed sir, I have received your kind letter, sent through Herr von Oliva. I am deeply thankful for the sentiments expressed therein, and can assure you that I sincerely return them, for I have never heard one of your works . . . without wishing that I could once admire you yourself sitting at the piano, and delight in your extraordinary talent. The good Bettina Brentano surely deserves the interest that you have shown in her. She speaks of you with rapture and the liveliest affection, and counts the hours that she spent with you among the happiest of her life.[48]

He looks forward to hearing the *Egmont* music, says he will use it in the court theater, hopes Beethoven will visit Weimar.

Beethoven's *Egmont* Overture and incidental music had been intended for a Vienna production of Goethe's play in May 1810. As it often transpired, he did not finish the music in time for the opening, even though the assignment from the imperial court theater had come the previous autumn and he had started it then. Here is an example of the difficulty he was having in those days getting serious pieces rolling, a situation his services to Archduke Rudolph did not help. He finished the *Egmont* music in June; it was premiered at the fourth performance of the play. He dispatched it to Breitkopf & Härtel for publication.[49]

This theater project had interested him for at least two reasons. The music published by the leading house in Europe would be his calling card to Goethe and he hoped the beginning of a friendship. From this connection, besides the satisfaction of being close to the great man, Beethoven hoped for an opera libretto — say, one drawn from the first part of Goethe's *Faust*, published in 1808, which was on Beethoven's mind as a possibility.[50] At the same time, *Egmont* was another story of the kind that always galvanized him: heroism, sacrifice, the shining idea of liberty. All the same, he had initially told the court theater he preferred to write music for a production of Schiller's *Wilhelm Tell*, the same sort of liberation story but with more action. He got assigned *Egmont* instead.[51]

Partly by chance, then, between the play and the songs this was a Goethe period for Beethoven. He hoped to parlay them into a friendship at least and a collaboration at best. This all transpired in the heart of what would eventually be named the *Goethezeit*, the age of Goethe in German culture. And like Beethoven, Goethe — poet, playwright, scientist, courtier, government minister, far-reaching polymath — joined an eighteenth-century sensibility to an art that not only pointed to the future but helped shape that future. In essence there were three German giants around the turn of the nineteenth century who served both as completions of the Aufklärung and prophets and instigators of Romanticism: Kant in philosophy, Goethe in letters, Beethoven in music. Romantics were in the process of making all of them into myths. Kant was recently dead, the other two still in the middle of their lives.

The *Egmont* music was one of Beethoven's major efforts in a time of slim pickings for him. Goethe's plot is based on a historical incident close to the heart of the Dutch people. It is set in the sixteenth century, when the Netherlands was ruled by Catholic Spain. The Spanish emperor Charles V had abolished the constitutional rights of the Dutch and used the Inquisition to suppress Protestants. The Flemish general Egmont, a national hero after his victories over the French, journeys to Madrid to plead with the court for tolerance. Speaking the truth to tyrants earns him a death sentence as a traitor. In the play his beloved Clärchen, failing in her attempts to rouse Egmont's countrymen to save him, kills herself in despair. Those two deaths begin a brutal Spanish suppression in Holland. But for Goethe this story does not end in defeat. On the eve of his execution Egmont dreams of an embodiment of Freedom with Clärchen's face, who places a laurel of victory on his head. Egmont goes to the scaffold exalted. For the end of the drama, after Egmont's execution, Goethe calls for a "symphony of victory."

With his concrete sense of things, Beethoven wrote on a sketch, "The main point is that the Netherlanders will eventually triumph over the Spaniards."[52] He also noted, "[P]erhaps the death could be represented by a rest."[53] He may or may not have remembered that he had done the same at the end of *Coriolan*. Here the martyrdom of the hero is not just a tragic end but also a new beginning, a prophecy of liberation.

The *Egmont* Overture and incidental music show how far Beethoven had come in finding his own theatrical voice since *Christus, Prometheus, Coriolan,* even *Fidelio* — or maybe how inspired he was by the first genuinely significant play he had worked with. Here in his theater music he frees himself of both Mozart and Cherubini. The orchestral sound is grand, rich, and colorful, distinct both from his symphonic orchestral voice and from his previous theater music. As in all his overtures, the one for *Egmont* amounts to a symphonic poem that follows the story.

As it needed to be, this is another outpouring of Beethoven's heroic style — one of the last. A stark orchestral unison begins the overture; then comes a darkly lumbering gesture in low strings, evoking the burden of oppression. The key is F minor, for Beethoven a tragic, death-tinted tonality. The introduction gathers to an Allegro that itself gathers steadily, like the impetus of revolt.[54] The stern second theme returns to the baneful opening idea sped up. As in *Coriolan,* the two themes of sonata form are used to represent contending forces in the story.

The music has an enormous forward thrust, always pointing ahead. After a short development, the recapitulation starts in the proper F minor then wanders in key, searching. It arrives back at F minor for the last hammer blows of tyranny and the short rest that stands for Egmont's death — short because it is not the end of the drama. The end is the "Victory Symphony," the prophecy of freedom the overture has been searching for. Here is another heroic piece of Beethoven's that ends with overflowing joy, as in the final moments of the *Eroica*, the Fifth Symphony, the *Leonore* overtures, and the opera itself. This is his most elemental joyful ending of all; through much of its pealing course, the "Victory Symphony" hardly moves off a triumphant F-major chord.[55]

The rest of the incidental music for *Egmont*, nearly half an hour of it, has the same rich and fresh sound as the overture. There are two songs for Clärchen, one a military march and the other a testament to love, neither of which owes anything overt to Mozart. The rest of the incidental music is entr'actes, the touching "Death of Clärchen," a melodrama, and the "Victory Symphony" heard again. There are passages like nothing else in Beethoven, such as the long, exquisite oboe solos of the third entr'acte. The several marches, by contrast, seem at once practiced (Beethoven wrote quite a few marches) and routine.

How Goethe responded to the *Egmont* music is not recorded. Among his many contradictory qualities, Goethe was a restlessly searching personality in his art and at the same time conservative in his politics, opinions, and tastes — except when he was not conservative, as in writing plainly of love and lust. His unpublished erotic poetry would have shocked Beethoven beyond words, but Clärchen and Egmont are chaste and heroic — Beethoven's kind of lovers.

Antonie Adamberger, who played Clärchen in this performance, recalled working with Beethoven on the music. With this actress noted for her beauty as much as her talent, he was in his most charming mode. "Can you sing?" he asked when she was brought to him.

"No!" she said.

Beethoven laughed. "No? But I'm supposed to compose the songs in *Egmont* for you!" She told him she had tried singing for a while but gave it up because it made her hoarse. "That'll be a fine how'd-you-do,"

Beethoven said jovially in Viennese dialect. He rummaged through the music on the piano and found something for her to sing as he accompanied. Pleased at what he heard, with a kind look he stroked her forehead and said, "Very well, now I know." Three days later he returned with the songs she had inspired and taught them to her. Finally he decreed, "There, that's right. So, so that's the way, sing it thus, don't let anybody persuade you to do it differently, and see that you don't put any ornaments in it."[56]

There were always these sorts of pleasant interludes, especially with singers and actresses. Otherwise it was a miserable period for Beethoven. An added misery, equal to any other for him, came to a head in February 1811. The Austrian inflation that had been speeding toward a gallop through the first decade of the century, spurred by war and by Napoleon's punitive demand for reparations, reached a climactic crash. The government declared bankruptcy and reduced the value of paper currency to a fifth of its former value. By that year the cost of living had gone up some 1,000 percent since 1795; in 1817, inflation would reach nearly 4,000 percent. The devaluation caused little stir among the aristocracy, most of whose wealth was in land. Government officials were given a raise to offset the devaluation. But many on a fixed income, including pensioners, and effectively including Beethoven with his yearly stipend, were devastated. A wave of bankruptcies and suicides broke out in the Austrian upper-middle class.[57]

As of the end of 1810, all three of Beethoven's contributing patrons — Archduke Rudolph and Princes Lobkowitz and Kinsky — had kept up on their contributions, even the dilatory Kinsky. That winter Rudolph was quick to increase his part of the stipend from 1,500 to 6,000 florins a year, to compensate for the devaluation. Kinsky eventually followed suit. But inflation was not Beethoven's only problem. Lobkowitz was on the verge of bankruptcy, mainly because of the acres of money he had spent on his musical passions. His livelihood on the line, Beethoven took none of this lying down; he went to the men or their representatives in person, and he went to the courts. But meanwhile, there was no money from Lobkowitz for three years, and payments from the Kinsky estate lapsed for two years.[58]

By the middle of 1811, Beethoven felt driven to distraction with his endless round of illness and frustration in love, and now anxieties over money. On doctor's orders he retreated to the spa at Teplitz, where Dr. Malfatti ordered him to suspend work and see to his recovery. That was the sort of medical direction the chronically ill Beethoven chronically ignored. In August, as he boarded the carriage for Teplitz, he received a parcel with a commission to write incidental music for two commemorative plays by August von Kotzebue, *King Stephan* and *The Ruins of Athens,* scheduled for the opening of a theater in Pest. The deadline was tight, but Beethoven was not about to pass up a commission. "Although my doctor has forbidden me to work," he wrote Gottfried Härtel concerning the Hungarian offer, "I sat down to do something for those mustachios, who are genuinely fond of me."[59]

Mounting one of his old-style marathons on the order of *Christus am Ölberge* and the *Choral Fantasy,* in his first three weeks in Teplitz he scribbled some thirty-five minutes of orchestral, choral, and solo music for the plays and put them in the mail on time — only to be notified that the opening had been postponed until the following year. At the same time he courted writer Kotzebue for an opera libretto: "Whether it be romantic, quite serious, heroic, comic or sentimental, in short, whatever you like . . . I must admit that I should like best of all some grand subject taken from history and especially from the dark ages, for instance, from the time of Attila or the like."[60] (Beethoven either did not know or did not care that Kotzebue's politics were notoriously reactionary, or that he was a fierce and vocal opponent of Goethe.)

Long-standing medical doctrine had it that one's health could be restored by taking the cure at a beautiful place in the country, preferably where springs gushed forth from the earth. Teplitz, near the Karlsbad spa and some thirty miles from Prague, was one of the celebrated hot springs in Europe. It offered tranquillity in the forms of a classical park, forests, and lakes. Also in Teplitz, brilliant company was reliably to be found. Goethe frequented the spa, likewise various aristocracy and royalty. Among the latter visitors this summer was Prince Kinsky, from whom Beethoven managed to extract the stipend money that had been in arrears.

One of those who made Beethoven's acquaintance on this visit to

Teplitz was diplomat, writer (later biographer of Goethe), and wounded veteran of the Austrian army Karl August Varnhagen von Ense. His impressions of Beethoven on this meeting, written to the poet Ludwig Uhland, stand as another high-Romantic paean to a demigod:

> I made the acquaintance of Beethoven and found this reputedly savage and unsociable man to be the most magnificent artist with a heart of gold, a glorious spirit and a friendly disposition. What he has refused to princes he granted to us at first sight: he played on the fortepiano. I soon was on intimate terms with him and his noble character, the uninterrupted flow of a godlike spirit which I always seemed to feel with an almost reverential awe when in his very silent presence . . . I spent the time entirely with him and his friend Oliva. The latter is one of the best of men . . . [Beethoven] is incredibly industrious and prolific. On his walks he seeks out distant places along the lonely paths between the mountains and through the forest, finding peace in the contemplation of the great features of nature . . . If I could only tell you how beautiful, how moving, devout, and serious, as if he had been kissed by a God, this man appeared as he played for us on the fortepiano some heavenly variations, pure creations granted by God to which the artist must give voice and, much as he would have wished, could not fix down on paper! At his request, my dear friend, I gave him all your poems.

Varnhagen got the full Beethoven treatment of puns, aphorisms, reminiscences, far-ranging observations, and complaints including diatribes against the French, plus admiration for the writer's fiancée, Rahel Levin, and a recollection of his 1806 fight with Lichnowsky: on one "fearful occasion a Prince [attempted] by physical force to make him play to his guests."[61] (Rahel, Varnhagen's "goddess of his heart's most dear delight," was a Jewish writer who kept a brilliant salon.[62] She and Varnhagen married in 1814, after she converted to Christianity.) Inevitably Beethoven turned their conversations toward an opera libretto.[63] In turn, Varnhagen introduced Beethoven to the philosopher and Kant disciple J. G. Fichte and to C. A. Tiedge, a poet and another Kantian, author of the lyric "An die Hoffnung" that Beethoven had set while courting Josephine. All members of this company were united in Francophobia. Beethoven took powerfully to Tiedge, and the two were quickly on a *du* intimacy. "Every day," Beethoven wrote the poet after he left Teplitz, "I berate myself for not having made your acquaintance at Teplitz sooner . . . Let us embrace like men who have cause to love and honor one another."[64] Inevitably, Beethoven saw Tiedge as not just a friend but also another potential librettist.

In fact, there is no record of any personal contact between Beethoven and Tiedge after this summer, and nothing else seemed to endure from the trip. No opera libretto appeared; in this period Beethoven said no to some dozen librettos submitted to him.[65] Meanwhile he and his new helpmate Oliva had a violent quarrel, which Varnhagen reported left the younger man "deeply depressed." They were soon reconciled and talked about going to England together — of which nothing came.[66]

The next meeting between Beethoven and Varnhagen was a couple of years later, in Vienna. On that occasion the writer found his demigod surly, unsociable, hostile toward the aristocracy, even uncouth, and declined to take him to see Rahel. Varnhagen would not have known that by that point Beethoven had suffered another failure in love, the worst yet.[67]

If Beethoven was ailing in 1811, however, his letters show a surprising lightness of spirit. His puckish imagination and rampant irony were running high. In a letter to Zmeskall, after a smeared line he finishes, "We make you a present of a few inkblots."[68] He wrote publisher Härtel another compendious letter, making excuses for *Christus* but trying to sell it anyway, and complained as usual about "those wretched r," meaning "reviewers" — he refused to write the word — who praised "the most contemptible bunglers." He ends with this sardonic melody: "You can't go on re-re-re-re-re-vi-vi-ew-ew-ew-ew-ing-ing to all eternity, that you can't do."[69] In the same letter he takes back the intended dedication of the Mass in C to Bettina Brentano, since "the lady is now married." It came out dedicated to Prince Kinsky, who had finally paid up his part of the stipend enhanced to account for inflation.

In one respect the Teplitz spa had its intended effect; for the moment, Beethoven felt healthier than he had in some time. He wrote Zmeskall in late October, "My feet are better, and the maker of the feet [presumably God] has promised the maker of the head [himself] a sound foot in eight days at latest."[70] The maker of the foot did not oblige.

On leaving Teplitz Beethoven visited Prince Lichnowsky at his estate in Graz, scene of their break five years earlier that had never completely healed. The once-lusty and -domineering Lichnowsky was failing, it was rumored from venereal disease. He had less than three years to live.[71] In nearby Troppeau Beethoven directed a performance of the Mass in C, of which he remained fond even if the world did not embrace it. After the mass he improvised on organ for a half hour — one of his last public performances. At the end of the year he wrote several versions of the lyric "An die Geliebte" (To the Beloved), perhaps with Antonie Brentano in mind: one version had an optional guitar part; she played the instrument.[72] It was the next spring when he gave the manuscript of one version to Antonie at her request. In it the poet imagines kissing a tear from his beloved's cheek, exclaiming, "[N]ow your sorrows are also mine!" To what extent this song, short in time but long in passion, was a testament of love for Antonie or only of empathy with that woman of constant sorrows is another of the mysteries of these days.

Back in Vienna he started his singing parties again, hoping for inspiration toward vocal works, and began sketching ideas for three new symphonies. On one page he jotted, "Freude schöner Götter Funken Tochter aus Elysium. Detached fragments, like princes are beggars, etc., not the whole ... Detached fragments from Schiller Freude brought together in a whole." Nearby in the sketchbook is a try at a melody for *An die Freude* and a note about a "Sinfonia in D moll."[73] So as of the turn of 1812 he was sketching what within the year became the Seventh and Eighth Symphonies, and what more than a decade later became the Ninth Symphony in D minor, which treats *An die Freude* just as he describes. These three symphonies amounted to the most ambitious slate of work he had planned in years.

But the work would never be unimpeded. The hopeful upturn in his health at Teplitz did not last. In November, he begged off a lesson with Archduke Rudolph, saying, "I was suddenly struck down by such a fever that I completely lost consciousness; an injured foot may have partly caused this feeling of faintness."[74] By now the foot infection, or whatever it was, had been torturing him for nearly a year.

Yet his creative energy was running relatively high, and also his kindness. This winter he began an extended correspondence with lawyer Joseph von Varena, whom he had met in Teplitz. Varena asked Beethoven for works to be done at charity concerts he was giving in Graz. Beethoven responded with great generosity and kept it up for years, donating to charities in Graz a stream of scores in print and manuscript.[75] "From my earliest childhood," he wrote Varena, "my zeal to serve our poor suffering humanity in any way whatsoever by means of my art has made no compromise with any lower motive . . . the only reward I have asked for was the feeling of inward happiness which always attends such actions."[76] The Graz charity concert of December 1811 included the *Choral Fantasy*; a seventeen-year-old pianist named Marie Koschak, whom Beethoven had recommended, scored a triumph with the solo part.[77]

In February the hastily assembled music for Kotzebue's *King Stephan* and *The Ruins of Athens* premiered with the plays in Pest. In comparison to its fellow quick productions such as *Christus am Ölberge* and *Prometheus*, this theater music seems closer to being truly Beethovenian, like the *Egmont* music. At the same time it was not so far from hackwork, written to please, in keeping with the Hungarian chauvinism of the plays. This theater music presaged a coming period of occasional pieces Beethoven turned out for the money.

In the end, of his more commercial items this music would stand as some of the more appealing, or anyway less notorious. The *Ruins of Athens* Overture is in his rich, fully developed theatrical style. Of the incidental pieces, the choral music is duly and conventionally inspiring, likewise a bass aria begotten by Mozart's Zarastro in *Die Zauberflöte*. There is an over-the-top male chorus that sounds rather like Mozart's Turks in *The Abduction from the Seraglio* singing from the fierce passions of opium. All this music for the "mustachios" of Hungary has a degree of exotic coloration; the evocative sonorities of the overture would have their impact, along with *Coriolan* and *Egmont*, on Romantic overtures and program music for many years to come. Best of all for Beethoven, this music went over nicely with audiences. From the Septet op. 20 onward, his most commercial pieces often turned out to be his most popular.

February 1812 also saw the Vienna premiere of the Fifth Piano Concerto, later dubbed *Emperor,* with Carl Czerny soloing. This concerto from 1809, which Beethoven wrote probably knowing he would never play because of his deafness, was not premiered until November 1811, in a Leipzig concert he did not attend. Like its predecessor, the *Emperor* is dedicated to Archduke Rudolph. The majestic quality that earned its name would be credited to the influence of its dedicatee, brother of the emperor. But there were many Beethoven dedications to Rudolph, and their characters range widely.

A more likely reason for the tone of the Fifth Concerto is simply that he had written nothing like it, and he wanted maximum contrast from his output in a given genre. As usual with Beethoven, the *Emperor* lays out its essential character and ideas in the first moments. It is in E-flat major, most often a heroic key for him, and so it is here. (It is his last heroic-style work in E-flat major.) We hear a *fortissimo* chord from the orchestra that summons bravura torrents of notes from the piano. The radical step is less the idea of beginning with the soloist (as he had already done in the Fourth Concerto) than the cadenza-like quality, which will mark much of the solo part (the reason he omits the usual concluding cadenzas). A second towering chord from the orchestra is answered by more heroic peals from the piano, this time sinking to some quiet *espressivo* phrases that foreshadow the second movement.

Only then does the orchestra set out on the leading theme, in a sweeping and imperious military style. By now it's clear that this piece is heroic in tone, symphonic in scope, and *the* hero is the soloist. The opening theme dominates the movement. The appearance of a softly lilting second theme in exotic E-flat minor presages a work marked by unusual key shifts, their effect ranging from startling to mysterious. At the end of the orchestral exposition the soloist returns on a rising chromatic dash that leads to a two-fisted proclamation of his own version of the orchestra's theme. It dissolves into flashing garlands of notes, continuing the endless cadenza in the solo part that persists through the course of an enormous movement.

After an opening more consistently militant in style than in any other Beethoven concerto, the second movement unfolds in a serenely spiritual atmosphere, beginning with an eloquent theme in muted strings that Czerny said was based on pilgrims' hymns. It echoes the quiet *espressivo* phrases of the first movement's opening. In turn, the spirituality of the second movement is punctuated with touches of the soloist's first-movement bravura.

Picking up directly from the end of the slow movement, the rondo finale begins with a lusty, offbeat theme in the piano. Call its tone playfully heroic. As in the first movement, the opening theme dominates. Toward the end, a thrumming martial timpani seems to herald the approach of the final cadenza. But once again there is no cadenza because the soloist has been showing off in a quasi-improvisatory fashion all along. The piece finishes with offbeat exclamations that land on the beat only at the last moment. So ends not the final work in Beethoven's heroic style but one of the last in which he seems to take the heroic mode at face value. He never completed another concerto.

Johann Friedrich Rochlitz, editor of the *Allgemeine Musikalische Zeitung* (so often maligned by Beethoven to its owner Härtel), called it "doubtless one of the most original, most inventive, most effective, but also most difficult of all existing concertos," and reported the audience at the Leipzig premiere to be "in transports of delight" at the end. The Viennese received it without enthusiasm.[78]

The two premieres, the slighter theater work receiving the most acclaim, ushered in an eventful, in some ways too eventful, year for Beethoven. His fame was secure, his earlier "revolutionary" works had settled into the repertoire, publishers were contending for his work (though not Breitkopf & Härtel anymore). In 1812, he completed the Seventh and Eighth Symphonies.

It could have been no surprise that in that year sculptor Franz Klein turned up at his door wanting to make a plaster life mask of the famous man. Partly because of the new quasi-science of phrenology—the theory that face and head reveal character, genius, what have you — molding the faces of the great had become fashionable. Goethe, George Washington, Keats, and many others submitted to the procedure. More practically, Klein and other artists wanted an objective record of a subject's "real" face on which to model paintings and sculptures. Klein's enthusiasm for taking casts of his subjects was reflected in his Viennese nickname of "Head Chopper." The impetus for this particular life mask came from piano maker Johann Andreas Streicher; he had commissioned Klein to make a bust of Beethoven to add to the distinguished company of busts in his private concert hall.

So one day Beethoven found himself lying face-up at an angle, his face and hair soaked in soapy water and oil, protective material covering his eyes, straws stuck up his nose to breathe through, while the Head Chopper slathered a thick mass of reeking wet gypsum over his face. As the procedure went on and on with excruciating slowness, Beethoven became increasingly fearful that he was going to suffocate. Suddenly in a spasm of anger and fear he jerked off the almost-set cast, threw it to the floor, and ran from the room.

The mask shattered into pieces. Klein was able to glue them together and so reconstructed the "true" face of the composer, down to his scars from smallpox or whatever it was. From there Klein made his soon-famous bust that, with the mask itself, became the model for most portraits of Beethoven from then on. The mask and those ensuing portraits show a small man with a formidable scowl turning down his protruding lips, his chin and brow fiercely clenched, his hair standing nearly on end. That was the image the Romantic world and later ages came to know Beethoven by. It was the face they wanted to see in their geniuses: fierce, bold, defiant, suffering, stormy up to the slant of his hair. So tormented did it look that for the rest of the century, many people assumed it was Beethoven's death mask.

With Klein's life mask and bust, the visual corollary of the Beethoven myth entered the zeitgeist. But no earlier portraits had that look, and neither did later ones done from life by artists who were observing what was actually in front of them, the man rather than the myth. Beethoven did not look like that bust most of the time. Except in his rages, his face was usually impassive, the major animation being in the eyes. The Klein mask and the bust he made from it are not a "real"

portrait of a genius. They are the face of a man scowling because he is ✳
angry and uncomfortable and frightened.[79]

Beethoven was perennially annoyed by the peripherals of fame, such
as the tribe of artists wanting him to sit still so they could capture his
face and his soul — though he sometimes liked the results. But there
were more serious things concerning him in 1812. He was still locked
in the grip of his ailments, but working on the Seventh and Eighth
Symphonies. "I have been constantly unwell and extremely busy," he
wrote his new friend Varena in Graz, offering him the first of the new
symphonies for a charity concert.[80]

At the end of July he left Vienna for his second Teplitz sojourn in
hope of a cure. Waiting to greet him there were Prince Lichnowsky;
Bettina von Arnim, formerly Brentano, with her new husband Achim,
and her brother Clemens; Karl August Varnhagen; Goethe; and a mysterious woman with whom Beethoven was desperately in love.

25

My Angel, My Self

ONLY TO YOUTH can love seem easy. With the years come losses that taint the yearning and the passion. From his twenties into his thirties Beethoven had been a lionized virtuoso, steadily but capriciously in love, and women showed up at his door. Then came Josephine Deym, beautiful and musical, whom he could not get off his mind. Her rejection devastated him but did not damp the fire of his work. In 1812, his desires were a different matter than his pursuit of Josephine five years before. It is as if after the creative climax at the end of 1808, when he put two new symphonies and the Fourth Piano Concerto before the public, he looked up from his labors and realized how miserably alone he had been. He courted Therese Malfatti, a girl of seventeen, and for his trouble gained only humiliation. But he did not give up, not yet. He had not forgotten Josephine. He had met Bettina Brentano and met or renewed his acquaintance with Antonie Brentano, and both women captivated him.

There was new urgency in his search now. This kind of desperation for love and companionship is a symptom of age, in Beethoven's case of passing forty alone and in bad health. And now a woman had appeared who had not drawn away from him, who for the first time in his life seemed prepared to return his love. But there was something awry between them.

He had to have been in a frantic state as he headed for the Teplitz resort at the end of June. He stopped in Prague and met with his dilatory patron Prince Kinsky, who gave him an advance of 600 florins on the next installment of the stipend.[1] On July 3, Beethoven failed to turn up for a planned evening with his earlier Teplitz acquaintance Karl Varnhagen. "I was sorry, dear V," he wrote later, "not to be able to spend my last evening at Prague with you . . . But a circumstance which I could not foresee prevented me."[2] He had received urgent news. Things were coming to a head.

Two days later, his coach struggling into Bohemia in miserably cold and rainy weather, Beethoven arrived in Teplitz.[3] The meeting of Goethe and Beethoven that Bettina had stage-managed was about to happen. But at that point Beethoven was thinking of another meeting, with a woman whom he believed to be nearby in Karlsbad. The next day he began to write her a letter in a mingling of love, hope, and despair, his words spilling onto the page like music with the surge of his passion. It is his only surviving letter to a woman that steadily uses the intimate *du*, "thou," a sign of intimacy between friends or lovers:

July 6
In the morning —

My angel, my all, my self. — only a few words today, in fact with pencil (with yours) — only tomorrow is my lodging positively fixed, what a worthless waste of time on such things — why this deep grief, when necessity speaks — Can our love exist but by sacrifices, by not demanding everything, can you change it, that you not completely mine, I am not completely yours — Oh God look upon beautiful nature and calm your soul over what must be — love demands everything and completely with good reason, so it is <u>for me with you, for you with me</u> — only you forget so easily, that I must live <u>for myself and for you,</u> were we wholly united, you would feel this painfulness just as little as I do —

my trip was frightful, I arrived here only at 4 o'clock yesterday morning, because they lacked horses . . . at the next to the last station they warned me about traveling at night, made me afraid of a forest, but this only provoked me — but I was wrong, the coach had to break down on the terrible route . . . still I had some pleasure again, as always whenever I fortunately survive something —

now quickly to interior from exterior, we will probably see each other soon, even today I cannot convey to you the observations I made during these last few days about my life — were our hearts always closely united, I would of course not have to . . . my heart is full of much to tell you — Oh — there are still moments when I find that speech is nothing at all —

cheer up — remain my faithful only treasure, my all, as I for you the rest of the gods must send, what must and should be for us — your faithful ludwig

Monday evening on July 6 —

You are suffering you my dearest creature — just now I notice that letters must be posted very early in the morning Mondays — Thursdays — the only days on which mail goes from here to K[arlsbad] — you are suffering — Oh, wherever I am, you are with me, I talk to myself and to you — arrange that I can live with you, what a life!!!! like this!!!! without you — Persecuted by the kindness of people here and there, which I think — I want to deserve just as little as I deserve it — Homage of man to man — it pains me —

and when I regard myself in the framework of the universe, what am I and what is he — whom one calls the Greatest — and yet — herein is again the divine spark of man — I weep when I think that you will probably not receive the first news of me until Saturday — as much as you love me — I love you even more deeply but — never hide yourself from me —

good night — since I am taking the baths I must go to sleep — Oh god — so near! So far! Is not our love a true heavenly edifice — but also firm, like the firmament —

good morning July 7

— while still in bed my thoughts rush toward you my Immortal Beloved now and then happy, then again sad, awaiting fate, if it will grant us a favorable hearing — I can only live either wholly with you or not at all

yes I have resolved to wander about in the distance, until I can fly into your arms, and can call myself entirely at home with you, can send my soul embraced by you into the realm of spirits — yes unfortunately it must be — you will compose yourself all the more, since you know my faithfulness to you, never can another own my heart, never — never — O God why have to separate oneself, what one loves so and yet my life in V[ienna] as it is now is a miserable life —

at my age now I need some uniformity and consistency of life — can this exist in our relationship? — Angel, right now I hear that the mail goes every day — and I must therefore close, so that you will receive the L[etter] immediately — be calm, only through quiet contemplation of our existence can we reach our goal to live together — be patient — love me — today — yesterday — What longing with tears for you — you — you — my love — my all — farewell — o continue to love me — never misjudge the most faithful heart of your beloved

L.

forever yours
forever mine
forever us[4]

This letter, written over the course of two days, is the only surviving part of an ongoing dialogue between Beethoven and his lover that had been carried on in letters and in person for some unknown length of time. Its contradictions echo his jumble of feelings. He was writing with her pencil, so they had been together not long before. The feelings revealed in his words are an excruciating mixture of yearning and uncertainty, of hope trying to overcome despair. Their dialogue had reached a point where, at either Teplitz or Karlsbad, they needed to reach a resolution.

The reason for his pain is adumbrated between the lines: "[C]an you change it, that you [are] not completely mine, I am not completely yours." He had fallen into his old pattern: his lover was married or betrothed or otherwise unavailable. The difference this time was that she reciprocated his love. Since it was some sort of forbidden relationship, the secrecy between them was so tight that no other letter between the two survives that clearly identifies her. For the rest of his life Beethoven kept these pages with him, hidden alongside the Heiligenstadt Testament and portraits of women he had loved, one of his collection of secret talismans. The letter may never have been mailed, or she may have returned it. He could keep it because it did not have her name on it. Deliberately, nothing was to be left for history to find her out. The future would know her only as *Unsterbliche Geliebte,* "Immortal Beloved."[5]

"[L]ove demands everything and completely with good reason, so it is for me with you, for you with me . . . I must live for myself and for you." They are united in love but not in life. How they are united cannot be gleaned from his words. Are they physically lovers or lovers in spirit, living in the hope of somehow being fully united? A plea for resignation, from himself and from her. He says fate must decide the issue, and for Beethoven fate was always a hostile power. And yet, he reminds her, in each of us there is a spark of the divine that cannot reach but can imagine God. "Is not our love a true heavenly edifice[?]" The love of man and woman, Mozart taught in *Die Zauberflöte* and Schiller in "An die Freude," is the earthly counterpart of divine love.

"I can only live either wholly with you or not at all." No more of this neither-nor; it must be one or the other. "[A]t my age now I need some uniformity and consistency of life — can this exist in our relationship?" He was forty-two, in his day much closer to the end than to the beginning. The letter speaks of his love in rapturous and anguished phrases, dogged by a sense of impossibility. At his age he can't live and love merely on hope. "[O]nly through quiet contemplation of our existence can we reach our goal to live together." Only in finding a way out of their dilemma. Now they must meet and decide whether there really can be a way, whether she is to be his Immortal Beloved forever or never.

Some of his letter is made of balanced phrases or antitheses, like a psalm: "you [are] not completely mine, I am not completely yours . . . for me with you, for you with me . . . you — you — you — my love — my all — farewell — o continue to love me." He finishes with the incantation, like a coda, "forever yours / forever mine / forever us," which is more music than sense.

The letter to the Immortal Beloved is the second great tragic aria of Beethoven's emotional life. The first was the Heiligenstadt Testament. That letter presaged defiance and an explosion of music. This second letter presaged suicidal depression and a sinking toward triviality and silence in his art.

Who was the Immortal Beloved? In the next two hundred years of speculation, history turned up no decisive answer, only a welter of tantalizing but inconclusive facts trailing off into uncertainties buttressed by guesses and suppositions. Still, there are essentially only three candidates.

In Beethoven's surviving correspondence the fierce, sometimes almost incoherent passion of his letter to the Immortal Beloved, its breathless phrases joined by dashes, connects it with only one person in his past: Josephine Deym. His letters to her have the same tone and style. When he wrote the letter to the Immortal Beloved, Josephine's two-year-old second marriage was already coming apart; the couple's first separation came in the next year.[6] But there is no evidence that Josephine was anywhere other than in Vienna at the time he wrote the letter, and no evidence of any connection either in person or in correspondence between them since their farewell letters of 1807.[7]

The other candidates are the two women Beethoven met in 1810 — unless he already knew Antonie Brentano from years before, through her family in Vienna. Antonie was miserable in her marriage. He was often at the Brentano house; she and Beethoven had formed a bond of mutual sympathy and affection. She was in Karlsbad when he wrote the Immortal Beloved letter to someone in that resort. Yet in contrast to Josephine's current husband, Antonie's husband was not cruel or indifferent; he was kind and patient with her. The trouble was that Franz Brentano was dull, always sunk in business. Antonie respected but did not love him, and she hated living in Frankfurt. But Beethoven was a man of rigid, almost puritanical ethics when it came to women and marriage — even if like most people he violated those ethics sometimes. He was friends with Franz Brentano and trusted him enough to borrow money from him and to ask his business advice. The couple had children; Antonie was pregnant for the fifth time when Beethoven wrote the Immortal Beloved letter.[8] After the sad denouement with the

Immortal Beloved, Beethoven actually went to stay with the Brentanos at Karlsbad and Franzenbad in August.[9]

It is hard to believe that Beethoven could have thought of breaking up Antonie's family, of taking on five children, of dealing such a blow to a man he liked and respected. Besides, if a pregnant Antonie had left her husband for Beethoven, the scandal would have been public and loud, reverberating between Vienna and Frankfurt.[10] It is equally hard to imagine that Beethoven would carry on a backstairs affair with a married woman at the same time that he socialized with the couple and enjoyed their children, who brought him fruit and flowers at his lodging in Vienna.[11]

The last candidate is, on the face of it, the most likely one: Bettina Brentano. She was young, fascinating, passionate, brilliant, talented, musical. She idolized Beethoven and plainly wanted to serve as his muse. It is hard to see Bettina as other than the kind of woman Beethoven had been searching for (except that Bettina conformed to no kind of woman other than herself). However, when they first met in 1810 and spent a few days closely in company, there was a barrier between them — at the time, Beethoven was courting Therese Malfatti. By the time he was disabused of that fantasy and had recovered his wits, Bettina was in the process of contemplating and finally accepting the proposal of Achim von Arnim.

To complicate the picture, there are reports that Bettina said her marriage was made not for love but because Arnim needed an heir to inherit some property, and it flattered her that a poet of his stature wanted to have a child with her.[12] (It was just before her engagement to Arnim that she paid her shattering visit to Goethe, when he suddenly began undressing her. Was this what Bettina wanted from Goethe? Now when it finally happened, she was about to be engaged. "The memory of it tears me apart," she wrote in describing the scene.)[13] Bettina had expected to be in Karlsbad and/or Teplitz around the time Beethoven wrote the Immortal Beloved letter, though her visit was delayed because she was recovering in Berlin from a nearly fatal first childbirth and accompanying depression. Still, she and Arnim went on to a long and affectionate marriage, with six more children.[14]

Around this point the facts about Bettina drift into speculation.

While Arnim was courting her, she and Beethoven exchanged any number of letters, of which only one of his survives (see chapter 24). In that letter, which refers to her lost letters, Beethoven does not seem crushed by the news of her marriage; his affection is strong but couched in terms more gallant than ecstatic. Bettina lived in Berlin. Could Beethoven have been courting a newly married and then pregnant woman at a distance? Could Bettina have reciprocated to the extent that she thought seriously of leaving Achim, with or without her newborn, and running off with Beethoven? Even somebody as unconventional as Bettina would have been daunted by that kind of scandal.

In 1816, Beethoven was reported to have told his nephew's schoolmaster that five years before he had met a woman who still obsessed him. If he meant the Immortal Beloved, and he probably did, that dating would apply to Bettina certainly, Antonie possibly, Josephine not at all.[15] As far as answering to Beethoven's statement "you are suffering," that applies to all three women. Bettina was gravely depressed. Antonie was chronically unhappy in her marriage and had been ill for some time. Josephine's second marriage was a disaster.

Josephine, Antonie, Bettina — each of those women was close to Beethoven, each of them had aroused his feelings and his sympathy, each of them was musical and admired him as much as anyone on earth. He loved each of them in some fashion and degree. Yet there appear to be unanswerable reasons why each of them could *not* have been the Immortal Beloved. He formed a friendship with Franz and Antonie Brentano, visited the family, enjoyed the children, borrowed money from Franz and asked for advice. His later letters to Antonie are warm but have not the slightest hint of simmering pain or regret.

As for Bettina, in the middle of her postpartum depression could she have contemplated leaving her new husband? Could Josephine Deym have been finding romantic feelings for Beethoven she never had before, making him promises during her second year of marriage, however much she regretted that marriage? Again, there is no record of Josephine being anywhere near Teplitz or Karlsbad when he wrote to the Immortal Beloved in Karlsbad.

All of it seems unbelievable. It makes no sense that any of these women is a credible candidate for the Immortal Beloved. *But life rarely makes sense.* It is close to certain that one of them was indeed the woman to whom Beethoven wrote his ecstatic and anguished letter of July 1812. Whoever she was, both of them covered their tracks thoroughly. In the next two centuries no unequivocal piece of evidence turned up.

Years later Bettina von Arnim published three letters from Beethoven: the one from 1811 that survived and the two that did not. The last nonsurviving one is full of surging feelings and virtual worship of Bettina. It ends, "God, how I love you." If it could be authenticated (not long after it was published it was questioned, the questioning growing into a chorus of condemnation over the years), the letter would go far to suggest that Bettina was the one. But missing letters cannot be authenticated.[16] Some of that letter seems more convincing, some of it less. In later years Bettina told Karl Varnhagen that Beethoven had loved and wanted to marry her. By then Varnhagen had known Bettina for a long time, and she was intimately close to his wife Rahel. Varnhagen did not remotely believe what Bettina told him about her and Beethoven.[17]

Yet Bettina can no more be dismissed than Antonie and Josephine. And, though it is far less likely, neither can some other unknown or unsuspected name be entirely ruled out. If the latter case was true, that woman has left no convincing traces at all. It may be that history will never know the identity of Beethoven's Immortal Beloved of 1812, who may well have sparked the rush of work that created the joyous Seventh Symphony and the comic and nostalgic Eighth, and afterward precipitated his decline toward silence. When he wrote the letter their relationship urgently had to be decided. Was it to be joining or parting, forever or never? By the time he left Teplitz it apparently had been decided. They must part.

There the mystery rests. What cannot be mistaken is the aftermath, the grinding depression that settled over Beethoven in the next two years. Added to his disappointment in love was a rankling loneliness. Old friends and patrons had fallen away: Prince Lobkowitz was struggling financially and not paying his part of the stipend; Prince Lichnowsky was dying; Baron Gleichenstein had angered Beethoven by declining to join him in Teplitz the previous year; in some degree he was estranged, for the moment, from his "father confessor," Countess Erdödy, and from Stephan von Breuning, one of his oldest friends; at the end of this year the Brentanos returned to Frankfurt and Beethoven never saw Antonie again, though they corresponded a few times. He had never felt so wounded, so alone, so uncertain of his direction in life or in art.

A week after writing his beloved, Beethoven wrote his note to Varnhagen in Prague, apologizing for missing their appointment: "There is not much to tell you about T[eplitz], for there are few people here and no distinguished ones . . . Hence I am living — alone — alone! alone!"[18]

A few days later, he wrote a singular letter to a stranger. Young pianist Emilie M. had sent him an admiring letter and enclosed the gift of a wallet she had made. It seems she had declared him to be as great as or greater than the masters of the past. In those days he was not feeling so great. His warm and kindly response to this child he probably never met is a sad meditation and confession, in a tone never seen anywhere else in his correspondence:

> My reply to your letter to me is late in arriving. My excuse must be a great amount of business and persistent illness . . . Do not rob Handel, Haydn and Mozart of their laurel wreaths. They are entitled to theirs, but I am not yet entitled to one.
>
> Your wallet will be treasured among other tokens of a regard which several people have expressed for me, but which I am still far from deserving.
>
> Persevere, do not only practice your art, but endeavor also to fathom its inner meaning; it deserves this effort. For only art and science can raise men to the level of gods.
>
> If, my dear Emilie, you should ever desire to have anything, do not hesitate to write to me. The true artist has no pride. He sees unfortunately that art has no limits; he has a vague awareness of how far he is from reaching his goal; and while others may perhaps be admiring him, he laments the fact that he has not yet reached the point whither his better genius only lights the way for him like a distant sun.
>
> I should probably prefer to visit you and your family than to visit

many a rich person who betrays a poverty of mind. If I should ever go to H., then I will call on you and your family. I know of no other human excellences than those which entitle one to be numbered among one's better fellow creatures. Where I find people of that type, there is my home.

If you want to write to me, dear Emilie, just address your letter to Teplitz where I am staying for four weeks. Or you may write to Vienna. It really doesn't matter. Look upon me as your friend and friend of your family.[19]

There are things in these pages that can be taken for more than passing notions. He writes that one's creations never come up to one's vision of what they can be. Art has no limits, the prize is never won, what one most hopes to achieve is always over the horizon. This is a rueful wisdom that most artists arrive at sooner or later. But in no other known place did Beethoven express it, or so firmly decline a laurel wreath for his own head. In his youth he had declared himself equal to anything. Now he saw his limits, or finally admitted them. A strain of self-abnegation creeps into his letters in these days. For Emilie he includes a credo: *Only art and science can raise men to the level of gods.* Not prayer, not miracle, not the church. Science and art both revelation, both divine. So he had learned in Bonn, and even in his suffering he never lost that faith.

The day after writing young Emilie, Beethoven met Goethe at last. The men had been circling one another warily at a distance for two years, since Bettina began her campaign to bring them together. But though Bettina was soon to arrive in Teplitz, she would not be permitted to join them for the great event. Recently at a picture exhibition she had gotten into a violent argument over a painting with Goethe's wife Christiane. It ended with Christiane ripping off Bettina's glasses and stamping on them.[20] As Bettina reported the fracas, she had been "bitten by a mad blood-sausage" — a pointed reference to Frau Goethe's weight, and the phrase got around.[21] Goethe had little choice. He banished Bettina from his presence; there were no more meetings or letters between them as long as Christiane lived. Bettina's husband

Achim, finding the situation as amusing as it was sad, wrote a friend from Teplitz, "Just imagine this, Goethe and Beethoven both here, and yet my wife is not enjoying herself! The first doesn't want to know her, and the second isn't able to hear her. The poor devil is getting deafer and deafer, and it's really painful to see the friendly smile he puts on it."[22] (If Bettina was the Immortal Beloved, they were meeting behind Achim's back to end their affair.)

In an already awkward situation, then, Goethe and Beethoven met. They spent the better part of a week together every day, walking and talking. Goethe made himself understood as best as he could. Beethoven played for the older man, asked for an opera libretto; Goethe promised one.[23] Beethoven felt honored, thrilled, at the same time disappointed by their encounter. Goethe felt great admiration for this artist nearly as legendary as himself, but he was not thrilled and in fact was considerably annoyed. They parted with assurances of friendship and collaboration. Then, nothing. No libretto, no exchange of letters. They may never have met again. The titans of their time could find no common ground.

This was not unusual, however. First meetings with Goethe often did not go well. He was firmly installed on his pedestal, he had nothing to prove to anybody, and in his work he did not need anybody. It was up to his admirers to make an impression. The first encounter between Goethe and Schiller, destined to be historic collaborators, had been an icy affair. Afterward the outraged Schiller declared that Goethe was "like a proud prude who has to be got with child so as to humiliate him before the world." With that unpleasantness out of the way, they began to find out how much they could give each other. Still, even through the historic years of their friendship, they never used the intimate *du*.[24]

For the rest of his life Beethoven proudly spoke of Goethe as his friend, but he was no such thing. Directly after their meeting Goethe wrote his wife, "More concentrated, more energetic and more intimate I have never yet seen an artist." But to his musical adviser Carl Friedrich Zelter, Goethe wrote, "I made Beethoven's acquaintance in Teplitz. His talent amazed me. However, unfortunately, he is an utterly untamed personality, who is not altogether in the wrong if he

finds the world detestable, but he thereby does not make it more enjoyable either for himself or others. He is very much to be excused,
on the other hand, and very much to be pitied, as his hearing is
leaving him, which, perhaps, injures the musical part of his nature
less than his social. He, by nature laconic, becomes doubly so because of this lack."[25]

What happened between them? It can be traced only in letters. The
context was that when he met Goethe, Beethoven had been in an agitated state, either reeling from the blowup of the Immortal Beloved
affair or anxious about its imminent outcome. But it meant a great deal
to him to have Goethe's friendship and collaboration, and he had the
capacity to win over people he needed, even when he was suffering.
Certainly he understood the challenge. He wrote Härtel, "If only I do
not have the same experience with him as others have with me!!!" He
asked the publisher for a presentation copy of his *Kennst du das Land?*
setting, adding, "and be sure to have it made on the thinnest and finest paper, for I am a poor Austrian musical bungler." He rarely wrote
self-deprecating words like that, still less like those he scratched out in
his subsequent phrase: "povero musico! (yet not in the manner — of a
castrato)."[26] In the tumult of the Immortal Beloved, the image of himself as a castrato had entered his mind.

It happened as he feared it would: he failed to impress Goethe, just
as most people failed to impress him. The main reason appears to have
been that he found Goethe's position as a courtier and his deference to
the aristocracy intolerable. Being Beethoven, he could not help saying
so. But his whole approach had been on the wrong foot.

The most famous stories about their meeting came from a letter of
Bettina's written years later. Beethoven had played piano for Goethe
and felt disappointed at the old man's moved but quiet response. To
Goethe he said, "'Once years ago I played well in Berlin and expected
great applause, but the only response from this oh-so-cultured audience was to wave handkerchiefs wet with tears. That was all wasted on
a rude enthusiast like me.'" Artists want applause, he told Goethe, the
longer and louder, the better. As in Berlin, with you I felt as if "'I had
merely a romantic, not an artistic audience before me. But I accept it
gladly from you, Goethe.'" But, Bettina reported, he did not accept it

gladly. "'You must know yourself how good it feels to be applauded by intelligent hands; if you do not recognize me and esteem me as a peer, who shall do so? By which pack of beggars shall I permit myself to be understood?'"

"Thus did he push Goethe into a corner," Bettina added after relating that moment. This is Bettina writing at a distance in time: whether reporting, gilding, or inventing is always the question with her. But the story rings true. Beethoven could not keep his mouth shut. And he needed Goethe more than Goethe needed him. He put his fellow titan on the spot, criticized not Goethe's lack of response but his way of responding—like a shallow and sentimental Romantic. This sounds more like Beethoven than like Bettina, the arch-Romantic. But that is not the most famous part of her report.

She painted a scene of the two walking in Teplitz and encountering the empress and a collection of archdukes. She said Beethoven had already lectured Goethe about his deference to the nobility: "'Nonsense, that's not the way . . . you must plainly make them understand what they have in having you or they will never find out . . . [They] can make a court councillor . . . but not a Goethe or a Beethoven.'" (Goethe in fact took pride in being a court official.) In Teplitz when the royal party reached them, Goethe stepped aside, took off his hat, and bowed his head in deference. Beethoven strode through the crowd, tipping his hat curtly. The party of nobles stepped aside to make room and greeted him. "'Well,'" he said to Goethe when the party had left, "'I've waited for you because I honor and respect you as you deserve, but you did those yonder too much honor.'" Afterward, Bettina reported, Beethoven came running to her and Arnim and gleefully reported the story. She in turn told Goethe's patron the duke of Weimar, who teased his resident genius about it.[27]

This incident may have transpired just as Bettina related it, or not. In any case, once again, she knew her men and had not departed entirely from reality. Something like that happened. Shortly after the meeting, Beethoven wrote Gottfried Härtel, "Goethe delights far too much in the court atmosphere, far more than is becoming to a poet. How can one really say very much about the ridiculous behavior of virtuosi in this respect [kowtowing to the nobility], when poets, who should be regarded as the leading teachers of the nation, forget everything else when confronted with that glitter —."[28]

In some form or other Beethoven had expressed his disappointments to Goethe. For his part, Goethe did not need to be lectured on his politics and behavior by anybody, even a Beethoven, or made fun of by his patron.

In short, Goethe found his fellow demigod to be a pain in the neck. Musically he never went beyond Haydn and Mozart. They give one room to feel for oneself, he said, rather than grabbing one's lapel. It is possible the two men got together when they were both in Karlsbad in the fall. In any case, after this year Goethe saw to it that they never met or exchanged letters again. So it happened that despite Bettina's best efforts, her titans went their ways separately. Later when the young Mendelssohn played the Fifth Symphony at the piano for Goethe, the old man was much agitated: "It's tremendous, quite mad; one could fear the whole house might collapse — imagine the lot of them playing it together!" He is reported to have enjoyed Beethoven's music for *Egmont*, but it seems Goethe never heard a Beethoven symphony from a full orchestra, and never wanted to.[29]

Part of Beethoven's despair that summer was that his health only declined as he took his daily baths and gulped the waters. (The medical effects of spas in those days were psychological at best, dangerous at worst. The mineral waters might contain lead, radioactivity, arsenic, and the like.) That summer he shuttled between spas, searching for healing and companionship. In Teplitz the year before, he had made the acquaintance of Amalie Sebald, a vivacious singer in her twenties, and they formed a flirtatious but not enduring relationship. Now from Karlsbad in September 1812, in response to some teasing letter of hers, he wrote Amalie in a mingling of banter and frustration: "I a tyrant? A tyrant to you! Only misjudgment of my character can make you say such a thing . . . Since yesterday I have not been feeling very well, and this morning my indisposition became more serious . . . All good wishes, dear A. If the moon seems to me to be brighter this evening than the sun has been during the day, then you will have a visit from a small person — from the smallest of small persons." In Karlsbad, staying in a guest house with Antonie and Franz Brentano, he began a long siege in bed. He invited Amalie to visit his bedside if she did not find that improper.[30] But mostly Beethoven lay alone in the trance of illness, music and pain and regret competing in his mind.

Before this new bout of debility, he had bestirred himself to play a concert with violin virtuoso Giovanni Battista Polledro. It was a benefit for his often-visited resort of Baden, where more than a hundred houses had been destroyed in a fire. Their concert brought in nearly 1,000 florins for relief of the homeless. Among other pieces the two played one of Beethoven's violin sonatas, and Beethoven improvised. He did not like the results, reporting it glumly as "a poor concert for the poor."[31]

His musical trials did not end there. In the summer of 1810, he had sent off fifty-three British Isles folk songs, arranged for voice, piano, violin, and cello, to publisher George Thomson in Edinburgh. He received a report from Thomson: "What delightful little conversations between the violin and violoncello. In a word, I am completely charmed by all of them." But not so charmed as not to demand that some of them be redone and simplified, to make them easier for the young Scottish ladies he hoped would buy them. When Haydn worked for Thomson, he reported, he "invited me to indicate to him frankly everything that would not please the national taste in the ritornellos and accompaniments." "Permit me to request," Thomson concludes, "that . . . you make the piano part completely simple, easy to read at sight, and easy to play." (In one accompaniment Beethoven had written a stretch of sixteenths in the right hand with triplets in the left — three against four, completely impractical for amateurs of modest ability.)[32] He instructs Beethoven how to write the arrangements, asking for more imitation between violin and cello and an independent violin line rather than one doubling the voice.[33]

There began a long exchange of mutual frustration. No one had ever subjected Beethoven to these kinds of nitpicking demands, but he kept his temper and tried to address Thomson's relentless refrains: Thomson couldn't provide Beethoven texts for the songs because he was commissioning new ones from poets (as he had done from Robert Burns);[34] Haydn did not ask for so much money; Haydn never ex-

pected more money for requested revisions. "In our country there is
not one pianist in a hundred who would like the ritornellos and accompaniments that I wish you [to] revise."[35]

Exasperated, Beethoven wrote back that he would not revise the accompaniments, "being convinced that any partial alteration changes
the character of the composition." Even in this piecework he was concerned with the total effect, and he called them "compositions" instead
of "arrangements." Rather than revising, he would do completely new
versions of the same tunes, but he expected to be paid for them: "I regret that you will suffer the loss; but you can scarcely put the blame on
me, since it ought to have been your affair to advise me more explicitly
of the taste of your country and small skill of your players." To provide
a positive note, he wrote that two of the songs Thomson sent "pleased
me very much," and he had done those settings "*con amore*."[36] He had
asked Thomson for 4 gold ducats (at that point about 30 florins) for
each song. If, as Thomson retorted, Viennese court composer Kozeluch was happy to receive only 2 ducats for each setting, Beethoven observed sardonically, "I must congratulate you and also the English and
Scottish audiences if they like [Kozeluch's settings]. I consider myself
twice as good in this genre as Mr Kozeluch," so he should be paid twice
as much.[37] Thomson stuck to 3 ducats per item. Meanwhile because
international postage was disrupted by the raging Napoleonic Wars,
the songs had to be mailed back and forth in multiple copies sent by
different routes. One package Beethoven posted via Malta took two
years to arrive in Scotland.[38]

Thomson did relent here and there, especially regarding Beethoven's
plea for texts. "I cannot understand," Beethoven wrote, "how you who
are a connoisseur cannot realize that I would produce completely different compositions if I had the text to hand, and the songs can never
become perfect products if you do not send me the text."[39] Thomson
later sent some words or at least summaries of the songs' topics: "*Dun-
can Gray*: A shepherd loving a village coquette is repulsed and becomes
disdainful in turn; but the village girl repents of her folly, is pardoned,
and they marry . . . *Auld Lang Syne*: A meeting of friends after several years of separation, recalling with delight the innocent pastimes
of their youth," and so on.[40] With these descriptions and/or evocative

song titles in hand, Beethoven could indulge in some expressive and pictorial touches, such as the turning of the mill wheel in *The Miller of Dee* and the evocation of a funeral march in *Fair Fidele's Grassy Tomb.*[41] His response to the title of *The Elfin Fairies,* however, was so subtly and freshly evocative that Thomson responded with dismay that this and some other settings were "too recherché, too bizarre, — in fact such as I dare not offer to the public."[42]

Whether more for *amore* or for money, Beethoven submitted to Thomson's hectoring and continued his piecework until 1820, setting around 125 folk songs in all, in total time amounting to one of the largest bodies of work in his life.[43] Thomson found less to complain about in the later settings, but his entreaties for simplicity never stopped. In fact Beethoven's settings tend to the plain, though never less than polished and individual. It is not that there are no gems in Beethoven's folk-song settings, only that there are surprisingly few.

Yet he found working with these tunes pleasant and profitable beyond the steady source of income. As a melodist Beethoven had never been as fluent and fertile as, say, Mozart. As has been noted before, part of the reason was that he insisted his instrumental and, to a degree, even vocal themes must submit to the motifs and the master plan of a piece. Now he steeped himself in tunes not his own, like found objects that he only needed to provide with support and atmosphere. Through the years he spent periodically working on the folk songs, the melodic element in his music evolved steadily toward the lyrical. There were more immediate implications in the Seventh Symphony that he finished in April 1812, whose finale resembles a Scottish reel. In the end it would be Thomson who broke off the project because, as he had preached for all those years, the settings were too much for his eternal young ladies. And Thomson never made a penny from Beethoven's arrangements.[44]

The aftermath of his last romantic failure saw another pattern returning for Beethoven: as fate heaped misfortune on him, he heaped on more by his own actions. In October, he rose from his sickbed and took a coach to Linz, where brother Nikolaus Johann lived, enjoying his wealth gained from selling medicines to the French army. In childhood, after the death of their mother and the collapse of their father, Ludwig had taken the role of his brothers' keeper. Since then he had never budged from that role, or rather from what he considered the sacred obligation to keep his siblings on the straight and narrow.

In Linz, Johann gave Ludwig a large, pleasant room with a view of the Danube. The local paper rhapsodized, "Now we have had the long wished for pleasure of having within our metropolis for several days the Orpheus and great musical poet of our time, Herr L. van Beethoven." There was charming and memorable music making. Beethoven improvised for dinner guests, then managed to knock over a table of plates. He befriended the *Kapellmeister* of Linz Cathedral and at his request wrote three equali for four trombones, modeled on traditional funeral pieces.[45] He finished the score of the Eighth Symphony.

But Ludwig was there on a mission. To his consternation he had learned that Johann was bedding his nominal housekeeper, Therese Obermeyer, who came equipped with an illegitimate daughter of five. Years before, over Ludwig's protests, their brother Carl had married the pregnant Johanna, a woman Ludwig considered (with some reason) a thief and a tart. Ludwig saw Johann's live-in mistress (again, with some reason) as a tramp and a gold digger. At thirty-five, the usually mild Johann did not remotely resemble his oldest brother. He was bony and graceless, with a cast in one eye and a turned-up corner to his mouth that gave him a strange, perpetually quizzical air.[46] In his newfound prosperity he had found no luck landing a more respectable mate. Ludwig was determined to put an end to this madness of his youngest brother's, whatever it cost. As usual, his meddling cost a great deal.

The matter came to a head in an ugly scene. Ludwig had demanded that Johann send Therese away. Johann refused and stormed into Beethoven's room in a fury. It came to shouts and punches. Moral and physical persuasion having failed, Ludwig complained to the local bishop, the civil authorities, and the police, finally obtaining a legal order kicking Therese out of town as an immoral woman.[47] Johann's defiant response was to make the affair respectable; he married the lady. Thereby Ludwig helped inflict on Johann what turned out a woeful marriage, which in turn Johann blamed Ludwig for getting him into.[48] So Ludwig watched both brothers marry women who, if hardly the incarnate evil he considered them to be, were still pieces of work, and that was to have long and bitter ramifications on his and his brothers' well-being.

Around this time, Beethoven heard a worse piece of news. On November 2, Prince Kinsky, the largest contributor to the yearly stipend, who had survived battles in the Napoleonic Wars, had been thrown from his horse and died from his injuries. Kinsky had been forgetful and dilatory in his payments when he was alive; could Beethoven hope for anything from his widow and his estate?

He did not let the issue lie. Less than two months after her husband's death, Princess Kinsky received the first letter from him: "The unhappy event — which has removed His Excellency . . . from our Fatherland, from his dear relations and from so many people whom he magnanimously supported . . . has also affected me in a manner as singular as it is painful. The bitter duty of self-preservation compels me to present to Your Excellency this most humble petition." Meticulously he reviews the history of the stipend and Kinsky's agreement to raise it to account for inflation.[49] It took years and more dogged pleas, but in 1815 the house of Kinsky resumed the payments.

Meanwhile Prince Lobkowitz, on the verge of bankruptcy, had stopped his contributions. Beethoven went after Lobkowitz too, personally and in the courts. The next year he wrote to Joseph von Varena in Graz about "the worries I am having here and the defense of my rights . . . as you know, I have to deal with a princely rogue, Prince Lobkowitz . . . What an occupation for an artist, whose most burning issue is his art! And it is H.R.H. the Archduke Rudolph who has plunged me into all these embarrassing situations —."[50] By then, in his desperation, he was ready to blame Rudolph for his efforts in arranging the stipend in the first place. At the same time he wrote Rudolph with a stunning show of false sympathy, saying that he needed to go to Baden for the cure but was being kept in Vienna "by the Lobkowitz and Kinsky affairs . . . Y.I.H. will have heard of Lobkowitz's misfortunes. He is to be pitied; and to be so rich surely does not spell happiness."[51]

But it was not as simple a matter as selfishness or greed. Beethoven was becoming chronically and irrationally anxious about money, and he had more than his own self-preservation to worry about now. In 1812, brother Caspar fell desperately ill with tuberculosis. From that point on, a good deal of Ludwig's earnings would go to Carl for doctors and family support — though their relations did not necessarily improve in the process and Beethoven still despised Carl's wife Johanna. To Varena, via whom Beethoven had been donating pieces for charity concerts in Graz, and who had offered money for the music, Beethoven wrote, "My circumstances on the whole happen to be the most unfavorable I have ever had to face . . . [I find] myself at the present moment, precisely owing to my great generosity [to Carl], in a position which . . . by reason of its very cause cannot make me feel ashamed." But he declined any payment from Graz unless "a wealthy third person" could be found to cover the costs.[52]

There was also his brother's young son Karl to worry about. Brother Carl's tuberculosis was virtually a death sentence, as it had been for their mother. The only question was when. Beethoven formed a determination to get his nephew out of his mother's clutches when Carl died. The next spring, pressured by Ludwig, his illness getting worse, Carl made a legal declaration: "Since I am convinced of the openhearted disposition of my brother Ludwig van Beethoven, I desire that, after my death, he undertake the guardianship of my surviving minor son, Karl Beethoven."[53] The next spring Carl rallied, and the matter of his son rested.

That spring Beethoven wrote his landlord Baron Pasqualati, "Please just let me know . . . what you have found out about the Lobkowitz affair in the matter of my salary, for I have not a farthing left. Furthermore, I beg your brother to write to Prague so that I may receive the Kinsky salary due to me."[54] He surely exaggerated about being down to his last farthing, but in one way and another he had gone through a great deal of money. Between March 1809 and November 1812, he received 11,500 florins from the stipend, the belated 200 pounds from his sale of works to Clementi in England, some 1,500 florins from Thomson for the folk songs, and several thousand from Breitkopf & Härtel. In a time when one could live well enough on 1,300 silver florins a year (paper florins were worth much less), he had made somewhere over 6,000 florins in each of the preceding three years. Yet by 1813 he had also borrowed some 1,100 florins from Franz Brentano; eventually his debt to Franz totaled 2,300.[55] Other than to brother Carl, there is no record of where it all went.

Despite everything, when the celebrated French violinist Pierre Rode arrived in Vienna, Beethoven responded to his presence — and to his admiration for the French violin school — with his first violin sonata in some eight years. It turned out to be his last. The piano part was written with Archduke Rudolph in mind; Rudolph and Rode premiered it at the Lobkowitz palace on December 29, 1812.

The four-movement Sonata for Violin and Piano in G Major, op. 96, is not Beethoven's grandest or most exciting in the medium and it may be technically his easiest to play, but it is surely his greatest. Here the qualities that would mark the late music begin to take focus: the subtlety of effect, the ability to turn suddenly from one idea to another with a mysterious purposefulness, the long-suspended harmonic periods, the melodic beauty, the deep-lying thematic integration based on a few motifs, the sometimes childlike simplicity that he makes touching and unforgettable. Beethoven's affection for Rudolph, his gratitude despite everything, surely colored the music. At the same time he tailored the piece to violinist Rode's style and taste. He wrote Rudolph, "In our finales we V[iennese] like to have fairly noisy passages, but R does not care for them — and so I have been rather hampered." (He wrote Rudolph in the same month, "Since Sunday I have been ailing, although mentally, it is true, more than physically. I beg your pardon a thousand times.")[56]

For Beethoven G major tended to be a gentle and pastoral key, and gentleness pervades this sonata. It begins with a little violin fillip of indefinite meter and tonality like a birdcall, introducing a movement of heart-filling warmth and charm conjuring the outdoors: reverie, birds, summer breezes. Nature was still Beethoven's cathedral; here is a fresh angle on a pastoral style. Nearly the entire first movement is marked *piano* or *pianissimo*. Figures evoking birdcalls and breezes will be abiding sources of material, as will the opening trill. Another idea that arrives later in the exposition is a poignant intrusion of notes borrowed from the minor, especially the flat sixth degree — and most especially

E-flat, the flat six of G major, which will play a role in the sonata both as a note (sometimes disguised as D-sharp) and as a key.

Formal outlines are on the whole simple and regular; the second movement Adagio espressivo is a straightforward ABA, the main theme one of his long-breathed lyrics, the middle section a blissful trance. The movement segues directly into a rough and ironic scherzo with jolting, offbeat accents; its trio has the lilt of a folk dance, say a German *Ländler*.

Another kind of folkish simplicity is the basis of the finale, Poco allegretto. (He had sketched the theme earlier, perhaps for the A Major Cello Sonata.)[57] Its theme suggests a little dance tune from a comic opera. The movement is continuous, the sections contrasting but flowing together, so it is not all that obvious that we are hearing a theme and six variations with a couple of interludes, one being a stretch of chromatic fugue whose apparently out-of-nowhere subject is actually a stretching out of the movement's opening theme. The coda gives us a bracing gust of wind, a warm reminiscence of the theme, and a jolly burst of final chords. All this is to say that the effect of the finale is less its nominal form, a theme and variations, than a stream of consciousness. That quality too will mark much of the late music: the old forms still functioning but sunk beneath the surface, a few seminal motifs flowering into a proliferation of melody, everything with an effect of transcendent, rhapsodic freedom.

This exquisite sonata shows that while life had assaulted Beethoven and he had faltered, his courage, his discipline, and his devotion to his craft had not deserted him completely. Here is the inner world of an aging, unhappy, chronically ailing composer who had increasing difficulty hearing anything but what sang in his head, but who remembered the sounds of nature and the feelings of exaltation and of love human and divine that he found there. These are things only an artist older and wiser, who has done much and suffered much, can fully understand and truly speak of.

Still, living back in the Pasqualati house overlooking the bastion in Vienna, his production slowed alarmingly. After the Violin Sonata in G Major, in the first half of 1813 he finished nothing else but some folk-

song settings and a piece for a play at the Burgtheater.[58] With few if any
friends left to unburden himself to, no shoulders to weep on, in 1812
he began to keep a *Tagebuch,* a diary. Its first entries reveal the rawest
anguish he had expressed since the Heiligenstadt Testament. This was
a private testament, addressed only to himself and to God:

> Submission, deepest submission to your fate . . . O hard struggle! . . .
> You must not be a human being, not for yourself, but only for others;
> for you there is no longer any happiness except within yourself, in your
> art. O God! give me strength to conquer myself, nothing at all must fet-
> ter me to life. In this manner with [A.] everything goes to ruin.[59]

> [Two entries later:] O terrible circumstances, which do not suppress
> my longing for domesticity, but [prevent] its realization. O God, God,
> look down upon the unhappy B., do not let it continue like this any
> longer.

The Heiligenstadt Testament had been written when he was younger,
healthier, in the middle of his fame as a virtuoso, his work running
strong and in demand, his wounds fresh, and there were fewer old
scars. Then his response to suffering had been defiance, not resignation, not submission. By the time of the *Tagebuch* submission was the
only path left for him. He did not believe in miracles, in God coming
down from the stars to answer his prayers, but he had no one but God
to pray to for an end to his suffering. As he had done in that earlier cry
from the cross, he threw himself on his art as the only meaning left in
his life. But in that earlier cry, when he feared never to feel joy again,
he had not given up on love and family. Now he was letting go of those
dreams too.

Every woman he had truly loved — including Julie Guicciardi, the
singer Magdalena Willmann, Josephine Deym, Therese Malfatti, his
Immortal Beloved — had rejected him or had been lost because of
forces outside his control. Now he gave up on women, gave up hopes
for love and romance and family. As he wrote in the *Tagebuch,* to give
up on love is close to giving up on life. Once again his art was all he had
left. But now, for the first time, his art was drifting.

Here was another turning point in his life, as the Heiligenstadt Testament had been, as the declaration of a new musical path had been before that. Beethoven had acted on those declarations with all the fierce power of his will. But his will was waning now; there is no decisiveness in his declaration of submission and withdrawal, only anguish. For the moment he did not have the energy and confidence to lift himself up. He was about to be very busy, in a time when the demand for his work heated up suddenly. But in spirit he was still on the way down.

Yet Beethoven, capricious in all things, was capricious even in his despair. Among those first anguished entries in the *Tagebuch* is a technical note: "The precise coinciding of several musical voices generally hinders the progression from one to the other." (He appears to mean that contrapuntal voices need to be rhythmically distinct.) And there would be few further cries from the soul like the ones that begin the diary. Nor did the *Tagebuch* become a record of daily events. The bulk of it is a collection of quotations Beethoven liked, from a great variety of literary sources, sprinkled with practical musical and household items, excerpts from potential opera librettos, and so on. "How should Eleison be pronounced in Greek?" runs one note. "E-le-i-son is correct." (That toward another try at a mass.) Authors quoted or referred to include Schiller (the most frequent), the philosophers Herder and Kant, the fantasist Gozzi, the Spanish dramatist Calderón, Pliny, Plutarch, Homer. He wrote down only a few entries about music and no quoted reviews of his work, good or bad. There is not a single entry about current events, which were in world-changing convulsions during the time of the *Tagebuch*.

The bulk of the entries are inspirational in one way or another. "Portraits of Handel, Bach, Gluck, Mozart, and Haydn in my room. They can promote my capacity for endurance." (In fact he had no pictures of those composers on his wall.) There were exhortations to stick to his last, to subdue his longings and transcend his pain and deafness: "Everything that is called life should be sacrificed to the sublime, and be a sanctuary of art. Let me live, even if by artificial means, if only they can be found!" He quoted a contemporary comment on artists: "'Unfortunately, mediocre talents are condemned to imitate the faults of the great masters without appreciating their beauties: from thence comes the harm that Michelangelo does to painting, Shakespeare to drama and, in our day, Beethoven to music.'"

The most unexpected collection of quotations shows that by the mid-1810s, Beethoven was reading Eastern religious texts and books about those religions, most having to do with Hinduism. His underlying concern was to broaden his conception of God. From a commentary on the *Rig-Veda:*

> Free from all passion and desire, that is the Mighty One. He alone. No one is greater than He. (Brahm.) His spirit, is enwrapped in Himself. He, the Mighty One, is present in every part of space. O God ... You are the true, eternally blessed, unchangeable light of all times and spaces ... You alone are the true (Bhagavan — the) blessed one, the essence of all laws, the image of all wisdom of the whole present world — You sustain all things.

> [Another entry, a paraphrase he had adapted to his own life and work:] All things flowed clear and pure from God. If afterwards I became darkened through passion for evil, I returned, after manifold repentance and purification, to the elevated and pure source, to the Godhead. — And, to your art.

> [From the Bhagavad Gita:] Blessed is (the man) who, having subdued all his passions, performeth with his active faculties all the functions of life, unconcerned about the outcome. Let the motive be in the deed, and not in the outcome. Be not one whose motive for action is the hope of reward.[60]

> [Regarding Indian music:] Indian scales and notes: *sa, ri, ga, ma, na, da, ni, scha.*

The final quotation in the *Tagebuch,* added years after it began, also concerns God. It is from Beethoven's favorite book of homilies and natural history, Christoph Christian Sturm's *Reflections on the Works of God and His Providence Throughout All Nature:* "Therefore, calmly will I submit myself to all inconstancy and will place all my trust in

Thy unchangeable goodness, O God! My soul shall rejoice in Thee, immutable Being. Be my rock, my light, my trust forever!"

In Schiller's essay "The Mission of Moses," Beethoven read inscriptions said to be found on Egyptian monuments:

> I AM THAT WHICH IS,
>
> I AM ALL, WHAT IS, WHAT WAS, WHAT WILL BE;
> NO MORTAL MAN HAS EVER LIFTED MY VEIL.
>
> HE IS ONLY AND SOLELY OF HIMSELF,
> AND TO THIS ONLY ONE ALL THINGS OWE THEIR
> EXISTENCE.

These evocations from ancient Egypt did not go into the *Tagebuch*. Beethoven copied them out on a sheet of paper and put them under glass on his writing table so they would be before his eyes as he worked. Those sublime sentiments would play their part in his late music too.

An undogmatic and unbigoted interest in non-Western religions was another part of the Aufklärung ethos Beethoven imbibed in Bonn. For deists, all religions worship the same things with different languages and images and traditions. Beethoven instinctively responded to poetic religious texts (after all, in large part religions are created and sustained by poetry). From these texts he wanted imagery, inspiration, broadening, not dogma. His most ambitious works from the *Eroica* onward had been involved with the world, the hero, the ideal society, joy, beauty, sorrow, personal struggle and triumph, and, so far, a frustrated search for a sacred style in music. Now in his anguish he turned his thoughts upward and beyond, reaching for a sense of the divine larger than any scripture or church. And he turned to God directly: neither the *Tagebuch* nor any of his letters or works to this time had any significant reference to Christ beyond his hasty oratorio *Christus am Ölberge*.

In his art Beethoven was reaching beyond the sorrows of lovers and friends, the rough jokes, the clashes of armies and exaltation of heroes that had inspired his work. Now for Beethoven, Sturm's book melding science and religion joined with a sense of primeval mystery. Beethoven was pulling away from the earth, to a higher angle of view. At the same time he was singing more within than ever, starting with the locked inwardness of the deaf man who can hear only the songs in his own head. No less was Beethoven headed for the childlike, the naive, the utterly simple, all these qualities more than ever. He had not given up his drive, seen from his earliest music, to do and to express and to feel *more* in every direction. It was these kinds of conceptions and images that helped create the music he was to write in his last years: humanity standing under the infinite canopy of the stars, no less human and concrete than before, with no heroes to exalt us but only ourselves, reaching toward one another and, in that, toward Elysium and toward God, to make a world whose order reflects the sublime order of the universe.

At the same time, the quotidian hounded Beethoven more than ever. As 1813 began, the element of the *Tagebuch* that prevailed in his external life was the despair of the first pages. Signs of desperation and loneliness were all over him. Occasionally in notes to his old bachelor friend and helper Baron Zmeskall, a new and peculiar term began to turn up, a shared code. In February, Beethoven wrote, "Be zealous in defending the Fortresses of the Empire, which, as you know, lost their virginity a long time ago and have already received several assaults —"; "Enjoy life, but not voluptuously — Proprietor, Governor, Pasha of various rotten fortresses!!!!"; "Keep away from rotten fortresses, for an attack from them is more deadly than one from well-preserved ones."[61]

The codes here are transparent enough. Beethoven is talking about prostitutes, solicitations, the threat of venereal disease. (A later conversation book cites the title of a French treatise on venereal diseases.)[62] Most bachelors in those days put off marriage until they were settled into a career, and patronized whores as a matter of course. It was estimated that in a population of around two hundred thousand Viennese in 1812, roughly 10 percent were full- or part-time prostitutes.[63] Once, violinist Ignaz Schuppanzigh took Beethoven to a brothel and had to avoid Beethoven's wrath for weeks. Still, it is likely Beethoven was acquainted with the institution before 1813. In these depressed years he began frequenting brothels more often, usually with old bachelor Zmeskall, his faithful helper in that as in much else.

His loneliness could not have been alleviated by these fleeting and tainted pleasures. All of it offended his spirit, his idealization of women and love, his puritanical instincts. The contrition shows up in the *Tagebuch:* "Sensual gratification without a spiritual union is and remains bestial, afterwards one has no trace of noble feeling but rather remorse."[64] Again: "From today on never go into that house — without shame at craving something from such a person."[65] At the same time, there is a commonsense acknowledgment of the inevitability of desire: "The frailties of nature are given by nature herself and sovereign Reason shall seek to guide and diminish them through her strength." From a Hindu text concerning the sacred image of the phallus, Beethoven copied, "To someone who was offended by the idea of the lingam, the Brahman uttered, 'Did not the same God who has created the eye also create the other human members?'"

If it were only a matter of everyday sins and regrets, all this might have been a passing symptom of lost love. But in addition Beethoven seemed visibly to be falling apart. Friends found him looking shockingly dirty and run-down. At the end of 1812, composer Louis Spohr met Beethoven at a restaurant, and they got together occasionally after. Beethoven knew of Spohr's work and was kindly toward him. Once, when Beethoven did not show up for several days, Spohr went to see him. Beethoven explained that his boots were in tatters and "as I have only one pair I am under house-arrest." His manners in those days, Spohr recalled, were "rough and even repulsive."[66]

Patrons in restaurants shied away from him. In Baden, piano maker Nannette Streicher and her husband found Beethoven in "the most deplorable condition ... He had neither a decent coat nor a whole shirt, and I must forbear to describe his condition as it really was."[67] This suggests that he was resorting to the bottle more than usual. The Streichers helped him as best they could.[68] It was as if Beethoven were sinking to where his father had been at nearly the same age. If he had not been one before, maybe in these years he became a functional alcoholic — impaired but still able to work, not out of control. At least, in contrast to his father's case, there are no stories of Beethoven being found rolling in the gutter. The Streichers' report, though, implies something in that direction.[69]

In his youth, Beethoven had known beyond doubt that he had great powers inside him. As the years brought their blows, whatever his anguish he sustained a conviction that he was equal to anything fate threw at him. After his youthful brashness left him, his essential confidence did not — though he had faltered in the aftermath of Josephine's withdrawal, in 1807. Now he was not so sure he was up to the blows. He wrote to Archduke Rudolph that "unfortunate incidents occurring one after the other have really driven me into a state bordering on mental confusion."[70] Eventually he hit bottom, then began to rise.

From now on, his mind and body, his inner creative tides and his external existence, which had always run on separate yet parallel tracks, were going to diverge more and more. It is as if the more anguish fate heaped on him, the more his rage and desperation and paranoia mounted, the brighter and purer his creative spirit burned. But not yet. That resolution would take the better part of a decade to gather. In 1813 and for some time after, the main thing he thought about was money.

Sunk more in grief than in art in those years, Beethoven never wrote of what was going on in the world, but he could not have been unaware of it, and in the end he profited from the results. In June 1812, Napoleon invaded Russia with a Grande Armée of nearly 700,000 men, the largest force in European history. Now the French were pursuing a dangerous two-front war; French forces were also fighting the British and Portuguese in Spain.

In Russia, nearly half Napoleon's troops were Poles and Germans from conquered territories. (One of his aims was to prevent Tsar Alexander I from invading Poland.) As the Russian army retreated before him, the world expected another conquest. At Borodino, on the road to Moscow, the Russians made a stand but retreated after bloody fighting. Napoleon's army swept into Moscow, only to find no troops defending it. Before long, a fire of mysterious origin burned much of the Russian capital to the ground. Tsar Alexander sat tight, refusing all peace overtures.

Finally, with no enemy to fight and winter coming on, Napoleon had no choice but to retreat with his gigantic and unwieldy army. Tsar Alexander enforced a ruthless and devastatingly effective scorched-earth policy in the path of the French as they struggled west in the brutal cold. The retreating troops began to die in the tens of thousands from freezing, starvation, disease, and enemy harassment. Napoleon had lost battles before, but by the time this campaign guttered out, the greatest self-made conqueror in history had directed, in statistical terms, one of the worst military debacles in history. As many as four hundred thousand of his army were dead. The conqueror was no longer invincible; he was running out of soldiers. His enemies stirred again.

In June 1813, Napoleon and the Austrian foreign minister, Clemens von Metternich, made an attempt at negotiation in Dresden. A few days before, a French army fleeing Madrid had been shattered near the town of Vittoria by the duke of Wellington's Anglo-Portuguese forces. The battle effectively marked the end of the Peninsular War that had been boiling since 1808, and so ended French rule in Spain. The constant drain of men and matériel in that war turned out, in the end, to be the main engine of Napoleon's downfall. "It was that miserable Spanish affair," he said later, "that killed me."[71]

Metternich knew his opponent intimately from his years as ambassador in Paris; that intimacy had included an affair with Napoleon's sister, among other adventures. Later as a minister back in Vienna, Metternich conceived and engineered the marriage of Napoleon and Marie-Louise, daughter of his emperor, which provided Napoleon with a son and heir. Metternich was not a general, but he was every bit as wily and treacherous a tactician as his opposite. In person and in power, Metternich would survive Napoleon by many years.

At this moment, Metternich knew something the Frenchman did not realize yet: in the game of conquest, Napoleon had put most of his remaining cards on the table in Spain and Russia, and he had lost. In Paris, Charles-Maurice de Talleyrand, a trusted adviser of Napoleon, had in fact been spying for the enemy for years; he assured Metternich of broad French support for Austrian demands. (Talleyrand had also been keeping Metternich apprised of secret military orders sent to French commanders.) No one could have precisely known or believed it yet, but Napoleon was headed on a trajectory toward a nondescript village near Brussels called Waterloo, whose absurd name was going to be, for the rest of history, a symbol of ultimate defeat.

The encounter in Dresden raged for nine hours and got nowhere. If France wanted a peace treaty, Metternich demanded, it would return Austrian and German territories that amounted to everything France had conquered since 1796. Pacing up and down, Napoleon ranted, bullied, cajoled. "So you want war? Well, you shall have it . . . I know how to die . . . but I shall never cede one inch of territory." Knowing he held the cards, Metternich stayed calm. In a transport of rage, Napoleon threw his hat across the room and cried, "You know nothing of what goes on in a soldier's mind! I grew up on the field of battle, and a man such as I cares little for the lives of a million men!" Metternich replied that he wished the whole of France could hear what Napoleon had just said. He reminded the general of his stupendous losses in Russia. Napoleon waved that away. Most of the dead, he declared, were only Poles and Germans, not French.

There Metternich lost his composure: "You forget, sire, that you are addressing a German!"

"I may lose my throne," Napoleon snarled, "but I shall bury the whole world in its ruins."

"Sire," replied Metternich, "you are a lost man."[72]

Having overseen a decade of negotiations with Napoleon including his marriage into the Austrian ruling family, the elegant, indolent, handsome, womanizing, utterly ruthless Clemens von Metternich was now going to lead the movement to erase Napoleon from power. Then he would lead the attempt to erase from the world everything Napoleon had done and stood for. The military part of it resolved the next October. In the Battle of Leipzig, Napoleon's 185,000 men fought off 320,000 allied troops for three days before being forced into retreat. Beethoven's old admirer and former French general Jean Bernadotte, now crown prince of Sweden, led the Swedish contingent against the French. This defeat was the end of the French Empire east of the Rhine and the effective deathblow for Napoleon's career as a conqueror. The next objective for the allies was Paris.

For Beethoven perhaps all this was mainly an annoyance that de-

Johann Nepomuk Maelzel

layed his mail and his annuity payments. But he entered this tide of history as a sideshow when a brilliant inventor and forthright huckster named Johann Nepomuk Maelzel approached him with a proposal to compose a piece for a mechanical instrument he had built. The music was to depict in the most graphic possible terms Wellington's victory over the French in Spain. Beethoven agreed immediately. In the abyss of the greatest depression of his life to date, this outlandish commission galvanized the period of his artistic nadir, and also the greatest triumph of his life.

26

We Finite Beings

THE YEARS 1814–15 would be splendid for Beethoven's fortune and fame, but his depression was hard to crack. He was still harried by illness, and his yearly stipend from the three aristocrats — Kinsky now dead, Lobkowitz teetering on bankruptcy — had become a millstone. "Oh, fatal decree, as seductive as a siren," he wrote in one of his laments to friends. "To resist it I should have had my ears plugged with wax and my arms bound fast, like Ulysses, to prevent me from signing."[1] The stipend that had been intended to give him freedom to work had become a snare preventing him from working.

Desperate for cash, Beethoven succumbed to Johann Nepomuk Maelzel's temptation of a battle piece, which as a genre was a cliché of clichés. In those days, major military engagements were regularly fought over again in the concert hall. Trained in music, Maelzel was the son of an organ builder, which perhaps explains his gift for mechanisms. The eighteenth century had seen a craze for "living machines," the most famous of them Vaucanson's mechanical duck, which appeared to eat food, then to digest and excrete it. After Maelzel came to Vienna in 1792, he taught music and pursued his mechanical inventions, including spectacular effects for local theaters. For a production of Haydn's *Seasons* he engineered snow, avalanches, rain, thunder, and lightning.[2] Maelzel purchased the celebrated chess-playing "Turk" of Wolfgang von Kempelen. This apparently all-but-supernatural machine was a fraud: the clockwork Turk could move chess pieces around a board well enough, but the actual playing was done by a small human chess master concealed in the base. After the Battle of Wagram, Napoleon had a round with the Turk at the Schönbrunn Palace.[3]

For years Maelzel experimented with devices for keeping time in music. For an article in a Vienna paper, his current version, called the chronometer, was endorsed by Beethoven, Hummel, and Salieri, among others.[4] It evolved into the classic Maelzel metronome, used under his name for the next two centuries. One of the most elaborate of his inventions was the Panharmonicon, a mechanical orchestra with imitations of strings, brass, winds, and percussion, powered by bellows and played by means of revolving cylinders, like a music box. Its first repertoire included pieces by Haydn, Handel, and Cherubini.[5] The device made Maelzel famous; he was named imperial court mechanician.

At some point Beethoven and Maelzel had gotten acquainted in Vienna. Beethoven liked to visit Maelzel's workshop and watch him fashion his contraptions.[6] For his new friend Maelzel made four ear trumpets, ranging from simple horns to more fanciful and probably useless designs. After the duke of Wellington's Anglo-Portuguese army ended French rule in Spain at the Battle of Vittoria, Maelzel primed Beethoven with the idea of writing a commemorative piece for his Panharmonicon. The result was a victory symphony that set Maelzel's machine whooping, piping, and drumming at the limit of its capacity. Contemplating the results, the two men settled on the idea of using that music as the conclusion of a more extensive orchestral piece whose instruments would include artillery and small arms. With the inevitable success of this orchestral *Wellington's Victory; or, The Battle of Vittoria* in hand, Maelzel could take the Panharmonicon on the road with the "Victory Symphony." Maelzel made various suggestions about the orchestral version, including its realistic bugle calls. How much of the final product was Maelzel's and how much Beethoven's is not clear. That question was a dispute waiting to happen, and soon enough it did.[7] "It is certain," Beethoven wrote in the *Tagebuch*, "that one writes most prettily when one writes for the public, also that one writes rapidly." He seemed not to mind composing the piece with Maelzel looking over his shoulder.

The premiere took place in December 1813, at a benefit concert for the war wounded that coincided with the approach of the largest diplomatic conclave in history, the Congress of Vienna. University Hall was crowded and ready for excitement, less for the new Seventh Symphony than for the patriotic pandemonium that *Wellington's Victory* promised. For another novelty, Maelzel's mechanical trumpeter played a couple of marches accompanied by the orchestra.[8] The musicians looked at the show as a grand lark. Beethoven's old friend and celebrated virtuoso Domenico Dragonetti stood in the bass section, longtime champion Ignaz Schuppanzigh headed the violins, Louis Spohr sat in the violin section. Composers Antonio Salieri and Johann Nepomuk Hummel handled the big drums that represented cannons, and future famed opera composer Giacomo Meyerbeer pounded a bass drum. Laughing, Beethoven recounted that he had to give Meyerbeer what for, because he was always late: "I could do nothing with him; he did not have the courage to strike on the beat!"[9] Besides the drums standing in for cannons, the performances also required special rattles that were used in theaters to represent musket fire.

The score was another of Beethoven's last-minute sprints in the tradition of *Christus am Ölberge* and the *Choral Fantasy*. In *Wellington's Victory*, two wind-and-brass bands plus strings represent the French and British forces. In the battle section, each side has its cannons and each its own tune: *Rule Brittania* in E-flat for the British, *Malbrouk* in C for the French.[10] One after another the armies are pictured marching into place announced by drums and fanfares and their respective marches (all realistic in the day of parade-ground battles). Then, insofar as is possible with an orchestra and a battery of drums and rattles, all hell breaks loose.

Call *Wellington's Victory* the ultimate parody and nadir of Beethoven's heroic style.[11] There are three phases to it: battle, charge, and "Victory Symphony." In the first two sections the muskets and cannons rattle and roar — each explosion precisely marked in the score — and meanwhile the orchestra rages, modulating furiously and making itself heard as best it can. It is a battle of guns and bands: in the course of the hullabaloo the British guns, march, fanfares, and key of E-flat major overcome the French equivalents, and the battle gutters to a close with scattered gunfire from the British. Call the ensuing "Victory Symphony" a low-rent rehash of the familiar Beethovenian joyous finish, featuring *God Save the King* in glory and, near the end, as a fugue. "I want to show the British what a treasure they have in 'God Save the King,'" Beethoven wrote in the *Tagebuch*. All in all, *Wellington's Victory* is a colossal piece of opportunistic, gimmicky, *fortissimo* hokum, which is to say that it is exactly what Beethoven intended it to be. He wrote most of the notes, but the inspiration and the spirit came from Maelzel the huckster. Beethoven remained the consummate professional; he knew how to produce twaddle on demand.[12] The Viennese went berserk over it.

While many of the cognoscenti took the piece as good patriotic fun, others were troubled by it. Czech pianist Johann Wenzel Tomaschek was present at the premiere and found himself "very painfully affected to see a Beethoven, whom Providence had probably assigned to the highest throne in the realm of music, among the rudest materialists. I was told, it is true, that he himself had declared the work to be folly, and that he liked it only because with it he had thoroughly thrashed the Viennese." Tomaschek voiced his regret to Beethoven's friend Sonnleithner, who replied that "the crowd would have enjoyed it even more if their own empty heads had been thumped the same way." In his usual laconic fashion, Beethoven largely declined comment on *Wellington's Victory* and promoted it vigorously to patrons and publishers. But he had no illusions about it. Years afterward he scrawled on a condemnation of the piece in a journal: "Nothing but an occasional work . . . Ah you pitiful scoundrel, my shit is better than anything you've ever thought."

If the applause for the Seventh Symphony at its premiere was less thunderous than that for *Wellington's Victory,* it was still received more noisily than any symphonic premiere of Beethoven's life to that time — part of the reason being that this time the orchestra was well prepared. During rehearsals, the violins had balked at a passage in the Seventh, called it too hard, refused to play it. Instead of erupting in rage, Beethoven told them to take the music home and practice, and it would work. The violinists did as directed, the next day the passage went well, and everybody was pleased with the results.[13]

Beethoven had finished the Seventh in 1812, four years after the Sixth. Since he required each symphony to be a leap in a new direction from what he had previously done, for the new one he again took a tack no one could have predicted. In the *Bonaparte/Eroica* Symphony he had attached a work to the dominating spirit of the age and to the coming of the ideal society as the gift of a benevolent despot. In the Fifth Symphony he turned his subject inward, to an evocation of each person's struggle and triumph. The Sixth was likewise inward, the experience of nature and its divine essence. If not the heroic or the sublime, what would he do for the Seventh? Less than at any point in his lifetime was there a progressive spirit alive in the age, a great hope to evoke in a great symphony. Beethoven was turning away from the heroic style and from that ethos — but turning toward what, he did not know yet.

In the Seventh Symphony in A Major, op. 92, he took another humanistic direction, not contemporary but eternal: a kind of Bacchic trance, dance music from beginning to end. By all accounts Beethoven was a laughable dancer in person, completely unable to stay on the beat, but here he proposed to dance for the ages. With that he again touched his roots in the Viennese Classical style, because the Seventh rises from something innate in it. The music of Haydn and Mozart and their time is often laid out in dance patterns, dance phrasing and rhythms.[14] But that hardly encompasses the Seventh. It dances unlike any symphony before, dances in obsessive rhythms fast and slow. Nothing as decorous as a minuet here. Rather it's shouting horns and strings skirling like bagpipes. The last movement resembles a Scottish reel. Whether there was a direct connection in Beethoven's mind of the dancing Seventh to the Viennese passion for dancing is impossible to say, but it turned out that quality and its general ebullience made the symphony a reflection of the celebrating and dancing Congress of Vienna.

The Seventh begins with an expansive, grandiose, even Napoleonic introduction, the longest Beethoven ever wrote. It is the magisterial overture for the dances to come. From the introduction's slow-striding opening theme many other melodies will grow. But mostly the introduction defines the symphony in brash and audacious harmonies, with a tendency to leap from key to key by nudging the bass up or down a notch. (The opening harmonic move from I to V6 will have echoes throughout in the symphony's massive bass lines. The moaning chromatic basses in the first-movement coda are an expansion of that opening move.)[15] The introduction defines key relationships striking for the time but by now thumbprints of Beethoven: around the central key of A major he places F major and C major, keys a third up and a third down. That group of keys will persist through the symphony, added to them D major, another third down from F.

A coy transition from the introduction leads into the first-movement Vivace, quiet at first but with mounting excitement. The Vivace is a titanic gigue. This is Beethoven's third symphony in a row whose first movement is dominated by a monorhythm. Its dotted figure is as relentless as the Fifth Symphony's tattoo, as mesmerizing as the Sixth's loping rhythms, but now the effect is propulsive and intoxicating rather than fateful like the Fifth or gentle like the Sixth. Rhythm plays a more central role than melody here, though there is a piping folk tune in residence. The second theme amounts to a passing interlude before the first theme is picked up again. The development proper has no real theme at all; it's scales, arpeggios, and rhythm. The music is steadily engaged in its quick changes of key in startling directions, everything propelled by the élan of the rhythm. From the first time one hears the symphony one never forgets the lusty and rollicking horns, which at the time were valveless instruments pitched high in A. Low, epic basses and shouting horns: these are the distinctive voices in an orchestral sound more massive and bright than in any of his earlier symphonies (each with its own orchestral color).

Also few listeners forget the first time they hear the stately and mournful, sui generis dance of the second movement, in A minor.[16] It was a hit from its first performance. Here commences, as much as in any single piece, the history of Romantic orchestral music. The idea is a process of intensification, adding layer on layer to the inexorably

[Handwritten marginalia: Lively, light, of music in the style of a dance (Renaissance or Baroque)]

marching chords in the low strings (with their poignant mix of major and minor) until the music rises to a sweeping, sorrowful lament. Once again, in a slowish movement now, the music is animated by an irresistible momentum. For contrast comes a sweet, harmonically stable B section in A major (plus C major, a third up). Rondo-like, the opening theme returns in variations, lightened, turned into a *fughetta*, the last variation serving as coda.[17]

The scherzo is racing, eruptive, giddy. Its main theme, beginning in F major and ending up a third in A, from one flat to three sharps in a flash, echoes harmonic patterns set up in the first pages of the symphony. The music is back to brash shifts of key animated by relentless rhythm. The trio, in D major (a third down from F), provides maximum contrast, presenting a kind of majestic tableau around an A drone, frozen in harmony and gesture like a painting of a ballroom. The trio returns twice and feints at a third time before Beethoven slams the door.

The intention of the Allegro con brio finale is to ratchet the energy higher than it has yet been. Few pieces attain the brio of this one. If earlier we had exuberance, stateliness, brilliance, those moods of dance, now we have something on the edge of delirium: a stamping, whirling two-beat reel, with the horns in high spirits again. Does any other symphonic movement sweep listeners off their feet and take their breath away so nearly literally as this one? Perhaps the most intoxicating moment in the finale is the closing section of the exposition in C-sharp minor, with its natural-minor B surging against the simultaneous harmonic-minor B-sharp. The symphony ends with the horns shouting for joy.

Among musicians the Seventh became famous for the daring and freshness of its modulations and the unity of its key scheme with its chain of thirds, C, A, F, and D major the central ones. Beethoven always had reasons for his keys in a piece, and this is one of his most subtle. Those four tonalities are chosen not just to make a dazzling effect. The keys C, A, F, and D major have *three and only three notes in common:* A, D, and E — the tonic, subdominant, and dominant notes of A major. Which is to say that Beethoven made his central complex of keys related by thirds into a symphonic expansion of the three most important notes in his home key of A major.[18] (Whether by coincidence or design, E, D, and A are also the first three downbeat notes in the *vivace* theme of the first movement.)

Among Beethoven's symphonies, the Seventh also marks the point when he largely left behind the heroic style and ethos. It is his first symphony since the Second to have no overt sense of dramatic narrative — something he was also slipping away from. Instead of narrative unity there is a unity of theme: the moods of dance.[19] One senses the influence of Beethoven's folk-song settings on the piece, including the "Scotch-snap" rhythm in the first-movement theme. More specifically, the main theme of the finale echoes his arrangement of the Irish tune *Nora Creina* that he made for Thomson. At the conclusion of that 6/8 folk tune — as much fiddle tune as song — Beethoven added this tag of his own:

From Travis, "Celtic Elements"

For the finale of the Seventh he turned that idea into 2/4 to make his main theme:

So the dozens of folk tunes Beethoven was "scribbling" — his term — in those years to pay the rent were also, surely as he hoped, turning out to be useful in his more ambitious music. Of course, for an artist anything is potential material: an emotion felt or endured, a book read, a person or a tune encountered, suffering emotional or physical.

The premiere of the Seventh and *Wellington's Victory* under Beethoven's baton was one of the most triumphant moments of his career before the public. For the first of many times, the audience demanded an encore of the slow movement of the Seventh. The orchestra was fiery and inspired, suppressing their giggles at Beethoven's antics on the podium. The paper reported from the audience "a general pleasure that rose to ecstasy." By popular demand, the concert was repeated four days later, with Maelzel's mechanical trumpeter again on hand. The celebratory music played into the celebration of Napoleon's fall and hopes for the end of so many years of war. The Seventh went on to become one of the most popular items in Beethoven's portfolio, issued in transcriptions for everything from two pianos and piano four hands to string quartet, piano trio, winds, and septet.[20] The two performances garnered 4,006 florins for wounded veterans.[21] Beethoven sent a copy of *Wellington's Victory*, with its hallelujahs for England and the king, to the prince regent in England with a dedication, hoping the future king would respond generously.[22]

True, the trashy and opportunistic *Wellington's Victory* got the most applause. It also set the tone of much of the music Beethoven was to write in the coming months. No amount of success could save him from rankling illness and creative uncertainty. Nor did the Seventh make clear the new path he was searching for. But for the moment he was not too proud to bask a little, to look forward to handsome proceeds from his own benefit concerts, even to enjoy with a sardonic laugh the splendid success of the bad piece and the merely bright prospects of the good one. The Seventh Symphony after all celebrates the dance, which lives in the ecstatic and heedless moment.

Beethoven told Goethe he believed that artists mainly want applause, and he was receiving extraordinary applause these days. It hardly lightened his mood. Soon after the triumphant charity concert he wrote yet another lawyer yet another rant about the stipend and the detestable Viennese and, for good measure, his brother Carl, over an issue that is not recorded:

> Many a time indeed I have cursed that wretched decree for having brought innumerable sorrows upon me . . . the best course would be to hand in the application first to the Landrechte [the court for the

nobility]. Please do your share and don't let me perish. In everything I undertake in Vienna I am surrounded by innumerable enemies. I am on the verge of despair — My brother, whom I have loaded with benefits, and owing partly to whose deliberate action I myself am financially embarrassed, is — my greatest enemy! Kiss Gloschek for me. Tell him that my experiences and my sufferings, since he last saw me, would fill a book.[23]

Around the same time, he wrote his old patron and delinquent stipend contributor Prince Lobkowitz, then the object of some of his legal initiatives, "The profound regard which for a very long time I have sincerely cherished for Your Highness, has in no wise been affected by the measures which dire necessity has compelled me to adopt."[24] In Beethoven's recent letters to others, Lobkowitz had been the "princely rogue" and "Prince Fizlypuzly."[25] Lobkowitz had known Beethoven long enough not to expect much gratitude.

Right after the premieres Beethoven got busy producing another concert, this one for his own benefit, in the large *Redoutensaal* of the Hofburg. It was to include a dramatic coup in the style of *Wellington's Victory*. "All would be well," he wrote Zmeskall, "if the curtain were there, but without it the aria will be a failure . . . Without a curtain or something of the kind its whole significance will be lost! — lost! — lost! . . . The Empress has not said yes [to attending] but neither has she said no — Curtain!!!!" For this concert of January 2, 1814, Beethoven included a bass aria from *The Ruins of Athens*. At the end of the aria a curtain was to sweep aside revealing a bust of Austrian emperor Franz I, the effect sure to bring down the house. The benefit repeated *Wellington's Victory*, already a sensation in Vienna.

This time Beethoven's berserk conducting nearly ran aground because he could hear so little of what he was directing. The orchestra had gotten used to the idea that he was going to swell up in the loud passages and more or less disappear under the music stand in soft ones. But when he got lost and jumped up at a soft moment and sank to his knee at a loud one, confusion and hilarity threatened. House *Kapellmeister* Michael Umlauf, prepared for this sort of thing, stepped behind Beethoven and restored order. When Beethoven realized the orchestra was not following him anymore, it is reported that he produced a smile. Amused? Embarrassed? Horrified? After the concert he placed a notice in the newspaper thanking "the most admirable and celebrated artists of the city" for their contribution to a splendidly successful evening.[26] Among the listeners at the concert was young violinist Anton Schindler, who met Beethoven this year when he delivered a note from violinist Ignaz Schuppanzigh. They met occasionally in the next years. It is not clear at what point Schindler determined to make a career out of his connection to the great man, to become what Beethoven called "an importunate hanger-on."[27]

This last concert produced considerable proceeds and inaugurated what in financial and critical terms became the most profitable year of Beethoven's life. The immediate practical result was that three singers from the court opera approached him about a revival of *Fidelio*, and George Friedrich Treitschke, manager of the Kärntnertor Theater, signed on to the idea. Treitschke had seen the first version, had been part of the group who pressured Beethoven to do the initial revision. Beethoven agreed to the revival but insisted on making many changes first, with Treitschke's help.[28] This time he found the ideal collaborator. Treitschke was a man of the theater; he had begun as an actor and went on to be a playwright and manager.[29] As usual the project mushroomed and became another cross for Beethoven to bear, but the results for his orphaned opera were enormous. At least now there appeared a detectable lightening in his mood. He wrote his friend Count Franz Brunsvik in Buda of the recent successes, declaring, "In this way I shall gradually work my way out of my misery . . . My opera is also going to be staged, but I am revising it a good deal . . . As for me, why good heavens, my kingdom is in the air. As the wind often does, so do harmonies whirl around me, and so do things often whirl about too in my soul."[30]

A new wrangle in his endless series of them was with Maelzel. Because the inventor had originated the idea for *Wellington's Victory* and contributed ideas for the orchestral version, he naturally felt that he had a stake in the music. When Beethoven refused to give him a score for out-of-town performances, Maelzel stole some orchestral parts and put on the piece in Munich. From his point of view, it was a matter of Beethoven's intending to keep all future profits from the orchestral version for himself—as indeed Beethoven did.[31] From Beethoven this sort of thing usually brought out the heavy artillery. First he cancelled a newspaper statement that included more thanks to Maelzel.[32] Then he went to the courts. To a lawyer in Vienna he sent a massive, point-by-point statement of the kind that was to become a specialty of his. Among other things, it claimed that Maelzel's hearing aids were useless; in fact Beethoven often used one or two of them.[33] In the end, the dispute with Maelzel stalled and never came to the dock.

The Beethoven vogue in Vienna continued to run high. While juggling his legal wrangles over Maelzel and the stipend, he continued to satisfy the demand. The end of February 1814 saw another successful concert for his own benefit, which like all his concerts (except the ones with Maelzel's help) he produced, financed, rehearsed, and conducted himself. It repeated the Seventh Symphony and *Wellington's Victory* and introduced the Eighth Symphony, op. 93.

Like the Sixth, the Eighth is a sort of vacation, this time into the past: a beautiful, brief, ironic look backward to Haydn and Mozart. Like the Sixth it is in F major, often a high-spirited key for Beethoven. Here is another symphony, like the Second and Fourth, with an operatic atmosphere. It begins with a grandly dancing 3/4 theme that sets up a movement relaxed and good-humored (it was originally a sketch for a piano concerto that he diverted into a symphony).[34] If the themes and style recall the eighteenth century, he made the orchestral sound big and rich—on the way toward the sound of his next symphony. In keeping, the forces he arranged for his February 1814 concert were huge: eighteen each at first and second violins, fourteen violas, twelve cellos, seven basses, and winds to match. As usual, about half were paid professionals, the rest amateurs who played for the pleasure of it.

Only part of the humor of the Eighth rests on its surface. Much of it is comedy for connoisseurs. The second theme takes the stage with a dancing gait on an inexplicable C-sharp, leading to a second theme in the (according to tradition) "wrong" key of D major. This is a third down from F, like the kinds of key relations by thirds he wielded in the

Seventh, but the game here is quite different. Soon the second theme rights itself into C major, the "proper" key for the second theme in an F-major piece, and the music proceeds with its lacy and ironic little tune. A development mainly given to *fortissimo* blasts of the opening theme on changing harmonies flows smoothly into a much-varied recapitulation and a long, developmental coda in which that errant C-sharp, sometimes masquerading as D-flat, keeps turning up.[35]

The short second movement is one of the most Mozartian outings he had written in years. Its ticktock tread and its theme conjure up Haydn's *Clock* Symphony and no less the gait and personality of one of Mozart's comic sidekicks — say, Leporello in *Don Giovanni*. That the third movement returns for the first time in a Beethoven symphony to the eighteenth-century minuet is another clue to his intentions. It looks back at the old courtly dance with music robust rather than delicate, freed of frills but still in the kind of trance of nostalgia that marks this symphony: Beethoven, with epics and tragedies behind him, looking over music itself with serene benevolence.

The lighthearted atmosphere carries into the scurrying, capering finale, in form a mingling of sonata and rondo. It includes one of the most elaborate of his jokes (again, a joke for the initiated). Having largely stayed out of sight in the middle movements, the errant C-sharp of the first movement returns as a rude offbeat blat in the basses.[36] Here, according to Beethovenian musical logic, is a gesture that must have consequences. The joke is that it has no consequences. It just keeps blundering into the main theme like a drunken uncle at a party. Which is to say, here Beethoven lampoons his own craftsmanship.

Still, the payoff has to come sooner or later. After an unprecedented second development section that continues to ignore the C-sharp, Beethoven convinces us that the piece is coming to a close. About the time the audience are reaching for their coats, the drunken uncle runs amok. The errant blat returns as D-flat, wrenching the music into the key of D-flat; then again as C-sharp, turning the music to C-sharp minor; then again as the dominant of F-sharp minor, forcing the music into a potentially catastrophic clash — because the brasses, still tuned to F major, are picking up their instruments. Just as a horrendous tonal pileup looms, the music simply slips down from F-sharp minor to F major with the entry of the brass. Much of the rest of the music is F-major chords rendered droll by what came before. Here in a comic context is another example of the way Beethoven invests a single element, this time a simple tonic chord, with a significance that resonates with everything that came before.

In its premiere, though, the Eighth did not find much resonance with listeners, especially in the company of the Seventh Symphony and *Wellington's Victory*. Those pieces played into the mood of celebration after decades of war. The audience was not in the mood for subtlety and nostalgia. The new symphony, reported the *Allgemeine Musikalische Zeitung*, "did not create a furor"; at the same time, the reviewer called the second movement of the Seventh "the crown of modern instrumental music." He was generous enough to suggest that if the Eighth were not presented following the more showy Seventh, it might succeed.[37] Czerny said that on hearing a report that the Eighth had not been received as well as the Seventh, Beethoven growled, "That's because it's so much better!"[38] Did he mean that? He probably meant it when he said it and contradicted it later. As for the audience response, besides the problem of the Eighth being flanked by more splashy works, his audience was apt to be disappointed now when they found Beethoven not being "Beethovenian" enough.

Still, he appreciated applause from whatever quarter. It became a favorite story of his that after the concert when he was walking on the Kahlenberg above Vienna, two young girls gave him some cherries, and when he offered to pay, one of them said, "I'll take nothing from you. We saw you in the *Redoutensaal* when we heard your beautiful music."[39]

In the spring of 1814, going furiously at the revision of *Fidelio* for its revival, Beethoven had little time to take note that on March 30 the French Senate, under duress by the allies, voted to dethrone Napoleon and place the Bourbon dynasty back on the throne. The porcine and obtuse Louis XVIII prepared to reclaim his dynasty's glory. Symbolically, the return of the French monarchy was the final negation of the Revolution that had tried to wipe aristocracy from the earth.

The previous autumn's Battle of Leipzig had been the defeat that appeared to finish off Napoleon. Paris was next. On March 31, Tsar Alexander I, dubbed "the Great Liberator" after the Russian campaign, rode with his teeming retinue through the streets of the French capital. First came the tsar's personal regiment, called the Red Cossacks, then royal Prussian hussars and the Russian Imperial Guard.[40] Finally Alexander appeared in the uniform of an officer of the guards, heavy gold epaulets across his shoulders, sporting an enormous hat with a cascade of feathers, his feet thrust in stirrups of wrought gold. He waved benevolently to the dazed Parisians as he headed to the house of the turncoat Talleyrand, who in a secret note had exhorted the hesitant allies to march on Paris immediately: "You are groping about like children . . . You are in the position to achieve anything that you wish to achieve."[41]

On April 12, Napoleon signed the Treaty of Fontainebleau, which mandated his unconditional abdication and banishment to the island of Elba, twelve miles from the Tuscan coast. There it was granted that he would reign as the sovereign of his own little principality, with extensive property, a division of sixteen hundred troops complete with artillery, and a toy navy of five ships. (He was disgusted when his promised stipend of 2 million francs a year from the restored French throne never appeared.) A few days after signing the treaty, he made a halfhearted attempt at suicide. His Austrian wife Marie Louise was spirited back to Vienna and never saw Napoleon again, despite his constant entreaties in letters. Marie Louise and their son were now held as family prisoners of the Habsburgs at the Schönbrunn Palace in Vienna. The ex-empress felt conflicting loyalties, but she had always done as she was told. Their son Napoléon François Joseph Charles Bonaparte, in his cradle named the king of Rome, would for the rest of his short life be officially a nonexistent person.

Austrian foreign minister Clemens Metternich had bitterly opposed the tsar's Elba plan, declaring that Napoleon would be back leading an army within two years.[42] As it transpired, Metternich understood the man better than anyone else. Marie Louise's letters to Napoleon he quietly intercepted and filed away.[43] With his usual attention to detail, Metternich picked out a new lover as solace for Marie Louise, from among the military nobility.

On April 11, Beethoven played piano in the premiere of the *Arch-duke* Trio. Composer Louis Spohr, who had been spending time with Beethoven, recalled it as "not a treat, for, in the first place, the piano was badly out of tune, which Beethoven minded little, since he did not hear it . . . Beethoven's continual melancholy was no longer a riddle to me."[44] Young pianist and composer Ignaz Moscheles, commissioned to do the piano and voice arrangement of *Fidelio,* found the playing "neither clean nor precise, yet I could still notice many traces of a once great virtuosity."[45] On the same day came the first hearing of a singspiel, *Die gute Nachricht* (The Good News), celebrating the fall of Paris. The music was the product of several composers; Beethoven contributed the final chorus, "Germania," another patriotic potboiler. The text was by playwright George Friedrich Treitschke, still working with Beethoven on the revision of *Fidelio.*

Early one morning Moscheles arrived to consult about his arrangement of the opera. Beethoven was still in bed but jumped up enthusiastically. To go over the music he stepped to the window overlooking the bastion. Soon he noticed that street urchins outside were raising a ruckus. "Those damned boys," he growled, "what do they want?" Moscheles smilingly pointed downward, reminding Beethoven that he was naked. "Yes, yes, you're right," Beethoven said, and put on a dressing gown. Later, when the arrangement was done, Beethoven found Moscheles had written on the last page, "Finished with the help of God." When the young man got the music back, he found Beethoven had scrawled under that: "O Man, help yourself." Beethoven did not believe that God directed one's writing hand.

In the middle of March, rehearsals began on the new version of *Fidelio,* still without its new overture and generally in flux. He had never struggled with a work as much as with this overhaul. To change something in one place meant he had to change things elsewhere. As he wrote his collaborator Treitschke, "I could compose something new far more quickly than patch up the old with something new, as I am now doing. For my custom even when I am composing instrumental music is always to keep the whole in view . . . I have to think out the entire work again . . . I assure you, dear T, that this opera will win for me a martyr's crown."[46] There is one of the most trenchant things

Beethoven ever said about his creative process: *Always keep the whole in view.* It is one of his laconic asides that speaks volumes. For him a work, from an opera to a symphony to a folk-song arrangement, was an organism of balanced parts, every part related to every other — and that to a degree even in the traditionally loose construction of operas.

Shortly before the *Fidelio* premiere he wrote Treitschke in continuing frustration, "This whole opera business is the most tiresome affair in the world . . . and — there is hardly a number in it which my present dissatisfaction would not have to patch up here and there."[47] His focus was still largely on the music rather than the dramatic pace and shape, but with Treitschke's expert help in the theatrical dimension he was determined to speed up the first act, which had always languished. The pacing would never entirely be fixed, but it ended up far tighter than in the first version.

A week before the premiere of the new *Fidelio,* Prince Lichnowsky died of a lingering illness, perhaps venereal. He had been Beethoven's first patron in Vienna and one of his most generous. After their quarrel of 1806, they had never been close again, but Lichnowsky maintained a kind of pathetic loyalty. It was reported that in his last years they had an agreement that the prince could stop in now and then and silently watch Beethoven at work. If the servant did not let him in, he would leave quietly without being admitted to the inner sanctum.[48]

The premiere of the not quite finished revision of *Fidelio* came on May 23 at the Kärntnertor Theater, where librettist Treitschke worked as a producer and dramatist. Standing in for the unfinished new overture was the old *Ruins of Athens* Overture. It went well, Beethoven conducting. Once again *Kapellmeister* Michael Umlauf sat behind him, ready to step in if there was trouble, because Beethoven could hear very little. The audience applauded stormily and called Beethoven before the curtain again and again.[49] A Viennese theatrical journal raved, "We were amazed at *Beethoven* in his entire greatness, and what was more, we were amazed at the master . . . who, before the *Battle of Vittoria,* had belonged to his antagonists. At last, the great genius has for once prevailed and is able to rejoice in his works . . . The music of this opera is a deeply thought-out, purely felt portrait of the most creative imagination, the most undiluted originality, the most divine ascent of the earthly into the incomprehensibly heavenly."[50] Among other things, this review reveals that there was still plenty of lingering anti-Beethoven sentiment in Vienna. To repeat: even paranoids have enemies.

The great disappointment of his career had finally paid him back for his trials. *Fidelio* went on to a long run and the applause only grew, both in the theater and in the press. In June a "K. B." wrote in the *Allgemeine Musikalische Zeitung,* "In the works of great poets there is an irony that gently hovers over the entire piece . . . Beethoven's compositions have not been considered enough from this point of view. But precisely from just this vantage many things that *appear* to be harsh and strange in him are recognized as exquisite and necessary. This pure, poetic irony, gentle, but often also piercing and terrible, hovers over many of his most splendid productions. Indeed, frequently a deep repressed rage speaks to us from his music, but let us not forget that it is a pure, holy rage." The process of mythologizing Beethoven is on extravagant display here. The elements of his music that had once been decried as "bizarre," critics now described with "harsh and strange," "rage," and "terrible" as terms of praise. E. T. A. Hoffmann had pioneered in these critical directions. The critic also mentions irony in connection with Beethoven. Presumably he meant the distinctively Romantic sense of irony in art as self-reflection, an author turning around in midcourse to view his creation from the outside, creating paradoxes, mirrors, doppelgängers, puncturing the illusion of reality by recognizing the work as artifice. How the critic saw that kind of irony in Beethoven's work so far is hard to discern; it would, if anything, be more relevant to the late works, which sometimes seem to be music about music. In any case, all these critical responses point to a generation finding its way to Beethoven by defining him in its own terms, as distinct from his terms (a process every artist is subject to). The Romantic portrait of Beethoven was falling into place.

Having posted a notice in the paper after the successful concert of the previous December, Beethoven put in another one after the success of *Fidelio.* He was on a winning streak in Vienna, and he wanted to enhance it with some public crowing.

A WORD TO HIS ADMIRERS

How often in your chagrin, that his depth was not sufficiently appreciated, have you said that van Beethoven composes only for posterity! You have, no doubt, been convinced of your error since if not before the general enthusiasm aroused by his immortal opera "Fidelio"; and also that the present finds kindred souls and sympathetic hearts for that which is great and beautiful without withholding its just privileges from the future.[51]

In July, *Fidelio* had a grand benefit concert before what the *Wiener Zeitung* reported as a full house — this after a long run — and earned "extraordinary applause . . . the enthusiasm for the composer, who has now become a favorite of the public, manifested itself in calls before the curtain after every act." He was still tinkering with the opera, restoring the "Gold" aria and writing a new aria for Anna Milder, his Leonore, having cut the first one after the performance. The new overture was in place. Czerny noticed that in these days Beethoven seemed to rise out of his funk of the last months and began to pay more attention to his appearance.[52]

In autumn 1814, he wrote to lawyer Johann Nepomuk Kanka, who was managing his lawsuits related to his yearly stipend:

You yourself know that a man's spirit, the active creative spirit, must not be tied down to the wretched necessities of life. And this business robs me of many other things conducive to a happy existence . . . I shall not say anything to you about our monarchs and so forth or about our monarchies and so forth, for the papers report everything to you — I much prefer the empire of the mind, and I regard it as the highest of all spiritual and worldly monarchies . . . To whatever height I feel uplifted when in happy moments I find myself raised to my artistic atmosphere, yet the spirits of this earth pull me down again . . . Thanks to my charming disciples and colleagues I have drunk to the full a cup of bitter sorrow and have already won the crown of martyrdom in art.[53]

In fact, what finally settled the stipend affair in Beethoven's favor was not the lawsuits that claimed so much of his time but the intervention of Archduke Rudolph. As Beethoven said, he lived in the empire of the mind, where he was of the highest nobility. But he was paying much attention to the kingdom of the world these days. His perennial bitterness remained. A month after his triumph at the Congress of Vienna with *Fidelio,* he wrote to lawyer Kanka, ranting about "the dishonest affair of the Kinsky family . . . If the affair turns out unfavorably by reason of the behavior of the K family, then I shall have this story published in all the newspapers . . . to the disgrace of the family."[54] The rift between the empire of the mind and his quotidian rage was widening steadily.

Beethoven's letter to Kanka mentioning "monarchies and so forth" shows that he had been reading the newspapers. Monarchs and monarchies were on everyone's mind these days. In the wake of Napoleon's fall, the crowned heads of Europe with their thousands of ministers, secretaries, courtiers, spies, minions, mistresses and lovers headed toward Vienna for a titanic convocation to decide how to put Europe back together. After twenty-five years of more war than peace, and enormous social changes, no one expected that the clock could be completely rolled back. There was, for example, no interest in reviving the Holy Roman Empire. But Austria wanted its old possessions returned and in the end got most of them. The deliberations and the festivities rolled into motion toward the end of September. The convocation was expected to last a few weeks. It lasted nine months.

The Austrian state bankrolled what was soon dubbed the Congress of Vienna. Over its course the state spent some 30 million florins to support and entertain the delegations.[55] The actual work was done largely by ministers, leaving the emperors and empresses and other distinguished hordes with little to do but enjoy themselves, in every fashion the human imagination could conceive and an ocean of money realize. The chronically overcrowded city of two hundred thousand was invaded by some one hundred thousand additional, mostly rich foreigners who had to be housed. But Vienna loved a show, and there was always somewhere for residents to double up and rent out their rooms or houses or palaces.

Musicians, actors, painters, caterers, landlords, blacksmiths, police, and prostitutes embraced the onslaught. The least chambermaid could go on the government payroll for ransacking the trash of the nobles and ministers for whom she cleaned house. Many hundreds had to be assembled to read every piece of trash with words on it and every piece of mail posted by anybody of interest. The police read and resealed some fifteen thousand letters a day.[56] (The investigative structures and techniques developed in Vienna were left in place after the congress, the spying now concentrating on citizens.) Each morning, Emperor Franz I received a distillation of the most suspicious and delicious bits of information gleaned from his army of spies: who was drinking, who was abstemious, who was talking to whom and sleeping with whom, and when and where and how much. One report noted that a Herr Mayer was doing nicely selling remedies for venereal disease to the distinguished visitors.[57] After the congress, the chief of police died of exhaustion.[58]

Altogether, representatives and hangers-on of about two hundred states were in attendance. Yet in fact there was hardly any congress at all — at least not of the political variety. The principals in the discussions were at first only four men, representing the leading powers: Foreign Minister Clemens Metternich of Austria, recently entitled prince by the emperor; Viscount Castlereagh of England (highly reserved but no pushover, later replaced by the duke of Wellington); King Frederick William III of Prussia; and Tsar Alexander I. Around these four men swarmed legions of schemers and petitioners and ministers and informants. Fractures formed right away. Metternich and Castlereagh were united in an obsession with order, peace, and stability at all costs; Alexander was determined to claim the whole of Poland for Russia; Frederick William deferred to the tsar almost slavishly. By this point, Metternich was essentially running the Austrian government for the shallow and indolent Austrian emperor Franz I, who was happiest out in the kitchen making toffee while obsessing about secret societies and subversion. Metternich, then forty-one, had no doubt of his capacity for this or any job. "Error," he reported of himself in later years, "has never crossed my mind."[59] More importantly to many in Vienna, Metternich and Castlereagh were called two of the handsomest men in Europe.[60]

France was represented by Charles-Maurice de Talleyrand. In the course of his career, Talleyrand had risen to power serving first the Bourbon throne, then the Revolution, then Napoleon, then the allies as a turncoat. As an English visitor described him, "He looks altogether like an old, fuddled, lame, village schoolmaster."[61] He hobbled about on a foot injured in childhood. All these appearances were deceiving. Talleyrand was the most cunning and ruthless man at the congress. Now he represented the restored Bourbon throne with the mission of making defeated France the equal of the other powers. He managed that mandate brilliantly; the Big Four became the Big Five. In the midst of this chaos of diplomats, these five men essentially decided the fate of Europe for the next century. The lesser powers, down to the smallest of the post-Napoleonic German states, schemed, bargained, pleaded, and hoped for scraps from the big table.

The more public endeavors of the congress caught most of the attention of Beethoven and the rest of the Viennese. Someone coined the famous summary: "The congress doesn't get on; it dances." More accurately, it danced, ate, chased kaleidoscopic amusements, flirted, made love. In town were more than two hundred heads of princely families, all touchy about precedence, none with any real function, all looking for fun.[62] Night and day there were balls, banquets, theatricals, operas, gala concerts, ballets, hunts, staged medieval jousts, picnics, sleigh rides, and *tableaux vivants* by aristocratic ladies ("Hippolytus Defending His Virtue Before Theseus").[63]

Countless smaller parties went on all over town, where much of the business of flirting and assignation was carried on along with informal intrigue and diplomacy. Russian ambassador Count Razumovsky, Beethoven's patron and dedicatee of the op. 59 Quartets, entertained on a stupendous scale in his nearly finished palace overflowing with art and finery. One of his dinners for 360 people included sturgeons from the Volga, oysters from Brittany and Belgium, truffles from Périgord, oranges from Sicily, pineapples from Moscow, strawberries from England, and cherries brought in the middle of winter from St. Petersburg at the cost of one ruble per cherry.[64] New and historic dishes were invented for the congress: beef Wellington, beef Stroganoff. From the sidelines, the Viennese watched the show and marveled. Day by day, gossip roiled through the streets and out the gates of the city into the suburbs.

The behavior and morality of the nobility were hardly expected to conform to the straight and narrow path demanded of commoners. Tsar Alexander's erratic behavior, boorishness, and bullying clogged the deliberations and finally left in ruins the almost-mythical stature he had gained as the Great Liberator.[65] Mystical, depressive, and unstable, Alexander began the congress idolized by the populace and ended it widely loathed, at least by those who had to deal with him. His beautiful and intelligent wife Elisabeth he treated with brutal disdain. The tsarina concentrated on entertainments, including music, and she was a fervent admirer of Beethoven.

In every way, the nobility of Europe came to Vienna to reclaim and reassert their ancient rights and privileges, including the right to do as they pleased. The art of excess reached perhaps unprecedented heights. In his free hours, Great Liberator Alexander turned out to be a heroic womanizer. Of the endless stories of trysting during the congress, one address can stand for all. In town there was a palace with two staircases leading to separate apartments that had been rented to two aristocratic visitors. The top of the left staircase was the domain of the Russian princess Katharine Bagration, whose lifestyle earned her the nickname "the Naked Angel." She established a virtual brothel for the aristocracy, with herself as open-armed proprietor. At one point a prince broke down a door in her flat to find his very young daughter in the arms of a Russian nobleman.[66]

Years before, Princess Bagration had enjoyed a heated fling with Clemens Metternich that produced a child whom she named, with incomparable cheek, Clementine. With this affair as with numberless later ones, Metternich's wife, slowly dying of tuberculosis, looked the other way and soldiered on in support of her husband. At the congress, Bagration became the tsar's favorite, though neither was remotely faithful. Many nights police spies observed the tsar trudging up the left-hand staircase. Emperor Franz would chortle over the reports at breakfast the next morning. One police report ran, "The porter rang four times to announce [the tsar], and the princess ... came out on the staircase dressed en négligé. She took Alexander into her boudoir where he at once noticed a man's hat. The princess gave an explanation that amused the Tsar. [She said it belonged to her decorator.] The Tsar stayed for two and a half hours."[67]

Above the right-hand staircase of the palace, meanwhile, resided Wilhelmine, duchess of Sagan — beautiful, twice divorced, and available. Metternich had known her slightly; now he fell helplessly in love with her. (A British diplomat at the congress reported Metternich as "most intolerably loose and giddy with women.")[68] Then, catastrophe: the duchess took a liking to the tsar. Soon spies were noting that the tsar's evening ascents went up the right-hand staircase more often than the left-hand one. Metternich was prostrate. For weeks he spent much of his time writing long, heartbroken letters to Wilhelmine. The congress languished while he wept. Much of Beethoven's conversation in the coming years concerned the frivolity, immorality, and excesses of the ruling class. The congress provided endless fuel for his outrage.

In this fashion the business and pleasures of the congress forged on. At the end of the year negotiations had become so poisonous that war threatened, but that was averted by Talleyrand's brilliant, two-faced negotiating. Among other things he engineered a secret treaty of France, England, and Austria against Russia and Prussia. After keeping Europe at war for most of a quarter century, France was now an equal among its former enemies.[69]

Citizens across Europe hoped the congress would bring peace, reform, a return to old borders and empires, a new age of *liberté, egalité,* and *fraternité* under the rule of enlightened monarchs. The people, including Beethoven, had not yet understood the implacable hostility of Metternich and many others to the least hint of democracy or constitutional government. The famously enlightened Tsar Alexander, who declared that he wanted to turn Poland into a republic attached to Russia, went home to devolve into an unstable, reactionary tyrant. The ruling class wanted its power, its privileges and fun secured forever. This continent-wide reassertion of power, excess, and reaction constituted the status quo against which Beethoven's last symphony was to propose an alternative.

• • •

In September 1814, as the Congress of Vienna began, Beethoven reported to Archduke Rudolph that "my health some time ago suffered a severe blow owing to an inflammation of my intestines, which brought me almost to death's door. But I am now much better." He had sent *Fidelio* to Prague, where Carl Maria von Weber conducted it in November.[70] The opera's popularity began to spread beyond Vienna. Despite everything, Beethoven managed to compose the Piano Sonata in E Minor, op. 90. Its two small movements are far from slight in effect. The opening alone has enough contrasting material for two or three movements.

The E Minor joins one of the most mercurial of movements to one of the most constant. It begins with a bluff striding three-beat; then follow without transition passages one could label tender, then poignant, then (after some fierce downward swoops and stabbing chords) a second-theme section suddenly driving and passionate, then fleet and urgent. Each of these ideas/moods will be developed in the movement, but by no means resolved.

The resolution, a kind of spiritual one, is the second movement. After one of the most fickle movements imaginable comes a sunny and songful E-major rondo whose delicately beautiful and a-touch-wistful theme comes back over and over, soothing moments of unease like a lullaby from which one does not want to stray for long.

Here is the first hint of the atmosphere of Beethoven's late piano music, including the long singing lines and the ability to touch the heart with moments that seem utterly ingenuous. He dedicated the sonata to Count Moritz Lichnowsky, brother of the recently passed Prince Karl. Count Moritz reported that Beethoven told him the sonata was a dialogue between "Head and Heart."[71] Beethoven wrote Moritz about the dedication, "I have never forgotten how much I owe you in general, although an unfortunate event produced conditions which prevented me from proving my gratitude as much as I should have liked." He probably meant the fight of 1806 with Karl Lichnowsky.

Even this lovely little outing, or rather its dedication to the count, had its practical ramifications for Beethoven. In the letter to Count Moritz Beethoven goes on to suggest, "I would say that it would be best for Lord Castlereagh not to write about this work on Wellington until the said lord has heard it here."[72] This refers to his campaign to get the prince regent of England to acknowledge the dedication of *Wellington's Victory,* which in fact the future King Georg IV never did. As part of that campaign, Beethoven was hoping to use Moritz to reach Viscount Castlereagh, head of the British delegation.

For artists as for diplomats and lovers, there was hay to be made in the Congress of Vienna, and plenty of dignitaries there knew Beethoven's name. He was quick to strike, pulling in his patrons and attaching himself to the hoopla. The congress was his apotheosis in the public eye. He would gain much, even if to most of the glittering personages at the congress he was still a sideshow, one entertainer among many. "There are two camps, pro and contra Beethoven," ran a police report to Prince Metternich. "Opposite Razumovsky, Apponyi and Kraft who idolize Beethoven, stands a much larger majority of connoisseurs who do not want any music by Beethoven."[73]

However accurate that might have been, Beethoven's ultimate glorification began in the first days of the congress, with a performance of *Fidelio* before a houseful of dignitaries. Already a sensation in town and now in its final form, it was the first grand opera to be heard at the congress. In 1805 it had been a fashionable "rescue opera" connected in the public mind with the spirit of the French Revolution — even if, to placate the censors, the libretto was set two centuries earlier. Now rescue operas were long out of fashion, but its story of triumph and jubilation fit the mood of the city and of the moment.

In his thoroughgoing revision, with a number of elements cut and rearranged and tweaked by Treitschke, Beethoven had fixed at least some of the first act's nagging problems of pace and mood. He wrote a new, fourth overture, this time not a tone poem tracing the story but a bustling curtain-raiser in E major, with only subtle relations to the opera: the opening fanfare foreshadows Leonore's E-major aria "Komm Hoffnung" (Come, Hope); the answering theme in horns foreshadows Florestan's heroic resignation.[74] As in the first version, the curtain opens on a mood of Mozartian light comedy in a dark setting: Leonore, suspecting her vanished husband Florestan is a political prisoner, has disguised herself as a man called Fidelio — fidelity — and gets a job in the prison. The idea of a woman disguised as a man was a familiar opera buffa and singspiel staple used by Mozart and many others. As tends to happen in these "pants roles," there comes a gender jumble, also returned from the earlier incarnation: the jailer's daughter Marzelline falls in love with Fidelio and pushes away Jaquino, the hapless turnkey who is courting her. Chief jailer Rocco approves of this prospective match for his daughter. Complications ensue.

With this libretto Beethoven had made his escape from Mozart, whom he could not equal as a theatrical soul and a painter of character, by embracing French opera and taking as a model its exemplar Cherubini. Having made his escape, he still needed Mozart as a foundation for the first act's banter and courtship and gender confusion. In tone and texture and rhythmic gait, the opening duet with Marzelline turning away Jaquino recalls the beginning of Mozart's *Marriage of Figaro* — except there sex is at the center of the banter between the lovers: Figaro is measuring the floor for their marital bed. Other than a few effusions from the besotted Marzelline, there is no sex in *Fidelio*. The quasi-comic bits and characterization in the first act Beethoven handles professionally enough, but only just. The low ebb of the buffa aspect is Rocco's wan "Gold" aria, which after much back-and-forth Beethoven put back in for good, further slowing down the first act.

The orchestra throughout the opera is richer in texture than Mozart's, from beginning to end marvelously varied and expressive in color. For all the dramatic deficiencies, this is Beethoven at the height of his powers, and there is going to be magic and splendor in it. The magic begins with one of the more beautiful and moving numbers in any opera: the quartet "Mir is so wunderbar." It is also the one moment in *Fidelio* where librettist and composer memorably paint a mingling of characters and feelings (something that came naturally to Beethoven in instrumental music, with difficulty in vocal music). In a gentle four-part canon, each picking up the theme in exactly the same notes as the others, Marzelline pines for Fidelio, Leonore/Fidelio grieves for the pain she is causing Marzelline, Jaquino writhes in jealousy, and Rocco looks forward to the wedding. Because of the canon and the filmy coloration of the orchestra based on low divided cellos and violas, there is an unforgettable, trancelike atmosphere. Here

Beethoven shows that if he cannot write an opera with characters who consistently cast a shadow, he can wield music to raise a pedestrian story to great heights — as Mozart did with the patchwork libretto of *The Magic Flute,* Beethoven's favorite Mozart opera.

The actual drama at hand, which has nothing to do with unrequited love, commences with the entrance of Pizarro, commandant of the prison, whose corruption Florestan has exposed. Now Pizarro has imprisoned his enemy and ordered him starved to death in the dungeon. Like the other characters, Pizarro is a familiar dramatic type. Leonore is the devoted and heroic wife, Marzelline the lovelorn teenager, Jaquino the rejected chump, Rocco the buffoon. If in the libretto Pizarro is a cardboard villain, in the music Beethoven makes him the embodiment of tyranny. Pizarro learns from Rocco that a minister, having heard of arbitrary incarcerations, will appear within a day to inspect the prison. If he is to complete his revenge, Pizarro must act immediately. "Ah, what a moment!" he cries in his *furioso* aria, "to murder the murderer myself!" His aria is riveted on the note D as he is riveted on his vengeance. Failing to recruit Rocco to dispatch the prisoner, Pizarro vows to put in the knife himself, so Florestan's last sight will be his enemy's triumph.

Leonore sings her heroic aria accompanied by a bravura trio of horns: "Come, hope, let the last star not forsake the weary! Love will reach it." She persuades Rocco to let the prisoners out for a few moments in the courtyard. Here is not only another supreme moment in opera but also the ethical and moral heart of *Fidelio.* As they emerge from the dungeons to music like a sunrise, the men whisper, "O what joy, to breathe with ease in the open air!" The first two notes in the violins are A and E-flat, forming a tritone, the ancient *diabolus in musica.* Those notes will return in the dungeon scene as the throb of despair.

The chorus of prisoners rises to a climax on the word *Freiheit:* "O freedom, freedom, will you return?" It is remarkable that that line was allowed to be sung in Austria, where the very word *Freiheit* was apt to be censored wherever it appeared. It could be argued to the censors that the chorus reflected Europe's release from the Napoleonic Wars, but with the prisoners' cries of "Freedom!" *Fidelio* reveals itself as what it is: a hymn to liberation from all tyranny.

The second act is set in the dungeon, the opening music a tone poem of darkness and desolation. It begins with a low unison F answered by a piercing chord in the winds. It is the same gesture that in Bonn began the *Joseph* Cantata, which celebrated Joseph II as a liberator, a bringer of light. Over and over the timpani strikes its eerie A–E-flat.[75] In the obscurity we see Florestan in chains. "God! What darkness here!" he groans. His laments and resignation give way to an aria of great, gentle beauty where he recalls the springtime of his life. That leads him to an ecstatic vision of Leonore as an angel who brings freedom. "Zur Freiheit!" ("To freedom!"), he cries over and over in spine-chilling high Gs. The larger resonance of *Freiheit* is again unmistakable. The aria is in A-flat major, Beethoven's key of noble resignation. Exhausted by his excitement, Florestan sinks into sleep.[76]

Leonore/Fidelio and Rocco enter the dungeon to dig the prisoner's grave before the appearance of Pizarro. At first she can't see the sleeping prisoner's face. The duet of the grave digging is presented in a texture of low strings with horns and trombones and contrabassoon, the sound baleful and archaic. Florestan raises his head; Leonore recognizes her husband and faints away with the horror of it. After she recovers, Pizarro appears. Still the archetypal villain, he snarls, "Let him die! But first he shall know who hacks his proud heart from him." As he strides toward Florestan with his dagger, Leonore throws herself between them. They struggle until she gives the shattering cry, "First kill his wife!" Astonishment all around, but Pizarro recovers himself and advances again. Leonore pulls out a pistol: "One more sound and you are dead!"

At that moment of maximum tension Beethoven unveils his coup, the moment the whole opera has been leading to: a trumpet fanfare. Pizarro had ordered a trumpeter to the ramparts to signal the approach of the minister, because Florestan must be dead and buried before the official arrives. *Always keep the whole in view,* Beethoven said. Only he would arrange the whole of an opera over a single moment that is at once a musical and a symbolic climax. The trumpet call is the sounding image of liberation. The minister arrives, shocked to find his old friend Florestan ravaged and enchained. Amid a throng in the town square the tyrant gets his just deserts, his prisoners are released. In a heartrending moment, Leonore unshackles her husband: general rejoicing in C major, the key that ends the Fifth Symphony so joyously. The music is full of shouts of "Retterin!" ("Savior!").[77] Near the end, probably at Beethoven's insistence, there is a quote from Schiller's "An die Freude": "He who has won a splendid wife may join our jubilation."[78]

Fidelio had first been created in the stupendous burst of creative energy and inspiration that followed the *Eroica,* when Beethoven first connected his Aufklärung ideals to his art. In the Third Symphony the bringer of liberation is Napoleon, the supposedly enlightened despot. In *Fidelio* it is a woman and wife who attains the summit of heroism, bringing down a tyrant by the power of her courage and her love.

Here *Fidelio* shows itself to be a descendent of Mozart's *Zauberflöte.*[79] That opera, steeped in Masonry and its humanistic ideals, is a fairy tale of love in all its manifestations: the earthy love of Papageno and Papagena, the exalted love of Tamino and Pamina, the divine love of Sarastro for all humanity. All contribute to the triumph over the tyrannous Queen of the Night. At the end of *Die Zauberflöte* Sarastro exalts the lovers as the crown of humanity: love between two people as the answer, the representative of divinity on earth. Beethoven in his own way, full of grand abstractions but animating them with all his powers in shaping tones, says the same in *Fidelio.* For listeners, much of what lingers in the mind from the opera are words and phrases he underlines in the music: "O what joy"; "Farewell, warm sunlight"; "What darkness here"; "May you be rewarded in better worlds"; "Savior!"; and above all "Freedom."

In the Ninth Symphony he would return to these matters again. *Fidelio* is another link in the chain of thought stretching from the Aufklärung spirit Beethoven imbibed in Bonn to the *Eroica* and *Fidelio* and the Fifth Symphony, to end in the Ninth, where all despots are put away. In its stylistic reach *Fidelio* stretches from the eighteenth-century buffa elements through the voice of the *Eroica* and Fifth Symphonies to prophecies of the Ninth and the *Missa solemnis.*[80] In other words, for Beethoven the final version of *Fidelio* became the bridge between the heroic and the post-heroic styles.

At the close of the performance in Vienna at the beginning of the congress, the cheers went on and on. The performance, conducted by Beethoven, was well done; *Kapellmeister* Umlauf again sat behind his back to deal with problems en route caused by Beethoven's deafness. Soprano Anna Milder, now Milder-Hauptmann, had been the first Leonore as a teenager with a big voice but little experience. Now as a mature singer and actress, she became the first great Leonore. Pizarro was Johann Michael Vogl; he went on to be an important champion of Schubert's songs.

It was librettist Treitschke who wrote the final and splendid new conclusion to Florestan's scene. He got a rare view of Beethoven composing when he presented him with the text:

> What I am now relating will live forever in my memory. Beethoven came to me about seven o'clock in the evening . . . [and] asked how matters stood with the aria. It was just finished, I handed it to him. He read, ran up and down the room, muttered, growled, as was his habit instead of singing — and tore open the pianoforte. My wife had often vainly begged him to play; today he placed the text in front of him and began to improvise marvelously . . . Out of it he seemed to conjure the motive of the aria. The hours went by, but Beethoven improvised on. Supper . . . was served, but — he would not permit himself to be disturbed. It was late when he embraced me, and declining the meal, he hurried home. The next day the admirable composition was finished.[81]

The key element here is music arrived at by improvisation in a deep *raptus,* when Beethoven forgot his mental and physical travails in the same way that he forgot to eat.

He had no time to rest after his labors finishing the new *Fidelio* and putting it onstage. Immediately he got to work on a cantata called *Der glorreiche Augenblick* (The Glorious Moment), a paean to the congress and its luminaries. Its text was by Salzburg surgeon and writer Alois Wiessenbach. He left his impressions of Beethoven at age forty-three:

> Beethoven's body has a strength and rudeness which is seldom the blessing of chosen spirits . . . The sturdiness of his body, however, is in

his flesh and bones only; his nervous system is irritable in the highest degree and even unhealthy. How it has often pained me to observe that in this organism the harmony of the mind was so easily put out of tune. He once went through a terrible typhus and from that time dates the decay of his nervous system and probably also his melancholy loss of hearing . . . It is significant that before that illness his hearing was unsurpassably keen and delicate, and that even now he is painfully sensible to discordant sounds . . . His character is in complete agreement with the glory of his talent. Never in my life have I met a more childlike nature paired with so powerful and defiant a will; if heaven had bestowed nothing upon him but his heart, this alone would have made him one of those in whose presence many would be obliged to stand up and do obeisance. Most intimately does that heart cling to everything good and beautiful by a natural impulse which surpasses all education . . . There is nothing in the world, no earthly greatness, nor wealth, nor rank, nor state can bribe it.[82]

The two men found some mutual sympathy partly because Wiessenbach was about as deaf as Beethoven. They conversed in shouts. In the same period came pianist Wenzel Tomaschek's visit to Vienna and Beethoven, about which he wrote a memoir. Tomaschek transcribed a bit of shoptalk, most of it devoted to putting down young Giacomo Meyerbeer as a pianist and composer — and timid bass drum player in *Wellington's Victory*. Tomaschek recalled Beethoven saying, "It has always been known that the greatest pianoforte players were also the greatest composers; but how did they play? Not like the pianists of today, who prance up and down the keyboard with passages which they have practiced — *putsch, putsch, putsch;* — what does that mean? Nothing! When true pianoforte virtuosi played it was always something homogeneous, an entity; if written down it would appear as a well-thought-out work. That is pianoforte playing; the other thing is nothing."[83] What Beethoven was talking about was not playing from score but rather improvisation. Czerny noted that Beethoven's more formal improvisations sounded like a published piece, just as Beethoven here said they should.

The triumphs kept coming. At the end of November there was a gala performance before dignitaries including the king of Prussia (he left early) and Tsar Alexander and his wife. *Wellington's Victory* and the Seventh Symphony were given another whirl, but the main event was the premiere of *Der glorreiche Augenblick,* the cantata Beethoven had whipped up over the previous month or so. If in moments here and there it presages the Ninth Symphony and the *Missa solemnis,* the cantata is mostly another testament to Beethoven's professionalism. When the occasion calls for bombastic hosannas to the ruling class, he is ready to oblige.

"Europe arises!" the cantata begins. A sample of its wretched couplets: "And Karl of Habsburg, ancient line, / Battled with trust in God divine. / Where Habsburg struck on the Danube's strands / There struck he him—and Austria stands."[84] Much brass and percussion, children adding their innocent voices to the rejoicing, "a wonderful, crowned figure bathed in light," figures representing Genius and Vienna in its moment of greatness, and so on. One listener was impressed by the music but found the text of the cantata "extremely mediocre": "All that it really contains is the fact that there are now many sovereigns in Vienna; exactly like so many poems written for occasions."[85] This was a charity concert, with a packed audience. It was repeated twice in December, first in a program for Beethoven's benefit, only half full, then again for charity, again packed.

Beethoven's old patron Count Razumovsky, Russian plenipotentiary to the congress, presented Beethoven to the assembled monarchs at the palace of Archduke Rudolph. Among them were the tsar and tsarina. Afterward Beethoven's physician friend Joseph von Bertolini suggested that he write a polonaise for the tsarina, since that dance was in fashion. Beethoven sat down and improvised several dances and asked Bertolini to pick one. The result was the op. 89 Polonaise for piano, which he presented to the tsarina at an audience. Delighted by the dedication, she in turn presented Beethoven with an equally welcome 50 ducats (about 450 florins). She asked if her husband, years before, had acknowledged Beethoven's dedication of the op. 30 Violin Sonatas. The tsar had not, Beethoven humbly admitted. The tsarina dutifully handed over another hundred ducats.[86]

In relating all this later, Beethoven scornfully noted that at the concert for his own benefit, the king of Prussia had done nothing but buy a 10-ducat ticket, while the tsar paid for his with 200 ducats.[87] The tsarina later received the dedication of the piano arrangement of the Seventh Symphony. He wrote a Baron von Schweiger, as a go-between, "Since the grand symphony in A can be regarded as one of the happiest products of my poor talents . . . I would take the liberty of presenting to Her Majesty the pianoforte arrangement of this work together with the polonaise . . . Should Her Majesty desire to hear me play, that would be the highest honor for me."[88]

The rampant gaiety of the congress inevitably led to disasters small and large. On the last day of 1814, Beethoven's patron Count Razumovsky gave a dinner in honor of the tsar for seven hundred guests in his almost-completed palace filled with almost-inconceivable fineries. At the congress Razumovsky was at the zenith of his prestige, at the top of his world. For days an army of cooks worked around the clock preparing the banquet. While they labored, a baking oven overheated unnoticed and fire got into the heating system. As the guests were eating, the palace erupted in flames.

By the time all the fire engines of Vienna arrived along with thousands of Viennese, who enjoyed a good fire, there was nothing to be done. Gone were three blocks of mansion, the great stables and riding school, the chapel, the carpets and tapestries, the old-master paintings, the hall of sculptures by Canova. Razumovsky was found sitting stunned on a bench on his grounds, wrapped in sables and wearing a velvet cap. Emperor Franz appeared to say what he could. When Razumovsky tried to kiss his hand, Franz snatched it away.[89] The tsar gave Razumovsky a loan of some 700,000 florins to recover, but he never did resurrect his palace, his fortunes, or his spirit. His string quartet headed by Schuppanzigh lingered for a while, but soon he had to give them up.

From late 1813 to the end of the next year, Beethoven had written two big patriotic potboilers, *Wellington's Victory* and *Der glorreiche Augenblick,* and a small one, *Germania.* He began 1815 with an ambitious slate of serious works planned: a sixth piano concerto in D major; an oratorio commissioned by the new Gesellschaft der Musikfreunde

(Association of the Friends of Music); an opera *Romulus and Remus* on a Treitschke libretto; a symphony; and a piano trio. The symphony, or something of that order, was the D-minor one he had been thinking about. On a sketch he wrote, "Freude schöner Götterfunken Tochter" ("Work out the overture!"). (At this point the idea may have been for a freestanding piece on Schiller's ode.) With the piano concerto he got nearly half a first movement in full-score draft and then gave up on it.[90] He finished no more concertos. None of the other planned pieces got far, either. His health, which had tormented him for years, was getting worse and likewise his hearing. If he had found ideas and directions that seized him, nothing would have stopped him from working, and the enthusiasm of the public for his music was the highest it had ever been. But nothing seized him.

In January 1814, the final settlement with the Kinsky estate returned to him the largest share of his annuity. Lobkowitz followed suit in April. The latter, fallen on hard times but still one of Beethoven's oldest and most devoted patrons, had no illusions left. In a rueful letter to Archduke Rudolph, Lobkowitz wrote, "Although I have reason to be anything but satisfied with the behavior of Beethoven toward me, I am nevertheless rejoiced, as a passionate lover of music, that his assuredly great works are beginning to be appreciated. I heard 'Fidelio' here and barring the book, I was extraordinarily pleased with the music, except the two finales, which I do not like very much. I think the music extremely effective and worthy of the man who composed it."[91] The gentle prince, who had nearly bankrupted himself because of his passion for music, died at the end of 1816, but his estate kept up the payments. No surviving letters of Beethoven memorialize either Prince Lobkowitz or Lichnowsky, the leading patrons of his first decades in Vienna.

That April Beethoven received a letter from his old friend and patron Countess Marie Erdödy, a peace offering after some quarrel had kept them apart for years. He responded: "I have read your letter with great pleasure, my beloved Countess, and also what you say about the renewal of your friendship for me. It has long been my wish to see you and your beloved children once again. For although I have suffered a great deal, yet I have not lost my former love for children, the beauties of nature and friendship." His brother Carl had apparently written her an entreaty. "I beg you," Ludwig wrote her, "to make allowances for him, because he is really an unhappy, suffering man."[92] He was bereft of many old friends now, and moved to hear from one of them. At the same time, he had to cultivate any potential patrons he had. Far gone were the brash days when he told off Prince Lichnowsky and laughed at losing an annuity. A note in his *Tagebuch* shows that the countess had sent a more tangible peace offering: "34 bottles [of wine] from Countess Erdödy."

Beethoven arranged a 1,500-florin loan to brother Carl from publisher Steiner, which was to be paid back in the form of rights to future pieces.[93] But even with his dying brother, Ludwig's capacity for rage had not mitigated. One day around this time, he burst into Carl's house at mealtime shouting, "You thief! Where are my notes?" He was referring to some score he thought Carl had lifted. Outraged, Carl took a pile of music from a drawer and threw it down on the table. Ludwig calmed down and apologized, but when he left Carl said he never wanted "that dragon" in the house again. All this was observed by the little boy Karl, seven then, who recalled the scene years later. Soon after, Ludwig saw his brother in town, looking very ill. Ludwig embraced him, covered him with kisses, and took him home in a cab, kissing him all the way.[94] His paroxysms erupted uncontrollably and passed. His later friend the playwright Franz Grillparzer said that in his rage "Beethoven became like a wild animal."

Beethoven had shared the general hope that the Congress of Vienna would turn out a progressive force in Europe. Before long he realized it had been one more failed hope, like the French Revolution, like Napoleon. Still keeping his lines open to Breitkopf & Härtel despite their not having taken anything from him in years, he wrote Gottfried Härtel in his usual confiding tone: "Since I last wrote to you . . . how much has happened — and far more evil than good! As for the demons of darkness, I realize that even in the brightest light of our time these will never be altogether chased away."[95]

Beethoven's Teplitz admirer Karl Varnhagen von Ense, now part of the Prussian diplomatic corps, found his hero had grown "uncouth . . .

Beethoven's French piano, an Érard, part of the inspiration of the *Waldstein* and *Appassionata* sonatas.

akg-images

First page of the *Waldstein* Sonata. Contrary to legend, by no means do all of Beethoven's manuscripts look like battle-fields. This sonata is copied cleanly from beginning to end, with few strikeouts or corrections.

Beethoven-Haus Bonn, Collection H. C. Bodmer

W. J. Mähler's 1804 portrait of Beethoven, who is holding the lyre of Apollo in one hand and conducting with the other; in the background, a sunlit Classical temple on the left and a Romantic dark forest on the right.

© Alfredo Dagli Orti / The Art Archive / Corbis

Napoleon's siege of Vienna in 1809.
Österreichische Nationalbibliothek

The Franz Klein life mask that created
the scowling-genius image of Beethoven
that the world wanted to see.

Beethoven-Haus Bonn

Beethoven in 1815, by Mähler, with the
fairly impassive face and intense eyes
those who knew him described.

Getty Images

LEADING CANDIDATES FOR THE IMMORTAL BELOVED

Josephine Deym in 1814

Beethoven-Haus Bonn

Antonie Brentano in 1808

Beethoven-Haus Bonn

Bettina Brentano in
her youth

Getty Images

Beethoven's demanding pupil and generous patron Archduke Rudolph, brother of Emperor Franz.

© Bettmann / Corbis

August von Klöber's sketch for a missing portrait of Beethoven and his nephew.

Beethoven-Haus Bonn

Joseph Karl Stieler's romanticized portrait of Beethoven holding the score of the *Missa solemnis.*

Beethoven-Haus Bonn

Karl van Beethoven in his cadet uniform.
Beethoven-Haus Bonn

Beethoven's youngest brother, Johann, in his prosperous later years.
Getty Images

A Romantic view of the Vienna Woods in Baden, with its ruins of castles on the heights. The tower on the right hilltop is where nephew Karl tried to shoot himself.
Land Niederösterreich, Landessammlungen, Niederösterreich

A stark portrait of Beethoven in old age by the fashionable Viennese painter Ferdinand Waldmüller.

akg-images

Beethoven's room at the time of his death.

Beethoven-Haus Bonn

The late composer.

Beethoven-Haus Bonn

The horde outside the Schwarzspanierhaus as Beethoven's funeral procession got under way.

Beethoven-Haus Bonn

he was particularly averse to our notables and gave expression to his repugnance with angry violence."[96] After the congress, rants against the aristocracy and their morality became a constant theme of Beethoven's conversation. Part of it at this point was his fury at Lobkowitz and the Kinsky estate over the stipend, and his general disgust at being dependent on aristocratic patronage. At the same time he knew that nearly all the notables in attendance at the congress, all those who had led the war against Napoleon, all those kings and emperors and princes and counts and dukes and archdukes and barons ruled the world not because of their skill or talent or labor but because of the titles before their names, glory they had been born to and never had to earn. The Enlightenment and the French Revolution had challenged that ancient network of privilege, but an ocean of blood had not succeeded in changing it.

As for Napoleon, exiled to the island of Elba, it turned out that he had one more grand trick up his sleeve. On March 7, as Prince Metternich headed for bed exhausted after a negotiating session that ended at 3 a.m., a valet handed him an envelope marked "Urgent." He threw it on the bedside table and tried to sleep. Failing that, he got up and opened the envelope. It was an inquiry from the English commissioner who oversaw Napoleon in exile, asking rather pathetically whether anyone had seen Napoleon in the Genoa harbor, because he was no longer to be found on Elba. Metternich, and soon the whole of Europe, was electrified and horrified. Napoleon had fled exile with his soldiers and horses and cannons in his ships, all conveniently supplied him by his conquerors.

Napoleon landed in the south of France. Onshore his first act was to declare the Congress of Vienna null and void. Over the next three months he made his way to Paris, gathering troops as he went, installed himself in the Tuileries (Louis XVIII having fled), and began to form a new government. The allied armies marched toward France. With his reconstituted army, Napoleon decided to strike north against the Prussians and the multinational forces of Wellington before they were joined by the Russians and Austrians.

After beating the Prussians at Ligny, Napoleon attacked Wellington's outnumbered forces at the village of Waterloo, near Brussels. The battle was tipping toward the French when the Prussians appeared and gave the victory to the allies. The battle had been, Wellington admitted, "a close-run thing." Back in Paris, Napoleon abdicated for the second and last time. Now there was no coddling from the allies. His second exile was to the remote South Atlantic island of St. Helena, where he lorded it over the locals, dictated his self-glorifying memoirs, and faded away with cancer. From his death in 1821, Napoleon ascended into myth and legend. As myths and legends tend to do, they mostly glossed over his crimes and despotism and reconstituted his glory. At least in terms of human freedom, Napoleon had surely been better than the leaders who followed him. The negation of what he achieved was accomplished with relentless repression on a cowed and exhausted European population.

During the sound and fury of Napoleon's last hurrah, Beethoven pursued his life of a composer barely composing. He occupied himself with business, fulminations, and abortive projects. His old friend Carl Amenda wrote from Courland, pushing an acquaintance's opera libretto, *Bacchus.* The success of *Fidelio* was bringing librettists flocking. Beethoven was interested in Amenda's idea. (One of the sketched titles for the Ninth Symphony was "Festival of Bacchus.")[97] He made a few sketches toward the Bacchus opera, one of which reveals some of his method of extracting and relating themes. Under a line of music he jotted, "It must be evolved out of the B.M. . . . Throughout the opera probably dissonances, unresolved or very differently, as our refined music cannot be thought of in connection with those barbarous times — Throughout the subject must be treated in a pastoral vein."[98] The "B.M." seems to mean "Bacchus motif," representing the main character, to be used in developing further themes in terms both abstract and symbolic. The harmonic style of the piece was to be expressive of the subject — breaking harmonic rules to symbolize barbarous times.

In April, he signed a major publishing contract with Steiner in Vienna, sending him the *Archduke* Trio, symphonies Seven and Eight, and *Wellington's Victory* as repayment for Steiner's loan to brother Carl.[99] He was already on warm, bantering terms with Steiner and his partner Tobias Haslinger, of whom Beethoven was particularly fond. He had given everybody joking military titles: Steiner the "Lieutenant General" and his shop in the middle of Vienna the "military headquarters." Haslinger was "Adjutant," himself "Generalissimo." The firm issued the Seventh and Eighth Symphonies in score and parts during 1816–17, their inevitable losses for that publication offset by sales of arrangements of the works for wind ensemble, string quintet, piano trio, piano duo, and so on.[100]

News of an unauthorized performance of *Wellington's Victory* in London again brought out his ire that the prince regent had not responded to his offer of a dedication: "All the papers were full of the praises and the extraordinary applause which this work had won in England. Yet no one [i.e., the prince regent] thought of me, its composer; nor did I receive the least mark of gratitude or acknowledgment of indebtedness."[101] Soon there was some gratitude from London, by way of an offer from the Philharmonic Society to compose three overtures. In earlier years Beethoven would have sat down and dashed them off. Instead, the next year he sent three overtures already composed, all of them minor, claiming they were new: *Die Ruinen von Athen, König Stephan,* and the relatively new *Namensfeier,* finished in March 1815 (this is a stately and slight overture based on sketches from years before).

Beethoven knew and was fond of the young composition student Charles Neate, who bought the overtures for the Philharmonic Society. When the society realized that for its commission of three new overtures it had been given used and not-all-that-excellent goods, its members were understandably put out. Beethoven made things worse with a sudden demand for an additional five pounds for expenses. When matters came to a head he blamed Neate, back in England, who had also tried, without success, to sell publishers the overtures and other pieces including the Seventh Symphony and the F Minor Quartet. Admitting that indeed the overtures were not exactly new and "do not belong to my best and greatest works," Beethoven insisted they had found considerable success and ought to fulfill the commission. Publishers did not share that opinion. His old pupil Ferdinand Ries, now living in London and championing Beethoven, found the *Ruinen* Overture in particular "unworthy of him."

When the overtures did not sell, Beethoven further blamed Neate for accepting them in the first place, and wrote some nasty words to his young British friend: "I swear that <u>you have done nothing</u> for me and that you will do nothing and again <u>nothing</u> for me, summa summarum, <u>nothing! nothing! nothing!!!</u>"[102] He got a hurt letter from Neate: "Nothing has ever given me more pain than your letter to Sir George Smart. I confess . . . that I am greatly at fault, but must say also that I think you have judged too hastily and too harshly of my conduct . . . What makes it the more painful is that I stand accused by the man who, of all the world, I most admire." Among other things, Neate explained, he'd had fiancée problems.[103] Touched and sympathetic, regretting his fury as he often did, Beethoven apologized: "What can I answer to your warm-felt excuses? Past ills must be forgotten and I wish you heartily joy that you have safely reached the long wished-for port of love."[104] From his futile efforts to sell Beethoven in Britain, Neate received a letter from one publisher saying, "For God's sake don't buy anything of Beethoven!" Another rejected the overtures with, "I would not print them if you would give me them gratis."[105] For some time after, the imbroglio soured British publishers on Beethoven.[106] His relations with publishers had always been forthright and more or less aboveboard, but a new element of fudging, manipulation, and finally outright deception had begun to creep in.

In June 1815, the Congress of Vienna signed the Final Act. Among its elements it created the German Confederation of thirty-eight states under the nominal leadership of the Austrian emperor. Sovereigns were placed back on their thrones. Russia did not get all of Poland, as Tsar Alexander had wanted, but got most of it; Poland was dismembered again. The pope got the Papal States back; Austria reclaimed much of northern Italy. This and other gains made Austria the second-most-populous state in Europe, after Russia.[107] Prussia got part of Saxony and Poland and became the de facto dominant German state, while Russia dominated eastern Europe. The agreements so painfully and intricately arrived at were a patchwork that had little to do with the wishes, languages, and traditions of the peoples involved. All the same, the agreement lasted for decades and inaugurated a century of relative peace in Europe.

In Germany and Austria it was to be a peace enforced by relentless repression. Metternich was determined to sacrifice liberty to stability, to the eternal "legitimacy" of thrones and aristocracies. In essence the state decreed that, to the greatest extent possible to enforce, history was to stop moving. The status quo was all. Politics were erased from public life. There were to be no more dreams or dreamers, only tranquil and submissive subjects. As Emperor Franz I informed a delegation of schoolmasters, "I have no use for scholars, but only for good citizens ... Whoever serves me, must teach what I order; whoever cannot do this or comes along with new ideas, can leave or I shall get rid of him."[108] While the Final Act of the congress turned out splendidly in terms of the peace and stability of Europe, likewise for the old thrones and aristocracies, for the people of Germany and Austria it represented the beginning of a spirit-killing twilight age: the bland, conformist, philistine era that came to be called the Biedermeier.

The position of Metternich and his emperor was that a single word of criticism of any ruling power, any aspiration to civil freedom or constitutional government, was an ember that could flare into revolution. Any club or assembly of persons could nurture subversion. As much as humanly possible every play, novel, poem, painting, every private letter, every conversation, every word or image written or uttered or pictured was scrutinized by spies and censors for political content, for the least whiff of any sentiment not endorsing the status quo. Police, spies, and censors were now a central part of the state budget. They inspected gravestones, cuff links, tobacco boxes for hints of secret societies and subversion. At one point crates of china passing through Vienna from France to Trieste were found to be labeled with the brand name Liberté. Officials eradicated the banned word from every box before sending them on.

As it had been for years, now more uncompromisingly than ever, each dramatic performance was watched by officials with a copy of the script in hand; extemporizing was forbidden. When the leading playwright Ferdinand Raimund apologized onstage for beating his mistress, he was clapped in irons for three days for departing from the script.[109] Said the author of an 1828 book, *Austria As It Is Observed,* "A writer in Austria must not offend against any Government; nor against any minister; nor against any hierarchy, if its members be influential; nor against the aristocracy. He must not be liberal — nor philosophical . . . nay, he must not explain things at all, because they might lead to serious thoughts."[110] Periodic student and worker movements across Europe were quickly suppressed.

Across the whole of life, German governments enforced a conformity and mediocrity of thought that led inescapably to an impoverishment of imagination and spirit. The elaborate bureaucracy created by Frederick the Great in Prussia and Joseph II in Vienna to serve the aims of benevolent despotism proved equally effective at sustaining naked despotism. To think or speak freely was something possible only in secret among trusted friends and family. The safest place was one's own home; the most characteristic designs of the Biedermeier age were parlor furniture. Enforcement was carried out not mainly in terms of executions or terror but by the constant threat of police and prison. After a while in the Biedermeier, the main enforcement was the beaten-down complacency of the population, who were tired of war and generally better off economically than their ancestors. In the long run repression bred revolution, but that did not flare in Europe until 1848, and those revolutions failed.

Again, all this amounted to the attempted negation of the French Revolution and of Napoleon — though in practice, elements of the Napoleonic Code survived in France and elsewhere, including greater freedom for Jews and reforms in government bureaucracy. Like many progressives Beethoven had been optimistic about the outcome of the Congress of Vienna, hoping for reform and peace. No more than anyone else could he have imagined the pall of repression that was about to settle over Austria, what had already been a police state turning into a more ruthless and efficient one. That had its implications on music as on the rest of life. After the congress, musical tastes turned to dance music, light opera, comic singspiels, Rossini operas. All this music, wrote Stendhal, "diverted the mind from politics and . . . was less troublesome to a government."[111] Beethoven was quick to understand the reality taking shape. Recall his letter of March 1815 to Härtel: "Since I last wrote to you . . . how much has happened, — and far more evil than good!"

At the same time, in that social, political, and intellectual wasteland, instrumental music, which could have a progressive and even radical frisson without actually saying anything censorable, flourished virtually unhindered. Music enjoyed the freedom of its mystery. And Beethoven, who loathed the new order and said so incessantly, had the relative freedom of his fame and, as far as the authorities were concerned, his madness.

Somehow Beethoven appeared in relatively good spirits as the summer of 1815 approached. Surely much of that had to do with money. During the congress he had made a great deal in his concerts, enough to salt some away, and his yearly stipend from the three nobles was back in place. There was a warm exchange of letters with Countess Marie Erdödy. She wrote him a poetic invitation to her estate at Jedlersee, with joking signatures: "Marie the Elder / Marie the Younger, Fritzi the Unique, August <u>ditto</u> [these are her children] . . . Violoncello of the Damned [Joseph Linke, Schuppanzigh's once and future cellist] / Old Baron of the Empire / Officious Steward."[112] Beethoven promised to visit the countess in Jedlersee but never made it; most of his life from here on was confined to Vienna, which he hated, and its rural suburbs, which he loved.

In another letter to Erdödy Beethoven returned to his old pattern of intimacy to his "father confessor." Consoling her about some travel miseries she had experienced, he wrote, "We finite beings, who are the embodiment of an infinite spirit, are born to suffer both pain and joy; and one might almost say that the best of us obtain joy through suffering."[113] Here he put forth a new credo, deeper than the aggressive defiance of the Heiligenstadt Testament, more heroic than resignation. He had arrived at a position that allowed him to exist and work through the endless pains of mind and body that fate inflicted on him and that he inflicted on himself. It enabled him to find joy in his very existence, and the strength of mind and musical imagination he still possessed in full measure. His earlier visions of joy had been simpler, more direct:

the pleasure of love and victory and celebration. In the Heiligenstadt Testament he had feared losing that kind of joie de vivre. Now he arrived at a new and terribly hard-won vision of joy within suffering. That philosophy was going to be necessary to sustain not only his music, but his life.

Again, all in all, despite ongoing illness and creative uncertainty, as 1815 wore on Beethoven seems to have been in some of his best spirits in years. But his brother Carl had again become desperately ill with tuberculosis. In October Carl received a minutely insulting letter from his superior at the Imperial Royal Treasury Office, where he worked as a cashier: "Neither from the most mediocre request for a leave of absence ... nor the hitherto submitted certificate from the ... Chief Surgeon ... is the cashier Carl von [sic] Beethoven to be seen as suffering from an incurable disease ... Rather one has much more sufficient reason to come to the last-named conclusion on the basis of his ... punishable disinclination for his duties; and on his customary negligence." The next month Carl wrote out his will. Beethoven put a note on the superior's letter: "This miserable bureaucratic product caused the death of my brother, since he really was so sick that he could not perform his duties."[114]

It was not brother Carl's death or his will that caused Beethoven hardly bearable suffering and distraction in the coming years, to the point of nearly driving him mad and finally all but killing him. It was the codicil to the will having to do with his brother's young son, Karl.

27

The Queen of the Night

CARL VAN BEETHOVEN died of consumption, the time's name for tuberculosis, on November 15, 1815. It was the same bleeding, choking nightmare that had claimed their mother. Carl's wife Johanna and son Karl could only watch, and wait for the aftermath. Somehow in his last days Carl managed to create an extensive will. It reveals that he and Johanna had battled a great deal about what was going to happen.[1]

"Certain that all must die," the will begins, "and feeling myself near this goal, I am, however, in full possession of my faculties, and freely and voluntarily deem it good to make the following, my last deposition." He commends his soul to the mercy of God, his body to the earth from whence it came. He leaves money for chanting four holy masses. He acknowledges that his wife will have the right to 2,000 florins in bonds she gave him at their marriage. Then he turns to the central issue:

5. I appoint my brother Ludwig van Beethoven guardian. Inasmuch as he, my deeply beloved brother, has often aided me with truly brotherly love in the most magnanimous and noblest manner, I expect, with full confidence and with full trust in his noble heart, that he shall

bestow his love and friendship that he often showed me, also upon my son Karl, and do all that is possible to promote the intellectual training and further welfare of my son. I know that he will not deny me this, my request.

7. . . . I designate my beloved wife Johanna . . . and my son Karl as universal heirs to all my property after the deduction of my existing debts and the above bequests, and that my entire estate shall be divided between them in equal portions.

What happened next can only be surmised but seems clear enough. Carl finalized item no. 5 without Johanna's knowledge. When she saw it she protested, there were shouts and tears, she reminded Carl how Ludwig had always despised her, she put her foot down. The result was the "Codicil to My Will":

Since I have observed that my brother, Herr Ludwig van Beethoven, desires after my eventual death to take wholly to himself my son Karl, and wholly to withdraw him from the supervision and training of his mother, and further, since the best of harmony does not exist between my brother and my wife, I have found it necessary to add to my will that I by no means desire that my son Karl be taken away from his mother, but that he shall always and as long as his future destiny permits remain with his mother, to which end she as well as my brother shall direct the guardianship over my son Karl. Only through harmony can the purpose that I had in appointing my brother guardian of my son be attained; therefore, for the welfare of my child, I recommend compliance to my wife and more moderation to my brother.

God permit the two of them to be harmonious for the welfare of my child. This is the last wish of the dying husband and brother.[2]

Still on the page at the beginning of the fifth item are four words that have been crossed out: "Along with my wife I appoint my brother Ludwig van Beethoven co=guardian." At some point before or after that was done, probably on Johanna's prodding, Carl added the codicil unequivocally calling for a dual guardianship and for the boy to live with his mother. Carl told his lawyer he made the codicil because "my brother is too much a composer and hence can *never* according to my idea, and with my consent, become my son's guardian."[3] But Ludwig was relentless. He wanted the boy for himself, Karl's connection to his mother completely under his control.

In a draft note Ludwig admitted his tampering with the will: "I knew nothing about the fact that a testament had been made; however, I came upon it by chance. If what I had seen was really to be the original text, then passages had to be stricken out. This I had my brother bring about, since I did not want to be bound up with such a bad woman in the matter of such importance as the education of the child."[4] He claimed that just before Carl died he changed his mind and sent his lawyer a message to delete the codicil, but the lawyer was not home and Carl died before it could be taken out. That may or may not be true. In any case, in his last hours of life Carl was thoroughly jerked back and forth by his brother and his wife.

For Ludwig, that his nephew Karl, then nine, had to be taken out of the clutches of a malignant mother was self-evident, something every right-thinking person would agree with. But the codicil remained. The discrepancy between the amended fifth item naming Ludwig as sole guardian and the codicil insisting that Karl should live with his mother was a legal fissure through which flowed years of misery for everybody concerned.

"My poor unfortunate brother has just died," Beethoven wrote Ferdinand Ries in London, to whom he was sending pieces to show publishers. "He had a bad wife. I may as well tell you that for some years he had suffered from consumption; and in order to make life easier for him, I must have given him 10,000 in Viennese currency . . . I may say that I mourn his loss with all my heart, and that I now rejoice at being able to feel sure that so far as his comfort was concerned I have nothing to reproach myself with." The support he gave Carl in his illness goes far toward explaining how Ludwig went through so much money in the last few years. He would not have kept track of those expenditures, so he may have given Carl a good deal less or a good deal more. In the letter to Ries, Beethoven pleaded "hardship for several years as well as the complete loss of my [stipend]."[5] In fact, in the last couple of years he *had* received his stipend and arrears, totaling 4,987 florins, had earned 7,441 florins from his 1814 concerts in Vienna, and had gotten payments from a row of publishers.[6]

In Carl's final days, Ludwig seems to have had no idea how critical his brother's condition was. So, since to him Carl appeared to have died unexpectedly (it had not been unexpected for Carl and Johanna), Ludwig immediately formed the idea that his brother had been poisoned by his wife. There was little evil he did not consider Johanna capable of. He demanded that a friend examine Carl's body for traces of poison. To his disappointment, nothing turned up.[7]

Two weeks after his brother died, Beethoven submitted a lengthy appeal to the Landrecht, the court of the nobility, to make him sole guardian of Karl. As reasons he cited the amended fifth article of the will as well as Johanna's conviction, some years before, for embezzlement, her history of infidelity, and the fact that she had been pregnant with Karl months before their marriage. The widow was therefore, he contended, a manifestly immoral and unworthy mother. That a child could be taken from a mother on such grounds was not unusual in those days.[8] Widows had scant legal power; any kind of taint could be reason for the court to name a guardian. Beethoven made his plea to the Landrecht rather than the Magistrat, the commoners' court. To him it was obvious that whatever the circumstances of his birth, he was no commoner. Meanwhile as far as the Landrecht was concerned, the *van* in his name indicated he was nobility; for the moment they did not inquire further.

On the nineteenth of January 1816, the Landrecht appointed Beethoven guardian. He appeared before the court and "vowed with solemn handgrasp before the assembled council to perform his duties." With that, the matter was apparently settled. To Antonie Brentano he sent a portrait of himself and added the sighing note of a beset but loving parent: "I have fought a battle for the purpose of wresting a poor, unhappy child from the clutches of his unworthy mother, and I have won the day — *Te Deum laudamus* — He is the source of many cares, but cares which are sweet to me."[9]

At the end of January, Beethoven placed Karl in a well-regarded local boarding school for boys operated by Cajetan Giannatasio del Rio.

"I am ready to give Karl to you at any time," he wrote Giannatasio. "In any case it will certainly be best to remove him later on from Vienna and send him to Mölk or somewhere else. There he will neither see nor hear anything more of his beastly mother."[10] There is no record of how Johanna, still in shock after her husband's death, responded at this point to having her son taken away. She probably expected to visit him in school at will.

A few days later Beethoven picked up Karl from the family home, writing schoolmaster Giannatasio, "It affords me much pleasure to inform you that at last I am bringing you tomorrow the precious pledge that has been entrusted to me . . . And now I beg you once more in no circumstances to allow his mother to influence him. How or when she is to see him, all this I will arrange with you tomorrow . . . but you yourself must have some sort of watch kept on your servant, for <u>she has already bribed my servant,</u> though for another purpose!"

Giannatasio had two musical daughters: Fanny, then twenty-five; and her younger sister Nanni, who was engaged to be married. The quieter and more serious of the sisters, Fanny suffered from periods of depression, including a recent months-long siege after the death of her fiancé.[11] The family had known a number of prominent people and Fanny idolized Beethoven, so she was duly thrilled to meet him. She wrote in her diary,

> What I have often vainly wished for, that Beethoven should come to our house, has at length happened. Yesterday afternoon he brought his little nephew to see the Institute; and today everything is arranged. Of my childish embarrassment I will say nothing . . . I cannot describe the delight I feel at being thus brought into communion with a man whom I honor so much as an artist, and esteem so highly as a man . . . How delighted I should be if we could really enter into friendly relations with Beethoven, and if I might hope to make a few hours of his life pleasant to him — to him who has banished so many dark clouds from mine.[12]

Fanny and her family could not have imagined what sort of saga they were entering into with the great man. As Beethoven's feelings surged up and down in the coming months, their feelings — and particularly Fanny's — were obliged to surge as well. Beethoven's intention was to control absolutely Johanna's access to her son, and as soon as possible to send him off to a boarding school far away from her. Soon it became clear that Johanna wanted to see Karl nearly every day, and for the moment Giannatasio had no authority to stop her.[13] "[After] the interview of the mother and your charming nephew today," the schoolmaster wrote, "I have to insist that you, as guardian, show me formal authority in a few lines, by which power I can . . . refuse to allow her to take the son with her . . . It will also not do for her to visit the child too much, for he always mourns her departure."[14]

Beethoven obliged: "Under no pretext whatsoever may Karl be fetched from the boarding school without his guardian's permission; and the mother is never to visit him there — if she desires to see him, she must apply to the guardian." Now he had given Johanna one of his nicknames: the "Queen of the Night," after the evil mother in Mozart's *Zauberflöte.* He continued to Giannatasio, "Last night that Queen of Night was at the Artists' Ball until three A.M. exposing not only her mental but also her bodily nakedness — it was whispered that she — was willing to sell herself — for 20 gulden! Oh horrible! And to such hands are we to entrust our precious treasure even for one moment?"[15]

Who was this woman whom Beethoven held in such holy horror? The most substantial testament to Johanna van Beethoven's person and personality to remain in the record is Beethoven's, and he was ready to believe anything about her: adulteress, thief, prostitute, poisoner of her husband, perverter of her child. The first two, at least, were probably true.

She was born Johanna Theresia Reiss, her father a well-to-do upholsterer. When she married, he gave her 2,000 florins as a dowry. In 1813, Johanna and Carl moved into a big house on the Alservorstadt that he bought with her father's money. The house had as many as a dozen rooms that they rented out.[16] Their son Karl grew up watching what had to have been a fractious marriage. Johanna was flighty and careless with money; Carl had an even more violent temper than Ludwig. He beat the boy, as his father had beaten him. Johanna would also not have escaped Carl's temper. Beethoven claimed to have protected Johanna from her husband's wrath, and that might well be true. There is a story that once during an argument at dinner, Carl drove a knife through Johanna's hand into the table. She liked to show off the scar.[17]

A few surviving stories leave some clues to her style. Later Karl recalled his mother saying that in her childhood her father would not give her any money, but she said that if she could steal it without his noticing, it was hers.[18] When she and Carl married, she was five months pregnant. Some four years before Carl died, she was convicted of embezzling a pearl necklace worth 20,000 florins. She tried to shift the blame to somebody else but was convicted and sentenced to a year in detention. After her husband's pleas to the court, the sentence was reduced to a month, most of which she never served.[19] In time, Karl's wife wrote of Johanna in her indigent later years, "By her letters she moved heaven and earth, and understood how to present her poverty and despair in burning colors and with dramatic effect."[20] Beethoven described her "sauciness and impertinence" when she first came to see him about Karl.[21] Those were the nicest terms he ever used about Johanna. Yet her letters and her appearances in court show her to be fairly articulate on the page and in person.

So Beethoven's sister-in-law seems to have been reasonably intelligent, also flighty, flirtatious, in some degree sexually loose — though when it came to the last, she was hardly in the virtuosic league of nobles at the Congress of Vienna. But Johanna wanted to be a mother to her boy. In those years she was fairly comfortable from her rentals, from what Carl had left her, and from her widow's pension, and she was entirely at leisure. When Beethoven tried to stand between her and Karl, she had nothing better to do than find ways to get around him. It appears that she made something of a game of it. At one point she apparently dressed as a man in order to see Karl on the school playground at Giannatasio's.

As for Karl himself, little record survives of what he was like in these years while his mother and his uncle battled over him. He had been traumatized watching his father die; he needed love and understanding. He got a boarding school and conflict and confusion. Beethoven's circle of friends largely took his side against Johanna and, eventually, against Karl as well. Johanna had her own champions. The only more or less objective observers of all this were the courts. For the moment the Landrecht accepted Beethoven's petition that the mother was unfit, and awarded the guardianship to him.

"You regard Karl as your own child," Beethoven jotted on a sketch. "Heed no gossip, no pettiness, in comparison with this sacred goal."[22] Why did he insist on claiming Karl and sticking to this decision whatever the cost to the boy, to his mother, to himself? At one point after Johanna had sent him a "disgusting scrawl" of an entreaty, he wrote Giannatasio, "I have replied to her this time not like a Sarastro but like a Sultan."[23] Here he identifies himself with two Mozart heroes: the exalted Sarastro in *Die Zauberflöte,* who kidnaps the daughter of the evil Queen of the Night out of disinterested concern for her welfare; and the Turkish pasha Selim in *The Abduction from the Seraglio,* who shows clemency to his Christian enemies.

The moral conceptions Beethoven imbibed in Bonn were still with him. "Nobility of character must in its turn produce what is noble," he wrote, "and virtue should not merely tolerate vice but not hesitate to check its evil effects."[24] The German Aufklärung believed that morality was an obligation, its cultivation a matter of will and reason. The laws of morality were self-evident; morality was the first measure of one's worth; self-improvement was every decent person's duty. One's personal morality was the foundation of value of one's task in life, whatever that might be: in order to be good at anything, one had first to be a good person. And these lessons were best imbibed in childhood. Beethoven had ambitions for Karl to become a good person and a figure in the world. He sent him to an excellent school, to piano lessons with Carl Czerny. He told a friend, "Karl must become an artist or scholar in order to live a high life."[25] For Beethoven, Karl was to be another creation of his own that would add luster to his name.

In his own mind Beethoven was like Sarastro, who does right not because it is expedient but because it is right. He felt a sacred duty — for him not an empty phrase but a binding imperative — to his departed brother to get Karl away from the Queen of the Night and to rear him properly. The poison of Karl's mother had to be purged from the boy's system. This was all a matter of ingrained conviction — the same conviction that informed Beethoven's music.

For well and ill, what Beethoven had been in his teens had not fundamentally changed. He had never grown into social maturity. He was not able to understand anything through another person's eyes, could see the world only through his own lens. When he made up his mind about a person or an issue, that was that, unless he could be persuaded that he had misjudged. There was no possible way Johanna could convince him he had misjudged her, so that was that. Just as in his music he demanded that the material must submit to his will, in his personal life he demanded that the world submit to his convictions about how things ought to be.

His solipsistic view of the world, his blinkered ethics, his ironclad sense of duty, his relentless discipline and tenacity of purpose had served him well as an artist. They had saved him from suicide, kept him working through times of physical and mental suffering. In the case of Karl, that same blinkered tenacity fueled a struggle that ate up years of his creative life.

Of course, there was more to what Beethoven was doing than what he claimed, what he believed he was doing. As with any person's life, much of this is unsearchable, but some of it seems evident. After the collapse of the Immortal Beloved affair, Beethoven gave up on the love of women, on companionship and family. This is a sad watershed in the life of a lonely man. He had little outlet for his sexual yearnings other than the grim solace of the brothel. Through Karl he could find companionship and family, fulfill his frustrated desire for fatherhood. Desperately he wanted love, the simple, elemental thing that had always escaped him. For all his paroxysms of emotion over women, true reciprocal love was something he had not experienced since his mother died, or at best had found only briefly in his affair with the Immortal Beloved.

Now for the first time since his childhood he believed he could have someone in the house whom he loved and who loved him in return. He loved Karl hopelessly. Over and over he said of his nephew, *Karl is my son, I am his true father.* The phrase "my son" moved him to his core. He tried to shape his son's life in the same way that he shaped a piece of music, because he did not truly understand the difference.

There is another element to this relationship, this perhaps the deepest-lying of all. Even though Beethoven remained physically robust when he was not actually prostrate in bed, for years he had been afflicted by a train of illnesses on top of his chronic digestive torments and the hopeless decline of his hearing. By 1816, he was not far from having sound and music entirely shut off from him. And again, as his fame reached new heights, his health declined and his creativity languished. If he had truly known where he wanted to go with his music, scarcely anything in heaven or earth could have stopped him. But in the years around 1815, he did not know where he was going, not yet.

So the problem with his music was only partly the result of pain and deafness and the endless career botherations that had been heaped on him, to which Karl now added a huge claim on his time and emotions. Added to all that was creative uncertainty. In his work he had reached the end of a train of thought he had once called the New Path, which had led him to the *Eroica* and beyond. Now that train of thought, with an image of the hero at the center of it, appeared to be played out. The benevolent despots he once exalted — Joseph II, Napoleon — had failed or betrayed his hopes. In German lands it was an era of mindless repression. The 1819 Carlsbad Decrees of the German Confederation deepened the reach of the police state, setting up a system of regulations and surveillance on all university students and faculties and suppressing political societies. Any professor removed for "subversive" opinions was banned from teaching for life, and no student expelled from one school could be accepted to any other university. Any published material more than twenty pages long had to be submitted to censors. A central investigating committee was set up with virtually Inquisitional powers.[26]

After the Congress of Vienna, the advent of the reactionary and conformist Biedermeier age across German lands and Metternich's police state in Austria, there were no heroes left. For Beethoven the end of heroes had arrived when his life appeared to be running out of hope. The Heiligenstadt crisis of 1802 had struck him when his creative juices were at high tide. Now a row of pieces had collapsed in the sketch stage: a piano concerto, a piano trio, an opera or two, and more. He cared about glory, and his glory had never ridden so high. But he had never been as sick, deaf, depressed, creatively uncertain, and perhaps suicidal as he was in the year his brother died.

A little boy gave Beethoven a reason to live. That inevitably meant, when he could get his feet under him again, that Karl gave him a reason to compose. His duty was clear to him, and it was unthinkable to neglect it. He had to live and he had to provide for his son. That could have meant more of what he called "scribbling," of the kind he had done in large and small forms for the last several years, from the folk-song settings to *Wellington's Victory* and *Der glorreiche Augenblick*. But there remained his ambition and his sense that his gift was owed to humanity. Now he needed to discover yet another new path, but until it presented itself he could only wait and feel his way toward it.

For Beethoven the fight for Karl, then, was in the most direct way a fight for his own life and work, even though he justified it in terms of his duty to his brother and the boy. He could not give up this connection to his life and work, no matter what it cost. But he never realized that a child cannot be shaped like a piece of music. He never understood that the world could never be malleable to his will. To the degree that the world was not as he demanded it to be, the world was contemptible.

But if Beethoven proved to be not the worst parent in the world, he was nearer the worst than the best. And though Johanna van Beethoven was something less than a paragon of motherhood, she was hardly the depraved beast her brother-in-law called her. Both of them loved Karl passionately and possessively, and neither of them would give him up.

To the people in Beethoven's circle, most of whom admired him more or less as much as any man who ever lived, he had always been a great musician and a great spirit. They discerned the generous, warm, world-embracing heart that lay under so much rage, cynicism, paranoia, solipsism, and human incapacity. A large part of that incapacity was an increasingly shaky self-knowledge, which allowed him to write to publisher Steiner, unbelievably, "[M]y character does not allow me to be distrustful."[27] Most who knew him were able to forgive all that. They forgave him, in other words, for never growing up in his relations with the world. He remained the child for whom the world was himself. The people around him were willing to take care of him and try to save him from himself. Often their efforts failed. He broke with one of his oldest friends, Stephan von Breuning, who entreated him not to take on the guardianship.

Karl was the first person in Beethoven's adult life who could neither get away from him nor understand him — nor, when Karl became a teenager, forgive him. The results were predictably terrible. Yet in the end Karl and his mother got out of it in one piece, if not unscathed. Beethoven did not. All this is to say that he had gotten himself and his nephew into a morass from which his needs and convictions appeared to allow them no escape except death.

As Fanny Giannatasio had hoped, when Karl started at her father's school, Beethoven embraced her family and became a regular visitor in the house. For a while they saw the best of him, the part that was open, voluble, funny, generous — even lovable. In the family parlor and around the table he reminisced, rhapsodized, dispensed his singular puns and verbal notions, talked music and politics, played with the children. Like many eccentrics Beethoven had his own language and his own humor. Everybody he knew got a nickname. Fanny was "the Lady Abbess" — presumably he found her to be sober as a nun. He told the family that he had received a commission from the new group of amateur enthusiasts in town called the Gesellschaft der Musikfreunde, Association of the Friends of Music. His name for them was the "Gesellschaft der Musikmörder," Association of the Murderers of Music.[28]

In her diary Fanny tracked Beethoven's visits and her burgeoning emotions:

January, 1816: Beethoven's appearance pleases me greatly . . . The day before yesterday he was with us in the evening and won all our hearts. The modesty and heartiness of his disposition please us extremely. The sorrow which his unhappy connection with the boy's mother entails preys upon his spirits. It afflicts me too, for he is a man who ought to be happy. May he attach himself to us, and by our warm sympathy and interest find peace and serenity! . . . I fear greatly that when I come to know this noble excellent man more intimately, my feelings for him will deepen into something warmer than friendship, and that then I shall have many unhappy hours before me. But I will endure anything, provided only I have it in my power to make his life brighter.

February 26th: He . . . allowed us to see in him the goodness of heart which is his special characteristic. Whether he spoke of his friends, or of his excellent mother, or gave his opinion on those who are contemporaries in art with himself, he proved to us that his heart is as well cultivated as his head . . . Has he already become so dear to me that my sister's laughing advice, not to fall in love with him, pains and troubles me beyond measure.

March 2nd: How can I be so vain as to believe or imagine that the power of captivating such a soul as his is reserved to me? Such a genius? and such a heart . . . Beethoven was with us the whole evening. In the afternoon he had been gathering violets for us, as he said himself, to bring spring to us . . . I spoke with him about walks, baths . . . and Karl's mother. His pure, unspoiled admiration for nature is very beautiful!

March: We entreated him so warmly to remain and take supper with us that he consented, and we intensely enjoyed listening to his rich, original remarks and puns. He gave us also many decided proofs that he is beginning to have confidence in us. He did not leave till nearly twelve o'clock.

March 21st: Yes, it must be confessed, Beethoven interests me to the selfish point of desiring, nay, longing, that I, and I alone may please him! . . . When I returned home, I found that Beethoven had passed the whole evening there. He had brought Shakespeare with him, and played with mother and the children at ninepins. He told them a great deal about his parents, as also of his grandfather, who must have been a true and honorable man.[29]

Fanny's diary records a young woman falling in love, imagining herself nurturing and rescuing one of the greatest of men. As a sign of the intensity of her feelings, Fanny is the only woman on record to declare that she liked how Beethoven looked. Otherwise she observed him astutely, noting among other things that his hearing had better and worse days. But as her feelings overcame her, Fanny could not fail to notice his attraction to her prettier and more vivacious sister Nanni, whose very presence could lighten his spirits. He passed over, in other words, the available sister for the more desirable but unavailable one —his old pattern.

> April 11th: I saw Beethoven again, for the first time since he has been suffering from the illness we feared was hanging over him. At first I was quite alone with him, but as nothing I said seemed to interest him, I began to feel discouraged. Presently Leopold [Nanni's fiancé], Nanni, and mother came in, and then he brightened up ... He remarked that one of those attacks of colic would carry him off some day; upon which I said that that must not happen for many a long year yet, and he replied, "He is a bad man who does not know how to die! I knew it when a lad of fifteen."

His charm and wit could burst out at any moment, even in the middle of practical matters. He wrote Frau Giannatasio, "The highly born and very well born Frau v G etc., is most politely requested to let me know very soon, so that I need not keep in my head so many pairs of trousers, stockings, shoes, pants, etc., I repeat, to let the undersigned know how many ells of cashmere my upstanding and worthy nephew requires for a pair of black trousers; and ... I ask her to reply without my having to remind her again. As to the Lady Abbess [Fanny], a vote is to be taken this evening about the question which concerns Karl, namely, whether he is to remain with you."[30] Despite the social pleasantries with the Giannatasios, his mood remained bitterly depressed. In the spring, he wrote Countess Erdödy:

> My brother's death caused me great sorrow; and then it necessitated great efforts to save my nephew ... from the influence of his depraved mother. I succeeded in doing this. But so far I have not yet been able to make a better arrangement for him than to place him at a boarding school, which means that he is separated from me; and what is a

boarding school compared with the immediate sympathetic care of a father for his child? For I now regard myself as his father ... Moreover, for the last six weeks I have been in very poor health, so much so that frequently I have thought of my death. I do not dread it. Yet I should be dying too soon so far as my poor Karl is concerned ... Man cannot avoid suffering; and in this respect his strength must stand the test, that is to say, he must endure without complaining and feel his worthlessness and then again achieve his perfection, that perfection which the Almighty will then bestow upon him.

Written to his old "father confessor," this is a point of honor that he meant seriously: endurance is the road to exaltation. As his mother had taught, "Without suffering there is no struggle, without struggle no victory, without victory no crown." But his prevailing depression remained, and that in turn afflicted the depressive Fanny. In her diary she began to confess her jealousy of her sister. By November 1816, she was enduring an archetypal turmoil:

I am childish enough to feel wounded because he seems to prefer Nanni to me, although I have told myself a thousand times that I have no right or pretensions to his showing a preference for me. I do not quite like his calling me the "Lady Abbess" when I am busy with my housekeeping ... It does not please me at all for him to regard me simply in the light of a good housekeeper ... He had been talking to me for about half an hour when she came in, and immediately he brightened up, and seemed to forget my presence. What more do I want, silly girl that I am? ... What I feel is the need of loving and being loved, the right of being sympathized with, my soul infused in another soul. That this wish should arise from knowing a man like Beethoven, seems a natural thing to me, and because the wish is there, I do not think I am so unworthy of him.[31]

By then, as they did sooner or later with nearly everybody, Beethoven's relations with the Giannatasio family had become fraught. The process began, as usual, with his becoming indecisive, going sour on people. Johanna kept finding ways to see Karl. The boy must be got out of town. "Beethoven's manner towards us has altered," a distraught Fanny wrote in her diary. "He is cold now for the first time, and I find myself grieving over it . . . His conduct is at times so very moody and unfriendly that I feel shy with him . . . He said his life was of no worth to himself, he only wished to live for the boy's sake."[32] Karl was his reason to live, his reason to compose. But composing was not going well. Ideas, rhymes and reasons, were eluding him.

That spring he wrote Ferdinand Ries in London, including one of the lists of his income and expenses that over time became a compulsion with him: "Until now he [Karl] has been at a boarding school. That costs up to 1,100 [florins] and, even so, it is not a good school. Hence I shall have to start a proper household where I can have him live with me." He ends, "My best greetings to your wife. Unfortunately I have no wife. I have found only one whom no doubt I shall never possess. Yet I am not on that account a woman-hater."[33]

If Karl was to live with him, he needed reliable servants. That became another obsession of the next months and years. "Please give up the idea," he pleaded to old friend Baron Zmeskall, "that no servant can ever put up with me."[34] This was a forlorn hope. Another request to Zmeskall for a male servant was symptomatic of his attitude: "He need not be physically attractive. Even if he is a bit hunchbacked I should not mind, for then I should know at once the weak spot at which to attack him."[35] This may have been a joke, but it was not far from the reality of how he managed servants. Meanwhile, in signing off letters he took to designating himself "a poor Austrian musical drudge."

This year Dr. Carl von Bursy, a friend of Beethoven's long-departed friend Karl Amenda, met Beethoven and contributed his impressions to the record. He found a man "small, rather stocky, hair combed back with much gray in it, a rather red face, fiery eyes which, though small, [were] deep-set and unbelievably full of life." Bursy had to shout to be heard and was often misunderstood.

By now Beethoven had a practiced line with visitors. "I never do anything straight through without pause," he told Bursy. "I always work on several things at once, and sometimes I work on this one and sometimes on that one." (This was neither untrue nor entirely accurate: the sketchbooks show he usually concentrated on one piece at a time, though others could be in progress and he might break off work on one piece for a more pressing project.) This stranger found Beethoven "venomous and embittered. He raged about everything, and is dissatisfied with everything, and he curses Austria and Vienna in particular. He speaks quickly and with great vivacity. He often banged his fist on the piano and made such a noise that it echoed around the room . . . He complains about the present age, and for many reasons . . . Art is no longer held in such high esteem and particularly not as regards recompense." Bursy found Beethoven's rooms pleasant, with a view out over the bastions. This visitor did not cite the usual squalor. He noted "two good oil portraits . . . on the wall, a man and a woman."[36] The man would have been his grandfather Ludwig. The identity of the woman did not turn up.

In the summer another crisis arrived when Karl developed a hernia that required an operation. In those days any operation was a great trauma, performed on a fully awake and usually writhing and screaming patient. The good surgeons were the ones who could work fast, before the patient died of shock. Beethoven arranged for the operation to be performed at Giannatasio's by Carl von Smetana, a leading Viennese surgeon; afterward Smetana became one of Beethoven's regular medical consultants.[37]

For some unexplained reason — possibly a "feverish cold" that struck him in October and lasted for months — Beethoven was in Baden and left it up to the Giannatasios to oversee Karl's operation and recovery. The procedure went blessedly well. After the operation Beethoven wrote Karl some practical items: "So far as I can see, there is still a certain amount of poison in your system. Hence I do entreat you to note down your mental and bodily requirements. The weather is becoming colder. Do you need another blanket or possibly your eiderdown? . . . The truss-maker has . . . promised to call again."[38]

But his relations with the boy were more emotional than practical. As always his feelings gushed out in a jumble, almost crazed sometimes, his mood depending on his health, his success in keeping the mother away, the state of Karl, all on top of his eternal capriciousness and volatility. His self-awareness, however inconstant, was one of the things that helped him survive and work. In July, he wrote to Frau Giannatasio, "I have all this time been really ill and suffering from a nervous breakdown."[39] His breakdowns tended to the manic more than depressive; he was rarely prostrate and helpless. Among the rants and paroxysms he tried to be a dutiful father, writing to the Giannatasios about Karl's shoes, stockings, coats, pants, and underwear. He did not ignore Fanny completely. In the summer his Lady Abbess was ill, and he went to visit her twice.[40] The sight of pain usually brought out his best.

In September 1816, Beethoven deposited 4,000 florins, earnings from his successes during the Congress of Vienna, with his publisher Steiner, with whom it would earn 8 percent interest. That money was earmarked for Karl's inheritance. In the coming years, however desperate for cash he became, however enraged toward the boy, he resisted touching it.

Surges of hope and high spirits were also part of his emotional tides. Fanny Giannatasio was buffeted by those tides again and again. She wrote in August that Beethoven came back from Baden "grumbling, as usual, over his expenses. When I saw him, and heard him speak so kindly of us, the wish of my heart again asserted itself that he would attach himself to us . . . He seems quite well, and says that he knows he shall be strong enough soon, his constitution is so healthy." She and her sister had visited him in Baden while he was taking the baths and peeked in his *Tagebuch,* the diary, which "appeared to contain many significant things." In that visit to Baden the sisters saw firsthand the kind of battles Beethoven was having with servants. He turned up with a scratch on his face, explaining that it had happened in an argument with one of them. "Look how he has marked me!" he cried.

As he had earlier to Ries that year, he told Fanny's father about the love of his life — surely the woman he had called Immortal Beloved. Fanny wrote, "Five years ago he made the acquaintance of a lady, whom to marry would have been the highest happiness life could have afforded him. It was not to be thought of, was quite impossible, in fact, and was a chimera. But still his feelings remain the same now as then. 'I cannot put her out of my thoughts,' were words which pained and hurt me beyond measure."[41]

•   •   •

In the spring of 1816, around the time Beethoven made that confession to Giannatasio and in a letter to Ries ("I have found <u>only</u> one whom no doubt I shall <u>never</u> possess"), he completed what amounted to a more lasting memorial to his lost love, a song cycle called *An die ferne Geliebte* (To the Distant Beloved). For all this work's unmistakable grounding in his own pain, however, he remained Beethoven. No matter how self-pitying he could be in person, he was not so in his art. In this work no less than in any earlier ones, he thought abstractly as well as emotionally, universally as well as personally.

Here in the guise of little tunes in folk style, in *An die ferne Geliebte* he created a new kind of unity, a cycle in which the story is unified and the whole greater than the parts. To take what on the surface appears to be a series of songs and make them into a structure of interdependent elements is an echt-Beethoven way to go about things, even when his own sorrows were involved. No song can be detached; each segues into the next. As in his instrumental music, there are internal motifs and interrelated keys and a return at the end.[42]

Beethoven had known folk music German and otherwise since his childhood, as well as songs written in folk style by composers including his teacher Christian Neefe. He had wielded the style himself here and there.[43] More recently he had made the dozens of folk-song arrangements for Thomson, which had recently departed from the original British Isles tunes to include Continental ones. Any effort that extensive was going to have an impact on his more ambitious work. He copied down a folk song, like a touchstone, on one of the sketches for *An die ferne Geliebte*.[44]

Part of the folk style he adopted for the cycle was a certain emotional restraint. The lyrics of true folk songs contain a full measure of passion and tragedy, but they do not treat those emotions operatically — especially since most folk songs are strophic, meaning each verse is sung to the same melody. In a strophic song one verse may concern love and another death, and the tune has to encompass them even-handedly. The first five of the six numbers in *An die ferne Geliebte* are strophic, varied en route; the variety is in the evolving piano accompaniment, in the contrast from song to song, in the unfolding of emotions from joy in nature to sorrow in love.

The verses came from a young Jewish medical student named Alois Jeitteles, who wrote poetry and plays with some success. How Beethoven ran across this cycle of six verses is not clear, but they could not have been better suited to his frame of mind at the time, or to his requirements as a composer.[45] The poems themselves enfold a pattern of echoes and returns and foreshadowings that are Beethovenian in their motivic structure.

For him *An die ferne Geliebte* was an address to his own distant, lost beloved, expressed in terms not of operatic anguish but of hope and gentleness, in the artless style of folk song: "What sounded from my overflowing heart, / Without the trappings of art, / Conscious only of its longing."[46]

The cycle begins with a simple E-flat chord and a simple strophic tune stretching over five stanzas. This will be one of his nonheroic works in E-flat. The evolving accompaniment subtly paints the poet's changing feelings: "I sit on the hill, peering / Into the blue mist-shrouded landscape, / Seeking those distant country pastures / Where I first found you, my beloved." Mountains, valleys, clouds, brooks, birds, longing in the midst of nature: those high-Romantic images return and develop through the course of the cycle. The end of the first number tells us that these are songs ultimately about songs — all songs, all music — and also about themselves as an emblem of love and remembrance: "For all space and time recedes / At the sound of songs, / And what a loving heart has consecrated / Will reach another loving heart." Here in essence is Beethoven's poetic definition of music itself. The composer's loving heart consecrates his gift to the world.

In the second number, as the poet looks out over the mountains the accompaniment conjures hunting horns and the singer's voice echoing in the cliffs. Again there is an underlying sympathy between nature and his feelings as he looks to the western horizon: "Where the sun's rays fade, / Where the clouds gather, / There I long to be!" The clouds return in the fourth song, gliding above birds whose calls drift into the music. (Here and in most of his vocal works, whatever his objections to literalistic tone painting, Beethoven paints every possible word, image, and feeling.) In the fifth number spring awakes, the swallow "busily fetches from every nook and cranny / Soft scraps aplenty for her bridal bed," and she and her mate make their nest. The music here is a beautiful, simple C major whose purity sets up the poignancy of a turn to C minor at the last words: "Our love alone beholds no spring, / And its net profit is tears."

The last song is no lament but rather returns to the gentle hope and resignation of the opening in the way it captures the potency and timelessness of music itself: "Accept them then, these songs / Which I sang for you, my love. / Then sing them again at eventide / To the sweet sound of the lute." That image of the singer's beloved taking up the melodies he has created leads to a heart-tugging *molto adagio* on "You sing what I sang." On a small scale, that is as distilled a musical and symbolic moment as the trumpet call that announces liberation in *Fidelio*. Two loving hearts drawn apart are united in music, the poet's song and his heart echoing in the song and heart of the beloved. In the most direct yet profound way, in that moment Beethoven is united with his own lost beloved in the only way he can be, and no less with all beloveds and all lost loves — which is to say, with all humanity.

At the last verse the opening melody of the cycle returns, and again we hear the consoling couplet that ended the first song: "What a loving heart has consecrated / Will reach another loving heart." As in all his best music, here is form at the service of intense emotion. With those lines the music speeds to a racing, almost operatic coda. From gentle beginning to triumphant end, *An die ferne Geliebte* is what its verses say it is: private anguish universalized and transcended in its singing.

The cycle is less than fifteen minutes long, its style deliberately simple and restrained. All the same, in conception and structure it is innovative unto revolutionary. *An die ferne Geliebte* marks the beginning of the integral Romantic *Liederkreis,* song cycle, as Beethoven dubbed it in his first edition. It was written when a young man named Franz Schubert had already written some of his first important freestanding lieder. This little set of songs by Beethoven would show Schubert the way toward his own song cycles — likewise toward the broadening possibilities of the new pianos as an accompanying instrument.[47]

For Beethoven, at the same time that one hopes this music helped put to rest an emotional calamity that still gnawed at him, it also played its part in his rebirth as a composer. Simplicity and directness had always been ideals for him, but here he expressed them in terms of folk music, of the kind that by now he had been working with for years in his folk-song arrangements. The folk style and a new emphasis on lyric melody were going to play a part in the complex of forces that shaped his late music. So was the kind of overt musical recall that happens at the end of the cycle.

Beethoven dedicated the songs to his old patron Prince Lobkowitz, who had returned to the fold paying his share of Beethoven's stipend. But by the time the music reached his house, Lobkowitz was dead at forty-four.[48] In any case, with *An die ferne Geliebte* Beethoven virtually said goodbye to lieder; he completed only two more substantial ones, *Resignation* in 1817 and *Abendlied* in 1820.[49]

For Beethoven the consolation of *An die ferne Geliebte* was spiritual at best. The miseries of his external life continued as before. Through 1816, he was determined to get Karl away from the Giannatasios to live with him, preparatory to sending the boy to a boarding school beyond the reach of his mother. By the end of the year he had for the moment given up on that dream. He could not shake the cold that had gotten into his lungs, and he had gone through a row of servants trying to find ones he could live with. As his music began to revive, everything else was falling apart. "My household is almost exactly like a shipwreck or tends to resemble one," he wrote Giannatasio. "In short, a soi-disant expert in such matters has cheated me over these [servants]. And, moreover, my health does not seem to be improving so very rapidly." So he says regretfully that the school is to keep Karl for another quarter. He directs the Giannatasios that the boy's piano lessons with Czerny should continue, three days a week. On a visit he brought up the idea of his coming to live with the Giannatasios, which made Fanny both excited and apprehensive.[50] It was another chimera; nothing came of it.

Toward the end of 1816, Beethoven wrote his nephew after they had visited his father's grave on the anniversary of Carl's death:

My dear Karl of my Heart!

I can't see you today, not yet, because I have a great deal to do! And, moreover, I am not completely recovered. But do not be anxious . . .

Indeed I too mourn for your father, but the best way for us both to honor his memory is for you to pursue your studies with the greatest zeal and to endeavor to become an upright and excellent fellow, and for me to take his place and to be in every way a father to you, and you see that I am making every effort to be all this to you.[51]

In juggling the contrapuntal demands of Karl's operation and school and lessons and overcoats and underwear, his own odious servants and the Queen of the Night, and his deteriorating health and hearing, it would seem that Beethoven would have had no time to think about business. But he never stopped thinking. Even in the times when he was bedridden in a filthy room, bleary with illness, his head lying on a sweat-soaked pillow, he was thinking, scheming, composing in his head.

Now he was sending a steady stream of letters to England, where his old student Ferdinand Ries and conductor Sir George Smart championed him. In London the Birchall publishing house accepted several pieces including the *Archduke* Trio and piano arrangements of the Seventh Symphony and *Wellington's Victory*, before a new owner took over who wanted nothing to do with Beethoven.[52] To help inspire Ries, Beethoven sent a compliment: "The Archduke Rudolph plays your works too, my dear Ries, and among these I find *Il Sogno* particularly delightful."[53]

After the breakup of Count Razumovsky's quartet following the burning of his palace, Beethoven lost two of the men from that quartet who numbered among his leading champions in Vienna. Violinist Ignaz Schuppanzigh had found work in Russia; he gave an all-Beethoven farewell concert in February 1816, the program including the third *Razumovsky* Quartet, the op. 16 Quintet, and the still-popular op. 20 Septet. A week later cellist Joseph Linke, living out of town at Countess Erdödy's estate, gave a concert that included a Beethoven cello sonata, perhaps one of the two new ones written for him, published as op. 102.[54]

At the Schuppanzigh concert Carl Czerny manned the piano in the op. 16 Quintet. In a spirit of youthful enthusiasm he added a number of his own flourishes to the part. It was an old and slight piece, but at the end of the concert Czerny got a royal chewing out from Beethoven in front of the other musicians. The next day came Beethoven's apology in a note: "Tomorrow I will call on you myself to have a talk with you. — I burst forth so yesterday that I was sorry after it had happened; but you must pardon that in a composer who would have preferred to hear his work exactly as he wrote it, no matter how beautifully you played in general. — I shall make amends *publicly* at [Linke's concert]. Be assured that as an artist I have the greatest wishes for your success." Beethoven kept his word about the public apology.[55]

During the same period, Johann Nepomuk Hummel left town. Once a Mozart student, he had found acclaim as a pianist and composer. After a shaky start to their relations, he and Beethoven had become rivals more friendly than otherwise. Happy to contribute, Hummel had directed the artillery in the *Wellington's Victory* performances. As a farewell gift Beethoven wrote Hummel a canon on *Ars longa, vita brevis* (Art is long, life is short). Beethoven was developing a habit of marking occasions or honoring visitors with little canons, most of them to ironic texts. As a sadly ironic echo of that text, Hummel did not see his friend again until Beethoven was on his deathbed.[56]

The op. 102 Cello Sonatas written for Linke were the last of Beethoven's essays in a genre he had essentially invented in op. 5. They also mark his farewell to chamber music with piano — that in part because he was no longer a performing pianist. In op. 102 appear more elements that will mark the late music, his second new path:

Lyric melody: Op. 102, no. 1, in C Major begins with a gentle, songful theme for cello alone.

Equality of voices: The piano enters on an echo of the melody, as if continuing the cello's thought. Nothing lingers of the eighteenth-century idea of a solo sonata as "piano with violin" or "with cello." In the C Major Sonata the two are like a couple who speak as one.

Harmonic suspension: There is no firm cadence onto C major until the third line, and barely then. Only at the end of the introduction does a prolonged C-major chord settle in.

Unconventional harmonic relationships and tonal structure in new directions: The quiet and lyrical C-major introduction prepares a driving, slightly demonic Allegro in A minor, a compact sonata-form movement that stays in the minor key to the end.

New subtlety in the handling of small motifs: The opening unaccompanied cello melody in the C Major Sonata serves as a kind of motto; the ensuing themes are based on motivic germs in the first bars: the fall from C down to G, the lift from C up to G in the second bar, and the echoed G–F–D figure between cello and piano. The singing second theme of the Allegro is made from these elements. Here more than before, Beethoven uses motifs as seeds to sprout themes, often within what sounds like a capricious drifting from one idea to another. Thus —

Poetic stream of consciousness: The impression of a clear dramatic narrative has receded, replaced by a sense of music seemingly capable of going anywhere from anywhere, changing direction in a second, the emotional effect powerfully evocative but often mysterious unto magical.

New angles on traditional formal patterns, with overt recalls of earlier movements: Following the first movement comes a swirling Adagio, not exactly a movement or an introduction either. All this is nominally in C major, but actually it sort of condenses in a C-major direction that melts unexpectedly into a varied recall of the opening page, now led by the piano — marked *dolce,* "sweetly." This recall of the opening barely departs from a C-major chord. Traditionally, long pieces had avoided literal recalls of music from earlier movements; until now Beethoven had shied away from it as well. Years before, the *Pathétique* was taken to task by a critic for its finale theme so clearly recalling a theme in the first movement. Thematic *connections* among movements were smiled on, *recalls* not. Now for Beethoven more or less literal recalls were going to be available as a device. (Eventually critics took to calling these kinds of pieces "cyclic" works.) Another feature of the late music —

Familiar forms still in place but often obscured, receding into the background, leaving more of an impression of fantasy and improvisation: In the C Major Cello Sonata, the second of two short virtual slow movements — or double introduction, or both — leads to the finale proper, a playful Allegro vivace, nominally in sonata form but almost monothematic with its little zipping figure.

Intensified contrasts: In the C Major and in the second work of op. 102, the D Major Cello Sonata, strong contrasts are often juxtaposed with little or no transition. The compact Allegro con brio of the D Major begins with a leaping and dynamic motto in piano, countered by a soaring lyric phrase in cello that seems to take up the piano's idea and lyricize it. Those two contrasting gestures are the central dichotomy of the piece. The dominant tone throughout, though, is ebullient and muscular, with lyrical interludes. In no. 2 of op. 102, the cooperation of cello and piano is as strong as in no. 1, but the terms are different, like two figures in a friendly and equal competition. In the D Major, the first-movement development is short, like that of the C Major, but both of them have a fresh tone; even though they develop material from the exposition, they sound more like an exposition than a development, because the music is made more of melody and counterpoint than of the usual accompanimental figuration.

Next, in the late music —

Long-breathed lyricism in slow movements: The lyrical trend in the D Major flowers in the remarkable second movement, marked Adagio con molto sentimento d'affetto, which sounds like an archaic, tragic aria. (If the mournful slow movement of the Piano Sonata in D Major, op. 10, is "prophetic," this movement is one of the things it prophesies.) We are close to the sublime slow movements of Beethoven's last years, with their long, time-stopping melodies. Here the music becomes ornamented, rhapsodic, finally slipping into an uncanny atmosphere prophetic of Schubert — his doppelgänger or his weird organ-grinder, in the song cycles.

A new emphasis on counterpoint in general and fugue in particular:
Beethoven is turning away from figuration and clear demarcations of
foreground and background, to a texture where all the voices are more
nearly equal and melody pervades the texture. The finale of the D Major is an energetic and dashing, also ironic, fugue. Later, Beethoven
said that if one were going to write fugues and other old forms in this
day and age (which by that point was the Romantic age), they must not
be rehashes of Bach and Handel; they needed to have, he said, something more "poetic," a new kind of expressiveness adapted to the forms
and norms of Viennese style. This poetic idea was going to pervade his
coming music.

The fugal finale of the D Major is an experiment in that direction. It
has a headlong, madcap drive full of rhythmic quirks that foreshadow
several of his fugal finales to come. Each of them will be a particular
rethinking of the fugue and of how it can be integrated into the late
eighteenth-century forms that Beethoven inherited. Classical form,
with its clear phrases and sections and thematic contrasts and developments, would seem to be antithetical to fugue, which is a sustained
contrapuntal procedure generally based on a single theme. (Fugal moments in the course of a movement in sonata form were common from
Haydn on, but whole fugal movements rare.) In other words, in his late
music Beethoven will be showing —

*A new historical awareness and integration of Classical, even Renais-
sance and Baroque forms and procedures — an integration of past and
present:* In shaping a series of individual approaches to that goal, he in
turn inflected the direction of music for a century and more.

These, then, were the new elements of the late music: unconventional
harmonic moves and tonal structures; long periods without harmonic
resolution; new angles on traditional formal patterns, sometimes with
overt recalls of earlier movements; familiar forms still in place but
often obscured; long-breathed lyricism; a new emphasis on counterpoint. With the latter Beethoven returned to the Baroque idea that
counterpoint is the heart of music. And when he wrote counterpoint,
Bach was usually in the front of his mind.

THIRD)
PHASE

POETIC

PERIOD

    None of these trends was entirely new for him, but all of them were expanded and intensified until the effect became quite new, more than the sum of its parts. The cello sonatas of op. 102 opened the gates to the late works, a second new path. Call this third phase of his music the Poetic Period.

In the autumn of 1816, in the wake of finishing *An die ferne Geliebte* and in the middle of a new piano sonata, Beethoven showed traces of his old rowdy high spirits. He wrote publisher Steiner, using his military designation, "With all my heart I embrace the L[ieutenant] G[eneral] and wish him the rod of a stallion."[57] Responding to a storm of mistakes in the Seventh Symphony engraving, he signed off to Steiner, "May God protect you — May the devil take you —."[58] And to Baron Zmeskall:

> You must know by now what sort of person more or less I should like my new servant to be, that is to say, good, orderly behavior, suitable references, married and without any murderous tendencies, so that my life may be safe. For although the world is full of rascals of all kinds I should like to live a little longer ... I will soon send you my treatise on the four violoncello strings, worked out very systematically; the first chapter is about guts in general — the second chapter deals with gut strings — and so forth.
>
> I need not warn you any more to take care not to be wounded near certain fortresses.[59]

The connection of the cello's gut strings (Zmeskall was a cellist), guts in general, and fortresses (prostitutes) is obscure but evocative. By now Beethoven seems to have gotten to some degree into the habit of visiting brothels, like most bachelors of his time. The moral anguish about it found earlier in the *Tagebuch* has disappeared. Now he is more concerned with the "rotten" fortresses — the prostitutes ready to give you venereal diseases. The next summer, Beethoven wrote Zmeskall, "I am always ready for it. The time I prefer most of all is at about half past three or four o'clock in the afternoon."[60]

1817   As 1817 arrived, his bad health and his other torments marched on, but at least they evolved. Beethoven was living in a high, narrow house on Sailerstätte. Its back looked out over the walls to the suburb of Landstrasse, where Giannatasio had recently moved his school. Karl having been secreted away in the school's new location, for the moment the Johanna problem receded. Apparently Beethoven also spent some time residing in the hotel Zum Römischen Kaiser.

C. F. Hirsch, grandson of Beethoven's old counterpoint teacher Albrechtsberger, lived near that hotel and his son made Beethoven's acquaintance. Somehow Hirsch persuaded Beethoven to give the boy lessons in harmony, meaning figured bass at the keyboard. Hirsch remembered of the lessons that Beethoven could essentially hear nothing but watched the boy's hands on the keys. Technical mistakes in voice leading threw him into a rage. When he detected a mistake he flushed red, pinched the boy hard, once went so far as to bite him on the shoulder. After the lessons, Beethoven became calm and friendly again. In his own work, after all, he often cursed the notes into place.

Hirsch's recollection of Beethoven's appearance recalls Burney's in the same period: ruddy complexion, hair going gray and standing up from his face, coarse hands with short fingers and close-cut nails. In the house he wore a flowery dressing gown, in the street a dark green or brown overcoat with dark trousers. In cold weather he sported a low top hat, in summer a straw hat, In all weathers he looked slovenly.[61]

During these months he was again feeling kindly toward the Giannatasios. In the middle of January, Fanny wrote in her diary that he had visited nearly every day for a week. "I am inexpressibly happy that he seems to cling to us. Little incidents often arouse within me bitter, sad feelings that might truly be termed jealous; as, for instance, his significant reply to Nanni's childish question . . . as to whether he loves anyone else besides his 'absent beloved one.'" Both sisters knew, in other words, about *An die ferne Geliebte* and its connection to Beethoven's own distant beloved. During one visit, father Giannatasio asked Fanny to accompany her sister in the songs. Beethoven ordered Fanny off the piano bench and accompanied Nanni himself. Fanny noted that he missed notes apparently without noticing, and it seemed that he could not hear Nanni at all.[62]

At the beginning of summer he and Nanni had a conversation about marriage that Fanny recorded, trying to contain her shock:

He is certainly a peculiar man in many things, and his ideas and opinions on [marriage] are still more peculiar. He declares that he does not like the idea of any indissoluble bond being forced between people in their personal relations to each other. I think I understand him to mean that man or woman's liberty of action ought not to be limited. He would much rather a woman gave him her love, and with her love the highest part of her nature, without . . . being bound to him in the relation of wife to husband. He believes that the liberty of the woman [in that situation] is limited and circumscribed.

He spoke of a friend of his who was very happy, and who had several children, who, nevertheless, held to the opinion that marriage without love was the best for man . . . As far as his experience went, he said that he did not know a single married couple who . . . did not repent the step he or she took in marrying; and that, for himself, he was excessively glad that none of the girls had become his wife whom he had passionately loved in former days.[63]

This appears a thought-out rather than spur-of-the-moment point of view, but to what degree did he actually mean it? Part of it was surely a rationalization, an attempt to convince himself that his disappointments in love had been after all for the best. In that respect it resembled what he wrote to Countess Erdödy about "joy through suffering." If he was to find any joy in the life fate had decreed for him, a path through suffering was the only available route. His old defiance had given way to resignation. If no one would marry him, to protect himself he rejected marriage. In the process, probably without realizing it, he echoed what his careworn, disillusioned mother Maria had said long before: "What is marriage but a little joy, then afterward a chain of sorrows." In those opinions and others, Beethoven appears to have taken for granted the equality of men and women — as usual, more in theory than in practice. But he never treated a woman other than with respect for her feelings and opinions, her autonomy — even when those feelings took her away from him.

WINTER 1817

This winter of 1817, Fanny Giannatasio was at the height of her infatuation and her sensitivity. In February Beethoven wrote her father a letter about Karl's new boots hurting his feet and about the boy needing more time to practice piano; he announced that he was coming to pick up Karl the next day, to take him to a concert. That letter, not warm but hardly angry, nonetheless put Fanny into a tizzy: "That Beethoven is vexed with us is a very great trial to me, but that he should show it in the way he does adds to its bitterness. It is true that father has not behaved very well to him; still, I think that Beethoven ought not to retort with biting sarcasm, when he knows how much affection and interest we have always had for him. I expect he wrote that letter in one of his misanthropical humors, and I forgive him for it." Two weeks later Fanny wrote with relief, "He has been to us, and we are friends again. It has pained me very deeply to be obliged to acknowledge how much Karl has been to blame in all these misunderstandings, and it grieved me still more deeply that we were forced to inform his uncle of several misdemeanors of his, which have angered him beyond measure."[64] Here a new theme entered the saga: the tendency of people around Beethoven to blame Karl for whatever problems arose. The boy was now eleven.

Piano maker Nannette Streicher had known Beethoven for a long time, possibly having met him in her teens. Now she started to advise him on domestic matters, especially concerning servants. He wrote her after an unpleasant encounter in February, "I ask you a thousand times to forgive me about yesterday. We had a meeting on the question of my nephew . . . and on such occasions I am really always in danger of losing my head. And that's what happened yesterday. I only hope that you may not have felt offended."[65]

Still on his campaign to find a reliable servant so he could bring Karl home, Beethoven wrote many letters to Nannette in these years. He dubbed her "my good Samaritan." "What does one give two servants for dinner and supper?" he asked her. He approached the question as if servants were domestic animals. "How often are they given roast meat . . . How much bread money for the housekeeper and maid per day?" Nannette answered in detail: no roast meat at night, cook their vegetables together to save fat, and so on and so on.[66] She and Zmeskall interviewed servants and sent them on to Beethoven. Sooner or later, usually sooner, he declared them beastly and threw them out. At one point he told Zmeskall he had found for a servant a former soldier who "wanted to devote himself entirely to me."[67] Within two weeks he had given the soldier notice: "He gets drunk and stays out of the house . . . and is so shockingly rude and insolent."[68]

Most of the female servants that came to him were older, but at one point Nannette found him a plump young woman named Peppi. "Ask if she is really a cook," he wrote Nannette. "If she is skilled with venison, fish., etc. Can she protect her 22-year-old virginity until we rightfully allow her to marry herself off? Boyfriends will not be allowed in the house."[69] Peppi turned out to be quite a good cook and lasted awhile. An older woman named Nanni also endured his treatment for some time. He wrote Nannette at the end of the year, "Things are really better — although today I had to put up with a good deal from N[anni] — But as a New Year wish I threw a half dozen books at her head."[70] He was not joking. "I don't think that Nanni is absolutely honest," he wrote Nannette, "apart from the fact that she is also a disgusting beast. I now realize quite clearly that people of that type must be ruled not by affection but by fear."[71] Later he accused the servants of being in collusion with Karl's mother, which drove him wild.

In practice, fear was one of his child-raising tools. He wrote Giannatasio, "As for Karl, I beg you to enforce the strictest obedience and to punish him immediately if he doesn't obey you . . . You will remember that I have already told you how during his father's lifetime he would only obey when he was beaten. Of course that was very wrong, but that was how things were done, and we must not forget it."[72] Here was another gap between theory and practice in Beethoven's life. He wrote Nannette, "I often give him a good shaking, but not without valid reason."[73] Karl would get his share of shaking and blows from his uncle.

In the spring of 1817, Beethoven lost another longtime friend and champion, Wenzel Krumpholz. The violinist fell dead in the middle of a walk on the Glacis outside the city walls. Around 1802, it was to Krumpholz that Beethoven had declared he was striking out on a new path. There is, remarkably, no record of a quarrel in their long friendship. Beethoven wrote a short *Song of the Monks* and inscribed it "In memory of the sudden and unexpected death of our Krumpholz."

Even good news tended to get tangled up in the general confusion and indecision. In London, Ferdinand Ries had been championing Beethoven to good effect. In June Ries relayed an invitation and commission from the Philharmonic Society: "My dear Beethoven, we would very much like to have you among us here in London next winter . . . I have been commissioned in the name of the Directorship to offer you 300 guineas on the following conditions."[74] He was to come to London the next winter and write two new symphonies. Everyone remembered Haydn's sojourns in England and how they had established the fame and fortune he enjoyed in his last years. Beethoven and everybody involved hoped for the same for him. He replied happily, adding some further stipulations (which the society declined to accept), and made a few sketches for a symphony in D minor. But the symphony and the commission and his promise of a visit languished for what turned out to be years.

An apparent resolution to some financial tangles appeared in the middle of 1817 when after extended negotiations Johanna van Beethoven signed a contract agreeing to pay Ludwig support for Karl, including an immediate 2,000 florins and thereafter half her yearly pension payments.[75] Lately Johanna had been less troubling and Beethoven more forgiving. He wrote Zmeskall, "It might hurt Karl's mother to have to visit her child at the house of a stranger; and in any case it is a less charitable arrangement than I like. So I am letting her come to me tomorrow."[76] He enjoyed being generous.

His *Tagebuch* shows the guilt Beethoven felt over Johanna's situation: "It would have been impossible without hurting the widow's feelings but it was not to be. And Thou, almighty God, seest into my heart, know that I have disregarded my own welfare for my dear Karl's sake, bless my work, bless the widow . . . God, God, my refuge, my rock. O my all, Thou seest my innermost heart and knowest how it pains me to have to make somebody suffer through my good works for my deal Karl!!! O hear, ever ineffable One, hear me, your unhappy, most unhappy of all mortals." Then he got wind that Johanna was spreading malicious gossip about him and peremptorily decreed that she could see Karl only twice a year.

Part of his depression in the summer of 1817 came from his inability to shake off the lung infection that had afflicted him since the previous October. He wrote Countess Erdödy that he had changed doctors from the "wily Italian" Malfatti, "who lacked both honesty and intelligence." He details his daily medical ordeal: From April 15 to May 4, "I had to take six powders daily and six bowls of tea . . . After that I had to take another kind of powder, also six times daily; and I had to rub myself three times a day with a volatile ointment. Then I had to come here [to Heiligenstadt] where I am taking baths. Since yesterday I have been taking another medicine, namely, a tincture, of which I have to swallow 12 spoonfuls daily."[77] His poor health he blamed on any number of causes, most often bad food (never the cheap wine he was fond of), but in a letter to Franz Brentano he came up with a new and perhaps not entirely fanciful reason: "My health has been undermined for a considerable time. The condition of my country has been partly responsible for this; and so far no improvement is to be expected, nay rather, every day there is a further deterioration."[78] The agenda of the Metternich regime was to draw the net tighter and tighter around any freedom of action, speech, thought. The police had begun going systematically through bookshops, confiscating any volume they deemed suspicious, sometimes destroying whole print runs.[79]

Yet these miseries and political and medical distractions could no longer restrain the tide of Beethoven's ideas. The cello sonatas had showed him more clearly where he wanted to go. Out of the same creative ferment that produced them, in November he finished a new piano sonata in A major, op. 101, that confirmed his second new path in the same way that the op. 31 Sonatas had done with the previous path. This first full bloom of what the future would call his Third Period begins with a short movement of ineffable, limpid beauty. The first and third movements will be quiet and inward; he called them "impressions and reveries."[80] These, note, are high-Romantic images. The second and fourth movements are as vigorous and outgoing as the others are gentle. That joining of apparent opposites, inward and outward, is another sign of his late music at its most poetic. Most of this sonata is contrapuntal. In a move he had been heading toward since at least the Fifth Symphony, the finale is the weightiest movement, a payoff of the gentle reverie of the opening. To reserve the climax of the piece for the finale, he lightens up the beginning.

The A Major begins as if in the middle of a thought, its singing 6/8 drifting gently upward and back down. The indication is *etwas lebhaft und mit der innigsten Empfindung,* somewhat lively and with the most intimate sentiment. In this movement one can make out on the page the familiar sonata-form elements: an exposition with two themes, development, recapitulation. But that is not the sounding impression. The landmarks are blurred, the second theme only a wisp, there is no repeat of the exposition, the recapitulation flows unnoticed from the development. The familiar form has receded under the surface, leaving a sense of a steady unfolding with little repeated exactly — like a fantasia. Though the sense of A major is clear enough, the music never cadences unequivocally on A until bar 93. As in the cello sonatas, the lack of resolution, the purposeful meandering of the harmony, creates not tension but rather a rapt suspension. As the harmony drifts like a summer cloud, likewise the sense of pulse and downbeat drift around the bar.

Now he is generating themes from primal motifs. The leading ones here are the four stepwise ascending notes of the first bar and especially the mellifluous fall of a third and a step in the second bar. The sonata will be permeated by both motifs, but the second one, a skip and a step, will be the most pervasive, the most essential to the tone of the whole (the third is sometimes expanded to a larger interval).

Second comes a jaunty march, or a dream of a march, the first of several in his late music. For all its lusty striding it integrates some of the drifting quality of the first movement. With its 2/4 march tempo it stands in for a scherzo and has the overall form of one, including a contrapuntal trio. The first movement's reveries and impressions are just over half the size of the march. Is that actually the opening movement, or is it the introduction to the march, which is the first movement proper? With Beethoven, harmony, rhythm, and form are all becoming more fluid. Part of that development is the receding presence of the old lucid, usually four-bar Classical phrasing that moved the music forward in clear segments.

In keeping with those kinds of ambiguities, the short slow movement of the A Major also serves as an introduction to the finale. It is another reverie, intensely inward, marked *langsam und sehnsuchtvoll,* slow and full of longing, the only time Beethoven ever used that last word (longing another high-Romantic sentiment) in a sonata. The tone of the movement has a touch of the archaic, like a Baroque lament with rich ornaments. It also sounds like a solemn reworking of the opening movement, and in fact after a chain of roulades it drifts into a brief recall of the opening that quickens into the finale. Now part of his old idea of drawing together the movements can be accomplished by more or less literal recalls and by blurring movement divisions, making the form more fluid and ambiguous. Are these interludes a two-part introduction to the finale, or if not, what? When Beethoven was young, critics called his sonatas too free, too much like fantasias. Now that the musical world had embraced his earlier work, he became more rhapsodic, more fantasy-like than ever.

For a second time he leaps from inward to outward, soulful to ebullient, now with a muscular and contrapuntal Allegro finale, whose angular theme mostly stays in the foreground. In the development, for the first time in his piano sonatas, that theme is turned into an extended *fugato.* In spirit, and covertly in the sound of the counterpoint, he is going back to Bach, whose *Well-Tempered Clavier* his fingers and musical mind learned in childhood. But as he did in the second cello sonata of op. 102, he integrates fugue into classical forms in new ways. Here the idea is *fugue as development section.* At the same time, in dealing with fugue and its contrapuntal elaboration of a subject he returns to Bach's sense of *inventio,* where the whole of a work is spun out of a single theme and a single character. Bachian counterpoint and Bachian invention: these no less than Haydn and Mozart were his foundations as a composer, but they had never expressed themselves more directly and cogently than here.

Beethoven's sonatas had always been distinct individuals, starting with their distinctive sonorities. With this one and after, that quality intensified: each sonata became in itself a legendary individual. In the history of piano sonatas, more than any other, op. 101 is *the* A Major. Neither he nor anyone else ever wrote one more subtly enrapturing, more beautifully enigmatic.

He dedicated the sonata to his admired Baroness Dorothea Ertmann, surely hoping it would particularly suit her to play. Who knows how much of it was not only a poem for but also a portrait of the baroness. Many musicians admired this "amateur" from the nobility. When composer and virtuoso Muzio Clementi heard her he could not help repeatedly calling out as she played, "She is a great master!" Composer J. F. Reichardt wrote, "Never have I encountered such power allied to such exquisite delicacy." The influence of Ertmann's playing spread around Vienna as well; Anton Schindler called her "a conservatory all by herself." Her playing, of course, took place entirely in private, because women soloists were not yet allowed on the concert stage and because piano sonatas were not yet played in public. Ertmann left Vienna in 1817 and returned, if at all, only for visits.[81] Wherever she went, she spread the gospel of Beethoven.

If op. 101 helped Beethoven to define a new path, it did not immediately lift him out of the most fallow period of his career. He was too busy, to distracted, too ill, too overwhelmed for sustained work.

Another musical effort of this year was the result of his continuing interest in using Maelzel's metronome to set tempos. (He and the inventor had reconciled, Maelzel hoping for a profitable venture together in England — one more scheme that never came to pass.) Earlier Beethoven had written to Viennese conductor and composer Ignaz Franz the kind of considered technical treatise he was still entirely capable of. This one was about tempo:

> I am heartily delighted to know that you hold the same views as I do about our tempo indications which originated in the barbarous ages of music. For, to take one example, what can be more absurd than Allegro, which really signifies merry, and how far removed [in expressive terms] we often are from the idea of that tempo. So much so that the piece itself means the very opposite of the indication . . . But the words describing the character of the composition [such as *con fuoco*,

giocoso] are a different matter. We cannot give these up . . . these certainly refer to the spirit of the composition — As for me, I have long been thinking of abandoning those absurd descriptive terms, Allegro, Andante, Adagio, Presto; and Maelzel's metronome affords us the best opportunity of doing so. I now give you my word that I shall never again use them in any of my new compositions —[82]

At the end of 1817, the *Allgemeine Musikalische Zeitung* published Beethoven's complete metronome markings for symphonies 1–8. At the same time he decreed that the A Major Piano Sonata should be designated not for the fortepiano but rather for the *Hammerklavier,* one of the German words for the piano (the more common name was *Flügel,* "wing," for the open lid). He began using German rather than Italian expressive terms — with a random sprinkling of the usual Italian ones. As a German, he wanted to use German rather than Italian terms, and he believed the metronome marks would be far more useful and precise than the vague traditional Italian indications like "Allegro." In fact, Beethoven did not stick with German terms in his music; before long he went back to the old Italian ones.

The relatively few metronome marks he issued — in the symphonies, the early and middle quartets, a few other pieces including the *Hammerklavier* Sonata — became a historic sticking point. Some of those tempos work, many of them are too fast, and some of them, mainly in the Ninth Symphony, are outlandish. A notorious example is the first movement of the *Hammerklavier,* whose pulse is given at 138.[83] What happened? Should performers attempt to observe Beethoven's tempo marks religiously for all times and places?

No. The ones that seem strangely fast are in fact too fast, and the reason is Beethoven's deafness. By and large, he could hear music now only in his head, and even the finest musician does not precisely hear acoustics and the physical weight of sound in the inner ear. The sounds in a musician's inner ear are literally lighter than air, weightless. They do not involve bows and lips and lungs physically putting air in motion. Also one cannot predict the physical resonance of rooms, each of which is different and each of which inflects the tempo of a performance. For that reason the tempos in one's head are usually too fast — say, two to four metronome clicks too fast. If Beethoven's given tempos are adjusted downward an average of two to four clicks, that will usually be a good starting place — except for the ones, as in the Ninth, that are just inexplicable.[84]

One example can stand for many — his 1817 metronome marks for the Sixth Symphony. For the first movement he gave half note = 66, which makes the quarter note 132, which is absurd. This tempo is not a matter of pleasant thoughts on arriving in the country; it is a brisk jog. In this case even four metronome clicks slower is still brisk, though at least imaginable. His second-movement tempo of dotted quarter = 50 is workable, though most conductors take it two or three clicks slower. His scherzo tempo, dotted half = 108, is likewise reasonable; most take it one or two clicks slower. His dotted quarter = 60 for the last movement is actually a notch slower than many performances. There is, in short, no detectable consistency in Beethoven's tempo markings.

At the same time, with his usual common sense regarding his craft, he also understood the limitations of metronome markings and tempered his initial enthusiasm. There are reports that in his performances he tended to speed up in crescendos, slow down in soft passages, and revert to the main tempo at structurally important points.[85] He wrote on a manuscript, "100 according to Mälzel, but this must be considered applicable only to the first bars, for sentiment also has its tempo and cannot be completely expressed by this number."[86] So in performance he believed in a nuanced, flexible tempo — the opposite of the metronomic tendencies of the next century. As Beethoven acknowledged, tempo is a matter of a performer's sensibility and musicality. One cannot put a metronome mark on feelings — or on the acoustics of every room.

As soon as Beethoven finished the A Major Piano Sonata he set out on another one in B-flat major, as expansive as the earlier one was intimate. He intended to make it his greatest sonata. If in the sorrows and tumults of the last years he had doubted whether he could find his stride again, he was no longer daunted by the intention of composing his "greatest" anything.

His creativity faced more grueling challenges than it ever had before. His body had been his first enemy. That was the most fundamental betrayal, the one that colored everything else. His friends saw how deafness affected his social being, soured him, stoked his paranoia and his rage. To have seized on Karl as his salvation when he was physically and mentally at his lowest ebb heaped on him another set of troubles. Even though he had plenty of real enemies (few of them able to do him harm anymore), he found them everywhere now, even among his friends.

Now his human incapacities, the worst of himself — his solipsism, suspicion, hotheadedness, and misanthropy — became his worst enemies, whether he was dealing with servants, with Karl, or with Karl's teachers. He was terrible at dealing with people in general, except publishers and lackeys, and terrible at dealing with the rest of life outside music. Now, starting with a young boy and his mother, he had no choice but to deal with people all the time, had to cope with the lives and needs of other people whom he could not begin to understand. He did it all badly.

His music and his *raptus* were his only escape, even though in his extremity he had taken to praying to God for help in a way he had not before. His prayers were not answered. In the time of the Heiligenstadt crisis he had seized his art like a drowning man. That had saved him, because then he saw in front of him a new path promising to take him to marvelous places. Now another creative path revealed itself, away from the heroic and toward at once the spiritual and the immediate, the quotidian and the childlike. As his miseries piled up unabated, the trajectories of his music and his life diverged more than ever. The courage demanded of him in order to work, which had seemed a crushing burden in 1802, was going to have to be stronger than ever. But his work was beginning to flow again, and his work fueled his courage.

He had always reached for *more*. Despite the most galling obstructions, by 1820 the tide of his creativity was rising and nothing could stem it. Now his work was going to enfold wider and deeper divides than ever: more seriously internal and more exuberantly external, a new transcendence and a new immediacy. In his music a more pervasive use of motifs underlay an atmosphere of improvisation. Narrative and drama were giving way to a sense of poetic fantasy. And given what Beethoven was enduring in his daily life, what he was going to achieve in the music of his last years would, to ordinary understanding, seem impossible, unbelievable.

28

What Is Difficult

IN JANUARY 1818, Beethoven's plan to bring Karl home to live with him was finally realized. The servant problem had receded to a degree, in that Nanni and Peppi were still with him and submitting to his little disciplines: "Fräulein N has been quite different since I threw those half dozen books at her head." More to the point, he wrote his domestic adviser Nannette Streicher, "If you happen to meet those Giannatasios at Czerny's, pretend to know nothing whatever about what is being done about my Karl . . . For those people might still like to interfere even more; and I don't want those commonplace people either for my Karl or for myself."[1]

Giannatasio had made an effort to keep Karl at the school by lowering the fee, but Beethoven was adamant, and Fanny Giannatasio crushed: "We shall have to part from the boy, and, with his departure, one of the links which bind us to our beloved friend, Beethoven, who has lately caused us a good deal of trouble . . . I did not recognize at first why this gives me such intense pain. I know now that it was the manner in which it was done, the cold and formal, but extremely polite letter, without one particle of affection or interest for us expressed in it."[2]

Beethoven did have some legitimate reason to be concerned about his ward's treatment at the school; in winter Karl's room had been so cold that he developed chilblains on his feet. But despite his astonishing words to Nannette, in a better moment Beethoven had written the Giannatasios, "Please accept my most sincere thanks for the zeal, integrity, and honesty with which you undertook the education of my nephew."[3] To Nannette he wrote delightedly, "Karl is arriving tomorrow, and I was mistaken in thinking that perhaps he would prefer to stay there. He is in good spirits and much livelier than he used to be; and every moment he shows his love and affection for me."[4]

Karl entered a situation that for a child was difficult from the ground up, because his guardian could hardly hear him speak. Beethoven's hearing still came and went, but overall it had declined to the point that he could only with difficulty make out music or even conversation shouted into an ear trumpet. Now others were going to have to write down their part of the dialogue. At home with Karl and the servants he used a slate and chalk. Outside the house he began to carry, in addition to his pocket music sketchbooks, notebooks of blank pages for conversation. As with his sketchbooks he never threw these conversation books away, and many survived. So from then on, history could eavesdrop on much of Beethoven's daily discourse—rather, other people's part of it, since he largely spoke his responses. Of the entries he wrote in the books, most were items for himself: musical sketches, marketing schemes, shopping lists, addresses, book recommendations. There were also rants concerning the government, the courts, and other things not safe to speak aloud in a police state.

In the first years of the conversation books the bulk of the encounters are with three friends, none of them aristocrats. Karl Joseph Bernard, as of 1819 editor in chief of the *Wiener Zeitung,* was a well-known and powerful man in Vienna; for Beethoven he had revised the text of the Congress of Vienna cantata, *Der glorreiche Augenblick.*[5] Karl Peters was an amateur painter and worked as a tutor to the Lobkowitz family, who had bestowed on him the coveted title, in that title-loving society, of *Hofrat,* privy councillor. Bookkeeper and amateur pianist Franz Oliva had been a factotum of Beethoven's since around 1810, in and out of his good graces and in and out of Vienna.[6] These men were all in their thirties, they had earned Beethoven's trust, they were able to advise and entertain him. For all his independence, Beethoven was sometimes too ready to take suggestions from anybody and everybody. Anton Schindler, his hanger-on of these years, once said that Beethoven was like "a ball thrown from one hand to the other — all his life the prey of conflicting advice."[7]

As the conversation books show, Bernard, Peters, and Oliva regularly dined with Beethoven in restaurants and inns. On his editor friend Beethoven bestowed the nickname "Bernard non sanctus," "unholy Bernard," to distinguish him from the church's St. Bernard. All three friends had pressing family and professional lives of their own, but they were prepared to give Beethoven a good deal of their time. All the same, they were no sycophants. The tone of their responses to Beethoven suggests they related on a relatively equal plane, even if none was on a *du* basis with him. One observer of his circle, probably at a restaurant, wrote, "Those about him contributed little, merely laughing or nodding their approval. He philosophized, or one might even say politicized, after his own fashion."[8] But there was more give-and-take than that. Based on his companions' responses in the conversation books, Beethoven did not always dispense sermons and rants but also joined in the ebb and flow of talk, except that responses to him had to be written down, and there was no question that he was the center of this particular circle. The others were the ones doing the favors.

In the first years the conversations were largely quotidian, ranging from the practical to the bawdy. The dominant theme was Karl and the legal processes that roiled around him. "As long as you are guardian and K is here," Bernard wrote, "not only will you have the same troubles as before, but will always have to struggle with his mother's intrigues." Bernard polished Beethoven's legal papers. Knowing that these were not his own strong suits, Beethoven relied on Bernard's judgment, his skill with words, his common sense. Oliva tended to advise on practical matters, from buying a heating stove to rentals, banks, investments, and interest.

Bernard and Peters were the more literary and imaginative companions of these years. Bernard was given to jotting down drinking songs and the like, including his own improvised poetry. At one point he wrote out a jovial lyric by Lessing that he wanted Beethoven to set, "In Praise of Laziness." Some of their humor concerned Peters's lively and lusty wife Josephine, a well-known singer in Vienna who presided over a group of friends interested in literature and the arts. Peters observed in the book, "Bernard thinks it's no good that I have a wife and want to be at home; I think he's jealous."

"He doesn't pay enough attention to his wife," Bernard responded. "She says I'm her vice-husband, and I always say if Peters dies I'll inherit her."[9]

It got more naughty sometimes. After all, there were virtually no women in the circle of people who dined with Beethoven and wrote in his conversation books. In the middle of winter Peters wrote, "Do you want to sleep with my wife? It's so cold."[10] This was presumably a joke. Beethoven knew Josephine, had probably accompanied her in private musicales. His reply to the offer was not written down. Beethoven thought well enough of Peters to make him at one point Karl's co-guardian. Oliva left Vienna in 1820 and the others drifted off in some degree, but there were no angry breaks as with many Beethoven acquaintances. One who appears less and less often in Beethoven's correspondence in these years is his old factotum Baron Zmeskall, who was afflicted with chronic gout, so could be of little service.

The first items in the first conversation book were sketches of Beethoven's, one of them putting a bass line under a natural minor scale. His friends were not given to flattery, and his music came up only now and then. Beethoven got reports on new plays and operas opening in town. Here and there word of a hearing remedy appears. Beethoven noted an "Electro Vibrations Machine" advertised to cure deafness.[11] Oliva reported a more outlandish cure: "You take fresh horseradish just as it comes from the ground, rub it on cotton, wrap it up and stick it in your ear." With this remedy, he assured Beethoven, the wife of a foreign count had regained her hearing.[12]

Each member of the circle had his quirks. Oliva generally noted when a name that came up was Jewish; when Ignaz Moscheles gave a recital, "the Jew played." At the same time Oliva was not particularly prone to gossip, though he heard one item he knew would please Beethoven concerning Karl's mother: "[Johanna] is lowdown riffraff.

Isn't it true that Karl knew she was sleeping with her lover when your brother was lying dead in the house?"[13] Meanwhile this was the Metternich era; any person young or old could be a spy working on commission. Oliva warned Beethoven, "Freedom — don't say it so loud . . . Everybody harks and listens."[14]

In the conversation books of the first years, Karl's hand shows up only occasionally — he probably wrote most of his responses on the slate at home. The boy's words in these days are mild, obedient, usually answering his uncle's questions. "I don't know where the lice are coming from. Anyway it's healthy to have lice." Already Karl keeps up with issues concerning his fate: "Have you asked Peters to be co-guardian?"[15] Peters in turn liked Karl and praised him to Beethoven: "Your nephew looks good, beautiful eyes, he's graceful, expressive physiognomy, excellent deportment." Others' testimonies also imply that Karl was an attractive and charming boy, and he had been doing reasonably well at school.

Beethoven wanted to make a great man of his nephew but did not particularly pressure him toward music beyond expecting him to keep up with his piano lessons. In the long run Karl did get around the keyboard a little and showed some sophisticated musical tastes. By his mid-teens he was correct and well spoken in the conversation books — as a writer, far more lucid and correct than his uncle — and he had the clear schoolboy hand Beethoven had possessed in his teens. To that point the impression Karl left to history was of a reasonably personable boy, intelligent but only so much, good at languages, more dutiful than many children his age but not at all ambitious. The tempests swirling around him did not overtly affect Karl for a while. In due course, they would.

Beethoven's domestic adviser Nannette Streicher crafted some of the most admired pianos in Vienna, which she signed "Streicher née Stein" to show her pedigree as daughter of the celebrated maker Johann Andreas Stein. Beethoven had preferred Stein pianos in his youth; later he liked Streichers even as he pressed the company to make its instruments stronger and louder.

In early 1818, he received exciting news: the British firm of John

Broadwood & Sons was sending him a piano as a gift. During his travels around the Continent, Thomas Broadwood, the current head of the firm, had met Beethoven. Broadwood recalled that he "was kind enough to play to me, but he was so deaf and so unwell."[16] The gift was a splendid six-octave, two-pedal instrument with a mahogany case. In a time of incessant experiment and evolution in design, Broadwoods were in the forefront of the art, but then and later, every piano from a given factory was different. This one had been tried out and signed by distinguished musicians including Muzio Clementi, John Cramer, and Beethoven's pupil Ferdinand Ries. Above the keys lay the Latin inscription *Hoc Instrumentum est Thomæ Broadwood (Londini) donum, propter Ingenium illustrissimi Beethoven.*

This Broadwood had to have been strongly made, to have survived its journey. On its way from London to Vienna it was sent to Trieste by boat, then carried 360 miles over the Alps on primitive roads.[17] When it arrived at the Streicher showroom in Vienna Beethoven was summering in Mödling. Concerned about its British action, heavier and with a bigger key dip than Viennese instruments, the Streichers had local pianist and Beethoven protégé Ignaz Moscheles try it out. He found it very hard to play. But the visiting British composer Cipriani Potter declared it top-notch, so it was sent on to Beethoven in Mödling.[18]

Potter was used to the British action; the Streichers worried that Beethoven was not going to be comfortable with it. Years before, he had tried to have the touch of his French Érard lightened, with little success. But he was delighted with the Broadwood. For one thing it was British, and he was an Anglophile hoping to enhance his reputation in that country. Most importantly, it was louder than Viennese instruments. He wrote the maker a delighted letter in French:

My very dear friend Broadwood — I have never felt a greater pleasure than in your honor's notification of the arrival of this piano, with which you are honoring me as a present. I shall look upon it as an altar upon which I shall place the most beautiful offerings of my spirit to the divine Apollo. As soon as I receive your excellent instrument, I shall immediately send you the fruits of the first moments of inspiration I gather from it, as a souvenir for you from me, my very dear

Broadwood; and I hope that they will be worthy of your instrument. My dear sir, accept my warmest consideration, from your friend and very humble servant — Ludwig van Beethoven.[19]

Before long he had some sort of metal chamber attached above the strings to amplify the sound. Potter told him the piano needed to be tuned. "That's what they all say," Beethoven growled. "They would like to tune it and spoil it, but they shall not touch it." Only when a tuner sent from Broadwood showed up did Beethoven allow it to be regulated and tuned — but like most of his pianos, even when he could hear them, this one would be habitually out of tune. When it arrived he had begun sketching a new piano sonata he intended to dedicate to Archduke Rudolph. Just as in the decade before his Érard had helped inspire the *Waldstein* and *Appassionata,* perhaps the Broadwood, the most robust piano in build and sound he had ever encountered, helped take him in the direction of writing the most massive piano sonata of his life.

Cipriani Potter became another in the string of foreigners who turned up at Beethoven's door and found themselves warmly received. Potter had hoped for composition lessons. As usual, Beethoven declined; he sent the young composer to his old string-quartet mentor Aloys Förster. Having looked over Potter's music, Förster told Potter that he didn't need teachers anymore. Potter relayed to him Beethoven's response to that: "Tell Förster he's an old flatterer." The quip got a laugh from the old man.

Beethoven invited the Englishman to join his rambles in the Vienna woods. To Ries in London Beethoven reported, "Botter [*sic*] visited me several times, he seems to be a good man and has talent for composition — I hope and wish that your prosperity may grow daily; unfortunately I cannot say that of myself. My unlucky connection with this Archduke has brought me to the verge of beggary. I cannot endure the sight of want."[20] The very generous Rudolph may have been leaning on Beethoven to give donations to the poor.

Potter was treated to the usual harangues. Still, if Beethoven complained incessantly, most of the time he did it with a certain entertaining gusto. They mostly conversed in Italian, in which Potter reported

Beethoven to be fluent. Their time together seems to have been jolly, yet in this same period Beethoven reported to Zmeskall, "Owing to a chill I am now feeling very much worse . . . I now know what it feels like to move daily nearer to my grave."[21] The next day, he thanked Zmeskall for the gift of a Maelzel chronometer: "We must see whether with its help one can measure all eternity."[22]

Potter noted Beethoven's Anglophilia and his determination to visit England. Among other things he wanted to see the Houses of Parliament. "You have heads on your shoulders in England," he told Potter; England, that is to say, was not a reactionary monarchy like Austria. There were the inevitable questions from the young musician. Potter asked about the new crop of virtuosos, among them Ignaz Moscheles, who had done the piano arrangement of *Fidelio*. Now Beethoven dismissed him: "Don't ever talk to me again about mere passage players." He declared the Englishman John Cramer — who he knew disliked his music — to be the finest pianist he ever heard. Outside yourself, Potter asked, whom do you call the greatest living composer? As usual, Beethoven answered Cherubini. And the ancestors? Once he had put Mozart first, Beethoven said, but now it was Handel.[23]

With the occasional socializing, Beethoven spent a productive, even relatively pleasant summer of 1818 in Mödling. He arrived in June in good spirits and feeling well, as shown in an outsize response he wrote his friend Vincenz Hauschka, a director of the new Gesellschaft der Musikfreunde. It was by way of agreeing to the society's offer of a commission for an oratorio, something the two had already discussed:

> Most Excellent Leading Member of the Club of the Enemies of Music [a pun: Gesellschaft der Musikfeinde] of the Austrian Imperial State! [Below he writes a Handelesque fugue subject to the text *Ich bin bereit!* —"I am ready!"] The only subject I have is a sacred one. But you want a heroic subject. Well, that will suit me too. But I think for such a mass of people [also a pun] it would be very appropriate to mix in a little sacred stuff. [He writes a fugue subject on "Amen."] Herr von Bernard would suit me [as librettist] quite well. But you must also pay him . . . Now all good wishes, most excellent little Hauschka. I wish you open bowels and the handsomest of close-stools. As for me, I

am rambling about in the mountains, ravines, and valleys here with a piece of music paper . . . In order to gain some leisure for a great work I must always scrawl a good deal beforehand for money so that I can stay alive while I am composing the great work. Let me add that my health has greatly improved and that if the matter is urgent I can easily contrive to serve you.[24]

He finishes the letter with a line of music combining *Ich bin bereit* and *Amen* in counterpoint.

The subject settled on for his friend Bernard's libretto was *Der Sieg des Kreuzes* (The Triumph of the Cross). It took Bernard years to finish the libretto,[25] after which Beethoven never got around to writing the oratorio. It is hard to imagine that that piously creaky subject would ever have inspired him. In June he received from the Gesellschaft an advance of 400 florins — in devalued paper currency — for the oratorio. The polite fiction that he was actually working on it was sustained for years.

The "scrawling" he refers to in the letter to Hauschka is more piece-work for Thomson in Scotland. "My songs with your ritornellos and accompaniments do not sell!" Thomson wrote Beethoven this summer. A friend of his in London had advised the publisher, "Although a great and sublime artist, Beethoven is <u>not understood,</u> and his arrangement of your songs is <u>much too difficult</u> for the public." In practice, Thomson had Beethoven's arrangements played over by his daughter Annie. If she found them too hard, he concluded they were too much for any young lady.[26] "Tell me, my dear sir," Thomson entreated, "is it not possible for you to demonstrate the enchanting power of your art in a simpler form?"[27] Yet he was willing to commission a new experiment, some sets of folk-song variations that Beethoven produced, and some easy quartets and trios that never came to pass.

Shortly after his rambunctious letter to Hauschka, Beethoven wrote an enormous one to Nannette Streicher telling her he'd chucked out the servants for colluding with Karl and even with his mother, who had bribed them with sugar, coffee, and cash. And so forth and so on, in page after page detailing with grim satisfaction the servants' "horrible treachery." (Yet Beethoven rather liked "elephantine" young Peppi and her cooking.) When Karl was not forthcoming about all the plots and treasons, "I pounced on him . . . I often give him a good shaking, but not without a valid reason."

Yet in his moil of feelings Beethoven adds about Johanna, "K[arl] has done wrong, but — a mother — a mother — a bad mother is still a mother." He was torn between dueling obligations: his duty to rear his nephew properly, and his and Karl's natural duty to a mother. That second duty explains his occasional spasms of generosity and regret concerning Johanna. It all weighed on him badly. He assures Nannette about the servant squabble, "This affair has given me a dreadful heart attack from which I am not yet completely recovered . . . Still it won't be necessary to take me to the madhouse . . . Please send us a comforting letter about the art of cooking, laundering, and sewing."[28] He announces he is sending Karl to a village parson for tutoring. His nephew was to be kept at his studies daily while Beethoven was busy working. He tells Nannette he has heard disturbing reports of this Parson Frölich but hopes for the best.

From there things took a precipitous turn downward. Beethoven got word from the parson that Karl was acting up, disturbing the other students. By this point Karl was revealing a gift for playing the people who were jerking him around. He told the parson that his uncle egged him on to revile his mother either by writing it down or by shrieking into his uncle's ear. Karl said further that he agreed to do this only to get in his uncle's favor and avoid punishment. In turn, Beethoven reported to the parson with "malicious joy" that Karl had picked up his uncle's term for Johanna, "raven-mother."

The parson was shocked at these violations of the fourth commandment, to honor thy father and mother. To Beethoven, meanwhile, Karl reported that Frölich would line up students on a bench and have them whipped by the strongest of their classmates.[29] Within a month the instruction with Frölich ended in mutual outrage. "There are human brutes indeed," Beethoven wrote Nannette, "and one of them is the parson here, who ought to be thrashed."[30] All three of these letters concerning the saga of Karl and the servants and the parson were produced in June 1818.

Nannette Streicher gave Beethoven patient-unto-heroic service in those years. She was, however, no blind acolyte. Nannette understood Beethoven at his best and his worst. Later she told the British publisher Novello, in her flavored English, "[A]s a beggar he was so dirty in his dress, and in manner like a bear sulky and froward, he laughed like no one else it was a scream, he would call people names as he passed them . . . he was avaricious and always mistrustful."[31]

Summer 1818

Yet somehow, again, that summer of 1818 was splendidly productive. Beethoven generally felt healthier and cheerier in the country. It was his first stay in picturesque Mödling, a medieval-to-Renaissance town south of Vienna, its hoary stone buildings arranged along a street that stretched up to hills topped with ruined castles. It was a prospect to inspire a Romantic, and a Beethoven. He became a regular at the Three Ravens pub, lived in the fifteenth-century Hafner-Haus on Herrengasse (later Haupstrasse). His flat had cozy, groin-vaulted rooms facing trees and vineyards in back, reached by an arched balcony that looked down on the courtyard. Mödling's hills and woods were a few minutes' walk away.

It was probably during this first of his three summers in Mödling that he was approached by another portrait painter. By then Beethoven, a man not enamored of his own physiognomy, looked at the species of painter as something to which he had to submit from time to time as a kind of penance for his fame. This artist, August von Klöber, left some sharp-eyed memories of their encounter. He had been advised by a Viennese musician who knew Beethoven that it was best to deal with this subject in the country, where he was usually more approachable. Beethoven agreed to the sittings if they did not take too long.

Klöber

Klöber was first shown into Beethoven's rooms by a servant; she said he could occupy himself with the resident books by Herder and Goethe until Beethoven got home. Finally Beethoven arrived with Karl. Klöber found he had to communicate by writing or via Karl, who shouted into his uncle's ear trumpet. Karl sat down at the piano to practice. Klöber noticed that deaf as he was, Beethoven could sense every mistake Karl made, corrected each one, and had him repeat passages.

The artist observed his subject professionally, as a figure he had to capture in his surface and in his essence. "Beethoven always looked very serious," Klöber recalled. "His extremely lively eyes usually wandered, looking upwards somewhat darkly and low-spiritedly, which I have attempted to capture in the portrait." Eventually that look became mythologized as Beethoven's *blick nach oben,* raising his eyes to heaven. In fact it was the characteristic stare of a deaf man straining to hear.[32] "His lips were shut, but the expression about the mouth was not unfriendly." Klöber noted that one of Beethoven's favorite topics was the overweening vanity and perverted taste of the Viennese aristocracy, "about whom he never had a good word to say, for he considered himself neglected by them, or not sufficiently understood." More and more as he got older, Beethoven despised the nobles he depended on to pay his rent. Archduke Rudolph, around whom there was no hint of scandal, was spared some of that contempt, but not all of it.

Klöber found that Beethoven could manage to sit still for only some three-quarters of an hour. The artist was agreeable to that, so Beethoven in turn became agreeable to him. That gave the painter a lot of free time. "You must have a good look at Mödling," Beethoven told him, "for it's quite lovely here, and as an artist you must certainly be a nature lover." Klöber took the advice. In his tramps around the countryside he occasionally saw Beethoven striding along with sketchbook in hand; he would stop as if listening, and with a stub of pencil jot down something on the page. Once, the artist caught sight of his subject climbing a hill across the valley, a broad-brimmed felt hat under his arm. At the top of the hill Beethoven lay down under a pine tree and watched the sky for a long time.

"Beethoven's dwelling in Mödling was quite simple," Klöber recalled, "as indeed was everything about him. In those days he wore a light blue frock-coat with yellow buttons, white waistcoat and a fashionable necktie," but all of them "in a quite neglected state. His complexion was healthy and robust, the skin somewhat pockmarked; his hair was the color of blued steel . . . When his hair was tossed about by the wind he had something absolutely Ossian-like [meaning bardic] and demoniacal about him. In friendly conversation, however, he took on a genial and mild expression . . . Every mood of his spirit was immediately and violently expressed in his countenance."[33]

Klöber's final oil portrait placed Beethoven, holding a sketchbook and pencil, in the Mödling countryside with Karl lying under a tree behind him. At some point that painting was lost. All that survived is a preparatory drawing Klöber made of Beethoven's head, the eyes looking into the distance, the hair wild. Despite a certain stiffness, it is one of the essential Beethoven renderings. He looks formidable but not forbidding — just as Klöber, Potter, and others found him in person. The portrait has none of the glowering scowl of the Klein life mask and the Romantic sculptures and paintings that followed from it. Klöber made Beethoven an imposing, powerful, utterly self-possessed presence, but also a person standing before you in the company of his nephew. It is one of the few renderings of Beethoven in the Romantic era that did not make him into a demigod. Beethoven complimented Klöber on the treatment of his hair. Most portraits, he said, made him look too tidy.[34]

That summer of 1818, Beethoven had his new Broadwood in Mödling to work on the piano sonata that was becoming Brobdingnagian. This year he also added to his sketches for two symphonies intended for the London Philharmonic Society. As always, he wanted to take the two works in contrasting directions. Some of his sketches had always been in the form of prose. A speculation toward one of the planned symphonies shows him improvising in words. It amounts to a portrait of the early, speculative stages of the creative process:

Adagio Cantique —

Solemn song in a symphony in the old modes — Lord God we praise you — alleluja — either as an independent piece or an introduction to a fugue. Perhaps the entire second symphony [the Tenth] will be characterized in this manner, whereby singing voices will enter in the finale, or even in the Adagio. The violins, etc., in the orchestra will be increased tenfold in the finale. Or the Adagio will in a distinct way be repeated in the finale, with the singing voices introduced one by one. In the Adagio text, a Greek myth, the text of an ecclesiastical song — in the Allegro, a celebration of Bacchus.[35]

This does not quite describe what became the Ninth Symphony, was perhaps intended for the Tenth that was never finished, but it still foreshadows elements of the Ninth and other works. By "a symphony in the old modes" he means the ancient church scales outside the usual major and minor scales; they go under the names Dorian, Lydian, Phrygian, and so on. The eighteenth century had abandoned all the church modes other than major and minor, but it was traditional to use the others in contrapuntal studies because they were based on modal sacred music going back to Palestrina. Beethoven wanted to draw Palestrina and the other Renaissance polyphonists within his grasp.

Moreover, the prose sketch shows he was thinking about a symphony with voices. Whether or not he already imagined them singing Schiller's "An die Freude" cannot be said at this point nor for a while to come. "Greek myth . . . a celebration of Bacchus": he had sketched ideas for an opera libretto concerning Bacchus, the Roman avatar of the Greek god Dionysus. Both of them were divinities not just of wine but of ecstasy, of being taken out of oneself, of possession with divine dancing joy. One can hear the eventual scherzo of the Ninth Symphony in those terms. His prose improvisation toward the new symphonies describes no specific piece to come but hints at several including the *Missa solemnis*.

In autumn 1818, Beethoven and Karl returned to Vienna, the twelve-year-old beginning at the Akademisches Gymnasium, with extra instruction in music, French, and drawing.[36] With Karl settling into a new situation, Beethoven finished the epic Piano Sonata in B-flat Major, op. 106, that he had been working on over the last two years. Having decided for both nationalistic and practical reasons to put away the standard Italian terms in music, he called it *Grosse Sonata für das Hammerklavier,* the latter a German name for *pianoforte,* which is Italian. (Beethoven believed, mistakenly, that the piano had been invented in Germany. In fact it was invented by the Italian Bartolomeo Cristofori, in the early eighteenth century.) He had directed that the title page of the previous sonata, op. 101, should also designate it as *für das Hammerklavier.* But the future would know op. 106 as the one and only *Hammerklavier,* because even in other languages that name seems to convey something of the formidable and intractable quality of the music. The first of his piano sonatas to use the four-movement pattern since op. 31, no. 3, this was Beethoven's ultimate hammer thrown at the pleasing, popular, amateur tradition of the piano sonata.

"What is difficult," he wrote to the publisher Haslinger about the far tamer (but still plenty difficult) op. 101, "is also beautiful, good, √ great and so forth. Hence everyone will realize that this is the most lavish praise that can be bestowed, since what is difficult makes one sweat."[37] Here is another moment in a letter where Beethoven revealed something essential about himself: *What is difficult is beautiful and good.* His life and career, his struggles with technique and with counterpoint, his struggles with his health were a testament to that credo. He found writing counterpoint, to name one example, supremely difficult. He never achieved true facility at it. Partly for that reason, as a challenge for himself and for listeners, in his last years he pursued counterpoint of burgeoning complexity and ambition.

The *Hammerklavier* was his supreme challenge to players and listeners alike. Counterpoint lies at its core, along with the ne plus ultra of his abiding determination to make the whole of a piece a single conception. The *Hammerklavier* is one of the most obsessive works anybody had ever attempted. The future would be duly obsessed with it. To the degree that *what is difficult is good* is true, this is the greatest of Beethoven's piano sonatas — just as he told Carl Czerny it was going to be, well before he finished it. Clearly part of "great" to Beethoven was its great size — this is the longest of his sonatas, at some forty-five minutes — and its outsize demands. The formula would be the same in his mass and his next symphony. Shrewd in his understanding of performers as he was in every other dimension of his craft, he knew the commitment, the intensity, even the anxiety that have to be marshaled for a performer to handle challenges like these. The trials inflicted on the performer become part of the music.

The *Hammerklavier* begins with a fanfare marked *impetuoso* that spans most of the keyboard; then comes an intimate contrapuntal answer that is in fact a flowing variation of the fanfare:

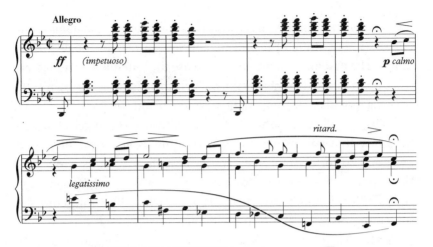

That fanfare seems to have begun as a sketch for a choral salute to Archduke Rudolph; proclaiming "Vivat Rudolphus!," it resembles the sonata's opening:

The phrase does not survive in the music, but the *vivat* quality does. From the outset the sonata was intended to be dedicated to Rudolph and presented to him on his name day—but like most promised Beethoven works now, it was not finished in time.[38] The dialogue of the first movement is between those initial gestures: full, heroic, and declamatory versus sparse, flowing, and contrapuntal. In the development section, the counterpoint blossoms into a stamping and pealing fugue. Here as in all his last sonatas he folds Baroque fugue into the modern structure of sonata form.

The particular tone of this movement and the *Hammerklavier* in general has little to do with the kind of implied narrative in instrumental music that was once a Beethoven staple. The first movement is not "expressive" in the usual sense, more a matter of indefatigable energy (all of it seriously fatiguing for the pianist), sometimes hard-edged and sometimes soaring. The singular world of the piece comes from its particular obsession, its way of joining content and form, microcosm and macrocosm. The opening *vivat* rhythm will be varied and fragmented throughout, as usual in Beethoven. In measures 2 and 4, the two sharp strokes of descending thirds, D–B-flat and F–D, will have their consequences, as also expected. It is the breadth and depth of those consequences that were new in Beethoven and new in music. This time those little melodic thirds are going to resonate at every level of the piece, governing the construction of themes, the harmonic sequences small and large, the sequences of keys, the keys of sections and movements. Instead of narrative in the outer movements, there is a depth of unity that goes beyond older conceptions and brushes aside centuries of tradition concerning key relations.[39] To a degree, in this sonata Beethoven obliterated the old dichotomy between melody and harmony: melody traditionally based mainly on scales, harmony on larger intervals that form chords. Here melody and harmony merge.

More than ever for him, from now on each major piece will be founded not on a novel formal or dramatic idea but on a rethinking of the nature of music and its genres, a search for fresh qualities and meanings that in turn reshapes the old formal models in more and more radical ways — without ever entirely departing from those models.[40] In this case, technique spills over into metaphysics. One ancient and abiding theory of the universe is that the smallest structures expand, level by level, into the largest. That is how the *Hammerklavier* works. Every melody in the piece is based on a scaffolding of descending thirds. The keys of the large sections in the first movement trace a descent in thirds: B-flat first theme, flowing second theme in G major, development beginning in E-flat. The fugue in the development section, its subject based in the *vivat* figure, marches downward athletically in thirds, sometimes in parallel-third lines:

Meanwhile, a modulatory scheme based on chains of thirds is theoretically endless. In contrast to the usual tonic–dominant–tonic closed system of diatonic music, it creates an open system that can conjure either gentle wandering or irresolvable tension. In the *Hammerklavier,* Beethoven exploits both those possibilities.

In the central part of the first movement, the Baroque procedure of *fugue* is wedded with the Haydn, Mozart, and Beethoven idea of *development.* The counterpoint of the development flows on into the *vivat* recapitulation and its answer, decorating them both. The end of the movement adds another element in the form of sustained trills; in the finale, trills are going to add a steady sparkle to the texture. The last moments form a giant stride of the *vivat* figure from nearly the top of the keyboard down to nearly the bottom.

Following the massive landscape of the first movement, a succinct scherzo, also in B-flat, takes up the *vivat* idea of that movement and turns it into light, lilting comedy. The form is entirely regular, on the old model of the minuet-scherzo. Its trio is a rolling B-flat-minor episode, Romantic unto bardic in tone, that foreshadows the next movement. With a scale that sweeps across the keyboard from bottom to top and a little giggle, we return to the scherzo proper.

After the comedy comes the tragedy, the longest slow movement Beethoven ever wrote, marked Appassionato e con molto sentimento, impassioned and with great feeling. The movement is in F-sharp minor (a third down from B-flat) and sonata form, but it feels like an endless song that encompasses the whole of a person's feeling life.[41] The music is constantly in evolution, like drifting through an endless dreamscape of sound and emotion. At the beginning it is marked *una corda,* meaning the muted effect of the hammers on one string, done with the soft pedal.[42] The second half of the first theme returns to *tre corde,* marked *con grand' espressione,* "with great expression." If it had been written for the stage it would be called one of the great tragic arias — except it is an aria only the piano can sing. In its course there are magical moments of G major that appear like sunlight breaking through clouds.

In Beethoven's work the harbinger of this movement is another minor-key slow movement he wrote in a piano sonata, the D-minor lament in op. 10, no. 3 — a work that like the *Hammerklavier* juxtaposes a comic movement with a tragic. As man and composer Beethoven had learned a great deal since op. 10, much of the human wisdom having to do with suffering. This movement laments and transcends the lamentation in the singing, above all at the recapitulation, where the theme is ornamented into spinning roulades like streams of tears. The slow movement of op. 10 sounds like sorrow itself; the slow movement of the *Hammerklavier* sounds like a sublime performance of sorrow and transcendence by a singer who has known every shade of grief and hope.

After Beethoven mailed the *Hammerklavier* to Ferdinand Ries in London, he sent an addition to the slow movement, a simple rising third, A–C-sharp, in octaves for the beginning, a one-bar introduction. Looking at it, Ries recalled, he wondered whether his old master had finally gone around the bend. Then he played it and discovered how those two notes color the whole of the gigantic movement. Like all great Beethoven, here are technique and expression joined: the added introduction is there partly to remind our ears of the primal significance of thirds in the sonata. The slow movement now begins with a simple gesture that is the distilled essence of the whole piece.

Like most of his late works, the *Hammerklavier* is aimed toward the finale, which is a prodigious fugue. But there needed to be a transition from the mournful canvas of the slow movement to a finale that takes up and pays off the dynamic energy of the first movement. For a solution Beethoven turned to tradition and in the process wrote one of the most striking pages of his life. The introduction takes up the old practice of preluding, in which an improviser plays free, drifting music figuratively or literally in search of an idea. To evoke that sense of protean exploring, Beethoven largely leaves out bar lines and erases any sense of beat — like some Baroque preludes. Within that freedom, a chain of thirds slowly wends its way downward through harmonies and keys until it reaches F, preparing the B-flat-major finale.

In the middle, when the chain reaches B major, there is a Bachlike eruption of imitative counterpoint that just as suddenly vanishes. Here is another feature of Beethoven's late music: *music about itself, a querying and questing evoking its process of being composed.* Now a question is posed: "How shall I write the fugue?" The prelude to the finale is an evocation of a composer searching for material, seizing on something and dropping it almost with a shake of the head, continuing the search until the solution is found (the finale of the Ninth Symphony will return to that notion). Much of the *Hammerklavier* has that quality of self-reflection, music observing and commenting on itself in the process of its unfolding.

So one of those as-if comments in the introduction is on the idea of fugue, which turns out to be what the prelude was searching for — prefigured by its abortive burst of Bachlike counterpoint. (For models, Beethoven copied out bits of fugues from *The Well-Tempered Clavier* alongside sketches for the finale.)[43] What is rejected at that point by the symbolic composer is not Bach or counterpoint but *old-style* counterpoint.[44] "The imagination, too, asserts its privileges," friends reported Beethoven saying, "and today a different, truly poetic element must be manifested in conventional form."[45] *Form informed by poetry.* He had begun thinking of his music in poetic terms. He wanted more feeling and evocation than drama and narrative. In keeping, he took to calling himself a *Tondichter,* tone poet, rather than a *Komponist.* In his always laconic comments on his music he spoke less of Aufklärung *reason,* more of Romantic *imagination, reverie,* and the like.[46] As his words to and about Goethe show, he believed poets to be the most significant of artists.

So for this fugal finale, involving that familiar Baroque genre, he intended to make something new, poetic, both Bach and not-Bach, starting with its long, amorphous, quite outlandish subject. Its primal features are a giant leap up of an octave and a third, a trill, and a babbling chain of sixteenths:

What happens to that theme in the course of the movement is going to spin out in two virtually contradictory directions. The fugue subject is treated to the old contrapuntal procedures of augmentation (stretching it out), inversion (turning it upside down), retrograde (backward), and stretto (theme entering on top of itself), all carried forth within the traditional outlines of fugal exposition and episode, subject and countersubject(s). At the same time, motifs from the subject are spun off as material for thematic variation and development, those sonata-like elements subsumed within the fugal texture. He pursues, in other words, a melding of apparently mutually exclusive genres, fugue and sonata. That serving of two masters at once is what creates some of the overheated quality of the music.

The keys of the finale's seven large sections form another descending chain of thirds: B-flat major–G-flat major–E-flat minor–B minor–G major–E-flat major. At that point, the music moves down a step to D major, from there falling a third to B-flat major in the return to the opening theme. This kind of complex and systematic modulation defining the sections of a piece is something sonatas can do that Baroque-style fugues do not. In other words, the fugal treatment is obsessively technical at the same time that the audible effect is of rhapsodic freedom.

So this is a fugue that unfolds like no other, in the large view also subsuming something like a combination of rondo (a traditional finale model) and variations.[47] As Beethoven admits above the opening measures (in Italian, despite his vow to use German terms), it is a *fuga a tre voci con alcune licenze,* "fugue in three voices with some license." (As he presumably knew, *con alcune licenze* was used as an indication in improvisatory pieces of the seventeenth and eighteenth centuries.) License, indeed. He sets forth a gigantic, manic fugue, or rather a teeming sonata/rondo/variation/fantasia on the idea of a fugue — again, Baroque fugue plus Aufklärung forms, including the thematic development that pervades the movement. Moments of comedy, pathos, and lyricism pass through the music like mists in wind. Often there are huge spaces between the hands, creating a singular sonority between the resonant bass and silvery and percussive high register.

Few listeners can follow all the twists and turns of the finale; most only try to take in what sounds like a churning dynamism glittering with trills, at the same time a kind of epic athletic contest for a performer struggling with piano keys and hammers and the limits of human endurance. *What is difficult is good,* and what is difficult is woven into the sounding impact of the *Hammerklavier:* a certain desperate quality in the performance is not only in some degree inevitable but necessary. This is a descendant of the end of the *Appassionata,* in which the assault on the player and instrument is part of the effect. The music seems to be tearing piano and performer apart.

Unlike some of his work of the previous decade, then, this is not music exalting a hero but rather music heroic in its essence. To a large extent, the hero in question is the performer, and after that the listener. Again, the piece exists on the other side of the eighteenth-century notion of piano sonatas and its notion of music in general as an elegant pleasure largely within the reach of amateur performers and listeners. The outer movements of the *Hammerklavier* are excessive beyond ease and beyond pleasure, sometimes nearly beyond human, though they enfold moments of wonderful beauty. The superhuman and the intimately human are both part of the *Hammerklavier.* Perhaps, given Beethoven's literary passions, is it relevant that the same can be said of Homer.

The listener experiences the whole of op. 106 as one takes in storms in the mountains and other forces of nature. For the strong of heart, *what is difficult is beautiful and good.*[48] "Now," Beethoven said, "I know how to compose." In fact, though the *Hammerklavier* informed virtually every piece he wrote afterward, he never wrote another one that sounds or works quite like this sonata. It was an experiment and an extreme. The works that followed, some even more gigantic, played out the sonata's implications in their own mostly gentler ways. Still, there would be a further enormous fugal finale to come, one that would set a new mark for excess and obsession not only in fugues but in the entirety of music. Beethoven would name that one the *Grosse Fuge,* the "Great Fugue."

As of 1818, Beethoven was not stone deaf and he never quite reached that point, but by then when he finished the most monumental of piano sonatas he was functionally deaf. How did he do his work? A professional composer can read and create music in his or her head without a piano, just as one reads and writes prose. Cultivating that inner ear is a basic skill for any trained musician, though some have a better inner ear than others. (It helps to have perfect pitch; there is no evidence as to whether or not Beethoven had it.) That was the foundation of how he worked in his deafness: he could compose away from the keyboard. All the same, in practice he had always done much of his work at the piano, making use of his facility as an improviser. Improvisation, again, was key to his process. What went down in his sketchbooks was shorthand for a great deal of work done at the piano and in his head, playing and revising. As his deafness shut him off from sound, he went to great lengths to hear the piano as well as he could — getting the louder Broadwood and the ear trumpets and the metal sound amplifier he attached to the piano. Apparently sometimes he held up an ear trumpet to the amplifier. (Neither that contraption nor a detailed description of it survives.)

The third means was more direct. He still spent a great deal of time improvising at the keyboard, even when he could hear nothing of what he played. When he improvised publicly in later life, the reported results ranged from splendid to pathetic; sometimes his hands got onto the wrong keys, and usually his pianos were out of tune. But after all his years as a virtuoso he had a sense of virtual hearing through his fingers. Maybe of the collection of stratagems he used to overcome his deafness, finger-pitch memory was the most useful. With it he could still draw on improvisation as his engine, his creative consciousness functioning through his fingers. Perhaps in the throes of improvisation it felt to him like he heard every note and nuance.

Did his deafness change his music? Of course it did, but *how* it did, how much of the late style had to do with his hearing, is not easy to discern. There are miscalculations, particularly in the late orchestration, but they are far outweighed by fresh and remarkable effects of spacing and color, in orchestra and piano and string quartet. Continuity is another matter. Czerny reported, secondhand, that Beethoven told a friend his deafness "prevented him from adhering, in his later works, to the consistent flow and unity of his earlier ones, for he had been accustomed to composing everything at the piano."[49] None of that is entirely accurate. Much of the late music has an unbroken flow and long-sustained arcs. Maybe here Czerny's own skepticism about the late period is speaking. Still, in one way and another Beethoven had to adapt his composing to his disability, mostly in ways only he would know.

Maybe the obsessive concentration on unity of material in the *Hammerklavier* was a way of attacking his disability. Having done it, he did not need that kind of obsession anymore. With the *Hammerklavier* he not only proved to the musical world that he was still capable of supremely ambitious works (even if some of the world considered this piece quite mad); he also proved it to himself. Now, seeing his new path clearly before him, there were no bounds to what he intended to do. But the fact that now he could hear music only in his head is surely what gave some of the late music an inward, ethereal, uncanny aura like nothing else. Some of the late music is like a memory of music sounding in the mind, with an ineffable beauty and poignancy. All his late music is pervaded with both loss and transcendence.

As Beethoven worked on the *Hammerklavier* in 1817–18, the Karl-and-Johanna troubles were in abeyance. With Karl living with him, sometimes in the country, there was less opportunity for Johanna to get at her son. But when they returned to Vienna, the struggle heated up again, toward its coming climax. Johanna had surely expected more access to Karl as a reward for contributing to his support. When Karl was back in Vienna that autumn of 1818, Johanna struck through the courts. She submitted to the Landrecht a petition to get the boy back. When that was rejected she applied to have Karl taken from the Gymnasium day school and placed in the Royal Imperial Convict, a boarding school —where she might be able to reach him. That too was rejected by the court. Meanwhile, probably to put pressure on Beethoven, she stopped paying support.

Somehow or other Johanna had been seeing or communicating with Karl, who at twelve was on the verge of sowing his oats as a teenager yet still somewhat pliable. Like a teenager too, he was becoming embarrassed to be seen in the company of his shabby, deaf guardian, who looked so peculiar that passersby gawked and street urchins heckled him. Beethoven habitually strode along quick-time, singing and mumbling to himself, muttering insults at passersby. He would not have moderated any of that when the boy was with him.

On December 3, Karl ran away to his mother. Distraught beyond words, Beethoven went to the Giannatasios. "Never shall I be able to forget," Fanny Giannatasio wrote in her diary, "the moment when he came and told us that Karl had left him, and had gone to his mother . . . To see this man weeping, who has already had so much sorrow to bear, was one of the saddest scenes I ever witnessed. I remember Beethoven's exclaiming, with the tears running down his cheeks . . . 'Ah, he's ashamed of me!'"[50]

But Beethoven dried his tears and next morning went to Johanna to fetch Karl home. She promised to send him back that night; to make sure, he summoned the police, who took the boy to the Giannatasios'. Immediately Johanna made another appeal to the Landrecht, complaining that Beethoven intended to send her son far away.[51] This time the court called for a hearing to interview all three principals: Beethoven, Karl, and his mother. It was in this round that Beethoven made a disastrous mistake involving a letter of the alphabet.

He turned up for the hearing with his editor friend Karl Bernard, who probably wrote down the judges' questions for him and provided advice. Whether or not Karl and Johanna had been coached, the court record shows their testimony was careful, coordinated, and effective. Examined first, Karl astutely played the middle. Was he getting good grades? Yes, between "eminent" and "first class." Why, the judges asked, did he leave his uncle? "Because his mother had told him she would send him to public school," Karl responded, "and he did not think he was getting on under private instruction." How was he treated by his uncle? "Well." Did he prefer to be with his mother or his uncle? "He would gladly remain with his uncle if he had someone with him, because his uncle is hard of hearing and he cannot talk with him." Did his mother persuade him to run away? "No." Has his uncle mistreated him? "He had often punished him but only when he deserved it . . . After his return [from his mother] his uncle had threatened to strangle him." Did his uncle encourage him to speak disrespectfully of his mother? "Yes, and it was in his uncle's presence, whom he thought he would please by it."

Did his uncle exhort him to pray? "Yes, he prayed with him morning and evening."[52]

Presumably the court was not too concerned about Beethoven's threat to strangle the boy; it was the kind of thing one said in angry moments, and no one expected he was serious. What Karl thought of it was not asked. To what extent his answers were inflected by fear of his uncle cannot be said.

Johanna testified last. Karl had come to her on his own accord, she said, "because he did not like to live with his uncle." She had advised Karl to go back, but he was afraid to. Had her brother-in-law forbidden her to see her son? He had told her to meet Karl at various places, then when she arrived he was not there. Had his uncle treated the boy well? Here, remarkably, Johanna did not condemn Beethoven at all — in fact, as far as the record shows, she never did. Echoing Karl's testimony, Johanna said that his deafness made it impossible for Karl to converse with him and except for the unreliable servants there was nobody who could properly take care of him: "His cleanliness was neglected and supervision of his clothing and washing; persons who had brought him clean linen had been turned back by his guardian." Had she heard of her son speaking disrespectfully of her? She had not. Was her husband of noble birth? "The documentary proof of nobility was said to be in the possession of the oldest brother, the composer . . . she herself had no document bearing on the subject." The last question was what, in fact, had already decided the matter for the Landrecht.

The judges asked the question because of what Beethoven had revealed in his testimony a few moments earlier. After asking him about the circumstances of Karl's flight, the court asked, In whose actual care was the nephew? Beethoven said he had arranged piano lessons and tutoring. "These studies occupied all the leisure time of his nephew so completely that he needed no care; moreover, he could not trust any of his servants with the oversight of his nephew, as they had been bribed by the boy's mother." Had the boy spoken disrespectfully of his mother in his uncle's presence? "No; besides, he had admonished him to speak nothing but the truth; he had asked his nephew if he was fond of his mother and he answered in the negative." Beethoven said he did not want Karl to be schooled in the Convict, as Johanna had petitioned for, because there were too many pupils there and too little supervision. For the moment, he said, he could only see hiring a tutor for the boy or sending him back to the Giannatasios' boarding school for the winter. After that he would send him to the Convict school in Mölk. Of course, he rambled on, ideally he would like to have Karl study at the excellent Theresianum in Vienna, "if he were but of noble birth."

Those few words let the cat out of the bag. It was a ruinous bit of information that Beethoven had volunteered unasked. The court pounced. *Were he and his brother of the nobility and did he have documents to prove it?* "Van," Beethoven replied, "was a Dutch predicate which was not exclusively applied to the nobility; he had neither a diploma nor any other proof of his nobility."

What made one noble was a rather informal matter; if one had a noble name, one was presumed to be so until and unless documents were required. All along, many people had assumed the *van* in Beethoven's name made him noble, because in Germany that was often the case: *van* was the equivalent of *von*. But as Beethoven admitted to the court before he thought better of it, that was not the case in Flanders, where his family was from.

A week later the Landrecht, reserved for the nobility, transferred his case to the commoners' court, the Magistrat.[53] Beethoven had to begin all over again.

That was going to be a dicey matter. The two courts had quite different frames of reference. Inevitably, the court for the nobles tended to favor the case of an aristocrat over that of a commoner, unless the situation was egregious. The Magistrat had no such bias. For this court it was a simple matter of a child being taken from home and from a mother who, though hardly a model parent, seemed to them neither indifferent nor incapable. Clearly Johanna loved her son and wanted him to be with her, as was her natural right. Her conviction for embezzlement from a few years before, the centerpiece of Beethoven's claim that she was unfit, the court declared to be an old matter for which she had paid her debt.

In January 1819, the Magistrat decreed that Beethoven was no longer his nephew's guardian and another had to be found. Meanwhile Karl was to be returned to his mother. Beethoven appealed. A friend of his, magistrate and musical amateur Mathias von Tuscher, agreed reluctantly to become co-guardian.

What had he been thinking in his testimony? He surely knew that because of the *van* many people, including the Landrecht, took him for aristocracy, and he had never felt it necessary to deny it. In dealing with the Landrecht he had a vital interest in keeping the question from coming up at all. But it was not simply a matter of deliberately misrepresenting himself. As far as Beethoven was concerned, by his own efforts he had raised himself above the common folk to virtual nobility. This was so ingrained in him that he got fatally careless in his testimony — or maybe he actually assumed that the court would accept his self-elevation. In a conversation book he wrote, "My nature shows that I do not belong among this plebian mass."[54] In a letter: "Since I have raised my nephew into a higher category, neither he nor I belong with the M[agistrat], for only innkeepers, cobblers, and tailors come under that kind of guardianship."[55] He felt himself to be of the aristocracy for *moral* reasons. That, of course, was absurd. Things had not changed because of the French Revolution and Napoleon. One was noble or common by birth or by royal decree. It was that way because it had always been that way. Napoleon had certified the system when he made himself emperor and set out to found a dynasty.

Beethoven's conception of himself as self-made nobility — like Napoleon — was inflected by another matter that on the face of it makes no sense at all. A rumor had gone around, including in print, that Beethoven was the bastard son of Prussian king Friedrich Wilhelm II, or even of Frederick the Great. In 1819, his friend Karl Peters wrote in a conversation book, "I asked Bernard if it hadn't been corrected that the Conversations-Lexicon said you were the natural son of the King of Prussia. Such things must be corrected, because it's not necessary for you to have that luster from the king, the reverse is the case."[56] The issue did not go any further at that point. Beethoven seems to have let the matter ride, despite the insult to his mother. (The insult to his drunken father would not have concerned him.) He did not specifically deny the rumor about his paternity until he was more or less on his deathbed. Here was another way for him to imagine himself an aristocrat, when all the rest of the world cared about was the *van* or the *von*.[57] A Napoleon could ennoble himself because he commanded a great many soldiers and guns. A Beethoven could not.

On New Year's Day of 1819, Beethoven wrote his patron and pupil Archduke Rudolph, "All that can conceivably be comprised in a wish, all that can conceivably be called profitable, such as welfare, happiness and blessings, are included in the wish I have expressed for Y.I.H. today." He touches briefly on his own concerns:

> A terrible event took place a short time ago in my family circumstances, and for a time I was absolutely driven out of my mind. To this alone you must ascribe the fact that I have not called upon Y.I.H. in person nor reported on the masterly variations of my highly honored and illustrious pupil who is a favorite of the Muses. I dare not express my thanks either verbally or in writing for this surprise and for the favor with which I have been honored. For I am too lowly placed and unable, however ardently I may intend to desire to do so, to repay you in the same coin . . . In a few days I hope to hear Y.I.H. yourself perform the masterpiece you have sent me; and nothing can delight me more than to assist Y.I.H. to take as soon as possible the seat on Parnassus which has already been prepared for Your Highness.[58]

The "too lowly placed" in his letter shows that Beethoven is still hurting from the Landrecht's demoting him to the Magistrat, which to him amounted to a humiliating public rebuke. The main point of the letter is to thank his patron for sending the new printing of Rudolph's magnum opus, *Forty Variations on a Theme by Beethoven*. For the purpose, the year before Beethoven had supplied the archduke with music and text of a four-bar, chorale-like theme called *O Hoffnung*: "O Hope! You steel the heart, you soften the pain." The melody has a distinct and maybe deliberate resemblance to the flowing second phrase in the beginning of the *Hammerklavier*.

His communications to Rudolph for a while hereafter would be full of paeans to his patron's great genius. Rudolph was a good pianist and a competent composer, though not a particularly imaginative, prolific, or ambitious one. By this point his piano playing had largely been wrecked by chronic gout. As a composer he never had the fertility and facility of somebody who has to make a living by his notes. And the archduke needed a leg up on his ascent to Parnassus: the manuscript of his variations shows extensive editing and correcting from Beethoven, the dozens of changes requiring five pages of sketched revisions. Many of the corrections concern mistakes of basic musical grammar and syntax.[59] Rudolph's variations end in high-Beethoven fashion, with a big fugue on the theme; Beethoven had to fix many problems there. All the same, his changes on the whole are in technical details; like any good teacher, he does not try to change his student's style.[60]

Now with the *Hammerklavier* going into print with its dedication to Rudolph, Beethoven had begun to think about writing a High Mass for the archduke's impending investment as archbishop of Ölmutz. Foreordained for that post, Rudolph had put it off in favor of his musical studies. For Beethoven, composing a mass could continue his long search for a new kind of sacred music. No less was it a practical project; he reasoned that the new archbishop ought to have a *Kapellmeister* for his ecclesiastical post. A big mass would be a tour de force to promote that idea. It could also crown his work with an ancient genre at the summit of sacred music. The Mass in C had been notable for its restraint. Now Beethoven wanted to expand everything to giant size and ambition.

The new project got no help from his life. He had finished the *Hammerklavier* with the Karl struggle in abeyance. Now with Johanna's determination reawakened, for him the situation was more dangerous and more maddening than ever. The Magistrat wanted to give the boy back to his raven-mother once and for all. Beethoven's main legal adviser now was a Vienna lawyer named Johann Baptist Bach — no relation to the famous musical Bachs but well placed, like most of Beethoven's friends, and an amateur cellist. He and Beethoven had an unclouded relationship to the end. On the same New Year's Day that Beethoven wrote his greetings to Rudolph, he wrote to Bach. He had drafted a long statement for the Magistrat, putting forth his case in detail:

> It is obviously of great importance to me that I should not be placed in a false position. That is why the written statement which I am de-

livering is so long-winded . . . There is no self-interest in my being a guardian. But I want by means of my nephew to establish a fresh memorial to my name. I do not need my nephew, but he needs me . . . The just man must be able to suffer injustice also, without swerving in the very least from what is right. In this spirit I will endure every test and no one shall make me waver — Whoever tries to remove my nephew entirely from me will have to shoulder a great responsibility. Disastrous consequences, both morally and politically, would be the result for my nephew . . . PS, As I have been very busy and also rather unwell, my document will surely be considered with indulgence.[61]

He knew the document he wanted Bach to submit to the court was "long-winded" and needed "indulgence"; there is his clear-sightedness. That there was no self-interest in his fight, that Karl needed him more than he needed Karl; there is his capacity for self-delusion. He believed that to rear Karl to a notable place in the world would add new luster to his own glory; there is his solipsism. As he prepared his blast to the Magistrat, Karl went back to his mother's and attended an institute run by Johann Kudlich, finally boarding there. Beethoven was at first satisfied with Kudlich's institution, but when he found that Johanna was being allowed access to Karl, this educator in turn became another "scoundrel or a weak person."[62]

His twelve-page report to the Magistrat dated February 1, 1819, was one of five documents he submitted to the court that year. That is what he was doing, rather than composing. This first is mostly a tempered and coherent statement that took him who knows how long to draft before he gave it to lawyer Bach for editing. But in the document he could not suppress his rage entirely. "I confess," he writes, "that I myself feel that I am better fitted than anyone else to inspire my nephew by my own example with a desire for virtue and zealous activity." As for his opponent,

If the mother could have repressed her wicked tendencies and allowed my plans [for Karl's education] to develop peacefully, then an entirely favorable result would have been the outcome of the arrangements I have so far adopted. But when a mother of that type tries to

initiate her child into the mysteries of her vulgar and even perverse
surroundings and in his tender years induces him . . . to bribe my servants, to tell lies, inasmuch as she laughs at him when he speaks the
truth, nay more, even gives him money in order to arouse lusts and
desires which are harmful to him . . . then this affair, which in itself is
difficult, becomes even more complicated and dangerous.[63]

Johanna had her own champion to represent her, civil servant Joseph
Hotschevar, husband of her mother's stepsister. Beethoven's statement
to the court responded to a comparably long-winded one of Hotschevar's in which he asserted that Karl could not remain with his uncle
"except at great risk to his well-being and with the danger of being
morally and physically warped." (That sounds rather like Beethoven's
terms.) As for Beethoven's relations with and responsibility to his
brother, Hotschevar continues, "It will not be asserting too much if
I say that Herr Carl v. Beethoven was only on good terms with his
brother . . . when he [Carl] was in need of money." Hotschevar claims
that Ludwig made a disreputable bargain, securing the 1,500-florin
loan to Carl from his publisher in return for the boy's going to Ludwig when Carl died. Hotschevar submitted a letter from Carl saying
he agreed to his brother's terms for the loan only out of desperation.
Hotschevar also submitted the codicil to the will, with its unequivocal
statement that Karl must not be taken from his mother. "The matter at
stake," Hotschevar concludes, "is the salvation of a talented boy."[64] (To
add to the shabbiness of the whole business, when Johanna turned up
pregnant in 1820, Hotschevar distanced himself from her.)[65]
    His petitions got Beethoven nowhere with the Magistrat. In April
he and new co-guardian Tuscher came up with another scheme, to
send Karl to the Bavarian town of Landshut and the school of the celebrated Catholic canon, liberal theologian, and teacher Johann Michael Sailer. Beethoven's distant friend Antonie Brentano knew Sailer
personally. On Beethoven's request she wrote a plea to the educator
asking him to accept Karl in his school. She cites the current "unfore-
seeable evil consequence upon morality throughout all the classes" in
her beloved Vienna. Karl is "an ardent boy, 10 to 12 years old, the only
son of parents without means — his father dead, his mother publicly

[known] as a thief, with a very low style of living." In reality Johanna did have means, and Antonie had never met either mother or son. As for Beethoven, she wrote, "This great, excellent man . . . is even greater as a human being than he is an artist. He has made it the greatest concern of his life to provide the best conditions possible" for Karl. She is sure Sailer will agree to take the boy, for his guardian "is natural, simple, and wise, with pure intentions; and the finest and surest approach would be if you write to him . . . as if you had known him for a long time, this singer of pious songs."[66]

Sailer agreed to accept Karl in his school, and around this time Beethoven bought two books of Sailer's for his library. He would have been particularly attracted to Sailer's belief that religious convictions must come from inside, not be imposed from outside: one must make faith one's own or it is empty orthodoxy.[67] The plan to enroll Karl with Sailer could have been an ideal solution all around, might have forestalled much misery. But Johanna vetoed it, and the Magistrat supported her. From there the situation deteriorated dangerously.

During an argument Beethoven jerked Karl out of a chair, injuring his groin still tender from the hernia operation. One imagines the boy rolling screaming on the floor, Beethoven standing over him in horror. To make sure Karl would not go to Landshut, Johanna apparently persuaded him to fail his spring examinations, which set his schooling behind for a year. In May the twelve-year-old was let out of boarding school to attend his mother's name-day celebration. He celebrated too much, spent the night at Johanna's, and in the morning made his way back to school nursing a miserable hangover. Finally he returned to his mother's house and stayed there in bed for three weeks. To the court, Johanna blamed his illness on the injury Beethoven had inflicted.[68]

Desperate, Beethoven declared, "I must now eat humble pie," and attempted to place Karl back in Giannatasio's boarding school. The schoolmaster said no.[69] In her diary, Fanny Giannatasio appears to have recovered from her infatuation. "Much as it pained us to refuse a request of Beethoven's," she wrote, "I am quite sure that we did the right thing, for we could have done no real good, and, perhaps . . . a great deal of harm."[70]

That these boundless admirers of Beethoven washed their hands of

Karl testifies to how frustrating their experiences had been. Beethoven had been especially attentive to the family lately, as always to daughter Nanni in particular. Earlier that year Nanni was married. When the family returned to the house they heard a song for voices and piano coming from musicians hidden in a corner. When the music was done Beethoven stepped out and presented the bride with the manuscript of the piece he wrote for her wedding.[71] There are his kindness and generosity, which were as constant as his wrath and paranoia.

In June, Beethoven's friend Mathias von Tuscher resigned the co-guardianship, saying he found it "in every respect burdensome and vexatious." The court appointed Johanna full guardian again. At the end of the year the Magistrat rejected two Beethoven pleas to be reinstated as guardian. Toward the end of 1819, the exasperated Magistrat declared that Karl had been "subject to the whims of Beethoven and had been tossed back and forth like a ball from one educational institution to another." In the wake of Tuscher's resignation, the court gave the co-guardianship to Johanna and a municipal employee named Leopold Nussböck. In January 1820, Beethoven and his legal adviser Johann Baptist Bach gave up on the Magistrat and petitioned the Appeals Court.

Meanwhile Karl was enrolled in a progressive school in Vienna run by Joseph Blöchlinger. This educator was a follower of Johann Heinrich Pestalozzi, whose progressive ideas on education were caught in his aphorisms "Learning by head, hand, and heart" and "The role of the educator is to teach children, not subjects." In those days Pestalozzi was virtually unique in deploring physical punishment in schools.

Beethoven approved the move, but it was not long before the conversation books began to ring with his denunciations of one more educator. To editor friend Bernard, who had approved of Blöchlinger, he cried, "You yourself a few days ago in the city gave me to understand clearly enough that my nephew hates me — oh, may the whole miserable mob be cursed and damned."[72] In the conversation books Blöchlinger was at first "the ice-house" and "that glacier."[73] Karl's reports picture him as stingy with food; he punished a student who had wet his bed with a beating and kept him on thin soup for days.[74] During an interview, Blöchlinger's mother was horrified to see Beethoven spit into a handkerchief and carefully examine the spittle.[75] Most likely, after losing a mother and brother to tuberculosis, he was looking for blood. Yet in the end Karl settled into the Blöchlinger institute, surely as good a school as could have been found for him in Vienna, and stayed there until 1823.

As the wrangles over schools receded, Karl's restlessness and distraction mounted, and his studies became more and more unsteady. "I had a terrible time with him," Blöchlinger reported to Beethoven in a conversation book, "getting him to stick to work again, good words are often fruitless with him and do not pull him out of his rut."[76] And worse: "The boy lies every time he opens his mouth. His laziness . . . leads him astray into everything . . . The boy will be and must be completely without character, even if we do manage to make him learn something worthwhile."[77] In the conversation books, Beethoven prepared lectures for himself or Blöchlinger to deliver to the boy: "You are little by little becoming habituated to abominable [things]."[78] One day the schoolmaster heard Beethoven shouting at Karl in the school: "I am known all over Europe! Don't you dare disgrace my name!"[79] What Karl became habituated to in practice was enduring his uncle's jeremiads and then going his own way.

All this trouble tempered but did not stem the creative wave Beethoven had been riding. His popularity in Vienna remained high. By now he had reached something of the status of a settled classic — at least, his more popular pieces had. He still went through the motions of conducting. A performance of the *Prometheus* Overture and the Seventh Symphony he conducted in early 1819 was received with shouts and tears. The new Vienna *Allgemeine Musikalische Zeitung* declared, "He who has not experienced Beethoven's symphony under his direction, cannot comprehend fully this major instrumental work of our time . . . Praise him and us! We name him *ours, Europe's* greatest composer, and Vienna recognizes thankfully what it possesses in him."[80] This from the Viennese whom Beethoven denounced every day. Another article, commemorating his forty-ninth birthday (correctly, despite Beethoven's own chronic confusion about his age), said that his works "belong completely to a poetic, primarily novel-like, fantastic world."

The old complaints about his tendencies to fantasy and bizarrerie were now resolved to a Romantic admiration of the same qualities.

In March came an invitation with great consequences. Anton Diabelli sent out a proposal to all the leading Vienna composers asking each to contribute one variation on a little waltz tune of Diabelli's own. The results were to be put out in a series of issues. Diabelli had worked for Steiner's publishing house, and now had set out with a partner as a publisher of works both serious and light — the latter including arrangements of popular tunes for piano and guitar. Among his discoveries was an obscure young phenomenon named Franz Schubert. Diabelli published Schubert's teenage efforts *Erlkönig* as op. 1 and *Gretchen am Sprinnrade* as op. 2; in the centuries to come, they would remain two of Schubert's most famous songs.[81]

The variations project, its contributors dubbed the Patriotic Society of Artists, constituted the opening gambit for Diabelli's firm. Being a small part of a patriotic artistic society was not Beethoven's style, but writing piano variations suited his present situation; they could be done in short bursts worked in around his physical and legal struggles. He notified Diabelli, whom he had dubbed "Diabolus diabelli," that he was on the job — not on a single variation but on a set of them. On the face of it, given the slightness of Diabelli's tune (Beethoven dismissed it as a *Schusterfleck*, a cobbler's patch), he appeared to be continuing the sort of lightweight folk-song variations he had lately been turning out for Thomson. But this project quickly spread into something enormously more ambitious.

By the beginning of summer Beethoven had sketched nearly two dozen variations on Diabelli's theme; at that point, as far as he was concerned, the piece was practically done. He put it aside for a bigger project, the mass for Archduke Rudolph's investment as archbishop. In June he wrote Rudolph from Mödling, "The day on which a High Mass composed by me will be performed during the ceremonies solemnized for Your Imperial Highness will be the most glorious day of my life; and God will enlighten me so that my poor talents may contribute to the glorification of that solemn day." The tone of the letter shows the two had already discussed the project together. The impetus came, presumably, from Beethoven, his rewards to be considered later.

The new mass was going to be exponentially more massive than the variations, though at this point Beethoven probably had little idea how massive. But he was ready to get going on major projects again. He got to work laying the foundation of the mass. He made a copy of the text, with parallel German translation, and began to study the pronunciation, accentuation, and shadings of meaning in the Latin. A minute concern for the text was going to be the foundation of what became the *Missa solemnis.* He began sketching the Kyrie, Gloria, and Credo, and jotted ideas for other segments.[82] At the same time he added sketches for a symphony in D minor. Now in a relatively short time, soon after finishing the monumental *Hammerklavier,* he had conceived the next three gigantic works of his last period: *Missa Solemnis,* Ninth Symphony, and *Diabelli* Variations.[¹]

Meanwhile he was doing better healthwise and working steadily, but his feelings had never been more tumultuous. Around the middle of summer he wrote a sulfurous letter to his friend Bernard:

> I heard from Oliva that Karl asked Blöch[linger] for permission to write me a letter in Latin for my name-day — I am of the opinion that you should make it clear to K[arl] in the presence of Herr B that I do not wish to receive any letter from him . . . His stubbornness, his ingratitude and his callousness have so got the better of him that when O[liva] was there he never once even asked for me . . . Away with him, my patience is at an end, I have cast him out of my heart. I have shed many tears on his account, that worthless boy . . . My love for him is gone. He needed my love. I do not need his.

He goes on venting in that vein for a while, yet by the end of the letter he has calmed down: "You understand, of course, that this is not what I really think (I still love him as I used to, but without weakness or undue partiality, nay more, I may say in truth that I often weep for him.)"[83]

On the same day that he wrote that letter in a blind rage to Bernard, Beethoven wrote to Archduke Rudolph as teacher to aristocratic pupil:

> I was in Vienna in order to collect in Y.I.H.'s library what was most useful for me, the chief purpose is rapid execution united to a better

understanding of art ... The older composers render us double service, since there is generally real artistic value in their works (among
them, of course, only the German Händel and Sebastian Bach possessed genius). But in the world of art, as in the whole of our great creation, freedom and progress are the main objectives. And although we
moderns are not quite as far advanced in solidity as our ancestors, yet
the refinement of our customs has enlarged many of our conceptions
as well. My eminent music pupil, who himself is now competing for
the laurels of fame, must not bear the reproach of being one-sided.[84]

There is no better illustration of how emotionally fickle Beethoven
could be, how intellectually and spiritually fickle, from moment to
moment.

Around this time younger brother Johann van Beethoven bought an
estate called Wasserhof near Gneixendorf, in the vineyard-rich Wachau Valley up the Danube from Vienna.[85] Johann was wintering in Vienna and had been spending time with Karl. Beethoven immediately
suspected treachery, that Johann was pushing Karl to become a mere
pharmacist like himself, that he was colluding with Karl's mother, that
he wanted the guardianship for himself. Beethoven's possessiveness toward Karl was boundless. Like a mother bear protecting her cubs, he
demanded total control of the boy and everything around him, wanted
no one else close to him. Once he arrived at that point, he was capable
of nearly any kind of jealous lashing out.

A month after he wrote the preceding letters, Beethoven drafted a
truly over-the-top one to Blöchlinger, who had allowed Johanna access
to Karl:

> I protest, first of all, against the letter which you have written to Fr[au]
> B[eethove]n without my approval — Secondly, I absolutely insist that
> ... the mother shall not be allowed to see K[arl] anymore. If she is,
> then legal proceedings will be taken against you as a seducer of my
> nephew into low company — Here is the letter which you wrote to
> me as if I were a schoolboy, thus displaying your ignorance of hu-
> man nature ... Men of high standing are not of your insignificant

opinion about miserable trifles . . . All kinds of people, and, I may say, several of the most eminent men show me their regard and affection. Among them are even several of the most distinguished and most worthy men of your native land, with whom, however, I would never associate you.[86]

And so forth. It appears that he never mailed the letter. It was private venting.

Karl stayed in the Blöchlinger institute for four more years. What most drove Beethoven to distraction now was Karl's not responding to him, not wanting to be with him. "He doesn't even express a wish to see me or speak to me," Beethoven cried to Bernard, "and indeed as long as I live he shall never see me again, for he is a monster."[87] That a teenager naturally rebels, pulls away from elders and especially from a demanding, suffocating love like Beethoven's, was hardly part of the understanding of adolescence in those days. Even if it had been, Beethoven still would have crucified himself. It is a reasonable guess that many of his excesses over Karl were fueled by wine. And through it all, he continued working doggedly on the mass, shaping some of the most remarkable creative conceptions of his life or anyone's life.

His affairs now were at loggerheads in a way that would have been fatal to most men and most artists. But not to him, though it certainly affected his production. Now and then he said, I am not crazy yet. Somehow he never was, not quite. And somehow in the throes of his suffering he never lost his kindness or his humor. From Mödling in the fall he wrote publisher Artaria in Vienna, "Most excellent Virtuosi *senza Cujoni* [without balls]! We inform you of this and of that and of other things as well, from which you must draw the best conclusions you can; and we request you to send us what is due to the composer, i.e., six . . . copies of the sonata in B♭."[88]

In autumn came another portraitist, Frederick Schimon. Heavily involved in the mass, Beethoven allowed the painter to set up his easel in an adjoining room and otherwise ignored him. Schimon worked at his leisure, finishing everything in the picture but the eyes, which were the most important part. He got his chance when Beethoven, pleased at how this artist had not discommoded him but came and went quietly, invited him to coffee. Schimon added the eyes: filmed, electric, and searching, the most striking part of an otherwise lumpy portrait, just as Beethoven's actual eyes were the most electrical part of his peasant's face.[89]

At the end of 1819, Beethoven offered to sell the new mass, "which will soon be performed," to Simrock in Bonn. The piece was far from finished — he had no idea how far. "My most gracious Lord," he wrote Simrock, "the Archbishop and Cardinal has not yet got enough money to pay his chief Kapellmeister what is right and proper . . . Therefore one must earn one's bread elsewhere." He was *Kapellmeister* in ironic terms only. If he hoped to secure a formal *Kapellmeister* position from Rudolph, that never came to pass. But the mass forged on. Meanwhile in March, as Beethoven worked on the Credo with a long way to go on the work, his only deadline passed when Rudolph was enthroned as archbishop of Ölmutz.

Beethoven spent much of the late winter preparing yet another legal memorandum, this one for the Appeals Court — forty-eight carefully argued pages, his longest one yet. It was written with the help of lawyer Bach, who urged Beethoven "to proceed as moderately as possible in all things so that it does not appear as if there were malice."[90]

Dated February 18, 1820, the draft of the memorandum begins, immoderately, "It is painful for a man like me to have to sully himself to the smallest extent with a person like fr[au] B[eethoven]. But since this is my last attempt to save my nephew, for his sake I am submitting to be so humiliated." He cites horrible crimes, nefarious purposes, unconscionable consequences. Meticulously he reviews the financial details. He admits that "once in a passion I dragged my nephew from the chair because he had done something very wicked; and since he has had to wear a truss ever since his hernia operation . . . the swift pulling consequently caused him some pain in the most tender place whenever he turned around quickly." The doctor, however, had assured him that "not the least damage was done."[91] He ends with an appeal to the Almighty.

Presumably Bach tempered the malice and bile in the document the court received, but there was plenty left. To add to the tragicomedy, it

was in this period that Johanna van Beethoven gave birth to an illegitimate daughter.[92] That may have been the last nail in the coffin for her
case. (In an utterly inexplicable footnote, Johanna named the daughter
Ludovica, the feminine form of Ludwig, presumably in honor of the
brother-in-law who loathed her and stole her son.)

This time, Beethoven's barrage of words worked. On April 8, 1820,
the Appeals Court issued a judgment in his favor. He and his friend
Karl Peters were named co-guardians, Johanna excluded. Beethoven
and his circle celebrated what seemed at last to be a final victory. But
the object of these years of struggle, Karl van Beethoven, had his own
life and agenda. To him, Uncle was becoming more a meddlesome nuisance than a guardian. And Karl had his own tricks in how he handled
adults.

Soon after the Appeals Court decree, Fanny Giannatasio and her
family visited Beethoven. "It was the first time we have seen him for a
year," she wrote in her diary. "I fancied he was very glad to see us. He
seemed tolerably well, and at all events, he has a respite from the worries and torment of Karl's mother. It pained me terribly to realize that
all our relations with this highly-gifted being are to a certain extent
ended . . . He made me a present of a new song of his, which gave me
immense pleasure."[93]

The song was *Abendlied unter'm gestirnten Himmel.* It is a vision of
the soul looking up at the starry night sky, where "no fear can torture it
any more, no power can give it orders; with transfigured countenance
it flies up to the heavenly light." Fanny's quietly regretful report of that
evening is the last time she mentions Beethoven in her journal.

29

The Sky Above, the Law Within

THE ROMANTICS SAID a genius is a person of a superhuman order who envisions and embodies worlds grander, more beautiful, more sublime, more terrifying than this one. Indeed Beethoven, by his late years already perceived as the quintessential Romantic genius, lived in another reality. Some territories of that reality were exalted, sublime, incomparably beautiful. Others were misanthropic, delusional, rationally and morally shabby. As an Aufklärer he believed in reason, while in his daily life he increasingly lost himself in unreason.

Still, somehow he never entirely lost himself. To be an artist is to be wholly committed to the products of your imagination. Some products of his imagination did him great harm — in the end, far more harm to him than to anyone else. But they did not wreck his art. It may appear too easy to say that the darkness never polluted the beauty and the beauty never illuminated the darkness, but that seems to have been what it was with him. His worlds contained irresolvable contradictions, warring territories, but he kept the boundaries intact and survived it all.

Toward the end of 1819, when he was still caught up in the legal wrangles over nephew Karl, in a newspaper he read a quotation from

Immanuel Kant that riveted him: "There are two things which raise [KANT] man above himself and lead to eternal, ever-increasing admiration: the moral law within me, and the starry sky above me." These were perhaps the most celebrated words Kant ever wrote — they are inscribed on his tomb. In a conversation book Beethoven condensed this vision to its essence: "'The moral law within us, and the starry sky above us.' Kant!!!"[1]

Like many things that inspire us, these words appeared when Beethoven was ready for them. They resonated with the whole of his life and music and helped point him toward the future. The important works of his middle years, starting with the *Eroica,* were largely humanistic: in rough terms, the conquering hero in the Third Symphony, the heroic individual in the Fifth. The Sixth Symphony and the Mass in C were steps toward a new sacred music, the Sixth more deistic in its sense of nature as divine revelation, the Mass in C a considered but provisional liturgical work. Now in his age, as many people do, Beethoven drew closer to God. As in all other things, he did it on his own terms.

In those words Kant had drawn closer to the divine as well. For him and his time, the starry sky was the external raiment of God, who lives beyond the stars, watching over His perfect universe. As Haydn sang in *The Creation,* "The heavens are telling the glory of God." Kant's philosophy notified humanity that as an infinite being, God was not available to finite human senses or reason, so here on earth we have to work out our happiness and morality for ourselves. As well as a humanistic moralist, Kant was a believer, so his words were personal for him: the moral law within *me,* the starry sky above *me.* For him God did not dictate moral law through scripture; rather the moral sense within each of us resonates with the unknowable but omnipresent divine order. The implication was the same in Beethoven's reverence toward nature as the true scripture, the immediate revelation of divine grace and order. It was partly in that sense that in regard to their work, Haydn and many others of the time referred steadily to the "natural." It was a matter of pursuing the rational and direct and unadorned, and in that way reflecting the divine order of nature.

What seems to have caught Beethoven about Kant's words was

that kind of conception. *The moral law within us, and the starry sky above us.* His obsession with moral imperatives, with the necessity of personal goodness and the iron sense of duty that Kant and his time preached, was in these words unified with God in a radiant interchange stretching between the earth and the heavens. These ideas were going to be central to the *Missa solemnis* Beethoven had been working on for nearly a year now, and the exalted and exalting idea of humanity standing on earth and raising its gaze to the stars was going to be a familiar image in the music he was to write for the rest of his life.

The gulf between Beethoven's music and his life, the exaltation and the darkness, only widened in his age. His projects were more ambitious than ever as he won the court battle over Karl's guardianship and directed his energies from his years-long legal struggles back to composition. In his daily life he remained as harassed, scattered, and earthbound as ever. His illnesses were more serious and prolonged, so more expensive. He was tumbling steadily deeper into debt.

He had long since lost his fees for performing. The yearly stipend from his patrons was not enough to support himself and Karl. Publications and commissions were now a life-and-death matter. In his later years he wrote more letters than ever to publishers and patrons — courting, cajoling, pitching, selling, demanding, complaining. He had become frantic about money, ransacking his trunk for pieces to sell no matter how old or how slight, composing one "trifle" after another in hope of quick cash. This was in part a matter of relentless mathematics: selling publishers the massive works that most concerned him now, a gigantic mass and a gigantic symphony, could not earn him enough to account for the time they cost (though he always maintained a forlorn hope that they would). He had to pay for the big pieces with trifles, and with serious smaller ones like piano sonatas and string quartets.

At least, with the guardianship settled, for the first time in years he could return to a semblance of routine in his work. Now he had a circle of friends influential in ways other than those of the aristocratic patrons he used to cultivate. If these friends could not shower him with money, they were ready to help out in other ways. He remained close to Karl Bernard, editor of the leading Viennese newspaper. Newer to

KANNE

the circle was Friedrich August Kanne, editor of the *Wiener Allgemeine Musikalische Zeitung,* a composer himself, encyclopedically learned, writer of a history of the Catholic Mass, alcoholic, and something of a grand eccentric.[2] Kanne and Beethoven consulted about the mass and about opera librettos; they had an ongoing debate about the emotional qualities of keys, which Beethoven believed in and Kanne did not.[3] That Kanne was becoming an important music critic in Vienna did not hurt.

KARL PETERS

Old friend Karl Peters, one of the first to write in the conversation books, remained in the circle. Beethoven had become close to lawyer Johann Baptist Bach, who helped him through the court case. He had *J B BACH LAWYER* finally befriended Joseph Blöchlinger, head of Karl's school; amid endless discussions of the boy, they often played chess together.[4] Among *JOSEPH BLÖCHLINGER* newer friends and sycophants were music publishers Antonio Diabelli, Sigmund Anton Steiner, and Tobias Haslinger, the latter an amiable young man who worked for Steiner. Beethoven was fond of Haslinger and amused them both with affectionate teasing. Beethoven regularly stopped by Steiner's music shop on the Graben, where he could visit with local musicians and where hopefuls like the young Franz Schubert observed him shyly from a distance.

Nearly all these men (Beethoven had no women confidants now) had some degree of expertise and influence in one area or another; all of them did him favors small and large. On the pages of the conversation books they could speak without worrying about prying ears. Politically they were progressive, which is to say that they hoped someday for the return of an enlightened emperor like Joseph II, or even Napoleon. In May 1820, Bernard wrote, "The whole of Europe is going to the dogs. N[apoleon] should have been let out for ten years." The boyish jokes and naughtiness continued: Beethoven discreetly jots down his admiration for a passing woman's backside; friend Janitschek teases him about trolling for whores and later cries on the page, "I salute you, O Adonis!"; Peters again offers his wife; Beethoven writes down the title of a French book on venereal diseases.[5]

Later in a conversation book, writing in French for privacy, Beethoven gave a sad summary of his old relationship with the teenage Julie Guicciardi, whose parents broke up their courtship (if that is what their relationship actually amounted to): "I was loved by her, and more than her husband ever was . . . She was already his wife before [they immigrated] to Italy — and she sought me weeping, but I rejected her . . . If I had wished to give the strength of my life to that life, what would have remained for the nobler, the better?"[6] With no women available to him now but prostitutes and (if it was not all joking) friends' wives for release, that idea was what he had retreated to, to armor his regrets. He had seized on Karl as someone to love, someone to love him. But with Karl he experienced family life mostly in its troubles, without the consolations of a wife who could understand and forgive him.

The court decision giving him Karl's guardianship was effectively final. Now the boy was largely insulated from his mother at Blöchlinger's boarding school. In summer 1820, Johanna made a last, desperate appeal directly to the emperor, and the official papers survived. They provide a view into how much the authorities in Metternich's police state knew about its citizens. The chief of the Royal Police and the Censor's Office reported to Emperor Franz II, "It is evident that this boy, now 13 years old . . . ran wild to some extent under the influence of his uneconomical mother, who did not have the best reputation. For a year now, at his uncle's expense, he has been in the private school of a certain Blöchlinger . . . His talent and his application are praised, and if he commits many thoughtless and youthful pranks . . . they are ascribed much more to his imprudence, combined with a passionate temperament and the habit of doing violence to obedience and decorum . . . than to ill will."[7] The emperor had plenty of reason to be suspicious of Beethoven — and his whole circle of liberals, for that matter — but he did not assent to Johanna's petition. She gave up trying to get her son back, but she never did lose contact with him. Meanwhile if she had in part lost a son, she had a new, illegitimate daughter for consolation.

Beethoven was desperate over money. Karl accounted for much of the drain, in addition to Beethoven's old carelessness with finances and the expense of spas and medical treatment. He still did not spend on luxuries, though his wine bills were high.[8] His habit of floating two or more flats at the same time still consumed a good deal of his income, likewise servants. His anxiety about money would never abate. Eventually some of his sketch pages were covered by numbers, obsessive financial figuring, written in long columns to be added up since he never learned to multiply. He composed more of the little piano pieces he called bagatelles, "trifles" intended for quick sale. At the same time he fell into the dangerous habit of promising unfinished, sometimes unbegun pieces to publishers who might give him an advance. There were other compromises. In 1819, he had directed Ries in London to try to sell a disjointed *Hammerklavier:* "Should the [*Hammerklavier*] not be suitable for London, I could send another one; or you could also omit the Largo and begin straight away with the Fugue, which is in the last movement, and then the Adagio, and then for the third movement the Scherzo — and omit entirely no. 4 . . . Or you could take just the first movement and Scherzo and let them form the whole sonata."[9]

In April 1820, he sent ten variations on national folk songs, eventually op. 107, to publisher Nikolaus Simrock in Bonn. He asked for 315 florins, telling Simrock, "I am not asking anything more for them since I have composed many of these trifles."[10] In another letter, he offered Simrock the enormous work he had only just set out on: "You will receive the Mass by the end of May or the beginning of June. So please remit the 100 Louis d'or to Herr F[ranz] Brentano, to whom I will send the work." Franz, the businessman husband of Beethoven's old friend (or lover) Antonie Brentano, was serving as middleman for some of his larger transactions.

To help keep the Brentanos on his team, he dedicated the new op. 109 Sonata to Maximiliane, the couple's piano-playing daughter. To Maxe he wrote a letter about it that was both sweet and disingenuous: "A dedication!!!! Well, this is not one of those dedications which are used and abused by thousands of people — it is the spirit which unites the noble and finer people of this earth and which time can never destroy. It is this spirit which . . . calls you to mind and makes me see you still as a child, and likewise your beloved parents, your most excellent and gifted mother, your father imbued with so many truly good and noble qualities."[11] To Franz he wrote, "I would like you to regard this work as a token of my lasting devotion to you and your whole family

— but do not put any wrong construction of this dedication, by fancy-ing that it is a hint to use your influence." Perhaps, but he depended on Franz for his good wishes and, in his service as a go-between, his reputation as a businessman.

Did Beethoven actually believe he would finish the mass this year? His old habit of excessive confidence about his output was accelerating — though at times in earlier years there appeared to be no limits to his productivity. Now if age and physical decline did not slow him down, deafness did. He could no longer work through pieces at the keyboard, so he had painstakingly to go through them note by note. Probably he was still feeling his way with the mass, did not yet envision its full scope. In any case, before long he took to deliberately misleading pub-lishers about works in the pipeline.

To add to his endless annoyances, another portrait painter showed up wanting him to sit still. This one was Joseph Karl Stieler, from Munich. He had been engaged in making pictures of great men, his catches including Goethe (for a painting eventually as famous as his Beethoven). He was also responsible for the notorious Gallery of Beau-ties, portraits of thirty-six women who had captured the eye of King Ludwig I of Bavaria. Stieler was, in other words, a successful artist for the high-placed, appreciated for turning out flattering images.

Stieler's portrait shows Beethoven in a grape arbor, holding a manu-script and pencil.[12] The manuscript is labeled "*Missa solemnis* in D#" (the strange key name was the German indication for D major). Here Beethoven is fierce and indomitable, his head tilting forward so he looks upward past the viewer, rapt in his genius. Stieler tidied up not only his subject's ungovernable hair but also his clothes and his face. This person is a roughly handsome, well-dressed man, which the ac-tual subject was not. For the next two centuries Stieler's painting en-dured as the ultimate Romantic image of Beethoven — which is to say, an icon in the cult of genius.

That spring of 1820, Beethoven sent a note to one of the prime archi-tects of the myth that was forming around him: the critic, composer, and fabulist E. T. A. Hoffmann, whose 1813 articles on the Fifth Sym-phony had placed Beethoven once and for all among the Romantic demigods. Hoffmann's name had come up in the conversation books:

"In the *Phantasie-Stücke* by Hoffmann," somebody wrote, "you are often spoken of." This elicited one of Beethoven's puns based on the meaning of the writer's name: "Hofmann [*sic*] you are no hope-man." By now Hoffmann had reached the summit of his fame with his tales of doppelgängers and automatons and other delirious fantasies. If he had not done so already, Beethoven perused the critic's writings about himself and probably sampled the tales as well, and sent off a letter of thanks. It was a tip of the hat from a living myth to his prime mythologizer: "I am seizing the opportunity . . . to approach a man so full of life and wit as you are — Also you have written about my humble self. Also our weak Herr Starke [another pun: *Stark* = 'strong'] showed me some lines of yours about me in his album. Thus I am given to believe that you take some interest in me. Allow me to say that this from a man with such distinguished gifts as yourself pleases me very much. I wish you everything that is beautiful and good."[13]

Meanwhile Beethoven had seized a new publisher, or rather two related ones. He sold Continental rights to twenty-five Scottish folk songs (op. 108), first arranged for Thomson in Scotland and now revised, to the house of Adolf Schlesinger in Berlin. The publisher's son Moritz ran an allied company in Paris. When the variations were dispatched he sketched some more piano bagatelles, which were a steady concern of his in these days — small pieces to be sold in sets. At the same time he agreed to write three new piano sonatas for Schlesinger. That commitment he kept. Though he was working away at the mass, between this summer and the end of 1821, the only major pieces he completed were the sonatas for Schlesinger, opp. 109–11. All three live among the legends of his late works.

In rural Mödling in the summer of 1820, his various initiatives continued, some of them trivial, some underhanded, some (the piano sonatas) with splendid outcomes. As always he rambled the hills and woods and gorges, sometimes with visitors. As he stood with his editor friend Bernard on a viewpoint looking out over the landscape, Bernard wrote in a conversation book phrases that must have echoed in Beethoven's feelings and fantasies: "One feels quite a different person in the country . . . Let's found an Institute for philology, philanthropy, poetry, and music here in Mödling — and have that cook to cook for us!"[14]

In autumn a Dr. Müller, visiting philologist from Bremen, noted like most visitors that Beethoven went on about "everything, the government, the police, the manners of the aristocracy, in a critical and mocking manner. The police knew it, but left him in peace either because he was a fantastic [i.e., crazy] or because he was a brilliant artistic genius." Likely there was one more reason the police let Beethoven alone: in dealing with an artist adopted by Archduke Rudolph, brother of the emperor, the police had to proceed with caution. If Beethoven was aware that his connection to Rudolph gave him a certain umbrella of protection in a repressive state, he did not appear to notice it. But unlike the fate of so many in Vienna, there was no record he was ever harassed or even visited by the police.

His friendships in these years tended to last, but publishers came and went. Beethoven and his Viennese publisher Steiner, whose house had printed his works great and small since the Seventh and Eighth Symphonies, were growing apart, partly because of Steiner's mounting impatience over the money Beethoven owed him — some 3,000 florins. Beethoven had been stalling Steiner for a long time, and not politely, meanwhile shopping his music elsewhere. The inevitable demand from Steiner to pay up arrived in late 1820: "I am not in a position to lend money without interest; I helped you as a friend in need; I relied upon and believed your word of honor . . . nor have I ever plagued you . . . and must therefore solemnly protest the reproaches made against me."[15] Meanwhile, the folk-song arrangements and variations that had earned Beethoven a steady trickle of income from George Thomson in Scotland dried up, after years of the publisher's entreating him to write more simply. Thomson had done nothing but lose money on Beethoven.

As for Karl, he remained the reasonably good student he had been, even with the increase in his laziness and acting out. If Beethoven had gained any understanding or tolerance regarding normal teenage foolishness, it is not evident in his dealings with his ward. In the summer Karl ran away from boarding school to his mother again. Beethoven wrote him, "Little by little you have become accustomed to horrible deeds . . . Now when you are more than 13 years old, goodness must establish itself anew in you. You should not hate your mother, but you cannot view her as another good mother. This is evident, and as long as you are guilty of further violations against me, you cannot become a good person; that is the same as if you rebelled against your father." The same day he wrote headmaster Blöchlinger detailed directions of what to say to the boy: "Lead back to the pain that he has caused me," and, "[T]he foundation of his moral improvement is to be based upon the recognition of his mother's true nature."[16]

Yet compared to the troubles of the immediate past, both Karl and his mother were going easy on Beethoven. His health was not going easy. In January 1821, he contracted a rheumatic fever that kept him in bed for six weeks with violent pain in his joints.[17] By March he was up and working, but then in July he came down with a jaundice that lasted some two months. This hepatitis was not painful, but he called it "a disease that is extremely loathsome to me." If the illness comes from a liver condition, as his likely did, it can lead to mental confusion and cause fluid to accumulate in the abdominal cavity. By this point Beethoven wore a body belt, "owing to the sensitive condition of my abdomen."[18] In the next few years his liver was going to be his undoing. Debility would come and go, but from this point illness would not relent for one day in carrying him toward his grave.

Beethoven's life in 1821 left relatively few traces in the record. For some reason no conversation books survived from this year, and relatively few letters. There is no extant response from him, for one example, to the passing of Josephine Deym-Brunsvik-Stackelberg, who had been his obsessive love in the first decade of the century and remained a candidate for his Immortal Beloved. Josephine died in Vienna in March after a miserable second marriage had left her alone and childless. Her sister Therese, once Beethoven's vivacious young pupil and now a pious old maid, had resisted their connection with all her influence. Yet when her sister died, Therese wrote in her journal, "If Josephine doesn't suffer punishment [after death] on account of Luigi's woe — his wife! what wouldn't she have made out of this hero!"[19] Did Beethoven feel any comparable regret at Josephine's passing?

But he composed, finishing the new piano sonatas for Schlesinger and adding forests of notes to the mounting pages of *Missa solemnis* sketches. In the summer he went to Baden for the cure, with its elaborate regime of bathing and medication.

This summer the local commissioner of police in Baden, dining with a party, was interrupted by a constable who advised him that they had a tramp in the jail who would not shut up. "He keeps on yelling that he is Beethoven; but he's a ragamuffin, has no hat, an old coat . . . nothing by which he can be identified." The commissioner said he would get to it in the morning. But in the middle of the night a policeman woke him up, saying the disturbance was unbearable. The tramp was demanding that Herr Herzog, a local music director, be called to identify him. Herzog was dragged out of bed and taken to the jail. "That *is* Beethoven!" he exclaimed. Herzog took Beethoven back to his own house and gave him his best room.

As the story emerged, the day before Beethoven had gone out for a walk and, lost in thought, strayed up the towpath of a canal. He kept going until he fell out of his trance and found himself lost and hungry. Trying to figure out where he was and where to find something to eat, he began peering in the windows of houses. This bedraggled Peeping Tom soon caught the attention of the police. "I'm Beethoven!" he told the constable who apprehended him. "Sure, why not?" the constable replied. "You're a tramp. Beethoven doesn't look like this," and hauled him off. Soon the mayor arrived to apologize and provided a state coach to take him back to Baden in style.[20]

Along with his burgeoning creative energy and eccentricity, his duplicitous business schemes also accelerated. In November 1821, having over the past year given his old Bonn friend Simrock repeated assurances that he and only he would have the *Missa solemnis,* he wrote Adolf Schlesinger in Berlin about corrections for the op. 109 Sonata and added, "I am taking this opportunity of writing you on the subject of the Mass about which you inquired. This is one of my greatest works and should you care to publish it, perhaps I might let you have it . . . And now let me ask you to keep this offer secret." He had meanwhile persuaded Franz Brentano, Antonie's husband, to advance him Simrock's offer of 900 florins out of Franz's own pocket. Certainly he did not want it to get around that he had offered the piece unequivocally to two publishers. Here he began a long, shabby game over selling the *Missa solemnis.*

So far he was only double-dealing. Eventually he worked his way up to quintuple-dealing. And eventually his friendship with Franz broke up over the loan, which Beethoven never paid back.[21]

After years of slow and erratic production, the course of 1822 was one of the astonishing periods of Beethoven's life, a creative flowering that would not have seemed possible if he had not done it. He greeted the new year not with optimism but with reports of a painful "gout in the chest." The condition bedeviled him for months. That summer another visitor, John Russell from England, added his impressions to the mounting record:

> Wild appearance . . . eye full of rude energy; his hair, which neither comb nor scissors seem to have visited for years . . . Except when he is among his chosen friends, kindliness or affability are not his characteristics . . . [in a cellar] drinking wine and beer, eating cheese and red herrings, and studying the newspapers . . . he must be humored like a wayward child . . . The moment he is seated at the piano, he is evidently unconscious that there is anything in existence but himself and his instrument; and, considering how very deaf he is, it seems impossible that he should hear all he plays. Accordingly, when playing very *piano,* he often does not bring out a single note . . . The muscles of his face swell, and its veins start out; the wild eye rolls doubly wild; the mouth quivers, and Beethoven looks like a wizard, overpowered by the demons whom he himself has called up.[22]

This account sounds suspiciously Romantic, the equivalent of the genius-scowl in so many Beethoven portraits. Earlier reports had his usual expression impassive most of the time, even when playing — except for the fiery eyes. But maybe in his age and in the isolation of deafness his feelings had made their way to his face.

Another visitor was Friedrich Rochlitz, a poet and writer who had edited Europe's leading musical journal, the *Allgemeine Musikalische Zeitung,* until 1817. Its critics were a frequent target of Beethovenian tirades, but the editor was a fervent if not slavish Beethoven admirer. Rochlitz's recollections of his visits in 1822 shed light less on

Beethoven's personality than on his personal style, his way of being in the world that made him endurable and even sometimes lovable, in spite of everything. He was always thinking, soliloquizing, making phrases when he was not making music: "His delivery was absolutely natural and free of any kind of restraint, and whatever he said was spiced with highly original, naïve judgment and humorous fancies. He impressed me as a man with a rich, aggressive intellect and a boundless, indefatigable power of imagination. He might have been a gifted adolescent who had been cast on a desert island and had there meditated on any experience or learning that he might have accumulated."

Rochlitz enjoyed listening to Beethoven sounding off. There was an ingenuous directness to his rants as he strode around the countryside in his shirtsleeves, his coat slung on a stick carried over his shoulder. "Even his barking tirades, such as those against his Viennese contemporaries, were only explosions of his fanciful imagination and his momentary excitement. They were uttered without any haughtiness, without any feeling of bitterness or resentment, simply blustered out lightly and good humouredly . . . He often showed . . . that to the very person who had grievously injured him, or whom he had just most violently denounced, he would be willing to give his last thaler, should that person need it."[23]

The latter hints that Rochlitz knew he himself was one of the people Beethoven regularly denounced — enough to earn him one of the composer's nicknames: "Mephistopheles," after Goethe's elegant demon.[24] In their last meeting Rochlitz noted that Beethoven was suddenly dressed cleanly and elegantly — he had begun a campaign to upgrade his wardrobe.[25]

Another visitor of 1822 was, as Beethoven knew painfully well, the only composer in the world who in many quarters put him in the shade. Gioachino Rossini's operas were as wildly popular in Vienna as they were in the rest of Europe. Stendhal, who published a biography of Rossini in 1824, declared, "During the last twelve years, there is no man who had been more frequently the subject of conversation, from Moscow to Naples, from London to Vienna, from Paris to Calcutta."[26] The Italian's first visit to Vienna in April raised the city's ongoing Rossini craze to a frenzy. Every important drawing room in town contended for his presence.

Beethoven and his circle, including Karl, regularly took snipes at this rival. "A pretty talent and pretty melodies by the bushel," Beethoven said. As for Rossini's celebrated facility, "His music suits the frivolous and sensuous spirit of the age, and his productivity is so great that he needs only as many weeks to write an opera as the Germans need years."[27] Both quips show that Beethoven had a good sense of the man who between 1815 and 1823 wrote twenty operas full of tunes that stick in the ears.

Rossini admired Beethoven's piano sonatas and quartets, as well as the *Eroica*. He was thirty in 1822, Beethoven fifty-one. The details of their meeting are hazy; it appears that publisher Dominico Artaria first brought Rossini to Beethoven, but he was sick that day and they did not succeed. A second attempt gained him entrance. Rossini was stunned by two things in that visit: the squalor of the rooms and the warmth with which Beethoven greeted this rival who he knew was eclipsing him. There was no conversation; Beethoven could not make out a word Rossini said.[28] But Beethoven congratulated him for *The Barber of Seville*: "It will be played as long as Italian opera exists." He had also looked over some of the serious operas. "Never try to write anything else but *opera buffa*," he continued. "Any other style would do violence to your nature." After a short meeting he sent him off with, "Write many more *Barbers*!"

Rossini left in tears. That night he was the prize guest of a party at Prince Metternich's. He pleaded with the assembled aristocrats, saying something must be done for "the greatest genius of the age." They brushed him off. Beethoven is crazy, misanthropic, they said. His misery is his own doing.[29]

In February 1822, Beethoven sent off the second two of the three piano sonatas Schlesinger had commissioned, opp. 110 and 111. Op. 109 was already engraved. Two months later Schlesinger got a revised finale for op. 111. In fact, Beethoven made a revised final version of one movement in each of the three sonatas.[30]

The last of Beethoven's thirty-two piano sonatas wrote the final chapters in his epochal series for the keyboard: his equivalent of *The Well-Tempered Clavier*. Here the divide between his painful and increasingly dismaying life and his increasingly spiritual art reaches an apogee. The last three sonatas mark an end point of his evolution in every dimension: technical, pianistic, expressive, spiritual. Each a distinct individual, the three still share a concern with counterpoint, a juxtaposition of extremes, a climactic finale, and an extraordinary variety combined with extraordinary integration. They combine a constant attention to minutiae in the developing of ideas while often giving the impression of rhapsodic improvisation. At other times they have an almost childlike simplicity and directness.

In character they range from earthy and comedic to ethereal and otherworldly. To repeat: Beethoven rarely compromised the technical for the expressive, or the expressive for the technical. In his late music he still submitted to the old forms established by his forebears, but now the forms are often sunk beneath the surface, still functioning but not breaking the impression of music unfolding in rhapsodic freedom. In the last sonatas, the technical and the expressive together reach an end point unlike anything before or since, perhaps at the end of what music can be and do — as can be said of *The Well-Tempered Clavier* as well.

The first movement of the E Major Sonata, op. 109, begins with a blithe, lilting tune marked Vivace ma non troppo. On an open harmony, as if in midthought, the music veers into a mysterious and improvisatory Adagio espressivo, which serves as the second theme of a tightly compressed sonata form:

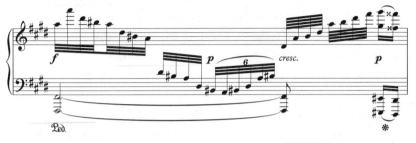

The leading idea apparently began as a bagatelle written for a piano anthology put together by his friend Friedrich Starke. Another friend, Franz Oliva, suggested that Beethoven use this idea for the commissioned sonata.[31] Now that theme begins the work on an artless and intimate note. In shape, dimensions, and impact, little op. 109 is the anti-*Hammerklavier*. Its opening fillip will be a largely constant presence, its "Scotch snap" rhythm contrasting with the pealing, rhythmically amorphous arpeggios of the second theme. The mercurial character established on the first page will persist throughout. The second theme flows directly (without repeating the exposition) into the development, in which the blithe opening idea becomes gradually vehement; that character phases imperceptibly into the recap. After a much-changed second theme, a quiet and touching coda suggests a joining of the themes. With a *fortissimo* and *prestissimo* eruption, the E-minor second movement breaks out with a driving, fiery-unto-alarming tarantella.[32]

Then comes a variation movement for the finale, the theme a solemnly beautiful sarabande, one of the long-breathed themes that exalt Beethoven's late music.[33] It is marked "Songful, with the most heartfelt expression." Haydn and Mozart had used variations as inner movements of sonatas, even occasionally as a first movement. Now Beethoven lifted variations (as in the *Eroica*) to a weight and finality beyond which nothing needed to be said in a work.[34] In keeping with what came before in the sonata, these variations have mercurial changes of speed and texture and character, from introspective to jovial to Baroquely contrapuntal.

In the final variation the music gathers into a shimmering texture of trills, conjuring something on the order of a divine radiance — say, Kant's starry sky. The trills gather slowly to an ecstatic climax, then the finale concludes with a simple recall of the theme, the effect of which summons a future poet's line that we return from a journey to where we began and know the place for the first time.[35]

All the late music was to take somewhere between decades and a century to emerge fully into the repertoire, free of questions of Beethoven's sanity and mutterings of the harm that deafness did to his work. In a time long distant from his, because of its warmth and lyricism, the Sonata in A-flat Major, op. 110, became the most popular of the late sonatas.

It begins with an almost childlike theme of surpassing tenderness, a voice clearly Beethovenian but never quite heard in the world before. To the tempo Moderato is added "songful and very expressive."[36] There follow four measures of a soft chordal theme marked "with amiability," then another expansive and beautiful melody that varies and expands the opening. (As in op. 26, internal variations in the themes foreshadow a later variation movement.) As in op. 109, the songful beginning gives way to rippling arpeggios, but here they are warm, and that warmth continues into the throbbing second theme. Except for a few bars of *forte* at the beginning of that second theme, the whole movement is soft, *piano* to *pianissimo*.

Here is an example of the capricious surface of much of the late music: from measure 30 there is a high-register, exquisite theme of two bars that is varied in the next two bars; then comes a slow shimmer of six beats, three bars of transition; then the second theme proper sings in the low register for three bars before giving way to another little new idea, then another. There is a sense of the composer picking up an idea, playing with it, then dropping it for a new one equally beautiful, like a child putting down a toy and reaching for another. Yet, unified by inner motifs, the kaleidoscopic train of melodies and textures and feelings does not fall apart but rather flows and sings ceaselessly. Beethoven the consummate master of form and continuity seems now to have the ability to go from anywhere to virtually anywhere else and make it work (a quality he shares with Mozart).

He continued to think of himself not just as a *Komponist* but as a *Tondichter,* a tone poet. The late sonatas and quartets are the distilled essence of his Poetic style, when the larger narrative and larger formal patterns are covered over by an intimate involvement with the moment — shifting ideas and shifting emotions, approaching at times the effect of a stream of consciousness. In the first movement, after that parade of some six distinct ideas in the course of a minute, suddenly without a repeat we begin the short development. It gives way almost undetectably to the recapitulation, which is transformed in its own development, its diaphanous arpeggios wafting over the whole of the keyboard.

From tender lyricism to farce: for the second movement a rambunctious two-beat scherzo based on two German folk songs — first, "My cat has had kittens," second and more intriguing, "I'm a slob, you're a slob." Another instant change of mood: a slow movement on the order of an operatic recitative and arioso, the beginning indescribably sorrowful, then a long-arched arioso in A-flat minor (and 12/16 time) marked "plaintive song."[37] Here is music rising from Beethoven's own sorrow to become universal, what the Romantics called *Weltschmerz,* "world-pain." It sinks to a whisper and a *pianissimo* pause.

The finale is fugal, the main subject based on the opening theme of the first movement. While the fugues in earlier sonatas were mostly robust unto aggressive, none more so than the *Hammerklavier,* this one flows like a choral work. As it reaches a climax comes another one of those startling but somehow inevitable turns that mark the late music: the fugue abruptly falls to pieces and we find ourselves back in the third-movement arioso, now in G minor, more devastated than before. After its gasping, sobbing song, it too seems to dissolve, and we return softly to another fugue, its theme the inversion of the first one. Its opening is marked "little by little coming back to life." The technique of thematic inversion, for centuries a staple of formal counterpoint, here is made into intense drama and emotion.[38] Soon the fugue theme returns triumphantly right side up, and the music gathers strength to the rippling arpeggios of the end.[39]

More than ever, the late sonatas seem to survey the entirety of life in one vision, from tragic to earthy to exalted, often shifting in the blink of an eye — just like Beethoven's own emotional life. That pattern is distilled further in the next sonata.

Beethoven may or may not have intended the two-movement op. 111 in C Minor to be his last piano sonata, but there is no question that it stands as a summation and apotheosis of the man and composer, of the late style, of the furthest potentials of expression in tone.

The overall form of the first movement is a Maestoso introduction and an Allegro that unites fugue and sonata form in yet another singular way. It is also the last appearance of Beethoven's "C-minor mood," with the intense-unto-demonic qualities that implies. On a sketch page for the movement he copied out fugue subjects from Mozart's Requiem and Haydn's early F Minor String Quartet.[40] So op. 111 is at once a return to models, a summation, and a radical reconception.

The introduction begins with pealing, ambiguous diminished chords, the effect recalling the introduction to the *Pathétique* — twenty-five years of growing and suffering later. That gives way to a low, snarling trill, then a roaring, striding C-minor theme breaks out. It starts, stops, stutters, trails off, sounding like a fugue subject that cannot find its footing, that struggles to become a fugue — which it finally achieves, briefly, on a variant of the theme. After a tender hint of a second theme and a repeat of the exposition, the music falls into another short but furious fugue in the development.[41]

In Baroque terms, that first movement of the C Minor is a sort of prelude leading to a sort of fugue. The movement proper, marked Allegro con brio ed appassionato ("fast and with fire and passion") rages to its end largely on the opening motif, sometimes varied and fragmented, most of it loud until a calming coda that seems to enfold the whole of the movement while preparing the next. The tempo is constantly in flux, slowing, speeding, lurching. This movement is the anti–opp. 109 and 110. Call it a representation of the turbulent, the disjointed, the furious: the manic, unheroic earthly.

The answer, perhaps Beethoven's ultimate answer, is transcendence. From furious and fragmented to a poignant song that seems to stop time in its course. The movement is labeled "Arietta," the tempo Adagio molto semplice e cantabile — very simply and songfully. It is as if C major were discovered for the first time, like a revelation. As in the op. 109 finale, here are variations on a simple and profound theme, but variations beyond any by anybody else: an unbroken flow that gradually increases in speed, by the third variation reaching a swirling, rhythmic gaiety. The music rises and speeds further, reaching magical shimmering realms high on the keyboard, until finally and unforgettably, the piano is alight with triple trills.

At the coda a specter of the original melody returns and with it the trills, the uncanny celestial light that shimmers on and on, finally making a slow descent back to earth and a simple conclusion.[42] These last pages are music beyond words, beyond poetry and philosophy, almost beyond earthly life, but encompassing them all.

In these incomparable pieces Beethoven largely left behind not only the heroic style of his middle music but also the heroic ideal, the dream of happiness bestowed from above by benevolent despots like Joseph II or conquerors like Napoleon — or by revolutions. In the late music power is overcome by tenderness and spirituality, narrative trumped by poetry.

Here then is his Poetic style. As with the Heroic style of his middle years, "poetic" describes some but not all of the music of the period, but it can be called the central current. In the *Eroica* Beethoven gave the responsibility for creating a new world to the conquering hero. Now in his mind the road to happiness, to Elysium, to the perfected society, has become inward, within the heart and soul of each man and woman.

Business under God's sky was a different matter. Beethoven had always been a shrewd and sharp dealer of his wares, but now his desperation over finances and his estrangement from reality, including the reality

Dos INESS

of his own actions, took him past any reasonable moral and ethical line — though it never shook his treasured but increasingly hazy sense of his own goodness. Again, though, part of his desperation was that works like the *Diabelli* Variations and especially the *Missa solemnis* could never pay him back for the time they cost. Any prospective publisher knew that bringing out the mass was going to be a money-losing proposition for many years to come, and the only reason to do it was for the prestige of bringing out what Beethoven was calling his magnum opus.

Another element of his dealings in the next years was that brother Johann had begun seeing to his interests. In the middle of 1822, Beethoven did what he could to reconcile with Johann, whose wife Therese he had long detested (not entirely without reason). Ludwig wrote Johann in May:

> I have made inquiries about apartments . . . the scheme [of living to-gether] would enable us both to save a good deal . . . I have nothing against your wife. I only hope that she will realize how much could be gained for you too by your living with me . . . Please, let us have peace. God grant that the most natural bond, the bond between brothers, may not again be broken in an unnatural way. In any case my life will certainly not last very much longer . . . owing to my indisposition which has now lasted for three and a half months [the "gout in the chest"] I am very sensitive and irritable . . . Away with everything that cannot promote my object, which is, that I and my good Karl may settle down to a kind of life that is particularly necessary and more suitable to me.[43]

Beethoven had, of course, a great deal against Johann's wife, and Therese soon gave him cause for further outrage. The idea of the brothers living together was absurd, and it appears Johann understood that. Still, they drew closer, for a while lived next door to each other in Vienna when Johann was wintering at the house of his baker brother-in-law.[44] This brother prosperous from the pharmacy trade began to advise Ludwig again and to carry on some dealings with publishers — just as their late brother Carl used to do but this time with better results.

Having bought his mansion in Gneixendorf, Johann had begun to play the man of property and leisure, but he seems to have fooled no one. Nephew Karl opined in a conversation book that while Johann might be "worldly, money-grubbing, and vain," he still had a genuine desire to help.[45] Johann had been kind to Karl, enough to arouse Ludwig's suspicion that his brother wanted the guardianship for himself.

Gerhard von Breuning, the son of Beethoven's old Bonn friend Stephan, remembered Johann cutting an outlandish figure, with his bony physique and out-of-plumb features, his clothes an attempt at elegance including white gloves that were always too long for his fingers, so the ends dangled. He was often seen in the Prater park joining the procession of the fashionable in his fancy carriage, sometimes with two liveried servants on board. "Everybody thinks him a fool," Count Moritz Lichnowsky wrote in a conversation book. "We call him the Chevalier . . . all the world says of him that his only merit is that he bears your name." Certainly Johann was proud of his connection to his famous brother. He attended concerts of Ludwig's music during which he applauded in his flapping gloves and attempted to shout the loudest bravos.[46]

At least partly as a result of Johann's advice, in 1822 Beethoven started promising the mass to a row of publishers. The year before, Nikolaus Simrock in Bonn had put his payment for it on reserve with Franz Brentano. In May Beethoven wrote Brentano, "The Mass will be with you in Frankfurt [for Simrock] at the end of next <u>month</u> at the latest." He had meanwhile offered the mass to Schlesinger in Berlin and now — along with smaller pieces — to C. F. Peters in Leipzig as well. Beethoven was at first uneasy about making the Peters offer, but Johann told him, "That's business."[47]

C. F. Peters aspired to have new Beethoven works in his catalog, and the mass seemed like a prestigious start. So began months of machinations by both of them. Since Beethoven acknowledged that he had shown the piece to others, Peters's main device in pushing his case was to run down the competition. He wrote Beethoven that Steiner "has dealt unfaithfully with me and has repaid my friendship with ingratitude."[48] In this he was surely playing on Beethoven's break with Steiner, who in turn advised Peters that Beethoven was "absolutely not to be dealt with."

When it came to the publishers Adolf Schlesinger in Berlin and his son Moritz in Paris, things got nastier. Shortly before he assured Simrock that he would have the mass in his hands in another month, Beethoven had written Adolf Schlesinger, "As to the Mass I have already agreed to let you have the work itself <u>together with the pianoforte arrangement</u> for an honorarium of 650 Reichsthaler in Prussian currency."[49] Knowing it had been offered to Schlesinger, Peters heatedly wrote Beethoven that "a Christian Mass composed by a Beethoven cannot come into the hands of a Jew," above all not "this Jew [Schlesinger], who is nowhere respected."[50]

With that cue, Beethoven responded to Peters in kind: soon after offering the mass to Schlesinger, Beethoven wrote Peters, "I <u>agree to give</u> you the Mass together with the pianoforte arrangement for — 1000 [florins] . . . You will receive a careful copy of the score by the end of July . . . In no circumstances will Schlesinger ever get <u>anything more from me,</u> because he too has played me a Jewish trick."[51] But Beethoven had his own tricks. Instead of the mass, whose final score was well in the future, Beethoven assembled a stack of lesser pieces to send to Peters: three small lieder including *Der Kuss,* more or less finished in 1798, six bagatelles, all but one from 1802 and earlier, and four marches for military band.[52] He touched up all the pieces before sending them, so it was some time before Peters got them.[53]

Beethoven had not needed much prodding to become disgusted with the Schlesingers. He wrote Moritz in Paris, "Apparently I am to have several unpleasant experiences with you and your father." They had fumbled his intended dedication of op. 110 to Antonie Brentano (it went to Archduke Rudolph), and he believed Moritz had shortchanged him by a dozen florins in the payment for opp. 110 and 111: "such insulting niggardliness, the like of which I have <u>never</u> experienced."[54]

Was Beethoven a habitual anti-Semite, as Peters seems to have been, in common with a large percentage of Germans? The record shows only a few Beethoven cracks about Jews, and the foregoing is one of the worst of them — in some ways still worse because it was done cynically to abet his courtship of a manifestly anti-Semitic publisher. Racial and ethnic bigotry was general in those days; another example appears in a Mozart letter to his father: "A charlatan, like all Italians." In the end, there is no indication that Beethoven had any more animus toward Jews than he had to the aristocracy, to the Viennese, to much of the rest of humanity. In any case, he kept submitting works to both Schlesingers, even after Moritz pirated some bagatelles.[55]

Likewise he kept dangling the mass in front of more publishers. Peters had offered 1,000 florins. Three weeks after receiving that offer, Beethoven wrote Artaria in Vienna that for the same fee, "All I can do is to give you the preference."[56] Why would he double-deal like this for the same fee? Perhaps because he owed Artaria money and he hoped he could fob off Peters with the "trifles" he intended to send.

By this point, Beethoven had unequivocally promised the mass to Simrock, Schlesinger, Peters, and Artaria, assuring them that the score would be immediately forthcoming. Those four houses would not be the last he courted and double-crossed, and in the end none of them got the piece.

Toward the end of 1822, he tried another and yet more dishonest gambit to keep publishers on the line. Now he said there were actually two masses under way; soon he was claiming three. To Peters in November: "In regard to the Mass things are as follows: I had already finished one long ago but I have not yet finished another . . . I do not yet know which of these two Masses you will receive."[57] By the "long ago" work he did not mean the already-published Mass in C but indeed the *Missa solemnis,* still not finished at all. The other mass he wrote of, which eventually metamorphosed into two, was bogus. True, for a while he did float the idea of writing a mass expressly for Franz II, and for it he made inquiries about the emperor's taste in masses. A few, very few, sketches survived for a mass in C-sharp minor.

To what extent do these promises represent deliberate lies, as opposed to an excess of optimism? Beethoven probably hoped to write two more masses, one of them for the emperor. If one wants to be generous, one can say that in his desperation he took the intention for the reality.

In spring 1823, an outraged Peters, having advanced Beethoven money, not only gave up on the mass but rejected all the miniatures he had received, starting with the bagatelles: "I have had several of them played but not one person wants to believe me that these are by you." He wanted, he wrote Beethoven heatedly, only "exceptionally" good pieces.[58] Beethoven was perhaps boggled by this response, since publishers were always plaguing him to write simpler and easier things.[59] Yet he doggedly kept after Peters. In the end nothing came of their years of negotiations. At some point, very apropos, Beethoven confessed in a letter to Peters, "Everything I do apart from music is badly done and stupid."[60]

Amid all this frustration, busywork, and chicanery, he kept composing and retained some of his high spirits. He wrote Johann gaily in autumn 1822, "Two women singers called on us today and as they absolutely insisted on being allowed to kiss my hands and as they were decidedly pretty, I preferred to offer them my mouth to kiss." The two singers were probably Henriette Sontag and Karoline Unger, both of them teenagers at the time, both of them to be involved in the premiere of his new symphony.[61] Later he passed on to both of them some wine given to him by an admirer. A friend reported that after drinking it, Sontag "vomited fifteen times the night before last . . . With Unger the effect was in the opposite direction. What a pair of heroines! . . . Both beauties send you their regards and ask for a better and more wholesome wine in future."[62]

Work continued on the mass and he made some sketches toward ninth and tenth symphonies. In early September he got word that the director of the newly built Josephstadt Theatre wanted him to adapt for its opening the *Ruins of Athens* incidental music, written for a similar opening in Pest and quite unknown in Vienna. Beethoven agreed. While a lyricist came up with new words for the existing vocal music, transferring the story from Hungary to Vienna, Beethoven mounted one of his old-style marathons. In a couple of weeks or so he wrote a new chorus, a ballet segment, and an overture he called *Die Weihe des Hauses* (The Consecration of the House) — having decided the old *Ruinin von Athens* Overture would not do for this occasion.[63] The grand and rather Handelian *Weihe des Hauses,* with stately trombone parts in the introduction and a fugue in the Allegro, showed that he still had his old professional skill at writing polished and effective occasional pieces in a hurry. For the premiere on October 3 the hall was packed with listeners primed for a new Beethoven sensation, but with the deaf composer directing and the orchestra uncertain, the response was muted.[64]

From that performance came an equally mixed result. Leading the violins in the house orchestra was Anton Felix Schindler. Then twenty-seven, he had played violin since childhood but studied philosophy and law at the University of Vienna. Schindler kept performing as an amateur, and in that capacity may have first met Beethoven in 1814 and occasionally encountered him thereafter — among the opportunities being the time he spent working as a clerk for Beethoven's lawyer and friend Johann Baptist Bach.

By the time the new theater opened in 1822, Schindler was accomplished enough to go professional and became concertmaster of the orchestra.[65] In his person Schindler was gaunt unto sepulchral, in manner dour and pretentious. He was an able musician and ambitious in other ways as well. By his own later account, he served as a confidant and unpaid secretary of Beethoven from 1819 to the end. Schindler's entries in the conversation books seem to bear out that claim.

But among Schindler's less admirable qualities was extravagant fabrication, most of it designed to convince the world and history that he was far closer and more indispensable to Beethoven, and for far longer, than he actually was. The first extant authentic letter from Beethoven to Schindler is dated June 1822, and that probably marks the actual beginning of their association. After Beethoven died, Schindler forged entries from himself in the conversation books dated before 1822 and some others dated afterward (having appropriated the books from the rooms where Beethoven died). He also invented any number of stories of things Beethoven said and did in those years. It is Schindler who reported that Beethoven said of the Fifth Symphony opening, "Thus fate knocks at the door!" and of the background of the op. 31, no. 2, piano sonata, "Read [Shakespeare's] *The Tempest.*" Both stories entered legend. Beethoven may have said them, he may not have.

Schindler went on to write the first major Beethoven biography, a work of the most remarkable mendacity and biographical incompetence. Hardly anything in it can be trusted on its own — a maddening predicament for future historians, because surely some of it is true. In later years, poet Heinrich Heine described Schindler as "a long black beanpole with a horrible white necktie and the expression of a funeral director," and noted that his business card read, *L'ami de Beethoven.*[66] Beethoven's old Bonn friend Franz Wegeler had some dealings with Schindler and detested him. Ferdinand Ries wrote in a letter, "From beginning to end he acted like an old house-nag . . . and wrote me a witty, dumb letter to cover it up. He can go to hell."[67] Over and over in their relations, Beethoven echoed that sentiment in one form and another.

Yet Schindler succeeded in attaching himself to Beethoven. As a sign of that, he began to acquire Beethovenian nicknames. He was *Lumpenkerl* ("Ragamuffin"), *Hauptlumpenkerl* ("Chief Ragamuffin"), *Samothracian Lumpenkerl* (referring to the Mysteries of Samothrace, i.e., member of an occult order). Most tellingly, Schindler was "Papageno," after Mozart's bumbling sidekick in *Die Zauberflöte.*[68] Clearly Beethoven understood Schindler's character. One did not have to be paranoid to dislike and distrust him.

The problem was that Beethoven badly needed an unpaid secretary and general factotum of the kind he had long relied on. Franz Oliva had filled that role for years before he left for Russia in 1820. Beethoven's longtime helper Baron Zmeskall was incapacitated with gout.[69] Brother Johann did a few services, but he had an estate far from town and an unfortunate family to occupy him. Karl helped out increasingly, but he was young and occupied with his studies. Schindler saw his chance, and he took it. He began his connection to Beethoven as the archetypal hanger-on. He ended by making Beethoven his career. In Schindler, Beethoven saw somebody prepared to jump at his beck and call. In Beethoven, Schindler saw his fortune and his immortality.

At least two good things can be said of Anton Schindler. He was a faithful errand boy to Beethoven for two or three of the last years, and Beethoven made good use of him — including borrowing money from him. And if Schindler put words in Beethoven's mouth, they were sometimes astute words. Schindler was an able musician and had good instincts about Beethoven's work — instincts that also illustrate the time's attitudes toward music. Whether Beethoven actually said "Thus fate knocks at the door" is unknowable, but as a succinct metaphor regarding the first movement of the Fifth Symphony, it survived because it could hardly be bettered.

By the middle of 1822, Beethoven's creative juices were flowing as they had not for a decade. He was about to return to the *Diabelli* Variations, begun in 1819. In July he wrote to Ferdinand Ries in London with his usual mix of affection, flattery, and business: "Have you any idea what fee the Harmony Society [he means the Philharmonic] would offer me for a grand symphony? I am still toying with the idea of going to London, provided my health permits it . . . You would find in me the just critic of my dear pupil who has now become a great master."[70] He already had some sketches toward two new symphonies. This small inquiry among many other schemes was going to have great consequences for Beethoven and for his art.

In July he wrote brother Johann, "As to my health, I feel better. For the last few days I have had to drink Johannesbrunnen water and take the powders four times a day; and now I am to go to Baden and take 30 baths . . . The Cardinal Archduke is here and I go to him twice a week. I have no hope of generous treatment or money, I admit. But I am on such a good, familiar footing with him that it would hurt me exceedingly not to be pleasant to him. Besides I do believe that his apparent niggardliness is not his fault."[71] A week later he asked "Most Excellent Little Brother! High and mighty landowner!" for a loan. He noted the 3,000 florins that he owed Steiner; the publisher was pushing him to pay up or make a deal for his complete works. Beethoven did not want to agree to that idea until Steiner canceled the debt. Having dealt with Beethoven, the publisher was not foolish enough to agree to that proposal. Karl, who wrote out the letter to Johann, ended, "I secretarius, embrace you too with all my heart and hope to see you again soon."[72] Karl was a sometime secretary for his uncle now, and to the job brought his fluency in French and English.

Throughout Beethoven's career, all the schemes and machinations on which he spent so much of his energy only occasionally bore fruit. Much of the time, the things that turned out to be important in his work were opportunities that fell in his lap. Another of those arrived in November 1822, in a letter from Prince Nicolai Galitzin in St. Petersburg. He was a cellist married to a pianist, and a Beethoven zealot. "As much a passionate amateur in music as a great admirer of your talent," he wrote, "I take the liberty of writing to you to ask if you would consent to compose one, two, or three new quartets."[73]

Here was a commission that arrived out of the blue that happened to be in tune with projects Beethoven wanted to do — he had already been working on a quartet, his first since the F Minor of 1810. Galitzin may have been inspired by the presence in St. Petersburg of Beethoven's champion Ignaz Schuppanzigh. If so, it added a chapter to the violinist's glory in history.[74] By the end of 1823, when he agreed to compose the three quartets for Galitzin, after more than a decade of creative searching, moneygrubbing, and comparative loose ends, Beethoven had in the pipeline most of the monumental works that were to occupy his last years: *Missa solemnis,* Ninth Symphony, *Diabelli* Variations, and now the set that came to be called the *Galitzin* Quartets.

Meanwhile he had agreed without enthusiasm to an offer of composing an oratorio for the Boston Handel and Haydn Society. He was pleased that his reputation had reached North America but no happier with this oratorio project than he had been with the one from the Gesellschaft der Musikfreunde in Vienna. Traditional oratorios did not inspire him. Neither piece would get even begun. In regard to the Boston offer he wrote in a conversation book, "I cannot write what I should like best to write, but that which the pressing need of money obliges me to write. This is not to say that I write only for money — when this period is past I hope to write what for me and for art is above all — Faust."[75]

With the *Missa solemnis* nearly done and two new symphonies still in the speculative stage, his supreme ambition had turned toward Goethe's towering drama of human ambition and frailty (no one except perhaps Goethe knew that the second half of *Faust* was yet to come). More immediately, Beethoven was interested in returning to opera. There had been an acclaimed revival of *Fidelio* in Vienna the previous year, and the Kärntnertor Theater wanted a new opera from him.

That 1822 performance marked the debut in the role of another of the first great Leonores, soprano Wilhelmine Schröder-Devrient, who was then seventeen. In a memoir she recalled her terror when Beethoven asked to take over the direction. She recalled the spectacle at the dress rehearsal: "With a bewildered face and unearthly inspired eyes, waving his baton back and forth with violent motions, he stood in the midst of the performing musicians and didn't hear a note!" She continued, "With each number, our courage dwindled further, and I felt as though I were watching one of Hoffmann's fantastic figures appear before me." Finally, inevitably, the orchestra fell apart and house *Kapellmeister* Umlauf had to tell him it was not going to work. At the performance the next evening, the singer saw Beethoven sitting behind the conductor, following the performance with his fierce gaze as if he were trying to hear it by force of will.[76]

The *Allgemeine Musikalische Zeitung* kept music lovers apprised of Beethoven's doings. In May 1822, the paper reported, "Our Beethoven seems to be becoming more receptive to music again, which he has shunned almost like a misogynist since his worsening hearing ailment. He has improvised masterfully a few times in a social gathering to everyone's delight and proved that he still knows how to handle the instrument with power, joy, and love. Hopefully the world of art will see the most exquisite fruits spring forth from these welcome changes."[77] No one could have had any idea of how lavish those fruits would be.

The year 1823 arrived with little to nothing of political importance happening around Europe. It remained that way for the rest of the decade, a testament to how thoroughly governments, above all in German lands, had shut down dissent, freedom of the press and of assembly, and as much as possible had drawn boundaries around speech, imagination, thought itself. In such times, instrumental music remained the only truly free art (only in the next century would demagogues address that matter as well). From the 1780s on, a generation had been inspired and troubled and devastated by a wave of revolution and war. That wave had crested and retreated. For artists, where was left to go but inward?

Despite his vocal hatred for the Metternich regime, Beethoven continued to go about his business without interference, his main order of business still taking the *Missa solemnis* to market. His first extant letter to Anton Schindler the previous June had included, "Please be so kind as to send me both the German and the French invitations to subscribe to the Mass." He had come up with a new scheme for getting money out of this unwieldy work: he would offer subscriptions to crowned heads, high aristocracy, any person or organization in Europe and Russia willing to part with the money. Each subscriber was to receive a deluxe hand-copied score, not made by the composer but autographed by him. His own final score was now getting done — though he tinkered with details for months to come.

It was an entirely legitimate idea, but to bring it off required further dissimulation. Beethoven had to assure his potential subscribers that the mass would not be published in the near future, if at all, while at the same time keeping his row of publishers on the hook. He wrote the subscription pitch letters himself, each carefully crafted for its recipient including lavish helpings of flattery. For this initiative he had plenty of incentive. His debts had gotten to the point that in early 1823 he cashed in one of his eight bank shares, which had been sacred, not to be touched, intended as a bequest for Karl. But he had to keep his creditors at bay. Publisher Steiner and a tailor had threatened to sue (the latter from Beethoven's recent campaign to upgrade his threadbare wardrobe). The 1,250 florins he claimed from the bank share did not all go to his debt, however — he needed some of it for the expenses of copying the enormous mass scores for the subscribers.[78] In March he formally made Karl his heir. From that point, no matter how desperate he was, he did not touch the remaining seven shares.

His pitch letters went to every acquaintance who was highly placed or knew somebody who was. He kept Schindler, Johann, and Karl busy collecting names and information and running chores. The conversation books buzzed with advice and plans among his circle. In February he wrote Goethe, telling him of his *Calm Sea and Prosperous Voyage* setting and asking humbly for any comment: "Indeed your criticism, which might almost be regarded as the very essence of truth, would be extremely welcome to me, for I love truth more than anything . . . How highly would I value a general comment from you on the composing of music or on setting your poems to music!" He went on to ask Goethe to propose to the Weimar court a subscription to the mass.[79] At that moment the titan of German letters was seventy-three and dangerously ill, his attention occupied by fever and delirium. Goethe recovered in the summer, but he never responded to Beethoven's letter.[80]

Beethoven wrote Carl Zelter in Berlin, Goethe's longtime musical adviser and now director of the celebrated Singakademie, asking him to put in a word with the Prussian court and suggesting that much of the mass could be done "almost entirely a la capella" — an absurd idea (the Singakademie performed only a cappella works).[81] Having just been named a member of the Royal Swedish Music Academy, Beethoven used that honor as part of a pitch to Karl XIV, the king of Sweden. Years before, the king had made Beethoven's acquaintance when he was Jean Bernadotte, an officer in Napoleon's army and disastrous French ambassador to Vienna. No offer came from Sweden.

Beethoven knew the secretary of the Privy Council of the Prussian court, Friedrich Duncker, author of the play *Leonore Prohaska*, to which Beethoven had contributed incidental music in 1815. In a long letter he gave Duncker details of his latest illnesses, complained of the expenses his nephew caused him, then got to the point with a touch of philosophy: "Although a man may find his greatest happiness in constantly looking upwards, yet in the end he too is obliged to pay attention to his immediate necessities . . . Well, I am now returning to the grand solemn Mass . . . which could also be performed as an oratorio." The Prussian king did smile on a subscription.

As he started thinking about the actualities of performance,

Beethoven began to promote the idea that the mass could be performed outside church, like an oratorio. This was a new conception for
liturgical pieces, and it was being done increasingly around Europe.
Though there were no reports of Beethoven attending a Mass in his
adulthood, surely he understood at some point that the *Missa solemnis* had grown beyond anything imaginable within a sacred service, so
secular venues were his best hope for performance.

By the end of his subscription campaign he had sent out about two
dozen proposals. The asking price for each score was 50 ducats, about
250 florins, of which some 85 went for copying. The legwork done by
his nephew and friends was, of course, free. In the end he sold ten
subscriptions, for a net profit of around 1,650 florins. Combined with
the eventual selling price of 1,000 florins from a publisher, his net for
the mass amounted to something less than three years of a lower-level
civil servant's income for his four years of labor. Among the subscribers were Tsar Alexander of Russia, the kings of Prussia and Denmark,
the grand dukes of Darmstadt and Tuscany, the Cäcelia Verein chorus in Frankfurt, and Prince Galitzin in St. Petersburg—the last of
whom actually arranged the premiere of the mass, that and a second
one in the city the only complete performances of it in Beethoven's lifetime. Louis XVIII of France not only subscribed but sent Beethoven a
commemorative gold medal, of which the recipient was inordinately
proud, pointing out to people that it contained half a pound of gold.[82]

During these efforts, his games with publishers continued. In February he assured Peters in Leipzig that "two or three Masses" were
forthcoming.[83] At about the same time he offered the mass to publisher
number five, Anton Diabelli's new house. Diabelli pressed him hard
about it but got only promises.[84]

In the middle of all this business Beethoven was still thinking about
future projects. In the spring he wrote Franz Grillparzer, Austria's leading playwright, "to ascertain the truth of the report that you had written an opera libretto in verse for me. How grateful I should be to you
for your great kindness in having this beautiful poem sent to me in
order to convince me that you really considered it worthwhile to offer

a sacrifice to your sublime Muse on your behalf."[85] Beethoven had approached his acquaintance Count Dietrichstein, head of the two court theaters, to query the writer.[86] Grillparzer had known about Beethoven since childhood, after his mother ran afoul of him in Heiligenstadt when she eavesdropped on his composing.

Grillparzer's well-known plays included *Sappho* and *The Golden Fleece* trilogy.[87] The names of Beethoven and Grillparzer would come to be linked in history, but the latter was never other than skeptical, maybe even scared, of Beethoven's music. The brooding and erratic writer's musical loyalties lay in the eighteenth century. In his journal he railed at Beethoven's "unfortunate" influence, his violations of "all conception of musical order and unity," his sacrifice of beauty to the "powerful, violent, and intoxicating."[88]

At the time Grillparzer and Beethoven communicated, the writer actually had two librettos available, one dark and one light. The serious one was *Drahomira,* from an old Bohemian legend,[89] but he submitted the light one first, saying later that he "did not want to give Beethoven the opportunity to step still closer to the extreme limits of music which lay nearby, threatening like precipices, in partnership with material that was semi-diabolical." So he put before Beethoven *Melusine,* from an old folk tale about a mermaid.

The two men had some memorable meetings that Grillparzer recalled. Arriving with Schindler for the first visit, he first found the composer "lying in soiled nightwear on a disordered bed, a book in his hand . . . As we entered Beethoven arose from the bed, gave me his hand, poured out his feelings of goodwill and respect and at once broached the subject of the opera. 'Your work lives here,' said he, pointing to his heart. 'I am going to the country in a few days and shall at once begin to compose it. Only, I don't know what to do with the hunters' chorus which forms the introduction. Weber [in *Der Freischütz*] used four horns; you see, therefore, that I must have eight. Where will this lead to?'"

Beethoven was joking, but Grillparzer apparently didn't get it.[90] He suggested that the hunters' chorus could be omitted. Here began months of consultations and revisions over the *Melusine* libretto that

ended up nowhere. Folk tales about mermaids were not in the least
Beethoven's style, and as he kept Grillparzer dangling for years he
hardly sketched a note for the opera. Still, the two men were able to
joke together, after a fashion. When Beethoven said he intended to
remain unmarried, old bachelor Grillparzer replied with an archetypal
male conceit: "Quite right! The intellects have no figures, and the figures have no intellect."[91]

On March 19, 1823, came a watershed moment in Beethoven's life,
when he presented a copy of the *Missa solemnis* to Archduke, now
also Cardinal, Rudolph, five years after he had proposed the idea.
There is no record that Rudolph paid Beethoven anything for the
mass or for the presentation copy, but Rudolph did write to the
Saxon court suggesting it buy a subscription, and it did. When the
cardinal was in Vienna now, he expected a three-hour composition
lesson every day, which all but precluded composing. Beethoven
felt frustrated but resigned. To Ries in London he wrote, "I am being shorn by the Cardinal more closely than I used to be. If I don't
go to him, my absence is regarded as a *crimen legis majestatus*,"
Beethoven's bad Latin for "high treason." He ends, naughtily, "Give
my best greetings to your wife until I arrive in London. Take care.
You think I am old, but I am a youthful old man."[92]
    In April there were two more watersheds. He finished the monu-
mental *Diabelli* Variations, most of which had been sketched in 1819
and then put aside for the mass and other projects. And his rotund
violinist and champion Ignaz Schuppanzigh returned to Vienna from
Russia, reconstituted his string quartet, and resumed concertizing.[93]
His first orchestral concert of 1824 in the Augarten included three
movements of the Fifth Symphony.[94]
    For the summer of 1823, Beethoven was invited to stay at the house
of a Baron von Prony at Hetzendorf. Perennially disgusted that his
noble patrons were not more generous with him and did not treat
him as an equal, he found this patron annoyingly worshipful, bowing
and scraping and following him around. Beethoven took to playing as
loudly as he could above the baron's bedroom at night, until his victim
regretfully sent him packing.[95]

From there, in mid-August Beethoven headed for Baden. Now, he was suffering from a painful and dangerous eye infection. In Baden his friends worried about that, and also that he was eating too much of his favorite fish with eggs and macaroni. His irritability with life in general and with Anton Schindler in particular led to a stern letter to Schindler in May: "When you write to me, just write in exactly the same way as I do to you, that is to say, without giving me a title, without addressing me, without signing your name . . . And you need not use figures of speech, but just say precisely what is necessary." Soon he was back to teasing Schindler as "Samothracian scoundrel!," sending him on errands, reporting his health: "I have to bandage my eyes at night and must spare them a good deal, for if I don't, as Smetana [his doctor] writes, I shall write very few more notes."[96]

More dissonance was on the way in the form of a new disaster from brother Johann and family. But amid the contrapuntal miseries, Beethoven had to have been satisfied that after so much trouble, so much illness, so much pain, near complete deafness, and years of rumors that he was crazy and written out — theories he at times had come close to believing himself — he had in a few months completed the mass and the *Diabelli* Variations, which he knew were among the crowning works of his life. The first was his magnum opus so far, the second the summit of his piano variations and somewhere near the summit of all his piano music. Both works involved old heroes and models. With the mass, he had put himself on the plane of Handel, with the op. 120 Variations on the plane of J. S. Bach.

The long genesis of op. 120 had begun in 1819, with Diabelli's little waltz and an invitation to join a collection of fifty composers in writing a single variation on it. This was a scheme to advertise Diabelli's new publishing house with miniatures composed by a row of famous names. For Beethoven, writing the requested variation could have been a throwaway or a source of quick cash. So why did he decide to make what he called this *Schusterfleck*, "cobbler's patch," the foundation of the most elaborate piano work of his life, one that, like the *Missa solemnis* and the *Hammerklavier* threatened to become unwieldy, impractical, hard to sell?

No matter how desperate Beethoven was, his artistic goals came first. With serious works, he wrote what he wanted, how he wanted, and then worried about how to sell it. Some of what lay behind the *Diabellis* seems simple enough. He had written variations since childhood, starting with his first published piece at age ten. Now if he was going to write a set, it was going to have the epic quality of most of his serious pieces in these years. As usual, this one was involved with models. To take something simple and inconsequential in itself and in a set of variations make it into something rich and unexpected was Haydn's game. Once again Beethoven took up his model and amplified it. As he became more concerned with the transcendent and sublime, he was also more concerned with the ordinary and everyday, like the raunchy folk tunes that followed the exquisite first movement of op. 110.

The ideal of simplicity had been with him from early on, something he learned from Handel and Haydn and Mozart, and from the folk music he had known from childhood and worked with later in his dozens of folk-song arrangements. "Please please please keep it simple," he wrote on a sketch for the Mass in C. The simple bass line in *The Creatures of Prometheus* represented the creatures unenlightened by art and feeling, mere moving clay. Like that commonplace bass line that became the germ of the *Eroica,* the creatures of Prometheus had infinite potential. Schiller said that every artist aspires to create form that transcends content. *Prometheus* and the *Eroica* exemplify that principle, using form to give meaning to the meaningless.

At times there is another side to Beethoven's concern with simplicity, pushing that concern a degree further into irony, parody, even a kind of aesthetic cynicism: the implication that the fundamental material of a piece is not so important, that it may as well be one thing as another. It was in this spirit that once in a soiree Beethoven took a cello part of his would-be rival Daniel Steibelt, turned it upside down, picked out a few notes at random, and on that foundation proceeded to improvise with his usual brilliance. In that same spirit of irony and bravado he seized Diabelli's *Schusterfleck: I can take anything at all, parody it, laugh at it, and still make something magnificent out of it, far beyond anything anybody including its originator could imagine doing with it.* Here he is close to mainstream Romantic irony, like those writers who in their works turned around to look at their material and themselves as if in a mirror, reminding the reader of the artifice before them, the artist grieving and laughing over his own creation.

There is a still-deeper layer to Beethoven's interest in taking up the ordinary and raising it toward the sublime. Apart from the grandfather he was named for, a first-rate musician, he came from ordinary people with ordinary jobs, ordinary troubles, ordinary tragedies. In the popular myth, so did Napoleon Bonaparte. Beethoven understood that, like Napoleon, he had on the foundation of his natural gifts lifted himself from the ordinary to the extraordinary by the forces of his labor, discipline, and vision. Both of them were men like the creatures of Prometheus, rising from the common clay of humanity, but in their case the rise was self-willed.

So Beethoven took up Diabelli's rattling little barroom tune with a certain cynical delight in its trashiness, and proceeded to transmute this ordinary dreck into gold. Ultimately, after all, as with Steibelt's cello part it didn't much matter where he started — and he wanted the world to understand that. The piece begins with nothing, just as he entered history as a mewling infant of a struggling family in a freezing church baptistery. What made the difference was what he did with his

life, and in this piece what makes the difference is what he does with a
meaningless waltz, to transmute it into meaning.

So parodistic intentions were part of the game from the beginning.
The fundamental tone of the work, like other of his piano variations
including the *Prometheus* set, is ironic and comic. Call the *Diabelli*
Variations a kind of sublime prank, in the sense of what Goethe called
Faust: "a very serious joke."

He sketched twenty-two variations in 1819, in the first burst of fervor for the work, but laid aside the piece to take up the *Missa solemnis,*
some new bagatelles, and the last three piano sonatas.[97] In 1819, a big
set of variations had been an ideal project for him, trying as he was to
get past years of relative inactivity by his standards, past his creative
uncertainty and struggles with health and courts. The *Hammerklavier*
had been a major sustained effort. The *Diabellis* were to be a series
of miniatures that could be discovered in improvisation, sketched
quickly, revised and polished in bits and pieces, arranged and rearranged like a collection of gems. Alone at the keyboard he probably
improvised dozens if not hundreds more variations that never reached
paper.

There is one metaphor for the *Diabellis*: a string of multicolored
gems. Or a parade of bagatelles, a galaxy of tiny worlds, a collection
of poems on a common theme. Or portraits of Beethoven himself,
who contained worlds. Or all of life and music in a series of lightning
flashes: here wistful, here absurd, here dancing, laughing, remember-
ing, weeping. Improvisation and variation had always been his wellspring, his engine. In the *Diabelli* Variations he made those inter-
twined arts the substance of the music. Perhaps more than anything
else, his first work on the project got his creative engine up to speed
again.

In the *Diabellis* we see a fundamental aspect of Beethoven's technique in a nutshell. *The beginning is central,* every part of that beginning: melodic, harmonic, rhythmic, coloristic, emotional. Now the
fundamental material is somebody else's tune, but the handling is the
same, carried to a new level. While every aspect of Diabelli's theme
is going to be grist for the mill, some elements will be steady leading
motifs:

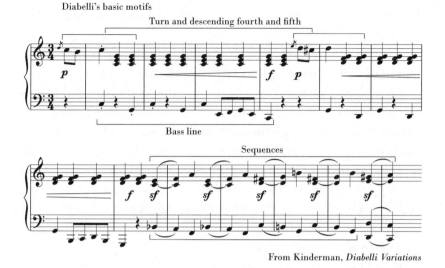

Diabelli's basic motifs

Turn and descending fourth and fifth

Bass line

Sequences

From Kinderman, *Diabelli Variations*

All Beethoven's variations have an overarching plan. The plan here is among his loosest but is still consistent, and it is made evident in the first three variations: Variation I is comically pompous, no. II light and mercurial, no. III lyric and pensive. As established in those first variations, the principle is going to be constant kaleidoscopic contrast. For the purpose of establishing that idea, the mercurial second variation was one of the last he composed, as he finally closed in on how to lay out the elements.[98] Beethoven surely knew Bach's *Goldberg* Variations, already famous and called a summit of the genre, likewise founded on a simple dance tune. The *Goldbergs* — and *The Well-Tempered Clavier* — were further models for the *Diabellis* in their conception and sometimes in their sound.

Beethoven was not interested in a structure like the *Goldbergs'* systematic one of groups of free variations regularly marked off by canonic ones. Here and there in the *Diabellis* two variations are joined, here and there one seems to be an answer to the previous, but mostly the order is loose, founded on contrasts calculated to sustain an impression of capriciousness and play.[99] All but two variations are in the C major of the theme (also including the familiar *minore*, a turn to C minor), but within each variation he went for maximum harmonic contrast, much chromaticism, internal modulations.[100] For one example of the tonal variety he injected into the theme, the C-minor

Variation XIV has a passage in D-flat major, which is nowhere hinted in the theme.

When Beethoven returned to the piece in 1823, he added eleven more variations, including the first two.[101] The final Variation I solved a problem he had left hanging in 1819, when the set started with the lyrical no. III: to follow the garishness of Diabelli's waltz with that quietly pensive and entirely Beethovenian variation was too big a jump. Instead, his new addition follows the theme with a faux-majestic march, forming a parody of the theme.[102] That march of Variation I is unlike anything else in the genre, in which the theme is always the beginning and, in a way, sole proprietor. Here Beethoven's first variation is more weighty, a second beginning, in which he lampoons the theme in his own voice.

Then the poems, the variegated gems, tumble out one after another, some breathlessly short like the scampering Variation II, some broad and inward, like no. III, some parodistic. Each of Beethoven's piano sonatas had been a distinctive individual with a distinctive handling of the instrument. Here that quality is boiled down to brief moments, each of them memorable. In this period Beethoven wrote Ferdinand Ries that the ideal for art was the combination of the beautiful and the unexpected. Here every moment is beautiful and unexpected.

Flowering and dancing and jumping, sparkling and singing, introverted and extroverted, the little worlds unfold. Variation XIII, with its jumpy starts and stops, is the most broadly comic yet in its parody of the theme. Next comes one of the surprises: no. XIV is in a richly chordal C minor with an ornamented melody marked Grave e maestoso, recalling the style of a Bach prelude.[103] For Beethoven, to write variations looks back to his first pieces, back to how he learned to compose by writing variations: taking a single piece of material through the most varied avatars. To pay homage to Bach is to look back at his childhood as well, when he grew up playing the *WTC*. It is also to look back at music itself. Here is another feature of Beethoven's late work: often it is *music about music*.[104]

There are further homages, more music about music, in unexpected ways. The somber slow chorale of Variation XX, recalling his equali for trombones, is answered by another parody emphasizing the rattling repeated chords of the theme. Variation XXII jumps in with the most startling moment in the piece: a quotation, in blank octaves, of "Notte e giorno faticar" from Mozart's *Don Giovanni,* the aria that introduces us to the don's comic sidekick Leporello. At some point Beethoven had realized that Mozart's tune has a similar harmonic structure to the Diabelli waltz, and it begins with a descending fourth, the leading melodic motif gleaned from the waltz. Woven into the piece, Mozart is another spirit hanging over the *Diabellis.*

That homage to Mozart is wry but not satirical, any more than is the Handelian fugue of Variation XXXII. Nothing overtly conjures Haydn, but the whole of the *Diabellis* is in effect a testament to what Beethoven's teacher did with variations. So the *Diabellis* are music about life, about the piano, and about the past of music, with homages to Handel, Bach, and Mozart, and tacitly to his rival Haydn.[105]

The Handelian fugue is preceded by the spiritual core of the *Diabellis:* Variation XXV, a magnificent tragic aria full of Baroque figuration that streams like tears. Then comes the big fugue, the climax but not the end. Instead he concludes the variations with a gentle farewell enfolding two final evocations — of Mozart again, and of himself.

Rather than a final cadence, the fugue falls into cadenza-like roulades, as if wiping away everything that came before. There is a muted, magical moment of transition. Then Variation XXXIII, an epilogue rather than a climax, takes shape as a little minuet looking back to Mozart. At the same time it has some of the exquisitely simple and ingenuous quality of the ending variations of op. 111, where Beethoven turned our eyes upward to the stars and said farewell to piano sonatas. Both that sonata's finale theme and the final variation of the *Diabellis* begin with a descending fourth; both are in an artless and supremely artful C major.

With the minuet the variations end on a gesture of wistful irony, of profound play. At the conclusion the minuet seems to dissolve, to evanesce, until the final *forte* thump in the middle of the bar. It is like a gentle wave of farewell, and a wink. The irony of the ending points to a fundamental quality of the genre. In a sonata, after the exposition and development and recapitulation, the piece comes to an end, with or without a coda. There is no such model for finishing variations, no predetermined conclusion. Ordinarily, when finished with a set of variations, the composer fashions an ad hoc conclusion — say, a vigorous fugue with a rousing final cadence. Otherwise, the music threatens to go on endlessly. Recall the time when painter W. J. Mähler visited Beethoven when he was finishing the *Eroica*. Beethoven played him the variation finale of the symphony and kept going with improvised variations for two hours.

So variations are in theory an infinite form, and Beethoven's ending ironically reminds us of that: *I could keep going at this forever, friends, and all of it would be marvelous. But I have to stop somewhere, so here it is: lebewohl. Ta-da!* His very serious joke ends the way life can, in the middle of a sentence. There is the final poetry of the *Diabelli* Variations. They were conceived in terms of radical contrasts from one to the next, and the last notes are contrasted to a silence on the brink of eternity.[106]

When Diabelli's house brought out the variations on the publisher's theme, in his advertisement he struck a note that must have made even Beethoven proud: "We present here to the world Variations of no ordinary type, but a great and important masterpiece to be ranked with the imperishable creations of the old Classics ... more interesting from the fact that it is elicited from a theme which no one would otherwise have supposed capable of a working-out of that character ... All these variations ... will entitle the work to a place beside Sebastian Bach's masterpiece [the *Goldberg* Variations]."[107] History thereafter hardly put it better.

The quotidian marched on. The tangle of Beethoven pieces in circulation, both sold and offered, became increasingly complicated. He had never juggled so many balls at once, in the moil of offering works large and small to a smorgasbord of publishers at the same time that he kept an eye out for others, and meanwhile composing at something close to his old heat. Peters turned down the bagatelles Beethoven sent him; Clementi published a set of them in England that was promptly pirated by Moritz Schlesinger and then by a publisher in Vienna. As a result, Beethoven ended up getting no money for the Continental edition of the bagatelles. This fee had been earmarked to pay off his debt to Johann. He had to write a new set of bagatelles to address his brother's loan.[108] Yet the next February he offered Moritz the *Missa solemnis* and the Ninth Symphony.[109]

In July he wrote Rudolph that his infection was improving — "I have been able to use my eyes again" — and he was composing the symphony for England that he hoped to finish in less than a fortnight. His outlandish misconceptions of the time he needed to finish big pieces continued, even when he was not writing publishers. Still, the Ninth Symphony would be done by early the next year.

A new pot of trouble arrived that month in an excruciatingly detailed letter from Schindler. Johann's wife and daughter were back to their amusements while Johann was laid up in bed:

> About your brother and the people dear to him, I shall confine myself to telling you as much as circumstances now allow.
>
> He is weak, unfortunately a far too weak man, though greatly to be pitied . . . He has two vipers at his side . . . These persons, despite their most venerable name, are worthy of being locked up, the older woman in prison, the younger in a correction house. How they can treat a husband and father in such a manner during his illness can only be imagined among barbarians . . . It is more than barbaric, when the wife, while her husband lies ill, leads her lover into his room to [meet] him, gets herself all gussied up like a sleigh horse in his presence, then goes driving with [the lover] and leaves her sick husband languishing at home.[110]

Schindler goes on to practical business and ends, "I am, in deepest submission, Your unalterably loyal, A. Schindler." Beethoven's hanger-on detested Johann, and here he was playing to Beethoven's prejudices about Therese and her daughter. Beethoven had dubbed them, respectively, "Fat Lump" and "Little Bastard." Still, storming over to Johann's house in Ludwig's usual fashion would not be advisable this time. In a conversation book, Schindler reported that Therese had declared that if Ludwig showed up at her house, she would be waiting for him in the hall with an iron poker in hand.[111]

Taking the route of discretion, Ludwig wrote Johann a stern letter:

Now you've gotten into a fine mess: I am informed of everything that Schindler has observed at your house. He was useful to me, so that I can learn about you and also help you.

You see how right I was to hold you back from this, etc. . . . I advise you to come out and stay here, and later to live with us all the time. How much more happily you could live with an excellent youth like Karl, and with me your brother.[112]

In August he returned to full big-brother mode: "However little you may deserve it so far as I am concerned, yet I shall never forget that you are my brother; and in due course a good spirit will imbue your heart and soul, a good spirit which will separate you from those two canailles, that former and still active whore, with whom her fellow miscreant slept no less than three times during your illness and who, moreover, has full control of your money, oh, abominable shame, is there no spark of manhood in you?!!!"[113]

Johann recovered from his illness and the issue died down without further theatrics from either side. From August 1823, Beethoven spent two months taking the cure in Baden. Shortly after he got there he received word that Wenzel Schlemmer, his main copyist for the last thirty years, had passed away. Schlemmer had possessed well-honed skills in divining the scrawls and blots and erasures of Beethoven's manuscripts. Beethoven had long counted on him for that so he did not have to recopy his more battle-scarred pages. (Contrary to legend, though, most of his final manuscripts are quite clean and clear.) Now to his longtime struggles with sloppy engravings from publishers were to be added struggles with underpaid and indifferent copyists.

He also wrote Johann, "I am delighted to hear that you are in better health. As for me, my eyes are not yet quite cured; and I came here with a ruined stomach and horrible cold, the former thanks to that arch-swine, my housekeeper, the latter handed on to me by a beast of a kitchen-maid."[114] In fact, Beethoven was in fairly fine fettle that summer, grousing away vigorously. The Ninth Symphony was going well. A British visitor found him capable of following conversation without an ear trumpet — so his hearing seemed to be in a relatively better phase.[115] Things were going better with his ward too. Beethoven's letters to Karl in these months are avuncular and affectionate: "Goodbye, little rascal, most excellent little rascal . . . Don't indulge in gossip at [Schindler's] expense, for it might injure him. Indeed he is sufficiently punished by being what he is."[116]

To Franz Grillparzer he wrote, "As you must have noticed at Hetzendorf, this obtrusive hanger-on of a Schindler has long ago become extremely odious to me."[117] Nonetheless, this summer Schindler was living in Beethoven's flat in Vienna.[118] Beethoven had come to rely on this coattail-hanger and for the moment did not want to send him away. For his part, Schindler also detested Karl, as he generally did anyone closer to Beethoven than himself. If it had not been so much the case before, with the advent of Schindler the dynamic of the circle around Beethoven began to be inflected by the question of who hated whom.

Grillparzer visited Beethoven in Hetzendorf to further share ideas for the *Melusine* libretto that neither man realized was foredoomed. In a conversation book the playwright made some suggestions about the music that foreshadow a composer of the next generation named Richard Wagner: "I have been thinking if it might not be possible to mark every appearance of Melusine or of her influence in the action by a recurrent and easily grasped melody. Might not the overture begin with this and after the rushing allegro the introduction be made out of the same melody." Their discussions were calm and professional, but Grillparzer still found their meeting odd in the extreme. At table with the playwright and, as it happened, Schindler, Beethoven left the room and returned with five bottles of wine. One flask he put before Schindler, three before Grillparzer. As the latter remembered, this was "probably to make me understand in his wild and simple way that I was master and should drink as much as I liked."

When Grillparzer had to return to town, Beethoven got in the open carriage with him and rode all the way to the gates of Vienna, where he got out to return to Hetzendorf on foot — a walk of some hour and a half. Seeing he had left some kind of paper on the seat, Grillparzer shouted at Beethoven, who turned with a laugh and sprinted away. A befuddled Grillparzer unrolled the paper to find the cab fare inside. "His manner of life," the poet concluded, "had so estranged him from all the habits and customs of the world that it probably never occurred to him that under other circumstances he could have been guilty of a gross offence."[119] In their meeting, Grillparzer recalled, Beethoven had told him *Melusine* was "ready." Again, not one note of sketch intended for the opera was ever found.[120] Beethoven had fallen into the habit of promising anything to anybody, trying to keep all his prospects on the hook.

In Vienna in the winter of 1823–24, Karl lived with his uncle as he began philology studies at the university, to make use of his gift for languages toward an academic career. As is familiar in teenagers, Karl was also turning his intelligence to manipulating his uncle, disparaging the people he knew Beethoven would enjoy hearing disparaged, flattering him about his adulation from the public.[121] Beethoven played Karl sketches and listened to his opinions. In 1823, when Beethoven was working on the slow movement of the Ninth Symphony, Karl wrote in a conversation book, "I'm glad that you have brought in the beautiful andante." It was the second theme of the movement, which Beethoven had sketched while he was working on the opening movement.[122]

Beethoven still felt relatively well, though in a letter he begged off lessons with Rudolph, saying he was weakened by the purgatives he was taking. He added some more inspirational words, of a kind he hardly wrote anybody but Rudolph: "There is nothing higher than to approach the Godhead more closely than other mortals and by means of that contact to spread the rays of the Godhead through the human race."[123] Here was a new or at least revised credo, confirming the turn from the humanism of the *Eroica* and Fifth Symphony to the atmosphere and ethos of the *Missa solemnis.*

Two pressing issues turned up that winter. After years of waiting, the Gesellschaft der Musikfreunde again made inquiries concerning its commissioned oratorio *The Victory of the Cross,* for which it had long since given him an advance of 400 florins. Surely by this point Beethoven had no illusions that he would ever actually produce the thing, but he was also not interested in returning the money. Instead, he pushed the mass on them: "The great Mass is really rather in the oratorio style and particularly adapted to the Society," which often mounted oratorios. He assured the group of "my zealous desire to serve the Society in whose benevolent deeds in behalf of art I always take the greatest interest." In the end, both parties let the commission slide, and the society never got its money back.

Around the end of the year Beethoven received a letter from his editor friend Berhard saying Johanna van Beethoven was ill and desperate. She had resumed sending half her pension for Karl's support. Beethoven's generosity to anyone in need came to the fore: "Assure her at once through her doctor," he wrote Bernard, "that from this month onwards she can enjoy her full pension <u>as long as I live</u> . . . I shall make a point of persuading my pigheaded brother also to contribute something to help her." He wrote a friendly New Year's greeting to Johanna, assuring her of "both my and Karl's sincerest wishes for her welfare."[124]

His beneficence didn't last. In another letter to Bernard, his moralistic dudgeon intervened: "Since Hofbauer . . . believes that he is the father of [Johanna's] child, <u>he is probably right.</u> And as she has become such a strumpet I consider that after all I should make Karl realize the guilt of <u>her wicked behavior</u>."[125] He had learned that the confessed father of her illegitimate daughter was paying her support for the child, so he rescinded his offer to let Johanna keep her whole pension. (Eventually her payments lapsed anyway.) These days Karl was running down his mother bitterly in the conversation books — whether from real disgust or by way of playing up to his uncle.[126]

In February 1824, Beethoven wrote out the final score of the Ninth Symphony. Then he got busy pitching it to publishers and planning a gala premiere of the symphony and the complete *Missa solemnis*. The conversation books broke out with schemes and proposals. Lying over the deliberations like a pall were Beethoven's indecisiveness and suspicion of everything and everybody. Among the voices trying to counter his resistance was alto Karoline Unger, who wrote in a conversation book in sopranoesque vexation, "If you give the concert, I will guarantee that the house will be full. You have too little confidence in yourself. Has not the homage of the whole world given you a little more pride? Who speaks of opposition? Will you not learn to believe that everybody is longing to worship you again in new works? O obstinacy!"[127]

Unger had no hope of cracking Beethoven's animus toward Vienna that had boiled in him for more than thirty years. He decided to make inquiries about holding the premiere in Berlin. When his friends and patrons in Vienna got wind of that, they realized something dramatic had to be done: they must prostrate themselves in the name of Music and of God and Country.

The circle drafted a long, flowery, abject letter begging Beethoven to keep the premiere in Vienna. It begins, "Out of the wide circle of reverent admirers surrounding your genius in this your second native city, there approach you today a small number of the disciples and lovers of art to give expression to long-felt wishes, timidly to proffer a long-suppressed request." They plead "in the name of all to whom art and the realization of their ideals are something more than means and objects of pastime." They plead in the names of Mozart and Haydn, "the sacred triad in which these names and yours glow as the symbol of the highest within the spiritual realm of tones, sprung from their fatherland." The thirty signers included publishers Artaria, Steiner, and Diabelli, Beethoven's onetime pupil Carl Czerny, the piano maker Streicher, Beethoven's old unpaid secretary Baron Zmeskall, and Count Moritz Lichnowsky, who had been the moving force in getting the signatures.

The letter was published in two journals. When he heard about it Beethoven responded furiously because he believed the public would think he was behind it. But he said he wanted to read the letter carefully, alone. Schindler wrote that he found Beethoven with the letter in hand, much moved. "It is very beautiful," he said. "It rejoices me greatly!"[128] It would be nice to believe that this time Schindler was telling the truth.

As of March Beethoven had agreed that the concert would be in Vienna. Then began the haggles and struggles over venue and arrangements. He wanted the Theater an der Wien, and the directorate was agreeable. But he also wanted Ignaz Schuppanzigh to head the violins. After all, Schuppanzigh had not only performed Beethoven's quartets from the beginning and championed his orchestral music, he had also headed the strings in the premiere of every Beethoven symphony so far. This request in favor of Schuppanzigh was entirely reasonable, a testament to an old colleague, but the management of the Theater an der Wien was not immediately agreeable. So speculation shifted to the barnlike Kärntnertor Theater, which had seen its share of Beethoven performances.

By that point Beethoven was waffling unbearably over arrangements, soloists, program, ticket prices. To get him back on track, Lichnowsky, Schindler, and Schuppanzigh cooked up a scheme to appear at his flat as if by accident and to prod and kid him into making some decisions in writing. This worked, until Beethoven realized he had been duped. Thereupon each of the friends received an insulting note canceling everything. The one to Count Moritz Lichnowsky read, "I despise treachery — Do not visit me anymore. There will be no concert —"[129] The count being high aristocracy, Beethoven could have been sent to jail for this insult, but the count retained his composure. The friends knew they were dealing with the most volatile of spoiled children. They let him calm down and went back. This time they had a cheery meeting commemorated by Schindler in a conversation book, starting with a list of those present:

> Herr L. van Beethoven, a *musikus* [the term for a workaday musician].
> Herr Count v. Lichnowsky, an amateur.
> Herr Schindler, a fiddler.
> Not yet present today:
> Herr Schuppanzigh, a fiddler representing Mylord Falstaff.[130]

As the conversation books spun out with plans, the Theater an der Wien offered generous terms, but the orchestra members declared they would play only under their concertmaster Franz Clement, an old Beethoven friend. That finished that venue. At virtually the last minute, just over a month before the mounting of what were intended to be the premieres of the gigantic Ninth Symphony and the *Missa solemnis,* the Kärntnertor was engaged. In the utmost haste, the soloists and a huge orchestra of amateurs and professionals were assembled.

None of that ended the discord. "After talks and discussions lasting for six weeks," Beethoven wrote Schindler, "I now feel cooked, stewed, and roasted."[131] He demanded unprecedented ticket prices, which the management resisted. The censors announced that the *Missa solemnis* could not be included because it was forbidden to perform sacred music in secular spaces. Beethoven hastily arranged a German text to replace the Latin and promised the mass sections would be listed as "hymns." When the rehearsals began he realized that attempting the complete mass would be impossible, so he cut it back to the first three movements. In a rehearsal of the symphony the lady soloists, alto Karoline Unger, then twenty-one, and soprano Henriette Sontag, eighteen, protested the high notes in their parts. Beethoven refused to budge. Unger called him a "tyrant over all the vocal organs." Turning to Sontag, she declared, "Well, then we must go on torturing ourselves in the name of God!" Just before the concert the bass soloist withdrew because he could not reach his high notes, and he had to be replaced.

Three rehearsals were planned, but because of a schedule conflict with a ballet performance only two were possible. Meanwhile there were sectional rehearsals with the orchestra and separate rehearsals for the choir and soloists. It was agreed that Michael Umlauf, who had served this function several times before, would be the actual conductor while Beethoven stood in front of him marking the tempos. As he had also done before, Umlauf told the orchestra to follow him and ignore Beethoven. At the last rehearsal Beethoven dissolved in tears at the performance of the Kyrie from the *Missa solemnis,* even though he likely could hear it only through his eyes. At the end he stood at the door and embraced all the amateurs who had donated their service.

Shortly after 7 p.m. on May 7, 1824, Umlauf and Beethoven together gave the first downbeat.

30

Qui Venit in Nomine Domini

THE KÄRNTNERTOR THEATER was full that May 7, 1824, when the Ninth Symphony was unveiled. Curiosity about the new symphony claimed most of the attention, even though three movements of the *Missa solemnis* were also to be heard. The turnout was a testament to how many Viennese still admired Beethoven, how many were ready to buy tickets for a big premiere. Beethoven's old devotee Baron Zmeskall, prostrate with gout, had himself carried into the hall in a sedan chair.[1] The imperial box lay empty, Archduke Rudolph absent, but the aristocracy was well represented, along with friends and patrons and enthusiasts, and a sprinkling of the random and the curious. The random and curious would not be the ones applauding wildly. They were bewildered by these works, as would be most of the musical world for a long time to come.

While Beethoven had his usual inflated expectations for the receipts, still it was remarkable that the hall was packed. The concert season was over, many Viennese off to their summer sojourns. Rossini fever still raged in the city, decimating the audience for any other music.[2] The Viennese appetite for pleasure was never more voracious than now, when entertainment helped keep a dark political reality at bay. With his string of operas filled with pretty tunes, Rossini satisfied that need. Beethoven, with his strange profundities and his overtones of bygone revolutionary times, was threatened with the most merciless of fates for an artist: being out of fashion.

The program began with the *Consecration of the House* Overture. During all the pieces, Beethoven stood somewhere in front of conductor Michael Umlauf. Accounts of the concert, most of them from years later, differ on whether he was directly in front of the orchestra or among the chorus. He was supposed to give the tempo for each movement, but Umlauf had told everyone to ignore him.

The performing forces were enormous for the time, the house orchestra filled out with less experienced amateurs from the Gesellschaft der Musikfreunde: twenty-four violins, ten violas, twelve each of basses and cellos, and doubled winds. The chorus for the mass and symphony numbered ninety, including some boy sopranos who had even more trouble with their part than the women.[3] At the head of the strings sat Ignaz Schuppanzigh. The two men still addressed each other as *er,* "he," like servant and master. But Beethoven had given up a better hall, the Theater an der Wien, and its house orchestra, partly because the management would not allow Schuppanzigh to lead the violins.

After the overture came the Kyrie, Gloria, and Credo of the *Missa solemnis,* translated into German to pacify the censors and billed as "Three Grand Hymns." There is little indication of how fared these movements of the mass. The Gloria and Credo are overwhelming in every respect, even more so than the Ninth Symphony. The slim response of critics and audience to the mass may have been a matter of something embarrassing being passed over in silence. The idea of mounting these movements and the Ninth with an amateur chorus and mostly amateur orchestra after a few rehearsals is painful to contemplate. Here could be at least one day in his life when Beethoven was lucky to be deaf.

Then came the Ninth Symphony, the inchoate whispers of its beginning coalescing into towering proclamations. The harmonic restlessness and formal vagaries of Beethoven's music of the last years had turned away even some of his devotees. This was the same on a gigantic scale. Though there were moments of fraught peace and desperate hope, the music of the first movement must at times have seemed like a physical assault. It ended, for some reason, with a funeral march.

But his devotees were there to cheer him, come what may. The stalwarts had come to accept like a force of nature the fact that this shoddy little man with the bulldog face, deaf and widely said to be half-mad at best, was one of the most remarkable figures of his time or of any time. Furious applause after the first movement of the symphony. When the second movement scherzo began, the orchestra's exclamations interrupted by timpani, the audience broke into delighted applause. At one point the scherzo was entirely interrupted by the commotion in the house. Frantic cheers after. The slow movement, with its languid beauty, may actually have been conveyed well enough by the orchestra, and surely the crowd was rapt.

Then it was as if after a sublime interlude of peace Beethoven unleashed a scream from the orchestra: the finale began with a brassy dissonance. The Ninth as a whole was the most formidable symphonic concoction Beethoven had issued since the *Eroica*. He had been accused of bizarrerie many times in the past, but nothing approached this finale. Even before it began, a good percentage of the audience had trickled away. The survivors heard something bizarre indeed: one after another, snippets of the previous movements were recalled, with the double basses of the orchestra seeming to dismiss each of them in gestures that sounded like an operatic recitative. In this performance, even that oddity was incomprehensible, because the basses had no idea what they were supposed to do and produced, a listener recalled, "nothing but a gruff rumbling."[4]

The soloists and chorus had been sitting waiting for their entrances, the audience waiting to hear what in the world the singers would do. There was no conception of what might happen because there had never before been voices in a symphony. After the orchestra had reviewed and dismissed the recalls of previous movements and presented a simple little theme, the dissonant fanfare broke out again. The bass soloist rose. "O friends, not these tones!" he cried. "Rather let us sing something more pleasing." He sounded like a fellow in a tavern, inviting his comrades to try a merrier tune. The men of the chorus obliged, shouting "Joy! Joy!" Whether or not they knew about the text in advance, many of the audience would have recognized Schiller's verses from their famous first lines: "Joy, thou lovely god-engendered Daughter of Elysium, Drunk with fire we enter, Heavenly one, thy holy shrine!" The older listeners knew what those verses stood for: the time of revolutionary fever, forty years before.

The choral finale ran its erratic course, fugues and perorations interrupted by a military march in Turkish style. Soloists Karoline Unger and Henriette Sontag, young and brilliant, both with splendid careers ahead of them, struggled to reach the high notes, or substituted lower ones. Some of the weaker string players were seen to put down their bows during the harder parts. The sopranos in the chorus simply left out many of the high notes. (The next two centuries would not suffice to render some of the vocal parts other than miserable to sing.) In the hall the ecstatic last pages rang out. A pandemonium of applause and cheers and *vivats*.

Through all this Beethoven stood in front of the conductor, dressed in a green frock coat because he didn't have a proper black dress coat, his eyes on the score that lay on a music stand, beating time, hearing nothing. Some described him as sunk in thought as he turned the pages. But violinist Joseph Böhm recalled, "Beethoven himself conducted, that is, he stood in front of a conductor's stand and threw himself back and forth like a madman. At one moment he stretched to his full height, at the next he crouched down to the floor, he flailed about with his hands and feet as though he wanted to play all the instruments and sing all the chorus parts."[5] That is closer to the usual reports of Beethoven's conducting.

Legend says that after the scherzo, or perhaps at the end of the symphony, he was still beating time, lost in the music in his head, when Karoline Unger pulled his sleeve to turn him around so he could see the ovation he could not hear.[6] It was as if the audience were breaking their voices to make him understand that this was a triumph in spite of everything — in spite of the incapable performance, the impossible music, the emptying seats, his lost hearing. However it happened, the thought of it is sad beyond description.

The immediate aftermath was unpleasant for everybody concerned. Friends walked Beethoven home after the concert. It fell to government minister Joseph Hüttenbrenner to present the report from the box office. Beethoven had tried to raise the usual ticket prices at the hall, but the management refused. He had banked on this concert to turn his finances around from years of disaster. When he read that despite the full house, after the enormous music-copying costs and other expenses his profit came to a measly 420 florins, he collapsed to the floor.

His friends carried him to the sofa and sat by him late into the night. He seemed stunned, did not ask for food, could not speak. Finally he fell asleep and was in the same position, still wearing his concert clothes, when his servants came in next morning.[7] From that point he built up toward the inevitable explosion. He was not interested in hearing facts and figures. In his mind, if the proceeds were that bad it had to be somebody's fault; he had to have been cheated, and that by his friends.

Next day Anton Schindler tried to fend off Beethoven's outrage and convince him that the concert had been a sensation. "Never in my life," Schindler wrote in a conversation book, "did I hear such frenetic and yet cordial applause. Once the second movement of the symphony was completely interrupted by applause, and there was a demand for a repetition. The reception was more than imperial for the people burst out in a storm four times. At the last there were cries of Vivat! . . . When the parterre broke out in applauding cries the 5th time the Police Commissioner yelled Silence!"

Certainly the ovations had been authentic, at least among the part of the audience who came to cheer and stayed to the end. Everyone knew Beethoven was chronically ill. Any work, any concert could be his last. He had always called the Viennese superficial, fickle, hostile to his music. In some degree the Viennese were all those things, but the city was no less the epicenter of his fame and the cult of genius that gathered around it. Could anyone in the hall have absorbed those

gigantic conceptions in those scrambling performances? Were the bravos for the music, or for the man and his legacy? Surely it was mostly
the latter. And perhaps in some quarters cheers for one more reason,
in those days nearly unspeakable: the connection of Schiller's poem to
the lost dream of liberty and revolution.

But no amount of testimonials to the premiere's success could clear
the clouds gathering around Beethoven. Two days after the concert he
invited Schindler, conductor Umlauf, and concertmaster Schuppanzigh to dine with him and Karl at Zum Wilden Mann in the Prater
park. He arrived first and ordered everyone an opulent dinner. When
his guests arrived they knew what was coming from the look on his
face. As soon as they sat down the accusations began. In a cold and biting voice he said he knew for a fact that the management and Schindler
had colluded to cheat him. Umlauf and Schuppanzigh tried to reason,
reminding him that Karl had overseen the box office.

Beethoven brushed them aside. He said he had been told of the
treachery by a reliable witness.[8] In these scenes with him over the years
there always seemed to be a reliable witness, and it generally seems to
have been one of his brothers. If there was anybody fanning the flames
in this case it was probably Johann van Beethoven, who detested
Schindler and it appeared was making a play to have him expunged
from the circle. Finally Beethoven's accusations drove Umlauf and
Schindler away, their dinners uneaten. Schuppanzigh made another
attempt to calm things, but after more insults flung at him he fled too.
Beethoven and Karl finished their bitter repast alone, with nobody to
rage at, Schindler recalled, but the waiters and the trees of the Prater.

Shortly after the concert Beethoven wrote to Schindler with a show
of temperance, but in humiliating terms:

I do not accuse you of having done anything wicked in connection
with the concert. But stupidity and arbitrary behavior have ruined
many an undertaking. Moreover I have on the whole a certain fear of
you, a fear lest someday through your action a great misfortune may
befall me . . . that day in the Prater I was convinced that in many ways
you had hurt me very deeply — In any case I would much rather try
to repay frequently with a small gift the services you render me, than

<u>have you at my table.</u> For I confess that your presence irritates me in so many ways . . . For owing to your vulgar outlook how could you appreciate anything that is not vulgar?![9]

Before long he permitted Schindler to serve him again, but the two were never fully reconciled.

Reviews of the music were largely sympathetic. After a cheerleading beginning, the critic in the new *Wiener Allgemeine Musikalische Zeitung* turned to the obvious deficiencies in the performance and the acoustics:

Beethoven's genius evidenced itself to us as entirely in its youth and original strength again in these grand, gigantic compositions. His rich, powerful fantasy holds sway with lofty freedom in the realm of tones familiar to it, and it raises the listeners on its wings into a new world that excites amazement . . . Neither the chorus nor the solo singers were sufficiently prepared for such difficult and deeply intricate music . . . the sound faded away and dissipated in the bare spaces [of the hall] between the wings to such an extent, that we could barely hear half of the noteworthy effects in the lively moving mass of sound.[10]

After the second performance, the same critic expanded his sense of the pieces:

Like a volcano [in the first movement] Beethoven's power of imagination makes the earth, which tries to impede the rage of his fire, burst, and with an often wonderful persistence, develops figures whose peculiar formation . . . not seldom expresses an almost bizarre character, but which become transformed under the artful master's skilled hand into a stream of graceful elaborations that refuse to end, swinging upward, step by step, into an ever more brilliant loftiness.[11]

The rest of that review proceeded in kind. It was written, however, by Friedrich August Kanne, now one of Beethoven's inner circle. Kanne had been primed, had perhaps looked over the score, and he did his duty toward his friend.

The Vienna correspondent for the older Leipzig *Allgemeine Musikalische Zeitung* was stunned but as positive as he could manage. Toward the end, this critic added a twist of the knife:

> But where can I find the words about these giant works to relate to my readers, especially after a performance that in no way could suffice in light of the extraordinary difficulties, especially in the vocal sections . . . And still the effect was indescribably great and magnificent, jubilant applause from full hearts was enthusiastically given the master, whose inexhaustible genius revealed a new world to us and unveiled never-before-heard, never-imagined magical secrets of the holy art! . . . The wildest mischief plays its wicked game in the Scherzo . . . What heavenly song [in the slow movement]; how overwhelming the variations and combining of motives, what artful and tasteful development . . . The finale (D minor) announces itself like a crushing thunderclap . . . Potpourri-like, in short phrases, all previously-heard principal themes are paraded before us once again . . . The critic now sits with regained composure at his desk, but this moment will remain for him unforgettable. Art and truth celebrate here their most glowing triumph . . . Even the work's most glowing worshipers and most inspired admirers are convinced that this truly unique finale would become more incomparably imposing in a more concentrated shape, and the composer himself would agree if cruel fate had not robbed him of the ability to hear his creation.[12]

Two weeks later, on May 23, the Ninth Symphony had its repeat in a concert at the big *Redoutensaal* in the Hofburg. Also on the program was the Kyrie of the mass without the other movements; a Beethoven Italian vocal trio, *Tremate, empi tremate,* from 1802; and, of all ironies, an aria by Rossini. But the concert started just after noon, the day was beautiful, many Viennese were already off to their summer retreats, and the hall was less than half full.[13] The concert lost money. At least the house manager honored a 500-florin guarantee he had promised Beethoven. There was talk of a third concert, but the idea evaporated.

At that point Beethoven had a number of plans for big pieces: the opera on Grillparzer's libretto, an overture on the notes B–A–C–H (in

German notation, B-flat–A–C–B) as a testament to that master, a tenth symphony, maybe even the oratorios for Vienna and Boston. None of them got off the ground. His epic phase and his orchestral music were both finished. Now he turned to an intimate medium he had neglected for years: the string quartet.

A review in the *Caecilia* noted, "In general . . . the interest in compositions of this genre [the symphony] is declining substantially, and the artistic disciple who travels this road . . . without profit, often without applause, must fight with unspeakable difficulties even to bring his work to performance." This, as history turned out, was the most prophetic notice. It took decades, and the advent of the modern specialist conductor, for the Ninth Symphony to be represented well and to enter the familiar repertoire. The *Missa solemnis* never did.

Missa solemnis

Why did Beethoven write the *Missa solemnis*? That he took up a second work on a far larger scale than the Mass in C without a commission is something he never entirely explained. That he planned it for the ceremony elevating Archduke Rudolph to archbishop of Ölmutz was his stated intention. That he hoped Rudolph might, by way of thanks, make him his *Kapellmeister* is a reasonable speculation. Given that his major projects of those years — the *Hammerklavier*, the *Diabelli* Variations, the Ninth Symphony — were carried out on a massive scale, the same tendency naturally affected the *Missa solemnis*. That the mounting ambitions of the piece meant that Beethoven missed the deadline of Rudolph's ceremony by three years was to be expected.

But there was more to it than that. There were two streams in Beethoven's music, the secular-humanist and the sacred, and the latter had never gotten its due. His main sacred works before, the oratorio *Christus am Ölberge* and the Mass in C, were respectively a rush job and a modest experiment. He had repented the operatic style of the oratorio. In its way, his most successful sacred work was the *Pastoral Symphony*.

Pious Haydn had once called Beethoven an atheist, and Beethoven once declared that Jesus was only a poor human being and a Jew.[14] Had he become more conventionally religious in his age, turning away from the personal deism of his younger years? Yes and no. In age one's thoughts turn toward the end, toward eternal things, often toward God. With death's breath at his shoulder closer and chillier than ever, Beethoven looked to the beyond more intently. At the same time, there is the psychological reality that when any artist takes up a work that is going to consume a large part of that person's life, the artist will become for the necessary time a believer in the project at hand.

Did Beethoven believe every word of the Latin Mass, including the ones that proclaim the one truth of the Holy Catholic and Apostolic Church? Certainly not, any more than the Lutheran Bach did when he wrote his B Minor Mass. In their settings both men raced through the more dogmatic parts of the text. Did Beethoven believe in eternal life? No unequivocal statement about that survives, but what he said in private is reflected in a conversation-book entry from his friend Karl Peters: "Even if you don't believe in it [religion, and/or immortality], you will be glorified . . . You will arise with me from the dead — because you must."[15] At one point when it was proposed he write a requiem, Beethoven said it should be a memorial for the dead and "the Last Judgment may be given a miss."[16]

There is also the question of Jesus. For Bach as for most Christians, Christ was the central figure in the faith. That was never true for Beethoven. He wanted to deal with God man to man. True, at one point in his last years he said, "My models are Socrates and Jesus." By that he meant Christ not necessarily as the literal Son of God but more likely as an ethical ideal, along with Socrates. Nonetheless, for the places in the Mass relating to Christ — the incarnation, the Eucharist — he made his music believe. He embodied that text and that faith, as was his job.

So in his age he returned to the ancient Latin rite of the kind he first heard, unknowing, at his baptism, when the priest touched his ear and proclaimed, "Adaperire." Be opened. Now, despite his prayers, God had let his ears close. And his religious opinions remained his own, his spirituality personal, emotional rather than dogmatic.

Worldly considerations played their usual part. He hoped to be named *Kapellmeister* for Cardinal Rudolph. There was also the matter of pride. As far as the musical world was concerned, the greatest contemporary masses were the six that Haydn wrote for the Esterházys in the last years of his productivity. Long after his death, Haydn remained a rival in Beethoven's mind, perhaps the only member of his central pantheon — Handel, Bach, Haydn, Mozart — whom he believed he could surpass. With the mass he could go up against Haydn on holy ground.

Another impulse lying behind the *Missa solemnis* was the challenge of mastering a towering tradition involving mass settings going back hundreds of years. In particular, the Viennese grand mass, called *Missa solemnis,* was a venerable genre. Now it meant simply a big piece with full orchestra in something approaching symphonic style. Since the mass had to do with faith, with the spirit, with God, it was a kind of work in some respects more exalted than any other. Bach and Beethoven wrote their most ambitious masses not only as a personal testament of faith but also because the mass was one of the supreme genres in music, something they wanted to leave for posterity.

Beethoven had already mastered opera, symphony, string quartet, and the other traditional media and genres. Now he added another one. That he was rarely found inside a church, that its rites and liturgies did not ordinarily inspire him, that if he had somehow witnessed his own baptism he might have been unmoved by the rituals and spells, did not deter him from taking up the words of the Latin ritual most central to the Catholic Church: the heart of every service, built around the moment of the Eucharist where Christ is present in body and blood. Still and all, Beethoven's Bonn-shaped indifference if not hostility to priests and ritual and dogma was inevitably going to inflect his mass. Because he was who he was, it could not be other than a personal statement.

For decades, Beethoven had wanted to find a new sacred style, far from opera, symphonic but only to a degree. He wanted to forge a sacred music never imagined before. Probably he did not realize it as he worked, but part of the solution had to be a new context. If as he worked he imagined the *Missa solemnis* performed as part of a church service, it was because that was the only familiar setting for a mass.

The practice of mounting liturgical pieces outside church was a recent development. When he was done with the mass, Beethoven seized on the idea. In fact, with a work of this size and difficulty, a concert-hall performance was the only kind remotely likely to happen. For more than a century it rarely happened at all.

As it took shape, the *Missa solemnis* in D Major, op. 123, is a work on the order of a five-movement choral symphony. Necessarily, though, it has to be laid out quite differently from a symphony. In that respect Beethoven worked, to a degree, in the formal traditions of the Viennese *Missa solemnis*, including calling his mass by that name. Like other Viennese masses, his forces are an orchestra, chorus, and four solo singers. There are no arias; the solo parts are involved in a steady dialogue with the choir. At one point he described it as "in oratorio style," and that is relevant as well. For him and his time the genre of oratorio was inextricably associated with Handel in general and *Messiah* in particular. That and Mozart's Requiem were the sacred works Beethoven most admired, and they would have their influences.[17] And *Messiah* is not liturgical music but a sacred work for the concert hall.

In every Catholic service, the Mass has two elements: the Ordinary, which is the same five-part text in nearly every service (Kyrie, Gloria, Credo, Sanctus, Agnus Dei); and the Proper, which is specific to that week in the liturgical calendar. Like most composers Beethoven set the Ordinary, which makes the piece appropriate throughout the year. He studied the Latin text minutely, annotating his copy with notes about proper pronunciation and the precise meanings of words. He wrote in his *Tagebuch*, "In order to write true church music . . . look through all the monastic church chorales and also the strophes in the most correct translations and perfect prosody in all Christian-Catholic psalms and hymns generally." With his well-thumbed Latin dictionary he traced the subtle differences between the various words for "born" and "begotten": *natum, genitum, incarnatus*.[18] He returned to the Renaissance theorist Zarlino to see what that authority said about the qualities of the archaic church modes: Dorian, Mixolydian, Lydian.

In Archduke Rudolph's enormous music library he looked through masses and Gregorian chants reaching back centuries. He studied sacred works by Mozart, Haydn, Handel, and Bach by copying out passages. He returned to Palestrina, whose austere a cappella polyphony from the sixteenth century Beethoven and his time still called the wellspring of polyphony and the purest and most spiritual of all sacred music.

All those elements made their way into the *Missa solemnis* in the course of its more than six hundred pages of sketches and drafts. Which is to say, Beethoven's mass is steeped in musical and liturgical traditions. It is at the same time sui generis. He remained an evolutionist, not a revolutionist. Now his evolution was more deeply than ever within himself, in his silent world.

He would pay dearly for the scope of his evolution. For nearly two centuries to come the *Missa solemnis* drifted around in the repertoire like an orphan. At nearly an hour and a half it is too big and too special for church, it is formidably difficult to mount in any circumstances, and with its enormous spans of time and kaleidoscopic contrasts of material without the familiar landmarks of musical forms — repeats and recapitulations and developments and codas — it is formidable to listen to as well.

Yet it is hard to put aside Beethoven's conviction that it was his greatest work. That it was his greatest challenge for himself and for everybody else was, for him, part of its significance: *What is difficult is good.* In many ways its essence is a phrase he wrote on the manuscript at the beginning of the Kyrie: "From the heart — may it return to the heart."[19] The *Missa solemnis* is a work from Beethoven's heart to the heart of his listeners, across time. As Beethoven himself wanted to deal with God man to man, there is no pious prayer to God to accept it, no "finished with God's help." This is one man's declaration of faith, in the form of the central liturgical text of the Catholic Church, and it is addressed not to congregants but to humanity.

Kyrie

The opening is marked *mit Andacht,* with reverence and devotion. The Greek words as a plea for mercy go back to deep antiquity: *Kyrie eleison, Christe eleison, Kyrie eleison,* Lord and Christ, have mercy on us. Usually each of the three phrases is repeated three times, symbolizing the Trinity. In Viennese mass settings the ABA of the text is usually reflected in the musical structure. Beethoven conforms to those traditions, the return of the A material resembling a sonata-form recapitulation.

He begins the *Missa solemnis* on a great D-major upbeat. That opening gesture begins to shape structure and symbol. The mass will be full of emphasized upbeats and notes held over the bar. Listeners do not immediately perceive the opening chord as an upbeat, or realize that the trumpets and timpani mark the downbeat, but the music settles into the bar line and the point is made, however subtly. The massive upbeat chord on *Kyrie* will return over and over.

Many resonances begin there. Beethoven knew that musicians will execute an upbeat, even a *tutti forte* one, differently than a downbeat; they will play it as though on a rising breath. The rhythm he gives the word *Kyrie* is the usual one in a musical setting, reflecting its spoken rhythm:[20]

But when the accented syllable is written as an upbeat, it is as if in its urgency to be heard the word has spilled over the bar line, come in early. That effect of spilling over will be heard myriad times in the mass, often at moments of greatest exaltation. A downbeat is an arrival; an upbeat points forward. It is that primal pointing forward, or more relevantly pointing upward, that Beethoven is concerned with. It begins on an upbeat pointing forward and upward. Later, the same idea will be heard in his strange repetition of the article *et,* "and." Articles are words that point forward.

As always with Beethoven, the beginning sets up a nexus of generating ideas and motifs for the work. But those leading ideas are not going to be handled as he usually does. Most of the mass text cannot be shoehorned into sonata form, rondo, and the like. The text allows sonata overtones in the Kyrie, and Beethoven handles it that way. But otherwise the form has to be shaped around the divisions and the implications of the text.

The Viennese mass had evolved various ways of structuring the sections, a sense of where the climaxes are, where material can return, where one can place a fugue, and so on. Beethoven conformed to much of that. But to an extraordinary degree, in the mass he let go of a lifetime of habits, of thinking in terms of regular returns of material, of motivic development, introductions, and codas. He also gave up the harmonic underpinnings of Classical form, with its center of gravity the tonic–dominant axis, and with major points in the structure marked by returns of the home key.

For the mass he put aside, in other words, the Classical coordination of theme and key geared to structure that one would hear in a symphony or the like. Here keys form patterns, but there is usually no regular structure for them to relate to — though all movements but the Credo begin and/or end in the home key of D. There is more a sense of evolving tonality that touches on some keys again and again, especially ones related by thirds: in the first *Kyrie* he surrounds D major with its mediants B minor and F-sharp major and minor. The dominant of D, A major, plays no part in the Kyrie at all. B-flat major will be a familiar secondary key (as it is in the D-minor Ninth Symphony). The harmony of much of the mass has the searching, restless quality of much of his late music, sometimes at the service of exaltation, sometimes conveying suffering.

Instead of Classical form and key relations, he decreed the absolute primacy of the text: the rhythms for both singers and orchestra are the rhythms of the text, the moods are the moods of the text, the ecstasies and moments of mystery explicate the text: *Gloria! Et resurrexit! Et incarnatus est.* As Beethoven pounded his hands and feet and bellowed as he worked, composing with his whole body, he wanted us not only to understand but to *feel* every phrase and every significant word, not only in our hearts and minds but also in our bodies, like the rocketing scales and ecstatic cries of *Gloria* and *Hosanna,* and the shuddering of the "Crucifixus." In theory he deplored overt pictorial representations in music, but he had enormous powers of musical description when he wanted to use them, and he had painted plenty of pictures in works including the *Pastoral* Symphony. In the mass there is not a single image suggested by the text that is not mirrored viscerally in the music: *ascendit* races up, *descendit* plunges down. That both gestures are clichés does not concern him. He is after bigger matters.[21] More than any other single element, the unity of music and text is the driving force, the form, the logic, the meaning of the *Missa solemnis*.

The melodic foundation in this work is not going to be themes subdivided into motifs and those motifs developed, but rather motifs that will be used to build themes and gestures in myriad forms and permutations. The first motif is the great D-major upbeat. From there the bass sinks from D to B: that descending third is another primal motif, first sung as *Kyrie*. The B-minor chord over that bass prophesies the B minor that is going to be a shadowy presence in the mass, including the bleak opening of the Agnus Dei. Dropping down another third, the next harmony is G major, the subdominant chord, setting up an emphasis on the subdominant throughout. Like most of the leading ideas, that harmonic tendency is both motivic and symbolic: the subdominant relationship is associated with gentleness and the pastoral topic (as in the *Pastoral* Symphony), and with harmonic ambiguity (because the tonic is dominant of the subdominant). At the same time, the subdominant–tonic harmonic cadence is the traditional musical setting of *Amen*. In a way, the whole of the *Missa solemnis* is a gigantic *Amen*.

In bars 3 and 4 there are brief chords on the downbeat and then silence. Beethoven was the first composer to make silence a thematic presence beyond a momentary effect, and so it will be in the mass. At the same time, in those two quiet chords placed on silence and the humble, head-bowed phrase that follows it, the violins trace a figure: F-sharp–B–A–G–F-sharp:

That is the prime generating motif of the *Missa solemnis*.[22] Its myriad forms and permutations are too many to cite, but here are a few:

As usual with Beethoven, the generating motif signifies both as a whole and in its parts. The rising fourth F-sharp to B will mark many themes; likewise the falling line B–A–G–F-sharp. Those last two notes, G and F-sharp, in themselves like a miniature *Amen*, will keep a regular presence. The descent down to F-sharp will echo all the way to the sopranos' last notes at the end: A–G–F-sharp on the word *pacem*, "peace." The notes A–G–F-sharp outline the primal falling third. So in its course the mass will present a cavalcade of themes, far beyond anything that would be coherent in a symphony. Instead of themes and developments, the music is made from these seed-motifs that continually sprout new themes.

After the opening gestures we hear three calls in the winds: first the clarinet's descending third D–B; in answer the oboe's poignant G–C-sharp; then the flute's A–G–F-sharp (the last notes of the generating motif). All these calls wordlessly intone *Kyrie.*

(The falling-third motif rises from the spoken inflection of the word *Kyrie*.) These woodwind figures establish the principle of imitation, of call-and-response becoming fugue and *fughetta* and *fugato* that enfolds the whole mass. Most of the music will be contrapuntal, the voices constantly echoing one another like an ongoing affirmation.

As far as the text is concerned, the Kyrie's three pleas for mercy from Lord and Christ have in themselves no particular context, dramatic overtones, or imagery. For that reason, composers were traditionally free to interpret them at will, in moods from anguished to magisterial. Meanwhile, in a *Missa solemnis* the Kyrie tends to serve as a kind of introduction to a grander Gloria. Beethoven gave his Kyrie a tone of ceremony and humble devotion — humility, but not submission. The big opening chord is *forte,* not *fortissimo;* it prefaces music of great gentleness in the first and last *Kyrie.* When the voices enter Beethoven sets up the call-and-response of soloists and choir, the individual and the group, that also will mark the piece.[23] The first section ends with the cadential G–F-sharp whispered on *eleison.*

The *Christe eleison* is marked by a new three-beat meter and faster tempo, its theme a flowing line based on the generating motif. Hereafter, Christ will tend to be represented in lines flowing up and down. The second *Kyrie* returns sounding like a sonata recapitulation, but varied and shortened. The movement ends in a tone of intense reverence, *pianissimo.*[24] In the last two bars Beethoven crossed out the original orchestral doubling and left the choir singing the last syllables quietly alone, an intimate, tender effect that will happen again and again.[25] Always it highlights and intensifies the words.

If the *Missa solemnis* is laid out on a gigantic scale, it is filled with intimate moments like that ending, dozens of them added as Beethoven returned to the nominally completed score. There is sometimes a great deal of complexity in the counterpoint, sometimes more than the ear can fathom, but the expression is always direct and unmistakable. Every note of the *Missa solemnis* is an avatar of the words. That too is symbolic. One ancient metaphor for Christ is *Logos,* "Word": *In the beginning was the Word, and the Word was with God, and the Word was God.*

Gloria

The essence of this movement is praise and exaltation: *Gloria in excelsis Deo, et in terra pax hominibus bonae voluntatis,* Glory to God in the highest, and on earth peace among men of goodwill. In the New Testament that is the song of the angels announcing the birth of Jesus, the moment of supreme joy in the faith. In this part of any mass the music must be as radiant as music can be. The text moves quickly from one idea to another, all of it addressed to God: We praise, glorify, acclaim, adore you, Lord God, King of Heaven, *Domine Deus, rex coelestis.* The middle, usually a separate and slower section, turns to pathetic entreaties: *Qui tollis peccata mundi, miserere nobis,* Who takes away the sins of the world, have mercy on us. Then, text and music return to praise: *Quoniam tu solus sanctus Dominus,* For You alone are holy, Lord. Often there is a big fugue on the final *Amen;* Beethoven follows that tradition. But after the *Amen* he returns to the *Gloria in excelsis,* partly as coda and partly as recapitulation.

These sections of text and their changing moods are the reason why a mass movement can't be encompassed by sonata form or any other conventional pattern, though it may involve repeated material.[26] Beethoven's layout of the Gloria movement is the traditional fast–slow–fast. Within that broad outline he presents a parade of ideas and themes, each part projecting its particular text: in all some nine distinct themes or ideas, the *Gloria* theme returning within the sections. Toward the end he piles climax on climax, ecstasy on ecstasy, the full orchestra roaring on for page after page. Here as elsewhere in the late music, Beethoven no longer feels obliged to give either performers or listeners a rest but rather mobilizes his singular skill in carrying us to a peak and then to a higher one.

The opening *Gloria* theme in 3/4 and D major is an explosion of exaltation, the horns and trumpets vaulting upward in a figure recalling Handel and the Baroque:[27]

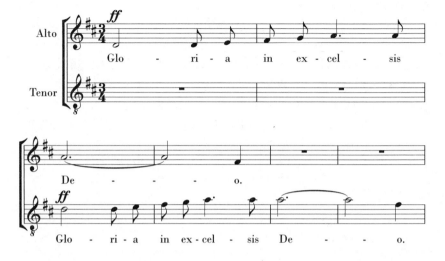

Had there ever been a more glorious Gloria? It begins full-blown, with a blaze of excitement, but that will be only a point of departure. The rising *Gloria* theme, meanwhile, pictures this moment in the service when the celebrant raises his arms to express joy. After spine-chilling pages, the music turns in a second to a soft and beautiful evocation of *pax hominibus,* peace to humankind. If the Kyrie amounted to an austerely devotional introduction to this quasi-symphonic mass, the blazing Gloria is the first movement proper. In its course, starting with the turn from *gloria* to *pax,* it reveals how Beethoven is going to build a sectional form founded on minute picturing of the text.

Laudamus te, we praise You, breaks out using the *Gloria* figure, now offset to begin on the third beat of the bar. *Adoramus te,* we adore You, is another sudden *pianissimo,* evoking the moment where the celebrant bows his head.[28] (If the mass ultimately goes beyond the church and its priests, aiming toward God without intervention, it nonetheless encompasses visceral images of the Catholic rite even as it transcends them.) *Glorificamus te,* we glorify You, is a short vigorous *fugato* on a leaping subject. With a hushed turn to B-flat major, the soloists lead a brief *Gratias agimus tibi,* we give thanks to You for Your great glory. With the arrival of *Domine Deus, rex coelestis,* Lord God, King of Heaven, Beethoven mobilizes the hard *d*'s of the Latin for cries of adoration, building to a tremendous triple-*forte* chord on *omnipotens,* omnipotent.[29]

The tempo slows to *larghetto* for the middle section, introduced by the winds to prepare pathos-filled entreaties: *Qui tollis peccata mundi,* Who takes away the sins of the world, Who sits at the right hand of God, have mercy on us. Here Beethoven concentrates on *miserere nobis.* The words are whispered over trembling figures in the strings and keened by the soloists; they mount to an anguished entreaty. *Quoniam tu solus sanctus Dominus,* For You alone are holy, Lord, starts the third section with a virile theme conjuring the power of God. In the climax the trombones — a sounding image of God's power — enter for the first time.[30]

In another quick turn of tempo and mood, the grandest and most vigorous fugue yet breaks out on *in gloria Dei patris,* in the glory of God the Father. (The choral lines are accompanied by trombones, the players' struggle to manage their scampering parts adding to the intensity.)[31] That fugue is marked *allegro, ma non troppo* — fast, but not too much — but even then it is plenty awkward for the singers. The climax of that section begins with an *Amen* marked *poco più allegro,* a little faster, at which point the music becomes manifestly too much: in a double fugue the *Amen* figure is combined with the *in gloria Dei patris* theme, both heard right-side up and inverted, at speeds verging on unsingable.[32] That mounts to yet another climax, vertiginous for listeners, its cries of *Amen!* playing dazzling tag with the meter.

Within the contrapuntal fabric of the Gloria we hear the upbeat motif, appearing much of the time as the old contrapuntal device of syncopations and suspensions tied over the bar. Here is another case in Beethoven of a familiar idea or device that was traditionally a local event — an arpeggio, a trill, a Neapolitan sixth, a suspension tied over the bar — turned into motif and expression by being treated as a theme. The *fortississimo* chord on *omnipotens* is a climactic example of the upbeat motif: the glory of the word comes in early on the third beat, ecstatically shattering the meter.

Ecstatic upbeats and displaced downbeats run riot in the apparently unsurpassable climax of the *Amen.* Then Beethoven surpasses it. He brings back the opening *Gloria* theme at a hair-raising pitch, the shouts of *Gloria!* seeming to fill heaven and earth, until his final coup: the last *Gloria* comes in on an upbeat, the orchestra plays a crashing *fortissimo* chord on the downbeat, and the choir alone finishes its triumphal shout in midbar, as upbeat to a breathtaking silence. The audience feels lifted, hearts pounding, into the air. In this mass full of thrilling visceral moments, in a work intended to raise us closer to God, this is the most exalting of all.

Credo

This part of the service is a series of avowals of belief, distilled in the two blunt syllables of the word *Credo* with which Beethoven begins the movement and punctuates much of it:

First proclaimed by the trombones in octaves, the theme is assertive, the word *Credo* repeated twice, the first as upbeat to the second, where its two syllables stride emphatically on the beat. This movement, with its proclamations of faith, will mostly stay rooted on the beat and within the meter. In its dimension as a quasi-symphonic mass, if the Kyrie is like an introduction and the Gloria a fast-tempo quasi–first movement, the Credo is a middle movement whose core tempo is moderate.

By now Beethoven's treatment of the text is established. At the outset he decided on the primacy of the word, in its sense and its sound. Like all composers in some degree or other, but with more intensity than most, he expresses the words in several dimensions at once.

First, there is the overall expressive atmosphere of the section at hand: the staunch assertion of the *Credo*, for example, sets the fundamental tone of the movement, and that enfolds the hushed mystery and awe of the *et incarnatus*.

Second, there is a constant attention to painting individual words and phrases: *omnipotens, invisibilium, ascendit, descendit, pacem.* Each word and phrase gets its distinctive melodic contour, rhythm, and color within the larger profile of the section and the movement. At times the orchestra does the word painting, or amplifies it, as in the trembling strings under the wailing lines of *miserere nobis.* All this word painting is firmly within the tradition of Handel in *Messiah* and elsewhere. (Recall, for one small example, how pictorially Handel sets the phrases "have gone astray" and "the crooked straight, and the rough places plain.")

Third, as noted before, Beethoven translates the spoken inflection and rhythm of the text into the music, then uses sound as expression: the hard *c* and *d* of *Credo* become a pounding affirmation; the *d*'s of *Deum de Deo* are set to a soaring line evoking divine power; *Et incarnatus est de Spiritu Sancto* is mystical starting in its *s*'s and open vowels. Because of the varying rhythms of the words, Beethoven never wields the monorhythmic effects he used in the Fifth through Seventh Symphonies. There is a constantly shifting rhythmic variety and forward drive, all of it founded on the text. Flexible, driving, constantly varied rhythm is one of the glories of the *Missa solemnis.*

Fourth, at times he inflects a word or a line with symbolic gestures, such as the flute's birdcalls behind the *et incarnatus.* At times he reinterprets a phrase in differing tones: in the Agnus Dei, the *dona nobis pacem* begins as a prayer in a pastoral mode; in the course of the movement, those words become a demand, a terrified entreaty, once again a prayer. Finally, at times he picks out a single unexpected word to make a point: the repeated *et* at several points in the Credo, all of them pointing forward to the most important *ands: et resurrexit, et ascendit.*

In the Credo Beethoven again reflected Viennese mass traditions and at the same time adapted and amplified them. He laid the movement out in the usual three sections, fast–slow–fast. The key is B-flat major, his leading secondary key (a mediant, not a dominant). The first section issues its assertions of belief: in one God, the son of God, true God, the Son consubstantial with the Father, the Son who descended from heaven for our salvation. Most of this is set in a forceful stride, *forte* to *fortissimo,* largely with full orchestra and staunch trombones. There are dizzying descents on the phrase *descendit de coelis,* came down from heaven. (The sopranos are required to make a cruel plunge of an octave and a half from a screaming high B-flat, then to leap back up to the B-flat.) In the middle of the first section there is a sudden turn to a hushed D-flat major, lines flowing up in a long ascent to herald the coming of Christ. Those long ascents will return memorably.[33] This is a movement full of foreshadowings, among them the winds' E-flat-major chord of the beginning, a high harmony that is going to emerge as another symbol of divinity.[34]

At the end of the first section comes a sudden hush to announce the central mystery of the faith: *Et incarnatus est.* To paint the sublime incarnation in the Virgin Mary, Beethoven takes up two ancient topics. The music is in Dorian mode, the old church scale whose character, he read in the work of the Renaissance theorist Zarlino, is "the donor of modesty and the preserver of chastity"[35] — fitting for Mary's immaculate conception. Beyond that he was interested in these modes for an antiquity that implies holiness. He wrote, "In the old church modes the devotion is divine . . . and [may] God let me express it someday."[36]

Hovering over hushed and mystical Dorian-mode phrases in the choir is a flute playing fluttering birdcalls. Here Beethoven paints an image that originated in scripture. After John the Baptist baptized Jesus, there was a vision of the Holy Spirit descending from heaven in the form of a dove. Another old tradition says that Jesus was conceived by that dove of the Spirit through Mary's ear — so by means of the Word. The holy dove turned up in Renaissance paintings portraying the incarnation. The flute's birdcalls here are not literally those of a dove or any other bird but imaginary birdcalls to conjure a spirit not of this earth. (Beethoven added the flute flutters as an afterthought to the "final" manuscript.)[37]

The incarnation, then the crucifixion. As the tragic center of the mass for many composers, including Bach, the "Crucifixus" is a movement in itself. Beethoven treats it relatively briefly, but distinctively: mostly inward, a spiritual as much as physical agony. At first the words are chanted by the choir in anguished harmonies while the strings play shuddering, piercing figures in accompaniment. The word *passus* brings a wailing line from bassoon and strings, the music finally falling to *pianissimo* darkness for the descent into the sepulchre.[38]

Many composers also make a whole movement of the joyous next section: *Et resurrexit,* And resurrected on the third day, according to the scriptures. Beethoven handles that announcement briskly in six bars of pealing declamation, first announced by the tenors on a high G and then in the choir in modal harmonies.[39]

More so than the resurrection, Beethoven is interested in the ascent to heaven: *et ascendit* in long, rocketing lines. Now comes the most dogmatic and troublesome part of the Credo. Christ sits at the right hand of God in judgment of the quick and the dead; then come the declarations of belief in the Trinity, in the one true church, in one baptism, in the resurrection of the dead. Again, it is not recorded precisely what Beethoven believed in regard to eternal life, likewise the celestial family and their cosmic courtroom. Of course, he could not presume to edit out the phrases dealing with these matters. Instead, he turned them to musical purposes: while the foreground takes up the opening *Credo* figure, in the background the dogmatic phrases are chanted like a priest rushing through the liturgy, creating a rhythmic energy that adds tremendous exhilaration to the cries of *Credo!* It comes down to the concluding "I look forward to the resurrection of the dead, and to life ever after," finished with mighty *Amens.*

But Beethoven is not finished with that last phrase, *et vitam venturi saeculi, amen.* On those words he erects a lilting, gentle tour de force of a fugue fleshed out with various contrapuntal devices: double fugue, inversion, stretto, diminution. The main theme is built on a chain of seven descending thirds that keep cycling in voice after voice, an evocation of eternity.[40] The fugue stretches out in a great arch, gathering and intensifying. Then with an *allegro con moto* injection it sprints forward, once again straining the limits of human voices. Once again, rhythms ecstatically spill over the bar line. As coda there is a slowing to *grave,* and amid chains of long scalewise ascents the music sinks to meditative exhaustion. Finally one more rising scale figure, the longest yet in the mass, starts from the bottom of the orchestra and flows upward until it reaches the flute that represented the holy dove. As scale figures rise up again and again, answered by scales sinking down, the movement ends on the same high E-flat chord it began with, now made ethereal. That coloration will soon return, unforgettably.

Here Beethoven reveals what he means by these lines flowing up and down. Recall Kant's words, in Beethoven's phrasing: "The moral law within us, and the starry sky above us." In the late music, in high and luminous sonorities Beethoven viscerally evokes that image of the divine — in the shimmering trills of the late piano sonatas, in the *Missa solemnis* and the Ninth Symphony, in the string quartets to come.[41] The long lines rippling up and down are another part of that image: the spirit of humanity reaching upward, the divine spirit descending. Christ stands as the prime avatar of that cosmic circuit. Here again is Kant's interchange of God and humanity, the order of nature and human morality being reflections of divine order.

Sanctus

The first words of the Sanctus are adapted from the Old Testament prophet Isaiah, who had a vision of God on His throne surrounded by six-winged seraphim eternally crying praises: *Sanctus, sanctus, sanctus, Dominus Deus Sabaoth!* Holy, holy, holy, Lord God of Sabaoth! Heaven and earth are full of thy Glory! Hosanna in the highest! For many composers, including Bach, the operative word is *glory:* the music evokes the majesty of God as He holds court from His throne.

Beethoven takes an entirely different path. It is in this and the next movement that he journeys the furthest from traditional interpretations of the text. He begins the Sanctus softly in D major, in a tone of solemn, ceremonial devotion. Much of it will be quiet, sung by the soloists rather than the full choir. He presumably had several reasons for this choice, including some needed calm and textural variety, but one choice is particularly meaningful. The central point of the Mass in church, and a central point of Catholic devotion, is the Eucharist. In a reenactment of the Last Supper, the celebrant raises the cup of wine, which is transubstantiated into the actual blood of Christ. Salvation depends on this sacrament, drinking the blood and eating the bread, which has become the body of Christ.[42] In the *Missa solemnis* that sacrament which occurs in the middle of the Sanctus casts its influence backward to the quiet orchestral beginning of the movement. The great perorations and towering climaxes that marked the Gloria and Credo will not be heard here.

The Sanctus begins with a sigh in the basses that rises to a texture of low strings with divided violas, horns, and low clarinets. The effect conjures the sound of an organ in quiet stops. The brass intone solemn chords, bringing in the soloists with their prayerful phrases.[43] The mood is the opposite of the glorious panoply often associated with this text. Beethoven was not so concerned with eternal salvation or six-winged seraphim. He was concerned with deeper mysteries. He aimed the movement toward its conclusion, the Benedictus.

The first section of the Sanctus ends with the soloists murmuring *Dominus Deus Sabaoth* at *pianissimo,* like priests at a distant altar. The *Pleni sunt coeli,* Heaven and earth are full of Thy glory, breaks out in a soaring fugue surrounded by racing strings. While the whole of the *Missa solemnis* is informed by Handel, this may be the most overtly Handelian moment.[44] The *Pleni* fugue is answered by a short, skipping fugue in 3/4 that dispenses briskly with *Hosanna in excelsis.* Many composers dwell on that line, but Beethoven wants to get on to his central section. From the *Hosanna* he shifts direction in seconds.[45]

The next pages, for orchestra alone, in a remarkable subdued organlike color, echo the beginning of the movement, with divided violas and cellos, the texture made ethereal by low flutes. In the event that this was an actual service, here the Eucharist would be celebrated. Beethoven labels the section *Präludium.* He has in mind the tradition in which organists would prelude, meaning improvise, during the Eucharist to join the Hosanna to the next section, the Benedictus.[46] So now he creates a searching, chromatic, quasi-improvisation in imitation of an organ. These pages are more a matter of mystery than practical musical continuity: in a sound and texture unique in music of its time, Beethoven conjures a tangible presence of the numinous, in preparation for what follows. Meanwhile, if with the *Dominus Deus* he supplied the chanting priests, here he supplies the church organist. In both respects, as in other parts of the mass, he subsumes the literal rite in the music.

In one of his quietly breathtaking moments, at the end of the *Präludium,* suspended high in musical space, comes another ethereal chord in two flutes and a violin. They begin the Benedictus with a long descent in a lilting, pastoral 12/8, in pure G major.[47] That heart-stopping high chord appears at the moment a candle would be lit on the altar to signify the moment of transubstantiation, when Christ becomes present in the bread and wine.[48]

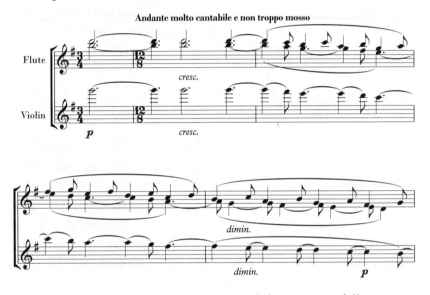

The Benedictus is marked *molto cantabile,* very songfully. Here is Beethoven's evocation and interpretation of the Eucharist, summoning Christ's descent from heaven onto the altar, into the bread and wine. It is a sui generis portrayal of that moment, that mystery, by way of an extended violin solo. Few things in music approach its gentle joy, its long-sustained beauty. Around the diaphanous singing and dancing of the Christ-violin, the choir chants, *Benedictus qui venit in nomine Domini,* Blessed is he who comes in the name of the Lord. Chorus and orchestra concentrate on the central word, *Benedictus* which goes on and on as an incantation under the endless song of the violin. It is a depiction of the divine presence as a vision of transcendent beauty, like a halo transmuted into sound. It is also the central movement downward in the dialectic of up and down, the human spirit reaching up and divine grace reciprocating. Staying close to a pure, pastoral G major, the music gathers to a tutti at the end of the movement, the violin singing over all and pronouncing the final benediction.[49]

Agnus Dei

The strangest and most haunting Agnus Dei written to its time begins in an atmosphere of stark tragedy in B minor, which Beethoven called a "black key." There are only a few words in this final segment of the Mass Ordinary: *Agnus Dei, qui tollis peccata mundi, miserere nobis. Dona nobis pacem,* Lamb of God, who takes away the sins of the world, have mercy upon us. Give us peace. The text comes from the words of John the Baptist when he first saw Jesus: "Behold the Lamb of God, who takes away the sins of the world." That image connects Christ, who sacrificed himself for the salvation of humanity, to the sacrificial lamb of Passover. Like any composer of an ambitious mass, Beethoven will have to repeat these words a good deal in order to fill out a substantial final movement. His approach will be to reinterpret the words en route. He breaks the text into the usual three segments, the first and second focused on *miserere nobis,* the third on *dona nobis pacem.* But in the end his Agnus Dei is a personal statement, rising from tradition but stretching beyond it.

Many Agnus Dei sections in masses begin with a gentle, pastoral evocation of Jesus as Lamb of God. Beethoven begins with a moaning, foreboding texture of bassoons, horns, and low strings as accompaniment to the prayer by the bass soloist and men's voices from the choir. The operative idea from the beginning is not Christ as savior but the words *miserere nobis,* have mercy on us, which the music portrays in swelling, funereal tones like a cry of suffering humanity.

The funeral tread stops, the music harkens. *Agnus Dei,* the choir chants, *pianissimo.* In piercing tones breaking out in the chorus in falling thirds we hear *Dona! Dona nobis pacem!* Give! Give us peace! Gentle music in D major and 6/8 begins, the string figures fluttering like the wings of the holy dove. We have awakened from a dolorous trance to a pastoral scene and a flowing and beautiful *fugato* whose theme sets the single word *pacem:*

At the head of this section, Beethoven placed in the score, *Bitte um innern and äußern Frieden*, "Prayer for inner and outer peace." The *fugato* is a pastoral idyll, the sounding image of peace, its meter and flowing lines recalling the violin solo that represents Christ in the Benedictus. The prayer swells, then the orchestra stops and leaves the chorus singing a cappella, with great simplicity and intimacy, *dona nobis pacem*. Beethoven has used this device of dropping out the instruments here and there throughout the mass, but this is the most poignant instance. He wants us to *feel* peace in our hearts and minds. Accompanied by figures dancing up in long ascents and down in descents, the choir sighs, *pacem, pacem*, in floating, archaic harmonies.

The yearning for peace intensifies; the pastoral and prayerful tone gives way to a demand: "Give us peace! Peace! Peace!" The music appears to be building toward a conclusion, a coda. But that is interrupted by something wrenchingly alien: throbbing drums, flurries of strings like gusts of wind presaging a storm. Suddenly out of nowhere there are bugle calls. The soloists take up a cry marked "anxiously": "Lamb of God! Have mercy on us!" The drums and bugles return, *fortissimo*, under which the soprano's cry for mercy can hardly be heard. In this moment Beethoven explodes the form, in the same way he did with the storm in the *Pastoral* Symphony.[50] Armies have disrupted the rite, destroyed the peace. It is war.

Even this shocking, high-Beethoven intrusion, though, had a precedent. As so often, that precedent was Haydn. In his *Mass in Time of War*, written in the midst of the Napoleonic Wars, Haydn's Agnus Dei is interrupted by trumpets and drums in the same place in the service, and in the same way: mounting drum taps and bugle calls, as if an army were surrounding the cathedral. In Haydn the choir's call for peace finally becomes militant, as does Beethoven's. But Haydn does not shatter the music as violently as Beethoven, does not break the form so completely, does not make the cries for mercy so anguished.

In Beethoven's Agnus Dei, the sounds of war recede, the music recovers. In a chain of falling thirds the chorus again intones, *Dona! Dona! Dona nobis pacem!*[51] But the pastoral mood, the idyllic vision of peace, is vanished for good. *Dona* becomes a surging *fugato* that leads to a return of the beautiful, sighing lines on *pacem*, which as before turn into a shouted demand. Yet again that is interrupted by an alien force. War overwhelms the music.

For this section Beethoven first sketched ideas for marches. Then he settled on something more ambiguous: a driving, militant fugue in gaunt colors, the fugue theme a mangling of the pastoral *pacem* theme:

Years before, he wrote over an idea in the *Eroica* sketches "a strange voice." Here is a truly foreign voice, cold, harsh, and bustling, like a bitter parody of his own heroic style (and this may be the point). In the *Eroica* and other pieces of his middle years, Beethoven hailed the enlightened leader, the benevolent despot, the military spirit. Now for him the military spirit is nothing but destruction. By the end of this section the bugles are raging, the drums roaring, the choir crying *Dona pacem!* in terror.

Now we understand what Beethoven meant by "prayer for inner and outer peace." The inner peace is that of the spirit. The outer peace is in the world. The fear and trembling in the *Missa solemnis* is not the fear of losing salvation in eternity; it is the human, secular fear of violence and chaos.

For a second time the music recovers. The intonations of *Dona nobis pacem* have gone from pastorally peaceful to demanding to fearful. Now prayers for peace break out again, and the flowing 6/8 returns — but it is not a real recapitulation, and still not with pastoral peace. In fact the texture is strangely broken up. The *fortissimo* demands of *pacem! pacem!* seem to fall apart. The music drifts.

Then in the distance, a war drum. The choir prays again: *pacem, pacem.* Again the drum interrupts, farther away, its alien B-flat almost out of hearing.[52] Staccato lines skitter up and down. The chorus makes a longer cry for peace, *forte* but not *fortissimo.* In this last choral phrase of the mass, the sopranos in their cadence again descend only to F-sharp, not all the way to a decisive finish on D. The orchestra gives a scant four bars of climactic music, ending on a staccato D-major chord. There the *Missa solemnis* finds its precipitous finish, in an atmosphere of fragmentation and irresolution.

What has happened? Generations will debate it, often trying to make the end into a pious and affirmative conclusion. But if Beethoven has put away many of his habits of development and musical logic in this work, he has not abandoned cause and effect, proportion, underlying logic, even when he intends to violate them. The war interludes break out around the rite, interrupt the service, shatter the peace, tear apart the form. The peace, the form, never recover their equilibrium.

In musical terms, with the sounds of war, Beethoven injects an alien and unprepared but overwhelming dramatic force into the music, in the same way that his thunderstorm once broke up a peasant dance in the *Pastoral.* This is a logic of image and narrative, not music. By the laws of music that Beethoven bent and adapted but never lost sight of, a new idea has to be integrated, the disruption it created has to be resolved. In the *Pastoral* Symphony the resolution is a peaceful, thankful finale. In the Eighth Symphony finale, the disruption of the intrusive C-sharps is resolved in a farcical outbreak of modulations at the penultimate moment.

In Beethoven's Agnus Dei, there is no integration and no resolution of the violence and disruption. The rumbling of drums at the end pictures war receding, at the same time reminds us of our terror. At one point Beethoven sketched a triumphant ending, labeled the receding-drum idea *peace.* Then he decided that, no, to finish this gigantic work of faith he wanted a curt, ambiguous, unresolved ending.

A work of faith it is. But in the end the *Missa solemnis* is Beethoven's personal faith as an individual reaching toward God, not an assertion of the credos and dogmas of the Holy Roman and Apostolic Church. He subsumes doctrine in some degree, as he must in order to write a mass at all, but he goes beyond doctrine into a unique mingling of faith, spirituality, and humanism. He created a mass that subsumed the doctrines and the physical rite of the church, the very gestures of the priests and the preluding of the organist, but he turns them into something both personal and universal.[53] Ultimately the *Missa solemnis* is a statement of faith and also of doubt, beyond the walls of any church. *From the heart, may it go to the heart*—person to person, without priests. The *Missa solemnis* is Beethoven's cathedral in sound. At the end there is no triumph of faith, no triumph of peace, no triumph at all. God has not answered humanity's prayers, its demands, its terrified pleas for peace. The drums have receded, but they are still out there, and they can come back. Beethoven's most ambitious work, his cathedral, the one he intended to be his greatest, ends with an unanswered prayer. What, then, is the answer? Whether he planned two successive works as a question and answer, or whether it happened because Beethoven was who he was and believed as he did, his answer was the Ninth Symphony.

31

You Millions

FOR BEETHOVEN THE Ninth Symphony in D Minor, op. 125, had a long background. It marked a return to roots in his life, his art, and his culture. Those roots reached back to his youth in Bonn during its golden years of Aufklärung, when he first determined to set "An die Freude," the Friedrich Schiller poem that in fiery verses embodied the spirit of the time. The intellectual atmosphere he breathed in Bonn included the philosophy of Kant, the Masonic ideal of brotherhood, the Illuminist doctrine of a cadre of the enlightened who will point humanity toward freedom and happiness. Passing through his life and awareness in the next decades were the French Revolution and its art, the funeral dirges and music for public festivals; then the wars and the burgeoning hopes of the Napoleonic years; then the destruction of those hopes and the end of the age of heroes and benevolent despots.

Also simmering within the Ninth Symphony as it took shape was the model and the threat of Haydn, who wrote *The Creation* and the song that became the unofficial Austrian national anthem. Beyond Haydn lay traditions and voices and models that Beethoven had always turned to for ideas and inspiration: Handel, Mozart, Bach, and the history of the symphony, including what he himself brought to that history.

Once, the threads of his early years had gathered into the *Eroica*, which secured the symphony for more than a century as the summit of musical genres. Now the accumulated threads of a lifetime converged to create the Ninth, the sister work to the *Missa solemnis*, the answer to the human and spiritual question that the mass left hanging: if God cannot give us peace, what can? Beethoven did not consider the mass and the Ninth his final statements, because he hoped to write still greater works if fate gave him the chance. Fate did not oblige. So if the mass and symphony were not the end, in many ways they were the summation and culmination of his life and work.

The Ninth itself took at least a decade to condense from its first vague imaginings, during anguished and drifting years, to the conception that it became: a monumental symphony whose culmination is a finale with the unprecedented inclusion of a choir and soloists singing verses from "An die Freude." As it took shape, the music of the symphony itself traces that same journey from vaporous beginnings through tragedy to triumph.

When in his teens Beethoven declared to friends his intention of setting the whole of Schiller's "To Joy," one of his adult admirers wrote to Schiller's wife, "I expect something perfect, for as far as I know him he is wholly devoted to the great and sublime." If Beethoven attempted that setting at all, any traces of it disappeared; several years later, he suppressed another setting that he had mentioned to a publisher. But he never stopped thinking about the poem — he remembered it after Napoleon betrayed the republican dream, and after Austria set out to erase the memory of that dream. Since the 1780s there had been some forty settings of "An die Freude," including one from 1815 by the young Franz Schubert.[1] They were widely sung in Masonic and Illuminati lodges. Most of these settings were, like the poem itself, in the tradition of the *geselliges Lied,* a social song intended to be sung by groups of friends.

Ideas about a "Freude" setting and/or a work with chorus, perhaps as part of a symphony or some sort of freestanding piece, began to turn

up in Beethoven's sketches of the middle teens. In early 1816 he added
one more sketch to his dozens of ideas for symphonies:

This is one of his few symphony sketches that eventually took wing.
It is recognizable as the opening of the eventual Ninth. More sketches
turned up in the winter of 1817–18, also involving what became central ideas. One of them was a string tremolo on the open fifth A–E,
the essential concept of the beginning. Loose, abortive ideas for the
second-movement scherzo appeared, written beneath one of them,
"Symphony at the beginning only 4 voices 2 Vln, Viol, Bass among
them forte with other voices and if possible bring in all the other instruments one by one." Sketches toward what became the slow movement may first have been intended for a different piece.[2]

By around 1818 he had fixed on the idea of a symphony with voices
to enter in the finale or earlier. He was also thinking about the archaic
church modes, though those ended up mainly in the mass and a late
quartet. He speculated about the music from a slow movement returning in the finale, also an ecclesiastical touch and a Bacchic (meaning
dancing and ecstatic) movement. Around the same time he wrote in
his *Tagebuch*, "To write a national song on the Leipzig October and
perform this every year. N.B. each nation with its own march and the
Te deum laudamus."[3] Here he imagined some sort of national work for
an international festival. In one way and another, all these ideas ended
up in the Ninth.

After what appears to be a long hiatus came a few bars of ideas in-

cluding, from 1822, a sketch toward variations on Handel's well-known
Funeral March from *Saul*. The snippet of the Handel march Beethoven
jotted down is a precursor of the coda of the Ninth's first movement:[4]

From Levy, *Beethoven*

That year he sketched a simple, almost chantlike setting of "An die
Freude" with this note: "Sinfonie allemand after which the chorus enters or also without variations. End of the Sinfonie with Turkish music
and vocal chorus."[5] So by that point he was thinking about a symphony
to end with a choral setting of "An die Freude" involving music in the
pseudo-Turkish style familiar in military music.

All these loose ideas, of the kind that characterize most of his jottings in the sketchbooks, precipitated into intensive work in the spring
of 1823. By then two things had happened. In November 1822, the Philharmonic Society in London accepted his proposal to write a symphony for it, offering 50 pounds; and he finished the *Diabelli* Variations
and had nothing else pressing to do. The London commission was yet
another impetus to go to England and see whether he could duplicate
Haydn's triumphs. Around April 1823, new sketches and drafts for the
symphony followed on the completion of the *Diabellis*.[6] Some eleven
months later, the Ninth was done.

When he got down to the job, he already had what amounted to a final conception of the opening. But he had a problem that needed to be
addressed before he went further. He was determined to make this an
end-directed symphony, that end being a choral finale involving voices

and "An die Freude." As he said, *Always keep the whole in view.* If the finale and its theme were to be a goal, the music needed to foreshadow it from the beginning. So before he got too far into the first movement, he had to find his finale theme. In that respect the symphony was going to be composed back to front, as the *Eroica* and the *Kreutzer* Sonata had been: the leading ideas of the beginning being developed from the main theme of the finale.

Quickly he found his opening phrase for the poem:

Freu-de, schö-ner   Göt-ter-fun-ken, Toch-ter aus E - ly - si - um,

wir be - tre - ten, feu - er -trun-ken, Himm-li-sche, dein Hei - lig - thum!

For the moment, though, that was all he found. The rest of the theme, which would encompass each of his chosen verses of the Schiller (selected from the much longer complete poem), would not come. But in fact the inception of the theme was all he needed, for the moment, to make his foreshadowings. The first phrase could stand for the whole of the *Freude* theme, just as the first notes of the *Eroica* theme often stood for the whole. He could finish the rest of the finale theme later.

At the same time, that first phrase, setting the first four lines of the Schiller, determined the style and direction of the *Freude* theme. It is above all simple, an ascent from the third degree of the scale to the fifth and back down to the first degree, all in quarter and half notes. Here Beethoven's longstanding concern with simplicity and directness found its ultimate distillation in a little ditty that was going to be the foundation of a monumental work. That ascent from the third degree to the fifth and scalewise back down to the first would be the essence of the foreshadowings in the symphony. So strong was that presence that it took him considerable pains, when he finally got to it, to finish the tune in the same plainspoken spirit while giving it at least a little seasoning.

Beyond that, what did he have in mind as he shaped the *Freude* theme from its seminal first phrase? He already understood that the finale and its theme were going be the goal, the destination. Which is to say, the symphony was going to be a journey toward joy, starting in despair. It was a familiar narrative for Beethoven; he had done something like it in the Fifth Symphony. And he knew what he was aiming for in the *Freude* theme itself: a tune in the simple, popular, rhythmically and harmonically straightforward style of a *geselliges Lied,* especially the kind the Freemasons used to sing (before they were banned in Austria).

In all this he was doing what he usually did, taking models and expanding them in his own directions, sometimes expanding them exponentially. One model was his own *Choral Fantasy* for piano, voices, and orchestra. Beethoven himself described the finale of the Ninth as in the vein of the *Choral Fantasy.* The leading themes for both pieces have the kind of straightforward, declamatory style of other of his songs on echt-Aufklärung texts going all the way back to *Who Is a Free Man?* from his youth (which his Bonn friend Wegeler turned into a Masonic song).

In turn, part of that style was the *geselliges Lied.* Those sociable songs, intended to be proclaimed in company with glass in hand, were always strophic, meaning each verse was sung to the same tune. Generally the songs exalted friendship, fellowship, brotherhood, and joy.[7] One example is Beethoven's own *Bundeslied* (Song of the Confederacy), on Masonic verses by Goethe. It begins: "Whenever the hour is good, / Inspired by love and wine, / Shall we, united, / Sing this song!" On the manuscript Beethoven noted it was to be sung "in companionable circles."[8]

On a larger scale was the memory of French revolutionary music that had been a major inspiration of the *Eroica.* These were pieces for public festivals that had a style at once popular and monumental. Here art became a communal ritual — in France largely to nationalistic and propagandistic ends, but artists had a deeper agenda. Poet Marie-Joseph Chénier wrote, "The ability to lead men is nothing else than the ability to direct their sensibilities ... the basis of all human institutions is morality, public and private, and ... the fine arts are essentially moral because they make the individual devoted to them better and happier. If this is true for all the arts, how much more evident is it in the case of music." Robespierre wanted to teach a specially written "Hymn to the Supreme Being" to every citizen so all Paris could sing it at an outdoor festival.[9]

Another piece of the background was the relatively new idea of national anthems, their tunes designed to be inspiring, memorable, easily singable by the multitudes. Haydn had been inspired by the British *God Save the King* when he was commissioned to write *Gott erhalte Franz den Kaiser,* which became the unofficial Austrian anthem. Haydn went on to write variations on the theme in his *Emperor* Quartet. (Beethoven also admired *God Save the King* and used it in piano variations and in *Wellington's Victory.*) Beethoven surely envied Haydn his anthem. Another model, most potent of all, was *La Marseillaise,* the indispensable song of the French Revolution that set feet marching to overthrow the ancien régime and attached itself to the revolutionary spirit everywhere. (That is why, after he crowned himself emperor, Napoleon banned the *Marseillaise.* Revolutions were to end with him.)

So a trajectory in Beethoven's work began in Bonn, rose to its apogee in the Third and Fifth Symphonies and in *Fidelio,* and came to rest in the Ninth Symphony, which resonated with the accumulated political and ethical ideas and energies of the previous decades. The *Eroica* exalts the conquering hero; *Fidelio* is a testament to individual heroism and liberation; the Fifth Symphony is an implicit drama of an individual struggling with fate. The *Eroica* and the Ninth have to do with the fate of societies. As to the road to an ideal society, the Ninth repudiates in thunder the answer of the *Eroica.*

No wonder that it cost Beethoven some trouble to finish the *Freude* theme after arriving at its opening phrase. By the time he needed the complete tune to compose the finale, he had gone through nineteen stages of work on it, mostly for the second part, which adds the seasoning of a leap to a note tied over the bar.[10] A great deal was riding on this theme, not only the direction and fate of his most ambitious symphony but matters well beyond that. He intended the theme to be his *God Save the King,* his Austrian anthem, his *Marseillaise.* But those anthems were devoted only to nations. His ambitions for his tune had expanded exponentially. He wanted to write a universal anthem, a *Marseillaise* for humanity.[11] To that end he demanded of himself that he create a popularistic theme like something that had written itself, an ingenuous little tune that everyone could remember and nearly anyone could sing.[12] He wanted a theme to conquer the world.[13]

The Ninth Symphony begins in mist and uncertainty, on a hollow open fifth and the wrong harmony: winds and string tremolos on A and E. The A seems to be the keynote, but it isn't. The sound of the beginning, like matter emerging out of the void and slowly filling space, had never been heard in a piece before. Yet its effect was familiar to the time: the beginning of the Ninth is a descendent of "Chaos" in *The Creation.* Haydn's "Chaos" resolves into the C-major revelation of *Let there be light!* The chaos of the Ninth's beginning resolves into a towering proclamation of forbidding import, the orchestra striding in militant dotted rhythms down a D-minor chord.[14] D minor for Beethoven was a rare key, usually fraught: the *Tempest* Sonata; the tragic slow movement of the Piano Sonata op. 10, no. 3; the *Ghost* Trio second movement.

In the Ninth, the gestures that emerge from the void are stern and heroic, at the same time gnarled, searching, nervous, remote. If this is some kind of heroic image, it is a hero whose proclamations are raging and indisputable. What will prove to be the leading theme and motifs are first heard in measures 19–20:

This is hardly a melodic idea; call it one of Beethoven's "speaking" themes. The rhythmic motif, *da-da-da-dum,* is of course essentially the same as that of the Fifth Symphony and any number of other Beethoven works. Another steady presence in the movement is the militant tattoo of dotted rhythms. The descending three-note bit of scale is the opening motif, inverted, of the *Freude* theme — a first, distant prophecy.

At the same time this beginning that emerges from nothing, filling in space, rising to a gigantic proclamation, suggests another metaphor that pervades the symphony. The beginning is an image of creation itself, of the creation of worlds, of societies, of individuals. It brought to music the idea that a work can evoke a self-creating cosmos. The beginning also involves *the creation of a theme,* which will eventually be the main business of the first part of the finale. Lying behind that is an image of the Ninth Symphony rising from silence *to create itself,* as a work rises from nothing in the mind of its creator. The last movement will return to that image. These images all work together. To say again: with Beethoven emotion, drama, image, and technique work in harmony (most of the time). Not only is the image of creation a fundamental idea and message of the Ninth Symphony, it is a central part of its effect.

This is the most complex first movement Beethoven had made since the *Eroica,* and a far more enigmatic opening than that symphony's. As in the earlier work, the first movement is based on fragments more than sustained themes. Here the texture is filled with bits of ideas constantly batted around the orchestra. Which is to say that, like the *Eroica,* it is developmental from the beginning, the exposition of the sonata form vibrating with the restlessness of a development section.

In keeping, it has the late period's tendency to float the harmony. After the first pages, there is no strong cadence to D minor until measure 429; this is the home key not as a foundation but as a long-awaited, hard-won goal. For long stretches there is no clear cadence at all. Such floating, unresolved harmony can create a feeling of suspension and reverie, but here it sustains an unrelenting tension.[15] Part of the effect is that much of the time the basses are restlessly in motion, in scales and arpeggios and melodic lines, so the harmony has no solid foundation. The movement avoids the usual secondary keys related to D minor — F major and A minor or major.

In their formal import the first two pages are ambiguous: is the A–E tremolo a theme or an introduction? What about the D-minor arpeggio theme? (As it plays out, the tremolo is not developed in the movement like a theme, but the arpeggio is.) The tremolo returns on D–A for a moment, stabilizing the harmony briefly, for the last time in a long time. Then two things of considerable import happen. First, the stern arpeggio theme recurs in B-flat. Second, the three-note descending motif from the speaking theme in measure 19 begins to be treated obsessively, first in a nervous alternation of D minor and D major. Those three tonalities — D minor, D major, B-flat major — are going to be the principal tonal areas of the symphony. Throughout there will be a dialectic between D minor and major. D minor was for Beethoven often an ominous key, D major associated with gaiety, comedy, joy. And as in the Fifth Symphony, major is destined to win out over minor in the finale.

In a sketch, the emotion Beethoven applied to the first movement was despair. Its tone is not like the portraits of despair in his music going back to *La Malinconia* in op. 18 and the *Pathétique* and *Appassionata*. In the Ninth the despair is something unfamiliar — unbending, elusive, relentlessly unstable. The tone of the music is close to Beethoven's heroic style, but the instability questions that style and that ethos.

As with the *Eroica*, the second-theme section of the sonata form is complex, full of ideas, ambiguous as to where it begins. Just before the second theme there is a sudden lyrical warming, a brief, harmonically stable moment in B-flat — unmistakably a moment of hope. Melodically and rhythmically, this is the first clear prophecy of the *Freude* theme, beginning with its three-note bit of ascending scale:

The warmth persists through the next phrases, the second theme proper. Then restlessness seeps back in. That moment of hope in lyrical B-flat is not truly part of the form; it is an interjection, an anomaly. It does not return until the recapitulation, and only that once.[16]

The end of the exposition is the down-striding dotted-arpeggio theme in B-flat. That is the first truly stable harmonic moment since the opening pages. From there we hear what seems to be the usual repeat of the exposition, returning to the tremolo strings on A–E. But it is a false repeat. For the first time in a symphony, Beethoven goes on without repeating the exposition.

The development section, usually the most turbulent part of a sonata-form movement, is here the most relatively calm — though there is still an undercurrent of tension. It begins with a look back at the descending-arpeggio figure, now quieted. Nearly every phrase is a tidy four bars. But from the exposition he has hardly any normal theme to develop, so now he uses the leading motifs to create more sustained themes. Between that and the lack of an exposition repeat, he is aiming for a through-composed effect, the material constantly in flux, forming and reforming in new directions, self-creating. There are loud, vigorous moments in the development, but no shattering climax as in the *Eroica*. The shattering moment is the recapitulation.

Still without a cadence, still in restless rhythms, the development settles down for a sustained stretch in D minor. From there without warning the recapitulation seems to erupt out of nowhere, assaulting the music with extraordinary effect: a *fortissimo* D-major chord with an F-sharp rather than a D in the bass. Beyond a harmony with an unstable note at its foundation, the D-major chord itself seems vertiginous and disorienting. In D major now, the falling-arpeggio theme breaks out. Here are a major chord and key violent in effect. The moment negates everything a recapitulation and a major chord are supposed to be — a release of tension, a homecoming. Here perhaps for the first time the movement clearly reveals its roots in violence and despair. It is one of the most original, unexpected, hair-raising moments Beethoven had created since the searing development climax and wrong-chord recapitulation in the *Eroica*. There the hero was triumphant. Here he is sowing ruin.

If the effect of the movement so far has been developmental and through-composed, the recapitulation is largely literal, settling down the explosion of the recapitulation. Then begins one of Beethoven's long codas, in length a quarter of the movement. It is a resumption of the development with some of its themes, but now as in the Fifth Symphony first movement, in the coda everything is made more intense, more forward-driving than the development proper.

At the end comes Beethoven's last shock in the movement. In the basses *pianissimo* begins an eerie chromatic moan. Above it the winds enact a striding theme that is unmistakably a funeral march — in fact, it is derived from the Handel "Dead March" that Beethoven jotted down as he worked on the Ninth. Like the opening of the symphony, the chromatic moan rises, fills up the space until it has virtually taken over the orchestra around the deathly stride of the march, with its relentless dotted rhythms, louder and louder. Abruptly, with a return to the D-minor down-striding theme that has become nothing but death, the movement is over.

Even here, in this web of puzzles and images, Beethoven thought of the technical and emotional and symbolic at the same time. Over the years as he redistributed the weights and balances of the musical forms he inherited, more and more he was interested in end-weighted pieces, especially in the symphonies. As said before, this is a particularly difficult thing to do, to write a weighty and compelling first movement and then top it in the finale. The *Eroica* was surely intended as a step in that direction, but in musical terms as distinct from symbolic, there the finale arguably does not pay off the weight and the implications of the first movement. The Fifth may have been intended to be end-directed as well, and the triumphant finale is splendid, but the first movement still claims most of the attention.

In the Ninth he wanted the choral finale to be the goal and glory of the symphony. To that end, then, he radically destabilized the first movement, kept it unresolved, searching and not finding all the way to its end. By the end of the movement, everything is in flux, unsettled, so a climactic finale becomes indispensable. Here Beethoven definitively solved the problem he had grappled with for decades, making the finale the principal movement.

Like all the late music, the Ninth was not a new direction for Beethoven as much as a continued deepening and expansion of trends that had been in his music all along: bigger pieces, more intense contrasts, more complexity and more simplicity. The instrumentation follows suit. The Ninth and the *Missa solemnis* have the most color-ful, variegated, innovative orchestration of his life. The Ninth's mas-sive sound reaches far beyond the modest colors and textures of the eighteenth-century orchestra that Beethoven wielded in the First Sym-phony. Symphonies of that earlier time were written mainly for private orchestras that might have five or six violins, two or three violas and cellos, one bass. In the Ninth, string lines are often doubled in octaves; there are four horns and, in the second and last movements, trom-bones. The premiere involved a string section two to four times bigger than that of the usual palace or theater orchestra; the music is geared for that size string section, plus doubled winds. Given Beethoven's evolution of orchestral technique and color since the middle sympho-nies, it is astounding how innovative and fresh are the orchestral styles of the mass and the Ninth, shaped when their composer was close to stone deaf. That orchestral sound was to be a prime model for the coming Romantic generations of composers. Inevitably, in the sym-phony there are mistakes and miscalculations that Beethoven was not able to hear and fix in rehearsals. At times, the winds sound thin and unbalanced amid the massive string and brass sonorities. But mostly the sound is powerful and brilliantly variegated.

Can we glimpse what sort of meanings are adumbrated here? The end of the first movement leaves everything unresolved, unsettled, and unsettling. But the unfolding of Beethoven's music over the decades suggests a trajectory of symbol and implication.

The end of the first movement is Beethoven's third and last funeral march. The first two, the op. 26 Piano Sonata's "Funeral March on the Death of a Hero" and the same on a grander scale in the *Eroica,* were high-humanistic, echt-revolutionary evocations written in the middle of the Napoleonic Wars, honoring a military hero as the highest exem-plar of human achievement. In the Ninth, with his last funeral march, Beethoven buries another hero but in a far different, far more bitter and disillusioned context.[17]

Written in the height of the idealism over Napoleon, the *Eroica* first movement depicted the creation of a hero, the other movements the aftermath of his triumph. In the wake of the fall of Napoleon, the de-struction of what he once appeared to stand for, came the police states that followed the Congress of Vienna. Across Europe, the age of heroes and benevolent despots was finished. So among its implications, the first movement of the Ninth Symphony depicts that bitter end — the deconstruction and burial of the heroic ideal, once and for all. That is the "despair" Beethoven wrote of. In the *Eroica* the conquering hero brought peace and happiness. In the Ninth the hero brings despair and death.[18] But within that despair are moments of hope, and it is those moments that prefigure the *Freude* theme.[19]

Each movement of the Ninth begins with not exactly an introduction but rather a kind of curtain-raiser. In the first movement it is the whispering emergence from the void. In the second movement it is bold, dancing, down-leaping octaves in strings and winds and, as an impudent interruption, crashing F-to-F octaves in timpani. Beethoven places the scherzo as the second movement instead of the usual third, something not unprecedented but new to his symphonies. Beethoven had stopped calling these movements "scherzo" after the Fourth Symphony, perhaps because he did not like the joking implication of the word, which is irrelevant to the tone of the Fifth Symphony scherzo.[20]

All the movements of the Ninth are grounded on D and the scherzo is in D minor, but not a tragic D minor. It is a vivacious, puckish, indefatigable *moto perpetuo*. Those qualities in a minor key give the scherzo a distinctive tone, a tinge of irony. At the same time there is a frenetic quality that recalls Beethoven's sketch years before, imagining "a celebration of Bacchus," something on the order of a revel, a drunken frenzy in manic counterpoint.

The movement is another of his graftings of fugue and sonata, the scherzo section a fully-worked-out sonata form. At the same time it has the familiar scherzo–trio–scherzo layout. The gist of the treatment is that the opening tune is both fugue subject and sonata-form first theme, introduced in a fugue and thereafter developed as a theme. This is Beethoven's most complexly contrapuntal scherzo — at the same time, with its kinetic and memorable subject, one of his most crowd-pleasing.

The harmony is far more stable than in the first movement, but from the beginning there is a wild card: the timpani, which is apt to barge in with its Fs in octaves rather than the time's almost unvarying D–A tuning of a movement in D.[21] Besides unsettling the D minor of the theme, in the development the timpani's Fs take the music into F and E-flat major, and they usher in the recapitulation.

After its short and explosive curtain-raiser, the fugue takes off as if it were already in stretto, the entrances of the subject coming in every four beats. The first-theme section ends with the theme in glory, the fugal treatment left behind in the mad rush:

The second theme arrives as a more lyrical interlude, its lines hinting at the *Freude* theme. The development begins with a droll harmonic sequence in falling thirds that starts on E-flat and ends when it reaches B major, the twelfth chromatic note in the bass. There follows a protean and indefatigable development section entirely given to the main theme, one part of the treatment being a switch between four-bar and three-bar phrasing of the one-beat meter — a novel effect in those days.

At the trio the D minor shifts to major, triple shifts to duple, complexity gives way to simplicity, and Beethoven commences one of his most delightful and surprising episodes: over a drone, a little wisp of folk song like you'd whistle on a sunny afternoon, growing through swelling repetitions into something hypnotic and monumental. It is recognizable as a musette, named for a droning folk bagpipe, a musical topic going back more than a century and always associated with an ingenuous and pastoral atmosphere. The theme enfolds the opening notes of the *Freude* theme in a different rhythm:

After the return of the scherzo, a largely literal recapitulation, Beethoven makes a feint at repeating the trio and then jokingly jumps into a mocking two-beat for a precipitous end.

So the second movement is made of complexity counterpoised by almost childlike simplicity. It is a striking choice to follow the deathly conclusion of the first movement. To say again, Beethoven has largely left behind the transparent dramatic arcs of his middle years, like the tragic one of the *Appassionata* and the triumphant one of the Fifth Symphony. Certainly the effect of the Ninth's second movement is different from Beethoven's other minor-key scherzo in the symphonies, the one in the Fifth with its touch of his C-minor demonic mood. Call the frenzied quality and the minor key of the Ninth's scherzo a fiercely seized Bacchic gaiety, a desperate forgetting, a mocking riposte to the dark D minor of the first movement.

Or call it an echo of the tarantella, in which you dance madly to survive the poison of the tarantula.

Every movement of the *Eroica* lies somewhere between ad hoc in form and a variant of a familiar form. Likewise in the Ninth. A stretch of sublime peace and reverie after the frenzied scherzo, the slow movement in B-flat — the other harmonic pole of the symphony — is founded on the idea of double variations, a genre shaped mainly by Haydn. The two themes, call them A and B, alternate and vary as they return. There ends the Haydnesque aspect of these double variations. For one thing, the themes in double variations are usually contrasting, often one in major and the other in minor. Here both themes are in major, the keys change, and the two themes contrast minimally: both have a long-breathed, lyrical beauty, the second more flowing and lilting.

Marked Adagio molto e cantabile, very slow and singing, the movement begins with a sighing curtain-raiser of two bars. The opening A theme in B-flat major is one of Beethoven's broad, ineffably noble melodies whose ancestors include the slow movement of the *Pathétique*. Its texture is intimate like that of a string quartet, the cellos alone on the bass line. In a long-unfolding melody of varying phrasing, without hurry it drifts down from B-flat to D below the staff, then over the next twelve bars slowly wends its way up to B-flat above the staff, then sinks down an octave. It is the kind of theme that in the next generation Wagner would name *unendliche Melodie*, floating free of the regular phrasing of Classical themes. Prophecies of the *Freude* theme are hinted in its three-note rising and falling figures. Also like the *Freude* theme, this one involves internal repeats of phrases, here in call-and-response between strings and winds.

With the briefest of transitions, the music slips into D major for the B theme — lilting, liquid, meandering, like trailing your hand in water beside a drifting boat on a summer's day. Another brief transition returns to B-flat major and the A theme, the tune having picked up the liquid sixteenths of the B theme. The B theme returns, varied mainly in being now in G major and in the winds rather than the strings. At that point the variations are put aside for an interlude like a free development of the A theme. It strays into the incredible key of C-flat major, where begins an enormous, rhapsodic horn solo.[22]

The A theme returns for the last time, back in B-flat, now ornamented into lacy sextuplets with little dance figures, everything unfolding in an atmosphere of exquisite, time-suspending reverie. The peace is broken by a stern fanfare whose pealing brass recall the first movement. The reverie returns; so does the fanfare. This time, at the end of the brassy interruption the music sinks from an F-major harmony down a third to D-flat, and for a moment the music takes on an uncanny aura. That drop of a third (which happened in similar ways in the *Missa solemnis*) is a prophecy of transcendent moments in the finale. Then, far longer than the theme calls for, as if it does not want to end, the music returns to reverie, swelling in waves. It ends *forte,* then *pianissimo.*

Surely in music there had never been a more beautiful, a more profound evocation of tranquillity and Arcadian peace, spun out in music of incomparable freshness and perfection of gesture and pace. There have been only those two interruptions, with their brassy fanfares. What follows is a rending scream.

Richard Wagner would name the brassy burst of fury that begins the finale the "terror fanfare." It shatters the peace of the slow movement, returns to the dissonance and despair of the first movement, and makes a new beginning with a new evocation of chaos. Now the unsettled first movement is going to find its goal, embodied in "An die Freude" (To Joy).

The threads in Beethoven's life gathered. Twenty years before, he anguished in his Heiligenstadt Testament, "Oh Providence — grant me at last but one day of pure joy — it is so long since real joy echoed in my heart — Oh when — Oh when, Oh divine One — shall I feel it again in the temple of nature and of mankind — Never? — No — Oh that would be too hard." In age we often return to the ideas and inspirations of our youth. In the Ninth Beethoven returned to Schiller's poem that had been a motif of his life since his teens, to the Enlightenment ideal of "life, liberty, and the pursuit of happiness." Rising from liberty, happiness transforms our lives and in turn transforms society.

That vision of happiness, of joy in the temple of nature and humankind, was what in the Heiligenstadt Testament Beethoven feared he had lost forever. At the end of a lifetime of pain, did he reclaim joy in the Ninth Symphony? In his life, no. His physical and emotional miseries only got worse, and his rage raged on. But here, in his art, he found overflowing joy—if not, when all was done, a finale that satisfied him.

In the first movement of the symphony, for the last time he buried the hero and the heroic ideal once exalted in the *Eroica*. Now through Schiller he replaced that ideal with a new one: the perfected society that begins in the freedom, happiness, and moral enlightenment of each person, growing from inside outward to brothers and friends and lovers, from there in a mounting chorus outward to universal brotherhood, the world Schiller named for the ancient Classical paradise: Elysium.[23]

Schiller spoke of love as "the bond that unites all men" and an eternal law that "establishes a correlation between individual happiness and the perfection of society."[24] When he wrote "An die Freude" in the revolutionary 1780s, Schiller was not a Mason or an Illuminatus but was close to those circles, particularly in the person of his Illuminatus friend Christian Gottfried Körner. "To Joy" was written for Körner, who first published it.[25] The poem encompassed the age, and the age embraced it. Of its Masonic and Illuminist echoes, the poem's journey from inside through friends and relations to a *Bund,* a confederation, and finally to a peaceful and happy world is like the agenda of the Illuminati, a secret brotherhood of the enlightened remaking society. Central to "An die Freude" is the echt-Masonic word *Brüder,* "brothers." A Masonic encyclopedia says, "The name of brother is the most universal and highest honorary title in every mystery cult and belongs to the essence of every religious alliance."[26]

In a commentary on "An die Freude," Schiller wrote, "Let us be conscious of a higher ideal unity and by means of brotherhood we will attain to this state . . . Joy is beautiful because it provides harmony; it is 'god-descended' because all harmony is derived from the Master of Worlds and flows back to him."[27] Here is an echo of Kant's circuit from divine to human, from the starry sky above to the moral law beneath.

Why did Beethoven proclaim joy and happiness, and not love, as the goal of human life and the path to Elysium? Perhaps because for an Aufklärer happiness is an end; freedom and love are completed in happiness. Love, in any case, had not treated Beethoven well. He was the son of a drunken father and a melancholic mother. He had extravagantly proclaimed his love to several women, to no end. He had subjected his nephew to a fierce and consuming passion that he called love, but it was something more troubled than that.

Did he have any real understanding of human love, the kind that is mutual and sharing? No one can say, but in any case as the central force in his most ambitious symphony, instead of Love he chose Joy —like Truth and Beauty, one of the personified qualities beloved of Aufklärers. All along, the only real fulfillment of Beethoven's life had been the joy of understanding his gift, of losing himself and his pain in the *raptus* of making music. In that dimension, the Ninth is a hymn not just to redeeming joy but to the redemption music itself can provide.

Schiller again: "All nations that have a history have a paradise, an age of innocence, a golden age . . . A state such as this is not merely met with before the dawn of civilization, it is also the state to which civilization aspires . . . The idea of a similar state, and the belief in the possible reality of this state is the only thing that can reconcile man with all the evils to which he is exposed in the path of civilization." In *Naïve and Sentimental Poetry,* Schiller wrote that humanity can no longer recover Arcadia, the primeval paradise in nature. In the modern world, the artist must lead humanity, "who no longer can return to Arcadia, forward to Elysium."[28]

Whether or not Beethoven knew these particular words of Schiller, they were ideas inherent in the poet's work and in the turn-of-the-century zeitgeist, and therefore part of what formed Beethoven. Perhaps here is the point of the slow movement of the Ninth: an evocation of lost Arcadian peace. The terror fanfare of the finale shatters that peace, because Arcadia is an illusion, a dream no longer possible in this world. The finale's opening blast marks the intrusion of reality, and a new beginning.

By now Beethoven had lived through the French Revolution and a relentless counterrevolution in the repressions of the last decade. Now in the finale of the Ninth Symphony, he mounted his counter-counter-revolution, to keep the hope of freedom alive.

He begins the finale with his terror fanfare in brass and winds and timpani, on a screaming chord: D minor with an added B-flat on the top, violently joining his two principal keys. It begins on an upbeat, doing violence to the meter, like a grotesque echo of the exalted upbeat that begins the *Missa solemnis*. The chaotic sound and effect are new in his work, new in music. But he had used that harmony before. In a different key, it is the same piercing chord that marks the climax of the *Eroica* development (in that case, A minor with F on top). There it was a representation of a catastrophe, say, a crux in a battle, out of which the hero sailed in a new theme. Here it is a return to the tumult and despair of the first movement.[29]

At the same time, the terror fanfare is another curtain-raiser. The movement proper begins with an idea incomprehensible to both listeners and orchestral players of the time: the double basses of the string section play a drifting, tonally wandering line recalling an operatic recitative. Beethoven had put recitative effects in instrumental works before, one of them the *Tempest* Sonata. But they had never been done in the orchestra. For years, players had no idea how to perform these passages.

The fanfare breaks out again, the basses answer again. At that point Beethoven, in the context of his time, plays one of his strangest cards yet. As if in a mangling of time we hear for a few seconds the mysterious A–E tremolos that began the symphony. The basses respond to this phantom with more wordless, chromatic recitative that seems to say, *No, not that*. Now there is a snippet of the scherzo and then of the slow movement, the scherzo rebuffed gruffly by the basses, the slow movement with wistful regret, growing to a *fortissimo* outburst.[30] That in turn gives rise to another snippet: it is the first phrase of the *Freude* theme in the winds, marked *dolce*, "sweetly." Now in a clear D major the basses wordlessly but unmistakably cry, *Yes! This is what we want!* In short, evocations of the first three movements have appeared in the finale, the basses have turned them away, and then they embrace the *Freude* theme.

In fact, Beethoven first roughed out those bass recitatives with words for a singer. In one sketch, after the quotation of the first movement the text of the recitative is "No, this would remind us too much of our despair." After the second movement snippet, "Nor this either, it is only sport, something more beautiful and better." After the third movement quotation, "Nor this, it is too tender, we must seek for something more animated." And after the bit of *Freude* theme, "This is it, Ha!, now it is found, I myself will intone it."[31] All these phrases evoke the setting of a *geselliges Lied,* one of the company searching for the best song for the occasion. But Beethoven was right to leave out words in the opening recitatives. After the initial shock of the time-warp return of the opening movements, the sentiments are entirely clear in the recitative of the double basses.

What has been sought since the first movement has been found. After their dismissing and then accepting recitatives, the basses quietly play through the *Freude* theme, unaccompanied — in the way that, say, a composer would write out the completed melody while rehearsing it in his head. Here again is the metaphor of creation, and of self-creation. In musical terms, two intersecting trains of thought have been set up. One is that the *Freude* theme is going to be the matter of the finale; everything will turn around it. Since it is based on a single theme rather than any ordinary finale pattern such as a rondo, the form is going to serve the theme rather than, as usual in music of the Classical period, the themes serving the form.

The second train of thought is that the form is going to be inflected as much by literary and symbolic forces as by "purely musical" ones. If it is true that Beethoven usually thought of the technical, the logical, the expressive, and the dramatic all at once and equally (except when he did not), here is one work where he places drama in equal possession of the musical dialogue — as he placed words in the forefront of the *Missa solemnis.* In the finale there is no "abstract" musical reason for the snippets of earlier movements.[32] Beethoven peremptorily placed them there to make a dramatic point. In musical terms, the movement so far is episodic, the unfolding imposed from without rather than generated from within. That will be true of much of the finale.[33]

After the ingenuous little *Freude* theme is rehearsed alone in the basses, as if teaching it to the orchestra, it is repeated, acquiring lovely contrapuntal accompaniments. On its fourth iteration/variation it becomes a grand military march. The march climaxes, the music sinks down to quiet fragments. At that point the terror fanfare bursts out again, more fiercely than before: now the first chord has every note of the D-minor scale smashed together. During it, the bass soloist rises.

If much of the matter is effectively as literary as it is musical, Beethoven has not forgotten musical logic. The orchestral bass recitative of the beginning implied words, to prepare us for the actual words to come. That was one solution to the problem of how to introduce the poem in some kind of organic way. Now instead of launching directly into the Schiller, the rest of the solution was to have the song introduced by a real recitative by a real singer.

The words Beethoven himself wrote for this recitative place the music in the context of a companionable gathering, the beginning of a *geselliges Lied*. As if with glass raised to us, the bass proclaims, "O friends, not these tones! Rather let's strike up something more pleasing, and full of joy." "Joy!" he cries again, and his brothers — the men in the choir — answer, "Joy! Joy!" Their leader peals out the tune as if firing them up and teaching it to them. All glasses raised now, the men join in lustily on the last lines (the altos doing service on the top part):

> *Joy, thou lovely god-engendered*
> *Daughter of Elysium,*
> *Drunk with fire we enter,*
> *Heavenly one, thy holy shrine!*
> *Thy magic reunites*
> *What fashion has broken apart;*
> *All men will become brothers*
> *Where thy gentle wing abides.*[34]

Having presented the lyric as it was intended, as a sociable song, Beethoven begins to move beyond that image. The theme is not only going to be varied in the usual way, by decorating it and using its melody and harmony to fashion music in new directions; it is also going to be redefined, has already been redefined, in terms of a series of styles and implied settings, what are sometimes called "character variations." So far we have heard the *Freude* theme naked, then clothed in counterpoint, then as a military march, then as a sociable song among comrades. The transformations of topic continue in that vein. The quartet of soloists gives us the next verse, decked out in terms so extravagantly florid as to be besotted. The chorus answers likewise:

[Solo quartet] Whoever has had the great success
To be a friend of a friend,
He who has won a sweet wife,
Join our jubilation!
Yes, whoever just one soul
In the round world can name his own!
And he who never could, he must
Weeping leave this fellowship!

[Chorus] All creatures imbibe joy
From the breasts of nature;
Everything good, everything bad
Follows her rosy path;
She gave us kisses and wine,
A friend proven even in death;
Ecstasy is given to the worm,
And the cherub stands before God.

By this point, with the first verses sung through, the finale is settled in as a train of variations on the *Freude* theme. But other formal models also find echoes: in one dimension it is a sort of cantata, or even a concerto (it has what amounts to a double exposition announced by the fanfares, the second exposition introducing soloists). There will be sonata-form echoes as well. At the same time, the movement resembles a miniature symphony in itself, with a scherzo and slow movement and jubilant finale. In this ad hoc form, all those elements are relevant. (What is not relevant is to try to boil down the unfolding into a single form.)

The first section or quasi-movement ends the "cherub" verse with a magical harmonic leap of a third down, from A major to F major, on *vor Gott*, before God. That harmonic shift was heard unforgettably in the third movement, from F to D-flat, and several times in the *Missa solemnis*. Always it evokes the divine. As it was in the mass, here that magical chord change will be joined by the God-texture of high harmonies. Beethoven wrote on a sketch in his matter-of-fact way, "The height of the stars [can be pictured] more by way of the instruments."[35] The implications of the shift, however, will have to wait, because something more worldly intervenes.

In a piece filled with shocks to the sensibilities and expectations of the time, what comes next is second to none. The music shifts to B-flat, the other harmonic pole of the symphony, as if to the key of a second theme in sonata form. We hear random grunts on bassoon and contrabassoon, with bass drum. They condense into a pulse that we take to be a downbeat but is an upbeat, so when the tune arrives we are jolted into the meter. It is another variation of the *Freude* theme, redefined into a "Turkish" march, the exotic Viennese military style. Its elements are less the melody in this case than the pounding, clanging "Turkish" percussion battery of bass drum, cymbals, and triangle. A swaggering, wine-inspired tenor takes the stage. He and the men of the choir give us the next verse, which reveals that the march illustrates a military metaphor in the text:

Happily, flying like God's suns
Through the splendorous battlefield of the heavens,
Brothers, run your course
Joyfully, like a hero to victory.[36]

That this Turkish march is another character variation puts it in the train of the previous ones: military, social song. But the import of the

Turkish march, the era's definition of a "bizarre" move in this context, is hard to pin down. What can be said is that this idea for the finale was there from early on: a sketch note from 1822 ran, "End of the Sinfonie with Turkish music and vocal chorus." In its tone the music is larky, satirical, verging on banal. Its implications in the context of the finale are symbolic, not musical. In a symphony intended to put aside the heroic ideal and replace it with an individual, spiritual, and sociable one, the military spirit here finds itself lampooned, the hero striding to his cosmic victory portrayed by a vulgar tune, a drunken tenor, tinkling triangle, and peeping piccolo. At the same time, to the contrary of satire, the Turkish march suggests an image of global brotherhood — as the Masonic song runs, "Mankind in East and West." This will not be the last appearance of the Turkish style in the movement, and the next one is not at all satirical in tone.[37]

There is another dimension to the march that enfolds both parody and seriousness. In Beethoven's mind as with most Viennese and most opera lovers, the Turkish style was wedded to a particular piece, which had been the greatest hit of Mozart's life and remained one of his most popular: his Turkish singspiel *Die Entführung aus dem Serail* (The Abduction from the Seraglio). When it was written, that production played into a fad for quasi-Turkish music and fashion in Vienna. The opera virtually enveloped the style, to the point that to think of one was to think of the other. Beethoven would not have cared about the *Abduction*'s exoticism as such, nor about its parodistic comedy at the expense of a "pagan" culture. What appealed to Beethoven was the serious, ethical part: at the end, Pasha Selim, who has bought an English girl as a slave from pirates, reveals himself as a man of enlightened empathy. Showing a clemency he has never received from his Christian enemy, the pasha lets the lovers go free. Among its dimensions, the Turkish march of the Ninth Symphony finale is Beethoven's echo of *Die Entführung*: humankind embraced in East and West.[38]

The deliberate triviality of the Turkish march is swept away by a dashing double fugue in triple time. This reveals the march as the beginning of the scherzo in the quasi-four-movement aspect of the finale. At the same time, in its driving minor-key lines and dazzling modulations it recalls the actual second-movement scherzo. The finale will be much involved in enfolding ideas from the whole symphony, and not only in the quoted bits at the beginning. The double fugue after the march recalls the scherzo, the terror fanfare recalls the atmosphere of the first movement. After a quiet, breath-catching moment, the choir breaks out to D major and belts out the first stanza and *Freude* theme straight, accompanied by the racing triplets of the fugue.

That climax reaches a sudden full stop. The next section, the quasi-slow movement, is announced by basses with trombones, the latter in their churchly mode. Here is music that was foreshadowed in the fall from A to F on *vor Gott,* before the march. The *Missa solemnis* was a sacred work troubled by a secular intrusion, the war music. The Ninth Symphony is a secular work with a sacred interlude in the middle of the finale. Here in Schiller's visionary stanzas and Beethoven's unforgettable setting, all humanity joins in a loving embrace:

> *Be embraced, you millions!*
> *This kiss for all the world!*
> *Brothers! over the starry canopy*
> *A loving Father must dwell!*
>
> *Do you prostrate yourselves, millions?*
> *Do you know the Creator, world?*
> *Search for Him over the starry canopy!*
> *He must live there beyond the stars!*

The music begins with its trombones and basses, the style stern and archaic, the tonality implying D Mixolydian. On the repeat of the words "be embraced," the Beethoven God-texture breaks out in high winds, with flashing string figures. As in *Fidelio* (*Freedom!*) and the mass (*Credo!*), Beethoven picks out the words he most cares about: *Millions! Brothers!* Here is another credo from Beethoven, a credo that does not negate the liturgical Credo in the mass but amplifies it with a humanistic one, under God's starry sky. To speak to the millions and name them brothers was the essence of what (as artist, as distinct from misanthropic man) Beethoven had been doing in all his creative life.

This is not the climax of the finale or of the entire work, but it is its

spiritual and ethical core, the credo of the Ninth Symphony. Here is
Beethoven's response to the unanswered prayer for peace that ended
the *Missa solemnis,* with the drums of war echoing in the distance. The
vision of the Ninth Symphony is that as loving brothers and sisters we
will find here on earth our joy and our peace. God cannot do that for
us. Conquering heroes and benevolent despots cannot do that for us.
We have to find Elysium for ourselves. As Beethoven wrote in slashing
words on a colleague's work that thanked God: *O Man, help yourself!*
Kant prepared the ground for that statement: What is Enlightenment?
To put away dogma and think for yourself.

The credo rises to "a loving Father must dwell." At that point
Beethoven again recalls the *Missa solemnis.* The harmony has the archaic, modal sound of some of the mass. The texture slips into the
remarkable organlike sound of divided violas and cellos and low flutes
and clarinets heard in the *Präludium* of the mass, which called forth
the descent of Christ into the bread and wine. That sacred communion
is echoed in this secular one. Together, in brotherhood, with kisses,
we acknowledge our creator and prepare to make our paradise. As in
many ways the Ninth has been a reflexive work, the first and last movements beginning as if they were creating themselves, here Beethoven
tells us what the Ninth is for him: *This kiss for all the world!* The credo
section ends in A major, *pianissimo,* in an uncanny texture evoking
the firmament, hanging over the words "he must live there beyond the
stars."

From that point the quasi-finale of the quasi-symphony breaks
out in a D-major explosion of joy, an exalted version of the *Freude*
theme and Schiller's first verse joined in a double fugue with the *Seid
umschlungen* ("be embraced") theme and its text. (In a sonata-form
interpretation of the movement, this is the recapitulation.)[39] This combination is full of meaning: the *Freude* theme and its text, the image of
Joy as a divine and magical presence on earth, to be celebrated among
companions, is joined to *Seid umschlungen,* the credo's ecstatic embrace of all humanity under God. With this double fugue, Beethoven
joins a humanistic and a spiritual vision, on the road to Elysium.[40]

After a climax that requires the sopranos to hold a high A for a brutal twelve bars, the double fugue sinks to more recollections of the "Do

you prostrate yourselves?" stanza, proclaiming those words in new forms centering on the word *Brothers!*, drifting away briefly from D major. From there, a new section begins, firmly back in D major, with its own skittering introduction. (Harmonically, the finale is as stable as the first movement was unstable.) This begins a gigantic coda.

Now the variations on the *Freude* theme have ended, and also all the verses of the poem that Beethoven chose to set. From here on, the musical material is developments and extrapolations of the *Freude* theme rather than the tune itself, and the verses are the two Beethoven wants to drive home: the initial *Freude, schöner Götterfunken* verse and the *Seid umschlungen* verse. The soloists rhapsodize on the first lines of the poem, "Thy magic reunites / What fashion has broken apart." By now that sentiment about reuniting what is broken has acquired a great deal of resonance in several kinds of uniting: East and West, sacred and secular, brother and brother, husband and wife. (This echoes the precursor of the Ninth, the *Choral Fantasy*, whose symbolic task was to unite love and strength through music.) In a pair of *poco adagios,* first the choir and then the soloists return in flowery ecstasies (straying into a brilliant B major) to the essential message, the central hope of the Ninth Symphony: "all men, all men, all men will become brothers, where thy gentle wing abides."

Then, in this gigantic movement to climax a gigantic symphony arrives the coda of the coda, an *allegro* directed to speed and intensity to the end. Both for excitement and for its symbolism, he brings back the Turkish battery; the total effect, including the melody, has the exotic, driving quality of the Turkish style. This time, it is an ecstatic celebration of humankind East and West. Now the central words are *Be embraced! Brothers! Above the stars must he dwell! This kiss for all the world! Joy! Joy!* It is the last of Beethoven's endings in overflowing jubilation, going back to the *Eroica* and the Fifth Symphony, to *Egmont* and *Fidelio.* The last words in the Ninth are "God-engendered!," completing the circle of human and divine but firmly planted on earth. In the *prestissimo* last bars, the Turkish battery clangs and thunders.

Humankind, help yourself! Beethoven shaped his last epic to that end, written in a dark time to keep alive Schiller's poem and its exaltation of freedom, without which there can be no true joy, no hope for a better world, no all-embracing brotherhood, no Elysium. In Austria, meetings of more than a few people outside one's family were forbidden, and one could be arrested for speaking the very word *freedom*.

The road to Elysium begins with the enlightenment of each individual, extends to one's brothers and lovers, and from there to the world. In addition to all the models and echoes that Beethoven infolded into the Ninth Symphony—Haydn's *Creation* and Austrian anthem, the *Marseillaise*, Handel and Bach, his own *Eroica* and *Fidelio* and Fifth Symphony, Mozart's *Abduction*—one more is significant. As I noted earlier, Beethoven's favorite Mozart opera, *Die Zauberflöte*, is among other things a parable of love: the earthy love of Papageno and Papagena, the exalted love of Pamina and Tamino, the divine and disinterested love of Sarastro for all humanity. The quarter-note simplicity of the *Freude* theme echoes Sarastro's sublime aria "In these hallowed halls." At the end of the opera, Sarastro and his *Bund* consecrate the lovers as the highest force on this earth: "May power be victorious / And crown as a reward / Beauty and Wisdom / With an eternal crown." Love was the vehicle of the lover's triumph, the meaning of their crown, the source of beauty and wisdom on this earth. With another metaphor but in the same spirit, Beethoven shaped the Ninth Symphony around Joy. It is his *Creation*, his *Marseillaise*, and also his *Zauberflöte*.

In the end, the Ninth Symphony presents us as many questions as answers. Its utopia is envisioned, not attained. It was neglected for decades before it found its triumph.[41] Yet the place in the world Beethoven intended the Ninth to inhabit is exactly where it ended up over the next two centuries: its *Freude* theme perhaps known to half of humanity, the symphony performed all over the globe, in East and West, often outside the concert hall as a great ceremonial work.

In an unprecedented way for a composer, far beyond the ambitions of the *Eroica*, Beethoven stepped into history with a communal ritual that does not simply preach a sermon about freedom and brotherhood but aspires to help bring them to pass. In the coming centuries, ideologies going by the names "democratic," "communist," "socialist," and "Nazi" would claim the Ninth as their own. It would be exalted by tyrannies and it would celebrate the downfall of tyrannies. How one viewed the Ninth, it turned out, depended on what kind of Elysium one had in mind, whether that all people should be brothers or that all nonbrothers should be exterminated. The *Freude* theme would end up as the anthem of a Europe united after centuries of war. All of this is as Beethoven surely hoped, in some degree even foresaw. If we want to conceive something in the direction of a universal artwork, here it is.

The Ninth emerges from a whispering mist to fateful proclamations. In the finale, the *Freude* theme, prefigured from the beginning, is almost constructed before our ears, hummed through, then composed and recomposed and decomposed. Which is to say, the Ninth is also music about music, about its own emerging, about its composer composing. And for what? "Be embraced, you millions! This kiss for all the world!" run the telling lines in the finale, in which Beethoven erected a movement of transcendent scope on a humble little tune that anybody can sing.

The Ninth Symphony, forming and dissolving before our ears in its beauty and terror and simplicity and complexity, is itself Beethoven's embrace for the millions, from East to West, high to low, naive to sophisticated. When the bass soloist speaks the first words in the finale, an invitation to sing for joy, Beethoven's words are addressed to everybody, to history. There's something singularly moving about that moment when this man — deaf and sick and misanthropic and self-torturing, at the same time one of the most extraordinary and boundlessly generous men our species has produced — greets us person to person, with glass raised, and hails us as friends.

❧

32

Ars Longa, Vita Brevis

FTER THE PREMIERES of the Ninth Symphony and parts of the *Missa solemnis,* Beethoven's financial and physical miseries harried him no less. But he did not take vacations from his work or from promoting his work. Somehow his energy for both remained strong. Medical science of the day could not discern that his liver was killing him, but the effects were clear enough. While he waited to see if he was dying, he turned his attention to smaller, more manageable but no less ambitious projects: the three string quartets commissioned by Russian Prince Nikolai Galitzin.

Meanwhile, after loosing the Ninth Symphony on the world, he did not consider that work a settled matter. At some point after the premiere, Beethoven told Carl Czerny that he had decided the choral finale was a mistake and he intended to replace it with a purely instrumental one.[1] What is to be made of this astonishing statement? The whole symphony was written toward the revelation of the finale, the Schiller ode, the *Freude* theme.

He did not explain his second thoughts about the finale. Presumably he would have spun it off as a freestanding piece, like a more elaborate *Choral Fantasy.* (He was to do the same with the finale of a string quartet.) One surmise is that he was not satisfied with its rambling and episodic course, its metaphorical gestures imposed from outside rather than motivated from inside the musical dialectic. In more pedestrian terms, he may have concluded that he had finally written something truly beyond the capacities of orchestras and choirs, given that the first three movements were already unprecedentedly difficult. Or perhaps the idea of redoing the finale reveals a touch of conservatism, a lingering uncertainty about the idea of sullying the instrumental, call it abstract, integrity of a symphony by putting in voices.

For whatever reason, in his notion about replacing the finale one sees Beethoven's integrity. He had envisioned setting "An die Freude" since his teens. The Ninth was his most ambitious symphony. It was a statement he wanted to give the world in a dark time. But if the finale did not work *musically* for him, he was ready to throw it out. In the end, of course, he did not write a replacement. He let the finale stand, and surely he was wise to. It has its issues, but its importance as an abiding image of freedom and fulfillment lifts it far beyond technical matters.

In May 1824, the same month as the premiere of the Ninth Symphony, a journal article in the new *Berlin Allgemeine Musikalische Zeitung* delved unprecedentedly into Beethoven's symphonies in their historical and technical dimensions. It was called "A Few Words on the Symphony and Beethoven's Achievement in This Field." The author was critic, theorist, and Beethoven devotee Adolph Bernhard Marx, who had founded the journal. In coming years he would be one of the men most responsible for naming and formalizing the idea of "sonata form." Like E. T. A. Hoffmann, Marx in his approach to music was a paradigm of his era, which is to say, Romantic in his sensibilities. At the same time he stands as a founder of the modern discipline of music theory. In other words, Marx was a product of a time and a culture in the process of developing a systematic and quasi-scientific study of history. In the German conception, history was logical and progressive. For Marx, while Beethoven was rooted in tradition he was superior to anything that came before.

Marx begins the article by reviewing the history of the symphonic genre, its relationship to the instrumental sonata, and the achievements of Mozart and Haydn. His language appears to be inspired in some degree by Hoffmann's rhapsodic musical writings. For Marx, Mozart's G Minor Symphony "demonstrates the expression of a restless, unsettled passion, of a struggling and fighting against a powerfully intruding agitation." Here is the Romantic atmosphere in music criticism: dramatic and expressive terms that could as well be applied to a play by Goethe or Shakespeare. When it comes to Haydn, Marx reflects the general decline of sympathy toward the symphonies, finding in them a certain impurity: "It seems as if [Haydn's] feeling, especially his childlike, untroubled joy . . . sometimes seizes upon certain extrinsic objects and blends their representation into the expression of the emotion itself."

He arrives at Beethoven, whose symphonies he views through the complementary lenses of the evocative and the technical: "In the areas of the sonata and the symphony, Beethoven began at Mozart's level . . . Even if many a moment shone forth more freshly and brightly than in the more gentle Mozart and echoed the Haydn school, and even if a greater, more deeply founded unity became manifest in Beethoven's compositions, the basic idea was, nevertheless, the same . . . His more advanced development led to a higher cultivation of the sonata form."

Probably for the first time in print, Marx takes note of Beethoven's expansion and intensification of the development section and the coda in sonata form, and his replacement of the minuet with the scherzo in the symphonies and elsewhere. He notes that the critical conceptions that grew up in the time of Mozart (here he leaves out Haydn) could not cope with Beethoven's innovations and his singular voice: "As long as Beethoven followed Mozart he received their applause. But in that period whenever they suspected the distinctive qualities of his music . . . it was considered to be an aberration or some kind of excess . . . Those arbiters stayed where they were, but art didn't, nor did Beethoven."

In this article Marx is more interested in expression than technique. His gist is that Beethoven always paints particular emotional states and often specific images. Years before, he had responded to the *Eroica* with a series of poems full of heroic imagery. Here he tours

symphonies 1–7 and their leading themes with evocative commentary: "Beethoven's Symphony in C Minor emerged from the indefinite lyricism that we believed to find in Mozart's earlier symphonies
. . . However, it does not exhibit a single feeling but rather a series of
spiritual conditions, with deep psychological truth. It is the struggle of
a strong being against an almost overwhelming fate." In the lyrical second subject he finds "the painful lament of a deeply wounded and yet
unweakened soul." And so on, through the symphony. He concludes,
"We could regard this symphony as the first to advance beyond the
Mozartian point of view."

He cites *Wellington's Victory,* with its portrait of a battle, and applies the same kind of narrative to the *Eroica.* By this point in history,
he writes, instrumental music was "no longer a dead artifice for expressing one's subjectivity and feeling . . . The orchestra became for
[Beethoven] an animated chorus engaged in dramatic action." With
the *Eroica,* "[e]verything now was united: *psychological development,*
connected to a series of *extrinsic* [i.e., extramusical] circumstances,
represented in a thoroughly *dramatic action* of those *instruments* that
form the orchestra." At the end of the article he concludes that whether
or not a given reader agrees with his particular interpretations, he will
have succeeded "if it is only recognized that a piece of [instrumental]
music was capable of stimulating an idea or definite representation."[2]

With Marx we approach the nineteenth-century elevation of music,
especially instrumental music, to the summit of creative endeavors,
"the art to which all other arts aspire." One of the reasons for that elevation, as exemplified in Marx, is that the perception of instrumental music began to subsume the qualities of literature, drama, poetry,
psychology, and philosophy. Music, especially instrumental music, became thereby the most all-embracing, the most universal art. At the
same time, instrumental music could achieve that status while remaining tantalizingly indefinable — the indefinable and unknowable being
echt-Romantic qualities. Music became a transcendently evocative
and emotional language beyond words.

By Marx's later writings, Beethoven had become not only the emperor of composers but the prime model for all future music, the stan-

dard against whom all others were to be judged. Through the nineteenth century and into the next, that was where Beethoven's legacy
rested, bestriding and virtually climaxing the history of his art. From
the throne others placed him on, he loomed intimidatingly over later
generations of composers. In that process, Mozart and Haydn were all
but delegated to the status of his precursors. At the same time, by calling all of Beethoven's work a series of virtual tone poems full of "dramatic action," Marx helped solidify the nineteenth-century triumph of
program music.

Beethoven himself was not particularly historically minded (as distinct from aware of the musical past) and too busy working out the
next piece to be steadily concerned about his influence. But he read
this article of Marx's and was impressed by it. There is no way to know
how much he felt the critic had read his mind, as such. Beethoven
had always been interested in creative responses to his work, in the
ways others made his music their own. Once in a letter he had thanked
E. T. A. Hoffmann for his poetic attentions. Now he thanked Marx.
Writing to publisher Adolph Schlesinger in Berlin, Beethoven sent
word that "I hope that he will continue to reveal more and more what
is noble and true in the sphere of art. And surely that ought gradually
to throw discredit upon the mere counting of syllables."[3] By the latter
he appears to mean critics who blandly cite musical themes and formal outlines, comparing them to people who analyze the meter of a
poem and think they know what it means. Beethoven preferred Marx's
more expressive and imaginative style. Later he wryly wrote to Adolph
Schlesinger's publisher son Moritz, "I request you to give my compliments to Herr Marx in Berlin and ask him not to be too hard on me
and to let me slip out occasionally through the back door." He had
some idea of how influential Marx was going to be, and he wanted to
prompt the critic to cut him some slack.[4]

Marx took his cue about revealing what was noble and true in art.
His article on the symphonies was only a middle stage in his journey
with Beethoven. He would spend the rest of his career exploring and
expanding his conceptions, which at once cinched Beethoven's triumph and put him into some tightly constrained and, for the future of

music, constraining boxes: Beethoven as not just an inspiration to the future but the model of models, a virtually unattainable ideal.[5]

Beethoven's concerns in these years were no longer his critics, good or bad, but rather the newest piece; a few friends (most of them serving in some degree as his lackeys); his ward Karl; illness; his disgusting servants; and money. Other than these things, there was little left in his life. Now alongside the notes in his sketches were long trains of sums added up — he still could not do multiplication. After promising the *Missa solemnis* to a row of publishers, in July 1824 he sold it and the Ninth Symphony to Schott and Sons for 1,000 and 600 florins, respectively.[6] At that point the Viennese publisher Diabelli still thought his house was in the running to get the mass.[7] Four months earlier, Beethoven had offered the Ninth to Moritz Schlesinger and to Schott on the same day.[8] He also heavily courted Probst, a new publisher for him, but after too many broken promises and pages-long excuses, Probst dropped out of the running. Beethoven was disgusted with his longtime Viennese house Steiner, mainly because he had long owed the publisher money and Steiner had been so contemptible as to press him about it. He paid the last 150 florins of his debt to Steiner in July 1824, and wrote Schott, "Steiner . . . is an out and out miser and a rogue of a fellow; that Tobias [Haslinger] is inclined to be weak and accommodating, yet I need him for several things."[9]

His letters to Tobias Haslinger himself (he was soon to take over the Steiner firm) had always been funny and affectionate. His hypocrisy in the letter to Schott lies probably not in that he was using Haslinger and had no respect for him but rather in that he was running down the competition to his now-preferred publisher, Schott, and downplaying his continuing involvement with Steiner and Haslinger. Even if he had turned to other houses, there was no complete break with Steiner. He still frequented Steiner's store on Paternostergasse; the publisher still did him favors and bid on pieces.

Beethoven innocently embarrassed himself to Haslinger directly, however, over an intricate piece of whimsy he wrote to Schott in the beginning of 1825. Here is Beethoven in what he called his "unbuttoned" mood. After another snipe at a rival publisher with whom he was involved ("Schlesinger is not to be trusted, for he filches wherever he can"), he concluded, in a flight of fancy subtle enough that it has to be annotated:

Here are a couple of canons for your journal [*Caecilia*] . . . as a supplement to a romantic biography of Tobias Haslinger of Vienna, consisting of three parts. Part 1 — Tobias appears as the apprentice of the famous Kapellmeister Fux [author of the excruciating counterpoint study *Gradus ad Parnassum*] . . . and he is holding the ladder to the latter's Gradus ad Parnassum. Then, as he feels inclined to indulge in practical jokes, Tobias by rattling and shaking the ladder makes many a person who has already climbed rather high up [in the craft of counterpoint] suddenly break his neck and so forth. He then says goodbye to this earth of ours but again comes to light in Albrechtsberger's time [this is Beethoven's old counterpoint teacher and Fux disciple].

Part 2. Fux's Nota cambiata [a musical ornament] which has now appeared is soon discussed with A[lbrechtsberger], the appoggiaturas [another ornament] are meticulously analyzed, the art of creating musical skeletons is dealt with exhaustively and so forth [a dig at Albrechtsberger's pedantry]. Tobias then envelops himself like a caterpillar, undergoes another evolution and reappears in this world for the third time.

Part 3. The scarcely grown wings now enable him to fly to the little Paternostergaße [home of Tobias's firm] and he becomes the Kapellmeister of the little Paternostergaße. Having passed through the school of appoggiaturas, all that he retains is the bills of exchange [a pun on *Wechselnote,* which means "appoggiatura," and *Wechsel,* "bill of exchange"]. Thus he . . . finally becomes a member of several homemade learned societies and so forth.[10]

This little fantasy shows that by this point Beethoven had acquired a good sense of what "Romantic" meant, enough so as to lampoon its tendency to the arcane and fantastic: Tobias twice dies and is reborn, and cocoons himself like a butterfly. Here particularly is the influence of a high-Romantic source, E. T. A. Hoffmann, whose stories were given to such magical metamorphoses. It appeared that Beethoven had been reading Hoffmann's tales. The clue to that connection is one of the canons Beethoven sent to Schott, the text of which involves a pun on the writer's name: "Hoffmann! You are no hope-man."[11]

Beethoven's immediate creative concerns after the premiere of the Ninth Symphony were two sets of piano bagatelles and the quartets for Galitzin. The piano pieces were the eleven of op. 119, pulled together between 1820 and 1822, and the six of op. 126. The first set had been intended to bring in money to help pay his debt to brother Johann. When the London edition of op. 119 was pirated by Moritz Schlesinger in Paris and then by another publisher in Vienna, Beethoven was left with no fees from European publication. In May and June 1824, he wrote the set of op. 126 to get the money for his brother.

The op. 33 Bagatelles had been popularistic pieces, each a delightful individual. As is noted about that set, here as much as anywhere begins the tradition of Romantic character pieces for piano. (By the time of Beethoven's op. 119, one of the other founders of that tradition, Franz Schubert, was already in his prime.) These pieces also played their part in the allied Romantic passion for fragments: small thoughts that are part of an implied larger picture. Examples in the next generation include Chopin's preludes. In a historical perspective, with the op. 119 Bagatelles it becomes far more imaginable that in another seven years the young Robert Schumann would publish *Papillons,* his wild, autobiographical collection of parti-colored miniatures evoking a masked ball.

The op. 119 Bagatelles are a more or less random assemblage, all of them tuneful, most under a minute and a half long, no. 9 lasting less than forty seconds. Five of them had been published before, donated as a favor to friend Friedrich Starke for his piano-pedagogy book. Some came from drafts going back as far as the 1790s.[12] They are arranged in terms of musical contrasts and a variety of keys, but really they are freestanding pieces, aimed more at the pleasure of an individual player than at public performance (which would have been unlikely in this period anyway). Most have a topic familiar to the time: no. 1 is a wistful dance, no. 5 a driving piece in Gypsy style, no. 9 an exquisite little waltz, and so on. All in all they constitute an echo of the kinds of pieces Beethoven could improvise on the spot, and likely began as improvisations that he touched up on the page.

Op. 126 is a different matter, what he called on the manuscript a *Ciclus von Kleinigkeiten,* a cycle of little things. They range from around a minute and a half to more than four minutes. He wrote publisher Schott that they were "probably the best I've written" of these kinds of pieces. No less than the others were these variegated, freestanding in effect. But the six still have the mark of a concentrated effort, and some of the atmosphere of the late music. The keys progress by thirds: G–g–E-flat–b–G–E-flat. No. 1 has the sublime and artless tunefulness of some of his late piano movements. No. 2 combines dashing bursts of toccata with cantabile phrases — the late propensity for juxtaposing high contrasts. No. 3 in E-flat major is a poignant stretch of cantabile that might have served as the basis of a slow movement in a late sonata. No. 4 begins as a Presto furioso in tone but has stretches of folkish musette. The set finishes with a flowing, introverted Quasi allegretto and a finale that begins and ends with a dashing Presto but is otherwise a kind of meditation in folk style. This set of small gems constitutes Beethoven's last opus for piano.

As each of the quartets for Prince Galitzin was finished, Beethoven bestirred himself to get it premiered and then to sell it. By now he was confirmed in his habit of promising works to more than one publisher, trying to keep all of them on the hook. Meanwhile he continued to promise the Gesellschaft der Musikfreunde its commissioned oratorio *The Triumph of the Cross,* which he never got around to. His letters to the society's cellist and concert organizer Vincenz Hauschka were invariably in his unbuttoned mood, and they use the intimate *du:* "While hailing you as the most powerful Intendant of all singing and growling clubs, the Imperial and Royal Violoncello in Chief, the Imperial and royal Inspector of all Imperial and Royal Hunts, and also the deacon of my most gracious lord, without domicile, without a roof over his head . . . I wish you this and that, from which you may select the best."[13]

While Beethoven was finishing the first of the *Galitzins,* the Quartet in E-flat Major, op. 127, Ignaz Schuppanzigh claimed the premiere of the quartet for his scheduled concert of January 25, 1825. Given the go-ahead, the violinist immediately placed a notice in the paper. With that, he hoped to forestall Beethoven's usual game of having second thoughts and giving it to somebody else — which Beethoven promptly did. He promised it to Joseph Linke, Schuppanzigh's cellist, for a benefit concert. There was a tense exchange between Beethoven and Schuppanzigh in a conversation book. "The affair with the quartet is accursed," Schuppanzigh began. He insisted he didn't want to fight with Linke over the premiere, but he still wanted the quartet: "I wouldn't say anything if it were not already in the newspaper."[14]

In the end, Schuppanzigh got his way. Beethoven treated Linke as he was doing with his stable of disappointed publishers, promising the cellist a future work, the premiere of the coming A Minor Quartet (Linke was duly annoyed over the whole matter). Then the E-flat Quartet was not ready in time for Schuppanzigh's January concert, and he had to substitute the op. 95 *Serioso.*

Schuppanzigh's next scheduled concert was on March 6. It appears that he got the music for the E-flat Quartet only two weeks before the date, so there was great anxiety on all sides. Beethoven needed strong premieres, and from op. 18 onward he had usually gotten them from Schuppanzigh. Meanwhile, for a performer at this point a new Beethoven quartet was a more loaded matter than it had been with the ones of a decade before. Now each premiere threatened to be a historic moment, therefore to have something to do with one's reputation not only in the present but potentially in the future. The E-flat Quartet, Beethoven's first since the *Serioso* of 1810, was as novel and difficult as any he had written. For performers and listeners it demanded whole new categories of understanding.

In hopes of inspiring the troops, Beethoven assembled the quartet players and asked them to sign a document of intent, joking in tone but serious in substance, concerning the premiere: "Best ones! Each one is herewith given his part and is bound by oath and indeed pledged on his honor to do his best, to distinguish himself and to vie each with the other in excellence." It was signed by everyone present, Linke with the ironic note, "The grand master's accursed violoncello," second violin

Karl Holz "the last, but only in signing," and Anton Schindler "secretarius."

There the jokes ended. Everyone's fears were confirmed. The premiere by Schuppanzigh's quartet was a scrambling affair, and Beethoven and everybody else blamed the violinist. The worst humiliation was that Beethoven used his brother Johann's critique of the performance to berate Schuppanzigh, when everybody knew Johann was a musical ignoramus.[15] Schuppanzigh protested as best he could, saying that he had needed more time to absorb the spirit of the music — a spirit as new to the medium as the *Razumovskys* had been.

Instead of waiting for a second try from Schuppanzigh, Beethoven recruited violinist Joseph Böhm to step in as first violin in a performance, with the same men in the other chairs. He hoped Böhm would be more diligent than Schuppanzigh, and indeed Böhm was. Beethoven attended their rehearsals, not hearing anything but following the players with his eyes and listening in his head. At one point, as they reached the ending Böhm felt that an indicated slowing of tempo was not working, so he signaled to keep the tempo steady to the end. Beethoven crouched in a corner, watching. When they finished he said only, "Let it remain so." Böhm's performance was received with stormy applause. Beethoven's old helper Baron Zmeskall reported, rather gleefully, to Therese Brunsvik: "Schuppanzigh received the disgrace and Böhm the victory."[16] The group repeated the quartet twice more that same March and again in April. Steiner, Beethoven's longtime principal publisher, now in disfavor, offered Beethoven 270 florins for it. Beethoven gave it to Schott.[17]

He was already at work on the next quartet for Galitzin. His labors and his general concentration were materially helped by the declining amount of time Cardinal Rudolph had to devote to music. After years of lessons that had taken up several days of the week when Rudolph was in town, Beethoven apparently gave his old patron the last lesson in December 1824.[18] Rudolph continued paying his part of Beethoven's annuity.

March 1825 saw the British premiere of the Ninth Symphony in London, conducted by Sir George Smart. Excitement ran high for the premiere, which was hoped to inspire Beethoven finally to make his

1825

long-delayed trip to London. But the performance turned out a scramble, the reception chilly. British enthusiasm for Beethoven languished from that point on.

On top of publishing, another chronic distraction, nephew Karl, only became more consuming. Karl was then seventeen and studying philology at the university. When he became guardian, Beethoven had declared he wanted to make his ward an artist or a scholar. It was a common sort of parental dictate in those days. Between his uncle and his other teachers, Karl had learned his way around the piano, but he was clearly not cut out for a musical career. The next choice was scholarship. Now, though he was bright enough, had a gift for languages, and studied well some of the time, he was not happy working toward an academic position.

In a conversation book of summer of 1824, Karl made an announcement. He told his uncle he wanted a job that he found more exciting, one that he could also start on sooner: "You will find my choice rather strange, but I will speak freely, nevertheless, as I prefer to do. The profession which I would like to choose is not a common one. On the contrary, it also demands study, only of a different kind; and one that is to my liking, I believe." What would that profession be? Uncle asked. "Soldier," Karl wrote.[19] Beethoven would have none of that, and there the matter rested.

As Karl reached his late teens he naturally yearned for independence, aspired to a few wild oats, cultivated a taste for beer and billiards.[20] Beethoven became more and more alarmed. He was especially terrified that the boy might be frequenting prostitutes, and that his mother Johanna might be procuring them for him. His concern was probably a mix of moral repugnance and his own fear of contracting venereal disease. Johanna was settled in as Beethoven's bête noire in chief, and she was still steadily scheming to reach her son. From Karl's point of view, his mother was far less judgmental, willing to let him have his fun. Now and then he ran away to her; a traumatic scene with his uncle invariably followed.

After one episode involving his mother or wine or both, and an aftermath that got verbally or physically violent, Karl wrote abjectly in a conversation book, "Dearest Father, you can be convinced that the hurt I caused you distresses me more than it does you. Anxiety has restored my reason to me, and I see what I have done . . . forgive me only this once! I will surely drink no more wine, it was all because of it that I could no longer contain myself."²¹ He was hardly sincere, and the effect of calming words never lasted long.

The older Karl got, the more Beethoven lost himself in suspicions, tried to control every part of the boy's life. Beethoven had a reflexive hatred and jealousy toward anyone else who had a connection to his nephew, saw everybody but himself as a corrupting influence. At one point Karl stood up for a servant Beethoven had mistreated, writing in a conversation book, "I don't know what you're angry about. I can't remember having laughed. At any rate, I must say that on the way she wept and complained that you torture her greatly and that she would rather go than to be so mistreated any longer in her old age. If you ordered her to wash, she only did her duty." Beethoven kept digging at Karl until he burst into tears. Finally Anton Schindler arrived and Karl fled. Beethoven told Schindler he believed that Karl was defending the old woman because he was sleeping with her.²²

Beethoven relentlessly attacked teenager Joseph Niemetz, Karl's friend since their time at the Blöchlinger institute. Niemetz was, Beethoven wrote to Karl, "completely lacking in decency and manners . . . rough and common . . . no friend for you."²³ It was true that Niemetz seemed to be the only person on Karl's side, which made them conspirators by necessity. At some point a note from Karl to Niemetz was discovered: "I had to write in such a great hurry for terror and fear of being discovered by the old fool."²⁴ Among the circle of acolytes around Beethoven, Karl had no defenders; all of them stoked Beethoven's suspicions and agreed with his strictures. Schindler, much given to jealously himself, had nothing but contempt for Karl.

Now the poles of Beethoven's rage and his smothering affection fell on the person who was least able to escape, understand, forgive. In October 1824, he wrote Karl, who had probably fled to his mother again, "As long as I live I shall cut myself off from you completely without forsaking you, of course, or failing to support you . . . Who will believe you or trust you who has heard what has happened and how you have mortally wounded and are daily wounding me?" A few days later: "My Beloved Son! Stop, no further—Only come to my arms, you won't hear a single hard word. For God's sake, do not abandon yourself to misery, you will be welcomed here as affectionately as ever . . . On my word of honor you will hear no more reproaches, since in any case they would no longer do any good."[25] This letter implies that Karl may have threatened to harm himself.

Between the two of them the road was all downhill. It was impossible for them to confront problems directly. In spring 1825, Karl did not study for his exams at the university. The potential mess was serious enough that Beethoven gave in at least one notch: he still would not accept Karl's going into the army but conceded that he could withdraw from the university and start studying business at the polytechnic institute.[26] Beethoven had given up the dream of his nephew's being an artist; now he gave up that of a scholarly career too.

After that Karl stayed in town to study during the summer. He roomed at the house of a Matthias Schlemmer, whom Beethoven expected to keep the boy on a short leash and to spy on him. In one letter he decreed that Schlemmer was "not to let Karl leave your house at night under any pretext whatever, unless you have received something in writing from me . . . Indeed one might be led to suspect that perhaps he really is enjoying himself in the evening or even at night in some company which is certainly not so desirable."[27] Later he asked Karl Holz, who had now edged out Schindler as Beethoven's main helper in Vienna, to play billiards with Karl to see how good the boy was at the game—so to assess how much time he was spending at it. Other friends got similar assignments. In a long, obsessive letter of summer 1825 asking editor friend Joseph Bernard to keep an eye on Karl, Beethoven wrote an archetypal complaint from the father of a teenager, segueing into his own obsessions:

> His manners are greatly deteriorating. His treatment of me is extremely offensive and is also having a bad effect on my health . . . Because I had to correct him on Sunday (and he absolutely refuses to be corrected) I had to face behavior on his part such as I have only

experienced in the case of his deceased father, an uncouth fellow, on whom, nevertheless, I showered benefits — I suspect that that monster of a mother is again involved in this little game and that it is partly an intrigue of that gentleman, my brainless and heartless brother, who is already planning to do business with him and who is also out to censure and instruct me . . . because I refuse to have anything to do with his overfed whore and bastard, and still less, to live with people who are so very much my inferiors.[28]

Four days after that letter to Bernard, he wrote mildly to Karl, "Dear Son! A little more or less than 21 gulden seems to me the best amount . . . It was hard work to raise it . . . By the way, do not wear your good clothes indoors. Whoever may call, one need not be fully dressed at home."[29]

When Beethoven went to the country in the warm months, he demanded that Karl visit on weekends. At the same time he turned his nephew into another of his Vienna lackeys, giving him shopping to do, music to copy, letters to write publishers. He expected Karl to study hard and at the same time to be at his beck and call. Most of the time Karl performed these chores as ordered. He still had a stratum of pride in his famous uncle. When Beethoven was out of Vienna, most of his constant letters were practical and affectionate. When they were together, there was trouble. In late 1824, when they were living on Johannesgasse in Vienna, the uproars of their arguments in addition to Beethoven's piano pounding were egregious enough that the landlord threw them out.[30]

Yet despite everything Beethoven was working, he reported to Karl, "tolerably well" at the string quartets for Galitzin.[31] Or he was until the spring of 1825, when his gut began to act up beyond his chronic episodes of vomiting and diarrhea. He developed a dangerous bowel inflammation. From Baden in April he wrote his doctor that he was bleeding from his mouth and nose.[32] By the next month he felt better, if still shaky. Since anything in an artist's life and health can be of use, he put this brush with death into the current string quartet: a hymn of thanksgiving by a convalescent.

His doctor at that point was Anton Braunhofer, professor of medicine at Vienna University and an exponent of the fashionable "Brunonian system" proclaimed by Scottish physician John Brown. The idea was to cure by opposites, attacking weaknesses of the body by stimulation, enemas, diet, and the like. In early 1826, Braunhofer ordered, "Two or three times a day you must syringe yourself with warm milk. Cream of rice and cream of cereal will do you much good." Beethoven should also avoid wine and coffee, which "augments and exaggerates the activity of the nerves."[33] In a time when the causes of disease remained virtually unknown, Beethoven was taken by Brunonian ideas and by Dr. Braunhofer, their distinguished exponent. He bestowed on the doctor one of his little canons on a punning text: "Doctor, close the door against Death; notes [*Noten*] will help him who is in need [*Not*]." History would credit Brunonian medicine with killing more people than the Napoleonic Wars.[34]

That spring and summer of 1825 Beethoven was taking the equally useless cure in Baden, living alone with an aged servant who was deaf and illiterate. He was working hard, otherwise sick and lonely and, as usual, disgusted with his servant. In August he wrote Johann, "Most Excellent and Worthy Brother! I request you, you you to come here as soon as possible, for I can't put up any longer with this old witch who 200 years ago would certainly have been burned . . . The evil nature of this female monster is the chief reason why she makes it impossible for herself to show the smallest sign of goodness — So I beg you to turn up in a few days. Otherwise I shall have again to take up with Herr Schott who has already been here and kissed <u>my hand</u> — But I should like to say again, like the Viennese, 'I kiss my hand' to Mr. <u>Shitting</u>."[35] Schott, the object of that pun making his name into defecation, remained Beethoven's main publisher. But as he wrote Karl Holz, as long as he got a good price he felt no loyalty to any publisher at all: "It is all the same to me what hellhound licks or gnaws away at my brain, since admittedly it must be so."[36]

Holz had largely replaced Schindler in Beethoven's affections and service because he was a livelier and more engaging companion — which included drinking companion. He was second violin in Schuppanzigh's quartet, an active conductor, and he was good at math, which was a gift to helpless Beethoven. Beethoven described Holz in a letter as a heavy drinker. Holz returned the compliment in describing Beethoven: "He was a stout eater of substantial food; he drank a great deal of wine at table, but could stand a great deal, and in merry company he sometimes became tipsy. In the evening he drank beer or wine . . . When he had drunk he never composed."[37] Since the name Holz means "wood," he had become the object of the inevitable Beethoven puns: "Most Excellent Piece of Mahogany!"; "Excellent Chip! Most Excellent Wood of Christ!"

As a function of his fame, Beethoven still had his string of visitors. Often as not he showed them a good time, especially if they visited him in the country, where he was usually in a better mood. Admirer Johann Andreas Stumpff, German born but living in London, turned up in Baden in September 1824. Much of Beethoven's line with visitors by this time had become routine. For Stumpff he rehearsed his humble admiration for Handel — dropping to his knee to illustrate — and for Mozart, and his contempt for the tastes of the Viennese. Hearing that Beethoven had seen no Handel scores outside *Messiah* and *Alexander's Feast* (he had surely seen others here and there), Stumpff secretly vowed to get his hero a complete Handel edition.[38] It took him years to find a copy; in the end, with those books Stumpff brightened Beethoven's last weeks of life.

Danish composer Friedrich Kuhlau visited Beethoven in Baden in autumn 1825 and found himself caught up in an eating-and-drinking fest. During it the conversation apparently got indecorous enough that several pages of the conversation book from the occasion were ripped out. The list of guests shows how widely sociable Beethoven could be in these days. At the table besides the visiting Dane were the Viennese piano maker Conrad Graf (who lent Beethoven one of his sturdy instruments), Haslinger, Holz, and a local oboe teacher. Beethoven led the party on a hike up and down the slopes of the Helenenthal, with its ruined castles. Then they all sat down in an inn and ordered champagne. In a conversation book Beethoven marked the occasion with a canon, beginning with the B–A–C–H motif, its text a pun in honor of Kuhlau: "Kühl, nicht lau," which means "Cool, not lukewarm." Next day Kuhlau had no recollection of how he got back to Vienna.[39] Beethoven wrote him, "I must admit that the champagne went too much to my head . . . I do not at all remember what I wrote yesterday." With that he enclosed the canon, which he had forgotten to give Kuhlau. Then to Holz, "Hardly had I got home when it occurred to me what stuff and nonsense I may have scribbled down yesterday." He added some advice for Holz about spying on Karl: it was always best to catch him in the act, which implies that Holz should be stalking the boy.[40]

British conductor and promoter Sir George Smart appeared in Vienna in autumn 1825, the main reason for his visit, he said, to get the tempos of the Ninth and other Beethoven symphonies from the horse's mouth. He arrived in time to hear the September 9 tryout of the A Minor String Quartet, the second of the Galitzin group. In his diary Smart left a recollection of the occasion. It was in the inn Zum Wilden Mann, in a room rented by Paris publisher Mortiz Schlesinger. (He wanted to hear the quartet before he bought it for his firm — but still he didn't get the piece.)

The room was stuffy and hot, occupied by what Smart described as "a numerous assembly of professors." He found the music "most chromatic and there is a slow movement entitled 'Praise for the recovery of an invalid.'" He understood that the invalid in question was Beethoven himself. Beethoven took off his coat and watched over the performers as they ran through the piece twice: "A staccato passage not being expressed to the satisfaction of his eye, for alas, he could not hear, he seized Holz's violin and played the passage a quarter of a tone too flat." Of those attending besides the players and professors, he notes nephew Karl, Tobias Haslinger, and Carl Czerny.[41] Holz recalled that at quartet rehearsals Beethoven usually sat between the first and second violinists, where he could hear some of the higher notes. He specified the tempos and tempo changes, and sometime demonstrated passages on the piano — or violin, as Smart witnessed. When Schuppanzigh struggled with the first-violin part, Beethoven might break into pealing laughter.[42]

A couple of days later Schlesinger hosted another performance and afterward invited some of the listeners and performers to dinner. Smart observed Schuppanzigh sitting at the head of the table: "Beethoven called Schuppanzigh Sir John Falstaff, not a bad name considering the figure of this excellent violin player." After dinner Beethoven improvised at the piano. At the end he rose, Smart said, "greatly agitated. No one could be more agreeable than he was — plenty of jokes. He was in the highest of spirits . . . He can hear a little if you halloo quite close to his left ear."[43] A few days later Smart visited Beethoven in Baden and got a dose of Beethovenian hospitality: a walk in the hills and, at lunch, a drinking contest. Smart reported with modest pride that Beethoven "had the worst of the trial." He did what he could to coax Beethoven to London, patiently answering his row of objections. As he left, Beethoven dashed off a canon for him on "Ars longa, vita brevis."[44] These days Beethoven appeared to be drinking more than usual, not the best course for a man with a bad liver.

In October 1825, Beethoven returned to Vienna from a long cure in Baden after sending more fulminations to Karl, who was moving their things to a new apartment: "Continue this way and you will rue the day! Not that I shall die sooner, however much this may be your desire; but while I am alive I shall separate myself completely from you."[45] In Vienna he had taken four spacious and attractive rooms in an apartment building called the Schwarzpanierhaus, fronting on the Alservorstadt Glacis outside the gates of the city. (It was called the Black Spaniard House because it had been built by black-robed Spanish Benedictines.) In the bedroom he installed his Broadwood and the new Graf piano. A maid and an old cook named Sali, a rare servant who seemed devoted to him, had a room for themselves. The floor of another room was piled with heaps of music in manuscript and print; its dust was rarely disturbed. After a lifetime of restless wandering, mostly within the confines of Vienna and its suburbs, the Schwarzpanierhaus was Beethoven's final residence.

His building lay diagonally across from the one where his childhood friend Stephan von Breuning lived, in the same flat the two had shared long ago before a fight broke up the arrangement. Since then there had been further breakups and reconciliations, the last estrangement flaring when Stephan objected to Beethoven's becoming Karl's guardian. Stephan worked in the Viennese bureaucracy as a councillor in the War Department, and he was ailing seriously. Now they had a warm reconciliation. The renewal of their friendship sparked Beethoven's nostalgia about Bonn, his yearning to see the Rhineland he left when he was twenty-two. He was fond of Stephan's son Gerhard, then on the verge of his teens. The boy got the inevitable Beethoven nicknames: *Hosenknopf* ("trouser-button"), because Beethoven said the boy stuck to him like one; and "Ariel," after Shakespeare's sprite in *The Tempest*, because Gerhard was given to capering about on their walks.

Gerhard von Breuning was with his father's famous friend often in his last years, and he left a trenchant and intimate memoir. He recalled that Beethoven commandeered Frau von Breuning to oversee his housekeeping and servants. There was only so much one could do. Beethoven's quarters remained a spectacle of dust and confusion, which is why Gerhard's mother resisted his invitations to meals at his flat. When walking with her husband's groaning and mumbling friend she was distressed to find that people took him for a tramp or a madman. Gerhard remembered that once, during a dinner at the Breuning flat, his sister let out a shriek over something, and Beethoven laughed with delight because he heard it. During walks with Gerhard, Beethoven commented on the sights. On a Versailles-style row of trees in the Schönbrunn Palace grounds: "All frippery, tricked up like old crinolines. I am only at ease when I am in unspoiled nature." On a passing soldier: "A slave who has sold his freedom for five kreuzers a day." Gerhard became familiar with Beethoven's sarcasm, in his words and his tone of voice. As visitors noticed, even in his fulminations and pontifications there was an energy, a gusto, a mind steadily and creatively at work.

Beethoven told Gerhard about his projects, among them the Tenth Symphony that existed mainly in his mind as he worked on his string quartets. There would be no chorus in this symphony, he said. With it

he wanted to create "a new gravitational force." History would like to
know what Beethoven meant by those words, if Gerhard remembered
them right (like most Beethoven anecdotes, this one was written down
years later).[46] Whatever that new gravitational force in a symphony
was to be, likely it came from what he had learned working on the new
quartets, each of which has its own gravity, its own mode of exploration.

If his rapprochement with Stephan von Breuning turned Beethoven's
mind back to his roots in Bonn, that nostalgia was amplified by a letter from another of his oldest friends, Franz Wegeler, now a much-
honored physician living in Koblenz. He was still married to Stephan's
sister Eleonore, one of Beethoven's early loves. They had both been
part of the artistic, intellectual, and progressive circle that gathered
around her and Stephan's mother, Helene von Breuning, who practically adopted the teenage Beethoven. Later it had been to Wegeler
that Beethoven first confessed his deafness. They had a friendship preserved by distance; there had never been a fight except for a short period of friction long before, when Wegeler was staying in Vienna. Yet
they had not corresponded in years. At the end of 1825, Wegeler's long,
affectionate, nostalgic letter arrived out of the blue. He addressed his
old friend by his first name in French, as he had done when they were
teenagers:

> My dear old Louis! I cannot let one of the 10 Ries children travel
> to Vienna without reawakening your memories of me. If you have
> not received a long letter every two months during the 28 years
> since I left Vienna, you may consider your silence in reaction to
> mine to be the first cause. It is in no way right and all the less so
> now, since we old people like to live so much in the past and es-
> pecially take delight in scenes from our youth. To me, at least, my
> acquaintance and my close youthful friendship with you, blessed by
> your kind mother, remains a very bright point in my life . . . Now I
> view you as a hero, and am proud to be able to say: I was not with-
> out influence upon his development; he confided to me his wishes
> and dreams; and when later he was so frequently misunderstood,

I knew well what he wanted. Thank God that I was able to speak about you with my wife and now later with my children, although my mother-in-law's house was more your residence than your own, especially after you lost your noble mother.

Wegeler's admiration for Maria van Beethoven echoed her son's; he does not mention father Johann. In the letter Wegeler catches Louis up on his doings since they were last in touch. He is sixty, the family is healthy, his daughter plays Beethoven on piano, his son studies medicine in Berlin. Mama Helene von Breuning is seventy-six, living in her parents' house in Cologne. Patriarchs Ries and Simrock are "two fine old men." Then Wegeler turns to a more serious matter, prodding his friend concerning the rumor that Beethoven was the bastard son of the king of Prussia. Beethoven knew about the story and had never publicly denied it. Wegeler asks, "Why have you not avenged the honor of your mother, when in the Conversations-Lexikon and in France, they make you out to be a love child? . . . If you will inform the world about the facts in this matter, so will I. That is surely one point at least to which you will reply."[47] The rumor about Beethoven's paternity had appeared first in a French historic dictionary of musicians, naming the father Prussian king Friedrich Wilhelm II. The Konversations-Lexikon in Leipzig changed the father to the even more absurd Frederick the Great.[48]

Wegeler enclosed a letter from his wife. Eleonore and Louis had parted on a sour note when he left Bonn in 1792. She entreats him to visit them and his homeland. Her mother Helene, she says, "is grateful to you for so many happy hours — listens so gladly to stories about you, and knows all the little details of our happy youth in Bonn — of the quarrels and reconciliations. How happy she would be to see you!" She downplays their daughter's musical talent but says the girl can play his sonatas and variations. She adds that Wegeler picks through his friend's themes for variations (the easiest part) "with unbelievable patience" at the piano, and he likes the old ones the best. "From this, dear Beethoven, you can see how you still live among us in these lasting memories. Just tell us once that this means something to you, and that you haven't completely forgotten us."[49]

Beethoven was surely pleased to get letters from his old friends, but he felt no haste about replying to them or about squelching the rumor concerning his paternity. He replied to Wegeler only a year later.

In January 1826, Beethoven sent the String Quartet in B-flat Major to Artaria for publication. It was the third and last of the *Galitzins* he finished. The B-flat ended up as op. 130, the second-finished A Minor as op. 132. With these three works he brought the Poetic style to the medium of string quartet and pushed the evolution of his late music into new territories. Part of what that says is that each of the quartets is even more a departure from tradition than the middle quartets and late piano sonatas. As a group they are distinct, and they are no less distinct from one another.

Still, there are threads holding the *Galitzins* together. One of those threads is the result of a change in working habit: having always sketched out pieces largely on a single line, for the late quartets Beethoven did the sketching on four staves.[50] That indicated his intention to be steadily contrapuntal and to find new textures and new kinds of part writing. On virtually every page, the quartets show that kind of attention to the individuality of the voices. At the same time that he sought a broader spectrum of color with the medium, Beethoven continued his quest for fresh ways of putting pieces together and, in keeping, new shades of feeling, new approaches to the human.

Among other developments as he made his way through these works, he veered further from the norms of logic and continuity he had learned from the Viennese Classical tradition, delved further into effects of juxtaposition and discontinuity. Here is a new intensification of the Poetic style, reaching toward conceptions that were to galvanize composers of the coming generation. In the *Galitzins* one finds more overt autobiography than before; finds Romantic irony of the self-reflecting kind (music about music, a theme about a theme); finds digressions and sudden passionate outbursts. In a review of op. 132, the critic called Beethoven "our musical Jean Paul," citing that Romantic writer noted for his volcanic fantasy, his formal and logical eccentricities. Along with Hoffmann, Jean Paul was a key inspiration of Robert Schumann and his generation.

QUARTET IN E FLAT MAJOR OP 127

The op. 127 Quartet is in E-flat major, the key purged of a heroic tone. It is a study in lyricism expressed in the most delicate and amiable passages — but they are new kinds of delicacy and amiability, with little trace of the eighteenth century. It begins with six bars of robust, bouncing chords in rich double-stops that in the first measures fool the ear about the meter — we hear a downbeat in the middle of the actual first beat:

Before the first theme proper, those six introductory bars embody another of Beethoven's games of these years with familiar formal functions: is this opening a theme or a micro-introduction? In practice it is more or less the latter, but it turns up a couple of times further in the movement, so it might better be called some sort of motto passage. The significant melodic element is the violin's rise of a sixth from E-flat to a trilled C in bar six. That sixth is going to be the compass of most themes to come, and C is going to be the main tonality of the development section. The first theme appears, warm and flowing, in the violin line, handed off to viola, with a fine lyrical charm. The rich contrapuntal web of these bars is going to return in various guises and permutations some two dozen times.[51]

In a compact exposition, the G-minor second theme flows lyrically like the first, and soon makes its way back to the first-theme idea. After

a brief closing section we find ourselves returned to the opening "introduction," as if the exposition has made the usual repeat back to the beginning. But the introductory idea is now in G major, and it ushers in the development without a repeat of the exposition. The development slips almost imperceptibly back into a transformed recapitulation, as if the recap were a continuation of the development. The coda, almost as long as the other sections, is pensive, to prepare the slow movement.

At one point in composing op. 127, Beethoven thought the quartet might have six movements, one of them called *La Gaieté* — as if in response to *La Malinconia* in op. 18. That plan receded to four move-

ments, and the lively *Gaieté* theme metamorphosed into the theme of
the Adagio.[52] That movement begins with a long, slow-arching theme
as subject for five gently beautiful variations. Here Beethoven's intensified focus on part writing comes to the front of the stage: unlike anything before, these verge on *texture variations,* some of those textures
made of several distinct figures in the instruments:

The fourth variation is an endless melody in the first violin, accompanied by pulsing chords. In the last variation the violin leads the way
into a liquid texture of sextuplets. While the first movement was just
over six and a half minutes, the variations are some sixteen and a half.
The next two movements will each be just under seven minutes, so the
slow movement is nearly as long as the other three combined.

The third movement is another of his sui generis outings. Marked
Scherzando vivace, lively and playful, it is therefore a scherzo, and
in scherzo–trio–scherzo form. Otherwise it sounds nothing like a
scherzo, or a minuet either, though it is in 3/4 and in minuet rather
than scherzo tempo. All of it is based on a bouncing and ironic tune
that goes in and out of fugue, like a parody of a fugue extended to
the point of seeming endless. The trio comes on in breathless triple
one-beat, like a manic scherzo. Here are the kind of instant changes
of direction that marked the late piano sonatas and some of the *Missa
solemnis,* now introduced to the string quartet.

In the finale, after another short, sort-of introduction (which char-
acterizes the beginning of all the movements), the first theme of the

sonata form is again warmly lyrical, like most of the quartet, and manifestly derived from the first theme of the first movement:

Here lines in long, flowing phrases alternate with dancing figures in
delicate staccato, especially the second theme. As in the first movement, a compact exposition slips without repeat into a compact development that continues unbroken into a highly varied developmental
recapitulation and finally into a long coda.[53] There is something magical about this coda, which transforms the main theme into passages
that recall the liquid last variation of the slow movement. It ends with
the kind of heart-filling affability that has marked the quartet from the
beginning.

   In its innovations, the wonderfully fresh and engaging op. 127 picks
up a little down the road from the two quartets of a decade before —
the *Serioso* and the *Harp*. Then in the *Galitzins* the serious deconstruction of forms and norms began.

                        •   •   •

A minor String Quartet, op 132

Another mark of Beethoven's late music is the union of mystery and surprise, even shock, with an inner logic that sinks traditional structure deeper beneath the fantasy-like surface. The quiet opening of the A Minor String Quartet, op. 132, presents us with an effect of a gnomic puzzle continually turning around on itself:

The four-note motive that is turned over and around — a half step up, a leap (primally a sixth) up and a half step down — is the fundamental motive of the quartet, both as intervals and as shape: step up–leap–step down. It will seed every theme, in ways both overt and subtle:

At the same time the opening implies most of the tonal centers in the quartet: the first four notes outline A minor, the first notes in the violin hint at E minor and then C major. The F–E of the second bar is another primal motif; here it foreshadows, among other things, the F major of the second theme. The opening phrase, in other words, virtually contains the quartet in embryo, including the austere contrapuntal texture that will flower in the third movement.

The tone of the first movement is peculiarly poignant; call it poised between yearning and hope. A minor was an unusual key for Beethoven. This quartet defines it not as a tragic tonality but rather as a key of Romantic passion, irony, and mystery. Call it a distant descendant, in another country, of an earlier rhapsodic work in A minor — the *Kreutzer* Sonata.

After the opening bars turning around the motto, there is a sudden skittering Allegro that as suddenly dissolves. Fragments of a breathless, yearning theme burst out, alternating with driving dotted descents on a B-flat triad. That phrase, constantly shifting among the instruments, is less a theme than a theme about a theme, or a gesture toward a theme that remains in potential. Yearning for the unrealizable: this is Romantic territory.

In its incompleteness the yearning phrase is nonetheless the main material of the movement, with new continuations in endless development. The rest of the matter is the skittering Allegro idea, the driving dotted figures, and a sweetly aching second theme in F major. These leaps among contrasting ideas, from quiet and austere to loud and passionate, foreshadow events all the way to the dichotomies of the third movement. There are no transitions, only sudden juxtapositions, like a character who is prey to manic emotions in a Sturm und Drang tale.

We are nominally in sonata form, though there is no repeat of the exposition, and the recapitulation apparently starts in the wrong key (E minor); a page later the music slips back into the proper A minor, but only briefly. From early on, Beethoven looked for fresh harmonic *EARLY* relationships within sonata form, turning away from the usual second theme in the dominant key to ones in mediants (III and VI), which became his norm. This fresh treatment of keys happened in the middle *MIDDLE* period, while his handling of formal outlines remained relatively traditional. Now, to say what he needs to say he has to bend the old forms *LATE* a great deal more, to more radical ends. Here, as in the E-flat Quartet but more thoroughly, he often departs from clear and regular Classical phrasing; he writes more than the usual four movements; he suppresses and rearranges familiar formal and tonal landmarks for a through-composed effect; he makes the recapitulation nearly as developmental as the development section.[54] In the A Minor the transformation of ideas is so constant from the beginning that it questions the very meaning of "exposition": when we first hear the yearning theme it enters the scene breathlessly, in fragments, as if it were already a recollection, a passionate wisp of memory known to the character onstage but not to us.

The second-movement scherzo is an ineffably zany interlude. It begins with rising figures based on the first movement's motto; over that phrase Beethoven places a swirling little waltz tune. This contrapuntal pair simply refuses to leave, dancing on chirpily through changes of key and texture in a display of Beethovenian minimalism. The middle-section trio is another instant shift of gears, its theme an ethereal musette.

In the third movement, like one of E. T. A. Hoffmann's imaginary authors who breaks into his own fiction, the composer steps from behind the curtain and reveals what this movement's bifurcating directions are about. It is labeled on the score *Heiliger Dankgesang eines Genesenen an die Gottheit, in der lydischen Tonart*, "Holy song of thanks to God from a convalescent, in Lydian mode." The joyful dance that twice interrupts the hymn is headed *Neue Kraft fühlend*, "Feeling new strength." The convalescent is, of course, Beethoven himself, recovered from a dangerous illness. Here too is Romantic territory: the artist as subject of his art.

In this movement Beethoven makes the most physical of human experiences, illness and recovery, into a sublime evocation of spiritual peace and thankfulness, then overflowing joy. It is nominally double variations, laid out ABABA, but the hymn is varied more, each time more melismatic, songful, gently ecstatic. The solemn and archaic *Heiliger Dankgesang* recalls Palestrina and other Renaissance sacred works. Beethoven's models were once contemporaries like Haydn, Mozart, Clementi, Cherubini. Now in the absence of great contemporaries, for inspiration he turned to composers of the past: Bach, Handel, Palestrina.[55] The drifting F-Lydian harmony and the austere texture of the *Heiliger Dankgesang* unfold in a prayerful trance.[56] Why Lydian mode?

The reason may be a passage in one of Beethoven's historical authorities, the sixteenth-century theorist Gioseffo Zarlino: "The Lydian mode is a remedy for fatigue of the soul, and similarly, for that of the body."[57] The dancing and ebullient *Neue Kraft* music breaks out in D major, its theme as vigorous and earthy as the hymn is ethereal and spiritual.

Beethoven spent months considering how to follow that uncanny movement. For a while he imagined a dance movement called "Alla allemande," but then he put that aside to be used in the op. 130 Quartet and replaced it with two movements. First, a short, jaunty Alla Marcia, assai vivace jolts us out of the song of thanksgiving. After what seems like only the first part of a march comes another startling and ironic turn: the march isn't finished, but that's enough of that. It dissolves, and the first violin gives out an impassioned quasi-recitative that serves as transition to an Allegro appassionato finale.

The last movement is a surging, sighing three-beat rondo, relatively straightforward in layout, merely unforgettably beautiful. The sustained singing line that eluded the first movement flows here in a long, steadily intensifying theme.[58] In the coda it climaxes in a breathless and breathtaking *presto,* the melody in a doubling of stratospheric cello and violin, the middle voices in a chattering accompaniment, and no bass line at all: the climax seems to be ascending into the air. The last pages are in a joyous A major.

The finale, like the whole of the quartet, is something that might have inspired E. T. A. Hoffmann to one of his crazed-by-love fantasies. The connection of the apparently distinct worlds of Beethoven and Hoffmann may not be coincidental. By now Beethoven had read Hoffmann and probably other Romantic writers, and he always had his creative antennae open to the zeitgeist.[59]

Whether or not the three *Galitzin* Quartets were designed with the possibility of being presented on a single program (it would be a frighteningly intense program for both players and listeners), there is no question that, for all their individuality, they took shape as some kind of unit — sharing material, forming a steady intensification of the principle of contrast until, with the String Quartet in B-flat Major, op. 130, contrast reached the verge of shattering the music.

The most obvious departure from convention in op. 130 is its six movements, each a distinct personality. Within each movement are further and more devious departures. The first page amounts to another ambiguous, not-quite introduction. It presents three disjunct ideas: an *adagio* chromatic moan that grows into chords that close in on F major; a pensive *fugato* on a figure that rises chromatically and then falls in a chain of thirds; then a sudden *allegro* burst of sixteenths, also based on a falling chain of thirds, over which is laid a little fanfare. This parade of contradictory gestures resembles the beginning of the A Minor Quartet, but here they are even more of a jolt:

   These are not just radically contrasting pieces of material; they are three distinct feelings — call them solemn, poignant, ebullient. By the usual Beethovenian/Classical logic, that beginning will set up themes, motifs, emotions, trains of thought that will unfold to the end of the piece. Even in the other late music, with its poetic rather than narrative frame of reference, much of that process still applies. But in the B-flat Quartet, the main thing that is going to apply is dissociation.[60] Having spent his life pushing the envelope of contrast in pieces, most radically in the A Minor Quartet, how far could he push the contrast before the music fell apart?

   Call the B-flat the trickster brother of the A Minor. For the ears and sensibilities of its time, op. 130 did fall apart, to a degree that suggested its composer was afflicted likewise. The outlandish finale was proof of the madness of the whole. To the ears of the distant future, though, this and all the late quartets would be signs not of madness but rather of prophecy, music as an occult puzzle, eternally modern. It must be added that in tone most of op. 130 is neither crazed nor despairing but instead ironic and comic, though the humor is subtle and one movement is inexpressibly tragic.

Beethoven called the first movement "a serious and heavy-going introduction" to a long quartet.[61] The three mutually exclusive worlds laid out on the first page are not themes as such; they are snippets that foreshadow themes to come. The nonintroduction is concluded by a frame, a return to the opening *adagio*. Then the *allegro* sixteenths break out again, becoming the first theme proper. They rocket on for a while, accompanied by the fanfare figure. That sequence is punctuated with a recall of the *fugato* figure from the first page, now speeded up to *allegro*.

Again we are in a warped sonata form, the solemn introduction popping up in various guises. There are more than a dozen changes of tempo and mood in the first movement. But the disruptions, on the whole, are in a spirit of irony and gaiety. The second theme turns up in G-flat major, a rare flat-side key for a second theme; partly because of its key, it offers a moment of lyrical calm before the chattering sixteenths return and lead to a subtheme that amounts to the sixteenth runs made legato, smoothing out the energy of the first theme. This is the only one of the *Galitzins* that calls for a repeat of the exposition.

The short, antidramatic development sounds like a haunting interlude on a hurdy-gurdy, obsessive harmonies pulsing under the little fanfare motif (the pulsation is based on an almost-absurd snippet, bar 4 of the opening) and a soaring legato line that comes and goes. This is one of the places in Beethoven, reaching back to his earlier works (such as the *Pastoral* Symphony) but more common in these years, in which for a space of time the music essentially does nothing, in a compelling way.[62] The trance of the development is broken by the rocketing sixteenths, the first theme returning; this is therefore the recapitulation, but hardly recognizable as such.

In the late works that are founded on sonata form, Beethoven was increasingly uninterested in Classical recapitulations that return to the home key and repeat earlier material literally. When previous material comes back it tends to be dynamic, in flux. That, combined with a preference for harmony that rarely cadences and a melodic bass line that does not firmly anchor the harmony, explains much of the fluid quality of the music.

The coda returns to the solemn opening idea of the movement, then the rocketing theme and the fanfare figure. So at the end the principal ideas are joined, but hardly in a sense of resolution. The coda falls into fragments, more dissociated even than in the beginning. In other words, the coda is not a resolution but rather questions whether anything has been resolved. Each bit of idea seems to run quickly out of breath, until a final four bars of racing sixteenths with the fanfare figure and a curt final cadence whose abruptness snubs a proper close.[63]

The odd-numbered movements of the quartet are expansive, the second and fourth compact, the second-movement scherzo compact to the point of intentional absurdity: two repeated phrases obsessing on a snide little motif, a helter-skelter trio, great sighs from the first violin, and a repeat of the scherzo, all adding up to about two hilarious minutes. We expect a slow movement to follow and we do get an Andante, but subtitled *poco scherzoso,* "a little jokingly." It begins with two bars of somber recollection of the first movement's chromatic beginning, but that is a misdirection. The ensuing movement is bustling and genial, involving some marvelously fresh sounds. It is laid out in sonata form, now as consistent and uniform in material as the first movement is the opposite.[64] In a section of the development marked *cantabile,* "singing," each of the four instruments has its own figure, the four fitting together like a mosaic of variegated colors.[65]

As fourth movement comes the lyrical three-beat lilt of the "Alla danza tedesca," a transposed (from A to G major) and renamed version of the "Alla allemande" that Beethoven dropped from the A Minor Quartet. The title relates it to a German dance. It is an artless dance, laid out in a scherzolike form with a trio in the middle, amounting to a gentle and faithful parody of its model. Ordinarily when Beethoven repurposed a movement like this it was because it had thematic, harmonic, or formal connections to the new piece — or, as in the *Kreutzer,* he developed the rest of the piece on ideas from the reused movement. But in this quartet, every movement is a distinct individual, as if it were a play with each act featuring a different character (and the overall plot remaining cryptic). Meanwhile, in the main themes of movements 2 to 5 lie four of the most memorable melodies Beethoven ever wrote, none of them more limpidly, wistfully lovely than the *tedesca.*

Again on display in the *tedesca* is the unprecedentedly varied scoring of all the *Galitzins,* encouraged by Beethoven's new process of sketching on four staves. The ingenuous principal theme begins in violin alone for four bars, the next phrase done by the violins in octaves; the consequent phrase again moves from first violin to violins in octaves, then the whole tune returns in octaves. The movement is an array of subtly mixed colors. The whole of the *Galitzins* expanded the palette of the string quartet in previously unimagined directions.

The first three movements of the quartet are comic/ironic in some degree. In most Beethoven, to say that would be to say that the core expression of the piece has these qualities, even though there may be shadowed episodes. To a degree this psychological pattern still applies to the late music at the same time that the music moved away from clear "narratives."

But in the B-flat, another Beethoven pattern is going to be put aside. After four movements, call them comic, ironic, dancing, and gently wistful, comes the "Cavatina," one of the most elegiac and tragic of all movements by Beethoven or anyone else. It is a song of endless heartbreak, the models for which in his life were endless. Beethoven said he had never been so moved in composing a movement; even the thought of it brought him to tears. In his youth he had laughed at the tears of his listeners when he improvised. Now the tears were his own, and he did not scorn them. Though the movement is some seven minutes it seems much longer, because it has another of the wide-arching melodies of the late slow movements. The manifestly sobbing last section, in dark C-flat major, is marked *Beklemmt,* "anguished."[66]

From comedy to anguish to what? A fugal finale as Beethoven was now given to, but a fugue like no other: what he called the *Grosse Fuge,* "Great Fugue." It is the one movement in all the late music that in the next two centuries never lost any of its reputation for strangeness. This music is eternally avant-garde. It may be that when Beethoven got to the finale of the quartet he had little idea of what he wanted. There are some twelve sketches for the finale theme. It may also be that even when he got rolling on the movement he did not realize how gigantic and relentless it was going to become.[67] However it happened, it turned out to be some sort of fugue to end all fugues; call it Beethoven's answer to Bach's giant *Art of Fugue* boiled down to a single movement. As with Bach, this construction is founded on a single motif, which is the same as the principal motif of the A Minor Quartet:[68]

As he worked on the A Minor, Beethoven tried out its opening motif as a fugue subject.[69] That was the germ of the *Grosse Fuge*. In its course that theme is transformed in character while being subjected to every traditional technical and thematic device that Beethoven had been drilled in years before by his contrapuntal master Albrechtsberger. As the old pedant laid them out in his treatise on composition, the theme of a fugue or other piece can be augmented (made longer rhythmically), diminished (made faster), shortened, syncopated, and used in stretto (the theme in quick entries, as if stepping on its own heels). After he lists these devices (he does not mention inversion of the theme), Albrechtsberger notes, "But one can rarely employ all of these together in one fugue." It is as if Beethoven remembered that sentence as a challenge. Now he determined to do just that, to wield all these devices in a single movement — in fugues of the last years having approached but never gone the full distance into this particular technical fanaticism.[70]

What emerged from this extravagant ambition grounded in tradition was a "revolutionary" work. In other words, in its hyperbolic and obsessive way the *Grosse Fuge* continued and intensified what Beethoven had been doing all his life. But nothing had approached its *fortissimo* ferocity, its manic and relentless counterpoint, its dissonance and aggression. The finale, like the Ninth Symphony's, is an ad hoc form seeming to enfold several movements in one: a fugue in B-flat as quasi–first movement, a second fugue in G-flat as slow movement, another in B-flat as scherzo. At that point, as with so many things in the B-flat Quartet, the analogy breaks down.[71]

The *Grosse Fuge* begins with what Beethoven called the "Overtura." With that designation he may have wanted to distinguish this intro- duction from a prelude, the usual preface to a fugue. In it the main theme is declaimed starting on an off-tonic G, starkly in four octaves, *fortissimo*, with explosive *sforzandos* on the middle notes. Thus he in- troduces each note of the theme individually, laying it before us like a building stone. Then, echoing the first movement, we hear a parade of snippets of music to come: the theme in lilting 6/8, then slow and soft with lacy figures woven around it. In the "Overtura," as in parts of the Ninth Symphony, we again find music about its own creation: a movement that begins by running through a kind of summary of its content.

Then the first fugue explodes in B-flat at a *fortissimo* whose rage never relents for four manic minutes. It has only one real harmonic cadence en route, to D minor. It is a double fugue, with a wildly leap- ing line in dotted rhythms serving as subject, the opening theme as countersubject. *What is difficult is good:* part of the effect of the mu- sic here is the suffering of the players. They have to contend with the awkwardness of the string writing, the constant leaps of more than an octave that require them to vault up and down over an intervening string while sustaining a fierce intensity for minute after minute.

The B-flat fugue is laid out in the traditional alternation of "expo- sition," sections with entries of the theme, and "episode," sections of free variation on the material. But the effect is of an almost featureless, harmonically chaotic rant. Everything gradually quickens and intensi- fies: triplets enter, then sixteenths, and then the theme begins to be syncopated, placed on the offbeat.

Again as in the B-flat Quartet's first movement, things will proceed in juxtapositions of disjunct material jammed together without transi- tions. The B-flat fugue stops almost as if hitting a wall. Then begins a *meno mosso, pianissimo* second fugue in G-flat major, its key echoing the second theme of the first movement. This section picks up the idea from the "Overtura," weaving flowing figures around the theme. The fugal treatment is looser here, and so it will be from now on. The *meno mosso* is more serene, amounting to a fuguelike interlude more than a full fugue.[72] Equally important is the character transformation, Beethoven taking his main theme in directions from ferocious to lyrical.

There follows a third section, in B-flat, beginning as an as-if fugue whose subject is another transformation of the main theme, picking up the lilting 6/8 fragment on the first page. Lyrical at first, the rhythm like a gigue or a scherzo, it segues into a new fugue in A-flat that builds to the ferocity of the first fugue as it rhythmically augments the main theme and adds trills. After this section builds to a gigantic, tortured climax, the *meno mosso* version of the fugue returns in A-flat, briefly, and likewise the 6/8 version in B-flat, no longer treated fugally but instead gentled into lyrical gaiety. It is as if in the *Grosse Fuge* the idea of fugue itself disintegrates en route. As Beethoven put it in the subtitle to the movement, *tantôt libre, tantôt recherchée*, "partly free, partly in strict counterpoint."[73]

Just before the coda everything dissolves into fragments, much like the end of the first movement: a recall of the opening *fortissimo* fugue, then a couple of bars of the *meno mosso* second fugue. The music seems to ask, Which will it be, fury or peace? The coda returns to the stern proclamation of the "Overtura," as if to look back across a journey that began on a distant peak. Then the fury drains out of the music, leaving delicate trills and a gentler recall of the theme that rises in a long crescendo from *pianissimo* to a *fortissimo* conclusion.

What does the *Grosse Fuge* mean to the whole of the Quartet in B-flat Major, this enigma that crowns the most enigmatic work of Beethoven's life? Many guesses would be proffered over the next two centuries. The more relevant ones would call the essence of the B-flat Major Quartet irony, disjunction, paradox. The fugue brings the climax of those qualities. Here Beethoven the supreme master of form and unity used all his craft to conjure a vision of disunity unto chaos,

comic in tone some of the time, in the end more provoking than joking, but with its own logic, however elusive.

Op. 130 had its premiere by the Schuppanzigh quartet in March 1826.
Because he could not hear the music and also perhaps sensing trouble,
Beethoven did not attend the concert. He waited at a tavern for a report. His friends arrived and assured him that much of the quartet had
pleased and in fact the second and fourth movements were encored.
What about the fugue? Beethoven demanded. One imagines hems and
haws, glances exchanged among the friends. It did not go well, they
admitted. "And why didn't they encore the Fugue?" he cried. "That
alone should have been repeated! *Cattle! Asses!*"

Soon his chosen publisher Artaria began a campaign to convince
Beethoven to spin off the finale as a separate piece and provide a
kinder and gentler alternative.[74] Artaria had paid some 400 florins,
unprecedented for a quartet, and was getting a work that threatened
to be unsalable. Realizing he had presented a challenge dangerous to
the future of the quartet, Beethoven, when Holz presented him with
the idea, took exactly one day to agree — and to name his price for the
alternate finale.[75] Artaria commissioned a four-hand piano arrangement to be published along with the separate string version. Thus the
Grosse Fuge would be saved, and at the same time the B-flat Quartet
saved from the *Grosse Fuge*. Beethoven lived just long enough to write
the new finale. The first publication of the quartet, in any case, had
the *Grosse Fuge*. Beethoven agreed to the alternative, but he did not
disavow the original version.

In any case the fugue is the true finale. However strangely, it enfolds motifs, rhythms, tonalities, gestures, styles from each of the other
movements. Most of all it pays off the contradictions that were first put
forth on the first page — though in the end, without trying to resolve
the dichotomies and ambiguities. But though the "Great Fugue" begins
in violence, as if a return and revenge of the old contrapuntalists, near
the end it arrives at its gentle and good-humored *allegro molto e con
brio*. The gentleness and brio last to the end, and maybe there is the
point: this epic, mad fugue begins in fury, but it ends in beauty.

What was Beethoven after in op. 130, his supreme enigma? Was he working toward some new kind of order in his music, in radically new, call them Romantic, directions? If so, in the time left to him he never wrote anything else like it.[76] Had he despaired of the models of organic form and logic he learned from the past? Surely not; in the next quartet he drew closer to those models again. The Quartet in B-flat Major stands as an ultimate, the furthest extension of the Poetic style, an unanswered question. One of the first reviewers called the fugue "incomprehensible, like Chinese."[77]

When he finished the three quartets for Prince Galitzin, Beethoven was not done with the medium. With no commission now, simply for himself, he went on to the Quartet in C-sharp Minor, which he intended to place at the opposite pole of the B-flat Major: after ultimate disintegration, ultimate integration. The opening fugue of the next quartet would be in itself the opposite pole of the *Grosse Fuge*. When he finished the B-flat Major he called it his favorite of his quartets.[78] When he finished the C-sharp Minor, he called it his greatest.

❧

33

Plaudite, Amici

A S THE END of 1825 approached, Beethoven seemed to have no awareness that his clock was running down, though it would hardly have surprised him. He had said long before that he knew how to die. He had come close any number of times, most recently from an inflamed colon. "Beethoven is now well again," his publisher friend Tobias Haslinger wrote composer Johann Hummel, "but he is aging very much."[1] If Beethoven noticed that, he did not mention it. He may not have owned a mirror anyway. Starting in December, his attention was taken up by the new string quartet, in C-sharp minor. Riding on the energy of the *Galitzin* Quartets, this one was done without commission, for himself.

In November he was made an honorary member of Vienna's leading musical organization, the Gesellschaft der Musikfreunde. It was a touching honor, especially since he had long owed the group either a refund of a commission or an oratorio to be titled *The Victory of the Cross*. (To try to accommodate him the directors suggested a new Biblical libretto, *Saul*.[2] It did no good.) The directors who approved his membership included composers Luigi Cherubini and Louis Spohr, neither of whom much approved of Beethoven's music, but they could not deny his position in the art.

Jan 1826

His health gave him no respite. By January his eye inflammation had returned, on top of abdominal troubles — either his long-standing ones or a new variety. In fact his liver was failing, an ailment to which he contributed by drinking more wine than usual. In that, he seems to have been abetted by Karl Holz, his current chief factotum. In other respects, Holz served Beethoven well. He was an able musician, second violin in the Schuppanzigh quartet, and a devoted and insightful friend.

Holz wrote in a conversation book, "I would explain the difference between Mozart's and your instrumental works in this way: For one of your works a poet could only write one poem; while to a Mozart work he could write three or four analogous ones."[3] Beethoven probably liked that. It speaks to the consistency of his narrative line — though it applies more to the early and middle music than to the late, which is more poetic than narrative. Mozart and Haydn are less allusive and more elusive. As Goethe observed, with works by "the newest composers" (mainly meaning Beethoven), "one cannot add anything more to such works from one's own spirit and heart."[4] He meant that Beethoven gave listeners less room to respond in their own terms, to find their own meanings and stories.

Holz recalled walking with Beethoven when he was working on the quartets, stopping to jot down an idea. Once Beethoven joked, "But that [idea] belongs to the quartet after the next one [the C-sharp Minor] since the next one [the B-flat] already has too many movements."

Holz admired the B-flat Major Quartet the most of the *Galitzins,* or at any rate told Beethoven he did, despite the *Grosse Fuge.* He asked which of them Beethoven liked most and got the reply, "Each in its own way! Art demands of us that we don't stand still . . . You'll find here a new kind of voice-leading, and, as to imagination, it will, God willing, be less lacking than ever before." This was spoken "in an imperial style."[5] Did Beethoven really worry that he had been deficient in imagination?

Beethoven sent the last quartet to Prince Galitzin in early 1826. He had gotten a partial advance, and waited for the 600 florins he was owed as final payment (it included 150 florins for a copy of the overture *Die Weihe des Hauses,* which Beethoven dedicated to Galitzin).

The money never came. When an emissary was deputized to ask for the payment in person in St. Petersburg, Galitzin put him off.[6] At the end of 1826, the prince wrote Beethoven a flowery excuse: "You must believe me very inconsistent and very thoughtless to leave you hanging for such a long time without a response, especially since I have received from you two new masterpieces of your immortal and inexhaustible genius."[7] Galitzin had suffered family losses and one of the extravagant bankruptcies aristocrats were given to. He finally paid his bill in 1852, to Karl van Beethoven. But he did not do it in good humor. Galitzin had arranged for the premiere of the *Missa solemnis* in St. Petersburg and after it reported to Beethoven, "I doubt if I exaggerate when I say that for my part I have never heard anything so sublime."[8] Years later the prince snarled, "Who acted more nobly, Beethoven or I? He sends me without warning a useless score [the mass] for which I had not asked. He then makes me pay fifty ducats for it when I could have bought a printed copy a few months later for only five thalers."[9]

In the world outside Beethoven's own labors and obsessions, Romanticism continued to define his music on its terms. In an *Allgemeine Musikalische Zeitung* article of January 1826, critic Gottfried Wilhelm Fink wrote an article titled with a perennial question: "Is It True That Our Music Has Declined So Far That It No Longer Can Stand Comparison with the Old and Oldest Music?" His review of the immediate past includes familiar tropes: "Haydn lifted up a great people into the new, friendly course of his life. Mozart arose with splendor. His light is clear like the light of reason, which, like a good father, allows the children of his heart to play around him." When the critic reaches Beethoven his metaphors reach for the mythological, while in their enthusiasm they threaten the incoherent: "Beethoven ascended like youth decorated with all the colors of spring. He seats himself upon mountains. Wildly his steeds rush forth. Brooding, he holds the reins firmly so that they rear at the precipice. He, however, peers into the abyss as if he had buried something down there. Then he bounds across the gaping crevices and proceeds home, playing as if in mockery or blustering as if in a storm. And that something in the depths strangely gazes after him — that is also life."[10]

In the spring Beethoven had a visit from piano pedagogue Friedrich

Wieck, who had decided before his daughter Clara was born that any child he fathered was going to be one of the greatest pianists in the world. (He later resisted but failed to prevent Clara, at eighteen already famous across Europe, from marrying Robert Schumann.) Wieck reported that Beethoven improvised for him for more than an hour on a piano with an amplifier on the sounding board. He listed the topics of Beethoven's conversation, or rather his soliloquies. They included his abominable housekeeper, music in Leipzig, the Leipzig *Allgemeine Musikalische Zeitung* editor Friedrich Rochlitz, walking, the Schönbrunn Palace and grounds, his idiot of a brother, "Viennese fools," the aristocracy, democracy, the French Revolution, Napoleon, the perfection of Italian opera, Cardinal Rudolph. As for his style, Wieck reported, "He expressed himself rather crudely, but gave the impression of being a noble, sympathetic, and sensitive character, friendly and enthusiastic in his attitude but politically a pessimist." Wieck noted that Beethoven often took his head or hair in his hands.[11] It is the posture of a man exhausted, or in pain.

Another visitor that summer reported Beethoven's punningly exclaiming over Sebastian Bach, "His name ought not to be Bach ['brook'] but Ocean, because of his infinite and inexhaustible wealth of combinations and harmonies." He declared that the purest church music should be a cappella, without instruments, and the highest example of that style was Palestrina. But he added, "It was folly to imitate [Palestrina] unless one had his genius and his religious beliefs."[12] Beethoven had made good use of the old polyphonist as a model, but he admitted by implication that even if he had the genius, he did not have that purity of faith.

Besides the Quartet in C-sharp Minor, more or less his only other project of this period involved the four-hand piano arrangement of the *Grosse Fuge,* commissioned from pianist Anselm Halm. When Beethoven received the arrangement, Halm enclosed a note saying that for the sake of convenience he had had to break up some of the lines among the hands. Beethoven was not interested in convenience. He rejected Halm's arrangement and did a new version himself. The manuscript shows massive revisions and struggles on the page; at some points the erasures have dug holes through the paper.[13] Publisher

Artaria was not pleased. He was expected to pay for the new finale, and when Beethoven threw out the keyboard arrangement of the fugue and redid it, Artaria had to pay for that too. In effect, the publisher paid for the unsalable *Grosse Fuge* three times.

Beethoven finished the C-sharp Minor String Quartet and went on to the next, in F major. During those months, relations between him and nephew Karl reached their inevitable smashup. For the first time since the 1790s, in the summer of 1826, Beethoven had stayed on in Vienna as the hot weather came on, mainly to keep an eye on his nephew. Karl, now nineteen and staying in a boarding house, had counted on his uncle's going away so he could have some relief from suspicions and accusations. At one point, Karl struck Beethoven and fled to his mother.[14] In June they had a violent argument over Karl's laundry bill.[15]

At the end of July 1826, around the time he finished the C-sharp Minor Quartet, Beethoven received a note from Karl's landlord, Wenzel Schlemmer: "I learned today that your nephew intended to shoot himself at latest next Sunday."[16]

Secretly Karl had been seeing his mother more often and carousing with his forbidden friend Niemetz. He told a teacher, "My uncle! I can do with him what I want, some flattery and friendly gestures make things all right again right away." He told Karl Holz that he could wrap his uncle around his finger.[17] In fact the nineteen-year-old was desperate, unraveling.

When Karl's landlord got wind that the boy was intending to shoot himself, he searched Karl's room. In a chest he found two pistols, one of them loaded, and lead and powder. Schlemmer reported to Beethoven, "I was given to understand only that it was to be on account of debts, but not quite for certain, he admitted them only in part, as the consequence of former sins." Beethoven dispatched Holz to fetch his nephew, but somehow Holz let him slip away. He reported to Beethoven, "I believe that if he intends to do himself harm, no one can stop him . . . He said, what good will it do you to keep me, if I do not get away today, it will happen another time."[18] Karl pawned his watch and bought another pair of pistols.

Soon after, Beethoven received word that Karl had disappeared. Frantic, he ran to Niemetz's house, then to Johanna's. There he found his ward lying in bed with a bullet lodged in the left side of his forehead. As the story trickled out, on August 6 Karl had gone to Baden and climbed to the ruins of Castle Rauhenstein on a cliff looking down into the Helenenthal. The wooded valley with its ancient ruins was a landscape he knew from walks with his uncle. Which is to say, Karl planned his end in a famous and picturesque setting: a Romantic suicide. He put one pistol to his head, shuddering, pulled the trigger, and missed or misfired. His feelings can be imagined as he raised the second pistol. That bullet knocked him down and out but did not penetrate his skull. A carter found him barely conscious. He asked to be taken to his mother's.

A later time would understand that a miss with two pistols indicates a cry for help rather than a determined attempt.[19] But in those days there were no such categories, and attempted suicide was a crime. The police were notified, as they had to be. Karl, slipping in and out of consciousness and effectively under arrest, was taken to the General Hospital. Under interrogation he told a policeman he had done it "because my uncle harassed me so."

Beethoven showed up at the hospital in a lather. "Is my nephew with you, the dissolute fellow, the scoundrel?" he demanded of a Dr. Seng, who reported his voice as "dull." Beethoven went on, "I really did not want to visit him, for he does not deserve it, he has made too much trouble for me." He told the doctor he had spoiled the boy. It appeared to Seng that Beethoven's main fear was that Karl would go to jail.[20]

The conversation books of the next weeks record Karl's responses to his uncle as he lay in bed. "Don't torment me now with reproaches and complaints. It is past," read one entry. When Beethoven began to berate his mother, Karl stood up for her: "I do not want to hear anything that is derogatory to her. It is not for me to be her judge. If I were to spend the little time I shall be here [in the hospital] with her, it would be only a small return for all that she has suffered on my account."[21] Beethoven could not allow that. He wrote a magistrate, "I urgently request you to arrange that my nephew, who will have recovered in a few days, shall not leave the hospital with anybody but myself and Herr von Holz — It is out of the question to allow him to be much in the company of his mother, that extremely depraved person. My anxieties and my request are warranted by her most evil, wicked and spiteful character, her enticement of Karl for the purpose of getting money out of me . . . and that she also was intimate with Karl's dissolute companion [meaning Niemetz]."[22] In the event, Karl was in the hospital for more than a month.

Beethoven ran into Stephan von Breuning's wife in town and cried to her, "Do you know what has happened to me? My Karl has shot himself!" Is he dead? Frau von Breuning asked. "No, he only grazed himself, he is still alive, there is hope that he can be saved — but the disgrace that he has caused me. I loved him so much!"[23] Schindler wrote that after the disaster Beethoven seemed overnight to look like a man of seventy. "To add to his suffering he was compelled to learn that many persons placed part of the blame for the rash act upon him." But his circle closed around him. Young Gerhard von Breuning wrote Beethoven, "You must come to us for all your meals so that you will not be alone."[24] Stephan von Breuning took over Karl's guardianship. Beethoven's friends blamed Karl alone.

These responses of Beethoven's are another testament to his incapacity to see the disaster beyond his own pain, his own reputation. Here is where the solipsism that had been with him since his youth, which his friends and admirers had always understood and largely forgiven, turned on him with devastating effect. And yet, now, finally, he bent. Holz and Stephan von Breuning pressed him to let Karl join the army as he wanted to. "A military life will be the best discipline for one who cannot endure freedom," Stephan told Beethoven. And Holz: "Here you see ingratitude as clear as the sun . . . A soldier at once!" Soon after this discussion, from his bed Karl wrote to his uncle in a conversation book, "My present condition is still such that I would ask you to make as little mention as possible of what has happened and cannot be altered. If my wish concerning a military career can be fulfilled I will be very happy, in any case I consider it the thing in which I could live and be satisfied."[25]

It had taken him a close encounter with death to achieve it, but now Karl knew he had the upper hand. Beethoven began to busy himself with arranging for his induction into the army, finding him a position, courting officers and officials to get a favorable situation. A hope of sending the boy to officer school did not pan out. He would have to start as a cadet. In one of his moments of calm common sense, Beethoven wrote to Breuning, now officially guardian, that in regard to the military accommodations, "I believe that there are three points to be observed with Karl. First, he is not to be treated as a culprit, which would have exactly the opposite result from what we want; second, in order to become promoted to a higher rank, one cannot live too modestly and meanly; third, too great a limitation on his eating and drinking might have a harsh effect upon him. I am not trying to obstruct you."[26]

Holz also began working on the military solution. Beethoven sadly wrote him, "On the whole I am not at all in favor of the army as a profession . . . I am worn out; and happiness will not be my portion again for a very long time . . . All my hopes have vanished, all my hopes of having near me someone who would resemble me at least in my better qualities!"[27] His hopes, his ideals, his convictions about self-improvement had been defeated by a teenage boy who aspired to little more than to be a teenage boy.

Everyone including Karl wanted him to sign up for the army right away, but that proved impossible — first, because he was confined to the hospital for weeks, and then because he had to wait until the wound had healed enough to be concealed. To avoid jail, meanwhile, he would have to submit to religious counseling.

Through it all, business went on. In the week after Karl shot himself, Beethoven dispatched the newly finished Quartet in C-sharp Minor to Schott, his letter including a joke that it was "patched together from pieces filched here and there." When he discovered that Schott had not understood the joke and was alarmed that the piece might not be entirely new, Beethoven had to send another letter to explain.[28] The quartet was anything but a patchwork. As much as anything he had ever written, it was made of whole cloth.

The C-sharp Minor Quartet, op. 131, begins with a keening melody on the middle strings of the violin — its most subdued register, in a shadowed key. The movement is headed Adagio ma non troppo, e molto espressivo. A second violin enters with the theme; a fugue begins to take shape. As the entries work their way down to the cello the texture remains austere, moving in simple quarter and half notes. The spareness and simplicity recall the *Heiliger Dankgesang* of the A Minor Quartet, but that was a hymn of thanks and this is a song of mourning. Both have an archaic feel, this one like a Renaissance ricercar.[29] Long before, Beethoven had begun to invest the old genre of fugue with more emotion than it had ever possessed.[30] Here is the climax of that investment. Richard Wagner was to say that he found this movement "the saddest thing ever said in notes." It is as if this music expressed the distillation of a minor key and its intrinsic sorrow, in the same way that the finale of the op. 111 Piano Sonata expresses some distillation of C major.

The singularity of this opening has to do with its being Beethoven's only first-movement fugue, and one of distinctive cast. Part of the effect is the rarity of its key. To find his only other work in C-sharp minor, and his last opening on a slow movement, one looks back to the *Moonlight* Sonata of 1801, with its haunting first movement. But C-sharp minor in piano and in strings are quite different matters. Its effect on keyboard has to do, if anything, with tunings in unequal temperament. In strings, the key is distinctively shadowed because it involves so few open strings — only A and E, the mediants of the scale. Partly for that reason, Beethoven picks out those notes and those keys in the quartet and begins a variation with them in the slow movement.[31]

The piece did not come easily. There were more than six hundred pages of sketches that included five sets of plans for the movements.[32] As it finally took shape, the quartet comprised seven numbered movements, each rising from the preceding one with little or no pause. He did not write the usual ending double bar until the conclusion of the piece. The whole is grounded on the beginning, the bare fugue theme that constitutes the *Thema*. The first three notes, G-sharp–B-sharp–C-sharp, form a head motif that will resonate all the way to the finale. The next two bars are the tail motif, whose scalewise flow will also have a long career. The first part of the *Thema* points to sorrow, the gently flowing last part to resignation and hope:

Adagio ma non troppo e molto espressivo

No less important is a single note invested with enormous consequence, the accented open-string A on the downbeat of the second bar. It sets up the importance of A major through the quartet — also D major, D being the accented note in the second violin's answer. In the opening bars, the A and the D are both heartrending.[33]

The second entry of the subject is not on the usual dominant key, G-sharp, but on F-sharp minor, the subdominant and the relative minor of A major. F-sharp minor will be another important key in the first movement, and at the end of the quartet F-sharp and C-sharp will still be contending.[34] The keys of the whole will be as unified as if they were a single movement. Most Classical works, including most by Beethoven, have two or at most three keys in their movements. The B-flat Major has four keys; the C-sharp Minor has six.

No fugal movements in late Beethoven are pure fugues. Each of them is a unique integration of Baroque and Classical models. The first movement of the C-sharp Minor begins with a full fugal exposition, but much of the rest is a contrapuntal and imitative development on the motifs of the theme, sonata-like, including a second-theme-like section in B major (not fugal) where the tail motif is diminished into eighth notes. After some exquisitely poignant echoing duets and more development, the last section before the coda is a fugue using an augmentation of the theme, each note doubled in length. The first clear cadence to C-sharp minor does not arrive until the end of the movement; the first truly firm cadence to that key is in the finale. The ending of the first movement, rich with double-stops, turns to C-sharp major, like one of Bach's lush conclusions. (Beethoven's fugue and its mood have a close affinity to the one in that key in *The Well-Tempered Clavier*.)[35]

Just before the final bars, the first violin reaches up achingly to D-natural, the gesture enfolding both feeling and logic: it makes a tonal transition to the second movement's nimble and dashing 6/8 gigue in D major, marked Allegro molto vivace. Deep darkness to light: part of the effect of the second movement's sudden brightening is the effect of D major in the instruments, that key ringing most of the open strings. Like all the movements, the second has a memorable leading theme, blithe and liquid. The movement is short and nominally in sonata form, though there is little trace of a development section. A big coda builds up to a stern, three-octave declamation that resurrects the serious side of the quartet. The sound remains open and simple; this quartet will not engage in the kinds of textural experiments Beethoven did in the *Galitzins*.

The coda of the second movement slips suddenly from *fortissimo* to soft sighs and fragments. What comes next is marked "No. 3," as if it were a movement, but really it is a short preface to the next movement—"preface" rather than "transition," because it amounts to brief skipping gestures and a sudden passionate burst of quasi-cadenza and quasi-recitative, each lasting a few seconds.

The central movement is marked Andante ma non troppo e molto cantabile, the last meaning "very songful." It is variations on a memorable and ingenuous tune that is presented in call-and-response between the violins. All is simple and transparent, the harmony placid, the rhythm gently striding, the focus on the tune but with melodic undercurrents in the accompaniment. The theme flows into the first variation, and all are linked. The variations contrast, but gently: the first flowery and contrapuntal, the second marchlike, and so on. The end of the movement is a train of vignettes: cadenzas for each of the instruments; a brief and breathless recollection of the theme in the wrong key (C major); a flowery, inexplicable processional full of trills that suddenly vanishes; another breathless recall of the opening theme; a zipping violin cadenza; for coda, fragmentary echoes of the theme.

Next is the scherzo proper, Presto in 2/2, in E major and with a trio in the middle. Here is comedy in rumbustious staccato, the tone somewhere between folklike and childlike, starting with the cello's gruff opening gesture like a clearing of the throat. This movement is as tuneful as the others, especially the lyrical musette-like theme of the trio, which has a giddy refrain that is one of Beethoven's most childlike, if not childish, moments. After a triple repeat of the scherzo, a double repeat of the trio, and a feint at a third repeat of the trio, the coda begins with the main theme returning in a remarkable guise: marked *sul ponticello,* an effect of playing next to the bridge of the instrument that produces a ghostly, metallic, from-afar quality. (Where had Beethoven heard this then-almost-unknown effect?)[36] The *ponticello* phrase is the perfect conclusion for a wonderfully wry movement.

Just as "movement" no. 3 was not really a movement but a preface for no. 4, no. 6 is a preface for no. 7, in the form of a somber, aria-like Adagio in G-sharp minor. Though it lasts a minute and a half, it amounts to yet another fragment. Its key of G-sharp minor prepares the C-sharp-minor finale — the first time that key has returned anywhere since the first movement — and its tone returns us to the seriousness, though not the sorrow, of the first movement. In effect it poses a question: at the end of this journey that started in tragedy and takes us through dance and grace and tenderness and laughter and nursery tunes, where do we end?

We end in a fierce march, the first movement in the quartet to have a fully decked-out sonata form. Its main theme sits on a C-sharp-minor chord for its first six bars, a definitive grounding on the tonic chord that the first movement never reached. From there the finale is broadly integrative, pulling together ideas from the whole. Here again is the D-natural whose interjection into the quartet's opening fugue contributed to that movement's feeling of sorrow. The finale theme's legato second section, too, returns to the head motif of the first fugue, first inverted and then right-side up:

A short but warmly lyrical second theme breaks out in a bright, breathtaking E major, its rising line recalling the trio theme of the scherzo, its resonant fifths in the cello recalling the end of the first movement and the fifth variation of the third movement. The driving staccato of the march recalls the staccato scherzo and the second variation of the second movement. The keys are the leading ones of the quartet: E and D major, F-sharp minor in the coda. The end barely makes it out of F-sharp minor to a quick, full-throated close on C-sharp major.

The earlier B-flat Major Quartet was the distillation of Beethoven's Poetic style: mercurial, fantasia-like, unpredictable from moment to moment in its mingling of light and dark. The C-sharp Minor is an integration of the Poetic style with the organic quality of his earlier music. Each movement is tightly made, with one or two leading ideas and contrasts subdued (except in the variations). The textures are simple and open, which is to say Classical. The movements flow together with little or no break between. The contrasts, deep ones, are mainly between rather than within the movements. There is no single dramatic unfolding but rather a mingling of qualities, as if the whole quartet were one variegated movement — and this is surely one of the reasons Beethoven called this his best quartet. Much of the overall effect has to do with the sound of its keys on the instruments: the darkness of C-sharp minor, F-sharp minor, and G-sharp minor with few open strings, while the other keys are the brightest ones on the instruments, resonating with open strings: A, D, E.[37]

As an answer to the suffering of the first movement, the finale is driving and dynamic but not heroic, not with the kind of triumph that ended the Third and Fifth and Ninth Symphonies, *Fidelio,* and *Egmont.* The overcoming of sorrow here is more subtle, shaded, hard won. Schiller wrote that in art suffering must be answered by a heroic overcoming, as an act of free moral will: "The depiction of suffering, in the shape of simple suffering, is never the end of art, but it is of the greatest importance as a means of attaining its end . . . This is effected in particular by tragic art, because it represents . . . the moral man, maintaining himself in a state of passion, independently of the laws of nature. The principle of freedom in man becomes conscious of itself only by the resistance it offers to the violence of the feelings."[38]

In his music Beethoven had largely treated tragedy in those terms. The heroic Fifth and the Ninth begin in darkness and end in triumph. (An exception is the *Appassionata* Sonata, where tragedy has the last word.) In the C-sharp Minor Quartet, the transcendence is deeper. In the first movement the formality of the fugal idea makes it something on the order of a ceremony carried out within the most profound grief. Transcendence is adumbrated in the moments of hope that temper the first movement, in the integral fabric that enfolds the whole quartet, in its emotional journey that enfolds so much of life. It is not a one-directional journey like that of the Fifth Symphony. Here light and shadow, comedy and tragedy, innocence and experience mingle as they do in life, as they mingled in Beethoven's own mercurial sensibility. The triumph in the C-sharp Minor Quartet is not in heroic gestures or in the kind of wild joy that ended *Fidelio* and the *Eroica*. As Beethoven's increasingly hard-won labors transcended the anguish of his life, the triumph of the C-sharp Minor Quartet, its answer to suffering, is the supreme poise and integration of the whole work.

With that, in effect, the course of Beethoven's art came to rest. What followed were aftereffects and asterisks.

Summer 1826

Still, in summer 1826, Beethoven had no plans to die and no thoughts of final statements. He had another quartet and a symphony to finish and a string quintet in sketches, and he needed to write the promised alternative finale for the B-flat Major Quartet. Having intended to dedicate the C-sharp Minor to a wealthy music fancier, at the last moment he changed the dedication to Lieutenant-Marshal Baron von Stutterheim, who agreed to accept Karl into his regiment despite the scandal of the suicide attempt.

For some time Beethoven's brother Johann had been trying to coax Ludwig out to his estate Wasserhof, in the little shabby hamlet of Gneixendorf, near Krems. (Beethoven said the name of his brother's village, with its crackling consonants, sounded like a breaking axle.)[39] Ludwig had been testily resisting the idea, knowing he would have to be around Johann's wife and daughter. For her part, wife Therese had not long ago threatened to brain him with an iron poker if he showed up to meddle. But now for Beethoven the idea of getting out of town was suddenly appealing, mainly because it would give Karl time to recover so he would be presentable for the army.

He and Karl left Vienna for Gneixendorf at the end of September

1826. With him he brought the string quartet in F major and the new finale for the B-flat Quartet, both of them nearly finished. Their journey of some fifty miles up the wandering Danube was the longest he had made in many years. It was the first time he had seen the lush landscape of the Wachau Valley since he first traveled to Vienna, in 1792, and then it had been wrapped in winter.

Just before they left, Beethoven hastily put down tempo markings for the Ninth Symphony, he sitting with music and a metronome dictating the numbers to Karl, who transcribed them as best he could, which was not entirely accurately. Publisher Schott did not help when it printed the starting tempo for the finale at dotted half = 66 (already too fast for the bass recitatives) with the first number upside down, 96. That absurd tempo remained in scores for two centuries.[40] Before the trip to his brother's, Beethoven also spent three days meticulously correcting a presentation score for Friedrich Wilhelm III, king of Prussia, to whom it was dedicated. Eventually the king wrote a chilly note of thanks and enclosed "a diamond ring as token of my sincere appreciation." Beethoven had the ring appraised. It turned out to be fake, an unidentifiable reddish stone. He had to be talked out of indignantly sending it back. It is at least possible that the original stone had been stolen en route and the imitation substituted.[41]

Beethoven had never been more attentive to Karl's needs as after the accident. His efforts included stroking officials to keep his nephew from prosecution. Just before the trip he wrote a magistrate, "Karl will have to spend a few days with me (before he leaves Vienna to join the army). His statements [to the police] are to be ascribed to the outbursts of anger caused by the impression made on him by my reprimands when he was thinking of taking his life. But even after that time he behaved affectionately to me. Rest assured that even in its fallen state humanity is always sacred to me."[42] He intended a week's trip, but they ended up staying in the country for two months, waiting for Karl's wound to heal enough to be hidden by his hair.

When Beethoven arrived at his brother's estate he was ailing with liverish symptoms: legs swollen, fluid accumulating in his abdomen so he had to wear a support around his bulging belly (it was not the first time he had to resort to that).[43] Johann gave his brother a suite of three rooms and assigned a servant to him. The center room featured an elaborate mural Johann had commissioned, depicting the Rhine country of their youth.[44] The only piano was in the parlor, where Beethoven only occasionally played it.

At the beginning he and Karl and Johann took some walks around the property. Johann owned four hundred acres, most of it leased to tenant farmers. Beethoven and Johann's wife largely avoided one another. Given her propensity for outside amusements, Johann had prevailed on Therese to sign a legal contract agreeing that if she took up with a lover, he could turn her out of the house without notice. This seedy expedient would not have made Beethoven happier. Therese did her best to be conciliatory, even trying to smooth things between Beethoven and Karl. "It seems that Karl has some of your rash blood," she wrote in a conversation book. "I have not found him angry. It is you that he loves, to the point of veneration."

Besides walks there were carriage trips to Krems; Johann sometimes had to go to Vienna on business, the fifty miles necessitating a two-day trip in each direction. From old habit the brothers were soon squabbling, partly over Johann's demand that Beethoven shell out a little for his board. At this point Johann, who was having trouble paying off his estate, was pressing his brother to live with him regularly in the warm months — again, for a modest rent.

Meanwhile despite everything, Beethoven had not changed his habit of riding Karl mercilessly. The boy had to fend off the attacks in the conversation books: "But why are you making such a scene today? Will you not let me go for a little now . . . I'll come back later. I only want to go to my room . . . Will you let me go to my room?" When he heard Karl had been playing piano duets with Therese, he accused him of sleeping with her. Further noisy scenes ensued. When Karl was sent to Krems to get writing supplies for his uncle, he would try to sneak in a little billiards. When he could get away from Uncle, the nineteen-year-old was all too obviously enjoying his first vacation in years from books and schoolmasters.

Beethoven finished the F Major Quartet and the alternate finale for the B-flat Quartet, then turned to a String Quintet in C Major. After breakfast he was out of the house, walking through the fields in his

usual style, shouting and singing and waving his arms conducting the
music in his head, stopping to write in a sketchbook. He returned for
lunch and a rest in his room, then went back out until dusk. At one
point his antics in the fields scared a team of oxen, which bolted down
a hill followed by their driver, a farm boy. When the boy had gotten
his team calmed down and back on the road, Beethoven once again
turned up waving and shouting and spooked them again. This time
the oxen ran all the way home. When the driver asked who this fool
was, he was told it was the famous brother of the landowner. "A hell of
a brother that is!" the boy exclaimed.[45]

This was not the only time when Beethoven was mistaken for a
tramp or a fool. At one point he accompanied Johann to a conference
with an official. The official's clerk noted the shabbily dressed person
standing motionless by the door during the long discussion, then
noted the low bows the stranger received from the official when the
two men left. The clerk, who was a music lover, asked his employer
who that imbecile was who received such a bow, and was astounded to
learn it was Beethoven.[46]

Neither work nor business slacked during his sojourn in Gneixendorf. Sending his metronome markings to Schott, he observed, "The
district where I am now staying reminds me to a certain extent of
the Rhine country which I so ardently desire to revisit." He offered
the coming string quintet to Diabelli and sent the F Major Quartet to
Moritz Schlesinger. At the end of November he sent the alternative
B-flat finale to Artaria. He wrote wry letters to friends in Vienna.

Then another disaster unfolded. This one was close to the last.

Ludwig received a letter from brother Johann, in whose house he was
living — though by this point he was eating in his rooms and hardly
speaking to the family. The subject of the letter was Karl. Johann
brought up the issue on paper in an attempt to forestall the blowup
he knew would happen if he presented it to his brother in person. But
the blowup was not to be avoided. "I cannot possibly remain quiet any
longer about the future destiny of Karl," Johann began. "He is getting
completely away from all activity, and will become so accustomed to
this life that he will be brought to work again only with the greatest dif-

ficulty, the <u>longer</u> he lives here so unproductively. Upon his departure, Breuning gave him only 14 days to recuperate, and now it is 2 months. You see from Breuning's letter that it is absolutely his intention [as now legal guardian] that Karl <u>shall hasten</u> to his profession; the longer he is here, the more unfortunate <u>for him,</u> because work will come all the harder to him, and therefore we may experience something else bad."[47]

Johann had always been the mildest of the brothers, also the least intelligent. But when Ludwig came to him in a fury over the letter, what ensued was a battle worthy of the old set-tos between Ludwig and Carl. The main issue was Ludwig's demand that Johann cut Therese out of his will and leave his considerable fortune to Karl. Johann would not be battered into submission. As for Karl, Johann was clearly right: the boy had recovered from his wound, he was getting lazy, it was time to join his regiment. Meanwhile Beethoven's physical condition was deteriorating. His stomach was bothering him, he had no appetite, his feet were swelling, his diarrhea acting up. He was meanwhile downing a good deal of wine.[48] His failing liver, his temper, and his drinking were working together now to bring him down.

For all those reasons on top of the blowup between the brothers, it was clearly time to go back to Vienna, where among other things Beethoven had his doctors. Karl resisted, saying his wound was still too obvious. But Beethoven wore him down, as Karl's entries in the conversation book show: "I beg of you once and for all to leave me alone. If you want to go, good . . . If not, good again . . . But I beg of you once more not to torment me as you are doing; you might regret it, for I can endure much, but too much I cannot endure. You treated your brother in the same way today without cause. You must remember that other people are also human beings . . . These everlastingly unjust reproaches!"[49]

Beethoven was determined to leave, come what may. Therese was going to Vienna in the comfortable family carriage and likely offered them a ride, but he refused.[50] He set Karl to checking coach schedules. There being nothing convenient, he decided they would catch a ride on a milk cart that was headed for Vienna. Perhaps he remembered the time years before, when he had fled from a row with Prince

Lichnowsky in an open cart in the rain and arrived back in Vienna laughing and healthy. But he had been two decades younger and stronger then. Nevertheless, on December 1, because of his argument with Johann and his hatred of Therese, both rising from his rage and his solipsism, Beethoven and his nephew climbed into the open milk cart in freezing weather. It took him back to Vienna and his deathbed.

Beethoven had only summer clothes with him. He and Karl stopped midway at an inn and got an unheated room in a tavern. In the middle of the night he fell into pleurisy: dry hacking cough, violent thirst, cutting pains in the side. He tried drinking ice water, which brought on pneumonia. In the damp and frosty morning he had to be lifted into the wagon.

Late in the day he arrived at his flat in the Schwarzpanierhaus in alarming shape. Braunhofer his doctor was summoned. He declined to come, pleading distance. The real reason was probably that Braunhofer knew what was coming and did not want to be the physician of record. After two more tries at finding a doctor, Karl Holz secured Andreas Wawruch, one of the most respected doctors in Vienna and a music lover who played the cello. When he arrived, on December 5, Wawruch declared to Beethoven, "I am a great admirer of yours and will do everything possible to help."[51]

Beethoven retired to his bed. It was a pattern familiar to him, had happened many times before. He had long known any illness might be his last, but he did not yet know that this would be the one. He never left his bedroom alive. But even in his extremity, Beethoven was the most stubborn and resilient of men. It took death a long time to catch him.

Beethoven did not expect the String Quartet in F Major, op. 135, to be his last completed work, but he did intend it to be his last string quartet, at least for as far in the future as he cared to imagine. Even if he did not anticipate how close the end was, he could not have expected to have much time left. He had written five quartets in two and a half years, and they were his only serious efforts in that time. The first three, the *Galitzins,* had traced a steady and deliberate disintegration of conventional norms of structure and logic. The C-sharp Minor had been a reintegration, but on a new plane rather than a return to the past.

The F Major Quartet is a look back, retrospective and essentially comic like the Eighth Symphony but again on a different plane than either Beethoven's past or the Classical past. The tone of this last work, written in a time of trauma when his body was sliding toward collapse, is full of laughter and irony as Haydn and Mozart expressed them, and in the middle lies a soulful song. Its laughter is hard to define, though — not exactly carefree, rather a performance by a clown old and tired, a final smiling doff of the cap, and an ironical exit from the stage.

It begins with a couple of questioning fillips, *piano,* answered by *pianissimo* hiccups. The three-note upswoop of grace notes that mark them all will be a motif. The fillips condense toward a graceful theme, but it is interrupted by a mock-solemn incantation in octaves.[52] A couple of bars of transition and we arrive precipitously at the second-theme section. What has been established is a tone wry and quirky, a texture as lucid and open as in Mozart and Haydn — and early Beethoven. If the rapid shifting of ideas in the first couple of lines reminds us that this is late Beethoven, the much longer second-theme section, with its parade of small themelets, adds up to a more sustained, lighthearted, Classical dancing stretch. After a short and unrepeated exposition comes a short development in which earlier ideas are woven together, all of it marked by the tipsy upswoop. The development includes a false recapitulation that leads to more excursions. That the recapitulation is developed and reconfigured might remind us of Haydn; the coda as long as the other sections reminds us this is Beethoven. In it the upswoops find their denouement. The brisk final cadence, *piano,* is without fuss.

The middle two movements are about as contrasting as contrast gets. The scherzo, placed second, is another of his short, minimal, more or less absurdist ones, the humor here perhaps the driest of all. It involves simple lines that seem to be devoted to three different downbeats. Occasionally an errant E-flat blurts in on the offbeat, without explanation.[53] The absurdity reaches its denouement in the trio, which begins racing crazily, traces keys upward from F to G to A (the notes of the scherzo's theme), and reaches a boggling moment when, under a screeching folk tune in the violin, the other instruments play a swirl-ing manic *fortissimo* figure in three octaves, unchanged, fifty times. The effect is outlandish, scarcely believable, and intended as such. The slow movement that follows is a transcendently songful theme and four gentle variations, all flowing together, in D-flat — as in the *Appassionata,* Beethoven's key of noble resignation. Here in a quartet whose texture and sound look back to Classical clarity and lightness, the scoring of this movement begins Romantically warm, in low strings with rich double-stops.

By the time he reached the finale, Beethoven was badly ill and perhaps weary of quartets. He confessed to publisher Moritz Schlesinger (to whom he had promised a new quartet to make up for losing the A Minor) that he had a lot of trouble finding ideas for the finale: "Here, my dear friend, is my last quartet. It will be the last; and indeed it has given me much trouble. For I could not bring myself to compose the last movement . . . And that is the reason why I have written the motto: The decision taken with difficulty — Must it be? — It must be, it must be! —"[54] That is one explanation of the mysterious inscription on the finale of the quartet, if not the only explanation. In effect, as a good Romantic would do, Beethoven picked up a story from his life and retold it with appropriate gaiety mixed with mock solemnity — appropriate both to the story and to the tone of the quartet.

The story went so: one Ignaz Dembscher, a rich music lover, had been hosting quartet parties at his house. Some players wanted to go through the B-flat Major at Dembscher's, but when he asked Beethoven for the parts, it came out that Dembscher had neglected to buy a ticket for Schuppanzigh's premiere of the quartet. Beethoven sent word that he would not supply the parts until the merchant shelled out the price of the ticket, a quite steep 50 florins. Hearing this, Dembscher laughed, "Must it be?" Hearing about this response, Beethoven gave a laugh and dashed off a canon on "It must be! Out with your wallet!"

That canon was what came to him to solve his finale problem in the F Major. It accounts for its mysterious preface: The finale is headed *Der schwere gefaßte Entschluss,* "The Hard-Won Resolution." Under it lies a *grave* musical question of G–E–A-flat noted *Muss es sein?,* "Must It Be?" Then a laughing *allegro* phrase is noted, *Es muss sein! Es muss sein!* Neither of these phrases is to be played; together they are a preface and program for the finale. Future generations would try to make this a metaphysical question and answer, appropriate to a man at the end of his life.[55] But in the movement proper, the solemn introductory music around the *Muss es sein?* phrase is part of the joke: it is the rhetoric of tragedy applied to comedy. The *allegro* is all swirling, dancing gaiety, the *Es muss sein!* figure its motto, and otherwise there are two delicious themes, one legato and the other bouncing, all of it laid out in lucid textures and equally lucid sonata form.

In his early and middle music Beethoven wrote a great many memorable pieces without particularly striking melodies, the fragmentary Hero theme of the *Eroica* an example. In all the late quartets and much other music of his last years, he produced one splendid melody after another. Here Beethoven made another mark on the rest of the century: the ascent of melody, especially singing melody, to a dominant position in the way music was heard and the way it was conceived in terms of form. As the marvelous mechanism of Classical form receded along with its foundation on key relations, melody stepped forward to take center stage. For theorist Adolph Marx, sonata form was above all a pattern of themes. That process was abetted by the leading younger composer in Vienna in those years, Franz Schubert, who happened to be one of the greatest born melodists who ever lived.

The end of the F Major Quartet, the end of the end for Beethoven (with two asterisks to follow), is a smiling pizzicato reminiscence of the bouncing second theme, the first violin then taking up the bow to render a squeaky version of it high above the staff, followed by a lusty and entirely unfraught final cadence. Whether or not Beethoven planned it this way, the retrospective, humorous, Haydnesque quality of the quartet rounded his career in the medium in a natural way. With op. 18, its first number also in F major, he began his journey with quartets grounded in the eighteenth century, but at moments looked ahead toward conceptions that had not yet fully taken shape; with op. 59 he put on the medium the stamp of his maturity and his most searching side; in the late quartets he reached for a more distant future but ended his journey with a look back at the beginning.

The F Major done and dispatched to Vienna, he finished the first asterisk in the conclusion of his life's work, the new finale — an alternative, not a substitute — for the B-flat Major Quartet. What his friends and publisher hoped for was something lighter and less bizarre than the *Grosse Fuge,* even something with the popular touch of the middle movements. Exhausted, depressed, his body failing, Beethoven agreed, or at least obliged. The new finale begins with a Haydnesque tick-tock on octave Gs and presents us a robust, perky, folkish tune that will never leave the scene for long. The theme, the texture, the general atmosphere have the light and dancelike quality of a Classical rondo finale. It is as if the new finale of the B-flat Major Quartet were conceived through the prism of the F Major Quartet. But these days Beethoven never took tradition whole; in practice the movement is a melding of sonata and rondo. The theme sounds, actually, like one of those ditties that in the late music he often takes up in a middle movement, plays with briefly, then drops. But here he needed a substantive finish, so this ditty dances on for more than seven minutes.

As a whole, the B-flat Quartet has two divergent tendencies: the dissociation and general eccentricity of the first movement, and the lyrical and popularistic qualities of the middle movements. Uniting them all were two more tendencies: an air of whimsy and irony to the proceedings (except the tragic "Cavatina"), and the intense individuality of each movement. The *Grosse Fuge* climaxed the eccentric strain of the quartet and took it to an almost unimaginable level. The new finale takes up the whimsical and ironic aspect and embodies it in another distinctive, quasi-freestanding individual. It has echoes of earlier movements, also echoes of the fugue — one example being the beginning, which begins, like the fugue, on an off-tonic G and falls by fifths until it reaches home on B-flat.

The exposition is, by Beethoven's present standards, shockingly regular: first theme (its second part repeated like a dance), second theme in the dominant, lively closing section in the dominant. It goes on to the development with no repeat. That development begins with a lyrical new theme that has the air of a B section in a rondo. Into it is woven a four-note figure that recalls the motto theme of the A Minor Quartet and main theme of the *Grosse Fuge* — the step–leap–step figure.[56] At the end of a long development there is a quiet false recapitulation in G minor that slips into the real recapitulation.

That long development was one means by which Beethoven expanded this rondo-like theme to the substantial movement he needed to make a balanced conclusion to the quartet. The other means was an enormous coda that amounts to a development of the development. It is as if Beethoven were reluctant to stop, perhaps wondering whether he was going to be writing his last concluding double bar. The coda builds to a *fortissimo* peroration, then calms to *pianissimo* and a poignant pause. At the end, two brisk and unexceptional bars of cadence.[57] And that was that.

With the F Major Quartet and this movement, at the end of his creative life Beethoven finished with a comedy, like Shakespeare in *The Tempest.* In the spectrum of his art one places the sixteen string quartets next to the thirty-two piano sonatas, both bodies of work incomparable journeys of growth and discovery enfolding the whole of life and feeling, and something like the whole potential of a medium and of music itself. The sonatas and the quartets are surveys of what music can be and do. In that achievement lies, to say it again, their kinship with another great synoptic work that had been part of Beethoven's musical consciousness from the beginning: Bach's *Well-Tempered Clavier.*

In *The Tempest* Shakespeare says good-bye to his art when he makes Prospero cast his magic staff into the sea. There is a valedictory quality to that play, which is as profound as comedy gets. In Beethoven's last movement there is no valediction. He was already at work on a new symphony and string quintet and had plans for more pieces, and no plans to retire until the pen fell from his hand.

When he got back to Vienna, despite his raging illness he sent Holz a four-bar canon, *Wir irren allesamt, ein jeder irrt anders,* "We all err, each one errs differently." That second, small asterisk was the last gasp.

At the end it was as it is with all such figures: to paraphrase a poet, a great mind and spirit fastened to a dying animal.[58] Few men's journeys to death have been so minutely and painfully chronicled as Beethoven's. His primary physician Dr. Wawruch wrote a report of the next months. He begins with a survey of his patient's deafness, his chronic digestive miseries; he notes that Beethoven slept only four to five hours a night. "He began to develop a liking for spirituous beverages, in order to stimulate his decreasing appetite and to aid his stomachic weakness by excessive use of strong punch and iced drinks." At Gneixendorf he had run around in all weathers, to the detriment of his health. Then, "as he himself jovially said, [he] used the devil's own most wretched conveyance, a milk-wagon, to carry him home."[59]

When Wawruch first arrived at the Schwarzpanierhaus he found Beethoven in frightening shape, lungs inflamed with pneumonia, choking, spitting blood, with shooting pains in his side that kept him from sleeping. Within a week that crisis passed and he was briefly out of bed, reading and writing. Then a fit of rage over his treatment by friends and family set off an attack of jaundice and vomiting and diarrhea that had him writhing in pain. His anger had now joined his train of enemies.

He lay in the big bedroom that held his two pianos, his bed facing the window. His cook and maidservant stayed on the job. Friends and relatives gathered: brother Johann, Karl Holz, publishers Diabelli and Haslinger, violinist Franz Clement.[60] Once again among the inner circle was the scorned Anton Schindler, who since Karl Holz was busy getting married had been returned to his place as Beethoven's lackey in chief. Gerhard, Stephan von Breuning's son, maintained a regular afternoon shift at the bedside. Stephan did what he could, but he was himself afflicted with a serious liver disease. There was, at last, a rapprochement between Beethoven and Karl. The conversation books show the now twenty-year-old helping to keep his uncle at his medical regimens, giving him enemas.[61] After Karl left for his regiment on January 2, 1827, he wrote a couple of letters but never saw his uncle again. In a letter to his lawyer on January 3, Beethoven named Karl his sole heir.[62]

Out of the blue, in the middle of December arrived the forty-volume set of Handel's works sent by his British admirer Johann Stumpff, who had been searching for the volumes for years. Beethoven was overjoyed. He pointed out to Gerhard the newly arrived stack of books: "I received these as a gift today; they have given me great joy with this . . . for Handel is the greatest, the ablest composer. I can still learn from him."[63] He wrote Stumpff a long letter of thanks, also asking him to propose to the Philharmonic Society that it give a concert for his benefit.

Several physicians were brought in for consultation, chief among them Dr. Johann Malfatti, uncle of the teenage Therese to whom Beethoven had proposed years before. Malfatti had been Beethoven's doctor for a time before Beethoven dismissed him as "a crafty Italian" and a quack. Now Beethoven had to be persuaded to accept Malfatti's treatment, and the doctor had to be mollified concerning the earlier insults he had been subjected to. Finally, Gerhard recalled, Beethoven "awaited Malfatti's visit as eagerly as the coming of the Messiah." Once when he was expecting Malfatti and Wawruch showed up instead, Beethoven turned to the wall and barked, "Ass!"[64]

In early December he penned a letter to Franz Wegeler in Bonn, finally replying to that old friend's nostalgic greeting of months before. He began with elaborate regrets for his delay in writing and all the things that had kept them separated: "Our drifting apart was due to the changes in our circumstances. Each of us had to pursue the purpose for which he was intended and endeavor to attain it. Yet the eternally unshakable and firm foundations of good principles continued to bind us strongly together." It was those Bonn-inspired principles he belabored Karl with, and they had turned back on him. He responded to Wegeler's query about the rumor that he was the son of the king of Prussia, and urged his friend to "Make known to the world the integrity of my parents, and especially of my mother." If Wegeler's son came to Vienna as planned, "I will be a friend and a father to him."

He said he still had a silhouette of Lorchen, Wegeler's wife, whom Beethoven had loved long ago. "So you see how precious to me even now are all the dear, beloved memories of my youth." He reviewed his latest honors and initiatives. He sent a portrait. He sighed, "I still hope to create a few great works and then like an old child to finish my earthly course somewhere among kind people." He succumbed to nostalgia: "My beloved friend! You must be content with this letter for today. I need hardly tell you that I have been overcome by the remembrance of things past and that many tears have been shed while the letter was being written. Still we have now begun to correspond and you will soon have another letter from me."[65]

Dr. Wawruch observed that when the jaundice set in, Beethoven's decline proceeded "with giant strides." He began to swell with edema, water building up in his abdomen from the effects of a deteriorating liver.[66] Finally Wawruch told Beethoven he had to be drained, which was not a simple matter. A specialist was called in. While Johann, Karl, and Schindler watched, the doctor cut into his abdomen and inserted a tube. Water spurted out, twenty-five pounds of liquid by Wawruch's estimation, and an afterflow from the tube several times that much. It was all perfectly ghastly, but Beethoven felt immediately better, enough to make a joke: "Professor, you remind me of Moses striking the rock with his staff."[67] At one point the incision became infected and gangrene was narrowly averted.[68] Gerhard discovered that Beethoven was being tormented with bedbugs and arranged to have his bedding changed. The edema continued, and three more tapping operations were performed over the next two months.

The dreary weeks stretched on in similar wretched scenes. To pass the hours, Beethoven leafed through the Handel volumes, read Walter Scott and Homer and other Greeks and Romans, made a pathetic attempt finally to learn the multiplication tables.[69] The ongoing train of visitors paid their respects, suspecting they were final ones. There were few if any attempts at musical sketches.

His letters continued, mostly dictated to Karl and Schindler, a mixture of business (including the eternal corrections of proofs) and pleas for favors. He wrote to publisher Schott asking for some Rhine or Mosel wine, hard to find in Vienna. Schott was remarkably slow to see to this request. On February 18 Beethoven wrote his old helper Baron Zmeskall, crippled with gout, "I do not despair. The most painful feature is the cessation of all activity . . . May heaven but grant you relief in your painful existence. Perhaps health is coming to both of us and we shall meet again in friendly intimacy."[70] His hopefulness may have been due to a letter from Wegeler dated February 1, in which his old friend gave his medical opinion that Beethoven would recover, and proposed they meet in the Karlsbad spa to complete his recovery and then revisit Bonn together.[71] If anything by then could have heartened

Beethoven enough to spark a recovery, the thought of seeing his physical and spiritual homeland would have.

His anxiety about money never abated. Among the letters were ones in February to onetime protégé Ignaz Moscheles and to conductor George Smart in London, both letters pressing their recipients to get him a loan from the Philharmonic Society. On February 22 Schindler wrote Moscheles, "As the matter presently stands with his illness, a recovery cannot be considered; although he does not know this for sure, he already suspects it."[72] Moscheles surely conveyed that to the society. The long-hoped-for Beethoven visit to London was never going to happen.

Hope rose and fell, but the slide was inexorable. After the third tapping drained his abdomen, he was hauled out of bed and propped in a tub for a sweatbath. Instead of easing him, this treatment made him swell up again with water. At the fourth tapping, the water from his belly soaked the bed and gushed across the floor. At that moment, Beethoven seemed to give up. Dr. Wawruch told him he would feel better now, but Beethoven replied, quoting a line from Handel's *Messiah,* "My day's work is finished. If there were a physician who could help me, 'his name shall be called Wonderful.'"[73]

Then his spirits rose again. He was excited when publisher Diabelli showed up to give him a framed picture of the humble cottage Haydn was born in. Beethoven directed it to be hung on the wall near his bed, and pointed it out to Gerhard: "Look, I got this today. See this little house, and in it so great a man was born!" The time for rivalry with his old teacher was past. Also hanging on the wall, as it had been for most of his adult life, was the portrait of grandfather Ludwig van Beethoven, whom he had hardly known, who was still his model of a musician's life.

On March 8 composer Johann Hummel turned up with his wife and young student Ferdinand Hiller. Given what they had heard, they were astonished to find Beethoven sitting by the window in a long gray dressing gown and high boots. He was skin and bones, but he managed to stand and greet them. The two onetime rivals embraced warmly. They had long been on a *du* intimacy. They settled down to talk, Hummel writing in a conversation book. Since Hummel was now the court

Kapellmeister in Goethe's town of Weimar, Beethoven asked after the old poet's health. As for himself, after his long siege in bed Beethoven felt more bored than tragic: "I have lain about for four months already, and one's patience finally wears out!" It is as if the pain meant nothing to him, that only the inability to compose hurt. (For Beethoven and for creators like him, not to work is barely to be alive. Virtually the only vacations he had ever taken from composing were when he was too sick to work.) With Hummel he went on to his usual complaints: the Viennese, the government. "Write a bookful of penitential songs and dedicate it to the Empress," he said with a bitter laugh. He was, for the moment with an old friend, more or less his usual self.

That was the last respite. Hummel visited three times more, each time the prospect sadder. The next time he found Beethoven in bed, groaning in pain. At the sight Hummel was about to burst into tears, but he was shushed by piano maker Johann Andreas Streicher. Yet Beethoven was still in control. He showed Hummel the picture of Haydn's birthplace, asked him to play in a benefit concert Schindler was giving (Hummel did, a week after Beethoven died). On the third visit Beethoven whispered, "I will probably be up above soon." (Was he finally convinced of immortality, or was he being metaphorical?) Yet he went on to talk about visiting London when he was well. Hummel saw that Beethoven's eyes were dull, and he could barely sit up.[74] On the last visit they found Beethoven lying sighing and mute in a haze of sweat. As they sat with him Hummel's wife took her handkerchief and wiped his brow. Hiller never forgot the grateful look Beethoven gave her.[75]

Then hope again. A bank official arrived to announce that the Philharmonic Society was sending him 100 pounds sterling, equivalent to around 1,000 florins. The official reported to Moscheles, "It was heartrending to see him, how he clasped his hands and almost dissolved in tears of joy and gratitude . . . I found poor Beethoven in the saddest state, more like a skeleton than a living being . . . Malfatti gives him little hope."[76] Beethoven roused himself to dictate a pitch to Moscheles, offering the Philharmonic Society a new overture or the tenth symphony, "sketches for which are already in my desk."[77] He was still making wild promises.

In fact, by then the doctors had given up. Malfatti, like Wawruch convinced that Beethoven was alcoholic, advised letting him have frozen punch in moderation, along with administering stomach rubs with ice water. It was a gesture at making him happier, not at healing. For the moment, it worked. After taking some punch, Beethoven became euphoric, writing Schindler, "Truly a miracle ∕. ∕∕. [the musical sign for repeating a figure]. Those very learned gentlemen have both been beaten; and it is only thanks to Malfatti's skill that my life is being saved. It is necessary that you should come to me this morning for a moment—" Schindler had been ill or injured and absent, but Beethoven had chores for him to do. Inspired by the punch, he began to joke again, to talk about writing the oratorio *Saul* for the Gesellschaft der Musikfreunde.

His euphoria lasted only a couple of days. He overdid the punch, fell into violent vomiting and diarrhea that weakened him further.[78] The condition of his body and bed by this point is painful to imagine. As best he could, declining day by day, he kept dictating letters and signing papers. On Stephan von Breuning's advice, he added a codicil to his will saying that until his maturity Karl could draw interest on his inheritance but not be able to touch the principal. Toward the end Gerhard remembered his father sitting on the bed beside a propped-up Beethoven, guiding his hand in signing document after document. At this point Beethoven could not manage to sign his name fully intact.[79]

Around March 22, Dr. Wawruch suggested to Beethoven that he allow a priest to administer last rites. By then he mostly lay in a stupor, staring emptily into space. But he extended his hand to Wawruch and said, "Let the priest be called." It was done. After the ceremony Beethoven joked to the priest, "I thank you, ghostly sir! You have brought me comfort!"[80] He dictated his last note, to his old landlord Baron Pasqualati:

> How can I thank you sufficiently for that excellent champagne which has so greatly refreshed me and will continue to! I need nothing more for today and I thank you for everything. — Please note down what further result you achieve in respect of the wines, for I would gladly

compensate you as much as my strength allows. — I cannot write any more today. May Heaven bless you in every way and reward you for your affectionate sympathy with your respectful and suffering BEETHOVEN.[81]

That note was surely touched up from Beethoven's rambles by Schindler or whoever wrote it down. The requested Rhine wines from Schott had still not arrived; he yearned to taste the vintages of his youth. The stupor deepened, yet he roused occasionally to mumble something about letters of thanks or proposals: "write . . . Smart . . . Stumpff."[82]

But the great mind and seething imagination were still at work. On March 24 he suddenly awoke and announced his own end, by way of a formula that was used to conclude ancient Roman comedies. In what Gerhard von Breuning remembered as "his favorite sarcastic-humorous manner as though to imply: nothing can be done," Beethoven declaimed in Latin: *Plaudite, amici, comoedia finita est.* Applaud, friends, the comedy is over.[83]

Later that day the Rhine wines finally arrived from Schott. Schindler put the dozen bottles on the table beside the bed. Beethoven opened his eyes and at the sight whispered, "Pity, pity, too late." He never spoke again.[84] They gave him a few spoonfuls of the wine. Then he fell into coma and delirium. As Gerhard and the others sat watching, the death rattle began. At times he rolled his eyes and beat his head on the pillow.[85] Outside, the sky was getting ominous, dark clouds gathering. The question of a grave arose. Gerhard suggested that they look in the village of Währing, where Stephan von Breuning's beloved first wife Julie von Vering was buried. Schindler and Stephan went to the graveyard there and found a spot near the Vering plot.

For two days Gerhard, Schindler, Johann, Stephan, the servants, and a few visitors came and went, watching over Beethoven. All were stunned and anguished that he was lasting so long. "His strong body and unimpaired lungs struggled titanically with approaching death," Gerhard recalled. "It was a terrible sight." On the afternoon of March 26 a violent thunderstorm broke out, pelting Vienna with snow and hail. "Just as in the immortal Fifth Symphony and the everlasting Ninth there are crashes that sound like a hammering on the portals of

Fate," Gerhard wrote, "so the heavens seemed to be using the gigantic drums to signal the bitter blow they had just dealt the world of art."[86]

At about 5:15 p.m. on March 26, Gerhard was called home to study, leaving in the room young composer Anselm Hüttenbrenner and a woman whom Hüttenbrenner remembered as "Frau von Beethoven," meaning Johanna. That Beethoven's most despised enemy attended his death would have been remarkable. But Hüttenbrenner probably remembered wrong; the woman was more likely Beethoven's maid Sali.

The circle around the deathbed had been counting days and then hours. Now they counted minutes. At 5:45, lightning lit up the chamber and there was a terrific clap of thunder. Suddenly Beethoven jerked into life, opened his eyes, raised his clenched fist into the air as if in defiance of it all, the whole mess of fate, the fickle gods, the worthless Viennese and corrupt aristocracy, the whole damned comedy. His hand fell, his eyes half closed. Hüttenbrenner had a hand under Beethoven's head, the other over his breast. He found no breath, no heartbeat.[87] Shortly after, when Gerhard, Stephan, and Schindler returned to the house they were told it was over.

Or so Hüttenbrenner reported the moment, many years later. Brother Johann gave a different version, saying Ludwig had died in his arms.[88] Inevitably history chose Hüttenbrenner's scene. His account is a death from myth, the last defiance of a demigod amid thunder and lightning. It may as well have happened that way as any other. What is certain is that Beethoven died the same death as any man, alone in his agony. But he was unafraid.

Then as later, Vienna loved a funeral and planned a grand occasion. The doctors were eager to get at him. When the body was lifted out of bed for the autopsy it was discovered Beethoven had terrible bedsores, about which he had hardly complained. The autopsy found his auditory nerves withered, his liver shrunken and diseased; he had cirrhosis, which usually results from long abuse of alcohol.[89] A painter made a plaster death mask, the features disfigured by the autopsy. Another artist drew the lifeless figure. Over the years Beethoven had suffered from deafness, colitis, rheumatism, rheumatic fever, typhus, skin disorders, abscesses, a variety of infections, ophthalmia, inflammatory degeneration of the arteries, jaundice, and at the end chronic hepatitis and cirrhosis of the liver.[90]

While the doctors cut at him, Johann, Schindler, Stephan, and Karl Holz began an anxious search for his papers. After some hours, they were about to give up when Holz pulled on a nail projecting from a cupboard. A collection of papers and other objects tumbled out of a hidden drawer.[91] As hoped, they included the bank shares left to Karl. The rest was his collection of talismans: the Heiligenstadt Testament, the letter to the Immortal Beloved, ivory miniatures of two young women. One portrait was identified as Julie Guicciardi. The other remained mysterious. If this was the face of the Immortal Beloved, her identity would never be fully resolved.[92] From that point, hour by hour, day by day, object by object that left the Schwarzpanierhaus, the tangible reality of Beethoven's life began to pass into legend.

In the confusion of the next day, Schindler spirited away a good deal of important material: four bundles of conversation books, manuscripts and letters, Beethoven's alabaster clock, his eyeglasses and ear trumpets.[93] In later years, before he sold the conversation books for a handsome price, Schindler forged a great many entries in the books to make it look like he was close to Beethoven years longer than he actually was. He also destroyed pages and perhaps whole books. All the same, if Schindler had not lifted those effects, they would have been scattered to all and sundry, as many of the musical manuscripts and sketchbooks were.

After the autopsy came the lying-in, in high style. In front of the door to his study, facing the door, the body was placed in a polished oak coffin resting on gilded supports. Beethoven's head was crowned by a wreath of white roses and laid on a white silk pillow; in the crossed hands were placed a cross and a white lily. All the hair on his head had been cut off by strangers, for souvenirs. Eight candles burned on each side of the coffin. And so on. Maid Sali, one of few servants he ever had whom he did not drive away with his violence and contempt, received the stream of visitors coming to view the body in state.[94]

The funeral of March 29 would be remembered as one of the grandest Vienna ever put on for a commoner. Schools were closed. The coffin was brought down to the courtyard of the Schwarzpanierhaus covered with a richly embroidered pall and laid with wreaths. Priests droned, and a choir sang. When the door of the courtyard was opened the press of people streaming in made it difficult to lift the coffin and start the procession. Finally it got under way. Among the pallbearers was Johann Hummel, among the torchbearers Carl Czerny, Franz Grill-parzer, Tobias Haslinger, Karl Holz, Ignaz Schuppanzigh, and Franz Schubert — the last destined to die the next year.

The cortege took shape among a welter of crosses, flowers, trombones, priests, singers, friends and members of the family, and a crowd of some ten thousand. As the procession turned onto the Alsergasse, brass instruments played the *Funeral March* from op. 26. At St. Stephen's Cathedral candles flickered in every altar, chandelier, and bracket. Again the press was so thick that friends and relatives had trouble getting inside.

After the service the procession to the cemetery began, thousands falling off but more thousands taking up the slow march. There was a stop at the parish church of Währing for more music and blessings. By now the procession included schoolchildren from the town and a convocation of the poor. Before the gates of the cemetery the coffin was laid down, and the tragedian Heinrich Anschütz stepped up to give the funeral oration written by Franz Grillparzer. Such orations were forbidden inside the cemetery. At the grave were more blessings, and the coffin descended into the ground. Johann Hummel dropped three flower wreaths on the coffin. By Viennese custom, friends and family threw handfuls of earth into the grave, and then it was done. The simple monument said only BEETHOVEN.[95] It needed no further inscription.

Then the aftermath and the legacy. Before Beethoven was buried, a grave digger in Währing came to Schindler and said he had been offered 1,000 florins for Beethoven's head. (After Haydn was buried, his body was exhumed and his head severed and spirited away by a phrenologist who wanted to study the skull.) The police were notified.[96] In November Beethoven's musical effects were auctioned off, bringing in a pathetic 1,140 florins. The autograph of the *Missa solemnis* sold for 7 florins, the score of his still-popular Septet for 18 florins. The total amount of his estate including Karl's bank shares was 10,000 florins. The bank official found the Philharmonic Society's 100-pound note intact. The society wanted its money back, but Moscheles persuaded its members to give up their claim, and the money was used for posthumous expenses.[97]

In April there were two memorial services packed with people, the music for one Mozart's Requiem and for the other Cherubini's Requiem. Beethoven would have approved of both. His family and circle went their ways, each to his or her own life and fate. At the Schwarzpanierhaus in April, an auction of his furnishings and belongings was chaos, used-clothes dealers pushing and shoving and the furniture jerked about. Graf reclaimed the piano he had lent Beethoven. After the stress and dismay of overseeing the auction, Stephan von Breuning suffered a relapse of his liver condition. In turn he took to his bed and never rose. He died two months and nine days after Beethoven and was buried steps from his childhood friend's grave.[98]

Karl van Beethoven left the military as a second lieutenant in 1832 and spent most of the rest of his life living comfortably in Vienna on the money he inherited from uncles Ludwig and, later, Johann. He married and he and his wife had five children; their only son Ludwig Johann died in America sometime after 1910. Karl died in 1858 at age fifty-two, from liver disease.[99] Johann van Beethoven's wife Therese died the year after Ludwig. She had secretly changed her will to leave her estate to her daughter, who therefore inherited half of Johann's estate — or at least the 41,000 florins he claimed at the time. In the winter months in Vienna over the next years, Johann became a familiar figure at concerts of his brother's music, sitting in the front row, at the end trying to cry the loudest bravos while he clapped in his oversize gloves with flapping fingers.[100] He lived on until 1848 and left his fortune of 42,000 florins to Karl as his brother had wanted him to. (That was worth more than 1 million in the dollars of a century later.)[101] Johanna van Beethoven, widow of brother Carl and Beethoven's bête noire, came into possession of the original Heiligenstadt Testament. In 1840, Franz Liszt helped her find a buyer for the letter. It eventually made its way to soprano Jenny Lind, herself a living legend. Johanna died destitute in 1868.[102]

In 1863, Beethoven's body was exhumed — along with Schubert's — studied by doctors, and reburied in a metal coffin, all financed by the Gesellschaft der Musikfreunde. In 1888, when the Währing cemetery was long deserted, he was exhumed again, and he and Schubert were given graves of honor side by side in the giant Zentralfriedhof, the city's main burial ground. In 1897, Brahms joined them.

After Beethoven died the first necrology appeared in the *Allgemeine Musikalische Zeitung,* written by its former editor Johann Friedrich Rochlitz. He had met Beethoven and long championed him, if not uncritically. "To him belong the greatest, richest, and most unusual qualities that modern instrumental music possesses," Rochlitz wrote.

> He is the foremost inventor of his contemporaries. In his works, so numerous and significant, he disdained to resemble even himself; rather, he wanted to appear as a new man in each work, even at the risk of making an occasional blunder, or of sometimes being scarcely understood by even a few people. Wherever his most bold, powerful, and energetic works are not yet revered, enjoyed, and loved, the reason is a lack of a noteworthy number of people who are capable of comprehending them and forming a public. The number will grow and with it his fame will increase . . .
>
> He did not understand people and for approximately the last fifteen years not even their words, and as he did not understand them, neither did they understand him, except in his musical notes . . . He created in his own world, wonderfully made up of musical notes that were only thought and not heard. He gave his world life and made it complete. That is truly the meaning of being what one can be through nature, providence, and one's own power of the will! . . .
>
> He will be remembered gloriously in every history of music . . . by having provided the essential content for its present period, and by having made it, this period and its history, his own personal domain.[103]

A longer and broader survey from Dr. Wilhelm Christian Müller in the May *AMZ* concludes,

He was called the Jean Paul of composers [which is to say, an echt Romantic]. We would rather compare him with Shakespeare in regard to original sublimity, profundity, strength, and tenderness with humor, wit, and his constant, new fantastic variations. Occasionally he also loses himself in excesses, but he is more organized and has more diverse character, and exhausts every idea: the most sublime majesty, the deepest melancholy, the warmest delicacy, the most capricious jesting, the most childlike simplicity, and the craziest merriment.[104]

The speech Franz Grillparzer wrote to be declaimed at the gates of the cemetery is more passionate and literary, as befit a poet and Austria's leading playwright. Grillparzer apparently held no resentment that Beethoven never got around to setting his opera libretto. But if the writer was fascinated by Beethoven the man, he never quite reconciled himself to the music, any more than he did to the whole of the Romantic era. Grillparzer's sensibility stayed in the eighteenth century. As he once wrote, "The path of modern culture leads from humanity, through nationalism, to bestiality."[105] For him, Beethoven was part of that modern culture.

But it was Grillparzer's job to pull out all the stops for the funeral, to wax enthusiastic about works he could not digest. He did his job memorably, sounding chords nationalistic, Romantic, and Aufklärung, and also slipped in his cautions and complaints. Grillparzer called Beethoven the last of his line, the extreme end of art, because he wanted him to be that.

Standing by the grave of him who has passed away we are in a manner the representatives of an entire nation, of the whole German people, mourning the loss of the only highly acclaimed half of . . . the fatherland's full spiritual bloom. There yet lives . . . the hero of verse in German speech and tongue [Goethe]; but the last master of tuneful song, the organ of soulful concord, the heir and amplifier of Handel and Bach's, of Haydn and Mozart's immortal fame is now no more, and we stand weeping over the riven strings of the harp that is hushed.

The harp that is hushed! Let me call him so! For he was an artist, and all that was his, was his through art alone. The thorns of life had wounded him deeply, and as the castaway clings to the shore, so did he seek refuge in thy arms, O thou glorious sister and peer of the Good and the True, thou balm of wounded hearts, heaven-born Art! . . .

He was an artist — and who shall arise to stand beside him? . . . from the cooing of doves to the rolling of thunder, from the craftiest interweaving of well-weighed expedients of art up to that awful pitch where planned design disappears in the lawless whirl of contending natural forces, he had traversed and grasped it all. He who comes after him will not continue him; he must begin anew, for he who went before left off only where art leaves off . . .

Because he withdrew from the world, they called him a man-hater, and because he held aloof from sentimentality, unfeeling . . . He fled the world because, in the whole range of his loving nature, he found no weapon to oppose it. He withdrew from mankind after he had given them his all and received nothing in return. He dwelt alone, because he found no second Self. But to the end his heart beat warm for all men, in fatherly affection for his kindred, for the world his all and his heart's blood . . .

He whom you mourn stands from now onward among the great of all ages, inviolate forever . . . And should you ever in times to come feel the overpowering might of his creations like an onrushing storm, when your mounting ecstasy overflows in the midst of a generation yet unborn, then remember this hour, and think, We were there, when they buried him, and when he died, we wept.

So Grillparzer performed his solemn task, adding his words and images to the growing myth. In the speech he never mentioned God. For him and his century, it was Art that was divine. His peroration "remember this hour, and think, We were there" echoes Shakespeare's Henry V before battle at Agincourt. The *Zeitung* critic had ended by comparing Shakespeare and Beethoven. That pairing had been made going back years, both in admiration and in censure. Beethoven's ironic penultimate words, "Applaud, friends, the comedy is over," were from classical Roman comedy but also essentially Shakespearean. They echo Prospero as he speaks to the audience at the end of the end for Shakespeare, *The Tempest:* "Release me from my bands with the help of your good hands." Beethoven had told Goethe that the main thing a rough artist like him wanted was applause, not tears.

Beethoven and Shakespeare: who better to compare? No composer before Beethoven would have fit that comparison. There was the breadth of human understanding and expression that sensitive listeners of his time came to understand in Beethoven, even when it scared them. These two creators shared a power of utterance, a wisdom and wit, a prodigal invention and reinvention, an incomparable depth and breadth of creative journey, and a joining of tragedy and comedy, the old and the new, strangeness and rightness. The sense of timelessness that comes from an eternal human essence shining through the garb of period and idiom and language itself. The transcendence of self in art. We hardly know who Shakespeare was. So much of what we know about Beethoven, we best forget when we come to his art. The limits and the pettiness of humanity held up against the illusion of the limitless in art were never more pointed as with him. He understood people little and liked them less, yet he lived and worked and exhausted himself to exalt humanity.

Over the centuries, Beethoven and Shakespeare were both elevated to classics, to virtual clichés, but both of them are too wild and strong to be bound in those chains. In the end they both went out with comedy, knowing that comedy is as deep as anything, that art is at the same time vaporous play and transcendent metaphor. "*Faust,*" Goethe said of his ultimate work, "is a very serious joke." These artists conjure worlds, and all of us can find a place in those worlds.

In looking back through the course of Beethoven's life as a man, what may be most astonishing about him is that he survived the burden of being Beethoven. So much weighed on him: so much music roiled inside, so much rage, so much delusion, so much anguish physical and mental. No wonder his time called him superhuman. But the truer and sadder reality is that Beethoven lived to the ultimate capacities of being human, and he encompassed that in his art. As one of the defining figures of a revolutionary age, he witnessed and spoke for all of us a new vision of what it means to be human.

Appendix

Beethoven's Musical Forms

Neither in Beethoven's day nor before did composers commonly set out on a piece without having in mind some traditional model of how its keys and melodic themes were going to be laid out. In modern parlance these models are all tidily labeled, the names including sonata form, sonata-rondo form, concerto-sonata form, theme and variations, ABA form, minuet-scherzo form, fugue and its derivations, canon, and so on. Some of these labels were known to Haydn, Mozart, and Beethoven (such as "fugue"), some were not (such as "sonata form").

That musical models were elaborately described by later-eighteenth-century theorists was due in part to the influence of the age of reason, which was given to rationalizations and classifications. By the later part of the century, understanding and mastering the various formal models was part of the job of every composer, and being able to understand and recognize them part of the skill of musical cognoscenti. For the purposes of this book, it will be useful to examine the main forms Beethoven composed with reference to.

SONATA FORM

This is the layout used for most first movements of multimovement instrumental works, sometimes for finales, now and then for slow movements, and for freestanding pieces such as overtures. What composers of Beethoven's day probably had in mind was an outline something like this:

EXPOSITION		DEVELOPMENT	RECAPITULATION	
|		|	|	
First theme section	Second theme section		First theme	Second theme

I ————►V———— :‖ X ————► I ———————— (I) ———— ‖

The Roman numerals refer to keys. I is the home key of the movement, called the *tonic.* V is the key of the fifth degree of that scale, called the *dominant.* For example, if the first theme and home key of a movement are in C major, the second-theme section will be in G major or in any case a new key. That first part of the movement is usually repeated.

In the middle section, the indication X should be read as "a collection of keys at will," in the course of what amounts to an as-if improvisation on the melodic themes of the first part. Eventually the tonic returns, and all the material of the movement is resolved into it. The modern terms for these sections are, for the first section, *exposition,* with its two theme sections; for the X section, *development;* and for the return of the opening key and material, the *recapitulation,* with its two theme sections now in the tonic key.

So the basic sections of a sonata-form movement are exposition, development, and recapitulation. The movement may be preceded by an *introduction,* usually slower than the rest of the piece. There may be an ending section, called the *coda.* Beethoven had his own terms for these sections: "first part" for the exposition, *Durchführung* ("working out") for the development, and *da capo* for the recapitulation. His term for the whole development and recapitulation section was "second part." When Beethoven created a movement in sonata form, he composed with reference to that outline.

Classical forms are all intensely concerned with keys and patterns of keys—that is the fundamental aspect of the forms. The essential practice in a sonata-form exposition is to move away from the tonic to a new key, which creates a sense of harmonic departure and therefore harmonic tension. That large harmonic move creates an exposition of two large parts called the first- and second-theme sections. In earlier Haydn, the musical themes associated with the two key areas were often closely related. In later Haydn and in Mozart and Beethoven, the exposition's two key areas are pointed up by different and contrasting themes (which are still subtly related). In order to create still more tension, the development often involves a number of keys, and an improvisatory atmosphere of searching and fragmentation and often drama, using material from the exposition (though sometimes a new theme turns up in the development). The idea of the recapitulation is to resolve the tension by returning everything to the home key, the tonic.

Most often in composing a piece, Beethoven first settled on its key. Then he found *das Thema*, the all-important opening theme that sets the mood, the leading motifs from which other themes will be made, and the general direction of the whole piece. Then he worked out the first-movement exposition, then the development, then the recapitulation and perhaps coda, then went on to the other movements in order. Often he sketched ahead, but still he tended to work out pieces one section and one movement at a time.

The formal outline we call sonata form is quite general and flexible, and it was treated with endless variety by composers. The handling of the form was adapted to the demands of the idea and material at hand. There may be subthemes within the first- and second-theme sections. Often the second key area is not the dominant but a more colorful substitute for it—the specific key is not as important as the idea of moving away from the home key to somewhere else. Some developments have a welter of keys, some relatively few. Some developments are dynamic and tumultuous, others calm. Sometimes the retransition to the recapitulation is dramatic, sometimes the moment of recapitulation is slipped into or even obscured. Rarely is the whole recapitulation actually in the tonic/home key; usually there is some amount of _modulation_ (change of key) for the sake of harmonic variety. Codas can be omitted, can be short, or (as sometimes in Beethoven) can be multipart sections in their own right, as long as the other sections.

Haydn and Mozart were usually interested in making their forms clear to the ears of the cognoscenti; here and there, Beethoven deliberately obscured or subverted formal outlines for expressive reasons. In any case, Haydn, Mozart, and Beethoven saw form as part of the expressive character of a piece: tumultuous or comic moods might warp the form in dramatic ways.

In many respects the essence of sonata form was a way of managing and controlling new kinds of _contrast._ Individual movements in the earlier Baroque period of the seventeenth and eighteenth centuries were largely based on a single melodic theme and a single emotional tone. Composers of the Classical era were interested in contrasting themes, contrasting emotions, rhythmic shifts of gear, sometimes violent changes of mood and direction. Beethoven stayed true to the traditional principles of sonata form throughout his life, but he pushed contrasts and disjunctions to a degree that bewildered many in his time.

Sonata form is the most complex and most flexible of traditional formal outlines. Composers made use of it well into the twentieth century. Often in Beethoven's era it was compared to the form of essays, sermons, stories, and dramas. It joined the idea of a clear presentation of ideas—the more or less predictable two theme sections of the exposition and recapitulation—to the unpredictable and quasi-improvisatory quality of the development. In the Romantic period of the nineteenth century, partly because of these connections to other artistic genres, sonata form and instrumental music in general came to be seen as subsuming literature, drama, poetry, even philosophy. That nineteenth-century exaltation of instrumental music started, above all, with Beethoven.

After Beethoven's day, theorists including Adolph Marx classified and categorized sonata form in a way that tended to freeze it into its simplest outline; often, nineteenth-century composers who used the form failed to understand the freedom with which earlier masters treated it. Some composers, above all Richard Wagner, decreed the old forms dead and buried. One of those who did understand their vitality and flexibility, and handled the traditional forms entirely creatively, was Johannes Brahms.

SONATA-RONDO FORM

The model of sonata form was so powerful to the eighteenth-century Classical period that its principles tended to invade other existing forms. The old idea of a *rondo* was a piece that went around and around a central theme, usually diagrammed ABACADA and so on: the A section being the main theme in the home key, the other sections containing contrasting ideas usually in new keys. The later eighteenth century integrated that model with sonata form, creating a hybrid we call *sonata-rondo.* One common outline for it is ABACABA. The A section functions like the first theme of a sonata form; the B section is like the second theme in a new key; the A comes back in the home key; the C section is like a development; the A returns like a recapitulation; and the rest of the piece is in the tonic key.

Again, composers handled this model with great freedom. The second A section was often shortened. The C section might be a new and contrasting idea (a "real" C section), a development of the A and B material, or a combination of the two. What happened after the C section was highly variable. Since a sonata-rondo movement was often lively, fast, sometimes comic, it was one of the common outlines for the finale of a multimovement work.

CONCERTO-SONATA FORM

In the Baroque period, the outline of a concerto movement was simple: a full-orchestra theme (called the *tutti*), a solo section with orchestral accompaniment, another orchestral interlude, another solo section, and so on as long as the composer liked: tutti, solo, tutti, solo, tutti, solo, etc. Once again, in the Classical period, sonata form invaded this model, creating a more complex hybrid involving a *double exposition.* In a Classical concerto, first the orchestra alone lays out the basic thematic material of the movement, as in a sonata-form exposition; then a variant of that exposition repeats, now with the soloist added, in alternating sections of tutti and solo. Then, again as in sonata form, there is a development section, recapitulation, and perhaps coda. The solo may introduce themes of its own. In any case, there is a constant sense of dialogue and interplay between solo and orchestra.

THEME AND VARIATIONS

This is a formal outline that can be used for a slow movement or a finale, even (though rarely) for a first movement. It can also be a freestanding piece, like Beethoven's *Diabelli* Variations. First there is a theme, a short piece either original or borrowed (such as a popular dance or opera tune). Then there is a series of variations that transform that theme. *What* is varied varies. The variations can be based on the melody, the harmony, the bass line, or a combination of these approaches. *Double variations* have two alternating themes, usually treated in alternation. The general idea is to take a piece of material, the theme, and make it into new and contrasting segments of music. Meanwhile there will be an overall shape imposed on the whole of the variations, often involving a gradually faster tempo.

ABA FORM

This is a simple outline often used for slow movements: A, a theme section perhaps with subthemes; B, a more or less contrasting middle section in a new key or keys; and a return to A in the tonic key, often ornamented or otherwise varied. Other versions of it might be ABABA or the like, and there may be a coda.

MINUET-SCHERZO FORM

Classical-era pieces tended to have a minuet movement, a kind of abstraction of the old three-beat popular dance. Most often this was the third of a four-movement piece, sometimes the second movement. One basic formal model was a large three-part form enclosing two smaller three-part forms: ABA minuet section; another ABA called the *trio*, usually lighter in texture; then a repeat of the minuet. So the large form is minuet–trio–minuet. Again, this general outline was varied at will.

The *scherzo*, a word meaning "joke," was an invention of Haydn. It speeds up the tempo of a minuet to make a new kind of racing, often high-spirited movement—the three-beat meter and formal outline being the same as the minuet, only the tempo faster and the mood lighter. Beethoven wrote many movements in scherzo form and fast tempo that were serious or even tragic, so he did not call those scherzos. He also wrote what amount to scherzos in two-beat meter.

The preceding are the main forms used in multimovement symphonies, concertos, solo sonatas, string quartets, and other chamber music. The overall idea has to do with contrasts of mood and tempo: a typical work might have a fast first movement in sonata form, a slow movement in ABA form, a medium-tempo minuet or racing scherzo, then a fast finale in sonata-rondo form. This pattern was, like all else, infinitely variable. Here and there in his work, Beethoven created new ad hoc or hybrid forms, such as the finales of the Third and Ninth Symphonies.

FUGUE

Fugue is a contrapuntal procedure that evolved in the early Baroque period and persisted through the Classical period and later. First, recall what *counterpoint* is: a superimposition of melodies, each line (called a *voice*, even in instrumental music) its own melody, yet the whole also creating effective harmony. (This is in contradistinction to other kinds of texture that involve a single melody with accompaniment.) In the Classical period and later, although fugues were still often composed, the idea had become a kind of self-conscious archaism. Because achieving a balance of good melody and good harmony in counterpoint is one of the most difficult skills in composition, usually involving concentrated study to master, the Classical period called fugue and overt counterpoint "the learned style."

A simple fugue is based around a single melodic idea called the *subject.* Counterpoint is woven around that subject, sometimes involving a consistent second thematic idea called a *countersubject.* A typical fugue begins like this: the subject is heard alone, then a second voice enters on the subject in the dominant key while the first voice continues in counterpoint (perhaps that being the countersubject); then a third voice enters in the tonic key while the other voices weave counterpoint around it. If it is a four-voiced fugue, there is a fourth entry of the subject while the other voices continue in counterpoint. Here is a typical opening of a three-voiced fugue:

SUBJECT —— Free counterpoint or countersubject   Free counterpoint
              SUBJECT ——   Free or countersubject
                                             SUBJECT ——

Collectively, a section with entries of the subject like this is called a *fugal exposition.* Then follows a section where there is a kind of as-if improvisation on the exposition material, that section called an *episode.* The whole of the fugue proceeds in an alternation of exposition (entries of the subject) and episode (free counterpoint on the material). At the end there may be a section called the *stretto* in which, as if in its eagerness to be heard, the subject enters in the voices in closer succession, each entry almost treading on the heels of the last.

There are infinite variations. A fugue can be in two voices or up to as many as you like (but rarely more than six). There may or may not be a countersubject, or a stretto at the end. The piece may be a *double fugue,* involving two more or less equal subjects. There are smaller named variants based on the fugal idea: a *fughetta* is a little fugue, often an episode in a larger movement; a *fugato* is a fuguelike section involving a subject but is less developed than a full fugue.

Beethoven was fascinated by the fugal idea and turned to it often, especially in the late music. But he was determined to adapt fugue to the demands of Classical-style movements, and constantly found new ways of integrating fugue and sonata or sonata-like forms, or creating new formal patterns based around fugue. Since the model of a fugue composer for Beethoven was J. S. Bach (mainly in *The Well-Tempered Clavier*), the style of Beethoven's fugues sometimes recalls Bach.

CANON

Canon resembles fugue in that it is a contrapuntal procedure based on a single subject, but it is a more rigid procedure than fugue. Think of canon as a grown-up form of "Row, Row, Row Your Boat": the beginning of a melody is heard alone, then a second voice begins the same tune while the first voice continues it, and the idea continues with as many voices as you like:

> MELODY————————————————————
>   MELODY————————————————————
>   MELODY———————————————— *etc.*

So the single tune is heard two or more times in overlapping entries and creates counterpoint with itself—in effective harmony. The canonic tune may or may not begin on the same pitches in each entry; there are other varieties, such as a *crab canon,* in which the second entry is the melody backward. Canons can't happen by accident; they have to be carefully composed. Bach was celebrated for the suppleness and beauty of his canons, qualities that are very hard to achieve in such a rigid form. Beethoven usually wrote freestanding canons only as jokes for friends, but some of his pieces have canonic episodes integrated into the larger form.

Works Cited

Albrecht, Theodore. *Letters to Beethoven and Other Correspondence.* 3 vols. Lincoln: University of Nebraska Press, 1996. In the notes, called "Albrecht."

Aldrich, Elizabeth. "Social Dancing in Schubert's World." In Erickson, *Schubert's Vienna.*

Alsop, Susan Mary. *The Congress Dances.* New York: Harper & Row, 1984.

Anderson, Emily. "Beethoven's Operatic Plans." *Proceedings of the Royal Musical Association, 88th Session (1961–1962).*

———, ed. and trans. *The Letters of Beethoven.* 3 vols. London: Macmillan, 1961. In the notes, called "Anderson."

———. *Mozart's Letters: An Illustrated Selection.* Boston: Little, Brown, 1990.

Andraschke, Peter. "Neefe's Volkstümlichkeit." In Loos, *Christian Gottlob Neefe.*

Arnold, Denis, and Nigel Fortune, eds. *The Beethoven Reader.* New York: Norton, 1971.

Baker, Nancy Kovaleff, and Thomas Christensen, eds. *Aesthetics and the Art of Musical Composition in the German Enlightenment: Selected Writings of Johann Georg Sulzer and Heinrich Christoph Koch.* Cambridge: Cambridge University Press, 1995.

Beahrs, Virginia Oakley. "The Immortal Beloved Riddle Reconsidered." *Musical Times,* February 1988.

———. "'My Angel, My All, My Self': A Literal Translation of Beethoven's Letter to the Immortal Beloved." *Beethoven Newsletter* 5, no. 2 (Summer 1990).

Beethoven, Ludwig van. "Beethoven's *Tagebuch.*" Translated by Maynard Solomon. In Solomon, *Beethoven Essays.*

———. *Ein Skizzenbuch zu Streichquartetten aus op. 18.* 2 vols., facsimile and transcription. Bonn: Beethovenhaus, 1972.

———. *Konversationshefte.* Edited by Karl-Heinz Köhler and Grita Herre. 11 vols. Leipzig: Deutscher Verlag für Musik, 1972.

Berlin, Isaiah. *The Age of Enlightenment: The Eighteenth Century Philosophers.* 1956. Reprint, Freeport, N.Y.: Books for Libraries Press, 1970.

Biba, Otto. "Concert Life in Beethoven's Vienna." In Winter and Carr, *Beethoven, Performers, and Critics,* 77–93.

Blanning, Tim. *The Pursuit of Glory: Europe, 1648–1815*. New York: Viking, 2007.

Bodsch, Ingrid. "Das kulturelle Leben in Bonn under dem letzten Kölner Kurfürsten Maximilian Franz von Österreich (1780/84–1794)." In Bodsch, *Joseph Haydn und Bonn*.

———, ed. *Joseph Haydn und Bonn: Katalog zur Ausstellung*. Bonn: StadtMuseum, 2001.

Bonds, Mark Evan. *Wordless Rhetoric: Musical Form and the Metaphor of the Oration*. Cambridge, Mass.: Harvard University Press, 1991.

Bonner Geschichtsblätter, herausgegeben von Stadtarchivar. Bonn: Der Verein, 1937–.

Bonner Intelligenzblätt. There is a selection of issues of this late eighteenth-century town paper on microfilm at the Bonn Stadtarchiv.

Botstein, Leon. "Beethoven's Orchestral Music." In Stanley, *Cambridge Companion*.

———. "The Patrons and Publics of the Quartets: Music, Culture, and Society in Beethoven's Vienna." In Winter and Martin, *Beethoven Quartet Companion*.

Brandenburg, Sieghard. "Beethoven's Op. 12 Violin Sonatas: On the Path to His Personal Style." In Lockwood and Kroll, *Beethoven Violin Sonatas*.

———. "Once Again: On the Question of the Repeat of the Scherzo and Trio in Beethoven's Fifth Symphony." In *Beethoven Essays: Studies in Honor of Elliot Forbes*, edited by Lewis Lockwood and Phyllis Benjamin, 146–98. Cambridge, Mass.: Harvard University Press, 1984.

Brandt, G. W. "Banditry Unleash'd; or, How *The Robbers* Reached the Stage." *New Theatre Quarterly* 22, no. 1 (2006): 19–29.

Braubach, Max, ed. *Die Stammbücher Beethovens und der Babette Koch, in Faksimile*. Bonn: Beethovenhaus, 1995.

———. "Von den Menschen und dem Leben in Bonn zur Zeit des jungen Beethoven und der Babette Koch-Belderbusch." *Bonner Geschichtsblätter* 23 (1969): 51.

Breuning, Gerhard von. *Memories of Beethoven*. Edited by Maynard Solomon. Translated by Henry Mins and Maynard Solomon. Cambridge: Cambridge University Press, 1995.

Brinkmann, Reinhold. "In the Time of the *Eroica*." In Burnham and Steinberg, *Beethoven and His World*.

Brion, Marcel. *Daily Life in the Vienna of Mozart and Schubert*. Translated by Jean Stewart. London: Weidenfeld & Nicholson, 1961.

Brophy, Brigid. *Mozart the Dramatist*. New York: Da Capo, 1988.

Brown, A. Peter. *The Symphonic Repertoire: The First Golden Age of the Viennese Symphony; Haydn, Mozart, Beethoven, and Schubert*. Bloomington: Indiana University Press, 2002.

Brown, Clive. "Historical Performance, Metronome Marks, and Tempo in Beethoven's Symphonies." *Early Music* 19, no. 2 (May 1991).

Broyles, Michael. *Beethoven: The Emergence and Evolution of Beethoven's Heroic Style*. New York: Excelsior Music, 1987.

Burnham, Scott. *Beethoven Hero*. Princeton: Princeton University Press, 1995.

Burnham, Scott, and Michael P. Steinberg, eds. *Beethoven and His World*. Princeton: Princeton University Press, 2000.

Cadenbach, Rainer. "Neefe als Literat." In Loos, *Christian Gottlob Neefe*.

Chua, Daniel K. L. *The "Galitzin" Quartets of Beethoven*. Princeton: Princeton University Press, 1995.

Clive, H. P. *Beethoven and His World: A Biographical Dictionary*. New York: Oxford University Press, 2001.

Closson, Ernest. "Grandfather Beethoven." *Musical Quarterly* 19, no. 4 (October 1933): 367–73.

Comini, Alessandra. *The Changing Image of Beethoven: A Study in Mythmaking.* New York: Rizzoli, 1987.

———. "The Visual Beethoven: Whence, Why, and Whither the Scowl?" In Burnham and Steinberg, *Beethoven and His World.*

Cook, Nicholas. *Beethoven: Symphony No. 9.* Cambridge: Cambridge University Press, 1993.

———. "Beethoven's Unfinished Piano Concerto: A Case of Double Vision?" *Journal of the American Musicological Society* 42, no. 2 (Summer 1989): 338–74.

Cooper, Barry. *Beethoven.* Oxford: Oxford University Press, 2000.

———. *Beethoven and the Creative Process.* Oxford: Clarendon, 1992.

———. *The Beethoven Compendium: A Guide to Beethoven's Life and Music.* New York: Thames & Hudson, 1992.

———. *Beethoven's Folksong Settings: Chronology, Sources, Style.* Oxford: Clarendon, 1994.

———. "The Compositional Act: Sketches and Autographs." In Stanley, *Cambridge Companion.*

Cooper, Martin. *Beethoven: The Last Decade, 1817–1827.* London: Oxford University Press, 1970.

Czerny, Carl. *On the Proper Performance of All Beethoven's Works for the Piano,* including "Reminiscences of Beethoven." Edited by Paul Badura-Skoda. Vienna: Universal Edition, 1970.

Dahlhaus, Carl. *Ludwig van Beethoven: Approaches to His Music.* Translated by Mary Whittall. Oxford: Clarendon, 1991.

Daschner, Hubert. *Musik für die Bühne.* Bonn: Beethoven-Archiv, 1969.

Davies, Peter J. *The Character of a Genius: Beethoven in Perspective.* Westport, Conn.: Greenwood, 2002.

Dean, Winton. "Beethoven and Opera." In Robinson, *Ludwig van Beethoven.*

Del Mar, Jonathan. "Del Mar's Musical Curiosities." Unpublished compilation.

———, ed. *Symphony No. 6 in F Major.* By Ludwig van Beethoven. Basel: Bärenreiter, 2001.

———, ed. *Violin Concerto, Piano Concerto.* By Ludwig van Beethoven. Basel: Bärenreiter, 2009.

DeNora, Tia. *Beethoven and the Construction of Genius: Musical Politics in Vienna, 1792–1803.* Berkeley: University of California Press, 1995.

———. "The Beethoven-Wölffl Piano Duel." In *Music in Eighteenth-Century Austria,* edited by David Wyn Jones. Cambridge: Cambridge University Press, 1996.

Donakowski, Conrad L. *A Muse for the Masses: Ritual and Music in an Age of Democratic Revolution, 1770–1870.* Chicago: University of Chicago Press, 1977.

Douël, Martial. "Beethoven's 'Adelaide.'" Translated by Fred Rothwell. *Musical Quarterly* 13, no. 2 (April 1927): 208–17.

Drabkin, William. *Beethoven: "Missa solemnis."* Cambridge: Cambridge University Press, 1991.

Drake, Kenneth. *The Beethoven Sonatas and the Creative Experience.* Bloomington: Indiana University Press, 1994.

Duffin, Ross W. *How Equal Temperament Ruined Harmony (and Why You Should Care).* New York: Norton, 2008.

Dülmen, Richard van. *The Society of the Enlightenment: The Rise of the Middle Class and Enlightenment Culture in Germany.* Translated by Anthony Williams. New York: St. Martin's, 1992.

E., F. G. "George P. Bridgetower and the Kreutzer Sonata." *Musical Times,* May 1, 1908.

Ehrlich, Cyril. *The Piano: A History.* Oxford: Clarendon, 1990.

Eisinger, Josef. "Was Beethoven Lead-Poisoned?" *Beethoven Journal* 23, no. 1 (Summer 2008): 15–17.

Erickson, Raymond, ed. *Schubert's Vienna.* New Haven: Yale University Press, 1997.

———. "Vienna in Its European Context." In Erickson, *Schubert's Vienna.*

Fiske, Roger. *Beethoven's "Missa solemnis."* New York: Scribner's Sons, 1979.

"Französische Ouvertüre." *Bonner Geschichtsblätter* 13 (1959): 17.

Friedenthal, Richard. *Goethe: His Life and Times.* Cleveland: World, 1963.

Gartenberg, Egon. *Vienna: Its Musical Heritage.* University Park: Pennsylvania State University Press, 1968.

Gay, Peter, ed. *Age of Enlightenment.* New York: Time-Life, 1966.

Geiringer, Karl, with Irene Geiringer. *Haydn: A Creative Life in Music.* 3rd ed. Berkeley: University of California Press, 1982.

Gladwell, Malcolm. "Late Bloomers." *The New Yorker,* October 20, 2008, 36–44.

Glauert, Amanda. "Beethoven's Songs and Vocal Style." In Stanley, *Cambridge Companion.*

Gordon, Philip. "Franz Grillparzer: Critic of Music." *Musical Quarterly* 2, no. 4 (October 1916).

Griffiths, Paul. *The String Quartet: A History.* New York: Thames & Hudson, 1983.

Gruneberg, R. "Karl van Beethoven's Suicide Attempt: A Re-assessment." *Musical Times,* March 1963.

Gutiérrez-Denhoff, Martella. *Die gute Kocherey: Aus Beethovens Speiseplänen.* Bonn: Beethoven-Haus, 1988.

Gutman, Robert W. *Mozart: A Cultural Biography.* New York: Harcourt Brace, 1999.

Gutzmer, Karl, et al. *Chronik der Stadt Bonn.* Dortmund, Ger.: Chronik Verlag, 1988.

Heartz, Daniel. *Mozart, Haydn, and Early Beethoven.* New York: Norton, 2009.

Helps, Arthur, and Elizabeth Jane Howard. *Bettina: A Portrait.* New York: Reynal, n.d.

Herriot, Edouard. *The Life and Times of Beethoven.* Translated by Adelheid I. Mitchell and William J. Mitchell. New York: Macmillan, 1935.

Hill, Cecil. *Ferdinand Ries: Briefe und Dokumente.* Bonn: Ludwig Röhrscheid Verlag, 1982.

Hofmann, Paul. *The Viennese: Splendor, Twilight, and Exile.* New York: Anchor, 1988.

Im Hof, Ulrich. *The Enlightenment.* Translated by William E. Yuill. Oxford: Blackwell, 1994.

Irmen, Hans-Josef. "Beethoven, Bach, und die Illuminaten." In *Beethoven und die Rezeption der alten Musik,* edited by Hans-Werner Küthen. Bonn: Verlag Beethoven-Haus, 2002.

———. "Neefe als Freimaurer und Illuminat." In Loos, *Christian Gottlob Neefe.*

Jackson, Myles W. "A Spectrum of Belief: Goethe's 'Republic' versus Newtonian 'Despotism.'" *Social Studies of Science* 24, no. 4 (November 1994).

Jander, Owen. "Exploring Sulzer's *Allgemeine Theorie* as a Source Used by Beethoven." *Beethoven Newsletter,* Spring 1987.

———. "The 'Kreutzer' Sonata as Dialogue." *Early Music* 16, no. 1 (February 1988).

———. "'Let Your Deafness No Longer Be a Secret—Even in Art': Self-Portraiture and the Third Movement of the C-Minor Symphony." In *Beethoven Forum* (University of Nebraska Press) 8 (2000).

Johnson, Douglas. "Decisive Years in Beethoven's Early Development." In Tyson, *Beethoven Studies*, vol. 3.

Johnson, Douglas P., Alan Tyson, and Robert Winter. *The Beethoven Sketchbooks: History, Reconstruction, Inventory.* 4 vols. Berkeley: University of California Press, 1985.

Johnston, William M. *The Austrian Mind: An Intellectual and Social History, 1848–1938.* Berkeley: University of California Press, 1972.

Jones, Timothy. *Beethoven: The "Moonlight" and Other Sonatas, Op. 27 and Op. 31.* Cambridge: Cambridge University Press, 1999.

Kagan, Susan. *Archduke Rudolph, Beethoven's Patron, Pupil, and Friend: His Life and Music.* Stuyvesant, N.Y.: Pendragon, 1988.

Kant, Immanuel. "What Is Enlightenment?" See Columbia University, Sources of Medieval History, Selected Texts, accessed December 20, 2013, http://www.columbia.edu/acis/ets/CCREAD/etscc/kant.html.

Kaufmann, Thomas Dacosta. "Architecture and Sculpture." In Erickson, *Schubert's Vienna.*

Kerman, Joseph. *"An die ferne Geliebte."* In Tyson, *Beethoven Studies*, vol. 1.

———. *The Beethoven Quartets.* New York: Knopf, 1967.

———, ed. *Ludwig van Beethoven: Autograph Miscellany from circa 1786 to 1799.* (The "Kafka Sketchbook.") Vol. 2. London: Trustees of the British Museum, 1970.

———. "Notes on Beethoven's Codas." In Tyson, *Beethoven Studies*, vol. 3.

Kinderman, William. *Beethoven.* Berkeley: University of California Press, 1995.

———. *Beethoven's Diabelli Variations.* Oxford: Clarendon, 1987.

———. "Beethoven's Symbol for the Deity in the 'Missa solemnis' and the Ninth Symphony." *Nineteenth-Century Music* 9, no. 2 (Autumn 1985).

———. "The Piano Music." In Stanley, *Cambridge Companion.*

Kinsky, Georg, and Hans Halm. *Das Werk Beethovens: Thematisch-Bibliographisches Verzeichnis Seiner Sämtlichen Vollendeten Kompositionen.* Munich: G. Henle Verlag, 1955.

Kirby, F. E. "Beethoven and the 'Geselliges Lied.'" *Music and Letters* 47, no. 2 (April 1966).

———. "Beethoven's Pastoral Symphony as a *Sinfonia caracteristica.*" In Lang, *Creative World.*

Kirkendale, Warren. "The 'Great Fugue,' op. 133: Beethoven's 'Art of the Fugue.'" *Acta Musicologica* 35 (1963): 15–24.

———. "New Roads to Old Ideas in Beethoven's 'Missa solemnis.'" *Musical Quarterly* 56, no. 4 (October 1970).

Kivy, Peter. *The Possessor and the Possessed: Handel, Mozart, Beethoven, and the Ideal of Musical Genius.* New Haven: Yale University Press, 2001.

Klapproth, John E. *Beethoven's Only Beloved: Josephine!* Self-published, 2011. Citations here come from a previous, unpublished version of the book.

Knight, Frida. *Beethoven and the Age of Revolution.* New York: International, 1973.

Knopp, Gisbert. "Die Stadtgestalt Bonns unter Kurfürst Max Franz." In Bodsch, *Joseph Haydn und Bonn.*

Kolisch, Rudolph. "Tempo and Character in Beethoven's Music." Pts. 1 and 2. *Musical Quarterly* 77, no. 1 (Spring 1993); no. 2 (Summer 1993).

Kolodin, Irving. *The Interior Beethoven: A Biography of the Music.* New York: Knopf, 1975.

Kramer, Richard. "Notes to Beethoven's Education." *Journal of the American Musicological Society* 28, no. 1 (Spring 1975): 72–101.

Kross, Siegfried. "Beethoven und die rheinisch-katholische Aufklärung." In *Beethoven: Mensch seiner Zeit.* Bonn: Röhrscheid, 1973.

Landon, H. C. Robbins. *Beethoven: A Documentary Study.* London: Macmillan, 1970. Note: This is an abridged edition, the source cited in most of the notes. When "unabridged" is added to a note, it means the unabridged edition, Macmillan, 1970.

———, with Henry Raynor. *Haydn.* New York: Praeger, 1972.

Lang, Paul Henry, ed. *The Creative World of Beethoven.* New York: Norton, 1970.

Levy, David B. *Beethoven: The Ninth Symphony.* Rev. ed. New Haven, Conn.: Yale University Press, 2003.

Lippman, Edward. *History of Western Musical Aesthetics.* Lincoln: University of Nebraska Press, 1994.

Lockwood, Lewis. "The Autograph of the First Movement of the Sonata for Violoncello and Pianoforte, Op. 69." In Lockwood, *Beethoven: Studies.*

———. *Beethoven: The Music and the Life.* New York: Norton, 2003.

———. *Beethoven: Studies in the Creative Process.* Cambridge, Mass.: Harvard University Press, 1992.

———. "Beethoven's *Leonore* and *Fidelio.*" *Journal of Interdisciplinary History* 36, no. 3 (Winter 2006).

———. "The Earliest Sketches for the *Eroica.*" In Lockwood, *Beethoven: Studies.*

———. "On the Beautiful in Music." In Lockwood and Kroll, *Beethoven Violin Sonatas.*

Lockwood, Lewis, and Mark Kroll, eds. *The Beethoven Violin Sonatas: History, Criticism, Performance.* Urbana: University of Illinois Press, 2004.

Loos, Helmut, ed. *Christian Gottlob Neefe (1748–1798): Eine eigenständige Künstlerpersönlichkeit.* Chemnitz, Ger.: Gudrun Schröder Verlag, 1999.

Lorenz, Michael. "Commentary on Wawruch's Report: Biographies of Andreas Wawruch and Johann Seibert, Schindler's Responses to Wawruch's Report, and Beethoven's Medical Condition and Alcohol Consumption." *Beethoven Journal* 22, no. 2 (Winter 2007): 44–52.

MacArdle, Donald W. "The Family van Beethoven." *Musical Quarterly* 35, no. 4 (October 1949): 528–50.

Mai, François Martin. *Diagnosing Genius: The Life and Death of Beethoven.* Montreal: McGill-Queen's University Press, 2007.

Marek, George R. *Beethoven: Biography of a Genius.* New York: Funk & Wagnalls, 1969.

Matthäus, Wolfgang. "Beiträge zur Musikgeschichte Bonns in den Jahren 1772–1791: Quellen und Berichte aus zeitgenössischen Tageszeitungen." *Bonner Geschichtsblätter* 21 (1967): 136.

May, Arthur J. *The Age of Metternich, 1814–1848.* Rev. ed. New York: Holt, Rinehart & Winston, 1961.

Monson, Dale E. "The Classic-Romantic Dichotomy, Franz Grillparzer, and Beethoven." *International Review of the Aesthetics and Sociology of Music* 13, no. 2 (December 1982).

Moore, Julia. "Beethoven and Inflation." In *Beethoven Forum* (University of Nebraska Press) 1 (1992).

Musulin, Stella. *Vienna in the Age of Metternich: From Napoleon to Revolution, 1805–1848.* Boulder, Colo.: Westview, 1975.

Newman, William S. "Beethoven's Pianos versus His Piano Ideals." *Journal of the American Musicological Society* 23, no. 3 (Autumn 1970).

Nicholls, David. *Napoleon: A Biographical Companion.* Santa Barbara, Calif.: ABC-CLIO, 1999.

Nicolson, Harold. *The Congress of Vienna: A Study in Allied Unity, 1812–1822.* London: Cassell, 1946.

Nohl, Ludwig. *An Unrequited Love: An Episode in the Life of Beethoven.* London: Bentley & Son, 1876. Reprint, n.p.: Nabu Public Domain Reprints, 2012.

Nottebohm, Gustav. *Beethoveniana: Aufsätze und Mittheilungen.* 2 vols. Leipzig: Verlag von C. F. Peters, 1872. Reprint, New York: Johnson Reprint Corp., 1970.

———. *Two Beethoven Sketchbooks: A Description with Musical Extracts.* Translated by Jonathan Katz. London: Gollancz, 1979.

Ohm, Gregor. "Zur Sozialpolitik in der Residenzstadt Bonn zur Zeit der Kurfürsten Max Friedrich und Max Franz." *Bonner Geschichtsblätter* 47–48 (1998).

Palisca, Claude V. "French Revolutionary Models for Beethoven's *Eroica* Funeral March." In *Music and Context: Essays for John M. Ward,* edited by Anne Dhu Shapiro. Cambridge, Mass.: Harvard University Department of Music, 1985.

Parsons, James. "'Deine Zauber binden wieder': Beethoven, Schiller, and the Joyous Reconcilation of Opposites." In *Beethoven Forum* (University of Illinois Press) 9, no. 1 (2002).

Pestelli, Giorgio. *The Age of Mozart and Beethoven.* Cambridge: Cambridge University Press, 1984.

Pfeiff, Ruprecht. *Bonn als Haupt- und Residenzstadt Kurkölns.* Puhlheim, Ger.: Rheinland-Verlag, 2000.

Plantinga, Leon. *Beethoven's Concertos: History, Style, Performance.* New York: Norton, 1999.

Ratner, Leonard G. *The Beethoven String Quartets: Compositional Strategies and Rhetoric.* Stanford, Calif.: Stanford Bookstore, 2001.

Raynor, Henry. *A Social History of Music / Music and Society.* 2 vols. in 1. New York: Taplinger, 1978.

Reid, Paul. *The Beethoven Song Companion.* Manchester: Manchester University Press, 2007.

Robinson, Paul A., ed. *Ludwig van Beethoven: Fidelio.* Translated by Annie Wood. Cambridge: Cambridge University Press, 1996.

Rolland, Romain. *Beethoven the Creator: The Great Creative Epochs, from the Eroica to the Appassionata.* Translated by Ernest Newman. New York: Dover, 1964.

Rosen, Charles. *Beethoven's Piano Sonatas: A Short Companion.* New Haven: Yale University Press, 2002.

———. *The Classical Style: Haydn, Mozart, Beethoven.* Expanded ed. New York: Norton, 1997.

Sachs, Harvey. *The Ninth: Beethoven and the World in 1824.* New York: Random House, 2010.

Scherer, F. M. *Quarter Notes and Bank Notes: The Economics of Music Composition in the Eighteenth and Nineteenth Centuries.* Princeton: Princeton University Press, 2004.

Scherman, Thomas, and Louis L. Biancolli., eds. *The Beethoven Companion.* Garden City, N.Y.: Doubleday, 1972. In the notes, called "Scherman and Biancolli."

Schiedermair, Ludwig. *Der junge Beethoven.* Leipzig: Verlag Quelle & Meyer, 1925.

Schiller, Friedrich. *On the Aesthetic Education of Man, in a Series of Letters.* Edited and translated by Elizabeth M. Wilkinson and L. A. Willoughby. Oxford: Clarendon, 1982.

Schindler, Anton. *Beethoven as I Knew Him: A Biography.* Edited by Donald W. Mac-Ardle. Translated by Constance S. Jolly. Chapel Hill: University of North Carolina Press, 1966.

Schloßmacher, Norbert. "Die Redoute in Bad Godesberg—Schauplatz einer denkwürdigen Begegnung zwischen Joseph Haydn und Ludwig van Beethoven im sommer 1792." In Bodsch, *Joseph Haydn und Bonn.*

Schmidt, James, ed. *What Is Enlightenment?: Eighteenth-Century Answers and Twentieth-Century Questions.* Berkeley: University of California Press, 1996.

Schwartz, Boris. "Beethoven and the French Violin School." *Musical Quarterly* 44, no. 4 (October 1958).

Senner, Wayne M., ed. and trans. *The Critical Reception of Beethoven's Compositions by his German Contemporaries.* 2 vols. Lincoln: University of Nebraska Press, 1999.

Simpson, Robert. "The Chamber Music for Strings." In Arnold and Fortune, *Beethoven Reader.*

Sipe, Thomas. *Beethoven: Eroica Symphony.* New York: Cambridge University Press, 1998.

Sisman, Elaine, ed. *Haydn and His World.* Princeton: Princeton University Press, 1997.

———. "'The Spirit of Mozart from Haydn's Hands': Beethoven's Musical Inheritance." In Stanley, *Cambridge Companion.*

Skowroneck, Tilman. *Beethoven the Pianist.* Cambridge: Cambridge University Press, 2010.

———. "Beethoven's Erard Piano: Its Influence on His Compositions and on Viennese Fortepiano Building." *Early Music* 30, no. 4 (November 2002): 523–38.

———. "Keyboard Instruments of the Young Beethoven." In Burnham and Steinberg, *Beethoven and His World.*

Solomon, Maynard. *Beethoven.* 2nd ed. New York: Schirmer, 1998.

———. *Beethoven Essays.* Cambridge, Mass.: Harvard University Press, 1988.

———. "Beethoven, Freemasonry, and the *Tagebuch* of 1812–1818." In *Beethoven Forum* (University of Nebraska Press) 8 (2000).

———. "Beethoven's 'Magazin der Kunst.'" *Nineteenth-Century Music* 7, no. 3 (April 1984).

———. "Beethoven's Productivity at Bonn." *Music and Letters* 53, no. 2 (April 1972): 165–72.

———. "Economic Circumstances of the Beethoven Household in Bonn." *Journal of the American Musicological Society* 50, nos. 2–3 (Summer–Fall 1997): 331–51.

———. *Late Beethoven: Music, Thought, Imagination.* Berkeley: University of California Press, 2003.

———. "The Masonic Thread." In Solomon, *Beethoven Essays.*

———. "The Ninth Symphony." In Solomon, *Beethoven Essays.*

Sonneck, Oscar G. T. *Beethoven: Impressions by His Contemporaries.* New York: Dover, 1967.

Specht, Richard. *Beethoven as He Lived.* New York: Smith & Haas, 1933.

Stader, Karl Heinz. "Bonn und der Rhein in der englischen Reiseliteratur." In *Aus Ge-*

schichte und Volkskunde von Stat und Raum Bonn: Festschrift Josef Dietz zum 80. Geburtstag, edited by Josef Dietz, Edith Ennen, and Dietrich Höroldt. Bonn: Röhrscheid, 1973.

Stanley, Glenn, ed. *The Cambridge Companion to Beethoven.* Cambridge: Cambridge University Press, 2000.

Steblin, Rita. *A History of Key Characteristics in the Eighteenth and Early Nineteenth Centuries.* 2nd ed. Rochester, N.Y.: University of Rochester Press, 2002.

Steinberg, Michael. "The Late Quartets." In Winter and Martin, *Beethoven Quartet Companion.*

Sterba, Editha, and Richard Sterba. *Beethoven and His Nephew: A Psychoanalytic Study of Their Relationship.* New York: Pantheon, 1954.

Stowell, Robin. *Beethoven: Violin Concerto.* Cambridge: Cambridge University Press, 1998.

Sturm, Christoph Christian. *Reflections on the Works of God and His Providence Throughout All Nature.* Mountain Valley, Va.: Funk & Sons, 1848.

Swafford, Jan. "In Search of Lost Sounds." *Slate,* March 2, 2010. http://www.slate.com/articles/arts/music_box/2010/03/in_search_of_lost_sounds.html.

———. "Silence Is Golden: How a Pause Can Be the Most Devastating Effect in Music." *Slate,* August 31, 2009. http://www.slate.com/articles/arts/music_box/2009/08/silence_is_golden.html.

———. "The Wolf at Our Heels." *Slate,* April 20, 2010. http://www.slate.com/articles/arts/music_box/2010/04/the_wolf_at_our_heels.html.

Teschner, Ulrike. "Bartholomäus Fischenich: Ein rheinischer Philosoph und Jurist der Aufklärungszeit." *Bonner Geschichtsblätter* 21 (1967): 17.

Thayer, Alexander W., et al. *Life of Beethoven.* 2 vols. Edited by Elliot Forbes. Princeton: Princeton University Press, 1964. In the notes, called "Thayer/Forbes."

Thompson, Bruce. *Franz Grillparzer.* Boston: Twayne, 1981.

Thomson, Katharine. "Mozart and Freemasonry." *Music and Letters* 57, no. 1 (January 1976): 25–46.

Travis, James. "Celtic Elements in Beethoven's Seventh Symphony." *Musical Quarterly* 21, no. 3 (July 1935).

Tusa, Michael C. "Music as Drama: Structure, Style, and Process in *Fidelio.*" In Robinson, *Ludwig van Beethoven.*

Tyson, Alan, ed. *Beethoven Studies.* 3 vols. Vol. 1, New York: Norton, 1973. Vol. 2, Oxford: Oxford University Press, 1977. Vol. 3, Cambridge: Cambridge University Press, 1982.

———. "Beethoven to the Countess Susanna Guicciardi: A New Letter." In Tyson, *Beethoven Studies,* vol. 1.

———. "The 1803 Version of Beethoven's *Christus am Oelberge.*" In Lang, *Creative World.*

———. "Notes on Five of Beethoven's Copyists." *Journal of the American Musicological Society* 23, no. 3 (Autumn 1970).

Valder-Knechtges, Claudia. "Andrea Luchesi, ein Italiener im Umkreis des jungen Beethoven." *Bonner Geschichtsblätter* 40 (1990): 29.

Walden, Edward. *Beethoven's Immortal Beloved: Solving the Mystery.* Lanham, Md.: Scarecrow, 2011.

Wallace, Robin. *Beethoven's Critics: Aesthetic Dilemmas and Resolutions During the Composer's Lifetime.* Cambridge: Cambridge University Press, 1986.

Walter, Horst. "Die biographischen Beziehungen zwischen Haydn and Beethoven." In Bodsch, *Joseph Haydn und Bonn.*

Webster, James. "The Falling-Out Between Haydn and Beethoven: The Evidence of Sources." In *Beethoven Essays: Studies in Honor of Elliot Forbes,* edited by Lewis Lockwood and Phyllis Benjamin, 3–29. Cambridge, Mass.: Harvard University Press, 1984.

Weck, Bernhard, "'Wer ist ein freier Mann?' Beethoven und universelle Freiheitsideen der Aufklärung: Ein Problemskizze." In *Verfassung im Diskurs der Welt: Liber Amicorum für Peter Häberle zum siebzigsten Geburtstag,* edited by Alexander Blankenagel, et al. Tübingen, Ger.: Mohr Siebeck, 2004.

Wegeler, Franz, and Ferdinand Ries. *Beethoven Remembered.* Arlington, Va.: Great Ocean, 1987. In the notes, called "Wegeler/Ries."

Wetzstein, Margot, ed. *Familie Beethoven im kurfürstlichen Bonn: Neuauflage nach den Aufzeichnungen des Bonner Bäckermeisters Gottfried Fischer.* Bonn: Verlag Beethoven-Haus, 2006. In the notes, called "Wetzstein/Fischer."

Will, Richard. "Time, Morality, and Humanity in Beethoven's *Pastoral* Symphony." *Journal of the American Musicological Society* 50, nos. 2–3 (Summer–Autumn 1997).

Winter, Robert, and Bruce Carr, eds. *Beethoven, Performers, and Critics.* Detroit: Wayne State University Press, 1980.

Winter, Robert, and Robert L. Martin, eds. *The Beethoven Quartet Companion.* Berkeley: University of California Press, 1994.

———. "Plans for the Structure of the String Quartet in C Sharp Minor." In Tyson, *Beethoven Studies,* vol. 2.

———. "The Quartets in Their First Century." In Winter and Martin, *Beethoven Quartet Companion.*

———. "The Sketches for the 'Ode to Joy.'" In Winter and Carr, *Beethoven, Performers, and Critics.*

Wolf, Christa. "Your Next Life Begins Today: A Letter about Bettina." In *Bettina Brentano-von Arnim: Gender and Politics,* edited by Elke P. Frederiksen and Katherine R. Goodman. Detroit: Wayne State University Press, 1995.

Wyn Jones, David. *Beethoven: "Pastoral" Symphony.* Cambridge: Cambridge University Press, 1995.

———. *The Life of Beethoven.* Cambridge: Cambridge University Press, 1998.

———. *The Symphony in Beethoven's Vienna.* Cambridge: Cambridge University Press, 2006.

Yates, W. E. "Cultural Life in Early Nineteenth-Century Vienna." In *Austrian Life and Literature, 1780–1938: Eight Essays,* edited by Peter Branscombe. Totowa, N.J.: Rowan & Littlefield, 1978.

Zehnder, Frank Günter, ed. *Die Bühnen des Rokoko: Theater, Music, und Literatur im Rheinland des 18. Jahrhunderts.* Vol. 7 of *Der Riss im Himmel: Clemens August und seine Epoche,* edited by Frank Günter Zehnder and Werner Schäfke. Cologne: Dumon, 2000.

Notes

1. Bonn, Electorate of Cologne

1. Thayer/Forbes, 1:44–45.
2. Ibid., 1:12.
3. Closson, "Grandfather Beethoven," 369.
4. MacArdle, "Family van Beethoven," 533.
5. Closson, "Grandfather Beethoven," 370; Clive, *Beethoven and His World,* 23.
6. Blanning, *Pursuit of Glory,* 366.
7. Pfeiff, *Bonn,* 25.
8. Wetzstein/Fischer, 5n12.
9. Pfeiff, *Bonn,* 32.
10. Zehnder, *Die Bühnen des Rokoko,* 157.
11. Pfeiff, *Bonn,* passim.
12. Knopp, "Die Stadtgestalt Bonns," 52–54.
13. Thayer/Forbes, 1:16.
14. *Siebengebirge* denotes "seven mountains," but they are mostly hills and there are more than forty of them, so one finds various theories about the origin of the name.
15. Victor Hugo, quoted in Scherman and Biancolli, 5.
16. Knopp, "Die Stadtgestalt Bonns," 51.
17. Stader, "Bonn und der Rhein," 122.
18. Thayer/Forbes, 1:40.
19. Madame de Staël, quoted in Knight, *Beethoven,* 10.
20. Marek, *Beethoven,* 26.
21. Raynor, *Social History,* 299. He gives 50,000 thalers as the cost of an opera production, which is about 75,000 florins. Here and throughout I will convert most sums to florins, for comparison.
22. This bon mot may be traditional or may be Thayer's.

23. Pfeiff, *Bonn,* 43.
24. Wetzstein/Fischer, 11nn33–34.
25. Thayer/Forbes, 1:17.
26. Ibid., 1:11.
27. Valder-Knechtges, "Andrea Luchesi," 46.
28. Wetzstein/Fischer, 13 and n42, 151.
29. Solomon, "Economic Circumstances," 334.
30. In Germany and Austria, the "first" floor of a building is the one above the ground floor. In American terms, then, the Beethovens rented the third floor of the Fischer house. Here, American floor numbers will be used.
31. Wetzstein/Fischer, 7.
32. Ibid., 27.
33. Thayer/Forbes, 1:18–19.
34. Wetzstein/Fischer, 14.
35. Ibid., 12n35.
36. Ibid., 12. As in much of Gottfried Fischer's memoir, this would have been his sister Cäcilie's recollection, because old Ludwig died before Gottfried was born.
37. Wegeler/Ries, 14.
38. Closson, "Grandfather Beethoven," 372.
39. Wetzstein/Fischer, 22.
40. Thayer/Forbes, 1:50–51.
41. Wetzstein/Fischer, 21–22.
42. Ibid., 29 and n113.
43. Ibid., 33.
44. Schiedermair, 97.
45. Wetzstein/Fischer, 28.
46. Thayer/Forbes, 1:23. In January 1773, a singer applying to fill Ludwig's place in the court choir describes him as "incapacitated." Wetzstein/Fischer, 7n18, says that Amelius is the painter's correct first name, not Thayer/Forbes's Johann.
47. The description of this painting is based on Owen Jander's article, "Let Your Deafness," 54–60. The detail concerning where Ludwig's finger points is mine. It seems significant that Ludwig points not toward the musical score but rather to his hand turning the page, which suggests that it was not only music itself that saved him but also his engagement with it.
48. Closson, "Grandfather Beethoven," 371.
49. Thayer/Forbes, 1:55.
50. Solomon, "Economic Circumstances," 337–38.
51. Davies, *Character of a Genius,* 4.
52. Solomon, "Economic Circumstances," 336n22.
53. Wetzstein/Fischer, 32n129.
54. Ibid., 27n107.
55. Zehnder, *Die Bühnen des Rokoko,* 153.

2. Father, Mother, Son

1. My sense of a prodigy's upbringing and the risks and problems it entails comes from a variety of sources about rearing children in exacting disciplines such as

music and athletics, but mainly from an interview of ca. 1984 with the celebrated violin teacher Dorothy DeLay about musical prodigies she had known and taught at Juilliard.

2. Wetzstein/Fischer, 45–46. Again, memories of Ludwig van Beethoven's first thirteen or so years that appear in Gottfried Fischer's memoir would have largely come from his sister Cäcilie, because Gottfried was born ten years after Ludwig, and Cäcilie eight years before.

3. To a degree, this is speculation about Johann's goals for his son, based on old Ludwig's training of Johann, which would have been his model — but with the added element that Ludwig the younger was far more talented than his father and was trained as a keyboard soloist rather than as a singer.

4. Wetzstein/Fischer, 46–47.

5. Skowroneck, "Keyboard Instruments," 154–57. He points out that Johann sometimes forced Ludwig to play in the middle of the night. This implies he was playing the quiet clavichord so as not to disturb the Fischer family one floor below.

6. Wetzstein/Fischer, 22.

7. Ibid., 57–58. This story also shows that Johann, like his son, honored old Ludwig's memory.

8. Ibid., 65–66.

9. Solomon, "Economic Circumstances," 11.

10. Wetzstein/Fischer, 36n140; Thayer/Forbes, 1:17. Belderbusch did not yet have the title *Graf,* or Count.

11. Ohm, "Zur Sozialpolitik," 193.

12. Quoted in Solomon, *Beethoven,* 47–48.

13. Im Hof, *Enlightenment,* 27.

14. Quoted in Marek, *Beethoven,* 145.

15. Blanning, *Pursuit of Glory,* 518.

16. Quoted in Brandt, "Banditry Unleash'd," 20.

17. Gutzmer, *Chronik der Stadt Bonn,* 76.

18. Pfeiff, *Bonn,* 47. Wetzstein/Fischer, 48, includes a contemporary print of the fire showing the injured and dead lying in the courtyard.

19. Wetzstein/Fischer, 50n183.

20. Quoted in Schiedermair, 173.

21. The story of the Electoral Residence fire is in Wetzstein/Fischer, 47–52.

22. Ibid., 30.

23. Solomon, "Economic Circumstances," 347–48.

24. Wetzstein/Fischer, 41.

25. The stories on these pages are from ibid., 37–42 passim.

26. Ibid., 57.

27. Zehnder, *Die Bühnen des Rokoko,* 162.

28. Thayer/Forbes, 1:57–58. Barry Cooper, in *Beethoven,* 4, notes that "concerto" in this case probably means a concerto arranged for one player, as was often done in those days. The "trios" are more puzzling unless there were other players involved.

29. Solomon doubts that Johann deliberately lied about Ludwig's age (*Beethoven,* 4). I am inclined to think Johann did, for three reasons: It is unlikely that both parents would lose track of their son's real age. When Ludwig later went to Holland with his mother and played at court in the Hague, his correct age was listed on the program.

And adjusting his son's age to make him look more Mozartian seems like a typical scheme of Johann's. Probably because of Johann's deception, for most of his life Beethoven himself was confused about his age.

30. Skowroneck, "Keyboard Instruments," 155, votes for early instruction in clavichord, then harpsichord, organ, and piano; Thayer/Forbes votes for piano.
31. Clive, *Beethoven and His World*, 99.
32. The Pfeifer stories are in Wetzstein/Fischer, 64–74. Cäcilie Fischer remembered the flutist fondly; there is much warmth in the stories recalled by Gottfried Fischer, who was born after Pfeifer left Bonn.
33. Schiedermair, 38. The Bonn court musical establishment was larger in the early 1700s than it was in Ludwig van Beethoven's childhood.
34. Gutzmer, *Chronik der Stadt Bonn*, 73.
35. Mozart, quoted in Sisman, "Spirit of Mozart," 46.
36. Thayer/Forbes, 1:37.
37. Bodsch, "Das kulturelle Leben," 68.
38. Christian Neefe report, in Thayer/Forbes, 1:37.
39. Braubach, "Von den Menschen," 109.
40. The public-versus-private performance equation varied from place to place: by the later eighteenth century, for example, England had a tradition of public performances of orchestra music, oratorio, and the like — some of that due to the efforts of producer Johann Peter Salomon — while in Vienna, musical life was still largely centered in private salons.
41. Sisman, "Spirit of Mozart," 46.
42. Gutzmer, *Chronik der Stadt Bonn*, 72.
43. Ibid., 79.
44. Landon, *Beethoven* unabridged, 24.
45. Matthäus, "Beiträge zur Musickgeschichte Bonns," 138–39.
46. Wetzstein/Fischer, 98.
47. Ibid., 41; B. Cooper, *Beethoven*, 4.
48. Wetzstein/Fischer, 98–100. Years later Cäcilie remembered Maria's words in detail — and Cäcilie never married.
49. Ibid., 58–59.
50. Ibid., 61.
51. Ibid., 63.
52. Ibid., 114.
53. Memory of court musician B. J. Mäurer, in ibid., 65n238.

3. Reason and Revolution

1. Wetzstein/Fischer, 54. The console and pedals and bench from the Minorite Church organ Beethoven played now reside in the Beethoven House in Bonn.
2. Thayer/Forbes, 1:58–59. It is not known exactly when Beethoven started school, but he likely attended five years at most. After he left the Tirocinium, someone named Zambona tutored him in Latin, logic, French, and Italian (Wetzstein/Fischer, 45n172). In adulthood his French was sketchy, his Italian reportedly fair.
3. Wetzstein/Fischer, 52.
4. Ibid., 91.

5. Gottfried Fischer's copious account of Johann's journeys with his son is in ibid., 90–98. (His spelling of Rovantini shows the Bonn pronunciation: Ruffangtini.) While he cites people and places in detail, Gottfried is probably enfolding a series of summer trips the Beethovens made in that period.

6. Gutiérrez-Denhoff. *Die gute Kocherey*, 33–34.

7. Wetzstein/Fischer, 100–102. Cäcilie Fischer said the kindly and handsome Rovantini was the only man she would ever have married.

8. Schiedermair, 140–41.

9. Andraschke, "Neefe's Volkstümlichkeit," passim.

10. Schiedermair, 151.

11. Ibid., 149; Weck, "Wer ist ein freier Mann?" 853.

12. Ohm, "Zur Sozialpolitik," 198.

13. Quoted in Cadenbach, "Neefe als Literat," 151. Cadenbach adds that Neefe in fact was "no matador" of the tonal art.

14. Schiedermair, 143.

15. Irmen, "Neefe," 179.

16. Marek, *Beethoven*, 5–8.

17. Berlin, *Age of Enlightenment:* "The unprecedented successes of the mathematical method in the seventeenth century left its mark on philosophy . . . This led to notable successes and equally notable failures, as the over-enthusiastic and fanatical application of techniques rich in results in one field, when mechanically applied to another . . . commonly does . . . The eighteenth century is perhaps the last period in the history of Western Europe when human omniscience was thought to be an attainable goal" (14). My overall conception of the Enlightenment here is close to the spirit of Berlin's conclusion: "The intellectual power, honesty, lucidity, courage, and disinterested love of the truth of the most gifted thinkers of the eighteenth century remain to this day without parallel. Their age is one of the best and most hopeful episodes in the life of mankind" (29). As we will see, Beethoven, for all his paranoia and bitterness, his lack of a coherent political agenda (except his admiration for the British parliamentary system), and his scarcely democratic contempt for most of the people around him, never really departed from the Aufklärung ideals of his youth.

18. The quotations and points from Kant are from his "What Is Enlightenment?" passim; and in Schmidt, *What Is Enlightenment?*

19. Berlin, *Age of Enlightenment*, 24.

20. Parsons, "Deine Zauber binden wieder," 5–7.

21. Blanning, *Pursuit of Glory*, 470.

22. Some of this paragraph derives from Gay, *Age of Enlightenment*, 11–12. As that book notes, even if the Enlightenment was not innately antireligious, there was a common belief among philosophers that "when science advanced, religion had to retreat" (20). Kant was troubled by the thought that his ideas might weaken religion partly because he insisted that humanity had to rely on itself rather than on God. In the end, Kant's ideas did often have the effect on philosophy that he feared.

23. Anderson, vol. 2, no. 376.

24. Quoted in Im Hof, *Enlightenment*, 270.

25. Quoted in Blanning, *Pursuit of Glory*, 296.

26. Dülmen, *Society of the Enlightenment*, 4. Dülmen views the German Aufklärung as largely a struggle for power and status by the new German bureaucratic middle

class — so it was an effort to challenge the hegemony of the aristocracy at the same time that the civil servant class diligently served the aristocracy.

27. Levy, *Beethoven*, 8.
28. Solomon, "Beethoven, Freemasonry," 108.
29. Quoted in Solomon, *Beethoven*, 47.
30. Quoted in Kross, "Aufklärung," 10.

4. Loved in Turn

1. A reproduction of the title page is in Lockwood, *Beethoven: Music*, 54. Forbes, in Thayer/Forbes, 1:66, notes that the countess was wife of Ignaz von Metternich, president of the High Court of Appeals.
2. Thayer/Forbes, 1:66.
3. The suggestion that the *Dressler* Variations may be a memorial for Franz Rovantini comes from Barry Cooper, in *Beethoven*, 7.
4. Bodsch, "Das kulturelle Leben," 68.
5. Schiedermair, 83–84.
6. Gutzmer, *Chronik der Stadt Bonn*, 77.
7. Wegeler/Ries, 13 and 17.
8. Thayer/Forbes, 1:92–93.
9. One of the startling things about the *Electoral* Sonatas is how many of Beethoven's future "innovations" are already in place in them. The "radical" idea in the *Pathétique* of repeating the introduction within the first movement he had already done in the F Minor *Electoral*. Meanwhile it is often noted that Beethoven expanded the frequency and variety of expression marks in music, especially in his piano music. He used more expressions than anyone ever had, and he made regular use of the extreme dynamic marks, *ff* and *pp*, which are infrequent in Mozart and Haydn. Yet Beethoven's mature piano music uses significantly *fewer* articulation elements and dynamic effects than the *Electoral* Sonatas. The difference is that in the mature works, these elements contribute to the total effect, whereas in the earlier ones, they often don't; they are forced attempts at idiomatic piano writing. Here as much as anywhere we are reminded that this is still a preteen boy composing his first pieces. There is also the question of how much his teacher Neefe helped Beethoven with these sonatas. One would expect Neefe to critique and edit them, but it is hard to imagine that the awkwardness of the markings would have escaped a professional like Neefe. Maybe that is something Beethoven did on his own. (It should be noted that some dynamic and articulation elements that are awkward to impossible on modern instruments may have been less so on the pianos of Beethoven's day.)
10. Translation based on the website of the Raptus Association for Music Appreciation, http://www.raptusassociation.org/sonindexe.html.
11. Wetzstein/Fischer, 102–3, text and notes. Gottfried and Cäcilie Fischer give an exhaustive account of the sightseeing of the trio. The identities of the wealthy widow and her daughter are not known.
12. Albrecht, vol. 1, no. 3, nn3–4. The concerto is WoO (work without opus) 4.
13. Ibid., no. 3.
14. Wetzstein/Fischer, 111–12.
15. Ibid., 72n261.
16. Solomon, *Beethoven*, 36.

17. Albrecht, vol. 1, no. 4.
18. Gutzmer, *Chronik der Stadt Bonn,* 78–80; Wetzstein/Fischer, 70 and n252.
19. Wetzstein/Fischer, 72n261; Thayer/Forbes 1:71.

5. Golden Age

1. Quoted in Landon, *Beethoven,* 32. There is no indication that Johann fell into debt or lived in desperate circumstances. The "respectable conduct" shows Johann was not yet given to extravagant public drunkenness.
2. Neefe's letter is in Schiedermair, 146–48. Though they were friends and colleagues, Neefe uses the formal *Sie* with Grossmann.
3. B. Cooper, *Beethoven Compendium,* 13.
4. Thomson, "Mozart and Freemasonry," 36 and 43.
5. G. E. Lessing, quoted in ibid., 25.
6. Quoted in Thomson, "Mozart and Freemasonry," 43.
7. Dülmen, *Society of the Enlightenment,* 55; Blanning, *Pursuit of Glory,* 332.
8. Dülmen, *Society of the Enlightenment,* 53.
9. Ibid., 64.
10. Irmen, "Neefe," 170.
11. Dülmen, *Society of the Enlightenment,* 108; ibid., 171. As is noted in Jackson, "Spectrum of Belief," 680, Goethe briefly became an Illuminatus in Weimar in 1783, but with his conservative temperament he soon turned vigorously against all secret societies as organizations that fomented revolution.
12. Quoted in Solomon, "Beethoven, Freemasonry," 119.
13. Adam Weishaupt, quoted in Dülmen, *Society of the Enlightenment,* 194n79.
14. Dülmen, *Society of the Enlightenment,* 113–14. Perhaps inevitably, the Order of Illuminati's secret agenda and its philosophy of covert infiltration soon gave birth to a vigorous and splendidly fanatical conspiracy theory that in its course, over the next two centuries and counting, would paint the order as a secret, evil, atheistic, fundamentally Jewish/Rothschild cabal that has essentially run the world ever since it incited the French Revolution. Today some members of the American religious right are of the conspiracy persuasion. Leaders of the John Birch Society discern the guiding hand of the Illuminati in the Communist revolution, the Vietnam War, and the Council on Foreign Relations. The reality of the Illuminati appears to be that they were a small, weak, short-lived movement, another case study in the Enlightenment's excesses of hope for human perfectibility. See Edward L. King, "The Illuminati," Anti-Masonry Points of View, http://www.masonicinfo.com/illuminati.htm.
15. Thomson, "Mozart and Freemasonry," 27. Thomson notes that while it is not clear whether Mozart was really an Illuminatus, several of his close friends were. These included Joseph von Sonnenfels, to whom later Beethoven dedicated his op. 28 Sonata, and scientist Ignaz von Born, a possible model for the godlike Sarastro in Mozart's *Die Zauberflöte.*
16. Ernst Wangermann, cited in Solomon, "Beethoven, Freemasonry," 126.
17. Irmen, "Neefe," 171.
18. Ibid., 187. Disparagement of female intellect and power was a feature of Freemasonry at the time, and turns up in *Die Zauberflöte* — though at the end Pamina is initiated as the equal of Tamino, a Mozartian touch contrary to Masonic practice.

19. Weck, "Wer ist ein freier Mann?" 853.

20. Kross, "Aufklärung," 16.

21. Irmen, "Neefe," 179n23.

22. Ibid., 171–80.

23. Weck, "Wer ist ein freier Mann?" 854.

24. Thayer/Forbes, 1:79.

25. Valder-Knechtges, "Andrea Luchesi," 49.

26. Both of the preceding Neefe quotations are from Schiedermair, 152–53.

27. Quoted in Baker and Christensen, *Aesthetics*, 31, 45–47, 64, 68, 77, 96, 100–101, respectively. It should be noted that any or all of these ideas from Sulzer were in the air in the eighteenth century and could have been gleaned from other sources. It's also true that most, if not all, of them would apply to the music of Haydn, Mozart, and other composers of the time. The direct echoes of those passages in Beethoven may be summarized thus: the manifest ethical intentions of his music; the concern with wholeness and the central importance of what he, like Sulzer, called *das Thema,* the opening idea; his statement, "It is my habit . . . always to keep the whole in view"; his program pieces and his observation that he always wrote with some sort of story or image in mind; the attention to the primary motifs and conceptions of a work in his sketches; the sense in his sketches, backed up by observers including Bettina Brentano, that from the beginning of work on a piece, he had a conception of the whole.

28. In saying Beethoven could not understand any path but his own, I'm not including his understanding of his musical models, which in technical terms he "understood" profoundly — as evidenced by how he absorbed, say, the motivic technique of Haydn and turned it to his own ends.

29. Scherman and Biancolli, 37–38. It is pointed out that Mozart's two piano quartets, the eighteenth century's masterpieces in this relatively uncommon genre, may not have been written when Beethoven's were done, and even if Mozart's were finished, they were too recent for Beethoven to have heard.

30. Another example of Beethoven's taking Mozart's model and ratcheting it up is in the matter of descending-third patterns in both C-major pieces. That pattern is a motif in the Mozart, as is seen in the two sets of descending chain-of-thirds outlines before and during the second theme, starting in m. 26. While Mozart never goes beyond five notes in the chain, Beethoven on his second page starts a wild and witty pattern of fifteen descending thirds, both covertly and overtly, in the melodic lines.

31. Barry Cooper, in *Beethoven*, 18, makes this point.

32. Lockwood, *Beethoven: Music,* 60. Lockwood notes (55–56) that when these quartets were published, after Beethoven's death, many people, including his one-time student Ferdinand Ries, did not believe they were by Beethoven. They simply could not accept that anyone at age fourteen, even Beethoven, could have written them. But the manuscript in Beethoven's hand exists, likewise his reuse of ideas from the quartets. On the manuscript, incidentally, Beethoven had first written his correct age and then changed it to thirteen. His uncertainty about his age was now ingrained and would stay that way for much of his life. Solomon's biography elevates that uncertainty to a major element of Beethoven's psyche, an identification with the Ludwig who was born and died the year before he was born.

33. Ibid., 59. Heartz, *Mozart,* 696, identifies the Mozart symphony as the *Linz.*

34. Irmen, "Neefe," 181–82.

35. Ibid., 188.
36. Solomon, "Beethoven's Productivity at Bonn," 165–66.

6. A Journey and a Death

1. Gutzmer, *Chronik der Stadt Bonn*, 82; Knight, *Beethoven*, 16.
2. Quoted in Kross, "Aufklärung," 15.
3. Gutzmer, *Chronik der Stadt Bonn*, 78 and 82.
4. Teschner, "Bartholomäus Fischenich," 28.
5. Bodsch, "Das Kulturelle Leben," 66.
6. Braubach, "Von den Menschen," 97.
7. Mozart, quoted in Clive, *Beethoven and His World*, 228.
8. Quoted in Irmen, "Neefe," 183.
9. Schiedermair, 56.
10. Knight, *Beethoven*, 16.
11. Albrecht, vol. 1, no. 5.
12. Solomon, "Economic Circumstances," 348–49.
13. Wetzstein/Fischer, 76.
14. B. Cooper, *Beethoven*, 31–32 and 23.
15. Ibid., 20–21. The Trio is WoO 37; the *Romance cantabile* survives only in a fragment.
16. Solomon, *Beethoven*, 27.
17. Thayer/Forbes, 1:108.
18. Davies, *Character of a Genius*, 10.
19. Irmen, "Neefe," 28–29.
20. Thayer/Forbes, 1:87.
21. Mozart, quoted in Gartenberg, *Vienna*, 45.
22. It is not known when Beethoven began the kind of improvisations that became legendary in his lifetime. His friend Wegeler said Count Waldstein encouraged the boy to start improvising, but when Beethoven met Mozart, Waldstein had not yet moved to Bonn. Barry Cooper, in *Beethoven*, 22, notes that soon after he met Beethoven, Mozart wrote his G Minor String Quintet, which twice touches on the rare key of E-flat minor, and that may indicate that Beethoven indeed showed Mozart the E-flat Major/Minor Piano Quintet.
23. Wetzstein/Fischer, 122.
24. Anderson, vol. 1, no. 1.

7. *Bildung*

1. Clive, *Beethoven and His World*, 385.
2. Wegeler/Ries, 19.
3. Ibid.
4. Schiedermair, 179, from the memoirs of Countess Lulu von Thürheim. Marek, *Beethoven*, 68, notes that Waldstein was a hotheaded Austrian patriot and a hater of the French, and that led to the break with Max Franz, who tried not to antagonize the French even after they beheaded his sister Marie Antoinette.
5. Solomon, "Beethoven, Freemasonry," 108.
6. Wegeler/Ries, 19–20. Wegeler and Ries are generally reliable but do make mistakes on details they are recounting from memory. They might be correct that Wald-

stein first encouraged Beethoven to improvise variations, but it is more likely that Beethoven gravitated to improvisation earlier on his own, with encouragement and stimulation from Waldstein.

7. Knight, *Beethoven*, 15.

8. Wegeler/Ries, 50. Schindler reported that Beethoven said Helene had kept him away from shady friends: "She knew how to keep the insects off the flowers." Schindler can never be trusted, but that sounds authentic.

9. Thayer/Forbes, 1:84.

10. Wegeler/Ries, 15.

11. Ibid., 25.

12. Schiedermair, 307.

13. As Brigid Brophy notes in *Mozart the Dramatist,* the misogynistic doctrines that defaced Masonry are on display in *Die Zauberflöte*: the evil Queen of the Night is denounced as a "proud woman" who wants to gain dominance over men. (She is surely also a representation of the anti-Masonic empress Maria Theresa.) Despite several antifemale rants in the opera, Brophy notes that Mozart manages to make the opera "feminist after all" by admitting Pamina into the brotherhood with Tamino.

14. Wegeler/Ries, 42n4.

15. Wetzstein/Fischer, 88.

16. Wegeler/Ries, 39.

17. Zehnder, *Die Bühnen des Rokoko,* 165.

18. Clive, *Beethoven and His World,* 279–80. Reicha's "fourteen years" of their friendship, if accurate at all, would have to include their years together in Vienna.

19. Thayer/Forbes, 1:95–96.

20. B. Cooper, *Beethoven,* 26.

21. The article on the Rombergs in *Grove Music Online* notes that they often made themselves out to be brothers rather than cousins, and they are often called brothers in the literature.

22. Thayer/Forbes, 1:96.

23. Clive, *Beethoven and His World,* 189; Braubach, "Von den Menschen," 81–82. Babette Koch was close friends with Lorchen von Breuning. Babette later married well, to Count Anton Belderbusch, nephew of Bonn's famous minister, who divorced his first wife to marry her. Her mother, Widow Koch, was close enough to the Beethoven family to serve as godmother to another of the children, who died soon after birth (Clive, 189).

24. Wegeler/Ries, 148.

25. *Bildung* is a German word that resists translation, with no standard definition. *The Oxford Duden German Dictionary* notes that it combines concepts of education and culture. My definition aims at an average of relevant concepts, taking into account that *Bildung* also involves experience in life and learning from it: thus the *Bildungsroman,* a novel whose narrative concerns the *Bildung* of its main character via a series of adventures. The model of the *Bildungsroman* is Goethe's *Wilhelm Meister,* equal in importance and popularity to his *Werther.* To a degree, both of those novels defined the age in German lands.

26. Blanning, *Pursuit of Glory,* 340.

27. Edmund Burke, quoted in Brinkmann, "Time of the *Eroica,*" 2.

28. Friedenthal, *Goethe,* 297.

29. Anderson, vol. 1, no. 3.
30. Albrecht, vol. 1, no. 7. Two hundred Reichsthalers equals 300 florins.
31. B. Cooper, *Beethoven,* 27. Certainly it is possible that Beethoven was writing pieces in these years that have not survived.
32. Brion, *Daily Life,* 19.
33. Johnston, *Austrian Mind,* 17.
34. Brion, *Daily Life,* 18.
35. See Clive on Schneider in *Beethoven and His World,* 320, and the entry on Schneider in *Biographisch-Bibliographisches Kirchenlexikon,* at http://www.bautz.de/bbkl/s/s1/schneider_eu.shtml.
36. Clive, *Beethoven and His World,* 10–11. Clive notes that Helene Averdonk, who became a singer in the *Kapelle,* must have remained close to the Beethoven family because she was godmother to Franz Georg, another of the ill-fated Beethoven children. She died in 1789, the year before her brother wrote the text to the *Joseph* Cantata.
37. Thayer/Forbes, 1:120.
38. Translation of the cantata text is on the website of the Raptus Association for Music Appreciation, http://www.raptusassociation.org/cantatas.html.
39. Brahms, when he examined the *Joseph* Cantata after its rediscovery in the 1880s, exclaimed in one of the most rhapsodic passages in all his letters, "Even if there were no name on the title page none other could be conjectured! — It is Beethoven through and through! The beautiful and noble pathos, sublime in its feeling and imagination, the intensity, perhaps violent in its expression, moreover the voice leading and declamation, and in the two outside sections all the characteristics which we may observe and associate with his later works" (quoted in Thayer/Forbes, 1:120). All the same, Brahms went on to say that he believed the cantata, because of its youthful excesses, should not be published.
40. Of the beginning of the *Joseph* Cantata, Barry Cooper writes, in *Beethoven,* 28, "No previous composer had exploited register as a compositional parameter to anything like the same extent, and the opening bars . . . provide a highly prophetic and striking example of his use of the technique."
41. In *The Classical Style,* 96, Charles Rosen makes the point that the style of the period of Haydn and Mozart was closer to comedy than tragedy: "The classical style . . . was, in its origins, basically a comic one . . . the pacing of classical rhythm is the pacing of comic opera, its phrasing is the phrasing of dance music, and its large structures are these phrases dramatized."
42. The chromaticism of the *Joseph* Cantata is complex and rambling, though mostly theoretically correct. It is based less on chromatic voice leading than on a steady diet of rapid modulation, altered chords, diminished sevenths, and the like. In other words, in the cantata Beethoven is thinking from chord to chord. Later, after he had studied counterpoint, he thought in terms of lines, which produce the harmony.

8. Stem and Book

1. Albrecht, vol. 1, nos. 10–11.
2. Thayer/Forbes, 1:111.
3. Mai, *Diagnosing Genius,* 20, notes that the apparent smallpox scars on Beethoven's face as an adult might have been from acne.

4. See the entry on Eulogius Schneider in the *Biographisch-Bibliographisches Kirchenlexikon,* at http://www.bautz.de/bbkl/s/s1/schneider_eu.shtml. It is not recorded whether Beethoven knew Schneider personally, but it seems likely that they met and even lifted a glass together in the small confines of Bonn, where nearly everybody artistic and politically progressive frequented the Zehrgarten.

5. Quoted in the *Wikipedia* entry for Eulogius Schneider, at http://en.wikipedia.org/wiki/Eulogius_Schneider.

6. Sipe, *Beethoven,* 3.

7. Saint-Just and Lebas, quoted in the *Wikipedia* entry for Eulogius Schneider, at http://en.wikipedia.org/wiki/Eulogius_Schneider.

8. Joseph Haydn, quoted in Gartenberg, *Vienna,* 46.

9. Landon, *Haydn,* 62.

10. Wyn Jones, *Life of Beethoven,* 20. Thayer/Forbes called March 6 Karneval Sunday, Schiedermair called it Shrove Tuesday. In fact it was a Friday.

11. Quoted in Thayer/Forbes, 1:98.

12. Maybe most startling of the Beethoven thumbprints in the *Righini* Variations is variation no. 4, its train of trills resembling the shimmering, uncanny textures in the late piano sonatas. The fading-into-the-distance ending sounds like a sketch for the coda of the first movement of the *Lebewohl* Sonata of nearly twenty years later. The contrapuntal variation no. 7 recalls his ongoing experience with Bach's *Well-Tempered Clavier.*

13. Thayer/Forbes, 1:125, notes that Czerny recalled that Beethoven used the *Righini*s to introduce himself in Vienna, which suggests that Beethoven intended them for a personal showpiece.

14. In 1809 Napoleon officially dissolved the Teutonic Knights and distributed their land to his allies, though the order lingered on.

15. The accounts of the trip are in Thayer/Forbes, 1:101–5; Wegeler/Ries, 23–24; and the Simrock account in Landon, *Beethoven* unabridged, 51. For his not being impressed, see the subsequent Junker account in the text.

16. Schiedermair, 213.

17. Nikolaus Simrock, quoted in Thayer/Forbes, 1:106.

18. Karl Ludwig Junker, quoted in Schiedermair, 90.

19. Ibid., 88–89; translation in Scherman and Biancolli, 30–31.

20. B. Cooper, *Beethoven Compendium,* 13.

21. B. Cooper, *Beethoven,* 36–37.

22. Landon, *Haydn,* 73.

23. Schloßmacher, "Die Redoute in Bad Godesberg," 108. Schloßmacher points out that the details of Haydn and Beethoven's encounters in Bonn are hazy, including whether they met at the beginning or end of Haydn's trip to England, and what music Beethoven showed Haydn. (Wegeler/Ries say it included one of the *Imperial* Cantatas.) Most scholars vote for the meeting on Haydn's return, because it had dramatic effects that were not seen earlier. The usual surmise is that of the cantatas it was most likely the *Joseph* that Beethoven showed Haydn, because he would have known it was the stronger of the two works, and its chief glory is the opening movement: he wanted to put his best foot forward. Schloßmacher notes that the Elector, who was fond of Godesberg, bought a house there and gave it to Count Waldstein as a sign of his favor and affection. Eventually, court concertmaster Franz Ries had a house on the main street; his son Ferdinand, Beethoven's pupil, retired there.

24. From Fischenich letter in Thayer/Forbes, 1:121.
25. Friedenthal, *Goethe*, 313.
26. The Beethovenhaus publication of the Beethoven *Stammbuch* (Braubach, *Die Stammbücher*) includes the one made for Babette Koch, which has far more and warmer entries than Beethoven's, each enlivened by a silhouette of the writer perhaps made by Babette. Given that the entries in the Beethoven *Stammbuch* are fewer and that some of his closest friends and mentors do not appear, I suspect the book was a last-minute affair at the time. Still, Beethoven thought enough of the *Stammbuch* to preserve it, in quite good condition.
27. Translations from Albrecht, vol. 1, no. 13 and 13n. Descriptions are based on Beethoven's *Stammbuch* in Braubach, *Die Stammbücher.*
28. Mark Evan Bonds, cited in Sisman, "Spirit of Mozart," 311n16.
29. Wetzstein/Fischer, 118.
30. Bartolomäus Ludwig Fischenich, quoted in Thayer/Forbes, 1:121.
31. Thayer/Forbes, 1:113.

9. Unreal City

1. Quoted in Knight, *Beethoven*, 24.
2. Wetzstein/Fischer, 124n456; Thayer/Forbes, 1:115–17; Guzmer, *Chronik der Stadt Bonn*, 84.
3. Thayer/Forbes, 1:258.
4. Specht, *Beethoven as He Lived*, 21.
5. Thayer/Forbes, 1:135.
6. Brion, *Daily Life*, 9.
7. Barry Cooper's *Beethoven Compendium*, 69, notes that the average income for a middle-class bachelor in Vienna in 1804 was 967 florins for basics, around 1,200 with luxuries and amusements. In calculating the practical value of Beethoven's earnings in this period, I'm assuming a round 1,000 florins as a minimal workable middle-class income.
8. Thayer/Forbes, 1:135 and 137.
9. As a doctor, Davies, in *Character of a Genius*, 14, interprets Johann's death as most likely alcoholic cardiomyopathy, though it could have been cirrhosis of the liver.
10. Wetzstein/Fischer, 132.
11. Thayer/Forbes, 1:136.
12. Anderson, vol. 1, no. 14.
13. Quoted in Kaufmann, "Architecture and Sculpture," 146.
14. Marek, *Beethoven*, 194.
15. Knight, *Beethoven*, 33; Erickson, "Vienna," 16.
16. Landon, *Beethoven*, 67.
17. Anderson, vol. 1, no. 12.
18. Gartenberg, *Vienna*, 69.
19. Aldrich, "Social Dancing," passim.
20. Solomon, *Beethoven*, 124.
21. Marek, *Beethoven*, 89.
22. Madame de Staël, quoted in Lockwood, *Beethoven: Music*, 77.
23. Quoted in Knight, *Beethoven*, 26–27.

24. Quoted in Solomon, *Beethoven*, 124.
25. Quoted in Landon, *Beethoven* unabridged, 52.
26. Solomon, *Beethoven*, 78.
27. Pestelli, *Age of Mozart and Beethoven*, 114.
28. Quoted in Biba, "Concert Life," 78.
29. Marek, *Beethoven*, 94. The statue of Schikaneder as Papageno remains today above the entrance of the Theater an der Wien.
30. Lockwood, *Beethoven: Music*, 74.
31. Landon, *Beethoven* unabridged, 52–53.
32. Geiringer, *Haydn*, 58 and 65; Raynor, *Social History*, 312.
33. Leopold Mozart, quoted in Scherer, *Quarter Notes*, 107.

10. Chains of Craftsmanship

1. Thayer/Forbes, 1:138.
2. DeNora, *Beethoven*, 96.
3. Copying music of other composers was a common way of studying in those days, as was demonstrated by J. S. Bach's copying and arranging of Vivaldi — which also handily produced scores to be used in performance. Among a great number of pieces, Beethoven twice copied out the contrapuntal development in Haydn's Symphony No. 99 (Walter, "Die biographischen Beziehungen," 116).
4. In various adaptations, the study of species counterpoint flourishes to this day in schools of music. For aspiring composers, it remains as difficult and as stimulating as ever.
5. Walter, "Die biographischen Beziehungen," 116.
6. Geiringer, *Haydn*, 121.
7. Ibid., 131.
8. Thayer/Forbes, 1:138.
9. B. Cooper, *Beethoven*, 44; Webster, "Falling-Out," 11–14. Cooper writes that it has not been determined who made the corrections on Beethoven's exercises, Haydn or somebody else, but most people assume the corrections are Haydn's. Later, Anton Schindler colluded with Schenk in the story, including forging entries about it in Beethoven's conversation books.
10. Walter, "Die biographischen Beziehungen," 116. Haydn did take a break from Eisenstadt in August; he and Beethoven may have gotten together then.
11. Solomon, *Beethoven*, 92.
12. Ibid., 89.
13. Anderson, *Mozart's Letters*, 169. One of the pianos in that duel was lent to Mozart by his friend Countess Thun, mother of Princess Christiane Lichnowsky.
14. Quoted in DeNora, *Beethoven*, 119–20. The Gelinek–Beethoven duel is generally agreed to have taken place in 1793, but the chronology of Gelinek's encounter is muddled in the elder Czerny's recall. He has Gelinek saying Beethoven was already a protégé of Karl Lichnowsky and had already studied with Johann Albrechtsberger. It's possible the duel took place later, but after 1793 it's hard to imagine Gelinek would not have known about Beethoven. Carl Czerny would have been told the story by his father years later; in 1793, the younger Czerny was only two.

15. Irmen, "Beethoven, Bach," 32. A French visitor, quoted in Landon, *Beethoven unabridged*, 68, notes his surprise to find that Lichnowsky, along with much of the high nobility in Austria, was sympathetic to the French Revolution.
16. Thayer/Forbes, 1:157.
17. Quoted in Marek, *Beethoven*, 107.
18. Irmen, "Beethoven, Bach," 32.
19. Wegeler/Ries, 33–34.
20. Landon, *Beethoven*, 46.
21. DeNora, *Beethoven*, 200n2.
22. Landon, *Beethoven* unabridged, 67.
23. Wegeler/Ries, 35–36.
24. Ibid., 32.
25. Thayer/Forbes, 1:220–22 and 262.
26. Irmen, "Beethoven, Bach," 40–41.
27. Solomon, *Beethoven*, 81.
28. Irmen, "Beethoven, Bach," 44.
29. Ibid., 40.
30. Thayer/Forbes, 1:157.
31. Albrecht, vol. 1, no. 18.
32. Anderson, vol. 1, no. 7.
33. Ibid., no. 9.
34. Albrecht, vol. 1, no. 16. Which pieces Beethoven sent to Bonn are uncertain, and the Oboe Concerto has not survived. The "Parthie" was probably the minor Wind Octet eventually published as op. 103. Haydn's citing the opinion of "connoisseurs and nonconnoisseurs" reflects the attitude of his time, that music should be written to appeal to all levels of taste and knowledge.
35. Albrecht, vol. 1, no. 17.
36. This point is made in Webster, "Falling-Out," 22. The gist of that article is that there is no reliable evidence for any significant break between Haydn and Beethoven, though Webster concedes that there was unquestionably tension and rivalry between them.
37. B. Cooper, *Beethoven*, 52. Beethoven jotted down this comment, which may have come from Haydn.
38. Ibid., 50.
39. Ibid., 50–51.
40. Kirkendale, "Great Fugue," 17. Kirkendale compares Beethoven's *Grosse Fuge* to Bach's *Art of Fugue*, which is also a compendium of fugal devices, such as combining a fugue subject with its mirror image and with faster and slower forms of itself.
41. Solomon, *Beethoven*, 98.
42. Anderson, vol. 1, no. 4.
43. B. Cooper, *Beethoven*, 49.
44. Quoted in ibid., 51.

11. Generalissimo

1. When I say Beethoven intended to write the first important piano "repertoire," I am using a modern conception. As I have noted before, the idea of a standing reper-

toire was only beginning to take shape in Beethoven's lifetime. But he would have been aware of a body of work in each of the various media by Haydn and Mozart.

2. Johnson, "Decisive Years," 17.
3. Wyn Jones, *Life of Beethoven*, 38.
4. Formed in 1792, the First Coalition against France included most of the German states, some Italian territories, Britain, Spain, and the Netherlands.
5. Thayer/Forbes, 1:168.
6. Anderson, vol. 1, no. 10. In 1793, Simrock had published Beethoven's Bonn-written variations on a theme from Dittersdorf's *Das rote Käppchen* (Little Red Riding Hood). In his spring 1794 letter, Beethoven chides him for sloppy proofreading and for giving him only one free copy.
7. Wegeler/Ries, 32. They say it was *sul G* (on the G string), but in the score it's *sul C*.
8. Solomon, *Beethoven*, 106.
9. Landon, *Beethoven*, 46.
10. Solomon, *Late Beethoven*, 136.
11. Knight, *Beethoven*, 33.
12. Anderson, vol. 1, no. 12.
13. Wetzstein/Fischer, 123nn453, 455.
14. Gutzmer, *Chronik der Stadt Bonn*, 83–87.
15. "Französische Ouvertüre," 17. The only recorded communication between Beethoven and Neefe after Beethoven left Bonn is the letter of thanks Beethoven wrote shortly after leaving.
16. Clive, *Beethoven and His World*, 389.
17. Wegeler/Ries, 24–25.
18. Anderson, vol. 1, no. 15.
19. B. Cooper, *Beethoven*, 53.
20. Senner, *Critical Reception*, vol. 2, no. 171n2.
21. Wyn Jones, *Symphony*, 43–44, 51, 58.
22. Clive, *Beethoven and His World*, 212–13.
23. Landon, *Beethoven*, 94.
24. Solomon, *Beethoven*, 86.
25. Thayer/Forbes, 1:156.
26. Wegeler/Ries, 38. Beethoven had been planning and sketching the C Major Concerto before the day he wrote out the score.
27. Thayer/Forbes, 1:175.
28. At some point, Beethoven wrote out cadenzas for the Mozart D Minor Concerto.
29. Landon, *Beethoven*, 44.
30. That concertos were practical items is the gist of Plantinga's view of the piano concertos in *Beethoven's Concertos*.
31. Ibid., 67. The early versions of the B-flat Concerto are lost, but the rondo that appeared as WoO 6 seems to have been the original finale (61).
32. The second theme of the B-flat Concerto's first movement is in D-flat, then G-flat in the recap; in the C Major, the second theme is in E-flat, and the recap drifts briefly into A-flat. So in both cases Beethoven surrounds the tonic of the work with flat submediant keys—prophetic of his later interest in mediant relationships.
33. Landon, *Beethoven* unabridged, 64–65.
34. B. Cooper, *Beethoven*, 55–56; Wyn Jones, *Life of Beethoven*, 43–44. Various sources cite a different sum as Beethoven's profit on op. 1.

35. Wegeler/Ries, 74. Ferdinand Ries was not yet in Vienna when the op. 1 Trios were first played and published, and his memoir was written decades later. As a result, it's not clear when Haydn actually first heard the trios — in earlier versions before he left for England, or the published versions after he returned. (At some point he may well have critiqued one or more of the trios as Beethoven worked on them.) Thus it's also unclear when Haydn gave Beethoven the advice about holding back the C Minor. Ries would have heard the story from Beethoven (not a particularly reliable source). Afterward, Ries asked Haydn personally about the matter. Haydn replied that "he had not imagined that this trio would be so quickly and easily understood nor so favorably received by the public."
36. Thayer/Forbes, 1:139.
37. Douglas Johnson, in "Decisive Years": "What the new works show . . . is a conflict between ambitious compositional technique . . . and not altogether suitable material, some of it borrowed from earlier works and some of it beefed up to approximate symphonic proportions" (26).
38. Solomon, *Beethoven*, 94.
39. An introduction to a work, especially a long and slow introduction to a first-movement Allegro, is a kind of exception to my rule that the beginning lays out the leading ideas of a piece, because a long, slow introduction is usually not the real *Thema*. Instead, the introduction tends, one way or another, to suggest the leading theme or themes of the following Allegro, as if it were the seedbed of the leading ideas. The theme following the introduction is treated in practice as *das Thema*. As for *das Thema* in music, the eighteenth- and nineteenth-century theorist H. C. Koch wrote, "Just as in speech the principal idea, or theme, provides the essential content of the same, and must contain the material for the development of principal and subsidiary ideas, so it is in music, with respect to the modifying of an emotion that is possible through the principal subject, and just as an orator moves on from his principal subject to subsidiary subjects, antitheses, dissections etc. . . . so the composer will act in the same manner in the treatment of a principal subject" (quoted in Dahlhaus, *Ludwig van Beethoven*, 121).
40. At various speeds and in various forms, the E-flat Trio's arpeggio motif turns up in Alberti-like figures through the first movement, in the B theme of movement 2, in the end of the A theme and the trio section of the scherzo, and in the finale from the main theme on.
41. From m. 299 of the finale, Beethoven provides, perhaps with tongue in cheek, a précis of his short–short–long rhythmic motif and, for that matter, his way of handling rhythmic motifs: first we hear it in quarters, then diminished in eighths, then in sixteenths. Then he neatly links the motif to the wry two-eighth-octave hiccup that opens the main theme.
42. The beginning of the slow movement takes a detour to the subdominant, just as the first movement did. Here Beethoven makes a recurring motif out of a modulation — but then, he eventually makes any recurring element a motif, including rests and single pitches.
43. Already in the C Minor Trio, Beethoven can wield the harmonic effect known as the "Neapolitan sixth" (N6) in dazzling ways. It feels not just like a fresh color in the harmony but like something breathtaking, almost vertiginous.
44. In the C Minor Trio, the tritone first shows up in the top piano line in mm. 7 and 9, followed by the violin solo emphasizing the same C–F-sharp tritone. Most of

the tritones in the trio resolve normally, but there is an unusual interest in them throughout. On the third page, all three instruments come to a weird, *pianissimo* pause on E-flat–A, which finally and furiously resolves *fortissimo*. Meanwhile, I think the first movement demonstrates that one of the ear-dazzling effects of the N6 chord is that its root forms a tritone with the dominant note to which it resolves. So, the Neapolitans in the C Minor Trio are another manifestation of the tritone motif.

45. Solomon, *Beethoven*, 101.

12. Virtuoso

1. Thayer/Forbes, 1:177; Landon, *Beethoven*, 49. The dances are WoO 7–8. Also this year, Beethoven wrote two other sets of six minuets. In *Beethoven*, 60, Barry Cooper details the striking sequence of tonalities in Beethoven's pension-fund-ball dances, the keys forming a chain of descending thirds and upward fourths, and compares them to the similar, if less exploratory, sequence in Haydn's dances for the 1792 ball. This is another case of Beethoven taking a model and elaborating on it.

2. Landon, *Beethoven*, 49. The headline dances for the November balls were by Franz Süssmayer, a prominent Mozart pupil best known for completing Mozart's unfinished Requiem.

3. Thayer/Forbes, 1:180–81.

4. Braubach, "Von den Menschen," 73.

5. Anderson, vol. 1, no. 16.

6. B. Cooper, *Beethoven*, 63–64. There is little documentation of these concerts or how they were received. Countess Clary was a well-known amateur singer.

7. The difficulties of *Ah! perfido* for the singer, probably coming no more from expressive intentions than from Beethoven's lack of experience writing for voice, are so fierce that there is no surprise in the report that one soprano "almost suffered a heart attack" from stage fright during the piece (Scherman and Biancolli, 367).

8. Thayer/Forbes, 1:183.

9. Important generating motifs of the F Minor Sonata include three elements of the beginning: the sixth from C to A-flat of the "rocket" motif (spread through two octaves), the turn figure of m. 2, and the first left-hand "&-2-&" rhythm. In mm. 7–8, the sixth motif is filled in to make a descending-sixth pattern that Kenneth Drake (*Beethoven Sonatas*, 88) calls the leading thematic idea in the sonata. Drake's examples showing how the descending-sixth idea is used are an excellent summary of the way Beethoven develops a motif: sometimes putting it on the surface, sometimes decorating it, sometimes making it a scaffolding on which to build a phrase or a new theme. Drake does not mention the main rhythmic motif (&-2-&) of the F Minor, but by and large nobody mentions Beethoven's steady use of rhythmic motifs (or Haydn's, or Mozart's).

10. The second theme of the A Major provides a good demonstration of the subtlety and discipline of Beethoven's handling of rhythmic motifs. The first gesture in the movement establishes the basic rhythmic idea, dotted rhythms creating *upbeats:* short upbeats like the beginning eighth, which is immediately decorated into a four-thirty-seconds upbeat, and in m. 11 extended into a three-eighths upbeat. In m. 58, the beginning of the second theme, the articulation implies a dotted quarter and then an eighth upbeat; two bars later, that idea is diminished into a dotted eighth

and two thirty-seconds; the articulation of mm. 60 and 61 implies a dotted half and quarter. In other words, the second theme is saturated with one dotted rhythmic figure expressed in three speeds. The main theme of the scherzo features a four-sixteenths upbeat; the main theme of the finale starts with a four-beat upbeat to the second bar. This kind of meticulous thematic work, in which an idea is expressed in a constant variety of ways both overt and covert, is common in Beethoven, even in the early opuses. He did not invent this kind of thematic work, but as with all his models, Beethoven took up ideas from the past and broadened and intensified them.

11. The rising fourth of bar 2 is an important motif in the Sonata in C Major, but the subtlest motif from the beginning is the implied turn figure D–E–F–E–(D) in the upper voice. It becomes a real turn in the beginning of the second theme, in m. 27, and starts the main theme of both middle movements. (A motif will routinely be inverted and/or retrograded, as in the second- and third-movement themes.) Spread out over two octaves, the opening theme of movement 1 is the scaffolding on which the scampering theme of the finale is constructed.

12. Skowroneck, *Beethoven the Pianist,* 68.

13. Anderson, vol. 1, no. 17. Johann Streicher was from childhood a friend of Schiller's, and would have spoken of him to Beethoven.

14. Ibid., no. 18. Note 4 identifies the young pianist as a Fräulein von Kissov, the trio movement she played probably the Adagio cantabile of op. 1, no. 1. Note 6 points out that, so far in letters, Beethoven uses both the terms *fortepiano* and *Klavier* referring to the instrument. Later he tended to use *Klavier,* but occasionally *Piano.*

15. While Beethoven was perennially dissatisfied with the pianos of his day, he also composed skillfully and idiomatically for them. A prime example is the first movement of the *Moonlight* Sonata, which works beautifully on period pianos but on modern instruments can't be played as written, with the sustain pedal held down throughout, because modern instruments sustain notes much longer.

16. Gutman, *Mozart,* 695. Mozart's tour of 1789 was his longest separation from his wife, Constanze. It was during the trip that he wrote the famous yearning and graphic letters to his wife back home. There was eventually a break between Mozart and Lichnowsky, who two years later sued Mozart over a loan made during the trip.

17. Thayer/Forbes, 1:187.

18. Ibid., 1:185.

19. In the next decade, Jean-Louis Duport would publish what became one of the most influential cello methods of the time, showing influences of the French school and using a new fingering system.

20. Landon, *Beethoven* unabridged, 91.

21. The Berlin stay is described in Thayer/Forbes, 1:184–87.

22. Kinderman, in *Beethoven,* 45, calls the introduction of the G Major prophetic of the beginning of the *Pathétique* and of *La Malinconia* in op. 18, no. 6.

23. Anderson, vol. 1, no. 19.

24. Wegeler/Ries, 156.

25. The full Schönfeld article is in Sisman, *Haydn.* History would not agree in the least with Schönfeld's skepticism about Haydn's late symphonies. That he called the symphonies Haydn's greatest works shows the current status of the genre.

26. Albrecht, vol. 1, no. 22.

27. Thayer/Forbes, 1:190.

28. Wegeler/Ries, 107–8.

29. B. Cooper (*Beethoven*, 60) points out how little *Adelaide* resembles other lieder of the time.
30. Anderson, vol. 1, no. 40. Other composers set "Adelaide," but in 1811, Matthisson belatedly named Beethoven's as his favorite. Schubert did several Matthisson settings. To later sensibilities, the poem "Adelaide" would seem sentimental and dated, but Matthisson's admirers of the time included Friedrich Schiller.
31. Wegeler/Ries, 42–43.
32. Douël, "Beethoven's 'Adelaide,'" 210–13.
33. Knight, *Beethoven*, 41.
34. Stendhal, quoted in ibid., 38.
35. Knight, *Beethoven*, 38–43.
36. Gutzmer, *Chronik der Stadt Bonn*, 87.
37. Blanning, *Pursuit of Glory*, 636.
38. Knight, *Beethoven*, 43.
39. Herriot, *Life and Times*, 68–70.
40. Nicholls, *Napoleon*, 24. Napoleon approved when, in 1810, Bernadotte was given virtual rule of Sweden, but later Bernadotte joined the coalition against Napoleon. In 1818, he succeeded to the thrones of Sweden and Norway as King Carl XIV and had a long and successful reign.
41. Knight, *Beethoven*, 45.
42. Broyles, *Beethoven*, 125.
43. Donakowski, *Muse*, 46–59.

13. Fate's Hammer

1. The darting, light-footed, entirely delightful finale of the op. 9, no. 1 Trio seems to prophesy the style of Mendelssohn's "fairy scherzos" decades later.
2. Solomon, *Beethoven*, 86.
3. Lockwood, *Beethoven: Music*, 125–27. The first two extant sketchbooks are known as Grasnick 1 and 2.
4. From an Amenda memoir quoted in Thayer/Forbes, 1:224–25.
5. Albrecht, vol. 1, no. 31.
6. Anderson, vol. 1, no. 30.
7. At this point Beethoven was not a beginner at writing for violin and piano. In his teens he had written or sketched a sonata and a rondo, and in Vienna finished the "Se vuol ballare" Variations as a duo. The Rondo survives as WoO 41, and the Variations are WoO 40.
8. Brandenburg, "Beethoven's Op. 12," 19–20.
9. C-flat major is a quite peculiar key to find oneself in, since it is enharmonically the same as the common B major. At the end of the development of no. 3, it is explained as a transition back to the recap: the C-flat becomes the root of a German sixth leading to V in E-flat.
10. Brandenburg, "Beethoven's Op. 12," 19. There is no specific record of what Beethoven and Schuppanzigh played in their March program, but op. 12 is the most likely. This concert was a benefit for Mozart's admired singer Josefa Duschek, for whom Beethoven had written *Ah! perfido*.
11. Perhaps the most famous example of descending half steps representing grief is the ostinato bass line in the "Crucifixus" of Bach's B Minor Mass.

12. To modern ears the kind of emotionalism heard in the *Pathétique* seems familiar, if not overfamiliar, on the border between drama and melodrama. Some find its effect more "rhetorical" than "real." If so, in its time it was a new kind of rhetoric. For all the traditional elements, to the ears of the late eighteenth century the piece seemed revolutionary.

13. Kinderman, "Piano Music," 115.

14. In recognition of the maturity of the "First Period" works, which have no apprentice pieces at all, Lewis Lockwood aptly calls this period the First Maturity. I am using the terms "New Path" and "full maturity" for the old "Second (or Heroic) Period," and generally am not using the old three-period terminology, because Beethoven and his time were not aware of it. He was aware, however, that around 1801–2 he was striking out on a new path, because he said so. When my subject supplies an apt term, I use it.

15. There is a long-standing debate about whether or not the exposition repeat in the first movement of the *Pathétique* includes the introduction.

16. Voices, strings, winds, and brass instruments playing without keyboard do not normally use equal temperament or anything other than their ears. A good violinist, for example, instinctively tunes each sonority individually, often without any rationalized system. That is why a string quartet can be more satisfyingly in tune than a piano. There have been myriad keyboard-tuning systems over the centuries. Recordings of works in traditional tunings have appeared, but not many; that remains a fertile field for scholarship and performance.

17. See Swafford, "Wolf at Our Heels."

18. Duffin points out (*Equal Temperament,* 87) that by 1818, equal temperament was dominant in keyboard and chamber music, but Beethoven was deaf by then and in his inner ear probably retained what he had grown up with, which was likely extended meantone temperaments. But he was vitally involved in his interpretation of the character of keys, which inevitably concerns tuning: claiming keys have individual characters on an equal-tempered keyboard makes no real sense. Meanwhile, for all the impact of equal temperament (ET) on the nineteenth century, mathematically correct ET was actually not attained until the early twentieth century. As Duffin and others note, tuners of the nineteenth century *thought* they were tuning equally, but they were actually shading toward well-temperament. As for Beethoven's favored tuning, there is no record of his talking about tuning at all.

19. Steblin, *History of Key Characteristics,* 78, quoting Abraham Peter Schulz, a student of leading theorist Johann Philipp Kirnberger.

20. Steblin, *History of Key Characteristics,* 118 (quoting Schubart).

21. Respectively, ibid., 105 (quoting Francesco Galeazzi), 109 (quoting Ribcock).

22. Ibid., 104–5 (quoting Galeazzi).

23. Compare Galeazzi's characterizations of the keys to, respectively, the First Symphony in C Major; most Beethoven pieces in C minor; the slow movement of op. 10, no. 3 in D Minor; the *Archduke* Trio in B-flat Major; the op. 14, no. 2 Sonata in E Major; most of his pieces in E-flat major; and the Seventh Symphony in A Major. All those are close to Galeazzi's characterizations, and plenty of other examples could be cited. In contrast, the *Waldstein* Sonata seems a deliberate essay in getting away from the usual character of C major, turning it in a more colorful and exciting direction than its traditional reputation would suggest.

24. Schulz, quoted in Steblin, *History of Key Characteristics,* 79.

25. Galeazzi, quoted in ibid., 105.

26. Schubart, quoted in ibid., 116.

27. Galeazzi, quoted in ibid., 104. In regard to Bach's expressive associations of keys in the *WTC,* it is worth noting that some of those pieces were first written in other keys and transposed to fit the scheme of the work.

28. Thayer/Forbes, 1:149.

29. Landon, *Beethoven* unabridged, 70–71.

30. Solomon, *Beethoven,* 160. This was a Beethoven memory of 1815 and was reported to Thayer long after by a second person, so it should be taken with due caution. But the details of the event are convincingly specific, and Beethoven would likely have had a vivid memory of the first time his hearing problems struck him. My surmise as to the year his hearing problems first appeared comes from his first recorded mention of it, in a letter to Franz Wegeler of June 1801 (Anderson, vol. 1, no. 51), where he says it happened three years before. Of the few extant letters from that year, 1798, the earlier ones are notably gay in tone (this was the time of Zmeskall as "Baron Muckcart-driver"). Letters later that year are sober and practically humorless. In fact, one of late 1798 to Zmeskall is a complaint over a misunderstanding that ends, "It is difficult for a friendship to thrive under such conditions" (Anderson, vol. 1, no. 31). The tone of that note is uniquely bristly among his surviving notes to Zmeskall. To the degree that notes to Zmeskall are a rough barometer of Beethoven's state of mind, it is significant that it is not until late 1802 that the notes return to their lighthearted and teasing tone: "sweetest and most extraordinary Count!" (Anderson, vol. 1, no. 65). It would be surprising if Beethoven's anxiety and depression over his hearing did not affect his letters. This evidence suggests it did, and implies a time of later 1798 when his hearing was first stricken.

31. Mai, *Diagnosing Genius,* 17.

32. Wenzel Johann Tomaschek, quoted in Thayer/Forbes, 1:207–8.

33. Beethoven, *Ein Skizzenbuch,* 1:8–9.

34. Johnson, Tyson, and Winter, *Beethoven Sketchbooks,* 1:87.

35. Senner, *Critical Reception,* vol. 1, no. 5. Senner (vol. 1, no. 3) calls the *AMZ* "the primogenitor of modern music criticism."

36. Tomaschek, quoted in DeNora, *Beethoven,* 154.

37. DeNora, "Piano Duel," 263–66; Clive, *Beethoven and His World,* 401.

38. Senner, *Critical Reception,* vol. 1, no. 4.

39. Sonneck, *Beethoven,* 36–37.

40. Charles Rosen, in *Classical Style:* the Classical style was "in its origins, basically a comic one . . . the pacing of classical rhythm is the pacing of comic opera, its phrasing is the phrasing of dance music, and its large structures are these phrases dramatized" (96).

41. Heinrich Christoph Koch, quoted in Jones, *Beethoven,* 57.

42. Mozart, quoted in Lockwood, *Beethoven: Music,* 169–70. This letter of Mozart's was probably intended to reassure his father, who always worried that his son was getting too arcane. It should not be taken for the whole of Mozart's attitude toward his work.

43. Senner, *Critical Reception,* vol. 1, no. 65.

44. Brandenburg, "Beethoven's Op. 12," 21.

45. Geiringer, *Haydn,* 355.

46. Landon, *Beethoven,* 97–98.

47. Albrecht, vol. 1, no. 29.
48. Thayer/Forbes, 1:209.
49. Ibid., 1:210.
50. Senner, *Critical Reception,* vol. 1, no. 63.
51. Ibid., no. 67. Oddly, in his review of the *Pathétique* the *AMZ* critic complains about a "reminiscence" in the third movement but can't figure out what it is. He is correct: the main theme of the rondo is based on the second theme of the first movement. The critic seems to feel that too overt a resemblance of themes between movements is a fault.
52. Czerny's account is in Thayer/Forbes, 1:225–28. Czerny taught Liszt and also taught Leschetizky, who taught Artur Schnabel, who as one of the premiere Beethoven pianists of his generation played and recorded in the first half of the twentieth century. Today Czerny is mainly known for his ubiquitous finger-training exercises, which were surely influenced by Beethoven's teaching.
53. Anderson, vol. 1, nos. 33–34. The current German edition of the complete letters speculates that the first letter may have been to Ignaz Schuppanzigh (because of the "he" form that Beethoven used with Schuppanzigh) and has no suggested recipient for the second, addressed as "Natzerl." Anderson assumes that to be a familiar diminutive for Ignaz, which is not Hummel's name. But the letter also uses the familiar *du,* "thou," and Beethoven did not appear to be on *du* terms with any of his friends named Ignaz. Sticking to the traditional addressee for both notes, I have used the form "'Nazy,'" another diminutive of Ignaz, which could be a pet name.
54. Clive, *Beethoven and His World,* 94. Dragonetti was associated with Beethoven's music for the rest of his life. He played in Beethoven's concert of December 1813 and years later played the finale bass recitatives of the Ninth Symphony as a solo in London performances. He used a three-stringed instrument, tuned A–D–G.
55. *Grove Music Online,* s.v. "Dragonetti, Domenico."

14. The Good, the Beautiful, and the Melancholy

1. Thayer/Forbes, 1:255. There is a long-standing debate about whether Beethoven played Concerto No. 1 or No. 2 in his 1800 concert. In *Beethoven,* 90, Barry Cooper notes that just before the concert, he copied out a new score of No. 1 in C Major, with accumulated revisions, so that suggests it was the one performed.
2. Senner, *Critical Reception,* vol. 1, nos. 162–63.
3. Anderson, vol. 1, no. 57.
4. Ibid., no. 50.
5. B. Cooper, *Beethoven,* 87.
6. *Grove Music Online,* s.v. "Punto, Giovanni." The Baroque style of extreme high horn and trumpet playing, which in Bach's day made melodic writing possible on those valveless instruments, had died out by the later eighteenth century.
7. Thayer/Forbes, 1:256–57.
8. Clive, *Beethoven and His World,* 273.
9. Landon, *Beethoven* unabridged, 163.
10. The account of Beethoven's encounters with Steibelt is in Wegeler/Ries, 70–71. Since the Trio is op. 11, Wegeler's memory may be faulty, or the encounters may have happened earlier.
11. Landon, *Beethoven* unabridged, 163.

12. Wegeler/Ries, 87–88.

13. Czerny, quoted in Drake, *Beethoven Sonatas,* 127: "One often finds in Beethoven's works that he bases the structure of his piece on single, seemingly unimportant notes, and insofar as one brings out these notes (as he himself used to do) one gives the whole piece proper color and unity." I have followed that principle here, though I differ with Czerny's "single" motif; I think there are several leading ideas in a given work.

14. Thayer/Forbes, 1:257.

15. Anderson, vol. 1, no. 40.

16. B. Cooper, *Beethoven,* 97.

17. Winter and Martin, *Beethoven Quartet Companion,* 10. Today Beethoven's quartet of instruments resides in a case at the Beethovenhaus, Bonn.

18. Kerman, *Beethoven Quartets,* 10.

19. Wyn Jones, *Life of Beethoven,* 51.

20. Winter and Martin, *Beethoven Quartet Companion,* 10; Thayer/Forbes, 1:262.

21. Anderson, vol. 1, no. 53.

22. Heartz, *Mozart,* 622. Griffiths, *String Quartet,* 81, cites Landon saying that Haydn may have failed to complete his Lobkowitz set of quartets because he did not want to compete with Beethoven. I suppose that's possible, but I think exhaustion and incipient senility were Haydn's main problems. He would not have found Beethoven a threat if he had had his full faculties. More likely, as he did with Mozart, he would have absorbed some of Beethoven's ideas into his own work.

23. Lockwood, *Beethoven: Music,* 162.

24. Heartz, *Mozart,* 749.

25. When I say that Beethoven in the *Pathétique* and here and there in other early opuses already had much of his voice but had not yet settled into it, or perhaps had not fully understood it, I'm thinking of artists in general, who do not necessarily have a eureka moment when they find their voice. Many of the larger issues of one's own creativity are seen through a glass darkly. They seem obvious only in retrospect, from the outside. In the same way, it is easy for a skilled mimic to imitate the style of distinctive artists like, say, Frost or Matisse or Beethoven. It was anything but easy for those men to create, because they were not imitating themselves but rather trying to do something fresh.

26. Kerman, *Beethoven Quartets,* 30.

27. Simpson, "Chamber Music," 250. In the first drafts, the opening movement, featuring the same motif, was actually in 4/4, not 3/4.

28. Kerman, *Beethoven Quartets,* 32. An example of a kind of thematic relationship that is not motivic or exactly tonal, which I call *gestural,* is seen in each of the movements' opening themes in the F-major quartet. In the beginning, after repeating his turn figure several times, starting on F, in the second line he climbs the figure upward by steps: F–G–A. The opening themes of the other three movements all have figures climbing by step. Meanwhile, all those movements start with some transformation of the opening turn motif.

29. Continuing his experiments with various kinds of relationships among themes beyond the usual motivic snippets, with the first chord in m. 3 of the D Major Quartet, Beethoven sets up the idea of strong-beat suspensions or appoggiaturas, especially 4–3 suspensions, as a leading motif of no. 3. This is another case of a gestural connection of themes.

30. Quartet No. 4 in C Minor is an example of what I call "ideas not up to the level of the craftsmanship" here and there in op. 18. Joseph Kerman writes, "The C-minor first movement is more crudely written than anything in the other Op. 18 Quartets" (*Beethoven Quartets,* 68). I abstain from voting on that question, but it's not one of his more striking movements. Yet here are the beginnings of ideas that will bear fruit in the Fifth Symphony in C Minor: the main motif in the quartet seems to be less the pitches or intervals of the beginning than the *shape* of the figure at the end of m. 1: C–E-flat–D, that is, leap up and step down. Expanded, that becomes the figure of the second phrase in m. 5, which in turn becomes the second theme in m. 34. By the bottom of the first page, the shape and its rhythm are being variously retrograded and diminished. The leading rhythmic motif is the &-2-&-1 of the first two bars — the same leading rhythmic motif as in the Fifth Symphony and other works.

31. Specifically in regard to the first movement of the C Minor, I mean what seems to my ear a too-abrupt transition to the second theme in m. 33 and an awkward harmonic jump from E-flat major to G minor in the second ending of the exposition.

32. Schiedermair, 152–53.

33. In *Beethoven Quartets,* Joseph Kerman finds La Malinconia interesting but in the end not entirely successful: "The mood of *La Malinconia* does not really seem to approach melancholy" (76). I don't completely disagree — Beethoven would advance in portraying emotion, as in all else — but I see the movement in the context of the whole, which adds to its impact. I also think that among other things Beethoven was looking (in contrast to the *Pathétique*) for an original way of depicting pathos and melancholy, one with no traditional musical topics representing sorrow. In that respect, the movement is a success.

34. Clive, *Beethoven and His World,* 167. Hoffmeister's publishing house would end up an acquisition of the still-extant C. F. Peters. As Wyn Jones details in *Symphony,* 30–31, Hoffmeister had great ambitions to publish symphonies in Vienna but gave them up because of lack of interest. By the time he sold out, in 1806, Beethoven's First was the only symphony he had published.

35. Anderson, vol. 1, no. 41. In the letter, in regard to all the instruments being obbligato (required) in the Septet, Beethoven says in passing, "As a matter of fact, I came into this world with an obbligato accompaniment." In regard to that sentence, Anderson notes an old story that Beethoven was born with a caul.

36. Charles Rosen (*Beethoven's Piano Sonatas,* 149) calls op. 22 Beethoven's "farewell to the 18th century" in the sonatas.

37. Scherer, *Quarter Notes,* 53–63.

38. Tyson, "Notes," 441–42.

39. Scherer, *Quarter Notes,* 52.

40. Arnold and Fortune, *Beethoven Reader,* 468.

41. Scherer, *Quarter Notes,* 170.

42. Anderson, vol. 1, no. 51.

43. Thayer/Forbes, 1:269.

44. See Solomon, "Beethoven's 'Magazin der Kunst.'"

45. Anderson, vol. 1, no. 44. Note that Beethoven refuses to write the whole word *Rezensenten,* "reviewers," because he is furious at them. This is another time when he cannot bring himself to write a name or even a word representing something or someone he is angry at.

46. Sipe, *Beethoven,* 12.

47. Clive, *Beethoven and His World,* 379–81.

48. Sipe, *Beethoven,* 13.

49. Schiller, *Aesthetic Education,* xvii.

50. Ibid., xv.

51. Ibid., 9.

52. This is from the later and more detailed description of the story in the appendix of Sipe, *Beethoven,* 118. No. 9, the murderous dance of Melpomene, begins with a quasi-recitative, followed by operatic *furioso* music. Thalia makes her deus-ex-machina entrance to a lilting pastoral tune.

53. Aldrich, "Social Dancing," 128. She notes that the democratic associations of the *englische* were enough to drive it out of favor in countries with a more rigid class structure than existed in Vienna.

54. Schiller, *Aesthetic Education,* 300, in the notes for letter 17. This letter was addressed to Schiller's close friend and confidant the former Illuminatus C. G. Körner, who had been an influence on "An die Freude."

55. Thayer/Forbes, 1:193.

15. The New Path

1. Landon, *Beethoven,* 80.

2. Senner, *Critical Reception,* vol. 1, nos. 215–16.

3. Landon, *Beethoven,* 79.

4. Geiringer, *Haydn,* 172. Haydn wrote in a letter, "This whole passage [in *The Seasons*] imitating a frog has not flowed from my pen. I was forced [by van Swieten] to write down this Frenchified trash."

5. Ibid., 179.

6. Anderson, vol. 1, no. 48.

7. Senner, *Critical Reception,* vol. 1, no. 174.

8. See Lockwood, "On the Beautiful."

9. What I'm calling the recapitulation on the "wrong" theme, on a V6 chord, in the first movement of op. 23 (after a hold) could also be considered a false recapitulation. The real one would then arrive later with the first theme, *fortissimo.* But then we'd have to declare a false recapitulation in the tonic key, which seems dubious. I think the real point is an ambiguous recapitulation that flows out of the development, and an experiment with the formal model, which is true, to some degree, of the whole sonata. The slow movement is an unusual full-scale sonata form with repeat of the exposition, the form of the last movement a complicated rondo. In other words, op. 23 is characterized by experiments with form throughout. That quality may be in response to a program of some sort, but here, as most of the time, Beethoven kept his programs to himself.

10. Anderson, vol. 1, no. 51.

11. Thayer/Forbes, 1:293–94.

12. Clive, *Beethoven and His World,* 284–85.

13. Czerny, *Proper Performance,* 9, 13.

14. Anderson, vol. 1, no. 51. Paragraph divisions added.

15. Ibid., no. 53.

16. Ibid., no. 54.

17. Landon, *Beethoven,* 80.

18. Landon, *Beethoven* unabridged, 137.

19. Landon, *Beethoven*, 82.

20. Thayer/Forbes, 1:292.

21. Quoted in Tyson, "New Letter," 9–10.

22. Czerny memoir, in B. Cooper, *Beethoven Compendium*, 17. Czerny puts the quote in 1803, but Lockwood corrects it to 1802, the year of op. 31. Common wisdom has it that the first unequivocal works on the New Path are the piano sonatas of op. 31, especially no. 2, misnamed *The Tempest*. I don't essentially disagree with that, but I feel that the first steps started in op. 26, which has the mature Beethoven voice. It is not certain when he announced the New Path to Krumpholz; it could have been before, during, or after the opp. 26–28 Sonatas of 1801. The New Path is, of course, what a later time would call the Second or Heroic Period, named for the *Eroica*. As is often noted, however, the music of the Second Period is not all in the heroic vein, and the symphony is not the first sign of his full maturity.

23. Drake, *Beethoven Sonatas*, 121–22.

24. Ironically, an orchestration of the op. 26 *Funeral March* was heard at Beethoven's funeral. He was already identified with the heroic images in his own music.

25. Lockwood, *Beethoven: Music*, 134–35.

26. Senner, *Critical Reception*, vol. 1, nos. 177–78n7.

27. If the atmosphere of the *Moonlight* Sonata was unique in its time, there is at least one likely precedent: the bubbling C Major Prelude of *The Well-Tempered Clavier*.

28. Modern pianos, with their longer sustain, cannot play with the pedal down throughout the first movement of the *Moonlight*. The effect has to be approximated. I've found that hearing the piece on a period piano, performed as directed, can be a stunning experience. Because of the short sustain, the overlap is subtle and beautiful. The main overlap on period pianos is in the longer-sustaining bass. See Swafford, "In Search."

29. Czerny, cited in Arnold and Fortune, *Beethoven Reader*, 109.

30. B. Cooper, *Creative Process*, 44.

31. The String Quintet in C Major is one of the works in the early opuses that to a modern ear, if not strongly "Beethovenian" in voice, is at the same time not particularly Mozartian or eighteenth-century either. From the perspective of the present, the most startling thing about it is how much the opening and a lot else about it sound like Brahms via Schubert. Besides the flowing theme and warm scoring, the opening resembles Brahms in its quick midphrase modulations. The piece is exceptionally unified in patterns of tonality and in its playful treatment of both key and form. The first movement, for example, has an unusual return to the opening theme, varied, at the end of the exposition; the effect is of an ABA exposition. The modulations throughout seem to turn mainly on the presence of a "sore" C-sharp/D-flat, and, as is usually the case in such situations, C-sharp is the first accidental in the piece. The Quintet is surely one of the most interesting of Beethoven's lesser-known works, compromised, to my ear, only by some themes on the bland side.

32. B. Cooper, *Beethoven*, 114.

33. Charles Burney, quoted in Lockwood, *Beethoven: Music*, 173.

34. Thayer/Forbes, 1:303.

35. Anderson, vol. 1, no. 58.

36. Albrecht, vol. 1, no. 38.

37. Anderson, vol. 1, no. 59.

38. Thayer/Forbes, 1:302.

39. Wegeler/Ries, 76–77 notes.

40. Thayer/Forbes, 1:318.

41. The C-sharp grace note at the beginning of the G Major Violin Sonata that I call the "hiccup" is echoed in the comical C-sharp grace notes in the theme of the finale. The C-sharps in the finale rondo theme also give it a bit of a Lydian feel.

42. Anton Schindler's report that Beethoven snapped, "Read Shakespeare's *Tempest!*" when asked what the D Minor Sonata was "about" can no more be relied on than anything else Schindler says. Which is to say that it might actually be true, but absent other evidence there is no way to know. Even if the story *is* true, it is by no means certain whether Beethoven was being ironic or serious. I think the efforts by Romain Rolland and others to connect this sonata to the play don't add up.

43. For a tour of contrasting theories on the form of *The Tempest,* see Jones, *Beethoven.* That Beethoven would make the idea of an arpeggio into a motif is characteristic of his drive to thematicize every element of music. He does the same here with the Neapolitan chord. Earlier in his music, as with most composers, N was a passing harmonic color. Now, it became a thematic element in some of his most fraught pieces. The exposition of the first movement of *The Tempest* climaxes on a hair-raising N chord folded into a chromatic-turn figure that is also a leading motif. If in theory the first theme proper is at m. 21, the reality is that the earlier Allegro passage sounds more like a theme than an introduction — so which is it? In the recapitulation, the first-theme section is elided and recomposed, further unsettling the expected formal outline. To repeat an earlier point: the driving and demonic quality of this work (Sturm und Drang, if you like) is amplified by compromising the formal model. For that reason, I submit that theoretical arguments over what the form of the movement "really" is miss the point. What the form really is, in this case, is intentionally, and expressively, ambiguous. Karl Dahlhaus: "The ambiguity should be perceived as an artistic factor — an attribute of the thing itself . . . The very contradictions of the form constitute its artistic character" (*Ludwig van Beethoven,* 170).

44. The warm opening chord of the E-flat Major is a ii 6/5, at that time considered a dissonance.

45. The nice thing about dancing a tarantella to keep from dying from the tarantula's bite was that it always worked, because the tarantula is not poisonous to humans.

46. The overall descending-third tonal progression of the op. 34 F Major Variations is foreshadowed in the opening phrase of the theme itself. The first chord change is to IV, prophesying the next two keys, D and B-flat. The following key, G, is the melodic goal of the first phrase, in bar four. By then the third bar has introduced an E-flat, the first accidental in the piece and the key of variation IV (the only one of the tonic notes in the piece not part of F major). So the keys of the theme itself descend in thirds.

47. The canonic variation 7 in the *Prometheus* Variations and their other echoes of Bach suggest that at this point Beethoven knew Bach's *Goldberg* Variations, which were already well known and much admired. Another point of resemblance is that Bach's and Beethoven's variations are both based on what would seem to be an insubstantial dance tune. The nostalgic appearance of the *englische* theme near

the end prophesies its similar but more impactful appearance near the end of the *Eroica*. Another *Eroica* prophecy is his extensive use of the three-note chromatic motif from the *Prometheus* bass as a melodic element.

48. Anderson, vol. 1, no. 62.
49. Ibid., no. 57.
50. Albrecht, vol. 1, no. 39.
51. Blanning, *Pursuit of Glory*, 348.
52. Nicholls, *Napoleon*, 62.

16. Oh, Fellow Men

1. Thayer/Forbes, 1:304–6. Paragraph divisions added.
2. What Beethoven was headed toward after the crisis embodied in the Heiligenstadt Testament was, of course, the *Eroica*. Long-standing common wisdom holds three things about the *Eroica* that I do not entirely subscribe to. One is that the Third Symphony is primarily about himself, his own heroism. As will be shown, it is about himself in part, but by no means entirely. Next, history has named his Second Period for the *Eroica* (though that is now understood to be dubious, since much of the Second Period music is not in his "heroic" style), so it is traditionally assumed that the Third Symphony inaugurated the Second Period. I think there is a grow-ing understanding that this period really started earlier, sometimes located at op. 31. Since I think the Second Period — here called the New Path — is more a matter of consolidation and intensification than of heroism, I've located its wellspring in the sonatas of opp. 26–28 and the next decisive step as op. 31. Finally, the Heiligen-stadt Testament is often assumed to have directly inspired or galvanized the *Eroica*. There is no way fully to know, but I doubt it. I think Beethoven was headed for the *Eroica* before his crisis, was planning it during the period of the *Prometheus* Varia-tions, and its roots go back to Bonn. In other words, I believe Beethoven would have written the *Eroica* in any case.
3. Thayer/Forbes, 1:309.
4. Anderson, vol. 1, no. 43n2.
5. Solomon, *Beethoven*, 165.
6. Senner, *Critical Reception*, vol. 1, no. 47.
7. Anderson, vol. 1, no. 53.
8. Senner, *Critical Reception*, vol. 1, no. 48.
9. Albrecht, vol. 1, no. 50. As per no. 52, Carl at this point was also handling pieces for Anton Reicha. There is no record of the fate of Carl's dog.
10. Wegeler/Ries, 107.
11. Jones, *Beethoven*, 62. Forbes questions Ries's memory of the Quintet imbroglio.
12. Albrecht, vol. 1, no. 49 and n3.
13. Wegeler/Ries, 77–78. The translation reads, "Where the devil . . . ," but I surmise that Beethoven, who swore lustily, would not have been so polite at that moment. Despite all this, Beethoven, who was somehow remarkably patient and forgiving with publishers, had later dealings with Nägeli.
14. B. Cooper, *Beethoven*, 127–28.
15. Thayer/Forbes, 1:326–27.
16. Moore, "Beethoven and Inflation," 202–4.
17. B. Cooper, *Beethoven*, 123.

18. Quoted in Thayer/Forbes, 1:324–25. Kotzebue also gives a nod to Baroness Dorothea Ertmann, who "plays with amazing precision, clearness, and delicacy."

19. Senner, *Critical Reception,* vol. 1, nos. 180–81.

20. Schiller, *Aesthetic Education,* 155–57. This is a more considered, if less forceful, translation than the one in Lippman, *History,* 134: "In a truly beautiful work of art the content should do nothing, the form everything . . . Therefore the real artistic secret of the master consists in his annihilation of the material by means of the form." I submit that the effect of Haydn, Mozart, and Beethoven, especially in sonata form and variation movements, is indeed to suppress the moment for the whole, to make the listener involved in the totality of the piece as if it were an experience in life. A work, that is to say, can be like a little life, every part of it dependent on the whole for its impact and "meaning." A theme and variations, for example, is involved with the moment, on what is happening to the theme, but there is still the cumulative effect (as Haydn regularly demonstrates) of an often-simple piece of material as foundation for a deepening unfolding of ideas.

21. Senner, *Critical Reception,* vol. 1, no. 29. One would like to ask this critic how a valley can be "laughing."

22. J. G. Sulzer, *Allgemeine Theorie der schönen Künste,* quoted in Brinkmann, "Time of the *Eroica,*" 12–13.

23. Wegeler/Ries, 65.

24. Thayer/Forbes, 1:329–30.

25. Senner, *Critical Reception,* vol. 1, no. 165. Tyson, in "1803 Version," 79, notes that the "just take a left" line was revised for the published score.

26. Clive, *Beethoven and His World,* 171.

27. Barry Cooper makes this point about Beethoven's personal relation to the text in *Beethoven,* 126, and he is generally positive about *Christus.* On the whole, I am less so. Certainly the oratorio has its virtues, including a strong introduction and final chorus. To my ears the orchestration is highly interesting: rich, varied, and colorful without being overscored like the *Joseph* Cantata and, arguably, the First Symphony. In general effect its scoring is distinct from the style of Beethoven's symphonies or his theater music. The treatment of trombones in particular is striking, more elaborate than in any work of his at least until the Fifth Symphony. After the premiere Beethoven added a chorus and did various tinkering over the years, but, as he admitted later, "I know that the text is extremely bad. But once one has thought out a whole work which is based even on a bad text, it is difficult to prevent this whole from being destroyed if individual alterations are made here and there. And although it may only be the case of a single word to which sometimes great significance has been attached, well then, that word must stand. And he is a poor composer who is neither able nor anxious to extract as much good as possible even from an inferior text." It would also be a poor composer who made revisions that were not consistent with the work's style, however unfortunate that style. To repeat what is said in the text, Beethoven had no illusions about *Christus,* but he did the best he could with it and hoped to profit from selling it. Moreover, when I call it his most misconceived and undigested large work, that is by no means to call it his worst.

28. Thayer/Forbes, 1:330.

29. Quoted in Lockwood, *Beethoven: Music,* 270.

30. Since much of the Second Symphony appears to be concerned more with color, mass, and kinetic energy than with the usual kind of themes, its material seems

more kaleidoscopic and diffuse than usual in Beethoven — in contrast, for example, to the motivically tight-woven C Minor Piano Concerto. Still, much of the thematic work draws on the three-note bit of scale from the second bar, and the startling diversion into B-flat on the second page finds many echoes. That note keeps turning up as part of various harmonies and keys (rather like A-flat in the C Minor Concerto). His sense of large-scale tonal dynamics can be seen in the finale: the "hiccup" opening figure repeatedly lands on the dominant in the A theme, but in the coda it is shifted to the tonic to make a large-scale resolution. Meanwhile, in calling the Second "operatic" in style, I am placing it with two other symphonies that seem similar, less in sound than in quasi-scenic effect: the Fourth and Eighth Symphonies (both of them also having buffa overtones). While the overall style of the Second is, I think, unique in Beethoven, there are certainly prophecies, one being the second, E-major theme of the second movement: for a moment in its expansive lyricism and elegant ornamentation, it looks forward to the slow movement of the Ninth Symphony.

31. Wegeler/Ries, 66–67.

32. The dates of composition of the C Minor Concerto are a matter of long debate. Kinderman (*Beethoven,* 65) votes for the traditional beginning date of 1800. In *Beethoven's Concertos,* Plantinga spends a chapter on the topic, "On the Origins of Piano Concerto No. 3," and concludes it was written ca. May 1802–March 1803, completed just before the benefit concert. In any case there was further refinement of the concerto after the premiere. For one thing, Beethoven did not write down the solo part until Ries played the concerto in 1804.

33. Some have questioned the connection of the Mozart and Beethoven C-minor concertos, but it seems manifest to me, and Plantinga, in *Beethoven's Concertos,* after noting the questions, concludes, "There may yet be hope for the argument from/for the Mozart connection" (158).

34. To repeat a point made earlier, in most Beethoven works, there is a pervading rhythmic motif. Some are overt, as in the Third Piano Concerto, the Violin Concerto, and the Fifth Symphony; more often, the rhythmic motif is covert but still important. Just as he develops melodic motifs by devices such as inversion, extension, ornamentation, and foreshortening, and uses them as a scaffolding to build new themes, he develops rhythmic motifs by augmentation, diminution, extension, and decoration, and in essence uses them as scaffolding — as with the implied dotted-half and -quarter phrasing of the violins in m. 9, an augmentation of the dotted rhythmic motif of mm. 2 and 3. An abiding gestural element in the C Minor Concerto is that its themes have internal repeats, starting with the opening figure repeated up a step in a call-and-response of strings and winds. Other cases of internal repeat are the double descent from G-sharp to E in m. 2 of the second movement, and the figure that repeats on different degrees in mm. 3 and 5. The rondo theme in the finale is a pattern of repeated figures. Call-and-response episodes between strings, winds, and soloist are another unifying idea.

35. The magical jump into G major in the second line of the second movement, and its pianistic scintillation on a C-major chord, refers us back to the tonic key of the concerto and helps integrate this highly stretched key scheme. As Czerny noted in relation to Beethoven's keeping the pedal down through the first theme, that is no longer practical on pianos of a decade and more later because their sustain is

longer. This is another version of the *Moonlight* Sonata problem: how to get the effect of a long-held pedal on a modern piano.

36. Quoted in Plantinga, *Beethoven's Concertos,* 146.
37. Thayer/Forbes, 1:331.
38. F. G. E., "George P. Bridgetower," 305. Also see Jander, "'Kreutzer' Sonata."
39. Anderson, vol. 1, no. 74.
40. Wegeler/Ries, 72.
41. Thayer/Forbes, 1:333.
42. The presence of F major as an important second key in this A-major work is one of the ideas that Beethoven picked up from the finale and transferred to the new movements. (As is noted before, in the Second Period he would be much interested in mediant relationships as substitutes for conventional tonic-dominant relations.) Another connection that has been noted in the literature is how the pounding theme at the beginning of the Presto relates to the 3–4-sharp–5 pattern over A in the opening theme of the finale. There is also the primal move E–F in the first movement (a dynamic gesture in itself, but also foreshadowing F major) and the resolving D-sharp–E in the finale, in both cases emphasizing a note a half step from the dominant. A deeper element, which as far as I know no one has noticed, is the rising chain of thirds Beethoven uses as a scaffolding for the first section of the finale, then uses to compose the beginning of the sonata. In the finale, it starts with the A and C-sharp between violin and piano in the first bars, adds E in bar 4, then moves on to G-natural and B in the piano, D and F-sharp in m. 11, A in the next measure, C-sharp in the violin, E and G in mm. 15–16, then B-flat to D in the piano, and F-sharp in the piano starting at m. 22. This F-sharp, the penultimate member in the chain, is prolonged and intensified in the next measures until the climactic arrival on A at m. 28. I think part of the exhilarating effect of that A is that it has been arrived at by a covert but still audible process of rising thirds: A–C-sharp–E–G–B–D–F-sharp–A–C–E–G–B-flat–D–F-sharp–A! In turn, Beethoven built the first movement's opening violin solo and answering piano phrases on a *descending* chain of thirds: A–F-sharp–D–B–G-sharp–E–C-sharp–A; that last violin A is picked up by the piano, which continues down the chain: A–F–D–B–G-sharp–E. From there, the chain starts to dissolve. Beethoven tends to be reliable about these matters, so the chain of thirds turns up in the slow movement, too: the top-voice E in m. 1, top-voice C in m. 2, then more directly A–F–D–B-flat–G–E–C in mm. 5–8. A worthwhile study waits to be written on Beethoven's interest in chains of thirds, already in evidence in his childhood Piano Quartets, which climaxed in the *Hammerklavier* Sonata.
43. The connection of sexuality and the *Kreutzer* reached a climax in Tolstoy's 1889 novella *The Kreutzer Sonata,* in which playing the piece incites a woman pianist and a male violinist to a fatal adulterous liaison. In turn, the novella inspired the kitschy but famous 1901 painting *Kreutzer Sonata,* by René François Xavier Prinet, which shows a male violinist impulsively seizing a young female from the piano in an embrace.
44. F. G. E., "George P. Bridgetower," 306.
45. Anderson, vol. 1, no. 99.
46. Schwartz, "French Violin School," 440.
47. Albrecht, vol. 1, no. 73.
48. Wegeler/Ries, 81–82.

49. Skowroneck, "Keyboard Instruments," 177, and "Beethoven's Erard Piano," 523–27. Beethoven's Érard (which still exists) has four pedals: una corda, dampers, and the extra stops known as a lute and a moderator. Its action was similar to the British Broadwood. Newman, in "Beethoven's Pianos," 488, notes that Beethoven was eventually dissatisfied with the heavier British-style action of the Érard. In 1805, piano maker Johann Andreas Streicher reported in a letter, "Beethoven certainly is a strong pianist, yet up to now he still is not able properly to manage his fortepiano received from Érard in Paris [based on English models], and has already had [the action] changed twice without making it the least bit better, since the construction of the same does not allow a different mechanism" (quoted in Newman, 498). Skowroneck, in *Beethoven the Pianist*, 86 (more recent than his articles), says there is evidence that the Érard was not a gift but Beethoven simply never paid for it. However, later Beethoven described the Érard in a letter as "a souvenir such as no one here has so far honored me with," which does imply it was a gift. Skowroneck says that the British and French pianos of the time were so close in sound that he considers them one tradition. I have referred to the "evolution" of the piano in this era, but Michael Frederick of the Frederick Collection noted in an interview that the reality in Beethoven's day was no unified evolution but a welter of makers and regions, each with its own style and innovations. The dominance in the modern era of one maker and style, Steinway, is a recent development in the history of the piano, and one some people are not happy with.
50. Albrecht, vol. 1, no. 67.
51. Anderson, vol. 1, no. 81.
52. Albrecht, vol. 1, no. 70. Carl's term is *Mist,* which is essentially "dung."
53. Ibid., no. 65.
54. Dalhaus, *Ludwig van Beethoven,* 22.
55. Lockwood, *Beethoven: Studies,* 135.

17. Heaven and Earth Will Tremble

1. Lockwood, *Beethoven: Studies,* 135–43. The sketchbook with work on opp. 34 and 35 and sketches toward the *Eroica* is called the "Wielhorsky." The sketchbook with most of the work on the symphony is called "Landesberg 6" or *Eroica.*
2. Thayer/Forbes, 1:335.
3. The eighteenth-century view of music as a kind of rational discourse is the main subject of Mark Evan Bonds's *Wordless Rhetoric: Musical Form and the Metaphor of the Oration.*
4. Hegel, quoted in Lockwood, "Beethoven's *Leonore* and *Fidelio,*" 479.
5. Sipe, *Beethoven,* 44.
6. Ibid., 46.
7. Napoleon Bonaparte, quoted in Marek, *Beethoven,* 190.
8. The idea that Napoleon was a product of the Enlightenment was not a myth. He had studied Rousseau, Voltaire, and the other philosophes. But his ambition and his cynicism far outrode his commitment to progressive philosophy.
9. Albrecht, vol. 1, no. 67.
10. See B. Cooper, *Creative Process,* 99. To summarize Beethoven's terminology, as seen in sketches, for the parts of what was later named "sonata form": *first part,* exposition; *second part,* development and recapitulation; *Durchführung,* devel-

opment; *Thema*, first theme; *mitte Gedanke* ("middle ideas"), second/subsidiary theme(s); *da capo*, recapitulation; *Schluss* or *coda*, coda. (I translate some terms and not others because the terms *Thema* ["*the* theme"] and *Durchführung* ["working-out"] have broader implications.) In recent times there has been a long debate as to whether sonata form is "really" binary or ternary. Clearly Beethoven saw it as binary: first part and second part. I am in the camp that sees the form as a joining of binary and ternary: exposition repeated, development, recapitulation (and in earlier sonata forms and a few of Beethoven's, the development and recapitulation are repeated as well).

11. My ongoing point is that while Beethoven and his time composed in terms of what we call sonata form and the other received formal outlines, the fundamental conception of a work was something other than that, beyond the intention of writing one more piece in sonata form. The conception was a dramatic or characteristic or metaphorical idea, or a broader musical one, to which the received form had to be shaped. The *conception,* the *idea,* comes first, then is mapped into a form as one composes the exposition, then the development, and so on. In the process the idea inflects the form, sometimes bending it almost beyond recognition. Now and then, as in three movements of the *Eroica* and in the Ninth Symphony, Beethoven was driven by the nature of his ideas to create virtually new, ad hoc forms.

12. In relation to Beethoven's creative process, I'm echoing some ideas of David Galenson, who proposes that geniuses (I would suggest most creative artists, genius or not) are what I call either planners or flounderers. Galenson's models are Picasso, a planner who started with a strong conception of what he was after in a painting, and Matisse, who floundered until he found a path. Both types can produce splendid work, but the planners tend to work faster and more confidently, and to mature earlier. (See Gladwell, "Late Bloomers.") I consider Beethoven the model of a planner, more of a conscious craftsman than most artists, and it is in those terms that I analyze his creative process. This is not to say, however, that there was not a good measure of floundering in his process, in some works more floundering and in some less. Some things simply take longer to ferment than others.

13. Some variations, including Bach's *Goldbergs,* are founded on the bass line of the theme, but it is not put forth nakedly, as Beethoven does in the *Prometheus* Variations and *Eroica.* As is reflected in the labels on the piano variations, Beethoven probably considered the *englische* tune the *Thema* proper of the finale. But in practice the bass line serves as the theme of the finale and underlies the whole symphony, so here I call it the main theme.

14. The pages are cited in Lockwood, "Earliest Sketches," 138–39, a classic sketch study.

15. To summarize the leading motifs of the *Eroica,* all exposed on its first page and more or less in order of importance: a triad, a chromatic slide, a C-sharp/D-flat "sore note," the G–A-flat pair. An important element is the contrast of the metrically regular "Hero" theme in mm. 3–6 and the pulse- and meter-erasing violin syncopations of mm. 7–8. The meter does not regain its footing until mm. 11–12. Clear meter and challenged meter will be a theme throughout the movement.

16. The harmony above the "sore" C-sharp on the first page is designed to be as ambiguous as a chord can get. It is spelled C-sharp–G–B-flat, constituting either an incomplete C-sharp o7 chord or a German sixth of iii without a root. In fact it functions as the latter, resolving to a iii 6/4 chord, G minor. In the recapitulation, the same ambiguous chord will resolve differently, more as if the C-sharp were D-

flat, but still not conventionally: to a C7 moving to F major. It's worth noting that there is a similar effect, with the same pitch, in the beginning of Haydn's late Sonata No. 62 in E-flat: a D-flat in the first bar that, as in the *Eroica,* throws the harmony into a tizzy and resonates throughout the piece. The "sore note" is one more device that Beethoven may have learned from Haydn, in person or through his music. Remarkably often, the sore note is D-flat/C-sharp — see the Eighth Symphony.

17. Nottebohm, *Two Beethoven Sketchbooks,* 52.

18. Dahlhaus, *Ludwig van Beethoven:* "The thematic configuration of the first movement of the *Eroica* is not 'given' anywhere, in the sense of a text set out for commentary; instead, it is entirely absorbed into the process for which it provides the substance" (175). He also notes that even at the end of the first movement, "the theme never appears in a 'real' or 'definitive' Gestalt." As I put it, the Hero is protean, always evolving. The new theme in the development is integrative but still not final.

19. I call the exposition development-like in its restlessness and in the fragmentary quality of its themes; at the same time it is like an exposition in being relatively stable harmonically: once it modulates to B-flat at the (veiled) second theme in m. 57, it essentially stays there.

20. Some might say that Beethoven's technique in regard to the varied handling of formal models might be true of him but not of Haydn and Mozart, who were more or less filling up assumed forms with material. I believe Haydn and Mozart *were* working in each piece (at least in their mature and more ambitious ones) with ideas particular to the piece, just as Beethoven was. Haydn's handling of sonata form in particular can be remarkably free (see the Sonata No. 62 in E-flat and the *Quinten* Quartet first movements). But in this too Beethoven pursued that idea *more* than his predecessors. He wanted to make works that were more strongly marked and individual than those of Haydn and Mozart, ones that generated and justified their forms from within — even when his form was closer to convention than some of Haydn's.

21. Marek, *Beethoven,* 188, notes that in 1795 Franz Wegeler turned Beethoven's line "Who is a free man?" with his friend's permission, into "What is the goal of a Mason?" with Wegeler's own text. The tone of the music and the sentiments of the original text were suitable for that.

22. In "The Compositional Act" (38–39) Barry Cooper notes that in Beethoven's mature sketches a given series of continuity drafts tend to get closer and closer to the final version, though there is some backtracking. Meanwhile it is usually not possible to trace the full development of a piece or movement because there are sketches missing. The sketches and drafts for the *Eroica* are unusually complete, but some are still missing — for example, most of the ones, if there were any, where Beethoven derived the opening Hero theme from the *englische* bass of the finale. There was also a great deal of work done at the keyboard and in his head, and never written down.

23. Nottebohm, *Two Beethoven Sketchbooks,* 62. As Nottebohm details (63–67), Beethoven struggled to base the closing section of the exposition mainly on the Hero theme but finally decided that would weaken its presence in the development (which by that point he was already working on). Finally he settled on a new chromatic motif (echoing the chromatic part of the Hero theme) and a brief touch of the triadic motif just before the development. Most of the ideas in this chapter regarding structure and logic are mine, but they form an ongoing dialogue with the

Eroica chapter in Nottebohm's classic essay "A Sketchbook of 1803." Nottebohm's study is pioneering and irreplaceable, but it has a well-known bias: from the welter of sketches for a work Nottebohm picks examples to fit his conception that the completion of a work had a steady evolution from rough to middling to finished. Lockwood and others have shown that Beethoven's process was not nearly so methodical and straight line. Some final manuscripts were still involved in floundering and sketching, and some of the most striking ideas in works came at the last minute. Behind the whole of this chapter is the reality that creating a work from the inside is a murkier and more fraught process than contemplating the finished work from the outside. Even for a supreme craftsman like Beethoven, much of the process of composing a work is a congeries of vague, unpolished, unfocused elements constantly threatening to fall apart.

24. As I say in the text, I think in the exposition Beethoven deliberately obscures the arrival of the second theme proper. The "real" second theme of the *Eroica* first movement has been a matter of long debate, not surprising given that Beethoven preceded it with twelve bars of transition (from m. 45) over a dominant (of B-flat) pedal, a moment that sounds less like a transition than like a theme, and a notably dancelike one. I call it theme 1B. It transitions into what I call the second theme proper at m. 57. In the exposition I call m. 57 the "proper" second theme partly because it is in the right key (B-flat, dominant) and in the right place in the exposition. As further evidence, the first continuity draft of the exposition (cited in the text, from Nottebohm) shows more clearly than the final version that this B-flat theme is intended as the beginning of the second-theme section (as Nottebohm calls it). What some scholars call the second theme, at m. 83, does not appear in that first long draft at all. But as I say, the clear arrival of the second-theme section is not the point; its *obscure* arrival is the point. Beethoven is looking for something different from the usual relatively lucid Classical exposition. He wants a constant dynamic flux with no clear signposts or points of arrival — that is, an effect more like a development. In general I'd say that the proliferation of themes and the ambiguity of the second theme's arrival are the main elements that make this exposition harder to follow than most. Still, despite how variegated the exposition is, when the key of B-flat arrives, it largely stays. In other words, the key layout of the exposition is conventional, but the way it is articulated and filled out with a plethora of themes and blurred boundaries is unusual and development-like. This is particularly true of the treatment of *das Thema,* which is handled developmentally from the beginning. The antiphonal theme 1B at m. 45, incidentally, is based on, and prophetic of, the *englische* theme of the finale — it has its lilting dotted rhythm and general outline, a series of descending three-note figures. (In the first movement, that theme displaces the sense of downbeat to the second beat of the measure.) Also incidentally, the end of the *Prometheus* bass, the cadential hook figures F–D–E-flat and E-flat–A–B-flat, is echoed a number of times in the first movement, starting with what I call theme 2B at m. 65. For another example, as said in the text, the trochaic figure of the Hero theme is like a 3/4 version of the *englische* rhythm. As often in Beethoven, these connections are more a matter of shape and/or rhythm than of intervals — but in all cases it is a figure he emphasizes. To summarize, the first movement is rich in motivic derivations from both the *Prometheus* bass and the *englische* tune, both melodically and rhythmically.

25. Nottebohm, *Two Beethoven Sketchbooks*, 71–72.

26. The superimposition of the recapitulation is the horn's Hero theme on the tonic triad against A-flat–B-flat in tremolo strings, representing a dominant seventh. *Grove Music Online* points out that the resulting dissonance of G and A-flat can be seen as another avatar of the primal melodic G–A-flat motif from the first page — in other words, a case of Beethoven's making a melodic figure into a harmonic one.

27. The apt adjective *evil* for the climactic harmony (an A-minor chord with added ♭6, scored to emphasize the E–F dissonance) is from Adolph Marx. My description aspires to convey the drama and intensity of these pages in the development, but as always there is a formal process going on too: those screaming tutti harmonies from m. 276 are a long windup to the "new" theme in E minor, a systematic preparation for that distant key. The bass line from m. 248 makes a long descent from D to B, the dominant of E minor. Meanwhile the "sore" C-sharp/D-flat is part of the new E-minor theme, as part of the three-note chromatic slide on its original pitches D-sharp/E-flat–D–C-sharp. The hair-raising climactic chord in the development, as should be expected in Beethoven, is foreshadowed earlier: in the lacerating A7–over–B-flat chord at the end of the exposition, m. 147. (The first long sketch for the development [Nottebohm, *Two Beethoven Sketchbooks*, 74–76] had a different bass descent, and the climactic harmony was on a diminished-seventh chord — dissonant, but far less shocking than the final version.)

28. See Nottebohm, *Two Beethoven Sketchbooks*, 81. Another detail of the development's new theme helps cement the connection of its descending three-note chromatic slide to the ones in the Hero theme. As was said in the previous note, in E minor, the development theme has in m. 286 the same enharmonic pitches as the Hero theme's chromatic slide on the first page: D-sharp–D–C-sharp. Meanwhile there is an intriguing divide between what I suspect most listeners hear as the essential new theme and the way Beethoven seems to have thought of it. All his sketches have only the *lower* line, the one derived from the Hero theme, standing in for the whole. Most listeners, however, naturally tend to hear the *upper* line (a foreshadowing of the second-movement dirge) as the "real" new theme. I think both lines contribute to the effect of what I call an integrative theme, at once looking backward to the Hero theme and forward to the *Funeral March*.

29. The new, double theme is heard four times in the development: in E minor, A minor, E-flat minor, and G-flat major (the last truncated). In the scoring Beethoven alternates emphasizing the lower and upper lines; the G-flat version is only the upper line.

30. The most common way for a coda to anticipate and/or prepare the next movement is tonally, an example being the way the final G-sharp of the middle movement of the Third Piano Concerto prepares the G–A-flat that opens the rondo theme. The idea of a coda foreshadowing *themes* of the next movement I have not found in the literature, but that happens sometimes in Beethoven, for example, in the first movement of the *Eroica* and, as we will see, in the first-movement recapitulation and coda of the Fifth Symphony.

31. Nottebohm, *Two Beethoven Sketchbooks*, 80.

32. My sense of the ending began with Brinkmann in "Time of the *Eroica*."

33. Burnham, in *Beethoven Hero*: "The final melodic utterance of the opening theme has thematic stability but no thematic closure . . . the unstable and volatile theme of the opening bars is now heard as a stable, indeed, potentially unending iteration"

(19). Burnham presents the progress of the first movement in structural terms as a series of upbeats and downbeats at various levels: the first presentations of the Hero theme, for example, form an upbeat to its *tutti fortissimo* eruption on the third page, but that presentation is also unfinished, forming an upbeat at a higher level.

34. Kramer, "Notes to Beethoven's Education," 99. There are sketches for *Eroica* horn passages on the same pages of Beethoven's notes from the horn article.

35. I see the *Eroica* as a narrative on the idea of the Hero in general, as embodied particularly in Bonaparte, but not as a "program" piece in the terms of the later nineteenth century. Neither here nor in most of Beethoven's other named pieces — especially the *Pastoral* Symphony and the *Lebewohl* Sonata — do I see a point-by-point narrative of events or ideas (though there is the all-too-blatant narrative of *Wellington's Victory*). His programs in symphonies and sonatas seem to me general, not specific. True, if it were discovered that, as a private device, Beethoven had modeled his first movement on, say, a particular battle or campaign of Napoleon's, I would not be particularly surprised. But in the absence of evidence I'm not inclined to speculate, and I don't hear that overtly suggested in the music. Perhaps my sense of the overall narrative will seem a stretch to some. But Beethoven conceived his works as wholes, and he would not give a piece a title and then drop the program after the first two movements. While I don't doubt that his "characteristic" conception covered the whole piece, then, there's no question that the narrative implications of the last two movements are more obscure than for the first two. I should mention that my programmatic narrative of the first two movements generally agrees with writers going back to Adolph Marx, who are the main subject of Burnham's *Beethoven Hero*.

36. Broyles, *Beethoven*, 123.

37. See Nottebohm, *Two Beethoven Sketchbooks*, 81–84.

38. Palisca, "French Revolutionary Models," 202. Even though Beethoven's phrase may well be based on Gossec, consciously or not, there is a significant difference in effect between the two marches. Only a close comparison of the notes reveals the similarities; the sound hardly does. Palisca cites possible connections to other pieces, especially by Cherubini. Czerny cites a model in a funeral march by Paer.

39. A summary of the form of the *Funeral March*:

> Part 1. A (dirge, C min.) B (E♭ maj.) A$_1$ (F min.) B$_1$ (E♭ maj.) A$_2$ (F min.) Closing (C min.)
>
> Part 2. C (Trio, C & F maj.) // A (C min.) Double Fugue (F & C min., E♭ maj.) Interlude (briefly A♭ maj.)
>
> Part 3. A$_3$ (C min.) B (E♭ maj.) A$_4$ (F min., C min.) Closing (C min.) CODA (D♭ maj.–C min.)

The second movement, like the others, has richly interwoven motivic and tonal relationships. The dirge *Thema*, besides its derivation from the end of the *Prometheus* bass, is built on an ascending triad (C minor), recalling the Hero theme. The middle theme begins with a simple ascending triad. The dirge melody meanwhile ascends first from G through C to G, sharing the tonic-dominant emphasis of the *Prometheus* bass opening and its main compass from dominant to dominant. The three-note chromatic motif is a feature of the B theme (first at mm. 21–22). Within the movement, the A-flat to E-flat descent in mm. 6–7 is augmented to make the beginning of the B theme from m. 17. That motif is inverted to make the imitative bass/viola accompaniment in the C section (from m. 69), which becomes the main fugue subject from m. 114. The symphony's home key of E-flat major turns up in the B theme and the fugue. Based on the first page of the symphony, the A-flat–G motif is featured throughout, likewise the primal C-sharp/D-flat sore note. One idea derived from the A-flat–G figure is the wailing appoggiaturas on those notes (also on F-sharp–G). One feature that unites the kaleidoscopic world of the second movement is the rhythmic motif quarter–eighth–eighth, which is implied in the dirge and overt in the B theme. The scoring is likewise kaleidoscopic, starting with the dark texture of the opening and then the rich B theme, with cellos and basses divided, all the strings in their lowest registers. The horns are brilliantly handled thoughout, with only a few stopped notes, carefully placed — above all, the piercing low B in m. 231, another of the small but powerful scoring details in the movement (which includes the oboe in its most poignant mode). On modern valved horns the piercing effect of the stopped horn near the end is lost — but I suggest that the low B should still be stopped.

40. For me and I suspect for many musicians the horn peroration at the climax of the fugue in the *Funeral March* is one of those moments that represent one of the highest, most heart-filling, most intensely humanistic summits that music is capable of. That moment is one of the reasons some of us are musicians in the first place. And yet, as I always say, it's all made of scales going up and down: just *scales*.

41. The surging bass line at the end of the *Funeral March* will be echoed in the bass line at the end of the Ninth Symphony first movement — likewise a funeral march.

42. Nottebohm, *Two Beethoven Sketchbooks*, 87–88.

43. Ibid., 88. Note bars 5–8 in the scherzo; they are derived from the "hook" motif in bars 7–8 of the *Prometheus* bass.

44. Ibid., 90.

45. The folkish theme of the scherzo is another one built on the scaffolding of the *Prometheus* bass. Its structural notes are the *basso*'s E-flat and B-flat, its main compass an octave — though from tonic to tonic rather than the bass's dominant to dominant.

46. My feeling is that Beethoven looked at the *Eroica* as an end-directed work, whose meaning and material are paid off in the finale. But in practice I think the finale lacks the weight and impact of the first movement, partly because much of it is in the light and rather conventional style of ballet music. Many people, and I am inclined to that camp, feel the finale does not work ideally for this symphony, because however beautifully conceived in both musical and symbolic terms, for all its gathering glories, the finale doesn't quite have the impact and scale to fulfill its function as the symphony's goal and apotheosis. The coda of the finale, however, is surely as glorious as it needs to be and forms a perfect conclusion to the symphony.

47. Schiller, *Aesthetic Education*, 300. I'm not suggesting that Beethoven knew this passage, from a letter of Schiller's to his friend C. G. Körner, but rather that this passage reflects the widespread reputation of the *englische* (see Aldrich, "Social Dancing").

48. It was Thomas Sipe's *Beethoven: Eroica Symphony* that pointed out for me the presence of the *englische* in the finale; its meaning was amplified by Aldrich's article on social dancing in Vienna and by Schiller's letter about the *englische*. Sipe relates the implied image of society in the finale to the Aesthetic State envisioned in Schiller's *Aesthetic Education* and provides a quite specific program relating to that social and philosophical work. Meanwhile, as Sipe notes, Constantin Floros has derived the whole of the *Eroica* from the story of the *Prometheus* ballet. Since, as I've said, it's likely that the ballet's story had some influence from the *Aesthetic Education*, Floros

and Sipe are on firm ground concerning influences on the finale, and certainly the scenario and ideas from the ballet contributed to the creation of the *Eroica*. But in regard to the finale I depart from Sipe's and Floros's interpretation, mainly for two reasons. First, as I said earlier, I don't think Beethoven wrote programs that specific or that abstractly philosophical. Second, their interpretations have little to do with Napoleon as the ideal of a benevolent despot, which I insist is the essential subject of the symphony from beginning to end. Beethoven would not switch programs in the middle of a program piece, or drop the program either. I think the main foundation of the *Eroica* was that image of Napoleon and ideals founded on Beethoven's *Bildung* in Bonn. In any case, generations of scholars and musicians have rarely if ever considered that this symphony was written from first note to last as a "characteristic" piece called, and in large part about, Bonaparte. As is clear, I'm proposing to put that fact back into the equation, without denying that the symphony is also about the heroic principle in a larger perspective — and no less is a triumph in "abstract" terms. Which is to say that Beethoven's later title *Eroica* was appropriate to the conception. Still, my interpretation is not entirely antithetical to that of Sipe and Floros. Sipe writes, "After the hero's military accomplishment and funeral solemnity, after the return of the troops to domestic concerns, Beethoven envisioned a new, peaceful political order. Schiller's idealism shaped that vision" (113). To that point we are in agreement and I have echoed his words — though I think the Schiller connection has more to do with "An die Freude," which Beethoven did read, than *Aesthetic Education,* which likely he did not (though ideas from it were present in the zeitgeist). But the *road* to Elysium in "An die Freude" is not the doing of a hero but rather something humanity achieves for itself. Beethoven will return to that question with the Ninth Symphony.

49. Nottebohm, *Two Beethoven Sketchbooks,* 94. I believe Beethoven's key choices (and for that matter Haydn's and Mozart's) have an internal reason as part of the overall structure of a work, so here are some ideas about why he begins the introduction of the finale in G minor (quickly modulating to E-flat). G minor has an important place in the development of the first movement and turns up in the scherzo. More immediately, the introduction of the finale foreshadows the G-minor military march in the middle of the finale. There may be more, if rather arcane, reasons. The C-sharp on the first page of the symphony resolves as if it were part of a German sixth on E-flat (that note is missing), to a G-minor chord. More significantly, the added note that makes the *Prometheus* theme into the Hero theme is G. The A-flat–G figure heard from the first page of the symphony forward may play a part as well. Meanwhile A-flat turns up as an emphasized key or chord several times in the finale (it is the dominant of D-flat); starting in m. 231, Beethoven makes a repeated point of A-flat as the Neapolitan chord of G minor.

50. The dit-dit-dit figure that serves as the refrain of the *basso* in the finale is another model of how Beethoven handles a rhythmic motif. It is a diminution of the three-quarter-note figure in bars 5 and 6 of the *englische*. Later he augments the figure to half notes.

51. Sipe, *Beethoven,* calls the C-major version of the *englische* a "false recapitulation" (111). It rather sounds that way, but things get unusual when the following section sets off in a return of the tonic E-flat (undercut by starting on I6) in a *fugato* that sounds nothing like a recapitulation.

52. In *Beethoven Hero,* Scott Burnham, like generations of scholars — Donald Francis

Tovey among them — is skeptical of the kind of long-range thematic and tonal relationships I'm talking about here, on the grounds that a listener who has not studied the score will never perceive them. I don't think that's an outlandish argument, though Tovey carries it to the extreme of avoiding most intermovement motivic relationships, and Heinrich Schenker ignores motifs altogether. But there's no question that Beethoven thought in these kinds of long-range terms; it is clear on the page, in his sketches, and in the stories of his improvisations on themes. Put another way, artists before the postmodern age had a horror of the arbitrary, and in composing music one holds the arbitrary at bay by having the piece feed on itself as it goes. To repeat a point made before, in the Classical period a piece mainly fed on its beginning: *das Thema, the* theme, as young Beethoven read in Sulzer's *Allgemeine Theorie.* (If the end comes first, as in the *Eroica* and the *Kreutzer,* Beethoven arranges for the piece to *seem* as if it feeds on its beginning.) As I say in the text, Beethoven composed his works based mainly on the governing theme in the same way an essayist or orator develops a theme or, as Sulzer says, a preacher expounds on a verse of scripture. I argue that the familiar sense of *rightness* in Beethoven's music — rightness even when he is being surprising or eccentric — has much to do, among other things, with underlying relationships that listeners sense but don't understand consciously. And by the time one has heard a work a few times, its web of relationships is embedded in one's perception of it as a sense of rightness. By *motif,* meanwhile, I mean not only melodic motifs but the whole range of thematic possibilities: a single pitch, a chord, a chord sequence, a silence, a texture, a color, and more — all the elements that Beethoven uses motivically in the direction of, as I call it, motivizing everything. It should not be forgotten, however, that a work can have elaborate patterns of relationships and still be entirely ineffective, boring, even incompetent. Again, a piece of music is not a logical or mathematical construction. A composer still has to make the music live and breathe, and that requires inspiration, not just calculation.

53. The apotheosis of the *basso* theme, a long *fortissimo* in a glorious E-flat major ringing with horns, would seem to be the climax of the movement, but Beethoven undercuts it with a long dominant pedal that points to the next section.

54. Here are some of the ways the finale's *poco andante* recalls the *Marcia funèbre,* which have to do not only with motifs but also with resemblances and analogies of color, texture, and mood. First, it begins, as in the second period of the second movement, with poignant wind music, the oboe as leading instrument. The answering string phrase at m. 357 is scored in the same color of low strings as the answering phrase in m. 17 of movement 2. The poignant accented appoggiaturas starting in m. 273 recall similar ones throughout the *Funeral March.* The arpeggio triplets in m. 365 recall the C section of movement 2 (m. 69) — and even more, the music at m. 397 recalls the C section of the *Funeral March.* The turn to a gentle, hopeful theme in A-flat at m. 404 recalls in key, color, and mood the beginning of the coda in the *Funeral March* (m. 209). The tremolos and quiet wind tattoos from m. 417 in the finale constitute a virtual quotation of the *Funeral March* from m. 160. Meanwhile the bass creeping up stepwise in triadic figures from m. 408 in the finale recalls the Hero theme doing likewise in much of the *first* movement. I note that there are no exact recalls of earlier movements in the finale — only similarities, analogies, subtle connections of mo-

tif, color, and shape. Beethoven at this point did not want literal intermovement returns; that attitude would change in his late music. I believe, though, that such relationships by analogy and underlying form are true to the way we perceive things. Nearly every new face we see reminds us of another face, and reflexively we categorize every new face by a row of criteria aesthetic, formal, racial, sexual, social, economic, and so on; but often we don't remember what that other face was. I suspect, in other words, that we tend to perceive things in analogies, and Classical thematic relations proceed as well not by literal repetition but by underlying similarities and analogies.

55. Again, another thematic element of the symphony has to do with its consistent tendency, starting with the first pages of the first movement, and seen in the third and fourth movements, to build a theme step by step from a quiet statement to what I call "the theme in glory." From beginning to end, the thematic treatment in the symphony is a forward-directed process of *becoming*. Only in the coda of the finale is there a sense of a final climax being reached.

56. The journey of Beethoven's vision of the Hero to *Beethoven Hero* is the main theme of Burnham's study.

57. To the clause "a new scope and ambition had entered the genre, and it would stay there" needs to be added a corollary: the model of the symphony Beethoven established may have done more harm than good to the symphony for generations after him. A new generation of great symphonists did not spring up — though there were certainly some worthy ones, including Schumann and Mendelssohn. After Beethoven, many composers avoided symphonies altogether. It was not until Brahms's symphonies decades later, which revived a genre by then nearly moribund, that the implications of what Beethoven made of the symphony truly took off. Schumann's symphonies, for one example, stand as the work of a composer trying to follow Beethoven's lead without being quite up to the job. Schubert came close with his Ninth and, if he had lived, might have fully inherited Beethoven's symphonic mantle. Berlioz never wrote a symphony in a truly Viennese-Classical spirit. The composer who followed up Beethoven's lead first, most deliberately, and most grandly was Wagner, on the stage.

58. Kerman makes this point about the intensified individuality of the New Path works in *Beethoven Quartets*. Interestingly, after writing my paragraph concerning Beethoven as a radical evolutionary, I ran across Kerman's reference to "the radical evolutionary curve of the corpus" (96) — a passing point in his case, but one that clearly grew in my mind since I had read it years before. Kerman is talking, however, about Beethoven's own oeuvre, while I use the phrase "radical evolutionist" to describe Beethoven's relationship to the whole of musical tradition.

59. This is a point elaborated in the "New Path" chapter of Dahlhaus, *Ludwig van Beethoven*. He calls the technique "less a 'theme' than a 'thematic configuration,' a grouping of elements . . . which are in effect 'pre-thematic' at the opening" (171). I call it "using a motif as a theme," the most distilled example being the Fifth Symphony first movement. Dahlhaus makes this a central marker of the New Path, but I'm not so sure. It is certainly a feature of the *Eroica, The Tempest,* the Fifth Symphony, and other works. At the same time, Beethoven does not abandon traditionally tuneful openings from which he extracts ideas for development, like the extended cello song that begins the first *Razumovsky* Quartet.

Also I don't see this special use of motif-as-theme as being entirely new in the Second Period; it is what happens, for example, in the first movement of the op. 18, no. 1 Quartet, dominated by its little turn figure. As Dahlhaus notes, pieces using this technique tend to be "processual," an ongoing process of developing protean bits of material taking the place of the usual exposition of themes. Like Dahlhaus, I see the first movement of the *Eroica* in those terms: more constant evolution and development than exposition.

60. Quoted in ibid., 26.

61. To say that Beethoven is the real hero behind the *Eroica* has been commonplace since his own lifetime. Commonplaces are not always wrong, but I stress that I think this is true only in part. As the text elaborates, there was a good deal more to the Second Period than that. The *Eroica* is not just about Beethoven himself; it is also about Napoleon, and about heroes and heroism in general; it is no less about form, development, innovation, ambition; it no less marks his discovery of how to embody his humanistic ideals in his music. As for his spiritual ideals, by and large that would be the concern of the late music.

62. Lockwood, *Beethoven: Music,* 156.

63. Barry Cooper makes this point in *Beethoven Compendium* (145) and in his biography.

64. Albrecht, vol. 1, no. 71. In addition to the 400 gulden (the equivalent of florins) that Lobkowitz donated to have the Third Symphony for six months, Beethoven offered the symphony to Simrock for 100 florins (a shockingly modest fee — he knew publishers' profit was much less for an orchestral piece). Symphonies in those days were published only in parts, not in a score, though Beethoven militated for scores and eventually got them.

18. *Geschrieben auf Bonaparte*

1. Thayer/Forbes, 1:336–37.

2. Czerny, *Proper Performance,* 16.

3. Landon, *Beethoven,* 8.

4. Skowroneck, *Beethoven the Pianist,* 113. Skowroneck notes that the *Waldstein* finale is the first sonata movement of Beethoven with extensive pedal markings. Though others have questioned it, Skowroneck believes the Érard did influence the *Waldstein* and *Appassionata.* I certainly agree.

5. Ibid., 99, quoting G. A. Griesinger. Given Beethoven's later disenchantment with the Érard, Skowroneck wonders whether his initial enchantment was due to his enthusiasm at the time for "matters French" (101). Perhaps that contributed, but also it was in Beethoven's nature to end up disenchanted with nearly everything and everybody. In any case, as Skowroneck notes, pianos were not very robust in those days, and after a few years Beethoven had probably worn it out.

6. From Anton Kuerti's note in his recording of the complete sonatas.

7. The sense of instant restless energy in the beginning of the *Waldstein* is created by several devices working together: The harmony hardly establishes C major before it deflects in the third bar to G major, then drops to B-flat immediately moving to F (this a function of the chromatically falling bass line). The rhythm is equally restless in its pounding energy, the right hand figure in sixteenths raising the tension

in the first two lines. Finally in the second line there is a crescendo that rises not to a *fortissimo* but to a decrescendo. Here is the dynamic pattern of the movement in a nutshell: The primary dynamic level of the exposition is *piano* to *pianissimo,* and there are several passages of a crescendo to a *subito piano.* The only *fortissimo* in the exposition starts in m. 62 — and that is a transition, not a point of arrival. The whole of the first movement demonstrates Beethoven's skill at managing a forward-driving rhythmic momentum: from the sudden slowing of the second theme, for example, there is a sustained rhythmic crescendo that stretches to the closing section at m. 74. Two motivic elements are notable. First, the little rise of E–F-sharp–G in the second measure is diminished and inverted in m. 3, then extended to a falling fifth in m. 4; that falling fifth, stretched out, is the essence of the E-major second theme in m. 35. The *rhythm* of the second theme (already in place from the first sketches), 1- 3 4, 1- 3-, is already implied in the way mm. 2–3 articulate the meter. Meanwhile the E major of the second theme is foreshadowed in the top-voice E of the first two measures. Beethoven was increasingly interested in mediant keys, but he did not throw them around arbitrarily. He prepares and justifies his keys in the context of the piece.

8. Wegeler/Ries, 89; Kinderman, "Piano Music," 106.
9. In *Beethoven the Pianist,* Skowroneck notes that in the *Waldstein* the effect of a trill in the last two fingers combined with a melody in the lower fingers (some of it having to be faked because the stretch is too big) goes back to figuration studies Beethoven did in Bonn: "[T]here survive at least ten pages of sketches that contain around eighteen examples of material with simultaneous trills and melodies for one hand . . . and cadential triple trills" (68).
10. Thayer/Forbes, 1:340; Wyn Jones, *Symphony,* 122.
11. Albrecht, vol. 1, no. 74.
12. Ibid., no. 75.
13. Anderson, vol. 1, no. 88.
14. Wegeler/Ries, 89–90.
15. Ibid., 101–3.
16. Ibid., 79–80.
17. Quoted in *Grove Music Online,* s.v. "Haydn, Franz Joseph."
18. Geiringer, *Haydn,* 338–39. Many of the later "Haydn" folk-song arrangements for Thomson were done by a pupil. These arrangements nominally from his pen totaled nearly 350.
19. Dean, "Beethoven and Opera," 26.
20. Robinson, *Ludwig van Beethoven,* 2.
21. Dean, "Beethoven and Opera," 29.
22. Thayer/Forbes, 1:346.
23. The influence of Cherubini on Beethoven's theatrical style was noted by critics of the time, including E. T. A. Hoffmann.
24. Dean, "Beethoven and Opera," 32–33.
25. Thayer/Forbes, 1:381.
26. Wyn Jones, *Symphony,* 164.
27. Clive, *Beethoven and His World,* 342; Thayer/Forbes, 1:345.
28. Anderson, vol. 1, no. 88.
29. Thayer/Forbes, 1:352.
30. Senner, *Critical Reception,* 1:190–92; Wallace, *Beethoven's Critics,* 11.

31. B. Cooper, *Beethoven Compendium*, 137.

32. Wegeler/Ries, 68.

33. Solomon, *Beethoven*, 176.

34. The article "Napoleon's Coronation as Emperor of the French," on the Georgian Index, at http://www.georgianindex.net/Napoleon/coronation/coronation.html, notes that Charlemagne's actual crown had been destroyed in the Revolution, so a new one was made in medieval style for the coronation.

35. Nicholls, *Napoleon*, 271–72.

36. Ibid., 58–60.

37. Thayer/Forbes, 1:355–56. Sketches for opp. 54 and 57 are shuffled into work on the opera.

38. Scholars have tended to brush aside the Triple Concerto, or to lavish on it assorted patronizing japes. Leon Plantinga calls it "an interlude in the French manner," Lewis Lockwood a "curiously passive work," Joseph Kerman a "Cinderella and ugly duckling." There is little question that it is uneven, discursive, and stylistically anomalous. It is also too attractive, expressive, and generally interesting to deserve its neglect. Recall that when seen in a good light, Cinderella was also attractive, expressive, and interesting. The reliably unreliable Schindler said that the concerto was written for and premiered by Archduke Rudolph, but that Beethoven pupil was only sixteen when it was written and probably had not yet started taking lessons.

39. Thayer/Forbes, 1:352.

40. The two letters quoted are Anderson, vol. 1, nos. 93 and 94.

41. Ibid., no. 98.

42. Albrecht, vol. 1, no. 90.

43. Thayer/Forbes, 1:356–57.

44. Wyn Jones, *Symphony*, 167. Senner, *Critical Reception*, 2:16n3, has a different chronology.

45. Thayer/Forbes, 1:350n9.

46. Ibid., 373.

47. Wegeler/Ries, 68–69.

48. Ibid., 104–6.

49. Rolland, *Beethoven the Creator*, 264.

50. Marek, *Beethoven*, 95.

51. Klapproth, *Beethoven's Only Beloved*, 22–23.

52. Clive, *Beethoven and His World*, 62; Anderson, vol. 1, no. 97n4.

53. Anderson, vol. 1, no. 97.

54. Thayer/Forbes, 1:358.

55. Quoted in Klapproth, *Beethoven's Only Beloved*, 21. Klapproth points out that Therese was in fact not beautiful and knew it; her "we" probably shows her intense closeness to Josephine, to whom she devoted herself.

56. Thayer/Forbes, 1:359.

57. Anderson, vol. 1, no. 103.

58. MacArdle, "Family van Beethoven," 537.

59. B. Cooper, *Beethoven*, 146–47.

60. Thayer/Forbes, 1:377.

61. As Wyn Jones details in *The Symphony*, 167–68, the tryouts of the *Eroica* Lobkowitz arranged are not entirely documented, and Beethoven was not present at private performances of the piece Lobkowitz arranged in Bohemia — which the prince

could arrange at will, since by contract he owned the piece for some months. Later he temporarily owned the Fifth and Six Symphonies.

62. Albrecht, vol. 1, no. 98.
63. Landon, *Beethoven*, 97.
64. Senner, *Critical Reception*, 1:168.
65. Thayer/Forbes, 1:375.
66. Senner, *Critical Reception*, 2:15–16.
67. Ibid., 2:17.
68. Thayer/Forbes, 1:376.
69. Senner, *Critical Reception*, 2:18.
70. Ibid., 2:19.
71. Ibid., 2:20–24.
72. Ibid., 2:32–33.
73. Ibid., 2:35–36.
74. Ibid., 2:37.

19. Our Hearts Were Stirred

1. Beahrs, "Immortal Beloved," 67. Beahrs and Klapproth (*Beethoven's Only Beloved*) believe Josephine Deym to be the "Immortal Beloved."
2. Anderson, vol. 1, no. 110, some paragraph breaks added. The exact dates of their letters in this period are uncertain. As will be noted again later, the tone of Beethoven's letters to Josephine Deym in this period is close to that of the later letter to the "Immortal Beloved" — except that here he uses the formal *Sie* for "you" and in the I. B. letter he uses the intimate *du*.
3. Ibid., no. 112.
4. Albrecht, vol. 1, no. 99.
5. Beahrs, "Immortal Beloved," 67. Beahrs and Klapproth call Josephine's words of this time love letters — something of a stretch.
6. Albrecht, vol. 1, no. 100. Beahrs ("Immortal Beloved," 66) questions Thayer's translation of Josephine's *heilige Bande* as "holy vows." She suggests "solemn obligations," referring to her children, and I have used that. A more literal translation is "sacred ties" — also likely referring to her children, who would lose their aristocratic privileges if she married a commoner. In any case, as Beahrs points out, Thayer was far off the mark when he suggested Josephine had taken some kind of vow of chastity. She bore at least two children out of wedlock.
7. Albrecht, vol. 1, no. 102. None in this exchange of letters between Beethoven and Deym of ca. spring 1805 have dates, the exact succession is conjectural, some letters exist in fragments, and likely some have been lost.
8. Ibid., no. 164.
9. Thayer/Forbes, 1:379.
10. B. Cooper, *Creative Process*, 51.
11. Senner, *Critical Reception*, 2:170.
12. Winter and Martin, "Quartets," 35.
13. Rosen, *Classical Style*, 143.
14. Albrecht, vol. 1, no. 104.
15. Anderson, vol. 1, no. 118.
16. Senner, *Critical Reception*, 2:224.

17. Thayer/Forbes, 1:400.

18. Franz Grillparzer reported that at the meeting, "Beethoven was full of attention and respect toward Cherubini" (quoted in Landon, *Beethoven*, 201).

19. Czerny, *Proper Performance*, 15.

20. Anderson, vol. 1, no. 119.

21. Landon, *Beethoven* unabridged, 202. This account from a Ries letter of roughly that time to critic and poet Heinrich Rellstab is significantly different from, and less dramatic than, the well-known later account in Ries's memoirs. I trust this one more because it was closer to the event (though Landon's date of 1804 for the letter is approximate).

22. Some details about the *Appassionata*: Like *The Tempest*, the *Waldstein,* the Fifth Symphony, and other of Beethoven's most overwhelming pieces, the *Appassionata* is tight in material and taut in construction — powerful emotion under relentless control. As in the *Waldstein,* in this sonata sonority is tied to structure: each section is defined not only by its material but also by a distinctive color and texture. Performances on period pianos reveal how much the music was inspired by the contrasts in registers of those pianos, from booming low to silvery high (see Swafford, "In Search"). In general, the pianism here is as radically new as in the *Waldstein.* In regard to form, technically speaking, the A-flat-major and A-flat-minor themes are both part of the second group, but I think in practice there is a sense of three themes (the A-flat-major being a late addition). By this sonata the Neapolitan chord has been decisively promoted from a local harmonic event to a full-fledged motif: the beginning idea in F minor is immediately repeated in the Neapolitan key of G-flat. That in turn is linked to the D-flat–C tattoo, which implies N of V. The hopeful moments in the outer movements tend to be extinguished in one way or another. An example is the A-flat-major second theme from m. 35; at the point when we expect a firm cadence, it strays into N at m. 42, followed by an E-flat seventh that resolves not to A-flat major but, at length, into the driving A-flat-minor theme at m. 51. It is often noticed that the four-note tattoo here is the same as the one in the Fifth Symphony; in both cases it has a fateful cast. Recall Ries's experience hearing Beethoven working on bits of the finale, improvising variations. That process seems to me to persist in the final version, which is virtually monothematic, the "whirlwind" idea constantly varied and redefined, as if the finale were in part about the process of composition itself. Finally, in material and tone there are interesting links from the *Appassionata* to two other well-known works: Beethoven's String Quartet in F Minor, op. 90, and Brahms's Piano Quintet in F Minor (the latter is Brahms's response, I think, to both the *Appassionata* and op. 90).

23. This is Donald Francis Tovey's memorable phrase for the *Appassionata* finale.

24. Hearing the *Appassionata* recorded by Stephen Porter on an 1827 Graf instrument from the Frederick Historic Piano Collection is unforgettable — in how the music utilizes the distinctive registers of the Viennese pianos of that time (lost on modern pianos), and in how the ending seems almost like an assault on the instrument, which struggles to contain the music.

25. Senner, *Critical Reception,* 2:168.

26. Thayer/Forbes, 1:380.

27. Heinrich Heine, quoted in Knight, *Beethoven,* 61. Napoleonic-era military garb, up to the plumed shakoes, survives in the uniforms of American marching bands. (The word for the hat came from the Hungarian *csákó,* "peaked cap.")

28. Anderson, vol. 1, no. 121.
29. Hill, *Ferdinand Ries*, 23; Thayer/Forbes, 1:382.
30. Wegeler/Ries, 90.
31. Anderson, vol. 1, no. 125.
32. Wyn Jones, *Life of Beethoven*, 87.
33. Albrecht, vol. 1, no. 105.
34. Ibid., no. 110.
35. Anderson, vol. 1, no. 124. "Colic" means fits of vomiting.
36. Knight, *Beethoven*, 62.
37. Landon, *Beethoven*, 107.
38. Knight, *Beethoven*, 61–62.
39. Thayer/Forbes, 1:384.
40. Ibid., 1:383. When Milder sang for Haydn in her teens, he exclaimed, "My dear child! You have a voice like a house!" It is reported that her age and inexperience showed at the premiere, but she later became a splendid Leonore.
41. Wyn Jones, *Life of Beethoven*, 89.
42. For a view of the final version of *Leonore/Fidelio*, see chapter 26. The overture for the original production was the one later known as *Leonore* No. 2. There is no surviving full score of the opera's first version.
43. Wegeler/Ries, 59–60.
44. Wyn Jones, *Life of Beethoven*, 90.
45. Senner, *Critical Reception*, 2:231.
46. Ibid., 2:173.
47. Thayer/Forbes, 1:399.
48. Joseph Röckel, cited in Landon, *Beethoven*, 107–8, and in Sonneck, *Beethoven*, 60–64. These are two accounts by Röckel that differ in details. I am mainly relying on the fuller account in Sonneck.
49. Anderson, vol. 1, no. 128.
50. B. Cooper, *Beethoven*, 153.
51. Czerny, *Proper Performance*, 14.
52. Röckel, in Sonneck, *Beethoven*, 64–65.
53. Senner, *Critical Reception*, 2:178.
54. Knight, *Beethoven*, 65.
55. Anderson, vol. 1, no. 130.
56. Robinson, *Ludwig van Beethoven*, 27–28.
57. Sonneck, *Beethoven*, 66–67.
58. Albrecht, vol. 1, no. 116.
59. Rev. Christian Sturm, quoted in Thayer/Forbes, 1:391–92. Though in theory Beethoven did not believe in miracles or a God who intervened to change our lives, he was at least as inconsistent as most people in the details of his beliefs. In any case, these words come from Sturm, not Beethoven.
60. Thayer/Forbes, 1:399.
61. Ibid., 1:408.
62. Ibid., 1:400.
63. Winter and Martin, "Quartets," 36.
64. Thayer/Forbes, 1:401.
65. Specht's characterization (*Beethoven as He Lived*, 146).
66. Landon, *Beethoven*, 112.

67. Specht, *Beethoven as He Lived,* 147.
68. Anderson, vol. 1, no. 132. As is noted earlier, Beethoven apparently began the first Razumovsky at the end of May 1806. He declared it finished to Härtel at the beginning of July — which was not likely.
69. B. Cooper, *Beethoven,* 158.
70. Clive, *Beethoven and His World,* 252.
71. Anderson, vol. 1, no. 125.
72. Ibid., no. 178. Oppersdorff was present for the blowup at Lichnowsky's in autumn 1806.
73. Various versions of the story are found in Thayer/Forbes, 1:403; and Landon, *Beethoven,* 115–18. The servant's story appears in Specht, *Beethoven as He Lived,* 20; Solomon, *Beethoven,* 190; and B. Cooper, *Beethoven,* 159.
74. Clive, *Beethoven and His World,* 365–66.
75. Quoted in Stowell, *Beethoven,* 22.
76. Ibid., 6–10; Schwartz, "French Violin School," 432, 446.
77. Winds are used prominently in the Violin Concerto, often scored with oboes rather than flute on top, producing a distinctively eighteenth-century sound.
78. As Stowell elaborates (*Beethoven,* 80–85), Owen Jander finds in the slow movement the atmosphere of a *Romanze,* of which Beethoven wrote two freestanding examples for violin. Plantinga among others is dubious about the connection. In general Plantinga finds more tension in the first movement than I do, using descriptions like "high pathos" and "insistent in the extreme." As he notes, though, the most common descriptor applied to the whole work is "serene." And as Plantinga also admits, most of the incipient disruptions are quickly restored to peace.
79. At the end of the finale Beethoven recalls the opening timpani tattoo, but I think that since the tattoo has not been around throughout, it's more a formal than an audible connection. In order to be meaningful, motifs have to keep happening. That the timpani tattoo largely gets lost after the first movement (though perhaps it survives in themes that tend to fall hard on the beat in duple patterns) and that the "sore" D-sharp near the beginning has only hazy implications later are, to me, signs of the haste in which the concerto was composed. The extreme regularity of the phrasing in the first movement may be another sign; likewise, that Beethoven used a perhaps-borrowed, at any rate conventional, theme for the finale. It took him time and energy to give fresh twists to ideas and their phrasing; his first thoughts were often more conventional and foursquare. My general sense is that the pieces he composed in a hurry have less pervasive and complex thematic, tonal, and rhythmic interrelationships, because there was not as much time to think, revise, and plan ahead.
80. Senner, *Critical Reception,* 2:68–69.
81. Stowell, *Beethoven,* 16–19, 24. Beethoven had heard Clement's Violin Concerto in D Major, because it premiered on an April 1805 concert in which Beethoven conducted the *Eroica.* Plantinga (*Beethoven's Concertos,* 233) notes that the violin writing in Beethoven's concerto is on the whole less adventurous than Viotti's.
82. Stowell says (*Beethoven,* 52–55) that in the manuscript of the Violin Concerto, there are multiple staves given to the solo part, and many passages have two or three different versions noted on those staves. The whole manuscript is much worked over by Beethoven, but it remains unclear how the final published version was arrived

at. As Plantinga writes (*Beethoven's Concertos,* 239), "the current form of the violin part bears an odd, fragmented relationship to the text of the autograph"; sometimes it follows the top line of the solo, sometimes the second, and sometimes it has a passage that does not appear on the autograph at all.

83. A paraphrase of Eugène Ysaÿe in Stowell, *Beethoven,* 20. It was mainly Joseph Joachim who placed the Violin Concerto in the repertoire, starting with a celebrated performance in 1844, when he was twelve.

20. That Haughty Beauty

1. Wyn Jones, *Life of Beethoven,* 92–93.
2. Thayer/Forbes, 1:427–28.
3. Senner, *Critical Reception,* 2:52–53.
4. *Grove Music Online,* s.v. "Schuppanzigh, Ignaz." As a historical footnote, Schuppanzigh also was one of only two men known to play in the premieres of every Beethoven symphony. The other was Anton Schreiber, the violist of his quartet.
5. Landon, *Beethoven,* 56–58.
6. Wegeler/Ries, 116.
7. Specht, *Beethoven as He Lived,* 42–43.
8. B. Cooper, *Beethoven Compendium,* 234.
9. Kerman, *Beethoven Quartets,* 59.
10. Part of the effect of the beginning of op. 59, no. 1, is that the cello solo mostly falls on the relatively milder middle G and D strings. The melody on the C string would have been stronger, on the A string more lyrical and sweet. Both were possible, but Beethoven chose the strings with the least distinctive character. Ratner, in *Beethoven String Quartets,* considers the tone of the movement "melancholy and nostalgic ... bittersweet in the touches of sharp dissonance" (106). Most commentators don't hear it in those terms. I find a certain expressive elusiveness in the F Major — part of its relatively undramatic quality.
11. Kerman in *Beethoven Quartets* emphasizes the individuality of the works. I'm concerned with how that individuality is expressed not only in the themes and forms but also in the colors and textures.
12. The opening of the F Major is made still more unstable, more strange, by its theme that turns around C, the fifth degree of the scale, treated as if it were the first degree, giving the cello theme a certain modal, Mixolydian flavor.
13. A few more elements unite the main theme of the first and last movements of the F Major Quartet. Both have a falling step on A–G that echoes the D–C motif, and the articulation of the finale theme has a resemblance to the 1234 1 rhythmic motif of the first movement: its implied phrasing is 1212 1. Also, both themes have a modal quality. The first segment of each transacts its main business within the compass of the sixth C to A. And, of course, both themes are presented by the cello, the main protagonist of the quartet, often involved in playing a melody rather than the usual bass line — which, as is noted, gives the whole quartet a bit of a suspended, modal quality (see Kerman, *Beethoven Quartets,* 93).
14. In characteristic Beethovenian fashion, the F Major's opening 1234 1 rhythmic motif is diminished from quarters to eighths in the third bar, augmented to whole notes in the violin from m. 16.

15. Kerman, *Beethoven Quartets,* uses "reinterpretation" for the effect I'm calling "re-definition" in the F Major, though he applies it only to the first movements of all three quartets. I think the most elaborate example of it is in the second movement of the F Major, with its constant reenvisioning of its opening rhythmic motif.

16. As late as the final manuscript, Beethoven had planned to repeat the entire development and recapitulation of the F Major Quartet first movement, but he finally struck it out (Lockwood, *Beethoven: Music,* 320). As Lockwood notes, even without the repeat this is still the longest quartet movement written to that time. Also, until late in the game he planned a similar repeat in the second movement, which is likewise enormous even without the repeat. If he had included the repeats, he would have ended up with a quartet as long as or longer than the *Eroica.* Lockwood concludes that the F Major "formed the primary model for quartet composers for the rest of the 19th century" (321), including Schumann, Mendelssohn, and Brahms.

17. The element that unifies the basketful of keys in the development of the F Major first movement is that most of them involve, and so constantly redefine, the note D: it is the sixth degree of the scale in F, the third degree in B-flat, the fifth degree in G minor, and so on, until it becomes the much-emphasized leading tone of E-flat minor.

18. Kerman, *Beethoven Quartets,* 109.

19. Regarding the form of the second movement of the F Major, see Ratner, *Beethoven String Quartets,* 117 and 119. He calls the total effect a "picaresque journey." It is in a barely noticeable sonata form with elements of rondo. "Drumbeat" and "pirouette" are Ratner's terms for the second movement's two leading ideas.

20. Landon, *Beethoven* unabridged, 208.

21. Kerman, *Beethoven Quartets,* 110.

22. Solomon, in "Beethoven, Freemasonry," 116, speculates that the "brother" involved in the slow movement of op. 59, no. 1, might have been a Masonic brother; the acacia is a Masonic symbol (though the willow is not). It is not likely that Beethoven was referring to a brother of his who died in infancy.

23. As is common in a slow-movement sonata form, there is no repeat of the exposition. The scalewise rising-fourth figure from the first movement turns up periodically, sometimes inverted, and there is a series of them in the first violin leading to the transitional violin solo, which has a series of fourth descents and ends with repeated D–C figures — the quartet's primal motif.

24. The primal D–C motif is very much around in the finale of the F Major — it arose from the first two notes of the *Thème russe* in the first place. As in the first movement, the keys tend to involve and redefine D (notably the redefining of D in the wrong-key recapitulation in B-flat), with one exception: there are excursions to D-flat in the developments of the first and third movements and a similar one to A-flat in the finale. All of them make a point of the D-flat becoming D-natural in modulating away from the flat key. I tend to agree with Kerman's and other scholars' feeling that the finale is not up to the level of the other movements. That is not an uncommon problem with Beethoven — and myriad other composers. Finales are a chronic headache.

25. Kerman, in *Beethoven Quartets,* 102, contrasts the F Major Quartet with the *Eroica* Symphony, saying the quartet "resists programmatic imaginings . . . breathes an abstract quality that sets it in a different emotional sphere from the symphony."

At some point I wrote in the margin of that page "don't agree!," but now, as the text reflects, I rather do agree. Kerman also notes, "Does not the piece as a whole tend towards a loose modality?" (103). As is noted in the text, I agree but don't see why he cites Lydian mode; the beginning actually has a Mixolydian feel, the finale's *Thème russe* tending to natural minor.

26. As is said in the text, the opening fifth in the violin and the cello's simultaneous E–D-sharp appear to be the primal motifs in the E Minor Quartet. Three measures later that B will rise a half step to C, then, in the turn to the Neapolitan, the E will rise to F. What seems to me to be the essential idea behind all this is *a fifth or other larger interval with a half step on each side*. The prime form of that motif is D-sharp–E–B–C, but its echoes are myriad throughout, and D-sharp/E-flat is the starring pitch. I think the presence of C major periodically in the piece and its sustained threat to E minor in the finale are partly explained by the figure D-sharp–E, the leading tone of the quartet's E minor rising to the third of C major. In its guise as E-flat, the starring pitch tends to relate to D, as in the cello in the beginning of the first-movement development. In other words, the D-sharp/E-flat is continually swinging one way or the other, relating to the keys E or D as the tonality goes — and thereby serves as a generating element of the tonal structure. So as D was the highlighted pitch in the F Major Quartet, in the E Minor it's D-sharp/E-flat — spelled out at the beginning of the development when E-flat–B-flat is respelled D-sharp–A-sharp, taking E-flat major into the beginning of a stepwise modulation scheme (echoing the first measures): B minor to C minor, A-flat major to B-flat minor, B minor to C major — and with that latter key another burst of ebullience. (C major will turn up in the same mood, same key, and same notes in the finale's *Thema*.) Meanwhile the presence of F major harks back to the first quartet in the set, the presence of C major to the next member of the set.

27. On the expressive effects of rests in music, see Swafford, "Silence Is Golden."

28. Both main themes of the E-minor second movement feature the primal E–D-sharp motif, the first theme beginning E–D-sharp and the second theme B–D-sharp–E (so also including the B–E fifth motif).

29. In the second movement of the E Minor, a *marcato* idea in horn fifths outlines the shape of the Russian theme to come in the scherzo, and the coda recalls the arpeggio themes of the beginning of the quartet.

30. The most famous use of the op. 56, no. 2, Russian folk song is the mighty coronation scene of Mussorgsky's *Boris Godunov*. Beethoven's treatment of it is joking, Mussorgsky's grand.

31. The shocking first chord of the C Major is a diminished seventh. Beethoven often does not resolve those kind of chords conventionally, and sometimes simply moves freely from one diminished seventh to another. This treatment is intended to erase a sense of tonality for a while; it is Beethoven's form of atonality.

32. Senner, *Critical Reception*, 2:172.

33. Ratner, in *Beethoven String Quartets*, 151, identifies the barcarole rhythm of the C Major Quartet's second movement.

34. Clive, *Beethoven and His World*, 31.

35. Thayer/Forbes, 1:413.

36. Clive, *Beethoven and His World*, 31.

37. Anderson, vol. 1, no. 138.

38. Ibid., nos. 138a and 139.

39. Thayer/Forbes, 1:416. It is possible these concerts were held in the Lichnowsky palace, but Thayer votes for Lobkowitz. There may have been a separate concert at Lichnowsky's, as Barry Cooper notes in *Beethoven Compendium*, 18–19.

40. Wegeler/Ries, 88–89.

41. Albrecht, vol. 1, no. 119.

42. B. Cooper, *Beethoven*, 167.

43. Clive, *Beethoven and His World*, 76.

44. Anderson, vol. 1, no. 143.

45. Ibid., no. 148.

46. Thayer/Forbes, 1:421–22.

47. Ibid., 1:423.

48. Anderson, vol. 1, no. 150; Albrecht, vol. 1, no. 122.

49. Gordon, "Franz Grillparzer," 555.

50. Albrecht, vol. 1, no. 124. This is noted in a letter from Prince Nikolaus to his vice-*Kapellmeister* Fuchs demanding to know why the altos were not at the rehearsal and saying that if Fuchs could not keep his singers in line, it would be on his head.

51. Anderson, vol. 1, no. 150. Here is one of the few cases of Beethoven saying something nice about Haydn during the old man's lifetime, though it is more a case of his being conventionally humble and deferential toward the prince.

52. Kinderman, *Beethoven*, 122.

53. Scherman and Biancolli, 495.

54. Kinderman, *Beethoven*, 122.

55. Hummel himself had provided a couple of masses for the princess's name day, so there actually may have been a little schadenfreude involved, but he was probably not gloating so much as tickled by his employer's response. On the whole, he and Beethoven got along well.

56. Albrecht, vol. 1, no. 124n4.

57. Anderson, vol. 1, no. 167.

58. Albrecht, vol. 1, no. 127.

59. Anderson, vol. 1, no. 151.

60. Ibid., nos. 154 and 156.

61. Solomon, *Beethoven*, 203. The report of Beethoven's suicide attempt comes not only from Schindler, who cannot be trusted, but also from tenor Joseph August Röckel, who is reasonably reliable. Schindler's account is quite specific as to the place and events, which adds some credence. Both are vague about the time, but Solomon suspects it was in the aftermath of the Josephine affair, and I agree.

62. Klapproth, *Beethoven's Only Beloved*, 84.

63. Quoted in ibid., 89. Klapproth assigns dates of 1809 to Beethoven's and Josephine's final surviving letters, without explanation. Albrecht and Anderson place them in 1807, the currently accepted dates (some of the extant parts of her side of their correspondence are things she wrote down as drafts — they are dated in relation to the Beethoven letters they seem to have responded to or inspired). It is suspicious of Klapproth not to have given reasons for his dates, yet more suspicious that in the case of Josephine's letter translated as no. 127 in Albrecht, Klapproth translates *mein Freund Beethoven* as "my boyfriend Beethoven" rather than the usual and far more likely "my <u>friend</u> Beethoven" (which I believe was intended to convey "my <u>friend</u> but not my <u>lover</u>"). I will leave these hairsplittings at this point, because they are

endless, but this kind of thing gives one pause about Klapproth's methods. At the same time, I am using some of his translations of material directly from Josephine and Therese. I also have to demur about Klapproth citing me in his acknowledgments, as if I somehow contributed to his book. I did nothing except to say I'd like to see it, thanks for sending it, and good luck. His fudging, meanwhile, does not mean Klapproth cannot be right about Josephine being the "Immortal Beloved." If nothing else, he fleshes out the fascinating story of Josephine's life and loves for English readers.

21. Schemes

1. Thayer/Forbes, 1:426.
2. From the *Oxford English Dictionary*, s.v. "genius": "This sense [of genius], which belongs also to F. *génie*, Ger. *genie*, appears to have been developed in the 18th c. (It is not recognized in Johnson's Dictionary.) ... The word had come to be applied with especial frequency to the kind of intellectual power manifested by poets and artists; and when in this application 'genius,' as native endowment, came to be contrasted with the aptitudes that can be acquired by study, the approach to the modern sense was often very close. [In] the further development of meaning ... the word had an especial fitness to denote that particular kind of intellectual power which has the appearance of proceeding from a supernatural inspiration or possession, and which seems to arrive at its results in an inexplicable and miraculous manner. This use ... came into great prominence in Germany, and gave the designation of *Genieperiode* to the epoch in German literature otherwise known as the 'Sturm und Drang' period. Owing to the influence of Ger. literature in the present century, this is now the most familiar sense of the Eng. word, and usually colours the other senses." See Peter Kivy's *The Possessor and the Possessed*, a study of the philosophy of genius.
3. Thayer/Forbes, 1:426.
4. Anderson, vol. 1, no. 164.
5. Wyn Jones, *Life of Beethoven*, 97.
6. Albrecht, vol. 1, no. 128.
7. Wyn Jones, *Beethoven*, 5.
8. Ibid., 9–10.
9. Thayer/Forbes, 1:444.
10. Anderson, vol. 1, no. 165.
11. Quoted in Geiringer, *Haydn*, 184.
12. Ibid., 185–86.
13. Kinsky and Halm, *Das Werk Beethovens*, 132.
14. The concert where the Fourth Symphony and *Coriolan* were first heard in Vienna comes from a review that mentions only the palace of "L.," which could represent either Lobkowitz or Lichnowsky. The balance of evidence points to Lobkowitz.
15. Lockwood, *Beethoven: Music*, 216.
16. A. Peter Brown calls the beginning of the Fourth one of Beethoven's several echoes of Haydn's "Chaos" in *The Creation* (*Symphonic Repertoire*, 476).
17. Tovey writes of the Fourth Symphony's "mastery of movement ... Mozart's freedom of movement reappears as one of the most striking qualities of the whole" (Scherman and Biancolli, 565).

18. Concerning the various expressive effects of pauses in music, see Swafford, "Silence Is Golden."
19. Senner, *Critical Reception*, 2:69.
20. Ibid., 2:43. The text has "the last of those," which I presume is a typo for "least."
21. See Lockwood, "Autograph." Most of the changes in the development have to do with redistributing material back and forth between cello and piano.
22. The D Major Trio is another work of ingenious unities. The stunning emotional turn of the second movement is prepared by the coda of the first. Each movement begins with an introductory gesture involving some kind of halt followed by a more sustained theme. Its world is also marked by a developmental approach, the ideas varying and metamorphosing constantly — which in the second movement is geared to an effect of something obsessive or inescapable.
23. Lockwood, *Beethoven: Studies*, 191–97.
24. Thayer/Forbes, 1:441–42.
25. Anderson, vol. 1, no. 167.
26. Ibid., no. 169; B. Cooper, *Beethoven Compendium*, 19, which reports 100 ducats, which is over 400 florins.
27. Anderson, vol. 1, no. 170.
28. Marek, *Beethoven*, 261–64; Clive, *Beethoven and His World*, 101–2.
29. Nicholls, *Napoleon*, 31–32; Clive, ibid., 39–40. The grandson of Jérôme Bonaparte's American wife, Charles Joseph Bonaparte, was secretary of the navy and attorney general under President Theodore Roosevelt.
30. Donakowski, *Muse*, 91.
31. Anderson, vol. 1, no. 166.
32. Ibid., no. 178.
33. Clive, *Beethoven and His World*, 252–53.
34. Anderson, vol. 1, nos. 180–81.
35. Landon, *Beethoven*, 124–25.
36. *Grove Music Online*, s.v. "Reichardt, Johann Friedrich."
37. Landon, *Beethoven* unabridged, 215.

22. Darkness to Light

1. Thayer/Forbes, 1:446.
2. Senner, *Critcal Reception*, 2:49. This account of what Beethoven said at the breakdown of the *Choral Fantasy* is from the newspaper report. Thayer/Forbes, 1:448–49, has a series of vaguely similar accounts of what happened and why. As conductor Seyfried recalled it, Beethoven forgot that he had told the orchestra not to make a repeat of the second variation, and they went on while he repeated.
3. Landon, *Beethoven*, 128.
4. Thayer/Forbes, 1:446–48.
5. To start a concerto with the soloist alone turns the classical concerto model upside down. Ordinarily the orchestra gives an exposition of the leading ideas, followed by the soloist entering to start the second part of the "double exposition." To begin with, the soloist creates formidable formal problems, in terms of the presentation of the main theme. Beethoven solves the problem with something that is also the dramatic essence of the Fourth Concerto: the soloist and orchestra never agree on

how the main theme goes. The piano has its version, the orchestra its version. Still, the orchestra's startling first entrance in B major is prepared in a characteristically Beethovenian way: B is the melody note the piano soliloquy begins on. (Similarly, in the *Waldstein* first movement, the E major of the second theme is prepared by the top-voice E of the first bar.)

6. There has been a great deal of commentary on the unusual opposition of solo and orchestra in the *second* movement of the Fourth Concerto. I have found no notice of the way the first page of the concerto and the whole first movement foreshadow that opposition. It is my position that Beethoven does not pull a new structural or dramatic idea out of a hat in the middle of a piece, but prepares all the important ideas from early on. (The rare exceptions are works like the Sixth and Eighth Symphonies, in which he deliberately breaks his own formal rules for realistic or expressive effect.) Which is to say, a major conception in a Beethoven second movement is going to be part of the conception and presentation from the beginning. The three movements of the Fourth Concerto present three kinds of bifurcation between solo and orchestra: in the first movement the soloist simply refuses to buy, and sometimes mocks, most of the orchestra's ideas; in the second movement the two are at loggerheads but come to a tentative reconciliation; in the third movement the same division is played as comedy and resolved harmoniously.

7. Plantinga, *Beethoven's Concertos*, 211.

8. Plantinga details Joseph Kerman's dissatisfaction with the piano's recapitulation: "I don't come up with any association to 'explain' it" (ibid., 200). My explanation makes sense to me, but it's more a dramatic than a "musical" explanation.

9. That the solo part in the first movement of the Fourth has been virtuosic, brilliant, and cadenza-like all along is my surmise for why the first of Beethoven's two cadenzas published a few years later, which is the one most often used, is so massive and elaborate: it has to be, to outdo what came before. My apologies for using "he" for the soloist. It's partly for the sake of simplicity, partly because I imagine the soloist as masculine but not at all aggressive. At times I find him Hamletlike, sunk in thought but not entirely oblivious to what is around him. Plantinga observes how Beethoven "luxuriates" in the new high notes available in the newest instruments. His old concertos went up to F above the treble staff; the Fourth reaches to C above that.

10. Jander has famously championed the idea that the second movement of the Fourth represents Orpheus taming the Furies. There is no evidence for Beethoven having had that in mind. At the same time, the few stories we know that lie behind his music, mainly ones he supplied himself, as in the *Lebewohl* Sonata and the *Eroica* and *Pastoral* Symphonies, are those kinds of narratives more often than ones from his own life (the *Lebewohl* turns an incident from his life into a larger human story). Note that all those stated programs apply to a whole piece, however, not just to a single movement.

11. The sudden interludes in flat keys in the finale of the Fourth — B-flat and E-flat — echo similar moments in the same keys in the first movement.

12. What I am saying about Beethoven's relationship to keys is that he had a core association of a given key with an expressive quality: the C-minor mood, the C-major mood, the E-flat-major mood, the E-flat-minor mood, and so on. At the same time, he liked to probe other qualities of a key. His works in E-flat major, for example, are by no means all heroic. A pointed example is with the *Waldstein:* C major is usually

a key implying a certain equanimity, but the C major of the *Waldstein* is searching and dynamic. To put it another way: never interested in repeating himself, when Beethoven picked up a key he had used before, he wanted to find a fresh angle on it.

13. Critic and theorist A. B. Marx, well before Schindler's line about fate appeared, portrayed the Fifth Symphony as an individual's struggle with fate. If Schindler fabricated Beethoven's observation, he could have gotten the idea from Marx.

14. As is said in the text, I think in the first five bars of the Fifth Symphony Beethoven intended to misdirect listeners about the key, expecting that we would hear the first four pitches, G–E-flat–F–D, in E-flat major. But I think the effect is lost with familiarity: anyone who knows the Fifth hears the first notes in C minor. It's a good question how many deliberate ambiguities intended by composers vanish with familiarity.

15. Beyond the rhythm and the S shape of the opening tattoo, every other element of it will be mined: the descending third of the first two notes is an important motif on its own (it becomes chains of descending minor thirds forming the o7 chords that mark structural junctions). The rising E-flat–F of notes 2 and 3 become the rising-step figure in the fog at the retransition. In addition, the A-flat–G in the violas at mm. 7 and 8 establish a falling-half-step motif that will have an important place.

16. The meter of the Fifth's first movement is a fast 2/4 conducted in one. Most of the phrases in the movement are four bars long, so it could have been written in 4/4. But Beethoven, a master of the psychology of notation, knew that for musicians a fast 2/4 has a nervous energy that 4/4 does not.

17. Kerman, in "Notes on Beethoven's Codas," 151, writes, "Thematic 'completion' . . . should be regarded as the centrally important feature in Beethoven's codas of the second period."

18. Kinderman, *Beethoven,* 126. He calls the brassy C-major perorations of the second movement "the distant premonition of a goal that cannot yet be attained" until the finale, and the third movement an "advance parody" of the finale.

19. Beethoven tinkered with the new pieces during rehearsals for the premiere and sent revisions to Breitkopf & Härtel afterward. In the process his intentions about the scherzo of the Fifth may have gotten lost in the shuffle. In the versions published first and afterward, there is only one round of the trio and no repeat of the original A section, only the varied, parodistic version of it. So what survived is a relatively conventional three-part scherzo form, A–B (trio)–A1 (the repeat varied and finally disappearing in fog). But it is possible that Beethoven, after much indecision, finally wanted the usual repeat back to the beginning and two rounds of the trio, making a five-part scherzo form: A–B–A–B–A1 (see Brandenburg, "Once Again"). The three-part version became established, but I argue that the five-part is preferable on musical grounds. For me the short version, even after decades of familiarity, does not leave the third movement expansive enough to balance the other movements. (In his notes to his Fifth Symphony edition, Jonathan Del Mar makes a meticulous case in favor of the three-part scherzo.)

20. Structurally speaking, what I'm calling the "fog" in the first three movements is an unusual kind of transition section. In the first movement it is the retransition to the recapitulation; in the second movement it marks the end of an A–B cycle in the double variations; in the third movement it is the transition to the finale, and the transition to the recapitulation after the return of the scherzo.

21. A. Peter Brown, *Symphonic Repertoire,* 489.

22. As of the turn of the nineteenth century, trombones were most familiar in church music and in opera and oratorio. Since they carried that association with the sacred, they also served to suggest the opposite: thus Mozart's demonic trombones at the end of *Don Giovanni,* and many similar effects since (see the "Witch's Round" in Berlioz's *Symphonie fantastique*). Remember that until the perfection of valves later in the century, trombones were the only chromatic brass instrument, and because of the slide they still retain the throaty quality of open horns. I am a former trombonist and have long considered the instrument a kind of muscular, working-class bloke in comparison to the more elegant and distinguished French horns, or the svelte and swashbuckling trumpets.

23. To reinforce a point made before: For clarity I sometimes present thematic relationships in place as they turn up in the music, but it is not really accurate to talk about relationships and echoes of themes as a looking backward. It is better to see them as the composer does, as a matter of the progression of ideas, of ongoing variation: taking a piece of material and making it into new things. So for Beethoven as for most composers, a thematic relation is not usually a matter of citing things backward but of the material at hand moving forward — though sometimes one will go back and rework something to make it more relevant to the leading ideas.

24. I am paraphrasing E. M. Forster on the Fifth Symphony in *Howards End.* Forster found the third movement more unequivocally demonic than I do; he calls it a "goblin." I find its import ambiguous, somewhere between comic and unsettling; thus my term *nonscherzo.*

25. Remarkably enough, the second performance of the Fifth Symphony was in Vienna on the night after its premiere, in a benefit for violinist Franz Clement (Wyn Jones, *Symphony,* 132).

26. Wyn Jones, *Beethoven,* 14–15. See also Kirby, "Beethoven's Pastoral Symphony." Kirby defines the Beethovenian sense of a "characteristic" piece as "a composition possessing certain typical features that mark it as belonging to a particular genre or type." Among the familiar types were the passionate Sturm und Drang, the pathetic, the melancholy, the military, the hunt, and the pastoral-idyllic.

27. Solomon points out in *Beethoven,* 266, that Beethoven seems to have adapted his movement titles in the *Pastoral* (not necessarily consciously, I add) from a symphony he heard in Bonn called *Le portrait musical de la nature,* by J. H. Knecht.

28. The development of the *Pastoral's* first movement is an example of the way Beethoven turns the conventions of sonata form inside out. The Fifth is the distillation of the drama inherent in the form; the Sixth is its negation, with the usually searching and dramatic development section the most placid part of the movement.

29. Thayer/Forbes, 1:438.

30. Botstein, "Beethoven's Orchestral Music," 172.

31. Wyn Jones, *Beethoven,* 38. In his Fifth Symphony edition, Jonathan Del Mar notes that the Sixth's familiar finale title was created by the publisher, so he restores the title on Beethoven's manuscript: "Shepherd Song / Benevolent feelings with thanks to the Divinity after the storm."

32. Kirby, in "Beethoven's Pastoral Symphony," 112, says the opening theme of the finale is a *ranz des vaches,* calling it a Swiss yodeling tune. It is more properly an alpenhorn call.

33. This evocation of the creative process of the *Pastoral* is from a compendium of sources, including the sketchbooks. See also Wyn Jones, *Beethoven,* 10–11. Wyn Jones details some echoes of Haydn's nature painting in the *Pastoral.*

34. Landon, *Beethoven,* 157.

35. Sturm, *Reflections,* passim.

36. Will begins his article "Time" citing Tovey's "peculiar claim": "Not a bar of the 'Pastoral' Symphony would be otherwise if its 'programme' had never been thought of." Obviously I find Tovey's claim more than peculiar — it is absurd. Meanwhile to see this, as most of the literature does, as a symphony that happens to have a pastoral atmosphere is to get it backward. As is detailed in the text, the idea for the symphony *began* with the program, which was then mapped into conventional forms that had to be bent and reshaped for the purpose. Every detail of the melody, harmony, rhythm, color, and form rose from the idea of the pastoral. But there are still familiar elements, among them the usual Beethovenian motivic relationships that enfold even the storm. Will gives a list of the "storm" motifs on p. 284, followed by the end of the scherzo. Note that his "storm" motif *b* echoes the theme of the scherzo on the next page. His motif *e,* the "lightning" figure from the storm, is prepared by the darting upward arpeggios in mm. 257–62 of the scherzo. Most intriguing is motif *d,* a rushing figure from the storm, which echoes the step up and sixth descent of, for example, mm. 240–44 of the scherzo (G–A–G–F–E–D–C). Augmented, that line will also be a leading idea in the finale.

37. Wyn Jones, *Beethoven,* 33–34.

38. Ibid., 36–37.

39. Senner, *Critical Reception,* 2:49.

40. Ibid., 2:50.

41. Basil Deane, in Arnold, *Beethoven Reader,* 297.

42. Knight, *Beethoven,* 73.

23. Thus Be Enabled to Create

1. Thayer/Forbes, 1:458.

2. Kagan, *Archduke Rudolph,* 12.

3. Wyn Jones, *Life of Beethoven,* 109.

4. Clive, *Beethoven and His World,* 295.

5. Kagan, *Archduke Rudolph,* 29.

6. Landon, *Beethoven,* 133–34.

7. Clive, *Beethoven and His World,* 183.

8. Solomon, *Beethoven,* 201. That Beethoven suspected Erdödy was paying the servant for sexual favors is a speculation of Solomon's.

9. Anderson, vol. 1, no. 208.

10. Ibid., no. 207.

11. Thayer/Forbes, 1:464. The date of the fracas between Breuning and Carl is not certain, but the leading guess is 1809.

12. Anderson, vol. 1, no. 216.

13. Clive, *Beethoven and His World,* 103. Anton Schindler was not a generous judge of Beethoven performers, but he admired Ertmann.

14. Albrecht, vol. 1, no. 78n1.

15. Thayer/Forbes, 1:412–13.

16. Ibid., 1:413.
17. Anderson, vol. 1, no. 202.
18. Brion, *Daily Life,* 149–50.
19. Herriot, *Life and Times,* 174.
20. Marek, *Beethoven,* 402.
21. Geiringer, *Haydn,* 189.
22. Knight, *Beethoven,* 76.
23. Marek, *Beethoven,* 402.
24. Sonneck, *Beethoven,* 68–75.
25. Marek, *Beethoven,* 407.
26. Anderson, vol. 1, no. 220.
27. Albrecht, vol. 1, no. 144.
28. B. Cooper, *Beethoven Compendium,* 20.
29. Albrecht, vol. 1, no. 145.
30. B. Cooper, *Beethoven,* 189–90.
31. Ibid., 192.
32. Anderson, vol. 1, no. 243.
33. Ibid., no. 235.
34. Kagan, *Archduke Rudolph,* 54.
35. Thayer/Forbes, 1:464.
36. Skowroneck, *Beethoven the Pianist,* 93. Skowroneck, 98, quotes a letter from Andreas Streicher saying that while he liked the sound of English and French pianos more than any others, he believed the action was "completely at odds with the structure of the hand" and so most people would not be able to play them. His goal was "to combine this [English/French] tone with our usual [Viennese] action." One should note that while his firm's pianos were usually formally attributed to Andreas, in fact his wife, Nannette, built them — as most musicians knew. Meanwhile, Skowroneck tentatively suggests that Reichardt overstated Beethoven's influence on Streicher. On the basis of existing letters, that could be said, but Beethoven also had plenty of personal contact with both Andreas and Nannette Streicher, which probably included much back-and-forth sharing of ideas, and Beethoven was never shy about expressing his opinions.
37. Rosen, in *Beethoven's Piano Sonatas,* 197, calls the beginning of the F-sharp Major Sonata "not an introduction at all, but a fragment of an independent slow movement . . . There are no models or precedents for these opening bars." Meanwhile, if the personality of op. 78 is gentle and charming, its key of F-sharp major makes it very hard for the fingers to get around. Surely this is one of the reasons this sonata is less well known than it might be. Drake in *Beethoven Sonatas* notes the prevailing B-sharp–C-sharp idea that underlies much of the material. The other leading motif is the three-note ascending (or descending) bit of scale heard in the introduction — the same motif as in the *Lebewohl* and any number of other Beethoven works.
38. Dahlhaus writes of the *Lebewohl* Sonata, in *Ludwig van Beethoven,* "The meaning expressed . . . does not lie in the extra-musical reality reflected in the work's themes, nor exclusively in the intra-musical structural coherence, but in the transformation of the one into the other" (41).
39. The introduction of the *Lebewohl* first movement is a prime example of Beethoven's way of suspending harmony: the *Lebewohl* motif is clearly in E-flat major, but the first full chord is C minor and there is no cadence to the tonic until the fifth bar

of the Allegro. There is a general tendency to aim for the dominant, and the Allegro begins strikingly on a subdominant sixth chord that slithers downward in chromatic thirds.

40. Anderson, vol. 1, no. 325.
41. Steinberg, "Late Quartets," 199.
42. The scherzo of the *Harp* Quartet clearly made a great impression on Mendelssohn; it is a virtual prototype of his "fairy" scherzos.
43. Anderson, vol. 1, nos. 251–52.
44. Ibid., no. 253.
45. Ibid., no. 258.
46. Some have questioned whether *Für Elise* was really written for Therese Malfatti. For one thing, of course, there is the name. As Barry Cooper points out in *Beethoven,* however, it was probably a pet name for Therese. Also the date of the composition is right, and when she died Therese had it in her possession, among other Beethoven manuscripts.
47. Thayer/Forbes, 1:490–91.
48. Anderson, vol. 1, no. 254. Anderson's dates of this letter and no. 265 are approximate; I have arranged them in what seems to be the correct order, showing the unraveling of Beethoven's hopes for Therese.
49. This is a supposition from Beethoven's note to Gleichenstein. A niece of Therese Malfatti later said of the proposal, "[H]er parents would never have given their consent" (Thayer/Forbes, 1:491).
50. Ibid., 1:490.
51. Anderson, vol. 1, no. 265.
52. Ibid., no. 256.
53. Kerman, *Beethoven Quartets,* 158.
54. Anderson, vol. 1, no. 263.
55. Senner, *Critical Reception,* 2:95–97, paragraph breaks added. I'm guessing that the Senner phrase "various simpletons make every drink" is a mistranslation for the archaic "various simples," which I've rendered as "various mysterious ingredients" in my third paragraph. I've also changed this translation's "interminable longing" at the end to the more familiar "infinite longing," because "interminable" has an inappropriate pejorative connotation.

24. Myths and Men

1. Sonneck, *Beethoven,* 85.
2. Friedenthal, *Goethe,* 131.
3. Helps and Howard, *Bettina,* 13–14.
4. Ibid., 76.
5. Wolf, "Your Next Life."
6. Helps and Howard, *Bettina,* 213.
7. Ibid., 28–30.
8. Ibid., 33.
9. Ibid., 80–81.
10. Wolf, "Your Next Life," 39.
11. Bettina Brentano, quoted in Walden, *Beethoven's Immortal Beloved,* 42.
12. Friedenthal, *Goethe,* 410.

13. Walden, *Beethoven's Immortal Beloved*, 30–31.

14. Marek, *Beethoven*, 277–78. The quotation is from Varnhagen von Ense.

15. Helps and Howard, *Bettina*, 204–5.

16. Ibid., 150.

17. Sonneck, *Beethoven*, 79–82.

18. If I am right that Beethoven in some unknowable degree allowed Bettina Brentano to put words in his mouth in her letters to Goethe, there are two possible and interlocking reasons for it. The obvious one is that he wanted to reach Goethe, and Bettina could write a more compelling letter than he could. The second reason is that, while Beethoven spoke very little about his music, he appreciated other people's rhapsodies inspired by his work, whether they came from critics like E. T. A. Hoffmann and Adolph Marx or from imaginative enthusiasts like Bettina.

19. Walden, in *Beethoven's Immortal Beloved*, 95–100, details the changes Bettina made in her published letters from Goethe by comparing them to the ones that still exist (nine of the sixteen in her book). He shows her changes to be relatively minor and most often the kind of political statements that would have been unwritable at the time, because they would have been censored. In regard to Goethe's letters to Bettina that are missing, Walden speculates on what additions may have been made. He also notes that she never claimed to have published his letters exactly as written, and that she likely took more liberties with *her* side of the correspondence. Bettina's defenders say that her collections of letters are actually epistolary novels, like Goethe's *Sorrows of Young Werther*.

20. B. Cooper, *Beethoven Compendium*, 20–21.

21. Thayer/Forbes, 1:490.

22. As an element in his thesis that Bettina Brentano was the "Immortal Beloved," whom Beethoven in a later conversation implied he met around 1810, Walden (*Beethoven's Immortal Beloved*) promotes a theory that Beethoven had known Antonie and her family since the 1790s. Walden's main source for that idea is Anton Schindler, a completely unreliable source. None of that is to say, however, that Beethoven did not know Antonie earlier, only that there is no clear record of it.

23. Solomon, *Beethoven*, 234–35.

24. Ibid., 235.

25. The portraits of Antonie are reproduced in ibid., 208.

26. Ibid., 233.

27. Ibid., 229.

28. Part of the tightly knit quality of the *Serioso* is the interrelationships of its key structure from beginning to end. The essence of that structure is the "sore" note D-flat in the beginning, part of the primal motif D-flat–C. (That in turn reveals the *Serioso* as the most important ancestor of Brahms's F Minor Quintet, which has, among other things, the same emphasis on D-flat, the same influence of D-flat on the harmonic structure, the same important D-flat–C motif, and a similar tragic tone throughout.) In the *Serioso* the keys of D-flat and G-flat turn up in later movements. For one example, the D-flat becomes C-sharp, the leading tone, in the D-major second movement. As Kerman and Ratner note, the quartet's abrupt opening move from I to N echoes the same harmonic move in the *Appassionata* and the E Minor *Razumovsky* Quartet.

29. The effect of the second theme, which I call unreal and evanescent, has to do not only with its startling contrast to the first theme but also with the highly unusual

harmonic move to the flat side, the subdominant direction, in a second theme. Even in the C-major *Waldstein* Sonata, in which nearly every tonal move starting from the opening bars is in the flat/subdominant direction, the second theme is in E, a dominant substitute.

30. The keys of the strange uprushing scales in the first movement form a pattern of rising fourths: A major, D major, G major. Each one is a violent jump from the key at hand (though D and A have an N relation to I and V in D-flat major). Meanwhile, note that A, D, and G are V, I, and IV of D major, the key of the second movement. To say again, part of the conception of this quartet is tightly interlocking keys among the movements.

31. The striking B-flat that inflects the D major of the second-movement theme is part of a flat-sixth motif in the piece, also part of its *moll-Dur* tendencies, such as the heart-tugging moment in mm. 40–41 of the first movement.

32. Wyn Jones, *Life of Beethoven,* 128.

33. Anderson, vol. 1, no. 283.

34. Solomon, *Beethoven,* 182.

35. Anderson, vol. 1, no. 294.

36. Ibid., no. 306.

37. Kinsky and Halm, *Das Werk Beethovens,* 773. Breitkopf & Härtel brought out *Christus am Ölberge* and the Mass in C as opp. 85 and 86.

38. Lockwood, *Beethoven: Music,* 308.

39. Anderson, vol. 1, nos. 300 and 301.

40. Albrecht, vol. 1, no. 157.

41. Some of Beethoven's on-the-surface-less-bold pieces have, like the *Archduke,* some of his more striking formal and tonal excursions. The scherzo is an example. It's based in B-flat major; the enormous, multipart trio begins in B-flat minor and goes on to D-flat major and E major, and arrives at B-flat major well before the return of the opening theme. Then comes the slow movement in D major. The harmonic peregrinations of the gentle *Archduke* rival those of the furious *Serioso,* and both are planned in terms of close tonal relationships among the movements.

42. Anderson, vol. 1, no. 295.

43. Marek, *Beethoven,* 258–59.

44. Walden, *Beethoven's Immortal Beloved,* 133–34.

45. For Walden (ibid.), the *du* and "with pain" — three words — in Beethoven's surviving letter to Bettina are central elements in his argument that she was the Immortal Beloved. The two letters from Beethoven that Bettina published, and which do not survive, are more unequivocally passionate. Yet others saw those missing letters and testified to their existence, and there is no doubt that Beethoven wrote Bettina more letters than the single one that survives — he refers to them. Meanwhile there is no evidence that Bettina destroyed his letters or any of Goethe's. For all she knew, in other words, the originals of Beethoven's letters would still be around to compare to her published versions. And so the speculations and ambiguities continue their rounds.

46. Anderson, vol. 1, no. 303.

47. Clive, *Beethoven and His World,* 251.

48. Albrecht, vol. 1, no. 155.

49. Kinsky and Halm, *Das Werk Beethovens,* 227.

50. Anderson, "Beethoven's Operatic Plans," 5.

51. B. Cooper, *Beethoven,* 195.

52. Lockwood, *Beethoven: Music,* 267.

53. Kinderman, *Beethoven,* 147.

54. Lockwood, *Beethoven: Music,* 267.

55. Burnham, in *Beethoven Hero,* writes that the coda of the *Egmont* Overture approaches naïveté, if not banality. I tend to agree.

56. Thayer/Forbes, 1:484–85.

57. Moore, "Beethoven and Inflation," 200–202.

58. Ibid., 212–13. Moore's figures about the stipend and its travails differ from Thayer/Forbes's (1:552–53). I am assuming hers are more up to date.

59. B. Cooper, *Beethoven,* 203. Cooper has doubts that the music for Pest was actually written in three weeks and suspects Beethoven began it earlier. But Beethoven's account to Breitkopf & Härtel less than a month later is unambiguous. Recall that he wrote the hour-long *Christus* in two weeks, or claimed to have.

60. Anderson, vol. 1, no. 344.

61. Landon, *Beethoven,* 142.

62. Thayer/Forbes, 1:512.

63. Clive, *Beethoven and His World,* 378.

64. Ibid., 368.

65. Anderson, vol. 1, no. 312.

66. Thayer/Forbes, 1:515, 531–32.

67. Clive, *Beethoven and His World,* 379.

68. Anderson, vol. 1, no. 340.

69. Ibid., no. 325.

70. Ibid., no. 328.

71. Lockwood, *Beethoven: Music,* 76.

72. B. Cooper, *Beethoven,* 205–6.

73. Thayer/Forbes, 1:519.

74. Anderson, vol. 1, no. 330.

75. Clive, *Beethoven and His World,* 377.

76. Anderson, vol. 1, no. 334.

77. Thayer/Forbes, 1:520.

78. Plantinga, *Beethoven's Concertos,* 272.

79. Comini, "Visual Beethoven," 287–90. Comini was the first to come to this commonsense understanding of why the Klein life mask turned out as it did and how that played into the Romantic cult of genius. It is the foundation of her *Changing Image of Beethoven: A Study in Mythmaking,* its subject Beethoven iconography.

80. Anderson, vol. 1, no. 369.

25. My Angel, My Self

1. B. Cooper, *Beethoven Compendium,* 22.

2. Anderson, vol. 1, no. 374.

3. Solomon, *Beethoven,* 215.

4. Based on the literal translation of Virginia Beahrs in "My Angel," with additions for the sake of clarity from the version in Anderson, vol. 1, no. 373, plus elements from the German. I have added some paragraph breaks, also for clarity. Beahrs is a leading champion of Josephine Deym as the Immortal Beloved, Maynard Solomon

(ibid.) of Antonie Brentano, Edward Walden (*Beethoven's Immortal Beloved*) of Bettina Brentano. The new entry in the debate by John E. Klapproth (*Beethoven's Only Beloved*) makes a book-length case for Josephine. In Klapproth I find dubious datings and translations and other fudging — see the final note for chapter 20 and note 6 below. My treatment of the Immortal Beloved mystery in this chapter gives an overview of the various theories, all of which amount to many pages of reasoning and speculation teetering on a handful of provable facts — some of those facts certainly tantalizing. As the text shows, I can't subscribe to any of the theories, even to the point of having a provisional favorite candidate, and after years of research and speculation I have no new theory to offer. Since I have no problem with mysteries — I am a musician, and music itself is a great mystery — I have kept my discussion to a summary of the more tangible and tantalizing aspects. Interested readers should examine Solomon, Walden, Beahrs, and Klapproth, for starters, with an open yet skeptical mind. Meanwhile, the George Marek biography votes for pianist Dorothea Ertmann, Romain Rolland (*Beethoven the Creator*) for Therese von Brunsvik, and Anton Schindler (*Beethoven*) for Giulietta Guicciardi. I don't believe any of those three are viable candidates.

5. *Unsterblich* is familiarly translated as "immortal," but the word can also mean "undying." As Anderson notes in *Letters of Beethoven,* the more literal sense of *Unsterbliche Geliebte* (usually the first word would be lowercase, but Beethoven capitalizes both) is "undying love." Since both translations are valid, I've used the familiar one.

6. Solomon, *Beethoven,* 222. The resemblance of the Immortal Beloved letter to the ones to Josephine Deym is the centerpiece of Klapproth's argument for her (*Beethoven's Only Beloved*). Solomon's detective work in *Beethoven* places Antonie Brentano definitely in Karlsbad when Beethoven wrote the letter saying his beloved was in that town; her presence in Karlsbad is Solomon's centerpiece. For Walden's part (*Beethoven's Immortal Beloved*), he shows that Bettina Brentano was *planning* to go to Karlsbad and/or Teplitz, and Beethoven may have believed she was in Karlsbad. Bettina's trip was delayed, and she arrived in Teplitz at the end of July — which is when Walden believes they met and Bettina told him she was staying with her husband. The centerpiece of Walden's argument is the two disputed letters from Beethoven that Bettina published but which no longer exist. I'll add that Walden does a far more respectable job of making his case than Klapproth, whose argument is at times forced and deceptive. Still, I think there is a case to be made for Josephine that makes roughly as much sense as the others.

7. Walden, *Beethoven's Immortal Beloved,* 4.

8. Ibid., 2.

9. Ibid., xiii.

10. Perhaps inevitably, there have been theories that the child Antonie Brentano was pregnant with in 1812 was Beethoven's. That is among the most unsupported and unlikely speculations in the debate — though, of course, unlikely things happen all the time.

11. Solomon, *Beethoven,* 234.

12. Walden, *Beethoven's Immortal Beloved,* 9. Walden notes that Bettina agreed to marry Arnim in December 1811 and was probably exchanging letters (now lost) with Beethoven at the time. Though Walden duly cites this notion, it makes for a problem in his thesis. If Bettina was marrying Arnim for practical reasons and not

love, and meanwhile she was in contact with Beethoven and they were falling or had fallen in love, why would she have gone ahead with the marriage? Soon after the wedding she wrote Goethe saying she was very happy with Arnim — though this was before her nearly fatal childbirth and subsequent depression.

13. Ibid., 30–31.

14. Bettina's four sons had the remarkable names of Siegmund, Friemund, Friedemund, and Huehnemund (Helps and Howard, *Bettina*, 134). The couple were often apart, and their letters are playful and intimate: "Farewell then, Arnim, but I am annoyed with you, you are not a bit affectionate, you hug me about once in a blue moon, and you don't kiss me as I should like to be kissed" (137). Bettina advocated giving children considerable freedom. In childhood, her daughter Gisela was given to crawling around under the table at dinner parties and biting the guests' ankles.

15. At the risk of adding another ambiguity to so many, Beethoven's statement that he had met his beloved five years before is a thirdhand account, from Fanny Giannatasio del Rio via her father's report from Beethoven. So Fanny's note of a *first* meeting five years before could easily have been mistaken.

16. Walden (*Beethoven's Immortal Beloved*, 76) notes that two independent witnesses in the nineteenth century said they examined the later-missing Beethoven letters that Bettina published, and testified that they were authentic. Secondhand testimony at that distance is tantalizing but, again, not the same thing as having the originals in hand, and the witnesses could not compare the printed versions word for word with the originals. Again: there clearly were more letters between Beethoven and Bettina than the single one of his that survives.

17. Marek, *Beethoven*, 282.

18. Anderson, vol. 1, no. 374.

19. Ibid., no. 376 (paragraph breaks added).

20. Walden, *Beethoven's Immortal Beloved*, 9.

21. Helps and Howard, *Bettina*, 130. These authors, incidentally, make no case for Bettina as the Immortal Beloved.

22. Knight, *Beethoven*, 84.

23. Anderson, vol. 1, no. 379.

24. "'Friendship Has to Be a Life's Work': Rüdiger Safranski on Goethe and Schiller," interview with Rüdiger Safranski by Sabine Tenta, January 2010, Goethe Institut, http://www.goethe.de/kue/lit/aug/en5583450.htm.

25. Sonneck, *Beethoven*, 88. Goethe's tone in complaining about Beethoven should be read in the context that he is playing to Zelter's aversion to Beethoven's work at this time. Zelter had gone so far as to declare that *Christus am Ölberge* was "suggestive of Greek vice" — i.e., homosexuality (Helps and Howard, *Bettina*, 130). Later Zelter became a fervent admirer of Beethoven and preached that gospel to his student Mendelssohn.

26. Anderson, vol. 1, no. 379.

27. Sonneck, *Beethoven*, 86–87.

28. Anderson, vol. 1, no. 380.

29. Friedenthal, *Goethe*, 412; Kerman, *"An die ferne Geliebte,"* 135. Kinderman, in *Beethoven*, 246, notes that in 1822, Mendelssohn did play for Goethe Beethoven's setting of "Wonne der Wehmut," and Goethe was delighted with it.

30. Anderson, vol. 1, nos. 377, 382, 388. After this summer it seems Beethoven and Amalie Sebald had no further contact.
31. Albrecht, vol. 1, no. 164.
32. B. Cooper, *Beethoven's Folksong Settings*, 16.
33. Albrecht, vol. 1, no. 163.
34. Ibid., no. 167.
35. Ibid., vol. 2, no. 170.
36. Anderson, vol. 1, no. 405.
37. Ibid., no. 352.
38. B. Cooper, *Beethoven's Folksong Settings*, 101.
39. Ibid., 73.
40. Ibid., 79.
41. Ibid., 83, 89.
42. Ibid., 164–65.
43. Ibid., 10.
44. Ibid., 43.
45. Thayer/Forbes, 1:541.
46. Landon, *Beethoven*, 190–92.
47. Solomon, *Beethoven*, 282.
48. B. Cooper, *Beethoven*, 212.
49. Anderson, vol. 1, no. 393.
50. Ibid., no. 428.
51. Ibid., no. 429.
52. Ibid., no. 411.
53. Albrecht, vol. 2, no. 171.
54. Anderson, vol. 1, no. 412.
55. Thayer/Forbes, 1:553–54.
56. Anderson, vol. 1, nos. 392, 394.
57. Kinderman, *Beethoven*, 163.
58. B. Cooper, *Beethoven's Folksong Settings*, 37.
59. I have not given page numbers for the *Tagebuch* entries. The "A" to whom Beethoven refers, Solomon reads as Antonie Brentano, his candidate for the Immortal Beloved. Walden (*Beethoven's Immortal Beloved*) and others question whether it refers to Antonie and/or whether in Beethoven's scrawl it was an *A* at all — the *Tagebuch* survives only in two copies made by others, and there are a number of places where the transcription either is clearly wrong or trails off because the original could not be read. Here are yet more ambiguities that keep the Immortal Beloved mystery afloat.
60. Beethoven, "Beethoven's *Tagebuch*," 268.
61. Anderson, vol. 1, no. 406; vol. 2, nos. 562, 681.
62. M. Cooper, *Beethoven*, 31.
63. Musulin, *Vienna*, 133.
64. Quoted in Solomon, *Beethoven*, 284, where Solomon details Beethoven's connection to prostitutes in this period.
65. Beethoven, "Beethoven's *Tagebuch*," 255.
66. Sonneck, *Beethoven*, 94–100.
67. Solomon, *Beethoven*, 284–85.
68. Thayer/Forbes, 1:554.

69. Mai, in *Diagnosing Genius,* 146–47, outlines the medical evidence for Beethoven's being "alcohol-dependent"—what I call a "functional alcoholic"—rather than showing "abuse," as his father had.
70. Anderson, vol. 1, no. 426.
71. Nicholls, *Napoleon,* 197–99.
72. This is Metternich's account of the meeting with Napoleon, which should be taken with several grains of salt.

26. We Finite Beings

1. Anderson, vol. 1, no. 427.
2. Knight, *Beethoven,* 159.
3. Scherman and Biancolli, 907n2.
4. Thayer/Forbes, 1:544.
5. Ibid., 1:560.
6. Marek, *Beethoven,* 455.
7. Ignaz Moscheles, who was working with Beethoven at the time, said that in fact much of the plan for *Wellington's Victory* and some of the military music came from Maelzel.
8. Thayer/Forbes, 1:566.
9. Scherman and Biancolli, 908.
10. Part of the impression of silliness that strikes Americans, at least, about *Wellington's Victory* is that in English *Malbrouk* (called "Marlborough" in the score) is also the tune of "For He's a Jolly Good Fellow" and "The Bear Came over the Mountain."
11. Dalhaus, *Ludwig van Beethoven,* 17.
12. Kinderman, in *Beethoven,* 170, has a discussion of how *Wellington's Victory* relates to kitsch.
13. Thayer/Forbes, 1:565.
14. Again, the connection of Classical-period music to dance is made in Rosen's *The Classical Style.*
15. The chromatically slithering bass of the Seventh's first-movement coda returns in a new guise in the coda of the finale.
16. Conductor James Sinclair notes that his and others' performances slightly over-dot the Seventh's first-movement rhythmic figure to give it more lightness. I see the three-note dactylic figure that dominates the second movement of the Seventh as an evening out of the dotted figure that dominates the first movement. The dotted figure returns in various augmentations in the scherzo, notably in the trio, but there are echoes of the dactyls in figures near the end of the scherzo. The dactylic figure is then diminished and intensified in the fiddle tune of the finale.
17. Famously, the second movement begins and ends on a i 6/4 chord that is a color rather than a functional harmony. In that it resembles Beethoven's use of diminished sevenths, which often are treated not functionally but rather as a color and a device for suspending tonality.
18. The way Beethoven develops an important pitch can be seen in the adventures of F and C in the first movement. F serves as N of V in A, as the third of D minor, the fifth of B-flat major, and so on.
19. The idea of the Seventh as unified by the moods of dance rather than a sense of

dramatic narrative is not an entirely new kind of thinking for Beethoven. The A-flat Major Piano Sonata, op. 26, for example, is held together not by narrative nor particularly by motifs but by *the idea of variation.*

20. Solomon, *Beethoven*, 276.
21. Thayer/Forbes, 1:566.
22. Clive, *Beethoven and His World*, 225.
23. Anderson, vol. 1, no. 441.
24. Ibid., no. 457.
25. Thayer/Forbes, 1:557.
26. Ibid., 1:571.
27. Clive, *Beethoven and His World*, 313.
28. Thayer/Forbes, 1:572.
29. Ibid., 1:571.
30. Anderson, vol. 2, no. 462.
31. Thayer/Forbes, 1:569.
32. Ibid., 1:567.
33. Anderson, vol. 1, no. 485.
34. Kinderman, *Beethoven*, 160.
35. For me, part of the humor in the Eighth is that the first three notes of the opening theme, C–A–B-flat, continually reshuffled, form the motivic foundation of all the themes in the Eighth. Another element holding together the themes is the idea of a prolonged upbeat: at the beginning, the first bar (as I think it should be phrased) is the upbeat to the second bar. The second-movement theme prolongs the upbeat idea, and the minuet comically extends it to seven beats. Meanwhile the first-movement development is a study in how to intensify a single sustained harmony through the course of a phrase, using texture, rhythm, and rising lines. The "errant" C-sharp in the Eighth is the same pitch as the "sore" C-sharp in the *Eroica*, but here it functions quite differently, more subtly and wittily.
36. As in the first movement, the second theme in the finale arrives in the "wrong" key, this time A-flat (with its D-flat as fourth degree) and then rights itself into the "proper" C major. From early in his work Beethoven used analogous harmonic moves in movements of a piece as a unifying element. (To concentrate only on pitch motivic relationships throughout a work is to miss half the kinds of relationships he is concerned with.) The D-flat-to-C-sharp intrusions near the end of the finale are a classic case of Beethoven "explaining" an underlying idea.
37. Thayer/Forbes, 1:575.
38. Lockwood, in *Beethoven: Music*, 234, observes that "the [Eighth Symphony's] delicate shading and subtle balances may have been harder for him to achieve than the direct outpouring of action in the Seventh."
39. Thayer/Forbes, 1:576.
40. Alsop, *Congress Dances*, 55.
41. Nicolson, *Congress of Vienna*, 85, 93.
42. Ibid., 93.
43. Musulin, *Vienna*, 136–37.
44. Thayer/Forbes, 1:578. Thayer implies, without quite saying so, that Schuppanzigh was the violinist at the premiere of the *Archduke,* and does not mention the cellist. According to Moscheles, Spohr was a bitter opponent of Beethoven's music.
45. Landon, *Beethoven*, 151.

46. Anderson, vol. 1, nos. 478–79.

47. Ibid., no. 481.

48. Thayer/Forbes, 1:563.

49. Ibid., 1:583.

50. Senner, *Critical Reception*, 2:180.

51. Thayer/Forbes, 1:586–87.

52. Ibid., 1:588–90.

53. Anderson, vol. 1, no. 502.

54. Ibid., no. 486.

55. Hofmann, *Viennese*, 97.

56. Knight, *Beethoven*, 94.

57. Brion, *Daily Life*, 165. It hardly needs to be said that in this period, "remedies" for venereal disease were fraudulent. There were no functional treatments at all.

58. Hofmann, *Viennese*, 105.

59. Nicolson, *Congress of Vienna*, 34.

60. Alsop, *Congress Dances*, 33.

61. Brion, *Daily Life*, 172.

62. Nicolson, *Congress of Vienna*, 159.

63. Ibid., 161.

64. Alsop, *Congress Dances*, 140.

65. Alexander's father, Tsar Paul I, was legendarily erratic. Alexander came to power when a group of officers murdered his father while Alexander sat downstairs listening to the screams. The old regimes were full of such stories, though the Russian ones tend to be more extreme.

66. Hofmann, *Viennese*, 97.

67. Alsop, *Congress Dances*, 124.

68. Ibid., 12.

69. Nicolson, *Congress of Vienna*, 177.

70. Anderson, vol. 2, nos. 493, 495n1.

71. Kolodin, *Interior Beethoven*, 224.

72. Anderson, vol. 2, no. 498.

73. Wyn Jones, *Life of Beethoven*, 123.

74. The main secondary key in the new *Fidelio* overture is C major, the key the opera ends in.

75. The eerie effect of the timpani A–E-flats in the dungeon has much to do with the tuning. Timpani in those days were almost invariably tuned on the tonic and dominant of the current key. Tuning them to a tritone was deliberately aberrational, also echt Beethoven in creating a powerful effect with simple means.

76. As B. Cooper notes in *Beethoven*, the imprisoned Florestan's vision of Leonore as the angel of freedom echoes the end of Goethe's *Egmont* — perhaps deliberately on the part of Treitschke, who conceived this new end of Florestan's aria.

77. The end of *Fidelio* is yet another of Beethoven's joyful endings, which for him meant mostly tonic and dominant harmonies, *fortissimo,* in simple textures and usually open keys between three flats and two sharps. I think here, as in the end of the *Egmont* Overture and even the Fifth Symphony, listeners by the end are left a bit battered. These endings lack, in a word, subtlety. For me the most successful and truly hair-raising of all Beethoven's joyful endings is the *Eroica's.*

78. Robinson (*Ludwig van Beethoven*) and others note that the theme of "O namenlose

Freude" comes from the sketches for the abortive *Vestas Feuer* and from a theme in the F-major Andante from the *Joseph* Cantata.

79. Tusa notes in "Music as Drama," 101, that Beethoven studied Mozart's operatic ensembles in preparing for *Fidelio* and copied out excerpts including ones from *Don Giovanni* and *The Magic Flute*. The canon *Mir ist so wunderbar* echoes one in Mozart's *Così fan tutte*.

80. Robinson, *Ludwig van Beethoven*, 69.

81. Georg Friedrich Treitschke, quoted in Thayer/Forbes, 1:573.

82. Alois Wiessenbach, quoted in ibid., 1:595.

83. Wenzel Tomaschek, quoted in ibid., 1:599. Once again, like most recollections of Beethoven, Tomaschek's was written years after the event, so it has the inevitable distortions of memory — as well as the distortions of the character and convictions of the person recollecting.

84. Scherman and Biancolli, 782.

85. Landon, *Beethoven*, 150.

86. Thayer/Forbes, 1:603.

87. Ibid., 2:645.

88. Anderson, vol. 1, no. 523.

89. Musulin, *Vienna*, 173.

90. Cook, "Unfinished Piano Concerto."

91. Thayer/Forbes, 1:611–12.

92. Anderson, vol. 2, no. 531.

93. B. Cooper, *Beethoven Compendium*, 24.

94. Thayer/Forbes, 1:551.

95. Knight, *Beethoven*, 101.

96. Thayer/Forbes, 1:602.

97. Albrecht, vol. 2, no. 200.

98. Thayer/Forbes, 2:618. The sketches are in Nottebohm's second volume of *Beethoveniana*.

99. B. Cooper, *Beethoven Compendium*, 24.

100. Wyn Jones, *Life of Beethoven*, 134–36.

101. Anderson, vol. 2, no. 546. Apparently the prince regent gave the score of *Wellington's Victory* Beethoven had sent to the Smart brothers, who performed it at the Drury Lane Theater.

102. Ibid., no. 778.

103. Albrecht, vol. 2, no. 234.

104. Anderson, vol. 2, no. 683.

105. Marek, *Beethoven*, 534.

106. Thayer/Forbes, 2:637–40.

107. May, *Age of Metternich*, 14.

108. Ibid., 79.

109. Musulin, *Vienna*, 259.

110. Yates, "Cultural Life," 12.

111. Stendhal, quoted in Knight, *Beethoven*, 103.

112. Albrecht, vol. 2, no. 208.

113. Anderson, vol. 2, no. 563.

114. Albrecht, vol. 2, no. 211.

27. The Queen of the Night

1. Kolodin (*Interior Beethoven*, 219n16) notes that Karl van Beethoven's death notice cites his age as thirty-eight, when in fact he was forty-one. That suggests Karl was as uncertain of his real age as Ludwig was.
2. Albrecht, vol. 2, no. 213.
3. Solomon, *Beethoven*, 314.
4. Thayer/Forbes, 2:624–25. The note is a handwritten fragment, perhaps a draft for a legal statement.
5. Anderson, vol. 2, no. 572.
6. Thayer/Forbes, 2:626.
7. Ibid., 2:625.
8. Wyn Jones, *Life of Beethoven*, 132.
9. Anderson, vol. 2, no. 607.
10. Ibid., no. 598.
11. Nohl, *Unrequited Love*, 4–6.
12. Ibid., 12–13.
13. Sterba and Sterba, *Beethoven and His Nephew*, 60. The Sterbas' thesis that Beethoven's attraction to Karl was homosexual is possible, because many things are possible. What is undoubtedly true of their thesis is that there is no evidence for it, and it is not necessary to explain Beethoven's obsession with Karl.
14. Albrecht, vol. 2, no. 220.
15. Anderson, vol. 2, no. 611.
16. Solomon, *Beethoven*, 300–301.
17. Sterba and Sterba, *Beethoven and His Nephew*, 46.
18. Ibid., 54.
19. Clive, *Beethoven and His World*, 14; B. Cooper, *Beethoven*, 213.
20. Solomon, *Beethoven*, 301.
21. Anderson, vol. 2, no. 612.
22. Sterba and Sterba, *Beethoven and His Nephew*, 55.
23. Anderson, vol. 2, no. 644.
24. Anderson, vol. 3, no. 967.
25. Nohl, *Unrequited Love*, 87.
26. The excuse for the Carlsbad Decrees was the murder of reactionary playwright August Kotzebue — with whom Beethoven had worked on *The Ruins of Athens* — by a member of a radical student group.
27. Anderson, vol. 2, no. 577.
28. Nohl, *Unrequited Love*, 62. Despite their mutual disappointments, the Gesellschaft der Musikfreunde gave twenty performances of Beethoven's symphonies between 1819 and 1827, including two movements of the Ninth (Wyn Jones, *Symphony*, 185).
29. Nohl, *Unrequited Love*, "Confessions."
30. Anderson, vol. 2, no. 718.
31. These quotations from Fanny's diary in 1816 are from Nohl, *Unrequited Love*, "Confessions."
32. Ibid., 77.
33. Anderson, vol. 2, no. 632.
34. Ibid., no. 648.

35. Ibid., no. 874.
36. Landon, *Beethoven,* 153–54. Unlike the usual memories of Beethoven from years later, Bursy's account is a diary entry, so it is probably more accurate than most.
37. Clive, *Beethoven and His World,* 340.
38. Anderson, vol. 2, no. 667.
39. Ibid., no. 710.
40. Nohl, *Unrequited Love,* 78.
41. Ibid., 96. As I noted in chapter 25, one has to remember that Fanny Giannatasio's account of Beethoven's love from "five years ago" is secondhand — or even third-hand, since it was gleaned from a conversation she overheard between Beethoven and her father, or from her father's report. That means her account is likely inaccurate in some way or other. It is not certain that Beethoven said, for example, that he had *met* the woman five years before; he may have meant that was the time of their closeness. If that part of Fanny's memory is correct, other parts will not be. That is why, for a biographer, firsthand accounts are the most reliable — though hardly completely reliable. We do not remember our own lives accurately or completely truthfully. A prime example is Beethoven, whose understanding of himself and his actions was sometimes astute, other times delusional. In any case, Fanny's recollection, which figures heavily in some Immortal Beloved theories, can't be assumed to be accurate.
42. The key sequence in *An die ferne Geliebte* is as patterned and interlocked as a Beethoven instrumental piece: 1. E-flat; 2. G (C) G; 3. A-flat–a-flat; 4. A-flat; 5. C (c F) C c; 6. E-flat (c B-flat) E-flat. The end of the last song returns to the melody and the concluding lines of the first song, like a recapitulation, and there is an extended coda. In other words, Beethoven applied aspects of instrumental composition to a song cycle — as he had done in smaller scale in *Adelaide.* If *An die ferne Geliebte* has not found the popularity of Schubert's lieder, the reason is mainly Schubert's phenomenal melodic gift, which was more fluid than Beethoven's, and which Schubert was able to give in to without being afflicted by Beethoven's incessant concern for form and logic. It insults neither man's achievement to say that Schubert was the more natural melodist — as Schiller would say, a "naive" creator, rather than a more self-conscious, laborious, "sentimental" one like Beethoven.
43. For Beethoven, folk music and poetry were not attached to nationalism in the way they became among Romantic artists and philosophers — in Germany, part of the ultimately destructive mythology of *das Volk.*
44. Kerman, "*An die ferne Geliebte,*" 133.
45. Some sources say Jeitteles's *An die ferne Geliebte* poems were never in print. Leslie Orrey in Arnold and Fortune, *Beethoven Reader,* 434, says they appeared in the journal *Selam.* Reid, in *The Beethoven Song Companion,* 47, leaves the question a bit vague.
46. Translations are from Reid, *Beethoven Song Companion.*
47. Ibid., 8.
48. Ibid., 48.
49. Kerman, "*An die ferne Geliebte,*" 157. A quotation from Beethoven in Glauert ("Beethoven's Songs") shows his discomfort with vocal music in general: "I know what to expect of instrumentalists, who are capable of almost everything, but with vocal compositions I must always be asking myself: can this be sung?" (192). In his

later vocal music, he largely, and unfortunately, stopped worrying about what was singable.

50. Nohl, *Unrequited Love,* 129–30.
51. Anderson, vol. 2, no. 673.
52. Albrecht, vol. 2, no. 235; B. Cooper, *Beethoven Compendium,* 24; Thayer/Forbes, 2:654.
53. Anderson, vol. 2, no. 624.
54. B. Cooper, *Beethoven Compendium,* 25.
55. Thayer/Forbes, 2:641.
56. Clive, *Beethoven and His World,* 172–74.
57. Anderson, vol. 2, no. 651.
58. Ibid., no. 675.
59. Ibid., no. 653.
60. Ibid., no. 846.
61. Thayer/Forbes, 2:664–65.
62. Nohl, *Unrequited Love,* 148.
63. Ibid., 165–66.
64. Ibid., 152, 156.
65. Anderson, vol. 2, no. 754.
66. Sterba and Sterba, *Beethoven and His Nephew,* 123.
67. Albrecht, vol. 2, no. 242.
68. Anderson, vol. 2, no. 802.
69. Albrecht, vol. 2, no. 245.
70. Anderson, vol. 2, no. 881.
71. Ibid., no. 884.
72. Ibid., no. 871.
73. Ibid., no. 904.
74. Albrecht, vol. 2, no. 239.
75. Thayer/Forbes, 2:672.
76. Anderson, vol. 2, no. 793.
77. Ibid., no. 783.
78. Ibid., no. 758.
79. Knight, *Beethoven,* 117.
80. Drake, *Beethoven Sonatas,* 135. Drake is quoting Anton Schindler on "impressions and reveries," so whether they were Beethoven's terms is suspect. But to repeat: even when Schindler put his own ideas into Beethoven's mouth, he was often astute.
81. Clive, *Beethoven and His World,* 103–4.
82. Anderson, vol. 2, no. 845.
83. Even Rudolph Kolisch, in his classic defense of Beethoven's tempos ("Tempo and Character"), can't quite believe Beethoven's *Hammerklavier* tempo.
84. My suggestion of two to four metronome clicks downward that should be applied to Beethoven's consistently hyperbolic tempo markings comes partly from the scores, partly from my experience as a composer, which I find echoed in the experience of other composers. Among others, I've found Brahms and Bartók disavowing their metronome marks. For some time I assumed that my own carefully done tempo markings were accurate. Then it occurred to me to check the tempos I had coached in my chamber and orchestral performances against my metronome markings on

the scores. I found my score markings to be consistently two to four metronome clicks too fast. I soon realized why: it was the difference between hearing music in one's head and hearing it in actual acoustic space. Thus my suggestion in the text about Beethoven's markings. All that, however (as Beethoven realized), is subject to the need for a nuanced and flexible tempo in performance, which (as Beethoven perhaps did *not* realize) is also subject to the acoustics of each hall. A "wet" room tends to require slower tempos, a "dry" room faster ones.

85. The information about Beethoven's tempo variations comes from the unreliable Schindler, but this point was seconded by the more reliable Ignaz Moscheles, who heard Beethoven conduct (Cook, *Beethoven*, 51).
86. Rosen, *Beethoven's Piano Sonatas*, 45.

28. What Is Difficult

1. Anderson, vol. 2, no. 885.
2. Nohl, *Unrequited Love*, 178–79.
3. Anderson, vol. 2, no. 887.
4. Ibid., no. 886.
5. Beethoven, *Konversationshefte*, 1:415n34.
6. The background on Bernard, Peters, and Oliva is from Clive, *Beethoven and His World*.
7. M. Cooper, *Beethoven*, 123.
8. Thayer/Forbes, 2:801.
9. Beethoven, *Konversationshefte*, 1:182.
10. Ibid., 1:184.
11. Ibid., 1:84.
12. Ibid., 1:100.
13. Ibid., 1:148.
14. Ibid., 1:146.
15. Ibid., 1:120.
16. Clive, *Beethoven and His World*, 58.
17. Ehrlich, *Piano*, 18.
18. Thayer/Forbes, 2:694–95. Beethoven's Broadwood ended up in the possession of Liszt.
19. Anderson, vol. 2, no. 891.
20. Thayer/Forbes, 2:696.
21. Anderson, vol. 2, no. 817.
22. Ibid., no. 818.
23. Thayer/Forbes, 2:682–83.
24. Anderson, vol. 2, no. 903.
25. Clive, *Beethoven and His World*, 29.
26. Albrecht, vol. 2, no. 255n3.
27. Ibid., no. 249.
28. Anderson, vol. 2, no. 904.
29. Thayer/Forbes, 2:700–701.
30. Anderson, vol. 2, no. 905.
31. Solomon, *Beethoven*, 333.

32. M. Cooper, *Beethoven*, 36n1.

33. Landon, *Beethoven*, 159–61.

34. Thayer/Forbes, 2:703.

35. Levy, *Beethoven*, 28.

36. Anderson, vol. 2, no. 976n4.

37. Ibid., no. 749.

38. B. Cooper, *Beethoven*, 261.

39. Much of my sense of the structure of the *Hammerklavier*, like that of most contemporary musicians, is founded on Charles Rosen's discussion of it in *The Classical Style*. As Rosen notes, the main key areas in the first movement run downward in thirds: B-flat, G, E-flat, B, all of them major keys. There is also a dialectic and/or struggle between the pitches and tonalities B and B-flat throughout the sonata; at the end of the scherzo, Beethoven spells out that idea with comical four-octave thumps back and forth on the two pitches. (As I have noted, he often "explains" his leading ideas like this.) B minor, which Beethoven called a "black key," turns up in each movement. Kinderman (*Beethoven*) writes, "B minor functions . . . like a focus of negative energy pitted against the B♭ major tonic" (202). The main elements I have added to Rosen's ideas are expressive descriptions, and my feeling that the *Hammerklavier* is not so much a departure for Beethoven as a condensation and intensification of things he had been doing all along. I add that another motif of the piece from the first measures onward is the contrast of full textures spanning the keyboard and sparse, usually contrapuntal textures. In regard to this and other works, thanks to friend Andrew Rangell, one of my favorite performers of Beethoven, who traded ideas with me.

    The *Hammerklavier* and other late Beethoven works remind me of a survey exhibition of Cézanne I once saw. It struck me that the painter's mature work, a precursor of cubism, was pictures of things built up from rectangles made with up-and-down squiggles of the brush. In the late paintings those squiggles grew broader and rougher, to the point that the painting became less *a picture of something made with particular strokes of the brush* than *strokes of the brush suggesting a picture of something*. In other words, what had once been a characteristic gesture making up a figurative painting had become, to some degree, the substance of the painting itself. In the *Hammerklavier* the kinds of small gestures — themes, motifs, chains of thirds — that Beethoven had always used to build pieces have become so pervasive at every level that they are no longer *a means of helping achieve logic and unity* but rather *the substance of the logic and unity*. (For example, the openings of the first movement and finale of the *Kreutzer* Sonata are based on a motif of chains of thirds, and they appear in the second movement; but they are not constantly present, not the overall substance of the music.)

40. As Rosen says in *Beethoven's Piano Sonatas*, the *Hammerklavier* was conceived as "an act of violence that sought paradoxically to reconquer a tradition in a time of revolution by making it radically new" (220). To add my own term, here again we find Beethoven not as a revolutionary but as a radical evolutionary.

41. Rosen in *Classical Style* shows that the main theme of the slow movement is also based on a scaffolding of descending thirds. The main secondary key is D major, a third down from F-sharp, though there are also the magical moments of G major.

42. As Rosen points out in *Beethoven's Piano Sonatas*, 225, modern pianos do not have

an *una corda* but only a two-string soft pedal, which does not achieve the intimacy of Beethoven's one-string pedal — though that effect might not project in a large modern concert hall.

43. Ibid., 227.

44. I find that Kinderman makes the same point about the introduction of the finale "rejecting" Bach-style counterpoint: the past is "transcended by the creation of a new contrapuntal idiom embodied in the revolutionary fugal finale of the sonata" (*Beethoven*, 207). Here is music that queries music. That in turn leads to Karl Dahlhaus's idea that late Beethoven has become "music about music," an idea that will come up in the text in due course.

45. Solomon, *Late Beethoven,* 99.

46. Ibid., 101.

47. Rosen, *Beethoven's Piano Sonatas,* 227.

48. After writing my own thoughts about the piece, I discover I've echoed or half-remembered Drake's summation in *Beethoven Sonatas,* 278.

49. Czerny, *Proper Performance,* 9. Czerny's lines about Beethoven being limited in his composing when he was completely deaf should be tempered by Czerny's ambivalence toward the late music, of which he wrote, "Considering his deafness, his last works are perhaps his most admirable, but they are by no means the most worthy of emulation."

50. Nohl, *Unrequited Love,* 189. I've substituted Thayer's translation "he's ashamed of me" for the incorrect translation from Nohl, "he makes me ashamed."

51. Thayer/Forbes, 2:706.

52. Sterba and Sterba, *Beethoven and His Nephew,* 142–43.

53. Thayer/Forbes, 2:710–11.

54. Ibid., 2:712.

55. B. Cooper, *Beethoven,* 268.

56. Beethoven, *Konversationshefte,* 1:179.

57. Solomon, *Beethoven,* 374. This is part of Solomon's elaborate thesis of a "nobility pretence" that Beethoven sustained until it was shot down by the Landrecht in the 1818 hearing.

58. Anderson, vol. 2, no. 933.

59. Kagan, *Archduke Rudolph,* 76–77.

60. Ibid., 106–8.

61. Anderson, vol. 2, no. 937.

62. Clive, *Beethoven and His World,* 198.

63. Beethoven's February 1819 statement to the Magistrat is in Anderson, vol. 3, nos. 1374–80.

64. Hotschevar's statement is in Sterba and Sterba, *Beethoven and His Nephew,* 313–19.

65. Clive, *Beethoven and His World,* 170–71. Remarkably, after Beethoven died, Hotschevar served for a while as Karl's guardian.

66. Albrecht, vol. 2, no. 256.

67. Lockwood, *Beethoven: Music,* 403.

68. B. Cooper, *Beethoven,* 273–74.

69. Anderson, vol. 2, no. 950.

70. Nohl, *Unrequited Love,* 195–96.

71. Thayer/Forbes, 2:732.

72. Ibid., 2:726–28.

73. Knight, *Beethoven,* 128.
74. Ibid., 130.
75. Sterba and Sterba, *Beethoven and His Nephew,* 78.
76. Joseph Blöchlinger, quoted in ibid., 189.
77. Ibid., 197–98.
78. Ibid., 199.
79. Solomon, "Beethoven and His Nephew," in *Beethoven Essays,* 145.
80. Wyn Jones, *Life of Beethoven,* 139.
81. Lockwood, *Beethoven: Music,* 391.
82. Drabkin, *Beethoven,* 12.
83. Anderson, vol. 2, no. 956.
84. Ibid., no. 955.
85. Thayer/Forbes, 2:739.
86. Anderson, vol. 2, no. 959.
87. Ibid., no. 960.
88. Ibid., no. 975.
89. Thayer/Forbes, 2:742.
90. B. Cooper, *Beethoven,* 276.
91. Thayer/Forbes, 2:750.
92. Ibid., 2:752.
93. Nohl, *Unrequited Love,* 200–201.

29. The Sky Above, the Law Within

1. B. Cooper, *Beethoven,* 275.
2. Kirkendale, "New Roads," 700–701.
3. Clive, *Beethoven and His World,* 181–82.
4. Ibid., 37.
5. Solomon, *Beethoven,* 334–39.
6. B. Cooper, *Beethoven,* 110.
7. Albrecht, vol. 2, no. 270.
8. Solomon, *Beethoven,* 334.
9. Anderson, vol. 2, no. 939.
10. Ibid., no. 1019.
11. Ibid., no. 1062.
12. Comini, *Changing Image,* 46–47.
13. Thayer/Forbes, 2:759.
14. Knight, *Beethoven,* 136.
15. Albrecht, vol. 2, no. 278.
16. Ibid., no. 271.
17. Anderson, vol. 2, no. 1051.
18. Ibid., no. 1041.
19. Thayer/Forbes, 2:775.
20. Ibid., 2:777–78.
21. Solomon, *Beethoven,* 355.
22. Landon, *Beethoven,* 177–79.
23. Friedrich Rochlitz, quoted in M. Cooper, *Beethoven,* 47–48. Solomon (*Beethoven*) has cast doubt on whether Rochlitz met Beethoven as frequently as he claimed, or

even at all, making Rochlitz another in the string of people who made fraudulent reports of their connection to Beethoven. Clive (*Beethoven and His World*), in his entry on Rochlitz, challenges Solomon's speculation. I find Rochlitz's observations astute and convincing in themselves — they are not a romanticized assemblage of common observations.

24. Solomon, *Beethoven,* 346.
25. Thayer/Forbes, 2:803.
26. Stendhal, *New York Times,* June 3, 2011, p. 16.
27. M. Cooper, *Beethoven,* 48.
28. Thayer/Forbes, 2:805.
29. Clive, *Beethoven and His World,* 292–93. One could argue that Beethoven's advice to Rossini to stick to comic opera was in fact a put-down, since Beethoven did not take comic opera seriously. At the same time, however, Beethoven was certainly right that comedy was Rossini's forte, the main thing in his work that would endure.
30. B. Cooper, *Beethoven,* 286.
31. Kinderman, *Beethoven,* 218; ibid., 279–80.
32. A look at the openings of all the movements of op. 109 shows how the themes rise from the third motif, rising and falling. For all its artless simplicity of effect, the opening theme outlines an intricate structure of voice leading in four parts.
33. The sarabande was a Baroque dance form that in Germany by the nineteenth century had become a slow, usually solemn dance in 3/4, with a characteristic emphasis, as in the op. 109 finale, on a dotted second beat.
34. Kinderman, *Beethoven,* 233.
35. The poet is T. S. Eliot, in *The Four Quartets.* The finale of the E Major Sonata ends with a descent from B to G-sharp, reversing the order of the first two notes in the piece in a cadential way — except that this cadence has the third in the soprano and moreover ends with the cadence to the tonic on the third beat. It is the gentlest, most unobtrusive ending imaginable. Of the last three sonatas, only op. 110 ends with the usual perfect authentic cadence, loud and on a downbeat.
36. The essence of the opening theme of op. 110 is two descending thirds joined by a step, C–A-flat–D-flat–B-flat — the same shape as the Fifth Symphony motif except the middle step moves hopefully upward rather than fatalistically downward. In the finale of op. 110 that down-up-down idea becomes the fugue theme. Meanwhile at the beginning the bass inverts the four-note motif, foreshadowing the inversion of the theme in the middle of the finale. Here is one of many examples in the late music in which all the lines, including the bass, tend more than ever to be contrapuntal and saturated with the leading motifs. Another steady connection of the themes in the sonata is that they involve the compass of a sixth — evolving slowly in the opening theme, more directly in the "I'm a slob" tune of the second movement. Beethoven did not throw ideas into a piece casually, even when, as here, they were quoted tunes done partly as a joke.
37. The middle of the introduction has a series of high A's joined with ties, with an indication to change fingers. This is the *Bebung* effect, which is associated with the clavichord: since a key on a clavichord is directly connected to the hammer, one can press on the key to make a vibrato-like pulsation while the hammer rests on the string. A piano cannot do that. See the "Piano Forum" of Piano Street, at http://www.pianostreet.com/smf/index.php?topic=26006.0, for pianists' ideas on

how a player can approximate the *Bebung*, which was also used by Chopin. Rosen (*Beethoven's Piano Sonatas,* 238) calls the *Bebung* in op. 110 "the representation of a cry of pain."

38. Rosen, *Beethoven's Piano Sonatas,* 240.

39. The fugue theme of op. 110 gets the usual Beethoven treatment of stretto, augmentation, and diminution. One commentator has said that older fugues might use one or two of these devices, but Beethoven rarely seems to consider a fugue complete until he has used all of them. Kinderman (*Beethoven,* 230) notes that the double diminution of the fugue subject from m. 165 distinctly recalls the "I'm a slob" tune from movement 2.

40. Lockwood, *Beethoven: Music,* 389.

41. Nottebohm points out that the op. 111 fugue theme, remarkably enough, appears in a sketch of 1801, perhaps intended for a violin sonata.

42. The final piano sonatas complete Beethoven's long development of the idea of a trill, from its Baroque function as a simple ornament, to a motif, to a pervasive presence that is at once a color, a texture, and an evocation of divine radiance.

43. Anderson, vol. 2, no. 1078.

44. Thayer/Forbes, 2:809.

45. Knight, *Beethoven,* 148.

46. Thayer/Forbes, 2:796–97.

47. B. Cooper, *Beethoven,* 298.

48. Albrecht, vol. 2, no. 294.

49. Anderson, vol. 2, no. 1074.

50. Albrecht, vol. 2, nos. 286, 290.

51. Anderson, vol. 2, no. 1083.

52. Thayer/Forbes, 2:813–14.

53. B. Cooper, *Beethoven,* 303.

54. Anderson, vol. 2, no. 1095.

55. Thayer/Forbes, 2:786; B. Cooper, *Beethoven,* 304.

56. Anderson, vol. 2, no. 1093.

57. Ibid., no. 1106.

58. Albrecht, vol. 2, no. 313.

59. B. Cooper, *Beethoven,* 303.

60. M. Cooper, *Beethoven,* 7.

61. Anderson, vol. 2, no. 1097. Clive (*Beethoven and His World*) casts some doubt on whether Sontag was one of the singers who visited Beethoven then.

62. Sachs, *Ninth,* 20.

63. Thayer/Forbes, 2:807.

64. Daschner, *Musik für die Bühne,* 224.

65. Clive, *Beethoven and His World,* 312.

66. Marek, *Beethoven,* 484.

67. Hill, *Ferdinand Ries,* 45.

68. Thayer/Forbes, 2:858n78.

69. Clive, *Beethoven and His World,* 404.

70. Anderson, vol. 2, no. 1084.

71. Ibid., no. 1086.

72. Ibid., no. 1087.

73. Albrecht, vol. 2, no. 299.

74. Kerman, *Beethoven Quartets,* 223–24.

75. Thayer/Forbes, 2:834.

76. Ibid., 2:811–12. Toward the end of Schröder-Devrient's long and illustrious career she created roles in Wagner operas including Venus in *Tannhäuser.*

77. Senner, *Critical Reception,* vol. 1, nos. 54–55.

78. Thayer/Forbes, 2:838–39.

79. Anderson, vol. 3, no. 1136.

80. Thayer/Forbes, 2:827.

81. Anderson, vol. 3, nos. 1135, 1161.

82. Thayer/Forbes, 2:829.

83. Anderson, vol. 3, no. 1145.

84. Ibid., no. 1162.

85. Ibid., no. 1169.

86. Monson, "Classic-Romantic Dichotomy," 171.

87. Thayer/Forbes, 2:842–43.

88. Solomon, *Late Beethoven,* 36.

89. Wyn Jones, *Life of Beethoven,* 165.

90. Thayer/Forbes, 2:844.

91. Gordon, "Franz Grillparzer," 556.

92. Anderson, vol. 3, no. 1175.

93. B. Cooper, *Beethoven Compendium,* 29.

94. Wyn Jones, *Symphony,* 207.

95. M. Cooper, *Beethoven,* 54.

96. Anderson, vol. 3, no. 1180.

97. Kinderman, *Beethoven's Diabelli Variations,* 34. Kinderman notes that the plan for the variations was on a large scale from the beginning: in a conversation-book entry from 1820, Franz Oliva refers to them as "the big variations" and says, "Diabelli will pay a lot."

98. Ibid., 85.

99. As Kinderman notes in ibid., several groupings have been proposed over the years, but he does not buy any of those theories and neither do I. My friend Andrew Rangell, who has made an outstanding recording of the *Diabellis,* treats each of them as a freestanding individual, except in the couple of cases where there is an *attacca* from one to the next. There is a quality of the mind, however, that likes to see patterns and groupings, so as listeners we tend to find questions and answers and groupings in the piece. Perhaps Beethoven understood that. But if he had wanted to group the variations, he would have done so clearly.

100. Variation I contains all twelve chromatic tones and touches briefly on G major, F major, A minor, and D minor. True, all but the D minor are already in Diabelli's theme, but Beethoven continually expands on the theme's collection of key allusions, and Diabelli's theme does not contain the keys or pitches E-flat or C-sharp/D-flat.

101. Kinderman, *Beethoven's Diabelli Variations,* 34.

102. Ibid., 72–73.

103. Specifically, Kinderman (ibid., 118–19) compares the C-minor Variation XIV with the E-flat Minor Prelude of Bach's *WTC*—the origin of what I've called Beethoven's "E-flat-minor mood," which is usually doleful.

104. The idea that much of late Beethoven is "music about music" is a point made ex-

pansively by Karl Dahlhaus in his writings on Beethoven, including *Ludwig van Beethoven.*

105. Kinderman (*Beethoven's Diabelli Variations,* 104): "Toward its close, the subject of the *Diabelli* Variations ceases to be merely the waltz, or even its possibilities . . . and becomes the entire musical universe as Beethoven knew it."

106. I am echoing Kinderman in ibid., where he ends his study of the sketches citing an unused, abortive sketch of Beethoven's with this splendid phrase: "[H]ere on the brink of eternity, the study of the genesis of the Diabelli Variations draws to a close." As Kinderman notes, a number of the late works, including the *Missa solemnis* and *Diabelli* Variations, conclude not with resolution but rather with "a pointed pregnancy of effect." The word *pregnancy* is the operative one: the works leave us not with a sense of finality but as matters to contemplate further. Two of the last three sonatas and the *Diabellis* all end with the third on top of the final tonic chord — not the usual perfect authentic cadence — so they subtly subvert the usual effect of an ending. The *Diabellis* also end on the second beat of a 3/4 bar, the weakest possible beat.

107. B. Cooper, *Beethoven,* 306–7.

108. Ibid., 304.

109. B. Cooper, *Beethoven Compendium,* 30.

110. Albrecht, vol. 2, no. 326.

111. M. Cooper, *Beethoven,* 53.

112. Albrecht, vol. 2, no. 327.

113. Anderson, vol. 3, no. 1231 and n4.

114. Ibid., no. 1231.

115. B. Cooper, *Beethoven,* 310.

116. Anderson, vol. 3, no. 1233.

117. Ibid., no. 1242.

118. B. Cooper, *Beethoven,* 309.

119. Thayer/Forbes, 2:861–62.

120. Ibid., 2:878.

121. Ibid., 2:882.

122. Ibid., 2:890.

123. Anderson, vol. 3, no. 1248. These inspirational words to Rudolph may be the closest Beethoven wrote in his own hand to the rhapsodic phrases attributed to him by Bettina Brentano in her letters to Goethe.

124. Ibid., no. 1257.

125. Ibid., nos. 1256, 1259.

126. M. Cooper, *Beethoven,* 46.

127. Thayer/Forbes, 2:896–97.

128. Ibid., 2:897–99.

129. Ibid., 2:901.

130. Ibid., 2:902.

131. Sachs, *Ninth,* 33.

30. *Qui Venit in Nomine Domini*

1. Marek, *Beethoven,* 594.

2. Levy, *Beethoven,* 124.

3. Ibid., 133.
4. Cook, *Beethoven*, 23.
5. Ibid., 22.
6. Some seventy years later, a singer from the chorus at the Ninth premiere told conductor Felix Weingartner, "Although Beethoven appeared to be reading along, he would continue to turn pages when the movement in question had already come to an end" (Sachs, *Ninth*, 22). If that was true of one or more of the movements, that means Beethoven was conducting through the music slower than the performance, much of which would also have been slower than his exaggeratedly fast metronome markings. Here is another piece of evidence that those markings are not reliable.
7. Landon, *Beethoven*, 182–83.
8. Ibid., 183–84.
9. Anderson, vol. 3, no. 1288.
10. Levy, *Beethoven*, 133–34.
11. Ibid., 138.
12. Ibid., 135–36.
13. B. Cooper, *Beethoven*, 318.
14. M. Cooper, *Beethoven*, 118–19.
15. Solomon, "Ninth Symphony," 28.
16. M. Cooper, *Beethoven*, 127.
17. Drabkin, *Beethoven*, 21. Lockwood (*Beethoven: Music*, 406) speculates that Beethoven may have known the Bach B Minor Mass, but if so I don't hear any echoes of that in the *Missa solemnis* — while in the *Diabelli* Variations there are audible echoes of the Bach *Goldbergs*. He did know Bach's mass existed, because at one point he queried a publisher about it, citing the bass line of the Crucifixus. Haydn owned a copy of it and would possibly have shown it to his student Beethoven. That Haydn looked over the Bach is shown in a quotation from the Kyrie, whether intentional or not, in the development of the earlier E-flat Major Piano Sonata.
18. Drabkin, *Beethoven*, 14–15.
19. Lockwood (*Beethoven: Music*, 407) speculates that the "from the heart" inscription may have been a private one directed to Archduke Rudolph. The phrase does not appear outside the autograph manuscript. I'm more inclined to give it a broader intention, even if it did not get into the printed score.
20. Kirkendale, "New Roads," 667.
21. As I said in the text, if the expression of the text happens to be conventional, as in *ascendit*, etc., Beethoven does it anyway. Species counterpoint and the whole of composing teaches the composer that he or she often needs to give up one desirable quality — say, originality — for a more important quality. Everything in music is relative. Here, for Beethoven, embodying and picturing the text override the threat of cliché.
22. The "germinal motive" F-sharp–B–A–G–F-sharp (I use the form "motif" here) was discovered and described briefly by Walter Riezler in the 1930s. It has since been generally acknowledged by scholars, though I think more tentatively than it deserves. As Drabkin notes, "Riezler's idea of motivic unity has not been developed by any subsequent writings on the Mass" (*Beethoven*). I hope I've begun to remedy that here, though in this book I don't have space to examine how thoroughly the motif pervades the music — especially since it subsumes the submotifs of the rising fourth, the falling third, and the G–F-sharp. It is also used in a kind of setlike

rearrangement, as in the G–F-sharp–B–A that forms the *eleison* figure in the first movement. In D major, the primal G–F-sharp motif can function and be resolved in three ways: as the seventh of an A7–D cadence, as part of a IV–I *Amen* cadence, and as a 4–3 suspension over a D in the bass. Beethoven uses all those flavors of the G–F-sharp motif.

23. In the chorus's third *Kyrie* the tenors and altos leap up in the middle of the chord: here and in other moments in the mass, Beethoven uses this novel and remarkable effect of intensifying a single chord from within.

24. The Kyrie, like the end of the whole mass in the choir, ends with the third of the chord in the soprano. Beethoven thereby avoids the effect of a final perfect authentic cadence, as he did in two of the last three piano sonatas. At the end of the Kyrie the basses trace the last part of the generating motif, falling from B down to F-sharp, then starting at C and tracing a long descent down to low D, with a lovely effect of homecoming after a harmonically searching movement that bypasses the dominant key of A. Still, when the basses reach the low D it is still not a perfect authentic cadence — there is a 4–3 suspension (G–F-sharp) above it.

25. Fiske, *Beethoven's Missa Solemnis,* 36.

26. Drabkin, *Beethoven,* 37.

27. In the brass writing of most of his orchestral music Beethoven stretched the capacities of French horns and largely wrote bland, ordinary trumpet parts — contributing more rhythm and volume than pitch, and usually conventionally allied with the timpani. Perhaps if he had encountered a trumpet virtuoso on the level of Punto with the horn and Dragonetti with the bass, he would have written more imaginatively for the instrument (as Haydn responded to his encounter with an experimental keyed trumpet by writing perhaps his finest concerto). The *Missa solemnis,* however, has some of the most elaborate and thrilling trumpet parts Beethoven wrote. The opening brass theme of the Gloria is in hemiola, its two-beat superimposed over the 3/4 creating tremendous energy. At the same time it has a dynamic harmonic and rhythmic shape, starting on the D tonic as an extended upbeat, racing up to the dominant, where the climax of the figure is on the hard *d* of *Deo,* which falls a third, from A to F-sharp, as it is inflected when spoken.

28. Kirkendale, "New Roads," 668.

29. The rising scale traversing a fifth that I call the *Gloria* figure is the leading thematic idea of the Gloria movement, in various guises more and less obvious. For example, the *Laudamus te* recycles and varies it, the *Domine fili unigenite* theme is a quiet version of it. While in the Gloria one can find echoes of the generating motif if one wishes, the falling-third motif is everywhere — as it is in the whole mass. Now the falling third begins to be extended into themes built on chains of falling thirds, such as the *glorificamus* theme, built on the scaffolding of C-sharp–A–C-sharp–A–F-sharp–D (on the downbeats).

30. The trombones do not appear in the manuscript scores and were added later by Beethoven by way of instructions to his copyists. Nonetheless, they are hardly an afterthought. They are the most elaborate trombone parts Beethoven ever wrote, and in their *soli* appearances they are indispensable. At other times they are used to double the vocal lines in figures of what must have been, to trombonists of the time, forbiddingly athletic. The same happens in the Ninth Symphony.

31. If one boils down the theme of the *in gloria dei Patris* fugue to its framework,

mostly on the strong beats, one gets D–G–E–A–F-sharp–B–A–G–F-sharp. So it is built on the generating motif. At the same time, that framework is precisely the theme — transposed — of the finale fugue of the op. 110 Piano Sonata. That thematic connection, I assume, for a change, was unconscious on Beethoven's part.

32. Fortunately, since the tempos in the mass are already hard enough to deal with, Beethoven did not add metronome markings.

33. From m. 86 in the Credo, what I call the "long ascent" is established as a musical and symbolic motif. There are a few answering descents, the main one being the long descent of the solo violin in the Sanctus.

34. See Kinderman, "Symbol for the Deity."

35. Kirkendale, "New Roads," 677.

36. Ibid., 676.

37. Ibid., 679.

38. Much of the effect of what I call the "wailing" line that accompanies the Crucifixus (from m. 167) comes from the piercing cross-relations of the theme's C-natural against C-sharp in the basses.

39. The *et resurrexit* proclamation is usually described as Mixolydian, but if so that amounts to C Mixolydian for three chords and G Mixolydian by the end — the final G-major chord sounds like an arrival, not a dominant. I'm calling the general effect "modal" mainly because of root-position chords moving by step — an archaic harmonic effect that Beethoven uses often in the mass and in the *Seid umschlungen* section of the Ninth Symphony finale.

40. As Kinderman points out ("Symbol for the Deity"), the *et vitam venturi* fugue theme in itself has seven descending thirds. However, the wind introduction and then the fugal entries are interlocked in a way that sustains a much longer descending chain. From m. 306, the oboe outlines G–E-flat–C–A (leaping up for the last). Then the sopranos enter a third down on F, their theme descending in thirds (some of them inverted to a sixth) down to F. At that point the fugal line always leaps up a sixth, here to D, so the next entry of the fugue theme enters a third down on B-flat and begins its descent of seven thirds. Beethoven would have laid out this pattern first and then composed the music around it — these things don't happen by accident, in the thickets of writing counterpoint. However, for harmonic reasons the entries on B-flat do not descend in thirds from that note, but from A — from which point the chain of thirds again connects the next two entries. What I am proposing here, with a necessary harmonic adjustment, is a quasi-endless chain of thirds. For Beethoven to use descending thirds as a metaphor for "life ever after" has a clear symbolism: that chain has no innate stopping point, can cycle endlessly as long one wants, in contrast to music built on a tonic–dominant axis. Descending thirds in themselves are also, of course, a primal motif in the mass.

41. Kinderman, in ibid., makes this connection of the Kant quotation and moments in the mass and the Ninth.

42. The relation of the Eucharist to salvation in Catholic doctrine is complex and much debated, so of course I don't propose to present the matter fully.

43. Kirkendale, in "New Roads" (686–87), writes that the quiet brass chorale that begins the Sanctus recalls the "tower music" tradition in German lands, in which

trombones and other brass intoned popular religious songs from town towers, their music sometimes compared to a chorus of angels. He notes that Beethoven wrote three chorale-like equali for trombones at the request of a towermaster in Linz. Here is another example of how the *Missa solemnis* is intimately involved with tradition while remaining unique.

44. The autograph calls for the soloists alone to sing the *Pleni sunt coeli* and *Hosanna*, but over the years most conductors have used the full choir. I vote for that, for several reasons: the chorus projects the splendor of the music better; soloists can't balance the orchestral tutti; and the movement needs the contrast of a choral section between two segments for soloists. There is a similar ambiguity about who sings the *et incarnatus*. I find it deeply moving with the tenors of the choir, unsatisfying with a tenor soloist in his relatively bland low register.

45. The *Pleni* and *Hosanna* fugues, both short and unrelated in theme, tempo, meter, and texture, form one of the most bewildering stretches of the mass. They obliterate every norm of Classical continuity, form, and relationship of material.

46. Kirkendale, "New Roads," 687–88. Kirkendale points out that Beethoven would have performed organ improvisations during the Eucharist in the church jobs of his teens. In the score Beethoven has an organ, so he could have used it for the *Präludium*, but he preferred to create an organlike effect in the orchestra —and the effect is quietly stunning. The scoring and the chromaticism of the *Präludium* are virtually proto-Wagnerian. Its central section emphasizes the generative motif.

47. From the beginning of the violin solo, there are sixteen measures of G major in slow tempo without an accidental. The first accidental is a chromatic appoggiatura on D-sharp. Finally there are some modulations, but mostly the music stays close to G major.

48. Kirkendale, "New Roads," 689.

49. The contrast of the searching, roaming harmonic style of much of the mass and the long dwelling on G major in the "Benedictus" is another example of what I mean about Beethoven's late style: he became both more complex and more simple.

50. When Beethoven "explodes" the form with the storm in the *Pastoral* Symphony and the war music in the *Missa solemnis*, he violates the form for a reason—for the sake of a dramatic, programmatic, pictorial effect that is, as the term goes, "extramusical." True, some have made efforts to integrate these moments into a logical, "purely musical" framework, including calling the storm the introduction to the symphony's finale, or a transition. In the case of the *Pastoral* these ideas are not entirely irrelevant, but what I am saying is that these theoretical constructs contradict what Beethoven intended, which is that these elements are *not* to be considered part of the form but rather do violence to it, for extramusical reasons. Again: for a composer of Beethoven's level, *form is another means of expression.* As I will show, in the finale of the Ninth he stretches the extramusical dimension still further, in the context not of a familiar formal outline but rather within an episodic, ad hoc form. In other words, in the finale of the Ninth there is no formal norm to break, so the programmatic elements (especially the recalls of earlier movements) take a further step toward what we might call the "purely extramusical." Perhaps the same could be said of the Agnus Dei in the mass, but

that has a simpler and less episodic formal layout than the finale of the Ninth. In the Agnus Dei, in other words, there is a clear-enough form to make breaking it meaningful.

51. In the choir, from the *tempo primo* at m. 190 Beethoven strings together fourteen falling thirds by m. 232.

52. M. Cooper, *Beethoven*, 272.

53. I would argue that all the greatest works of religious art are, in the end, universal, because they move us in human terms whether or not we subscribe to their faith. Bach's *St. Matthew Passion* is the archetypal example. I will speculate that the *Missa solemnis* is personal because Beethoven, being who he was, could not make it otherwise. Bach, by contrast, seems to me to be more conscious —perhaps with the support of his sect—of making biblical stories and religious doctrine universally human: the *St. Matthew Passion* is immediately about the death of Christ, but also about the universal experience of death and loss. There is the way that in his sacred music Bach subsumed the emotions of opera, the genre he never got around to writing.

31. You Millions

1. Levy, *Beethoven*, 20.

2. Cook, *Beethoven*, 11. One of those sketches is highly reminiscent of the slow movement of the *Pathétique*.

3. B. Cooper, *Beethoven*, 264–65.

4. Levy, *Beethoven*, 28.

5. Cook, *Beethoven*, 14.

6. Winter, "Sketches," 182–84.

7. Kirby, "Beethoven and the 'Geselliges Lied,'" 120.

8. Solomon, "Masonic Thread," 151.

9. Donakowski, *Muse*, 50–51.

10. Winter, "Sketches," 183. As Winter notes, those nineteen stages of sketching the *Freude* theme did not necessarily take much time. Six or eight attempts at a theme can be the work of an hour or less.

11. Cook, *Beethoven*, 94. "A *Marseillaise* for humanity" was the apt phrase of Edgar Quinet in the nineteenth century—though he also spread the erroneous rumor that Schiller's censored original poem was "An die Freiheit" (To Freedom).

12. Winter, in "Sketches," calls the *Freude* theme a "synthetic folk song" and places it in the tradition of folk roots in Haydn and Mozart. Without entirely disagreeing, I am more inclined to place it in the popularistic tradition of the *geselliges Lied,* the social song, which may subsume folk music but has its own tradition. Also I think national anthems are a relevant model, and they are not usually folk songs, though they may utilize one. I'll opine that in comparison to *An die Freude*, Haydn's anthem is the better tune, arguably the finest of all national anthems. In comparison, the American *Star-Spangled Banner* is notoriously awkward to sing, with too wide a range.

13. There is an often-repeated story that even as Beethoven planned the *Freude* theme as the focus of the choral Ninth, he also resisted the idea and sketched a purely instrumental finale. That idea is attractive given that, in the end, as the text will ad-

dress, Beethoven had second thoughts about the finale. But Winter, in "Sketches," gives a convincing rebuttal to Nottebohm and later writers who thought a sketch marked *Finale instrumentale* was intended as an alternative for the Ninth finale. (That theme ended up in op. 132.)

14. One of the most striking things about the Ninth's beginning is how A sounds like the tonic until, at the end of the first tremolo section, Beethoven adds a D against the A and E, anticipating the D-minor arpeggio and undermining the A in a quite disorienting way.

15. After the return of the tremolo idea on D–A in the beginning, there is no real cadence to D minor until the D pedal of m. 328, and that is a weak cadence. The first strong cadence after the opening is to B-flat at the closing section of the exposition. There is no true perfect authentic cadence to D until the return of the closing section just before the coda.

16. After the moment of lyrical warmth in B-flat, there is an echoing phrase in a sudden magical turn to B major a couple of pages later.

17. Solomon, in *Beethoven*, writes about the dissolution of the heroic style, after which "[t]he task he would set himself in his late music would be the portrayal of heroism without heroics, without heroes" (295). I don't, however, find much implied "portrayal of heroism" in the late music. The centrality of brotherhood in the Ninth and the spirituality of much of the late music are not concerned with heroic ideals at all.

18. Note that Wagner, for whom the Ninth was an obsession and in many ways a starting point, in the *Ring* cycle depicts the failure of the masculine principle of power and heroism, embodied in the heroic fool Siegfried, and the triumph of the feminine principle of compassion, embodied in Brünnhilde. In that, then, he also echoes the Ninth. The beginning of the *Ring*, that enormous, slow-unfolding E-flat-major chord that evokes the Rhine, is one of many descendants of the Ninth's opening, others to be found in Bruckner and Mahler.

19. Tovey never more clearly revealed his willful hostility to fundamental thematic relationships than when he wrote of the B-flat interlude in the first movement of the Ninth that its resemblance to the *Freude* theme is "superficial and entirely accidental."

20. Lockwood, *Beethoven: Music*, 430–31.

21. The scherzo of the Ninth is one of Beethoven's excursions in unusual timpani tunings, another striking example being the tritone tuning at the beginning of the dungeon scene in *Fidelio*.

22. A long-standing and unresolved question over the fourth horn solo in the movement debates whether Beethoven had an early valved horn available, or whether he wanted a great many stopped notes — the solos are possible to play on an open horn, but barely.

23. Solomon has called the Ninth "an extended metaphor of a quest for Elysium." What defines that search is the way the *Freude* theme is foreshadowed from the beginning. That is the kind of foreshadowing Beethoven usually did, but this time it involves a text in the finale and thus more tangible images, all the prefiguring at the service of shaping an absolutely end-directed symphony.

24. Cook, *Beethoven*, 101.

25. Levy, *Beethoven*, 20. It was to his Illuminatus friend Körner that Schiller wrote about "An die Freude" in 1800: "It still remains a bad poem and represents a stage

of my development that I have since left behind in order to produce something respectable." All the same, because everybody already knew it, Schiller published it in his collected poems, but deleted some of its more extravagant prerevolutionary sentiments, among them "beggars become brothers of princes."

26. Solomon, "Beethoven, Freemasonry," 113.

27. Lockwood, *Beethoven: Music*, 422.

28. Friedrich Schiller, *Naïve and Sentimental Poetry*, quoted in Solomon, *Beethoven Essays*, 11.

29. My score of the finale has the tempo of the opening as dotted half = 90, which is a long-standing engraver's mistake. Beethoven's actual intended tempo was dotted half = 66, which is awkward but at least performable for the opening fanfare. But that tempo is unworkably fast for the bass recitatives, which Beethoven insisted he wanted done in strict time. In strict time, a pulse of 66 for the bar would turn the recitatives into waltzes. At the same time, 66 for the fanfare buzzes past the opening harmony so fast as to negate its impact — even more so when it comes back later as a crunch of all the notes in the scale. In contrast, Beethoven's tempo of quarter = 88 is entirely reasonable for the first movement (one often hears faster performances), likewise 116 for the second movement (again, modern performances are sometimes faster). Metronome 60 and 63 for the third movement are reasonable, but many take it slower and I prefer it that way — Beethoven's metronome mark seems to me to damage the sense of reverie and timelessness in the slow movement. For a survey of problems in these and other metronome indications in the symphonies, see C. Brown, "Historical Performance."

30. None of the earlier movements recalled in the opening section of the finale are quoted literally: the first adds C-sharp to the first movement's A–E tremolo; rather than a false tonic, the harmony now sounds vaguely like the dominant seventh of D, which it actually is. The bit of the second movement is in A minor, not D minor; the beginning of the third movement is properly in B-flat, but in winds rather than strings. All those changes help integrate the snippets into the tonal and timbral spectrum of the D-major finale, with its stretch of B-flat and its frequent emphasis on the wind band (all but one of the recollections are mainly in winds).

31. Thayer/Forbes, 2:892–93.

32. When I say there is no "abstract" point to the recalls of earlier movements in the finale, I mean that their impression mainly conveys a narrative logic. At least in one "abstract" dimension, they are an extension of Beethoven's constant habit of keeping the whole in view and basing a whole work on one set of ideas. This usually involves themes or motifs recurring throughout the piece, only not to the extent of more or less literal quotations as in the Ninth and other late works. As I said in a note in the previous chapter, at times the finale of the Ninth approaches the opposite of the "purely musical": the "purely extramusical."

33. That the form of the finale is unprecedented is in keeping with the rest of the symphony. The first movement has a development that is the least dramatic part of the movement and a recapitulation that does violence to the idea of a recapitulation. The second movement is an amalgam of fugue, sonata, and scherzo. The third movement comprises unusual double variations. The finale is an ad hoc form based around variations. Once again, in the symphonies only the *Eroica* has this kind of bending and tinkering with traditional outlines in every movement.

34. Translations of "An die Freude" here are based on the ones in Levy, *Beethoven,* but are largely my own.
35. Kinderman, *Beethoven,* 281. Kinderman first examined what I am calling the "God-texture" in the *Missa solemnis* and the Ninth, and explored how the two relate.
36. In my translation of the Schiller, I am assuming that "his suns" in the text means God's suns, God having ended the previous verse. I'm translating the obscure German *Plan* in context with its military sense of "battlefield" rather than the usual "firmament," which is not a standard sense of the word. Levy (*Beethoven,* 107) notes echoes of Psalm 19 in the Schiller verse.
37. Beethoven's metronome marking for the Turkish march is dotted quarter = 84. In contrast to his penchant for exaggeratedly fast markings, this one is bizarrely slow. Only perhaps in a funeral would a military band march so slow, and that tempo would ruin the energy of the fugue that follows. Even in the present time, when many conductors give lip service to Beethoven's metronome markings (mainly the fast ones), I have never heard anyone conform to that tempo for the Turkish march. It's always taken some five to seven clicks faster, as I think it clearly should be.
38. To say that in the finale Beethoven symbolically embraces the East, via the Turkish march, is not to make him some sort of modern multiculturalist. It is rather to say that this echoes his interest in Eastern religions and the like. Turkey was an old enemy of Austria, meanwhile, and partly for that reason an object of Austrians' fascination. In any case, Beethoven's knowledge of Eastern cultures would have been severely limited.
39. Levy, in *Beethoven,* writes, "Beethoven had recognized that the theme for '*Seid umschlungen, Millionen*' was contrapuntally compatible with the '*Freude*' theme" (115), as if the combination were a happy accident. But there are few happy accidents in counterpoint. The uniting of the two themes in a double fugue reveals that this section had to have been sketched first. A successful combination of the *Freude, schöner Götterfunken* and *Seid umschlungen* themes had to be composed that way. Then the *Seid umschlungen* theme was retroactively placed first, on its own, in the credo. In fact, on p. 37, Levy reproduces a sketch where Beethoven worked out the double fugue in strict counterpoint, right out of Fux.
40. Ibid., 115.
41. When I say the Ninth was "neglected for decades," I mean in the mainstream concert repertoire, which by the middle of the nineteenth century was becoming the museum that it has remained since. Among other things, it needed the new specialized conductors to shape performances. At the same time, in score and in its occasional performances, from the outset the Ninth had enormous impact on composers including Berlioz, Wagner, and Brahms.

32. *Ars Longa, Vita Brevis*

1. Cook, *Beethoven,* 119n25. Czerny is usually a reliable witness, so his story of Beethoven's planning to replace the Ninth Symphony finale has reasonable credibility. True, there is at least a possibility that Czerny made up the story to discredit the finale because he didn't approve of it. As has been seen, this was a common practice in memoirs of the time, Schindler being the prime example.
2. Adolph Bernhard Marx, "A Few Words on the Symphony and Beethoven's Achieve-

ment in This Field," in Senner, *Critical Reception*, 1:59–75. Note that Marx had already arrived at the term "sonata form," though this was before the full development of his conceptions in his theoretical writings.

3. Anderson, vol. 3, no. 1403. History calls Hoffmann and Marx the most important of Beethoven's contemporary critics, and they are the only two critics he ever thanked. Even in that, he was prophetic.

4. Botstein, in "Patrons and Publics," says that through the journal *Prometheus* Beethoven was aware of "the claims of the early German romantics" including Schlegel, and his friends attended Schlegel's famous lectures (103).

5. The "constraining boxes" I mean in relation to Marx's writings and influence are mainly three. First, he made Beethoven the unquestioned king of composers and the virtual standard by which all music was to be judged. I suspect that did Beethoven's reputation — and Western music itself — more harm than good. (Later in life, Marx wrote a biography of Beethoven.) Second, there is Marx's rigid and oversimplified model of sonata form, which, as Charles Rosen has written, was put forth not as a description of what Beethoven, Mozart, and Haydn actually did (which was far freer than Marx's outline) but rather as a model for how composers should use the form. Marx's influence had much to do with what Karl Dahlhaus (*Ludwig van Beethoven*) called the "ossified" handling of form in the later nineteenth century. (It was also what Wagner and his followers wanted to escape from. Of those who stayed true to the old forms, especially sonata form, it was mainly Brahms who understood how freely they were treated in the past and how pernicious was Marx's ossification of them.) Third, in his writing Marx treats formal organization as largely a matter of themes, which is a distortion; Classical forms were more fundamentally a matter of key structure. Both for well and ill, Marx's ideas dominated his time and soldiered on through most of the twentieth century. In large measure, his conception of Beethoven became *the* conception. In the late-century postmodern reaction against such norms, Beethoven himself was blamed for his dominance, as if he had deviously shaped his own future historical reputation. None of this, however, is really meant to blame Marx either, who was a brilliant theorist and, like Beethoven, not responsible for the historical consequences of his influence.

6. B. Cooper, *Beethoven Compendium*, 30. It is not clear which of the two Schott brothers Beethoven corresponded with.

7. Anderson, vol. 3, no. 1301.

8. B. Cooper, *Beethoven*, 320.

9. Anderson, vol. 3, nos. 1300, 1349.

10. Ibid., no. 1345 (paragraphs added).

11. Kinderman, *Beethoven*, 327.

12. Lockwood, *Beethoven: Music*, 396.

13. Clive, *Beethoven and His World*, 154.

14. Thayer/Forbes, 2:938–39.

15. Ibid., 2:940.

16. Winter, "Quartets," 40.

17. Thayer/Forbes, 2:938–41.

18. B. Cooper, *Beethoven Compendium*, 31.

19. Thayer/Forbes, 2:917.

20. MacArdle, "Family van Beethoven," 543.

21. Sterba and Sterba, *Beethoven and His Nephew,* 238.
22. Ibid., 233.
23. M. Cooper, *Beethoven,* 63.
24. Sterba and Sterba, *Beethoven and His Nephew,* 277.
25. Anderson, vol. 3, nos. 1440, 1445.
26. B. Cooper, *Beethoven,* 343.
27. Anderson, vol. 3, no. 1380.
28. Ibid., no. 1387.
29. Ibid., no. 1389.
30. Thayer/Forbes, 2:922–23.
31. Anderson, vol. 3, no. 1390.
32. Thayer/Forbes, 2:946.
33. Mai, *Diagnosing Genius,* 127.
34. M. Cooper, *Beethoven,* 444.
35. Anderson, vol. 3, no. 1408.
36. Ibid., no. 1415.
37. Thayer/Forbes, 2:942–43.
38. Ibid., 2:919–20.
39. Ibid., 2:958.
40. Anderson, vol. 3, nos. 1427, 1428.
41. Landon, *Beethoven,* 190.
42. Lockwood, *Beethoven: Music,* 545n35.
43. Landon, *Beethoven,* 169.
44. Thayer/Forbes, 2:963–65.
45. Ibid., 2:954.
46. Breuning, *Memories of Beethoven,* passim.
47. Albrecht, vol. 3, no. 422.
48. Ibid., no. 422, notes.
49. Ibid., no. 423.
50. B. Cooper, *Beethoven,* 323.
51. Ratner, *Beethoven String Quartets,* 196.
52. Lockwood, *Beethoven: Music,* 446.
53. The recapitulation proper of the E-flat Major finale is preceded by a huge false recap in A-flat, the subdominant — an echo of the main theme, which twice jumps from the tonic to an accented subdominant on the second beat.
54. Ratner, in *Beethoven String Quartets,* does not want to call the middle of the A Major's first movement a development at all. He calls it "X (a parenthesis in the form)" (263). After it he places not a recapitulation but a second exposition, starting in E minor. Since I find the movement developmental from the beginning, I leave the usual designations in place but add a question that the piece seems to present us: is there really *any* exposition, in the usual sense of presenting well-defined ideas as a subject for musical discussion and eventual recapitulation? A frequent analogy of the Classical era was to compare musical form to an essay, which begins with a clear exposition of ideas and, toward the end, returns to them in summary. By the late quartets, that analogy has broken down. Beethoven is heading toward, I would not say true stream of consciousness as a retreat to the irrational, but rather an impression of free rhapsody anchored on covert rather than overt forms.
55. Solomon, *Beethoven,* 295.

56. As has been noted by various writers, the *Heiliger Dankgesang* does not entirely succeed in making its nominal tonic, F, sound like a tonic chord — at least, not until the end of the movement. In practice, to the ear the music tends to sound like an endlessly unresolved C major — which is part of its unique effect of suspension. Descendants of the *Heiliger Dankgesang* include the long string chorale in the Sibelius Seventh Symphony and the string background of the Ives *Unanswered Question*.

57. Kolodin, *Interior Beethoven*, 290.

58. The opening-motto theme of the A Minor — two half steps joined by a leap, usually of a sixth — often becomes not just line but counterpoint, all the way to the figure in m. 42 of the finale. That climactic figure joins, from the bottom, G-sharp–A, F–E, and D-sharp–E, which can be found, respectively, in bars 1, 2, and 3 of the quartet. Meanwhile the primal half step of the quartet, F–E, is all over the finale, starting with the accompaniment figure of the beginning in second violin and in the violins in the penultimate system of the coda.

59. I find Chua's book on the *Galitzin* Quartets an interesting and worthwhile study, even if he is too beholden, for my taste, to fashionable academic theory. Rather than relating the quartets to the Romantic spirit and/or to the tumult in Beethoven's life, he makes the *Galitzins* a deliberate critique of the norms of Classical discourse in music, and thereby makes Beethoven into a virtual poststructuralist: "By setting their own agenda of disruption and disorder, [the *Galitzins*] detail theory in a way that exposes its limitations . . . they constantly undermine analysis." Therefore, his analysis will be "deconstructive" (9). All the same, if Chua is at pains to show how Beethoven deconstructs norms and models and traditions, he still has trenchant things to say about the construction of the quartets, including their motivic structure.

60. *Dissociation* is perhaps the single most common word applied by commentators concerning the B-flat Quartet, starting with Kerman in his book *Beethoven Quartets*. Kerman's chapter on the B-flat and A Minor Quartets is titled "Contrast."

61. Lockwood, *Beethoven: Music*, 444.

62. "Trance" is Kerman's term in *Beethoven Quartets* for the central section of the A Minor's first movement, which he calls "the most eccentric [development] Beethoven ever wrote." But there is a reason behind it. As happens now and then but more often in late Beethoven, the development has to find its own ideas, because the rest of the movement is already developmental. The spreading of development out of the development section proper, thereby compromising the meaning and purpose of that section, was a problem that bedeviled composers for the rest of the century — at least among composers still using sonata form, notably Brahms.

63. In *Beethoven*, Barry Cooper tacitly accounts for the vagaries of the B-flat Quartet by citing the sketches, which imply that Beethoven set out on the piece with few plans: "[T]he quartet was thus being created as a kind of narrative, rather than a canvas where the overall outline is clear from the start" (330). I presume Cooper means a kind of narrative of its own compositional process. Cooper also says that after some dozen sketches for the theme of the finale, the *Grosse Fuge* took shape as it did "almost by accident." While this smacks of Cooper trying to rationalize his own discomfort with the quartet or at least the finale, it also is a possible explanation, though others note that Beethoven had the final version of the finale theme early on (see Kinderman, *Beethoven*, 303). As is seen in the text, I'm more inclined

to see Beethoven as deliberately pushing boundaries to the limit here, if not past it. That in turn may have been allied to a compositional process that deliberately avoided his usual habit of starting with a firm, if flexible, plan for the work. One clue in that direction is the coda of the first movement. In it I don't hear Kerman's sense that the reconciliation of the coda is "forced." In the coda I hear Beethoven reviewing all the leading ideas, presenting them first in an even more fragmentary way than they were at the beginning, then smoothing them out at the very end. In light of thematic integration and general resolution as a goal of Classical style and of Beethoven himself, the open question of the end is whether anything in that direction has been achieved. Fragmentation, nonintegration, is the character not only of the first movement but of the whole quartet.

64. Kerman, *Beethoven Quartets*, 315.

65. Having found a tendency to build the themes of the first movement of the B-flat in descending chains of thirds, I expected Beethoven to stick to that idea as he ordinarily does — one example being the ascending and descending chains of thirds in each movement of the *Kreutzer*. But I don't find those thirds in the scherzo. The main theme of the third movement is built on a scaffolding of thirds climbing by step: D-flat–F, F–A-flat, B-flat–D-flat–F. The *tedesca* theme is a simple third descent of D–B–D–G. As Kerman details (ibid.), there are other motivic, gestural, and tonal echoes throughout the piece, but it is hard to make a case for any particular three or four ideas living up to my (loose) requirement of a fundamental idea in a piece: it must keep happening. At the same time, that elusiveness of overriding ideas does conform to one überidea: dissociation.

66. Kerman's excellent summation of the B-flat Quartet: "The first movement ... is Beethoven's *most* contrasty and enigmatic ... the second movement stands out as his *most* precipitous and ill-behaved, the fourth movement as his *most* innocently dance-like. The *Cavatina* is his *most* emotional slow movement ... As for the Finale, the Great Fugue, it not only beggars superlatives but obviously was written with the express purpose of beggaring superlatives (which is not to say that this was its exclusive purpose)" (ibid., 320). In describing the fugue, adjectives can only scramble to approach the reality. I confess I am embarrassed to try to write about it at all; I do it because it is my job. Two students of mine, in two different schools, seemed to be on the verge of breakdown when they gave class presentations on the *Grosse Fuge*. One of them had obsessed over the piece for months, among other things making it the ringtone on his cell phone. Needless to say, the *Grosse Fuge* was a favored work of Stravinsky and a row of other twentieth-century composers and music theorists. In a memorable concert of the James Levine years with the Boston Symphony, a string-orchestra arrangement of the *Fuge* began and ended a program, framing the Beethoven and Schoenberg Violin Concertos. The point was that the *Fuge* was the most avant-garde work of the evening, and the point was made.

67. B. Cooper, *Beethoven*, 332–33, 344.

68. If one wants, one can find the theme of the *Grosse Fuge* buried in the opening of the quartet, in the notes A-flat–G–E-flat–D, but to make the connection the first two notes have to be reversed, and the middle interval is a fifth rather than the fugue's sixth. For all my motif hunting, I'm not convinced by this connection. One interesting attempt at drawing the quartet together under some rubric comes from Ratner in *Beethoven String Quartets*: "*The chief connection between the Great Fuge and Op. 130 is topical.*" Certainly some of the quartet falls clearly into topics:

the "Cavatina" operatic, the *tedesca* a German dance. But Ratner believes there is virtually no moment in Beethoven and the Classical style that is *not* in some topic or other, a doctrine I don't subscribe to. Still, I think Ratner's ideas about topics in general are a unique and valuable contribution to understanding Beethoven and his predecessors.

69. Kerman, *Beethoven Quartets*, 269.
70. Kirkendale, "Great Fugue," 17.
71. Ratner rather tortuously calls the form of the *Grosse Fuge* a "Fantasia along the lines of a *variation-canzona*" and sees it as a sequence of topics: the B-flat fugue a march, the G-flat fugue an arioso, the 6/8 fugue a gigue (*Beethoven String Quartets*, 284). This is more specific than but similar to Kerman's view of the movement as a progression of character changes.
72. Kerman, *Beethoven Quartets*, 279.
73. Lockwood, *Beethoven: Music*, 459.
74. Publisher Artaria showed a certain instinct for the nature of the B-flat Quartet when Beethoven considered publishing each movement separately, though nothing came of the idea (ibid., 460).
75. Ibid.
76. Kerman, *Beethoven Quartets*, 322.
77. Lockwood, *Beethoven*, 460.
78. Kinderman, *Beethoven*, 304.

33. *Plaudite, Amici*

1. Albrecht, vol. 3, no. 419. In this letter to Hummel, Haslinger notes that his publishing partner Steiner is "elderly and also somewhat strange."
2. B. Cooper, *Beethoven Compendium*, 32.
3. Lockwood, *Beethoven: Music*, 350.
4. Goethe, quoted in Botstein, "Patrons and Publics," 77.
5. Lockwood, *Beethoven: Music*, 442.
6. Beethoven's final appeal about the Galitzin debt was issued five days before Beethoven died.
7. Albrecht, vol. 3, no. 444.
8. Marek, *Beethoven*, 603–5.
9. Fiske, *Beethoven's Missa solemnis*, 21.
10. Gottfried Wilhelm Fink, "Is It True That Our Music Has Declined So Far That It No Longer Can Stand Comparison with the Old and Oldest Music?," in Senner, *Critical Reception*, vol. 1, no. 87.
11. M. Cooper, *Beethoven*, 75.
12. Thayer/Forbes, 2:956. From the relatively little J. S. Bach that Beethoven was acquainted with, it is remarkable that he understood Bach's inexhaustible imagination.
13. *New York Times* and *The Guardian*, October 13, 2005 — soon after Beethoven's lost manuscript of the *Grosse Fuge* four-hand arrangement was rediscovered in, of all places, the town King of Prussia, outside Philadelphia.
14. Solomon, *Beethoven*, 368–69.
15. Albrecht, vol. 3, no. 433n4.
16. Sterba and Sterba, *Beethoven and His Nephew*, 278.
17. Thayer/Forbes, 2:994–95.

18. Sterba and Sterba, *Beethoven and His Nephew,* 277–79.

19. Gruneberg's "Suicide Attempt" summarizes the "cry for help" interpretation. It points out that nearly all genuine suicide attempts succeed on the first try.

20. Sterba and Sterba, *Beethoven and His Nephew,* 279–84.

21. Thayer/Forbes, 2:998–1003.

22. Anderson, vol. 3, no. 1502.

23. Breuning, *Memories of Beethoven,* 83.

24. Thayer/Forbes, 2:1000.

25. Ibid., 2:1001–3.

26. Ibid., 2:1004.

27. Anderson, vol. 3, no. 1521.

28. Ibid., no. 1498.

29. Ratner, *Beethoven String Quartets,* 238.

30. When I say Beethoven invested fugue with more emotion than anybody had, that is not to say that I believe he wrote the greatest fugues. For me, Bach did. Part of the reason I say that is that Bach seems to me a born contrapuntalist in a way Beethoven never quite was, for all his labors in counterpoint. Certainly Bach wrote expressive, even tragic fugues, but it was not his style to invest them with the full Beethovenian intensity of emotion, which rose from the Classical sonata style. Meanwhile, Baroque fugues do not have the variety of keys that Beethoven's do, which is also the influence of the sonata style.

31. As the text notes, keys like C-sharp minor are "shadowed" in strings, because they involve few open strings. The standard string keys are bright ones between one flat and three sharps, which have the most open strings. The keys of C, G, and F major contain every open string on every instrument. Even when the open strings are not used for those notes in playing, they resonate with the pitches. When the young Brahms drafted a piano trio in C-sharp minor, his violinist friend Joachim told him that was an awkward and ungrateful key for strings and he should take it down to C minor — which Brahms did, in the C Minor Piano Quartet. As I have said before, from the evidence of his first chamber opuses, I think from early on Beethoven had learned to make good use of the timbral contrast of bright and dark string keys. There is also the issue of which degrees of the scale the open strings fall on. In C-sharp minor the open strings are E and A — the mediant degrees. It's clear in the C-sharp Minor Quartet that Beethoven was aware of this and made use of it as part of the significance especially of the notes A and D, both in the fugue and in the tonal plan of the whole quartet. The first answer in the fugue is in the subdominant partly to emphasize D, another open string. The second movement emerges from dark C-sharp minor to D major, the Neapolitan, one of the brightest string keys. Harmonic C-sharp minor also includes a B-sharp, enharmonically a C, and in the first movement Beethoven makes memorable use of the cello's lowest note in its B-sharp incarnation. In contrast to the present, orchestral players in Beethoven's day regularly used open strings when those pitches came up. I've never seen a study of whether chamber players of the time did the same, though I suspect they did and that Beethoven expected the A in the fugue theme to be an open string, likewise the D in the answer and the E at the top of the line.

32. Winter, "Plans for the Structure," 136; Lockwood, *Beethoven: Music,* 471.

33. As is often noted, the configuration of the beginning, B-sharp–C-sharp, A–G-sharp, two semitones joined by a leap, is yet another version of the leading motif of the A

Minor Quartet and the *Grosse Fuge* motif — so it is shared by three quartets. Chua (*"Galitzin" Quartets,* 7) relates these to the "notorious B–A–C–H motif," which I find a bit of a stretch, though they all involve two semitones separated by some sort of leap. I also don't see why the Bach motif is "notorious" rather than "famous."

34. Given the importance of the subdominant in the C-sharp Quartet and the significance of D and A as N and N of V, Ratner (*Beethoven String Quartets*) calls the presence of the Neapolitan a "deep subdominant."

35. Lockwood, *Beethoven,* 473.

36. In his "Musical Curiosities," Beethoven editor Jonathan Del Mar traces the *ponticello* effect back to a few uses in Telemann and Boccherini, and in Haydn's Symphony No. 97 — the latter the most likely place Beethoven heard it.

37. The key relations in the quartet all stress subdominants in relation to C-sharp minor: F-sharp minor and the "deep subdominants" of A and D. This creates a unique tonal world, largely avoiding more dramatic and dynamic dominant relationships except within the subdominant areas. The first movement also avoids E, the relative major of C-sharp minor. E major finally turns up in the scherzo. Most of the last page of the quartet is in F-sharp minor, turning to C-sharp major only in the last six bars. To my ear, the final cadence to C-sharp is detectably compromised.

38. From Schiller's essay "The Pathetic."

39. Solomon, *Beethoven,* 370.

40. B. Cooper, *Beethoven,* 345–46.

41. Thayer/Forbes, 2:1002.

42. Anderson, vol. 3, no. 1533.

43. Sterba and Sterba, *Beethoven and His Nephew,* 293.

44. John Suchet, "Therese van Beethoven (1787–1828): Beethoven's Sister-in-Law," Classic FM, accessed December 20, 2013, http://www.classicfm.com/composers/beethoven/guides/therese-beethovens-sister-in-law/. The winegrowers who currently own Wasserhof have preserved Beethoven's rooms and filled them with original or period furniture.

45. Thayer/Forbes, 2:1008–9. The translation given is Thayer's archaic "A pretty brother, that he is!" I've updated it.

46. Ibid., 1007.

47. Albrecht, vol. 3, no. 446.

48. Thayer/Forbes, 2:1013.

49. Ibid., 2:1015.

50. Sterba and Sterba, *Beethoven and His Nephew,* 293.

51. Mai, *Diagnosing Genius,* 90–91.

52. The solemn incantation on the first page of the F Major becomes a more chromatic cantus firmus–like figure later in the movement. That version happens to be, yet again, the motto and leading motif that open the A Minor Quartet and the theme of the *Grosse Fuge.*

53. I think the E-flat in the scherzo is intentionally a non sequitur in effect, but it was elaborately foreshadowed in the coda of the first movement, which is full of out-of-key E-flats.

54. Anderson, vol. 3, no. 1538A.

55. One memorable creative use of the *Muss es sein?* idea in the quartet is in Milan Kundera's *The Unbearable Lightness of Being.* Kundera, who studied music, makes

the quartet finale a motif in the book, tying its question and answer into his grand theme of heaviness (the question) and lightness (the answer).

56. Another idea that the new finale takes up from earlier movements of the B-flat Quartet, mainly the first movement, is chains of thirds, which are all over the movement starting with the third-based main theme. The dashing sixteenths of the second theme recall a similar effect in the first movement, but that theme is also founded on a long train of rising thirds that climb, bar by bar: F–A / C–E–G–B-flat / D–F / A–C–E-flat–G / B-flat–D / F–A / C–E. The second phrase of sixteenths starts a new rising chain of thirds. The *fortissimo* climax of the coda features a sequence of triads descending by thirds in the lower voice, echoed a beat later in the upper voice. There is a worthwhile study to be done of Beethoven's use of themes and passages based on chains of thirds, going back past the *Hammerklavier* and *Kreutzer* Sonatas all the way to the *Electoral* Sonata.

57. For all my fondness for the alternative finale, I am inclined to agree with Kerman, in *Beethoven Quartets,* who essentially finds the fugue too much and the substitute finale too little, neither entirely satisfactory. In practice I vote for the *Grosse Fuge* because it crowns an enigmatic work with a climactic enigma of overwhelming power. Kerman finds the B-flat Quartet, on the whole, a not entirely successful stage of a journey in some new direction that Beethoven did not live to define. I tend to agree with that, too. I wonder whether the direction may have had something to do with the "new kind of gravity" Beethoven planned for the Tenth Symphony. If the B-flat is neither my favorite Beethoven quartet nor the one I find his "greatest," for me it is the most fascinating one. It also contains some of the most beautiful and moving music he ever wrote.

58. Yeats: "sick with desire / and fastened to a dying animal," from "Sailing to Byzantium."

59. Wawruch, quoted in Mai, *Diagnosing Genius,* 217–18.

60. Breuning, *Memories of Beethoven,* 101.

61. Thayer/Forbes, 2:1022–23.

62. Clive, *Beethoven and His World,* 19.

63. Breuning, *Memories of Beethoven,* 96.

64. Ibid., 95.

65. Anderson, vol. 3, no. 1542.

66. Wawruch, quoted in Mai, *Diagnosing Genius,* 217–19.

67. Thayer/Forbes, 2:1022–23.

68. Mai, *Diagnosing Genius,* 219.

69. Thayer/Forbes, 1:942.

70. Ibid., 2:1034.

71. Albrecht, vol. 3, no. 459.

72. Ibid., no. 460.

73. Thayer/Forbes, 2:1033–38.

74. Hiller account in Landon, *Beethoven,* 199–200.

75. Thayer/Forbes, 2:1047.

76. Albrecht, vol. 3, no. 468. Years later Schindler and Anselm Hüttenbrenner reported that Schubert visited Beethoven on his deathbed, but there is no evidence for it — or that Beethoven and Schubert ever met, though Beethoven surely knew the younger man's reputation and had likely seen some songs.

77. Anderson, vol. 3, no. 1566.
78. Wawruch, cited in Mai, *Diagnosing Genius,* 220.
79. Breuning, *Memories of Beethoven,* 103.
80. Thayer/Forbes, 2:1049.
81. Anderson, vol. 3, no. 1570. The original of the note does not survive.
82. Albrecht, vol. 3, no. 469.
83. Breuning, *Memories of Beethoven,* 101–2.
84. Albrecht, vol. 3, no. 479.
85. Ibid., no. 472.
86. Breuning, *Memories of Beethoven,* 104.
87. Thayer/Forbes, 2:1050–51.
88. Ibid., 2:1051n61. Johann's account of his brother dying in his arms is presumably a fabrication — there is no record that he was present.
89. I have concluded that Beethoven was a functional alcoholic, but many over the years have disputed the idea that he was so much a drinker as that. Given the primitive state of medicine in those days, no doctor's conclusions can be fully trusted. But doctors Wawruch and Malfatti both considered Beethoven alcoholic, and Lorenz's article "Commentary on Wawruch's Report" concludes that alcoholic cirrhosis is a strong, if not unassailable, possibility. This is also the conclusion of several doctors cited in Mai (*Diagnosing Genius,* 141). Mai's chapter 4 reviews questions concerning alcohol, hearing, and lead poisoning, and the possibility that Beethoven had inflammatory bowel disease. Not all cirrhosis is caused by alcohol. Likewise, there is a good deal of evidence for lead poisoning, but some, including Eisinger ("Was Beethoven Lead-Poisoned?"), conclude he was not afflicted with it. Like Beethoven's deafness and every other aspect of his health, these questions likely will never be answered for certain. What I say in the text is that Beethoven may have had lead poisoning from early in life, but if that was not the cause, he had some other chronic condition that afflicted his digestive system.
90. M. Cooper, *Beethoven,* 439.
91. Breuning, *Memories of Beethoven,* 106.
92. Solomon (*Beethoven,* 383) says the second medallion is Antonie Brentano, his nominee for the Immortal Beloved.
93. Ibid.
94. Breuning, *Memories of Beethoven,* 108; Thayer/Forbes, 2:1053.
95. Thayer/Forbes, 2:1054–56.
96. Albrecht, vol. 3, no. 477.
97. Ibid., no. 491n2.
98. Breuning, *Memories of Beethoven,* 113–14.
99. Clive, *Beethoven and His World,* 20; John Suchet, "Karl van Beethoven (1806–58): Beethoven's Nephew," Classic FM, accessed October 23, 2013, http://www.classicfm.com/composers/beethoven/guides/karl-van-beethoven-nephew/.
100. Breuning, *Memories of Beethoven,* 114. Gerhard's deploring description of Johann van Beethoven was probably inflected by Schindler, who despised Johann.
101. Clive, *Beethoven and His World,* 26; Albrecht, vol. 3, no. 446n4.
102. Clive, *Beethoven and His World,* 15–17.
103. Johann Friedrich Rochlitz, in Senner, *Critical Receptions,* vol. 1, no. 43.
104. Wilhelm Christian Müller, in Senner, *Critical Receptions,* vol. 1, no. 45.
105. Thompson, *Franz Grillparzer,* 86.

Index

⟨≈⟩

ABA form, 942

Adelaide (Beethoven), 200–201, 239, 240, 248

Albrechtsberger, Johann Georg, 163–64, 173, 198–99, 685, 893

Alexander I, Tsar/Tsarina, 294, 420, 425, 479, 523, 609–10, 627, 633, 635–36, 645–46, 652

Allgemeine Musikalische Zeitung (AMZ/ General Musical Magazine), 229, 230, 231, 233–34, 238, 243, 244, 264, 269, 271, 272, 290, 310, 312–13, 318–19, 323, 329, 351, 382–83, 397, 399–401, 407, 408, 412, 417, 426, 437, 471, 472, 513–14, 540, 542, 577, 626, 630, 694, 731, 749, 767, 796, 900, 901, 933–34

Amenda, Karl Friedrich
background, 209–10
Beethoven and, 210–12, 227, 236, 249, 251, 252, 278–79, 283, 388, 650, 672

American Revolution, 26, 49, 102

AMZ. See Allgemeine Musikalische Zeitung (AMZ/General Musical Magazine)

An die ferne Geliebte/To the Distant Beloved (Beethoven), 675–78, 684

Appassionata Sonata (Beethoven), 326, 374, 410–12, 429, 448, 460, 499, 530, 531, 556, 559, 703, 718, 835, 841, 910–11, 918

Archduke Trio, 534, 561–63, 628, 650, 679

Arnim, Achim von, 564–65, 579, 586, 587, 588

"art" definition/description, xvi, xvii, xviii

Artaria publishing house, 159, 166, 169, 178–79, 234, 309–10, 735, 751, 761, 786, 879, 896, 901–2, 914

Aufklärung. See Enlightenment

Austria
French occupations/book bans, 168, 171, 200, 203, 524, 525
wars with France, 202–3, 262–63, 523–24, 526–27
See also specific individuals

Averdonk, Johanna Helene, 30, 107

Averdonk, Severin Anton, 107

Bach, C. P. E., 33, 44–45, 59, 117, 149, 154, 158, 195

Bach, J. C., 44, 45, 158

Bach, J. S., 43, 44, 45, 56, 97, 149, 157, 158, 271, 381, 780, 901, 945

Bach, Johann Baptist (lawyer), 726, 727, 730, 736–37, 741, 763
Bagration, Katherine, Princess, 635–36
"baroque" defined, 231–32
Baroque period (music)
  concerto-sonata form, 941–42
  fugue form, 943, 944
  musical form and, 940, 941–42, 943, 944
Battle of Vittoria (Beethoven). *See Wellington's Victory* (Beethoven)
bedbugs, 924
"Beethoven" name
  origins, 3
  spelling variations, 3
Beethoven, Anna Maria Franziska van, 35
Beethoven, Caspar Anton Carl van
  christening, 24
  description, 186–87, 328–29, 388, 520
  Heiligenstadt Testament/letter and, 301–6
  illness/death, 600, 648, 656, 657, 659–60
  Johanna/child and, 424, 598, 600, 662–63
  as Ludwig's agent, 168, 188, 291–93, 297, 309, 310, 328–29, 375, 388, 395, 396, 407–8, 418, 452
  music and, 99
  relationship with Ludwig, 454, 455, 520–21, 523, 611–12, 648, 650, 659–60
  rheumatic fever, 311
  will, 656–59
Beethoven, Cornelius van, 3
Beethoven family
  deaths of infants/children, 2, 35, 64, 99
  home locations/moves following grandfather's death, 28
  home on Wenzelgasse, 87
  See also Fischer house/surroundings
Beethoven, Franz Georg van, 64
Beethoven, Johann van
  attempts to become *Kapellmeister*, 19, 88
  Beethoven's name day, 2
  Belderbusch and, 19, 20, 88

birth/childhood, 13–14
bribes to Belderbusch, 19–20, 88
Caspar Carl/music and, 36
Christmas celebrations, 24
court chapel choir and, 2, 12, 13, 16, 24, 29, 99
death/funeral, 135
description/character, 28–29, 36, 113
exile decree and, 104–5
father's debtors and, 18
father's inheritance and, 18, 19, 28–29, 88
favorite food, 42
marriage to Maria, 14–15, 18
Max Franz regime and, 69
money and, 16, 18, 24
music and, 2, 12, 13, 15, 23–24, 29, 35–36
relationship with father, 14, 15, 31
salary raise and, 16, 18
teaching music, 24, 29
wife's illness/death and, 92, 93, 99
wine business/drinking problems, 13, 67, 88, 92, 99, 104–5, 127, 135
Beethoven, Johann van/Ludwig's music
  clavier and, 22
  Cologne performance (1778), 30–31
  discipline methods, 21–22, 79
  finding other teachers, 31–33
  goals, 22
  Mozart inspiration and, 23, 30
  parties/celebrations and, 23–24
  promotion, 29–31
  Rhineland tour (1781), 42
  son composing and, 22–23
  son's age at beginning, 22
  violin/viola, 22
Beethoven, Johanna
  background/description, 424, 660, 662–63, 700–701
  daughter of, 736–37, 742, 785, 932
  death, 932
  Ludwig and, 424, 598, 600, 659, 660, 662, 663–65, 667, 689–90, 706, 727–28, 734, 736, 737, 785, 868
  marriage to Carl/son, 424, 598, 600, 657, 660, 662–63

son and (after husband's death),
658, 661, 662, 663–64, 667, 671,
689
See also Beethoven, Karl/Ludwig; Reis,
Johanna
Beethoven, Karl
birth/life with parents, 424, 600, 648
description, 701, 731
hernia/surgery, 673
life/death after Ludwig, 932
military career and, 868, 870, 904–5,
911, 914–15, 922, 932
on mother, 785, 868, 903
Schindler and, 783, 869
Stephan von Breuning as guardian,
904, 905, 915, 927
Beethoven, Karl/Ludwig
boarding school, 660–62, 663, 668,
671–72, 673, 674, 678, 688, 697–98,
730–31, 734–35, 741, 742, 746
commoner's court/decision and,
723–24
conflict with Karl's mother, 600,
658–59, 660–62, 663–64, 673
finances/inheritance and, 674, 740, 742,
768, 922, 927, 932
Karl running away to mother, 721,
746–47, 868, 902
Karl's suicide attempt/arrest and,
902–5, 912
Landrecht court/Ludwig as "nobility"
and, 660, 721–23, 724
legal battles (Ludwig/Johanna), 660,
721–24, 726–31, 736–37, 742
living together, 698, 701, 707, 720–21,
784, 875
Ludwig again as co-guardian, 737
Ludwig spying on nephew, 870–71,
874
Ludwig's deafness and, 698, 707,
722
Ludwig's servants and, 672, 678,
687–88, 697, 705–6, 869, 875
Niemetz and, 869, 902, 903, 904
parson's tutoring and, 706
reasons for Ludwig's actions, 664–68,
696, 742

relationship, 673–74, 678–79, 688, 701,
706, 733, 734, 735, 751, 764, 766,
782–83, 784, 845, 868–71, 874, 875,
922
school in Vienna (1818), 710
visit with Johann/conflict, 911–16
Beethoven, Ludwig Maria van, 2
Beethoven, Ludwig van
1796 tour/music, 193–98, 199–200
attitudes toward aristocracy, 41, 52, 65,
96, 128–29, 144, 761
attitudes toward women, 74, 98, 391–92
Bigot friendship and, 448–51
comparisons to Haydn/Mozart, 900
comparisons to Shakespeare, 935–36
conducting style, 485–86, 622–23, 792
descriptions, xiii, xiv, 41, 60–61, 96,
97–98, 128, 153, 169–70, 184–85,
196, 202, 223, 240, 281, 282, 377,
421, 522, 525, 572, 573, 591–92, 608,
643–44, 648–49, 672–73, 699, 707,
708, 709, 749, 750, 751, 873
grandfather/grandfather's portrait and,
16–18, 61, 278
"Immortal Beloved," 579, 581–89, 603,
674, 930
legacy/significance, xi–xii, 933–36
metronome markings, 694–95, 912, 914
mistaken as tramp, 748, 914
Napoleon and, 299, 334–45, 366–67,
384–85, 386, 421, 526
"new path" decision, 283
Oberdöbling house and, 328, 333, 335,
390
Paris move and, 329–30, 334–35, 387
patterns of falling in love, 201–2, 280,
391–93
politics of, 366
Prague trip/musical work, 187–89
raptus/trances, 98–99, 112–13, 128, 227,
278, 335, 404, 427, 545, 552, 643,
696, 748, 845
relationship patterns/themes, 61, 94,
126, 160, 172–73, 282, 520, 521,
904
relationship with brothers, 31, 99, 104,
127, 135, 187–88

Beethoven, Ludwig van (*cont.*)
  religion and, 2, 50–51, 129, 305–6,
    458, 605–7, 729, 739–40, 797–98,
    824–25
  routine with visitors, 873–75
  rumor of noble father, 734, 878
  self-concept of nobility, 724–25
  sense of duty and, 31, 44, 77, 99, 128,
    275, 369, 404, 528, 664, 665, 740
  solitude and, 39, 64, 89, 112–13, 128
  stories/images and music, 227–28
  talismans of, 17, 82, 281, 301, 584, 930
  trends of late music, 680–84
  See also specific works
Beethoven, Ludwig van, and Bonn
  age fifteen–sixteen and music, 88–89
  birth date, 2
  childhood play, 37–38, 41
  composition return, 116
  court music/pay, 60, 66–67, 69, 75, 99,
    100, 104, 105
  early loves/women admired, 98, 101,
    112, 201
  education (nonmusical), 41, 101
  first portrait, 97
  foundation/beliefs, 127–30
  house music vs. public concerts, 34
  leaving Bonn for Vienna, 123–30
  name day, 1–2
  piano playing expertise, 83, 89
  relationship with father, 31, 41, 61,
    103–5, 127, 135
  relationship with mother, 36, 41, 61,
    92–94, 878
  reviews of first published
    compositions, 66
  social life (late teens), 101–2
  teachers, summary, 40
  See also Fischer house/surroundings;
    *specific individuals/teachers;
    specific works*
Beethoven, Ludwig van, and health/
    hearing problems
  in 1797, 207
  in 1804, 383, 387, 389, 390
  in 1805, 402
  in 1817, 690

  in 1821/1822, 747, 749
  in 1825, 871–72, 898, 899
  in 1826/1827 illness/death, 916, 921–29
  alcohol and, 608–9, 872, 873, 875, 899
  begging off giving lessons and, 560–61,
    574–75, 784
  causes and, 130, 224
  composing only and, 307, 436
  composing process, 718–20, 744
  conversation books and, 698, 699, 700,
    701, 730, 739, 741–42, 744–45, 759,
    784, 785, 787, 903, 913, 922, 930
  death of those near him and, 225
  digestive tract, 130, 175, 225, 226, 262
  doctors/medicine and, 224, 225, 276,
    277, 278, 279, 291, 303–4, 455, 537,
    571, 690, 872
  ear trumpets and, 614, 624, 698, 707,
    719, 782, 930
  friends/family at deathbed, 922, 924,
    925–26, 927, 928–29
  hearing problems, 130, 223–26, 262,
    276, 277, 278, 279–80, 291, 300,
    302–8, 614, 624, 698, 707
  Heiligenstadt Testament/letter, 301–6
  Heiligenstadt "vacation"/work (1802),
    291, 292–300
  hiding deafness, 225, 303
  lead poisoning and, 130, 224, 225
  letter to Wegeler, 276–77, 279–80
  liver problems, 747, 857, 875, 899, 912
  medicine in late 1770s/early 1800s, 130,
    224, 225, 857, 872
  spa at Teplitz and, 571–74, 579, 581,
    589–90, 591–93, 594
  summary, 929–30
  telling friends of deafness, 276–77, 278,
    279–80
  tinnitus, 224, 226
  travels/visit with Johann (1826), 912,
    915–16
  winter of 1800–1801, 262, 266–67
  See also death of Beethoven
Beethoven, Ludwig van, and Vienna
  1795 music/events, 186
  1796 tour/music, 193–98, 199–200
  1797 music/events, 200–202, 205–9

1798 tour, 226–27
1800 music events, 242–48
1803 benefit concert, 315–24
arrest/jailing, 748
becoming composer/technique,
    147–48, 149–50
Beethoven's attitude toward Vienna/
    Viennese, 52, 134, 138, 144, 465,
    470, 561, 616, 621, 708, 731, 761,
    785–86, 793, 873, 901, 926
Beethoven's trip/move to (1792), 127,
    132–33
Bonn/Bonn friends and, 158–61, 164
Bonn court collapse and, 173
Congress of Vienna and, 638–46,
    648–49, 654–55, 666, 674
courting (1810), 536–40
early days/finances, 133–36, 145
early patrons, 153–58
finances/problems (1807), 436
finances/problems (1809), 530
finances/problems (1811), 570
finances/problems (1812–1813), 599–601
finances/problems (1814–1815), 613,
    621–22, 623
finances/problems (1820s), 740, 742–43,
    768–69, 793, 794–95, 796, 862
folk song arrangements/Thomson
    publisher, 528–29, 595–97
last residence, 875–76
Lorchen correspondence/music
    dedication, 158–61
marriage/wife views, 170, 460, 522, 686
music of 1809–1810, 531–34
music of revolution and, 205–6
musical duels, 153, 229–31, 247–48
opera preparations, 222–23, 311, 314–15
piano sonatas/experimenting (1798),
    213–15
public debut/preparations, 174–75
resolutions, 165, 173
singers visiting/wine and (1822), 762
sketchbook use beginnings, 209
string instruments gift to, 249, 303,
    304
students/young female students, 173,
    207–8, 236, 280–82

as teacher, 173, 207–8, 236, 280, 281,
    685
"van" in name and, 154
Vienna at time of, 136–44
war/patriotic songs, 203
Beethoven, Ludwig van (grandfather)
    becoming *Kapellmeister*, 11–12
    Belderbusch and, 11
    birth/childhood, 3
    business and, 12
    death, 17
    description/character, 14, 16, 17, 18, 42
    as Flemish, 3
    as godfather, 2
    home/Fischer family, 12–13
    as *Kapellmeister*, 2, 11–12, 17
    marriage to Maria Josepha Poll, 3, 12
    music and, 2, 3–4, 11–12, 13–14, 17, 18
    parents/siblings, 3, 12
    portrait of, 16–17, 45, 278
    relationship with son, 14, 15
    salary/duties as *Kapellmeister*, 12
    as wine dealer, 12
Beethoven, Maria Josepha (Poll)
    alcoholism and, 12, 13–14
    marriage, 3, 12
Beethoven, Maria Margaretha Josepha
    van, 87–88, 99
Beethoven, Maria van (Keverich)
    background, 14–15, 132
    Beethoven's name day, 2
    Bonngasse house, 15, 16
    children/infants' deaths, 2, 15, 35, 64,
        99
    description/character, 15, 29, 36–37
    "dowry" and, 18
    first husband/death, 2, 14–15
    Frau Fischer and, 29
    health problems/death, 67, 87–88, 90,
        92–93, 274
    home moves and, 28
    on marriage, 15, 36–37, 42
    mother of, 18, 37
    name day celebrations, 23
    Rovantini/Rovantini's sister and, 33, 43,
        64–65
Beethoven, Michael van, 3

Beethoven, (Nikolaus) Johann van
arriving in Vienna, 186–87
childhood accident/abscess, 29, 37
christening/godparents, 24
daughter of Therese, 781–82
description/character, 29, 36, 37,
186–87, 598, 759, 867
Heiligenstadt Testament/letter and,
301–6
illness/Therese and daughter, 781–82
Karl (nephew) and, 734, 759
life/death after Ludwig, 932
Ludwig and, 597–99, 758, 759, 762, 764,
765, 766, 780–82, 872
Ludwig dying/death and, 922, 928, 929
Ludwig's debt to, 454, 765, 780–81, 864
Ludwig's visit/conflict with (in Linz),
597–99
Ludwig's visit/conflict with (Wasserhof
estate), 911–16
mistress/wife (Therese), 598–99, 758,
781–82, 911, 913, 915, 916, 932
pharmacy/French army, 527, 597
Schindler and, 794
Wasserhof estate and, 734, 759
Beethoven, Therese, 598–99, 758, 781–82,
911, 913, 915, 916, 932
Belderbusch, Caspar Anton von
Beethoven family and, 11, 19, 20, 24, 67
Clemens August's debt and, 10–11
death, 66, 67
Elector of Cologne and, 10–11
French and, 34
government style/Enlightenment,
24–25
Max Friedrich successor/money and,
34–35
music and, 33
rumors on, 27–28
theater of Electoral Residence/National
Theater, 60, 66
Bernadotte, Jean, 204, 205, 206, 327, 611,
769
Bernard, Karl Joseph, 698, 699–700, 704,
705, 721, 724, 730, 733, 735, 740,
741, 745, 785, 870–71
Bernhard, Frau von, 169–70

Bigot, Paul/Marie, 429, 448–51
bigotry (racial/ethnic) in Beethoven's
time, 260, 760–61
biographies on Beethoven, xii–xiii, xix
"biography" description, xv–xvi
Blöchlinger, Joseph, 730–31, 734–35, 741,
742, 747, 869
Böhm, Joseph, 792, 867
Bonaparte, Jérôme
background, 478–79, 523
Kapellmeister offer to Beethoven, 478,
479–80, 482, 516
Bonaparte, Napoleon. *See* Napoleon
Bonaparte
Bonaparte Symphony. *See Eroica*
Symphony (Beethoven)
Bonn
Archbishop of Cologne residence and,
4
Beethoven's attitudes toward, 94
Cologne and, 5
description, 7–8
dysentery epidemic (1781), 42–43
electorates history, 5
Enlightenment, 25, 49, 51–52, 54, 75, 83,
85–86, 101, 131
famine (Max Friedrich's regime), 67
fire at Electoral Residence (1777),
27–28, 67
flood (1784), 67–68
French occupation/war and, 168, 171,
200, 203
French Revolution/Terror and, 113–14
golden age, 85, 87
holidays/celebrations and, 9
Illuminati and, 74–75, 82–83, 84
Kapelle breakup, 200
Kapelle Mergentheim trip, 118–21
music/dance importance, 9, 33–34,
116–17
people of (1700s), 5, 8–9
Rhine importance, 7–8
University of Bonn, 84–85, 87, 113–14
See also Beethoven, Ludwig van, and
Bonn; *specific individuals*
Boston Massacre (1770), 15
Bouilly, J.-N., 378, 379, 414

Braun, Peter Anton, Baron, 292, 381, 382,
    416, 423–24, 436–37
Braunhofer, Anton, 872, 916
Breitkopf & Härtel publisher, 229, 234,
    270–72, 284–85, 291–92, 297–98,
    308, 309, 310, 329, 374–75, 384–85,
    396, 407, 408, 426, 427, 457, 458,
    476–77, 512, 527–28, 534, 560, 567,
    577, 600, 648
    *See also Allgemeine Musikalische
    Zeitung (AMZ/General Musical
    Magazine)*
Brentano, Antonie
    background/description, 554–55
    Beethoven and, 554, 555–56, 574, 595,
        660, 728–29, 760
    Bettina and, 550
    "Immortal Beloved" and, 585–86, 587
Brentano, Bettina
    Achim von Arnim marriage, 564–65,
        579, 586, 587, 588
    background/description, 543, 545–49
    Beethoven and, 550–53, 563–65
    Beethoven meeting, 544–45, 549–50
    conflict with Goethe's wife, 590–91
    Goethe and, 544, 546, 547–49, 551–53,
        565, 586
    on Goethe/Beethoven meeting, 592–93
    "Immortal Beloved" and, 586–87, 588
    letters/publications and truth, 548, 550,
        551–53
Brentano, Clemens, 546, 547, 549, 554,
    564, 565, 579
Brentano family, 546, 547
Brentano, Franz, 550, 554, 556, 585–86,
    595, 743–44, 748–49, 759
Breuning, Christoph von, 62, 97, 163, 187
Breuning, Eleonore (Lorchen) von, 61, 97,
    98, 112, 125, 158–61, 278, 923
    marriage to Wegeler, 98, 877, 878, 923
Breuning, Emanuel Joseph von, *Hofrat*,
    27, 61
Breuning family
    Beethoven/*Bildung* and, 61–62, 97–98
    house/visitors, 61–62, 98
Breuning, Gerhard, 876–77, 904, 922, 923,
    924, 925, 927, 928, 929

Breuning, Helene von
    background, 61
    Beethoven and, 61–62, 97, 113, 125, 273,
        278, 877, 878
Breuning, Lorenz (Lenz) von, 61, 200, 388
Breuning, Lorenz von, Canon, 61, 97
Breuning, Stephan von
    Beethoven and, 62, 97, 125, 187, 199,
        273–74, 370, 382, 387–89, 418, 419,
        424, 539, 589, 875–76, 877, 904,
        922, 927, 928
    death, 932
    first love, 98
    first wife's death/burial place, 521, 928
    as Karl Beethoven's guardian, 904, 905,
        915, 927
    quarrel/reconciliation with Beethoven,
        387–89, 875–76
Bridgetower, George, 324–25, 327, 431
Browne, Count/Countess, 179, 200, 209,
    328, 376–77
Brunsvik, Anna von, Countess, and
    daughters, 236, 280, 393–94
Brunsvik, Charlotte von, 236, 392–93,
    394, 395
Brunsvik, Franz von, 393, 394, 453–54,
    460
Brunsvik, Josephine von, 236, 280. *See
    also* Deym, Josephine, Countess
Brunsvik, Therese von, 236, 392–93, 394,
    405, 460–61, 532, 563, 747, 867
Bureau des arts et d'industrie, 381, 408,
    454, 455
Burggraf, C. J. M., 42
Burke, Edmund, 102
Burney, Charles, 232, 290, 685
bust/life mask of Beethoven (Klein),
    577–79, 709

Calvinism, 45, 69
canon, 945
*Cantata on the Accession of Emperor
    Leopold II* (Beethoven), 110, 111,
    116, 146
*Cantata on the Death of Emperor Joseph
    II* (Beethoven), 108–10, 111, 116,
    119–20, 123, 146, 225, 318, 344

Castlereagh, Viscount, 633, 637–38

Catherine the Great, 294, 425

Catholicism
  Beethoven and, 2
  newborn name day rituals, 1, 2
  See also specific individuals

cello sonata of op. 102 (Beethoven), 692–93

Charlemagne, 4

Chénier, Marie-Joseph, 205, 831

Cherubini, Luigi
  background/music, 378, 379, 417, 423, 431, 434, 470, 471, 614, 898, 932
  Beethoven and, 116, 378, 380, 409, 525, 639, 704, 886, 898
  Lodoïska, 116, 308, 378

Choral Fantasy (Beethoven), 202, 485, 486–88, 514, 571, 575, 615, 831, 854, 857

Christus am Ölberge (Beethoven), 311, 315–16, 317–19, 379, 380, 407, 408, 427, 451, 456, 458, 481, 513, 568, 571, 573, 575, 606, 615, 797

Classical period (music)
  description, xvii
  Enlightenment and, 54
  fugue form, 943
  musical form and, 940, 943

Classical style (music)
  creation of, 44
  description, 33, 149

clavichord vs. harpsichord, 22

"clavier," 22

Clemens August, Archbishop Elector of Cologne
  ancestors/family of, 5–6
  Beethoven (grandfather) and, 3
  Bonn makeover and, 4, 6–7
  Bonn residents employment and, 9–10
  childhood/education, 5–6
  death, 10
  debt, 10, 86
  description/character, 6
  music/art and, 6, 9
  positions before Elector, 6
  residences and, 6, 7

Clement, Franz, 396, 418, 430, 431, 433, 434, 435, 485, 787, 922

Clementi, Muzio
  Beethoven and, 91, 119, 167, 213, 452–53, 454, 455, 529, 531, 600, 780, 886
  music/background, 59, 91, 152, 167, 237, 452–53, 693, 702

coda, 350, 938, 939, 940, 942

Coleridge, Samuel Taylor, 5

Collin, Heinrich von, 418, 437, 464, 465, 469, 477–78, 481–82. *See also Coriolan* (Beethoven's music for Collin's play)

Cologne
  archbishop (1257) and, 5
  Bonn and, 5
  as "free city," 5

Concerto No. 3 in C Minor (Beethoven), 321–24

concerto-sonata, 941–42

Concerts for Enthusiasts, 464–65

Congress of Vienna
  Beethoven and, 638–46, 648–49, 654–55, 666, 674
  description, 632–37, 638
  Final Act/consequences, 652–55, 666, 838–39
  spies/censorship following, 653–55, 746

contra dance, 139, 267–68

Coriolan (Beethoven's music for Collin's play), 437, 451, 452–53, 467, 469–73, 480, 482–83, 568, 575

crab canon, 945

Cramer, Carl Friedrich, 45, 56

Cramer, Johann Baptist, 237–38

criticism/reviews of Beethoven's work
  Beethoven reading reviews/responding, 234, 271–72, 426
  examples, 237–38, 312, 313–14, 316–17, 382–83
  "fantastic" sonatas, 232
  late-eighteenth-century taste and, 231–33
  provocation and, 227
  review of first published compositions, 66

Braun, Peter Anton, Baron, 292, 381, 382, 416, 423–24, 436–37

Braunhofer, Anton, 872, 916

Breitkopf & Härtel publisher, 229, 234, 270–72, 284–85, 291–92, 297–98, 308, 309, 310, 329, 374–75, 384–85, 396, 407, 408, 426, 427, 457, 458, 476–77, 512, 527–28, 534, 560, 567, 577, 600, 648
  See also Allgemeine Musikalische Zeitung (AMZ/General Musical Magazine)

Brentano, Antonie
  background/description, 554–55
  Beethoven and, 554, 555–56, 574, 595, 660, 728–29, 760
  Bettina and, 550
  "Immortal Beloved" and, 585–86, 587

Brentano, Bettina
  Achim von Arnim marriage, 564–65, 579, 586, 587, 588
  background/description, 543, 545–49
  Beethoven and, 550–53, 563–65
  Beethoven meeting, 544–45, 549–50
  conflict with Goethe's wife, 590–91
  Goethe and, 544, 546, 547–49, 551–53, 565, 586
  on Goethe/Beethoven meeting, 592–93
  "Immortal Beloved" and, 586–87, 588
  letters/publications and truth, 548, 550, 551–53

Brentano, Clemens, 546, 547, 549, 554, 564, 565, 579

Brentano family, 546, 547

Brentano, Franz, 550, 554, 556, 585–86, 595, 743–44, 748–49, 759

Breuning, Christoph von, 62, 97, 163, 187

Breuning, Eleonore (Lorchen) von, 61, 97, 98, 112, 125, 158–61, 278, 923
  marriage to Wegeler, 98, 877, 878, 923

Breuning, Emanuel Joseph von, *Hofrat*, 27, 61

Breuning family
  Beethoven/*Bildung* and, 61–62, 97–98
  house/visitors, 61–62, 98

Breuning, Gerhard, 876–77, 904, 922, 923, 924, 925, 927, 928, 929

Breuning, Helene von
  background, 61
  Beethoven and, 61–62, 97, 113, 125, 273, 278, 877, 878

Breuning, Lorenz (Lenz) von, 61, 200, 388

Breuning, Lorenz von, Canon, 61, 97

Breuning, Stephan von
  Beethoven and, 62, 97, 125, 187, 199, 273–74, 370, 382, 387–89, 418, 419, 424, 539, 589, 875–76, 877, 904, 922, 927, 928
  death, 932
  first love, 98
  first wife's death/burial place, 521, 928
  as Karl Beethoven's guardian, 904, 905, 915, 927
  quarrel/reconciliation with Beethoven, 387–89, 875–76

Bridgetower, George, 324–25, 327, 431

Browne, Count/Countess, 179, 200, 209, 328, 376–77

Brunsvik, Anna von, Countess, and daughters, 236, 280, 393–94

Brunsvik, Charlotte von, 236, 392–93, 394, 395

Brunsvik, Franz von, 393, 394, 453–54, 460

Brunsvik, Josephine von, 236, 280. *See also* Deym, Josephine, Countess

Brunsvik, Therese von, 236, 392–93, 394, 405, 460–61, 532, 563, 747, 867

Bureau des arts et d'industrie, 381, 408, 454, 455

Burggraf, C. J. M., 42

Burke, Edmund, 102

Burney, Charles, 232, 290, 685

bust/life mask of Beethoven (Klein), 577–79, 709

Calvinism, 45, 69

canon, 945

Cantata on the Accession of Emperor Leopold II (Beethoven), 110, 111, 116, 146

Cantata on the Death of Emperor Joseph II (Beethoven), 108–10, 111, 116, 119–20, 123, 146, 225, 318, 344

Castlereagh, Viscount, 633, 637–38
Catherine the Great, 294, 425
Catholicism
  Beethoven and, 2
  newborn name day rituals, 1, 2
  See also specific individuals
cello sonata of op. 102 (Beethoven),
    692–93
Charlemagne, 4
Chénier, Marie-Joseph, 205, 831
Cherubini, Luigi
  background/music, 378, 379, 417, 423,
    431, 434, 470, 471, 614, 898, 932
  Beethoven and, 116, 378, 380, 409, 525,
    639, 704, 886, 898
  Lodoïska, 116, 308, 378
Choral Fantasy (Beethoven), 202, 485,
    486–88, 514, 571, 575, 615, 831, 854,
    857
Christus am Ölberge (Beethoven), 311,
    315–16, 317–19, 379, 380, 407, 408,
    427, 451, 456, 458, 481, 513, 568,
    571, 573, 575, 606, 615, 797
Classical period (music)
  description, xvii
  Enlightenment and, 54
  fugue form, 943
  musical form and, 940, 943
Classical style (music)
  creation of, 44
  description, 33, 149
clavichord vs. harpsichord, 22
"clavier," 22
Clemens August, Archbishop Elector of
    Cologne
  ancestors/family of, 5–6
  Beethoven (grandfather) and, 3
  Bonn makeover and, 4, 6–7
  Bonn residents employment and,
    9–10
  childhood/education, 5–6
  death, 10
  debt, 10, 86
  description/character, 6
  music/art and, 6, 9
  positions before Elector, 6
  residences and, 6, 7

Clement, Franz, 396, 418, 430, 431, 433,
    434, 435, 485, 787, 922
Clementi, Muzio
  Beethoven and, 91, 119, 167, 213, 452–53,
    454, 455, 529, 531, 600, 780, 886
  music/background, 59, 91, 152, 167, 237,
    452–53, 693, 702
coda, 350, 938, 939, 940, 942
Coleridge, Samuel Taylor, 5
Collin, Heinrich von, 418, 437, 464, 465,
    469, 477–78, 481–82. *See also*
    Coriolan (Beethoven's music for
    Collin's play)
Cologne
  archbishop (1257) and, 5
  Bonn and, 5
  as "free city," 5
Concerto No. 3 in C Minor (Beethoven),
    321–24
concerto-sonata, 941–42
Concerts for Enthusiasts, 464–65
Congress of Vienna
  Beethoven and, 638–46, 648–49,
    654–55, 666, 674
  description, 632–37, 638
  Final Act/consequences, 652–55, 666,
    838–39
  spies/censorship following, 653–55,
    746
contra dance, 139, 267–68
Coriolan (Beethoven's music for Collin's
    play), 437, 451, 452–53, 467,
    469–73, 480, 482–83, 568, 575
crab canon, 945
Cramer, Carl Friedrich, 45, 56
Cramer, Johann Baptist, 237–38
criticism/reviews of Beethoven's work
  Beethoven reading reviews/
    responding, 234, 271–72, 426
  examples, 237–38, 312, 313–14, 316–17,
    382–83
  "fantastic" sonatas, 232
  late-eighteenth-century taste and,
    231–33
  provocation and, 227
  review of first published compositions,
    66

See also Allgemeine Musikalische Zeitung (AMZ/General Musical Magazine); duels (musical); *specific individuals; specific works*
Czerny, Carl
  background/music, 248, 274, 420, 438
  Beethoven/Beethoven's music and, 196, 239–40, 295, 323, 397–98, 409, 438, 444, 491, 532, 577, 631, 644, 679–80, 719–20, 786, 874, 931
  father of, 152–53, 239

de Staël, Madame, 9, 33, 140
deafness. *See* Beethoven, Ludwig van, and health/hearing problems
death of Beethoven
  AMZ on Beethoven, 933–34
  auction of effects, 931–32
  autopsy/death mask, 929
  body exhumed/reburials, 933
  burial, 931
  friends/family at deathbed, 922, 924, 925–26, 927, 928–29
  funeral, 929, 930–31
  funeral oration, 931, 934–35
  last days, 916, 921–29
  lying-in, 930
  materials found after death, 930
  memorial services, 932
  monument, 831
  offer to gravedigger, 931
  pallbearers/torchbearers, 931
Declaration of Independence (Jefferson), 49
Degenhart, Johann Martin, 124, 125
deism, 50–51
Dembscher, Ignaz, 918
Description of a Girl (Beethoven), 58
Deym, Joseph, Count, 236, 393–94
Deym, Josephine, Countess
  Beethoven and, 236, 392–93, 394–96, 402–6, 411, 413–14, 428, 458–61, 478, 537, 554, 563, 564, 565, 580, 585, 587, 603, 747
  Beethoven's songs for, 395, 396, 403, 406

Count Deym and, 236, 393–94
  death, 747
  "Immortal Beloved" and, 585, 587, 588, 747
  marriage to Stackelberg, 460–61, 563, 747
  sisters Charlotte/Therese and, 394
  See also Brunsvik, Josephine
Diabelli, Anton/publisher, 732, 741, 770, 862, 914, 922, 925
Diabelli Variations (Beethoven), 732, 733, 758, 765, 766, 772, 773–80, 797, 829–30, 942
diary (*Tagebuch*) of Beethoven
  entries in, 604–6, 608, 614–15, 616, 648, 674, 684, 689–90, 800, 828
  giving up on love/family, 603–4
Diderot, Denis, 46–47
Dietrichstein, Moritz, Count, 480–81, 771
"dominant" defined, 938
Dragonetti, Domenico, 240–41, 247, 615
Dressler Variations (Beethoven), 57, 58, 62, 66
duels (musical), 152–53, 229–31, 247–48
Duport, Jean-Louis/Jean Pierre, 195, 196–97

Egmont music (Beethoven), 539, 553, 556, 560, 564, 566, 567–70, 575, 594, 854, 910
Eichoff, Joseph, 82
Eighth Symphony (Beethoven)
  performances/publications, 624
  writing/description, 574, 577, 579, 588, 624–26, 626
Elector title, 4
Electoral Sonatas (Beethoven)
  composition style and, 62–64
  D Major Sonata, 64
  F Minor Sonata, 62–63
  Max Friedrich and, 62, 64
  review, 66
Electorate of Cologne
  end of, 171
  fire at Electoral Residence (1777), 27–28, 67

Electorate of Cologne (*cont.*)
  history, 4
  music and, 33
  See also specific individuals
Emilie M.'s letter from Beethoven,
  589–90
Emperor Concerto/Fifth Piano Concerto
  (Beethoven), 519, 521, 527, 528,
  576–77
Empfindsamkeit aesthetic/cult, 44
englische described, 359–60
Enlightenment
  1780s and, 43–44, 102–3
  Beethoven and, 50–51, 52, 79, 265, 335
  Bonn and, 25, 49, 51–52, 54, 75, 83,
    85–86, 101, 131
  church/state separation, 50
  deism, 50–51
  description/views, 46–52
  education and, 25
  Electorate of Cologne government
    style changes, 25
  geographical differences, 51–52
  German literature/philosophy and,
    25–26
  Germany and, 25–26, 51–52, 53–54
  happiness/joy and, 49, 53–54, 305
  Leipzig and, 43–44
  reason/science and, 8, 26, 46, 47, 48,
    50, 51, 52
  religion and, 46–48, 50
  *See also specific events; specific
    individuals*
Erdödy, Anna Marie, Countess, 460, 478,
  482, 516, 519–20, 588–89, 647–48,
  655, 670–71, 679, 686, 690
Eroica Symphony (Beethoven)
  Beethoven as hero, 363
  Beethoven conducting, 397
  Beethoven planning/motives, 332–35
  englische/*Prometheus* theme and,
    331–32, 333, 337–39, 341, 349, 353,
    359–60, 361, 362–63
  hero/Napoleon and, 332, 333, 334, 336,
    337, 338, 339, 341, 342, 344, 345,
    346, 347, 349, 350–51, 352, 357–58,
    359–60, 361–63, 365, 368

musical form and, 365–66
  Napoleon becoming emperor and,
    384–85, 386
  New Path and, 364, 365, 366, 368–69
  Oberdöbling house and, 333, 335
  performances, 464
  premiere, 396, 397–98
  private readings, 390–91, 396
  publishing of, 363
  reception, 363–65, 366, 368–69, 396–97,
    398–401
  writing/description, 222, 335–64, 439,
    468, 469, 504, 505, 507, 508, 513,
    617
Ertmann, Dorothea von, Baroness, 521,
  522, 555, 693
Esterházy, Nikolaus, Prince, 151, 161, 179,
  203, 451, 455, 456, 457–58, 464, 466

"Farewell, The"/*Das Lebewohl*
  (Beethoven), 228, 523, 531,
  533–34
Fidelio (Beethoven)
  Beethoven/Braun quarrel and
    consequences, 423–24
  censors and, 414–15
  description, 110, 416–17, 556, 832
  French army occupation and, 415–16,
    419
  premiere of reworked version/
    performances, 421–23
  premiere performance, 416–17
  revisions/revival, 623, 626, 628–31, 637,
    638–43, 650, 767
  reworking, 417–19, 435
  story, 378–80
  title change from *Leonore*, 416
  writing/rehearsals, 381, 382, 409–10,
    412, 413, 415, 416
Fifth Piano Concerto/*Emperor* Concerto
  (Beethoven), 519, 521, 527, 528,
  576–77
Fifth Symphony (Beethoven)
  dedication, 480
  description, 411, 489–90, 495–505, 508,
    513, 514, 617
  writing, 461, 476

First Symphony (Beethoven), 221, 242, 243, 244–45, 260, 273, 289–90, 291, 292, 315, 316, 319, 320, 364, 481, 838

Fischenich, Bartholomäus Ludwig, 85, 101, 131

Fischer, Cäcilie
Beethoven family and, 14, 32, 36–37, 41, 93
Johann Beethoven and, 32
Ludwig and, 41, 98–99
Maria Beethoven and, 36–37, 42
Pfeifer and, 32
Rovantini and, 33, 36, 42–43

Fischer, Gottfried
as baker, 12–13
on Beethoven family, 12–13, 28, 38, 135

Fischer house/surroundings
Beethoven brothers play and, 29, 37–38
description, 28, 29
flood (1784) and, 67–68
Rhine and, 28, 38
telescopes and, 38

Fischer, Johann, 12

Fischer, Theodor
as baker, 12
Beethoven family and, 15, 28, 36, 37, 87
children, 29

Forbes, Elliot, xiii

Förster, Emanuel Aloys, 249, 251, 425, 703

Fourth Piano Concerto (Beethoven), 367, 427, 432, 435, 451, 453, 481, 488–89, 490, 517, 580

Fourth Symphony (Beethoven), 430, 435, 445, 451, 452–53, 467–69, 480, 490–95

France
Revolution and Terror, 43, 51, 102–3, 110, 113, 114, 116, 124, 137, 170, 171, 205, 263, 265, 267, 378
wars (1790s/early 1800s), 122, 124, 168, 171, 200, 202–4, 213, 262–63, 412–13, 420–21
See also specific individuals

Franklin, Benjamin, 50, 71, 393

Franz II, Holy Roman Emperor
France/war and, 168, 202, 204, 334, 420–21
reign, 122, 137, 138, 140, 168, 170, 202, 203, 334, 385, 420–21, 742, 761

Frederick the Great, King of Prussia, 25, 52, 71, 87, 97, 195, 336, 654, 724, 878

Frederick William II, King of Prussia, 195, 196, 197

Freemasons
banning, 170
Beethoven and, 78, 90, 335
as elite, 72
Enlightenment ideals and, 72, 827, 844
members/membership, 71, 72
Schiller's "Ode to Joy," 54
society description/agenda, 71–72

Freymüthige (journal), 312, 398, 417

Friedrich Wilhelm II/III, kings of Prussia, 724, 878, 912

Fries, Count, 247, 309

fugue
overview, 943–45
sections/components, 944–45
types, 944–45

funeral of Beethoven. *See* death of Beethoven

Für Elise (Beethoven), 538, 553

Fux, Johann Joseph, 148–50, 163

Galeazzi, Francesco, 220–22

Galitzin, Nicolai, Prince, 766, 770, 899

Galitzin Quartets (Beethoven)
B-flat Major/alternative finale for, 879, 887–90, 892, 920–21
description, 879–97, 916
Grosse Fuge, 718, 892–97, 899, 901, 902, 920–21
payment and, 899–900

Gelinek, Joseph, Abbé, 152–53

Gellert, Christian Fürchetegott, 44, 87, 289

General Musical Magazine. See
Allgemeine Musikalische Zeitung
(*AMZ/General Musical Magazine*)

genius
  definitions/descriptions, xiv–xv, xix
  use of term, xiv
Genzinger, Marianne von, 150
Germany
  "benevolent despots" and, 52, 103
  government and, 51–52, 103
  social songs, 53
Gesellschaft der Musikfreunde, Vienna,
    646–47, 668, 704, 766, 784, 790,
    865, 898, 927, 933
Gewandhaus (Leipzig) concerts, 43, 141
Ghost Trio (Beethoven), 474, 475, 477,
    833. *See also* Piano Trios, op. 70
    (Beethoven)
Giannatasio, Cajetan/family, 660–62, 673,
    674, 685–86, 687, 688, 697–98, 721,
    729–30, 737
Giannatasio, Fanny
  Beethoven and, 661–62, 668–70,
    671–72, 674, 685, 687, 697, 721,
    729, 737
  illness, 674
Gleichenstein, Ignaz von, Baron, 454, 455,
    516, 517, 521, 522, 536, 537, 538–40,
    554, 588
Gluck, 71, 86, 109, 205, 419, 428, 604
Goethe, Johann Wolfgang von
  Beethoven and, 565–67, 579, 581,
    590–92, 621, 769
  Freemasons and, 71
  influence/significance, 26, 49, 87, 196,
    312, 744
  meeting Beethoven, 591–94
  wife's conflict with Bettina, 590–91
  work/views of, 26, 27, 45, 71, 74, 98, 103,
    112, 116, 124, 188, 228, 335, 524, 537,
    538, 539, 544, 545, 546, 547–49,
    551–53, 556, 564, 565–68, 569, 767,
    936
  See also Egmont music (Beethoven)
"Good, the True, and the Beautiful, the,"
    44, 49, 98, 266
Gossec, F. J., 204, 205, 354
Graf, Conrad/piano, 873, 875, 932
Griesinger, George August, 374, 377,
    396

Grillparzer, Franz, 476, 648, 770–72,
    783–84, 796, 931, 934–35
Grosse Fuge (Beethoven), 718, 892–97,
    899, 901, 902, 920–21
Grossmann, Gustav F. W.
  background, 32, 43, 60, 68
  Illuminati, 74
  leaving Bonn, 68
  Neefe and, 43, 70, 71, 74
  recommendations for teachers, 32, 38,
    43
Grossmann-Hellmuth Company, 60
Guarneri instruments, 249, 431
Guicciardi, Julie, 280–82, 286–87, 393,
    603, 741–42
Guicciardi, Susanna, Countess, 280,
    281–82, 325

Hammerklavier Sonata (Beethoven)
  Beethoven's deafness and, 720
  publications and, 743
  writing/description, 710–18, 720, 725
Handel
  death, 157
  music/significance, 157, 158, 178, 195,
    234, 235, 238, 249, 318, 434, 469,
    505, 511, 529, 589, 614, 683, 704,
    734, 773, 774, 779, 799, 800–801,
    809, 813, 817, 826–27, 829, 837, 855,
    873, 886, 922–23, 924, 925, 934
Hansmann, Father, 40–41
Harp Quartet (Beethoven), 534–36, 556,
    560, 883
harpsichord vs. clavichord, 22
Härtel, Gottfried, 272, 308, 309, 329, 377,
    396–97, 407, 426, 476–77, 527–28,
    559–60, 571, 593–94, 655
  See also Breitkopf & Härtel
Haslinger, Tobias/publisher, 650–51, 711,
    741, 862, 863, 864, 873, 874, 898,
    922, 931
Hauschka, Vincenz, 704–5, 865
Haydn, Joseph
  Beethoven and, 59, 98, 123, 147, 159, 167,
    179–80, 184–85, 192, 208, 213, 222,
    235–36, 269, 350, 376–77, 524, 797
  Beethoven on studying with, 147, 150

Beethoven studying with/relationship,
123–24, 145, 146–47, 150–52
Beethoven's C Minor Trio and, 179–80,
184
Bonn visits, 114–16, 122–23
correspondence with Max Franz,
161–62
Creation, The, 180, 234–36, 242, 263,
270, 318, 464, 465–66, 488, 505,
507, 511, 524, 739, 826, 833
decline, 376–77, 430, 465–66, 524
description/as teacher, 145–46
England trip (1794–1795), 162–63, 168,
178
Freemasons and, 71, 72, 115, 122
Marx on, 859, 861
mistresses/Genzinger and, 150
Mozart and, 115, 121, 122, 123
musical form and, 939, 940, 943
Seasons, The, 270, 505, 507, 511, 613–14
status, 34, 115–16, 123, 170, 203, 409
works/views of, 26, 34, 43, 44–45, 123,
142, 143, 149, 178, 192, 203–4, 227,
250–51, 262, 390, 429
See also specific works
hearing loss. *See* Beethoven, Ludwig van,
and health/hearing problems
Heiligenstadt Testament/letter
background/text, 301–6
fate of, 932
Heine, Heinrich, 412, 764
Hiller, Ferdinand, 925, 926
Hiller, J. A., 43, 45
Himmel, Friedrich Heinrich, 195, 197
Hoffmann, E. T. A.
background/views, 540, 858, 879
Beethoven/reviews and, 52–53, 540–43,
545, 630, 744–45, 859, 861
writings, 52–53, 859, 863–64, 886, 887
Hoffmeister, Franz Anton, 259–60,
263–64, 270, 271, 298–99
Holy Roman Empire
Archbishop Electors and, 4, 5, 6
"Austria" (1700s), 4
description (1700s), 4–5, 55
emperor selection, 4, 5–6
emperor's residence, 136

end of, 420–21
"Germany" (1700s), 4
government/rule and, 4–5
Habsburgs and, 4
Rhine and, 5
Holz, Karl
alcohol/Beethoven and, 872, 873, 899
background/music, 866–67, 872–73
Beethoven and, 870, 872–73, 874, 896,
899, 902, 903–4, 905, 916, 921, 922,
924, 930, 931
on Mozart/Beethoven music, 899
horse of Beethoven, 200
Hugo, Victor, 8
Hume, David, 49
Hummel, Johann Nepomuk, 240, 312, 457,
614, 615, 680, 898, 925–26, 931

Illuminati
Beethoven and, 74, 79, 129, 335
beginnings, 43, 73
Bonn lodge, 74–75, 82–83, 84
collapse/banning, 83
description, 72–76, 77, 78, 79, 87, 90,
98, 153, 171, 173, 266, 335, 368, 479,
826, 827, 844
Freemasons and, 73, 74
"Immortal Beloved," 579, 581–89, 603,
674, 930
industrial revolution beginnings, 15
Intelligenzblatt (newspaper), 26, 47, 74

Jan Sobieski, King of Poland, 6
Jefferson, Thomas, 49, 50
Jesuits
education and, 25
pope's dissolution of (1773), 25
revival after dissolution, 25
John Broadwood & Sons gift to
Beethoven, 701–3, 709, 719, 875
Joseph II, Holy Roman Emperor
death, 105
decrees/reign, 43, 60, 105–7, 136, 137,
139, 140, 151, 152, 334
description, 35, 52, 85, 103, 336, 366,
393, 641, 654, 666, 741, 757
Enlightenment, 84, 87, 92

Joseph II, Holy Roman Emperor (*cont.*)
  Freemasons and, 106
  memorial/cantata and, 107–10
  relatives, 34, 84, 105–6
Josephstadt Theatre opening (1822),
  762–63
Junker, Karl Ludwig, 120, 121

Kanne, Friedrich August, 741, 795–96
Kant, Immanuel
  influence/significance, 49, 101, 367
  as professor, 15–16, 87
  University of Bonn and, 85
  works/views of, 43, 47–49, 102–3, 567,
    738–40, 816, 826, 844, 853
Kapellmeister offer to Beethoven (in
    Cassel), 478, 479–80, 482, 516
Keglevics, Babette, 207–8
Keverich, Maria Magdalene, 2, 14–15.
    See also Beethoven, Maria van
    (Keverich)
keys
  emotional resonance and, 219, 220–22
  temperament and, 219–20
  tuning and, 219–20, 221
Kielmansegge, Countess von,
    commission offer, 298–300
King Stephan music (Beethoven), 571, 575
Kinsky, Caroline, Princess, 530
Kinsky, Ferdinand, Prince, 518, 519, 529,
    570, 571, 581, 599
Klein, Franz, 577–79, 709
Klinger, Friedrich Maximilian, 26
Klöber, August von, 707–9
Klopstock, Friedrich Gottlieb, 98, 102,
    103, 124–25
Knight's Ballet (Beethoven), 116–18
Koch family/Zehrgarten, 75, 101, 124, 125,
    126–27, 187
Koch, Willibald, Friar, 40
Körner, Christian Gottfried, 74, 844
Kotzebue, August, 312, 571, 575
Kraft, Nikolaus, 169, 521, 638
Kreutzer, Rodolphe, 204, 205, 206, 216,
    327, 330, 352–53, 431, 434
Kreutzer Sonata (Beethoven), 325–27, 337,
    408, 431, 435, 830, 885, 892

Krumpholz, Wenzel, 239, 282–83, 324, 375,
    420, 688–89
Kügelgen brothers, painters, 86, 101
Kuhlau, Friedrich, 873–74

lead poisoning possibilities, 130, 224,
    225
Lebewohl, Das/"The Farewell"
    (Beethoven), 228, 523, 531, 533–34
Leipzig and Enlightenment, 43–44
Leonore (Beethoven). *See Fidelio*
    (Beethoven)
Leopold II, Holy Roman Emperor, 105,
    110, 122, 137
Les adieux. See Lebewohl, Das/"Farewell,
    The" (Beethoven)
*Lesegesellschafts/*reading societies, 83, 87,
    102, 107, 108
Lessing, Gottfried Ephraim, 26, 71,
    699–700
Leym, Johann Georg, 14–15
Leym, Maria Magdalene, 2, 14, 15. *See also*
    Beethoven, Maria van (Keverich)
Lichnowsky, Karl, Prince
  background/description, 153, 154–55,
    174
  Beethoven and, 153, 154–56, 158, 166,
    168, 169, 179, 180, 212, 248–49, 324,
    413, 416, 418, 426–27, 579, 915–16
  illness/death, 574, 588, 629
  practical joke/consequences, 375–76
  quarrel with Beethoven/consequences,
    428–29, 448, 450–51, 478, 519
  string instruments gift to Beethoven,
    249
  trip with Beethoven, 187
Lichnowsky, Maria Christine, Princess
  background, 153–55
  Beethoven and, 153–55, 158, 166, 169,
    275, 278, 418–19
Lichnowsky, Moritz
  background, 154
  Beethoven and, 154, 155, 156, 158, 166,
    169, 204, 637–38, 759, 786, 787
life mask/bust of Beethoven (Klein),
    577–79, 709
Lind, Jenny, 932

ppersdorff, Count, 427, 428, 455, 461, 479, 480

er, Ferdinando, 379–80, 416, 421
aine, Thomas, 103, 116
asqualati, Baron/house, 390, 391, 600, 602, 927–28
assavanti, Candidus, 27
Pastoral Sonata (Beethoven), 287–88
Pastoral Symphony/Sixth Symphony (Beethoven)
  dedication, 480
  premiere/performances, 483, 486
  reviews, 513–14
  Sturm's writings and, 509–11
  writing/description, 228, 476, 505–8, 511–13, 617
Pathétique/Grande Sonate Pathétique (Beethoven), 63, 207, 217–19, 221, 238, 239, 240, 245, 259, 321, 411
patrons' contract with Beethoven (1809)
  description, 516, 517–19, 522, 529
  Kinsky's death/Lobkowitz financial problems and, 599, 613, 621–22, 631–32, 647, 649
patrons' expectations, 561
Pergolesi, Giovanni, 17
Peters, C. F./publisher, 759–60, 761, 762, 770, 780
Peters, Karl, 698–99, 700, 701, 724, 737, 741, 798
Petrovna, Elizabeth, 425
Pfeifer, Tobias Friedrich
  background, 32
  Cäcilie Fischer and, 32
  Johann and, 32, 38
  leaving Beethoven family, 38
  as Ludwig's teacher, 32–33, 38, 40
  residence with Beethovens, 32
Piano Concerto No. 1 in C Major (Beethoven), 177–78
Piano Concerto No. 2 in B-flat (Beethoven), 176–77
piano/pianoforte
  1770s and, 22
  1780s and, 59
  Beethoven in mid-teens and, 59–60

Beethoven's favorite makers of, 90, 193
Érard of Paris piano, 328, 378, 532, 559, 702, 703
Graf, Conrad/piano, 873, 875, 932
John Broadwood & Sons gift to Beethoven, 701–3, 709, 719, 875
significance, 59
See also Streicher, Johann Andreas; Streicher, Nannette
Piano Quartets WoO 36, 79–82, 83
Piano Sonata in A-flat Major (Beethoven), 754–56
Piano Sonata in A Major (Beethoven), 690–92
Piano Sonata in C Minor (Beethoven), 756–57
Piano Sonata in E Major (Beethoven), 751–54
Piano Sonata in E Minor (Beethoven), 637–38
Piano Sonatas, op. 2 (Beethoven), 189–93
Piano Sonatas, op. 31 (Beethoven)
  description, 294–96
  Nägeli changing, 310
  See also Tempest, The (Beethoven)
Piano Sonatas, opp. 26–28 (Beethoven), 283–87, 288, 290. *See also Moonlight* Sonata (Beethoven)
Piano Trios, op. 1 (Beethoven), 166, 167–68, 179–84, 185
Piano Trios, op. 70 (Beethoven), 473–76
  See also Ghost Trio (Beethoven)
Piano Variations, opp. 34 and 35 (Beethoven), 296–98
pirated/stolen work, 261–62, 298, 308, 309–10, 375, 453, 761, 780–81, 864
Pius VI, Pope, 106
Pius VII, Pope, 299, 385, 523
Pleyel, Ignaz, 409, 429
Poll, Maria Josepha, 3
Pope, Alexander, 50
Poppelsdorf Palace/Allée, 7
portraits of Beethoven
  first portrait, 97
  Klöber, 707–9
  Mähler, 371–72

Linke, Joseph, 655, 679, 680, 866–67
Liszt, Franz, 546, 932
"living machines" craze, 613–14
  See also Maelzel, Johann Nepomuk
Lobkowitz, Prince
  background/description, 174, 250–51, 421
  Beethoven and, 173–74, 179, 209, 212, 216, 369, 382, 387, 390, 391, 416, 451, 480, 483, 486, 490, 518–19, 570, 622, 647
  Concerts for Enthusiasts and, 464–65
  financial problems of, 570, 588
Lobkowitz quartets (Beethoven), 209, 227, 237, 249–59
Lorenz, Canon, 61
Louis XVI, King of France, 15, 85, 103, 124, 137, 265
Louis XVIII, King of France, 626, 770
Luchesi, Andrea, *Kapellmeister,* 19, 20, 59, 86
"Ludwig" spelling variations, 3

Maelzel, Johann Nepomuk, 612, 613–15, 616, 621, 623–24, 693, 694, 704
  stealing Beethoven's music/ unauthorized performances, 623–24
Magazin der Musik, 45, 56
Mähler, Willibrord Joseph, 370–71
Malfatti, Johann, 536–37, 571, 690, 923, 926, 927
Malfatti, Therese/family and Beethoven, 536–39, 543, 553–54, 586, 603, 923
Maria Theresa, Empress, 85, 106, 157
Marie Antoinette, 15, 85, 103, 105, 171
Marseillaise, La, 107, 204, 205, 832, 855
Marx, Adolph Bernard
  Beethoven's response to, 861
  elevating Beethoven and music, 858–62
  "sonata form" and, 858, 919, 940–41
Masons. *See* Freemasons
Mass in C (Beethoven/Esterházy commissioned), 451, 455–58, 477, 485, 797

Mastiaux, J. G. von, 34
Matthisson, Friedrich von, 200, 201, 248, 249, 268
Maximilian Franz
  austerity and, 86
  Beethoven and, 86, 89, 92, 94, 129, 135–36, 195
  Bonn spa, 122–23
  as coadjutor of the Electorate of Bonn, 34–35
  death, 273
  description, 85–86
  as Elector of Bonn, 68, 84, 85–87, 89, 92, 94, 95, 99, 107, 113, 118–21, 122–23, 124, 131, 135–36, 168, 170–71, 334
  Enlightenment and, 84, 85, 86–87, 107
  family of, 34, 84, 85
  Joseph II and, 34, 84, 85, 105
  Kapelle/music and, 69, 86, 99–101, 118–21
  Mozart and, 85–86
  war/departures from Bonn and, 124, 131, 135, 168, 170–71
Maximilian Friedrich, Archbishop Elector of Cologne
  Belderbusch and, 10–11, 34, 67
  death, 68
  description/character, 24
  Electoral Sonatas (Beethoven) and, 62, 64
  government style/Enlightenment, 24–25, 54
  mistress of, 24
  music and, 33
  Neefe and, 60
  rebuilding residence following fire (1777), 28
  successor, 34–35
Méhul, E. N., 204, 330, 434
Meinertzhagen family, 42
Mendelssohn, Felix, 451, 522, 594
Mergentheim trip, 118–21
Messiah (Handel), 234, 505, 511, 800, 813, 873, 925
metronome (Maelzel), 614, 693, 694

Metternich, Clemens von
background, 610
Napoleon and, 610, 611, 627, 649
regime of, 633, 635, 636, 638, 653, 666, 690, 701, 742, 751, 768
Metternich family, 33–34
Meyer, Friedrich, 415, 417–18, 422
Meyerbeer, Giacomo, 615, 644
Milder, Anna, 416, 481, 485, 631, 643
Minorite order, 40–41
minuet-scherzo, 943
Missa solemnis (Beethoven)
Agnus Dei, 819–24
background/Beethoven's views of, 797–801
begging Beethoven for Vienna premiere, 785–86
Credo, 812–16
Gesellschaft der Musikfreunde and, 784–85
Gloria, 809–12
Kyrie, 801–8
performances and, 769–70
preparations for premiere/premiere (parts of), 786–89, 790
presentation to Rudolph, 772
publishers and, 748–49, 759–60, 761, 767, 770, 781, 862
Sanctus, 816–19
subscribers/subscriptions and, 768, 769, 770, 772
writing/description, 726, 732–33, 735, 736, 740, 741, 744, 747–48, 766, 772, 797, 801–25
Molière, 60
Moonlight Sonata (Beethoven), 286–87, 290, 529, 533, 906
Moscheles, Ignaz, 628, 700, 702, 704, 925, 926, 932
Mozart, Leopold
children/music and, 30, 31, 33
health problems/death, 90
as violinist, 30
Mozart, Wolfgang Amadeus
Beethoven meeting/myth, 89–92
criticism of others, 91

death, 121, 122
description, 91
Freemasons and, 71, 72, 90, 115, 153, 205, 332
wife/children, 90
Mozart, Wolfgang Amadeus/music
1770s, 23, 30
Beethoven and, 59, 80–81, 82, 89–91, 97, 98, 147, 149, 167, 175, 176, 181, 183, 192, 207, 208, 213, 321, 379
Beethoven on, 91
Bonn family performance (1763), 30
on composing, 362
Don Giovanni, 90, 100, 187, 207, 625, 779
Jupiter Symphony, 468
Magic Flute, The/Die Zauberflöte, 71, 116, 177, 195, 205, 222, 318, 332, 375, 477, 488, 575, 584, 640, 642, 662, 664, 764, 855
Marriage of Figaro, The, 100, 106, 159, 242, 639
Marx on, 859, 861
on music listeners, 33
musical duel, 152
musical form and, 939, 940
as prodigy, 23, 30, 31
Requiem, 109, 524, 756, 800, 932
sister and, 30
status/works, 43, 90, 149, 195, 231, 232–33, 320, 390
music composers
dichotomy, 33
stolen/pirated work, 261–62, 298, 308, 309–10, 375, 453, 761, 780–81, 864
See also specific individuals
music listeners dichotomy, 33
musical forms (overview)
ABA form, 942
background, 937
canon, 945
coda and, 350, 938, 939, 940, 942
concerto-sonata, 941–42
fugue, 943–45

minuet-scherzo, 943
sonata, 938–41
sonata-rondo, 941
theme and variations, 942

Nägeli publisher, 292, 293, 310
name day of Beethoven
baptism, 1–2
exorcisms/anointings, 1, 2
Napoleon Bonaparte
Beethoven and, 299, 334–45, 366–67, 384–85, 386, 421, 526
Code Napoleon, 386
Concordat (1801) and, 299
descriptions, 333
dethroning/exile of, 626, 650
as emperor, 384–86, 420, 421, 523–24, 526–27
end/defeat of, 609–11, 614, 627, 649–50
as First Consul, 241, 299, 334, 336
leaving Elba and, 649–50
marrying into Habsburg family/son, 527, 627
relatives as rulers, 523
rise of, 206, 333, 421
as "self-made," 366–67
wars and, 189, 202, 203, 204, 213, 285, 420, 421, 523–24, 526–27, 609–11
See also Eroica Symphony (Beethoven)
Neefe, Christian Gottlob
attitudes toward women, 74
background, 43–44, 57
Beethoven learning composition and, 62–64
collection of sketches, 75–77
court music/theater and, 60, 66, 68, 69, 75, 83, 86, 98, 100
criticism of, 82
description, 46, 79, 549
Dilettanterien, 75–77, 82
at end of life/death, 171
Enlightenment and, 38, 71
Freemasons and, 71, 72
Illuminati and, 73, 74, 75, 82
Leipzig and, 43–44, 57

as Ludwig's teacher/m[...]
46, 54, 56–57, 58–
66–67, 77, 78, 79,
191, 253, 314, 335
Max Franz regime and[...]
Mozart inspiration and[...]
portrait of, 45–46
publication promoting[...]
56–57
Reading Society, 83
religion and, 45
reputation, 45
as *Schwärmer*, 46, 71, 75
Nelson, Horatio, 203, 213, 4[...]
Newton, Isaac, 50
Niemetz, Joseph, 869, 902, 9[...]
Ninth Symphony (Beethove[...]
background/influences ov[...]
826–29, 858
begging Beethoven for Vie[...]
premiere, 785–86
British premiere, 867–68
description/meanings, 830–[...]
943
Freude/Joy theme, 826, 827–[...]
832, 833, 835, 839, 841, 8[...]
844, 846–47, 848, 849, 8[...]
853, 854, 855, 856, 857, 85[...]
legacy/significance, 797, 855–[...]
performances, 785, 796
preparations for premiere/pre[...]
786–89, 790–93
profit from premiere concert/[...]
Beethoven's reaction, 793, [...]
publishers and, 781, 862
reception/reviews, 792–93, 795–[...]
revising thoughts, 857–58
Schiller's poem and, 164, 826, 82[...]
843–44, 845, 848, 852, 853, 8[...]
857
tempo markings, 912, 914
writing, 733, 766, 782, 785, 790–92[...]
Novalis, 51, 368

Oberthür, Bonifaz, 74, 84
Oliva, Franz, 566, 572, 573, 698–99, 700–701, 733, 753, 764

Schimon, 735–36
Stieler, 744
Potter, Cipriani, 702, 703–4, 709
prejudice (racial/ethnic) in Beethoven's
    time, 260, 760–61
Probst publisher, 862
Prometheus ballet/music (Viganò/
    Beethoven), 264–65, 266–70
prostitutes and Beethoven, 391, 607–8,
    684, 742, 868
public performance scheduling, 436–37
publishers of music
    finances and, 261–62
    See also specific publishers
publishers of music and Beethoven
    anti-Semitism and, 760–61
    Beethoven and Clementi/Britain,
        452–53
    "exclusive" offers to multiple
        publishers, 748–49, 759–60, 761,
        862
    money owed Steiner, 746, 765–66, 768,
        862
    "new" overtures/British publishers,
        651–52
    promises/lies, 761, 770
    public fight with, 308–10
    publication against Beethoven's wishes,
        166, 168–69
    See also specific publishers
Punto, Giovanni (Wenzel Stich), 246–47,
    263, 351

Radoux, Amelius, 16
Razumovsky, Count
    background/description, 154, 425–26,
        465
    Beethoven and, 154, 179, 425, 429, 437,
        448, 480, 634, 645
    palace fire/consequences, 646, 679
    publishing/Britain, 453
Razumovsky, Countess, 179
Razumovsky Quartets, 426, 427, 435, 437,
    438, 439–48, 450, 452, 453, 454,
    472, 488, 535, 536, 679, 867
    description, 439–48
reading societies, 83, 87, 102, 107, 108

Reicha, Anton, 100, 194, 273–74, 525
Reicha, Joseph, 100
Reichardt, Johann Friedrich, 438, 482–83,
    486, 517, 521, 532, 693
Reis, Johanna, 424–25, 662–64
    See also Beethoven, Johanna
Renaissance-Palestrina style, 148–50
rescue opera, 378, 379. *See also Fidelio*
    (Beethoven)
Rhine, 5, 8
Ries, Ferdinand
    Beethoven/Beethoven's music and, 179,
        248, 274, 291, 292, 293, 294, 310,
        315, 321, 328–29, 369, 375–77, 384,
        388, 390, 391–92, 401, 410, 438,
        511, 545, 651–52, 659, 672, 674, 675,
        679, 703, 715, 743, 772
    conscription into French army and, 413
    practical joke/consequences, 375–76,
        413
Ries, Franz Anton, 62, 74, 93, 100–101,
    119, 274
Righini Variations (Beethoven), 117–18,
    119, 153
Robespierre, 114, 205, 832
Rochlitz, Johann Friedrich, 229, 312–13,
    378, 577, 749–50, 901, 933
Röckel, Joseph August, 418, 419, 421, 423,
    424, 481
Rode, Pierre, 601
Rolland, Romain, xix
Romance cantabile (Beethoven), 89
Romantics/Romantic period
    Beethoven myth and, xii, xix, 51, 53, 54,
        182, 217, 233, 326, 363, 367–68, 371,
        399, 474, 542, 567, 578, 630, 738,
        744, 918, 934
    description/views, 8, 27, 51, 52–53, 54
    sonata and, 940
Romberg, Andreas, 100, 120, 200
Romberg, Bernhard, 100, 112, 118, 120,
    442
Rossini, Gioachino, 750–51, 789–90, 796
Rotterdam trip (Ludwig/mother, 1783)
    Beethoven on, 65–66
    Beethoven performing/payment, 65,
        66

Rovantini, Franz Georg
  Beethoven family and, 32–33, 35
  Cäcilie Fischer and, 33, 36, 42–43
  death, 42–43
  description/character, 33
  Johann and, 42
  as Ludwig's teacher, 32–33, 40, 42, 58
  sister visiting grave, 64–65
Rudolph, Archduke
  as archbishop/cardinal, 726, 732, 736,
    772
  background/music, 516–17, 725–26
  as Beethoven patron, 516, 517–19, 531,
    560–61, 570, 576, 599, 609, 631–32,
    647, 703, 725, 733–34, 746, 800–801
  Beethoven planning mass for, 726,
    732–33, 735, 797, 798–99
  Beethoven protection and, 746
  dedications (Beethoven), 516
  piano lessons/Beethoven, 516–17, 530–
    31, 560–61, 574–75, 772, 784
  See also Missa solemnis (Beethoven)
Ruins of Athens, The (Beethoven), 571,
    575, 622, 629, 762–63
rumor of Beethoven's noble father, 734,
    878

Salieri, Antonio, 170, 208, 222–23, 311, 318,
    379, 391, 466, 614, 615
Salomon, Johann Peter, 114–16, 122, 243
Satzenhoven, Caroline von, 24
Schall, August von, 82, 135, 195
Schenk, Johann Baptist, 150–51
"scherzo" defined, 943
Schikaneder, Emmanuel
  background, 142
  Beethoven/operas and, 311, 312, 328,
    330, 369, 374, 375, 378, 379, 381–82,
    391
Schiller, Friedrich
  Freemasons and, 71
  Goethe and, 591
  Illuminati and, 74
  influence/significance of, 87
  Kant and, 85
  "Ode to Joy"/*An die Freude,* 53–54, 87,
    103, 265, 266, 335

  wife, 131
  work/views of, 26, 27, 43, 53–54, 60,
    102–3, 124–25, 164, 218, 265–66,
    268, 305, 313, 335, 359, 845
  See also Ninth Symphony (Beethoven)
Schimon, Frederick, 735–36
Schindler, Anton
  background/music, 623, 693, 763,
    866–67
  Beethoven and, 764–65, 768, 769, 771,
    773, 781, 783, 786, 787, 790, 793,
    794–95, 869, 922, 924, 925, 926,
    927, 928, 929, 931
  on Beethoven/Beethoven's music,
    495–96, 699, 763–64, 904
  description, 763–64
  Holz replacing, 870, 872
  on relationship with Beethoven,
    763–64, 765, 930
  taking material after Beethoven's death,
    930
Schlemmer, Wenzel, 260, 782, 902
Schlesinger, Adolf/Moritz publishers, 745,
    747, 748, 751, 759, 760–61, 780, 861,
    862–63, 864, 874, 875, 914, 918
Schmidt, Johann, 291, 303–4, 455, 537
Schneider, Eulogius, 85, 87, 107–8,
    113–14
Schott and Sons publishers, 862, 864,
    865, 867, 872, 905, 912, 914, 924,
    928
Schröder-Devrient, Wilhelmine, 767
Schubert, Franz, xix, 515, 643, 677, 682,
    732, 741, 827, 864, 919, 931, 933
Schumann, Robert, 864, 879, 901
Schuppanzigh, Ignaz
  background/music, 156, 242, 324, 437,
    438, 485, 521, 623, 679, 873, 874,
    896, 918
  Beethoven and, 158, 169, 212, 216, 239,
    240, 242, 251, 278, 279, 312, 324,
    376, 407, 437–38, 442, 454, 465,
    607, 615, 646, 655, 679, 766, 772,
    786–87, 790, 794, 866, 867, 872–73,
    874, 875, 896, 899, 918, 931
  description, 156, 437–38
Schwärmer defined, 46

Sebald, Amalie, 594, 595
Second Symphony (Beethoven), 291, 300,
    315, 316, 319–21, 382–83, 427
Septet, op. 20 (Beethoven), 209, 243–44,
    245, 260, 263, 292, 309, 399, 434,
    576, 679, 931
Serioso Quartet (Beethoven), 534, 556–58,
    562, 563, 866, 883
Seventh Symphony (Beethoven)
    performances/publications, 615, 626,
        645, 651, 679, 684, 731, 746
    writing/description, 258, 574, 579, 588,
        597, 616–21, 624, 626, 646
Seyfried, Ignaz von, 230–31, 233, 316, 422,
    465, 485
Shakespeare/works, 60, 156, 215, 295, 320,
    412, 469–70, 474, 538, 763–64, 876,
    921, 935–36
Simrock, Nikolaus/publisher, 74, 119–20,
    138, 168–69, 170, 291, 293, 310, 327,
    329, 369, 453, 736, 743, 759, 761
Sixth Symphony. *See* Pastoral Symphony/
    Sixth Symphony (Beethoven)
Smart, Sir George, 652, 679, 867, 874, 875,
    925, 928
Sobieski, Jan, King of Poland, 6
sonata
    Baroque period, 940
    Classical era, 940, 941, 942
    classifying and, 940–41
    overview, 938–41
    Romantic period, 940
    sections/components, 938–39
"sonata form" and Marx, 858, 919, 940–41
sonata-rondo, 941
Sonnleithner, Joseph von, 381, 382, 408,
    409, 413, 414–15, 419, 454, 476,
    616
Sontag, Henriette, 762, 788, 792
Spohr, Louis, 608, 615, 628, 898
Stackelberg, Christoph von, 460–61, 563,
    747
Stackelberg, Josephine. *See* Deym,
    Josephine, Countess
Stamitz, Carl, 65
Stammbuch (stem-book), 124–27, 163
Starke, Friedrich, 745, 753, 864

steam power beginnings/effects, 15
Steibelt, Daniel, 247–48, 409, 775
Stein, Johann Andreas, 90, 193
Stein, Nannette (Maria Anna), 90, 193
    See also Streicher, Nannette
Steiner, Sigmund Anton/publisher, 560,
    648, 650–51, 667, 674, 684, 732,
    741, 746, 759–60, 765–66, 768,
    862, 867
Stendhal, 202, 654–55, 750
Sterkel, Abbé, 59, 119
Stich, Wenzel (Giovanni, Punto), 246–47,
    263, 351
Stieler, Joseph Karl, 744
Streicher, Johann Andreas, 193–94, 427,
    532, 558–59, 578, 926
Streicher, Nannette, 608–9, 687–88, 697,
    702, 705–7
    See also Stein, Nannette (Maria Anna)
String Quartet in C-sharp Minor
    (Beethoven), 898, 899, 901, 902,
    905–11, 916–17
String Quartet in F Major (Beethoven),
    902, 912, 913, 914, 916, 917–19
String Quintet in C Major, op. 29
    (Beethoven), 288–89, 292
Stumpff, Johann Andreas, 873, 922–23,
    928
Sturm, Christoph Christian, 509–11,
    606–7
Sturm und Drang (Storm and Stress),
    26–27, 43, 45, 52, 235, 885
Sulzer, Johann Georg, 76, 77–78, 314
Swieten, Gottfried van
    background/description, 157, 158, 234,
        270
    Beethoven and, 157, 273

Tagebuch. See diary (*Tagebuch*) of
    Beethoven
Talleyrand, Charles-Maurice de, 610, 627,
    634, 636
Tempest, The (Beethoven), 294–96, 328,
    365, 833, 846
Tenth Symphony plans, 876–77
Teutonic Knights, 95, 118
Thayer, Alexander Wheelock, xii–xiii

Theater an der Wien
  Beethoven and, 311, 312, 328, 363, 370,
    381–82, 391, 436–37, 457, 480–81,
    484–86
  Beethoven's letter/petition to directors
    of, 462–64
  Eroica premiere and, 396, 397–98
  Fidelio and, 416
  Schikaneder and, 142, 328, 381, 391
theater of Electoral Residence/National
    Theater
  Belderbusch and, 60, 66
  closing/job loses (1784), 69, 70
  as National Theater, 60, 66
  productions (1780s), 60
  reopening/reviving, 86, 99–100
theme and variations
  Beethoven and, 57, 58, 942
  description, 57–58, 942
Third Piano Concerto (Beethoven), 195,
    315, 316, 376, 467, 468, 488
Third Symphony (Beethoven). *See Eroica*
    Symphony (Beethoven)
Thomson, George/publisher, 328, 378,
    429–30, 528, 529, 561, 595–97, 600,
    620, 675, 705, 732, 745, 746
thoroughbass, 31–32, 147, 149
Thun, Countess, 154, 169, 179, 425
Thürheim, Lulu von, Countess, 155, 174
Tiedge, C. A., 396, 572–73
To an Infant (Beethoven), 58
*To the Distant Beloved/An die ferne
    Geliebte* (Beethoven), 675–78, 684
Tomaschek, Wenzel Johann, 226–27, 229,
    248, 616, 644
"tonic" defined, 938
Touchemoulin, *Kapellmeister,* 11
Treitschke, G. F., 418, 623, 628, 629, 638,
    643, 647
Trémont, Baron de, on Beethoven/
    Beethoven's house, 525–26
Trio for Piano and Winds (Beethoven),
    105
Trio for Piano, Clarinet, and Cello
    (Beethoven), 215–16, 247
Trio for Piano, Flute, and Bassoon
    (Beethoven), 112

Triple Concerto, op. 56 (Beethoven), 387
Triumph of the Cross, The (Beethoven),
    704–5, 865
Tuscher, Mathias von, 723–24, 728, 730

Umlauf, Michael, 622, 629, 643, 767, 788,
    790, 794
Unger, Karoline, 762, 785–86, 788, 792
University of Cologne, 85

van den Eaden, Gilles
  death, 60
  as Ludwig's teacher, 31–32, 40
"van" vs. "von," 3, 154, 723–24
Varena, Joseph von, 575, 579, 599, 600
Varnhagen, Karl, 572, 573, 579, 581, 588,
    589, 648–49
venereal disease, 574, 607, 629, 633, 684,
    741, 868
Vering, Julie von, 521, 928
Vermeer, 158
Vestas Feuer, 328, 369, 374–75, 378, 379,
    382
Victory of the Cross, The (commissioned
    oratorio), 784, 898
Vienna
  fear of "Jacobins," 137–38
  French occupation (1805), 415–16,
    419–20
  French/war and, 203–5
  music/dance, 136–37, 138–44, 464–65
  See also Beethoven, Ludwig van, and
    Vienna
Vienna trip (1787) of Beethoven
  Beethoven's letter to von Schaden,
    93–94
  mother's illness and, 92
  Mozart meeting/myth and, 89–92
  overview, 89–92
  Vienna description, 91–92
Viennese Classical style, 149
Viganò, Salvatore, 264–65, 266, 267, 269
Violin Concerto (Beethoven), 430, 431–
    34, 435, 445
Violin Sonata in G Major (Beethoven),
    601–2
Violin Sonatas (Beethoven), 216, 233–34

Violin Sonatas, op. 30 (Beethoven), 293–94
Viotti, Giovanni Battista, 176, 324, 431, 434
Vivaldi, Antonio, 97
Voltaire
  Joseph II and, 52
  works/views of, 46, 50, 60
von Schaden, Joseph, *Hofrat*
  Beethoven and, 90, 92, 93–94
  Beethoven's letter to, 93–94
  Freemasons and, 90
von Schaden, Nannette, 90
"von" vs. "van," 3, 154, 723–24

Wackenroder, Wilhelm, 290
Wagner, Richard, 783, 842, 843, 906, 941
Waldstein, Count
  background/career, 95, 96, 116, 117, 118, 154
  as Beethoven's mentor/champion, 95–96, 98, 99, 113, 116, 125–26, 164, 372
  Bonn/court and, 95, 96, 97
  Freemasons and, 96
Waldstein Sonata (Beethoven), 326, 369, 372–74, 410, 411
Washington, George, 71, 103, 393, 578
Wawruch, Andreas, 916, 921–22, 923, 924, 925, 927
Wegeler, Franz
  on Beethoven, 61, 95, 97–98, 201, 545
  Beethoven and, 61, 85, 95, 101, 119, 125, 172–73, 187, 200, 273, 275–78, 388, 389, 424, 536, 539, 877–78, 879, 923–24
  University of Bonn, 85
  wife (Lorchen), 98, 877, 878, 923

Weishaupt, Adam, 73–74
Well-Tempered Clavier, The (J. S. Bach)
  Beethoven and, 45, 56, 57, 59, 81, 109, 154, 193, 692, 716, 751, 752, 777, 907, 921, 945
  keys/tuning system and, 220, 222
  "well-tempered" defined, 220
Wellington's Victory (Beethoven)
  publishing, 650–51, 679
  unauthorized performances, 651
  writing/description, 614, 615–16, 620–21, 622, 623, 624, 626, 629, 638, 644, 645, 646, 650, 651, 667, 680, 832, 860
Westerholt, Maria Anna von, 89, 112
"Who Is a Free Man?" (*Wer ist ein freier Mann?*) (Beethoven), 114, 344, 487
Wieck, Friedrich/Clara, 900–901
Wiessenbach, Alois, 643–44
Willmann, Magdalena, 201–2, 603
Wittelsbachs of Bavaria, 6
Wölffl, Joseph, 229–31, 233, 247
women instrumentalists (early 1800s), 521–22

Zehrgarten/Beethoven's friends, 75, 101, 124–25, 126–27, 187
Zelter, Carl Friedrich, 196, 553, 591–92, 769
Zmeskall, Nikolaus, Baron
  background/description, 156–57, 700, 764, 789, 924
  Beethoven and, 157, 158, 198, 212–13, 235, 278, 279, 403, 409, 520, 530, 536, 540, 556, 573–74, 608, 622, 672, 684, 687–88, 689, 700, 704, 764, 786, 789, 867, 924